on Internet

D1490374

INTERNET WORLD'S

on INTERNET 94

AN INTERNATIONAL

GUIDE TO

ELECTRONIC JOURNALS,

NEWSLETTERS, TEXTS,

DISCUSSION LISTS,

AND OTHER RESOURCES

ON THE INTERNET

edited by Tony Abbott

Editorial Board

PAT ENSOR, University of Houston Libraries
RICHARD GARTNER, Bodleian Library, Oxford University
MARK HINNEBUSCH, Florida Center for Library Automation
ELIZABETH LANE LAWLEY, Internet Training & Consulting Services
RALEIGH MUNS, University of Missouri, St. Louis, Libraries
GORD NICKERSON, University of Western Ontario

with a Preface by DANIEL P. DERN

TK
5105.875
.I57
I588
1994

Indiana University
Library
Northwest

Mecklermedia
Westport • London

First printing December 1993
Second printing April 1994

ISSN 1066-9973
ISBN 0-88736-929-4

Copyright © 1994 Mecklermedia. All rights reserved. No part of this publication may be reproduced in any form by any means without prior written permission from the publisher, except by a reviewer who may quote brief passages in review.

The publisher does not assume and hereby disclaims any liability to any party for any loss or damage caused by errors or omissions in *On Internet*, whether such errors or omissions result from negligence, accident, or any other cause.

Mecklermedia, 11 Ferry Lane West, Westport, CT 06880.
Mecklermedia Ltd., Artillery House, Artillery Row, London SW1P 1RT, UK.

Printed and bound in the United States of America.

Contents

Preface

W elcome to ON INTERNET, a book intended to help you locate and use Internet resources that are appropriate to your activities and needs. Before you launch yourself into the Internet's firehose-spray of information and resources, here are a few tips on how to search and use Internet resources effectively — and how to use them in a socially responsible manner that minimizes unnecessary impact to Internet resources and users. First, however, a few quick words synopsizing the Internet are in order.

THE INTERNET TODAY

The roots of the Internet and its resources go back ten, twenty, even thirty or more years depending on what aspects you look at — to the general deployment of the TCP/IP protocol stack in the early 1980s, the creation of the ARPAnet in 1969, and to the use of electronic mail and computer-mediated discussions even earlier — systems like PLATO and CAUCUS which pre-saged today's BBSs, Usenet Newsgroups, CompuServe Forums, and groupware like Lotus NOTES.

The Internet today has truly become a global information and communications resource, comparable in scope and importance to the phone system for voice and facsimile, the government and private postal carriers for hardcopy, and the print and electronic media for information dissemination.

The Internet connects Fortune 100 corporations and small businesses, government agencies, college and K12 academic institutions, libraries, private individuals, computer user groups, professional societies and more. The Internet community comprises an estimated ten to twenty or thirty million people spanning every continent and time zone. Factoring in the global e-mail and messaging communities that interact with full Internet sites — the entity dubbed "Matrix" by John Quarterman in his seminal book of the same name — brings the total to thirty or more millions across over 100 countries.

The Internet's tendrils also reach out to commercial online services, including America OnLine, CompuServe, DELPHI, and GEnie, to thousands of Bulletin Board Systems on FidoNet and elsewhere, to commercial information services like Dialog and Dow Jones, to tourist bureaus, bookstores, magazine tables of contents and partial text . . . there's probably one new major Internet service or site appearing roughly every hour, and a new user joining perhaps every minute, maybe even every few seconds. Your challenge, as an Internet user, is to find and locate those specific resources of value to you among the myriad virtual haystacks in the fields of cyberspace.

WHERE ON THE INTERNET IS WALDO, CARMEN SANDIEGO, ETC?

The Internet is home to a mind-boggling array of information, services and re-sources...millions of retrieveable files, thousands of libraries and other free-for-use or pay-for-use on-line facilities, and thousands of public and private topical discussions. These are often referred to in the context of the primary search and retrieval tool associated with them, e.g.,

- 2,000+ anonymous-FTP sites holding several million files, with a searchable index available through several dozen archie servers
- 2,000+ Gopher servers with an estimated 1-2 million file and menu items, with searchable global and local indexes through numerous VERONICA and JUGHEAD servers
- 3,000+ electronic mailing list discussion groups
- 3-5,000 Usenet Newsgroups
- Several hundred WAIS databases
- 700 - 1,000 library catalogs listed through tools such as HYTELNET or LIBS
- Dozens to hundreds of commercial on-line services, "free-nets," government and private BBSs, typically organized through Gopher menus

In olden times — up to say 1990 — the majority of users and organizations on the Internet knew 'who they were and why they were there.' You probably knew who the other network users in your field were, their e-mail addresses, the names of the relevant discussion groups, the locations of important sites, and where the files and programs were stored.

Today, the reverse is more likely to be true. New users hop on the Internet hoping to learn what it's good for, where the hot collections of files are, what's available for their interests and needs. As you can see from this book's different sections, there's a lot there — the challenge is as much to pick the best selections as to find anything.

Using the Internet well requires a combination of knowledge about the network, skill with its tools, and a good feel for "network etiquette," a.k.a. netiquette. Let's take a look at "how to be a good Internet user" before you launch yourself face-first onto the Information Highway.

THINK GLOBALLY BUT START BY ACTING LOCALLY

Whether you're looking for a popular file or want to join a disussion group, always start locally, at your system, LAN or site, before moving "outwards" beyond your organization into the rest of the Internet. Like Dorothy in the Land of Oz, what you're looking for may be right in your own back yard after all.

For example, suppose you want to subscribe to the RISKS Digest, a popular discussion of the risks and implications of technology. It is available from a central site on the Internet — but before you send a 'subscribe message' (and we'll talk more about this in a moment) — see if it's available locally:

- If you have Usenet Newsgroups within your site, RISKS should be available as comp.risks — use your Usenet Newsreader to follow this group. (By adding "comp.risks" to your .newsrc or other Usenet profile, or, if it's already there, indicating this is a Newsgroup you do want to follow.) RESULT: No additional "copies" of RISKS needed. Many discussions are available as both Usenet Newsgroups and Internet mailing lists.
- If your site performs "local redistribution" of mailing lists, "subscribe" through your local postmaster. This helps avoid the need for another copy of each RISKS message to be sent across the Internet to you. If your site doesn't, consider suggesting this to your site or system administrator.

Similarly, suppose you're looking for a copy of a file, e.g., a version of the Eudora mailreader program. Before conducting an Archie search, determine if your site maintains local source archives; if it does, copies of many popular programs may already be available in-house.

Check the public directories; ask your system administrators; post a query to a local BBS or Newsgroup. There's no point in downloading and installing additional copies.

If this search fails, then try an Archie search. Do your best to identify the site "nearest" to you in terms of highbandwidth links — it's not appropriate to drag megabytes of files across a 9600 or 56kbps link belonging to another network if you don't need to. If the files are big and you're not in a hurry, consider delaying your retrieval until after primary working hours.

Also be ready to consider other retrieval methods, such as FTP — mail servers, dial-up UUCP retrieval — or finding a System Administrator willing to download the files to a disk for you. If you want more than a certain volume of files, consider obtaining them by ordering a magtape, or on CD-ROM. Several gigabytes of "Internet archives" are available this way; if you access the Internet through a by-the-hour dial-up connection, the cost may well be less than prolonged downloading — and will definitely be easier.

Similarly, before asking a question to a public forum such as a mailing list or Newsgroup:

• Be sure to look for and read its FAQ (Frequently-Asked Questions) or other introductory message. If it seems like a relatively basic question, like "Can I telnet to CompuServe?" or "Where are popular FTP sites for Windows software and information?" the odds are good that the question's been answered in the appropriate FAQ. (This suggests that one of your first tasks will be to locate an available, ideally searchable FAQ archive.)

• If possible, read any group for at least two weeks, preferrably four, before posting any messages of your own to the group. Remember you're "new in town;" sit back and wait until you've gotten a sense of who's who, who knows what, etc. It's possible you'll NEVER post messages to many mailing lists or Newsgroups you follow. That's OK — do you feel obligated to write letters to all the magazines and newspapers you read or radio shows you listen to?

HOW TO JOIN, PARTICIPATE IN, AND LEAVE A LIST

One of the most frustrating aspects of using the Internet can be trying to join — and leave — a mailing list or other discussion group. You'll get used to seeing other people make these mistakes — try not to be one of them.

Part of the challenge is that there are many similar but not quite identical facilities, making it easy to get wrong. The larger part, however, is that people often forget the right way to do it — or make simple but high-impact mistakes in using e-mail.

Joining and Leaving:

The two most common mailing membership methods are "-request" — also called "Internet" or "Arpanet" style -- and "listserv".

In the first, all "administrative" messages are sent to

```
listname-request@listsite
```

e.g., administrative messages for the list dos-lovers go to

```
dos-lovers-request@lezner.ize.edu
```

and messages intended to go to participants on the list go to the list-address, e.g.,

```
dos-lovers@lezner.ize.edu
```

These "-request" addresses typically — but not universally — are processed by a person, rather than a program, capable of interpreting messages such as

```
please add me to this list -- thanks
```

or

```
please take me off this list
```

or

```
help! unsubscribe me! joe@llama.nyzoo.org
```

or even

```
I'll be away all summer; turn me off and I'll let you
know when I'm back -Thanks!
```

Increasingly, however, more mailing list owners are turning to programs to handle the administrative traffic. Here, messages are received by the program, rather than a person; the mailing list management program does its best to interpret the contents of your message and process it.

For example:

```
subscribe thomas jefferson
subscribe jefferson thomas
subscribe constitution-l jefferson
unsubscribe thomas jefferson
unsubscribe
```

One of the oldest and best known such programs is one named LISTSERV, prevalent at BITNET sites. There is also a varient commonly identified as ListServ, which runs on Unix machines. Other popular "list management" programs include procmail and major-domo.

Each program may have different syntax; when in doubt, send as a first message simply:

```
help
```

in the Subject and body. Unfortunately, there is no one standard for these mailing list programs. Some will take commands in the Subject, in the message body, or in both; some only in one or the other, and so on. Some expect you to put your lastname first, others the other way around; some require your e-mail address in your command and others will take it from your message. Get used to this cyber-anarchy; that's the way it is.

Many lists, when you join, send you a message containing key addresses, rules, syntax and command summaries, and other basic information — be sure to save these messages in a file for future reference! All the messages in the world to the central maintainer asking to be deleted won't help if you've joined through a local redistribution — or if you can't remember the correct command syntax.

Always bear in mind that each mailing list program at a site may be managing more than one mailing list, in which case your message must identify the desired list by name. Or, there may be a different administrative mail name for each list — in which case you may not need to include a list's name in your message.

Some programs, such as the BITNET LISTSERV facilities, can even route your request from any LISTSERV program to the one in charge of the mailing list your message is for.

Participating: Once your name has been added to a list, you send messages intended for all members to the appropriate address, e.g.,

```
constitution-l@camel.uzoo.org
```

Replying to an Individual, Replying to the List or Group:

Along with sending administrative messages to the entire list, the other common mistake you'll see — and probably do at least once — is a message being sent to all members of a list instead of to a single user. Sometimes these messages are innocuous, such as "Hey, Fred, let's meet for lunch" — but it's just as easy to broadcast highly embarrassing or career-limited messages which, once sent, can't be called back.

In e-mail, this frequently happens because the user has specified the "reply' command, and didn't notice that the reply message has been addressed to the list instead of to the individual who wrote the to-be-replied-to message. The only reliable answer here is: *Always check your reply message's TO field before sending it.*

Similarly, when answering a posting in a Usenet Newsgroup, be sure you're REPLYing to an individual versus doing a FOLLOW-UP to the entire Newsgroup — unless, of course, that's what you mean to do.

FINAL REMINDERS

There are a number of defintive essays on how to participate properly in Usenet Newsgroups — which also apply to participating in mailing lists — which are part of the "Periodic Postings" regularly made available through the Usenet news.announce.newusers Newsgroup and from popular FAQ archive sites.

"Periodic Posting" Usenet articles you should read include:

"What is Usenet?"
"A Primer on How to Work With the Usenet Community"
"Rules for posting to Usenet"
"Answers to Frequently Asked Questions"
"Emily Postnews Answers Your Questions on Netiquette"
"Hints on writing style for Usenet"
"Introduction to the news.answers newsgroup"

Read them carefully before you launch into the Internet — and reread them at least once a month later (you'll be amazed how much more sense they'll make at this point!).

Once you've read these, depending on what you're interested in, see "Further Periodic Usenet Articles Worth Reading." These articles include things like lists of Usenet Newsgroups with one-line explanations, lists of mailing lists available via e-mail, etc.

(You probably don't want to read any of these messages in their entirety — but it's worth becoming familiar with them, and the types of information they offer. Then, at later dates, when you're looking for information about Usenet Groups, mailing lists, etc., you'll remember to go locate current versions of these messages and read/search through them.)

Also consider reading "Netiquette" sections in one or more Internet user guides — and be sure to read and familiarize yourself with any local usage policies and agreements regarding e-mail, Usenet, and other Internet activites!

Happy cyber-hunting!

—Daniel P. Dern (ddern@world.std.com)
author, The Internet Guide for New Users (McGraw-Hill, 1994).
© Copyright 1993 Daniel P. Dern

Introduction

The type and variety of information resources available on the Internet — the worldwide matrix of interconnected computer networks — is expanding at a phenominal rate. Knowing where to turn for an authoritative guide to what is available and how to get it is a challenging enterprise, even for the most veteran of Internet searchers. That is why we have created ON INTERNET.

ON INTERNET is your guide to a full range of Internet-accessible data files — from artificial intelligence to women's studies, from space exploration to rock music, from environmental studies to AIDS research. Listed in this book are nearly 6,000 special-interest mailing lists, electronic journals, text and software archives, community-wide information systems, and that new area of Internet activity — commercial companies offering electronic shopping and other products and services over the net.

The thousands of resources listed here (many of which point the user to hundreds and even thousands of other resources) make ON INTERNET the most comprehensive volume in your Internet reference bookshelf.

THE ARRANGEMENT OF THIS BOOK

1. Discussion Lists and Special Interest Mailing Lists

This book is arranged in nine basic sections organized around types of information resources available online. The first of these is Discussion Lists and Special Interest Mailing Lists. Discussion lists are ongoing fora for communication and interaction related to a particular topic or group of topics. From AIDS to zoology, nearly every conceivable subject area has a discussion list and most of them are quite open and welcome new subscribers to their ranks.

The mailing list idea is a simple one. Just as you can send multiple copies of an e-mail message to a list of recipients, so can a powerful computer (often called a listserver) send multiple messages to diverse groups of subscribers on a constant basis.

Lists can be moderated or unmoderated. A moderated list means that a human editor reviews all messages intended for the list members to decide whether they are appropriate to the discussion underway on that list. An unmoderated list, on the other hand, is one in which all messages intended to be read by the list's subscribers are electronically forwarded to the subscribers without intervention. This latter type of list is the more common of the two and, for obvious reasons, requires less day to day involvement from the list administrator.

Some etiquette is necessary in dealing with messages sent to lists. First of all, it is important to remember that there are different mailing addresses for different kinds of messages. If you are already a subscriber to a list or several lists, you will know that all too often a request to be added to or dropped from a particular mailing list will be forwarded automatically to every member of the list. What the requestor should have done was to send a standard listserv subscribe or unsubscribe message directly to the listserver (the computer maintaining the list), or to send a similar message privately to the listowner (a person). List members themselves, of course, can do nothing to actually subscribe or unsubscribe a person from the list.

In ON INTERNET we have attempted wherever possible to list all the relevant addresses. In some cases, where such information was not available, or if you are unsure, it is best to send a private message to the listowner or other contact person associated with a list. That individual will let you know if you must send a listserv-directed message and how to accomplish that.

2. Electronic Journals and Newsletters

Similar to discussion lists are electronic journals and newsletters, featuring news and/or articles on a particular topic and periodically published to a list of subscribers. All ejournals have editors at their helms and some have full advisory boards with manuscript referral and acceptance policies akin to traditional printed periodicals. A number of ejournals, such as the Online Journal of Current Clinical Trials, Psycoloquy, and Interpersonal Computing and Technology: An Electronic Journal for the 21st Century, are at the forefront of efforts to "legitimate" the ejournal in this way and establish the genre as a successful method of research-based scholarship. The vast majority of ejournals and newsletters, do not fit this model, however. Taken as a whole ejournals represent the full range of interests from the mainstream to the quirky.

3. Electronic Texts, Text Archives, Selected FTP Sites, and Internet Resource Guides

This broad group of resources contains a variety of individual types of information in a range of subject areas. Included here are lists of online public access library catalogs; electronic text archives such as the Gutenberg Project, the Center for Electronic Texts, and others; a very selected list of several of the hundreds of FTP sites worldwide; and a fairly comprehensive listing of Internet resource guides that are themselves available through FTP, telnet, or via e-mail. The factor determining an item's inclusion in this section of the directory is that, unlike either discussion lists or ejournals which are sent periodically to your computer after you subscribe to them, these are items which must be retrieved from a remote computer's database. As such, this section acts as a pointer to vast additional resources available at hundreds of sites across the net.

4. Freenets and Other Community-Based Information Services

The community information system represents one of the most forward-looking and democratic (though perhaps the most underfunded) models for getting the Internet to the people. Most such systems provide a range of free and useful information to their communities and seem to presage one aspect of how a totally wired nation might work. To quote from the Triangle (NC) Freenet information brochure:

> Free-Nets are similar to ordinary electronic bulletin boards in that both require a computer with modem, and both are accessed with a telephone line. Both provide information and allow a user to interact with other participants. But a Free-Net typically covers a wider spectrum of community information than the hobbyist or commercial BBS, and it puts you and your family in direct communication with the community's officials and leaders. Most Free-Nets also provide access to the worldwide computer network called the Internet.

> To access a Free-Net, you need a computer and a modem hooked to your telephone, or similar computer-to-computer communications. (Computers with direct connections to the Internet have direct access to most Free-Nets.) You dial a local telephone number that connects you to the Free-Net computer, and then follow the simple instructions and "menus" that take you to the information you seek. So to send a message to a friend, for instance, you'd simply go to the e-mail area, write your message, and "mail" it. It's really that simple!

5. Campus-Wide Information Systems

Rather like community information systems, Campus-Wide Information Systems (or CWISs) are a growing phenomenon and are being established on more and more campuses nationally and internationally. This list of gopher- and telnet-accessible systems has been graciously provided by Judy Hallman of UNC-Chapel Hill. Like many other such lists of resources, this list is updated on a regular basis online. Interested CWIS searchers and administrators should also consider joining the discussion list CWIS-L to keep current on all aspects of establishing and running a campus system.

6. Commercial Services on the Internet

No other area of Internet activity has been as controversial as the growing commercialization of the net. With governmental funding ebbing quickly and Internet-related business opportunities arising seemingly daily, it is little wonder that a number of companies are offering fee-based services over the net, testing traditional acceptable-use policies. A recent electronic colloquium on the Coalition for Networked Information's discussion list CNI-MODERNIZATION (on the modernization of the net) featured an extended debate on the methodology of advertising on the network, a hitherto unmentionable topic. The companies whose services are listed in this section of the directory represent the first few pioneers in what will undoubtedly become a vast base of commercial offerings.

7. Usenet Newsgroups and Other Mailing Lists

The Usenet has been described as an international network of electronic bulletin board systems linked to the Internet. Its most significant feature is its huge sea of messages from hundreds of thousands (millions?) of users worldwide. These messages are arranged topically and the whole corpus of Usenet Newsgroups (and such similar mailing lists as the commercial ClariNet groups described in this section) add some 3,500 topic-related fora to the universe of the Internet.

The term "news" is defined broadly as anything anyone has to contribute on a topic, items circulated and shared and read and added to constantly by the Usenet community worldwide. Like traditional Internet and Bitnet discussion lists, Newsgroups can be moderated or unmoderated, and digests of news messages collected by a moderator can be distributed periodically (daily, weekly, monthly, etc.) Your Internet host, the computer through which you receive your net connection, must be a Usenet newsfeed site for you to access the Newsgroups. Contact your local system administrator for details.

8. WAIS-Accessible Databases

The five-hundred plus databases profiled in this section (themselves including tens of thousands of discrete documents and files) are searchable through Wide-Area Information Servers (WAIS), a proprietary client-server program that features cross-database keyword searching of subject terms. This swiftly growing universe of text-searchable files (with dozens of new databases mounted monthly) represents an exceptionally user-friendly aspect of Internet resource sharing.

Appendix: List Review Service

In this section we offer critical reviews of discussion lists conducted by the List Review Service, an ejournal edited by Raliegh C. Muns of the University of Missouri-St. Louis Libraries. These reviews, of twenty-five discussion lists on a variety of topics, make a useful archive of list activity and diversity and point the way toward qualifying and quantifying the extreme range of interest that is represented on the Internet. See the instructions in the Appendix for subscribing to the List Review Service to ensure that you receive the latest reviews in this growing database.

Subject Index

This subject index covers resources listed in sections 1, 2, 3, 4, and 6. Sections 5, 7, and 8 are condensed lists of hundreds of diverse individual archives crying out for adequate subject management. One element of our editorial plan for subsequent editions is to provide detailed subject access to these resources.

The hundreds of category terms in this index are visible proof of the diversity of interest and activity on the net. It should be recalled, too, that although the items listed in these categories are digital entities (lists, journals, computer archives), each of them represents the result of ardent and mostly uncompensated human endeavor.

CONNECTING TO THE RESOURCES IN THIS DIRECTORY

For many of the resources listed in this book you will need a full Internet account, one that allows not only e-mail traffic to and from your workstation, but also file transfer capabilities (ftp), login to remote computers (telnet), and access to gopher and WAIS servers.

While use of ON INTERNET assumes a basic knowledge of how to accomplish these Internet communications functions (and there is a growing list of books addressing these tasks — see the Bibliography at the end of this introduction), some brief explanation here of the basic functions may serve as a handy guide to finding one's way around the Internet.

E-mail-Based Subscription Requests

To subscribe to a discussion list or electronic journal or newsletter, you must send an e-mail message requesting to be added to the subscribership of the list or journal. In some cases, noted in the entries in this directory, you will address your request to a human listowner or editorial contact. In other cases, you will be sending your message directly to a computer. Your message to the computer must be worded in the correct fashion or it will not be interpreted correctly. If your subscription request has been recieved properly, you may (sometimes) receive a simple computer-generated confirmation of this.

As an example, let us look at requesting a subscription to the ejournal Psycoloquy, whose entry in this directory contains a nicely worded description of the proper way to subscribe.

> To subscribe to Psycoloquy send an e-mail message to: listserv@pucc.bitnet or listserv@pucc.princeton.edu containing the following one-line message (without a message header or topic, i.e., leave "Subject" line blank): sub psyc Firstname Lastname (substituting your first and last name, of course). (These instructions DO work, so please follow them faithfully! If for some reason you still do not succeed, send e-mail to psyc@pucc.bitnet or psyc@pucc.princeton.edu and we will subscribe you by hand.)

Thus, at your system prompt (usually %, :, >, or $), to engage the e-mail function, type the word mail followed by a space and then the listserv address noted in the instructions above (from the Bitnet network use the Bitnet address, from the Internet use the address ending in edu). Then hit return or enter:

```
system% mail listserv@pucc.princeton.edu [enter]
```

The Subject line of your e-mail message appears. This is overlooked by the listserv computer so it should contain no data. In the body of the e-mail type the subscribe command message and end your e-mail.

```
sub psyc John Public [enter]
```

If everything has gone well, you should be a subscriber. A look at the introductory notes to Section 7 of this book covering Usenet Newsgroups offers subscription procedures specific to those lists.

Telnet

The telnet function allows Internet users from their own workstations to login to a remote computer and browse its files as if that workstation were actually connected via a local-area network to that remote computer host. Many library online public access catalogs and other online databases are telnet accessible. If you have only e-mail capabilities (if you access the Internet, for example, through a bulletin board system, a commercial communications service like America Online, Prodigy, or CompuServe, among others), you may not have the telnet option available to you. If you do, however, the function is essentially quite simple in operation. At your system prompt (usually %, :, >, or $), type the word telnet followed by a space and the resource Internet host address. For instance, a login to NASA's Spacelink database would be initiated by the following command:

```
system% telnet spacelink.msfc.nasa.gov [enter]
```

This will bring you into the Spacelink system where you will be asked a number of questions requiring a response, then you will enter the database. Most telnet-accessible databases can be connected to following this simple procedure. Check the listings in this directory for more specific logon procedures and examples.

Gopher

Gopher is an Internet searching utility that offers a helpful and friendly interface to a vast array of different types of information, from library catalogs to campus information services to government databases. It is built on the standard client-server relationship where a client program communicates to a similar server program to effect a connection. Within the Gopher system, information files are set up in hierarchical menu-like fashion. And access to one Gopher server gives you access to all (or nearly all) the Gopher servers worldwide.

If you have a local Gopher client available to you through the frontend system you have your Internet account on, you can access what has become known as Gopherspace at your system prompt by simply entering gopher followed by a return. If, like many users, however, you don't have a local client, you will use the Telnet feature to reach public-access gopher addresses. At your system prompt, then, you would type telnet followed by a space and the address of the remote Gopher server. Greeting you will be a menu-system in which you use the arrow keys to highlight and the return key to select different options.

File Transfer Protocol—FTP

The sometimes confusing but usually quite rewarding FTP function allows one to logon to to a remote computer host and retrieve files from that host, downloading them to one's own workstation. There are hundreds of FTP sites throughout the world containing thousands of free software programs, electronic texts, image and data files of all types, and other information that can be retrieved and brought to your own computer. There are many pitfalls to FTPing that can quickly befuddle an Internet beginner, so it is best to read about the function in one of the many good books currently available (see Bibliography below).

In brief, however, you initiate an FTP session at your system prompt, by typing ftp followed by a space and the name of the host maintaining the files you need. When you receive a login prompt, type anonymous. When a password is requested, convention has it that you type in your e-mail address. Once connected, you should then be presented with an FTP prompt (ftp>). If you wish to review the FTP commands, type help at this prompt and you will be shown a list. An ls command (list) will list the files and the subdirectories in the current directory. Using the cd command at this point allows you to change directories (cd) to the one that you are seeking. Once you have located the desired file in that directory, you may initiate a retrieval procedure by typing get followed by a space and the filename exactly as written in the directory. The binary command alters the file transfer mode from standard text or ascii to binary; this is necessary for successful transfer of certain types of files. Similarly, the ascii command alters the transfer mode to straight ascii text. Once the transmission has been effected, you may type quit or bye at the FTP prompt to close out your session.

A NOTE ABOUT DATA GATHERING FOR ON INTERNET 1994

After a lengthy questionnaire had been finalized in May 1993, we e-mailed it over the course of three months to approximately 3,500 Internet, Bitnet, and Mailbase addresses, and began receiving their responses almost immediately. The entries in ON INTERNET reflect in many cases the words of the respondents. Additional information for entries was gathered from numerous sources, provided by a great many individuals, some of whom are mentioned in the acknowledgments below. Daily scouring of the net, multiple subscriptions to lists and ejournals, printed resources, and word of mouth contributed to increasing our universe of records. Data gathering ceased November 3rd.

The descriptions for most of the resources in this book came from the owners and managers of those resources themselves. While necessary editing has trimmed and somewhat homogenized these distinctive voices, we trust that our editorial voice will not be confused with theirs.

As with any printed directory covering a field that is changing and expanding at an incredible rate, this book will have omissions. Happily, ON INTERNET is not so much a source as a finger pointing to sources — sources which are in a constant state of being updated, revised, and enhanced. It is a directory; that is, it directs the reader to something, it is not the thing itself. On the other hand, as someone has wisely said, no one first learns about the Internet by being online. We are still dependent to a great extent on printed explanations, references, sources — witness the ever increasing number of books about the net from every major technology publisher. So, clearly there is a need for information that can sit on your desk. ON INTERNET will annually address that need as a tool for all Internet users, whether you are "just looking" or whether you need the net to get you through the day.

We herewith invite your comments and suggestions to help us in updating for next year's edition. Send any new information, queries, requests for inclusion, and other communication to the editor at meckler@jvnc.net. We are beginning work on ON INTERNET 95 already.

A SHORT NOTE ABOUT THE TITLE OF THIS BOOK

When we originally proposed this book, it carried the title ON INTERNET 1993, since we hoped it would appear in mid-year 1993. Vain hope. The immensity of the goal we had set ourselves — to publish a more comprehensive directory to a wider range of Internet resources than had yet been published — was more formidable a challange than any of the staff had anticipated. Data collection and input began in May and continued to October, resulting in a directory carrying nearly 6,000 individual entries. Our apologies to all who (rightly) expected the book earlier. We have a sober admiration for all who attempt to catalog and quantify the ocean of information that is the Internet.

—Tony Abbott
meckler@jvnc.net

BIBLIOGRAPHY

Here follows a brief and selective list of books dealing with the Internet. The user of this directory is urged to read one or more of these books in order to get a solid grounding in Internet concepts.

Dern, Daniel P. *The Internet Guide for New Users*. New York, NY: McGraw-Hill, Inc., 1993, 570pp.

Gibbs, Mark and Richard Smith. *Navigating the Internet*. Carmel, IN: SAMS Publishing, 1993, 500pp.

Gilster, Paul. *The Internet Navigator*. New York, NY: John Wiley & Sons, Inc., 470pp.

Engle, Mary E. Marilyn Lutz, Williams W. Jones, Jr., and Genevieve Engel. *Internet Connections: A Librarian's Guide to Dial-Up Access and Use*. Chicago, IL: American Library Association (Library and Information Technology Association), 1993, 166pp.

Internet World: The Magazine for Internet Users, monthly. Westport, CT: Mecklermedia, 1993- .

Krol, Ed. *The Whole Internet User's Guide & Catalog*. Sebastopol, CA: O'Reilly & Associates, Inc., 1992, 376pp.

Lane, Elizabeth and Craig Summerhill. *Internet Primer for Information Professionals*. Westport, CT: Mecklermedia, 1993, 182pp.

LaQuey, Tracy with Jeanne C. Ryer. *The Internet Companion*. Reading, MA: Addison-Wesley Publishing Company, 1993, 196pp.

McClure, Charles R., ed. *Libraries and the Internet/NREN*. Westport, CT: Mecklermedia, 1994, 300pp.

Newby, Gregory. *Directory of Directories on the Internet*. Westport, CT: Mecklermedia, 1993, 186pp.

Notess, Greg R. *Internet Access Providers: An International Resource Directory*. Westport, CT: Mecklermedia, 1994, 325pp.

Tennant, Roy, John Ober, and Anne G. Lipow. *Crossing the Internet Threshold: An Instructional Handbook*. San Carlos, CA: Library Solutions Press, 1993, 134pp.

Veljkov, Mark and George Hartnell. *Pocket Guides to the Internet (Volume 1: Telneting; Volume 2: Transferring Files with File Transfer Protocol; Volume 3: Using and Navigating Usenet; Volume 4: The Internet E-Mail System; Volume 5: Basic Internet Utilities; Volume 6: Terminal Connections)*. Westport, CT: Mecklermedia, 1993, 64+pp. each.

Acknowledgments

T he editor would like to acknowledge the seminal participation of a great many people in the conception, creation, and editing of this first annual directory. First and foremost are the members of the editorial advisory board whose suggestions and input at the initial stages of work on the book, and whose assistance in gathering data and in providing hard information, directions, and lists of Internet addresses all the way through the project, made this endeavor both easier and more challenging, as the staff at Meckler hustled to keep up with the load of incoming data. A special nod of thanks in this regard goes to Richard Gartner and to Gord Nickerson for their lists and lists and more lists. Next, the in-house staff, beginning with Johanna Selles-Roney, and continuing with Kelly Jensen and Andrew Shriver, deserves commendation for their tireless editorial contribution from the book's initial stages all the way through to its completion.

Individually, a number of people went further than they had to to support our endeavor and to provide us information: Amanda Barrett for providing numerous lists of women's studies and related discussion groups and ejournals; Daniel P. Dern for his fine preface and nod of approval; Thomas Grundner of National Public Telecomputing Corporation for a starter list of Freenets and associated information systems; Judy Hallman for providing her list of campus-wide information systems; Michael Hart for assistance with data about Project Gutenberg and for moral support; Richard Jensen for his aid in providing data on the growing inventory of H-based history discussion lists; Brewster Kahle and Dia Cheney of WAIS, Inc., for their permission and assistance in allowing use of their directory of WAIS databases; David Lawrence of Uunet for his contributions to and their permission to use the annotated list of Usenet newsgroups; Chris Lynch of Clari-Net for allowing us to print their annotated list of ClariNet newsgroups; Dennis Nicholson of BUBL for pointing to UK sources of information; Allison Pihl of GES/JvNCnet for assistance in helping to organize the electronic distribution of the questionnaire; Gene Spafford for his amusingly annotated lists of Usenet Newsgroups; and Robert Zakon for access to his database of choice Internet items.

Finally, a hearty thanks must go to all the people who completed the longish questionnaire which is the backbone of this directory. Without their participation, support, and enthusiasm for our efforts, this book would not have have seen the light of day.

Section 1. Discussion Lists and Special Interest Mailing Lists

78-L
Description: 78-L is a forum for the discussion of the pre-LP record era.
Subjects covered: music
List moderated: No.
Editorial contact: Doug Elliot
Internet: de3@cornellc.cit.cornell.edu
How to access: Send subscribe message to listserv@cornell.edu
How to unsubscribe: Send unsubscribe message to listserv@cornell.edu

9NOV-89-L
Description: 9NOV-89-L is a forum for discussing German re-unification.
Subjects covered: political science; history; Germany
List moderated: No.
Editorial contact: Axel Mahler
Internet: axel@avalanche.cs.tu-berlin.de
How to access: Send subscribe message to listserv@utdallas or listserv%utdallas.bitnet@vm1.nodak.edu
How to unsubscribe: Send unsubscribe message to listserv@utdallas or listserv%utdallas.bitnet@vm1.nodak.edu
Archives: Archives are developed weekly; apply to listowner for details.

AAUA-L
Description: AAUA-L is a forum on university administration.
Subjects covered: colleges and universities
Host: American Association of University Administrators
List moderated: No.
Editorial contact: Jerry Neuner
Bitnet: neuner@canisius
How to access: Send subscribe message to listserv@ubvm or listserv@ubvm.cc.buffalo.edu
How to unsubscribe: Send unsubscribe message to listserv@ubvm or listserv@ubvm.cc.buffalo.edu
Archives: Archives are developed monthly; apply to listowner for details.

AAVLD-L
Description: AAVLD-L is a forum about veterinary diagnostics.
Subjects covered: veterinary science
Host: AAVLD
List moderated: No.
Editorial contact: James T. Case, DVM, Ph.D.

Bitnet: jcase@ucdcvdls
How to access: Send subscribe message to listserv@ucdcvdls
How to unsubscribe: Send unsubscribe message to listserv@ucdcvdls
Archives: Archives are developed monthly; apply to listowner for details.

ABC@CWI.NL
Description: ABC@CWI.NL is a forum on the ABC programming language and its implementations.
Subjects covered: computer science
List moderated: No.
Editorial contact: Steven Pemberton
Internet: abc-list-request@cwi.nl
How to access: Contact the Editor
How to unsubscribe: Contact the Editor
Archives: Yes; Send anonymous FTP to mcsun.eu.net and cd programming/languages/abc/abc.intro

ACADEMIC-INDUSTRY-RELATIONS@MAILBASE.AC.UK
Description: ACADEMIC-INDUSTRY-RELATIONS is a mailbase discussion group on the topic of academic-industry re-lations.
Subjects covered: human resources
List moderated: No.
Internet: academic-industry-relations-request@mailbase.ac.uk
How to access: Send subscribe message to mailbase@mailbase.ac.uk in the following format: join academic-industry-relations Yourfirstname Yourlastname
Archives: Archives are developed monthly; apply to listowner for details.

ACADV@NDSUVM1
Description: ACADV@NDSUVM1 offers a forum for academic advisory professionals.
Subjects covered: education
List moderated: Yes.
Editorial contact: Dr. Harold L. Caldwell
Internet: 00hlcaldwell%bsuvax1.bitnet@vm1.nodak.edu
Bitnet: 00hlcaldwell%bsuvax1
How to access: Send subscribe message to listserv@ndsuvm1 or listserv@vm1.nodak.edu
How to unsubscribe: Send unsubscribe message to listserv@ndsuvm1 or listserv@vm1.nodak.edu

Archives: Yes; Private

ACES-L (ATLANTIC CONGRESS OF ENGINEERING STUDENTS FORUM)

Description: ACES-L provides a forum for all Atlantic Canadian engineeering students to discuss current topics relating for the most part to the field of engineering, engineering education, the engineering image and engineering activities/events in Atlantic Canada. ACES is the Atlantic Region of the Canadian Federation of Engineering Students. All students in accredited engineering institutions are members of the Canadian Federation of Students (CFES). The CFES provides a voice for all engineering students. Through the use of ACES-L, all students can easily participate in the goings-on of the Federation, and enables them to find out what the CFES National Executive and Atlantic Regional Representatives are doing. It also allows students to prepare for the annual atlantic region meeting and the annual national meeting of the Federation: The Congress of Canadian Engineering Students - Conference.
Subjects covered: engineering; education; colleges and universities
Net address for operations: LISTSERV@UNB.CA
Net address for questions or submissions: ACES-L@UNB.CA
Established: January 1993
Subscribers: 20
Sponsor: University of New Brunswick Fredericton, New Brunswick, Canada.
Host: Same as above
List moderated: List is unmoderated, but is monitored by the Canadian Federation of Engineering Student's Commissioner of Electronic Communication.
Editorial contact: Troy Morehouse, CFES Commissioner of Electronic Communication Room H-223, Sir Edmund Head Hall, University of New Brunswick, Fredericton, New Brunswick, Canada.
Tel: (506) 453-3534
Fax: (506) 453-4569
Internet: cfes@jupiter.sun.csd.unb.ca
Bitnet: cfes@unb.ca
How to access: Send the following one line e-mail message to LISTSERV@UNB.CA SUB ACES-L your-name-and/or-affilliation
Access policy: Anybody who is interested in engineering and engineering education are invited to participate (being an engineering student is not a pre-requisite).
How to unsubscribe: Send e-mail message to LISTSERV@UNB.CA
How to submit: Send any submissions (postings) to ACES-L@UNB.CA
Submission policy: Postings of a slanderous, sexist, racist, or homophobic nature will not be tolerated on ACES-L. Doing so will result in immediate removal from subscription.
Archives: None currently provided, but may be in the future.
Related files: CFES and ACES-L have related documentation (i.e. minutes, policy manuals, bylaws, logos, addresses, etc) available via anonymous FTP at jupiter.sun.csd.unb.ca, and can be found in the /pub/cfes directory. An incoming directory is provided for site submissions.

ACM-L

Description: ACM-L is a discussion list of the Association for Computing Machinery.

Subjects covered: computer science
Host: Association for Computing Machinery
List moderated: No.
Editorial contact: Duane Weaver
Internet: weaver@ohstvma.acs.ohio-state.edu
Bitnet: weaver@ohstvma
How to access: Send subscribe message to listserv@ohstvma or listserv@ohstvma.acs.ohio-state.edu
How to unsubscribe: Send unsubscribe message to listserv@ohstvma or listserv@ohstvma.acs.ohio-state.edu

ACQNET@CORNELLC

Description: ACQNET is a discussion list for acquistion librarians.
Subjects covered: library and information science
List moderated: No.
Editorial contact: Christian Boissonnas
Bitnet: cri@cornellc
How to access: Contact the Editor
How to unsubscribe: Contact the Editor

ACRLNY-L

Description: Acrlny-L is a list posting library events.
Subjects covered: library and information science
List moderated: No.
How to access: Send subscribe message to listserv@nyuacf
How to unsubscribe: Send unsubscribe message to listserv@nyuacf

ACSOFT-L

Description: Acsoft-L is a discussion forum covering all aspects of academic software development.
Subjects covered: computer science; computer hardware and software; colleges and universities
List moderated: No.
Editorial contact: Timothy Bergeron
Bitnet: c09615tb@wuvmd
How to access: Send subscribe message to listserv@wuvmd or listserv@wuvmd.wustl.edu
How to unsubscribe: Send unsubscribe message to listserv@wuvmd or listserv@wuvmd.wustl.edu

ACT-UP@WORLD.STD.COM

Description: ACT-UP@WORLD.STD.COM is a forum for discussion of AIDS activism.
Subjects covered: political science; AIDS/HIV studies; activism
List moderated: No.
How to access: Send subscribe message to ACT-UP-REQUEST@WORLD.STD.COM
How to unsubscribe: Send unsubscribe message to ACT-UP-REQUEST@WORLD.STD.COM

ACTIV-L

Description: ACTIV-L provides news, information, and resources of interest to activists and anyone interested in promoting peace; economic, legal, and social justice and equality; a clean environment and safe workplace; democratic control over domestic and foreign policy, and other issues of concern to the

progressive community. Also included are daily forwards of articles from the IGC Networks PeaceNet, EcoNet, and LaborNet (with full permission); selected articles from The Nation; Z magazine; New Liberation News Service (NLNS) Multinational Monitor (MM); Lies of Our Times (LOOT); Left Business Observer (LBO); Covert Action Information Bulletin (CAIB); Mother Jones (MJ); etc. Among other features are auto-posts of resource file listings of progressive/independent newspapers; audio-cassettes and videos; organizing resources; speakers and Speakers Bureaus; Books; Catalogs; Socially-responsible investing, etc., also of telephone/fax numbers and addresses for Congress, White House, media, etc. The Popular Quote of the Day ("Today's Quote...") provides inspiration, agitation, and/or humor.
Subjects covered: human rights; environmental studies; third world studies; political activism
Net address for operations: LISTSERV@MIZZOU1.BITNET
Net address for questions or submissions: activ-l@mizzou1.bitnet
Established: Spring 1990
Subscribers: 1,000 +. Some 700 "direct" subscribers, including many "nodes" which forward in turn to other mailing lists reaching hundreds more.
List moderated: Yes.
Moderation procedure: Email submissions to "activ-l@mizzou1.bitnet"
Editorial contact: Rich Winkel
Route 1 Box 193, Harrisburg, MO USA 65256
Tel: (314) 882-4356
Internet: rich@pencil.cs.missouri.edu; mathrich@mizzou1.missouri.edu
Bitnet: mathrich@mizzou1.bitnet
Review: "Misc.activism.progressive (MAP) is the most informative, progressive, moderated newgroup on InterNet.'-- Hank Roth, Facilitator of pnews conferences, PeaceNet, FidoNet, & InterNet. <pnews@igc.apc.org>; <odin@world.std.com>
How to access: Email to "activ-l@mizzou1.bitnet"
Archives: GESend 1-line email message:
GET ACTIV-L ARCHIVE ACTIV-L
to LISTSERV address given above for a listing of the "library" and instructions for using the general GET command for retrieving other files/articles. Send 1-line email message:
GET AMLDBASE DOC ACTIV-L to the same address for a tutorial on using the more comprehensive database searches.
T ACTIV-L ARCHIVE ACTIV-L
Related files: Available ftp from: pencil.cs.missouri.edu:/usr/users/ftp/pub/map/ (log into pencil.cs.missouri.edu as "anonymous" and give name as password; then type "cd LOOKEE__HERE/map" and then "dir" for the directory listing)
Additional information: Additional editor: Harel Barzilai, 112 Sapsucker Woods Road, Ithaca NY 14850; tel 607-257-7057; Internet: harelb@math.cornell.edu

ACTIVIST@ GUVM

Description: ACTIVIST@ GUVM is a forum on personal activism.
Subjects covered: activism; psychology
List moderated: No.
How to access: Send subscribe message to listserv@guvm
How to unsubscribe: Send unsubscribe message to listserv@guvm

ACTNOW-L (COLLEGE AND ORGANIZATIONAL ACTIVISM LIST)

Description: ACTNOW-L features free-form discussion on a variety of topics (generally) dealing with activism.
Subjects covered: political activism
Net address for operations: listserv@brownvm.brown.edu
Net address for questions or submissions: actnow-l@brownvm.brown.edu
Established: January 31, 1991
Host: Brown University, Providence RI 02912 USA
List moderated: Yes, informally.
Moderation procedure: List owner checks list to keep topics inline with list goals. Otherwise participants can discuss freely.
Editorial contact: David B. O'Donnell
15 Everett Ave, Providence, RI USA 02906-3321
tel + 1 401 453 3886
Tel: (401) 453-3886
Internet: atropos@netlab.cis.brown.edu
Bitnet: el406006@brownvm.brown.edu
How to access: Send e-mail article to 'ACTNOW-L@brownvm.brown.edu'
How to unsubscribe: Send 'UNSUB ACTNOW-L' to listserv@brownvm.brown.edu
Archives: List is archived automatically by listserv on a monthly basis. Send 'INDEX ACTNOW-L' in e-mail to listserv@brownvm.brown.edu to receive a copy of available archive names.
Related files: Files are available to subscribers through LISTERV@KENTVM

ADA-SW@WSMR-SIMTEL20.ARMY.MIL

Description: ADA-SW is a list covering software in the Ada Repository on SIMTEL20.
Subjects covered: computer science
List moderated: No.
How to access: Send subscribe message to ADA-SW-REQUEST@WSMR-SIMTEL20.ARMY.MIL
How to unsubscribe: Send unsubscribe message to ADA-SW-REQUEST@WSMR-SIMTEL20.ARMY.MIL
Archives: Yes; Send anonymous FTP to WSMR-SIMTEL20.ARMY.MIL

ADAPT-L@AUVM

Description: ADAPT-L is a list covering topics related to library adaptive technology.
Subjects covered: disabilities; library and information science
Net address for questions or submissions: LISTSERV@AUVM
How to access: Send subscribe message to LISTSERV@AUVM
How to unsubscribe: Send unsubscribe message to LISTSERV@AUVM

ADDICT-L

Description: ADDICT-L includes discussion around all areas of addictive behavior. Emphasis on behavioral addictions (e.g., gambling, sex, eating). Academic and research oriented discussion. Although recovery is not the main theme, recovering individuals are welcome to add opinions and thought to discussions.

Not used as support group, but rather supporting research and academia in addictionology.

Subjects covered: addiction studies; substance abuse
Net address for operations: LISTSERV@KENTVM
Established: January 1992
Sponsor: Kent State University-120 Library, Kent, Ohio 44242
Host: Kent State University-120 Library, Kent, Ohio 44242
List moderated: No.
Technical contact: David Delmonico
310 White Hall, Kent, Ohio 44242
Tel: (216) 672-2662
Fax: (216) 672-3407
Internet: Ddelmoni@kentvm.kent.edu
Bitnet: Ddelmoni@kentvm
How to access: Send message to LISTSERV@KENTVM with no subject. Include the words ''SUB ADDICT-L <First name> <Last name>'' as the first and only line of text in the body of the message.
Access policy: Open List - Not to be used as a support/therapy type group, although recovering individuals are welcome to subscribe.
How to unsubscribe: Send message to LISTSERV@KENTVM with no subject. Include the words ''UNSUB ADDICT-L'' as the first and only line of text in the body of the message.
How to submit: File section available - send all submissions to listowner (ddelmoni@kentvm) which will be reviewed and posted as appropriate.
Submission policy: Files should be related to the area of addiction and be of interest to researchers and other subscribers interested in the theory, cause, or related area of addictionology.
Archives: Archives are available of past messages since conception of ADDICT-L.
Related files: Files are available to subscribers through LISTERV@KENTVM

ADLTED-L

Description: The ADLTED-L list contains a discussion of adult education topics pertinent to Canada. Examples of the discussion in the past year include: public policy and adult education, the federal funding of adult education in Canada, resources in adult education, and reports of the implementation of national policies concerning adult education.
Subjects covered: adult education; education; policy planning and analysis
Net address for operations: LISTSERV@MAX.UREGINA.CA
Net address for questions or submissions: ADLTED-L@MAX.UREGINA.CA
Established: Spring 1991
Subscribers: 106
Sponsor: Department of Adult Education, The Ontario Institute for Studies in Education, 225 Bloor Street West, Toronto, Ontario, Canada M5S 1V6.
Host: University of Regina, Regina, Saskatchewan, Canada.
List moderated: The discussion on the list is not moderated, but the list is maintained as a private list for adult educators. Membership is open to anyone in Canada with an interest in adult education. Requests for membership from outside of Canada are asked to supply information about their interest or involvement in adult education.
Moderation procedure: Send message to Listserv. If additional information is required a message from one of the list owners will be sent.
Editorial contact: Lynn Davie

Department of Adult Education, The Ontario Institute for Studies in Education, 225 Bloor Street West, Toronto, Ontario, Canada M5S 1V6.
Tel: (416) 923-6641, ext. 2355
Internet: LDAVIE@OISE.ON.CA
Bitnet: LDAVIE@UTOROISE
How to access: Send the message Subscribe Your Full Name (Example: Subscribe Lynn Davie) to:
LISTSERV@MAX.UREGINA.CA
Access policy: Must be an adult educator or have a substantial interest in issues concerning adult education.
How to unsubscribe: Send the message Leave to:
LISTSERV@MAX.UREGINA.CA
Submission policy: Any member of the list may send messages on any pertinent topic.
Archives: Archives of past discussions are available from the listserv for any member.
Additional information: Additional editors: Alan Thomas,Department of Adult Education, The Ontario Institute for Studies in Education, 252 Bloor Street West Toronto, Ontario, Canada M5S 1V6; tel (416) 923-6641; ATHOMAS@OISE.ON.CA; ATHOMAS@UTOROISE; Larry Hein, University of Regina, Regina, Sasketchewan, Canada; LIHEIN@MAX.UREGINA.CA; LIHEIN@UREGINA1

ADQ@UQUEBEC

Description: ADQ@UQUEBEC is a forum for the Association des Demographes du Quebec.
Subjects covered: demography
Host: Association des Demographes du Quebec
List moderated: Yes.
Editorial contact: Pierre J. Hamel
Internet: hamel@inrs-urb.uquebec.ca
Bitnet: hamel@uquebec
Archives: Yes; Apply to listowner for details.

ADV-ELI

Description: ADV-ELI is a discussion group related to the latest advances in electrical engineering.
Subjects covered: electronics; computer hardware and software; telecommunications; electrical engineering
Net address for operations: ADV-ELI@UTFSM.BITNET or ADV-ELI@LOA.DISCA.UTFSM.CL
Net address for questions or submissions: LISTSERV@UTFSM.BITNET or LISTSERV@LOA.DISCA.UTFSM.CL
Established: January 1993
Sponsor: Federico Santa Maria University, Valparaiso, Chile.
Editorial contact: Francisco J. Fernandez M. Murphy 321 Apt 107A, Ed. Costa Azul, Vina del Mar, Chile.
Tel: +56 32 662729
Fax: +56 32 660471
Internet: FFERNAND@LOA.DISCA.UTFSM.CL
Bitnet: FFERNAND@UTFSM.CL
How to access: Send mail to LISTSERV@LOA.DISCA.UTFSM.CL with a SUB ADV-ELI <full name> in the body of the letter.
Access policy: Open to all the people interested in the topic.
How to unsubscribe: Send a SIGNOFF ADV-ELI to the listserv.
How to submit: Automatic submission.
Submission policy: All interested people.

Related files: There are also two more lists managed by me on the same listserv. They are ADV-ELO and ADV-INFO, related to the latest advances on electric engineering and computing, respectively. To subscribe, participate, etc., to the lists you have to use the same instructions as outlined above.

ADV-ELO

Description: Adv-Elo is a distribution list posting the latest advances in electronic engineering and topical discussions and questions on developments in electronics and related fields.
Subjects covered: electronics; computer hardware and software; telecommunications; electrical engineering
Net address for operations: ADV-ELO@UTFSM.BITNET or ADV-ELO@LOA.DISCA.UTFSM.CL
Net address for questions or submissions: LISTSERV@UTFSM.BITNET or LISTSERV@LOA.DISCA.UTFSM.CL
Established: January 1993
Subscribers: 93
Sponsor: Federico Santa Maria University, Valparaiso, Chile.
List moderated: No.
Editorial contact: Francisco J. Fernandez M.
Murphy 321 Apt 107A, Ed. Costa Azul, Vina del Mar, Chile.
Tel: +56 32 662729
Fax: +56 32 660471
Internet: FFERNAND@LOA.DISCA.UTFSM.CL
Bitnet: FFERNAND@UTFSM.CL
How to access: Send mail to LISTSERV@LOA.DISCA.UTFSM.CL with a SUB ADV-ELO <full name> in the body of the letter.
Access policy: Open to all the people interested in the topic.
How to unsubscribe: Send a SIGNOFF ADV-ELO to the listserv.
How to submit: Automatic submission.
Submission policy: All interested people.
Archives: A list logbook will be held on the listserv files. Send a INDEX ADV-ELO to listserv to see the log files list. Send a FET ADV-ELO <Filename> <Filetype> to retrieve the file.
Related files: There are also two more lists managed by me on the same listserv. They are ADV-ELI and ADV-INFO, related to the latest advances on electric engineering and computing, respectively. To subscribe, participate, etc., to the lists you have to use the same instructions as outlined above.

ADV-INFO

Description: ADV-INFO is an electronic discussion list related to the latest advances in computing.
Subjects covered: electrical engineering; computer hardware and software
Net address for operations: ADV-INFO@UTFSM.BITNET or ADV-INFO@LOA.DISCA.UTFSM.CL
Net address for questions or submissions: LISTSERV@UTFSM.BITNET or LISTSERV@LOA.DISCA.UTFSM.CL
Established: January 1993
Sponsor: Federico Santa Maria University, Valparaiso, Chile.
List moderated: No.
Editorial contact: Francisco J. Fernandez M.
Murphy 321 Apt 107A, Ed. Costa Azul, Vina del Mar, Chile.
Tel: +56 32 662729
Fax: +56 32 660471
Internet: FFERNAND@LOA.DISCA.UTFSM.CL

Bitnet: FFERNAND@UTFSM.CL
How to access: Send mail to LISTSERV@LOA.DISCA.UTFSM.CL with a SUB ADV-INFO <full name> in the body of the letter.
How to unsubscribe: Send a SIGNOFF ADV-INFO to the listserv.
How to submit: Automatic submission.
Submission policy: All interested people.
Related files: There are also two more lists managed by me on the same listserv. They are ADV-ELI and ADV-ELO, related to the latest advances on electric engineering and computing, respectively. To subscribe, participate, etc., to the lists you have to use the same instructions as outlined above.

ADVANC-L

Description: Advanc-L covers the GEAC Advance Library System.
Subjects covered: library and information science
List moderated: No.
Editorial contact: Daniel Lester
Internet: alileste@idbsu.idbsu.edu
Bitnet: alileste@idbsu
How to access: Send subscribe message to listserv@idbsu or listserv@idbsu.idbsu.edu
How to unsubscribe: Send unsubscribe message to listserv@idbsu or listserv@idbsu.idbsu.edu
Archives: Archives are developed monthly; apply to listowner for details.

ADVISE-L

Description: Advise-L is a discussion forum for professional advisors and counselors.
Subjects covered: colleges and universities
List moderated: No.
Editorial contact: Taras Pryjma
Bitnet: taras@utorgpu
How to access: Send subscribe message to listserv@uga
How to unsubscribe: Send unsubscribe message to listserv@uga
Archives: Archives are developed monthly; apply to listowner for details.

AEDNET DISCUSSION LIST

Description: The Adult Education Network (AEDNET) is an international electronic network. The network is operated through a listserv that enables subscribers to share information. Researchers, practitioners, and graduate students in adult and continuing education are provided with opportunities to discuss important topics and concerns in an online environment. AEDNET is operated by the Adult Education Program of the Programs for Higher Education of the Abraham S. Fischler Center for the Advancement of Education at Nova University located in Fort Lauderdale, Florida. AEDNET activities include network-wide discussions and information exchanges on topics and queries, conferences and special events, of interest to adult and continuing educators. Also, a refereed electronic journal, New Horizons in Adult Education, is distributed through AEDNET.
Subjects covered: adult education; education; distance education
Net address for operations: listserv@alpha.acast.nova.edu

How to access: Send the message subscribe aednet Your__ Name to listserv@alpha.acast.nova.edu The subject line doesn't matter. There should be no other text in the message (e.g., your signature block). Give the listserv a couple of minutes to respond. You should receive a return mail message welcoming you to the AEDNET subscription list.

How to unsubscribe: You can unsubscribe to the AEDNET by sending a message to: listserv@alpha.acast.nova.edu In the body of the message please type: unsubscribe aednet your__name where your__name is the name you used originally to subscribe. For example, I would type: unsubscribe aednet Sue Spahn. Give the listserv a few minutes to respond. You should receive a message notifying you that you have successfully unsubscribed.

How to submit: Send all messages to: aednet@alpha.acast.nova.edu not to listserv. The subject line should indicate what your message is about. The body of your message can be anything you like, just as in a regular email message. By default, you will not get a copy of your message sent back to you (although you can change this). However, you can be sure your message was received if others reply.

Related files: You may want to receive the latest email INDEX or ISSUE of the New Horizons In Adult Education journal, the AEDNET Newsletter, or the latest jobs listing from the Chronicle of Higher Education. Each of these items can be obtained by mailing a request to the listserv and placing your request in the body of the mail message.

AELFLOW@TECHNION

Description: AELFLOW@TECHNION is a forum on aerospace engineering fluids.
Subjects covered: engineering
List moderated: No.
Editorial contact: Dr. Yakov Cohen
Bitnet: aer8601@technion
How to access: Send subscribe message to listserv@technion or listserv@technion.technion.ac.il
How to unsubscribe: Send unsubscribe message to listserv@technion or listserv@technion.technion.ac.il
Archives: Archives are developed yearly; apply to listowner for details.

AERONAUTICS@RASCAL.ICS.UTEXAS.EDU

Description: AERONAUTICS@RASCAL.ICS.UTEXAS.EDU covers aspects of aviation.
Subjects covered: engineering; aeronautics; aviation
List moderated: Yes.
How to access: Send subscribe message to AERONAUTICS-REQUEST@RASCAL.ICS.UTEXAS.EDU
How to unsubscribe: Send unsubscribe message to AERO-NAUTICS-REQUEST@RASCAL.ICS.UTEXAS.EDU

AESRG-L

Description: AESRG-L is a list of the Applied Expert Systems Research Group.
Subjects covered: artificial intelligence; computer science
List moderated: No.
Editorial contact: Tim Patrick
Bitnet: cs201@mizzou1l
How to access: Send subscribe message to listserv@mizzou1
How to unsubscribe: Send unsubscribe message to listserv@mizzou1

Archives: Archives are developed yearly; apply to listowner for details.

AFAM-L

Description: AFAM is a list covering African-American research.
Subjects covered: African-American studies; history
Net address for operations: LISTSERV@UMCVMB
Net address for questions or submissions: AFAM-L@UMCVMB
How to access: Send message to listserv: SUBSCRIBE <listname> <your name>

AFAS-L

Description: AFAS-L is a roundtable discussion among librarians and other interested people on topics relating to African American Studies and Librarianship. Topics can include peripheral issues such as race relations and multicultural diversity. AFAS-L uses LISTSERV software at Kent State University. It is owned and moderated by members of the ACRL Afro-American Librarians' Section.
Subjects covered: African-American studies; race relations; library and information science
Net address for operations: listserv@kentvm or listserv@kentvm.kent.edu
Net address for questions or submissions: afas-l@kentvm or afas-l@kentvm.kent.edu
Established: May 1, 1992
Subscribers: 265
Sponsor: ACRL Afro-American Studies, Librarian Section, Kent State University, Kent, Ohio 44242.
Host: Kent State University, Kent, OH 44242.
List moderated: Yes.
Moderation procedure: Messages posted to AFAS-L are first sent to moderator for review before forwarding to list.
Editorial contact: Gladys Smiley Bell
Kent State University, Kent State University Libraries and Media Services, Room 161, Library Building, Kent, OH 44242.
Tel: (216) 672-3045
Fax: (216) 672-2265
Internet: gbell@kentvm.kent.edu
Bitnet: gbell@kentvm
How to access: SEND COMMANDS TO LISTSERV, NOT TO AFAS-L. Send commands as the text of an e-mail message. Do not include a subject line and do not add any other information except for the command in the text of the e-mail message.
Access policy: The purpose of AFAS-L is to facilitate discussion of African American Studies and Librarianship. Messages on this list should relate directly to this issue. Topics can include related issues such as the impact of electronic dissemination of information on minorities. The AFAS-L moderators reserve the right to reject any posting that we decide is inappropriate for AFAS-L. When the moderators decide not to post a message, they will send an explanation to the sender. The sender may be given the option of altering the message so that it can be posted to the list by the moderators. Personal messages, including those that offer criticism of a person instead of a person's statement, should not be sent to the list and will be rejected. While the purpose of the list is to facilitate discussion of African American studies and librarianship, there may be times when professional librarians need to draw upon the expertise of AFAS-L subscribers to answer reference questions. Ref-

erence questions may be posted to the list only by subscribers and only when other resources have been exhausted. Responses to reference questions should be sent to the person who asked the question. The person who asked the question is strongly encouraged to inform the list of the results of their query. The moderators will handle all questions about the functions of LISTSERV as it pertains to AFAS-L, as well as any mailing errors. Any comments on the operation of the list should be sent to a moderator for our consideration, rather than to the list itself.

How to submit: AFAS-L@KENTVM is the Bitnet address of the discussion list itself. AFAS-L@KENTVM.KENT.EDU is the Internet address of the discussion list. All mail sent to either AFAS-L@KENTVM or AFAS-L@KENTVM.KENT.EDU is directed to the moderator who then reviews messages for forwarding to all subscribers to the list. Not all messages sent to AFAS-L will be forwarded by the moderator.

Archives: There are two ways to search the archives of LISTSERV based discussion lists. If your email address is on the BITNET and you have interactive messaging capability you can search interactively using a program that you retrieve from the LISTSERV. If your email address is on the Internet or you do not have interactive messaging, you can search the archives in ''Batch'' mode via email. To learn to effectively search you will need to read the manual. To retrieve the manual for LISTSERV database searching, send a message via e-mail to LISTSERV@KENTVM (Internet: LISTSERV@KENTVM.KENT.EDU). Leave the subject line blank and the text should read INFO DATABASE.

Additional information: Additional editors: Rochelle Redmond Ballard, University of Central Florida, P. O. Box 25000, Orlando, Florida 32816-0666; tel407-823-5049; fax407-823-5865; Internetfdballar@ucf1vm.cc.ucf.edu; Bitnetfdballar@ucf1vm; Stanton F. Biddle, City University of New York, Baruch College Library, 17 Lexington Avenue, Box 317, New York, NY 10010; tel212-447-3881; fax212-447-3705; Internet Bitnet sfbbb@cunyvm; Gerald Holmes; Internetgholmes@kentvm.kent.edu; Bitnetgholmes@kentvm; Carol Ritzen Kem, Department of Collection Management, The George A. Smathers Libraries, University of Florida, Gainesville, FL 32611; tel904-392-4919; fax904-392-7251; Bitnet carokem@nervm; Mark G. R. McManus, Simpson Library, Mary Washington College, 1801 College Avenue, Fredericksburg, VA 22401-4664; tel703-899-4591; fax703-899-4499; Internetmmcmanus@s850.mwc.edu; Michael Walker, Librarian, Reference Services Department, Virginia Commonwealth University, Box 2033, 901 Park Avenue, Richmond, VA 23284-2033; tel804-367-1103; fax804-367-0151; Bitnet mwalker@vcuvax; William Welburn, University of Iowa, University of Iowa Libraries, Iowa City, IA 52242; tel319-335-6155; Internet william-welburn@uiowa.edu; Bitnet cadlwwts@uiamvs

AFRICA-L

Description: Africa-L focuses on African peoples.
Subjects covered: Africa; political science
List moderated: No.
Editorial contact: Carlos Fernando Nogueira
Bitnet: ctedtc09@brufpb
How to access: Send subscribe message to listserv@brufmg
How to unsubscribe: Send unsubscribe message to listserv@brufmg

AFRICANA@WMVM1

Description: AFRICANA@WMVM1 is a forum on information technology in Africa.
Subjects covered: information technology
List moderated: No.
Editorial contact: Paa-Bekoe Welbeck
Internet: pbwelb@wmvm1.cc.wm.edu
Bitnet: pbwelb@wmvm1
How to access: Send subscribe message to listserv@wmvm1 or listserv@wmvm1.cc.wm.edu
How to unsubscribe: Send unsubscribe message to listserv@wmvm1 or listserv@wmvm1.cc.wm.edu
Archives: Archives are developed monthly; apply to listowner for details.

AFROAM-L

Description: AFROAM-L is a discussion list focusing on critical issues in African-American life and culture.
Subjects covered: African-American studies; sociology
Net address for operations: AFROAM-L@HARVARDA
Subscribers: 190+
Editorial contact: Lee D. Baker
Bitnet: LDBaker@HARVARDS
Review: Reviewed by List Review Service edited by Raleigh Muns: see appendix.
How to access: Send an email message wth blank subject line to LISTSERV@HARVARDA. Message should consists solely of the line: SUBSCRIBE AFROAM-L your__name
Archives: No searchable archives are avialable.

AG-EXP-L

Description: Ag-exp-l is a list dealing with expert systems in agriculture.
Subjects covered: agriculture; artificial intelligence; computer science; expert systems
Net address for operations: listserv%ndsuvm1.bitnet@cunyvm.cuny.edu
Net address for questions or submissions: ag-exp-l%ndsuvm1.bitnet@cunyvm.cuny.edu
How to access: Send a message to the Internet address listserv%ndsuvm1.bitnet@cunyvm.cuny.edu The body of the message should consist of: subscribe AG-EXP-L <your full name>

AGOCG-ANIMATION@MAILBASE.AC.AK

Description: AGOCG-ANIMATION@MAILBASE.AC.AK provides a forum for discussing all aspects of animation.
Subjects covered: animation; graphics
List moderated: No.
Internet: agocg-animation-request@mailbase.ac.uk
How to access: Send subscribe message to mailbase@mailbase.ac.uk in the following format: join agocg-animation Yourfirstname Yourlastname
How to unsubscribe: Send unsubscribe message to mailbase@mailbase.ac.uk.
Archives: Archives are developed monthly; apply to listowner for details.

AGOCG-IP@MAILBASE.AC.AK

Description: AGOCG-IP@MAILBASE.AC.AK provides a forum for discussing all aspects of image processing.
Subjects covered: image processing; graphics
List moderated: No.
Internet: agocg-ip-request@mailbase.ac.uk
How to access: Send subscribe message to mailbase@mailbase.ac.uk in the following format: join agocg-ip Yourfirstname Your last name
How to unsubscribe: Send unsubscribe message to mailbase@mailbase.ac.uk
Archives: Archives are developed monthly; apply to listowner for details.

AGRIC-L

Description: Agric-L is a general discussion on agriculture.
Subjects covered: agriculture
List moderated: No.
Editorial contact: Harold Pritchett
Bitnet: harold@uga
How to access: Send subscribe message to listserv@uga or listserv@uga.cc.uga.edu
How to unsubscribe: Send unsubscribe message to listserv@uga or listserv@uga.cc.uga.edu
Archives: Archives are developed monthly; apply to listowner for details.

AGRIS-L

Description: Agris-L is the electronic forum of the United Nations' Food and Agriculture Organization.
Subjects covered: agriculture; library and information science
Host: Food and Agriculture Organization of the U.N.
List moderated: No.
Editorial contact: A. Lebowitz
Internet: gilsn2@irmfao01
How to access: Send subscribe message to listserv@irmgao01
How to unsubscribe: Send unsubscribe message to listserv@irmgao01
Archives: Archives are developed monthly; apply to listowner for details.

AHC-L

Description: AHC-L is the list of the (European) Association for History and Computing
Subjects covered: computer science; history
Net address for operations: LISTSERV@DGOGWDG1
Net address for questions or submissions: AHC-L@DGOGWDG1
How to access: Send message to listserv: SUBSCRIBE <listname> <your name>

AI-CHI@LLL.LLNL.GOV

Description: AI-CHI is a forum for discussing the use of artificial intelligence theories in human/computer interface design.
Subjects covered: artificial intelligence; computer science
List moderated: No.
Editorial contact: Dr. Sherman Tyler
Internet: wiley!sherman@lll-lcc.llnl.gov
How to access: Send subscribe message to WILEY!AI-CHI-REQUEST@LLL.LCC.LLNL.GOV
How to unsubscribe: Send unsubscribe message to WILEY!AI-CHI-REQUEST@LLL.LCC.LLNL.GOV
Archives: Yes; Apply to listowner for details

AI-ED@SUN.COM

Description: AI-ED@SUN.COM provides a forum for discussion of artificial intelligence applications for education.
Subjects covered: education; artificial intelligence; computer science
Net address for questions or submissions: ai-ed-request@sun.com
List moderated: No.
Editorial contact: J. R. Prohaska
Internet: prohaska@sun.com
How to access: Send subscribe message to AI-ED-REQUEST@SUN.COM
How to unsubscribe: Send unsubscribe message to AI-ED-REQUEST@SUN.COM

AI-KAPPA-PC

Description: The list is intended to be a forum for discussion for Kappa PC users. Subjects could therefore include problems, queries, cries for help and hopefully tips and solutions. It would also be nice if the users of Kappa started to talk about programming styles in Kappa, and possibly the question of documenting applications. Kappa PC seems to be evolving quite rapidly and it would be good if we could discuss things and suggest them to Intellicorp rather than having them take the initiative. This list is intended for those with an interest in Kappa PC, the MS Windows KBS and OOP tool. Discussion need not be entirely about the tool itself - related subjects would also be welcome.
Subjects covered: computer hardware and software; Kappa PC; computer science
Net address for operations: mailbase@mailbase.ac.uk
Net address for questions or submissions: ai-kappa-pc@mailbase.ac.uk
Established: February 1993
Subscribers: 39
Sponsor: Joint Information Systems Committee of the UK Higher Education Funding Councils
Host: University of Newcastle, Newcastle Upon Tyne, UK.
List moderated: No.
Editorial contact: Andy Vann
Department of Civil Engineering, Univesity of Bristol, Queen's Building, University Walk, Bristol BS8 1TR, UK.
Tel: +44 272 303279
Fax: +44 272 303889
Internet: A.M.Vann@bristol.ac.uk
Copyright statement: Authors of accepted contributions assign to ai-kappa-pc the right to publish the text electronically in screen-readable ASCII and to make it available permanently in electronic archives. Authors do, however, retain copyright to their contributions and may republish them in any form that they choose, so long as they clearly acknowledge ai-kappa-pc@mailbase.ac.uk as the original source of publication.
How to access: Send message to mailbase@mailbase.ac.uk containing the single line join ai-kappa-pc <first name> <last name> where <first name> and <last name> should be replaced with your first and last names.

How to unsubscribe: Send the message leave ai-kappa-pc to mailbase@mailbase.ac.uk
How to submit: Send your message to ai-kappa-pc@mailbase.ac.uk
Archives: Message archive files are stored as MM-YYYY where MM is the month number and YYYY is the year number. These can be retrieved by anonymous ftp or by sending a message to mailbase@mailbase.ac.uk containing the line send ai-kappa-pc <filename> where <filename> should be replaced by the name of the file required.
Related files: Additional files stored with the list can be retrieved in the same way as the archive files. An index to files stored with the list can be retrieved by sending a message to mailbase@mailbase.ac.uk containing the single line index ai-kappa-pc
Gopher accessibility: Mailbase can be accessed by gophering to mailbase.ac.uk
Additional information: One last word - if you think you've found a bug in Kappa or you have a similar technical problem please ring Intellicorp first. It's important for all our sakes that they find out about bugs quickly and can then do something about them. Also, if you're paying for technical support you might as well get your money's worth. Once you have rung them it would be good to notify the list to warn others - especially if you manage to find a workaround!

AI-MEDICINE (ARTIFICIAL INTELLIGENCE IN MEDICINE)

Description: Ai-medicine (Artificial Intelligence in Medicine) features discussions and announcements relating to artificial intelligence in medicine, with emphasis on knowledge-based systems as applied to medical domains.
Subjects covered: artificial intelligence; medicine
Net address for operations: ai-medicine-request@med.stanford.edu
Established: September 1990
Host: Knowledge Systems Laboratory, Stanford Univ., Stanford, CA 94305.
List moderated: pseudo-moderated
Moderation procedure: List coordinator reviews all incoming messages and redistributes messages to the mailing list only if they are relevant to the topic. This procedure is devised to filter out misdirected (e.g., subscription requests) and irrelevant (e.g., wrong target audience, "junk mail") messages.
Editorial contact: Serdar Uckun, MD, PhD.
Knowledge Systems Laboratory, Stanford University, 701 Welch Road Bldg, C., Palo Alto, CA 94304
Tel: (415) 723-1915
Fax: (415) 725-5850
Internet: uckun@hpp.stanford.edu
How to access: Send requests (in plain English) to ai-medicine-request@med.stanford.edu
How to submit: Send submission to ai-medicine@med.stanford.edu
Archives: Archives of the mailing list, including related dissertation abstracts and medline search results, are available via anonymous ftp from lhc.nlm.nih.gov under /pub/ai-medicine, or via the ai-medicine e-mail server from ai-medicine-server@med.stanford.edu (send a message to his address with a subject line of "HELP" for instructions).
Related files: Related bibliography files, conference announcements, etc.

Gopher accessibility: Archives accessible via the Stanford Camis gopher on a trial basis (not announced to public).

AIBI-L

Description: Aibi-L discusses computerized analysis of Biblical and related texts.
Subjects covered: linguistics; Bible studies
List moderated: No.
Editorial contact: Gregory Bloomquist
Internet: gbloomq@acadvm1.uottowa.ca
Bitnet: gbloomq@uottowa
How to access: Send subscribe message to listserv@uottowa or listserv@acadvm1.uottowa.ca
How to unsubscribe: Send unsubscribe message to listserv@uottowa or listserv@acadvm1.uottowa.ca
Archives: Archives are developed weekly; apply to listowner for details.

AIDS-STAT@WUBIOS.WUSTL.EDU

Description: AIDS-STAT@WUBIOS.WUSTL.EDU is a forum on AIDS research.
Subjects covered: AIDS/HIV studies; medicine
List moderated: No.
Editorial contact: David Dodell
Internet: ddodell@stjhmc.fidonet.org
How to access: Send subscribe message to AIDS-STAT-REQUEST@WUBIOS.WUSTL.EDU
How to unsubscribe: Send unsubscribe message to AIDS-STAT-REQUEST@WUBIOS.WUSTL.EDU

AIDS@RUTVM1

Description: The AIDS list mirrors postings from the Usenet newsgroup "sci.med.aids". We do not recommend that you subscribe to the AIDS mailing list if you already have access to the sci.med.aids newsgroup. Both size and frequency of articles appearing in this forum are high.
Subjects covered: AIDS/HIV studies; medicine
Net address for operations: listserv@rutvm1.rutgers.edu
Net address for questions or submissions: aids@rutvm1.rutgers.edu AIDS@RUTVM1.BITNET
Established: 1986
Subscribers: 205 members of the list proper as of May 17, 199. 19000 estimated readers of sci.med.aids as of May 17, 1993
Sponsor: UCLA Computer Science Department
List moderated: Yes.
Moderation procedure: Prohibited postings:
1. no ad hominem arguments (i.e., "you are a bozo, therefore you are wrong.") 2. unusual technical claims must be accompanied by references. 3. no insults. We especially encourage technical contributions. If a particularly unenlightening interaction has been continuing for a long time, the moderators reserve the right to stop a topic.
Editorial contact: Professor J. Philip Miller
Biostatistics Department Washington University St. Louis, MO
Tel: (314) 362-3617
Internet: phil@wubios.wustl.edu
Technical contact: Dan R. Greening
Software Transformation, Inc., Suite 100 1601 Saratoga, Sunnyvale Rd., Cupertino, CA 95014
Tel: (408) 973-8081 X313
Fax: (408) 973-0989

Internet: dgreen@cs.ucla.edu
Sample contents: Contents include news excerpts, electronic copies of several newsletters, drug and vaccine protocol announcements, technical discussions, and personal stories.
Review: In proceedings{aids:gree89a, author = "Daniel R. Greening and Alan D. Wexelblat", title = "Experiences with Cooperative Moderation of a USENET Newsgroup", booktitle = "Proceedings of the 1989 ACM/IEEE Workshop on Applied Computing", year = 1989}
Copyright statement: Copyright 1993, Dan R. Greening. Non-commercial reproduction allowed.
How to access: Send the following message to listserv@rutvm1.rutgers.edu or listserv@rutvm1.bitnet: subscribe aids. NOTE: the aids-d mailing list is for discussion of moderation policies only. Very few people will be interested in this list.
How to unsubscribe: Send the following message to listserv@rutvm1.rutgers.edu or listserv@rutvm1.bitnet: unsubscribe aids
How to submit: Send the article (with no special messages or comments to the moderators) to aids@rutvm1.bitnet or aids@rutvm1.rutgers.edu.
Submission policy: Send the message to aids-d@sti.com.
Archives: No archive currently available. Contact dgreen@sti.com if you would like to offer an internet archive site. (We need one!)

AIL-L

Description: AIL-L is a conference dealing with artificial intelligence and law.
Subjects covered: artificial intelligence; law and legal studies
Net address for operations: listserv@austin.onu.edu
List moderated: No.
Editorial contact: David R. Warner, Jr.
Internet: warner@austin.onu.edu
How to access: Send subscribe message to listserv@austin.onu.edu
How to unsubscribe: Send subscribe message to listserv@austin.onu.edu

AILIST@DB0TUI11

Description: AILIST@DB0TUI11 is a discussion forum on the topic of artificial intelligence.
Subjects covered: artificial intelligence; computer science
List moderated: Yes.
Editorial contact: Gerald Gschwind
Internet: gschwind@dbotui11
How to access: Send subscribe message to listserv@dbotui11 or listserv@vm1.nodak.edu
How to unsubscribe: Send unsubscribe message to listserv@dbotui11 or listserv@vm1.nodak.edu
Archives: Archives are developed weekly; apply to listowner for details.

AIRLINE@CUNYVM

Description: AIRLINE@CUNYVM is a discussion on prototyping.
Subjects covered: science and technology
List moderated: Yes.
Editorial contact: Geert K. Marien
Internet: gkmqc@cunyvm.cuny.edu

Bitnet: gkmqc@cunyvm.bitn
How to access: Send subscribe message to listserv@cunyvm or listserv@cunyvm.cuny.edu
How to unsubscribe: Send unsubscribe message to listserv@cunyvm or listserv@cunyvm.cuny.edu
Archives: Archives are developed weekly; apply to listowner for details.

AJBS-L

Description: AJBS-L is a forum of the Association of Japanese Business Studies.
Subjects covered: business; Japan
List moderated: Yes.
Editorial contact: James W. Reese
Internet: r505040@univcsvm.csd.scarolina.edu
Bitnet: r505040@univcsvm
How to access: Send subscribe message to listserv@ncsuvm or listserv@ncsuvm.cc.ncsu.edu
How to unsubscribe: Send unsubscribe message to listserv@ncsuvm or listserv@ncsuvm.cc.ncsu.edu
Archives: Archives are developed monthly; apply to listowner for details.

ALBION-L

Description: Albion-L focuses on British and Irish history.
Subjects covered: history
List moderated: No.
Editorial contact: Joe Coohill
Bitnet: gd03jtc@ucsbvm
How to access: Send subscribe message to listserv@ucsbvm
How to unsubscribe: Send unsubscribe message to listserv@ucsbvm

ALCTS@UICVM

Description: ALCTS@UICVM is the publication of the Association for Library Collections and Technical Services (ALCTS).
Subjects covered: library and information science
List moderated: Yes.
Bitnet: u34261@uicvm or u19466@uicvm
How to access: Send subscribe message to listserv@uicvm
How to unsubscribe: Send unsubscribe message to listserv@uicvm

ALEPHINT@TAUNIVM

Description: ALEPHINT@TAUNIVM is a list for users of ALEPH system software.
Subjects covered: library and information science
List moderated: No.
Editorial contact: Dorit Mendil
Internet: masterm@tauvax.tau.ac.il
How to access: Send subscribe message to listserv@taunivm
How to unsubscribe: Send unsubscribe message to listserv@taunivm
Archives: Archives are developed monthly; apply to listowner for details.

ALF-L (ACADEMIC LIBRARIAN'S FORUM)

Description: ALF-L is concerned with exploring the working conditions of academic librarians, and welcomes news of developments in the status of the profession in colleges and universities. It was originally set up as a result of a conference of librarian members of the Canadian Association of University Teachers.
Subjects covered: academic libraries; library and information science; colleges and universities; workplace studies
Net address for operations: ALF-L@YorkVM1
Net address for questions or submissions: ALF-L@YorkVM1
Established: December 1990
Subscribers: 706
Host: Universite York University
List moderated: No.
Editorial contact: Tiit Ko(tilde)dar
203M Scott, Universite York University
Tel: (416) 736-2100 XT33527
Fax: (416) 736-5358
Internet: tkodar@vm2.yorku.ca
Bitnet: tkodar@yorkvm2
How to access: Tell listserv at yorkvm1 sub alf-l your-full-name (or send a mail message to: LISTSERV@YORKVM1 with the one-line message: subscribe ALF-L your-full-name).
Access policy: At present, open to all, wherever they're located geographically.
How to unsubscribe: Tell listserv at yorkvm1 unsub alf-l your-full-name (or send a mail message to: LISTSERV@YORKVM1 with the one- line message: subscribe ALF-L your-full-name).
How to submit: Send to: ALF-L@yorkvm1
Submission policy: Limited to subscribers only. Submissions from non- subscribers should be sent directly to the List-Owner.
Archives: Messages to the list are stored, & available to subscribers.

ALGERIA-NET

Description: ALGERIA-NET discusses cultural and political elements of Algerian society.
Subjects covered: political science; cultural studies; current events; Algeria
List moderated: No.
Editorial contact: Nasr Belkheir
Internet: belk@pyr.gatech.edu
How to access: Contact the Editor
How to unsubscribe: Contact the Editor

ALIFE@COGNET.UCLA.EDU

Description: The alife mailing list is for communications regarding artificial life, a formative interdisciplinary field involving computer science, the natural sciences, mathematics, medicine and others.
Subjects covered: artificial intelligence; computer science; medicine
Net address for questions or submissions: alife-request@cognet.ucla.edu
How to access: Send mail to alife-request@cognet.ucla.edu to be added to the list.

ALLMUSIC@AUVM

Description: ALLMUSIC@AUVM is a forum for discussing the broadest range of musical interests.

Subjects covered: music
List moderated: No.
Editorial contact: Mike Karolchik
Internet: u6183@wvnvm.wvnet.edu
Bitnet: mike@wvnvm
How to access: Send subscribe message to listserv@auvm or listserv@auvm.auvm.edu
How to unsubscribe: Send unsubscribe message to listserv@auvm or listserv@auvm.auvm.edu
Archives: Archives are developed weekly; apply to listowner for details.

ALLSTAT

Description: Allstat is a broadcast system for the UK statistical community. The list is operated by the ''Computers In Teaching Initiative'' Centre for Statistics, although the broadcasts need not be concerned with teaching.
Subjects covered: statistics; education; mathematics; medicine
Net address for operations: mailbase@mailbase.ac.uk
Net address for questions or submissions:
allstat@mailbase.ac.uk
Established: 1988
Subscribers: 600
Sponsor: Joint Information Systems Committee of the UK Higher Education Funding Councils.
Host: University of Newcastle Upon Tyne, UK.
List moderated: No.
Editorial contact: Stuart G. Young
Dept of Statistics, Mathematics Building, University of Glasgow, GLASGOW G12 8QQ
Scotland, UK.
Tel: 041-339-8855, ext. 4386
Fax: 041-330-4814
Internet: stuart@stats.gla.ac.uk
How to access: Send message to mailbase@mailbase.ac.uk containing the single line join allstat <firstname> <lastname> where <firstname> and <lastname> should be replaced with your first and last names.
How to unsubscribe: Send message to mailbase@mailbase.ac.uk containing the single line leave allstat
How to submit: Send your message to allstat@mailbase.ac.uk
Archives: Message archive files are stored as MM-YYYY where MM is the month number and YYYY is the year number. These can be retrieved by anonymous ftp or by sending a message to mailbase@mailbase.ac.uk containing the line send allstat <filename> where <filename> should be replaced by the name of the file required.
Related files: Additional files stored with the list can be retrieved in the same way as the archive files. An index to files stored with the list can be retrieved by sending a message to mailbase@mailbase.ac.uk containing the single line index allstat. There is also a sublist for those interested in medical statistics, and this is called medstat. It currently has 207 subscribers. The above information applies equally to this sublist, with ''allstat'' replaced by ''medstat'' where appropriate.
Gopher accessibility: Mailbase can be accessed by gopher.
Additional information: There is also a sublist for those interested in medical statistics, and this is called medstat. It currently has 207 subscribers. The above information applies equally to this sublist, with ''allstat'' replaced by ''medstat'' where appropriate.

ALTLEARN
Description: Altlearn is a discussion list covering alternative approaches to education for the educationally disabled.
Subjects covered: learning disabilities; disabilities; developmental disabilities; education
Net address for operations: listserv@sjuvm.bitnet
Net address for questions or submissions: altlearn@sjuvm.bitnet
Established: September 1990
Subscribers: 160
Sponsor: St. John's University, Jamaica, NY.
Host: St. John's University, Jamaica, NY.
List moderated: No.
Technical contact: Dr. Robert Zenhausern
St. John's University, Jamaica, NY 11439.
Tel: (718)-990-6447
Fax: (718)-990-6705
Internet: drz@sjuvm.stjohns.edu
Bitnet: drz@sjuvm.bitnet
How to access: Send mail to listserv@sjuvm.bitnet with the message: sub altlearn Firstname Lastname
Access policy: Subscription is automatic.
How to unsubscribe: Send mail to listserv@sjuvm.bitnet with the message: signoff altlearn
How to submit: Send mail to altlearn@sjuvm.bitnet
Archives: Logs of all messages available in the form: altlearn log9305 (logs of altlearn for May, 1993).

AMALGAM@DEARN
Description: AMALGAM@DEARN is a forum on the use of dental amalgams.
Subjects covered: medicine
List moderated: No.
Editorial contact: Siegfried Schmitt
Bitnet: uj21@dkauni2
How to access: Send subscribe message to listserv@dearn or listserv@vm.gmd.de
How to unsubscribe: Send unsubscribe message to listserv@dearn or listserv@vm.gmd.de
Archives: Archives are developed yearly; apply to listowner for details.

AMERCATH
Description: AMERCATH is a forum for debate, discussion, and the exchange of ideas on topics surrounding the history of Catholocism in the United States.
Subjects covered: American Catholicism; religion
Net address for operations: LISTSERV@UKCC.UKY.EDU
Net address for questions or submissions: AMERCATH@UKCC.UKY.EDU
Established: 1991
Subscribers: 148
Host: Jefferson Community College-University of Kentucky
List moderated: No.
Editorial contact: Anne Kearney
Jefferson Community College-University of Kentucky
109 East Broadway Louisville, KY 40202
Tel: (502)584-0181, ext. 353
Fax: (502) 585-4425
Internet: JCCANNEK@UKCC.UKY.EDU
Bitnet: JCCANNEK@UKCC

Technical contact: Same as above
Sample contents: Job announcements, research requests, current topics of interest.
How to access: Tell listserv@UKCC.UKY.EDU SUB AMERCATH Your first name Your last name
How to unsubscribe: Tell listserv@UKCC.UKY.EDU SIGNOFF AMERCATH
How to submit: Mail to AMERCATH@UKCC.UKY.EDU
Submission policy: Send to listowner. No submissions of a commercial or personally derogatory nature, no obscenities. ALWAYS put your name and e-mail address at the end of every posting. (It is important that people be able to contact you privately if they wish, and some mail systems do not identify the writer anywhere in the header.) Also, if you are replying to someone else's posting, briefly quote or summarize that posting before you offer your reply. Doing so will make your message clearer and avoid confusion. You can indicate the message you are replying to by using a < before each line. On some systems, you can use the command ''reply text''. You should send replies to AMERCATH when the contents are likely to be of interest to a number of subscribers. Comments directed at a particular person should be sent privately, NOT to AMERCATH.

AMERICA
Description: AMERICA is a forum for the discussion of aspects pertaining to US foreign trade policies.
Subjects covered: political science; trade and economic data
List moderated: Yes.
Internet: SUBSCRIBE@XAMIGA.LINET.ORG
How to access: Send subscribe message to SUBSCRIBE@XAMIGA.LINET.ORG in the format: #america username@domain

AMERICAN-STUDIES@MAILBASE.AC.UK
Description: AMERICAN-STUDIES@MAILBASE.AC.UK is a forum for American Studies.
Subjects covered: colleges and universities
List moderated: No.
Internet: american-studies-request@mailbase.ac.uk
How to access: Send subscribe message to mailbase@mailbase.ac.uk in the following format: join american-studies Your first name Your last name
Archives: Archives are developed monthly; apply to listowner for details.

AMERSTDY@MIAMIU
Description: AMERSTDY@MIAMIU is a forum for American Studies education.
Subjects covered: American studies; education
List moderated: No.
Editorial contact: Barbara Gribbin
Bitnet: bgribbin@miamiu
How to access: Send subscribe message to listserv@miamiu
How to unsubscribe: Send unsubscribe message to listserv@miamiu
Archives: Archives are developed monthly; apply to listowner for details.

AMLIT-L (AMERICAN LITERATURE DISCUSSION LIST)

Description: AMLIT, the American Literature Discussion List, has been created for the discussion, deliberation, and debate of topics and issues in the vast and diverse field of American Literature, among a world wide community of those with a shared interest in this subject. Consultations, conferences, and an ongoing exchange of information between both scholars and students of American Literature is certainly to be expected on this list. Relevant postings for announcements of conferences and calls for papers are welcome here.
Subjects covered: language and literature; American literature and language; cultural studies
Net address for operations: Listserv@Mizzou1.Missouri.Edu
Established: Summer 1992
Subscribers: 235
Sponsor: English Department, Univ. of Missouri, Columbia 107 Tate Hall Columbia, MO 65205
Host: University of Missouri, Columbia
List moderated: No.
Editorial contact: Michael O'Conner
107 Tate Hall, UMC, Columbia, MO 65205
Tel: (314) 882-2339
Internet: Engmo@Mizzou1.Missour.Edu
(or)C359452@Mizzou1.Missouri.Edu
Bitnet: Engmo@Mizzou1
Technical contact: Same as above
How to access: Usual Listserv procedures.
Access policy: This list is open to anyone.
How to unsubscribe: Usual Listserv procedures.
How to submit: Usual Listserv procedures

AMP-L

Description: AMP-L is a list covering atomic and molecular physics.
Subjects covered: physics
List moderated: No.
Editorial contact: Henrik Zawischa
Internet: f41zaw@dhhdesy3
How to access: Send subscribe message to listserv@dearn
How to unsubscribe: Send unsubscribe message to listserv@dearn

AMWEST-H@USCVM

Description: AMWEST-H@USCVM is a forum for the discussion of the opening of the American West.
Subjects covered: history
List moderated: No.
Editorial contact: Valentine Smith
Internet: cdell@vax1.umkc.edu
How to access: Send subscribe message to listserv@uscvm
How to unsubscribe: Send unsubscribe message to listserv@uscvm

ANCHODD (AUSTRALIAN NATIONAL CLEARINGHOUSE ON DRUG DEVELOPMENT)

Description: ANCHODD (Australian National Clearinghouse on Drug Development) is an electronic discussion list covering any topic of interest to drug scientists, whether experimental or clinical.
Subjects covered: pharmacology; health sciences; medicine
Net address for operations: listserv@cc.utas.edu.au
Net address for questions or submissions: anchodd@cc.utas.edu.au
Established: 1990
Subscribers: 150
Sponsor: Centre for Pharmacology, Medicinal Chemistry and Toxicology, University of Tasmania, PO Box 252 C, Hobart 7001, Australia.
Host: Centre for Pharmacology, Medicinal Chemistry and Toxicology, University of Tasmania, PO Box 252 C, Hobart 7001, Australia.
List moderated: No.
Editorial contact: Stuart McLean
Centre for Pharmacology, Medicinal Chemistry and Toxicology, University of Tasmania, PO Box 252 C, Hobart 7001, Australia.
Tel: (002) 202199(International callers: please use 61 02 in place of 002)
Fax: (002) 202870
Internet: S.McLean@pharm.utas.edu.au
Bitnet: Description of list contents: messages requesting information or other assistance, making announcements, etc.
How to access: End the message "subscribe anchodd name" to listserv@cc.utas.edu.au
How to unsubscribe: Send "unsubscribe anchodd" to listserv@cc.utas.edu.au
How to submit: Send message to anchodd@cc.utas.edu.au
Archives: anchodd archives are most accessible at the Gopher site: Australian sources/Austin Hosp ital/Medicine, Medical Science Information and Resources/anchodd
Gopher accessibility: anchodd archives are most accessible at the Gopher site: Australian sources/Austin Hosp ital/Medicine, Medical Science Information and Resources/anchodd

ANCIEN-L

Description: ANCIEN-L is a forum for debate, discussion, and the exchange of information by students and scholars of the history of the Ancient Mediterranean. ANCIEN-L is ready to distribute newsletters from study groups, and to post announcements of meetings and calls for papers, short scholarly pieces, queries, and other items of interest. ANCIEN-L is associated with the general discussion list HISTORY, the History Network, and co-operates fully with other lists similarly associated.
Subjects covered: history; archaeology; cultural studies
Net address for operations: LISTSERV@ulkyvm.louisville.edu
Established: 1992
Sponsor: Univ. of Louisville, Louisville, KY 40292
Host: Univ. of Louisville, Louisville, KY 40292
List moderated: No.
Editorial contact: James A. Cocks Information Technology, Univ. of Louisville, Louisville, KY 40292
Tel: (502) 588-6303
Internet: jacock01@ulkyvm.louisville.edu
Bitnet: JACOCK01@ULKYVM
How to access: Subscriptions should be made by sending the command: SUB ANCIEN-L your first name your last name to either: Internet: LISTSERV@ulkyvm.louisville.edu or BITNET: LISTSERV@ULKYVM
How to unsubscribe: To unsubscribe send the command: UNSUB ANCIEN-L to either: Internet:

LISTSERV@ulkyvm.louisville.edu or BITNET:
LISTSERV@ULKYVM
Archives: Log files for 1 year.
Related files: See History Network

ANEST-L
Description: Anest-L is an alectronic conference on anesthesiology and computers.
Subjects covered: medicine; health sciences; computer science
Host: Dept. of Anesthesiology, SUNY Health Science Center
List moderated: No.
Editorial contact: Andrew M. Sopchak
Internet: sopchaka@vax.cs.hscsyr.edu
Bitnet: sopchaka@snysyrv1
How to access: Send subscribe message to listserv@ubvm or listserv@ubvm.cc.buffalo.edu
How to unsubscribe: Send unsubscribe message to listserv@ubvm or listserv@ubvm.cc.buffalo.edu

ANET-L
Description: Anet-L is the forum of the Alberta Post-Secondary Education Network.
Subjects covered: education
List moderated: No.
How to access: Send subscribe message to listserv@ualtavm or listserv@vm.ucs.ualberta.ca
How to unsubscribe: Send unsubscribe message to listserv@ualtavm or listserv@vm.ucs.ualberta.ca

ANGLICAN (EPISCOPAL MAILING LIST)
Description: The ANGLICAN mailing list is a forum to provide a non-hostile environment for discussion among Christians who are members of the Holy Catholic Church in the Anglican Communion or who are simply interested in Episcopal beliefs and practices.
Subjects covered: Anglicanism; religion
Net address for operations: LISTSERV@AMERICAN.EDU
Net address for questions or submissions: ANGLICAN@AMERICAN.EDU
Established: February 1990
Subscribers: 130
Sponsor: dragon.com
Host: American.edu
List moderated: No.
Editorial contact: Cynthia M. Smith
2710 Regal Way, Tucker, GA 30084.
Internet: cms@dragon.com
Technical contact: Charles Smith
2710 Regal Way, Tucker, GA 30084.
Internet: cts@dragon.com
How to access: Send message to LISTSERV@AMERICAN.EDU containing the single line: Subscribe ANGLICAN ''FirstName LastName''
Access policy: List subscription is open to all.
How to unsubscribe: Send message to LISTSERV@AMERICAN.EDU containing the single line: unsubscribe ANGLICAN
How to submit: Send message to ANGLICAN@AMERICAN.EDU
Submission policy: Submissions are open to all.
Archives: This list is archived; apply to listowner for details.

ANIME-L
Description: Anime-L is a list covering animedia (Japanese animation studies).
Subjects covered: animation; graphics
List moderated: Yes.
Editorial contact: Ron Jarrel
Internet: raa-gate-@vtserf.cc.vt.edu
Bitnet: jarrell@vtm1
How to access: Send subscribe message to listserv@vtvm1
How to unsubscribe: Send unsubscribe message to listserv@vtvm1
Archives: Archives are developed weekly; apply to listowner for details.

ANN-LOTS@NDSUVM1
Description: ANN-LOTS is an announcements forum for computer researchers.
Subjects covered: information technology
List moderated: No.
Editorial contact: John Cane
Internet: j__kane@unhh.unh.edu
How to access: Send subscribe message to listserv@ndsuvm1 or listserv@vm1.nodak.edu
How to unsubscribe: Send unsubscribe message to listserv@ndsuvm1 or listserv@vm1.nodak.edu
Archives: Archives are developed monthly; apply to listowner for details.

ANSAX-L
Description: Ansax-L is a discussion group about Anglo-Saxon England.
Subjects covered: history
List moderated: Yes.
Editorial contact: Patrick W. Conner
Internet: u47c2@wvnvm.wvnet.edu
Bitnet: u47c2@wvnvm
How to access: Contact listowner
How to unsubscribe: Contact listowner
How to submit: Contact listowner

ANSFORTH
Description: ANSFORTH is a discussion list supporting ongoing review and development of standards for the Forth Programming Language by the X3/J14 Technical Committee. Focuses on timely production of useful documents, as opposed to advocacy or philosophy.
Subjects covered: Forth Language Standards; computer hardware and software
Net address for operations: ansforth-request@minerva.com
Net address for questions or submissions: ansforth@minerva.com
Established: March 1993
Subscribers: 35
Sponsor: X3/J14 ANS Forth Technical Committee c/o FORTH, Inc. 111 N. Sepulveda Blvd Suite 300 Manhattan Beach, CA 90266.
Host: ATHENA Programming, Inc. 24680 NW Dixie Mountain Road Hillsboro, OR 97124.
List moderated: Yes.
Moderation procedure: Moderator controls flow of postings.
Editorial contact: Greg Bailey

ATHENA Programming, Inc., 24680 NW Dixie Mountain Road, Hillsboro, OR 97124.
Tel: (503) 621-3215
Fax: (503) 621-3954
Internet: gvb@minerva.com
How to access: Mail prose to ansforth-request@minerva.com
Access policy: For formal review a form must be completed and a voluntary fee may be paid to the X3 Secretariat.
How to unsubscribe: Mail prose to ansforth-request@minerva.com
How to submit: Mail to ansforth@minerva.com
Submission policy: We welcome postings made in good faith that are relevant, concise, and constructive. Site and list shall not be abused. Usenet newsgroup comp.lang.forth for traffic not appropos here.
Archives: Subject to change; check with ansforth-request.
Related files: Subject to change: check with ansforth-request.
Additional information: Practical membership limits apply. Subscriptions for exploders/secondary lists, BBS's, and reposters welcomed.

ANSI-ART
Description: ANSI-ART is a forum for the compilation and dissemination of ANSI and ASCII art forms.
Subjects covered: art; graphics
List moderated: No.
Editorial contact: Christopher Davis
Internet: ddbag256f@sa.birmp.ac.uk
How to access: Send subscribe message to DDBAG256F%SA.BIRMP.AC.UK@NSF.AC.UK
How to unsubscribe: Send unsubscribe message to DDBAG256F%SA.BIRMP.AC.UK@NSF.AC.UK

ANTHRO-L
Description: Anthro-L is an electronic discussion group centering on anthropology.
Subjects covered: anthropology
List moderated: No.
Editorial contact: Ezra Subrow
Internet: apyezra@ubvmsc.cc.buffalo.edu
Bitnet: apyezra@ubvmsc
Review: Reviewed by List Review Service edited by Raleigh Muns: see appendix.
How to access: Send subscribe message to listserv@ubvm or listserv@ubvm.cc.buffalo.edu
How to unsubscribe: Send unsubscribe message to listserv@ubvm or listserv@ubvm.cc.buffalo.edu
Archives: Archives are developed monthly; apply to listowner for details.

ANU-NEWS
Description: ANU-NEWS is a discussion list for the discussion of the use, bugs, and fixes for ANU-NEWS software, a USENET News transport and reader for VMS. Discussion is oriented towards administration, but users are also allowed.
Subjects covered: Internet; telecommunications; computer hardware and software
Net address for operations: LISTSERV@VM1.NODAK.EDU
Net address for questions or submissions: LISTSERV@NDSUVM1
Established: July 1, 1989

Subscribers: 74
Sponsor: University of Kansas Computer Ctr, Lawrence, KS 66045.
Host: North Dakota State University, Computer Center, PO Box 5164, Fargo, ND 58105.
List moderated: No.
Editorial contact: Bob Sloane
University of Kansas Computer Center, Lawrence, KS 66045.
Tel: (913) 864-0444
Fax: (913) 864-0485
Internet: sloane@kuhub.cc.ukans.edu
Bitnet: sloane@ukanvax
Technical contact: Bob Sloane
University of Kansas Computer Center, Lawrence, KS 66045.
Tel: (913) 864-0444
Fax: (913) 864-0485
Internet: sloane@kuhub.cc.ukans.edu
Bitnet: sloane@ukanvax
How to access: Send the command ''SUB ANU-NEWS your name'' to LISTSERV at NDSUVM1. Please note: listserv commands go to the listserv ID, not the list!
Access policy: Anyone interested can subscribe.
How to unsubscribe: To UNsubscribe send the command ''SIGNOFF ANU-NEWS'' to LISTSERV at NDSUVM1. Please note: listserv commands go to the listserv ID, not the list!
How to submit: Send email to ANU-NEWS@VM1.NODAK.EDU or ANU-NEWS@NDSUVM1.
Submission policy: Submissions should be related to ANU-NEWS.
Archives: Monthly notebooks will be kept. For a list send LISTSERV @ NDSUVM1 the command INDEX ANU-NEWS

APASD-L
Description: Apasd-L is a list of current policy decisions and legislation affecting psychologists.
Subjects covered: psychology
Host: American Psychological Association
List moderated: Yes.
Editorial contact: Deborah Segal
Bitnet: apasddes@wuvm
How to access: Send subscribe message to listserv@vtvm2
How to unsubscribe: Send unsubscribe message to listserv@vtvm2
Archives: Yes.

APB-L
Description: Apb-L is a forum for the advancement of behaviorist psychologies.
Subjects covered: psychology
List moderated: Yes.
Internet: RDAVID@LAVALVM1
How to access: Send subscribe message to listserv@lavalvm1
How to unsubscribe: Send unsubscribe message to listserv@lavalvm1
Archives: Yes.

APB-UL-L
Description: Apb-ul-L is a forum for the advancement of behavioral psychologies.
Subjects covered: psychology
List moderated: No.

How to access: Send subscribe message to listserv@lavalvm1
How to unsubscribe: Send unsubscribe message to
listserv@lavalvm1
Archives: Archives are developed monthly; apply to listowner
for details.

APEX-L

Description: APEX-L, The Asia-Pacific EXchange, is an electronic forum to promote international and multicultural education on college campuses, with a special focus on Asian and Pacific curricula, instructional strategies, and campus-wide activities.
Subjects covered: Asia-Pacific studies; colleges and universities; education
Editorial contact: James N. Shimabukuro
University of Hawaii-Kapiolani CC, 4303 Diamond Head Road,
Honolulu, HI 96816
Internet: jamess@uhunix.uhcc.hawaii.edu
How to access: Send a message to
jamess@uhunix.uhcc.hawaii.edu

APF@VULCAN

Description: APF@VULCAN is a philosophy forum for the
Australasian region.
Subjects covered: philosophy; ethics
Host: Philosophy Program, Research School of Social Sciences,
Australian National University
List moderated: No.
Editorial contact: Robin Davies
Internet: rad@vulcan.anu.edu.au
How to access: Send subscribe message to
apf@vulcan.anu.edu.au with the string ''admin'' in the ''Subject:'' line.
How to unsubscribe: Send unsubscribe message to
apf@vulcan.anu.edu.au with the string ''admin'' in the ''Subject:'' line.
Archives: Yes; Contact the Editor

APL-L

Description: APL-L is a conference on the APL computer programming language.
Subjects covered: computer science
List moderated: No.
Editorial contact: David G. MacNeil
Internet: DGM@UNB.CA
How to access: Send subscribe message to listserv@unb.ca
How to unsubscribe: Send unsubscribe message to
listserv@unb.ca

APSCNET@MCGILL1

Description: APSCNET@MCGILL1 is a forum for students of
behavioral science.
Subjects covered: psychology
Host: American Psychological Student Caucus
List moderated: No.
Editorial contact: Zografos Cavamanos
Internet: aps-aki@ego.psych.mcgill.ca
How to access: Send subscribe message to listserv@mcgill1
How to unsubscribe: Send unsubscribe message to
listserv@mcgill1

AQUA-L

Description: Aqua-L is a forum dealing with raising aquatic
species.
Subjects covered: aquaculture; zoology
List moderated: No.
Editorial contact: Ted White
Internet: zoowhite@vm.uoguelph.ca
Bitnet: zoowhite@uoguelph
How to access: Send subscribe message to listserv@uoguelph
or listserv@vm.uoguelph.ca
How to unsubscribe: Send unsubscribe message to
listserv@uoguelph or listserv@vm.uoguelph.ca
Archives: Archives are developed monthly; apply to listowner
for details.

AQUIFER@IBACSATA

Description: AQUIFER@IBACSATA is a forum on water pollution.
Subjects covered: ecology; environmental studies
List moderated: No.
Editorial contact: Prof. S. Troisi
Bitnet: 1026tro@icsuniv
How to access: Send subscribe message to listserv@ibacsata
How to unsubscribe: Send unsubscribe message to
listserv@ibacsata
Archives: Archives are developed monthly; apply to listowner
for details.

AR-ALERTS@NY.NEAVS.COM

Description: AR-ALERTS@NY.NEAVS.COM is a forum for
animal rights groups.
Subjects covered: activism; animal rights
List moderated: No.
Editorial contact: James Corrigan
Internet: james@ny.neavs.com
How to access: Send subscribe message to
MAJORDOMO@NY.NEAVS.COM
How to unsubscribe: Send unsubscribe message to
MAJORDOMO@NY.NEAVS.COM

AR-TALK@THINK.COM

Description: AR-TALK@THINK.COM is a forum covering animal rights.
Subjects covered: animal rights
List moderated: No.
Editorial contact: David Taylor
Internet: taylor@think.com
How to access: Send subscribe message to AR-Talk-Request@Think.com
How to unsubscribe: Send unsubscribe message to AR-Talk-Request@Think.com

ARACHNET@UOTTOWA

Description: ARACHNET is an association of electronic lists
and journals on electronic publishing topics.
Subjects covered: electronic publishing
List moderated: No.
Editorial contact: Diane Kovacs
Internet: dkovacs@kentvm.kent.edu

How to access: Contact the Editor
How to unsubscribe: Contact the Editor
Archives: Archives are developed monthly; apply to listowner for details.

ARCANA@UNCCVM

Description: ARCANA@UNCCVM is a forum centering on occult topics.
Subjects covered: religion; occult; philosophy
List moderated: No.
Editorial contact: Leonard Roberts
Bitnet: acc00ltr@unccvm
How to access: Send subscribe message to listserv@unccvm
How to unsubscribe: Send unsubscribe message to listserv@unccvm
Archives: Archives are developed monthly; apply to listowner for details.

ARCH-L

Description: Arch-L is a list covering archaelogical topics, including research, site information, bibliographic data, etc.
Subjects covered: archaeology
List moderated: No.
Editorial contact: Sebastian Rahtz
Internet: spqr@minster.york.ac.uk
How to access: Send subscribe message to listserv@dgogwdgl
How to unsubscribe: Send unsubscribe message to listserv@dgogwdgl
Archives: Yes, archives are available; apply to listowner for details.

ARCHIVES@INDYCMS

Description: ARCHIVES@INDYCMS is a forum covering archival theory and practice.
Subjects covered: library and information science; archival theory
List moderated: No.
Editorial contact: Donna B. Harlan
Internet: harlan@ucs.indiana.edu
Bitnet: harlan@iubacs
How to access: Send subscribe message to listserv@indycms or listserv@indycms.iupui.edu
How to unsubscribe: Send unsubscribe message to listserv@indycms or listserv@indycms.iupui.edu
Archives: Archives are developed monthly; apply to listowner for details.

ARCLIB-L

Description: Arclib-L is an electronic discussion list for Irish and UK architectural librarians.
Subjects covered: library and information science; architecture
List moderated: No.
Editorial contact: Julia Barrett
Internet: jbarrett@irlearn
How to access: Send subscribe message to listserv@irlearn or listserv@irlearn.ucd.ie
How to unsubscribe: Send unsubscribe message to listserv@irlearn or listserv@irlearn.ucd.ie
Archives: Yes; Monthly, Private

ARGENTINA@OIS.DB.TORONTO.EDU

Description: ARGENTINA@OIS.DB.TORONTO.EDU is a forum for discussion of Argentina.
Subjects covered: Argentina
List moderated: No.
Editorial contact: Carlos G. Mendioroz
Internet: tron@db.toronto.edu
How to access: Send subscribe message to ARGENTINA-REQUEST@OIS.DB.TORONTO.EDU
How to unsubscribe: Send unsubscribe message to ARGENTINA-REQUEST@OIS.DB.TORONTO.EDU

ARIE-L

Description: Arie-L is a forum covering use of the Ariel document transmission system developed by RLG.
Subjects covered: library and information science; document delivery
List moderated: No.
Editorial contact: Dan Lester
Bitnet: alileste@idbsu
How to access: Send subscribe message to listserv@idbsu
How to unsubscribe: Send unsubscribe message to listserv@idbsu
Archives: Archives are developed monthly; apply to listowner for details.

ARJUNA@MAILBASE.AC.UK

Description: ARJUNA is a mailbase discussion list on the Arjuna programming system.
Subjects covered: computer hardware and software
List moderated: No.
Internet: arjuna-request@mailbase.ac.uk
How to access: Send subscribe message to mailbase@mailbase.ac.uk in the following format: join arjuna Yourfirstname Yourlastname
Archives: Archives are developed monthly; apply to listowner for details.

ARLIS-L

Description: ARLIS-L is an electronic forum for art and other visual resource information professionals. ARLIS-L is affiliated with Art Libraries Society of North America (ARLIS/NA). Subjects covered include items of interest to art, architecture, and other visual resource librarians, as well as, reference queries, job announcements, conference announcements, cataloging issues, trades of materials, reviews of books and products, etc.
Subjects covered: art; library and information science; fine arts
Net address for operations: LISTSERV@UKCC.uky.edu
Net address for questions or submissions: ARLIS-L@UKCC.uky.edu
Established: September 1990
Subscribers: 600
Sponsor: University of Kentucky Libraries
Host: University of Kentucky, Lexington, Kentucky
List moderated: Yes.
Moderation procedure: Postings are automatically submitted to the moderator before distribution.
Editorial contact: Mary Molinaro
Library Microlabs, 213A King South, University of Kentucky, Lexington, KY 40506-0039.

Tel: (606) 257-6199
Fax: (606) 257-8379
Internet: molinaro@uklans.uky.edu
Bitnet: molinaro@ukcc
How to access: Send mail to LISTSERV@ukcc.uky.edu with the following message as the ENTIRE message (no subject line, please!) subscribe ARLIS-L Your Name
Access policy: Subscription is open to anyone.
How to unsubscribe: Send mail to LISTSERV@ukcc.uky.edu with the following message as the ENTIRE message (no subject line, please!): UNSUB ARLIS-L
How to submit: Send mail to ARLIS-L@ukcc.uky.edu
Submission policy: All messages are submitted to ARLIS-L moderator for posting to ARLIS-L.
Archives: All messages are archived and are searchable through LISTSERV. For information send mail to LISTSERV@ukcc.uky.edu with the following message: INFO DATABASE

ARMS-L
Description: Arms-L is a forum for discussion of peace and war-related issues.
Subjects covered: activism; peace studies
List moderated: Yes.
Editorial contact: Rob Gross
Bitnet: gross@bcvms
How to access: Send subscribe message to listserv@buacca or arms-d-request@xx.lcs.mit.edu
How to unsubscribe: Send unsubscribe message to listserv@buacca or arms-d-request@xx.lcs.mit.edu
Archives: Contact the Editor

AROMA-TRIALS@MAILBASE.AC.UK
Description: AROMA-TRIALS@MAILBASE.AC.UK is a conference on olfaction and related research.
Subjects covered: health sciences; medicine
List moderated: No.
Internet: aroma-trials-request@mailbase.ac.uk
How to access: Send subscribe message to mailbase@mailbase.ac.uk in the following format: join aroma-trials Your first name Your last name
Archives: Archives are developed monthly; apply to listowner for details.

ART-SUPPORT@MAILBASE.AC.UK
Description: ART-SUPPORT is a forum for discussing art-related items.
Subjects covered: art
List moderated: No.
Internet: art-support-request@newcastle.ac.uk
How to access: Send subscribe message to mailbase@newcastle.ac.uk
How to unsubscribe: Send unsubscribe message to mailbase@newcastle.ac.uk

ARTCRIT@YORKVM1
Description: ARTCRIT@YORKVM1 is a forum for the discussion of the visual arts.
Subjects covered: art
List moderated: Yes.

Editorial contact: Michele Macaluso
Internet: macal@nexus.yorku.ca
How to access: Send subscribe message to listserv@yorkvm1 or listserv@vm1.yorku.ca.
How to unsubscribe: Send unsubscribe message to listserv@yorkvm1 or listserv@vm1.yorku.ca.
Archives: Archives are developed monthly; apply to listowner for details.

ARTNET@MAILBASE.AC.UK
Description: ARTNET is a forum for discussion of various art/computer-related topics.
Subjects covered: art
List moderated: No.
Internet: artnet-request@mailbase.ac.uk
How to access: Send subscribe message to mailbase@mailbase.ac.uk in the following format: join artnet Yourfirstname Yourlastname
How to unsubscribe: Send unsubscribe message to mailbase@mailbase.ac.uk in the following format: join artnet Yourfirstname Yourlastname
Archives: Archives are developed monthly; apply to listowner for details.

ASCII-ART
Description: ASCII-ART is a forum for the compilation and dissemination of ASCII artforms.
Subjects covered: art
List moderated: No.
Editorial contact: Christopher Davis
Internet: dzza1005f@sa.birmp.ac.uk
How to access: Send subscribe message to DZZA1005F@SA.BIRMP.AC.UK
How to unsubscribe: Send unsubscribe message to DZZA1005F@SA.BIRMP.AC.UK

ASEH-L
Description: ASEH-L is the discussion list of the American Scoiety of Environmental Historians.
Subjects covered: environmental studies; history
Net address for operations: LISTSERV@TTUVM1
Net address for questions or submissions: ASEH@TTUVM1
How to access: Send message to listserv: SUBSCRIBE <listname> <your name>

ASHE-L
Description: Ashe-L discusses issues pertaining to the Association for the Study of Higher Education.
Subjects covered: education
Host: Association for the Study of Higher Education
List moderated: No.
How to access: Send subscribe message to listserv@mizzoui
How to unsubscribe: Send unsubscribe message to listserv@mizzoui

ASIS-L
Description: ASIS-L is an electronic discussion list of the American Society for Information Science posting announce-

ments of national, regional, and local ASIS activities and programs; recruitment of volunteers for ASIS offices and projects; and discussion of information science topics.
Subjects covered: library and information science; science and technology
Net address for operations: ASIS-LISTSERV@UVMVM or LISTSERV@UVMVM.EDU
Net address for questions or submissions: ASIS-L@UVMVM or ASIS-L@UVMVM.UVM.EDU
Established: May 1992
Subscribers: 475
Sponsor: American Society for Information Science, 8720 Georgia Avenue, Suite 501, Silver Spring, MD 20910.
Host: University of Vermont, Libraries & Media Services, Burlington, VT 05405-0036.
List moderated: No.
Editorial contact: Merri Beth Lavagnino
117 Bailey/Howe Library, University of Vermont, Burlington, VT 05405-0036.
Tel: (802) 656-1369
Fax: (802) 656-4038
Internet: MLAVAGNI@UVMVM.UVM.EDU
Bitnet: MLAVAGNI@UVMVM
How to access: Send electronic mail message to LISTSERV@UVMVM. Leave the subject line blank. Enter as the text of your message "SUBSCRIBE ASIS-L <YOUR FULL NAME>
How to unsubscribe: Send electronic mail message to LISTSERV@UVMVM. Leave the subject line blank. Enter as the text of your message, "UNSUBSCRIBE ASIS-L"
How to submit: Send electronic mail message to ASIS-L@UVMVM

ASKERIC

Description: AskERIC is an Internet-based question-answering service for teachers, library media specialists, and administrators. Anyone involved with K-12 education can send an e-mail message to AskERIC. Drawing on the extensive resources of the ERIC system, AskERIC staff respond with an answer within 48 working hours. Questions include all areas of K-12 education. AskERIC also provides the "AskERIC Electronic Library," a Gopher/FTP site of selected electronic full-text resources and database citations. The address of this site is: ericir.syr.edu (port# 70). AskERIC is a pilot Internet development & research project funded in part by the U.S. Department of Education as part of the ERIC program and SMARTLINE initiative. AskERIC is also part of a series of Internet projects at Syracuse University seeking to explore Internet usefulness and accessibility. The specific purpose of AskERIC is to develop and study Internet-based education information services, systems, and resources that best meet the needs of K-12 end users.
Subjects covered: education; ERIC
Editorial contact: Nancy Morgan, Richard Tkachuck, AskERIC Coordinators, ERIC Clearinghouse on Information and Technology, Syracuse University, Syracuse, NY 13244-4100.
Technical contact: David Lankes, AskERIC Researcher, ERIC Clearinghouse on Information and Technology, Syracuse University, Syracuse, New York 13244
Tel: (315) 443-9114
Fax: (315) 443-5448
Internet: rdlankes@ericir.syr.edu
How to access: To use the AskERIC email question-answering service, send a question to: askeric@ericir.syr.edu

How to submit: Please send any questions or comments to: askeric@ericir.syr.edu
Submission policy: To use the AskERIC email question-answering service, send a question to: askeric@ericir.syr.edu

ASMICRO-L

Description: ASMICRO-L is a discussion forum on the design and use of application-specific microprocessors.
Subjects covered: engineering; computer science
List moderated: No.
Editorial contact: Pedro Luis Prospero Sanchez
Internet: pl@vm131.lsi.usp.ansp.br
How to access: Send subscribe message to asmicro-request@vme131.lsi.usp.ansp.br
How to unsubscribe: Send unsubscribe message to asmicro-request@vme131.lsi.usp.ansp.br

ASSESS@UKCC

Description: ASSESS@UKCC is a forum for discussing issues related to higher education.
Subjects covered: education; colleges and universities
List moderated: No.
Editorial contact: Thomas E. Kunselman
Internet: vaatek@ukcc.uky.edu
Bitnet: vaatek@ukcc
How to access: Send subscribe message to listserv@ukcc or listserv@ukcc.uky.edu
How to unsubscribe: Send unsubscribe message to listserv@ukcc or listserv@ukcc.uky.edu

ASTR-O@BRFAPESP

Description: ASTR-O@BRFAPESP is a conference on astronomy.
Subjects covered: astronomy; events listings
Host: Socieadade Astronomica Brasileira (SAB)
List moderated: No.
Editorial contact: Augusto Daminelli
Internet: daminelli@iag.usp.ansp.br
Bitnet: daminelli%iagusp@brfapesp
How to access: Send subscribe message to mailserv@brfapesp or mailserv@brfapesp.ansp.br
How to unsubscribe: Send unsubscribe message to mailserv@brfapesp or mailserv@brfapesp.ansp.br

ASTRA-UG

Description: ASTRA-UG is a list featuring discussions on and questions about modifications on the NJE distributed database service ASTRA.
Subjects covered: computer science; computer hardware and software
Net address for operations: LISTSERV@ICNUCEVM.CNUCE.CNR.IT
Net address for questions or submissions: ASTRA-UG@ICNUCEVM.CNUCE.CNR.IT
Established: 1990
Subscribers: 69
Sponsor: CNUCE-CNR, Via S. Maria 36 Pisa 56127 Italy
Host: Same
List moderated: No.
Editorial contact: Esra Delen

Ege Univ. Bilgisayar Ar. ve Uyg. Mrk. 35100 Bornova Izmir Turkey
Tel: 90-51-887221
Fax: 90-51-887230
Internet: ESRA@EGE.EDU.TR
Bitnet: ESRA@TREARN
Technical contact: Daniele Vannozzi CNUCE-CNR Via S.Maria 36, Pisa 56127 Italy
Tel: 39-50-593111
Internet: VANNOZZI@ICNUCEVM.CNUCE.CNR.IT
How to access: Tell Listserv at ICNUCEVM SUB ASTRA-UG fullname
How to unsubscribe: Tell Listserv at ICNUCEVM SIGNOFF ASTRA-UG
How to submit: By mailing to ASTRA-UG@ICNUCEVM
Archives: Available via LOG files on LISTSERV.
Gopher accessibility: Yes
WAIS accessibility: Yes
WorldWideWeb accessibility: Yes

ASTRONOMY@BBN.COM

Description: ASTRONOMY@BBN.COM is a list of scheduled events of interest to astronomers.
Subjects covered: astronomy; events listings
Host: BBN Systems & Technologies
List moderated: No.
Editorial contact: Dick Koolish
Internet: koolish@bbn.com
How to access: Send subscribe message to ASTRONOMY-RE-QUEST@BBN.COM
How to unsubscribe: Send unsubscribe message to ASTRON-OMY-REQUEST@BBN.COM

AT-FINANCE-BOARD@INVNEXT.WORLDBANK.ORG

Description: The Advanced Technology for Finance Special Interest Group of the INNS maintains the AT-Finance mailing list for discussions of financial or economic applications of advanced technology. Discussion sometimes involves Neural Networks, Genetic Algorithms, Fuzzy Logic, Statistics, Complexity theory, Artificial Life, and Nonlinear and Chaos Theory.
Subjects covered: artificial intelligence
How to access: Send mail to at-finance-request@invnext.worldbank.org
How to submit: Send mail to the AT-Finance administrator at <at-finance@invnext.worldbank.org>

ATLAS-L

Description: ATLAS-L is a listserv list dealing with the library automation package ATLAS from Data Research Inc.
Subjects covered: computer hardware and software; library and information science; library automation
Net address for operations: LISTSERV@TCUBVM.BITNET
Net address for questions or submissions: ATLAS-L@TCUBVM.BITNET
Established: Summer 1990
Subscribers: 344
Sponsor: Texas Christian University
Host: Texas Christian University
List moderated: No.
Editorial contact: James L. Mayne

PO Box 32883, Fort Worth TX, 76129.
Tel: (817) 921-7695 x6843
Fax: (817) 921-7110
Internet: mayne@gamma.is.tcu.edu
Bitnet: mayne@tcucvms
Technical contact: James L. Mayne
PO Box 32883, Fort Worth TX, 76129.
Tel: (817) 921-7695 x6843
Fax: (817) 921-7110
Internet: mayne@gamma.is.tcu.edu
Bitnet: mayne@tcucvms
How to access: Send the command ''subscribe atlas-l your-name'' to the BITNET address listserv@tcubvm, where your-name is your full name.
Access policy: Subscriptions are open to any interested persons.
How to unsubscribe: Send the command ''signoff atlas-l'' to the BITNET address listserv@tcubvm
How to submit: Send an e-mail message to the BITNET address atlas-l@tcubvm
Archives: Past postings can be retrieved using the standard means for BITNET listservs. The command is send atlas-l.logxxyy where xx is the year such as 93 and yy is the month such as 02 for February.

AUSTEN-L

Description: Austen-L is an edited digest for students of Jane Austen.
Subjects covered: English language and literature; Austen, Jane
List moderated: No.
Editorial contact: Dr. Jacqueline Reid-Walsh
Bitnet: michael@vm1.mcgill.ca
How to access: Send subscribe message to listserv@mcgill1
How to unsubscribe: Send unsubscribe message to listserv@mcgill1
Archives: Archives are developed monthly; apply to listowner for details.

AUTISM

Description: AUTISM is an electronic discussion list covering autism and developmental disability from a scientific and phenomonlogical perspective. Support group for parents and teachers of individuals with autism.
Subjects covered: autism; developmental disabilities; disabilities
Net address for operations: autism@sjuvm.bitnet
Established: April 1992
Subscribers: 153
Sponsor: St. John's University, Jamaica, NY.
Host: St. John's University, Jamaica, NY.
List moderated: No.
Technical contact: Dr. Robert Zenhausern
St. John's University Jamaica, NY 11439.
Tel: (718)-990-6447
Fax: (718)-990-6705
Internet: drz@sjuvm.stjohns.edu
Bitnet: drz@sjuvm.bitnet
How to access: Send mail to listserv@sjuvm.bitnet with the message: sub autism Firstname Lastname
Access policy: Subscription is not automatic and your request will be forwarded to the listowner.
How to unsubscribe: Send mail to listserv@sjuvm.bitnet with the message: signoff autism

How to submit: Send mail to autism@sjuvm.bitnet
Archives: Logs of all messages available in the form: autism log9305 (logs of altlearn for May, 1993). Other files available. For a complete list of files send mail to listserv@sjuvm.bitnet with the message: index autism

AUTOCAT@UVMVM
Description: AUTOCAT@UVMVM is a forum for discussion of library cataloging and authority control.
Subjects covered: library and information science
List moderated: No.
Editorial contact: Judith Hopkins
Lockwood Library, SUNY-Buffalo, Buffalo, NY 14260-2200
Internet: ulcjh@ubvm.cc.buffalo.edu
Bitnet: bhutchin@uvmvm
How to access: Send subscribe message to listserv@ubvm or listserv@ubvm.cc.buffalo.edu
How to unsubscribe: Send unsubscribe message to listserv@ubvm or listserv@ubvm.cc.buffalo.edu
Archives: Archives are developed weekly; apply to listowner for details. For a complete list of files, send mail to listserv with the message: index autocat

AVIATION-THEORY@MC.LCS.MIT.EDU
Description: AVIATION-THEORY@MC.LCS.MIT.EDU covers aerospace engineering.
Subjects covered: engineering; aerospace
List moderated: No.
Editorial contact: Rob A. Vingerhoeds
Internet: rob%bgerug51.bitnet@mitvma.mit.edu
Bitnet: rob@bgerug51
How to access: Send subscribe message to AVIATION-THEORY-REQUEST@MC.LCS.MIT.EDU
How to unsubscribe: Send unsubscribe message to AVIATION-THEORY-REQUEST@MC.LCS.MIT.EDU

AXSLIB-L@BITNIC
Description: AXSLIB-L is the list of Project EASI: Library Access for Persons with Disabilities
Subjects covered: disabilities; library and information science
Net address for questions or submissions: LISTSERV@BITNIC
How to access: Send subscribe message to LISTSERV@BITNIC
How to unsubscribe: Send unsubscribe message to LISTSERV@BITNIC

AYN-RAND@UA1VM
Description: AYN-RAND@UA1VM is a forum for the discussion of philosophical aspects of Objectivism.
Subjects covered: philosophy; Rand, Ayn
List moderated: Yes.
Editorial contact: Jimmy Wales
Bitnet: jwales@iubvm
How to access: Send subscribe message to listserv@ua1vm or listserv@ua1vm.ua.edu
How to unsubscribe: Send unsubscribe message to listserv@ua1vm or listserv@ua1vm.ua.edu
Archives: Archives are developed monthly; apply to listowner for details.

BAGPIPE@SUNAPEE.DARTMOUTH.EDU
Description: BAGPIPE@SUNAPEE.DARTMOUTH.EDU is a forum covering bagpipes and related instruments.
Subjects covered: music; musical instruments
List moderated: No.
Internet: pipes-request@sunapee.dartmouth.edu
How to access: Send subscribe message to PIPES-REQUEST@SUNAPEE.DARTMOUTH.EDU
How to unsubscribe: Send unsubscribe message to PIPES-REQUEST@SUNAPEE.DARTMOUTH.EDU

BAHAI-FAITH@ONEWORLD.WA.COM
Description: BAHAI-FAITH@ONEWORLD.WA.COM is a forum on the Baha'i religion.
Subjects covered: religion
List moderated: No.
Editorial contact: Charles W. Cooper II
Internet: bahai-faith-request@oneworld.wa.com
How to access: Contact the Editor
How to unsubscribe: Contact the Editor

BALLROOM
Description: Ballroom is an electronic discussion group covering any aspect of Ballroom and Swing dancing, and related activities, including but not limited to: requests and posting of places to dance; announcements of special events; discussions of technique, styles, customs, etiquette; exchange of information about clubs; ballroom dance music; discussion of dances, steps, etc.
Subjects covered: dance; music; sports
Net address for operations: ballroom-request@athena.mit.edu
Net address for questions or submissions: ballroom@athena.mit.edu
Established: December 1990
Subscribers: 150 direct subscribers; estimated 500+ through sub-lists and gateways.
Sponsor: MIT Ballroom Dance Club, MIT Room W20-401, Cambridge, MA 02139.
Host: MIT Ballroom Dance Club, MIT Room W20-401, Cambridge, MA 02139.
List moderated: No.
Editorial contact: Shahrukh Merchant
182 Winding Pond Road, Londonderry, NH 03053.
Tel: (603) 437 1357
Internet: ballroom-request@athena.mit.edu
Copyright statement: Since this is a public unmoderated list, it is only a distribution medium; accordingly, submitters of articles are responsible for ensuring that no copyright-protected works are submitted without permission of the copyright owner. Neither the list administrator nor sponsoring institution claims general copyrights to articles posted to the list, although individual postings may have their own copyright statements.
How to access: E-mail to ballroom-request@athena.mit.edu
Access policy: Anyone may join; the following information is required: Full name; Internet-compatible e-mail address; Affiliation with ballroom/dance organization, if any; Postal or ZIP code and country; Whether subscriber has access to Netnews (Usenet News) (Yes/No/Yes but rarely use/Don't know); and (Optional) How the subscriber found out about this list. Allow up to 2 weeks for addition.
How to unsubscribe: E-mail to ballroom-request@athena.mit.edu requesting deletion

How to submit: E-mail to ballroom@athena.mit.edu
Submission policy: No official policy, but adherence to the following "common sense" rules are requested. (1) Contents should be on Ballroom/Swing and related subjects (2) No copyright-protected works without permission from the copyright owner (3) Use a descriptive title in the "Subject:" field (4) Understand that this is a resource for all to enjoy, so use common sense and good taste.
Related files: The mailing list ballroom@athena.mit.edu is connected via a bidirectional gateway to the Netnews newgroup rec.arts.dance. Anything mailed to the mailing list is automatically posted to rec.arts.dance. Since rec.arts.dance covers non-ballroom topics also, the gateway in the reverse direction is filtered, so that only those articles posted to rec.arts.dance with "ballroom" or the name of a ballroom dance in the "Subject:" or "Keywords:" field are mailed to the mailing list.

BALT-INFO

Description: BALT-INFO, an electronic network of Baltic librarians, will help participating libraries exchange information and concerns related to acquisitions, cataloging, reference services, and any other aspect of librarianship. BALT-INFO will also try to help researchers locate Baltic-related bibliographic citations or library resources as well as attempt to answer relevant reference requests. BALT-INFO will also serve as a forum for announcing Baltic-related conferences, grants, and other possible funding sources for librarians and researchers in the field. Whenever possible, information about any identifiable Baltic-related INTERNET resources or databases will also be posted. The BALT-INFO Project will last for about one year (until September 30, 1994). During this time, IREX funding will be used to upgrade or establish INTERNET links for participating research libraries in the Baltic. IREX funding for INTERNET training has also been made available, and Dawn Mann of RFE-RL will conduct three three-day workshops (one each in Tallinn, Riga, and Vilnius). She will also visit BALT-INFO participants in Tartu (Estonia) and Kaunas (Lithuania).
Subjects covered: Estonia; Lithuania; Latvia; library and information science
Net address for questions or submissions:
MANND@RFERL.ORG
Editorial contact: Dawn Mann
Internet: MANND@RFERL.ORG

BALT-L

Description: BALT-L, an electronic discussion group relating to the interests of Baltic librarians, is intended to help participating libraries exchange information and concerns related to acquisitions, cataloging, reference services, and any other aspect of librarianship.
Subjects covered: Estonia; Lithuania; Latvia; library and information science
Net address for questions or submissions:
MANND@RFERL.ORG
Editorial contact: Dawn Mann
Internet: MANND@RFERL.ORG

BALTUVA@MCGILL1

Description: BALTUVA@MCGILL1 is a forum covering issues of the Jewish faith.
Subjects covered: religion; Judaica

List moderated: No.
Editorial contact: Claire Austin
Internet: czca@musica.mcgill.ca
How to access: Send subscribe message to listserv@mcgill1 or listserv@vm1.mcgill.ca
How to unsubscribe: Send unsubscribe message to listserv@mcgill1 or listserv@vm1.mcgill.ca

BALZAC-L

Description: BALZAC-L is a discussion list covering announcements, discussions, requests and sharing of information on the study and teaching of French literature. It is the first French language list on the Internet as well as the first French literature list.
Subjects covered: French language and literature; language and literature; cultural studies
Net address for operations: BALZAC-L-REQUEST@CC.UMONTREAL.CA
Net address for questions or submissions: BALZAC-L@CC.UMONTREAL.CA
Established: OCTOBER 1991
Subscribers: 175
Sponsor: Departement D'Etudes Francaises, University de Montreal, Pavillon Lionel-Groulx 3150, Rue Jean-Brillant, Montreal, Quebec Canada H3C 3J7.
Host: Universite de Montreal, C.P. 6128, Succursale a Montreal, Quebec, Canada H3C 3J7.
List moderated: Subscriptions moderated, submissions not moderated.
Editorial contact: Christian Allegre
Department D'etudes Francaises, Universite de Montreal, Pavillon Lionel-Groulx, C.P. 6128, Succursale a Montreal, Quebec, Canada H3C 3J7.
Tel: (514) 343-6623
Fax: (514) 343-2256
Internet: ALLEGRE@ERE.UMONTREAL.CA
How to access: Send subscribe note to: BALZAC-L-REQUEST@CC.UMONTREAL.CA
Access policy: Send brief note requesting subscription from your Internet address with full name, position, name & address of department and university, telephone, fax.
How to unsubscribe: Send note to: BALZAC-L-REQUEST@CC.UMONTREAL.CA
How to submit: Send submissions to:
BALZAC-L@CC.UMONTREAL.CA
Submission policy: Since Balzac-L is not moderated, all submissions are immediately forwarded to all members. Submissions must not be of a commercial nature. In case of hesitation, please write to: ALLEGRE@ERE.UMONTREAL.CA (Christian Allegre) OR PIERSENS@ERE.UMONTREAL.CA (Michel Pierssens).
Additional information: Second editor: Michel Pierssens (Founding Editor and Co-Owner), Department D'etudes Francaises, Universite de Montreal, Pavillon Lionel-Groulx, C.P. 6128, Succursale a Montreal, Quebec, Canada H3C 3J7 and Co-owner), tel. (514) 343-6378; fax (514) 343-2256; Piersens@ere.umontreal.ca Lanuages currently used are 1) French [db1] 2)English.

BARBERSHOP

Description: Barbershop offers general discussion about barbershop singing and the activities of the various barbershop singing

organizations such as the S.P.E.B.S.Q.S.A., Sweet Adelines, and Harmony, Inc. Typical topics might include results from chorus and quartet contests, sources for barbershop arrangements, and reviews of barbershop recordings.
Subjects covered: barbershop singing; music
Net address for operations: barbershop-request@bigd.cray.com
Net address for questions or submissions: barbershop@bigd.cray.com
Established: July 1991
Subscribers: 80
Sponsor: Cray Research, Inc., 655F Lone Oak Dr., Eagan, MN 55121
List moderated: No.
Technical contact: David Bowen
655F Lone Oak Dr., Eagan, MN 55121
Tel: (612) 683-5094
Fax: (612) 683-5599
Internet: david.bowen@cray.com
How to access: Send mail to barbershop-request@bigd.cray.com.
Access policy: No restrictions on subscribers. The list is purged of invalid addresses on a periodic basis.
How to unsubscribe: Send mail to barbershop-request@bigd.cray.com.
How to submit: Send to barbershop@bigd.cray.com
Submission policy: Submissions should pertain to barbershop singing and likely to be of general interest to the group at large.
Archives: An archive of past contest results is available by e-mail to barbershop-request@bigd.cray.com [db1]

BEE-L

Subjects covered: beekeeping
Net address for questions or submissions: mts@gnv.ifas.ufl.edu, mts@ifasgnv.bitnet
Host: University of Florida
Editorial contact: Malcolm T. Sanford
Building 970, Box 119620, University of Florida, Gainesville, FL 32611-0620.
Internet: mts@gnv.ifas.ufl.edu, mts@ifasgnv.bitnet
How to access: Send message to mts@gnv.ifas.ufl.edu or mts@ifasgnv.bitnet

BEHAVIOR@ASUACAD

Description: BEHAVIOR@ASUACAD is a forum for the discussion of behavioral disorders in children.
Subjects covered: psychology
List moderated: No.
Editorial contact: Samuel A. DiGangi
Bitnet: atsad@asuacad
How to access: Send subscribe message to listserv@asuacad or listserv@asuvm.inre.asu.edu
How to unsubscribe: Send unsubscribe message to listserv@asuacad or listserv@asuvm.inre.asu.edu
Archives: Archives are developed monthly; apply to listowner for details.

BELIEF-L (PERSONAL IDEOLOGIES DISCUSSION LIST)

Description: Discussion on BELIEF-L centers on religious and philosophical topics.
Subjects covered: religion; philosophy; ethics; political science

Net address for operations: listserv@brownvm.brown.edu
Net address for questions or submissions: BELIEF-L@brownvm.brown.edu
Established: June 1989
Subscribers: 307
Host: Brown University, Providence RI (brownvm.brown.edu)
List moderated: Yes, informally.
Moderation procedure: List owner handles subscription problems, monitors list activity with assistance from 'quiet' owners. Subscribers are generally given free reign but are expected to follow rules outlined in list header. Subscribers failing to do so are given three warnings before removal (to date, no one has been removed by this fashion).
Editorial contact: David B. O'Donnell
15 Everett Ave, Providence RI USA 02906-3321
Tel: (401) 453-3886
Internet: atropos@netlab.cis.brown.edu
Bitnet: EL406006@brownvm
Technical contact: Same as above
How to access: Send 'SUB BELIEF-L user name' in e-mail to listserv@brownvm.brown.edu
How to unsubscribe: Send 'UNSUB BELIEF-L' in e-mail to same listserv.
How to submit: Send article as e-mail to belief-l@brownvm.brown.edu
Archives: Archived weekly via normal Listserv program. Archives are maintained for up to three months. Send 'INDEX BELIEF-L' to listserv@brownvm.brown.edu to get a list of archives. List is also digested weekly; to receive the digested form, subscribe (see above) and then send 'SET BELIEF-L NOMAIL DIGEST' in e-mail to listserv@brownvm.brown.edu

BETA@MJOLNER.DK

Description: BETA@MJOLNER.DK is a forum for users of BETA computer programming language.
Subjects covered: computer science
List moderated: No.
Editorial contact: Elmer Soerensen Sandvad
Internet: usergroup-request@mjolner.dk
How to access: Contact the Editor
How to unsubscribe: Contact the Editor

BGRASS-L BLUEGRASS MUSIC DISCUSSION LIST

Description: BGRASS-L is an electronic discussion list devoted to Bluegrass and Old Time Music. The purpose of BGRASS-L is to be a forum for discussion of: 1. Issues related to the International Bluegrass Music Association (IBMA); 2. BG and OT music in general, including but not limited to recordings, bands, individual performers, live performances, publications, business aspects, venues, history, you-name-it. Early commercial country music is also an acceptable topic.
Subjects covered: music; bluegrass music
Net address for operations: LISTSERV@UKCC.UKY.EDU
Net address for questions or submissions: BGRASS-L@UKCC.UKY.EDU
Established: November 22, 1991
Subscribers: 313
Sponsor: University of Kentucky
Host: University of Kentucky
List moderated: No.
Editorial contact: Frank Godbey

University of Kentucky, Computing Center, 128 McVey Hall, Lexington, KY 40506-0045.
Tel: (606)257-2362
Fax: (606)258-1978
Internet: UKA016@UKCC.UKY.EDU
Bitnet: UKA016@UKCC
Technical contact: Sashi Sathaye
Tel: (606)257-2247
Internet: SYSSASH@UKCC.UKY.EDU
Bitnet: SYSSASH@UKCC
Copyright statement: Copyright to submissions to BGRASS-L is retained by the person writing the message. Messages distributed by BGRASS-L may be freely forwarded electronically or in hard-copy but may not be accumulated, extracted, quoted from, or otherwise used in any form in any commercial or non-commercial venture, whether for profit or not, without written permission from each message writer whose work is so used.
How to access: Send e-mail to: LISTSERV@UKCC or LISTSERV@UKCC.UKY.EDU with the following command in the BODY of the mail (NO subject:): SUB BGRASS-L your full name
Access policy: BGRASS-L is open to anyone with an interest in the music and network access.
How to unsubscribe: To unsubscribe, send e-mail from the address to which your subscription is distributed to: LISTSERV@UKCC or LISTSERV@UKCC.UKY.EDU with the following command in the BODY of the mail (NO subject:): UNSUB BGRASS-L
How to submit: To communicate, send e-mail to: BGRASS-L@UKCC or BGRASS-L@UKCC.UKY.EDU
Submission policy: Try to keep communications within the general subjects covered by the list. If replies or messages are intended for only one person, please take them off-list.
Archives: LISTSERV has access to archives from the beginning of the list. To find out what files are available send e-mail to the LISTSERV at one of the addresses above, with the following command as the only message line: GET BGRASS-L FILELIST Then decide what you want and send another message in the form GET BGRASS-L <filename> (Note: retrievals are subject to a 256k daily limit to any address.)
Related files: Archives of BGRASS-L are also available via anonymous ftp as follows:
FTP to hypatia.gsfc.nasa.gov, log in as anonymous, give your e-mail address as the password, then change to the directory /pub/logs/BGRASS-L. (Note: ftp space is maintained by Archie Warnock, Internet: warnock@hypatia.gsfc.nasa.gov)
Gopher accessibility: Via "gopher" select: "WAIS Based Information" "byletter" "B" (Note: WAIS-based files are maintained by Archie Warnock, see ftp, above).

BI-L (BIBLIOGRAPHIC INSTRUCTION DISCUSSION LIST)

Description: BI-L is an international computer conference dedicated to discussing ways of assisting library users in effectively and efficiently exploiting the resources available through the libraries of the 1990s. Contributors to the forum deal with the practical, theoretical, and technical aspects of what has been called Bibliographic Instruction, Library Use Instruction, Library Orientation, and several other names. We examine, explore, critique, appraise, and evaluate strategies, programs, and equipment that we have found to be valuable (or not) in working toward the goal of the self-sufficient library user.

Subjects covered: library and information science; bibliographic instruction
Net address for operations: LISTSERV@bingvmb.BITNET
Net address for questions or submissions:
BI-L@bingvmb.BITNET
Established: April 26, 1990
Subscribers: 1500
Sponsor: Binghamton University, Binghamton, NY 13902-6012.
Host: Binghamton University, Binghamton, NY 13902-6012.
List moderated: Yes.
Moderation procedure: Moderator eliminates messages that contain obvious errors or that are outside the scope of the list's purpose.
Editorial contact: Martin Raish
Box 6012, Main Library, Binghamton Universit, Binghamton, NY 13902-6012.
Tel: (607) 777-4385
Fax: (607) 777-4848
Internet: mraish@bingvmb.cc.binghamton.edu
Bitnet: mraish@bingvmb
Technical contact: Brian Frederick
Computer Center, Binghamton University, Binghamton, NY 13902.
Tel: (607) 777-6129
Internet: frederic@bingvaxa.cc.binghamton.edu
Bitnet: frederic@bingvaxa
Review: BI-L: An Electronic Discussion Group for IME Medical Reference Services Quarterly 11(2) (Summer 1992):79-88.
How to access: Send the following command to LISTSERV@bingvmb sub BI-L <yourfirstname> <yourlastname>
Access policy: The forum is available to anyone with an e-mail account on a computer connected to BITNET, or to networks that are linked to BITNET. Messages sent to BI-L are reviewed by the moderator, who distributes appropriate items to all conference participants. BI-L subscribers normally receive about 5 messages per day.
How to unsubscribe: Send the following command to LISTSERV@bingvmb unsub BI-L
How to submit: Send your message to BI-L@bingvmb
Archives: Postings are archived for six months.
Related files: Network Knowledge for the Neophyte; The Image of the Librarian in Commercial Motion Pictures; other files will be added during the latter part of 1993.

BIBLE

Description: BIBLE is an electronic conference designed to provide a forum for anyone interested in learning to study the Bible. Anyone interested in studying the Bible together is invited to subscribe, but the list will assume that the participants consider the Bible authoritative. Experts and professionals are welcome to provide wisdom and insight, but those interested in an exclusively academic approach to Bible study should join either the NT-GREEK list (NT-GREEK-REQUEST@VIRGINIA.EDU) or the OT-HEBREW list (OT-HEBREW-REQUEST@VIRGINIA.EDU).
Subjects covered: Bible studies; religion; Christianity
Net address for operations: BIBLE on BIBLE-REQUEST@VIRGINIA.EDU
BIBLE on BIBLEREQ@VIRGINIA.BITNET
Sponsor: The list is supported by the University of Virginia. The list is sponsored by the the Center for Christian Study, an independent Christian ministry at the University of Virginia. For

more information about the Center for Christian Study contact: The Center for Christian Study, 128 Chancellor Street, Charlottesville, VA 22903 (804) 295-2471.

How to access: You may subscribe by sending an e-mail message to BIBLE-REQUEST@VIRGINIA.EDU BIBLEREQ@VIRGINIA.BITNET if your account is on the internet, with the following request as the text of the message. SUB BIBLE Your First name Your Last name This, the 'SUB ...,' must be part of the message; the subject line will be ignored.

Access policy: Subscription to this conference is open to anyone interested.

How to unsubscribe: You may leave the list at any time by sending a ''UNSUBscribe BIBLE'' request to BIBLE-REQUEST@VIRGINIA.EDU. Please note that this request must NOT be sent to the list address (BIBLE@VIRGINIA.EDU) but to the REQUEST address (BIBLE-REQUEST@VIRGINIA.EDU). You are currently subscribed to receive messages immediately as they arrive. This volume of mail may prove annoying. There is an alternative of receiving periodic digests of the list's activity. To receive only the digested format of BIBLE send the message: DIGEST BIBLE to the REQUEST address (BIBLE-REQUEST@VIRGINIA.EDU). To change back to the immediate format of BIBLE send the command: IMMEDIATE BIBLE to the REQUEST address (BIBLE-REQUEST@VIRGINIA.EDU). If you want to receive both the immediate messages of BIBLE and their digested format send the command: IMMEDIATE-AND-DIGEST BIBLE to the REQUEST address (BIBLE-REQUEST@VIRGINIA.EDU).

How to submit: Remember two simple rules-of-thumb: If it's a request (SUBscribe, UNSUBscribe), send it to the list requester: BIBLE-REQUEST@VIRGINIA.EDU(Internet) BIBLEREQ@VIRGINIA .BITNET(Bitnet) If it's a message for general distribution to the members of the list, send it to the list: BIBLE@VIRGINIA.EDU(Internet) BIBLE@VIRGINIA.BITNET(Bitnet)

Submission policy: Contributions sent to this list are automatically broadcast to everyone else on the list. If you wish to reply to an individual member of the list please send that person mail directly. If you use your systems automatic REPLY feature your message will get sent only to the individual member and not broadcast to the entire list.

BIBSOFT@INDYCMS

Description: BIBSOFT@INDYCMS is a forum on bibliographic database management software.

Subjects covered: computer hardware and software

List moderated: No.

Editorial contact: Jim Morgan

Internet: morganj@indyvax.iupui.edu

Bitnet: morganj@indyvax

How to access: Send subscribe message to listserv@indycms or listserv@indycms.iupui.edu

How to unsubscribe: Send unsubscribe message to listserv@indycms or listserv@indycms.iupui.edu

BICOMPAL

Description: Bicompal is a list designed to search relationships between older and younger individuals with physical and educational handicaps. The goal is to develop a Big Brother/Sister relationship across the computer networks.

Subjects covered: disabilities; education; sibling studies

Net address for operations: listserv@sjuvm.bitnet

Established: February 1992

Subscribers: 85

Sponsor: St. John's University, Jamaica, NY.

Host: St. John's University, Jamaica, NY.

Technical contact: Dr. Robert Zenhausern St. John's University Jamaica, NY 11439.

Tel: (718)-990-6447

Fax: 718-990-6705

Internet: drz@sjuvm.stjohns.edu

Bitnet: drz@sjuvm.bitnet

How to access: Send mail to listserv@sjuvm.bitnet with the message: sub bicompal Firstname Lastname

Access policy: Subscription is open to anyone.

How to unsubscribe: Send mail to listserv@sjuvm.bitnet with the message: signoff bicompal

How to submit: Send mail to bicompal@sjuvm.bitnet

Archives: Logs of all messages available in the form: bicompal log9305 (logs of altlearn for May, 1993). Other files available. For a complete list of files send mail to listserv@sjuvm.bitnet with the message: index bicompal

BIFEM-L

Description: BIFEM-L is a moderated list established in order to offer bisexual women a place for discussion.

Subjects covered: gay and lesbian topics; feminism; women's studies

Net address for operations: LISTSERV@BROWNVM, LISTSERV@BROWNVM.BROWN.EDU

List moderated: Yes.

How to access: Send subscription messages to LISTSERV@BROWNVM (Bit.) or LISTSERV@BROWNVM.BROWN.EDU

Access policy: Open to women only.

BIG-DB@MIDWAY.UCHICAGO.EDU

Description: BIG-DB@MIDWAY is a forum on large database management.

Subjects covered: computer science

List moderated: No.

How to access: Send subscribe message to big-DB@midway.uchicago.EDU

How to unsubscribe: Send unsubscribe message to big-DB@midway.uchicago.EDU

BIG-LAN@SUVM.ACS.SYR.EDU

Description: BIG-LAN discusses design and implementation implementation issues related to campus-wide networks.

Subjects covered: electronic networking; campus-wide information systems

List moderated: No.

Editorial contact: John Wobus

Internet: jmwobus@suvm.acs.syr.edu

Bitnet: jmwobus@suvm

How to access: Send subscribe message to listserv@suvm or listserv@suvm.acs.syr.edu
How to unsubscribe: Send unsubscribe message to listserv@suvm or listserv@suvm.acs.syr.edu
Archives: Archives are developed monthly; apply to listowner for details.

BILLING@HDETUD1

Description: BILLING@HDETUD1 discusses billing and chargeback of computing resources.
Subjects covered: campus-wide information systems
List moderated: No.
Editorial contact: Rob van Hoboken
Internet: rcoprob%hdetud1.bitnet@cunyvm.cuny.edu
How to access: Send subscribe message to listserv@hdetud1 or listserv%hdetud1.bitnet@cunyvm.cuny.edu
How to unsubscribe: Send unsubscribe message to listserv@hdetud1 or listserv%hdetud1.bitnet@cunyvm.cuny.edu
Archives: Archives are developed monthly; apply to listowner for details.

BIOMED-L

Description: Biomed-L is a forum focusing on ethics in medicine.
Subjects covered: medicine; ethics
List moderated: No.
Editorial contact: Bill Sklar
Internet: e1406007@brownvm.brown.edu
Bitnet: e1406007@brownvm
How to access: Send subscribe message to listserv@ndsuvm1 or listserv@vm1.nodak.edu
How to unsubscribe: Send unsubscribe message to listserv@ndsuvm1 or listserv@vm1.nodak.edu
Archives: Archives are developed weekly; apply to listowner for details.

BIOPI-L

Description: Biopi-L is a list covering secondary education relating to biology.
Subjects covered: education; biology
List moderated: No.
Bitnet: TMANNEY@KSUVM
How to access: Send subscribe message to listserv@ksuvm
How to unsubscribe: Send unsubscribe message to listserv@ksuvm
Archives: Archives are developed monthly; apply to listowner for details.

BIOSPH-L

Description: Biosph-L is a forum for discussion of the Earths' ecology.
Subjects covered: environmental studies; ecology
List moderated: No.
Editorial contact: Dave Phillips
Internet: davep@acsu.buffalo.edu
How to access: Send subscribe message to listserv@ubvms or listserv@ubvm.cc.buffalo.edu
How to unsubscribe: Send unsubscribe message to listserv@ubvms or listserv@ubvm.cc.buffalo.edu

Archives: Archives are developed weekly; apply to listowner for details.

BIRD—RBA@ARIZVM1

Description: BIRD—RBA is a forum for birding.
Subjects covered: ecology; environmental studies
List moderated: No.
Editorial contact: Charles B. Williamson
Internet: chuck%evax2@arizona.edu or cwilliamson@pimacc.pima.edu
How to access: Send subscribe message to listserv@arizvm1 or listserv@arizvm1.bitnet@cunyvm.cuny.edu
How to unsubscribe: Send unsubscribe message to listserv@arizvm1 or listserv@arizvm1.bitnet@cunyvm.cuny.edu
Archives: Archives are developed weekly; apply to listowner for details.

BISEXU-L

Description: BISEXU-L is a moderated list established for the exchange of ideas and opinions relevant to the topic of bisexuality.
Subjects covered: gay and lesbian topics; feminism; women's studies
Net address for operations: LISTSERV@BROWNVM, LISTSERV@BROWNVM.BROWN.EDU
List moderated: Yes.
How to access: Send subscription messages to LISTSERV@BROWNVM (Bit.) or LISTSERV@BROWNVM.BROWN.EDU

BNFNET-L

Description: Bnfnet-L is an electronic conference on biological nitrogen fixation.
Subjects covered: agriculture
Host: UNESCO's Microbiological Resource Center
List moderated: No.
Editorial contact: Roger Harper
Bitnet: harper@finfun or harper@finuha
How to access: Send subscribe message to listserv@finhutc
How to unsubscribe: Send unsubscribe message to listserv@finhutc
Archives: Archives are developed monthly; apply to listowner for details.

BONSAI-L

Description: Bonsai-L is a forum dedicated to the horticultural artform of bonsai.
Subjects covered: horticulture; art
List moderated: No.
Editorial contact: Daniel Cwiertniewicz
Internet: dan@foghorn.pass.wayne.edu or dcwiert@cms.cc.wayne.edu
Bitnet: dcwiert@waynest1
How to access: Send subscribe message to listserv@waynest1 or listserv@cms.ss.wayme.edu
How to unsubscribe: Send unsubscribe message to listserv@waynest1 or listserv@cms.ss.wayme.edu
Archives: Archives are developed monthly; apply to listowner for details.

BORIKEN@ENLACE

Description: BORIKEN@ENLACE is a discussion list about Puerto Rico.
Subjects covered: Puerto Rico
List moderated: No.
Editorial contact: Roberto Loran
Internet: r__loran@racin.clu.net
How to access: Send subscribe message to listserv@enlace
How to unsubscribe: Send unsubscribe message to listserv@enlace
Archives: Archives are developed monthly; apply to listowner for details.

BR DOMAIN

Description: BR Domain is a server containing information on Brazilian mailing lists and Brazilian networks.
Subjects covered: Internet; Brazil
List moderated: No.
Bitnet: gomide@brfapesp
Additional information: This is not an electronic conference, only a source for information.

BRAIN-L

Description: BRAIN-L carries open discussion of all topics generally related to mind/brain questions.
Subjects covered: medicine; psychology
Net address for operations: LISTSERV@VM1.MCGILL.CA
Net address for questions or submissions: brain-l@vm1.mcgill.ca
Established: 1989
Subscribers: 225
List moderated: No.
Editorial contact: Chris F. Westbury, The Department Of Psychology, McGill University, 205 Doctor Penfield Avenue, Montreal, QuebecH3A 1B1 CANADA.
Tel: (514) 398-6132
Internet: chris@ego.psych.mcgill.ca
How to access: Send a note with the content 'subscribe BRAIN-L<your name>' to LISTSERV@VM1.MCGILL.CA
How to unsubscribe: Send a note with the content 'unsubscribe BRAIN-L' to LISTSERV@VM1.MCGILL.CA
How to submit: Send messages to brain-l@vm1.mcgill.ca
Additional information: The list is run on McGillUniversity computers, but was started and is currently operated by a group of graduate students with an interest in mind/brain issues....so there's no 'address' (either physical or e-mail) which can be said to be the address of the sponsoring institution in any relevant sense.

BRAS-NET

Description: Bras-net is an electronic forum for communications and discussions by Brazilian Students.
Subjects covered: Latin America; education; colleges and universities
Technical contact: Walter Morales
Internet: walter@psg.com
Bitnet: walter@pccvm.bitnet
How to access: LISTSERV@PCCVM.BITNET and send your complete name
Access policy: Subscription entitles access to information on Bras-net.

How to unsubscribe: LISTSERV@PCCVM.BITNET and state SIGNOFF BRAS-NET
How to submit: BRAS-EUA-OESTE@CS.UCLA.EDU

BRASS

Description: Brass is a discussion list for players of brass instruments.
Subjects covered: music; musical instruments
Net address for operations: brass-request@geomag.gly.fsu.edu
Net address for questions or submissions: brass@geomag.gly.fsu.edu
Established: 1988
Subscribers: 140
Host: Florida State University Geology Dept.
B-160, FSU Tallahassee, FL 32306
List moderated: No.
Editorial contact: Ted Zateslo
Geology B-160, Florida State Univ., Tallahassee, FL 32306
Tel: (904) 644-7817
Fax: (904) 644-4214
Internet: zateslo@geomag.gly.fsu.edu
How to access: E-mail to brass-request@geomag.gly.fsu.edu
Access policy: Anyone with an interest in brass playing is welcome to join the list.
How to submit: E-mail to brass-request@geomag.gly.fsu.edu
Submission policy: No policy aside from relevance to list topic.
Archives: Available for anonmyous ftp from geomag.gly.fsu.edu:/pub/brass
Related files: Anonymous ftp from geomag.gly.fsu.edu:/pub/brass

BRIDGES

Description: BRIDGES is a moderated list focusing on Jewish feminist identity.
Subjects covered: Judaica; feminism; activism; women's studies
Net address for operations: LISTSERV@ISRAEL.NYSERNET.ORG
List moderated: Yes.
How to access: Send subscription messages to LISTSERV@ISRAEL.NYSERNET.ORG

BRINE-L

Description: Brine-L is a list discussing brine shrimp.
Subjects covered: aquaculture; zoology
List moderated: No.
Editorial contact: Lamar Jackson
Bitnet: ljackson@uga
How to access: Send subscribe message to listserv@uga or listserv@uga.cc.uga.edu
How to unsubscribe: Send unsubscribe message to listserv@uga or listserv@uga.cc.uga.edu
Archives: Archives are developed monthly; apply to listowner for details.

BRS-L

Description: BRS-L is a forum discussing all aspects of the BRS/Search software.
Subjects covered: library and information science; BRS Information Technologies

List moderated: No.
Editorial contact: Karl P. Geiger
Bitnet: brsadm@uscvm
How to access: Send subscribe message to listserv@uscvm or listserv@vm.usc.edu
How to unsubscribe: Send unsubscribe message to listserv@uscvm or listserv@vm.usc.edu
Archives: Archives are developed monthly; apply to listowner for details.

BRSZ@CNI.ORG
Description: BRSZ@CNI.ORG covers information relating to the BRS Z39.50 project.
Subjects covered: library and information science; telecommunications
Host: Coalition for Networked Information
List moderated: Yes.
Editorial contact: Craig A. Summerhill
Internet: craig@cni.org
How to access: Send subscribe message to listserv@cni.org
How to unsubscribe: Send unsubscribe message to listserv@cni.org

BRUNONIA@BROWNVM
Description: BRUNONIA@BROWNVM is a discussion list for alumni of Brown University.
Subjects covered: colleges and universities
List moderated: Yes.
Editorial contact: Anne Diffily
Internet: adbam@brownvm.brown.edu
Bitnet: adbam@brownvm
How to access: Send subscribe message to listserv@brownvm or listserv@brownvm.brown.edu
How to unsubscribe: Send unsubscribe message to listserv@brownvm or listserv@brownvm.brown.edu
Archives: Yes.

BUDDHIST@JPNTOHOK
Description: BUDDHIST@JPNTOHOK is a forum for Buddhist and Indian studies.
Subjects covered: religion
List moderated: No.
Editorial contact: Yoshiyuki Kawazoe
Internet: KAWAZOE@JPNTOHOK
How to access: Send subscribe message to listserv@jpntohok
How to unsubscribe: Send unsubscribe message to listserv@jpntohok
Archives: Archives are developed monthly; apply to listowner for details.

BUILDING-MODELS-COMBINE@MAILBASE.AC.UK
Description: BUILDING-MODELS-COMBINE is a mailbase discussion list on data modeling.
Subjects covered: physics
List moderated: No.
Internet: building-models-combine-request@mailbase.ac.uk

How to access: Send subscribe message to mailbase@mailbase.ac.uk in the following format: join building-models-combine Your first name Your last name
Archives: Archives are developed monthly; apply to listowner for details.

BUSLIB-L
Description: Buslib-L is an electronic forum for business librarians.
Subjects covered: library and information science
List moderated: No.
Editorial contact: Barbara Butler
Internet: butler@equinox.unr.edu
How to access: Send subscribe message to listserv@idbsu or listserv@idbsu.idbsu.edu
How to unsubscribe: Send unsubscribe message to listserv@idbsu or listserv@idbsu.idbsu.edu
Archives: Archives are developed monthly; apply to listowner for details.

C+HEALTH@IUBVM
Description: C+Health@IUBVM discusses issues related to computers and health.
Subjects covered: computer hardware and software; medicine; health sciences
List moderated: No.
Editorial contact: Judy Smith
Internet: smithj@a1.relay.upenn.edu

C18-L
Description: C18-L is a non-specific discussion for events and history of the 18th century.
Subjects covered: history
List moderated: No.
Editorial contact: Kevin Berland
Internet: bcj@psuvm.psu.edu
Bitnet: bcj@psuvm
How to access: Send subscribe message to listserv@psuvm or listserv@psuvm.psu.edu
How to unsubscribe: Send unsubscribe message to listserv@psuvm or listserv@psuvm.psu.edu
Archives: Archives are developed monthly; apply to listowner for details.

CAACSALF@UQUEBEC
Description: CAACSALF is a forum for discussion of the French language.
Subjects covered: linguistics; sociology
Host: Association Canadienne des Sociologues et des Anthropologues de Langue Francaise
List moderated: Yes.
Editorial contact: Pierre J. Hamel
Internet: hamel@inrs-urb.uquebec.ca
Bitnet: hamel@uquebec
How to access: Send subscribe message to listserv@uquebec
How to unsubscribe: Send unsubscribe message to listserv@uquebec
Archives: Archives are developed monthly; apply to listowner for details.

CAAH@PUCC

Description: CAAH@PUCC is a list covering the discussion of art history.
Subjects covered: art history
Host: Consortium of Art and Architectural Historians
List moderated: No.
Editorial contact: Marilyn Louis
Bitnet: MALAVIN@PUCC
How to access: Send subscribe message to listserv@pucc or listserv@pucc.princeton.edu
How to unsubscribe: Send unsubscribe message to listserv@pucc or listserv@pucc.princeton.edu
Archives: Archives are developed monthly; apply to listowner for details.

CABOT@SOL.CRD.GE.COM

Description: CABOT@SOL.CRD.GE.COM covers studies related to Sebastian Cabot.
Subjects covered: history; Cabot, Sebastion
List moderated: No.
Editorial contact: Richard Welty
Internet: cabot-request@sol.crd.ge.com
How to access: Send subscribe message to cabot-request@sol.crd.ge.com
How to unsubscribe: Send unsubscribe message to cabot-request@sol.crd.ge.com

CACI-L

Description: CACI-L is a list of the Canadian Academic Centre in Italy.
Subjects covered: colleges and universities
Host: Canadian Academic Centre in Italy
List moderated: No.
Internet: CACI@IRMUNISA
How to access: Send subscribe message to listserv@ualtavm or listserv@vm.ucs.ualberta.ca
How to unsubscribe: Send unsubscribe message to listserv@ualtavm or listserv@vm.ucs.ualberta.ca

CADUCEUS--HISTORY OF MEDICINE COLLECTIONS FORUM

Description: CADUCEUS--History of Medicine Collections Forum is a forum for discussion of history of the health sciences and the administration of special collections in the history of medicine.
Subjects covered: library and information science; medicine; administration
Net address for operations: CADUCEUS@Beach.UTMB.Edu
Net address for questions or submissions: CADUCEUS@Beach.UTMB.Edu
Established: May 19, 1992
Subscribers: 140
Sponsor: Moody Medical Library, The University of Texas Medical Branch, 9th & Market Streets, Galveston, TX 77555.
Host: Moody Medical Library, The University of Texas Medical Branch, 9th & Market Streets, Galveston, TX 77555.
List moderated: Yes.
Moderation procedure: Postings are compiled/edited and distributed once or twice a week, depending on volume.
Editorial contact: Inci Bowman

Moody Medical Library, The University of Texas Medical Branch, Galveston, TX 77550-1035.
Tel: (409) 772-2397
Internet: IBOWMAN@Beach.UTMB.Edu
Bitnet: IBOWMAN@UTMBeach
Technical contact: Molly Hamilton
Office of Academic Computing, The University of Texas Medical Branch, Galveston, TX 77550.
Internet: Z919016@Beach.UTMB.Edu
Bitnet: Z919016@UTMBeach
How to access: Send e-mail to CADUCEUS, include first and last name. (CADUCEUS is not on a Bitnet Listserv.)
Access policy: Open to anyone interested in history of medicine.
How to unsubscribe: Send e-mail to CADUCEUS
How to submit: Send postings to CADUCEUS
Archives: Back files, CADUCEUS Contents (Index) and Subscription list are available via anonymous FTP. Host: Beach. UTMB.Edu. Sub directory: CADUCEUS

CALL-L

Description: CALL-L is a discussion list for members of the group of Canadian Academic Law Libraries.
Subjects covered: library and information science; law and legal studies
List moderated: No.
Editorial contact: John Sadler
Internet: jsadler@unb.ca
How to access: Send subscribe message to listserv@unbvm1 or listserv@unb.ca
How to unsubscribe: Send unsubscribe message to listserv@unbvm1 or listserv@unb.ca
Archives: Archives are developed monthly; apply to listowner for details.

CAMEL-L

Description: Camel-L is a forum discussing camels.
Subjects covered: zoology
Host: Camel Research Center, King Faisal University, Saudi Arabia
List moderated: Yes.
Editorial contact: Abdullah Altaher
Bitnet: facmab76@sakfu00
How to access: Send subscribe message to LISTSERV@SAKFU00
How to unsubscribe: Send unsubscribe message to LISTSERV@SAKFU00

CAMELOT@CASTLE.ED.AC.UK

Description: CAMELOT@CASTLE.ED.AC.UK is a forum discussing the legends and myths of King Arthur.
Subjects covered: English language and literature; Medieval studies; Celtic studies
List moderated: No.
Editorial contact: Chris Thornborrow
Internet: ct@castle.edinburgh.ac.uk
How to access: Send subscribe message to CAMELOT-REQUEST@CASTLE.ED.AC.UK
How to unsubscribe: Send unsubscribe message to CAMELOT-REQUEST@CASTLE.ED.AC.UK

Archives: Yes; send anonymous FTP to sapphire.epcc.ed.ac.uk (129.215.56.11) and cd pub/camelot

CANADIAN ASSOCIATION FOR UNIVERSITY CONTINUING EDUCATION ELECTRONIC NETWORK

Description: The purpose of CAUCE-L is to provide an electronic forum where issues broad, narrow, practical, theoretical, controversial or mundane) related to university continuing education can be disussed. While list is open its membership is currently largely Canadian.
Subjects covered: education; continuing education; colleges and universities
Net address for operations: UREGINA1.UREGINA.CA Max.CC.URegina.ca
Net address for questions or submissions: CAUCE-L@MAX.CC.UREGINA.CA
Established: November 1989
Subscribers: 82
Sponsor: CAUCE, 1001 - 151 Slater Street, Ottawa, Ontario, Canada K1P 5N1.
Host: University Extension, University of Regina, Regina, SK Canada S4S 0A2.
List moderated: No.
Editorial contact: Dr. Larry I. Hein
University Extension, University of Regina
Regina, Sask. Canada S4S 0A2
Tel: (306) 779 4892
Fax: (306) 779 4825
Internet: LIHEIN@max.cc.uregina.ca
Bitnet: LIHEIN@URegina1.Bitnet
Technical contact: Dale Anderson
Computing Services, University of Regina
Tel: (306) 585 4686
Fax: (306) 585 4878
Internet: nderson@max.cc.uregina.ca
How to access: Send the following message to the listserv: SUBscribe cauce-l full__name
Access policy: Subscription is open to those interested or involved in university continuing education.
How to unsubscribe: Send the following message to the listserv: signoff cauce-l
How to submit: Send mail to cauce-l@max.cc.uregina.ca or cauce-l@uregina1.bitnet
Submission policy: Postings are open to subscribers only.
Archives: Yes. Apply to moderator for more details.

CANCER-L

Description: Cancer-L is a discussion list on cancer and related issues.
Subjects covered: medicine; cancer
List moderated: No.
Editorial contact: Susan Rodman
Bitnet: u0ac3@wvnvm
How to access: Send subscribe message to listserv@wvnvm or listserv@wvnvm.wvnet.edu
How to unsubscribe: Send unsubscribe message to listserv@wvnvm or listserv@wvnvm.wvnet.edu

CANSPACE (CANADIAN SPACE GEODESY FORUM)

Description: The Canadian Space Geodesy Forum (CANSPACE) is a computer-communications-based information dissemination and discussion group that was established several years ago as an aid to improving communication among scientists and engineers working with the techniques of space geodesy. Among topics discussed are the Navstar Global Positioning System (GPS), Glonass, Transit, very long baseline interferometry, satellite laser ranging, satellite altimetry, etc. Daily postings of information bulletins include GPS satellite constellation status reports (Department of Defense Notice Advisories to Navstar Users) and reports of solar and geomagnetic field activity. Information concerning satellite launches and orbital elements is posted regularly. Although initially intended to link Canadian geodesists and geophysicists together, CANSPACE now has a wide international subscriber list and is open to all. Questions are particularly encouraged.
Subjects covered: space and space exploration; Canada; astronomy; navigation; satellites
Net address for operations: CANSPACE@unb.ca
Established: June 1989
Subscribers: 341
Sponsor: University of New Brunswick, P.O. Box 4400, Fredericton, N.B. E3B 5A3 Canada.
Host: Geodetic Research Laboratory, Department of Geodesy and Geomatics Engineering, University of New Brunswick, P.O. Box 4400, Fredericton, N.B. E3B 5A3, Canada.
List moderated: Yes.
Moderation procedure: Any CANSPACE subscriber may post directly to the list; however, the postings are closely monitored by the moderator.
Editorial contact: Richard B. Langley
Geodetic Research Laboratory, Department of Geodesy and Geomatics Engineering, University of New Brunswick, P.O. Box 4400, Fredericton, N.B. E3B 5A3 Canada.
Tel: (506) 453-5142
Fax: (506) 453-4943
Internet: lang@unb.ca
Bitnet: lang@unb
Technical contact: Terry Arsenault, Department of Surveying Engineering, University of New Brunswick, P.O. Box 4400, Fredericton, N.B. E3B 5A3 Canada.
Tel: (506) 453-4698
Fax: (506) 453-4943
Internet: se@unb.ca
Bitnet: se@unb.ca
Copyright statement: Everything posted is believed to be in the public domain. Reference to CANSPACE would be appreciated in subsequent re-postings.
How to access: Send an e-mail message to listserv@unb.ca (or listserv@unbvm1.bitnet but NOT to the CANSPACE address itself) with the following text in the message body: SUB CANSPACE your name Once you are a subscriber, you may post a message to CANSPACE simply by sending the message to canspace@unb.ca. The message will be automatically distributed.
Archives: All CANSPACE messages are archived in monthly notebooks that may be retrieved or searched using the LISTSERV database function. An archive of related information files is also maintained on a computer at UNB (not the computer running LISTSERV). Among the many files included are a brief description of GPS, tables showing the present status of

the GPS and Glonass satellite constellations, and a 1,000 item GPS bibliography. Files may be retrieved via anonymous FTP. Connect to unbmvs1.csd.unb.ca (131.202.1.2) and change the working directory to PUB.CANSPACE.
Related files: Related files include those available under PUB.CANSPACE. Among these are: $INDEX--The index file $README--Introduction to CANSPACE, the Canadian Space Geodesy Forum ARCHIVES--Information on accessing the CANSPACE archives.
Additional information: The address of the Canadian Space Geodesy Forum is canspace@unb.ca (or canspace@unbvm1.bitnet).

CAP-L (COMPUTER-AIDED PUBLISHING)
Description: CAP-L is a list to encourage technical communication students from several universities to discuss topics of technical, political, economic, and ethical importance in the area of computer-assisted publishing.
Subjects covered: computer hardware and software; electronic publishing; science and technology; telecommunications
Net address for operations: majordomo@mtu.edu
Net address for questions or submissions: cap-l@mtu.edu
Established: 1991
Subscribers: 40
Sponsor: Michigan Technological University, 1400 Townsend, Houghton, MI 49931.
List moderated: No.
Editorial contact: Dickie Selfe
138 Walker, MTU-Humanities Dept., Houghton, MI 49931.
Tel: (906) 487-3225
Internet: rselfe@mtu.edu
Technical contact: Mark Mach
113 Walker, MTU-Humanities Dept., Houghton, MI 49931.
Tel: (906) 487-2582
Internet: mrmach@mtu.edu
Copyright statement: Please do not quote any posting without authorization of author that has been forwarded to the list manager.
How to access: Send ''subscribe__cap-l'' <your e-mail address>'' to ''majordomo@mtu.edu''
Access policy: Open to anyone.
How to unsubscribe: Send ''unsubscribe__cap-l'' <your e-mail address>'' to ''majordomo@mtu.edu''
How to submit: Send mail to ''cap-l@mtu.edu''

CAPDU-L
Description: Capdu-L is an electronic conference among members of the Canadian Association of Public Data Users.
Subjects covered: demographics; government information
Host: Canadian Association of Public Data Users
List moderated: No.
Editorial contact: chumphre@ualtavm
How to access: Send subscribe message to listserv@ualtavm or listserv@vm.ucs.ualberta.ca
How to unsubscribe: Send unsubscribe message to listserv@ualtavm or listserv@vm.ucs.ualberta.ca
Archives: Archives are developed yearly; apply to listowner for details.

CARISUSE@SUN1.COGS.NS.CA
Description: CARISUSE@SUN1.COGS.NS.CA is a forum for CARIS users.
Subjects covered: geographic information systems; computer hardware and software
List moderated: No.
Editorial contact: Roger Mosher
Internet: roger@sun1.cogs.ns.ca
How to access: Send subscribe message to roger@sun1.cogs.ns.ca in the following format: subscribe CarisUse <your internet address>
How to unsubscribe: Send subscribe message to roger@sun1.cogs.ns.ca in the following format: unsubscribe CarisUse <your internet address>

CARL-L
Description: CARL-L is the CARL Users Information List, providing information on the Colorado Alliance of Research Libraries and its services.
Net address for operations: LISTSERV@UHCCVM
Editorial contact: Judith Hopkins
Technical Services Research and Analysis Officer, Central Technical Services, Lockwood Library Building, State University of New York at Buffalo, Buffalo, NY 14260-2200
Tel: (716) 645-2796
Fax: (716) 645-5955
Internet: ulcjh@ubvm.cc.buffalo.ed
Bitnet: ulcjh@ubvm
How to access: Send your subscription request to LISTSERV@UHCCVM with message text: Subscribe CARL-L Firstname Lastname

CARR-L
Description: CARR-L is a discussion list covering computer-assisted reporting and research.
Subjects covered: computer hardware and software; journalism; education
Net address for operations: LISTSERV@ULKYVM or @ULKYVM.LOUISVILLE.EDU
Net address for questions or submissions: CARR-L@ULKYVM
Established: October 1992
Subscribers: 275
Sponsor: University of Louisville
Host: University of Louisville
List moderated: No.
Editorial contact: Elliott Parker
Journalism Dept., Central Michigan University, Mt. Pleasant, MI 48859.
Tel: (517) 774-3196
Fax: (517) 774-7805
Internet: 3ZLUFUR@CMUVM.CSV.CMICH.EDU
Bitnet: 3ZLUFUR@CMUVM
How to access: LISTSERV@ULKYVM
SUB CARR-L <real__name>
Access policy: This list is open to anyone.
How to unsubscribe: Send SIGNOFF CARR-L message to LISTSERV@ULKYVM
How to submit: Send email to CARR-L@ULKYVM
Submission policy: Open, but must be related to list topic.
Archives: Full archives are available. Contact list moderator.
Related files: Related files are accessible in associated filelist.

CASE-L

Description: Case-L is a discussion forum on computer-aided systems analysis.
Subjects covered: computer science; engineering
List moderated: No.
Editorial contact: Richard Hintz
Internet: spgrjh@accvma.ucop.edu
How to access: Send subscribe message to listserv@uccvma or listserv@uccvma.ucop.edu
How to unsubscribe: Send unsubscribe message to listserv@uccvma or listserv@uccvma.ucop.edu
Archives: Archives are developed monthly; apply to listowner for details.

CASID-L

Description: Casid-L is a list covering international development.
Subjects covered: demographics; political science
Host: Canadian Association for the Study of International Development
List moderated: No.
Editorial contact: Myron Frankman
Internet: inmf@musicb.mcgill.ca
How to access: Send subscribe message to listserv@mcgill1
How to unsubscribe: Send unsubscribe message to listserv@mcgill1
Archives: Archives are developed monthly; apply to listowner for details.

CATALUNYA@CS.RICE.EDU

Description: CATALUNYA@CS.RICE.EDU is a forum for discussing the region of Catalan, its language and culture.
Subjects covered: language and literature; cultural studies
List moderated: No.
Internet: Send subscribe message to catalunya-request@cs-rice.edu
How to access: Send subscribe message to catalunya-request@cs-rice.edu

CAUSERIE@QUEBEC

Description: CAUSERIE@UQUEBEC is a forum at the University of Quebec.
Subjects covered: language and literature
List moderated: No.
Editorial contact: Pierre Chenard
Internet: uqpsgen@uqss.uquebec.ca
Bitnet: uqpsgen@uquebec
How to access: Send subscribe message to listserv@uquebec or listserv@uquebec.ca
How to unsubscribe: Send unsubscribe message to listserv@uquebec or listserv@uquebec.ca

CBEHIGH@BLEKUL11

Description: CBEHIGH@BLEKUL11 provides discussion on the use of computers in higher education.
Subjects covered: education; education technology; computer-assisted instruction (CAI)
Host: Computer Based Education, University Computing Centre, University of Leuven

List moderated: No.
Editorial contact: Peter Arien
Internet: laaaa43@cc1.kuleuvenac.be
Bitnet: laaaa43.blekuii
How to access: Send subscribe message to listserv@blekul1 or listserv@cci.kuleuven.ac.be
How to unsubscribe: Send unsubscribe message to listserv@blekul1 or listserv@cci.kuleuven.ac.be
Archives: Yes.

CCES-L (CONGRESS OF CANADIAN ENGINEERING STUDENTS FORUM)

Description: CCES-L, known by its subscribers as "the Link," provides a forum for all Canadian engineering students to discuss current topics relating for the most part to the fields of engineering, engineering education, and the engineering image. All students in accredited engineering institutions are members of the Canadian Federation of Students (CFES). The CFES provides a voice for all engineering students. Through the use of CCES-L, all students can easily participate in the goings-on of the Federation, and enables them to find out what the CFES National Executive are doing. It also allows students to prepare for the annual national meeting of the Federation: The Congress of Canadian Engineering Students - Conference.
Subjects covered: engineering; education; colleges and universities
Net address for operations: LISTSERV@UNB.CA
Net address for questions or submissions: CCES-L@UNB.CA
Established: March 1990
Subscribers: 160
Sponsor: University of New Brunswick, Fredericton, New Brunswick, Canada.
Host: University of New Brunswick, Fredericton, New Brunswick, Canada.
List moderated: List is unmoderated, but is monitored by the Canadian Federation of Engineering Student's Commissioner of Electronic Communication.
Editorial contact: Troy Morehouse
CFES Commissioner of Electronic Communication Room H-223, Sir Edmund Head Hall, University of New Brunswick, Fredericton, New Brunswick, Canada.
Tel: (506) 453-3534
Fax: (506) 453-4569
Internet: cfes@jupiter.sun.csd.unb.ca
Bitnet: cfes@unb.ca
How to access: Send e-mail message to LISTSERV@UNB.CA
Access policy: Postings of a slanderous, sexist, racist, or homophobic nature will not be tolerated on CCES-L. Doing so will result in immediate removal from subscription.
How to unsubscribe: Send e-mail message to LISTSERV@UNB.CA
How to submit: Send any submissions (postings) to CCES-L@UNB.CA
Archives: No archives are currently provided, but may be in the future.
Related files: CFES and CCES-L have related documentation (i.e. minutes, policy manuals, bylaws, logos, addresses, etc) available via anonymous FTP at jupiter.sun.csd.unb.ca, and can be found in the /pub/cfes directory. An incoming directory is provided for site submissions.

CCHD-L

Description: CCHD-L is a forum for the Carolina Consortium for Human Development.
Subjects covered: psychology
List moderated: No.
Editorial contact: Doug Cutlar
Bitnet: uncdwc@uncvm1
How to access: Send subscribe message to listserv@uncvm1 or listserv@uncvm1.oit.unc.edu
How to unsubscribe: Send unsubscribe message to listserv@uncvm1 or listserv@uncvm1.oit.unc.edu

CDPLUS-L

Description: CDPLUS-L is a discussion list of the CDPLUS software users group.
Subjects covered: CD-ROM; library and information science
Net address for questions or submissions: LISTSERV@UTORONTO
How to access: Send subscribe message to LISTSERV@UTORONTO
How to unsubscribe: Send unsubscribe message to LISTSERV@UTORONTO

CDROM-L

Description: CDROM-L is a discussion list on all aspects of CD-ROM usage.
Subjects covered: computer hardware and software; library and information science
List moderated: No.
Editorial contact: Rich Hintz
Internet: opsrjh@uccvma.ucop.edu
Review: Reviewed by List Review Service edited by Raleigh Muns: see appendix.
How to access: Send subscribe message to listserv@uccvma or listserv@uccvma.ucop.edu
How to unsubscribe: Send unsubscribe message to listserv@uccvma or listserv@uccvma.ucop.edu

CDROMLAN@IDBSU

Description: CDROMLAN offers a general discussion on CD-ROM products.
Subjects covered: computer hardware and software
List moderated: No.
Editorial contact: Dan Lester
Internet: alileste@idbsu.idbsu.edu
Bitnet: alileste@idbsu
Review: Reviewed by List Review Service edited by Raleigh Muns: see appendix.
How to access: Send subscribe message to listserv@idbsu or listserv@idbsu.idbsu.edu
How to unsubscribe: Send unsubscribe message to listserv@idbsu or listserv@idbsu.idbsu.edu

CDS-ISIS@HEARN

Description: CDS-ISIS is a discussion group on UNESCO's CDS/ISIS text retrieval software.
Subjects covered: computer hardware and software; library and information science

Net address for questions or submissions: LISTSERV@HEARN
How to access: Send subscribe message to LISTSERV@HEARN
How to unsubscribe: Send unsubscribe message to LISTSERV@HEARN

CEC@QUCDN

Description: CEC@QUCDN is a forum for members of the Canadian Electro-accoustics community.
Subjects covered: engineering
List moderated: No.
Editorial contact: Peter Gross
Bitnet: grosspa@qucdn
How to access: Send subscribe message to listserv@qucdn or listserv@qucdn.queensu.ca
How to unsubscribe: Send unsubscribe message to listserv@qucdn or listserv@qucdn.queensu.ca
Archives: Archives are developed monthly; apply to listowner for details.

CED-COURSEWARE

Description: ced-courseware is a discussion forum and bulletin board for members of a UK consortium producing Windows-based courseware for the teaching of Biomedical practicals.
Subjects covered: Microsoft Windows; computer hardware and software; biomedicine
Net address for operations: mailbase
Net address for questions or submissions: ced-courseware@mailbase.ac.uk
Established: 1992
Subscribers: 20
List moderated: No.
Editorial contact: G.Donaldson
Dept. of Physiology, Queen Mary and Westfield College, Mile End Road, London, E1 4NS, UK.
Tel: 071-982-6274
Fax: 081-983-0467
Internet: G.Donaldson@qmw.ac.uk
How to access: Send email to G.Donaldson@qmw.ac.uk
Access policy: List is open to any person or UK institution who applies to and is approved by the consortium or its management group.
How to unsubscribe: Send email to G.Donaldson@qmw.ac.uk
How to submit: Email to ced-courseware@mailbase
Gopher accessibility: Yes, apply to listowner for details.

CELLULAR-AUTOMATA@THINK.COM

Description: cellular-automata@think.com is a list focusing on artificial intelligence.
Subjects covered: artificial intelligence
How to access: All requests to be added to or deleted from this list, problems, questions, etc., should be sent to cellular-automata-request@think.com.
Archives: Archived messages may be found at ftp.think.com in the files: mail/ca.archive*

CEM-L

Description: CEM-L is a forum on engineering mathematics.
Subjects covered: engineering; mathematics

Host: University of Texas at Dallas
List moderated: No.
Editorial contact: David Lippke
Bitnet: lippke@utdallas
How to access: Send subscribe message to listserv@utdallas or listserv%utdallas.bitnet@vm1.nodak.edu
How to unsubscribe: Send unsubscribe message to listserv@utdallas or listserv%utdallas.bitnet@vm1.nodak.edu
Archives: Archives are developed monthly; apply to listowner for details.

CENSUS-ANALYSIS@MAILBASE.AC.UK
Description: CENSUS-ANALYSIS@MAILBASE.AC.UK is a discussion of data from UK census reports.
Subjects covered: demographics; government information
List moderated: No.
Internet: census-analysis-request@mailbase.ac.uk
How to access: Send subscribe message to mailbase@mailbase.ac.uk in the following format: join census-analysis Your first name Your last name
Archives: Archives are developed monthly; apply to listowner for details.

CENSUS-NEWS@MAILBASE.AC.UK
Description: CENSUS-NEWS@MAILBASE.AC.UK is a forum covering information about UK census data.
Subjects covered: demographics; government information
List moderated: No.
Internet: census-news-request@mailbase.ac.uk
How to access: Send subscribe message to mailbase@mailbase.ac.uk in the following format: join census-news Your first name Your last name
Archives: Archives are developed monthly; apply to listowner for details.

CENSUS-PUBLICATIONS@MAILBASE.AC.UK
Description: CENSUS-PUBLICATIONS@MAILBASE.AC.UK is a forum covering information about UK census data.
Subjects covered: demographics; government information
List moderated: No.
Internet: census-publications-request@mailbase.ac.uk
How to access: Send subscribe message to mailbase@mailbase.ac.uk in the following format: join census-publications Yourfirstname Yourlastname
Archives: Archives are developed monthly; apply to listowner for details.

CENTAM-L
Description: Centam-L covers Central America.
Subjects covered: Central America
List moderated: No.
Editorial contact: John Schonholtz
Internet: JMS@NETCOM.COM
How to access: Send subscribe message to listserv@ubvm or listserv@ubvm.cc.buffalo.edu
How to unsubscribe: Send unsubscribe message to listserv@ubvm or listserv@ubvm.cc.buffalo.edu

CERRO-L
Description: Cerro-L focuses on Central Europe.
Subjects covered: Central Europe; political science; current events
Host: Univ. of Economics and Business Admin., Vienna, Austria; Slovak Academy of Sciences, Bratislava; CSFR, Univ. of North Carolina at Chapel Hill, NC
List moderated: No.
Editorial contact: Gerhard Gonter
Bitnet: gonter@awiwuwii
How to access: Send subscribe message to listserv@aearn or listserv@aearn.edvz.uni-linz.ac.at
How to unsubscribe: Send unsubscribe message to listserv@aearn or listserv@aearn.edvz.uni-linz.ac.at
Archives: Yes; Send anonymous FTP to: ftp.wu.wien.ac.at and cd pub/cerro

CETH (CENTER FOR ELECTRONIC TEXTS IN THE HUMANITIES DISTRIBUTION LIST)
Description: CETH posts announcements relating to the work of the Center for Electronic Texts in the Humanities, which involves bibliographic control of electronic texts, education and information in the area of humanities computing, and development of an online text collection and search and retrieval software.
Subjects covered: humanities; electronic texts
Net address for operations: listserv@pucc, listserv@pucc.princeton.edu
Established: 1992
Sponsor: Center for Electronic Texts in the Humanities, Rutgers and Princeton Universities, 169 College Avenue, New Brunswick, NJ 08903.
Host: Princeton University, Computing and Information Technology, 87 Prospect Avenue, Princeton, NJ 08544.
List moderated: Yes.
Moderation procedure: This list is the electronic distribution list of the Center for Electronic Texts in the Humanities (CETH). Only the list owner can post to this list. Postings are infrequent and irregular, and contain mostly announcements relating to the work of CETH.
Editorial contact: Christine Bohlen
Center for Electronic Texts in the Humanities, 169 College Avenue, New Brunswick, NJ 08903
Tel: (908) 932-1384
Fax: (908) 932-1386
Internet: ceth@zodiac.rutgers.edu
Bitnet: ceth@zodiac
How to access: To listserv send the message subscribe ceth firstname lastname
Access policy: The list is open to all.
How to unsubscribe: To the listserv send the message unsubscribe ceth
Archives: Contents are archived at the listserv address according to regular LISTSERV software practices.
Additional information: CETH has established an open electronic discussion list on electronic text centers, ETEXTCTR@RUTVM1 (see entry elsewhere). More information is available at hoogcarspel@zodiac or hoogcarspel@zodiac.rutgers.edu.
CETH maintains an inventory of electronic texts on RLIN (Research Libraries Information Network), the Rutgers Inventory of Machine-Readable Texts in the Humanities. Information about

its contents at hoogcarspel@zodiac.rutgers.edu (CETH); information about access at bl.ric@rlg or bl.ric@rlg.stanford.edu (RLIN Information Center).

CFS-L (CHRONIC FATIGUE SYNDROME)
Description: CFS-L (Chronic Fatigue Syndrome) is a discussion list seeking to serve the needs of persons with chronic fatigue syndrome by enabling a broad discussion of CFS-related topics. CFS is an illness characterized by debilitating fatigue and a variety of flu-like symptoms. The condition is also known as chronic fatigue immune deficiency syndrome (CFIDS), myalgic encephalomyelitis (ME) and by other names, and in the past has been known as chronic Epstein-Barr virus (CEBV).
Subjects covered: chronic fatigue syndrome; myalgic encephalomyelitis; health sciences; medicine
Net address for operations: LISTSERV@LIST.NIH.GOV or LISTSERV@NIHLIST.BITNET
Net address for questions or submissions: CFS-L@LIST.NIH.GOV
or CFS-L@NIHLIST.BITNET
Established: August 1992
Subscribers: 193
List moderated: No.
Editorial contact: Roger Burns
2800 Quebec St. NW, #1242, Washington, DC 20008.
Tel: (202) 966-8738
Internet: cfs-news@list.nih.gov
Bitnet: cfs-news@nihlist Fidonet: 1:109/432
How to access: Send the command SUB CFS-L <your> <name> to the Internet address LISTSERV@LIST.NIH.GOV or to BITNET address LISTSERV@NIHLIST
Access policy: Subscription is open to all.
How to unsubscribe: Send the command UNSUB CFS-L to either of the LISTSERV addresses described above.
How to submit: cfs-l@list.nih.gov or cfs-l@nihlist.bitnet
Archives: There are monthly logs at the listserv. To get the log for August, 1992, i.e. for year 92 month 8, send the command GET CFS-L LOG9208 as an e-mail message to LISTSERV@LIST.NIH.GOV or to LISTSERV@NIHLIST.BITNET .
Related files: There are many files about CFS available at the Albany LISTSERV. Send the command GET CFS-D FILELIST to the BITNET address LISTSERV@ALBNYDH2 or to the Internet address LISTSERV%ALBNYDH2.BITNET@ ALBANY.EDU in order to obtain a listing of files currently available. Note also Internet lists CFS-NEWS (electronic newsletter), CFS-D (notice of updates to CFS information files at Albany LISTSERV), and CFS-MED (medical discussion) The file CFS-RES.TXT describes most electronic sources of CFS information. Send the command GET CFS-RES TXT to the Albany LISTSERV (addresses given above under "Related files" section).
Additional information: Please note that any advice which may be given on this list regarding diagnoses or treatments, etc., reflects only the opinion of the individual posting the message; people with CFS ought to consult with a licensed health care practitioner who is familiar with the syndrome.

CFS-MED (CHRONIC FATIGUE SYNDROME MEDICAL LIST)
Description: The moderated CFS-MED (Chronic Fatigue Syndrome) list enables physicians to discuss medical research and

clinical issues regarding chronic fatigue syndrome (CFS). CFS is an illness characterized by debilitating fatigue and a variety of flu-like symptoms. The illness is also known as chronic fatigue immune deficiency syndrome (CFIDS), and outside of the USA is usually known as myalgic encephalomyelitis (ME). In the past the syndrome has been known as chronic Epstein-Barr virus (CEBV). Patients who need advice about their individual cases are urged to consult with a licensed health care practitioner who is familiar with the syndrome. Note that CFS-NEWS (electronic newsletter) and CFS-L (CFS general discussion) are also available on this LISTSERV.
Subjects covered: chronic fatigue syndrome; myalgic encephalomyelitis; health sciences; medicine
Net address for operations: LISTSERV@LIST.NIH.GOV or LISTSERV@NIHLIST.BITNET
Net address for questions or submissions: CFS-MED@LIST.NIH.GOV
Established: March 1993
Subscribers: 100
List moderated: Yes.
Moderation procedure: Messages for posting to the list will be sent to the list address where the moderator may forward or edit the message for actual posting to the list.
Editorial contact: Roger Burns
2800 Quebec St. NW, #1242, Washington, DC 20008.
Tel: (202) 966-8738
Internet: cfs-med@list.nih.gov
Bitnet: cfs-med@nihlist Fidonet: 1:109/432
How to access: Send the command SUB CFS-MED <your> <name> to the Internet address LISTSERV@LIST.NIH.GOV or to BITNET address LISTSERV@NIHLIST
Access policy: List is open to all.
How to unsubscribe: Send the command UNSUB CFS-MED to either of the LISTSERV addresses described above.
How to submit: cfs-med@list.nih.gov or cfs-med@nihlist.bitnet
Archives: There are monthly logs at the listserv. To get the log for March, 1993, i.e. for year 93 month 3, send the command GET CFS-MED LOG9303 as an e-mail message to LISTSERV@LIST.NIH.GOV or to LISTSERV@NIHLIST.BITNET .
Related files: There are many files about CFS available at the Albany LISTSERV. Send the command GET CFS-D FILELIST to the BITNET address LISTSERV@ALBNYDH2 or to the Internet address LISTSERV%ALBNYDH2.BITNET@ ALBANY.EDU in order to obtain a listing of files currently available.
Additional information: Note Internet lists CFS-NEWS (electronic newsletter), CFS-D (notice of updates to CFS information files at Albany LISTSERV), and CFS-L (general discussion) The file CFS-RES.TXT describes most electronic sources of CFS information. Send the command GET CFS-RES TXT to the Albany LISTSERV (addresses given above under "Related files" section).

CGE@MARIST
Description: CGE@MARIST is a forum covering the use of computer graphics in education.
Subjects covered: computer graphics; education
List moderated: Yes.
Editorial contact: Willam J. Joel
Internet: jzem@maristvm.marist.edu
Bitnet: jzem@marist

How to access: Send subscribe message to listserv@marist or listserv@maristvm.marist.edu
How to unsubscribe: Send unsubscribe message to listserv@marist or listserv@maristvm.marist.edu
Archives: Archives are developed monthly; apply to listowner for details.

CHAIRS-L

Description: Chairs-L is the Academic Chairpersons Discussion List, an unmoderated discussion list dealing with issues and problems that an academic chairperson faces daily. Discussion topics include the chairperson's role and power, faculty development, annual evaluation, tenure and promotion, budgetary problems, affirmative action, grievances, recruitment procedures, and personnel matters. Membership is open free of charge to all interested individuals or organizations.
Subjects covered: management; colleges and universities
Net address for operations: Chairs-Request@Acc.Fau.Edu
Net address for questions or submissions: Chairs-L@Acc.Fau.Edu
Established: 3rd quarter 1991
Subscribers: 193
Sponsor: Florida Atlantic University, 500 NorthWest 20th Street, Boca Raton, FL 33431-0991.
Host: Florida Atlantic University, 500 NorthWest 20th Street, Boca Raton, FL 33431-0991.
List moderated: No.
Editorial contact: M. Yasar Iscan, Dept of Anthropology, FAU, Boca Raton, FL
Tel: (407) 367-3230
Fax: (407) 367-2744
Internet: ISCAN@ACC.FAU.EDU
Bitnet: ISCAN@FAUVAX
Technical contact: Ralph P Carpenter
Department of Psychology, Florida Atlantic University, Boca Raton, FL 33431-0991.
Tel: (407) 367-2616
Fax: (407) 367-2749
Internet: Ralpho@Acc.Fau.Edu
Bitnet: Ralpho@FauVax
How to access: Email to Chairs-Request@Acc.Fau.Edu (BITNET-restricted users send to Chairs-Request@FAUVAX) The sole content of the message BODY must be: Subscribe Chairs-L John Q Public
Access policy: This discussion list is open to all interested individuals or organizations.
How to unsubscribe: From EXACTLY the same address from which the original subscription was requested, Email to Chairs-Request@Acc.Fau.Edu (BITNET-restricted users send to Chairs-Request@FauVax) The sole content of the message BODY must be: Unsubscribe Chairs-L
How to submit: Email to Chairs-L@Acc.Fau.Edu (BITNET-restricted users send to Chairs-L@FauVax)
Submission policy: This discussion list is open to all interested individuals or organizations.

CHAUCER@SIUCVMB

Description: CHAUCER@SIUCVMB is a forum on Medieval English literature.
Subjects covered: English language and literature; Chaucer, Geoffrey
List moderated: No.

Editorial contact: Jeff Taylor
Bitnet: gr4302@siucvmb
How to access: Send subscribe message to listserv@siucvmb or listserv@siucvmb.siu.edu
How to unsubscribe: Send unsubscribe message to listserv@siucvmb or listserv@siucvmb.siu.edu

CHAUCERNET@UNLINFO.UNL.EDU

Description: CHAUCERNET@UNLINFO.UNL.EDU is a forum discussing Chaucer and other aspects of his language and culture.
Subjects covered: English language and literature; Chaucer, Geoffrey; history
Host: New Chaucer Society
List moderated: No.
Editorial contact: Thomas H. Bestul
Internet: tbestul@crcvms.unl.edu
Bitnet: tbestul@unlvax1
How to access: Send subscribe message to listserv@siucvmb or listserv@unlinfo.unl.edu
How to unsubscribe: Send unsubscribe message to listserv@siucvmb or listserv@unlinfo.unl.edu

CHEM-COMP@MAILBASE.AC.UK

Description: CHEM-COMP@MAILBASE.AC.UK is a forum on computational chemistry.
Subjects covered: chemistry
List moderated: No.
Internet: chem-comp-request@mailbase.ac.uk
How to access: Send subscribe message to mailbase@mailbase.ac.uk in the following format: join chem-comp Yourfirstname Yourlastname
Archives: Archives are developed monthly; apply to listowner for details.

CHEM-MOD@MAILBASE.AC.UK

Description: CHEM-MOD@MAILBASE.AC.UK is a forum for discussion of modelling in computational chemistry.
Subjects covered: chemistry
List moderated: No.
Internet: chem-mod-request@mailbase.ac.uk
How to access: Send subscribe message to mailbase@mailbase.ac.uk in the following format: join chem-mod Yourfirstname Yourlastname
Archives: Archives are developed monthly; apply to listowner for details.

CHEM-TALK

Description: CHEM-TALK is a discussion list for chemists.
Subjects covered: chemistry
List moderated: No.
Editorial contact: Dr. Manus Monroe
How to access: Contact the Editor
How to unsubscribe: Contact the Editor

CHEME-L

Description: Cheme-L covers chemical engineering.
Subjects covered: chemistry

List moderated: No.
Editorial contact: Raul Miranda
Bitnet: r0mira01@ulkyvm
How to access: Send subscribe message to listserv@psuvm or listserv@psuvm.psu.edu
How to unsubscribe: Send unsubscribe message to listserv@psuvm or listserv@psuvm.psu.edu

CHEMED-L
Description: Chemed-L is a forum for chemistry education.
Subjects covered: chemistry; education
List moderated: No.
Editorial contact: Bill Halpern
Bitnet: whalpern@uwf
How to access: Send subscribe message to listserv@uwf or listserv%uwf.bitnet@cunyvm.cuny.edu
How to unsubscribe: Send unsubscribe message to listserv@uwf or listserv%uwf.bitnet@cunyvm.cuny.edu
Archives: Archives are developed monthly; apply to listowner for details.

CHEMIC-L
Description: Chemic-L covers information on chemistry research in Israel.
Subjects covered: chemistry
List moderated: Yes.
Editorial contact: Jo van Zwaren
Internet: jo%ilncrd.bitnet@cunyvm.cuny.edu
Bitnet: jo@ilncrd
How to access: Send subscribe message to listserv@taunivm or listserv@taunivm.tau.ac.il
How to unsubscribe: Send unsubscribe message to listserv@taunivm or listserv@taunivm.tau.ac.il

CHEMISTRY@OSC.EDU
Description: CHEMISTRY@OSC.EDU covers computational chemistry.
Subjects covered: chemistry
Host: Ohio Supercomputer Center
List moderated: No.
Editorial contact: Dr. Jan K. Labanowski
Internet: jkl@osc.edu
Bitnet: jkl@ohstpy
How to access: Send subscribe message to CHEMISTRY-REQUEST@OSCSUNB.OSC.EDU
How to unsubscribe: Send unsubscribe message to CHEMISTRY-REQUEST@OSCSUNB.OSC.EDU
Archives: Archives are developed daily; apply to listowner for details.

CHEMSERV@UKANVM
Description: CHEMSERV@UKANVM is a forum for members of the American Chemical Society.
Subjects covered: chemistry
List moderated: No.
How to access: Send subscribe message to listserv@ukanvm or listserv@ukanvm.cc.ukans.edu
How to unsubscribe: Send unsubscribe message to listserv@ukanvm or listserv@ukanvm.cc.ukans.edu

CHICLE@UNMVMA
Description: CHICLE@UNMVMA is a discussion list on Chicano literature.
Subjects covered: literature; Chicano literature
List moderated: Yes.
Editorial contact: Teresa Marquez
Bitnet: tmarquez@unmb
How to access: Send subscribe message to chicle@unmvm or chicle@unmvma.edu
How to unsubscribe: Send unsubscribe message to chicle@unmvm or chicle@unmvma.edu
Archives: Yes, apply to listowner for details.

CHILE-L
Description: Chile-L is an electronic conference on Chile.
Subjects covered: Chile
List moderated: No.
Editorial contact: Antonio Mladinic
Bitnet: mlad@purccvm
How to access: Send subscribe message to listserv@purccvm
How to unsubscribe: Send unsubscribe message to listserv@purccvm
Archives: Archives are developed weekly; apply to listowner for details.

CHILENET@UCHCECVM
Description: CHILENET@UCHCECVM is an electronic conference on networking in Chile.
Subjects covered: Chile; electronic networking
List moderated: No.
Editorial contact: Enrique OlivaresCanouet
Bitnet: eolivar@uchcecvm
How to access: Send subscribe message to listserv@uchcecvm
How to unsubscribe: Send unsubscribe message to listserv@uchcecvm
Archives: Archives are developed monthly; apply to listowner for details.

CHIMIECH@FRMOP11
Description: CHIMIECH covers molecular chemistry.
Subjects covered: chemistry
List moderated: No.
Editorial contact: Jean-Marie Teuler
Bitnet: ucir044@frors31
How to access: Send subscribe message to listserv@frmop11 or listserv%frmop11.bitnet@vm1.nodak.edu
How to unsubscribe: Send unsubscribe message to listserv@frmop11 or listserv%frmop11.bitnet@vm1.nodak.edu
Archives: Archives are developed monthly; apply to listowner for details.

CHIMIECT@FRMOP11
Description: CHIMIECT covers molecular chemistry.
Subjects covered: chemistry
List moderated: Yes.
Editorial contact: Jean-Marie Teuler
Bitnet: ucir044@frors31
How to access: Send subscribe message to listserv@frmop11 or listserv%frmop11.bitnet@vm1.nodak.edu

How to unsubscribe: Send unsubscribe message to listserv@frmop11 or listserv%frmop11.bitnet@vm1.nodak.edu
Archives: Archives are developed monthly; apply to listowner for details.

CHIMIEGS@FRMOP11

Description: CHIMIEGS is a conference on molecular chemistry.
Subjects covered: chemistry
List moderated: No.
Editorial contact: Jean-Marie Teuler
Bitnet: ucir044@frors31
How to access: Send subscribe message to listserv@frmop11 or listserv%frmop11.bitnet@vm1.nodak.edu
How to unsubscribe: Send unsubscribe message to listserv@frmop11 or listserv%frmop11.bitnet@vm1.nodak.edu
Archives: Archives are developed monthly; apply to listowner for details.

CHINA-ND@KENTVM

Description: CHINA-ND is a forum of the China News Digest.
Subjects covered: current events; China
List moderated: Yes.
Internet: ASMXY@ASUACVAX
How to access: Send subscribe message to listserv@kentvm or listserv@kentvm.kent.udu
How to unsubscribe: Send unsubscribe message to listserv@kentvm or listserv@kentvm.kent.udu
Archives: Archives are developed weekly; apply to listowner for details.

CHINA@PUCC

Description: CHINA@PUCC is a forum for Chinese Studies.
Subjects covered: China; education
List moderated: Yes.
Editorial contact: Tom Nimick
Internet: q4356@pucc.princeton.edu
Bitnet: q4356@pucc
How to access: Send subscribe message to listserv@pucc or listserv@pucc.princeton.edu
How to unsubscribe: Send unsubscribe message to listserv@pucc or listserv@pucc.princeton.edu
Archives: Archives are developed monthly; apply to listowner for details.

CHINANET@TAMVM1

Description: CHINANET@TAMVM1 discusses networking issues in China.
Subjects covered: electronic networking
List moderated: No.
Editorial contact: Butch Kemper
Bitnet: x040bk@tamvm1
How to access: Send subscribe message to listserv@tamvm1
How to unsubscribe: Send unsubscribe message to listserv@tamvm1
Archives: Archives are developed monthly; apply to listowner for details.

CHMINF-L (CHEMICAL INFORMATION SOURCES DISCUSSION LIST)

Description: CHMINF-L is a discussion list about information sources (including books, databases, and software) of relevance to chemistry.
Subjects covered: chemistry; library and information science
Net address for operations: LISTSERV@IUBVM.UCS.INDIANA.EDU
Net address for questions or submissions: CHMINF-L@UCS.UCS.INDIANA.EDU
Established: May 1991
Subscribers: 650 as of July 1, 1993
Sponsor: Indiana University, Chemistry Library, Bloomington, IN 47405.
Host: Indiana University
List moderated: No.
Editorial contact: Gary Wiggins
Chemistry Library, Indiana University, Bloomington, IN 47405.
Tel: (812) 855-9452
Fax: (812) 855-6611
Internet: WIGGINS@UCS.INDIANA.EDU
Bitnet: WIGGINS@IUBACS
How to access: Send message SUB CHMINF-L to LISTSERV@IUBVM.UCS.INDIANIA.EDU.
Access policy: There are no restrictions to subscribing to this list. Submissions of a blatent marketing nature are prohibited.
How to unsubscribe: Send message UNSUB CHMINF-L to LISTSERV@IUBVM.UCS.INDIANIA.EDU.
How to submit: Send email message to CHMINF-L@IUBVM.UCS.INDIANA.EDU.
Archives: Archives are updated monthly.

CHPOEM-L

Description: Chpoem-L is a forum for discussion of Chinese poetry.
Subjects covered: Chinese language and literature; poetry
List moderated: Yes.
Editorial contact: Xiao Fei Wang
Internet: xiaofei@einstein.physics.buffalo.edu
Bitnet: v118raga@ubvms
How to access: Send subscribe message to listserv@ubvm or listserv@ubvm.cc.buffalo.edu
How to unsubscribe: Send unsubscribe message to listserv@ubvm or listserv@ubvm.cc.buffalo.edu
Archives: Archives are developed weekly; apply to listowner for details.

CHUG-L

Description: Chug-L is a forum for Brown Univeristy humanities computing issues.
Subjects covered: humanities
List moderated: Yes.
Editorial contact: Elli Mylonas

Bitnet: elli@brownvm
How to access: Send subscribe message to listserv@brownvm or listserv@brownvm.brown.edu
How to unsubscribe: Send unsubscribe message to listserv@brownvm or listserv@brownvm.brown.edu
Archives: Yes; apply to listowner for details.

CINEMA-L
Description: Cinema-L is a forum on cinema.
Subjects covered: theater; cinema studies
List moderated: No.
Editorial contact: Mike Karolchik
Bitnet: mike@wvnvm
How to access: Send subscribe message to listserv@auvm or listserv@auvm.auvm.edu
How to unsubscribe: Send unsubscribe message to listserv@auvm or listserv@auvm.auvm.edu
Archives: Archives are developed weekly; apply to listowner for details.

CIRCPLUS@IDBSU
Description: CIRCPLUS@IDBSU is an electronic discussion on circulation issues for libraries.
Subjects covered: library and information science
List moderated: No.
Editorial contact: Daniel Lester
Internet: alileste@idbsu.idbsu.edu
Bitnet: alileste@idbsu
How to access: Send subscribe message to listserv@idbsu or listserv@idbsu.idbsu.edu
How to unsubscribe: Send unsubscribe message to listserv@idbsu or listserv@idbsu.idbsu.edu
Archives: Archives are developed weekly; apply to listowner for details.

CIRCUITS-L
Description: Circuits-L covers electronic engineering.
Subjects covered: engineering; electrical engineering
List moderated: No.
Editorial contact: Paul E. Gray
Internet: gray@uwplatt.edu
Bitnet: gray@uwplatt
How to access: Send subscribe message to CIRCUITS-RE-QUEST@UWPLATT.EDU with the following information: name; e-mail address; home, business and fax phone number; U.S. postal address.
How to unsubscribe: Send subscribe message to CIRCUITS-REQUEST@UWPLATT.EDU

CIT$W
Description: CIT$W is the Cracow Institute of Technology open discussion list, accessible to everyone interested in CIT's activity. Cracow Institute of Technology (CIT) is the very first private technological institute established in the Central-European post-communist countries. Located in the more than one thousand year old city of Cracow, former Polish capital, CIT has an excellent Faculty which provides high - quality teaching (postgraduate and doctoral studies) to individual students and small groups, in Aerodynamics and Aeroelasticity, Applied Mathematics, Applied Physics and Metrology, Artificial Intelli-gence, Chemical Engineering, Computer Science, Computer Aided Engineering, Coupled Fields, Dynamics of Constructions, Energy Technology, Environmental Science and Engineering, Laser Technology, Management, Material Science, Motor Vehi-cle Engineering, Robotics, Technical Cybernetics, Telecommuni-cations. The tuition fees are much lower than at most Western universities. Free room and board. Free textbooks. Language of instruction is English.
Subjects covered: engineering; aerodynamics; telecommunications; computer science
Net address for operations: LISTSERV@PLEARN.BITNET or LISTSERV@PLEARN.EDU.PL
Net address for questions or submissions: CIT$W@PLEARN.BITNET
Established: May 1992
Host: Cracow Institute of Technology, Makowa 16, PL 30-650 Krakow, Poland.
List moderated: No.
Editorial contact: WACLAW PRZYBYLO MAKOWA 16, PL 30-650 KRAKOW, POLAND
Tel: (48-12) 55-50-51
Fax: (48-12) 21-75-77 or 22-36-06
Internet: ZTPRZYBY@KRAK.CYF-KR.EDU.PL
Bitnet: ZPPRZYBY@PLKRCY11.BITNET
Technical contact: VLADIMIR KLONOWSKI 1055 - 606 LUCKNOW ST., HALIFAX, NS, CANADA B3H 2T3
Tel: (902) 422-7111
Fax: (902) 422-7111
Internet: KLONOWSK@AC.DAL.CA
How to access: Listserv commands should be used (Revised LISTSERV version 1.7f) Postmasters are: LISTMNT@PLEARN.BITNET
How to unsubscribe: Send to LISTSERV@PLEARN.BITNET command (in the body) UNSUBSCRIBE CIT$W or SIGNOFF CIT$W or TELL LISTSERV AT PLEARN UNSUBSCRIBE CIT$W
How to submit: Send e-mail message to CIT$W@PLEARN.BITNET with the text you want to submit in the body.
Archives: A list of the available archive files may be obtained by sending and e-mail message IND CIT$W (in the body) to LISTSERV@PLEARN.BITNET ; monthly NOTEBOOK archives files are available under names LOGyymm, e.g., LOG9303 for March 1993.
Related files: CIT$P - the private list of Cracow Institute of Technology Faculty and Staff; subscribtion is provided by the owners of CIT$W.

CIVIL-L
Description: Civil-L is a forum focusing on civil engineering research and education.
Subjects covered: engineering; education
List moderated: No.
Editorial contact: Eldo Hildebrand
Internet: eldo@unb.ca
Bitnet: eldo@unb
How to access: Send subscribe message to listserv@unbvm1 or listserv@unb.ca
How to unsubscribe: Send unsubscribe message to listserv@unbvm1 or listserv@unb.ca
Archives: Archives are developed daily; apply to listowner for details.

CJUST-L
Description: Cjust-L is a list focussing on criminal justice.
Subjects covered: law and legal studies
List moderated: Yes.
Bitnet: flood@iubvm
How to access: Send subscribe message to listserv@iubvm or listserv@iubvm.ucs.indiana.edu
How to unsubscribe: Send unsubscribe message to listserv@iubvm or listserv@iubvm.ucs.indiana.edu

CLAN@FRMOP11
Description: CLAN@FRMOP11 is a conference covering cancer research.
Subjects covered: medicine; cancer
List moderated: No.
Editorial contact: Jean-Claude Salomon
Bitnet: salomon@frmop11
How to access: Send subscribe message to listserv@frmop11 or listserv%frmop11.bitnet@vm1.nodak.edu
How to unsubscribe: Send unsubscribe message to listserv@frmop11 or listserv%frmop11.bitnet@vm1.nodak.edu
Archives: Archives are developed monthly; apply to listowner for details.

CLASS-L
Description: CLASS-L is a mailing list and file server for researchers in classification, clustering, phylogenetic estimation, and related areas of data analysis.
Subjects covered: data analysis; artificial intelligence
Net address for questions or submissions: class-l%sbccvm.bitnet@cunyvm.cuny.edu
How to access: Send a message to the internet address listserv%sbccvm.bitnet@cunyvm.cuny.edu The body of the message should consist of:
subscribe CLASS-L <your full name>
How to unsubscribe: Send a message to the internet address listserv%sbccvm.bitnet@cunyvm.cuny.edu The body of the message should consist of: signoff CLASS-L

CLASSICS
Description: CLASSICS is an unmoderated list for discussing ancient Greek and Latin subjects. This list is open to everyone interested in Classics, and prospective members are warmly welcomed. The discussions assume a background in ancient Greek and/or Latin. The list is neither run by nor directly affiliated with the University of Washington Classics Department.
Subjects covered: Greek language and literature; Latin language and literature; classical studies; philology
Net address for operations: LISTSERV@UWAVM.U.WASHINGTON.EDU
Net address for questions or submissions: CLASSICS@UWAVM.U.WASHINGTON.EDU
Established: April 17, 1992
Sponsor: u.washington.edu
Host: uwavm.u.washington.edu
List moderated: No.
Editorial contact: Linda Wright
Univ of Wash JE-20, 4545 - 15th Ave NE, Seattle, WA 98105
Tel: (206) 543-5128
Internet: lwright@u.washington.edu
Bitnet: lwright@CAC

Technical contact: Doug Luft
Univ of Wash JE-30, 4545 - 15th Ave NE, Seattle, WA 98105
Tel: (206) 543-3087
Fax: (206) 685-4044
Internet: dbluft@cac.washington.edu
Bitnet: dbluft@UWAVM
Copyright statement: none
How to access: SUB CLASSICS <your name>, sent to listserv address (see above).
How to unsubscribe: UNSUB CLASSICS, sent to listserv address.
How to submit: Send email to CLASSICS@UWAVM.U.WASHINGTON.EDU
Submission policy: Normal email etiquette, remain within list subjects.
Archives: The list is archived in monthly logs.
Related files: From ftp.u.washington.edu in pub/classics. Contains several texts and Latin workbook.

CLASSM-L
Description: Classm-L is an e-conference on classical music.
Subjects covered: music
List moderated: No.
Editorial contact: Catherine Yang
Internet: cyang@brownvm.brown.edu
Bitnet: cyang@brownvm
How to access: Send subscribe message to listserv@brownvm or listserv@brownvm.brown.edu
How to unsubscribe: Send unsubscribe message to listserv@brownvm or listserv@brownvm.brown.edu
Archives: Archives are developed weekly; apply to listowner for details.

CLAYART@UKCC
Description: CLAYART@UKCC is a forum for those interested in the fields of pottery and the ceramic arts.
Subjects covered: art; pottery
List moderated: No.
Editorial contact: Joe Molinaro
Bitnet: artmolin@eku
How to access: Send subscribe message to listserv@ukcc or listserv@ukcc.uky.edu
How to unsubscribe: Send unsubscribe message to listserv@ukcc or listserv@ukcc.uky.edu
Archives: Archives are developed monthly; apply to listowner for details.

CLIMLIST
Description: CLIMLIST is a moderated international electronic mail distribution list for climatologists and those working in closely related fields. It is primarily intended for persons undertaking research in climatology, teaching climatology and providing services of a climatological nature. It is not intended for those with a general or avocational interest in climatology. Students undertaking research for a degree are encouraged to subscribe. The list is used to disseminate notices regarding conferences and workshops, data availability, calls for papers, positions available etc, as well as requests for information. In addition, an updated directory of email addresses for the subscribers to the list is distributed every month (usually on the 15th).

Subjects covered: climatology; education; science and technology
Net address for operations: LISTSERV@PSUVM.PSU.EDU
Net address for questions or submissions: aja+@osu.edu (Internet) or AJA+@OHSTMAIL (BITNET)
Established: October 1988
Method of issuance: CLIMLIST subscriptions are available in two formats: by default, subscribers receive mailings as distributed to the listserver. On request, a 'digest' version is available, in which mailings are accumulated and distributed on a weekly basis.
Subscribers: 510
Sponsor: Department of Geography, The Ohio State University, 103 Bricker Hall, 190 North Oval Mall, Columbus, OH 43210-1361.
Host: The Pennsylvania State University, University Park, Pennsylvania.
List moderated: Yes.
Moderation procedure: Mailings intended for CLIMLIST should be sent to List Owner John Arnfield (aja+@osu.edu or AJA+@OHSTMAIL.BITNET). They are reviewed for compatibility with CLIMLIST's policies and purpose and, if appropriate, are edited to a standard format and sent to LISTSERV@PSUVM.PSU.EDU for distribution to subscribers.
Editorial contact: John Arnfield
Department of Geography, The Ohio State University, 103 Bricker Hall, 190 North Oval Mall, Columbus, OH 43210-1361.
Tel: (614) 292-7954
Fax: (614) 292-6213
Internet: aja+@osu.edu
Bitnet: AJA+@OHSTMAIL
Technical contact: John Arnfield
Department of Geography, The Ohio State University, 103 Bricker Hall, 190 North Oval Mall, Columbus, OH 43210-1361.
Tel: (614) 292-7954
Fax: (614) 292-6213
Internet: aja+@osu.edu
Bitnet: AJA+@OHSTMAIL
How to access: Subscription is not automated but is controlled by the list moderator. Persons interested in subscribing should send email to John Arnfield (aja+@osu.edu on internet, AJA+@OHSTMAIL on BITNET) providing the following information: 1.The name, as it should appear in the directory; 2.The email address or addresses; 3.The affiliation (department and institution or equivalent); 4.A statement as to whether the email address is a personal one or is shared (e.g., it is for a group); and 5. The area(s) of interest, expertise or responsibility in the field of climatology.
Access policy: All persons engaged actively in research and/or teaching in climatology or related scientific areas or persons providing climatological services are welcome to subscribe. Persons with a casual or avocational interest in climatic issues or persons with a meteorological (rather than climatological) orientation should not subscribe. In addition, this is not a list for 'chatting' - it is a medium for the distribution of information relating to climatology.
How to unsubscribe: Send email to the list moderator, John Arnfield, at either of the email addresses given under subscription information, requesting deletion.
How to submit: Items for distribution should be sent to the list moderator, John Arnfield, at aja+@osu.edu (internet) or AJA+@OHSTMAIL (BITNET). If the item is consistent with the purpose of CLIMLIST (see policy statements above), it will be edited to a standard format and forwarded to the listserver for distribution.
Submission policy: All submissions must be consistent with the aims of the list. Conference announcements, research reports, jobs available, data source information, degree program descriptions, non-trivial requests for information, various climate-related newsletters, personal statements etc are all acceptable.
Archives: CLIMLIST mailings are archived monthly on LISTSERV@PSUVM.PSU.EDU and can be retrieved by CLIMLIST subscribers only using conventional VM LISTSERV procedures.

CLP.X@XEROX.COM
Description: CLP.X@XEROX.COM is a forum for discussion of computer programming languages.
Subjects covered: computer science; conferences and conference listings
List moderated: No.
Editorial contact: Jacob Levy
Internet: jlevy.pa@xerox.com
How to access: Send subscribe message to CLP-REQUEST.X@XEROC.COM or JLEVY.PA@XEROX.COM
How to unsubscribe: Send unsubscribe message to CLP-REQUEST.X@XEROC.COM or JLEVY.PA@XEROX.COM

CLU-SW@SEISMO.CSS.GOV
Description: CLU-SW is a discussion list covering topics related to CLU software.
Subjects covered: computer hardware and software
List moderated: No.
Editorial contact: Matti Jokinen
Internet: jokinen@cs.utu.fi
How to access: Send subscribe message to clu-sw-request@cs.uta.fi
How to unsubscribe: Send unsubscribe message to clu-sw-request@cs.uta.fi

CMSUG-L
Description: CMSUG-L is a discussion list on CMS.
Subjects covered: computer hardware and software
List moderated: No.
Editorial contact: Gary Samek
Internet: c133ges@utarlvm1.uta.edu
Bitnet: c133es@utarlvm1
How to access: Send subscribe message to listserv@utarlvm1 or listserv@utarlvm1.uta.edu
How to unsubscribe: Send unsubscribe message to listserv@utarlvm1 or listserv@utarlvm1.uta.edu

CMU-TEK-TCP@CS.CMU.EDU
Description: CMU-TEK-TCP is a discussion list on the CMU-TEK TCP-IP package for VAX/VMS.
Subjects covered: computer hardware and software
List moderated: No.
Editorial contact: Dale Moore
Internet: dale.moore@ps1.cs.cmu.edu
How to access: Send subscribe message to CMU-TEK-TCP-REQUEST@CS.CMU.EDU
How to unsubscribe: Send unsubscribe message to CMU-TEK-TCP-REQUEST@CS.CMU.EDU

CNEDUC-L

Description: Cneduc-L is a forum discussing aspects of computer networking education.
Subjects covered: education; education technology
List moderated: No.
Editorial contact: Lynn Burlbaw
Bitnet: lmb2379@tamrigel
How to access: Send subscribe message to LISTSERV@TAMVM1
How to unsubscribe: Send unsubscribe message to LISTSERV@TAMVM1
Archives: Archives are developed monthly; apply to listowner for details.

CNI-ANNOUNCE@CNI.ORG

Description: CNI-ANNOUNCE@CNI.ORG is a forum of the Coalition for Networked Information announcing news of its activities.
Subjects covered: Internet
Host: Coalition for Networked Information
How to access: Send subscribe message to listserv@cni.org
How to unsubscribe: Send unsubscribe message to listserv@cni.org

CNI-ARCH@UCCVMA

Description: CNI-ARCH is a conference of the Coalition for Networked Information's working group on network architectures and standards.
Subjects covered: computer science; electronic networking
Host: Coalition for Networked Information
List moderated: No.
Editorial contact: Clifford Lynch
Internet: calur@uccmvsa.ucop.edu
How to access: Send subscribe message to listserv@uccvma or listserv@uccvma.ucop.edu
How to unsubscribe: Send unsubscribe message to listserv@uccvma or listserv@uccvma.ucop.edu

CNI-BIGIDEAS@CNI.ORG

Description: CNI-BIGIDEAS@CNI.ORG is a forum of the Coalition for Networked Information for big ideas, i.e., large concepts and strategies about the future of the National Research and Education Network (NREN)
Subjects covered: Internet; NREN
Host: Coalition for Networked Information
How to access: Send subscribe message to listserv@cni.org
How to unsubscribe: Send unsubscribe message to listserv@cni.org

CNI-COPYRIGHT@CNI.ORG

Description: CNI-COPYRIGHT@CNI.ORG is a forum of the Coalition for Networked Information discussing copyrights and intellectual property.
Subjects covered: copyright; intellectual property; Internet
Host: Coalition for Networked Information
List moderated: Yes.
Editorial contact: Mary Brandt Jensen
Internet: mjensen@charlie.usd.edu
How to access: Send subscribe message to listserv@cni.org

How to unsubscribe: Send unsubscribe message to listserv@cni.org

CNI-DIRECTORIES@CNI.ORG

Description: CNI-DIRECTORIES@CNI.ORG is a forum on directory and information resource services on networks.
Subjects covered: electronic networking; Internet
Host: Coalition for Networked Information
List moderated: Yes.
Editorial contact: George Brett
Internet: ghb@concert.net
How to access: Send subscribe message to listserv@cni.org
How to unsubscribe: Send unsubscribe message to listserv@cni.org
Archives: Yes.

CNI-LEGISLATION@CNI.ORG

Description: CNI-LEGISLATION@CNI.ORG is a forum discussing CNI legislation and policies regarding the Internet.
Subjects covered: electronic networking; Internet
Host: Coalition for Networked Information
List moderated: Yes.
Editorial contact: Richard G. Akeroyd, Jr.
Bitnet: rakeroyd@wesleyan
How to access: Send subscribe message to listserv@cni.org
How to unsubscribe: Send unsubscribe message to listserv@cni.org

CNI-MANAGEMENT@CNI.ORG

Description: CNI-MANAGEMENT is a forum on management issues in the Coalition for Networked Information.
Subjects covered: electronic networking; Internet
Host: Coalition for Networked Information
List moderated: Yes.
Editorial contact: Lee Alley
Bitnet: iadlra@asuacad
How to access: Send subscribe message to listserv@cni.org
How to unsubscribe: Send unsubscribe message to listserv@cni.org

CNI-MODERNIZATION@CNI.ORG

Description: CNI-MODERNIZATION@CNI.ORG is a forum discussing the network-assisted modernization of scholarly publishing.
Subjects covered: electronic networking; Internet
Host: Coalition for Networked Information
List moderated: Yes.
Editorial contact: James Williams
Internet: williams-j@cubldr.colorado.edu
How to access: Send subscribe message to listserv@cni.org
How to unsubscribe: Send unsubscribe message to listserv@cni.org

CNI-PUBINFO@CNI.ORG

Description: CNI-PUBINFO@CNI.ORG is a forum on the CNI Public Information Working Group.
Subjects covered: electronic networking; Internet
Host: Coalition for Networked Information

List moderated: Yes.
Editorial contact: Barbara von Wahlde
Internet: unlbvw@ubvm.cc.buffalo.edu
How to access: Send subscribe message to listserv@cni.org
How to unsubscribe: Send unsubscribe message to listserv@cni.org

CNI-TEACHING@CNI.ORG

Description: CNI-TEACHING@CNI.ORG is a forum of the Coalition for Networked Information's Teaching and Learning Working Group.
Subjects covered: Internet
Host: Coalition for Networked Information
How to access: Send subscribe message to listserv@cni.org
How to unsubscribe: Send unsubscribe message to listserv@cni.org

CNI-TRANSFORMATION@CNI.ORG

Description: CNI-TRANSFORMATION@CNI.ORG is a forum discussing the transformation of scholarly and academic communication.
Subjects covered: electronic networking; Internet
Host: Coalition for Networked Information
List moderated: Yes.
Editorial contact: Charles Henry
Bitnet: chhenry@vassar
How to access: Send subscribe message to listserv@cni.org
How to unsubscribe: Send unsubscribe message to listserv@cni.org

CNSF-L

Description: CNSF-L posts activities and events related to the Cornell National Supercomputing Facility.
Subjects covered: campus-wide information systems; colleges and universities
List moderated: No.
Editorial contact: Tom Britt
Bitnet: brittt@snysyrv1
How to access: Send subscribe message to listserv@ubvm or listserv@ubvm.cc.buffalo.edu
How to unsubscribe: Send unsubscribe message to listserv@ubvm or listserv@ubvm.cc.buffalo.edu
Archives: Yes.

COCAMED (COMPUTERS IN CANADIAN MEDICAL EDUCATION)

Description: COCAMED (Computers in Canadian Education) is a discussion list covering Computers in Canadian Medical Education. It serves as an information exchange between medical educators and those working in medical informatics areas. Subjects covered are software, computer-aided learning, standards, medical informatics, organizational impact of medical informatics, hardware, techniques, conferences, pedagogy, medical databases, shareware, information servers, internet, medical vocabularies, medical decision support tools, and micrcomputer enhanced teaching in medical education.
Subjects covered: medicine; computer hardware and software; education; library and information science
Net address for operations: utoronto.bitnet

Net address for questions or submissions: cocamed@utoronto.bitnet
Established: October 22, 1990
Subscribers: 136
Sponsor: Dalhousie Medical School, Halifax NS Canada.
Host: University of Toronto, Toronto, ON Canada.
List moderated: No.
Editorial contact: Grace Paterson, Medical Education Unit, Office of the Dean, Faculty of Medicine, Tupper Building, Dalhousie University, Halifax NS B3H 4H7.
Tel: (902) 494-1764
Fax: (902) 494-7119
Internet: grace@tupdean1.med.dal.ca
Bitnet: gpaterso@dalac
How to access: To listserv send the following message: subscribe COCAMED your name
Access policy: This list is open to all.
How to unsubscribe: To listserv send the following message: unsubscribe COCAMED
How to submit: Send a posting to COCAMED@UTORONTO.BITNET
Archives: CAMIS gopher (Center for Advanced Medical Informatics at Stanford) archived at UTORONTO
Gopher accessibility: Yes, this is accessible on the gopher at CAMIS (Center for Advanced Medical Informatics at Stanford).

COG-SCI-L

Description: COG-SCI-L is a discussion group covering cogntive sciences.
Subjects covered: cognitive science
Host: Cognitive Science Centre, McGill University
List moderated: Yes.
Bitnet: INAMC@MUSICB.MCGILL.CA
How to access: Send subscribe message to listserv@mcgilli
How to unsubscribe: Send unsubscribe message to listserv@mcgilli

COGNEURO@PTOLEMY.ARC.NASA.GOV

Description: COGNEURO@PTOLEMY.ARC.NASA.GOV is a forum covering cognitive science and neuroscience.
Subjects covered: psychology
List moderated: No.
Internet: cogneuro-request@ptolemy.arc.nasa.gov
How to access: Send subscribe message to COGNEURO-REQUEST@PTOLEMY.ARC.NASA.GOV
How to unsubscribe: Send unsubscribe message to COGNEURO-REQUEST@PTOLEMY.ARC.NASA.GOV

COLEXT@ANDESCOL

Description: COLEXT@ANDESCOL is an electronic conference on Colombia.
Subjects covered: Colombia
List moderated: No.
Editorial contact: Juan Felipe Arjona
Bitnet: jfarjona@andescol
How to access: Contact the Editor
How to unsubscribe: Contact the Editor
Archives: Archives are developed weekly; access from CUVMB node

COLLDV-L (LIBRARY COLLECTION DEVELOPMENT LIST)

Description: COLLDV-L (Library Collection Development List) is a list offering primarily specialized queries and responses from collection development librarians, along with professional announcements and relevant job postings.

Subjects covered: library collection development; library management

Net address for operations: LISTSERV@USCVM or LISTSERV@VM.USC.EDU

Established: August 1, 1992

Subscribers: 1,141

Sponsor: University of Southern California, Los Angeles

Host: University of Southern California, Los Angeles

List moderated: Yes.

Moderation procedure: Postings are forwarded by the local listserv to the moderator for approval. Moderator reformats messages and forwards to the list. Like messages are grouped together. Original posting is repeated when a response is being provided.

Editorial contact: Lynn Sipe, Assistant University Librarian for Collection Development, University of Southern California Library

Tel: (213) 740-2929

Fax: (213) 749-1221

Internet: LSIPE@CALVIN.USC.EDU

Bitnet: LSIPE@USCVM

Technical contact: IBM Mainframe Consulting U.S.C. University Computing Services

Tel: (213) 740-555

Internet: ACTION@VM.USC.EDU

Bitnet: ACTION@USCVM

How to access: Send mail or interactive message to Listserv: LISTSERV@USCVM OR LISTSERV@VM.USC.EDU WITH COMMAND 'SUBSCRIBE COLLDV -L first name last name

Access policy: Subscription open to anyone.

How to unsubscribe: SEND MAIL OR INTER-ACTIVE MESSAGE TO LISTSERV@USCVM OR LISTSERV@VM.USC. EDU WITH COMMAND 'UNSUBSCRIBE C OLLDV-L first name last name

How to submit: SEND MAIL TO COLLDV-L@USCVM OR COLLDV-L@VM.USC.EDU

Archives: List has been archived from March 22, 1993 onward. Standard LISTSERV protocols apply.

COLLIB-L

Description: COLLIB-L is open to the networking community. Its primary role is to serve as a means of communication among members of the ACRL's College Libraries Section. It is also intended to serve as a forum for the discussion of issues relevant to other college librarians and staff who serve primarily 4-year undergraduate institutions. Please note that COLLIB-L is not a BITNET Listserv. Ground rules: COLLIB-L is not a chat line. Personal messages should be addressed to an individual, not broadcast to all subscribers. All subscribers are asked to show courtesy and exercise tolerance in their postings.

Subjects covered: electronic networking; library and information science; colleges and universities

Net address for operations: listserv@willamette.edu

Net address for questions or submissions: collib-l@willamette.edu

Established: March 1, 1993

Subscribers: 600

Sponsor: Willamette University Library

List moderated: Yes.

Editorial contact: Larry R. Oberg, Willamette University Library, 900 State Street, Salem, OR 97301

Tel: (503) 370-6312

Fax: (503) 370-6141

Internet: loberg@willamette.edu

Technical contact: Sara Amato Willamette University Library, 900 State Street, Salem, OR 97301

Tel: (503) 370-6312

Fax: (503) 370-6141

Internet: samato@willamette.edu

How to access: Anyone may subscribe to the list by sending a <sub collib-l your name> command to <listserv@willamette.edu>. For example <sub collib-l sue smith>. It is presently possible for anyone to determine that you are a COLLIB-L subscriber through the use of the <rev collib-l> command, which returns the network addresses and names of all subscribers.

How to unsubscribe: You may leave the list at any time by sending a <signoff collib-l> command to <listserv@willamette.edu>.

Archives: Postings to COLLIB-L will be archived once a month with a filename for that month and year, e.g., march1993. To retrieve a list of available archives send the command <index> to <listserv@willamette.edu>. Files for collib-l will be listed under the 'Subarchive: collib-l' section. To retrieve an archive file, sent the following the command <get collib-l filename> to <listserv@willamette.edu>. For example <get collib-l march1993>.

WAIS accessibility: Plans for WAIS access summer 1993.

COLOR AND VISION NETWORK

Description: CVNet maintains a list of email addresses of biological vision scientists. It also distributes weekly updates of these addresses, distributes announcments pertaining to jobs, scientific meetings, and other information related to vision research. This is not a BBS in the usual sense. CVNet does not accept commercial messages, help-me messages, or messages that pertain only to very local events. CVNet addresses an international constituency. Scientists from over two dozen countries have registered with CVNet.

Subjects covered: biology; vision research

Net address for operations: CVNet@vm1.yorku.ca

Net address for questions or submissions: Same as above

Established: 1986

Subscribers: 1302

Sponsor: York U, North York, Ontario

Host: Same as above

List moderated: Yes.

Moderation procedure: All information is sent to CVNet@vm1.yorku.ca

Editorial contact: Dr. Peter K. Kaiser, Dept. of Psych. York U 4700 Keele St. North York Ont. M3J 1P3

Tel: (416) 736-2100 ext. 66335

Fax: (416) 736-5814

Internet: cvnet@vm1.yorku.ca

Bitnet: cvnet@yorkvm1

Technical contact: Same as above

How to access: Send message to CVNet

How to unsubscribe: Send message to CVNet

How to submit: Send message to CVNet

Submission policy: Send message to CVNet

COM-ALG@NDSUVM1
Description: COM-ALG@NDSUVM1 is a forum on commutative algebra.
Subjects covered: mathematics
List moderated: No.
Editorial contact: Joseph Brennan
Internet: brennan@plains.nodak.edu
Bitnet: nu160025@ndsuvm1 or brennan@plains
How to access: Send subscribe message to listserv@ndsuvm1 or listserv@vm1.nodak.edu
How to unsubscribe: Send unsubscribe message to listserv@ndsuvm1 or listserv@vm1.nodak.edu
Archives: Archives are developed monthly; apply to listowner for details.

COM-PRIV@PSI.COM
Description: COM-PRIV@PSI.COM is a forum on the commercialization of the Internet.
Subjects covered: Internet; information technology
List moderated: No.
How to access: Send subscribe message to COM-PRIV-REQUEST@UU.PSI.COM
How to unsubscribe: Send unsubscribe message to COM-PRIV-REQUEST@UU.PSI.COM
Archives: Yes; Send anonymous FTP to com-priv uu.psi.com and cd /archive/com-priv/

COMENIUS@CSEARN
Description: COMENIUS@CSEARN information services in libraries.
Subjects covered: library and information science
List moderated: No.
Editorial contact: Alexandra Cernochova
Internet: alexaprg@csearn
How to access: Send subscribe message to listserv@csearn
How to unsubscribe: Send unsubscribe message to listserv@csearn
Archives: Archives are developed monthly; apply to listowner for details.

COMLAW-L
Description: Comlaw-L is a forum centering on computers and legal education.
Subjects covered: law and legal studies; education
List moderated: Yes.
Editorial contact: John Boeske
Bitnet: jboeske@ualtavm
How to access: Send subscribe message to listserv@ualtavm or listserv@vm.ucs.ualberta.ca
How to unsubscribe: Send unsubscribe message to listserv@ualtavm or listserv@vm.ucs.ualberta.ca
Archives: Archives are developed weekly; apply to listowner for details.

COMMCOLL
Description: COMMCOLL is a discussion list covering topics related to community colleges and/or junior colleges.
Subjects covered: education; colleges and universities
Net address for operations: Jefferson Community College, University of Kentucky
List moderated: No.
Editorial contact: Anne Kearney
Jefferson Community College-University of Kentucky, 109 East Broadway, Louisville, KY 40202
Tel: (502) 584-0181, ext. 353
Fax: (502) 585-4425
Internet: JCCANNEK@UKCC.UKY.EDU
Bitnet: JCCANNEK@UKCC
Technical contact: Same as above
How to access: Tell listserv@UKCC.UKY.EDU SUB COMMCOLL Your first name Your last name
How to unsubscribe: Tell listserv@UKCC.UKY.EDU SIGNOFF COMMCOLL
How to submit: Mail to COMMCOLL@UKCC.UKY.EDU
Submission policy: No submissions of a commercial or personally derogatory nature, no obscenities. ALWAYS put your name and e-mail address at the end of every posting. (It is important that people be able to contact you privately if they wish, and some mail systems do not identify the writer anywhere in the header.) Also, if you are replying to someone else's posting, briefly quote or summarize that posting before you offer your reply. Doing so will make your message clearer and avoid confusion. You can indicate the message you are replying to by using a < before each line. On some systems, you can use the command "reply text". You should send replies to COMMCOLL when the contents are likely to be of interest to a number of subscribers. Comments directed at a particular person should be sent privately, NOT to COMMCOLL.

COMP-ACADEMIC-FREEDOM-TALK@EFF.ORG
Description: COMP-ACADEMIC-FREEDOM-TALK is a forum discussing academic freedom.
Subjects covered: colleges and universities; intellectual freedom; computer privacy
Host: Electronic Frontier Foundation
List moderated: Yes.
Editorial contact: Carl Kadie
Internet: kadie@eff.org
How to access: Send subscribe message to LISTSERV@EFF.ORG including line: add name-of-version.
Archives: Yes; Send anonymous FTP to eff.org uu.psi.com and cd /pub/academic directory

COMP-CEN@UCCVMA.UCOP.EDU
Description: COMP-CEN discusses operation of mid- to large-sized computer facilities.
Subjects covered: campus-wide information systems; computer science
List moderated: No.
Editorial contact: Rich Hintz
Internet: opsrjh@uccvma.ucop.edu
How to access: Send subscribe message to listserv@uccvma or listserv@uccvma.ucop.edu
How to unsubscribe: Send unsubscribe message to listserv@uccvma or listserv@uccvma.ucop.edu

COMP-PRIVACY@PICA.ARMY.MIL

Description: COMP-PRIVACY is a discussion on the effects of technology on privacy.

Subjects covered: computer privacy; information technology

List moderated: Yes.

Editorial contact: Dennis G. Rears

Internet: drears@pica.army.mil

How to access: Send subscribe message to comp-privacy-request@pica.army.mil

How to unsubscribe: Send unsubscribe message to comp-privacy-request@pica.army.mil

COMP-SOC@LIMBO.INTUITIVE.COM

Description: COMP-SOC@LIMBO.INTUITIVE.COM is a forum for discussing the impact of science and technology on society.

Subjects covered: information technology; philosophy; sociology; ethics

List moderated: No.

Editorial contact: Dave Taylor

Internet: taylor@limbo.intuitive.com

How to access: Contact the Editor

How to unsubscribe: Contact the Editor

COMPIL-L

Description: COMPIL-L is an electronic forum for discussion of compilers, interpreters, and other language processors and related topics such as assemblers, debuggers, and language design. Questions, comments, conference reports, CFPs, book reviews, etc., are welcome.

Subjects covered: computer science; computer language processors; computer hardware and software

Net address for operations: listserv@american.edu

Net address for questions or submissions: compilers@iecc.cambridge.ma.us or compil-l@american.edu

Established: 1986

Subscribers: On usenet, over 20,000. Via direct subscription, under 100 (anyone who can get it on usenet shouldn't ask for a direct sub).

Sponsor: I.E.C.C., PO Box 349, Cambridge, MA 02238-0349.

Host: The American University in Washington, DC, handles the gateway from news to mail. Moderation and archives are at I.E.C.C.

List moderated: All submissions are read by the moderator, rejected if inappropriate, and lightly edited (especially for authors who don't speak English well). Turnaround time is usually a day or two.

Editorial contact: John Levine, I.E.C.C., PO Box 349, Cambridge MA 02238-0349.

Tel: (617) 492-3869

Fax: (617) 492-4407

Internet: compilers-request@iecc.cambridge.ma.us

Bitnet: OWNER-COMPIL-L@AUVM

Copyright statement: All items may be reproduced without restriction. No compilation copyright claimed.

How to access: Mail ''SUB COMPIL-L your real name to LISTSERV@AMERICAN.EDU Users of MVS or VM/370 may use standard listserv commands.

Access policy: This list is open to anyone.

How to unsubscribe: Mail ''SIGNOFF COMPIL-L your real name'' to LISTSERV@AMERICAN.EDU Users of MVS or VM/370 may use standard listserv commands.

How to submit: E-mail to compilers@iecc.cambridge.ma.us or COMPIL-L@AUVM

Submission policy: Any germane contribution welcomed.

Archives: Complete archives and related files for FTP at primost.cs.wisc.edu or mail server at compilers-server@iecc.cambridge.ma.us. Files include compiler bibliographies, machine readable grammars for popular languages, source code for compiler tools, and other random compiler related stuff.

Gopher accessibility: FTP archive probably known to Gopher.

COMPMED

Description: COMPMED is an Internet/Bitnet mailing list for discussing the topics of comparative medicine and the veterinary specialty of laboratory animal medicine (all species). This discussion group is primarily intended to provide a forum for information exchange among professionals working in the field of biomedical research.

Subjects covered: medicine; career opportunities; veterinary science

Net address for operations: LISTSERV@WUVMD (Bitnet) or LISTSERV@WUVMD.WUSTL.EDU (Internet)

Net address for questions or submissions: COMPMED@WUVMD (Bitnet) or COMPMED@WUVMD.WUSTL.EDU (Internet)

Established: 1992

Subscribers: 450

Sponsor: Division of Comparative Medicine Washington University Box 8061, 660 South Euclid Ave. St. Louis, MO 63110

Host: Washington University

Editorial contact: Ken Boschert, DVM
Washington University, Division of Comparative Medicine
Box 8061, 660 South Euclid Ave., St. Louis, MO 63110

Tel: (314) 362-3700

Fax: (314) 362-6480

Internet:
KEN@WUDCM.WUSTL.EDUKEN@WUDCM.BITNET

Copyright statement: Reproduction of COMPMED postings is prohibited without prior consent of the list owner, Ken Boschert (ken@wudcm.wustl.edu).

How to access: To subscribe to the COMPMED mailing list, send Bitnet e-mail to: LISTSERV@WUVMD or Internet e-mail to: LISTSERV@WUVMD.WUSTL.EDU with the BODY of the mail consisting of the following:
SUBscribe COMPMED first name last name

How to unsubscribe: You may leave the list at any time by sending the following command (in the body of your e-mail message): SIGNOFF COMPMED to: LISTSERV@WUVMD (Bitnet) or LISTSERV@WUVMD.WUSTL.EDU (Internet).

How to submit: To send a message to the list, so that everyone can read it, send mail to:
COMPMED@WUVMD.WUSTL.EDU (Internet) or COMPMED@WUVMD (Bitnet)

Archives: Contributions to this list are automatically archived. You can obtain the available archive file (containing messages from the past month by sending the command: INDEX COMPMED to LISTSERV@WUVMD (Bitnet) or to LISTSERV@WUVMD.WUSTL.EDU (Internet).

Related files: FTP WUARCHIVE.WUSTL.EDU /doc/techreports/wustl.edu/compmed

Gopher accessibility: Not yet, but coming soon!

COMPOS01@ULKYVX
Description: COMPOS01@ULKYVX is a forum for writing professionals.
Subjects covered: writing
List moderated: No.
How to access: Send subscribe message to listserv@ulkyvx
How to unsubscribe: Send unsubscribe message to listserv@ulkyvx

COMPUTATIONAL CHEMISTRY LIST
Description: Computational Chemistry List is an electronic forum for the discussion of Computational Chemistry. Among topics covered are: chemistry software, announcements, description, bug reports and workarounds, computational chemistry workshops and symposia, computational chemistry methodology, hardware related issues, opinions on products and services, and approaches to molecular simulations. The list is not organized for particular software package or specific discipline. Discussions on all topics of computer applications in chemistry are encouraged, though the most popular topics are: quantum chemical calculations, molecular mechanics and dynamics calculations, molecular modeling, molecular graphics, molecular spectroscopy computations.
Subjects covered: chemistry; molecular mechanics; science and technology; computer hardware and software
Net address for operations: chemistry-request@osc.edu
Net address for questions or submissions: chemistry@osc.edu
Established: January 1991
Subscribers: 1418 (however, many addresses on the list are the local lists, to save the bandwidth) from over 30 countries.
Sponsor: Ohio Supercomputer Center, 1224 Kinnear Road, Columbus, OH 43212-1163.
Host: Ohio Supercomputer Center, 1224 Kinnear Road, Columbus, OH 43212-1163.
List moderated: No.
Moderation procedure: However, the software has few filters. One of them is to block messages from some addresses (i.e., prevent internet jerks from posting charismatic messgaes to the list). Another is detecting subscription/unsubscription messages. You need not to be subscribed to the list to post, however, most of the responses are sent to the list, so you would miss your answers if you were not subscribed. Messages without Subject: line are rejected.
Editorial contact: Jan K. Labanowski
Ohio Supercomputer Center, 1224 Kinnear Road, Columbus, OH 43212-1163.
Tel: (614) 292-9279
Fax: (614) 292-7168
Copyright statement: No copyright restrictions, however, the list of subscribers is not distributed and not available on request.
How to access: Send a short message to the list administrator (chemistry-request@osce.du) stating your: name, address, institution and electronic mail address.
Access policy: Anyone can subscribe.
How to unsubscribe: Send a short message to the list administrator (chemistry-request@osc.edu) requesting insubscription. Usually the message header provides enough information to unsubscribe.
How to submit: Send a message to chemistry@osc.edu as you would send an ordinary e-mail message. When your message is received, a confirmation message is returned to the author.

Submission policy: Before your submit your message, you should read the rules of the list which are spelled in the "help" file available from the archived.
Archives: All messages posted to the list are archived on the anonymous ftp site: kekule.osc.edu [128.146.36.48] (this address may change in a month or so). They can be also obtained via e-mail. For more information on the list archives and rules send a message: send help from chemistry to OSCPOST@osc.edu or OSCPOST@OHSTPY.BITNET
Related files: Beside archived messages, the archives for CCL list on anonymous ftp on kekule.osc.edu [128.146.36.48] contain many programs, documents, announcements, etc. The top directory is /pub/chemistry for the computational chemistry related materials. Another activity is the "Computational Chemistry Job Market". The files /pub/chemistry/positions.offered and /pub/chemistry/positions.wanted contain job opening annouecements, and resumes of people looking for a job, respectively. These are most frequently accessed files. The archives can be alsa search by keywords and reqular expressions. The instructions are given in the file /pub/chemistry/help.search on anon. ftp kekule.osc.edu.
Gopher accessibility: Gopher to be introduced shortly.

COMSERVE@RPITSVM
Description: COMSERVE@RPITSVM plays host to various discussion lists covering communication and related fields.
Subjects covered: communications
List moderated: No.
Editorial contact: Comserve Staff
Internet: comserve@vm.its.vpi.edu
Bitnet: comserv@rpitsvm
How to access: Send message "Show Hotlines" to comserv@rpitsvm or comserve@vm.its.vpi.edu to show a description of the hotlines. Send a subscribe message in the form of "Join Hotline name Your name"

COMSOC-L
Description: Comsoc-L covers issues related to the computer and society.
Subjects covered: sociology; computer science
List moderated: Yes.
Editorial contact: Greg Walsh
Internet: socicom@auvm.american.edu
How to access: Send subscribe message to listserv@auvm or listserv@auvm.american.edu
How to unsubscribe: Send unsubscribe message to listserv@auvm or listserv@auvm.american.edu

COMTEN-L
Description: COMTEN-L is a forum for discussion of all types of networking hardware and software.
Subjects covered: computer hardware and software; electronic networking
List moderated: No.
Editorial contact: Dwight M. McCann
Bitnet: dwight@uscbvm
How to access: Send subscribe message to listserv@ucsbvm or listserv%ucsbvm@cunyvm.cuny.edu
How to unsubscribe: Send unsubscribe message to listserv@ucsbvm or listserv%ucsbvm@cunyvm.cuny.edu

CONFER-L

Description: Confer-L is a discussion list covering the academic uses of interactive messaging systems.
Subjects covered: electronic networking; colleges and universities
List moderated: No.
Editorial contact: Mary Beth Green
Internet: tsumbgo1@asntsu.asn.net
How to access: Send subscribe message to listserv@ncsuvm or listserv@ncsuvm.cc.ncsu.edu
How to unsubscribe: Send unsubscribe message to listserv@ncsuvm or listserv@ncsuvm.cc.ncsu.edu
Archives: Archives are developed monthly; apply to listowner for details.

CONFOCAL@UBVM

Description: CONFOCAL@UBVM is a forum on confocal microscopy.
Subjects covered: chemistry
List moderated: No.
Editorial contact: Robert Summers
Internet: summers@ubmed.buffalo.edu
Bitnet: anargs@ubvms
How to access: Send subscribe message to listserv@ubvm or listserv@ubvm.cc.buffalo.edu
How to unsubscribe: Send unsubscribe message to listserv@ubvm or listserv@ubvm.cc.buffalo.edu
Archives: Archives are developed monthly; apply to listowner for details.

CONNECTIONISTS@CS.CMU.EDU

Description: connectionists@cs.cmu.edu is a mailing list focusing on artificial intelligence
Subjects covered: artificial intelligence
How to access: All requests to be added to or deleted from this list, problems, questions, etc., should be sent to connectionists-request@cs.cmu.edu.

CONS-L

Description: Cons-L is a list for consultants on campus-wide information services.
Subjects covered: campus-wide information systems
List moderated: No.
Editorial contact: Michael Walsh
Internet: ccmw@musica.mcgill.ca
How to access: Contact the Editor
How to unsubscribe: Contact the Editor

CONSALD

Description: CONSALD was created by and for the members of the Committee on South Asia Libraries and Documentation (CONSALD), a consortium of librarians and scholars of South Asian Studies. List membership is open to any interested persons, and, in addition to the members of CONSALD itself, members include scholars, researchers and academic program administrators. List contents include all aspects of libraries, books, scholarly materials, and research-support resources relating to the study of South Asia (any field), as well as policy issues regarding their acquisition, distribution, and access.

Subjects covered: South Asia; library and information science; library collection development
Net address for operations: listserv@utxvm
Net address for questions or submissions: CONSALD@utxvm
Established: 1992
Subscribers: 49
Sponsor: University of Texas at Austin, Austin, Texas 78713.
List moderated: Yes.
Moderation procedure: Submissions automatically forwarded to one of the moderators, who can either approve a posting in entirety, edit the posting, or reject it. Listserv software distributes the postings.
Editorial contact: Merry Burlingham
University of Texas at Austin, South Asia Librarian, General Libraries PCL 5.108, Austin, TX 78713-7330.
Tel: (512) 495-4329
Fax: (512) 495-4269
Internet: LLMLB@UTXDP.DP.utexas.edu
Bitnet: LYAA101@UTXVM orllmlb@utxdp ormerry.b@utxvm
Technical contact: David Magier
Director, Area Studies Library Services, Columbia University Libraries, 304 International Affairs, 420 West 118th Street New York, NY 10027.
Tel: (212) 854-8046
Fax: (212) 854-2495
Internet: magier@columbia.edu
How to access: Send an email message to: listserv@utxvm the message should read SUBSCRIBE CONSALD <your full name>
Access policy: This list is open to anyone.
How to unsubscribe: Send an email message to: listserv@utxvm the message should read SIGNOFF CONSALD
How to submit: Send your posting to: CONSALD@utxvm
Submission policy: Submissions are reviewed by the moderators for accuracy, conciseness, and appropriateness to the subject area of the list (see above). Submissions are occasionally edited by the moderators, but are usually posted verbatim.

CONSERVATION DISTLIST

Description: Conservation DistList is a discussion centering on the preservation of library materials.
Subjects covered: library and information science
List moderated: No.
Editorial contact: Walter Henry
Internet: whenry@lindy.stanford.edu
How to access: Send subscribe message to WHENRY@LINDY.STANFORD.EDU
How to unsubscribe: Send unsubscribe message to WHENRY@LINDY.STANFORD.EDU

CONTENTS@UOTTOWA

Description: CONTENTS@UOTTOWA is a forum discussing newly published material on religious studies and related areas.
Subjects covered: religion
List moderated: Yes.
Editorial contact: Michael Strangelove
Internet: 441495@acadvm1.uottowa.ca
Bitnet: 441495@uottowa
How to access: Send subscribe message to listserv@uottowa listserv@acadvm1.uottowa.ca
How to unsubscribe: Send unsubscribe message to listserv@uottowa listserv@acadvm1.uottowa.ca

Archives: Archives are developed monthly; apply to listowner for details.

CONTEX-L

Description: Contex-L is a discussion on past societies as revealed through old texts from the Hebrew, Christian and Greco-Roman cultures.
Subjects covered: linguistics; religion; classical studies
List moderated: Yes.
Editorial contact: Michael Strangelove
Internet: 441495@acadvm1.uottowa.ca
Bitnet: 441495@uottowa
How to access: Send subscribe message to listserv@uottowa or listserv@acadvm1.uottowa.ca
How to unsubscribe: Send unsubscribe message to listserv@uottowa or listserv@acadvm1.uottowa.ca
Archives: Archives are developed monthly; apply to listowner for details.

COOPCAT@NERVM

Description: COOPCAT@NERVM is a clearinghouse for information on cooperative cataloging projects.
Subjects covered: library and information science
List moderated: No.
Editorial contact: Carol Walton
Bitnet: carwalt@nervm
How to access: Send subscribe message to listserv@nervm
How to unsubscribe: Send unsubscribe message to listserv@nervm
Archives: Archives are developed monthly; apply to listowner for details.

COPYEDITING-L

Description: COPYEDITING-L is a discussion group for editors and other defenders of the Queen's English.
Subjects covered: English grammar; writing; editing
Net address for operations: listserv@cornell.edu
Established: December 1992
Subscribers: 350
Editorial contact: Beth Goelzer Lyons
1353 Slaterville Rd., Ithaca, NY 14850-6275
Tel: 607 255-9451
Fax: 607 255-5684
Internet: bg11@cornell.edu
Internet: listmgr@cornell.edu
How to access: Send to listserv@cornell.edu the following command: >subscribe COPYEDITING-L <your first name> <your last name>
Access policy: This list is open to anyone.
How to unsubscribe: Send to listserv@cornell.edu the following command: >unsubscribe COPYEDITING-L
How to submit: Send your posting to COPYEDITING-L@cornell.edu
Submission policy: This is an unmoderated list, so posters are asked to keep postings more-or-less editing-relevant .

CORMOSEA (COMMITTEE ON RESEARCH MATERIALS ON SOUTHEAST ASIA)

Description: CORMOSEA is a discussion list of the Committee on Research Materials on Southeast Asia covering all aspects of research into historical and political issues related to Southeast Asia.
Subjects covered: Southeast Asia
How to access: Send a subscription request to Kent Mullinger at MULLINER@OUVAXA.CATS.OHIOU.EDU

CORPORA@400.HD.UIB.NO

Description: CORPORA@400.HD.UIB.NO covers information and questions regarding text corpora.
Subjects covered: linguistics
Host: Norwegian Computing Centre for the Humanities.
List moderated: No.
Editorial contact: Knut Hofland
Internet: knut@x400.hd.uib.no
How to access: Send subscribe message to CORPORA-REQUEST@X400.HD.UIB.NO
How to unsubscribe: Send unsubscribe message to CORPORA-REQUEST@X400.HD.UIB.NO

CORRYFEE

Description: The aim of CORRYFEE is to provide an online information service for researchers in the fields of "Economics, Econometrics and Management Science" The list is intended as a bulletin board for exchanging information between researchers. Furthermore, the listgives you an opportunity to raise questions to the subscribers of the list. CORRYFEE is supported by the Faculty of Economics andEconometrics of the University of Amsterdam, the Netherlands.
Subjects covered: economics; econometrics
Net address for operations: listserv@hasara11.bitnet
Net address for questions or submissions: corryfee@hasara11.bitnet
Established: 1991
Subscribers: 1000
Sponsor: University of Amsterdam
Host: Academic Computer Center Amsterdam (SARA)
List moderated: Yes.
Moderation procedure: Editor examines if contribution fits profile of list
Editorial contact: Hans Amman
Dept Macroeconomics,University of Amsterdam,Roeterstraat 11, El 911 1018 WB Amsterdam, the Netherlands
Tel: 31-20-5254203
Fax: 31-20-5255280
Internet: amman@sara.nl
Bitnet: a608hans@hasara11
Sample contents:
How to access: Send mail to amman@sara.nl
How to unsubscribe: Send mail to amman@sara.nl
How to submit: Send mail to amman@sara.nl

COSNDISC@BITNIC

Description: COSNDISC@BITNIC is the discussion forum of the Consortium for School Networking.
Subjects covered: education technology

List moderated: Yes.
Editorial contact: John Clement
Bitnet: jrc@bitnic
How to access: Send subscribe message to listserv@bitnic or listserv@bitnic.educom.edu
How to unsubscribe: Send unsubscribe message to listserv@bitnic or listserv@bitnic.educom.edu
Archives: Archives are developed monthly; apply to listowner for details.

CPE-LIST@UNCVM1.OIT.UNC.EDU
Description: CPE-LIST is a discussion on large-scale computing machines.
Subjects covered: computer science; engineering
Host: Information Services Division, University of North Carolina Hospitals
List moderated: No.
Editorial contact: Lyman A. Ripperton
Internet: lyman@unchmvs.unch.unc.edu
How to access: Send subscribe message to listserv@uncvm1 or listserv@uncvm1.oit.unc.edt
How to unsubscribe: Send unsubscribe message to listserv@uncvm1 or listserv@uncvm1.oit.unc.edt

CPSR@GWUVM
Description: CPSR@GWUVM is a discussion forum of Computer Professionals for Social Responsibility.
Subjects covered: information technology; intellectual freedom; computer privacy
Host: Computer Professional for Social Responsibility
List moderated: Yes.
Editorial contact: Paul Hyland
Internet: phyland@gwuvm.edu
Bitnet: phyland@gwuvm
How to access: Send subscribe message to listserv@gwuvm or listserv@gwuvm.edu
How to unsubscribe: Send unsubscribe message to listserv@gwuvm or listserv@gwuvm.edu
Archives: Yes.

CREA-CPS@NIC.SURFNET.NL
Description: CREA-CPS@NIC.SURFNET.NL is a forum for discussion of creative problem solving.
Subjects covered: psychology
List moderated: No.
Editorial contact: Bram Donkers
Internet: n.a. donkers@io.tufelft.nl
How to access: Send subscribe message to listserv@nic.surfnet
How to unsubscribe: Send unsubscribe message to listserv@nic.surfnet

CREAD (LATIN AMERICAN & CARIBBEAN DISTANCE AND CONTINUING EDUCATION)
Description: CREAD is an electronic discussion group focusing on distance education in Latin America and the Caribbean.
Subjects covered: Latin America; distance education; Caribbean; colleges and universities
Net address for operations: listserv@yorkvm1.bitnet

How to access: Send message to listserv.

CRETA-PILOT@MAILBASE.AC.UK
Description: CREAT-PILOT is a list covering electronic translation software among European languages.
Subjects covered: language and literature; computer hardware and software; translation studies
Host: CRETA, Commission of the European Economic Community
List moderated: No.
Internet: creta-pilot-request@mailbase.ac.uk
How to access: Send subscribe message to mailbase@mailbase.ac.uk in the following format: join creta-pilot Yourfirstname Yourlastname
How to unsubscribe: Send subscribe message to mailbase@mailbase.ac.uk in the following format: join creta-pilot Yourfirstname Yourlastname
Archives: Archives are developed monthly; apply to listowner for details.

CREWRT-L
Description: Crewrt-L is a forum on writing education at higher learning institutions.
Subjects covered: writing; education; colleges and universities
List moderated: No.
Editorial contact: Eric Crump
Internet: lceric@mizzou1.missouri.edu
Bitnet: lceric@mizzou1
How to access: Send subscribe message to listserv@mizzou1 or listserv@mizzou1.missouri.edu
How to unsubscribe: Send unsubscribe message to listserv@mizzou1 or listserv@mizzou1.missouri.edu
Archives: Archives are developed weekly; apply to listowner for details.

CRIN@FRMOP11
Description: CRIN@FRMOP11 covers superconductivity.
Subjects covered: engineering
List moderated: No.
How to access: Send subscribe message to listserv@frmop11 or listserv%frmop11.bitnet@vm1.nodak.edu
How to unsubscribe: Send unsubscribe message to listserv@frmop11 or listserv%frmop11.bitnet@vm1.nodak.edu

CRO-NEWS
Description: CRO-NEWS distributes news and information on and about Croatia.
Subjects covered: current events; Croatia
List moderated: No.
Editorial contact: Nino Margetic
Internet: cro-news-request@mph.sm.ucl.ac.uk
How to access: Contact the Editor
How to unsubscribe: Contact the Editor

CROATION-NEWS/HRVATSKI-VJESNIK
Description: CROATION-NEWS/HRVATSKI-VJESNIK is a bi-lingual (English/Croatian) listing for news on and about Croatia.

Subjects covered: current events; Croatia
Internet: croation-news-request@andrew.cmu.edu

CROMED-L

Description: Cromed-L is an international e-conference on medical issues in Croatia.
Subjects covered: medicine; Croatia
Host: Ministry of Health, Rep. of Croatia, Office for Cooperation between WHO and the Rep. of Croatia.
List moderated: Yes.
Internet: IVAN.MARIC@UNI-ZG.AC>MAIL.YU
How to access: Send subscribe message to listserv@aearn
How to unsubscribe: Send unsubscribe message to listserv@aearn
Archives: Archives are developed monthly; apply to listowner for details.

CRYONICS

Description: CRYONICS is a forum that discusses aspects of cryonics.
Subjects covered: medicine
List moderated: Yes.
Editorial contact: Kevin Q. Brown
Internet: kqb@whscad1.att.com
How to access: Contact the Editor
How to unsubscribe: Contact the Editor
Archives: Yes; Apply to listowner for details

CRYPTO-L

Description: Crypto-L is a forum focusing on cryptology and related mathematics coding techniques.
Subjects covered: mathematics
List moderated: No.
How to access: Send subscribe message to listserv@jpntohok
How to unsubscribe: Send unsubscribe message to listserv@jpntohok

CSA-DATA@UICVM

Description: CSA-DATA@UICVM is a conference on Chinese statistical archives.
Subjects covered: mathematics; statistics
List moderated: No.
Bitnet: u11370@uicvm or u22378@uicvm
How to access: Send subscribe message to listserv@uicvm or listserv@uicvm.uic.edu
How to unsubscribe: Send unsubscribe message to listserv@uicvm or listserv@uicvm.uic.edu
Archives: Yes.

CSEMLIST

Description: The aim of csemlist is to provide an online information service for researchers in the field of ''Computational methods in Economics and Econometrics.'' The list is intended as a bulletin board for exchanging information between researchers. Furthermore, the list gives the reader an opportunity to raise questions to the subscribers of the list.
Subjects covered: economics; econometrics
Net address for operations: listserv@hasara11.bitnet

Net address for questions or submissions:
csemlist@hasara11.bitnet
Established: 1991
Subscribers: 1000
Sponsor: University of Amsterdam
Host: Academic Computer Center Amsterdam (SARA)
List moderated: Yes.
Moderation procedure: Editor examines if contribution fits profile of list
Editorial contact: Hans Amman
Dept Macroeconomics,University of Amsterdam,Roeterstraat 11, E1 911 1018 WB Amsterdam, the Netherlands
Tel: 31-20-5254203
Fax: 31-20-5255280
Internet: amman@sara.nl
Bitnet: a608hans@hasara11
Technical contact: Same as above
Review: Reviewed by List Review Service edited by Raleigh Muns: see appendix.
How to access: Send mail to amman@sara.nl
How to unsubscribe: Send mail to amman@sara.nl
How to submit: Send mail to amman@sara.nl

CSP-L

Description: CSP-L is a list featuring discussion of and questions about modifications on the CSP: IBM's Cross System Product.
Subjects covered: computer science; computer hardware and software
Net address for operations: CSP-L@TREARN.BITNET
Net address for questions or submissions: CSP-L@TREARN.BITNET
Established: 1990
Subscribers: 82
Sponsor: Ege Univ. Bilgisayar Ar. ve Uyg. Mrk.35100 Bo
Host: Same as above
List moderated: No.
Editorial contact: Esra Delen, Ege Univ. Bilgisayar Ar. ve Uyg. Mrk. 35100 Bornova Izmir Turkey
Tel: 90-51-887221
Fax: 90-51-887230
Internet: ESRA@EGE.EDU.TR
Bitnet: ESRA@TREARN
Technical contact: Same as above
How to access: Tell Listserv at TREARN SUB CSP-L fullname
How to unsubscribe: Tell Listserv at TREARN SIGNOFF CSP-L
Archives: Available via LOG files on LISTSERV.

CSRNOT-L

Description: Csrnot-L is an electronic conference for the Center for the Study of Reading.
Subjects covered: education
Host: The Center for the Study of Reading, University of Illinois, Chicago
List moderated: No.
How to access: Send subscribe message to listserv@uiucvmd or listserv@vmd.cso.uiuc.edu
How to unsubscribe: Send unsubscribe message to listserv@uiucvmd or listserv@vmd.cso.uiuc.edu

CTF-DISCUSS@CIS.UPENN.EDU

Description: CTF-DISCUSS is a forum for discussion of computer science issues.
Subjects covered: computer science
List moderated: No.
Editorial contact: Dave Farber
Internet: ctf-discuss-request@cis.upenn.edu
How to access: Contact the Editor
How to unsubscribe: Contact the Editor

CTI-ACC-AUDIT@MAILBASE.AC.UK

Description: CTI-ACC-AUDIT is a mailbase list for auditors.
Subjects covered: business
Host: CTI Centre for Accounting Finance and Management, School of Information Systems, University of East Anglia
List moderated: No.
Internet: cti-acc-audit-request@mailbase.ac.uk
How to access: Send subscribe message to mailbase@mailbase.ac.uk in the following format: join cti-acc-audit Your first name Your last name
Archives: Archives are developed monthly; apply to listowner for details.

CTI-ACC-BUSINESS@MAILBASE.AC.UK

Description: CTI-ACC-BUSINESS is a mailbase list focusing on computers and accounting.
Subjects covered: business
Host: CTI Centre for Accounting Finance and Management, School of Information Systems, University of East Anglia
List moderated: No.
Internet: chem-mod-request@mailbase.ac.uk
How to access: Send subscribe message to mailbase@mailbase.ac.uk in the following format: join chem-mod Your first name Your last name
Archives: Archives are developed monthly; apply to listowner for details.

CTI-COMPLIT@MAILBASE.AC.UK

Description: CTI-COMPLIT@MAILBASE.AC.UK discusses computer literacy in education.
Subjects covered: education; computer science; colleges and universities
Host: CTI Centre for Accounting Finance and Management, School of Information Systems, University of East Anglia
List moderated: No.
Internet: cti-complit-request@mailbase.ac.uk
How to access: Send subscribe message to mailbase@mailbase.ac.uk in the following format: join cti-complit Your first name Your last name
Archives: Archives are developed monthly; apply to listowner for details.

CTI-ECON@MAILBASE.AC.UK

Description: CTI-ECON is a mailbase list for academic economists.
Subjects covered: economics
Host: CTI Centre for Accounting Finance and Management, School of Information Systems, University of East Anglia
List moderated: No.

Internet: cti-econ-request@mailbase.ac.uk
How to access: Send subscribe message to mailbase@mailbase.ac.uk in the following format: join cti-econ Your first name Your last name
Archives: Archives are developed monthly; apply to listowner for details.

CTI-GEOG@MAILBASE.AC.UK

Description: CTI-GEOG@MAILBASE.AC.UK is a forum discussing uses of IT in teaching geography in higher education.
Subjects covered: geography
List moderated: No.
Internet: cti-geog-request@mailbase.ac.uk
How to access: Send subscribe message to mailbase@mailbase.ac.uk in the following format: join cti-geog Your first name Your last name
Archives: Archives are developed monthly; apply to listowner for details.

CTI-L

Description: The CTI-L list was formed to accommodate anyone interested in computer-based training, computer-aided learning, or instruction.
Subjects covered: education; computer-assisted instruction (CAI)
Net address for operations: CTI-L@IRLEARN.UCD.IE
Net address for questions or submissions: CTI-L@IRLEARN.UCD.IE
Established: May 1992
Subscribers: 300
Sponsor: University College, Dublin
Host: University College, Dublin
List moderated: No.
Editorial contact: Claron O'Reilly
Computer Centre, UCD, Ireland
Tel: 706 2005
Fax: 283 7077
Internet: claron@irlearnarn.ucd.ie
Bitnet: arn.ucd.ie
Technical contact: Same as above
How to access: Tell listserv@irlearn.ucd.ie add cti-l FIRST__NAME LAST__NAME
Access policy: This list is open to anyone.
How to unsubscribe: Tell listserv signoff cti-l
How to submit: Mail cti-l@irlearn.ucd.ie
Submission policy: Postings must not be offensive.

CTI-MATHS

Description: cti-maths is an electronic discussion group for mathematicians, particularly those interested in the use of computers or the teaching of mathematics in higher education in the United Kingdom.
Subjects covered: mathematics; education; computer hardware and software
Net address for operations: mailbase@mailbase.ac.uk
Established: March 1992
Subscribers: 163
Sponsor: CTI Centre for Maths and Stats, Centre for Computer-Based Learning, The University of Birmingham, Edgbaston, Birmingham B15 2TT.
List moderated: No.

Technical contact: Pam Bishop, Centre Manager
CTI Centre for Maths and Stats
Tel: +44 (0)21 414 4800
Fax: +44 (0)21 414 4865
How to access: Send a message to mailbase@mailbase.ac.uk as
follows: join cti-maths first name surname
How to unsubscribe: Send a message to
mailbase@mailbase.ac.uk as follows: leave cti-maths
How to submit: Send your message to cti-
maths@mailbase.ac.uk

CTI-MUSIC

Description: cti-music is an electronic forum for discussion of
any aspects of the use of computers in the teaching of music in
higher education. Included is news from the CTI Centre for Mu-
sic.
Subjects covered: music; computer hardware and software;
education
Net address for operations: mailbase@mailbase.ac.uk
Net address for questions or submissions: cti-mu-
sic@mailbase.ac.uk
Established: April 1993
Subscribers: 34
Sponsor: Joint Information Systems Committee of the UK
Higher Education Funding Councils.
Host: University of Newcastle Upon Tyne.
List moderated: No.
Editorial contact: Lisa Whistlecroft
CTI Centre for Music, Music Department, Lancaster University,
Lancaster LA1 4YW, UK.
Tel: (0524) 593776
Fax: (0524) 847298
Internet: CTImusic@lancaster.ac.uk
Technical contact: Lisa Whistlecroft
CTI Centre for Music, Music Department, Lancaster University,
Lancaster LA1 4YW, UK.
Tel: (0524) 593776
Fax: (0524) 847298
Internet: CTImusic@lancaster.ac.uk
How to access: Send message to mailbase@mailbase.ac.uk con-
taining the single line join cti-music <firstname> <lastname>
where <firstname> and <lastname> should be replaced with
your first and last names.
How to unsubscribe: Send message to
mailbase@mailbase.ac.uk containing the single line leave cti-
music
How to submit: Send your message to cti-mu-
sic@mailbase.ac.uk
Archives: Message archive files are stored as MM-YYYY
where MM is the month number and YYYY is the year number.
These can be retrieved by anonymous ftp or by sending a message to mailbase@mailbase.ac.uk containing the line send cti-
music <filename> where <filename> should be replaced by
the name of the file required.
Related files: Additional files stored with the list can be retrieved in the same way as the archive files. An index to files
stored with the list can be retrieved by sending a message to
mailbase@mailbase.ac.uk containing the single line index cti-
music
Gopher accessibility: Mailbase can be accessed by gopher.

CUMREC-L

Description: CUMREC-L is a discussion list about all types of
administrative computer use. Computer programmers and pro-
fessionals as well as administrators are encouraged to ask ques-
tions and share experiences with all types of hardware and soft-
ware as it relates to college and university administration.
Subjects covered: computer hardware and software; colleges
and universities; administration
Net address for operations: LISTSERV@VM1.NODAK.EDU
Net address for questions or submissions: CUMREC-
L@VM1.NODAK.EDU
Established: January 1989
Subscribers: 1050
Sponsor: South Dakota State University, Brookings, SD 57007.
Host: North Dakota State University, Fargo, ND 58105.
List moderated: No.
Editorial contact: Joe Moore
SDSU Computing Services, Bldg. 2201, Brookings, SD 57007.
Tel: (605) 688-4678
Fax: (605) 688-5014
Internet: moorej@cc.sdstate.edu
Bitnet: cc19@sdsumus
How to access: Send to LISTSERV@vm1.nodak.edu:
sub cumrec-l your name
Access policy: Stay on topic and follow general nettiquette
Archives: Send to listserv@vm1.nodak.edu: get cumrec-l index

CUPLE-L

Description: CUPLE-L is a discussion list covering Compre-
hensive Unified Physics Learning Environment software.
Subjects covered: physics; computer hardware and software
List moderated: No.
Editorial contact: Jack Wilson
Internet: jack_wilson@mts.rpi.edu
How to access: Send subscribe message to listserv@ubvm or
listserv@ubvm.cc.buffalo.edu
How to unsubscribe: Send unsubscribe message to
listserv@ubvm or listserv@ubvm.cc.buffalo.edu
Archives: Archives are developed monthly; apply to listowner
for details.

CVNET@YORKVM1

Description: CVNET@YORKVM1 is a forum of the Color and
Vision Network.
Subjects covered: physics; biology, physiology, psychology
List moderated: Yes.
Editorial contact: Peter K. Kaiser
Internet: pkaiser@vm1.yorku.ca
Bitnet: pkaiser@yorkvm1
How to access: Send subscribe message to cvnet@yorkvm1 or
cvnet@vm1.yorku.ca
How to unsubscribe: Send unsubscribe message to
cvnet@yorkvm1 or cvnet@vm1.yorku.ca

CW-L

Description: CW-L is a forum about computers and writing.
Subjects covered: writing; computer science
List moderated: No.
Editorial contact: Fred Kemp
Internet: ykfok@ttacs1.ttu.edu
Bitnet: ykfok@ttacs

How to access: Send subscribe message to listserv@ttuvml
How to unsubscribe: Send unsubscribe message to listserv@ttuvml

CW-MAIL@TECMTYVM

Description: CW-MAIL discusses campus-wide mail systems.
Subjects covered: Internet; campus-wide information systems
List moderated: No.
Editorial contact: Juan M. Courcoul
Internet: postmast@tecmtyvm.mty.itesm.edu
Bitnet: postmast@tecmtyvm
How to access: Send subscribe message to listserv@tecmtyvm or listserv@tecmtyvm.mty.itesm.mx
How to unsubscribe: Send unsubscribe message to listserv@tecmtyvm or listserv@tecmtyvm.mty.itesm.mx
Archives: Archives are developed monthly; apply to listowner for details.

CWIS-L

Description: CWIS-L is an electronic discussion group on all aspects of the creation and maintenance of campus-wide information systems.
Subjects covered: library and information science; campus-wide information systems; colleges and universities
Net address for questions or submissions: CWIS-L-request@wuvmd.Wustl.edu
How to unsubscribe: Send a message to the "request" address: CWIS-L-request@wuvmd.Wustl.edu or send an unsubscribe request to the listserver to which you originally sent a subscribe request. You can determine which listserver is sending you the message by examining the message header.

CYAN-TOX@GREARN

Description: CYAN-TOX@GREARN is a forum for disussion of toxins.
Subjects covered: biology; biochemistry
List moderated: No.
Editorial contact: Tom Lanaras
Bitnet: cdaz02@grtheun1
How to access: Send subscribe message to listserv@grearn
How to unsubscribe: Send subscribe message to listserv@grearn
Archives: Archives are developed monthly; apply to listowner for details.

CYBSYS-L

Description: CYBSYS-L is an electronic discussion group relevant to the fields of academic cybernetics and systems science.
Subjects covered: cybernetics; computer science; science and technology; computer hardware and software
Net address for operations: LISTSERV@BINGVMB.BITNET
Net address for questions or submissions: CYBSYS-L@BINGVMB.BITNET
Established: 1988
Subscribers: 600
Sponsor: SUNY-Binghamton
Host: Systems Science, SUNY-Binghamton, Binghamton, NY 13902.
List moderated: Yes.

Moderation procedure: Moderator edits out only "junk" messages: e.g., innapropriate requests to subscribe/unsubscribe; and posts not relevent to cybernetics or systems science.
Editorial contact: Cliff Joslyn
327 Spring St., # 2, Portland, ME 04102.
Technical contact: Same as above
Internet: cybsys@bingsuns.cc.binghamton.edu
How to access: Send message "sub cybsys-l Your Full Name" to LISTSERV@BINGVMB.BITNET
Access policy: List is open to anyone.
How to unsubscribe: Send message "unsub cybsys-l" to LISTSERV@BINGVMB.BITNET
How to submit: Mail message to CYBSYS-L@BINGVMB.BITNET
Submission policy: Posts relevant to cybernetics and systems science.
Related files: Newsgroup sci.systems

DAI-LIST

Description: DAI-List focuses on distributed artificial intelligence.
Subjects covered: artificial intelligence
Net address for questions or submissions: DAI-List-request@mcc.com
How to access: Send requests to DAI-List-request@mcc.com

DAIRY-L

Description: Dairy-L covers topics related to the dairy industry.
Subjects covered: agriculture
List moderated: No.
Editorial contact: Mark Varner
Internet: varner@umd5.umd.edu
How to access: Send subscribe message to listserv@umdd or listserv@umdd.umd.edu
How to unsubscribe: Send unsubscribe message to listserv@umdd or listserv@umdd.umd.edu
Archives: Archives are developed weekly; apply to listowner for details.

DANCE-L

Description: Dance-L is a forum for discussing all aspects of folk and traditional dancing.
Subjects covered: dance
List moderated: No.
Editorial contact: Les A.M. Van der Heijden
Bitnet: XYZ@RCL.WAU.NL
How to access: Send subscribe message to listserv@hearn or listserv%hearn.bitnet@cunyvm.cuny.edu
How to unsubscribe: Send unsubscribe message to listserv@hearn or listserv%hearn.bitnet@cunyvm.cuny.edu
Archives: Archives are developed monthly; apply to listowner for details.

DARGON-L

Description: Dargon-L is a forum for writers.
Subjects covered: writing
Host: Dargon Writers Project
List moderated: No.
Editorial contact: Dafydd, Dargon Project Director
Bitnet: white@duvm

How to access: Send subscribe message to listserv@ncsuvm or listserv@ncsuvm.cc.ncsu.edu
How to unsubscribe: Send unsubscribe message to listserv@ncsuvm or listserv@ncsuvm.cc.ncsu.edu

DASP-L
Description: DASP-L is a forum on digital accoustic signal processing.
Subjects covered: physics
List moderated: No.
Editorial contact: Frantisek Kadlek
Internet: fkadlec@csearn
How to access: Send subscribe message to listserv@csearn
How to unsubscribe: Send unsubscribe message to listserv@csearn
Archives: Archives are developed monthly; apply to listowner for details.

DCRAVES
Description: dcraves is a chatty free form list discussing raves in the Washington D.C./Baltimore area. A weekly calender of events is produced.
Subjects covered: events listings; music; Washington, D.C.
Net address for operations: listserv@american.edu
Net address for questions or submissions: dcraves@american.edu
Established: December 1992
Subscribers: 80
Sponsor: American Univeristy, 4400 Massachussetts Avenue NW, Washington, DC 20016.
List moderated: No.
Editorial contact: Susan Kameny
330 Moncada Way, San Francisco, CA 94127.
Tel: (415) 334 8421
Internet: sk2479a@american.edu
Bitnet: Douglas Zimmerman
Internet: dz5401a@american.edu
How to access: Send email to listserv@auvm.american.edu and in the first line of your letter type SUB DCRAVES (name)
Access policy: Be respectful of everyone.
How to unsubscribe: Send email to listserv@auvm.american.edu and in the first line type del dcraves (name)
Related files: Email dcraves-request@auvm.american.edu for more information on related files.
Additional information: Second editor: Thomas Edwards tedwards@wam.umd.edu

DE MONTFORT UNIVERSITY
Description: Pharmacy Mail Exchange is a discussion list on pharmacological topics.
Subjects covered: pharmacology
Net address for operations: uk.ad.dmu
Editorial contact: Paul Hodgkinson
Pharmacy Mail Exchange, Department of Pharmacy, De Montfort University, Leicester LE1 9BH, UK.
Tel: +44 533 577285
Fax: +44 533 577287
Internet: phh@dmu.ac.uk, phh@uk.ac.dmu (Janet)
How to access: Send an email message to phh@dmu.ac.uk

Additional information: The abbreviation 'Pharmex' for our list Pharmacy Mail Exchange must NOT be used. It was dropped a year ago following complaints from a US company who use it as a trade name.

DE.SCI.KI
Description: de.sci.ki is an International Usenet newsgroup on artificial intelligence.
Subjects covered: artificial intelligence

DE.SCI.KI.ANNOUNCE
Description: de.sci.ki.announce is an International Usenet newsgroup on artificial intelligence.
Subjects covered: artificial intelligence

DE.SCI.KI.DISCUSSION
Description: de.sci.ki.discussion is an International Usenet newsgroup on artificial intelligence.
Subjects covered: artificial intelligence

DE.SCI.KI.MOD-KI
Description: de.sci.ki.mod-ki is an International Usenet newsgroup on artificial intelligence.
Subjects covered: artificial intelligence

DEFENCE-SCI-AND-TECH-POLICY@MAILBASE.AC.UK
Description: DEFENCE-SCI-AND-TECH-POLICY is a mailbase list covering European defense and industrial technology.
Subjects covered: science and technology
List moderated: No.
Internet: cti-econ-request@mailbase.ac.uk
How to access: Send subscribe message to mailbase@mailbase.ac.uk in the following format: join cti-econ Yourfirstname Yourlastname
Archives: Archives are developed monthly; apply to listowner for details.

DENTAL-L@IRLEARN.UCD.IE
Description: Dental-L is an electronic discussion list for the exchange of information between researchers in the field of oral health and dental research.
Subjects covered: health sciences; dental sciences; medicine
Net address for operations: LISTSERV@IRLEARN.BITNET
Net address for questions or submissions: DENTAL-L@IRLEARN.UCD.IE
Established: June 1992
Subscribers: 8
Sponsor: Oral Health Services Research Centre, University College, Dental School, Cork, Ireland.
Host: University College Dublin, Dublin, Ireland.
List moderated: No.
Editorial contact: Dr. Ruben Keane
Oral Health Services Research Centre, University College, Dental School, Cork, Ireland.
Tel: +21 276871, ext. 2761

Fax: +21 545391
Internet: IN%'STPD8008@IRUCCVAX.UCC.IE
Technical contact: Ms. Kathryn Neville
Oral Health Services Research Centre, University College, Dental School, Cork, Ireland.
Tel: +21 276871, ext. 2761
Fax: +21 545391
Internet: IN%'STPD8008@IRUCCVAX.UCC.IE
How to access: Send the following commands to LISTSERV@IRLEARN.UCD.IE: SUBSCRIBE DENTAL-L <firstname secondname>
How to unsubscribe: Send the following commands to LISTSERV@IRLEARN.UCD.IE: SIGNOFFDENTAL-L <firstname secondname>
How to submit: Messages for distribution via the list should be sent to IN%'DENTAL-L@IRLEARN.UCD.IE"

DENTALMA@UCF1VM

Description: DENTALMA@UCF1VM is a list covering dental-related information.
Subjects covered: medicine
List moderated: No.
Editorial contact: Karl-Johan Soderholm
Bitnet: soderhol@uffsc
How to access: Send subscribe message to listserv@ucf1vm or listserv@ucf1vm.bitnet@cunyvm.cuny.edu
How to unsubscribe: Send unsubscribe message to listserv@ucf1vm or listserv@ucf1vm.bitnet@cunyvm.cuny.edu
Archives: Archives are developed monthly; apply to listowner for details.

DEOS-L

Description: DEOS-L is an international forum for disucssion of distance learning.
Subjects covered: distance education; colleges and universities; education
Net address for operations: listserv@psuvm.bitnet
Subscribers: 1325
How to access: Send message to listserv.

DERRIDA@CFRVM

Description: DERRIDA@CFRVM focuses on Jacques Derrida and deconstruction philosophies in general.
Subjects covered: linguistics; Derrida, Jacques; literary theory and criticism
List moderated: No.
Editorial contact: David L. Erben
Internet: dqfacaa@cfrvm.cfr.usf.edu
Bitnet: dqfacaa@cfrvm
Review: Reviewed by List Review Service edited by Raleigh Muns: see appendix.
How to access: Send subscribe message to listserv@cfrvm. cfr. usf.edu or listserv@cfrvm
How to unsubscribe: Send unsubscribe message to listserv@cfrvm. cfr. usf.edu or listserv@cfrvm
Archives: Archives are developed monthly; apply to listowner for details.

DERYNI-L

Description: Deryni-L is a forum for discussion of the writings of Katherine Kurtz.
Subjects covered: science fiction; Kurtz, Katherine
List moderated: No.
Editorial contact: Edward J. Branley
Internet: elendil@mintir.new-orleans.la.us
How to access: Send subscribe message to mail-server@mintir.new-orleans.la.us
How to unsubscribe: Send unsubscribe message to mail-server@mintir.new-orleans.la.us

DESIGN-L

Description: Design-L serves as a forum for topics related to design in art and architecture.
Subjects covered: design; art; architecture
List moderated: No.
Editorial contact: Howard Ray Lawrence
Bitnet: hrl@psuvm or hrl@psuarch
How to access: Send subscribe message to listserv@psuvm or listserv@psuvm.psu.edu
How to unsubscribe: Send unsubscribe message to listserv@psuvm or listserv@psuvm.psu.edu
Archives: Archives are developed monthly; apply to listowner for details.

DEUTSCHE-LISTE@CCU.UMANITOBA.CA

Description: deutsche-liste is a discussion list covering German literature and culture.
Subjects covered: German language and literature; history
Net address for operations: listserv@ccu.umanitoba.ca
Net address for questions or submissions: collape@ccu.umanitoba.ca
How to access: Send message to listowner at colappe@ccu.umanitoba.ca

DEVEL-L

Description: Devel-L is an electronic disussion on technology transfer.
Subjects covered: technology transfer; political science
Host: Volunteers in Technical Assistance (VITA)
List moderated: No.
Editorial contact: Rafe Ronkin
Bitnet: vita@gmuvax
How to access: Send subscribe message to listserv@auvm or listserv@auvm.auvm.edu
How to unsubscribe: Contact the Editor
How to submit: Contact the Editor
Archives: Archives are developed weekly; apply to listowner for details.

DIABETES@IRLEARN

Description: DIABETES@IRLEARN is a list covering diabetes research.
Subjects covered: medicine
List moderated: No.
Editorial contact: Martin Wehlou
Internet: wehlou@fgen.rug.ac.be

How to access: Send subscribe message to listserv@irlearn or listserv@irlearn.ucd.ie
How to unsubscribe: Send unsubscribe message to listserv@irlearn or listserv@irlearn.ucd.ie
Archives: Archives are developed monthly; apply to listowner for details.

DIARRHOE@SEARN

Description: DIARRHOE@SEARN is a discussion on conditions that cause diarrhoea in humans and animals.
Subjects covered: medicine
Sponsor: UNESCO Microbial Resources Center, Karolinska Institute, Stockholm, Sweden
List moderated: No.
Editorial contact: Eng-leong Foo
Internet: eng-leong__foo__mircen-ki%micforum@mica.mic.ki.se
How to access: Send subscribe message to listserv@searn or listserv@searn.sunet.se
How to unsubscribe: Send unsubscribe message to listserv@searn or listserv@searn.sunet.se
Archives: Archives are developed monthly; apply to listowner for details.

DIBUG@COMP.BIOZ.UNIIBAS.CH

Description: DIBUG@COMP.BIOZ.UNIBAS.CH is a forum for discussion of biochemical topics.
Subjects covered: biophysics; biochemistry
List moderated: No.
How to access: Send subscribe message to DIBUG-REQUEST@COMP.BIOZ.UNIBAS.CH
How to unsubscribe: Send unsubscribe message to DIBUG-REQUEST@COMP.BIOZ.UNIBAS.CH

DIS-L

Description: DIS-L is an electronic forum carrying announcements, requests for materials, materials available, database information, genetic notes, technical notes, etc., on topics related to drosophila (fruit flies).
Subjects covered: drosophila; fruit flies; biology
Net address for operations: LISTSERV@IUBVM.UCS.INDIANA.EDU
Net address for questions or submissions: MATTHEWK@INDIANA.EDU or CTHUMMEL@HMBGMAIL.MED.UTAH.EDU
Established: JANUARY 1991
Sponsor: Dept. of Biology, Indiana University, Bloomington, IN 47405.
Host: Indiana University
List moderated: Yes.
Moderation procedure: Submission deemed appropriate by the editors are compiled and distributed as a quarterly newsletter.
Editorial contact: Kathleen Matthews
Department of Biology, Indiana University, Bloomington, IN 47405.
Tel: (812) 855-2577
Fax: (812) 855-2577
Internet: MATTHEWK@INDIANA.EDU
Bitnet: MATTHEWK@IUBACS
Technical contact: Carl Thummel

Dept. of Human Genetics, HHMI, University of Utah, 5200 Eccles Inst., Bldg. 533, Salt Lake City, UT 84112.
Tel: (801) 581-2937
Fax: (801) 581-5374
Internet: CTHUMMEL@HMBGMAIL.MED.UTAH.EDU
Review: Extract published in annual Drosophila Information Service (ed., James Thompson Jr.).
How to access: Send the following e-mail message from the account at which you wish to receive DIN:
To: LISTSERV@IUBVM.UCS.INDIANA.EDU (or LISTSERV@IUBVM via Bitnet) Subject: Message: SUB DIS-L Firstname Lastname
Access policy: List is open to all.
How to unsubscribe: Substitute UNSUB in the above message
How to submit: Technical notes should be sent to CTHUMMEL@HMBGMAIL.MED.UTAH.EDU
All other submissions to MATTHEWK@INDIANA.EDU
Submission policy: E-mail only, no research reports, no commercial material.
Archives: Back issues are available by anonymous FTP or gopher from ftp.bio.indiana.edu in flybase/news
Gopher accessibility: Yes (gopher ftp.bio.indiana.edu).

DISARM-D@ALBNYVM1

Description: DISARM-D@ALBNYVM1 is a disgest on peace and war-related issues.
Subjects covered: activism; peace studies
List moderated: Yes.
Editorial contact: Donald Parsons
Internet: dfp10@uacsc2.albany.edu
Bitnet: dfp10@albnyvm1
How to access: Contact the Editor
How to unsubscribe: Contact the Editor
Archives: Archives are developed monthly; apply to listowner for details.

DISASTER RESEARCH

Description: Disaster Research (DR) is a moderated bulletin for creators and users of information regarding hazards and disasters. DR comprises timely articles on recent disaster events; developments at the local, federal, and international levels regarding hazards and hazards management, disaster response, and mitigation; new resources available to hazards managers; upcoming conferences and training; and, perhaps most importantly, queries, messages, and comments from DR's many subscribers. Through this last service, researchers and hazard managers can quickly query their peers for information regarding any aspect of disasters.
Subjects covered: disaster research
Net address for operations: MAILSERV@VAXF.COLORADO.EDU
Net address for questions or submissions: HAZARDS@VAXF.COLORADO.EDU
Established: January 1989
Subscribers: 400
Sponsor: Natural Hazards Information Center, IBS #6 Campus Box 482, University of Colorado at Boulder, Boulder, CO 80309-0482
Host: Same as above
List moderated: Yes.
Moderation procedure: Submissions are saved then reformatted and sent out to the list approximately every two weeks in

the form of a newsletter. Urgent requests are sent out immediately.
Editorial contact: David L. Butler
Natural Hazards Information Center,
IBS #6 Campus Box 482, University of Colorado at Boulder,
Boulder, CO 80309-0482
Tel: (303) 492-4180
Fax: (303) 492-2151
Internet: hazards@vaxf.colorado.edu
Technical contact: Same as above
Copyright statement: No copyright - reproduction and retransmission is encouraged.
How to access: Either send a request to: David Butler, Natural Hazards Research and Applications Information Center, Institute of Behavioral Science #6, Campus Box 482, University of Colorado, Boulder, Colorado 80309-0482; telephone: (303) 492-6818; fax: (303) 492-2151; hazards@vaxf.colorado.edu
Or send an e-mail message with the single word SUBSCRIBE in the body of the message to: mailserv@vaxf.colorado.edu
Access policy: All interested persons welcome.
How to unsubscribe: As above, except say UNSUBSCRIBE
How to submit: Send submissions to: David Butler, Natural Hazards Research and Applications Information Center, Institute of Behavioral Science #6, Campus Box 482 University of Colorado Boulder, Colorado 80309-0482 USA Telephone: (303) 492-6818 Fax: (303) 492-2151 hazards@vaxf.colorado.edu
Submission policy: All submissions will be considered. Virtually all have been posted in the past. However the moderator reserves the right to either edit (i.e. shorten) submissions or reject them altogether.
Archives: For back issues of Disaster Research, send one of the following commands to the MAILSERV address above: SEND [HAZARDS]INDEX.LIS for a list of available DR issues; SEND [HAZARDS]DR##.TXTfor a specific back issue - substitute the number of the issue you want (01 - 116) for the ## in the command.

DISC-L

Description: Disc-L accesses advanced listings and curriculum materials for educational cable TV programming, specifically the Discovery channel.
Subjects covered: curriculum; education
List moderated: No.
Gleason Sackmann
Internet: sackmann@sendit.nodak.edu
How to access: Send subscribe message to listserv@sendit.nodak.edu
How to unsubscribe: Send unsubscribe message to listserv@sendit.nodak.edu

DISC-NORDLIB

Description: The DISC-NORDLIB discussion list has been established to serve humanities and social science librarians, archivists and others with interest in collections and services related to Nordic area studies. Discussion, comments and questions will focus on issues of access to research materials, cooperative collection development and shared resources and the study of the five Nordic countries of Denmark, Norway, Sweden, Finland and Iceland. The perceived need for this list grew out of discussions over th epast year amongst librarians at SASS conferences and in the Scandinavian Discussion Group of the Western Euro-

pean Area Studies Section of the Association of College and Research Libraries (American Library Association).
Subjects covered: cultural studies; library and information science; archivism; Nordic studies
Editorial contact: Charles G. Spetland
180 Wilson Library, University of Minnesota, Minneapolis, MN 55455.
Tel: (612) 624-7854
Fax: (612) 626-9353
Bitnet: c-spet@uminn1
How to access: DISC-NORDLIB-REQUEST@MAIL.UNET.UMN.EDU (be sure to include your e-mail address).
How to submit: Messages to be posted to the group should be sent to: DISC-NORDLIB@MAIL.UNET.UMN.EDU
Submission policy: Comments or questions on the adminstration or policies of the list should be sent to: Charles Spetland at C-SPET@VM;.SPCS.UMN.EDU
After subscribing, you will automatically receive a monthly posting outlining these procedures.

DISCIPLINE

Description: Discipline is an electronic forum covering discussion of anything related to Robert Fripp's musical activity, King Crimson, and related music and musicians, with reviews, articles, questions and answers, debate, news, announcements, discographies, etc.
Subjects covered: music; Fripp, Robert; King Crimson; rock music
Net address for operations: toby@c.man.ac.uk
Net address for questions or submissions: toby@c.man.ac.uk
Established: June 1992
Subscribers: 340
List moderated: Yes.
Moderation procedure: All submissions are mailed to moderator.
Editorial contact: Toby Howard
Department of Computer Science, University of Manchester' Oxford Road, Manchester, M13 9PL, UK.
Tel: +44 61-275-6274
Fax: +44 61-275-6236
Internet: toby@c.man.ac.uk
How to unsubscribe: Address all queries to the moderator at toby@c.man.ac.uk
How to submit: Address all queries to the moderator at toby@c.man.ac.uk
Archives: The Discipline archives are available on ftp.uwp.edu, in /pub/music/lists/discipline.

DISSPLA@TAUNIVM

Description: DISSPLA@TAUNIVM is a forum on Display Integrated Software System and Plotting Language.
Subjects covered: computer hardware and software
List moderated: No.
Editorial contact: Zvika Bar-Deroma
Internet: er7101%technion.bitnet@vm1.nodak.edu
Bitnet: er7101@technion
How to access: Send subscribe message to listserv@taunivm or listserv@taunivm.tau.ac.il
How to unsubscribe: Send unsubscribe message to listserv@taunivm or listserv@taunivm.tau.ac.il

DISTOBJ@HPLB.HP.COM
Description: DISTOBJ is a discussion list on distributed object systems.
Subjects covered: computer science
List moderated: No.
Editorial contact: Harry Barman
Internet: hjb@hplb.hpl.hp.com
How to access: Send subscribe message to distobj-request@hplb.hpl.hp.com
How to unsubscribe: Send unsubscribe message to distobj-request@hplb.hpl.hp.com

DISTRIBUTED-AI@MAILBASE.AC.UK
Description: DISTRIBUTED-AI is a mailbase discussion forum on distributed artificial intelligence systems.
Subjects covered: artificial intelligence; computer science
List moderated: No.
Internet: distributed-ai-request@mailbase.ac.uk
How to access: Send subscribe message to mailbase@mailbase.ac.uk in the following format: join distributed-ai Yourfirstname Yourlastname
How to submit: Send contributions to distributed-ai@mailbase.ac.uk
Archives: Archives are developed monthly; apply to listowner for details.

DIV28@GWUVM
Description: DIV28@GWUVM is a forum for members of the APA's Division 28.
Subjects covered: psychology
Host: American Psychologcal Association
List moderated: No.
Editorial contact: Cheri Fullerton
How to access: Send unsubscribe message to listserv@gwuvm
How to unsubscribe: Send unsubscribe message to listserv@gwuvm

DIVERS-L
Description: Divers-L is the list of the Diversity Concerns Exchange and covers multicultural and gender studies.
Subjects covered: gender studies
List moderated: No.
Editorial contact: Howard Lawrence
Bitnet: hrl@suarch
How to access: Send subscribe message to listserv@psuvm or listserv@psuvm.psu.edu
How to unsubscribe: Send unsubscribe message to listserv@psuvm or listserv@psuvm.psu.edu

DJ-L (CAMPUS RADIO DISK JOCKEY DISCUSSION LIST)
Description: DJ-L Campus Radio Disk Jockey Discussion List is a general discussion of topics of interest to campus radio disk jockeys.
Subjects covered: music; radio and television; colleges and universities
Net address for operations: LISTSERV@NDSUVM1.BITNET
LISTSERV@VM1.NoDak.edu

Net address for questions or submissions: DJ-L@NDSUVM1.BITNET
DJ-L@VM1.NoDak.edu
Established: January 1990
Subscribers: 153
Editorial contact: Douglas J. Coffman
432 East Coed Hall, 1801 Townsend Drive,
Houghton, MI 49931-1195.
Tel: (906) 487-1196
Internet: lefty@mtu.edu
Technical contact: Marty Hoag
Internet: INFO@VM1.NoDak.edu
Bitnet: INFO@NDSUVM1
How to access: Via Bitnet: Send and interactive command to LISTSERV@NDSUVM1 containing sub DJ-L (Your Full Name); Via mail:Send e-mail to LISTSERV@VM1.NoDak.edu The first line of the BODY of the mail file should say: sub DJ-L (Your Full Name) Do not include a .sig file.
Access policy: No restrictions on subscribers.
How to unsubscribe: Send the command "unsub DJ-L" to the same address as you sent your subscription.
How to submit: Send submissions to DJ-L@NDUSVM1.BITNET or to DJ-L@VM1.NoDak.edu
Submission policy: Restrictions explained in List Welcome File
Archives: Available from LISTSERV@NDSUVM1 or LISTSERV@VM1.NoDak.edu

DKB-L
Description: DKB-L is a forum dedicated to the use of DKB Ray Tracer software originated by David Buck.
Subjects covered: art; graphics
List moderated: No.
Editorial contact: David Buck
Internet: dbuck@ccs.carleton.ca
How to access: Send subscribe message to listserv@trearn or listserv%trearn.bitnet@cunyvm.cuny.edu
How to unsubscribe: Send unsubscribe message to listserv@trearn or listserv%trearn.bitnet@cunyvm.cuny.edu
Archives: Archives are developed monthly; apply to listowner for details.

DNH-PILOT
Description: The Diet, Nutrition and Health project covers sociology, food science and technology, agricultural economics, and psychology. Researchers in academic institutions across the European Community, together with industrial partners, and with some external funding, are involved.
Subjects covered: food science; agricultural economics; nutrition and health
Net address for operations: mailbase@uk.ac.mailbase
Net address for questions or submissions: mailbase@uk.ac.mailbase
Established: 1992
Subscribers: 19
Sponsor: Dept of Sociology, University of Reading, Whiteknights, Reading, RG6 2AA
Host: The NISP Team, Computing Laboratory, The University, Newcastle upon Tyne, NE1 7RU, UK.
List moderated: No.
Editorial contact: Malcolm Hamilton

Dept of Sociology, University of Reading, Whiteknights, Reading, RG6 2AA, UK
Tel: 734 875123 x7510
Fax: 734 318922
Internet: m.b.hamiton@reading.ac.uk
Bitnet: lpshamlt@cms.am.reading.ac.uk
How to access: Send e-mail message to
mailbase@uk.ac.mailbase stating join dhn-pilot firstname
lastname
Access policy: List is open to anyone.
How to unsubscribe: Send e-mail message stating leave dnh-pilot firstname lastname
How to submit: Send e-mail to dhn-pilot@uk.ac.mailbase

DOCDIS@UA1VM

Description: DOCDIS@UA1VM is an e-conference for doctoral students in library and information science.
Subjects covered: library and information science
List moderated: No.
Editorial contact: Virginia Young
Bitnet: vyoung@ua1vm
How to access: Send subscribe message to listserv@uaivm
How to unsubscribe: Send unsubscribe message to listserv@ua1vm
Archives: Archives are developed monthly; apply to listowner for details.

DOROTHYL@KENTVM

Description: DOROTHYL@KENTVM is a forum on the works of Dorothy L. Sayers and on mystery literature in general.
Subjects covered: English language and literature; mysteries; Sayers, Dorothy L.
List moderated: Yes.
Editorial contact: Kara L. Robinson
Internet: krobinso@kentvm.kent.edu
Bitnet: krobinso@kentvm
How to access: Send subscribe message to listserv@kentvm.kent.edu
How to unsubscribe: Send unsubscribe message to listserv@kentvm.kent.edu
Archives: Archives are developed daily; apply to listowner for details.

DPMAST-L

Description: DPMAST-L is a forum of the Data Processing Management Association.
Subjects covered: computer science
List moderated: No.
Editorial contact: Ross Doepke
Bitnet: ed6704@cmsuvmb
How to access: Send subscribe message to listserv@cmsuvmb
How to unsubscribe: Send unsubscribe message to listserv@cmsuvmb

DRUGABUS

Description: DRUGABUS is an electronic forum covering general discussion about substance abuse.
Subjects covered: substance abuse
Net address for operations: DRUGABUS@UMAB.BITNET

Net address for questions or submissions:
DRUGABUS@UMAB.BITNET
Established: 1989
Subscribers: 150
Sponsor: UMAB Office of Substance Abuse Studies,
20 N. Pine Street, Room 224 Baltimore, MD 21201-1180.
Host: University of Maryland at Baltimore, School of Pharmacy, 20 N. Pine Street, Baltimore, MD 21201-1180.
List moderated: No.
Editorial contact: Trent Tschirgi
OSAS, 20 N. Pine Street, Rm. 224, Baltimore, MD 21201-1180.
Tel: (410) 706-7513
Fax: (410) 706-7184
Internet: TTSCHIRG@UMAB.BITNET.EDU
Bitnet: TTSCHIRG@UMAB
Technical contact: Elizabeth Brindley
IRMD, 100 N. Greene St, RM.524, Baltimore, MD 21201.
Tel: (410) 706-6146
Internet: EBRINDLE@UMAB
Copyright statement: All postings become the copyrighted property of UNAB office of substance abuse studies unless previously copyrighted. Contents may be reproduced in full without express permission for not-for profit purposes.
How to access: Tell LISTSERV at UMAB SUBSCRIBE DRUGABUS YOURID@YOURNODE (FIRSTNAME MI LASTNAME)
Access policy: Subscription by request.
How to unsubscribe: Tell Listserv at UMAB DELETE DRUGABUS YOURID@YOURNODE
How to submit: DRUGABUS@UMAB
Archives: 3 months of postings are archived. Apply to moderator for details.

DTP-L

Description: Dtp-L is a forum covering the desktop publishing field.
Subjects covered: writing; desktop publishing
List moderated: No.
Editorial contact: Jeff Wasilko
Internet: jjwcmp@ultb.isc.rit.edu
How to access: Send subscribe message to listserv@yalevm or listserv@yalevm.ycc.yale.edu
How to unsubscribe: Send unsubscribe message to listserv@yalevm or listserv@yalevm.ycc.yale.edu

DTS-L (DEAD TEACHERS SOCIETY LIST)

Description: DTS-L is the Dead Teachers Society list covering discussions of a wide variety of teaching and learning topcs.
Subjects covered: education
Net address for operations: listserv@iubvm.bitnet
Review: Reviewed by List Review Service edited by Raleigh Muns: see appendix.
How to access: Send message to listserv.

DYNIX-L

Description: Dynix-L is a forum for users of DYNIX system software.
Subjects covered: library and information science; DYNIX
List moderated: No.
Editorial contact: Todd D. Kelley
Internet: kelley@oyster.smcm.edu

How to access: Send subscribe message to kelley@
oyster.smcm.edu
How to unsubscribe: Send unsubscribe message to kelley@
oyster.smcm.edu

DYNSYS-L
Description: Dynsys-L is a forum for discussion of dynamical systems.
Subjects covered: engineering
List moderated: No.
Editorial contact: Karl Petersen
Internet: unckep%unc.bitnet@cunyvm.cuny.edu
Bitnet: unckep@unc
How to access: Send subscribe message to newserv@uncvml or ultima%unc.bitnet@cunyvm.cuny.edu
How to unsubscribe: Send unsubscribe message to newserv@uncvml or ultima%unc.bitnet@cunyvm.cuny.edu

E-EUROPE@PUCC
Description: E-EUROPE@PUCC is a discussion list focusing on business topics in Eastern Europe.
Subjects covered: business; Eastern Europe
Net address for operations: LISTSERV@PUCC, E-EUROPE@PUCC.PRINCETON.EDU
How to access: Send a standard subscribe request to the listserv.
How to unsubscribe: Send a standard unsubscribe request to the listserv.

EADP-PILOT@MAILBASE.AC.UK
Description: EADP-PILOT@MAILBASE.AC.UK is a forum for European researchers in human development.
Subjects covered: psychology
Host: European Association of Developmental Psychologists
List moderated: No.
Internet: eadp-pilot-request@mailbase.ac.uk
How to access: Send subscribe message to mailbase@mailbase.ac.uk in the following format: join eadp-pilot Yourfirstname Yourlastname
Archives: Archives are developed monthly; apply to listowner for details.

EARAM-L
Description: EARAM-L is the discussion list of the Society of Early Americanists.
Subjects covered: American history; history
Net address for operations: LISTSERV@KENTVM
Net address for questions or submissions: EARAM-L@KENTVM
How to access: Send message to listserv: SUBSCRIBE <listname> <your name>

EARLYM-L
Description: Earlym-L is a forum for music of the Medieval and Renaissance periods.
Subjects covered: music; Renaissance studies; Medieval studies
List moderated: No.
Editorial contact: Gerhard Gonter

Internet: gonter@awiwuwll
How to access: Send subscribe message to listserv@aearn
How to unsubscribe: Send unsubscribe message to listserv@aearn
Archives: Archives are developed weekly; apply to listowner for details.

EASTLIB
Description: EASTLIB is a discussion forum of the Committee on East Asian Libraries on issues centering on East Asian librarianship.
Subjects covered: East Asia; library and information science
How to access: Send the following message to LISTSERV@MENTO.OIT.UNC.EDU: SUBSCRIBE EASTLIB <yourfirstname yourlastname>

EBCBCAT@HDETUD1
Description: EBCBCAT@HDETUD1 is a biotechnology software catalog.
Subjects covered: biophysics; biochemistry; computer hardware and software
List moderated: No.
How to access: Send subscribe message to listserv@hdetud1 or listserv@hdetud1.tudelft.nl
How to unsubscribe: Send unsubscribe message to listserv@hdetud1 or listserv@hdetud1.tudelft.nl

EC@INDYCMS
Description: EC@INDYCMS is a forum for discussion of the European Community.
Subjects covered: political science
List moderated: No.
Editorial contact: John B. Harlan
Internet: ijbh200@indyvax.iupui.edu
Bitnet: ijbh200@indyvax
How to access: Send subscribe message to listserv@indycms or listserv@indycms.iupui.edu
How to unsubscribe: Send unsubscribe message to listserv@indycms or listserv@indycms.iupui.edu
Archives: Archives are developed monthly; apply to listowner for details.

ECIXFILES@IGC.ORG
Description: ECIXFILES@IGC.ORG is a list and distribution service of files related to energy and climate information.
Subjects covered: environmental studies; climatology
Host: Energy and Climate Information Exchange
List moderated: No.
Editorial contact: Lelani Arris
Internet: larris@igc.org
How to access: Send subscribe message to ecixfiles@igc.org and cd p:ecixfiles
Archives: Yes; Send anonymous FTP to: 192.82.108.1

ECONED-L
Description: Economic Education Computer Discussion Group is a forum for discussing issues in economic education over Bitnet and other computer networks nationwide has been estab-

lished. There is no cost involved for using the service. The idea behind the discussion group is that individuals working in the area may easily transmit messages to others working in the area. The types of messages may include, but are not limited to, seeking input on current research projects of a general nature, asking for help or ideas on theoretical or empirical topics, expressing concerns and opinions about current policy directions, announcing conferences, support groups, or the like. In short, anything that has to do with the topic of economic education, whether opinion, fact, or the usual combination of the two is welcome.

Subjects covered: economics; education
Net address for operations: LISTSERV@UTDALLAS
Net address for questions or submissions:
LISTSERV@UTDALLAS
Established: 1990
Subscribers: 159
Sponsor: The University of Texas at Dallas
Host: The University of Texas at Dallas
List moderated: No.
Editorial contact: Kurt Beron
The University of Texas at Dallas
PO Box 830688,GR 31 Richardson, TX 75083
Tel: (214) 690-2920
Fax: (214) 690-2735
Internet: beron@utdallas.edu
Bitnet: KBERON@UTDALLAS
How to access: Use TELL or SEND or TRANSMIT command, as appropriate, to LISTSERV@UTDALLAS with the command SUB ECONED-L your name VIA MAIL: Send mail to LISTSERV@UTDALLAS with the first text line being SUB ECONED-L your name
Access policy: There are no restrictions to subscriptions.
How to unsubscribe: In place of ''SUB'' in the above put ''SIGNOFF''
How to submit: Send mail to ECONED-L@UTDALLAS
Submission policy: The only restrictions are good taste and the knowledge that everyone subscribing to the discussion group will see the posted message.
Archives: Past mail available to subscribers.

ECONET@IGC.ORG
Description: ECONET@IGC.ORG is a service for people working in the environmental preservation field.
Subjects covered: environmental studies
How to access: $50 signup fee. Monthly subscription of $10. Connect charges are: $10/hr for peak times, $5/hr for off-peak. Access of service is accomplished by simple login procedures (i.e. telnet igc.org OR rlogin igc.org)

ECONET@MIAMIU
Description: ECONET@MIAMIU is a forum covering environmental topics.
Subjects covered: environmental studies
List moderated: No.
Editorial contact: Jianguo Wu
Bitnet: jwu@miamiu
How to access: Send subscribe message to listserv@miamu
How to unsubscribe: Send unsubscribe message to listserv@miamu
Archives: Archives are developed monthly; apply to listowner for details.

ECONOMY@TECMTYVM
Description: ECONOMY@TECMTYVM is a discussion forum on all aspects of economics.
Subjects covered: economics
List moderated: Yes.
Editorial contact: Alejandro Ibarra
Internet: 5343tbit@tecmtyvm.mty.itesm.mx
Bitnet: 5343tbit@tecmtyvm
How to access: Send subscribe message to listserv@tecmtyvm or listserv@tecmtyvm.mty.itesm.mx
How to unsubscribe: Send unsubscribe message to listserv@tecmtyvm or listserv@tecmtyvm.mty.itesm.mx
Archives: Archives are developed monthly; apply to listowner for details.

ECPR-ECO
Description: ECPR-ECO is an electronic discussion list for researchers interested in the subject of ecological analysis of election results. Topics covered include geographical mapping of election results, ecological analysis of election results.
Subjects covered: environmental studies; political science; international studies
Net address for operations: mailbase@mailbase.ac.uk
Net address for questions or submissions: ecpr-eco@mailbase.ac.uk
Established: April 1993
Sponsor: European Consortium for Political Research
Host: Institute of Political Science, University of Aarhus Universitetsparken, DK-8000 Aarhus C, Denmark.
List moderated: No.
Editorial contact: Soren Thomsen
Institute of Political Science, University of Aarhus, Universitetsparken, DK-8000 Aarhus C, Denmark.
Tel: +45 89 42 11 33
Fax: +45 86 13 98 39
Internet: ifskris@ecostat.aau.dk
Internet: mailbase-helpline@mailbase.ac.uk
Copyright statement: Copyright is held either by the authors or by the UK Networked Information Services Project (NISP).
How to access: Send the message join ecpr-eco My Name to mailbase@mailbase.ac.uk (please note that Mailbase will only accept your name as two words).
Access policy: No special limitations to membership.
How to unsubscribe: Send the message leave ecpr-eco to mailbase@mailbase.ac.uk
Archives: Archives are available. Apply to listowner for details.
Related files: You can retrieve a manual for use of the mailbase system by sending the following message to mailbase@mailbase.ac.uk: send mailbase user-guide
Additional information: Second editor: Clive Payne, Social Studies Faculty Centre, University of Oxford, George Street, Oxford OX1 2RL, UK; tel +44-865-278713; fax +44-865-278725; Internet nuff@vax.ox.ac.uk

ECPR-PILOT@MAILBASE.AC.UK
Description: ECPR-PILOT@MAILBASE.AC.UK is a forum for discussing aspects of teaching of political science in Europe.
Subjects covered: education; political science; politics
Host: European Consortium for Political Research
List moderated: No.
Internet: ecpr-pilot-request@mailbase.ac.uk

How to access: Send subscribe message to mailbase@mailbase.ac.uk in the following format: join ecpr-pilot Yourfirstname Yourlastname
Archives: Archives are developed monthly; apply to listowner for details.

ECS-HELPDESK
Description: ECS-HELPDESK is a forum of the European Cetacean Society.
Subjects covered: communications; zoology
Host: European Cetacean Society
List moderated: No.
Internet: ecs-helpdesk-request@mailbase.ac.uk
How to access: Send subscribe message to mailbase@mailbase.ac.uk in the following format: join ecs-helpdesk Yourfirstname Yourlastname
Archives: Archives are developed monthly; apply to listowner for details.

ECS-NEWS@MAILBASE.AC.UK
Description: ECS-NEWS@MAILBASE.AC.UK is a forum of the European Cetacean Society.
Subjects covered: zoology
Host: European Cetacean Society
List moderated: No.
Internet: ecs-news-request@mailbase.ac.uk
How to access: Send subscribe message to mailbase@mailbase.ac.uk in the following format: join ecs-news Yourfirstname Yourlastname
Archives: Archives are developed monthly; apply to listowner for details.

ECTL@SNOWHITE.CIS.UOGUELPH.CA
Description: ECTL@SNOWHITE is a discussion on computer speech interfaces.
Subjects covered: computer science; engineering
List moderated: No.
Editorial contact: David Leip
Internet: david@snowhite.cis.uoguelph.ca
How to access: Send subscribe message to ectl-request@ snowhite.cis.uoguelph.ca
How to unsubscribe: Send unsubscribe message to ectl-request@ snowhite.cis.uoguelph.ca

ECUADOR@NERS6KI.NCSU.EDU
Description: ECUADOR@NERS6KI.NCSU.EDU is a forum on Ecuador.
Subjects covered: Ecuador
List moderated: No.
Editorial contact: G. Ivan Maldonado
Internet: ivan@neptj.ncsu.edu
How to access: Contact the Editor
How to unsubscribe: Contact the Editor

ED2000-EUROPE
Description: ED2000-EUROPE lists the schools participating in the ED-2000 program.

Subjects covered: education
List moderated: No.
Internet: ed2000-europe-request@mailbase.ac.uk
How to access: Send subscribe message to mailbase@mailbase.ac.uk in the following format: join ed2000-europe Yourfirstname Yourlastname
Archives: Archives are developed monthly; apply to listowner for details.

ED2000-PILOT@MAILBASE.AC.UK
Description: ED2000-PILOT@MAILBASE.AC.UK is an e-conference covering computer-assisted instructional techniques and practices.
Subjects covered: distance education; education; computer-assisted instruction (CAI)
List moderated: No.
Internet: ed2000-pilot-request@mailbase.ac.uk
How to access: Send subscribe message to mailbase@mailbase.ac.uk in the following format: join ed2000-pilot Yourfirstname Yourlastname
Archives: Archives are developed monthly; apply to listowner for details.

EDAD-L
Description: Edad-L is an electronic conference for educational administrators.
Subjects covered: education
List moderated: No.
Editorial contact: Ed Lilley
Bitnet: u5b35@wvnvm
How to access: Send subscribe message to listserv@wvnvm or listserv@wvnvm.wvnet.edu
How to unsubscribe: Send unsubscribe message to listserv@wvnvm or listserv@wvnvm.wvnet.edu

EDINFO-L
Description: Edinfo-L is a forum focusing on educational information.
Subjects covered: education
List moderated: No.
How to access: Send subscribe message to listserv@iubvm or listserv@iubvm.ucs.indiana.edu
How to unsubscribe: Send subscribe message to listserv@iubvm or listserv@iubvm.ucs.indiana.edu

EDISTA@USACHVM1
Description: EDISTA@USACHVM1 is a list on distance education.
Subjects covered: education; distance education; Chile
Net address for operations: listserv@usachuvm1
Host: University Distance Program, University of Santiago, Chile
List moderated: No.
Editorial contact: Prof. Jorge Urbina Fuentes
Bitnet: unidis@usachvm
How to access: Send subscribe message to listserv@usachvm1
How to unsubscribe: Send unsubscribe message to listserv@usachvm1

EDLAW@UKCC

Description: EDLAW@UKCC is a forum for educators in the field of law in public and private education, colleges and universities.
Subjects covered: law and legal studies; education
List moderated: Yes.
Editorial contact: Virginia Davis-Nordin
Internet: nordin@ukcc.uky.edu
How to access: Send subscribe message to LISTSERV@UKCC
How to unsubscribe: Send unsubscribe message to LISTSERV@UKCC

EDMAC@MAILBASE.AC.UK

Description: EDMAC@MAILBASE.AC.UK is a discussion on the development of TEX macros.
Subjects covered: linguistics
List moderated: No.
Internet: edmac-request@mailbase.ac.uk
How to access: Send subscribe message to mailbase@mailbase.ac.uk in the following format: join edmac Yourfirstname Yourlastname
Archives: Archives are developed monthly; apply to listowner for details.

EDNET

Description: EDNET covers the use of the Internet in education.
Subjects covered: Internet; education; distance education
Net address for operations: listserv@nic.umass.edu
Internet: PGSMITH@UCSVAX.UCS.UMASS.EDU
How to access: Send message to listserv@nic.umass.edu.
How to unsubscribe: Send message to listserv@nic.umass.edu.

EDNET6-L

Description: Ednet6-L discusses network planning management from grades K-12.
Subjects covered: education
List moderated: No.
How to access: Send subscribe message to listserv@iubvm or listserv@iubvm.ucs.indiana.edu
How to unsubscribe: Send unsubscribe message to listserv@iubvm or listserv@iubvm.ucs.indiana.edu

EDPOLYAN

Description: EDPOLYAN is a list covering discussion of education policy.
Subjects covered: education; comparative education; colleges and universities; administration
Net address for operations: LISTSERV@ASUACAD.BITNET
Net address for questions or submissions: EDPOLYAN@ASUACAD.BITNET
Established: January 1990
Subscribers: 600
Sponsor: Arizona State University
Host: Arizona State University
List moderated: Yes.
Moderation procedure: List is private. User must be a subscriber to post to List moderator/manager.
Editorial contact: Gene V. Glass

College of Education, Arizona State University, Tempe, AZ 85287-2411.
Tel: (602) 965 2692
Internet: Glass@asu.edu
Bitnet: Glass@asu
Review: Reviewed by List Review Service edited by Raleigh Muns: see appendix.
How to access: Send message to LISTSERV@ASUACAD.BITNET SUB EDPOLYAN name
How to unsubscribe: Send message to LISTSERV@ASUACAD.BITNET SIGNOFF EDPOLYAN
How to submit: Send message to EDPOLYAN@ASUACAD.BITNET
Archives: Notebooks are archived at LISTSERV@ASUACAD.BITNET
Gopher accessibility: Files are accessible through the Gopher at ASKERIC Syracuse University.

EDSTAT-L

Description: Edstat-L is a forum covering teaching statistics on a college level.
Subjects covered: mathematics; statistics
List moderated: No.
Editorial contact: Tim Arnold
Internet: arnold@stat.ncsu.edu
Bitnet: arnold@ncsustat
How to access: Send subscribe message to listserv@ncsuvm or listserv@ncsuvm.cc.ncsu.edu
How to unsubscribe: Send unsubscribe message to listserv@ncsuvm or listserv@ncsuvm.cc.ncsu.edu
Archives: Archives are developed monthly; apply to listowner for details.

EDSTYLE

Description: EDSTYLES is an electronic discussion list on learning styles.
Subjects covered: education; distance education
Net address for operations: listserv@sjuvm.bitnet
How to access: Send standard subscribe request to listserv@sjuvm.bitnet
How to unsubscribe: Send standard unsubscribe request to listserv@sjuvm.bitnet

EDTECH@OHSTVMA

Description: EDTECH@OHSTVMA centers on educational technology.
Subjects covered: computer-assisted instruction (CAI)
List moderated: No.
Editorial contact: Vickie Banks
Internet: 21602vb%msu.bitnet@vm1.nodak.edu
Bitnet: 21602vb%msu
How to access: Send subscribe message to listserv@ohstvma or listserv@ohstvma.acs.ohio-state.edu
How to unsubscribe: Send unsubscribe message to listserv@ohstvma or listserv@ohstvma.acs.ohio-state.edu

EDUC@QUEBEC

Description: EDUC@QUEBEC is an education forum.
Subjects covered: education
List moderated: No.

How to access: Send subscribe message to listserv@quebec
How to unsubscribe: Send unsubscribe message to listserv@quebec

EDUCAI-L
Description: Educai-L is a discussion on the use of expert systems and artificial intelligence in the development of educational programs.
Subjects covered: education technology
List moderated: No.
Editorial contact: John T. Grasso
Bitnet: u5521@wvnvm
How to access: Send subscribe message to listserv@wvnvm or listserv@wvnvm.wvnet.edu
How to unsubscribe: Send unsubscribe message to listserv@wvnvm or listserv@wvnvm.wvnet.edu

EDUCOM-W
Description: EDUCOM-W is a moderated discussion list centering on issues in technology and education of interest to women.
Subjects covered: education; feminism; science and technology; women's studies
Net address for operations: LISTSERV@BITNIC, LISTSERV@BITNIC.EDUCOM.EDU
List moderated: Yes.
How to access: Subscription messages should be sent to LISTSERV@BITNIC (Bitnet) or LISTSERV@BITNIC.EDUCOM.EDU (Internet).

EDUSIG-L
Description: Edusig-L discusses the DEC hardware and education.
Subjects covered: education technology; Digital Equipment Corporation
Host: Digital Equipment Corporation
List moderated: No.
Editorial contact: Jim Gerland
How to access: Send subscribe message to listserv@ubvm or listserv@ubvm.cc.buffalo.edu
How to unsubscribe: Send unsubscribe message to listserv@ubvm or listserv@ubvm.cc.buffalo.edu
Archives: Archives are developed monthly; apply to listowner for details.

EDUTEL@RPITSVM
Description: EDUTEL covers computer-mediated communication and instruction.
Subjects covered: education technology; computer-assisted instruction (CAI)
Host: Comserve
List moderated: No.
Editorial contact: Staff
Internet: support@vm.its.vpi.edu
Bitnet: support@rpitsvm
How to access: Send subscribe message to comserve@rpitsvm or comserve@vm.its.vpi.edu
How to unsubscribe: Send unsubscribe message to comserve@rpitsvm or comserve@vm.its.vpi.edu

ELDNET-L
Description: ELDNET-L is an electronic discussion list addressing issues related to or of interest to engineering and related subject area libraries and librarians.
Subjects covered: engineering; library and information science; education; physical sciences
Net address for operations:
LISTSERV@VMD.CSO.UIUC.EDU or
LISTSERV@UIUCVMD
Net address for questions or submissions: ELDNET-L@VMD.CSO.UIUC.EDU or ELDNET-L@UIUCVMD
Established: August 1991
Subscribers: 203
Sponsor: Engineering Libraries Division, American Society for Engineering Education, 11 Dupont Circle, Suite 200 Washington, DC 20036.
Host: University of Illinois at Urbana-Champaign, Grainger Engineering Library, Information Center, 1301 W. Springfield Ave., Urbana, IL 61801.
List moderated: Yes.
Moderation procedure: All messages addressed to the list are received by the editor/moderator who determines whether the message meets all criteria required for forwarding to the list subscribers (these criteria are spelled out in a welcome message sent to all new subscribers). If all criteria are met, the editor/moderator forwards the message to the list subscribers.
Editorial contact: Mel DeSart
Grainger Engineering Library Information Center 1301 W. Springfield Ave. Urbana, IL 61801.
Tel: (217) 244-4426
Internet: DESART@VMD.CSO.UIUC.EDU
Bitnet: DESART@UIUCVMD
How to access: Address e-mail to
LISTSERV@VMD.CSO.UIUC.EDU or
LISTSERV@UIUCVMD. Leave subject line blank. Text of message should be SUBSCRIBE ELDNET-L yourfirstname yourlastname. Send message.
Access policy: List is open to anyone.
How to unsubscribe: Address e-mail to
LISTSERV@VMD.CSO.UIUC.EDU or
LISTSERV@UIUCVMD. Leave subject line blank. Text of message should be UNSUBSCRIBE ELDNET-L. Send message.
How to submit: Address e-mail to ELDNET-L@VMD.CSO.UIUC.EDU or ELDNET-L@UIUCVMD. Please include a descriptive subject line. Send message.
Submission policy: All submissions should address list subjects. No ads or listings of items for sale will be accepted. Constructive criticism will be accepted. Open attacks on individuals, topics, or prior submissions may be returned by the editor/moderator, particularly if not designated as a flame.
Archives: List is archived. Ease of access is determined by subscriber's e-mail software.
Related files: There are FTP-able files available to those list subscribers who are also members of ELD/ASEE. No files available to other list subscribers.
Additional information: Additional information or comments: U.S. mail addresses listed above do not take effect until January 1994 when library moves into a new building. Current U.S. mail address for contact is: Mel DeSart, Engineering Library, 221 Engineering Hall, 1308 W. Green Street, Urbana, IL 61801.

ELEASAI (THE OPEN FORUM ON LIBRARY AND INFORMATION SCIENCE RESEARCH)

Description: ELEASAI is a Listserv conference on research in library and information science. It concerns current research in progress or in planning stages, methodological and statistical issues, funding for research, computing as a research tool, broad trends in scientific research as they affect library and information science, and similar research-oriented topics. ELEASAI's address is ELEASAI@ARIZVM1. It is a companion conference to JESSE, which focuses on teaching and educational concerns in library and information science. JESSE concerns curricula, educational methodologies and issues, courses in development, resources, computing as a teaching tool, broad trends in education as they affect library and information science education, and similar education- oriented topics. JESSE's address is JESSE@ARIZVM1. Two separate conferences are maintained at user request: while participants agree and maintain that research and teaching are inextricably linked together, and that work in one area naturally flows into the other, separate lists enable participants to manage the ever-increasing flow of information over the net a little better. Users can subscribe to one or the other or both. ELEASAI is strictly focused on research issues; JESSE is broadly concerned with issues of interest to the academic and may appear to drift from time to time.

Subjects covered: library and information science; computer hardware and software; education; colleges and universities

Net address for operations: LISTSERV@ARIZVM1

Net address for questions or submissions: ELEASAI@ARIZVM1

Established: January 1992

Subscribers: 435

Sponsor: School of Library Science, University of Arizona, 1515 East First St., Tucson, AZ 85719.

List moderated: No.

Editorial contact: Gretchen Whitney, Asst. Prof.
University of Arizona, 1515 East First Street, Tucson, AZ 85719

Internet: GWHITNEY@CCIT.ARIZONA.EDU

Bitnet: GWHITNEY@ARIZVMS

Technical contact: Charles Seavey, Assoc. Prof.
School of Library Science, University of Arizona, 1515 East First Street, Tucson, AZ 85719

Tel: 602-621-3957

Fax: 602-621-3279

Internet: DOCMAPS@CCIT.ARIZONA.EDU

Bitnet: DOCMAPS@ARIZVMS

Copyright statement: The University of Arizona Graduate Library School provides ELEASAI and JESSE as a public service. It does not verify the accuracy of submitted messages nor does it endorse the opinions expressed by message authors. Authors of ELEASAI and JESSE messages are solely responsible for content of their messages. The conferences are moderated only in that the moderators encourage participation in the conferences, assist users with questions regarding the mechanics of the conference, and generally try to keep things on track.

How to access: Send message to listserv@arizvm1.bitnet with no header and only subscribe eleasai melvil dewey replacing melvil's name with your own.

Access policy: Subscriptions are open to anyone.

How to unsubscribe: Send message to listserv@arizvm1.bitnet with no header and only unsubscribe eleasai in the message.

How to submit: Send message with meaningful header and whatever text desired to eleasai@arizvm1

Submission policy: Same as above

Archives: Archived monthly on listserv@arizvm1

Gopher accessibility: This list is rumored to be on a German gopher somewhere; have not located.

THE ELECTRIC ECLECTIC DISCUSSION LIST

Description: The Electric Eclectic is a multimedia Internet magazine, featuring sound and image files in addition to text files. This mailing list has been formed for those interested in discussing the development of multimedia applications on the Internet.

Subjects covered: Internet; multimedia computing

Editorial contact: Nathaniel Borenstein
Bellcore Corp., Morristown, NJ

How to access: Send an email message to ee-discuss-request@eitech.com, with the word subscribe in the subject line of the message.

ELECTRONIC COLLEGE OF THEORY

Description: Electronic College of Theory is an electronic conference on literary theory. It includes discussions of topics in theory, announcements of conferences, publications, calls for papers, and reports of the business of the Society for Critical Exchange.

Subjects covered: literary theory and criticism; cultural studies; language and literature

Net address for operations: xx124@po.cwru.edu

Net address for questions or submissions: xx124@po.cwru.edu

Established: 1990

Subscribers: 154

Sponsor: Society for Critical Exchange, Guilford House, Case Western Reserve University, Cleveland, OH 44106-7117.

Host: Case Western Reserve University

List moderated: Yes.

Moderation procedure: E-mail submissions bundled and sometimes lightly edited (especially headers and such) by the moderator.

Editorial contact: Gary Lee Stonum
English Department, Case Western Reserve University, Cleveland, OH 44106-7117.

Tel: 216-368-3342

Fax: 216-368-2216

Internet: gxs11@po.cwru.edu

Bitnet: gxs11!po.cwru.edu@cunyvm

How to access: Send e-mail to xx124@po.cwru.edu including in body of the message name and postal address and mentioning whether currently belong to the Society for Critical Exchange.

Access policy: Subscription initially open to anyone requesting it. However, we ask that after a month or so of the person either join the Society for Critical Exchange (annual dues, $15) or sign off.

How to unsubscribe: Send mail to xx124@po.cwru.edu. If this is only a hiatus, include restartdate.

How to submit: By e-mail to xx124@po.cwru.edu

Submission policy: Submissions welcome from anyone, including non-subscribers. However, moderator reserves right to edit for appropriateness. Edited copy not posted without the author's specific approval.

Archives: Not currently available by ftp or similar methods. However, the moderator maintains issue archives privately, so write to gxs11@po.cwru.edu for information about searching back issues.

ELENCHUS@UOTTOWA
Description: ELENCHUS@UOTTOWA is a forum on early Christian thought and literature.
Subjects covered: religion; Christianity
List moderated: No.
Editorial contact: L. Gregory Bloomquist
Internet: gbloomq@acadvm1.uottowa.ca
Bitnet: gbloomq@uottowa
How to access: Send subscribe message to listserv@uottowa listserv@acadvm1.uottowa.ca
How to unsubscribe: Send unsubscribe message to listserv@uottowa listserv@acadvm1.uottowa.ca

ELLASBIB@GREARN
Description: ELLASBIB@GREARN is a conference covering the Greek Library Automation System.
Subjects covered: library and information science
List moderated: No.
Editorial contact: Giannis Kosmas
Internet: op1@grearn
How to access: Send subscribe message to listserv@grearn
How to unsubscribe: Send unsubscribe message to listserv@grearn
Archives: Archives are developed monthly; apply to listowner for details.

ELLHNIKA@DHDURZ1
Description: ELLHNIKA@DHDURZ1 is a forum for Greek TEX software issues.
Subjects covered: linguistics; computer hardware and software
List moderated: Yes.
Editorial contact: Yannis Haralambous
Bitnet: yannis@frcitl81
How to access: Send subscribe message to listserv@dhdurz1
How to unsubscribe: Send unsubscribe message to listserv@dhdurz1

THE EMBEDDED DIGEST
Description: The Embedded Digest carries discussions of interest to embedded computer system developers. Embedded systems are special-purpose computer systems that are incorporated into a product.
Subjects covered: computer science; computer hardware and software
Net address for operations: embed-request@synchro.com
Net address for questions or submissions: embed@synchro.com
Established: April 1993
Subscribers: 192
Sponsor: Riverside Garage & Brewery, 16A Jay St, Cambridge, MA 02139.
Host: SynchroSystems, 16A Jay St, Cambridge, MA 02139.
List moderated: Yes.
Moderation procedure: The digest is edited before distribution to the list.

Editorial contact: Chuck Cox, BJCP Master Beer Judge Riverside Garage & Brewery, 16A Jay St, Cambridge, MA 02139.
Tel: (617) 547-5113
Internet: chuck@synchro.com
How to access: Send Internet address to: embed-request@synchro.com
How to unsubscribe: Send Internet address to: embed-request@synchro.com
How to submit: Send submission to: embed@synchro.com

EMBINFO@IBACSATA
Description: EMBINFO@IBACSATA is a forum the European Molecular Biology Network.
Subjects covered: biology
List moderated: No.
Editorial contact: Giovanni Turso
Bitnet: turso@ibacsata
How to access: Send subscribe message to listserv@ibacsata
How to unsubscribe: Send unsubscribe message to listserv@ibacsata
Archives: Archives are developed monthly; apply to listowner for details.

EMEDCH-L
Description: Emedch-L covers the study of early medieval China.
Subjects covered: history; China
List moderated: Yes.
Editorial contact: Ken Klein
Bitnet: kklein@uscvm
How to access: Send subscribe message to listserv@uscvm or listserv@vm.usc.edu
How to unsubscribe: Send unsubscribe message to listserv@uscvm or listserv@vm.usc.edu

EMFLDS-L
Description: EMFLDS-L is a forum on electromagnetics in medicine, communications, and science.
Subjects covered: medicine; science and technology
List moderated: No.
Editorial contact: David J. Rodman, M.D.
Bitnet: oopdavid@ubvms
How to access: Send subscribe message to listserv@ubvms or listserv@ubvm.cc.buffalo.edu
How to unsubscribe: Send unsubscribe message to listserv@ubvms or listserv@ubvm.cc.buffalo.edu
Archives: Archives are developed monthly; apply to listowner for details.

EMHIST-L
Description: EMHIST-L is a list covering early modern Europe.
Subjects covered: Early Modern Europe; history
Net address for operations: LISTSERV@uscvm
Net address for questions or submissions: EMHIST-L@uscvm
How to access: Send message to listserv: SUBSCRIBE <listname> <your name>

EMULPC-L

Description: EMULPC-L is a discussion list on PC emulation software and hardware.
Subjects covered: computer hardware and software
List moderated: No.
Editorial contact: Pedro Sepulveda
Bitnet: psepulve@usachvm1
How to access: Send subscribe message to listserv@usachvm1 or listserv%usachvm1.bitnet@vm1.nodak.edu
How to unsubscribe: Send unsubscribe message to listserv@usachvm1 or listserv%usachvm1.bitnet@vm1.nodak.edu

EMUSIC-D

Description: EMUSIC-D is used to announce the availability of new archives on the EMUSIC-L anonymous ftp server (castrovalva.gsfc.nasa.gov).
Subjects covered: electronic music; music
Net address for operations: listserv@auvm.american.edu
Net address for questions or submissions: emusic-d@auvm.american.edu
Established: January 1989
Subscribers: 612 on EMUSIC-D
Sponsor: The American University (auvm.american.edu)
Host: The American University (auvm.american.edu)
List moderated: No. Subscribers expected to follow specified canons of behavior.
Moderation procedure: Warnings for first two offenses, removal from list thereafter.
Editorial contact: Joe McMahon
Code 931, NASA/GSFC, Greenbelt, MD 20771.
Tel: (301) 286-8090
Internet: xrjdm@twinpeaks.gsfc.nasa.gov
Bitnet: xrjdm@gibbs
Copyright statement: This list has no specific copyright policy. Subscribers retain the rights to their postings
How to access: Send mail to listserv@auvm.american.edu with the text ''subscribe emusic-d <your name>''; ''<your name>'' should be replaced with your actual first and last name. Two names are required at minimum by the list server software. If there are problems, send mail to the list's technical contact.
Archives: Back issues are available for anonymous ftp from castrovalva.gsfc.nasa.gov in the directory /EMUSIC-L/back-issues as separate issues within directories named by volume (e.g., /EMUSIC-L/back-issues/vol45 would contain the files index. and issue01, issue02, etc.).
Related files: castrovalva.gsfc.nasa.gov contains miscellaneous documents pertaining to discussions, past and present. A copy of the complete MIDI specification, a number of Macintosh software items (THINK C/MIDI Manager interface code, some MAX objects), and test documents containing recommendations on how to buy one's first keyboard, signon/signoff procedures for EMUSIC-L, schematics for a primitive, do-it-yourself analog synthesizer, and a listing of the items currently available through the EMUSIC-L music exchange.

EMUSIC-L

Description: EMUSIC-L is a list carrying reviews of music, questions-and-answer exchanges, reports on subscriber performances, and discussions of musical technique. EMUSIC-L exists to provide a forum for the discussion of music made by elec-tronic means. The actual means are secondary. What we are concerned with is the music, composing, and related topics. A companion list, EMUSIC-D, is used to announce the availability of new archives on the EMUSIC-L anonymous ftp server (castrovalva.gsfc.nasa.gov).
Subjects covered: electronic music; music; computer hardware and software
Net address for operations: listserv@auvm.american.edu
Net address for questions or submissions: emusic-l@auvm.american.edu
Established: January 1989
Subscribers: 323
Sponsor: The American University (auvm.american.edu)
Host: The American University (auvm.american.edu)
List moderated: No. Subscribers expected to follow specified canons of behavior.
Moderation procedure: Warnings for first two offenses, removal from list thereafter.
Editorial contact: Joe McMahon
Code 931, NASA/GSFC, Greenbelt, MD 20771.
Tel: (301) 286-8090
Internet: xrjdm@twinpeaks.gsfc.nasa.gov
Bitnet: xrjdm@gibbs
Copyright statement: This list has no specific copyright policy. Subscribers retain the rights to their postings.
How to access: Send mail to listserv@auvm.american.edu with the text ''subscribe emusic-l <your name>''; ''<your name>'' should be replaced with your actual first and last name. Two names are required at minimum by the list server software. If there are problems, send mail to the list's technical contact. Those wishing to subscribe to EMUSIC-D should substitute ''emusic-d'' for ''emusic-l'' in the above procedure.
Access policy: EMUSIC-L is meant to be for the discussion of electronic music, in the studio, the classroom, in performance, and on recordings, including techniques, resources, user reviews and experiences, and speculation on futures. Some divagations will be tolerated; however, the list owner maintains final say as to the subject matter on the list and will move to terminate off-topic, pointless, and (especially) rancorous discussions.
How to unsubscribe: Send mail to listserv@auvm.american.edu with the text ''unsub emusic-l''. If there are problems, send mail to the list's technical contact.
Archives: Back issues are available for anonymous ftp from castrovalva.gsfc.nasa.gov in the directory /EMUSIC-L/back-issues as separate issues within directories named by volume (e.g., /EMUSIC-L/back-issues/vol45 would contain the files index. and issue01, issue02, etc.).
Related files: castrovalva.gsfc.nasa.gov contains miscellaneous documents pertaining to discussions, past and present. A copy of the complete MIDI specification, a number of Macintosh software items (THINK C/MIDI Manager interface code, some MAX objects), and test documents containing recommendations on how to buy one's first keyboard, signon/signoff procedures for EMUSIC-L, schematics for a primitive, do-it-yourself analog synthesizer, and a listing of the items currently available through the EMUSIC-L music exchange.
Additional information: Subscribers who wish to receive only a single daily message consisting of all postings each day may, after initially subscribing, send mail to listserv@auvm.american.edu with the body ''set emusic-l digest''.

ENDNOTE@UCSBVM

Description: ENDNOTE is a discussion group for users of EndNote/EndLink software.
Subjects covered: computer hardware and software; library and information science
Net address for questions or submissions: LISTSERV@UCSBVM
How to access: Send subscribe message to LISTSERV@HEARN
How to unsubscribe: Send unsubscribe message to LISTSERV@HEARN

ENERGY-L

Description: Energy-L is a forum on all aspects of energy in Israel.
Subjects covered: engineering; Israel
List moderated: Yes.
Editorial contact: Dr. M.Wolff
Bitnet: wolff@ilncrd
How to access: Send subscribe message to listserv@taunivm or listserv@taunivm.tau.ac.il
How to unsubscribe: Send unsubscribe message to listserv@taunivm or listserv@taunivm.tau.ac.il

ENGINEERING-CASE@MAILBASE.AC.UK

Description: ENGINEERING-CASE is a forum on the uses of computers in control systems engineering.
Subjects covered: engineering; computer-assisted design (CAD)
List moderated: No.
Internet: engineering-case-request@mailbase.ac.uk
How to access: Send subscribe message to mailbase@mailbase.ac.uk in the following format: join engineering-case Yourfirstname Yourlastname
Archives: Archives are developed monthly; apply to listowner for details.

ENGINEERING-DESIGN@MAILBASE.AC.UK

Description: ENGINEERING-DESIGN is a forum for researchers at the (UK) national Engineering Design Centres.
Subjects covered: engineering
List moderated: No.
Internet: engineering-design-request@mailbase.ac.uk
How to access: Send subscribe message to mailbase@mailbase.ac.uk in the following format: join engineering-design Yourfirstname Yourlastname
Archives: Archives are developed monthly; apply to listowner for details.

ENGLMU-L

Description: Englmu-L is a discussion list on using electronic media in English literature education.
Subjects covered: information technology; English language and literaure
List moderated: No.
Editorial contact: Eric Crump
Bitnet: lcerice@mizzou11
How to access: Send subscribe message to listserv@mizzou11

How to unsubscribe: Send unsubscribe message to listserv@mizzou11
Archives: Archives are developed yearly; apply to listowner for details.

ENVBEH-L

Description: Envbeh-L is a forum for the discussion of behaviorism and physical environments.
Subjects covered: psychology
List moderated: No.
Editorial contact: Tony Monteiro
Internet: monteiro%polygraf.bitnet@mitva.mit.edu
Bitnet: monteiro@polygraf
How to access: Send subscribe message to listserv@polyvm or listserv%polygraf.bitnet.mitvma.mit.edu
How to unsubscribe: Send unsubscribe message to listserv@polyvm or listserv%polygraf.bitnet.mitvma.mit.edu
Archives: Archives are developed monthly; apply to listowner for details.

ENVIROLINK

Description: EnviroLink is a list covering environmental news, information, actions, etc.
Subjects covered: environmental studies
Net address for operations: env-link+forms@envirolink.org
Net address for questions or submissions: env-link+@envirolink.org
Established: Sept 1991
New postings are announced on Usenet newsgroups as well as on every major computer network.
Available in other media: EnviroDisk and Printouts available (call for more info).
Subscribers: 430,000 people, 93 countries
Sponsor: The EnviroLink Network, 4551 Forbes Ave. 3rd Floor, Pittsburgh, PA 15213.
List moderated: Yes.
Moderation procedure: This is a moderated distribution list.
Editorial contact: Josh Knauer
4551 Forbes Ave. 3rd Floor, Pittsburgh, PA15213.
Tel: (412) 681-8300
Fax: (412) 681-6707
Internet: josh@envirolink.org
Indexed or abstracted: Yes, EnviroGopher (envirolink.hss.cmu.edu)
How to access: Send mail to: env-link+forms@andrew.cmu.edu and ask to be subscribed.
Access policy: Anyone can subscribe.
How to unsubscribe: Same as above
How to submit: Send message to env-link+@andrew.cmu.edu
Archives: To read our archives on EnviroGopher, telnet to: envirolink.org login: gopher password: envirolink *send mail to: admin@envirolink.org*
Related files: Telnet to: envirolink.hss.cmu.edu login id: gopher password: envirolink
Gopher accessibility: Yes, these files are accessible on EnviroGopher.

ENVST-L

Description: Envst-L is a forum on environmental studies.
Subjects covered: environmental studies
List moderated: No.

Editorial contact: Harold Ward
Bitnet: halward@brownvm
How to access: Send subscribe message to listserv@brownvm or listserv@brownvm.brown.edu
How to unsubscribe: Send unsubscribe message to listserv@brownvm or listserv@brownvm.brown.edu
Archives: Archives are developed weekly; apply to listowner for details.

EOCHR (EASTERN ORTHODOX CHRISTIAN DISCUSSION LIST)

Description: EOCHR is an electronic forum for discussion of Eastern Orthodox religions.
Subjects covered: religion; Eastern Orthodox religions; Christianity
How to access: Send an email message to DRAGIC.VUKOMANOVIC@QUEENSU.CA
How to unsubscribe: Send an email message to DRAGIC.VUKOMANOVIC@QUEENSU.CA

EP-LIST

Description: EP-List is a digest intended to promote discussions on a wide range of technical issues in evolutionary optimization, as well as provide information on upcoming conferences, events, journals, special issues, and other items of interest to the EP community. Discussions on all areas of evolutionary computation are welcomed, including artificial life, evolution strategies, and genetic algorithms. The digest is meant to encourage inter-disciplinary communications.
Subjects covered: evolutionary programming; artificial intelligence; computer science
Net address for questions or submissions: ep-list-request@magenta.me.fau.edu
Editorial contact: N. Saravanan
Florida Atlantic University
Internet: saravan@amber.me.fau.edu
How to access: To subscribe to the digest, send mail to ep-list-request@magenta.me.fau.edu and include the line ''subscribe ep-list'' in the body of the text. Further instructions will follow your subscription.

EPP-L

Description: EPP-L is a discussion list related to the Einstein Papers Project.
Subjects covered: physics; science and technology
List moderated: No.
Editorial contact: Adam Bryant
Internet: adb@bv-it.bv.edu
How to access: Send subscribe message to listserv@buacca
How to unsubscribe: Send unsubscribe message to listserv@buacca
Archives: Yes; Contact the editor

EQUILIBRN

Description: equilibrn is an electronic forum for discussion of library issues of concern to librarians of color.
Subjects covered: library and information science; race relations
Net address for operations: listserv@fullerton.edu

Net address for questions or submissions: equilibrn@fullerton.edu
Editorial contact: Ron Rodriguez
Internet: rrodrqu@fullerton.edu
How to access: Send a messages to listserv@fullerton.edu and in the body of the message state: subscribe EQUILIBRN <your name>

EQUINE-D@PCCVM

Description: EQUINE-D@PCCVM is a Bitnet redistribution of the Usenet newsgroup rec.equestrian.digest on horses.
Subjects covered: zoology
List moderated: Yes.
Editorial contact: W. K. (Bill) Gorman
Internet: 34aej7d@cmuvm.csv.cmich.edu
Bitnet: 34aej7d@cmuvm
How to access: Send subscribe message to listserv@pccvm
How to unsubscribe: Send unsubscribe message to listserv@pccvm

EQUINE-L

Description: Equine-L is a forum centering on horses.
Subjects covered: zoology
List moderated: Yes.
Editorial contact: W. K. (Bill) Gorman
Internet: bj496@cleveland.freenet.edu
Bitnet: 34aej7d@cmuvm
Review: Reviewed by List Review Service edited by Raleigh Muns: see appendix.
How to access: Send subscribe message to listserv@pccvm
How to unsubscribe: Send unsubscribe message to listserv@pccvm

ERASMUS@VM.EPAS.UTORONTO.CA

Description: ERASMUS@VM.EPAS.UTORONTO.CA provides a forum for discussion of all aspects pertaining to the Renaissance and the Protestant Reformation.
Subjects covered: religion; art; history
List moderated: Yes.
Editorial contact: Prof. William Bowen
Internet: bowen@epas.utoronto.ca
How to access: Send subscribe message to BOWEN@VM.EPAS.UTORONTO.CA
How to unsubscribe: Send unsubscribe message to BOWEN@VM.EPAS.UTORONTO.CA

ERIC-L

Description: Eric-L covers the use of literature in education
Subjects covered: education; language and literature
List moderated: Yes.
Editorial contact: Edinfo Administrator
Bitnet: EDINFO@IUBVM
How to access: Send subscribe message to listserv@iubvm or listserv@iubvm.ucs.indiana.edu
How to unsubscribe: Send unsubscribe message to listserv@iubvm or listserv@iubvm.ucs.indiana.edu
Archives: Yes; Separate, Private

ERL-L

Description: ERL-L is a list on education research
Subjects covered: education
Net address for operations: listserv@asuacad.bitnet
How to access: Send standard subscribe request to listserv.
How to unsubscribe: Send standard unsubscribe request to listserv.

ERMIS

Description: ermis is a list covering topics of interest to people of Greek descent.
Subjects covered: Greek politics; Greek language and literature
Net address for operations: listserv@cs.bu.edu
Net address for questions or submissions: ermis@cs.bu.edu
Established: April 1989
Subscribers: 35
Sponsor: Boston University, 111 Cummington St., Boston MA 02215.
List moderated: No.
Moderation procedure: Only subscribers can submit to the list through electronic mail.
Editorial contact: Nicos Kontopoulos
15 North Beacon St., Apt. UL-04, Boston, MA 02134.
Tel: (617) 787-1780
Fax: (617) 787-1339
Internet: nicos@cs.bu.edu
Bitnet: nicos%cs@buacca
Technical contact: Anastasios Kotsikonas
Advanced Visual Systems, 300 Fifth Ave., Waltham, MA 02154.
Tel: (617) 890-4300 x2250
Fax: (617) 890-8287
Internet: tasos@cs.bu.edu
Bitnet: tasos%cs@buacca
How to access: Send electronic mail to listserv@cs.bu.edu with the request "subscribe ermis NAME_OF_SUBSCRIBER"
Access policy: Open, some discussion will be in Greek.
How to unsubscribe: Send electronic mail to listserv@cs.bu.edu with the request "unsubscribe ermis"
How to submit: Automatic, send submission through electronic mail to ermis@cs.bu.edu
Submission policy: Open to all subscribers of the list.
Archives: Available through the listserver; send electronic mail to listserv@cs.bu.edu with the requests "index" and then "get ARCHIVE_NAME FILE_NAME"
Related files: Listserver software available through ftp on cs.bu.edu, directory /pub/listserv

EROFILE@UCSBUXA

Description: EROFILE@UCSBUXA offers reviews of French and Italian literary works.
Subjects covered: French language and literature; Italian language and literature; literary theory and criticism
Host: Department of French and Italian, University of California, Santa Barbara
List moderated: Yes.
Editorial contact: Charles La Via and Jonathan Walsh
Internet: erofile@ucsbuxa.ucsb.edu
Bitnet: erofile@ucsbuxa
How to access: Send subscribe message to erofile@ucsbuxa or erofile@ucsbuxa.ucsb.edu

How to unsubscribe: Send unsubscribe message to erofile@ucsbuxa or erofile@ucsbuxa.ucsb.edu
Archives: Yes; apply to listowner for details.

ESE-L

Description: ESE-L is a discussion forum on the development of expert systems databases.
Subjects covered: computer science; artificial intelligence
List moderated: No.
Editorial contact: Sanjay Kapur
Bitnet: sk@sbccvm
How to access: Send subscribe message to listserv@sbccvm
How to unsubscribe: Send unsubscribe message to listserv@sbccvm
Archives: Archives are developed daily; apply to listowner for details.

ESPERANTO@RAND.ORG

Description: ESPERANTO@RAND.ORG is a forum covering Esperanto.
Subjects covered: language
List moderated: No.
Editorial contact: Mike Urban
Internet: esperanto-request@rand.org
How to access: Send subscribe message to ESPERANTO-REQUEST@RAND.ORG
How to unsubscribe: Send unsubscribe message to ESPERANTO-REQUEST@RAND.ORG

ESPORA-L

Description: Espora-L is a forum on the history of the Iberian Peninsula.
Subjects covered: history; Spain; Portugal
List moderated: Yes.
Editorial contact: Richard Clement
Bitnet: rclement@ukanvm
How to access: Send subscribe message to listserv@ukanvm or listserv@ukanvm.cc.ukans.edu
How to unsubscribe: Send unsubscribe message to listserv@ukanvm or listserv@ukanvm.cc.ukans.edu
Archives: Yes; Send anonymous FTP to: kuhub.cc.ukans.edu

ETEXTCTR@RUTVM1

Description: ETEXTCTR@RUTVM1 is an electronic discussion group on electronic text centers. It is a moderated list, meant to cover broad issues: budgets, acquisitions, cataloging, public services, management, training and staff development, etc., but to be focused initially on full-text files that are primarily monographic in nature rather than e-journals or numeric data files.
Subjects covered: electronic texts; Internet
Editorial contact: Annelies Hoogcarspel
Center for Electronic Texts in the Humanities, 169 College Avenue, New Brunswick, NJ 08903
Tel: (908) 932-1384
Fax: (908) 932-1386
Internet: hoogcarspel@zodiac.rutgers.edu
Bitnet: hoogcarspel@zodiac
How to access: Send a message to listserv@rutvm1 (bitnet address) OR listserv@rutvm1.rutgers.edu (internet address). Leave

the subject line blank, and send as the body of the message the following line: subscribe etextctr Firstname Lastname
How to submit: Send your postings to etextctr@rutvm1 (bitnet) OR etextctr@rutvm1.rutgers.edu

ETHCSE-L

Description: ETHCSE-L is a forum covering ethics issues in the software engineering community.
Subjects covered: ethics; engineering; computer software
List moderated: No.
Editorial contact: Don Gotterbarn
Internet: i01gbar@etsu
Bitnet: i01gbarn@etsu
How to access: Send subscribe message to listserv@utkvm1 or listserv@utkvm1.utk.edu
How to unsubscribe: Send unsubscribe message to listserv@utkvm1 or listserv@utkvm1.utk.edu

ETHICS-L

Description: Ethics-L is a forum on ethics in computing.
Subjects covered: ethics; philosophy; computer science
List moderated: No.
Editorial contact: Jane Robinett
Bitnet: jrobinet@polytech
How to access: Send subscribe message to listserv@twnmoe10
How to unsubscribe: Send unsubscribe message to listserv@twnmoe10
Archives: Archives are developed monthly; apply to listowner for details.

ETHMUS-L

Description: ETHMUS-L is a discussion list related to ethnomusicology and includes news, research, works-in-progress, dissertation abstracts, and country research reports.
Subjects covered: ethnomusicology; music
Net address for operations: LISTSERV@UMDD (Bitnet), LISTSERV@UMDD.UMD.EDU (Internet)
Established: December 10, 1989
Subscribers: 284
Sponsor: University of Maryland, College Park, Maryland 20742 U.S.A.
Host: Same as above
List moderated: Yes.
Editorial contact: Dr. Karl Signell
Center for Turkish Music, Music Department, University of Maryland, Baltimore County Baltimore, MD 21228
Tel: (410) 455-2489
Fax: (410) 455-1070
Internet: signell@umdd.umd.edu
Bitnet: signell@umdd
Technical contact: Ira Gold
Computer Science Center
University of Maryland College Park MD 20742 U.S.A.
Tel: (301) 405-3040
Internet: igold@umdd.umd.edu
Bitnet: igold@umdd
How to access: SUB ETHMUS-L <firstname lastname>sent to LISTSERV@UMDD or LISTSERV@UMDD.UMD.EDU SUB command gets application form. Potential subscriber fills in form, sends it to listowner, who screens for policy requirements.

Access policy: Restricted to those with a professional interest in ethnomusicology: scholars, teachers, librarians, graduate students, and scholars in related disciplines. Submission content must relate to ethnomusicology: news, research, works-in-progress, dissertation abstracts, country reports, etc.
How to unsubscribe: UNSUB ETHMUS-L sent to LISTSERV@UMDD or LISTSERV@UMDD.UMD.EDU
How to submit: Upload to ETHMUS-L@UMDD or ETHMUS-L@UMDD.UMD.EDU
Submission policy: Questions should be directed to signell@umdd.umd.edu
Archives: All past issues of Ethnomusicology Research Digest, major documents, databases, multimedia software, etc., are available from the listserv. Complete index of all archived materials: ARCHIVE INFO file. Subset list SEM-L for members in good standing of the Society for Ethnomusicology. Current Bibliography, SEM Newsletter, and other SEM materials accessible to SEM-L members.
Related files: All ETHMUS-L archived files except those with personal information and those restricted to SEM members, are available via telnet or FTP at inforM.umd.edu, /inforM/Educational-Resources/ReadingRoom/etc. When telnetting, select Search Files option from first menu, and enter ''ethnomusicology'' string (without quotes) to go directly to that directory.

ETHNO@RPITSVM

Description: Ethno@RPITSVM provides a forum for ethnomethodology and conversation analysis.
Subjects covered: anthropology
Host: Comserve
List moderated: No.
Editorial contact: Comserve Editorial Staff
Internet: support@vm.its.vpi.edu
Bitnet: support@rpitsvm
How to access: Send subscribe message to comserve@rpitsvm or comserve@vm.its.vpi.edu
How to unsubscribe: Send unsubscribe message to comserve@rpitsvm or comserve@vm.its.vpi.edu

ETHNOHIS@HEARN

Description: ETHNOHIS is a list covering ethnology and history.
Subjects covered: history; anthropology; ethnology
List moderated: No.
Editorial contact: Fred Melssen
Internet: u211610@hnykun11.urc.kun.nl
How to access: Send subscribe message to listserv@hearn or listserv@nic.surfnet.nl
How to unsubscribe: Send unsubscribe message to listserv@hearn or listserv@nic.surfnet.nl

ETHOLOGY@SEARN

Description: ETHOLOGY@SEARN is a forum on animal behavior.
Subjects covered: zoology
List moderated: No.
Editorial contact: Jarmo Saarikko
Internet: saarikko@finuh
Bitnet: saarikko@cc.helsinki.fi
How to access: Send subscribe message to listserv@searn or listserv@searn.sunet.se

How to unsubscribe: Send unsubscribe message to listserv@searn or listserv@searn.sunet.se
Archives: Yes; apply to listowner for details

EUEARN-L
Description: EUEARN-L is a list focusing on computer technology and telecommunications in Eastern Europe.
Subjects covered: telecommunications; Eastern Europe; computer hardware and software
Net address for operations: LISTSERV@UBVM
How to access: Send a standard subscribe request to the listserv.
How to unsubscribe: Send a standard unsubscribe request to the listserv.

EV@SJSUVM1.SJSU.EDU
Description: EV@SJSUVM1.SJSU.EDU is a forum on electric vehicles.
Subjects covered: science and technology
List moderated: No.
Editorial contact: Clyde R. Visser
Internet: cvisser@ucrmath.ucr.edu
How to access: Send subscribe message to listserv@sjsuvm1 or listserv@sjsuvm1.sjsu.edu
How to unsubscribe: Send unsubscribe message to listserv@sjsuvm1 or listserv@sjsuvm1.sjsu.edu
Archives: Archives are developed monthly; apply to listowner for details.

EWM@ICNUCEVM
Description: EWM@ICNUCEVM is a forum on European women in mathematics.
Subjects covered: mathematics
List moderated: No.
Editorial contact: Laura Tedeschini Lalli
Bitnet: laurated@itcaspur
How to access: Contact the Editor
How to unsubscribe: Contact the Editor

EXLIBRIS@RUTVM1.RUTGERS.EDU
Description: EXLIBRIS@ZODIAC.RUTGERS.EDU covers topics related to special library collections.
Subjects covered: library and information science; rare books
List moderated: No.
Editorial contact: Peter Graham
Internet: graham@rutvm1.rutgers.edu
How to access: Send subscribe message to EXLIBRIS-REQUEST@RUTVM1.RUTGERS.EDU
How to unsubscribe: Send unsubscribe message to EXLIBRIS-REQUEST@RUTVM1.RUTGERS.EDU

EXPRESS-USERS@CME.NIST.GOV
Description: EXPRESS-USERS is a forum on the EXPRESS information modeling language.
Subjects covered: computer science
List moderated: No.
Editorial contact: Steve Clark
Internet: express-users-request@cme.nist.gov
How to access: Send subscribe message to EXPRESS-USERS-REQUEST@CME.NIST.GOV
How to unsubscribe: Send unsubscribe message to EXPRESS-USERS-REQUEST@CME.NIST.GOV

EYEMOV-L
Description: Eyemov-L is a forum for the discussion of eye movement.
Subjects covered: medicine
List moderated: Yes.
Editorial contact: Dennis Carmody
Internet: carmody__d@spcvxa.spc.edu
Bitnet: carmody__d@spcvxa
How to access: Send subscribe message to eyemov-r@spcvxa or eyemov-r@spcvxa.spc.edu
How to unsubscribe: Send unsubscribe message to eyemov-r@spcvxa or eyemov-r@spcvxa.spc.edu
Archives: Archives are developed monthly; apply to listowner for details.

F-EMAIL
Description: F-EMAIL is for information and discussion on gender differences in use of computer communication, noting both a prevalent view that internetworking is a predominantly male domain, but also some suggestions that females may in fact be better suited to computer mediated communication (CMC).
Subjects covered: gender studies; communications; cultural studies; women's studies
Net address for operations: mailbase@mailbase.ac.uk
Net address for questions or submissions: f-email@mailbase.ac.uk
Established: June 1, 1993
Sponsor: Queen Margaret College,Clerwood Terrace, Edinburgh, ScotlandEH12 8TS.
Host: The NISP Project,Computing Service, The University,Newcastle upon Tyne, UK NE1 7RU.
List moderated: No.
Editorial contact: Chris Gunn
Dept Communication & Information Studies, Queen Margaret College,Clerwood Terrace, Edinburgh, ScotlandEH12 8TS.
Tel: (4431) 031 317 3000
Fax: (4431) 031 317 4156
Internet: cs0gunn@cis.qmced.ac.uk
Bitnet: chris__gunn@hicom.org
How to access: Send a message to: mailbase@mailbase.ac.uk Subj: <anything - gets ignored> ... with text: join f-email <firstname> <surname> eg: join f-email Chris Gunn
How to unsubscribe: Send a message to: mailbase@mailbase.ac.uk Subj: <anything - gets ignored>
How to submit: Send a message to: f-email@mailbase.ac.uk Subj: <as appropriate> <your message text>
Archives: Messages to the list are archived monthly and may be retrieved by e-mail. For an index of available e-mail archives (and other files associated with the F-EMAIL list ...)
Send a message to: mailbase@mailbase.ac.uk Subj: <anything - it gets ignored> ... with text: index f-email
To obtain a file in the filelist returned by the INDEX command ... Send a message to: mailbase@mailbase.ac.uk Subj:

<anything - it gets ignored> ... with text send f-email <name-of-file-wanted>

Related files: The Mailbase system on JANET, through which F-EMAIL is provided, is also an online service, and details of lists, archived e-mail, and files associated with lists, can be browsed interactively ... Telnet to:mailbase.ac.uk (or 128.240.2.118) Login as:guest Password:mailbase

Gopher accessibility: The Mailbase system now also has a Gopher interface ... Name = Mailbase Gopher Type = 1 Host = mailbase.ac.uk Port = 70 Path =

FACSER-L

Description: Facser-L is a discussion forum on topics related to facilities and services on college and university campuses.

Subjects covered: colleges and universities

List moderated: No.

Editorial contact: Kate Bingham

Bitnet: u42b5@wvnvm

How to access: Send subscribe message to listserv@wvnvm or listserv@wvnvm.wvnet.edu

How to unsubscribe: Send unsubscribe message to listserv@wvnvm or listserv@wvnvm.wvnet.edu

FACXCH-L

Description: Facxch-L is a forum for faculty members in art, design, and architecture.

Subjects covered: art; architecture

List moderated: No.

Editorial contact: Howard Ray Lawrence

Bitnet: hrl@psuarch

How to access: Send subscribe message to listserv@psuvm or listserv@psuvm.psu.edu

How to unsubscribe: Send unsubscribe message to listserv@psuvm or listserv@psuvm.psu.edu

Archives: Archives are developed monthly; apply to listowner for details.

FAMCOMM@RPIECS

Description: FAMCOMM@RPIECS is a discussion list on marital, family, and relational communications.

Subjects covered: gender studies; communications

How to access: Send message to COMSERVE@RPIECS.BITNET or COMSERVE@VM.ECS.RPI.EDU

FAMILY-L

Description: Family-L is a forum for the discussion of family medical practice.

Subjects covered: medicine; education

List moderated: No.

Editorial contact: Joe Stanford

Bitnet: fcmjoe@mizzou1l

How to access: Send subscribe message to listserv@mizzou1

How to unsubscribe: Send unsubscribe message to listserv@mizzou1

Archives: Archives are developed monthly; apply to listowner for details.

FAMLYSCI@UKCC

Description: FAMLYSCI@UKCC is a forum discussing the psychology of the family.

Subjects covered: psychology

Host: Department of Family Studies at the University of Kentucky

List moderated: No.

Editorial contact: Greg Brock

Internet: gwbrock@ukcc.uky.edu

Bitnet: gwbrock@ukcc

How to access: Send subscribe message to GWBROCK@UKCC.UKY.EDU

How to unsubscribe: Send unsubscribe message to GWBROCK@UKCC.UKY.EDU

Archives: Archives are developed weekly; apply to listowner for details.

FASE@CS.UH.EDU

Description: FASE the Forum for Academic Software Engineering covers software engineering instruction.

Subjects covered: computer science; engineering

List moderated: No.

How to access: Send subscribe message to fase@cs.uh.edu

How to unsubscribe: Send unsubscribe message to fase@cs.uh.edu

FASTBS-L

Description: FASTBS-L is a conference on the FASTBUS data bus system.

Subjects covered: computer science

List moderated: No.

Editorial contact: Robert G. Skegg

Internet: rosk@dave.triumf.ca

Bitnet: rosk@triumfcl

How to access: Send subscribe message to listserv@ualta vm or listserv@vm.ucs.ualberta.ca

How to unsubscribe: Send unsubscribe message to listserv@ualta vm or listserv@vm.ucs.ualberta.ca

FAU-L

Description: FAU-L is an unmoderated discussion list dealing with issues, concerns, and news related to Florida Atlantic University, its alumni, students, faculty, visitors, and friends. FAU is located in Boca Raton, Florida, halfway between the cities of West Palm Beach and Ft. Lauderdale, and two miles inland from the Atlantic shore. It is one of the state's nine public universities, and has both undergraduate and graduate programs in liberal arts & sciences, engineering, business, urban and regional planning, and education. The discussion list exists to facilitate the exchange of ideas, information, and experiences between its subscribership.

Subjects covered: Florida Atlantic University; colleges and universities; events listings

Net address for operations: Fau-Request@Acc.Fau.Edu

Net address for questions or submissions: Fau-L@Acc.Fau.Edu

Established: Late 1991

Subscribers: 202

Sponsor: Florida Atlantic University, 500 NorthWest 20th Street, Boca Raton, FL 33431-0991.

Host: Florida Atlantic University, 500 NorthWest 20th Street, Boca Raton, FL 33431-0991.
List moderated: No.
Editorial contact: M. Yasar Iscan
Dept of Anthropology, FAU, Boca Raton, FL 33431.
Tel: (407) 367-3230
Fax: (407) 367-2744
Internet: ISCAN@ACC.FAU.EDU
Bitnet: ISCAN@FAUVAX
Technical contact: Ralph P. Carpenter
Department of Psychology, Florida Atlantic University, Boca Raton, FL 33431-0991.
Tel: 407/367-2616
Fax: 407/367-2749
Internet: Ralpho@Acc.Fau.Edu
Bitnet: Ralpho@FauVax
How to access: Email to Fau-Request@Acc.Fau.Edu (BITNET-restricted users send to Fau-Request@FAUVAX). The sole content of the message BODY must be: Subscribe FAU-L John Q Public
Access policy: This discussion list is open to all interested individuals or organizations.
How to unsubscribe: From EXACTLY the same address from which the original subscription was requested, Email to Fau-Request@Acc.Fau.Edu (BITNET-restricted users send to Fau-Request@FauVax). The sole content of the message BODY must be: Unsubscribe FAU-L
How to submit: Email to Fau-L@Acc.Fau.Edu (BITNET-restricted users send to Fau-L@FauVax)

FAXONEDI

Description: FAXONEDI is intended as a forum for the implementation of standard Electronic Data Interchange among the Faxon Company, Faxon trading partners (client sites, suppliers, and financial institutions), and other involved parties (standards associations, value-added networks, etc.) As such, it primarily concerns the implementation of such messages as claims, responses, invoices, prices, and shipping information as ecoded according to the ANSIX12 standards.
Subjects covered: EDI (electronic data interchange); Faxon Company; library-vendor relations; computer hardware and software
Net address for operations: MAILSERV@FAXON.COM
Net address for questions or submissions: FAXONEDI@FAXON.COM
Established: 1993
Subscribers: 200
Sponsor: The FaxonCompany, 15 Southwest Park, Westwood, MA 02090.
Host: The Faxon Company, 15 Southwest Park, Westwood, MA 02090.
Commercial organization: Yes.
List moderated: Yes.
Moderation procedure: All messages are routed by the mail server to the moderator, who then either broadcasts the message, directly replies, or in turn routes the message to someone who can reply.
Editorial contact: Fritz Schwartz
The Faxon Company, 15 Southwest Park, Westwood, MA 02090.
Tel: 617-329-3350 (X334)
Fax: 617-329-9875
Internet: SCHWARTZ@FAXON.COM

Bitnet: SCHWARTZ@FAXON
Technical contact: Kathy Coghlan
The Faxon Company, 15 Southwest Park, Westwood, MA 02090.
Tel: 617-329-3350 (X739)
Fax: 617-329-9875
Internet: COGHLAN@FAXON.COM
Bitnet: COGHLAN@FAXON
How to access: Send the following message to MAILSERV@FAXON.COM: SUBSCRIBE FAXONEDI [SUBSCRIBER NAME]
Access policy: Subscription is limited to the membership described above and FAXON encourages all within that community to self-subscribe. However, subscribers should note that all not meeting those criteria will regularly be removed from the list.
How to unsubscribe: Send the following message to MAILSERV@FAXON.COM: UNSUBSCRIBE FAXONEDI [SUBSCRIBER NAME]
How to submit: Send any appropriate message to FAXONEDI@FAXON.COM
Submission policy: All questions, comments, and general information on the implementation of EDI among Faxon and trading partners is welcome.

FEDSIG-L

Description: Fedsig-L is a list centering on discussion of Federal electronic information.
Subjects covered: library and information science; government information
List moderated: No.
Editorial contact: Richard S. Little
Bitnet: un072147@wvnvms
How to access: Send subscribe message to listserv@wvnvm or listserv@wvnvm.wvnet.edu
How to unsubscribe: Send unsubscribe message to listserv@wvnvm or listserv@wvnvm.wvnet.edu

FEDTAX-L

Description: FEDTAX-L is a public forum discussing Federal tax legislation. It is not a US government sponsored list.
Subjects covered: taxes; government information
Net address for operations: LISTSERV@SHSU.EDU
Host: Sam Houston State University
How to access: Send an email message with a blank subject line to LISTSERV@SHSU.EDU. The message should consist solely of the line: SUBSCRIBE FEDTAX-L your__name.

FEMAIL

Description: FEMAIL is a moderated discussion list on topics related to feminism around the world. The list is open to both men and women.
Subjects covered: gender studies; feminism; women's studies
Net address for operations: FEMAIL-REQUEST@LUCERNE.ENG.SUN.COM
List moderated: Yes.
How to access: Send subscription requests to FEMAIL-REQUEST@LUCERNE.ENG.SUN.COM

FEMECON-L

Description: FEMECON-L is an electronic discussion group for feminist economists.
Subjects covered: economics; feminism; women's studies
Net address for operations: LISTSERV@BUCKNELL.EDU
List moderated: Yes.
How to access: Send subscription messages to LISTSERV@BUCKNELL.EDU

FEMINISM-DIGEST

Description: FEMINISM-DIGEST is a digest of the Usenet newsgroup soc.feminism.
Subjects covered: gender studies; feminism; women's studies
Net address for operations: FEMINISM-DIGEST@NCAR.UCAR.EDU, FEMINISM-DIGEST%NCAR.UCAR.EDU@NCARIO
List moderated: No.
How to access: Send a request to FEMINISM-DIGEST@NCAR.UCAR.EDU (Internet) or FEMINISM-DIGEST%NCAR.UCAR.EDU@NCARIO (Bitnet).
How to submit: Recipients of FEMINISM-DIGEST can respond to postings by sending messages to FEMINISM@NCAR.UCAR.EDU (Internet) or FEMINISM%NCAR.UCAR.EDU@NCARIO (Bitnet).

FEMINIST

Description: feminist is a discussion list covering informatoin on women and libraries, announcements of Feminist Task Force activities, discussion of feminism and librarianship, feminism in the workplace, etc.
Subjects covered: feminist; library and information science; workplace studies
Net address for operations: listserv@mitvma.mit.edu
Net address for questions or submissions: feminist@mitvma.mit.edu
Established: Fall 1991
Subscribers: 405
Sponsor: American Library Association, Social Responsibilities RoundTable, Feminist Task Force. Coordinator, Theresa A. Tobin, MIT Humanities Library, Room 14S-226, Cambridge, MA 02139.
Host: MIT, Cambridge, MA 02139.
List moderated: No.
Editorial contact: Theresa A. Tobin
MIT Humanities Library, 14S-226, Cambridge, MA 02139.
Tel: (617) 253-5674
Fax: (617) 253-3109
Internet: tat@athena.mit.edu
How to access: Send this message: subscribe feminist your full name to: listserv@mitvma.mit.edu
Access policy: All are welcome to participate in this list.
How to unsubscribe: Send this message: unsubscribe feminist to: listserv@mitvma.mit.edu
How to submit: feminist@mitvma.mit.edu
Submission policy: There are no formal restrictions; a welcome letter is sent out upon subscribing which describes typical discussion topics to date.

FEMISA

Description: FEMISA is a disussion list for issues surrounding feminism, gender, women and international politics, etc.

Subjects covered: gender studies; feminism; women's studies; political science
Net address for operations: LISTSERV@CSF.COLORADO.EDU
List moderated: No.
How to access: Send subscription requests to COMSERVE@RPITSVM (Bitnet) or COMSERVE@VM.ITS.RPI.EDU (Internet).

FEMREL-L

Description: FEMREL-L focuses on women and religion and on feminist theology.
Subjects covered: religion; feminism; women's studies
Net address for operations: LISTSERV@MIZZOU1
List moderated: No.
How to access: Send subscription messages to LISTSERV@MIZZOU1

FET-NET@HEARN

Description: FET-NET@HEARN is a conference providing discourse on research of fetal/perinatal physiology.
Subjects covered: medicine
List moderated: No.
Editorial contact: Bouke Woudstra or Jan Aarnoudse
Bitnet: xpvkbouke@rug.nl
How to access: Send subscribe message to listserv@hearn
How to unsubscribe: Send unsubscribe message to listserv@hearn
Archives: Archives are developed monthly; apply to listowner for details.

FEUSERS

Description: FEUSERS is a mailbase-list serving the researchers, teachers, and groups active in using and developing FINITE ELEMENTS and FINITE DIFFERENCE software. Code developers and vendors of finite element and finite difference packages are particularly encouraged to be involved in FEUSERS. Users and developers of graphical pre- and post-processing systems (with solid modelling) and CAD/CAM interfaces for finite elements and finite difference applications software are also encouraged to participate. Industries and industrial participants with a solutions approach would be highly appreciated in this forum. The FEUSERS forum aims to encourage discussion and free exchange of ideas amongst the members of the list. As a list member, you are free to raise a topic and express your views on it, invite other views and even summarise them. You can also respond to a topic currently in discussion. All postings to the group are distributed to all the list-members, and the list will not initially be moderated. Discussion topics on finite element and finite difference applications areas such as structural and mechanical engineering analysis and design, aerospace engineering, electronics and electrical engineering, computational fluid dynamics, heat and thermal analysis, impact analysis, chemical engineering, nuclear and solid state physics, etc. are highly desirable. Specific suggestions and questions on various packages (e.g. ideas, patran, abaqus, nastran, lusas, emas, fidap, phoenics, etc) could be beneficial for many finite element and finite difference users and developers.
Subjects covered: mathematics; engineering; computer hardware and software
Net address for operations: mailbase@mailbase.ac.uk

Net address for questions or submissions:
feusers@mailbase.ac.uk
Established: May 15, 1993
Subscribers: 128
Host: The JNT Networked Information Services Project, The Computing Service, University of Newcastle upon Tyne, Newcastle upon Tyne, UK.
List moderated: No.
Editorial contact: Minaz Punjani
Engineering Computing, University of London Computer Centre, 20 Guilford Street, London WC1N 1DZ UK.
Tel: [+44] 071 405 8400
Fax: [+44] 71 242 1845
Internet: m.punjani@ulcc.ac.uk or m.punjani@uk.ac.ulcc (janet)
Copyright statement: Copyright (c) 1993, feusers@mailbase.ac.uk
How to access: Send message to mailbase@mailbase.ac.uk: JOIN feusers <YOUR__Firstname> <Your__Surname>
How to unsubscribe: Send message to mailbase@mailbase.ac.uk: LEAVE feusers <YOUR__ Firstname> <Your__Surname>
How to submit: Send e-mail to feusers@mailbase.ac.uk
Archives: Archives are available; apply to listowner.
Related files: Files are available through ftp; apply to listowner.

FICINO
Description: FICINO is a discussion forum posting notices, queries, and information covering all aspects of the field of Renaissance and Reformation Studies.
Subjects covered: Renaissance studies; Reformation studies; religion; philosophy
Net address for operations: Editor@epas.utoronto.ca
Net address for questions or submissions:
listserv@vm.utcc.utoronto.ca
Established: September 28, 1990
Subscribers: 185
Sponsor: Centre for Reformation and Renaissance Studies, Victoria University in the University of Toronto, Toronto, Ontario, Canada.
Host: University of Toronto, Computing Services (Victoria University is a federated institution of the University of Toronto).
List moderated: No, but subscribers must submit a biography before being added to the list.
Moderation procedure: All initial requests should be sent to Editor@epas.utoronto.ca A biography will be requested. When it is returned, subscriber will be added to the list.
Editorial contact: Germaine Warkentin
English Section, Victoria College, University of Toronto, Toronto M5S 1K7 Canada
Tel: (416) 585-4483
Fax: (416) 585-4584
Internet: warkent@epas.utoronto.ca
How to access: Send a message to Editor@epas.utoronto.ca
How to unsubscribe: Send a message to Editor@epas.utoronto.ca
How to submit: Send a message to Editor@epas.utoronto.ca
Archives: Archives are available; apply to listowner.
Additional information: Second editor: William Bowen, Humanities (Music,) Scarborough College, University of Toronto: (416) 287-7194; bowen@epas.utoronto.ca

FICTION-WRITERS%STUDGUPPY@LANL.GOV
Description: FICTION-WRITERS is a forum covering fiction writing.
Subjects covered: writing
List moderated: No.
Editorial contact: Doug Roberts
Internet: roberts%studguppy@lanl.gov
How to access: Send subscribe message to WRITERS-REQUEST%STUDGUPPY@LANL.GOV
How to unsubscribe: Send unsubscribe message to WRITERS-REQUEST%STUDGUPPY@LANL.GOV

FILM-L
Description: Film-L is a forum for the discussion of cinema.
Subjects covered: theater; cinema studies
List moderated: No.
Editorial contact: Alejandro S. Kurczyn
Internet: 499229%vmtecmex.bitnet@vm1.nodak.edu
Bitnet: 499229@vmtecmex
How to access: Send subscribe message to listserv@vmtecmex
How to unsubscribe: Send unsubscribe message to listserv@vmtecmex

FILMMAKERS
Description: The Filmmakers mailing list is a technical discussion forum for filmmakers. Discussions primarily revolve around technical issues dealing with 16mm production work, although other subjects are welcome. Video is not covered.
Subjects covered: filmmaking
Net address for operations: filmmakers-request@grissom.larc.nasa.gov
Net address for questions or submissions:
filmmakers@grissom.larc.nasa.gov
Established: 1986
Subscribers: 106
Host: NASA/Langley Research Center
List moderated: No.
Editorial contact: Scott Dorsey
217 Thomas Nelson ln., Williamsburg, VA 23185
Internet: kludge@grissom.larc.nasa.gov
How to access: Send mail to the request address.
Access policy: Be a nice person with an interest in film work.
How to unsubscribe: Send mail to the request address.
How to submit: Send mail to the network address.
Submission policy: Have something relevant to film work.

FINAID-L
Description: Finaid-L is a forum discussing topics related to student finacial aid.
Subjects covered: colleges and universities
List moderated: Yes.
Editorial contact: Robert E.Quinn
Bitnet: req1@psuadmin
How to access: Send subscribe message to listserv@psuvm or listserv@psuvm.psu.edu
How to unsubscribe: Send unsubscribe message to listserv@psuvm or listserv@psuvm.psu.edu
Archives: Yes.

FINEART@RUTVM1

Description: FINEART@RUTVM1 is a forum whose goal is to promote communication among artists and scientists internationally.

Subjects covered: art; computer science; science and technology; fine arts

Host: Society for the Arts, Science, and Technology (ISAST)

List moderated: No.

Editorial contact: Ray Lauzzana

Tel: (413) 545-1902

Internet: lauzzana%ecs.umass.edu@relay.cs.net

How to access: Send subscribe message to listserv@rutvm1 or listserv@rutgers.edu

How to unsubscribe: Send unsubscribe message to listserv@rutvm1 or listserv@rutgers.edu

FIREARMS0POLITICS@CS.CMU.EDU

Description: FIREARMS0POLITICS@CS.CMU.EDU is a forum for discussion of gun legislation.

Subjects covered: government information; activism; firearms

List moderated: No.

Editorial contact: Karl Kleinpaste

Internet: karl_kleinpaste@n2.sp.cs.cmu.edu

How to access: Send subscribe message to FIREARMS-POLITICS-REQUEST@CS.CMU.EDU

How to unsubscribe: Send unsubscribe message to FIREARMS-POLITICS-REQUEST@CS.CMU.EDU

Archives: Yes; Send anonymous FTP to: archive.cis.ohio-state.edu and cd pub/firearms

FIREWALLS@GREATCIRCLE.COM

Description: FIREWALLS is a forum covering Internet security systems.

Subjects covered: Internet; computer privacy

List moderated: No.

Editorial contact: Brent Chapman

Internet: brent@greatcircle.com

How to access: Send subscribe message to Majordomo@GreatCircle.com with "subscribe firewalls" in the body

How to unsubscribe: Send unsubscribe message to Majordomo@GreatCircle.com

FIRSTSEARCH-L

Description: Firstsearch-L is a discussion list carrying machine-readable news articles and information of interest to users of OCLC's FirstSearch Catalog.

Subjects covered: OCLC; FirstSearch Catalog; library and information science; computer hardware and software

Net address for operations: listserv@oclc.org

Net address for questions or submissions: For disssemination of information only; submissions are not accepted.

Established: November 1992

Subscribers: 183

Host: OCLC, Inc., 6565 Frantz Road, Dublin, OH 43017 (614) 764-6000 (tel); (614) 764-6096 (fax).

List moderated: Yes.

Moderation procedure: Submissions from subscribers are not redistributed to the list.

Editorial contact: Ken Thomas
OCLC, Inc., 6565 Frantz Road, Dublin, OH 43017.

Tel: (614) 761-5016

Fax: (614) 761-5047

Internet: ken_thomas@oclc.org

Technical contact: Laura Toms
OCLC, Inc., 6565 Frantz Road, Dublin, OH 43017.

Tel: (614) 761-5016

Fax: (614) 761-5047

Internet: ltoms@oclc.org

How to access: Send a message to listserv@oclc,org and include the following string in the message body: subscribe firstsearch-1 Your Name replacing "Your Name" with the subscriber's name.

Access policy: Anyone may subscribe; no approval is required.

How to unsubscribe: Send a message to listserv@oclc.org and include the following string in the message body: unsubscribe firstsearch-1

How to submit: Submissions are ignored and are not redistributed to the list.

Archives: Database descriptions (ASCII files).

Additional information: Second technical contact: George Pallas, OCLC, Inc., 6565 Frantz Road, Dublin, OH 43017. tel (614) 764-6301 Fax (614) 761-5047. List service provided by UNIX-LISTSERVER version 5.5.

FISC-L

Description: Fisc-L is discussion list on fee-based information centers.

Subjects covered: library and information science

Host: American Library Association

List moderated: Yes.

Editorial contact: Diane Richards

Internet: nu146901@vm1.nodak.edu

How to access: Send subscribe message to listserv@ndsuvm1 or listserv@vm1.nodak.edu

How to unsubscribe: Send unsubscribe message to listserv@ndsuvm1 or listserv@vm1.nodak.edu

Archives: Archives are developed monthly; apply to listowner for details.

FISICA-L

Description: Fisica-L is a list for the exchange of physics data.

Subjects covered: physics

List moderated: No.

Editorial contact: Miguel Tostes Ribeiro

Internet: migueltr@brufmg.anmg.br

Bitnet: migueltr@brufmg

How to access: Send subscribe message to listserv@brufmg or listserv@brufmg.anmg.br

How to unsubscribe: Send unsubscribe message to listserv@brufmg or listserv@brufmg.anmg.br

Archives: Archives are developed monthly; apply to listowner for details.

FIST

Description: FIST (Feminism in/and Science and Technology) is an unmoderated list for discussion of feminism and science and technology.

Subjects covered: science and technology; feminism; women's studies

Net address for operations:
LISTSERV@DAWN.HAMPSHIRE.EDU

List moderated: No.
How to access: Send subscription messages to
LISTSERV@DAWN.HAMPSHIRE.EDU

FKFIC-L
Description: FKFIC-L was created for those who wanted to post stories based on the television show Forever Knight. The television show is centered around the life of an 800-year-old vampire who lives in Toronto and works as a homocide detective to 'pay back society' for the evil he's done in the past. The show itself is based on a TV-pilot by the name of Nick Knight, starring Rick Springfield, although the series stars Welsh-born Geraint Wyn Davies as the enigmatic vampire.
Subjects covered: Forever Knight; television; writing
Net address for operations: LISTSERV@psuvm.psu.edu
Net address for questions or submissions: FKFIC-L@psuvm.psu.edu
Established: December 1992
Subscribers: 129
Host: Center for Academic Computing, Pennsylvania State University, 134 Computer Building, University Park, PA 16802.
List moderated: No.
Editorial contact: Jean Prior
RD 2 Box 630, Port Matilda, PA 16870.
Tel: (814) 692 - 4846
Internet: jap8@psuvm.psu.edu
Bitnet: jap8@psuvm
Technical contact: William Verity
215A Computer Bldg., University Park, PA 16802.
Tel: (814) 865 - 4758
Internet: whv@psuvm.psu.edu
Bitnet: whv@psuvm
How to access: Send mail to listserv@psuvm.psu.edu with SUB FKFIC-L user's name in the body of the mail.
How to unsubscribe: Send mail to listserv@psuvm.psu.edu with UNSUB FKFIC-L user's name in the body of the mail.
How to submit: Send mail to FKFIC-L@psuvm.psu.edu
Submission policy: Members are requested to keep their posts relevant to the lists' topics, but no action is taken unless this request is flagrantly violated.

FLAIRS@UCF1VM
Description: FLAIRS is a discussion list of the Florida Artificial Intelligence Research Symposium.
Subjects covered: computer science; artificial intelligence
List moderated: No.
Bitnet: ucfown@ucf1vm
How to access: Send subscribe message to listserv@ucf1vm or listserv%ucf1vm.bitnet@cunyvm.cuny.edu
How to unsubscribe: Send unsubscribe message to listserv@ucf1vm or listserv%ucf1vm.bitnet@cunyvm.cuny.edu
Archives: Archives are developed monthly; apply to listowner for details.

FLEXWORK@PSUHMC
Description: FLEXWORK@PSUHMC is a forum discussion on the topic of flexible work environments.
Subjects covered: business
List moderated: No.
Editorial contact: Maria Holcomb
Bitnet: mholcomb@psuhmc

How to access: Send subscribe message to listserv@psuhmc
How to unsubscribe: Send unsubscribe message to listserv@psuhmc
Archives: Archives are developed monthly; apply to listowner for details.

FNORD-L
Description: Fnord-L is a forum for discussion of philosphical topics.
Subjects covered: philosophy
List moderated: No.
Editorial contact: Patrick G. Salsbury
Internet: salsbury@acsu.buffalo.edu
How to access: Send subscribe message to listserv@ubvm or listserv@ubvm.cc.buffalo.edu
How to unsubscribe: Send unsubscribe message to listserv@ubvm or listserv@ubvm.cc.buffalo.edu
Archives: Archives are developed weekly; apply to listowner for details.

FOLKLORE@TAMVM1
Description: Folklore@TAMVM1 is a forum for discussion of topics in folklore.
Subjects covered: folklore
List moderated: No.
Editorial contact: Mark Glaser
Bitnet: mg6be8@panami
How to access: Send subscribe message to listserv@tamvm1 or listserv@tamvm1.tamu.edu
How to unsubscribe: Send unsubscribe message to listserv@tamvm1 or listserv@tamvm1.tamu.edu
Archives: Archives are developed monthly; apply to listowner for details.

FOLK—MUSIC@NYSERNET.ORG
Description: FOLK—MUSIC@NYSERNET.ORG is a forum for listing information on the folk music scene.
Subjects covered: music
List moderated: No.
Editorial contact: Alan Rowoth
Internet: alan@lpl.org
How to access: Send subscribe message to sub—folk@lpl.org
How to unsubscribe: Send unsubscribe message to sub—folk@lpl.org
Archives: Yes; send anonymous FTP to nysernet.org and cd FOLK—MUSIC

FOLLAC
Description: FOLLAC is devoted to the folklore, traditional and expressive culture of Latinos, Latin Americans and people from the Caribbean. The list owner is convener of a section of the American Folklore Society called FOLLAC (Folklore Latino, Latinoamericano y Caribeno), and many of the list members are also members of that society.
Subjects covered: folklore; anthropology; Latin America; Caribbean
Net address for operations: OWNER-FOLLAC@CCWF.CC.UTEXAS.EDU
Net address for questions or submissions: FOLLAC@CCWF.CC.UTEXAS.EDU

Established: March 1993
Subscribers: 98
Sponsor: Folklore Latino, Latinoamericano y Caribeno, American Folklore Society
Host: University of Texas
List moderated: No.
Editorial contact: Emily Socolov
1505 Rabb Road, Austin, TX 78704.
Tel: (512) 444-3990
Fax: (512) 471-6535
Internet: SOCOLOV@CCWF.CC.UTEXAS.EDU
Technical contact: Johan Van Zanten
Tel: (512) 471-0251
Fax: (512) 471-1582
Internet: johan@ccwf.cc.utexas.edu
Review: A forthcoming review is to appear in the Bytelore Column of the American Folklore Society's Newsletter.
How to access: Send message to OWNER-FOL-LAC@CCWF.CC.UTEXAS.EDU
How to unsubscribe: Send message to OWNER-FOLLAC@CCWF.CC.UTEXAS.EDU
How to submit: Send message to FOL-LAC@CCWF.CC.UTEXAS.EDU
Gopher accessibility: Files accesible via Gopher.

FOODWINE

Description: FOODWINE is an academic and interdisciplinary forum for the discussion of food and beverages.
Subjects covered: food science
Net address for operations:
LISTSERV@CMUVM.CSV.CMICH.EDU
Net address for questions or submissions:
FOODWINE@CMUVM.CSV.CMICH.EDU
Established: October 1992
Subscribers: 310
Sponsor: Central Michigan University, Mt. Pleasant, MI 48859.
Host: Central Michigan University
List moderated: No.
Editorial contact: Musa Knickerbocker
Registrar's Office, Journalism Dept., Central Michigan Univeristy, Mt. Pleasant, MI 48859.
Tel: (517) 774-7228 or (517) 774-3196
Internet: 32HYFEV@CMUVM.CSV.CMICH.EDU
How to access: Email to
LISTSERV@CMUVM.CSV.CMICH.EDU with the message
SUB FOODWINE <real_name>
Access policy: List is open to anyone.
How to unsubscribe: Email to
LISTSERV@CMUVM.CSV.CMICH.EDU with the message
SIGNOFF FOODWINE
How to submit: FOODWINE@CMUVM.CSV.CMICH.EDU
Archives: Full archives are available. Apply to listowner for details.
Additional information: Co-editor: Elliott Parker, Registrar's Office, Journalism Dept., Central Michigan U. Mt. Pleasant, MI 48859; tel.: (517) 774-7228 or (517) 774-3196; Internet:3ZLUFUR@CMUVM.CSV.CMICH.EDU; Bitnet: 3ZLUFUR@CMUVM

FORENS-L

Description: The Forensic Medicine and Sciences Interest Group Discussion List Forens-L is an unmoderated discussion list dealing with forensic aspects of anthropology, biology, chemistry, odontology, pathology, psychology, serology, toxicology, criminalistics, and expert witnessing and presentation of evidence in court. Membership to this discussion list is open free of charge to all interested individuals or organizations.
Subjects covered: forensic medicine; science and technology; medicine
Net address for operations: Forens-Request@Acc.Fau.Edu
Net address for questions or submissions: Forens-L@Acc.Fau.Edu
Established: 3rd quarter 1991
Subscribers: 195
Sponsor: Florida Atlantic University, 500 NorthWest 20th Street, Boca Raton, FL 33431-0991.
Host: Florida Atlantic University, 500 NorthWest 20th Street, Boca Raton, FL 33431-0991.
List moderated: No.
Editorial contact: M. Yasar Iscan
Dept of Anthropology, FAU, Boca Raton, FL 33431.
Tel: 407-367-3230
Fax: 407-367-2744
Internet: ISCAN@ACC.FAU.EDU
Bitnet: ISCAN@FAUVAX
Technical contact: Ralph P Carpenter
Department of Psychology, Florida Atlantic University, Boca Raton, FL 33431-0991.
Tel: (407) 367-2616
Fax: (407) 367-2749
Internet: Ralpho@Acc.Fau.Edu
Bitnet: Ralpho@FauVax
How to access: Email to Forens-Request@Acc.Fau.Edu (BITNET-restricted users send to Forens-Request@FAUVAX) The sole content of the message BODY must be: Subscribe Forens-L John Q Public
Access policy: This discussion list is open to all interested individuals or organizations.
How to unsubscribe: From EXACTLY the same address from which the original subscription was requested,
Email to Forens-Request@Acc.Fau.Edu (BITNET-restricted users send to Forens-Request@FauVax) The sole content of the message BODY must be: Unsubscribe Forens-L

FORKNI-L

Description: FORKNI-L is a discussion list posting messages relating to the television program, Forever Knight. The television show is centered around the life of an 800-year-old vampire who lives in Toronto and works as a homocide detective to 'pay back society' for the evil he's done in the past. The show itself is based on a TV-pilot by the name of Nick Knight, starring Rick Springfield, although the series stars Welsh-born Geraint Wyn Davies as the enigmatic vampire.
Subjects covered: Forever Knight; television; writing
Net address for operations: LISTSERV@psuvm.psu.edu
Net address for questions or submissions: FORKNI-L@psuvm.psu.edu
Established: December 1992
Subscribers: 129
Host: Center for Academic Computing, Pennsylvania State University, 134 Computer Building, University Park, PA 16802.
List moderated: No.
Editorial contact: Jean Prior
RD 2 Box 630, Port Matilda, PA 16870.
Tel: (814) 692 - 4846

Internet: jap8@psuvm.psu.edu
Bitnet: jap8@psuvm
Technical contact: William Verity
215A Computer Bldg., University Park, PA 16802.
Tel: (814) 865 - 4758
Internet: whv@psuvm.psu.edu
Bitnet: whv@psuvm
How to access: Send mail to listserv@psuvm.psu.edu with SUB FORKNI-L user's name in the body of the mail.
How to unsubscribe: Send mail to listserv@psuvm.psu.edu with UNSUB FORKNI-L user's name in the body of the mail.
How to submit: Send mail to FORKNI-L@psuvm.psu.edu
Submission policy: Members are requested to keep their posts relevant to the lists' topics, but no action is taken unless this request is flagrantly violated.

FORUMBIO@BNANDP11

Description: FORUMBIO@BNANDP11 is a forum on molecular biology.
Subjects covered: biology; biochemistry; biophysics
Host: Unite d'Informatique Scientifique, Institut Oasteur Foundation, Paris, France
List moderated: No.
Editorial contact: Bruno Durasse
Bitnet: durasse@bnandp11
How to access: Send subscribe message to listserv@bnandp11
How to unsubscribe: Send unsubscribe message to listserv@bnandp11
Archives: Archives are developed monthly; apply to listowner for details.

FRAC-L

Description: FRAC-L is a forum for discussion of fractals and chaos; computer programs; applications in multiple disciplines, including art, engineering, music, and social disciplines.
Subjects covered: fractals; computer hardware and software; computer science; chaos theory
Net address for operations: LISTSERV@GITVM1
Net address for questions or submissions: FRAC-L@GITVM1 or FRAC-L@GITVM1.GATECH.EDU
Established: 1988
Subscribers: 604
Sponsor: Georgia Institute of Technology, Atlanta, GA.
Host: Georgia Institute of Technology, Atlanta, GA.
List moderated: No.
Editorial contact: Ermel Stepp
Marshall University
Tel: (304) 696-2949
Fax: (304) 696-6565
Internet: ESTEPP@WVNVM.WVNET.EDU
Bitnet: ESTEPP@WVNVM
How to access: Send email to LISTSERV@GITVM1 or LISTSERV@GITVM1.GATECH.EDU with the sole line of text: subscribe FRAC-L Your-Full-Name Your-Full-Name is your real name.
Access policy: List is open to anyone.
How to unsubscribe: Send email to LISTSERV@GITVM1 or LISTSERV@GITVM1.GATECH.EDU with the sole line of text: signoff FRAC-L Your-Full-Name
How to submit: Send email message to FRAC-L@GITVM1 or FRAC-L@GITVM1.GATECH.EDU

Archives: Related files and logs are available from LISTSERV@GITVM1 or LISTSERV@GITVM1.GATECH.EDU. To get index send email to LISTSERV@GITVM1 or LISTSERV@GITVM1.GATECH.EDU with the sole line of text: INDEX FRAC-L.
Related files: Host byrd.mu.wvnet.edu, login anonymous, password: user's email address, cd /pub/estepp/fracha. Usenet accessibility: bit.listserver.frac-l and sci.fractals

FRALL-L

Description: Frall-L is a list covering funding resources.
Subjects covered: colleges and universities
List moderated: Yes.
Editorial contact: Cody R. Nivens
Bitnet: 9531nive@ucsbvm
How to access: Send subscribe message to listserv@uscbvm
How to unsubscribe: Send unsubscribe message to listserv@uscbvm
Archives: Archives are developed monthly; apply to listowner for details.

FRANCEHS@UWAVM

Description: FranceHS@UWAVM is a discussion list centering on topics in French history.
Subjects covered: French language and literature; history; France
Net address for operations: listserv@UWAVM
Net address for questions or submissions: FranceHS@UWAVM
How to access: Send message to listserv: SUBSCRIBE <listname> <your name>

FREE-L

Description: FREE-L is an electronic forum for discussion of parental rights issues.
Subjects covered: family studies; parenting; parents' rights
Net address for operations: listserv@iupui.edu or listserv@indycms.iupui.edu
Editorial contact: Aaron L. Hoffmeyer
Internet: tr@cbnea.att.com
How to access: Send standard email request to listserv
How to unsubscribe: Send standard email request to listserv

FUNDLIST@JHUVM

Description: FUNDLIST covers academic fund raising programs.
Subjects covered: colleges and universities
List moderated: No.
Internet: jwm@jhudev.dev.jhu.dev
Bitnet: ecf-gjwm@jhuvms
How to access: Send subscribe message to listserv@jhuvm
How to unsubscribe: Send unsubscribe message to listserv@jhuvm
Archives: Archives are developed monthly; apply to listowner for details.

FUSION

Description: fusion is an email-distributed version of the Usenet newsgroup sci.physics.fusion.
Subjects covered: cold fusion; nuclear science; physics; science and technology
Net address for operations: fusion-request@zorch.sf-bay.org
Net address for questions or submissions: fusion@zorch.sf-bay.org
Established: April 1989
Subscribers: 140
List moderated: No.
Editorial contact: Scott Hazen Mueller
4108 Killigrew Drive
Tel: (209) 545-9417
Internet: scott@zorch.sf-bay.org
How to access: Send mail to fusion-request@zorch.sf-bay.org
How to unsubscribe: Send mail to fusion-request@zorch.sf-bay.org
How to submit: Send mail to fusion-request@zorch.sf-bay.org
Archives: fusion is archived at vm1.nodak.edu

FUTURE-L

Description: Future-L is a list covering future studies.
Subjects covered: futurism
Host: EDUCOM
List moderated: No.
Bitnet: LISTMGR@BITNIC
How to access: Send subscribe message to listserv@bitnic or listserv@bitnic.educom.edu
How to unsubscribe: Send unsubscribe message to listserv@bitnic or listserv@bitnic.educom.edu
Archives: Archives are developed monthly; apply to listowner for details.

FUTURE@NYX.CS.DU.EDU

Description: FUTURE@NYX.CS.DU.EDU is a forum on cyberculture/technoculture.
Subjects covered: science and technology; futurism; popular culture
List moderated: No.
Editorial contact: Andy Hawks
Internet: ahawks@nyx.cs.du.edu or ahawks@mindvox.phantom.com
How to access: Send subscribe message to FUTURE-REQUEST@NYX.CS.DU.EDU
How to unsubscribe: Send unsubscribe message to FUTURE-REQUEST@NYX.CS.DU.EDU
Archives: Yes; Send message to: FUTURE-REQUEST@NYX.CS.DU.EDU

FUZZY-MAIL

Description: FUZZy-MAIL is the Technical University of Vienna's fuzzy logic mailing list.
Subjects covered: fuzzy logic; artificial intelligence; computer science
Net address for questions or submissions: fuzzy-mail@vexpert.dbai.tuwien.ac.at
How to access: Send the following command to listserv@vexpert.dbai.tuwien.ac.at:
SUB FUZZY-MAIL your__full__name where ''your__full__name'' is your real name, not your login Id.

FWAKE-L

Description: FWAKE-L is a list covering the works of James Joyce and specifically Finnegan's Wake.
Subjects covered: Joyce, James; language and literature; Irish language and literature
Net address for operations: LISTSERV@IRLEARN.UCD.IE
Net address for questions or submissions: LISTSERV@IRLEARN.UCD.IE
Established: 1989
Subscribers: 138
Sponsor: University College Dublin, Belfield, Dublin 4, Ireland.
List moderated: No.
Editorial contact: Michael O'Kelly
5, Walker's Cottages, Dublin 6, Ireland.
Tel: Dublin 966985
Internet: MOKELLY@IRLEARN.UCD.IE
Review: Reviewed by List Review Service edited by Raleigh Muns: see appendix.
How to access: TELL LISTSERV@IRLEARN.UCD.IE SUBSCRIBE FWAKE-L
How to unsubscribe: TELL LISTSERV@IRLEARN.UCD.IE UNSUBSCRIBE FW
How to submit: MAIL FWAKE-L

FWAKEN-L

Description: FWAKEN-L is a list posting annotations to Finnegan's Wake by Irish author James Joyce.
Subjects covered: Joyce, James; language and literature; Irish language and literature
Net address for operations: LISTSERV@IRLEARN.UCD.IE
Net address for questions or submissions: LISTSERV@IRLEARN.UCD.IE
Established: 1989
Subscribers: 13
Sponsor: University College Dublin, Belfield Dublin 4, Ireland.
Host: University College Dublin, Belfield Dublin 4, Ireland.
List moderated: Yes.
Moderation procedure: Submissions are selected and formatted by the editor.
Editorial contact: Michael O'Kelly
5, Walker's Cottages, Dublin 6, Ireland.
Tel: Dublin 966985
Internet: MOKELLY@IRLEARN.UCD.IE
How to access: TELL LISTSERV@IRLEARN.UCD.IE SUBSCRIBE FWAKEN-L
Access policy: Submit 2 original annotations to Finnegan's Wake.
How to unsubscribe: TELL LISTSERV@IRLEARN.UCD.IE UNSUBSCRIBE FW
How to submit: Send to MOKELLY@IRLEARN.UCD.IE who distributes.

GA-LIST

Description: GA-List is a moderated, digest format mailing list covering genetic algorithms and genetic programming.
Subjects covered: genetics; artificial intelligence
Net address for questions or submissions: GA-List@AIC.NRL.NAVY.MIL
How to access: Send subscription requests to the -request form of the list or to gref@aic.nrl.navy.mil

Archives: Past copies of the digest are archieved on ftp.aic.nrl.navy.mil in the /pub/galist directory. Some software is also archived there.

GARDENS

Description: The purpose of Gardens & Gardening is to promote and exchange information about home gardening. Everyone is welcome to participate, especially the novice gardener. Topics include vegetable gardens, herbs, flowers, ornamental gardening, container gardening, outdoor gardening, and so on.
Subjects covered: gardening; herbs; flowers
Net address for operations: Listserv@ukcc.uky.edu
Net address for questions or submissions: Gardens@ukcc.uky.edu
Established: Spring 1992
Subscribers: 642
Sponsor: University of Kentucky; ukcc.uky.edu
List moderated: No.
Technical contact: Bob Crovo
128 McVey Hall, University of Kentucky Computing Center, Lexington, KY 40506-0045.
Tel: (606) 257-2258
Fax: (606) 258-1978
Internet: Crovo@ukcc.uky.edu
Bitnet: crovo@ukcc
How to access: Send mail to Listserv@ukcc.uky.edu with this message: SUB GARDENS Your Name
How to unsubscribe: Send mail to Listserv@ukcc.uky.edu with * divide the list into various groups, such as indoor and outdoor, etc.
How to submit: Send mail to gardens@ukcc.uky.edu
Archives: Archives are available via the listserv. Apply to listowner for more details.

GATED-PEOPLE@DEVVAX.TN.CORNELL.EDU

Description: GATED-PEOPLE is a discussion forum on Cornell's GateDeamon networking software.
Subjects covered: computer hardware and software
List moderated: No.
Editorial contact: Jeffrey C. Honig
Internet: jch@devvax.tn.cornell.edu
How to access: Send subscribe message to GATED-PEOPLE-REQUEST@DEVVAX.TN.CORNELL.EDU
How to unsubscribe: Send unsubscribe message to GATED-PEOPLE-REQUEST@DEVVAX.TN.CORNELL.EDU
Archives: Yes; Send anonymous FTP to DEVVAX.TN.CORNELL.EDU cd pub/lists/gated-people

THE GAY/LESBIAN/BISEXUAL LIBRARIANS NETWORK

Description: GAY-LIBN is an electronic forum for discussions of interest to gay, lesbian, and bisexual librarians (and friends). Discussions on the list are often directly related to libraries, library associations, and new publications of interest to the group. Since the list is devoted to the general concerns of LesBiGay librarians, however, many of the exchanges on the list are of a more general nature.
Subjects covered: gay and lesbian topics; library and information science

Net address for operations: LISTSERV@USCVM, LISTSERV@VM.USC.EDU
Net address for questions or submissions: LIBN@USCVM, GAY-LIBN@VM.USC.EDU
Established: December 12, 1992
Subscribers: 540
Host: University of Southern California, Los Angeles, CA.
List moderated: No.
Editorial contact: Keith R. Trimmer
Catalog Department, University Libraries, University of Southern California, Doheny Memorial Library, Room 110, University Park, Los Angeles, CA 90089-0182.
Tel: (213) 740-8408
Fax: (213) 749-1221
Internet: trimmer@vm.usc.edu, trimmer@charon.usc.edu
Bitnet: trimmer@uscvm
Technical contact: IBM Mainframe General Information & Consulting University Computing Center, 1010 West Jefferson Boulevard, Los Angeles, CA 90089.
Tel: (213) 740-5555
Internet: action@vm.usc.edu
Bitnet: action@uscvm
Copyright statement: No formal policy. However, due to the potentially sensitive nature of the list, it is requested that messages not be x-posted without the permission of the original poster, or that they be x-posted only after stripping data identifying the original sender from the message.
How to access: From Bitnet nodes, send an interactive message or mail to LISTSERV@USCVM with the text SUB GAY-LIBN Firstname Lastname. From other hosts, send mail to LISTSERV@VM.USC.EDU with the text SUB GAY-LIBN Firstname Lastname
Access policy: Subscription requests are forwarded by LISTSERV to the list owner. Requests identified as originating from NETNEWS SERVERs are rejected. Requests from group accounts are discouraged, but are not automatically rejected. Occasionally, the list owner may inquire about the nature of an account prior to processing the subscription request.
How to unsubscribe: Send mail to LISTSERV@USCVM or to LISTSERV@VM.USC.EDU with the text UNSUB GAY-LIBN
How to submit: Send mail or non-mail files to GAY-LIBN@USCVM // GAY-LIBN@VM.USC.EDU
Submission policy: Only subscribers are permitted to post to the list. Messages received from non-subscribers are automatically returned to the sender by LISTSERV.
Archives: Posts to the list are archived, and full-text keyword searching is available via the LISTSERV database functions. (Access to the database is restricted to subscribers only.)
Related files: As with the LOGfiles (the archive of postings to the list), other files available via the Listserv GET command are restricted to subscribers only. Currently available are a LesBiGay discography, the Bisexual Resource List (updated monthly), the Bear Code, the Twink Code, and the MuffDiva Index. It is hoped that the American Library Association Gay and Lesbian Task Force Clearinghouse files will be added in the near future.
Additional information: The list currently averages 24 messages per day. The total number of lines posted per day is usually less than 1400, but there are occasional exceptions when there are more than 40 messages posted, and the volume has run to as many as 4000 lines in a single day.

GAYNET
Description: GAYNET is a discussion list on gay and lesbian topics related to life on college and university campuses.
Subjects covered: gay and lesbian topics; colleges and universities
Net address for questions or submissions: GAYNET-RE-QUEST@ATHENA.MIT.EDU
List moderated: Yes.
How to access: Send subscription messages to GAYNET-RE-QUEST@ATHENA.MIT.EDU

GENDER
Description: GENDER is a moderated list focussing on discussion of issues related to the study of communication and gender.
Subjects covered: gender studies; feminism; communications
Net address for operations: COMSERVE@RPITSVM, COMSERVE@VM.ITS.RPI.EDU
List moderated: No.
How to access: Send subscription requests to COMSERVE@RPITSVM (Bitnet) or COMSERVE@VM.ITS.RPI.EDU (Internet).

GENETICS@INDYCMS
Description: GENETICS@INDYCMS is a discussion list on clinical human genetics.
Subjects covered: genetics
List moderated: No.
Editorial contact: Luis Fernando Escobar, MD
Internet: ized100@indyvax.iupui.edu
Bitnet: ized100@indyvax
How to access: Send subscribe message to listserv@indycms or listserv@indycms.iupui.edu
How to unsubscribe: Send unsubscribe message to listserv@indycms or listserv@indycms.iupui.edu
Archives: Archives are developed monthly; apply to listowner for details.

GEOCAL@MAILBASE.AC.UK
Description: GEOCAL is a list on teaching geography.
Subjects covered: geography; computer-assisted instruction (CAI)
List moderated: No.
Internet: geocal-request@mailbase.ac.uk
How to access: Send subscribe message to mailbase@mailbase.ac.uk in the following format: join geocal Yourfirstname Yourlastname
Archives: Archives are developed monthly; apply to listowner for details.

GEODESIC@UBVM
Description: GEODESIC is a forum for the discussion of the works and theories of Buckminster Fuller.
Subjects covered: engineering
List moderated: No.
Editorial contact: Patrick G. Salsbury
Internet: salsbury@acsu.buffalo.edu
Bitnet: v291nhtp@ubvmsd

How to access: Send subscribe message to listserv@ubvm or listserv@ubvm.cc.buffalo.edu
How to unsubscribe: Send unsubscribe message to listserv@ubvm or listserv@ubvm.cc.buffalo.edu
Archives: Archives are developed monthly; apply to listowner for details.

GEOFEM
Description: GEOGFEM is devoted to feminist and gender-related issues in geography.
Subjects covered: geography; feminism; women's studies
Net address for operations: LISTSERV@UKCC, LISTSERV@UKCC.UKY.EDU
List moderated: No.
How to access: Send subscription messages to LISTSERV@UKCC (Bitnet) or LISTSERV@UKCC.UKY.EDU (Internet).

GEOGRAPH@FINHUTC
Description: GEOGRAPH@FINHUTC is a Finnish discussion list covering geography.
Subjects covered: geography
List moderated: No.
Editorial contact: Mervi Pyyhtia
Bitnet: pyythia@finuha, or pyythia@finuhb
How to access: Send subscribe message to listserv@finhutc or listserv%finhutc. bitnet@cunyvm.cuny.edu
How to unsubscribe: Send unsubscribe message to listserv@finhutc or listserv%finhutc. bitnet@cunyvm.cuny.edu
Archives: Archives are developed daily; apply to listowner for details.

GEONET-L
Description: Geonet-L is an e-conference for geoscience librarians.
Subjects covered: library and information science; geography; science and technology
List moderated: Yes.
Editorial contact: Lois Heiser
Internet: heiser@ucs.indiana.edu
Bitnet: heiser@iuvbm
How to access: Send subscribe message to listserv@iubvm
How to unsubscribe: Send unsubscribe message to listserv@iubvm
Archives: Yes; Yearly, Private

GERINET@UBVM
Description: GERINET@UBVM is an electronic conference on geriatric health concerns.
Subjects covered: medicine
List moderated: No.
Editorial contact: J. Phillip Miller
Internet: phil@wubios.wuslt.edu
How to access: Send subscribe message to listserv@ubvms or listserv@ubvm.cc.buffalo.edu
How to unsubscribe: Send unsubscribe message to listserv@ubvms or listserv@ubvm.cc.buffalo.edu
Archives: Archives are developed monthly; apply to listowner for details.

GERLINGL@UIUCVMD

Description: GERLINGL@UIUCVMD is a forum dedicated to the discussion and study of older Germanic languages.

Subjects covered: Old German language and literature; philology

List moderated: No.

Editorial contact: James Marchand

Internet: marchand@ux1.cso.uiuc.edu

Bitnet: marchand@uiucvmd

How to access: Send subscribe message to listserv@uiucvmd or listserv@vmd.cs.uiudc.edu

How to unsubscribe: Send unsubscribe message to listserv@uiucvmd or listserv@vmd.cs.uiudc.edu

Archives: Archives are developed monthly; apply to listowner for details.

GIS-ARTICLES

Description: GIS-ARTICLES is an electronic publishing opportunity, a chance to circulate Geographic Information Systems (GIS) and related research papers in machine readable form for comment. There are currently no papers on the list.

Subjects covered: geography; geographic information systems; Internet

Net address for operations: GIS-ARTICLES@mailbase.ac.uk

Established: April 1992

Subscribers: 36

Sponsor: The JNT Networked Information Services, Project 1992, The Computing Service, University of Newcastle upon Tyne, Newcastle, UK NE1 7RU.

Host: Networked Information Services Project (NISP,) University of Newcastle upon Tyne, Newcastle, UK NE1 7RU.

List moderated: No.

Moderation procedure: Mail sent to this list is automatically forwarded to each list member.

Editorial contact: Christine Hobson
Dept of Town and Regional Planning, University of Sheffield, Western Bank, Sheffield S10 2TN UK.

Tel: 44 742 826185

Fax: 44 742 722199

Internet: c.hobson@sheffield.ac.uk

Technical contact: Cliff Spencer
The Computing Service, University of Newcastle upon Tyne, Newcastle, UK NE1 7RU.

Tel: 44 91 222 6000

Internet: mailbase-helpline@mailbase.ac.uk

How to access: Send email to GIS-ARTICLES@mailbase.ac.uk with the following command: join <listname> <your-email-name> <your firstname> <your lastname> E.g. join GIS-AR-TICLES 123abc@univ.sysa Chris Hobson

Access policy: Please use this list as a vehicle for discussing your work.

How to unsubscribe: Send email to GIS-ARTI-CLES@mailbase.ac.uk with the following command: leave <listname> e.g. leave GIS-ARTICLES

How to submit: Just send an email with your submission to GIS-ARTICLES@mailbase.ac.uk

Archives: All archive files are kept for one year by date order. Files which have been submitted using the list owners' template will be available by requesting the named file. (The list owner can forward files on behalf of the list members). To receive an archive file, send an email to GIS-ARTICLES@mailbase.ac.uk with the command: send <listname> <filename> E.g. send GIS-ARTICLES 05-1993 or send GIS-ARTICLES introduction

Related files: All available by using the Index command - index <listname> There are none at present.

GIS-CONFERENCES

Description: GIS-CONFERENCES contains details of as many worldwide Geographic Information Systems (GIS)-related conferences as moderators are aware of.

Subjects covered: geography; conferences and conference listings; geographic information systems

Net address for operations: GIS-CONFER-ENCES@mailbase.ac.uk

Net address for questions or submissions: GIS-CONFERENCES@mailbase.ac.uk

Established: April 1992

Subscribers: 26

Sponsor: The JNT Networked Information Services, Project 1992, The Computing Service, University of Newcastle upon Tyne, Newcastle, UK NE1 7RU.

Host: Networked Information Services Project (NISP,) University of Newcastle upon Tyne, Newcastle, UK NE1 7RU.

List moderated: No.

Moderation procedure: Mail sent to this list is automatically forwarded to each listmember.

Editorial contact: Christine Hobson
Dept of Town and Regional Planning, University of Sheffield, Western Bank, Sheffield, UK S10 2TN.

Tel: 44 742 826185

Fax: 44 742 722199

Internet: c.hobson@sheffield.ac.uk

Technical contact: Cliff Spencer
The Computing Service, University of Newcastle upon Tyne, Newcastle, UK, NE1 7RU.

Tel: 44 91 222 6000

Internet: mailbase-helpline@mailbase.ac.uk

How to access: Send email to GIS-CONFER-ENCES@mailbase.ac.uk with the following command: join <listname> <your-email-name> <your firstname> <your lastname> E.g. join GIS-CONFERENCES 123abc@univ.sysa Chris Hobson

Access policy: Useful for all those who spend much of their time travelling between various conferences, workshops, etc.

How to unsubscribe: Send email to GIS-CONFER-ENCES@mailbase.ac.uk with the following command: leave <listname> E.g. leave GIS-CONFERENCES

How to submit: Just send an email with your submission to GIS-CONFERENCES@mailbase.ac.uk

Archives: All archive files are kept for one year by date order. Files which have been submitted using the list owners' template will be avai lable by requesting the named file. (The list owner can forward fil es on behalf of the list members). To receive an archive file, send an email to GIS-CONFERENCES@mailbase.ac.uk with the command: send <listname> <filename> E.g. send GIS-CONFERENCES 05-1993 or send GIS-CONFERENCES introduction

Related files: All available by using the Index command - index <listname>

Gopher accessibility: Gopher to mailbase@ac.uk

GIS-HELP

Description: GIS-HELP has been created so that people can discuss with other users their technical difficulties, problems, solutions and general experience of Geographic Information Systems (GIS) hardware and software.

Subjects covered: geography; geographic information systems; computer hardware and software

Net address for operations: GIS-HELP@mailbase.ac.uk

Net address for questions or submissions: GIS-HELP@mailbase.ac.uk

Established: April 1992

Subscribers: 27

Sponsor: The JNT Networked Information Services, Project 1992, The Computing Service, University of Newcastle upon Tyne, Newcastle, UK NE1 7RU.

Host: Networked Information Services Project (NISP,) University of Newcastle upon Tyne, Newcastle, UK NE1 7RU.

List moderated: No.

Moderation procedure: Mail sent to this list is automatically forwarded to all list members.

Editorial contact: Christine Hobson
Dept of Town and Regional Planning, University of Sheffield, Western Bank, Sheffield, UK S10 2TN.

Tel: 44 742 826185

Fax: 44 742 722199

Internet: c.hobson@sheffield.ac.uk

Technical contact: Cliff Spencer
The Computing Service, University of Newcastle upon Tyne, Newcastle, UK, NE1 7RU.

Tel: 44 91 222 6000

Internet: mailbase-helpline@mailbase.ac.uk

How to access: Send email to GIS-HELP@mailbase.ac.uk with the following command: join <listname> <your-email-name> <your firstname> <your lastname> E.g. join GIS-HELP 123abc@univ.sysa Chris Hobson

How to unsubscribe: Send email to GIS-HELP@mailbase.ac.uk with the following command: leave <listname> E.g. leave GIS-HELP

How to submit: Just send an email with your submission to GIS-HELP@mailbase.ac.uk

Archives: All archive files are kept for one year by date order. Files which have been submitted using the list owners' template will be avai lable by requesting the named file. (The list owner can forward fil es on behalf of the list members). To receive an archive file, send an email to GIS-HELP@mailbase.ac.uk with the command: send <listname> <filename> E.g. send GIS-HELP 05-1993 or send GIS-HELP introduction

Related files: All available by using the Index command - index <listname>

Gopher accessibility: Gopher to mailbase@ac.uk

GIS-JOBS

Description: GIS-JOBS contains details of jobs available within the Geographic Information Systems field (mainly in the UK, but a few worldwide ones occasionally).

Subjects covered: career opportunities; geography; geographic information systems

Net address for operations: GIS-JOBS@mailbase.ac.uk

Net address for questions or submissions: GIS-JOBS@mailbase.ac.uk

Established: April 1992

Subscribers: 38

Sponsor: The JNT Networked Information Services, Project 1992, The Computing Service, University of Newcastle upon Tyne, Newcastle, UK NE1 7RU.

Host: Networked Information Services Project (NISP,) University of Newcastle upon Tyne, Newcastle, UK NE1 7RU.

List moderated: No.

Moderation procedure: Mail sent to this list is automatically forwarded to all list members.

Editorial contact: Christine Hobson
Dept of Town and Regional Planning, University of Sheffield, Western Bank, Sheffield, UK S10 2TN.

Tel: 44 742 826185

Fax: 44 742 722199

Internet: c.hobson@sheffield.ac.uk

Technical contact: Cliff Spencer
The Computing Service, University of Newcastle upon Tyne, Newcastle, UK, NE1 7RU.

Tel: 44 91 222 6000

Internet: mailbase-helpline@mailbase.ac.uk

How to access: Send email to GIS-JOBS@mailbase.ac.uk with the following command: join <listname> <your-email-name> <your firstname> <your lastname> E.g. join GIS-JOBS 123abc@univ.sysa Chris Hobson

How to unsubscribe: Send email to GIS-JOBS@mailbase.ac.uk with the following command: leave <listname> E.g. leave GIS-JOBS

How to submit: Just send an email with your submission to GIS-JOBS@mailbase.ac.uk

Archives: All archive files are kept for one year by date order. Files which have been submitted using the list owners' template will be avai lable by requesting the named file. (The list owner can forward fil es on behalf of the list members). To receive an archive file, send an email to GIS-JOBS@mailbase.ac.uk with the command; send <listname> <filename> E.g. send GIS-JOBS 05-1993 or send GIS-JOBS introduction

Related files: All available by using the Index command - index <listname>

Gopher accessibility: Gopher to mailbase@ac.uk

GIS-L

Description: GIS-L is a forum for the discussion of Geographical Information Systems.

Subjects covered: geographic information systems

List moderated: No.

Editorial contact: David M. Mark

Bitnet: gismgr@ubvms

How to access: Send subscribe message to listserv@ubvm or listserv@ubvmcc.buffalo.edu

How to unsubscribe: Send unsubscribe message to listserv@ubvm or listserv@ubvmcc.buffalo.edu

Archives: Yes.

GIS-NEWS

Description: GIS-NEWS is a public discussion list to which anyone can subscribe and contribute. It is intended as a forum for distributing any newsworthy indormation relevant to the UK Geographic Information Systems community.

Subjects covered: geographic information systems; geography

Net address for operations: GIS-NEWS@mailbase.ac.uk

Net address for questions or submissions: GIS-NEWS@mailbase.ac.uk

Established: April 1992

Subscribers: 38

Sponsor: The JNT Networked Information Services, Project 1992, The Computing Service, University of Newcastle upon Tyne, Newcastle, UK NE1 7RU.
Host: Networked Information Services Project (NISP,) University of Newcastle upon Tyne, Newcastle, UK NE1 7RU.
List moderated: No.
Editorial contact: Christine Hobson
Dept of Town and Regional Planning, University of Sheffield, Western Bank, Sheffield, UK S10 2TN.
Tel: 44 742 826185
Fax: 44 742 722199
Internet: c.hobson@sheffield.ac.uk
Technical contact: Cliff Spencer
The Computing Service, University of Newcastle upon Tyne, Newcastle, UK, NE1 7RU.
Tel: 44 91 222 6000
Internet: mailbase-helpline@mailbase.ac.uk
How to access: Send email to GIS-NEWS@mailbase.ac.uk with the following command: join <listname> <your-email-name> <your firstname> <your lastname> E.g. join GIS-NEWS 123abc@univ.sysa Chris Hobson
How to unsubscribe: Send email to GIS-NEWS@mailbase.ac.uk with the following command: leave <listname> E.g. leave GIS-NEWS
How to submit: Just send an email with your submission to GIS-NEWS@mailbase.ac.uk
Archives: All archive files are kept for one year by date order. Files which have been submitted using the list owners' template will be avai lable by requesting the named file. (The list owner can forward fil es on behalf of the list members). To receive an archive file, send an email to GIS-NEWS@mailbase.ac.uk with the command; send <listname> <filename> E.g. send GIS-NEWS 05-1993 or send GIS-NEWS introduction
Related files: All available by using the Index command - index <listname>
Gopher accessibility: Gopher to mailbase@ac.uk

GIS-UK

Description: GIS-UK is the superlist within which the following discussion lists are nested. Geographic Information Systems (GIS) and related research, conferences, etc.
Subjects covered: geography; computer hardware and software; computer science; geographic information systems
Net address for operations: GIS-UK@mailbase.ac.uk
Net address for questions or submissions: GIS-UK@mailbase.ac.uk
Established: April 1992
Subscribers: 52
Sponsor: The JNT Networked Information Services, Project 1992, The Computing Service, University of Newcastle upon Tyne, Newcastle, UK NE1 7RU.
Host: Networked Information Services Project, (NISP) University of Newcastle upon Tyne, Newcastle, UK, NE1 7RU.
List moderated: Yes.
Moderation procedure: Mail sent to this list is automatically forwarded to the list owner. Listowner decides whether this particular list is the right one for the type of message, or whether to suggest one of the sub lists. Listowner either forwards it to the list or returns it to the sender.
Editorial contact: Christine Hobson
Dept of Town and Regional Planning, University of Sheffield, Western Bank, Sheffield, UK S10 2TN.
Tel: 44 742 826185

Fax: 44 742 722199
Internet: c.hobson@sheffield.ac.uk
Technical contact: Cliff Spencer
The Computing Service, University of Newcastle upon Tyne, Newcastle, UK NE1 7RU.
Tel: 44 91 222 6000
Internet: mailbase-helpline@mailbase.ac.uk
How to access: Send email to gis-uk@mailbase.ac.uk with the following command: join <listname> <your-email-name> <your firstname> <your lastname> E.g. join gis-uk 123abc@univ.sysa Chris Hobson
Access policy: Only subscribe to this list if you are prepared to get multiple copies of all postings.
How to unsubscribe: Send an email to gis-uk@mailbase.ac.uk with the following command: leave <listname> E.g. leave gis-uk
How to submit: Just send an email with your submission to gis-uk@mailbase.ac.uk
Submission policy: The submission will be scanned for libellous statements. Then it will either be forwarded to the most appropriate list, or returned to the sender.
Archives: All archive files are kept for one year by date order. Files which have been submitted using the listowners' template will be available by requesting the named file. (The listowner can forward files on behalf of the list members). To receive an archive file, send an email to gis-uk@mailbase.ac.uk with the command send <listname> <filename> E.g. send gis-uk 05-1993 or send gis-uk introduction
Related files: All related files are available by using the Index command - index <listname>
Gopher accessibility: Gopher to mailbase@ac.uk

GLB NEWS

Description: GLB-NEWS (Information Repository for News of Interest to GLB Folk) is a discussion group centering on topics related to the gay community. Subjects covered include (mainly political) news items of interest to gay men, lesbians, bisexuals, transvestites, transgendered persons and others friendly and/or sympathetic to those groups. The list header can be acquired by sending 'REVIEW GLB-NEWS' in email to listserv@brownvm.brown.edu.
Subjects covered: gay and lesbian topics
Net address for operations: listserv@brownvm.brown.edu
Net address for questions or submissions: glb-news@brownvm.brown.edu
Established: January 1993
Host: Brown University, Providence RI (brownvm.brown.edu)
List moderated: Yes.
Moderation procedure: List Editor-at-large receives submissions from list members or other sources, determines relevance to list and posts them. List is not for open discussion.
Editorial contact: David B. O'Donnell
15 Everett Ave, Providence RI USA 02906-3321
Tel: (401) 453-3886
Internet: atropos@netlab.cis.brown.edu
Bitnet: EL406006@brownvm
Technical contact: same
How to access: Send 'SUB GLB-NEWS user name' in e-mail to listserv@brownvm.brown.edu
How to unsubscribe: 'UNSUB GLB-NEWS' in e-mail to same listserv.

How to submit: Send article as e-mail to GLB-NEWS@brownvm.brown.edu or EL406006@brownvm.brown.edu (first address is preferred)
Archives: Archived weekly via normal Listserve program. Archives are maintained for up to three months. Send 'INDEX GLB-NEWS' to listserv@brownvm.brown.edu to get a list of archives. List is also digested weekly; to receive the digested form, subscribe (see above) and then send 'SET GLB-NEWS NOMAIL DIGEST' in e-mail to listserv@brownvm.brown.edu
Additional information: NOTE that GLB-News, while accepting subscriptions from anyone, does not allow subscribers to get a list of other subscribers. This is to maintain the confidentiality of list members and protect them from heterosexist attacks. The list editor(s) can and will take steps to keep the list from being submitted to heterosexism and homophobia, including forwarding information to site administration.

GLOSAS-L

Description: GLOSAS-L publishes contributions dealing with the practical applications of telecommunications in education. We lay particular emphasis on global cooperative gaming, simulations, and educational exchanges as well as initiatives to broaden network access on a global scale. Our ultimate objective is to see the establishment of a global (electronic) university which would offer universal access to quality education. There are two GLOSAS News bulletins - Global Education (GN/GE) and Global Peace Gaming (GN/GPG). Both are labelled accordingly on the subject line. For example, an issue of the Global Education bulletin would be labelled GN/GPG/Vxx/Nyy (V = Volume and N = Number). For added convenience, the subject line also shows the approximate size of the file. This is generally kept under 33 Kbytes. GN/GE appears 4-5 times and GN/GPG 5-6 times annually. GLOSAS is a non-profit, publicly supported international research and development organization dedicated to the development of channels and infrastructure for a global university. It also acts as an advocate of worldwide access to global distance-education services. GLOSAS has conducted numerous Global Lecture Hall (TM) teleconferences during which novel technologies and modes of communication are tested.
Subjects covered: education; telecommunications; colleges and universities; distance education
Net address for operations: LISTSERV@acadvm1.uottawa.ca
Established: 1991
Subscribers: 50
Sponsor: GLOSAS/USA
Host: University of Ottawa
List moderated: No.
Editorial contact: Prof. Anton Ljutic
Champlain College, 900 Riverside Dr., St. Lambert, Quebec J4P 3P2 Canada.
Tel: (514) 672-7360 x280
Fax: (514) 672-9299
Internet: anton@vax2.concordia.ca; anton@carleton.ca
Sample contents: CONTENTS OF GN/GPG: The Global Peace Gaming edition of GN is largely based on materials sent to us by John and Suzette McLeod, Editors of ''Simulation in the Service of Society'' (S3), a special section of the technical journal SIMULATION published by the Society for Computer Simulation International (SCSI). It may be reproduced only for personal use or for the use of students. In either case full credit

must be given to the original source of publication: SIMULATION (Volume, Number and Date as indicated).
Copyright statement: We reserve copyright but encourage redistribution of our materials with proper credit given. Please ask the author's permission if you wish to redistribute an entire article.
How to access: If you know someone who wishes to subscribe please have that person send the following message to the same address: SUB GLOSAS Firstname Lastname.
How to unsubscribe: In order to get OFF this list, please send the message UNSUB GLOSAS to: Listserv@vm1.mcgill.ca or contact the editor.
Archives: Monthly archives are kept, with a 12 month total.
Additional information: We have about 450 email subscribers and over 500 subscribers by fax in over thirty countries (April 1993). Our address lists are confidential, we do not share them. In order to receive additional information about GLOSAS and a membership application form please send an email message to the editor.

GOLF-L

Description: GOLF-L is a discussion group focusing on discussion of the sport of golf.
Subjects covered: golf; sports
Net address for questions or submissions: GOLF-L@UBVM
Established: August 1992
Subscribers: 120+
Host: University of Buffalo, Buffalo, NY.
List moderated: No.
Editorial contact: Chris Tanski
730 Bowling Green Road, Cortland, NY.
Tel: 607-756-8229
Internet: CAPTANSKI33@SNYCORVA.CORTLAND.EDU
Bitnet: CTANSKI@ONONDAGA
How to access: Send message to LISTSERV@UBVM
How to unsubscribe: Send message to LISTSERV@UBVM
How to submit: Send message to GOLF-L@UBVM
Submission policy: Send mail to GOLF-L-REQUEST@UBVM.CC.BUFFALO.EDU

GOVDOC-L

Description: Govdoc-L is a conference on isuues related to government documents.
Subjects covered: library and information science; government information
List moderated: Yes.
Editorial contact: Duncan Aldrich
Internet: duncan@equinox.unr.edu
Review: Reviewed by List Review Service edited by Raleigh Muns: see appendix.
How to access: Send subscribe message to listserv@psuvm or listserv@psuvm.psu.edu
How to unsubscribe: Send unsubscribe message to listserv@psuvm or listserv@psuvm.psu.edu
Archives: Archives are developed weekly; apply to listowner for details.

GRAD-ADV@ACS.UNC.EDU

Description: GRAD-ADV@ACS.UNC.EDU covers topics related to advising students about graduate school.
Subjects covered: education

List moderated: No.
How to access: Send subscribe message to listserv@unc or listserv@acs..unc.edu
How to unsubscribe: Send unsubscribe message to listserv@unc or listserv@acs.unc.edu

GRAFOS-L

Description: Grafos-L is a Spanish language forum on graphic mathematics.
Subjects covered: mathematics
List moderated: No.
Editorial contact: Marcia Cerioli
Bitnet: cerioli@ufrj
How to access: Send subscribe message to listserv@ufrj or listserv%ufrj.bitnet@cunyvm.cuny.edu
How to unsubscribe: Send unsubscribe message to listserv@ufrj or listserv%ufrj.bitnet@cunyvm.cuny.edu
Archives: Archives are developed monthly; apply to listowner for details.

GRANTS-L

Description: Grants-L distributes grant-related information from the National Science Foundation.
Subjects covered: colleges and universities
List moderated: Yes.
Bitnet: jimj@jhuvm
How to access: Send subscribe message to listserv@jhuvm or listserv@vms.cis.pitt.edu
How to unsubscribe: Send unsubscribe message to listserv@jhuvm or listserv@vms.cis.pitt.edu
Archives: Archives are developed monthly; apply to listowner for details.
Additional information: For additional information on NSF Grants and Contracts BBS, contact Mary Ann Messier at (202) 357-7880

GRAPH-L

Description: Graph-L is a forum for graphics students and faculty primarily at Yale University.
Subjects covered: graphics; computer graphics
List moderated: No.
Editorial contact: Peter Fox
Bitnet: fox@yalastro
How to access: Send subscribe message to listserv@yalevm or listserv@yalevm.ycc.yale.edu
How to unsubscribe: Send unsubscribe message to listserv@yalevm or listserv@yalevm.ycc.yale.edu
Archives: Archives are developed monthly; apply to listowner for details.

GRAPHICS@OHSTVMA

Description: GRAPHICS@OHSTVMA is a graphics forum based at Ohio State University.
Subjects covered: graphics; computer graphics
List moderated: No.
Editorial contact: Duane Weaver
Bitnet: weaver@ohstvma
How to access: Send subscribe message to listserv@ohstvma or listserv@ohstvma.acs.ohio-state.edu

How to unsubscribe: Send unsubscribe message to listserv@ohstvma or listserv@ohstvma.acs.ohio-state.edu
Archives: Archives are developed monthly; apply to listowner for details.

GRAPHIX@UTFSM

Description: GRAPHIX@UTFSM is a forum that covers all aspects of the computer graphics field, including hardware/software issues.
Subjects covered: computer graphics; computer hardware and software; graphics
List moderated: No.
Editorial contact: Douglas Sargent
Bitnet: dsargent@utfsm
How to access: Send subscribe message to listserv@utfsm
How to unsubscribe: Send unsubscribe message to listserv@utfsm
Archives: Archives are developed monthly; apply to listowner for details.

GRAPHNET

Description: GRAPHNET is a list covering topics in graph theory and applications. Subjects covered include Hamilton graphs, chromatic graph theory, domination theory, digraphs, hypergraphs, matroids, etc.
Subjects covered: mathematics; graph theory
Net address for operations: LISTSERV@vm1.nodak.edu
Net address for questions or submissions: GRAPHNET@vm1.nodak.edu
Established: February 1990
Subscribers: 215
Sponsor: North Dakota Higher Education Computer Network, University Computer Center, IACC Building, North Dakota State University Fargo, ND 58105.
Host: North Dakota State University, Fargo, ND 58105.
List moderated: No.
Editorial contact: Warren E. Shreve
Math Dept, NDSU, Box 5075, Fargo, ND 58105-5075.
Tel: (701)237-7707
Fax: (701) 237-7589
Internet: shreve@plains.nodak.edu
Bitnet: shreve@plains.bitnet
Technical contact: Marty Hoag
University Computer Center, NDSU, Fargo, ND 58105.
Tel: (701) 237-8639
Internet: hoag@plains.nodak.edu
Bitnet: hoag@plains.bitnet
How to access: Send message: join graphnet to listserv@vm1.nodak.edu or to listserv@ndsuvm1.bitnet
Access policy: Those who are willing to identify themselves and submit only appropriate messages are welcome to subscribe.
How to unsubscribe: Send message: leave graphnet to listserv@vm1.nodak.edu or to listserv@ndsuvm1.bitnet
How to submit: Send message to graphnet@vm1.nodak.edu or to graphnet@ndsuvm1.bitnet
Submission policy: Messages will be considered appropriate if they are of interest to researchers in the area of graph theory, including such topics as Hamiltonian graphs, chromatic graph theory, domination theory, digraphs, hypergraphs, matroids, etc.
Archives: Archive information is available through listserv@vm1.nodak.edu

Related files: Technical information available through listserv@vm1.nodak.edu

GRAVITY@UWF
Description: GRAVITY@UWF is a forum on gravity and spacetime physics.
Subjects covered: astronomy; physics
List moderated: No.
Editorial contact: Dick Smith
Bitnet: spacemgr@uwf
How to access: Send subscribe message to listserv@uwf or listserv@uwf.bitnet@cunyvm.cuny.edu
How to unsubscribe: Send unsubscribe message to listserv@uwf or listserv@uwf.bitnet@cunyvm.cuny.edu
Archives: Archives are developed monthly; apply to listowner for details.

GRMNHIST: GERMAN HISTORY FORUM
Description: GRMNHIST is an electronic discussion list for historians and others interested in German history.
Subjects covered: history; Germany
Net address for operations: GRMNHIST@VM.USC.EDU
Subscribers: 161
List moderated: No.
Editorial contact: Thomas Zielke
Bitnet: TZIELKE@DGOGWDG1
Review: Reviewed in List Review Service edited by Raleigh Muns: see appendix.
How to access: Send an e-mail message with blank subject line to: LISTSERV@USCVM (Bitnet address) or LISTSERV@VM.USC.EDU (Internet address). Message should consist solely of: SUBSCRIBE GRMNHIST your__name
Archives: Yes, archives are avialable; contact listowner.
Related files: Related files include the History Network, a collection of history-related resources. (Telnet to hnsource.cc.ukans.edu / login: history - no password is required.)

GUTNBERG@UIUCVMD
Description: GUTNBERG@UIUCVMD is a discussion list centering on the Gutenberg Project of electronic texts.
Subjects covered: electronic texts; full text
List moderated: Yes.
Editorial contact: Michael Hart
Internet: HART@VMD.CSO.UIUC.EDU
Review: Reviewed by List Review Service edited by Raleigh Muns: see appendix.
How to access: Send subscribe message to listserv@uiucvmd or listserv@vmd.cso.uiuc.edu
How to unsubscribe: Send unsubscribe message to listserv@uiucvmd or listserv@vmd.cso.uiuc.edu
Archives: Archives are developed weekly; apply to listowner for details.

GWMON@SH.CS.NET
Description: GWMON@SH.CS.NET is a forum on management of computer gateways and networks.
Subjects covered: electronic networking; computer science
List moderated: No.
Editorial contact: Craig Partridge

Internet: craig@loki.bbn.com
How to access: Send subscribe message to GWMON-RE-QUEST@SH.CS.NET
How to unsubscribe: Send unsubscribe message to GWMON-REQUEST@SH.CS.NET

GYMN
Description: GYMN is a discussion lists on all aspects of gymnastics.
Subjects covered: gymnastics; sports
Net address for operations: owner-gymn@athena.mit.edu
Net address for questions or submissions: gymn@athena.mit.edu
Established: summer 1992
Subscribers: 80
Host: Massachusetts Institute of Technology
List moderated: No.
Technical contact: Robyn Kozierok
MIT, 20 Ames St. Rm. 401c, Cambridge, MA
Tel: (617) 253-0116
Fax: (617) 258-6264
Internet: owner-gymn@athena.mit.edu
How to access: Email to owner-gymn@athena.mit.edu
Access policy: Anyone may join -- takes 24 hours to process.
How to unsubscribe: Email to owner-gymn@athena.mit.edu
How to submit: Email to owner-gymn@athena.mit.edu
Archives: Past digests have been stored, but we are currently working out arranging an ftp site for them.
Additional information: Both a normal email list and a digest form are available.

H-AMSTDY@UICVM
Description: H-Amstdy aims to act as a conduit for information relating to American Studies. The main focus of the list will be interdisciplinary discussion of American experience, but the list will strive to become a virtual institution linking American Studies organizations throughout America and overseas.
Subjects covered: American studies; history
Net address for operations: Listserv@uicvm.uic.edu
Net address for questions or submissions: H-Amstdy@uicvm.uic.edu or H-Amstdy@uicvm
Established: July 5, 1993
Subscribers: 222
Sponsor: University of Illinois at Chicago, History Department (M/C 198), 723 SEO 851 S. Morgan St., Chicago, IL 60607-7049.
List moderated: Yes.
Moderation procedure: All messages for H-Amstdy received by moderator; generally released without any change; occasionally delayed due to volume of messages.
Editorial contact: Jeff Finlay
31-48 31st Street, Astoria, NY 11106.
Tel: (718) 545-9013
Internet: finlay__j@spcvxa.spc.edu
Bitnet: finlay__j@spcvxa
How to access: Send note to listserv@uicvm.uic.edu or listserv@uicvm with message Subscribe H-Amstdy Firstname Lastname School/Organization
Access policy: All welcome; prefer faculty, professional, graduate students.
How to unsubscribe: Send note to listserv@uicvm.uic.edu or listserv@uicvm with message Signoff H-Amstdy

How to submit: Send note to H-Amstdy@uicvm.uic.edu or H-Amstdy@uicvm.uic.edu

Submission policy: All posts will be accepted provided they are they are non-inflammatory and make an attempt to address the interdisciplinary concerns of the list.

Archives: H-Amstdy maintains a Listserv fileserver which is attempting to build up a database of important texts for American Studies. To obtain the list of documents, send a note to Listserv@uicvm or Listserv@uicvm.uic.edu with the message "Index H-Amstdy" to obtain a file, send a note to Listserv@uicvm or Listserv@uicvm.uic.edu with the message Get "Filename Filetype"

H-CIVWAR@UICVM

Description: H-CivWar@uicvm is a discussion list covering the American Civil War.

Subjects covered: American studies; history; Civil War

Net address for operations: listserv@uicvm

Net address for questions or submissions: H-CivWar@uicvm

How to access: Send message to listserv: SUBSCRIBE <listname> <your name>

H-DIPLO

Description: H-DIPLO is a discussion list covering issues in diplomatic history, international relations and foreign affairs. It includes research advice, bibliographies, syllabi, etc. Review of list (citation or extract): Subjects covered: Diplomatic history, international relations, foreign affairs

Subjects covered: diplomatic history; history; political science; international studies

Net address for operations: LISTSERV@UICVM

Net address for questions or submissions: H-DIPLO@UICVM

Established: June 1993

Subscribers: 82

Sponsor: University of Illinois, Chicago

Host: University of Illinois, Chicago

List moderated: Yes.

Moderation procedure: Postings are collected manually into daily digests.

Editorial contact: Michael J. McCarthy

Dept. of History, Marshall University

Tel: 304/696-6372

Fax: 304/696-6277

Internet: mmccarth@muvms6.wvnet.edu

Bitnet: mmccarth@muvms6

Technical contact: Jim Mott

Internet: jimmott@spss.com

Copyright statement: All posters retain copyright to material. Posting does not preclude other publication.

How to access: Send email message to LISTSERV@UICVM with blank subject line and the following as the only text: SUB H-DIPLO firstname lastname school For example: SUB H-DIPLO Chris Smith Marshall Univ.

Access policy: All interested individuals are welcome, but list will cater to serious scholars. Subscribers can be removed by moderator.

How to unsubscribe: Send email message to LISTSERV@UICVM with blank subject line and the following as the only text: UNSUB H-DIPLO

How to submit: Send an email message to H-DIPLO@UICVM

Archives: Archives are available on LISTSERV@UICVM

Related files: Related files available via anonymous FTP to byrd.mu.wvnet.edu in the pub/history/diplomatic/h-diplo subdirectory

H-ETHNIC@UICVM

Description: H-Ethnic@uicvm is a discussion list covering ethnicity and immigration.

Subjects covered: ethnicity; history; immigration

Net address for operations: listserv@uicvm

Net address for questions or submissions: H-Ethnic@uicvm

How to access: Send message to listserv: SUBSCRIBE <listname> <your name>

H-FILM

Description: H-FILM is a free international forum to promote the scholarly study of film history, mass communication, and popular culture and the use of media in teaching. The primary purpose of H-FILM is to enable scholars to communicate their current research and teaching interests and test new ideas. H-FILM will feature: reviews of books, films, and documentaries; announcements of grants, conferences, and jobs; course outlines, class handouts, syllabi, bibliographies, and other teaching resources; discussion of film history, mass communication, popular culture, and the use of media in teaching.

Subjects covered: cinema studies; popular culture

Net address for operations: LISTSERV@uicvm.uic.edu or LISTSERV@uicvm.BITNET

Net address for questions or submissions: H-FILM@uicvm.BITNET or H-FILM@uicvm.uic.edu

List moderated: Yes.

Moderation procedure: H-FILM will be moderated to filter out extraneous messages (like requests for subscription) and items that do not aid the scholarly dialogue. All contributions will be part of the public domain and can be freely used, printed, copied or retransmitted if credit is given the original author.

Editorial contact: Steven Mintz

Tel: 713-743-3109

Fax: 713-743-3216

Internet: hist4@Jetson.uh.edu

How to access: Send this message to LISTSERV@uicvm.uic.edu or to LISTSERV@uicvm.BITNET: SUB H-FILM Firstname Surname, Your School

How to submit: Send posts directly to: H-FILM@uicvm.BITNET or H-FILM@uicvm.uic.edu

To respond to an H-FILM post, use the REPLY command.

Related files: H-Film is a part of the H-Net family of scholarly discussion groups, which is endorsed by the American Historical Association, the Organization of American Historians, and the Southern Historical Association.

Additional information: Advisory Board: Tino T. Balio, University of Wisconsin; David Burner, SUNY-Stony Brook; Gregory Bush, University of Miami; David H. Culbert, Louisiana State University; Leslie Fishbein, Rutgers University; Don Graham, University of Texas; Garth Jowett, University of Houston; Douglas Kellner, University of Texas; Leonard J. Leff, Oklahoma State University; Charles Musser, Yale University; Randy W. Roberts, Purdue University; Peter C. Rollins, Oklahoma State University; Roy Rosenzweig, George Mason University; Ken Short, University of Houston; Richard Slotkin, Wesleyan University; Julian Smith, University of Florida; Thomas Sobchack, University of Utah; Vivian Sobchack, UCLA; June Sochen, Northern Illinois University; Donald Staples, University of North Texas; Paul J. Vanderwood, San Diego State University; Daniel Walkowitz, New York University.

H-GRAD

Description: H-Grad enables graduate students in history-related fields to easily communicate about graduate school -- taking courses, teaching, TAing, passing exams, writing papers, and basic survival. H-grad will facilitate discussion on a wide range of issues involved in the graduate school experience at the college and university level. H-Grad will be especially interested in all facets of graduate school, including life both in and out of the department. Special attention will be paid to use of new technologies in history related fields. H-Grad will publish tips basic to survival in graduate school, such as: how to choose and get along with your mentor, how to navigate department politics, how to prepare for papers and exams, dealing with living and working arrangements, managing a loving relationship while in school, etc. Additionally, special attention will be given to coursework and teaching, such as bibliographies, syllabi, historiography, etc. H-Grad will also post announcements of conferences, fellowships, grants, and jobs. Subscribers will write in with questions, comments, and reports. H-Grad will carry publisher's announcements of new books and will commission book reviews.
Subjects covered: education; colleges and universities; graduate education; history
Established: September 1993
List moderated: Yes.
Moderation procedure: H-Grad will be moderated to filter out extraneous messages (like requests for subscription) and items that do not belong on H- Grad. They may belong somewhere else, or in the comoderator's judgement do not aid the dialogue. The comoderators will not alter the substance of anyone's missive. All contributions to H-Grad will be part of the public domain and can be freely used, printed, copied or retransmitted if credit is given the original author.
Editorial contact: Kelly Richter
University of Illinois, Chicago
Bitnet: u59611@uicvm
How to access: To subscribe on BITNET, send this message to LISTSERV@uicvm: sub H-Grad firstname surname, school (example: sub H-Grad Jane Doe, Central Delaware State); to subscribe on INTERNET, send the same message to LISTSERV@uicvm.uic.edu
How to submit: All posts should be sent directly to H-GRAD@uicvm. To answer an H-GRAD post, use the REPLY command. Long documents should be sent via Bitnet.
Additional information: Additional editor: Robert A. Harris, Binghamton University, Binghamton, NY; bb05196@bingvmb. H-Grad has an editorial board entirely comprised of graduate students. In order that subscribers to this list may converse (and carp) openly, this discussion group will be limited to people currently enrollled in a graduate program.

H-LAW@UICVM

Description: H-Law@uicvm is a discussion group centering on U.S. legal and constitutional issues.
Subjects covered: law and legal studies; history; political science
Net address for operations: listserv@uicvm
Net address for questions or submissions: H-Law@uicvm

How to access: Send message to listserv: SUBSCRIBE <listname> <your name>

H-POL

Description: H-POL enables political historians and historically-oriented scholars in political science, political sociology, and related disciplines to easily communicate current research and research interests; to discuss new articles, books, papers, approaches, methods and tools of analysis; to test new ideas and share comments and tips on teaching. There are no geographical or chronological boundaries. H-POL will try to stimulate dialogues among scholars who study political history worldwide. It will publish syllabi, outlines, handouts, bibliographies, guides to termpapers, listings of new sources and archives, and reports on new software, datasets and cd-roms. Subscribers will write in with questions, comments, and reports. H-POL will post announcements of conferences, fellowships and jobs. We are especially interested in reaching college faculty who already have, or plan to teach courses on political history. H-POL will therefore actively solicit syllabi, reading lists, termpaper guides, ideas on films and slides, and tips and comments that will be of use to the teacher who wants to add a single lecture, or an entire course. The moderators will solicit postings (by email, phone and even by regular mail), will assist people in subscribing and setting up options, will handle routine inquiries, and will consolidate some postings. The moderators will solicit and post newsletter type information (calls for conferences, for example, or listings of sessions at conventions.) They will also commission book and article reviews, and to post book announcements from publishers. Anyone with suggestions about what H-POL can and might do is invited to send in the ideas.
Subjects covered: political science; history
Sponsor: H-POL is sponsored by the H-Net project of the UIC History department, with support from the College and ACLS.
List moderated: Yes.
Moderation procedure: H-POL will be moderated to filter out extraneous messages (like requests for subscription) and items that do not belong on H-POL. They may belong somewhere else, or in the judgment of the moderators they do not aid the scholarly dialog. The moderators will not alter the meaning of the message (but will, if necessary, add name and e-address). All contributions to H-POL will become part of the public domain and can be freely used, printed, copied or retransmitted if credit is given to the original author.
Editorial contact: Jim Mott
SPSS Inc., 444 N. Michigan Avenue, Chicago, IL 60611.
Tel: 312-329-3542
Internet: JimMott@spss.com
How to access: Send this email message via Internet to LISTSERV@uicvm.uic.edu: sub H-POL firstname surname, school Example: sub H-POL Leslie Jones, Southern Jersey U. If you use Bitnet instead of Internet, the same message goes to LISTSERV@uicvm [capital or lower case does not matter, but spelling does. Note "LISTSERV"]. There are no dues or fees of any kind. Subscribers only need an address on Bitnet or Internet, which is provided to faculty and students by campus computer centers. The consultants there, or your departmental guru, can explain how to send an email message via Bitnet or Internet.
How to unsubscribe: Send this message to LISTSERV@uicvm.uic.edu UNSUB H-POL
How to submit: Send an email note directly to H-POL@UICVM.uic.edu (Internet) or H-POL@UICVM (Bitnet).

Longer messages will also be accepted, but may be stored on a fileserver for interested subscribers to access if they choose, rather than having them sent to everyone.

Archives: Documents of interest--bibliographies, book and article reviews, announcements, teaching materials, and descriptions of tools, techniques, and computer software and hardware, plus the weekly files of messages--will be made available from the H-POL fileserver. To obtain a list of available documents, send a note to Listserv@uicvm.uic.edu (or Listserv@uicvm) with the following command: Index H-POL To obtain a specific document, send Listserv the command GET filename filetype Contributions to the archive are welcome, and should be sent as files to H-POL@UICVM.uic.edu.

Additional information: Additional editor: Mark Kornbluh; Hpol@artsci.wustl.edu.

H-RHETORIC

Description: H-RHETORIC is a discussion list covering the history of rhetoric, writing, and communication.

Subjects covered: rhetoric; writing; language and literature; communications

Net address for operations: LISTSERV@UICVM

Net address for questions or submissions: H-RHETORIC@UICVM

Established: 1993

Sponsor: H-Net, Dept of History, m/c 198, 851 South Morgan St., SEO 723, Chicago, IL 60607-7049.

Host: University of Illinois-Chicago, Dept of History, m/c 198, 851 South Morgan St., SEO 723, Chicago, IL 60607-7049.

List moderated: Yes.

Moderation procedure: Moderator examines all messages.

Editorial contact: Gary L. Hatch
3146 JKHB, English Department, Brigham Young University, Provo, UT 84602

Tel: 801-378-2402

Fax: 801-378-4649

Internet: gary__hatch@byu.edu

Technical contact: Wendy Plotkin
Dept of History, m/c 198, 851 South Morgan St., SEO 723, Chicago, IL 60607-7049.

Tel: 312-996-3141

Fax: 312-996-6377

Internet: u15608@uicvm.uic.edu

Bitnet: u15608@uicvm

Copyright statement: All postings are in the public domain.

How to access: Send this message to LISTSERV@UICVM; sub H-RHETORIC Firstname Lastname, School or Affiliation

Access policy: This list is open to all historians of rhetoric.

How to unsubscribe: Send this message to LISTSERV@UICVM: unsub H-RHETORIC

How to submit: Send submission to h-rhetoric@uicvm

Submission policy: Moderator selects postings of interest to scholars in history of rhetoric; news items especially welcome. All items must be signed.

Archives: Monthly logs stored and open.

Related files: FILESERVER files available.Request by sending message INDEX h-rhetoric to LISTSERV@UICVM

H-RURAL@UICVM

Description: H-Rural@uicvm is a discussion group centering on rural and agricultural history.

Subjects covered: rural studies; history; agriculture

Net address for operations: listserv@uicvm

Net address for questions or submissions: H-Rural@uicvm

How to access: Send message to listserv: SUBSCRIBE <listname> <your name>

H-SOUTH@UICVM

Description: H-South@uicvm is a discussion group centering on the southern United States.

Subjects covered: rural studies; history

Net address for operations: listserv@uicvm

Net address for questions or submissions: H-South@uicvm

How to access: Send message to listserv: SUBSCRIBE <listname> <your name>

H-TEACH

Description: H-Teach is an electronic discussion group intended to enable historians to easily communicate about teaching approaches, methods, problems, and resources. H-Teach will facilitate discussion on the wide range of policy issues involved in teaching history at the college and university level. H-Teach will be particularly interested in methods of teaching history to graduate and undergraduate students in diverse settings. Special attention will be paid to use of new technologies in and outside of the classroom. H-Teach will also provide a forum for exchange of information about specific teaching tools including texts, videos, exams, and assignments. H-Teach will publish syllabi, outlines, handouts, bibliographies, guides to termpapers, listings of new sources, library catalogs and archives, and reports on new software, datasets and cd-roms. H-Teach will also post announcements of conferences, fellowships, and jobs. Subscribers will write in with questions, comments, and reports. H-Teach will carry publisher's announcements of new books, and we will commission book reviews.

Subjects covered: education; distance education; library and information science; colleges and universities

Net address for operations: LISTSERV@uicvm, LISTSERV@uicvm.uic.edu

List moderated: Yes.

Moderation procedure: H-Teach will be moderated to filter out extraneous messages (like requests for subscription) and items that don't belong on H-Teach. They may belong somewhere else, or in the moderator's judgment they do not aid the scholarly dialogue. The moderator will not alter anyone's meaning (but will, if necessary, add name and e-address). All contributions to H-Teach will become part of the public domain and can be freely used, printed, copied or retransmitted if credit is given to the original author.

Editorial contact: Mark Kornbluh
Washington University, St Louis

Internet: H-Teach@Artsci.wustl.edu

How to access: Send this email message to LISTSERV@uicvm or LISTSERV@uicvm.uic.edu: sub H-Teach firstname surname, school [i.e. sub H-Teach Leslie Jones, Southern Jersey U.]

How to submit: Send an email note directly to H-TEACH@UICVM

Related files: Documents of interest--bibliographies, book and article reviews, announcements, teaching materials, and descriptions of tools, techniques, and computer software and hardware, plus the weekly files of messages--will be made available from the H-Teach fileserver. Contributions to the archive are welcome, and should be sent as files to H-TEACH@UICVM.

H-URBAN

Description: H-URBAN is a new international electronic discussion group. It has been set up at the University of Illinois at Chicago (UIC) in order to provide a forum for scholars of Urban History. There are no geographical or chronological boundaries. Subscription is free, and subscribers will automatically receive messages in their computer mailboxes. Messages can be saved, discarded, copied, printed out, or relayed to someone else. It's like a newsletter that is free and published daily. The primary purpose of H-URBAN is to enable historians to easily communicate current research and teaching interests; to discuss new approaches, methods and tools of analysis; to test new ideas and share comments on current historiography. H-URBAN will be especially interested in methods of teaching history to graduate and undergraduate students in diverse settings. H-URBAN will have an editorial board broadly representative of the state of scholarship. 2. H-URBAN will feature dialogues in the discipline among historians of women across the world. It will publish syllabi, outlines, handouts, bibliographies, guides to termpapers, listings of new sources and archives, and reports on new software, datasets and cd-roms. Subscribers will write in with questions, comments, and reports. H-URBAN will post announcements of conferences, fellowships and jobs. We expect many messages at first will be of the ''how can I do this with my computer?'' variety and also ''where can I locate such-and-such?'' Please send them in, for someone on the list will be able to help.
Subjects covered: urban history; history; technology education
Net address for operations: Listserv@uicvm.uic.edu
Net address for questions or submissions: H-Urban@uicvm.uic.edu, H-Urban@uicvm
Established: February 1993
Subscribers: 188
Sponsor: University of Illinois at Chicago, History Department, (M/C 198), 723 SEO, 851 S. Morgan St., Chicago, IL 60607-7049.
Host: University of Illinois at Chicago, History Department, (M/C 198), 723 SEO, 851 S. Morgan St., Chicago, IL 60607-7049.
List moderated: Yes.
Moderation procedure: All messages for H-Urban received by moderator; generally released without any change; occasionally delayed due to volume of messages.
Editorial contact: Wendy Plotkin
University of Illinois at Chicago, History Department, (M/C 198), 723 SEO, 851 S. Morgan St., Chicago, IL 60607-7049.
Tel: (312) 996-3141
Fax: (312) 996-6377
Internet: U15608@uicvm.uic.edu
Bitnet: U15608@uicvm
How to access: Send note to listserv@uicvm.uic.edu or listserv@uicvm with message Subscribe H-Urban Firstname Lastname School/Organization
Access policy: All welcome; prefer faculty, professional, graduate students.
How to unsubscribe: Send note to listserv@uicvm.uic.edu or listserv@uicvm with message Signoff H-Urban
How to submit: Send note to H-Urban@uicvm.uic.edu or H-Urban@uicvm.uic.edu
Submission policy: Should be addressed to academic discussion or announcement of resources; submitters should realize that scholars have many demands on time, and submittals should be something that will add to ability of urban historians to teach or conduct research. Majority of submissions should be related to urban history; however, more general interest messages will be distributed in moderation.
Archives: H-Urban maintains a Listserv fileserver which is attempting to include all messages as files, grouped together and indexed by subject. To obtain the list of documents, send a note to Listserv@uicvm or Listserv@uicvm.uic.edu with the message ''Index H-Urban''; to obtain a file, send a note to Listserv@ uicvm or Listserv@uicvm.uic.edu with the message Get ''Filename Filetype''
Gopher accessibility: An urban history gopher linked to HNServer at University of Kansas will be in place by end of July 1993.
Additional information: The H-URBAN Editorial Board comprises: Burton Bledstein, UIC; William Crozier, St. Mary's College, MN; Perry Duis, UIC; Daniel Greenstein, U of Glasgow; James Grossman Newberry Library; Michael H. Ebner, Lake Forest College, Exec. Secretary, Urban History Association; David Jordan, UIC; Louise Kerr, UIC; Eric Monkkonen, UCLA; Janice Reiff, UCLA.

H-WOMEN

Description: H-WOMEN is a forum for scholars and teachers of women's history, centering on the social history of women.
Subjects covered: history; feminism; women's studies
Net address for operations: LISTSERV@UICVM, LISTSERV@UICVM.UIC.EDU
Established: 1993
Subscribers: 350
Sponsor: H-Net, Dept of History, m/c 198, 851 South Morgan St., SEO 723, Chicago, IL 60607-7049.
Host: University of Illinois-Chicago, Dept of History, m/c 198, 851 South Morgan St., SEO 723, Chicago, IL 60607-7049.
List moderated: Yes.
Moderation procedure: Moderator examines all messages.
Editorial contact: Richard Jensen
H-Net, Dept of History, m/c 198, 851 South Morgan St., SEO 723, Chicago, IL 60607-7049.
Tel: 312-996-3140
Fax: 312-996-6377
Internet: u08946@uicvm.uic.edu
Bitnet: u08946@uicvm
Technical contact: Wendy Plotkin
Dept of History, m/c 198, 851 South Morgan St., SEO 723, Chicago, IL 60607-7049.
Tel: 312-996-3141
Fax: 312-996-6377
Internet: u15608@uicvm.uic.edu
Bitnet: u15608@uicvm
Copyright statement: All postings are in the public domain.
How to access: Send this message to LISTSERV@UICVM sub H-WOMEN Firstname Lastname, School or Affiliation
Access policy: This list is open to all historians of women.
How to unsubscribe: Send this message to LISTSERV@UICVM unsub H-WOMEN
How to submit: Send submission to h-women@uicvm
Submission policy: Moderator selects postings of interest to scholars in women's history; news items especially welcome. All items must be signed.
Archives: Monthly logs stored and open.
Related files: FILESERVER files available. request by this message to LISTSERV@UICVM INDEX h-women

HABSBURG@PURCCVM

Description: HABSBURG@PURCCVM is a discussion group on Austrian history since 1500.
Subjects covered: Austria; history
Net address for operations: LISTSERV@PURCCVM
Net address for questions or submissions: HABSBURG@PURCCVM
How to access: Send message to listserv: SUBSCRIBE <listname> <your name>

HARP-L

Description: Harp-L is a forum covering harmonica playing.
Subjects covered: music; musical instruments
List moderated: No.
Editorial contact: Chris Pierce
Bitnet: pierccm@wkuvx1
How to access: Send subscribe message to listserv@wkuvx1
How to unsubscribe: Send unsubscribe message to listserv@wkuvx1

HCFNET@UCSBVM

Description: HCFNET covers humanities computing centers on college campuses.
Subjects covered: humanities; colleges and universities; computer hardware and software
List moderated: Yes.
Editorial contact: Eric Dahlin
Bitnet: hcfidahl@ucsbuxa
How to access: Send subscribe message to listserv@ucsbvm
How to unsubscribe: Send unsubscribe message to listserv@ucsbvm
Archives: Archives are developed monthly; apply to listowner for details.

HDESK-L

Description: Hdesk-L is a discussion group for managers and staff of computer-related academic help desks.
Subjects covered: campus-wide information systems
List moderated: No.
Editorial contact: Roman J. Olynyk
Internet: u0ba9@wvnvm.wvnet.edu
Bitnet: u0ba9@wvnvm
How to access: Send subscribe message to listserv@wvnvm or listserv@wvnvmwvnet.edu
How to unsubscribe: Send unsubscribe message to listserv@wvnvm or listserv@wvnvmwvnet.edu

HEADER-PEOPLE@MC.LCS.MIT.EDU

Description: HEADER-PEOPLE is a discussion on topics related to network messaging technology and standardization.
Subjects covered: computer science; electronic networking; electronic mail
List moderated: No.
Editorial contact: Pandora B. Berman
Internet: cent@ai.ai.mit.edu
How to access: Send subscribe message to HEADER-PEOPLE-REQUEST@MC.LCS.MIT.EDU
How to unsubscribe: Send unsubscribe message to HEADER-PEOPLE-REQUEST@MC.LCS.MIT.EDU

Archives: Yes; For recent files, send FTP to MIT-MC (MC.LCS.MIT.EDU) file KSC;HEADER MINS, or, for older files, KSC;HEADER MINS00 through MINS15

HEALTH-L

Description: Health-L is a conference on health research.
Subjects covered: health sciences; medicine
List moderated: No.
Editorial contact: Jill Foster
Internet: jill.foster@newcastle.ac.uk
How to access: Send subscribe message to listserv@irlearn or listserv@irlearn.ucd.ie
How to unsubscribe: Send unsubscribe message to listserv@irlearn or listserv@irlearn.ucd.ie
Archives: Archives are developed monthly; apply to listowner for details.

HEBLANG

Description: HEBLANG is a list centering on discussions of Hebrew Etymology, and Grammar.
Subjects covered: Hebrew language and literature; Semitic language and literature
Net address for operations: LISTSERV@israel.nysernet.org
Net address for questions or submissions: HEBLANG@israel.nysernet.org
Established: April 1993
Subscribers: 94
Sponsor: Israel.Nysernet.Org
Host: Israel.Nysernet.Org
List moderated: No.
Editorial contact: Benjamin Kite
3838 East Grant Avenue, Terre Haute, Indiana 47805
Tel: (812) 466-3262
Internet: ajax@judy.indstate.edu
Bitnet: FLKITE@INDSVAX1
Sample contents: The Etymology and Grammar of Modern, Biblical, Tiberian, Medieval, and most other forms of Hebrew, with some branching into other Semitic languages, such as Aramaic or Arabic.
How to access: Send the words ''SUBSCRIBE HEBLANG <firstname> <lastname>'' on the first line of an otherwise blank e-mail message addressed to <LISTSERV@israel.nysernet.org>.
Access policy: Subscription is only restricted to those who have not kept their postings civil and germane in the past.
How to unsubscribe: Send the words ''UNSUBSCRIBE HEBLANG'' on the first line of an otherwise blank e-mail message addressed to <LISTSERV@israel.nysernet.org>.
How to submit: Send e-mail directly to HEBLANG@israel.nysernet.org. That mail will become your submission.
Submission policy: Submissions will not be refused, however, a persistent stream of irrelevant, rude or otherwise inappropriate postings will instigate removal from the list for the user.
Archives: Archived at Israel.Nysernet.Org
Related files: HEBLANG.STANDARDS (Availible through ajax@judy.indstate.edu or from <FLKITE@INDSVAX1.BITNET>
Gopher accessibility: See <warren@israel.nysernet.org>

HEBREW-L
Description: Hebrew-L is a forum for Jewish studies.
Subjects covered: Judaica
List moderated: Yes.
Editorial contact: Prof. Tzvee Zahavy
Bitnet: maic@uminn1
How to access: Send subscribe message to listserv@uminn1
How to unsubscribe: Send unsubscribe message to listserv@uminn1
Archives: Yes.

HEGEL@VILLVM
Description: HEGEL@VILLVM is a forum studying the works of the German philosopher, G. W. F. Hegel (1770-1931).
Subjects covered: philosophy; Hegel, G. W. F.
Host: Hegel Society of America
List moderated: No.
Editorial contact: Dr. Lawrence S. Stepelevitch
Bitnet: stepelev@vuvaxcom
How to access: Send subscribe message to listserv@villvm
How to unsubscribe: Send unsubscribe message to listserv@villvm
Archives: Archives are developed monthly; apply to listowner for details.

HELLAS@AUVM
Description: HELLAS@AUVM covers Greek topics (in Greek language).
Subjects covered: communications; Greece
List moderated: Yes.
Editorial contact: Spiros Liolis
Bitnet: sliolis@auvm
How to access: Send subscribe message to listserv@auvm or listserv@auvm.auvm.edu
How to unsubscribe: Send unsubscribe message to listserv@auvm or listserv@auvm.auvm.edu
Archives: Yes; Weekly, Private

HELP-NET@TEMPLEVM
Description: HELP-NET@TEMPLEVM is a forum providing assistance with software and utilities for users of the Internet and Bitnet networks.
Subjects covered: electronic networking; Internet
List moderated: No.
Editorial contact: Jeff Linder
Internet: jeff@monet.ocis.temple.edu
Bitnet: v5057u@templevm
How to access: Send subscribe message to listserv@templevm or listserv@vm.temple.edu
How to unsubscribe: Send unsubscribe message to listserv@templevm or listserv@vm.temple.edu

HELPNET@NDSUVM1
Description: HELPNET@NDSUVM1 is a forum on how global networks may help in times of disasters (i.e. hurricanes, earthquakes, etc.)
Subjects covered: electronic networking; information technology
List moderated: Yes.

Editorial contact: Marty Hoag
Internet: mhoag@vm1.nodak.edu
Bitnet: info@ndsuvm1
How to access: Send subscribe message to listserv@ndsuvm1 or listserv@vm1.nodak.edu
How to unsubscribe: Send unsubscribe message to listserv@ndsuvm1 or listserv@vm1.nodak.edu
Archives: Archives are developed weekly; apply to listowner for details.

HELWA-L
Description: HELWA-L is a list for discussion of concerns related to Malaysian women in the U.S. and Canada.
Subjects covered: Malasia; feminism; women's studies
Net address for operations: LISTSERV@PSUVM
List moderated: No.
How to access: Send subscription messages to LISTSERV@PSUVM

HEPNET-J@JPNKEKVM
Description: HEPNET-J is the Japanese HEPnet.
Subjects covered: physics
List moderated: No.
Editorial contact: Yukio Karita/KEK
Bitnet: karita@jpnkekvx
How to access: Send subscribe message to listserv@jpnkekvm
How to unsubscribe: Send unsubscribe message to listserv@jpnkekvm
Archives: Archives are developed monthly; apply to listowner for details.

HEPROC-L (HIGHER EDUCATION PROCESSES DISCUSSION LIST)
Description: HEPROC-L is a new list that brings together diverse members of the higher education community in order to probe questions, problems, and solutions within higher education (HE), and to electronically publish at no cost the results of that probing. Careful facilitation will allow the list to accurately reflect the true knowledge of its membership and to enjoy a reasonable mail volume.
Subjects covered: education; colleges and universities
Editorial contact: Carl Reimann
PO Box 480, Clarksburg, MD 20871-0480.
Tel: (301) 972-1155
Fax: (301) 972-1144
Internet: p00714@psilink.com
How to access: Send SUB HEPROC-L <YOUR NAME> to LISTSERV@AMERICAN.EDU or @AUVM.BITNET

HERB
Description: HERB is a discussion group on herbs and plants in medicine and related fields.
Subjects covered: medicinal plants; gardening
Net address for operations: LISTSERV@TREARN.BITNET
Net address for questions or submissions: HERB@TREARN.BITNET
Established: 1990
Subscribers: 350

Sponsor: Ege Univ. Bilgisayar Ar. ve Uyg. Mrk. 35100 Bornova Izmir Turkey
Host: Same as above
List moderated: No.
Editorial contact: Esra Delen
Ege Univ. Bilgisayar Ar. ve Uyg. Mrk. 35100 Bornova Izmir Turkey
Tel: 90-51-887221
Fax: 90-51-887221
Internet: ESRA@EGE.EDU.TR
Bitnet: ESRA@TREARN
How to access: Tell Listserv at TREARN SUB HERB fullname
How to unsubscribe: Tell Listserv at TREARN SIGNOFF HERB
How to submit: Mail to HERB@TREARN
Archives: Available via LOG files on LISTSERV.

HESSE-L
Description: Hesse-L is a forum covering the life and works of Hermann Hesse.
Subjects covered: German language and literature; Hesse, Herman
List moderated: Yes.
Editorial contact: Gunther Gottschalk
Internet: gs01gott@humanitas.ucsb.edu
Bitnet: hcf2hess@ucsbuxa
How to access: Send subscribe message to listserv@ucsbvm
How to unsubscribe: Send unsubscribe message to listserv@ucsbvm
Archives: Archives are developed monthly; apply to listowner for details.

HILAT-L
Description: HILAT-L (Higher Education in Latin America) is a discussion group centering on research into education in Latin American countries.
Subjects covered: Latin America; education
Net address for operations: listserv@bruspvm.bitnet
How to access: Send standard subscribe request to listserv.
How to unsubscribe: Send standard unsubscribe request to listserv.

HIM-L (HEALTH INFORMATION MANAGEMENT)
Description: The purpose of HIM-L is to: facilitate the transition of ''medical record'' practitioners to ''health information managers''; discuss current legislative, accreditation, and regulatory issues affecting the HIM field; provide a forum for health information management educators to share educational strategies; develop joint student projects within and between HIM programs; provide interaction for HIM students with educators and students from other HIM programs; and provide an opportunity for HIM students to practice using a listserv.
Subjects covered: health sciences; administration; management
Net address for operations: listserv@fiona.umsmed.edu
Net address for questions or submissions: him-l@fiona.umsmed.edu
Established: June 1993
Sponsor: University of Mississippi Medical Center, 2500 N. State Street, Jackson, MS 39216.

Host: University of Mississippi Medical Center, 2500 N. State Street, Jackson, MS 39216.
List moderated: No.
Editorial contact: Ann H. Peden
University of MS Med. Ctr. -SHRP,
2500 N. State St., Jackson, MS 39216.
Tel: (601) 984-6305
Fax: (601) 984-6344
Internet: apeden@fiona.umsmed.edu
Technical contact: Daryl Rester
Systems Programme, University of MS Med. Ctr., 2500 N. State St., Jackson, MS 39216.
Tel: (601) 984-1162
Internet: rester@fiona.umsmed.edu
How to access: Send command to listserv@fiona.umsmed.edu: SUBSCRIBE HIM-L Your Full Name
Access policy: Subscription is open to all interested in the purposes of the list.
How to unsubscribe: Send command to listserve@fiona.umsmed.edu: UNSUBSCRIBE HIM-L
How to submit: Mail message to him-l@fiona.umsmed.edu
Submission policy: This is an unmoderated list.

HIRIS-L
Description: HIRIS-L is a list for high resolution infrared spectroscopy.
Subjects covered: chemistry
List moderated: Yes.
Editorial contact: Alberto Gambi
Bitnet: g1wudo32@icineca
How to access: Send subscribe message to listserv@iveuncc
How to unsubscribe: Send unsubscribe message to listserv@iveuncc
Archives: Archives are developed yearly; apply to listowner for details.

HISLAW-L
Description: Hislaw-L provides a forum for discussion on the history of law.
Subjects covered: law and legal studies
Host: University of Louisville
List moderated: No.
Editorial contact: James A. Cocks
Internet: jacock01@ulkyvm.louisville.edu
Bitnet: jacock01@ulkyvm
How to access: Send subscribe message to listserv@ulkyvm or listserv@ulkyvm.louisville.edu
How to unsubscribe: Send unsubscribe message to listserv@ulkyvm or listserv@ulkyvm.louisville.edu

HISTEC-L
Description: Histec-L is a discussion list on evangelical Christianity.
Subjects covered: religion; Christianity
List moderated: Yes.
Editorial contact: Daniel H. Bays
Bitnet: bays@ukanvm
How to access: Contact the Editor
How to unsubscribe: Contact the Editor
Archives: Yes; Send anonymous FTP to: kuhub.cc.ukans.edu and cd malin.histec

HISTORY-ECON@MAILBASE.AC.UK

Description: HISTORY-ECON@MAILBASE.AC.UK is a forum covering economic history.
Subjects covered: economics; history; education
List moderated: No.
Internet: history-econ-request@mailbase.ac.uk
How to access: Send subscribe message to mailbase@mailbase.ac.uk in the following format: join history-econ Yourfirstname Yourlastname
Archives: Archives are developed monthly; apply to listowner for details.

HISTORY-METHODS@MAILBASE.AC.UK

Description: HISTORY-METHODS@MAILBASE.AC.UK is an electronic conference discussing computer-based historical methodologies.
Subjects covered: history; information technology
List moderated: No.
Internet: history-methods-request@mailbase.ac.uk
How to access: Send subscribe message to mailbase@mailbase.ac.uk in the following format: join history-methods Yourfirstname Yourlastname
Archives: Archives are developed monthly; apply to listowner for details.

HISTORY-TEACHING@MAILBASE.AC.UK

Description: HISTORY-TEACHING@MAILBASE.AC.UK covers the use of computers in teaching.
Subjects covered: education; computer-assisted instruction (CAI)
Host: Computers in Teaching Initiative, Centre for History
List moderated: No.
Internet: history-teaching-request@mailbase.ac.uk
How to access: Send subscribe message to mailbase@mailbase.ac.uk in the following format: join history-teaching Yourfirstname Yourlastname
Archives: Archives are developed monthly; apply to listowner for details.

HISTORY-VASCO@MAILBASE.AC.UK

Description: HISTORY-VASCO@MAILBASE.AC.UK is an electronic forum for dicussing the discoveries of Portuguese explorers in the 15th and 16th centuries.
Subjects covered: history; Portugal; exploration
Host: Centre for the Study of the Portuguese Discoveries, Linacre College, Oxford
List moderated: No.
Internet: history-vasco-request@mailbase.ac.uk
How to access: Send subscribe message to mailbase@mailbase.ac.uk in the following format: join history-vasco Yourfirstname Yourlastname
Archives: Archives are developed monthly; apply to listowner for details.

HISTORY@PSUVM

Description: history@psuvm is a discussion group focusing on general history topics.
Subjects covered: history
Net address for operations: listserv@psuvm

Net address for questions or submissions: history@psuvm
Subscribers: 480
Editorial contact: Thomas Zielke
Bitnet: TZIELKE@DGOGWDG1
How to access: Send an e-mail message with blank subject line to: LISTSERV@PSUVM (Bitnet address) or LISTSERV@PSUVM.PSU.EDU (Internet address). Message should consist solely of: SUBSCRIBE HISTORY your__name
Related files: Related files include:HISTORY@DGOGWDG1 (ARCHIVES); HISTORY@IRLEARN (ARCHIVES); HISTORY@RUTVM1 (ARCHIVES); HIST-L@UKANVM (ARCHIVES); HISTORY@UMRVMB (ARCHIVES); HISTORY@UBV; HISTORY@MCGILL1; HISTORY@CSEARN

HISTORYA@UWAVM

Description: HISTORYA@UWAVM is an electronic discussion centering on history.
Subjects covered: history
List moderated: No.
Internet: kamai@milton.u.washington.edu
How to access: Send subscribe message to listserv@uwavm
How to unsubscribe: Send unsubscribe message to listserv@uwavm
Archives: Yes; Monthly, Private

HISTOWNR@UBVM

Description: HISTOWNR@UBVM is a forum for all history-related discussion-list owners.
Subjects covered: history
Host: Historisches Seminar, Universitat Oldenburg
List moderated: No.
Editorial contact: Thomas Zielke
Internet: 113355@doluni1
How to access: Send subscribe message to listserv@ubvm.cc.buffalo.edu
How to unsubscribe: Send unsubscribe message to listserv@ubvm.cc.buffalo.edu

HIT@UFRJ

Description: HIT@UFRJ, or Highly Imaginative Technology and Science Fiction, is an e-conference which discusses future technology and science fiction.
Subjects covered: science and technology; futurism; science fiction
List moderated: No.
Editorial contact: Geraldo Xexeo
Internet: xexeo@rio.cos.ufrj.nr
Bitnet: gxexeo@cernvm
Review: Reviewed by List Review Service edited by Raleigh Muns: see appendix.
How to access: Send subscribe message to listserv@ufrj or listserv%ufrj.bitnet@cunyvm.cuny.edu
How to unsubscribe: Send unsubscribe message to listserv@ufrj or listserv%ufrj.bitnet@cunyvm.cuny.edu
Archives: Archives are developed monthly; apply to listowner for details.

HL-7

Description: HL-7 is an electronic conference designed to foster communication concerning technical, operational, and business

issues involved in the use of the HL-7 interface protocol. It is also intended as a forum for the HL-7 Working Group members who are participating in the specification of the interface protocol. Health Level Seven is an application protocol for electronic data exchange in health care environments. It is called level seven because the protocol assumes the underlying network support of levels one through six of the Open Systems Interconnection (OSI) network model of the International Standards Organization (ISO). The HL-7 standard is specified at the seventh level, which is the application level. This HL-7 (Health Level Seven) Conference is not an offical part of the HL-7 Working Group and Executive Committee.
Subjects covered: Health Level Seven; electronic data exchange; computer hardware and software; telecommunications
Net address for operations: HL-7-REQUEST@VIRGINIA.EDU: HL-7 HL-7-REQ@VIRGINIA.BITNET
Host: University of Virginia
Editorial contact: David John Marotta
Medical Center Computing, Stacey Hall, University of Virginia, Box 512 Med. Cntr., Charlottesville, VA 22908
Tel: (804) 982-3718
Fax: (804) 296-7209
Internet: djm5g@virginia.edu
Bitnet: djm5g@virginia
How to access: You may subscribe by sending an e-mail message to: HL-7-REQUEST@VIRGINIA.EDU(Internet); HL-7-REQ@VIRGINIA.BITNET(Bitnet) with the following request as the text of the message. SUB HL-7 YourFirstname YourLastname This, the 'SUB ...,' must be part of the message; the subject line will be ignored. Remember two simple rules-of-thumb: If it's a request (SUBscribe, UNSUBscribe), send it to the list requester: HL-7-REQUEST@VIRGINIA.EDU(Internet) HL-7-REQ@VIRGINIA.BITNET(Bitnet).
Access policy: In accordance with current CREN regulations, commercial activity (such as the selling of software) will be prohibited. Subscription to this conference is open to anyone interested.
Additional information: Official inquiries concerning HL-7 (Health Level Seven) should be sent directly to: Health Level Seven, 900 Victors Way, Suite 122, Ann Arbor, MI 48108; voice: (313) 665-0007, and fax: (313) 665-0399.

HLIST@ONEB.ALMANAC.BC.CA
Description: HLIST@ONEB.ALMANAC.BC.CA is an electronic conference on the Holocaust.
Subjects covered: history; Holocaust studies
List moderated: No.
How to access: Send subscribe message to listserv@oneb.almanac.bc.ca
How to unsubscribe: Send unsubscribe message to listserv@oneb.almanac.bc.ca

HN-ASK-L
Description: HN-Ask-L is a discussion group focusing on information on history lists and communications.
Subjects covered: history; communications
Net address for operations: LISTSERV@ukanvm
Net address for questions or submissions: HN-Ask-L@ukanvm
How to access: Send message to listserv: SUBSCRIBE <listname> <your name>

HOLOCAUST@UICVM
Description: HOLOCAUST@uicvm is a discussion group centering on Holocaust research and information.
Subjects covered: Holocaust studies; history
Net address for operations: LISTSERV@uicvm
Net address for questions or submissions: HOLOCAUST@uicvm
How to access: Send message to listserv: SUBSCRIBE <listname> <your name>

HOME-ED@THINK.COM
Description: The Home Education mailing list is a forum for everyone interested in children learning at home. Many of us are parents or thinking about becoming parents. Some are not. Some of us are already educating our children at home, others planning to, others just curious. We come from all walks of life, from across the United States (and at least one person each from Canada, U.K., Australia, New Zealand, and Malaysia), and from many different philosophical backgrounds. Everyone is welcome, as long as they are willing to engage in polite (if occasionally animated) discussion with people holding other beliefs. This is a place to share information, to ask questions, to discuss problems and successes; it is an electronic general store, post office, village green, or whatever metaphor you like, where people interested in educating their children come together. Children are welcome on the list. If your child is able to use a computer well enough to read our postings and respond, they are mature enough to participate in the discussion. We use the term ''Home Education'' to try to encompass all approaches to children learning at home, whether by schooling, child-directed learning or any other process.
Subjects covered: education; home education
Net address for operations: home-ed-request@think.com
Net address for questions or submissions: home-ed@think.com
Established: Early 1991
Subscribers: 271
List moderated: No.
Editorial contact: David Mankins
Thinking Machines Corporation, 245 First St., Cambridge, MA 02142.
Internet: home-ed-request@think.com
How to access: Send a request to home-ed-request@think.com
How to unsubscribe: Send a request to home-ed-request@think.com
How to submit: Send a message to home-ed@think.com
Submission policy: We frown on overtly political discussions.

HOPOS-L
Description: HOPOS-L is a discussion list for members of HOPOS, the History of Philosophy of Science Working Group. Principle focus is on the history of the philosophy of science, but discussion ranges widely over topics in the history of science, the philosohpy of science, the sociology of science, science education, and related topics.
Subjects covered: science and technology; history of science; philosophy; education
Net address for operations: LISTSERV@UKCC.UKY.EDU
Net address for questions or submissions: HOPOS-L@UKCC.UKY.EDU
Established: July 1992
Subscribers: 400

Sponsor: Department of Philosophy, University of Kentucky, Lexington, KY 40506-0027.
Host: Department of Philosophy, University of Kentucky, Lexington, KY 40506-0027.
List moderated: Yes.
Moderation procedure: List is monitored by listowner. In those rare instances when problems arise, the listowner communicates directly with the parties involved the correct the problem.
Editorial contact: Don Howard
Department of Philosophy, University of Kentucky, Lexington, KY 40506-0027.
Tel: 606-257-4376
Fax: 606-258-1073
Internet: einphil@ukcc.uky.edu
Bitnet: einphil@ukcc
How to access: Send one-line message of the form subscribe hopos-l Your Name to listserv@ukcc.uky.edy
Access policy: This list is open to the public.
How to unsubscribe: Send one-line message of the form unsubscribe hopos-l to listserv@ukcc.uky.edu
How to submit: Send message to hopos-l@ukcc.uky.edu
Archives: For list of archive files, send one-line message of the form: index hopos-l to listserv@ukcc.uky.edu.
Related files: See HOPOS subdirectory under Science Studies at gopher kasey.umkc.edu

HORROR@PACEVM

Description: HORROR@PACEVM is a forum for discussion of horror films and literature.
Subjects covered: horror fiction; science fiction; cinema studies
List moderated: No.
Editorial contact: Cliff Brenner
Bitnet: vman@pacevm
How to access: Send subscribe message to listserv@pacevm
How to unsubscribe: Send unsubscribe message to listserv@pacevm
Archives: Archives are developed monthly; apply to listowner for details.

HORT-L

Description: Hort-L covers horticulture.
Subjects covered: horticulture
Host: Horticulture Dpartment, Virginia Polytechnic Institute
List moderated: Yes.
Editorial contact: Diane Relf
Bitnet: pdrelf@vtvm1
How to access: Send subscribe message to listserv@vtvm1
How to unsubscribe: Send unsubscribe message to listserv@vtvm1

HOUNDS OF THE INTERNET

Description: Hounds of the Internet is a list discussing Sherlock Holmes and anything relating to him and his times.
Subjects covered: Holmes, Sherlock; language and literature; Doyle, Sir Arthur Conan; English language and literature
Net address for operations: hounds@beloit.edu
Net address for questions or submissions: hounds@beloit.edu
Established: October 1992
Subscribers: 57
Sponsor: Beloit College, 700 College St. Beloit WI 53511

Host: Same as above
List moderated: Yes.
Moderation procedure: Messages not meant for the entire list or that are garbage characters are weeded out
Editorial contact: Alan Block
700 College Street, Beloit WI 53511
Tel: (608) 363-2464
Internet: blocka@beloit.edu
How to access: Send a request to hounds@beloit.edu
Access policy: Anyone who requests gets on.
How to submit: Send mail to hounds@beloit.edu
Submission policy: Anything that is about Holmes and is not attacking any individual or espousing any views outside of the purview of the list's mission.
Archives: Some archives are available on request.
Related files: Gopher access to all Holmes texts in electronic form.
WAIS accessibility: Limited WAIS available.

HPSST-L

Description: Hpsst-L discusses the relationships between history and the philosophy of science.
Subjects covered: philosophy; history of science
List moderated: No.
Editorial contact: Doug Farquhar
Internet: farquadad@qucdn.queenssu.ca
How to access: Send subscribe message to listserv@qucdn
How to unsubscribe: Send unsubscribe message to listserv@qucdn
Archives: Archives are developed monthly; apply to listowner for details.

HRD-L

Description: HRD-L is a discussion forum on topics related to human resource development.
Subjects covered: human resources
List moderated: No.
Editorial contact: John Cofer
Bitnet: cofer@utkvx
How to access: Send subscribe message to LISTSERV@MIZZOU1
How to unsubscribe: Send unsubscribe message to LISTSERV@MIZZOU1
Archives: Archives are developed yearly; apply to listowner for details.

HRI-L

Description: HRI-L is a forum for high-resolution imaging in astronomy.
Subjects covered: astronomy
List moderated: No.
Editorial contact: Marco de Vos
Internet: devoscm@hgrrug5
How to access: Send subscribe message to listserv@hearn or listserv%hearn.bitnet@cunyvm.cuny.edu
How to unsubscribe: Send unsubscribe message to listserv@hearn or listserv%hearn.bitnet@cunyvm.cuny.edu

HRIS-L
Description: HRIS-L is a Canadian forum on human resources issues.
Subjects covered: human resources
List moderated: No.
Editorial contact: Dee Shriver
Bitnet: dschrive@ualtvm
How to access: Send subscribe message to listserv@ualtavm or listserv@vm.ucs.ualberta.ca
How to unsubscribe: Send unsubscribe message to listserv@ualtavm or listserv@vm.ucs.ualberta.ca
Archives: Archives are developed monthly; apply to listowner for details.

HSPNET-L
Description: Hspnet-L is a conference which discusses rural hospitals.
Subjects covered: medicine
List moderated: Yes.
Editorial contact: Donald F. Parsons, M.D.
Bitnet: dfp10@albnydh2 or dfp10@albnyvm1
How to access: Send subscribe message to DFP10@ALBNYDH2
How to unsubscribe: Send unsubscribe message to DFP10@ALBNYDH2
Archives: Yes; Separate

HTECH-L@SIVM
Description: HTech-L is a discussion list covering the history of technology.
Subjects covered: science and technology; history
Net address for operations: LISTSERV@SIVM
Net address for questions or submissions: HTech-L@SIVM
How to access: Send message to listserv: SUBSCRIBE <listname> <your name>

HUMANIST@BROWNVM
Description: HUMANIST is a list covering computer use in the humanities.
Subjects covered: humanities; computer hardware and software
List moderated: Yes.
Editorial contact: Allen Renear and Ellen Brennan
Internet: editors@brownvm.brown.edu
Bitnet: editors@brownvm
How to access: Send subscribe message to listserv@brownvm or listserv@brownvm.brown.edu
How to unsubscribe: Send unsubscribe message to listserv@brownvm or listserv@brownvm.brown.edu
Archives: Archives are developed weekly; apply to listowner for details.

HUMBIO-L
Description: Humbio-L is an unmoderated discussion list dealing with biological anthropology, adaptation, environmental stress, biological race, growth, genetics, paleoanthropology, skeletal biology, forensic anthropology, paleodemography, paleopathology, primate biology & behavior.
Subjects covered: biology; anthropology; genetics
Net address for operations: HumBio-Request@Acc.Fau.Edu

Net address for questions or submissions: HumBio-L@Acc.Fau.Edu
Established: Late 1991
Subscribers: 220
Sponsor: Florida Atlantic University, 500 NorthWest 20th Street, Boca Raton, FL 33431-0991.
Host: Florida Atlantic University, 500 NorthWest 20th Street, Boca Raton, FL 33431-0991.
List moderated: No.
Editorial contact: M. Yasar Iscan
Dept of Anthropology, FAU, Boca Raton, FL 33431.
Tel: 407-367-3230
Fax: 407-367-2744
Internet: ISCAN@ACC.FAU.EDU
Bitnet: ISCAN@FAUVAX
Technical contact: Ralph P. Carpenter
Department of Psychology, Florida Atlantic University, Boca Raton, FL 33431-0991.
Tel: 407/367-2616
Fax: 407/367-2749
Internet: Ralpho@Acc.Fau.Edu
Bitnet: Ralpho@FauVax
How to access: Email to HumBio-Request@Acc.Fau.Edu (BITNET-restricted users send to HumBio-Request@FAUVAX). The sole content of the message BODY must be: Subscribe HumBio-L John Q Public
Access policy: This discussion list is open to all interested individuals or organizations.
How to unsubscribe: From EXACTLY the same address from which the original subscription was requested, Email to HumBio-Request@Acc.Fau.Edu (BITNET-restricted users send to HumBio-Request@FauVax). The sole content of the message BODY must be: Unsubscribe HUMBIO-L
How to submit: Email to HumBio-L@Acc.Fau.Edu (BITNET-restricted users send to HumBio-L@FauVax)

HUMBUL (HUMANITIES BULLETIN BOARD)
Description: HUMBUL is an online bulletin board project aimed principally at the arts and humanities community. The project is funded by the British Library R&D Department. Hosted by Oxford University's Computer Services on the VAXcluster, HUMBUL is administered by the CTI Centre for Textual Studies and the Office for Humanities Communication. Users may access HUMBUL at Oxford University Computing Services via the Joint Academic Network (JANET) or by means of two direct-dial PSTN lines.
Subjects covered: fine arts; humanities; computer science; language and literature
Net address for operations: HUMBUL@VAX.OX.AC.UK
Net address for questions or submissions: HUMBUL@VAX.OX.AC.UK, STUART@VAX.OX.AC.UK
Established: 1985
Subscribers: 4500
Sponsor: Office for Humanities Communication, OUCS, 13 Banbury Road, Oxford OX2 6NN, UK (funded by the British Library).
Host: Oxford University Computing Services, 13 Banbury Road, Oxford OX2 6NN, UK.
List moderated: Yes, weekly.
Moderation procedure: Editor monitors discussion lists, other bulletin boards, printed journals etc. Material is then placed on HUMBUL under different sections.

Editorial contact: Dr Stuart Lee
Research Officer, CTI Centre for Textual Studies, Oxford University Computing Services, 13 Banbury Road, Oxford OX2 6NN, UK.
Tel: 0865-273221/283282
Fax: 0865-273221
Internet: STUART@UK.AC.OX.VAX
How to access: The JANET X.29 call addresses are as follows: The NRS name is UK.AC.HUMBUL (standard form) or HUMBUL (abbreviated form). If you are unable to use either of these names, the number you should call is: 00005020010002 For those who have difficulty in accessing the Joint Academic Network (JANET), HUMBUL may also be accessed via a dial-up line as follows: (0865) 722311 (V21 300 bps full duplex) (V22 1200 bps full duplex) (V22bis 1200 bps full duplex) (V23 1200 bps half duplex) (V23 1200/75 bps full duplex) To the 'Which Service' prompt reply PAD. To the 'PAD'> prompt reply HUMBUL. In case of difficulty, further advice may be obtained by telephone to the OUCS Humanities Section during office hours on Oxford (0865) 273221.
Access policy: Open to anyone interested in humanities computing.
How to submit: Send message to HUMBUL or editor.
Archives: HUMBUL holds its own (limited) archive

HUMEVO@GWUVM

Description: HUMEVO@GWUVM is a forum on human evolution.
Subjects covered: biology; anthropology
List moderated: Yes.
Editorial contact: Noel T. Boaz
Bitnet: boaz@gwuvm
How to access: Send subscribe message to listserv@gwuvm
How to unsubscribe: Send unsubscribe message to listserv@gwuvm
Archives: Archives are developed monthly; apply to listowner for details.

HUMGRAD

Description: Humgrad is an electronic mailing list for postgraduates working in the humanities. It is a forum for the exchange of ideas, information and comment on any humanities subject and the work and problems of postgraduates. It aims to be less formal than other humanities lists in order to avoid the inhibitions some postgraduates and computing novices can feel when interacting with those who may be their academic and computational superiors.
Subjects covered: humanities; language and literature; colleges and universities; education
Net address for operations: mailbase@mailbase.ac.uk
Net address for questions or submissions: humgrad@mailbase.ac.uk
Established: February 1992
Subscribers: 200
Sponsor: Oxford University Computing Services, 13 Banbury Road, OXFORD OX2 6NN, UK
List moderated: No.
Editorial contact: Gavin Burnage
Oxford University Computing Services, as above
Tel: 0865 273280
Fax: 0865 273275
Internet: gburnage@natcorp.ox.ac.uk Bitnet

How to access: Join Humgrad Your Name to this address mailbase@mailbase.ac.uk
Access policy: Open to all those interested in the humanities and postgraduate study. when you decide to send a contribution, try to write as you would like to be written to, no matter what the provocation to do otherwise. The only other rule of note is that over-lengthy contributions should be avoided. If you write a long article or report, send it to the listowners rather than to the list -- we will place it in the mailbase archive while you send a short summary of its contents to the list.
How to unsubscribe: Send this command: leave humgrad to this address: mailbase@mailbase.ac.uk
How to submit: Send your message to this address: humgrad@mailbase.ac.u
Submission policy: All messages relevant to humanities subjects and postgraduate issues are welcome. Longer messages or articles can be archived.
Archives: The Humgrad archive at mailbase contains monthly log files of all mail sent to the list in the preceeding 14 months (old log files are removed once a month. Also available in the archive is the CTI Centre for Textual Studies Resources Guide, information about HUMBUL, and personal biographies submitted by some subscribers. Other articles can be archived. To review the archive material available, send this message index humgrad to this address: mailbase@mailbase.ac.uk To retrieve an archive file send this message: send humgrad filename to this address: mailbase@mailbase.ac.uk
Additional information: Stuart Lee, Oxford University Computing Services, as above. Tel. 0865 283282; fax 0865 273275

HUMSPC-L

Description: Humspc-L is a private list for special mailings related to the Humanist list.
Subjects covered: humanities
Editorial contact: Allen Renear and Ellen Brennan
Internet: Allen Renear and Ellen Brennan
Bitnet: editors@brownvm
How to access: Send subscribe message to listserv@brownvm or listserv@brownvm.brown.edu
How to unsubscribe: Send unsubscribe message to listserv@brownvm or listserv@brownvm.brown.edu
Archives: Archives are developed monthly; apply to listowner for details.

HUNGARY@GWUVM

Description: HUNGARY@GWUVM is a discussion list focusing on a wide range of issues related to Hungary.
Subjects covered: Hungary; Eastern Europe
How to access: Send a standard subscribe request to LISTSERV@GWUVM
How to unsubscribe: Send a standard unsubscribe request to LISTSERV@GWUVM

HY-PEOPLE@ORVILLE.ARC.NASA.GOV

Description: HY-PEOPLE is a discussion list on hyperchannel networkings related to Internet Protocol networks.
Subjects covered: computer hardware and software; electronic networking
List moderated: No.
Editorial contact: John Lekashman
Internet: lekash@orville.arc.nasa.gov

How to access: Send subscribe message to BY-PEOPLE-RE-QUEST@ORVILLE.ARC.NASA.GOV
How to unsubscribe: Send unsubscribe message to BY-PEO-PLE-REQUEST@ORVILLE.ARC.NASA.GOV

HYPBAR-L
Description: Hypbar-L is a conference on hyperbaric medicine.
Subjects covered: medicine
List moderated: No.
Internet: al@ccvs4.technion.ac.il
How to access: Send subscribe message to listserv@technion or listserv@technion.technion.ac.il
How to unsubscribe: Send unsubscribe message to listserv@technion or listserv@technion.technion.ac.il
Archives: Archives are developed monthly; apply to listowner for details.

HYPERMED@UMAB
Description: HYPERMED@UMAB is a forum on hypermedia instruction in the biomedical sciences.
Subjects covered: education; health sciences; medicine
List moderated: No.
Editorial contact: Kent Hisley
Bitnet: khisley@umab
How to access: Send subscribe message to listserv@umab or listserv@umab.umd.edu
How to unsubscribe: Send unsubscribe message to listserv@umab or listserv@umab.umd.edu
Archives: Archives are developed monthly; apply to listowner for details.

HYTEL-L (HYTELNET UPDATES DISTRIBUTION LIST)
Description: Hytel-L is a moderated list offering periodic postings regarding new versions of the HYTELNET program, plus updates and new files. HYTELNET is a program allowing easy communications with Internet sites reachable via Telnet.
Subjects covered: online public access catalogs; computer hardware and software; library and information science
Net address for operations: listserv@kentvm.kent.edu
Net address for questions or submissions: aa375@freenet.carleton.ca
Established: March 1993
Subscribers: 870
Sponsor: Kent State University, Kent, OH
Host: Kent State University, Kent, OH
List moderated: Yes.
Moderation procedure: Posting allowed only by moderator
Editorial contact: Peter Scott
324 8th St. E., Saskatoon, SA, Canada, S7H0P5
Tel: 306-244-8761
Internet: aa375@freenet.carleton.ca
How to access: Send e-mail message "subscribe hytel-l FirstName Lastname" to listserv@kentvm.kent.edu
How to unsubscribe: Send e-mail message "unsubscribe hytel-l" to listserv@kentvm.kent.edu
How to submit: Send e-mail to aa375@freenet.carleton.ca
Related files: For related files, ftp to access.usask.ca Files are stored in the pub/hytelnet/pc directory.
Gopher accessibility: Name = HYTELNET - All new files & updates since Version 6.3 Type = 1 Port = 70

Path = ftp:access.usask.ca@/pub/hytelnet/pc/
Host = access.usask.ca
Additional information: Postings are gatewayed to the Usenet group bit.listserv.hytel-l

I-FINGER@SPCVXA
Description: I-FINGER@SPCVXA is a forum for finger programming.
Subjects covered: computer hardware and software
List moderated: No.
Editorial contact: Terry Kennedy
Internet: terry@spcvxa.spc.edu
Bitnet: terry@spcvxa
How to access: Send subscribe message to i-finreq@spcvxa or finreq@spcvxa.spc.edu
How to unsubscribe: Send unsubscribe message to i-finreq@spcvxa or finreq@spcvxa.spc.edu
Archives: Yes; Apply to listowner for details.

I-REDES@UTFSM
Description: I-REDES@UTFSM is a Spanish language list centering on computer networking topics.
Subjects covered: computer science; electronic networking
List moderated: No.
Editorial contact: Hernan Lobos Mitzio
Bitnet: hlobos@@utfsm
How to access: Send subscribe message to listserv@utfsm
How to unsubscribe: Send unsubscribe message to listserv@utfsm
Archives: Archives are developed monthly; apply to listowner for details.

I-VIDTEK@UIUCVMD
Description: I-VIDTEK@UIUCVMD focuses on video technology in education.
Subjects covered: science and technology
List moderated: Yes.
Bitnet: VIDEOTECHREQUEST@WSMR-SIMTEL20.ARMY.MIL
How to access: Send subscribe message to listserv@uiucvmd or listserv@vmd.cso.uiuc.edu
How to unsubscribe: Send unsubscribe message to listserv@uiucvmd or listserv@vmd.cso.uiuc.edu
Archives: Archives are developed weekly; apply to listowner for details.

IAMEX-L
Description: IAMEX-L is a list administered by the AI Investigation Center in Instituto Tecnologico y de Estudios Superiores de Monterrey (ITESM) in Monterrey, N.L.
Subjects covered: artificial intelligence
Net address for questions or submissions: pl500368@tecmtyvm.bitnet
How to access: Send email message to: pl500368@tecmtyvm.bitnet (Juana Maria Gomez Puertos) or pl157961@tecmtyvm.bitnet (Fernando Careaga Sanchez)

IAMSLIC@UCSD CONFERENCE

Description: IAMSLIC@UCSD CONFERENCE is an international email conference for discussion of information-related topics in freshwater, marine, and brackishwater sciences.
Subjects covered: marine sciences; biology; environmental studies
Net address for operations: istserv@ucsd.edu, listserv@ucsd.bitnet
Net address for questions or submissions: iamslic@ucsd.edu, iamslic@ucsd.bitnet
Established: 1991
Subscribers: 132
Sponsor: International Association of Aquatic and Marine Science Libraries and Information Centers (IAMSLIC), c/o Library Harbor Branch Oceanographic Institution, Inc., 5600 Old Dixie Highway, Fort Pierce, FL 34946.
Host: Scripps Institution of Oceanography Library, University of California, San Diego, 9500 Gilman Drive, San Diego, CA 92093-0175.
List moderated: No.
Editorial contact: Peter Brueggeman
Scripps Institution of Oceanography Library, University of California, San Diego, 9500 Gilman Drive, San Diego, CA 92093-0175.
Tel: 619-534-1230
Fax: 619-534-5269
Internet: PBRUEGGEMAN@UCSD.EDU
Copyright statement: Messages sent to the IAMSLIC@UCSD CONFERENCE are distributed automatically and not edited. The conference is provided as a public service for those interested in aquatic and marine information. Authors of messages are solely responsible for the content of their messages. IAMSLIC does not verify the accuracy of submitted messages nor endorse the opinions expressed.
How to access: Send the following email message to listserv@ucsd.edu or listserv@ucsd.bitnet : subscribe <your Internet or Bitnet email address> iamslic
Access policy: Membership in this list is open to anyone.
How to unsubscribe: Send the following email message to listserv@ucsd.edu or listserv@ucsd.bitnet : delete <your Internet or Bitnet email address> iamslic
How to submit: Send your email message to iamslic@ucsd.edu or iamslic@ucsd.bitnet; please note that this is a different address than the subscription address.
Additional information: IAMSLIC sponsors a similar aquatic sciences information bulletin board on Omnet's ScienceNet email system on SprintMail. Messages originating from IAMSLIC's Omnet bulletin board are posted onto the IAMSLIC@UCSD conference. Some Omnet-origin messages are best answered by responding to the person at the Omnet address since they are not on the Internet. Internet-to-Omnet addressing instructions are posted with eearch Omnet-origin message that need a specific response.

IAPSY-L

Description: Iapsy-L is a forum for the Interamerican Psychologists (SIPNET) organization.
Subjects covered: psychology
Host: Interamerican Society for Psychology
List moderated: No.
Editorial contact: Bernardo M. Ferdman
Internet: bmf13@uacsc2.albany.edu
Bitnet: bmf13@albnyvm1

How to access: Send subscribe message to listserv@albnyvm1 or listserv@uacsc2.albany.edu
How to unsubscribe: Send unsubscribe message to listserv@albnyvm1 or listserv@uacsc2.albany.edu
Archives: Archives are developed monthly; apply to listowner for details.

IBERIAN—ISSUES

Description: IBERIAN—ISSUES is a forum about Latin America.
Subjects covered: Latin America
List moderated: No.
Bitnet: nicbbs@bitnic
How to access: Send subscribe message to nicbbs@bitnic in the following format: BBOARD SUBSCRIBE IBERIAN—ISSUES Yourfirstname Yourlastname

IBJ-L (THE INTERNET BUSINESS JOURNAL DISTRIBUTION LIST)

Description: IBJ-L is an electronic distribution list which distributes selected portions of the hardcopy Internet Business Journal. Under the sponsorship of the Wladyslaw Poniecki Foundation, the list distributes only the table of contents, article abstracts, editorial, letter from the publisher, and the column, Access--Ability, by Dr. Norm Coombs. This e-version is freely available in low ascii text and will soon be available as a PostScript file. The IBJ e-version will also soon be available via ftp and gopher.
Subjects covered: business; Internet; telecommunications; computer hardware and software
Editorial contact: Michael Strangelove
177 Waller, Ottawa, Ontario K1N6N5 CANADA
Tel: (613) 747-0642
Fax: (613) 564-6641
Internet: 441495@Acadvm1.Uottawa.CA
Bitnet: 441495@Uottawa
How to access: To subscribe to the Internet Business Journal Distribution List, send the command:
SUB IBJ-L your name to listerv@poniecki.berkeley.edu. Send the command in the body of the mail message, not in the subject line. Replace "your name" with your full name. Subscribers to IBJ-L will receive notice of new table of content/abstract editions, new online documents relevant to th ebusiness community, and related information. There is no subscription fee for IBJ-L. Please note that IBJ-L is not a conversational list. Only the list owner will post to IBJ-L.
Archives: IBJ-L will archive unique resources relevant to the business community, but will not mirror (duplicate) resources already available elsewhere via the Internet.
Additional information: IBJ-L is intended to be very low volume in the number of postings. General informational items, press releases, conference announcements, and so forth will NOT be posted. Items that inform subscribers of new Internet business community resources, services and online documents WILL be announced through IBJ-L. IBJ-L will archive unique resources relevant to he business community, but will not mirror (duplicate) resources already available elsewhere via the Internet.

IBYCUS-L@USCVM

Description: IBYCUS-L is a discussion list covering Ancient Greece.
Subjects covered: Greek language and literature; history
Net address for operations: Listserv@uscvn
Net address for questions or submissions: IBYCUS-L@uscvm
How to access: Send message to listserv: SUBSCRIBE <listname> <your name>

ICECA@RUTVM1

Description: ICECA@RUTVM1 is a conference focusing on AIDS.
Subjects covered: AIDS/HIV studies; medicine
Host: International Committee for Electronic Communication on AIDS
List moderated: No.
Editorial contact: Michael Smith
Bitnet: mnsmith@umaecs
How to access: Send subscribe message to listserv@rutvm1 or listserv@rutgers.edu
How to unsubscribe: Send unsubscribe message to listserv@rutvm1 or listserv@rutgers.edu
Archives: Yes.

ICEN-L

Description: ICEN-L is a discussion forum covering issues on international careers and related issues.
Subjects covered: human resources
List moderated: Yes.
Editorial contact: Susan Snider Salmon
Bitnet: icenl@indiana.edu
How to access: Send subscribe message to listserv@iubvm or listserv@iubvm.ucs.indiana.edu
How to unsubscribe: Send unsubscribe message to listserv@iubvm or listserv@iubvm.ucs.indiana.edu
Archives: Archives are developed monthly; apply to listowner for details.

ICON-GROUP@ARIZONA.EDU

Description: ICON-GROUP is a forum about the Icon programming language.
Subjects covered: computer science
List moderated: No.
Editorial contact: Bill Mitchell
Internet: whm@arizona.edu
How to access: Send subscribe message to Icon-Group-Request@ARIZONA.EDU
How to unsubscribe: Send unsubscribe message to Icon-Group-Request@ARIZONA.EDU

ICS-L

Description: ICS-L is a forum of the International Chemometrics Society.
Subjects covered: chemistry
List moderated: No.
Editorial contact: Tom O'Haver
Internet: thomas__c__ohaver@umail.umd.edu
How to access: Send subscribe message to listserv@ummd or listserv@ummd.umd.edu

How to unsubscribe: Send unsubscribe message to listserv@ummd or listserv@ummd.umd.edu
Archives: Archives are developed monthly; apply to listowner for details.

ICU-L

Description: Icu-L contains articles and topics related to computers in education.
Subjects covered: education technology
List moderated: No.
Editorial contact: Jim Gerland
Internet: listmgr@ubvm.cc.buffalo.edu
Bitnet: listmgr@ubvm
How to access: Send subscribe message to listserv@ubvm or listserv@ubvm.cc.buffalo.edu
How to unsubscribe: Send unsubscribe message to listserv@ubvm or listserv@ubvm.cc.buffalo.edu

IDANET

Description: IDANET (Individual Differences and Assessment Net) is a network of academic researchers and professionals involved in the definition, design, and application of individual differences measurement. The net members are drawn from the areas of experimental, occupational, and educational research. The purpose of the net is to provide an information conduit between disparate workers and investigators in the area of individual differences. Since this area includes the assessment of personality, intelligence, and motivation, both at the biological, psychometric, and social levels, the net is expected to provide an attractive focus for individuals working in any of these areas, at either a clinical, research, or applied level. Software news, programs, measurement problems and solutions, and other relevant information would also be expected to be broadcast via the net. The net might also be used for conference and workshop announcements, calls for papers, notifications, book listings/reviews, job advertisements, and advertisements for student placements etc. IDANET will also be supporting the new hardcopy International Journal of Human Assessment by providing an on-line forum and filestore for dissemination of statistical and psychometrics software, algorithms, and commentaries on articles in the journal or issues raised by an article.
Subjects covered: measurement studies; psychometrics; psychology; computer hardware and software
Net address for operations: mailbase@mailbase.ac.uk
Net address for questions or submissions: idanet@mailbase.ac.uk
Established: May 1993
Subscribers: 42
Sponsor: University of Surrey
Host: Newcastle Network Information Services Project
List moderated: Yes.
Editorial contact: Paul Barrett
University of Surrey, Department of Psychology, Guildford, Surrey GU2 5XH, UK.
Tel: 0483-509175
Fax: 0483-32813
Internet: pss1pb@surrey.ac.uk
How to access: Send any message to idanet-request@mailbase.ac.uk
How to unsubscribe: Send a message to idanet@mailbase.ac.uk containing the following line: leave idanet
How to submit: Send a message to idanet@mailbase.ac.uk

Archives: Yes, archives are stored monthly.
Related files: Ftp files are available (via anonymous - ASCII or RTF format only). Also, email file retrieval facility.

IDFORM

Description: IDFORM is the monthly newsletter of the IDFORUM list whose subscribers automatically receive it. It publishes material related to industrial design.
Subjects covered: industrial design
Net address for operations: LISTSERV@VM1.YORKU.CA
Editorial contact: Maruice Barnwell
Multidisciplinary Studies, Glendon College, York University, 2275 Bayview Avenue, Toronto, Ontario, Canada M4N 3M6.
Internet: GL250267@VENUS.YORKU.CA
How to access: Send a mail message to: LISTSERV@VM1.YORKU.CA with the one line message: SUBSCRIBE IDFORUM your full name.

IDFORUM

Description: IDFORUM is the first and only list for all involved in the world of industrial and product design. IDFORUM provides worldwide access to design institutions and research centres--the list operates as an open forum for "news & views" from the world of industrial design. Since it's inception, over two years ago, IDFORUM has attracted users from more than 30 countries, including Argentina, Australia, Austria, Belgium, Brazil, Canada, Columbia, Costa Rica, the Czech Republic, Egypt, Finland, France, Great Britain, Hungary, Ireland, Italy, Japan, Korea, Mexico, Netherlands, Norway, Portugal, Spain, Sweden, Tunisia, Turkey and the U.S.A.
Subjects covered: industrial design
Net address for operations: LISTSERV@VM1.YORKU.CA
Editorial contact: Maruice Barnwell
Multidisciplinary Studies, Glendon College, York University, 2275 Bayview Avenue, Toronto, Ontario, Canada M4N 3M6.
Internet: GL250267@VENUS.YORKU.CA
How to access: Send a mail message to: LISTSERV@VM1.YORKU.CA with the one line message: SUBSCRIBE IDFORUM your full name.
Related files: Each month subscribers receive IDFORM a moderated electronic newsletter.

IDFORUM@YORKVM1

Description: IDFORUM@YORKVM1 is an international electronic forum in the field of industrial design.
Subjects covered: design
List moderated: Yes.
Editorial contact: Maurice Barnwell
Internet: g1250267@venus.yorku.ca
Bitnet: g1250267@yuvenus
How to access: Send subscribe message to listserv@yorkvm1 or listserv@vm1.yorku.ca
How to unsubscribe: Send unsubscribe message to listserv@yorkvm1 or listserv@vm1.yorku.ca
Archives: Archives are available; apply to listowner for details.
Related files: Related files include an electronic journal, Voice of Industrial Design, which list subscribers automatically receive. Apply to listowner for further details.

IDRISI-UK@MAILBASE.AC.UK

Description: IDRISI-UK@MAILBASE.AC.UK is a list for membership of the UK IDRISI users group. It covers geographic information systems.
Subjects covered: geographic information systems
Host: UK IDRISI Users Group
List moderated: No.
Internet: idrisi-uk-request@mailbase.ac.uk
How to access: Send subscribe message to mailbase@mailbase.ac.uk in the following format: join idrisi Yourfirstname Yourlastname
Archives: Archives are developed monthly; apply to listowner for details.

IE-DIGEST

Description: The IE-digest aims to act as a forum to exchange ideas on using 'intelligent' techniques to model economic and financial systems. Calls for papers, paper announcements and queries are welcome.
Subjects covered: artificial intelligence; economics
Net address for questions or submissions: IE-list@cs.ucl.ac.uk
Editorial contact: Suran Goonatilake
Dept. of Computer Science, University College London, Gower St., London WC1E 6BT, UK.
Internet: surang@cs.ucl.ac.uk
How to access: Send mail to IE-list-request@cs.ucl.ac.uk
Archives: An archive of back issues of the digest, as well as papers, bibliographies and software, may be obtained by anonymous ftp from cs.ucl.ac.uk:ie (128.16.5.31).

IECC: INTERNATIONAL E-MAIL CLASSROOM CONNECTIONS

Description: IECC, the International E-Mail Classroom Connections mailing list serves as a meeting place for teachers seeking partner classes for international and cross-cultural electronic mail exchanges. A variety of mailing lists already exist that facilitate traditional, one-on-one pen-pal communication. This list is different, in that subscribers and contributors are looking for an entire class of e-mail partners in an international or cross-cultural context. Guidelines: IECC should not be used to find individual penpals; the use of any language is acceptable; and IECC is not a moderated list-- postings to the list are distributed automatically to all subscribers.
Subjects covered: education
Net address for questions or submissions: iecc-request@stolaf.edu
How to access: Send a message containing the word "subscribe" to iecc-request@stolaf.edu
How to submit: To contribute send a message to iecc@stolaf.edu

IEEE-L

Description: IEEE-L is a forum catering to IEEE student members.
Subjects covered: engineering
Host: IEEE
List moderated: No.
Editorial contact: Paul D. Kroculick or Charles Elliott
Bitnet: tjw0465@bingtjw

How to access: Send subscribe message to listserv@bingvmb or listserv@bingvmb.cc.binghamton.edu
How to unsubscribe: Send unsubscribe message to listserv@bingvmb or listserv@bingvmb.cc.binghamton.edu

IEEE@USACHVM1

Description: IEEE@USACHVM1 is a Spanish language forum catering to all IEEE student members.
Subjects covered: engineering
List moderated: Yes.
Editorial contact: Eric Soto-Lavin
Bitnet: ieeesb@usachvm1
How to access: Send subscribe message to listserv@usachvm1
How to unsubscribe: Send unsubscribe message to listserv@usachvm1
Archives: Archives are developed monthly; apply to listowner for details.

IFDO-L

Description: IFDO-L is a discussion list of the International Federation of Data Organizations (IFDO). Subscription is open to all organizations participating in IFDO. The purpose of IFDO-L is to support the exchange of information between IFDO members and to facilitate mailings to IFDO members.
Subjects covered: computer hardware and software; data acquisition and organization; science and technology
Net address for operations: listserv@nic.surfnet.nl
Net address for questions or submissions: ifdo-l@nic.surfnet.nl
Established: July 1993
Subscribers: 11
Sponsor: International Federation of Data Organizations, IFDO Secretariat, Danish Data Archives - DDA, att. Per Nielsen, Munkebjergvaenget 48 DK-5230, Odense M, Denmark; tel: (+45) 66 15 79 20; fax: (+45) 66 15 83 20 E-mail: ifdo@dda.dk
Host: Steinmetz Archive, Herengracht 410-412, 1017 BX Amsterdam, The Netherlands; tel: (+31) 20 622 50 61; fax: (+31) 20 623 83 74; E-mail: steinm@swidoc.nl
List moderated: Yes.
Moderation procedure: Contributions to the file server with filename IFDO-L are moderated by the list manager in consultation with the IFDO secretariat.
Editorial contact: Harry Heemskerk
Steinmetz Archive, Herengracht 410-412, 1017 BX Amsterdam, The Netherlands.
Tel: (+31) 20 622 50 61
Fax: (+31) 20 623 83 74
Internet: hheemskerk@swidoc.nl
Technical contact: Cor van der Meer
Steinmetz Archive, Herengracht 410-412, 1017 BX Amsterdam, The Netherlands.
Tel: (+31) 20 622 50 61
Fax: (+31) 20 623 83 74
Internet: cor@swidoc.nl
Copyright statement: Copyright statements are left to contributors. None of the elements of the list are necessarily sanctioned by IFDO.
How to access: Send SUBSCRIBE IFDO-L institution name to LISTSERV@NIC.SURFNET.NL
Access policy: Subscription is open to IFDO members only. Contributors are requested to restrict their messages to IFDO

related matters only. Duplication of messages broadcasted on generally accessible lists such as IASSIST and SOS-DATA should be avoided. Contributions to the file server are moderated by the list manager in consultation with the IFDO secretariat.
How to unsubscribe: Send SIGNOFF IFDO-L to LISTSERV@NIC.SURFNET.NL
How to submit: Send messages to IFDO-L@NIC.SURFNET.NL For contributions to the file server contact the list manager.

IFIP-DIALUP@ICS.UCI.EDU

Description: IFIP-DIALUP covers issues related to network dialup systems and X.400 and X.500 hosts.
Subjects covered: computer science; electronic networking; electronic mail
List moderated: No.
Editorial contact: Einar Stefferud
Internet: stef@nma.com
How to access: Send subscribe message to IFIP-DIALUP-REQUEST@ICS.UCI.EDU
How to unsubscribe: Send unsubscribe message to IFIP-DIALUP-REQUEST@ICS.UCI.EDU
Archives: Yes.

IFIP-GTWY@ICS.UCI.EDU

Description: IFIP-GTWY covers issues related to X.400 and non-X.400 MHS environments.
Subjects covered: computer science; electronic networking
List moderated: No.
Editorial contact: Tim Kehres
Internet: kehres@tis.llnl.gov
How to access: Send subscribe message to IFIP-GTWY-REQUEST@ICS.UCI.EDU
How to unsubscribe: Send unsubscribe message to IFIP-GTWY-REQUEST@ICS.UCI.EDU
Archives: Yes; Send anonymous FTP to ICS.UCI.EDU in directory mhs, file ifip-gtwy

IFPHEN-L

Description: IFPHEN-L is a forum on interfacial phenomena.
Subjects covered: chemistry
Host: American Institute of Chemical Engineers
List moderated: Yes.
Editorial contact: Richard L. Zollars
Bitnet: scef0002@wsuvms1
How to access: Send subscribe message to listserv@wsuvm1 or listserv%wsuvm1.bitnet@cunyvm.cuny.edu
How to unsubscribe: Send unsubscribe message to listserv@wsuvm1 or listserv%wsuvm1.bitnet@cunyvm.cuny.edu
Archives: Archives are developed monthly; apply to listowner for details.

IFREEDOM

Description: The Forum on Censorship and Intellectual Freedom has been established to serve as a national registry of censorship challenges in Canada, and as an open forum on matters pertaining to censorship and intellectual freedom.
Subjects covered: intellectual freedom; censorship; human rights

Net address for operations:
LISTSERV@SNOOPY.UCIS.DAL.CA
Net address for questions or submissions:
IFREEDOM@SNOOPY.UCIS.DAL.CA
Established: January 1993
Subscribers: 208
Host: School of Library and Information Studies
Dalhousie University Halifax, N.S. Canada B3H 4H8
List moderated: Yes.
Moderation procedure: Through NSTN Operations Centre List
Editorial contact: Larry Amey
School of Library and Information Studies,
Dalhousie University, Halifax, N.S. Canada B3H 4H8
Tel: (902) 494-2488
Fax: (902) 494-2451
Internet: AMEY@AC.DAL.CA
Technical contact: Daniel MacKay
NSTN Operations Centre,Communications Services, Killam Library, Dalhousie University, Halifax, N.S. Canada B3H 4H8
Tel: (902) 494-NSTN
Fax: (902) 494-2319
Internet: daniel@nstn.ns.ca Bitnet
How to access: Send message to:
LISTSERV@SNOOPY.UCIS.DAL.CA SUBJECT: (do not enter anything, carriage return) MESSAGE: SUBSCRIBE IFREEDOM YOUR NAME
How to unsubscribe: Send message to: IFREEDOM-REQUEST@NSTN.NS.CA
SUBJECT: (do not enter anything, CR)
MESSAGE: UNSUBSCRIBE YOUR NAME
Archives: Soon to be archived.

III-OPEN@MAILBASE.AC.UK

Description: III-OPEN@MAILBASE.AC.UK is a forum for discussing issues related to the SERC Image Interpretation Initiative.
Subjects covered: colleges and universities
List moderated: No.
Internet: iii-open-request@mailbase.ac.uk
How to access: Send subscribe message to mailbase@mailbase.ac.uk in the following format: join iii-open Yourfirstname Yourlastname
Archives: Archives are developed monthly; apply to listowner for details.

IIRS@TAUNIVM

Description: IIRS@TAUNIVM is a conference for Israeli information retreival specialists.
Subjects covered: information technology
List moderated: No.
Editorial contact: Miriam Farber
Bitnet: rafarber@weizmann
How to access: Send subscribe message to listserv@taunivm or listserv@taunivm.tau.ac.il
How to unsubscribe: Send unsubscribe message to listserv@taunivm or listserv@taunivm.tau.ac.il
Archives: Archives are developed monthly; apply to listowner for details.

IIS-SCOTLAND

Description: IIS-Scotland is a list for facilitating discussion and information exchange on matters relevant to Scottish information scientists. In addition, it will be specifically used to publicly disseminate non-confidential documents of the Scottish branch of the Institute of Information Scientists.
Subjects covered: library and information science; computer hardware and software
Net address for operations: mailbase@mailbase.ac.uk
Net address for questions or submissions: iis-scotland@mailbase.ac.uk
Established: January 14, 1993
Subscribers: 47
Sponsor: Queen Margaret College, Clerwood Terrace, Edinburgh, Scotland EH12 8TS.
Host: The NISP Project, Computing Service, The University, Newcastle upon Tyne, UK NE1 7RU.
List moderated: No.
Editorial contact: George McMurdo
Department of Communication & Information Studies, Queen Margaret College, Clerwood Terrace, Edinburgh, Scotland EH12 8TS.
Tel: (4431) 031 317 3505
Fax: (4431) 031 316 4165
Internet: cimmu@cis.qmced.ac.uk, geo__mcmurdo@hicom.org
Technical contact: Chris Gunn
Department of Communication & Information Studies, Queen Margaret College, Clerwood Terrace, Edinburgh, Scotland EH12 8TS.
Tel: (4431) 031 317 3000
Fax: (4431) 031 317 4156
Internet: cs0gunn@cis.qmced.ac.uk, chris__gunn@hicom.org
How to access: Send a message to: mailbase@mailbase.ac.uk Subj: <anything - gets ignored> ... with text: join iis-scotland <firstname> <surname> (eg: join iis-scotland George McMurdo).
How to unsubscribe: Send a message to: mailbase@mailbase.ac.uk Subj: <anything - gets ignored> ... with text: leave iis-scotland
How to submit: Send a message to: iis-scotland@mailbase.ac.uk Subj: <as appropriate> <your message text>
Archives: Messages to the list are archived monthly and may be retrieved by e-mail. For an index of available e-mail archives (and other files associated with the IIS-Scotland list) send a message to: mailbase@mailbase.ac.uk Subj: <anything - it gets ignored> ... with text: index iis-scotland. To obtain a file in the filelist returned by the INDEX command ... Send a message to: mailbase@mailbase.ac.uk Subj: <anything - it gets ignored> ... with text send iis-scotland <name-of-file-wanted>
Related files: The Mailbase system on JANET, through which IIS-Scotland is provided, is also an online service, and details of lists, archived e-mail, and files associated with lists, can be browsed interactively ... Telnet to: mailbase.ac.uk (or 128.240.2.118) Login as:guest Password:mailbase
The Mailbase system now also has a Gopher interface:
Name = Mailbase Gopher Type = 1 Host = mailbase.ac.uk
Port = 70

ILAS-NET@TECHNION

Description: ILAS-NET is a forum for the study of linear algebra.
Subjects covered: mathematics

Host: International Linear Algebra Society
List moderated: No.
Editorial contact: Danny Hershkowitz
Internet: mar23aa@technion.technion.ac.il
Bitnet: mar23aa@technion
How to access: Send subscribe message to listserv@technion or listserv@technion.technion.ac.il
How to unsubscribe: Send unsubscribe message to listserv@technion or listserv@technion.technion.ac.il
Archives: Yes; Send anonymous FTP to: 132.68.1.6 and cd MAT

ILL-L

Description: ILL-L was established to serve as an informal electronic forum for all aspects of interlibrary loan and document delivery.
Subjects covered: library and information science; document delivery; interlibrary loan; library collection development
Net address for operations: ILL-L@uvmvm
Net address for questions or submissions: ILL-L@uvmvm
Established: November 1990
Subscribers: 1301
Sponsor: University of Vermont, Burlington, VT 05405.
Host: University of Vermont, Burlington, VT 05405.
List moderated: No.
Editorial contact: Patricia Mardeusz
Interlibrary Loan Dept., Bailey/Howe Library, University of Vermont, Burlington, VT 05405.
Tel: (802) 656-2242
Fax: (802) 656-4238
Internet: pmardeus@uvmvm.uvm.edu
Bitnet: pmardeus@uvmvm
How to access: Tell listserv at uvmvm subscribe ill-l <e-mail addres s> <full name> [e.g., tell listserv at uvmvm subscribe ill-l jdoe@bqg joe doe]
Access policy: This list is open to parties interested in ILL and document delivery.
How to unsubscribe: Tell listserv at uvmvm signoff ill-l <full name>
How to submit: Mail ill-l@uvmvm
Submission policy: Anyone may submit a question or comment dealing with interlibrary loan or document delivery. No advertisements or personal messages are allowed.
Archives: Yes, archives are available; apply to listowner.

IMAGE-L

Description: Image-L iprovides a forum for discussing image processing, multimedia, computer video and related topics.
Subjects covered: multimedia computing; graphics; computer software and hardware; computer graphics
List moderated: No.
Editorial contact: Yusuf Ozturk
Bitnet: bilyoz@trearn
How to access: Send subscribe message to listserv@trearn or listserv%trearn.bitnet@vmi.nodak.edu
How to unsubscribe: Send unsubscribe message to listserv@trearn or listserv%trearn.bitnet@vmi.nodak.edu
Archives: Archives are developed monthly; apply to listowner for details.

IMMUNE@WEBER.UC SD.EDU

Description: IMMUNE@WEBER.UC SD.EDU is a conference on the human immune system.
Subjects covered: medicine
List moderated: No.
Editorial contact: Cyndi Norman
Internet: cnorman@ucsd.edu
Bitnet: cnorman@ucsd
How to access: Send subscribe message to IMMUNE-RE-QUEST@WEBER.UCSD.EDU
How to unsubscribe: Send unsubscribe message to IMMUNE-REQUEST@WEBER.UCSD.EDU
Archives: Archives are developed monthly; Send anonymous FTP to: WEBER.UCSD.EDU and cd /pub/immune

IMUG-L (INNOPAC MUSIC USERS GROUP)

Description: IMUG-L is a technical discussion group by music librarians who use the Innopac electronic library catalog at their institutions, marketed by Innovative Interfaces Inc. of Berkeley, CA.
Subjects covered: music; library and information science; computer hardware and software
Net address for operations: LISTSERV@OHSTVMA.BITNET
Net address for questions or submissions: IMUG-L@OHSTVMA.BITNET
Established: August 1992
Subscribers: 120
Host: Ohio State University Music Library, 166 Sullivant Hall, 1813 N. High St., Columbus, OH 43210-1307.
List moderated: No.
Editorial contact: Alan Green
Ohio State University Music Library, 166 Sullivant Hall, 1813 N. High St., Columbus, OH 43210-1307.
Tel: 614-292-2319
Fax: 614-292-7859
Internet: green.200@osu.edu
Bitnet: green+@ohstmail.bitnet
How to access: Send the following command to address LISTSERV@OHSTVMA.BITNET: sub imug-l <firstname> <lastname> >
Access policy: Subscriptions are open to anyone.
How to unsubscribe: Standard bitnet signoff, or send message to listowner Alan Green.
How to submit: Send email to address: imug-l@ohstvma.bitnet
Archives: All messages are archived.

INDEX-L

Description: Index-L is a discussion forum for indexers.
Subjects covered: library and information science
List moderated: Yes.
Editorial contact: Charlotte Skuster
Bitnet: skuster@bingvmb
How to access: Send subscribe message to listserv@bingvmb
How to unsubscribe: Send unsubscribe message to listserv@bingvmb
Archives: Archives are developed monthly; apply to listowner for details.

INDIA-L@UKCC

Description: INDIA-L@UKCC is the University of Kentucky forum on India.
Subjects covered: India; cultural studies
Host: University of Kentucky
List moderated: Yes.
Editorial contact: K. Vaninadha Rao
Internet: kvrao@andy.bgsu.edu
Bitnet: kvrao@trapper
How to access: Send subscribe message to listserv@ukcc
How to unsubscribe: Send unsubscribe message to listserv@ukcc
Archives: Archives are developed weekly; apply to listowner for details.

INDIA-L@UTARLVM1

Description: INDIA-L@UTARLVM1 is the Univ. of Texas at Arlington forum on India.
Subjects covered: India; cultural studies
Host: University of Texas at Arlington
List moderated: Yes.
Editorial contact: K. Vaninadha Rao
Internet: kvrao@andy.bgsu.edu
Bitnet: kvrao@trapper
How to access: Send subscribe message to listserv@utarlvm1 or add@andy.bgsu.edu
How to unsubscribe: Send unsubscribe message to listserv@utarlvm1 or add@andy.bgsu.edu
Archives: Archives are developed weekly; apply to listowner for details.

INDIA-L@UTEMPLEVM

Description: INDIA-L@UTARLVM1 is the Temple University forum on India.
Subjects covered: India; cultural studies
Host: Temple University
List moderated: Yes.
Editorial contact: K. Vaninadha Rao
Internet: kvrao@andy.bgsu.edu
Bitnet: kvrao@trapper
How to access: Send subscribe message to listserv@utemplevm
How to unsubscribe: Send unsubscribe message to listserv@utemplevm
Archives: Archives are developed weekly; apply to listowner for details.

INDIA@PCCVM

Description: INDIA@PCCVM is a forum for discussions related to India and the region.
Subjects covered: cultural studies; India
List moderated: Yes.
Editorial contact: Geert K. Marien
Bitnet: indiamgr@pccvm, or gkmlc@cunyvm
How to access: Send subscribe message to listserv@pccvm
How to unsubscribe: Send unsubscribe message to listserv@pccvm
Archives: Archives are developed weekly; apply to listowner for details.

INFED-L

Description: INFED-L is a discussion list on the uses of computers (or what is usually called Informatics) in Education, broadly conceived. The list is unmoderated. Contributions may deal with the various uses of computers in higher, secondary, elementary or informal education and may cover topics such as development and authoring tools, programming languages (Prolog, Logo, etc.), specific applications, generic approaches (such as Artificial Intelligence and education, for example), computer-based communications, etc. Discussion of the philosophical and sociological implications of computer-aided teaching and learning is also welcome.
Subjects covered: education; computer hardware and software; computer-assisted instruction (CAI)
Net address for questions or submissions: INFED-L@CCSUN.UNICAMP.BR
List moderated: No.
Editorial contact: Eduardo Chaves
Internet: CHAVES@CCVAX.UNICAMP.BR
Bitnet: CHAVES@BRUC.BITNET
How to access: Send a message to LISTSERV@CCSUN.UNICAMP.BR and include the following in the body of the message: SUB INFED-L Your full name
How to submit: To send a message to the list, address the message to: INFED-L@CCSUN.UNICAMP.BR

INFO + REF@INDYCMS

Description: INFO + REF@INDYCMS is a conference fo rreference librarians and consultants.
Subjects covered: library and information science
List moderated: No.
Editorial contact: John B. Harlan
Internet: ijbh200@indyvax.iupui.edu
Bitnet: ijbh200@indyvax
How to access: Send subscribe message to listserv@indycms or listserv@indycms.iupui.edu
How to unsubscribe: Send unsubscribe message to listserv@indycms or listserv@indycms.iupui.edu
Archives: Archives are developed monthly; apply to listowner for details.

INFO-ADA@AJPO.SEI.CMU.EDU

Description: INFO-ADA is a forum about the Ada programming language.
Subjects covered: computer science
List moderated: No.
Editorial contact: Karl A. Nyberg
Internet: karl@grebyn.com
How to access: Send subscribe message to listserv@ndsuvm1 or info-ada-request@ajpo.sei.cmu.edu
How to unsubscribe: Send unsubscribe message to listserv@ndsuvm1 or info-ada-request@ajpo.sei.cmu.edu
Archives: Yes; Send anonymous FTP to AJPO.SEI.CMU.EDU and cd ftp/public/infoada

INFO-ANDREW-BUGS@ANDREW.CMU.EDU

Description: INFO-ANDREW-BUGS is a discussion list on problems in the ANDREW environment.

Subjects covered: computer hardware and software; electronic networking
List moderated: No.
Editorial contact: Adam Stoller
Internet: ghoti + @andrew.cmu.edu
How to access: Send subscribe message to INFO-ANDREW-BUGS-REQUEST@ANDREW.CMU.EDU
How to unsubscribe: Send unsubscribe message to INFO-ANDREW-BUGS-REQUEST@ANDREW.CMU.EDU

INFO-ANDREW@ANDREW.CMU.EDU

Description: INFO-ANDREW is a discussion forum on the ANDREW development project of Carnegie-Mellon University and IBM.
Subjects covered: computer hardware and software; electronic networking
List moderated: Yes.
Editorial contact: Adam Stoller
Internet: ghoti + @andrew.cmu.edu
How to access: Send subscribe message to INFO-ANDREW-REQUEST@ANDREW.CMU.EDU
How to unsubscribe: Send unsubscribe message to INFO-ANDREW-REQUEST@ANDREW.CMU.EDU

INFO-C@RESEARCH.ATT.COM

Description: INFO-C is a forum on C programming.
Subjects covered: computer science
List moderated: No.
Editorial contact: Mark Plotnick
Internet: info-c-request@research.att.com
How to access: Send subscribe message to listserv@ndsuvm1 or info-c-request@research.att.com
How to unsubscribe: Send unsubscribe message to listserv@ndsuvm1 or info-c-request@research.att.com

INFO-FRAME@AEROSPACE.AERO.ORG

Description: INFO-FRAME is a forum on system frameworks.
Subjects covered: computer science
List moderated: No.
Editorial contact: Louis MacDonald
Internet: louis@aerospace.aero.org
How to access: Send subscribe message to INFO-FRAME-REQUEST@AEROSPACE.AERO.ORG
How to unsubscribe: Send unsubscribe message to INFO-FRAME-REQUEST@AEROSPACE.AERO.ORG

INFO-FUTURES@ENCORE.COM

Description: INFO-FUTURES@ENCORE.COM is a forum for speculation of current and likely events in the field of computer research and technology.
Subjects covered: computer science; information technology; futurism
List moderated: No.
Editorial contact: Barry Shein
Internet: bzs@encore.com
How to access: Send subscribe message to INFO-FUTURES-REQUEST@ENCORE.COM
How to unsubscribe: Send unsubscribe message to INFO-FUTURES-REQUEST@ENCORE.COM

INFO-GCG

Description: INFO-GCG is a discussion list providing a forum for scientists to share experiences, ideas, problems, solutions and queries relating to GCG software and/or research utilizing GCG software. INFO-GCG/bionet.molbio.gcg is a place where users and administrators of the GCG software system can discuss how to best use this software tool to accomplish research objectives. The list should not be used to contact GCG Inc, report software bugs to GCG Inc, or request assistance from GCG Inc. There is an existing e-mail address established by GCG Inc for this purpose.
Subjects covered: genetics; science and technology; computer hardware and software
Net address for operations: info-gcg@net.bio.net
Net address for questions or submissions: info-gcg@net.bio.net
Established: 1988
Subscribers: 300
Sponsor: BIOSCI/bionet (Intelligenetics)
List moderated: No.
Editorial contact: John Cargill
Manager of Research Computing, Ontario Cancer Institute, 500 Sherbourne Street, Toronto, Ontario Canada M4X 1K9
Tel: (416) 924-0671
Fax: (416) 926-6529
Internet: cargill@ocicl.oci.utoronto.ca
Bitnet: cargill@utoroci
Copyright statement: Non Commercial Use Only
How to access: Send mail to info-gcg-request@net.bio.net
How to unsubscribe: Send mail to info-gcg-request@net.bio.net
How to submit: Send mail to info-gcg@net.bio.net
Additional information: The list is available on Usenet as "bionet.software.gcg". The list is maintained through the generosity of Dave Kristofferson of Intelligenetics, and is part of the BIOSCI/bionet hierarchy of mailing lists/newsgroups.

INFO-GNU-MSDOS@WUGATE.WUSTL.EDU

Description: INFO-GNU-MSDOS is a discussion group of the GNUISH MS-DOS Development Group.
Subjects covered: computer hardware and software
List moderated: No.
Editorial contact: Mr. David J. Camp
Internet: david@wubios.wustl.edu
How to access: Send subscribe message to listserv@wugate or listserv@wugate.wustl.edu
How to unsubscribe: Send unsubscribe message to listserv@wugate or listserv@wugate.wustl.edu

INFO-KERMIT@WATSON.CC.COLUMBIA.EDU

Description: INFO-KERMIT@WATSON.CC.COLUMBIA.EDU is a discussion forum on the Kermit file transfer protocol.
Subjects covered: computer hardware and software; telecommunications
List moderated: Yes.
Editorial contact: Christine Gianone
Internet: cmg@watson.cc.columbia.edu
How to access: Send subscribe message to listserv@cuvma or info-kermit-request@watson.cc.columbia.edu

How to unsubscribe: Send unsubscribe message to listserv@cuvma or info-kermit-request@watson.cc.columbia.edu
Archives: Yes; Send anonymous FTP to WATSON.CC.COLUMBIA.EDU

INFO-LAW@BRL.MIL

Description: INFO-LAW@BRL.MIL focuses on computers and law.
Subjects covered: law and legal studies; computer science
List moderated: Yes.
Editorial contact: Mike Muuss
Internet: info-law-request@brl.mil
How to access: Send subscribe message to INFO-LAWREQUEST@BRL.MIL
How to unsubscribe: Send unsubscribe message to INFO-LAWREQUEST@BRL.MIL

INFO-M2@UCF1VM.CC.UCF.EDU

Description: INFO-M2 is a forum on the Modula 2 programming language.
Subjects covered: computer science
List moderated: No.
Editorial contact: UCF Postmaster
Internet: postmast@ucf1vm.cc.ucf.edu
Bitnet: postmast@ucf1vm
How to access: Send subscribe message to listserv@ucf1vm or listserv@ucf1vm.cc.ucf.edu
How to unsubscribe: Send unsubscribe message to listserv@ucf1vm or listserv@ucf1vm.cc.ucf.edu

INFO-MACH@CMU.EDU

Description: INFO-MACH@CMU.EDU is a forum on the MACH operating system.
Subjects covered: computer hardware and software
List moderated: No.
Editorial contact: Doug Orr
Internet: doug.orr@cs.cmu.edu
How to access: Send subscribe message to INFO-MACH-REQUEST@CMU.EDU
How to unsubscribe: Send unsubscribe message to INFO-MACH-REQUEST@CMU.EDU

INFO-MICRO@WSMR-SIMTEL20.ARMY.MIL

Description: INFO-MICRO offers a general discussion of microcomputers.
Subjects covered: computer hardware and software
List moderated: Yes.
Editorial contact: Keith Petersen
Internet: W8SDZ@WSMR-SIMTEL20.ARMY.MIL
How to access: Send subscribe message to INFO-MICRO-REQUEST@WSMR-SIMTEL20.ARMY.MIL
How to unsubscribe: Send unsubscribe message to INFO-MICRO-REQUEST@WSMR-SIMTEL20.ARMY.MIL
Archives: Yes; Send anonymous FTP to WSMR-SIMTEL20.ARMY.MIL

INFO-MINIX@UDEL.EDU

Description: INFO-MINIX is a discussion list on the Minix operating system.
Subjects covered: computer hardware and software
List moderated: No.
Editorial contact: Glen Overby
Internet: minix@plains.nodak.edu
How to access: Send subscribe message to listserv@ndsuvm1 or listserv@vm1.nodak.edu
How to unsubscribe: Send unsubscribe message to listserv@ndsuvm1 or listserv@vm1.nodak.edu
Archives: Yes; Send anonymous FTP to VM!.NODAK.EDU cd listserv

INFO-MODEMS@WSMR-SIMTEL20.ARMY.MIL

Description: INFO-MODEMS@WSMR-SIMTEL20.ARMY.MIL is a discussion list on modems.
Subjects covered: computer hardware and software; telecommunications
List moderated: Yes.
Editorial contact: Keith Petersen
Internet: W8SDZ@WSMR-SIMTEL20.ARMY.MIL
How to access: Send subscribe message to INFO-MODEMS-REQUEST@WSMR-SIMTEL20.ARMY.MIL
How to unsubscribe: Send unsubscribe message to INFO-MODEMS-REQUEST@WSMR-SIMTEL20.ARMY.MIL
Archives: Yes; Send anonymous FTP to WSMR-SIMTEL20.ARMY.MIL

INFO-NETS@THINK.COM

Description: INFO-NETS@THINK.COM is a general discussion list on networking topics.
Subjects covered: electronic networking
List moderated: No.
Editorial contact: Robert L. Krawitz
Internet: rlk@think.com
How to access: Send subscribe message to listserv@bitnic or listserv@bitnic.educom.edu
How to unsubscribe: Send unsubscribe message to listserv@bitnic or listserv@bitnic.educom.edu
Archives: Archives are developed monthly; apply to listowner for details.

INFO-ODA+@ANDREW.CMU.EDU

Description: INFO-ODA+ is a forum for discussion of all topics covering ISO standard 8613 on open data architecture.
Subjects covered: computer science
List moderated: No.
Editorial contact: Mark Sherman
Internet: mss+@andrew.cmu.edu
How to access: Send subscribe message to INFO-ODA-REQUEST+@ANDREW.CMU.EDU
How to unsubscribe: Send unsubscribe message to INFO-ODA-REQUEST+@ANDREW.CMU.EDU

INFO-PASCAL@BRL.MIL

Description: INFO-PASCAL is a forum on the PASCAL programming language.

Subjects covered: computer science
List moderated: No.
Editorial contact: Herman Lobos
Bitnet: hlobos@utfsm
How to access: Send subscribe message to listserv@utfsm or info-pascal-request@brl.mil
How to unsubscribe: Send unsubscribe message to listserv@utfsm or info-pascal-request@brl.mil
Archives: Yes; Send anonymous FTP to WSMR-SIMTEL20.ARMY.MIL and cd /PD2:ARCHIVES.PASCAL

INFO-RUSS

Description: INFO-RUSS is a discussion list covering the Russian emigre community worldwide.
Subjects covered: Russia; political science
Editorial contact: Alexander Kaplan
Internet: SASHA@SUPER.ECE.JHU.EDU
How to access: Send an email message to SASHA@SUPER.ECE.JHU.EDU
How to unsubscribe: Send an email message to SASHA@SUPER.ECE.JHU.EDU

INFO-TANDEM

Description: info-tandem is an electronic forum for discussion of computer systems from Tandem Computers Inc.
Subjects covered: Tandem Computers Inc.; computer hardware and software; computer science
Net address for operations: info-tandem-request@zorch.sf-bay.org
Net address for questions or submissions: info-tandem@zorch.sf-bay.org
Established: March 1992
Subscribers: 40
List moderated: No.
Editorial contact: Scott Hazen Mueller
4108 Killigrew Drive
Tel: (209) 545-9417
Internet: scott@zorch.sf-bay.org
How to access: Send mail to info-tandem-request@zorch.sf-bay.org
How to unsubscribe: Send mail to info-tandem-request@zorch.sf-bay.org
How to submit: Send mail to info-tandem@zorch.sf-bay.org

INFO-TEX@SHSU

Description: INFO-TeX is a forum on the TeX document processing system.
Subjects covered: computer hardware and software
Host: Sam Houston State University
List moderated: No.
Editorial contact: George D. Greenwade, Ph.D.
Internet: bed__gdg@shsu.edu
Bitnet: bed__gdg@shsu
How to access: Send subscribe message to listserv@shsu or listserv@shsu.edu
How to unsubscribe: Send unsubscribe message to listserv@shsu or listserv@shsu.edu
Archives: Yes; Located at fileserv@shsu or fileserv@shsu.edu

INFO-UNIX@BRL.MIL

Description: INFO-UNIX offers an advanced and administrative-related discussion of microcomputers.
Subjects covered: computer hardware and software
List moderated: No.
Editorial contact: Mike Muuss
Internet: mike@brl.mil
How to access: Send subscribe message to INFO-UNIX-REQUEST@BRL.MIL
How to unsubscribe: Send unsubscribe message to INFO-UNIX-REQUEST@BRL.MIL

INFO-V@PESCADERO.STANFORD.EDU

Description: INFO-V is a discussion list covering the V distributed operating system.
Subjects covered: computer hardware and software
List moderated: No.
Editorial contact: Keith A. Lantz
Internet: lantz@gregorio.stanford.edu
How to access: Send subscribe message to INFO-V-REQUEST@PESCADERO.STANFORD.EDU
How to unsubscribe: Send unsubscribe message to INFO-V-REQUEST@PESCADERO.STANFORD.EDU

INFO-VLSI@THINK.COM

Description: INFO-VLSI is a forum covering the design and production of inegrated circuitry.
Subjects covered: engineering; computer science
List moderated: No.
Editorial contact: Bruce Walker
Internet: bruce@think.com
How to access: Send subscribe message to INFO-VLSI-REQUEST@THINK.COM
How to unsubscribe: Send unsubscribe message to INFO-VLSI-REQUEST@THINK.COM
Archives: Yes; Archives are located at Think.com in the files: mail/info-vlsi.archive*

INFO-VM@UUNET.UU.NET

Description: INFO-VM@UUNET is a discussion list centering on the GNU Emacs VM mail reader.
Subjects covered: computer hardware and software
List moderated: No.
Editorial contact: Kyle Jones
Internet: info-vm-request@uunet.uu.net
How to access: Send subscribe message to INFO-VM-REQUEST@UUNET.UU.NET
How to unsubscribe: Send unsubscribe message to INFO-VM-REQUEST@UUNET.UU.NET

INFO-ZIP@WSMR-SIMTEL20.ARMY.MIL

Description: INFO-ZIP is a forum on ZIP-related programs.
Subjects covered: computer hardware and software
Editorial contact: Keith Petersen
Internet: w8sdz@wsmr-simtel20.army.mil
Bitnet: w8sdz@ndsuvm1
How to access: Send subscribe message to INFO-ZIP-REQUEST@WSMR-SIMTEL20.ARMY.MIL

How to unsubscribe: Send unsubscribe message to INFO-ZIP-REQUEST@WSMR-SIMTEL20.ARMY.MIL
Archives: Yes; Send anonymous FTP to WSMR-SIMTEL20.ARMY.MIL cd listserv

INFORMATION RETRIEVAL
Description: Information Retrieval is a list covering library and information science and computer science.
Subjects covered: library and information science; computer science
Net address for operations: mailbase@newcastle.ac.uk
Established: 1990
Subscribers: 200
List moderated: No.
Editorial contact: John Lindsay
School of Information Systems, Kingston University, Kingston Upon Thames KT1 2EE, UK.
Tel: 081 547 2000 x 2699
Fax: 081 547 1457
Internet: is__s377@kingston.ac.uk
How to access: Send message to is__s377@kingston.ac.uk
How to unsubscribe: Send message to is__s377@kingston.ac.uk
How to submit: Send message to is__s377@kingston.ac.uk

INFOSYS@HDETUD1
Description: INFOSYS@HDETUD1 is a forum covering a wide range of information systems issues.
Subjects covered: information technology
List moderated: No.
Internet: winfave@hdetud1.tudelft.nl
Bitnet: winfave@hdetud1
How to access: Send subscribe message to listserv@hdetud1
How to unsubscribe: Send unsubscribe message to listserv@hdetud1

INGRAFX@PSUVM
Description: INGRAFX is a conference covering information graphics matters.
Subjects covered: information technology
List moderated: Yes.
Internet: WHY@PSUVM
How to access: Send subscribe message to listserv@psuvm
How to unsubscribe: Send unsubscribe message to listserv@psuvm
Archives: Archives are developed weekly; apply to listowner for details.

INMYLIFE@WKUVX1
Description: INMYLIFE@WKUVX1 forum for discussing the popular culture of the 1960s.
Subjects covered: music; political science; cultural studies; popular culture
List moderated: No.
Editorial contact: Matt Gore
Bitnet: goremh@wkuvx1
How to access: Send subscribe message to listserv@wkuvx1
How to unsubscribe: Send unsubscribe message to listserv@wkuvx1

INNOPAC@MAINE
Description: INNOPAC@MAINE provides a forum for discussion of Innovative Interfaces' Online Public Access Catalog software.
Subjects covered: library and information science; Innovative Interfaces
List moderated: No.
Editorial contact: Marilyn Lutz
Bitnet: lutz@maine
How to access: Send subscribe message to listserv@maine
How to unsubscribe: Send unsubscribe message to listserv@maine
Archives: Archives are developed monthly; apply to listowner for details.

INNS-L
Description: INNS-L posts announcements and inquiries related to neural networks.
Subjects covered: neurology; medicine; biology
Net address for operations: UMDD.umd.edu bitnet
Net address for questions or submissions: INNS-L@UMDD.umd.edu
Established: December 1991
Subscribers: 376
Sponsor: Facilities donated to the International Neural Network Society by University of Maryland UMCP, College Park, MD.
Host: University of Maryland UMCP, College Park, MD.
List moderated: Yes.
Moderation procedure: INNS-L distributes announcements from the International Neural Network Society and other items submitted by members and non-members. Submitted items are usually announcements or inquiries. The moderator distributes submissions according to a liberal criterion of whether they are of interest to the members of the International Neural Network Society.
Editorial contact: Mary Ann Metzger
INNS-L Coordinator, Department of Psychology, University of Maryland, UMBC, Baltimore, MD 21228.
Tel: (410) 455-2657
Fax: (410) 455-1055
Internet: metzger@umbc.edu
Bitnet: metzger@umbc
How to access: Send message to listserv@UMDD or to listserv@UMDD.umd.edu with the command: subscribe INNS-L Your Name Here
Access policy: Subscriptions are currently open to the public.
How to unsubscribe: Send message to listserv@UMDD or to listserv@UMDD.umd.edu with the command: signoff INNS-L Your Name Here
How to submit: Send message to listserv@UMDD or to listserv@UMDD.umd.edu with the command: signoff INNS-L Your Name Here
Submission policy: Announcements and inquiries of interest to the members of the International Neural Network Society will be distributed.
Archives: Distributed items are retained in listserv archives at UMDD.
Additional information: Second editor: James Wesolowski, INNS-L Moderator, International Neural Network Society, 1250 24th Street, NW Suite 300, Washington, DC 20037; tel (202) 466-4667; fax (202) 466-2888; 70712.3265@compuserve.com

INSTITUTE FOR COMPUTERS AND WRITING

Description: Institute for Computers and Writing is a list centering on the impact of computers on writing and the teaching of writing.

Subjects covered: computer science; language and literature; writing; education

Net address for operations: listserv@ttuvm1

Net address for questions or submissions: ICW-L@ttuvm1

Established: May, 1993

Subscribers: 15

Sponsor: Texas Tech University, Lubbock, TX 79409

Host: Texas Tech University, Lubbock, TX 79409

List moderated: No.

Editorial contact: Fred Kemp

Department of English, Texas Tech University, Lubbock, TX 79409-3091

Tel: (806) 742-2501

Fax: (806) 742-0989

Internet: YKFOK@ttacs1.ttu.edu

Bitnet: YKFOK@ttacs

Technical contact: John Halbert

University Computing Facility, 9 Computer Center, Texas Tech University, Lubbock, TX 79409-3051

Tel: (806) 742-3619

Internet: SNAHAL@TTUVM1.TTU.EDU

Bitnet: SNHAL@TTUVM1.TTU.EDU

How to access: Send the email message: subscribe mbu-1 yourfirstname yourlastname to listserv@ttuvm1

Access policy: MBU-L accepts all subscribers interested in computers and writing and willing to maintain reasonable network decorum. Subscription is open and all submissions are accepted.

How to unsubscribe: Send the email message: signoff mbu-1 to listserv@ttuvm1

How to submit: Send e-mail to mbu-1@ttuvm1

Submission policy: All e-mail is accepted automatically.

INT-LAW

Description: INT-LAW is a discussion group covering topics, issues pertaining to foreign, comparative, and international law librarianship.

Subjects covered: law and legal studies; international studies; library and information science

Net address for operations: LISTSERV@UMINN1

Net address for questions or submissions: INT-LAW@UMINN1

Established: April 30, 1991

Subscribers: 422

Sponsor: University of Minnesota, Minneapolis, MN 35455.

List moderated: Yes.

Moderation procedure: Co-moderators monitor postings, confer on questionable ones, and deal with respective answers accordingly.

Editorial contact: Mila R. Rush

U. of MN Law Library, 229 19th Ave. S., Minneapolis, MN 33455.

Tel: (612) 625-0793

Fax: (612) 625-3478

Internet: M. Rush@VM1.SPCS.UMN.EDU.

Bitnet: M.Rush@UMMN1

How to access: Send message to LISTSERV@UNINN1: sub INT-LAW first second name

How to unsubscribe: Send message to LISTSERV@UMINN1: uns INT-LAW

How to submit: Send message to INT-LAW@UMINN1

Archives: Full archives are stored at LISTSERV@UMINN1

Gopher accessibility: FATTY, LAW, Cornell

Additional information: Co-moderator: Lyonnette Louis-Jacques, U. of Chicago, D'Angelo Law Library, 1121 2 60th. St., Chicago, IL 60637.

INTECH-L

Description: Intech-L covers computers in education.

Subjects covered: education technology; computer-assisted instruction (CAI)

List moderated: No.

How to access: Send subscribe message to listserv@ulkyvm

How to unsubscribe: Send unsubscribe message to listserv@ulkyvm

INTERCUL@RPITSVM

Description: Intercul@RPITSVM is a forum for discussion of intercultural communication.

Subjects covered: anthropology

Host: Comserve

List moderated: Yes.

Editorial contact: Comserve Support Staff

Internet: comserve@vm.its.vpi.edu

Bitnet: comserve@rpitsvm

How to access: Send subscribe message to comserve@rpitsvm or comserve@vm.its.vpi.edu

How to unsubscribe: Send unsubscribe message to comserve@rpitsvm or comserve@vm.its.vpi.edu

INTERCULTURAL COMMUNICATION PRACTICUM

Description: Intercultural Communication Practicum (Xcult-X) is an electronic discussion list focusing on issues related to communication philosophy in the twenty-first century. Xcult-X attempts to follow a completely open policy. Concealed subscriptions are strongly discouraged.

Subjects covered: communications; futurism; philosophy

Net address for operations: LISTSERV@UMRVMB

Net address for questions or submissions: Xcult-X@UMRVMB

Established: January 1991

Subscribers: 104

Host: University of Missouri-Rolla

List moderated: No.

Moderation procedure: Xcult-X is completely unmoderated. The Listowner refers individual concerns/complaints to the list group for discussion.

Editorial contact: W. Lance Haynes

215 Humanities, UMR, Rolla, MO 65401.

Tel: 314-341-4803

Fax: 314-341-6312

Bitnet: LANCE@UMRVMB

Copyright statement: As far as the owner is concerned, anything sent to the list is public domain.

How to access: Tell LISTSERV@UMRVMB Subscribe Xcult-X Your Name

Archives: Archived at UMRVMB.

Gopher accessibility: Gopher access is available.

INTERF-L

Description: The Israeli Interest Group on ''Interfacial Phenomena'' (INTERF-L) is intended for physicists, chemists, biologists and engineers whose research interests lie within the broad area of physics and chemistry of Interfacial Phenomena. In particular: Liquids at Interfaces, Wetting and Adhesion Phenomena, Capillarity. Complex and Macromolecular Fluids: Structure, Phase Transitions and Interfaces. Thermodynamics and Hydrodynamics of Polymer Melts and Solutions, Microemulsions, Colloids, Emulsions and Foams, Suspensions, Surfactants in Solutions, Membranes, Amphiphilic Monolayers and Bilayers, Gels, Liquid Crystals, Porous Media, The INTERF-L Interest Group will provide the following functions: Increase the communication between members of this inter-disciplinary community in Israel. Announcements of seminars, conferences, scientific programs, grants and other items of common interest. In the future, we hope that other workshops, meetings and special seminars could be organized with the help of INTERF-L.
Subjects covered: interfacial phenomena; complex fluids
Net address for operations: listserv@taunivm.tau.ac.il
Net address for questions or submissions:
listserv@taunivm.tau.ac.il
Established: 1989
Host: Tel Aviv University, Ramat Aviv 69978 Israel
List moderated: Yes.
Editorial contact: Prof. David Andelman
School of Physics, Tel Aviv University,
Ramat Aviv 69978 Israel
Tel: (972)-3-6419529
Fax: (972)-3-6422979
Internet: andelman@taunivm.tau.ac.il
Bitnet: andelman@taunivm
How to access: Send a one line e-mail item to
listserv@taunivm sub interf-l ''your name''
Access policy: Subscription is open to all although the list mainly provides information to the Israeli community (conferences, seminars, etc.).
How to unsubscribe: Send a one line e-mail to
listserv@taunivm
signoff interf-l
How to submit: Send an e-mail item to interf-l@taunivm
Submission policy: Only items of common interest to the Israeli community of Interfacial Phenomena and Complex Fluids will be posted.

INTERFACES-P-M@CRIM.CA

Description: INTERFACES-P-M is a discussion list on computer interface design.
Subjects covered: computer science
List moderated: No.
Editorial contact: Julian Lebensold
How to access: Send subscribe message to INTERFACES-P-M-REQUEST@CRIM.CA
How to unsubscribe: Send unsubscribe message to INTERFACES-P-M-REQUEST@CRIM.CA

THE INTERNATIONAL HEALTH COMMUNICATION HOTLINE

Description: The International Health Communication Hotline is an electronic list carrying international and interdisciplinary discussion of health communication and related issues.
Subjects covered: health sciences; medicine; education

Net address for operations: InHealth@Jaguar.Uof S.Edu
Net address for questions or submissions:
InHealth@VM.ITS.RPI.Edu
Established: February 1992
Subscribers: 150
Host: University of Scranton and Bloomsburg University
List moderated: Yes.
Moderation procedure: Seek information to post, moderators provide dbase functions.
Editorial contact: Leonard Assante
Dept of Communication, University of Scranton, Scranton, PA 18510-4592.
Tel: (717) 941-6164
Fax: (717) 941-6164
Internet: AssanteLi@Jaguar,UofS.edu
Bitnet: AssanteLi@Scranton
Technical contact: Tim Stephens
Dept. of Comm., RPI, Albany, NY.
Internet: support@vm.its.rpi.edu
How to access: Join InHealth Your Name send to:
Comserve@VM.ITS.RPI.edu
Access policy: List is open to anyone.
How to unsubscribe: Send message to listserv: Dropout Your Name
How to submit: Send to InHealth@VM.RPI.ITS.edu
Additional information: Part of COMSERVE network of communication-related lists.

INTERNET FAX BYPASS SERVICE MAILING LIST

Description: The Internet Fax Bypass Service is an experiment in remote printing, using the Internet to address fax machines as remote printers. The mailing list has been established to discuss the experiment.
Subjects covered: Internet; telecommunications
Net address for questions or submissions: tpc-rp-request@aarnet.edu.au
How to access: Send an email message requesting to be added to the list to: tpc-rp-request@aarnet.edu.au

INTERNIC NET-HAPPENINGS

Description: InterNIC Net-Happenings is a discussion list carrying Internet-related news, conference reports, information about new Internet resources, and other announcments.
Subjects covered: Internet
Net address for operations: listserv@is.internic.net
How to access: Send an email message to
listserv@is.internic.net with the message subscribe net-happenings <firstname lastname>
Archives: The list is archived daily and available in digest form. The archives can be searched by email through the listserv rogram (send the command ''help'' for information).
Gopher accessibility: Yes, the archives are searchable through the InterNIC gopher server in the directory named is.internet.net Everybody/Network Resources/Internet Information

INTERNIC NET-RESOURCES

Description: InterNIC Net-Resources is a discussion list carrying Internet-related news and announcments.
Subjects covered: Internet
Net address for operations: listserv@is.internic.net

How to access: Send an email message to listserv@is.internic.net with the message subscribe net-resources <firstname lastname>
Archives: The list is archived daily and available in digest form. The archives can be searched by email through the listserv rogram (send the command "help" for information).
Gopher accessibility: Yes, the archives are searchable through the InterNIC gopher server in the directory named is.internet.net Everybody/Network Resources/Internet Information

INTERSCRIPTA@MORGAN.UCS.MUN.CA

Description: Interscripta is a discussion list covering medieval seminar topics.
Subjects covered: Medieval studies; history
Net address for operations: Listserv@morgan.ucs.mun.ca
Net address for questions or submissions: Interscripta@morgan.ucs.mun.ca
How to access: Send message to listserv: SUBSCRIBE <listname> <your name>

INTUDM-L

Description: Intudm-L is a forum covering the study of intuition.
Subjects covered: psychology
List moderated: No.
Editorial contact: Weston H. Agor
Bitnet: hy00@utep
How to access: Send subscribe message to listserv@utepa
How to unsubscribe: Send unsubscribe message to listserv@utepa
Archives: Yes.

IOOB-L

Description: IOOB-L is a discussion forum on industrial psychology and organizational behavior topics.
Subjects covered: human resources
List moderated: Yes.
Editorial contact: John L. Cofer
Internet: cofer%utkvx.bitnet@cunyvm.cuny.edu
Bitnet: cofer@utkvx
How to access: Send subscribe message to listserv@uga or listserv@uga.cc.uga.edu
How to unsubscribe: Send unsubscribe message to listserv@uga or listserv@uga.cc.uga.edu
Archives: Archives are developed monthly; apply to listowner for details.

IOUDAIOS@YORKVM1

Description: IOUDAIOS is the international forum for scholarship on early Judaism and Christian origins. Discussion is focussed on first century Judaism, but ranges widely over from the Maccabean period up to the early Rabbinic period (ca. 200 B.C.E. to 400 C.E.). Discussion often involves the relationship of nascent Christianity to Judaism.
Subjects covered: Judaica; language and literature; Hebrew language and literature; Christianity
Net address for operations: LISTSERV@YORKVM1 listserv@vm1.yorku.ca
Net address for questions or submissions: IOUDAIOS@YORKVM1

Established: April 25, 1990
Subscribers: 600
Sponsor: York University, 4700 Keele Street North, York, ON, Canada M3J 1P3
List moderated: No.
Editorial contact: David Reimer
Regent's Park College, Oxford OX1 2LB, England
Tel: (0865) 59887
Internet: dreimer@vax.ox.ac.uk (dreimer@mach1.wlu.ca until 1 July 1993)
Review: David J. Reimer, "A LISTSERV Case Study: IOUDAIOS@YORKVM1" Journal ARC: The Journal of Religious Studies, McGill University Journal 20 (1992) 112-114.
How to access: Send message "SUB IOUDAIOS Your Name" to LISTSERV@YORKVM1 or listserv@vm1.yorku.ca.
Access policy: Subscription is open to any interested individual. Discussion assumes acquaintance with hellenistic Greek and classical Hebrew languages and the relevant primary sources.
How to unsubscribe: Send message "UNS IOUDAIOS" to LISTSERV@YORKVM1 or listserv@vm1.yorku.ca.
How to submit: Send messages to IOUDAIOS@YORKVM1 or ioudaios@vm1.yorku.ca
Submission policy: Submissions should be within the parameters of the group as set out in E-MANUAL IOUDAIOS (see below). IOUDAIOS Review is a review journal for books primarily in the field of early Judaism (200 B.C.E. - 200 C.E.) and secondarily in the relation of early Judaism to Christian origins.
Archives: Two foundation documents (the manual: E-MANUAL IOUDAIOS; and the etiquette rules: 7QASKY IOUDAIOS) are available from the YorkVM1 fileserver. Complete weekly logs of past discussion are stored under filenames in the form: IOUDAIOS LOGyymmw, where yy = the year, mm = the month (numeric), and w = the week, specified by the letters A - E (for weeks 1 - 5).
Related files: IOUDAIOS also makes available electronic preprints; a directory of holdings is available in the file FILELIST IOUDIAOS.
Gopher accessibility: IOUDAIOS is at present exploring the possibility of making its archive available on a gopher site.
Additional information: IOUDAIOS (and IOUD-REV) are in the process of relocating. Contact David Reimer (addresses above) for further developments.

IPCT-L (INTERPERSONAL COMPUTING AND TECHNOLOGY LIST)

Description: The Interpersonal Computing and Technology List (IPCT-L) was created February 1992 by the Center for Teaching and Technology (CTT) at the Academic Computer Center, Georgetown University. A special effort will be made to promote an international forum for pedagogical issues important to higher education involving teaching with technology, and especially with connectivity and networking. A goal is to create a forum for the discussion of computing and other technology that can be used to promote learning. Topics may involve teaching and training; collaboration; the development of partnerships among learners, faculty or teachers, and other interested persons in the educational community; research that reflect these interests, and the fostering of collegial relationships within the context of the other goals of this list. The decade of the 1980s was characterized by the personal computer, and development of individual productivity. The focus of the IPCT-L, as we move toward the 21st century, is that interpersonal computing and technology will tie persons together throughout the world -- to share ideas and solve problems.

Subjects covered: telecommunications; Internet; communications

Net address for operations: LISTSERV@GUVM.GEORGETOWN.EDU

Net address for questions or submissions: IPCT@CAC.PSU.EDU

Established: February 1992

Subscribers: 1100+

List moderated: Yes.

Moderation procedure: The moderators reserve the right to make all decisions regarding the posting of messages. Those that are judged to fall outside the mission statement of this list will be returned to the sender, with an explanation for the rejection; or with a suggestion to 'revise and resubmit' or a request for clarification. All messages not returned will be posted. No messages will be posted anonymously.

Editorial contact: Mauri Collins

Internet: mauri@cac.psu.edu

Bitnet: mmc7@psuvm

Technical contact: Zane Berge

Internet: BERGE@GUVAX.GEORGETOWN.EDU

Bitnet: BERGE@GUVAX

Review: Reviewed by List Review Service edited by Raleigh Muns: see appendix.

Copyright statement: Copyright of individual postings to, and archived files of, IPCT-L are retained by the original author unless specifically transferred. Copying, modification, publication or distribution of postings, or archives, of Interpersonal Computing and Technology Discussion List (IPCT-L) are not permitted except by the written permission of the original author(s) or the party to whom he/she has transferred copyright unless the author grants such permission within the original posting. In keeping with the spirit of free distribution of information over the net, individual authors are encouraged to grant such permission at the time of posting. This might be done as follows: Copyright [NAME] 1992. Permission is hereby granted for the redistribution of this material over electronic networks so long as this item is redistributed in full and with appropriate credit given to the author. All other rights reserved.

How to access: Send the following one-line message in the body of an email message to LISTSERV@GUVM or LISTSERV@GUVM.GEORGETOWN.EDU; SUBSCRIBE IPCT-L YOURFIRSTNAME YOURLASTNAME

How to unsubscribe: Send the following one line message to LISTSERV@GUVM or LISTSERV@GUVM.GEORGETOWN.EDU as an interactive message or (in the body, not the Subject: line of the email note): SIGNOFF IPCT-L

Related files: IPCT-J, Interpersonal Computing and Technology: An Electronic Journal for the 21st Century (Subscribers to IPCT-L automatically receive IPCT-J).

IPENET (INTERNATIONAL POLITICAL ECONOMY)

Description: IPEnet is an electronic discussion list that facilitates discussion from people around the world interested in International Political Economy. Since its inception in early November 1992, IPEnet has grown to over 300 subscribers from more than twenty countries around the world (Australia to Zimbabwe). IPE is an unmoderated and open list. This means that all messages posted to the list will be automatically redistributed

around the world. Topics for discussion on the list include, but are not limited to, the following: 1. Substantive discussion over topics such as NAFTA, regional trading blocs, trade regimes, international debt, indigenous persons, and IPE, women, structural adjustment and export led growth, longcycles, historical world systems, EEC, currency and market crises, democracy and governance in Latin and South America, Africa and Asia, commocity negotiations, the political economy of IMF structural adjustment loans. Comment and contributions on curriculum questions; suggested texts, new articles of common interest for course-related adoption. Circulation of draft articles for comments and discussion (an archive area is accessible via ftp or gopher-pipe csf.colorado.edu). Personal exchanges in the effort to develop a greater sense of community among IPE colleagues.

Subjects covered: political science; economics; commerce

Net address for operations: listserv@csf.colorado.edu

Net address for questions or submissions: ipe@csf.colorado.edu

Established: November 1992

Subscribers: 395

Sponsor: Wilfrid Laurier University (Waterloo, Ontario)

Host: Communications for Sustainable Future (Colorado)

Editorial contact: Lev Gonick
Dept. of Political Science, Wilfrid Laurier University, Waterloo, Ontario N2L 6H4 Canada.

Tel: (519) 884-1970 ext. 3860

Fax: (519) 884-8854

Internet: lgonick@mach1.wlu.ca

How to access: Mail to: listserv@csf.colorado.edu SUB ipe yourname (ex.sub ipe Lev Gonick)

How to submit: lgonick@mach1.wlu.ca

Archives: Accessible via ftp or gopher: p ipe csf.colorado.edu

IPR-SCIENCE

Description: ipr-science is a list covering intellectual property in science, academic-industry links, sociological/ethical/legal analyses, inventiveness and exploitability (e.g., via patents). Information, bibliographies, news, research-in-progress, information on meetings, etc., are all welcome.

Subjects covered: science and technology; technology transfer; intellectual property

Net address for operations: mailbase@mailbase

Net address for questions or submissions: ipr-science@mailbase

Established: 1992

Subscribers: 55

Sponsor: SATSU, Anglia Polytechnic University, East Road, Cambridge, CB1 IPT, UK.

List moderated: No.

Editorial contact: Kathryn Packer
SATSU, Anglia Polytechnic University, East Road, Cambridge, CB1 IPT, UK.

Tel: + 44 223 63271

Internet: kpacker@mailbase

Technical contact: Andrew Webster
SATSU, Anglia Polytechnic University, East Road, Cambridge, CB1 IPT, UK.

How to access: Send the following message: join <first name> <last name> ipr-science to mailbase@mailbase (JANET)

Access policy: Subscriptions are open to anyone.

How to unsubscribe: Send the following message: leave ipr-science to mailbase@mailbase

How to submit: Send message to ipr-science@mailbase

Archives: Archives are stored monthly.

IR-L
Description: IR-L is a discussion covering information retreival topics.
Subjects covered: library and information science; information technology
List moderated: Yes.
Editorial contact: Mary Engle
Bitnet: issmee@uccvma
How to access: Send subscribe message to listserv@uccvma or listserv@uccvma.ucop.edu
How to unsubscribe: Send unsubscribe message to listserv@uccvma or listserv@uccvma.ucop.edu
Archives: Archives are developed monthly; apply to listowner for details.

IR@MAILBASE.AC.UK
Description: IR@MAILBASE.AC.UK is a discussion list covering topics related to information retrieval.
Subjects covered: information technology; library and information science
List moderated: No.
Internet: ir-request@mailbase.ac.uk
How to access: Send subscribe message to mailbase@mailbase.ac.uk in the following format: join ir Yourfirstname Yourlastname
Archives: Archives are developed monthly; apply to listowner for details.

IRL-NET@IRLEARN
Description: IRL-NET@IRLEARN is a forum for people working in Ireland.
Subjects covered: Ireland
List moderated: No.
Editorial contact: Fionn D. Murtagh
Bitnet: fionn@dgaeso51
How to access: Send subscribe message to listserv@irlearn or listserv@irlearn.ucd.ie
How to unsubscribe: Send unsubscribe message to listserv@irlearn or listserv@irlearn.ucd.ie

IRL-POL@IRLEARN
Description: IRL-POL@IRLEARN is a discussion forum for Irish politics.
Subjects covered: Ireland; political science
List moderated: No.
Editorial contact: James P. McBride
Internet: bridec92@irlearn.ucd.ie
Bitnet: bridec92@irlearn
How to access: Send subscribe message to listserv@irlearn
How to unsubscribe: Send unsubscribe message to listserv@irlearn
Archives: Archives are developed monthly; apply to listowner for details.

IRNES@MAILBASE.AC.UK
Description: IRNES@MAILBASE.AC.UK is a forum of the Interdiscipliary Research Network on the Environment and Society.
Subjects covered: ecology; environmental studies
Host: Interdisciplinary Research Network on the Environment and Society
List moderated: No.
Internet: irnes-request@mailbase.ac.uk
How to access: Send subscribe message to mailbase@mailbase.ac.uk in the following format: join irnes Yourfirstname Yourlastname
Archives: Archives are developed monthly; apply to listowner for details.

IRVC-L (FORUM FOR RESEARCH ON VIRTUAL CULTURE)
Description: The Institute for Research on Virtual culture (IRVC) aims to foster, encourage, advance, and communicate research and scholarly inquiry on virtual culture. IRVC-L is a virtual forum of IRVC to conduct substantive discourse on research and scholarly inquiry to create and develop knowledge about virtual culture. Substantive discourse is encouraged on topics such as: 1. Conceptualization of virtual culture (alternative philosophic, metatheoretical, and theoretical paradigms, principles, assumptions, propositions, and problems); 2. Alternative futures orientation, change, transformation, reform, and restructuring: conservative, liberal, or radical; 3. Review and critique of literature, including articles in refereed scholarly journals; 4. Alternative designs and methodologies for research and scholarly inquiry on virtual culture; 5. Findings, conclusions and implications for education; 6. Research in progress on virtual culture; 7. Collaborative research by subscibers; 8. Setting the research agenda on virtual culture; 9. Institute for Research on Virtual Culture; 10. Relevant announcements, events, and issues.
Subjects covered: virtual culture; cyberspace; Internet; telecommunications
Net address for questions or submissions: IRVC-L@byrd.mu.wvnet.edu
List moderated: Yes.
Ermel Stepp
Tel: Institute for Research on Virtual Culture, Marshall University, Huntington WV 25755-2440.
How to access: Send a message to listserv@byrd.mu.wvnet.edu with the line of text: subscribe IRVC-L Yourfirstname Yourlastname
Access policy: Subscription to IRVC-L is open, but the list is private and subscription is required to post messages to the forum and access listserv archives.
How to submit: Messages sent to the forum will be automatically distributed to all subscribers. Such messages should be within the scope of the purposes of the forum: Substantive discourse of virtual culture, related research issues (e.g., design and/or methodology) relevant announcements, and other messages pertinent to the forum. To send a message to the forum, address the message to IRVC-L@byrd.mu.wvnet.edu. [Do not sent a message intended for the forum to the listserv.]
Archives: IRVC maintains archives, including research papers and reports, dissertations, conference proceedings, journals, and other information about IRVC and virtual culture. The archive may be accessed by anonymous FTP to byrd.mu.wvnet.edu in /pub/estepp/IRVC in various subdirectories. Research scholars

and writers may submit documents to be archived. Retrieve file archive.submission from /pub/estepp/IRVC and follow the instructions in it.

Related files: The Electronic Journal on Virtual Culture (EJVC) is a refereed, scholarly journal published by Arachnet, with the cooperation of the Kent State University and the Institute for Research on Virtual Culture, Marshall University. The EJVC is archived at byrd.mu.wvnet.edu in /pub/ejvc, and it is retrievable via anonymous FTP. Get EJVC.ARCHIVES from the archives via FTP. Articles published in the EJVC will be discussed on IRVC-L.

ISDN@ABALL.IN-BERLIN.DE

Description: ISDN@ABALL is a conference on ISDN in Europe.

Subjects covered: computer science; electronic networking

Editorial contact: Per Sigmond

Internet: per.sigmond@teknologi.agderforskning.no

How to access: Contact the Editor

How to unsubscribe: Contact the Editor

ISDS@UIUCVMD

Description: ISDS@UIUCVMD is the discussion list of the Illini Space Development Society.

Subjects covered: astronomy

Host: Illini Space Development Society

List moderated: No.

Editorial contact: Bennett Crook

Bitnet: bcrook@waynest1

How to access: Send subscribe message to listserv@uiucvmd or listseerv@vmd.cso.uiuc.edu

How to unsubscribe: Send unsubscribe message to listserv@uiucvmd or listseerv@vmd.cso.uiuc.edu

Archives: Archives are developed weekly; apply to listowner for details.

ISLAM-L

Description: Islam-L is a discussion list about the history of Islam.

Subjects covered: religion

Host: University of Louisville

List moderated: Yes.

Editorial contact: James A. Cocks

Internet: jacock01@ulkyvm.louisville.edu

Bitnet: jacock01@ulkyvm

How to access: Send subscribe message to listserv@ulkyvm or listserv@ulkyvm.louisville.edu

How to unsubscribe: Send unsubscribe message to listserv@ulkyvm or listserv@ulkyvm.louisville.edu

Archives: Archives are developed monthly; apply to listowner for details.

ISO10646@JHUVM

Description: ISO10646@JHUVM is a conference discussing issues related to multi-byte coded character sets.

Subjects covered: computer science

List moderated: No.

Editorial contact: Edwin F. Hart

Internet: hart%aplvm.bitnet@vm1.nodak.edu

Bitnet: hart@aplvm

How to access: Send subscribe message to listserv@jhuvm or listserv@jhuvm.hcf.jhu.edu

How to unsubscribe: Send unsubscribe message to listserv@jhuvm or listserv@jhuvm.hcf.jhu.edu

ISO@NIC.DDN.MIL

Description: ISO@NIC.DDN.MIL covers issues related to the ISO protocol stack.

Subjects covered: computer science

List moderated: No.

Internet: iso-request@nic.ddn.mil

How to access: Send subscribe message to ISO-RE-QUEST@NIC.DDN.MIL

How to unsubscribe: Send unsubscribe message to ISO-RE-QUEST@NIC.DDN.MIL

ISODE@NIC.DDN.MIL

Description: ISODE@NIC.DDN.MIL covers issues related to the ISO development environment.

Subjects covered: computer science

List moderated: No.

Internet: isode-request@nic.ddn.mil

How to access: Send subscribe message to ISODE-RE-QUEST@NIC.DDN.MIL

How to unsubscribe: Send unsubscribe message to ISODE-RE-QUEST@NIC.DDN.MIL

ITALIC-L

Description: Italic-L is a discussion group covering TeX and LATeX related software issues.

Subjects covered: computer hardware and software

List moderated: No.

Editorial contact: Peter Flynn

Bitnet: cbts8001@iruccvax

How to access: Send subscribe message to listserv@irlearn or listserv@irlearn.ucd.ie

How to unsubscribe: Send subscribe message to listserv@irlearn or listserv@irlearn.ucd.ie

Archives: Archives are developed monthly; apply to listowner for details.

ITEX-L

Description: Itex-L is a forum of the Israel Technology Exchange.

Subjects covered: science and technology

List moderated: Yes.

Editorial contact: Dr. Menachem Fishbein

Internet: fishb@iljct

How to access: Send subscribe message to listserv@taunivm or listserv@taunivm.tau.ac.il

How to unsubscribe: Send unsubscribe message to listserv@taunivm or listserv@taunivm.tau.ac.il

Archives: Yes; Apply to listowner for details

ITRDBFOR@ASUACAD

Description: ITRDBFOR@ASUACAD is a discusion list of the International Tree Ring Data Bank.

Subjects covered: ecology; plant biology

List moderated: No.
Editorial contact: Dr. Tom Nash
Bitnet: atthn@asuacad
How to access: Send subscribe message to listserv@asuacad or listserv@asuvm.inre.asu.edu
How to unsubscribe: Send unsubscribe message to listserv@asuacad or listserv@asuvm.inre.asu.edu
Archives: Archives are developed monthly; apply to listowner for details.

IUIC-HYPER@MAILBASE.AC.UK
Description: IUIC-HYPER is a mailbase discussion group on IUIC Hypermedia.
Subjects covered: information technology
List moderated: No.
Internet: iuic-hyper-request@mailbase.ac.uk
How to access: Send subscribe message to mailbase@mailbase.ac.uk in the following format: join iuic-hyper Yourfirstname Yourlastname
Archives: Archives are developed monthly; apply to listowner for details.

IUIC-INFS@MAILBASE.AC.UK
Description: IUIC-INFS is a mailbase discussion list on IUIC campus-wide information services.
Subjects covered: campus-wide information systems; electronic networking
List moderated: No.
Internet: iuic-infs-request@mailbase.ac.uk
How to access: Send subscribe message to mailbase@mailbase.ac.uk in the following format: join iuic-infs Yourfirstname Yourlastname
Archives: Archives are developed monthly; apply to listowner for details.

IUIC-LIBS@MAILBASE.AC.UK
Description: IUIC-LIBS@MAILBASE.AC.UK is a discussion group focusing on cooperation with libraries.
Subjects covered: library and information science
List moderated: No.
Internet: iuic-libs-request@mailbase.ac.uk
How to access: Send subscribe message to mailbase@mailbase.ac.uk in the following format: join iuic-libs Yourfirstname Yourlastname
Archives: Archives are developed monthly; apply to listowner for details.

IUIC-NEWSLETTER@MAILBASE.AC.UK
Description: IUIC-NEWSLETTER is a mailbase list for editors of computing service newsletters.
Subjects covered: electronic networking
List moderated: No.
Internet: iuic-newsletter-request@mailbase.ac.uk
How to access: Send subscribe message to mailbase@mailbase.ac.uk in the following format: join iuic-newsletter Yourfirstname Yourlastname
Archives: Archives are developed monthly; apply to listowner for details.

IVRITEX@TAUNIVM
Description: IVRITEX@TAUNIVM is a discussion list on the Hebrew Tex document processing system.
Subjects covered: computer hardware and software; Hebrew language and literature
List moderated: No.
Editorial contact: Don Hosek
Bitnet: dhosek@hmcvax
How to access: Send subscribe message to listserv@taunivm or listserv@taunivm.tau.ac.il
How to unsubscribe: Send subscribe message to listserv@taunivm or listserv@taunivm.tau.ac.il
Archives: Archives are developed monthly; apply to listowner for details.

JACK-LONDON@SONOMA.EDU
Description: JACK-LONDON@SONOMA.EDU is a forum for discussion of the works of Jack London.
Subjects covered: American literature and language; London, Jack
List moderated: No.
Editorial contact: Claire Stasz
Internet: stasz@sonoma.edu
How to access: Send subscribe message to JACK-LONDON-REQUEST@SONOMA.EDU
How to unsubscribe: Send unsubscribe message to JACK-LONDON-REQUEST@SONOMA.EDU

JAMIE-L
Description: Jamie-L is a forum about acoustic guitarist Jamie Notarthomas.
Subjects covered: music; Notarthomas, Jamie
List moderated: No.
Editorial contact: Jeffrey Anbinder
Internet: bory@cornella.cit.cornell.edu
How to access: Send subscribe message to listserv@cornell.edu
How to unsubscribe: Send subscribe message to listserv@cornell.edu

JANET@GWUVM
Description: JANET@GWUVM is a discussion list covering the IBM version of Waterloo Janet network software.
Subjects covered: computer hardware and software; electronic networking
List moderated: No.
Editorial contact: Jonathan M. Lang
Internet: jmlang@gwuvm.gwu.edu
How to access: Send subscribe message to listserv@gwuvm or listserv@gwuvm.gwu.edu
How to unsubscribe: Send unsubscribe message to listserv@gwuvm or listserv@gwuvm.gwu.edu

JCMT-L
Description: JCMT-L is a list for affiliated networks for the James Clerk Maxwell Telescope.
Subjects covered: astronomy
List moderated: Yes.
Editorial contact: Russell O. Redman
Internet: redman@hiaras.hia.nrc.ca

How to access: Send subscribe message to listserv@ualtavm or listserv@vm.ucs.ualberta.ca
How to unsubscribe: Send unsubscribe message to listserv@ualtavm or listserv@vm.ucs.ualberta.ca
Archives: Archives are developed yearly; apply to listowner for details.

JDOCS-DB@TEMPLEVM

Description: JDOCS-DB@TEMPLEVM is an electronic document database for journalism.
Subjects covered: journalism
List moderated: No.
Editorial contact: John L. Center
Bitnet: v2097a@templevm
How to access: Send subscribe message to listserv@templevm or listserv%templevm.bitnet@vm1.nodak.edu
How to unsubscribe: Send unsubscribe message to listserv@templevm or listserv%templevm.bitnet@vm1.nodak.edu

JESSE

Description: JESSE is a Listserv conference which focuses on teaching and educational concerns in library and information science. JESSE concerns curricula, educational methodologies and issues, courses in development, resources, computing as a teaching tool, broad trends in education as they affect library and information science education, and similar education-oriented topics. JESSE's address is JESSE@ARIZVM1. It is a companion conference to ELEASAI, which focuses on research in library and information science. It concerns current research in progress or in planning stages, methodological and statistical issues, funding for research, computing as a research tool, broad trends in scientific research as they affect library and information science, and similar research-oriented topics. ELEASAI's address is ELEASAI @ARIZVM1. Two separate conferences are maintained at user request: while participants agree and maintain that research and teaching are inextricably linked together, and that work in one area naturally flows into the other, separate lists enable participants to manage the ever-increasing flow of information over the net a little better. Users can subscribe to one or the other or both. ELEASAI is strictly focused on research issues; JESSE is broadly concerned with issues of interest to the academic and may appear to drift from time to time. While many users are library school faculty, JESSE also serves computer specialists, practicing librarians, consultants, organizational leaders, and others in the US and abroad. ELEASAI was founded in January 1992, and JESSE in April of 1992, JESSE by Gretchen Whitney and Charley Seavey. The University of Arizona Center for Computing and Information Technology provides technical support for the conference.
Subjects covered: library and information science; colleges and universities; education
Net address for operations: LISTSERV@ARIZVM1
Net address for questions or submissions: JESSE@ARIZVM1
Established: April 1992
Subscribers: 433
Sponsor: School of Library Science, University of Arizona, 1515 East First St., Tucson, AZ 85719
Host: Same as above
List moderated: No.
Editorial contact: Gretchen Whitney, Asst. Prof.

University of Arizona, 1515 East First Street, Tucson, AZ 85719
Tel: (602) 621-3491
Fax: (602) 621-3279
Internet: GWHITNEY@CCIT.ARIZONA.EDU
Bitnet: GWHITNEY@ARIZVMS
Copyright statement: The University of Arizona Graduate Library School provides ELEASAI and JESSE as a public service. It does not verify the accuracy of submitted messages nor does it endorse the opinions expressed by message authors. Authors of ELEASAI and JESSE messages are solely responsible for content of their messages. The conferences are moderated only in that the moderators encourage participation in the conferences, assist users with questions regarding the mechanics of the conference, and generally try to keep things on track.
How to access: Send message to listserv@arizvm1.bitnet with no header and only subscribe jesse melvil dewey replacing melvil's name with your own.
Access policy: This list is open to anyone.
How to unsubscribe: Send message to listserv@arizvm1.bitnet with no header and only unsubscribe jesse
How to submit: Send message with meaningful header and whatever text desired to jesse@arizvm1
Submission policy: See above description
Archives: The list is archived monthly on listserv@arizvm1
Additional information: Additional editor: Charley Seavey, Assoc. Prof. address School of Library Science, University of Arizona, 1515 East First Street, Tucson, AZ 85719; tel 602-621-3957; fax 602-621-3279; Internet DOCMAPS@CCIT.ARIZONA.EDU Bitnet DOCMAPS@ARIZVMS.

JEWISHNT-GLOBAL JEWISH INFORMATION NETWORK PROJECT

Description: Jewishnt at BGUVM is a discussion forum on all things concerning the establishment of the Global Jewish Information Network. The network will cater specifically to the information and communication needs of the Jewish communities all over the world. This network will be readily accessible from every Jewish congregation, institute, school and home and will provide the following services: Worlwide Electronic Mail facilities; Jewish Directories and Nameservers; Easy access to Jewish databases; Electronic newspapers, Bulletin Boards and conferences; Access to libraries of software on Jewish subjects; Jewish educational services; and a Jewish Electronic University.
Subjects covered: Judaica; distance education; electronic networking
Net address for operations: LISTSERV@bguvm.bgu.ac.il, LISTSERV@bguvm.BITNET
Net address for questions or submissions: JEWISHNT@bguvm.bgu.ac.il
Established: October 1991
Subscribers: 350
Sponsor: Ministry of Communications (Israel), Division of Information Technologies, 9 Ahad HaAm St., Tel Aviv, Israel.
Host: Ben Gurion University, Computer Center, Beer Sheva, Israel.
List moderated: Yes.
Moderation procedure: All messages to the list are directed to the moderator. The moderator applies an editorial policy that keeps the discussion and contributions within the framework of the list's aims: the establishment of the Global Jewish Information Network.

Editorial contact: Dov Winer
P.O.B. 151, Dor Haela 99875, Israel.
Tel: (972) 2 - 332286
Fax: (972) 2 - 332286
Internet: dovw@vms.huji.ac.il, viner@bguvm.bgu.ac.il
Bitnet: viner@bguvm.BITNET
Technical contact: Pini Albilia
Computer Centre, Ben Gurion University, Beer Sheve, Israel
Tel: (972) 57-461154
Internet: maint1@bguvm.bgu.ac.il
Bitnet: maint1@bguvm.BITNET
Review: From the paper: ''Electronic Documentation in Israel'' by Elhanan Adler, Head, School of Librarianship, University of Haifa (ELHANAN@LIB.HAIFA.AC.IL) at the conference: ''Documenting Israel'' - May 1993 - Harvard University: ''Selected Israeli Electronic Information Services, Suppliers and Sources of Information: JEWISHNT - Jewish Global Information Network Project: An electronic distribution list for information regarding networking and access to Jewish and Israeli information worldwide, at all levels - from academic and scientific data to Jewish community and educational networks. The best single source for up-to-date information regarding network-accessible information and services (but does not include acquirable data - CDROMS, etc.)''
Copyright statement: Copyright on the proceedings of the conference are reserved for the moderator. Reproduction of this material is authorized and encouraged provided that citation of the source is included in the reproduction.
How to access: Send the following message to the address: LISTSERV@bguvm.bgu.ac.il
Access policy: The list is open to everybody with a positive and legitimate interest in the aims of the list.
How to unsubscribe: Send the following message to the address: LISTSERV@bguvm.bgu.ac.il UNSUBscribe JEWISHNT
How to submit: Send messages with the submission to: JEWISHNT@bguvm.bgu.ac.il
Submission policy: Messages are posted by moderators if they fall within the framework of the purpose of the list.
Archives: To receive an updated files list of the archives send the following message to: LISTSERV@bguvm.bgu.ac.il INDEX JEWISHNT as a one line message of an email message. Then you will be able to retrieve the files listed by sending email messages of the type: GET filename filetype to the same address (LISTSERV@bguvm.bgu.ac.il).

JEWSTUDIES

Description: Jewstudies is an ejournal of ongoing research in Jewish studies, including shared reference, bibliographical, and research sources, conference information, and short research notes.
Subjects covered: Judaica
Net address for operations: LISTSERV@NYSERNET.ORG
Net address for questions or submissions: JEWSTUDIES@NYSERNET.ORG
Established: 1993
Subscribers: 200+
Host: NYSERNET.ORG
List moderated: Yes.
Moderation procedure: Individuals submit material which is almost universally accepted but often slightly edited.
Editorial contact: Avi Jacob Hyman

Department of History, Ontario Institute for Studies in Education, 252 Bloor Street West, Toronto, Ontario, Canada M5S 1V6.
Tel: 416-781-5017
Internet: AJHYMAN@oise.utoronto.ca
Bitnet: AJHYMAN@UTorOISE.bitnet
Internet: Chaim@Nysernet.Org
How to access: Send the message SUBSCRIBE JEWSTUDIES <your_name> to LISTSERV@NYSERNET.ORG
How to unsubscribe: Send the message SIGNOFF JEWSTUDIES to LISTSERV@NYSERNET.ORG
How to submit: Send to JEWSTUDIES@NYSERNET.ORG
Submission policy: ALL SUBMISSIONS MUST INCLUDE E-MAIL ADDRESS of SENDER
Related files: Related files accessible at LISTERV/NYSERNET/ORG

JMBA-L

Description: JMBA-L is a discussion group for those wishing to discuss issues related to being Jewish and in an MBA program or being Jewish and in business. This would include such issues as discrimination, Israel-American Trade, job hunting, etc.
Subjects covered: Judaica; business
Net address for operations: listserv@israel.nysernet.org
Net address for questions or submissions: jmba@israel.nysernet.org
Established: August 1993
Subscribers: 4+
Sponsor: Nysernet
List moderated: No.
Editorial contact: Michael Rand
285 Riverside Drive, New York, NY 10025.
Tel: 212 749 6766
Internet: rand@gursey.baruch.cuny.edu
How to access: Use standard listserv signup procedures.
Access policy: This list is open to anyone interested.
How to unsubscribe: Use standard listserv signoff procedures.
How to submit: Send email to jmba@israel.nysernet.org
Submission policy: Open to all submissions
Archives: Archived at Israel.nysernet.org

JOBLIST@FRORS12

Description: JOBLIST posts career information to EARN network members.
Subjects covered: colleges and universities
Host: European Academic Research Network
List moderated: No.
Editorial contact: Hans Decker
Internet: deck@frors12
How to access: Send subscribe message to listserv@frors12
How to unsubscribe: Send unsubscribe message to listserv@frors12
Archives: Archives are developed monthly; apply to listowner for details.

JOBPLACE@UKCC

Description: JOBPLACE is a forum discussing carreer education and placement issues.
Subjects covered: colleges and universities
List moderated: No.
Editorial contact: Drema Howard

Internet: dkhowa01@ukcc.uky.edu
Bitnet: dkhowa01@ukcc
How to access: Send subscribe message to listserv@ukcc or listserv@ukcc.uky.edu
How to unsubscribe: Send unsubscribe message to listserv@ukcc or listserv@ukcc.uky.edu
Archives: Archives are developed monthly; apply to listowner for details.

JOURNET@QUCDN

Description: JOURNET@QUCDN covers journalism educators.
Subjects covered: journalism
List moderated: No.
Editorial contact: George Frajkor
Internet: gfrajkor@ccs.carleton.ca
How to access: Send subscribe message to listserv@qucdn or listserv@qucdn.queensu.ca.
How to unsubscribe: Send unsubscribe message to listserv@qucdn or listserv@qucdn.queensu.ca.
Archives: Archives are developed monthly; apply to listowner for details.

JPINFO-L

Description: Jpinfo-L is a discussion list about Japan.
Subjects covered: Japan
List moderated: No.
Editorial contact: Koki Higashida
Bitnet: koki@jpnsut10
How to access: Send subscribe message to listserv@jpnsut10
How to unsubscribe: Send unsubscribe message to listserv@jpnsut10
Archives: Archives are developed monthly; apply to listowner for details.

JTTAG

Description: The Job Transfer Technical Advisory Group (JTTAG) of the UK Academic Community is an experts group convened to provide a forum for discussion of all technical aspects of ISO JTM and Red Book JTMP. It may also consider any other standard that relates to job transfer.
Subjects covered: science and techology; job transfer
Net address for operations: mailbase-helpline@mailbase.ac.uk
Net address for questions or submissions: jttag@mailbase.ac.uk
Established: Early 1990
Subscribers: 19
List moderated: No.
Editorial contact: Phil Chambers
University of Exeter, Computer Unit, Laver Building, North Park Road, Exeter EX4 4QE, England.
Tel: +44 392 263956
Fax: +44 392 211630
Internet: P.A.Chambers@ex.ac.uk, jttag-request@mailbase.ac.uk
How to access: Send an email message with the body consisting of one line: join jttag <firstname> <lastname> to mailbase@mailbase.ac.uk
How to unsubscribe: Send an email message with the body consisting of one line: leave jttag to mailbase@mailbase.ac.uk
How to submit: Send your contribution to jttag@mailbase.ac.uk

Additional information: Additional editor: Janusz Lukasiak, University of Manchester Computer Centre, Oxford Road, Manchester M13 9PL England; tel: +44 61 275 6007; fax: +44 61 275 6040; Internet: J.Lukasiak@mcc.ac.uk, jttag-request@mailbase.ac.uk

JUDAICA@TAUNIVM

Description: JUDAICA@TAUNIVM is a forum for discussion of Judaica.
Subjects covered: Judaica
List moderated: No.
Editorial contact: Avrum Goodblat
Internet: heasif@shum.huji. ac.il
How to access: Send subscribe message to listserv@taunivm or listserv@taunivm.tau.ac.il
How to unsubscribe: Send unsubscribe message to listserv@taunivm or listserv@taunivm.tau.ac.il
Archives: Archives are developed monthly; apply to listowner for details.

JUDAICA@UMINN1

Description: JUDAICA@UMINN1 focuses on Jewish topics.
Subjects covered: Judaica
List moderated: Yes.
Editorial contact: Tzvee Zahavy
Bitnet: maic@uminn1
How to access: Send subscribe message to listserv@uminn1
How to unsubscribe: Send unsubscribe message to listserv@uminn1
Archives: Archives are developed monthly; apply to listowner for details.

JUDGENET: THE BEER JUDGE DIGEST NETWORK

Description: JudgeNet carries discussions of interest to beer judges and brewing competition organizers.
Subjects covered: beer; contests and competitions
Net address for operations: judge-request@synchro.com
Net address for questions or submissions: judge@synchro.com
Established: November 1991
Subscribers: 128
Sponsor: Riverside Garage & Brewery, 16A Jay St, Cambridge, MA 02139.
Host: SynchroSystems, 16A Jay St, Cambridge, MA 02139.
List moderated: Yes.
Moderation procedure: The digest is edited before distribution to the list.
Editorial contact: Chuck Cox, BJCP Master Beer Judge
Riverside Garage & Brewery, 16A Jay St, Cambridge, MA 02139.
Tel: (617) 547-5113
Internet: chuck@synchro.com
How to access: Send Internet address, name, and judging rank & organization (if any) to: judge-request@synchro.com
How to unsubscribe: Send request to: judge-request@synchro.com
How to submit: Send submission to: judge@synchro.com
Archives: New subscribers receive instructions for accessing the JudgeNet archives.

Related files: The latest edition of the Beer Judge Certification Exam Study Guide is available in the JudgeNet archives.
Additional information: While most subscribers are BJCP (USA) certified beer judges, we also have judges from other countries as well as apprentice judges who are seeking certification. Anyone with an interest in judging or organizing beer competitions in any country is encouraged to subscribe.

K12ADMIN

Description: K12ADMIN is a world-wide discussion group for K-12 school administrators set up to provide a discussion base for K-12 school administrators: principals, vice principals, superintendents, assistant superintendants, central and county office administrators, and others involved with K-12 school administration. Conversation on this list will focus on the topics of interest to the school administrator community, including the latest on school management, curriculum, services, operations, technology and activities. K12ADMIN is a discussion group for administrative practitioners helping other administrative practitioners, sharing ideas, helping to solve problems, telling each other about new publications and up-coming conferences, asking for assistance or information, and linking administrators for information and resource sharing. This discussion is open to ALL school administrators and people involved with the school administration field worldwide. We want to keep the activity and discussion focused on school administration, K-12. But, the group can be used by members for many different things -- to ask for input, share ideas and information, link programs that are geographically remote, make contacts, etc.
The K12ADMIN list is operated by several volunteers, including Mike Eisenberg, Director of the ERIC Clearinghouse on Information Resources at Syracuse University, Mary Lou Finne, User Services Coordinator of the ERIC Clearinghouse on Educational Management at the University of Oregon, and Peter Milbury, Librarian of Pleasant Valley High School, Chico, California.
Subjects covered: school management; curriculum; educational technology; education
Net address for operations: listserv@suvm.syr.edu
Net address for questions or submissions: k12admin@suvm.syr.edu
Established: May 5, 1993
Subscribers: 177
Sponsor: ERIC Clearinghouse on Information Resources Syracuse University Syracuse, New York 13244
List moderated: No.
Editorial contact: Mike Eisenberg
ERIC Clearinghouse on Information Resources at Syracuse University
Internet: ERIC04@SUVM.SYR.EDU
How to access: 1. Address an e-mail message to: listserv@suvm.syr.edu 2. Type the message: subscribe k12admin Your Name
Example: subscribe k12admin Jane Doe 3. Send the message 4. You will receive a subscription confirmation from K12ADMIN
How to unsubscribe: 1. Address an e-mail message to: listserv@suvm.syr.edu
2. Type the message: unsubscribe k12admin
3. Send the message 4. You will receive a unsubscription confirmation from K12ADMIN
How to submit: 1. Address an e-mail message to: k12admin@suvm.syr.edu 2. Compose your message 3. Send the message

Archives: K12ADMIN is archived at the "AskERIC Free Library", a gopher site of K-12 educational resources.
Gopher accessibility: Gopher to: ericir.syr.edu (port# 70). For more information, email a question to: askeric@ericir.syr.edu
Additional information: Co-owners/technical contacts: (1) Mary Lou Finne (ERIC Clearinghouse on Educational Management at the University of Oregon) MARY__LOU__FINNE__AT__CATE@CCMAIL.UOREGON.EDU; (2) Peter Milbury (Pleasant Valley High School, Chico, California) PMILBUR@EIS.CALSTATE.EDU

KATALIST

Description: KATALIST is a computerized discussion forum started in 1992 to catalyze the information flow among the Hungarian librarians about library automation and electronic information services. Topics covered by KATALIST include developing and maintaining online library catalogs (OPACs; library automation questions; interlibrary loan and other library services via e-mail; information sources on the international computer networks; online and CD-ROM databases. etc. The language of the list is Hungarian, but there are materials in English (information from other sources like PACS-L, ComServe, MeckJournal) and users are free to post letters written in English to the list.
Subjects covered: online public access catalogs; library and information science
Net address for operations: LISTSERV@HUEARN
Net address for questions or submissions: KATALIST@HUEARN
Established: January, 1992
Subscribers: 96
Sponsor: University of Miskolc Central Library
H-3515 Miskolc-Egyetemvaros, Hungary
Host: Information Infrastructure Development Program, H-1132 Budapest XIII. Victor Hugo u. 18-22. Hungary
List moderated: No.
Editorial contact: Laszlo Drotos
Univ. of Miskolc Central Library
H-3515 Miskolc-Egyetemvaros, Hungary
Tel: (36) 46-365-111/13-27
Fax: 36) 46-369-554
Internet: h1192dro@ella.hu
Bitnet: h1192dro@huella
Technical contact: Sandor Aranyi
Information Infrastructure Development Program, Computer and Automation Institute, H-1132 Budapest XIII. Victor Hugo u. 18-22. Hungary
Tel: (36) 1-1497-532
Bitnet: ib001ara@huearn
How to access: Send a SUBSCRIBE KATALIST Lastname Firstname message to the LISTSERV@HUEARN address
How to unsubscribe: Send a SIGNOFF KATALIST message to the LISTSERV@HUEARN address
Archives: Archived and searchable with the listserv at the HUEARN host.

KIDCAFE@NDSUVM1

Description: KIDCAFE@NDSUVM1 is a forum for communication between young people.
Subjects covered: youth
List moderated: Yes.
Editorial contact: Dan Wheeler

Internet: dan.wheeler@uc.edu
How to access: Send subscribe message to listserv@ndsuvm1
or listserv@vm1.nodak.edu
How to unsubscribe: Send unsubscribe message to
listserv@ndsuvm1 or listserv@vm1.nodak.edu
Archives: Archives are developed weekly; apply to listowner
for details.

KIDLINK

Description: The KIDLINK Society was formed to create a
global dialog among the 10 to 15-year-olds of the world. Our
efforts have been organized into a series of year-long projects,
beginning with KIDS-91. KIDS-94 began in May 1993 and will
continue until May 1994. In order to accomplish the goal of
creating a global dialog, the KIDLINK Society runs several
mailing lists, each with distinct purpose and procedures. Some
the lists are for kids only, others are for the teachers and other
adult volunteers who coordinate the project. There are several
different kinds of activities for kids within the 10 to 15 age
limits. These range from open discussion to structured projects.
The KIDLINK list carries the newsletters and official announcements about the project; there is no discussion. All project participants are required to subscribe to this list. Subscribers to
KIDLINK will receive information about the other lists operated
by the Society. There is also a KIDNEWS list for those who
just want to receive the newsletters.
Subjects covered: education; children; telecommunications
Net address for operations: listserv@vm1.nodak.edu or
listserv@ndsumv1.bitnet
Established: October 1990
Subscribers: 700+
Sponsor: KIDLINK Society, 4815 Saltrod, Norway; email:
kidlink-info@vm1.nodak.edu or kidlink-info@ndsuvm1.bitnet
List moderated: Yes.
Editorial contact: Odd de Presno
4815 Saltrod, Norway
Fax: +47 41 27111
Internet: opresno@external.uio.no
Technical contact: Dan Wheeler
Mail Location 2, University of Cincinnati, Cincinnati, OH
45221-0002.
Tel: 513-556-3607
Internet: Dan.Wheeler@uc.edu
Bitnet: wheeler@ucbeh
How to access: Send an email message to:
LISTSERV@VM1.NODAK.EDU or:
LISTSERV@NDSUVM1.BITNET containing the command:
SUB KIDLINK <your-first-name> <your-last-name>
Access policy: We welcome everyone who shares our goal to
subscribe to KIDLINK.
How to unsubscribe: Send the command: SIGNOFF KIDLINK
to the LISTSERV address.
Archives: All of our lists are archived on the LISTSERVer. In
addition, there is a large collection supporting files. We suggest
that interested persons begin by sending these two commands to
the LISTSERVer: GET KIDLINK GENERAL GET KIDLINK
MASTER
Related files: Files are also available via anonymous FTP from
vm1.nodak.edu: CD KIDLINK GET KIDLINK.GENERAL etc.
Gopher accessibility: The KIDLINK Gopher carries most of
our files: kids.duq.edu

KIDPLAN@NDSUVM1

Description: KIDPLAN is a list discussing planning for the
KIDLINK project.
Subjects covered: youth
List moderated: Yes.
Editorial contact: Dan Wheeler
Internet: DAN.WHEELER@UC.EDU
How to access: Send subscribe message to listserv@ndsuvm1
or listserv@vm1.nodak.edu
How to unsubscribe: Send unsubscribe message to
listserv@ndsuvm1 or listserv@vm1.nodak.edu
Archives: Archives are developed weekly; apply to listowner
for details.

KIDS-92@NDSUVM1

Description: KIDS-92@NDSUVM1 is a global network used
by children (aged 10-15).
Subjects covered: education; youth
List moderated: No.
Editorial contact: Odd de Presno
Internet: opresno@coma.uio.no
How to access: Send subscribe message to listserv@ndsuvm1
or listserv@vm1.nodak.edu
How to unsubscribe: Send unsubscribe message to
listserv@ndsuvm1 or listserv@vm1.nodak.edu

KIDS-ACT@NDSUVM1

Description: KIDS-ACT@NDSUVM1 is a general forum for
children.
Subjects covered: education; youth
List moderated: Yes.
Editorial contact: Dan Wheeler
Internet: dan.wheeler@uc.edu
How to access: Send subscribe message to listserv@ndsuvm1
or listserv@vm1.nodak.edu
How to unsubscribe: Send unsubscribe message to
listserv@ndsuvm1 or listserv@vm1.nodak.edu
Archives: Archives are developed weekly; apply to listowner
for details.

KIDSNET@PITTVMS

Description: KIDSNET@PITTVMS is a global network for
teachers and students in grades K-12.
Subjects covered: education; education technology
List moderated: No.
Editorial contact: Bob Carlitz
Internet: carlitz@vms.cis.pitt.edu
How to access: Send subscribe message to joinkids@pittvms or
kidsnet-request@vms.cis.pitt.edu
How to unsubscribe: Send unsubscribe message to
joinkids@pittvms or kidsnet-request@vms.cis.pitt.edu

KLARINET@VCCSCENT

Description: KLARINET@VCCSCENT is a forum for clarinet
players and enthusiasts.
Subjects covered: music; musical instruments
List moderated: No.
Editorial contact: Jim Fay
Bitnet: nvfayxj@vccscent

How to access: Send subscribe message to listserv@vccscent
How to unsubscribe: Send unsubscribe message to listserv@vccscent
Archives: Archives are developed monthly; apply to listowner for details.

KOL-ISHA

Description: KOL-ISHA is a moderated list for questions and issues concerning women's roles in Judaism.
Subjects covered: Judaica; feminism; women's studies
Net address for operations:
LISTSERV@ISRAEL.NYSERNET.ORG
List moderated: Yes.
How to access: Send subscription messages to
LISTSERV@ISRAEL.NYSERNET.ORG

KONFER-L

Description: KONFER-L is a list covering conference, workshop, and seminar announcements.
Subjects covered: conferences and conference listings
Net address for operations: LISTSERV@TREARN.BITNET
Net address for questions or submissions: KONFER-L@TREARN.BITNET
Established: 1990
Subscribers: 133
Sponsor: Ege Univ. Bilgisayar Ar. ve Uyg. Mrk.35100 Bornova Izmir Turkey
Host: Same
List moderated: No.
Editorial contact: Esra Delen
Ege Univ. Bilgisayar Ar. ve Uyg. Mrk. 35100 Bornova Izmir Turkey
Tel: 90-51-887221
Fax: 90-51-887230
Internet: ESRA@EGE.EDU.TR
Bitnet: ESRA@TREARN
Technical contact: Same as above
How to access: TELL LISTSERV AT TREARN SUB KONFER-L fullname
How to unsubscribe: TELL LISTSERV AT TREARN SIGNOFF KONFER-L
How to submit: Mail to KONFER-L@TREARN
Archives: Available via LOG files on LISTSERV

KURT GOEDEL SOCIETY MAILING LIST

Description: The Kurt Goedel Society is an international organization for the promotion of research in all areas of logic, in philosophy and the history of mathematics, above all in connection with the biography of Kurt Goedel, and in other areas to which Goedel made contributions, especially mathematics, physics, theology, philosophy, and Leibnitz studies. It was founded in 1987 and is chartered in Vienna. Its founding president was Prof. Hao Wang. The Kurt Goedel Society distributes information about its activities, in particular announcements of conferences, lectures, seminars, and publications, and calls for papers. In certain cases, announcements by other institutions may be forwarded to the list as well. The list is not intended for discussion of any nature.
Subjects covered: Goedel, Kurt; mathematics; philosophy; Leibnitz, Gottfried Wilhelm
Net address for operations: kgs@logic.tuwien.ac.at

Net address for questions or submissions:
kgs@logic.tuwien.ac.at
Established: 1992
Subscribers: 444
Sponsor: Kurt Goedel Society, Institut fuer Computersprachen E185/2, Technische Universitaet, Wien, Resselgasse 3/1 A-1040, Vienna, Austria.
List moderated: Yes.
Moderation procedure: The list distributes material pertaining to the interests of members of the Kurt Goedel Society, i.e., symbolic logic and theoretical computer science, in particular announcements of conferences sponsored by the KGS, announcements of lectures and seminars, publications, calls for papers. It is not intended for discussion, although requests for information from individuals may be forwarded at the moderator's discretion.
Editorial contact: Richard Zach
Kurt Goedel Society, Institut fuer Computersprachen E185/2, Technische Universitaet, Wien, Resselgasse 3/1 A-1040, Vienna, Austria.
Tel: (+43 1) 588 01 x 4088
Fax: (+43 1) 504 15 89
Internet: kgs@logic.tuwien.ac.at
How to access: Send email to kgs@logic.tuwien.ac.at
Access policy: There are no restrictions to list membership.
How to unsubscribe: Send email to kgs@logic.tuwien.ac.at
How to submit: Send email to kgs@logic.tuwien.ac.at
Submission policy: This list is restricted to announcements of interest to members of the Kurt Goedel Society, at moderator's discretion. We are trying to keep this list low volume and generally do not forward announcements of other institutions unless they are of significant interest to all subscribers.
Archives: Membership information, programs, announcements, etc., of the Kurt Goedel Society are available by ftp from logic.tuwien.ac.at in directory /pub/kgs
Additional information: The Kurt Goedel Society is an international organization for the promotion of research in all areas of logic, in philosophy and the history of mathematics, above all in connection with the biography of Kurt Goedel, and in other areas to which Goedel made tributions, especially mathematics, physics, theology, philosophy and Leibnitz studies. It was founded in 1987 and is chartered in Vienna.

KUTUP-L

Description: Kutup-L is an e-conference among Turkish libraries.
Subjects covered: library and information science
List moderated: No.
Editorial contact: Huryasa Aslan
Bitnet: huryasa@tranavm1
How to access: Send subscribe message to listserv@trmetu
How to unsubscribe: Send unsubscribe message to listserv@trmetu
Archives: Archives are developed monthly; apply to listowner for details.

L-ARTECH@UQAM

Description: L-ARTECH@UQAM is a forum for organizations/indiviuals interested in the fields of art and technology.
Subjects covered: art; science and technology
List moderated: No.
Editorial contact: Andre Planke

Bitnet: c1040@uqam
How to access: Send subscribe message to listserv@uqam
How to unsubscribe: Send unsubscribe message to listserv@uqam
Archives: Archives are developed yearly; apply to listowner for details.

L-CHA@UQAM

Description: L-CHA@UQAM is a conference for the Canadian Historical Association.
Subjects covered: history
List moderated: Yes.
Editorial contact: Jose Igartva
Internet: R1227@UQAM
How to access: Send subscribe message to listserv@uqam
How to unsubscribe: Send unsubscribe message to listserv@uqam
Archives: Yes; Yearly, Private

L-ETHO@UQAM

Description: L-ETHO@UQAM is a forum for ethologists.
Subjects covered: zoology
List moderated: Yes.
Editorial contact: Jacques Beauregard
Bitnet: r20370@uqam
How to access: Send subscribe message to listserv@uqam
How to unsubscribe: Send unsubscribe message to listserv@uqam
Archives: Archives are developed yearly; apply to listowner for details.

L-HCAP@NDSUVM1

Description: L-HCAP@NDSUVM1 discusses issues related to handicapped persons in the educational environment.
Subjects covered: disabilities; education
List moderated: No.
Editorial contact: Bill McGarry
Bitnet: wtm@bunker
Review: Reviewed by List Review Service edited by Raleigh Muns: see appendix.
How to access: Send subscribe message to listserv@ndsuvm1 or listserv@vm1.nodak.edu
How to unsubscribe: Send unsubscribe message to listserv@ndsuvm1 or listserv@vm1.nodak.edu

L-OHACAD@AKRONVM

Description: L-OHACAD is a forum of the Ohio Higher Education Computer Council.
Subjects covered: education; education technology
Host: Ohio Higher Education Computer Council
List moderated: No.
Editorial contact: Al Herbert
Bitnet: herbert@akronvm
How to access: Send subscribe message to listserv@akronvm
How to unsubscribe: Send unsubscribe message to listserv@akronvm
Archives: Archives are developed monthly; apply to listowner for details.

LABMGR

Description: LABMGR is a forum for the discussion of issues concerning administration of computer labs in colleges and universities.
Subjects covered: computer hardware and software; colleges and universities; management
Net address for operations: LISTSERV@UKCC.uky.edu
Net address for questions or submissions: LABMGR@UKCC.uky.edu
Established: February 1992
Subscribers: 798
Sponsor: University of Kentucky Libraries, University of Kentucky, Lexington, Kentucky.
Host: University of Kentucky, Lexington, Kentucky.
List moderated: Yes.
Moderation procedure: Posting automatically submitted to moderator.
Editorial contact: Mary Molinaro
Library Microlabs, 213A King South, University of Kentucky, Lexington, KY 40506-0039.
Tel: 606-257-6199
Fax: 606-257-8379
Internet: molinaro@uklans.uky.edu
Bitnet: molinaro@ukcc
How to access: Send mail to LISTSERV@ukcc.uky.edu with the following message as the ENTIRE message (no subject line, please!) subscribe LABMGR Your Name
Access policy: Subscription is open to anyone.
How to unsubscribe: Send mail to LISTSERV@ukcc.uky.edu with the following message as the ENTIRE message (no subject line, please!): UNSUB LABMGR
How to submit: Send mail to LABMGR@ukcc.uky.edu
Submission policy: All messages are submitted to LABMGR moderator for posting to LABMGR
Archives: All messages archived and are searchable through LISTSERV. For information send mail to LISTSERV@ukcc.uky.edu with the following message: INFO DATABASE
Additional information: LABMGR is also available as the newsgroup info.labmgr

LACTACID@SEARN

Description: LACTACID@SEARN is a forum for discussion of lactic acid bacteria.
Subjects covered: biology; biochemistry
Sponsor: UNESCO Microbial Resources Center, Karolinska Institute, Stockholm, Sweden
List moderated: No.
Editorial contact: Eng-leong Foo
Internet: eng-leong__foo__mircen-ki%micforum@ mica.mic.ki.se
How to access: Send subscribe message to listserv@searn or listserv@searn.sunet.se
How to unsubscribe: Send unsubscribe message to listserv@searn or listserv@searn.sunet.se
Archives: Archives are developed monthly; apply to listowner for details.

LANG-LUCID@CSL.SRI.COM

Description: LANG-LUCID is a forum on the computer programming language Lucid.
Subjects covered: computer science

List moderated: No.
Editorial contact: R. Jagannathan
Internet: lang-lucid-request@csl.sri.com
How to access: Send subscribe message to LANG-LUCID-RE-QUEST@CSL.SRI.COM
How to unsubscribe: Send unsubscribe message to LANG-LU-CID-REQUEST@CSL.SRI.COM

LANGIT@IVEUNCC
Description: LANGIT@IVEUNCC is list centering on the Italian language and linguistics.
Subjects covered: Italian language and literature; linguistics
List moderated: No.
Editorial contact: Roberto Dolci
Bitnet: dolci@iveuncc
How to access: Send subscribe message to listserv@iveuncc or listserv@iveuncc.unive.it
How to unsubscribe: Send unsubscribe message to listserv@iveuncc or listserv@iveuncc.unive.it
Archives: Archives are developed yearly; apply to listowner for details.

LANTRA-L
Description: Lantra-L is a list covering natural language translation work.
Subjects covered: language; translation studies
List moderated: No.
Editorial contact: Helge Niska
Internet: helge.niska@dafa.se
How to access: Send subscribe message to listserv@searn
How to unsubscribe: Send unsubscribe message to listserv@searn
Archives: Archives are developed monthly; apply to listowner for details.

LASMED-L
Description: Lasmed-L is a conference on medical lasers in Israel.
Subjects covered: medicine; Israel
List moderated: Yes.
Editorial contact: Joseph van Zwaren
Internet: jo%ilncrd.bitnet@cunyvm.cuny.edu
Bitnet: jo@ilncrd
How to access: Send subscribe message to listserv@taunivm or listserv@taunivm.tau.ac.il
How to unsubscribe: Send unsubscribe message to listserv@taunivm or listserv@taunivm.tau.ac.il

LASNET@EMX.UTEXAS.EDU
Description: LASNET@EMX.UTEXAS.EDU is a list covering Latin American topics.
Subjects covered: Latin America
List moderated: No.
Editorial contact: Ning Lin
Internet: ilasut@emx.utexas.edu
Bitnet: ilasut@utxvm
How to access: Send subscribe message to LASNET-RE-QUEST@EMX.UTEXAS.EDU
How to unsubscribe: Send unsubscribe message to LASNET-REQUEST@EMX.UTEXAS.EDU

LASPAU-L
Description: Laspau-L (Latin American Scholarship Program of American Universities) provides a forum for discussing issues related to Latin America.
Subjects covered: Latin America
List moderated: Yes.
Editorial contact: Cesar Galindo-Legaria
Bitnet: cesar@husc9
How to access: Send subscribe message to listserv@harvarda or listserv@harvard.harvard.edu
How to unsubscribe: Send unsubscribe message to listserv@harvarda or listserv@harvard.harvard.edu
Archives: Archives are developed monthly; apply to listowner for details.

LATAM-INFO
Description: LATAM-INFO provides a forum for the disemmination of information and discussion of matters of common concern amongst subject specialists, librarians, academic staff, postgraduate students, and others in the field of Latin American studies.
Subjects covered: Latin America; language and literature
Net address for operations: MAILBASE@MAILBASE.AC.UK
Net address for questions or submissions: LATAM-INFO@MAILBASE.AC.UK
Established: November 1991
Subscribers: 55
Sponsor: British Library, Hispanic Section, Great Russell Street, London WC1B 3DG, UK, and the Society for Latin American Studies, Dr. Ann Varley, Secretary, Department of Geography, University College, 26 Bedford Way, London WC1H 0AP, UK.
List moderated: No.
Technical contact: Pat Noble, Joint Listowner
University of London Library, Senate House, Malet Street, London WC1E 7HU, UK.
Tel: 071-636-4514 ext 5040
Fax: 071-436-1494
Internet: PNOBLE@CONSULL.LON.AC.UK
How to access: Send to mailbase@mailbase the following one-line message: JOIN LATAM-INFO <yr firstname> <yr lastname>
Access policy: No restrictions on subscribing.
How to unsubscribe: Send to mailbase@mailbase the following one-line message: LEAVE LATAM-INFO
How to submit: Send messages to: LATAM-INFO@MAILBASE.AC.UK
Archives: Messages are archived by mailbase for one year, then deleted.
Related files: Some information files may be archvied and associated with the list on mailbase.
Additional information: Joint Listowner: Rory Miller, Institute of Latin American Studies, 86/88 Bedford Street South, P.O. Box 47, Liverpool L69 3BX, UK; tel: 051-794-3079; fax: 051-794-3080; RORY@UXB.LIVERPOOL.AC.UK

LATCO LIST
Description: LATCO is a free e-mailing list devoted to the exchange of information, ideas and discussion of Business and Trade with Latin America. It is administered by the Latin American Trade Council of Oregon (LATCO), a private, non-profit

trade association located at the World Trade Center in Portland, Oregon. LATCO is pleased to host an open discussion about Latin American business and international trade where businessmen and professionals can learn from each other about business, the business climate, and aspects of doing business in Latin America.
Subjects covered: Latin America; business; trade and economic data
Sponsor: Latin American Trade Council of Oregon (LATCO)
Editorial contact: Tom Miles
Internet: tmiles@well.sf.ca.us
Technical contact: Walter Morales
Internet: (walter@psg.com)
Bitnet: (walter@pccvm.bitnet)
How to access: Send a message to the following e-mail address: lserv@psg.com One single line containing the following message: subscribe latco <your e-mail address>
How to unsubscribe: If you ever want to remove yourself from this mailing list, send a message to the following e-mail address: lserv@psg.com
One single line containing the following message: unsubscribe latco <yourname@youraddress>
How to submit: Messages to members: latco@psg.com
Always remember to write a subject on your messages. That saves readers a lot of time screening messages.
Submission policy: Trade and economic data, analysis, opinions and experience, sources of information about Latin American business and industry and announcements of events, courses or seminars are welcome. Languages: English, Spanish or Portugese. When possible, please include an English summary or abstract for articles in Spanish or Portugese. Cultural/geographical region: Mexico, Caribbean, Latin America.
Additional information: It is not a commercial forum. Advertising or offers to buy/sell merchandise are not permitted. There are commercial networks for that purpose.

LAW-LIB@UCDAVIS.EDU
Description: LAW-LIB@UCDAVIS.EDU is a conference covering topics of interest to law librarians.
Subjects covered: library and information science; law and legal studies
List moderated: No.
Editorial contact: Elizabeth St. Goar
Internet: estgoar@ucdavis.edu
How to access: Send subscribe message to law-req@ucdavis.edu
How to unsubscribe: Send unsubscribe message to law-req@ucdavis.edu

LAWSCH-L
Description: Lawsch-L is a list for students of law.
Subjects covered: law and legal studies
Host: American University Law School
List moderated: No.
Editorial contact: Ed Kania
Internet: ekania@auvm.auvm.edu
Bitnet: ekania@auvm
How to access: Send subscribe message to listserv@auvm or listserv@auvm.auvm.edu
How to unsubscribe: Send unsubscribe message to listserv@auvm or listserv@auvm.auvm.edu

LDBASE-L
Description: Ldbase-L is a listserv database search list.
Subjects covered: computer hardware and software
List moderated: No.
Editorial contact: Phil Endacott
Internet: endacott@kuhub.cc.ukans.edu
Bitnet: endacott@ukanvax
How to access: Send subscribe message to listserv@ukanvm or listserv@ukanvm.cc.ukans.edu
How to unsubscribe: Send unsubscribe message to listserv@ukanvm or listserv@ukanvm.cc.ukans.edu

THE LEARNING LIST
Description: THE LEARNING LIST focuses on a variety of philosophies of learning.
Subjects covered: education
List moderated: No.
Editorial contact: Rowan Hawthorne
Internet: learning-request@sea.east.sun.com
How to access: Contact Editor
How to unsubscribe: Contact Editor

LIBADMIN
Description: LIBADMIN is an electronic discussion group devoted primarily to discussion of issues dealing with library administration and management.
Subjects covered: library and information science; management; administration
Net address for operations: LISTSERV@UMAB
Net address for questions or submissions: LIBADMIN@UMAB
Established: 1991
Subscribers: 1512
Host: University of Maryland at Baltimore, 100 North Greene St., Baltimore, MD 21201.
List moderated: No.
Editorial contact: Pamela Bluh
Marshall Law Library, University of Maryland School of Law, 20 North Paca Street, Baltimore, MD 21201.
Tel: (410) 706-7400
Fax: (410) 706-8354
Internet: PBLUH@UMAB.UMD.EDU
Bitnet: PBLUH@UMAB
Technical contact: John Culshaw
Library, University of Colorado, Boulder, CO.
Internet: CULSHAW__J@UCBLDR.COLORADO.EDU
How to access: Tell listserv@umab subscribe LIBADMIN your name
How to unsubscribe: Tell listserv@umab sunsub LIBADMIN

LIBER-PILOT@MAILBASE.AC.UK
Description: LIBER-PILOT@MAILBASE.AC.UK is a forum for European research libraries.
Subjects covered: library and information science
List moderated: No.
Internet: liber-pilot-request@mailbase.ac.uk
How to access: Send subscribe message to mailbase@mailbase.ac.uk in the following format: join liber-pilot Yourfirstname Yourlastname
Archives: Archives are developed monthly; apply to listowner for details.

LIBER@UVMVM

Description: LIBER@UVMVM is a list covering media services in libraries.
Subjects covered: library and information science
List moderated: No.
How to access: Send subscribe message to listserv@uvmvm or listserv%uvmvm.bitnet@vm1.nodak.edu
How to unsubscribe: Send unsubscribe message to listserv@uvmvm or listserv%uvmvm.bitnet@vm1.nodak.edu

LIBERNET

Description: Libernet is intended to be a forum for high-quality, real-world oriented presentation of information of interest to classical liberals, libertarians, objectivists, and anyone else interested in applying the philosophy of liberty to the problems of our day. It is also intended for the rapid dissemination of news items that friends of liberty might be interested in. Accordingly, the following topics are appropriate for postings to Libernet: 1) News items: quotes/articles from major newspapers relating to market-oriented approaches to social problems, support for civil liberties, etc. 2) Book reviews 3) Election results 4) Personal stories about campaigning, convincing others about the merits of liberty, etc. 6) Copies of letters to the editor 7) Conference/seminar announcements 8) Upcoming media events of interest 9) Questions about any of the above.
Subjects covered: libertarianism; philosophy; political science
Net address for operations: libernet-request@dartmouth.edu
Net address for questions or submissions: libernet@dartmouth.edu
Sponsor: Dartmouth College, Hanover NH 03755
List moderated: No.
Editorial contact: Barry Fagin
Thayer School of Engineering, Dartmouth College, Hanover NH 03755
Tel: (603) 646-3060
Fax: (603) 646-3856
Internet: barry.fagin@dartmouth.edu
How to access: Email to libernet-request@dartmouth.edu and follow instructions.
Access policy: The overriding principle of Libernet is that is not to be used as a forum for interactive discussion. Questions are perfectly appropriate, provided their answers are suitable material for Libernet. Within this context, readers are asked to use their judgement.

LIBEVENT@USCVM

Description: LIBEVENT@USCVM lists library events in Southern California.
Subjects covered: library and information science
List moderated: Yes.
Editorial contact: Karen Howell
Bitnet: khowell@uscvm
How to access: Send subscribe message to listserv@uscvm or listserv@vm.usc.edu
How to unsubscribe: Send unsubscribe message to listserv@uscvm or listserv@vm.usc.edu
Archives: Archives are developed monthly; apply to listowner for details.

LIBEX-L

Description: Libex-L is a discussion list on exhibits.
Subjects covered: library and information science
List moderated: Yes.
Editorial contact: Christine Whittington
Bitnet: christin@maine
How to access: Send subscribe message to listserv@maine
How to unsubscribe: Send unsubscribe message to listserv@maine
Archives: Archives are developed monthly; apply to listowner for details.

LIBMASTR@UOTTOWA

Description: LIBMASTR@UOTTOWA carries information about the Library Master bibliographic database.
Subjects covered: library and information science
List moderated: Yes.
Editorial contact: Michael Strangelove
Bitnet: 441495@uottowa
How to access: Send subscribe message to listserv@uottowa
How to unsubscribe: Send unsubscribe message to listserv@uottowa
Archives: Yes; Monthly, Private

LIBPER-L

Description: Libper-L is a list discussing personnel issues for libraries.
Subjects covered: library and information science
List moderated: No.
Editorial contact: M. Jean McDonald
Bitnet: mcdonald@ksuvm
How to access: Send subscribe message to listserv@ksuvm
How to unsubscribe: Send unsubscribe message to listserv@ksuvm
Archives: Archives are developed monthly; apply to listowner for details.

LIBPLN-L

Description: Libpln-L focuses on academic library planning.
Subjects covered: library and information science; colleges and universities
List moderated: No.
Editorial contact: W. Bernabei
Bitnet: bernabei@qucdn
How to access: Send subscribe message to listserv@qucdn or listserv@qucdn.queensu.ca
How to unsubscribe: Send unsubscribe message to listserv@qucdn or listserv@qucdn.queensu.ca
Archives: Archives are developed monthly; apply to listowner for details.

LIBRARY@INDYCMS

Description: LIBRARY@INDYCMS contains general news for library employees and users.
Subjects covered: library and information science
List moderated: No.
Editorial contact: Donna B. Harlan
Internet: harlan@ucs.indiana.edu
Bitnet: harlan@iubacs

How to access: Send subscribe message to listserv@indycms or listserv@indycms.iupui.edu
How to unsubscribe: Send unsubscribe message to listserv@indycms or listserv@indycms.iupui.edu
Archives: Archives are developed monthly; apply to listowner for details.

LIBREF-L

Description: LIBREF-L is an electronic forum for the discussion of library reference issues. LIBREF-L is a roundtable discussion among reference librarians and other interested people that takes place across computer networks. LIBREF-L uses LISTSERV software at Kent State University. It is owned and moderated by reference librarians at Kent State University Libraries.
Subjects covered: library and information science; library reference
Net address for operations: listserv@kentvm or listserv@kentvm.kent.edu
Net address for questions or submissions: libref-l@kentvm
Established: November 1991
Subscribers: 2795
Sponsor: Kent State University Libraries, Kent, OH 44242.
List moderated: Yes.
Moderation procedure: Postings to the list are first received by its moderators and if appropriate are posted to LIBREF-L.
Editorial contact: Laura Bartolo
Room 161, Library Building, Reference Department, Kent State University Libraries and Media Service, Kent State University, Kent, Ohio 44242.
Tel: 216-672-3045
Fax: 216-672-2265
Internet: lbartolo@kentvm.kent.edu
Bitnet: lbartolo@kentvm
Review: Robinson, Kara and Diane Kovacs. "LibRef-L, Sharing Reference Expertise over the Academic Networks." Wilson Library Bulletin 67/5 (January 1993): 47-50.
How to access: SEND COMMANDS TO LISTSERV, NOT TO LIBREF-L. Send commands as the text of an e-mail message. Do not include a subject line and do not add any other information except for the command in the text of the e-mail message.
How to unsubscribe: SEND COMMANDS TO LISTSERV, NOT TO LIBREF-L. Send commands as the text of an e-mail message. Do not include a subject line and do not add any other information except for the command in the text of the e-mail message.
How to submit: Send an e-mail note addressed to LIBREF-L@KENTVM (if your e-mail address is on the BITNET) or LIBREF-L@KENTVM.KENT.EDU (if your e-mail address is on the Internet) exactly as you would send an e-mail note to a person. The LISTSERV will "read" LIBREF-L's mail and pass it on to the moderator for possible distribution to everyone who is subscribed. The moderators reserve the right to reject any posting that we decide is inappropriate for LIBREF-L. When the moderators decide to reject a message, they will send an explanation to the sender. The sender may be given the option of altering the message so that it can be posted to the list by the moderators. The moderators reserve the right to reject any posting that is of a personal nature.
Archives: Because of limited space on our fileserver, only 6 months of LIBREF-L archives are currently available. The moderators are looking at various ways to make earlier archives available to our subscribers. If you have any questions, please contact the moderators and we will be happy to answer them. There are two ways to search the archives of LISTSERV based discussion lists. If your email address is on the BITNET and you have interactive messaging capability you can search interactively using a program that you retrieve from the LISTSERV. If your email address is on the Internet or you do not have interactive messaging, you can search the archives in "Batch" mode via email. To learn to effectively search you will need to read the manual. To retrieve the manual for LISTSERV database searching, send a message via email to LISTSERV@KENTVM (Internet: LISTSERV@KENTVM.KENT.EDU). Leave the subject line blank and the text should read INFO DATABASE.
Additional information: Additional editors: Gladys Smiley Bell, gbell@kentvm.kent.edu (Internet), gbell@kentvm (Bitnet); Mary Du Mont, mdumont@kentvm.kent.edu (Internet), mdumont@kentvm (Bitnet); Leslie Haas, lhaas@kentvm.kent.edu (Internet), lhaas@kentvm (Bitnet); Carolyn Radcliff, radcliff@kentvm.kent.edu (Internet), radcliff@kentvm (Bitnet); Kara Robinson, krobinso@kentvm.kent.edu (Internet), krobinso@kentvm (Bitnet); Barbara Schloman, bschloma@kentvm.kent.edu (Internet), bschloma@kentvm (Bitnet)
Address: Room 161, Library Building, Reference Department, Kent State University Libraries and Media Services, Kent State University, Kent, Ohio 44242; tel: 216-672-3045; fax: 216-672-2265.

LIBRES@KENTVM

Description: LIBRES@KENTVM is a list used to distribute LIBRES, the Library Research ejournal.
Subjects covered: library and information science
List moderated: Yes.
Editorial contact: LIBRES Editors
Internet: editors@kentvm.kent.edu
Bitnet: editors@kentvm
How to access: Send subscribe message to listserv@kentvm or listserv@kentvm.kent.edu
How to unsubscribe: Send unsubscribe message to listserv@kentvm or listserv@kentvm.kent.edu
Archives: Yes; Monthly, Private

LIBSUP-L

Description: Libsup-L focuses on issues of interest to library support staff.
Subjects covered: library and information science
List moderated: No.
Editorial contact: Mary Kalnin
Internet: kalnin@carson.u.washington.edu
How to access: Send subscribe message to listserv@uwavm
How to unsubscribe: Send unsubscribe message to listserv@uwavm
Archives: Archives are developed monthly; apply to listowner for details.

LINGUIST

Description: LINGUIST is a discussion and information list on academic linguistics. The list is oriented towards those who study language as a profession, not towards those non-professionally interested in languages, nor towards those who teach languages.

Subjects covered: language and literature; linguistics
Net address for operations: listserv@tamvml.tamu.edu
Net address for questions or submissions:
linguist@tamvml.tamu.edu
Established: December 1990
Subscribers: 3509
Sponsor: Texas A&M University, College Station, TX 77843
and Eastern Michigan University, Ypsilanti, MI.
Host: Texas A&M University, College Station, TX 77843.
List moderated: Yes.
Moderation procedure: Mail is received and reviewed by moderators and editors. Flames and inappropriate (i.e., non-linguistic) messages are sent back. The remaining mail is sorted into topics and posted to the list in a standard LINGUIST mail-envelope.
Editorial contact: Anthony Aristar
Dept. of English, Texas A&M University, College Station, TX 77843.
Tel: (409) 845-3452
Fax: (409) 862-2292
Internet: aristar@tamuts.tamu.edu
How to access: Send the message: sub linguist first-name last-name to the address: listserv@tamvml.tamu.edu (Internet) LISTSERV@TAMVM1 (Bitnet)
Access policy: Subscription is open to all involved in the teaching of linguistics or in research in that field.
How to unsubscribe: Send the message: unsub linguist to the address: listserv@tamvml.tamu.edu (Internet) LISTSERV@TAMVM1 (Bitnet)
How to submit: Send postings to the address: linguist@tamvml.tamu.edu (Internet) LINGUIST@TAMVM1 (Bitnet)
Submission policy: Only postings which are directly related to the academic field of linguistics are accepted. Postings are expected to show a reasonable level of linguistic sophistication.
Additional information: Additional editor: Helen Dry, Dept. of English, Eastern Michigan University, Ypsilanti, MI 48197; tel (313) 487-0145; Internet hdry@emunix.emich.edu

LIS

Description: LIS, or Lesbians in Science, is a list for lesbians in various scientific professions, colleges and universities, government, etc.
Subjects covered: gay and lesbian topics; colleges and universities; workplace studies; science and technology
Net address for questions or submissions:
ZITA@JUNO.PHYSICS.WISC.EDU,
LIS@JUNO.PHYSICS.WISC.EDU
List moderated: Yes.
How to access: Send subscription messages to ZITA@JUNO.PHYSICS.WISC.EDU
How to submit: Send postings to LIS@JUNO.PHYSICS.WISC.EDU

LIS-BAILER

Description: LIS-BAILER carries messages from teaching and research staff in institutions of information and library studies in the U.K. and overseas.
Subjects covered: library and information science
Net address for operations: LIS-BAILER@MAILBASE.AC.UK

Net address for questions or submissions: LIS-BAILER@MAILBASE.AC.UK
Established: 1992
Subscribers: 68
Sponsor: British Association of Information & Library Educators and Researchers
Host: Mailbase
List moderated: No.
Editorial contact: David Stoker
Department of Information & Library Studies, University of Wales, Aberystwyth, SY23 3AS, UK.
Tel: 0970 622178
Fax: 0970 622190
Internet: das@aber.ac.uk
How to access: Send the following message subscribe lis-bailer <firstname> <lastname> to mailbase@mailbase.ac.uk
How to unsubscribe: Send message to mailbase@mailbase.ac.uk
How to submit: Send message to mailbase@mailbase.ac.uk
Submission policy: Send message to mailbase@mailbase.ac.uk

LIS-ENQUIRIES

Description: LIS-Enquiries is the main forum for libraries on JANET to distribute surveys and information: most libraries have at least one member. It is also the communication channel for the JANET User Group for Libraries (JUGL). It was set up by SCONUL's ACIS to provide a cumulating index to email surveys.
Subjects covered: library and information science; Janet User Group
Net address for operations: mailbase@mailbase.ac.uk
Net address for questions or submissions: LIS-Enquiries@mailbase.ac.uk
Established: May 1990
Subscribers: 335
Sponsor: Networked Information Services Project (NISP) at Newcastle University Computing Service.
List moderated: Yes.
Moderation procedure: Messages addressed to LIS-Enquiries@mailbase.ac.uk are routed automatically to moderator.
Editorial contact: Adrian Peasgood
University of Sussex Library, Brighton, BN1 9QL, UK.
Tel: (0) 273 678158
Fax: (0) 273 678441
Internet: a.n.peasgood@central.sussex.ac.uk
Internet: mailbase@mailbase.ac.uk
How to access: Email mailbase@mailbase.ac.uk with the message Join LIS-Enquiries <yourfirst name> <your surname>
Access policy: One subscriber at each institution assumes responsibility for disseminating messages and co-ordinating responses, but others are welcome to subscribe.
How to unsubscribe: Email mailbase@mailbase.ac.uk with the message Leave LIS-Enquiries
How to submit: Send to LIS-Enquiries@mailbase.ac.uk
Submission policy: The list's remit covers surveys and general information of interest to the academic community.
Archives: Monthly archives retained for two years.
Related files: ftp:mailbase.ac.uk (in directory /pub/lis-enquiries); gopher:mailbase.ac.uk

LIS-LINK

Description: LIS-link is a forum for those providing computer-based information and reference services in libraries, covering, in particular: access, training, and pricing of on-line databases; CD ROM; JANET [e.g. BIDS]; IXI; the Internet; commercial hosts on public networks. It is also a forum for news and discussion on the development of library and information services through computing technology and networking, covering, in particular: research; practice; the convergence of academic services on campus. In addition is serves as a forum for news and discussion on items of general interest to LIS professionals in U.K. higher education/research institutions.

Subjects covered: library and information science
Net address for operations: Mailbase@uk.ac.mailbase
Net address for questions or submissions: LIS-Link@uk.ac.mailbase
Established: March 29, 1991
Subscribers: 896
Sponsor: Systems Division, Strathclyde University Library, 101 St James' Road, Glasgow, Scotland.
Host: JNT Networked Information Services Project, Computer Centre, University of Newcastle, Newcastle Upon Tyne, UK.
List moderated: No.
Editorial contact: Dennis Nicholson
Systems Division, Strathclyde University Library, 101 St James' Road, Glasgow, Scotland.
Tel: 041 552 3701 ext 4132/4118
Fax: 041 552 3304
Internet: cijs24@vaxa.strath.ac.uk
Internet: mailbase-helpline@mailbase.ac.uk
How to access: Send the message: Join Lis-link Yourfirstname Yourlastname to: mailbase@uk.ac.mailbase
How to unsubscribe: Send the message: Leave Lis-link to: mailbase@uk.ac.mailbase
How to submit: Send your message to: lis-link@uk.ac.mailbase
Archives: Short term archive only.
Related files: Various files in the lis-link archive, for details send the message: index lis-link to: mailbase@uk.ac.mailbase
Gopher accessibility: Name = Mailbase Gopher Type = 1 Host = mailbase.ac.uk Port = 70
Additional information: Additional editors: Jean Shaw and Kenneth McMahon; same address information as above.

LIS-MEDICAL@MAILBASE.AC.UK

Description: LIS-MEDICAL@MAILBASE.AC.UK is an electronic forum for members of the University Medical Schools Library Group.
Subjects covered: library and information science; health sciences
List moderated: No.
Internet: lis-medical-request@mailbase.ac.uk
How to access: Send subscribe message to mailbase@mailbase.ac.uk in the following format: join lis-medical Yourfirstname Yourlastname
Archives: Archives are developed monthly; apply to listowner for details.

LIS-RAREBOOKS

Description: LIS-rarebooks is a forum for the discussion of rare books librarianship and its special requirements for standards and systems. This list will discuss how these requirements are being met. Initial discussion will focus on the Library Associa-tion's RBG survey, Rare books cataloguing in the British Isles (Ann Lennon and David Pearson, BL Research Paper, 94, 1991).

Subjects covered: rare books; library and information science
Net address for operations: mailbase@mailbase.ac.uk
Net address for questions or submissions: lis-rarebooks@mailbase.ac.uk
Established: 1991
Subscribers: 64
Sponsor: Joint Information Systems Committee of the UK Higher Education Funding Councils.
Host: University of Newcastle Upon Tyne, UK
List moderated: No.
Editorial contact: Michael Smallman
Main Library, Queen's University of Belfast
Tel: 0232-245133 ext. 3604
Internet: lbg0456@v2.qub.ac.uk
Copyright statement: Authors of accepted contributions assign to <listname> the right to publish the text electronically in screen-readable ASCII and to make it available permanently in electronic archives. Authors do, however, retain copyright to their contributions and may republish them in any form that they choose, so long as they clearly acknowledge <listname>@mailbase.ac.uk as the original source of publication.
How to access: Send message to mailbase@mailbase.ac.uk containing the single line: join lis-rarebooks <firstname> <lastname>
How to unsubscribe: Send message to mailbase@mailbase.ac.uk containing the single line: leave lis-rarebooks
How to submit: Send your message to lis-rarebooks@mailbase.ac.uk
Archives: Message archive files are stored as MM-YYYY where MM is the month number and YYYY is the year number. These can be retrieved by anonymous ftp or by sending a message to mailbase@mailbase.ac.uk containing the line: send lis-rarebooks <filename> where <filename> should be replaced by the name of the file required.
Related files: Additional files stored with the list can be retrieved in the same way as the archive files. An index to files stored with the list can be retrieved by sending a message to mailbase@mailbase.ac.uk containing the single line: index lis-rarebooks
Gopher accessibility: Mailbase can be accessed by gophering to mailbase.ac.uk.

LIS-RESEARCH@MAILBASE.AC.UK

Description: LIS-RESEARCH@MAILBASE.AC.UK is a forum for discussing topics related to the UK Research Council libraries.
Subjects covered: library and information science
List moderated: No.
Internet: lis-research-request@mailbase.ac.uk
How to access: Send subscribe message to mailbase@mailbase.ac.uk in the following format: join lis-research Yourfirstname Yourlastname
Archives: Archives are developed monthly; apply to listowner for details.

LIS-SCOTLAND@MAILBASE.AC.UK
Description: LIS-SCOTLAND@MAILBASE.AC.UK is a discussion list on libraries in Scotland.
Subjects covered: library and information science
List moderated: No.
Internet: lis-scotland-request@mailbase.ac.uk
How to access: Send subscribe message to mailbase@mailbase.ac.uk in the following format: join lis-scotland Yourfirstname Yourlastname
Archives: Archives are developed monthly; apply to listowner for details.

LIS-X500@MAILBASE.AC.UK
Description: LIS-X500@MAILBASE.AC.UK is a discussing of topics on the development of library-specific applications for the X.500 protocol.
Subjects covered: library and information science
List moderated: No.
Internet: lis-x500-request@mailbase.ac.uk
How to access: Send subscribe message to mailbase@mailbase.ac.uk in the following format: join lis-x500 Yourfirstname Yourlastname
Archives: Archives are developed monthly; apply to listowner for details.

LISABEN
Description: LISABEN is a discussion list covering lesbianism and related topics.
Subjects covered: gender studies; gay and lesbian topics
How to access: Send message to lisaben-request@athena.mit.edu

LIST OF LISTS
Description: The List of Lists is a Dartmouth-maintained merged list of the LISTSERV and manually maintained discussion lists on Bitnet and the Interest Group lists on the Internet. It is a single file with one line for each mailing list. The list has been updated monthly for the last year and has a stable format. It currently contains information on about 3,500 lists. Although it is possible to retrieve the Dartmouth list-of-lists and examine it with a text editor, the file has a line length of 614 bytes and is hard to read with some editors. To releave this problem, we have written a search-and-display application for most common operating systems: Macintosh, MS-DOS, Unix, VAX/VMS, and VM/CMS. If you don't want to bother with installing these applications, we supply a short text version of the data file that omits the long description of the list, but is easier to use in an editor.
Subjects covered: discussion lists; Bitnet; Internet
Net address for operations: LISTSERV@DARTCMS1
How to access: The full data file and all applications are available from DARTCMS1 by mail via LISTSERV and by anonymous FTP. Once you have the appropriate application installed, you should enter an FUI or AFD subscription to the datafile so you will receive the monthly updates. To receive an application and current datafile by mail, send email to LISTSERV@DARTCMS1 with the contents:
SEND MACSIG PACKAGE to get the Macintosh application;
SEND PCSIG PACKAGE to get the MS-DOS application;
SEND UNIXSIG PACKAGE to get the Unix application; SEND VAXSIG PACKAGE to get the VAX/VMS application; SEND

CMSSIG PACKAGE to get the VM/CMS application; SEND LISTSHRT PACKAGE to get the short data file for use via editor; SEND LISTTEXT PACKAGE to get the full data file broken in six pieces; SEND LISTSERV LISTS to get the full data file with Bitnet addresses; SEND INTERNET LISTS to get the full data file with Internet addresses. The full data file is 750k bytes. If you are connected to the Internet it is better to get it by anonymous FTP than by mail. A typical FTP session would consist of: FTP DARTCMS1.DARTMOUTH.EDU ANONYMOUS CD SIGLISTS GET READ.ME GET LISTSERV.LISTS QUIT

LIST-MANAGERS@GREATCIRCLE.COM
Description: LIST-MANAGERS covers issues related to managing Internet mailing lists.
Subjects covered: Internet
List moderated: No.
Editorial contact: Brent Chapman
Internet: brent@greatcircle.com
How to access: Send subscribe message to Majordomo@GreatCircle.COM
How to unsubscribe: Send unsubscribe message to Majordomo@GreatCircle.COM

LISTSERV@DEAKIN.OZ.AU
Description: LISTSERV@DEAKIN.OZ.AU is a forum for discussion of information technology in education.
Subjects covered: education technology
Host: Deakin University
List moderated: No.
How to access: Send subscribe message to listserv@deakin.oz.au
How to unsubscribe: Send unsubscribe message to listserv@deakin.oz.au

LITERA-L
Description: Litera-L is a forum focusing on literature in general.
Subjects covered: language and literature
List moderated: Yes.
Editorial contact: Fernando Careaga Sanchez
Internet: pl157961@tecmtyvm.mty.itesm.mx
Bitnet: pl157961@tecmtyvm
How to access: Send subscribe message to listserv@tecmtyvm or listserv@tecmtyvm.mty.itesm.mx
How to unsubscribe: Send unsubscribe message to listserv@tecmtyvm or listserv@tecmtyvm.mty.itesm.mx

LITERARY@UCF1VM
Description: LITERARY@UCF1VM is a general forum for literature.
Subjects covered: language and literature
List moderated: No.
Editorial contact: Lois Buwalda
Bitnet: lois@ucf1vm
How to access: Send subscribe message to listserv@ucf1vm
How to unsubscribe: Send unsubscribe message to listserv@ucf1vm
Archives: Archives are developed monthly; apply to listowner for details.

LITPROG@SHSU.EDU

Description: LITPROG@SHSU.EDU is a discussion list on literate programming and related issues.
Subjects covered: computer science
List moderated: No.
Editorial contact: George D. Greenwade, Ph.D.
Internet: bed__gdg@shsu.edu
Bitnet: bed__gdg@shsu
How to access: Send subscribe message to listserv@shsu or listserv@shsu.edu
How to unsubscribe: Send unsubscribe message to listserv@shsu or listserv@shsu.edu
Archives: Yes; Available from fileserv@shsu or fileserv@shsu.edu

LITSCI-L

Description: Litsci-L is a list on science fiction topics.
Subjects covered: literature; science fiction
List moderated: No.
Editorial contact: Joe Amato
Internet: jamato@ux1.cso.uiuc.edu
Bitnet: jamato@uiucvmd
How to access: Send subscribe message to listserv@uiucvmd
How to unsubscribe: Send unsubscribe message to listserv@uiucvmd
Archives: Archives are developed monthly; apply to listowner for details.

LITURGY

Description: LITURGY is a discussion list centering on topics in liturgical research. The list maintains a file of members' research interests as well as a number of files associated with liturgical studies. It is the aim of the list to build up a database of liturgical texts in electronic form. Discussion in recent issues has included a diverse number of liturgy-related subjects from the place of the creed and the Lord's Prayer in the liturgy, liturgy and ecumenism, the early liturgy of Jerusalem, the Easter Vigil through to the Anglican Book of Common Prayer. LITURGY is intended as a discussion on all aspects of the academic study of Christian liturgy. The list does not confine itself to any single historical period, geographical area or denomination. Contributions are therefore welcome from scholars in all fields of theology and history.
Subjects covered: liturgy; religion; Christianity
Net address for operations:
MAILBASE@MAILBASE.AC.UK
Established: October 2, 1992
Subscribers: 140
Sponsor: University of Durham, UK
Host: Mailbase, NISP Team, University of Newcastle, UK
List moderated: Not generally
Moderation procedure: The list only becomes moderated as a last resort in striving to maintain serious academic discussion.
Editorial contact: Michael A. Fraser
Department of Theology,
University of Durham, Abbey House, Palace Green, DURHAM DH1 3RS United Kingdom

Fax: +44 91 374 4744
Internet: m.a.fraser@durham.ac.uk
Bitnet: m.a.fraser@durham.ac.uk
How to access: Send, via email, to the address: mailbase@mailbase.ac.uk the command:
subscribe liturgy Your-Full-Name (E.g. Joan Smith)
Access policy: Open to all who are interested in contributing to an academic discussion of the history, theology, and practice of the Christian liturgy.
How to unsubscribe: Send, via email, the following command to: mailbase@mailbase.ac.uk unsubscribe liturgy
How to submit: Send items intended for the discussion group to the address: liturgy@mailbase.ac.uk
Submission policy: We welcome all items for discussion that fall into the broad category of liturgy. Our only condition is that submissons are academic and objective in nature. We especially welcome contributions from scholars researching in the field of liturgical studies.
Archives: All contributions to the group are archived for up to twelve months. They can easily be retrieved via email from the Mailbase server.
Related files: At present there is no FTP access to the Liturgy group files. However, we have a limited amount of storage space for text files which can be retrieved via email. These include a file of biographical details of subscribers to the group.
Additional information: As part of our wider aim of making easier the exchange of ideas we are contemplating setting up the first electronic journal in liturgical studies. Subscribers to the group include members of the North American Academy of Liturgy and Societas Liturgica. We hope to form electronic links with similar societies and institutions across the globe.

LIVE-EYE@YORKVM1

Description: LIVE-EYE@YORKVM1 is a conference on color science and vision studies.
Subjects covered: medicine
List moderated: No.
Internet: cvnet@vm1.yorku.ca
How to access: Send subscribe message to listserv@yorkvm1 or listserv@vm1.yorku.ca
How to unsubscribe: Send unsubscribe message to listserv@yorkvm1 or listserv@vm1.yorku.ca
Archives: Archives are developed monthly; apply to listowner for details.

LM__NET

Description: LM__NET is a world-wide discussion group on school library media topics started in June 1992. It has grown to over 875 members since then. Members come from most states and several countries. Approximately 10-15 messages are posted per day on a variety of topics related to school librarianship. We are hoping that with the start of the new semester many new school library media people will join us. Conversation on LM__NET should focus on the topics of interest to the school library media community, including the latest on school library media services, operations, and activities. It is a list for practitioners helping practitioners, sharing ideas, solving problems, telling each other about new publications and upcoming conferences, asking for assistance or information, and linking schools through their library media centers. The LM__NET listserv is open to ALL school library media specialists worldwide and people involved with the school library media field. It is not for general librarians or educators. We want to keep the activity and discussion focused on school library media. But, the listserv can be used by library media people for many different things—to ask for input, share ideas and information, link programs that are geographically remote, make contacts, etc.

Subjects covered: school libraries; education
Net address for operations: listserv@suvm.bitnet or listserv@suvm.syr.edu
Established: June 1992
Subscribers: 875
Sponsor: ERIC Clearinghouse on Information Resources and the School of Information Studies, Syracuse University.
Host: Syracuse University
List moderated: No.
Editorial contact: Peter Milbury
Tel: (916) 891-3060
Fax: (916) 891-3166
Internet: pmilbur@eis.calstate.edu
Technical contact: Peter Milbury
Pleasant Valley High School, 1475 East Avenue, Chico, CA 95926
Tel: (916) 891-3060
Fax: (916) 345-3308
Internet: PMILBUR@EIS.CALSTATE.EDU
How to access: To join, send an email request to either: Peter Milbury: PMILBUR@EIS.CALSTATE.EDU or Mike Eisenberg: MIKE@ERICIR.SYR.EDU
It's important to include your full userid/address and your firstname lastname, so that we have you entered properly. For example: ''Add to LM—NET JDoe@lmc.mystate.edu name: Jane Doe'' [quotes unnecessary].
Access policy: Members only. How do you send a message to all of the other subscribers of LM—NET? It's easy. Just send an e-mail message as you would to anyone else with an electronic mail address. Send to: LM—NET@SUVM.BITNET
If you post a message to LM—NET, please note that you WILL NOT receive a copy of your message from the listserv. You might want to send yourself a copy as a reminder that you posted the message: i.e., so you don't sit around wondering if you really DID post that important bit of information to all your LM—NET friends. The amount of acknowledgment you wish to receive from LM—NET upon completion of a mailing posting can be changed by means of a ''SET LM—NET option'' command, where ''option'' may be either ''ACK'' (mail acknowledgement), ''MSGACK'' (interactive messages only) or ''NOACK''. Send the command of your choice by e-mail to: LISTSERV@SUVM.BITNET
How to unsubscribe: You may leave the LM—NET at any time by sending a ''SIGNOFF LM—NET'' command by e-mail to LISTSERV@SUVM.BITNET Please note that this command is sent only to the listserv address: LISTSERV@SUVM.BITNET [It must NOT be sent to the membership list address: LM—NET@SUVM.BITNET]
In the event that you want to unsubscribe/sign off from LM—NET.... All you have to do is send the message signoff lm—net to listserv@suvm.bitnet Leave the Subject line of your message blank.)
How to submit: More information on LISTSERV commands can be found in the ''General Introduction Guide'', which you can retrieve by sending an ''INFO GENINTRO'' command by e-mail to LISTSERV@SUVM.BITNET This is an excellent way to learn about listservers, an important part of Internet services and resources.

Archives: The LM—NET Archives are now available at the AskERIC Gopher site. The quickest way to find them is to use Telnet to go to a Gopher server, and then, by going through a series of menus, you will reach the LM—NET Archives, at the AskERIC (ERIC-IR) Gopher. For example: Telnet to a Gopher server on the Internet, as in the following: Telnet to> consultant.micro.umn.edu (or other Gopher following: Telnet to consultant.micro.umn.edu (or other Gopher address) At the login prompt, type: gopher (or other specified login). At the TERM = (vt100) prompt hit return or enter your terminal type. LM—NET is found by moving through the directories, which are given as menu choices through the main Gopher menu.
Gopher accessibility: See above description, under Archives.

LN

Description: LN is a forum for discussion of Natural Language Processing. It includes announcements and reports on conferences, calls for papers, job announcements, and other discussion about NLP, with a particular attention to the French research community.
Subjects covered: natural language processing; language and literature; French language and literature; computer science
Net address for operations:
LISTSERV@FRMOP11.CNUSC.FR
Net address for questions or submissions:
LN@FRMOP11.CNUSC.FR
Established: 1991
Subscribers: 486
Sponsor: GDR-PRC Communication Homme-Machine Pole Langage Naturel LLAOR-CNRS, 250, Av. Albert Einstein F-06560, Sophia-Antipolis, France.
Host: LLAOR-CNRS, 250, Av. Albert Einstein F-06560, Sophia-Antipolis, France.
List moderated: Yes.
Moderation procedure: Each mail message sent to LN is submitted to the moderators (one for discussions, one for all the other information).
Editorial contact: Philippe Blache
LLAOR-CNRS, 250, Av. Albert Einstein, F-06560, Sophia-Antipolis, France.
Tel: +33/93.95.43.46
Fax: +33/92.96.07.55
Internet: pb@llaor.unice.fr
Technical contact: Pierre Zweigenbaum
INSERM, 91, Bd de l'Hopital, F-75634 Paris Cedex 13.
Tel: +33/45.83.67.28
Fax: +33/45.86.56.85
Internet: pz@biomath.jussieu.fr
How to access: Send following message to listserv: SUBSCRIBE LN <First Name> <Name>
How to unsubscribe: Send following message to listserv: UNSUBSCRIBE LN
How to submit: Send mail to LN@FRMOP11.CNUSC.FR
Archives: Send the mail message: GET LN LOG<yy><mm> to: LISTSERV@FRMOP11.CNUSC.FR This file contain the mails sent during the month <mm> of the year <yy>.

LOJBAN-LIST@SNARK.THYRSUS.COM

Description: LOJBAN-LIST@SNARK.THYRSUS.COM is a conference on artificial language called Lojban.
Subjects covered: language
List moderated: No.

Editorial contact: John Cowan
Internet: lojban-list-request@snark.thyrsus.com
How to access: Send subscribe message to lojban-list-request@snark.thyrsus.com
How to unsubscribe: Send unsubscribe message to lojban-list-request@snark.thyrsus.com

LORE@NDSUVM1

Description: Lore is a list for discussion of folklore.
Subjects covered: folklore
List moderated: No.
Editorial contact: Pat Carey
Internet: carey@plains.nodak.edu
Bitnet: carey@ndsuvml
How to access: Send subscribe message to listserv@ndsuvml or listserv@vml.nodak.edu
How to unsubscribe: Send unsubscribe message to listserv@ndsuvml or listserv@vml.nodak.edu
Archives: Archives are developed weekly; apply to listowner for details.

LPN-L

Description: LPN-L distributes Laboratory Primate Newsletter.
Subjects covered: zoology; primates
List moderated: Yes.
Editorial contact: Judith Schrier
Bitnet: primate@brownvm
How to access: Send subscribe message to listserv@brownvm or listserv@brownvm.brown.edu
How to unsubscribe: Send unsubscribe message to listserv@brownvm or listserv@brownvm.brown.edu
Archives: Archives are developed monthly; apply to listowner for details.

LS2K

Description: LS2K is a discussion forum of the LS/2000 (library integrated system software) users group.
Subjects covered: library and information science; computer hardware and software
How to access: Send subsciption requests to: LS2K-REQUEST@CC.UTAH.EDU

LSTOWN-L

Description: LSTOWN-L is a conference for VM istserv e-conference listowners.
Subjects covered: Bitnet; electronic networking; Internet
List moderated: No.
Editorial contact: John B. Harlan
Internet: ijbh200@indyvax.iupui.edu
How to access: Send subscribe message to listserv@indycms or listserv@indcms.iupui.edu
How to unsubscribe: Send unsubscribe message to listserv@indycms or listserv@indcms.iupui.edu

LUTE

Description: Lute is a discussion group concerning all aspects of lutes.
Subjects covered: music; musical instruments; lutes

Net address for operations: lute-request@cs.dartmouth.edu
Net address for questions or submissions: lute@cs.dartmouth.edu
Established: September, 1991
Subscribers: 94
Sponsor: Dartmouth College, Hanover N.H. 03755
List moderated: No.
Editorial contact: Wayne Cripps
c/o CS Dept, Bradley Hall, Dartmouth College, Hanover, NH 03755.
Tel: (603) 646-3198
Fax: (603) 646-1312
Internet: wbc@cs.dartmouth.edu
How to access: Send email message to: lute-request@cs.dartmouth.edu
Access policy: Anyone can join. Anything related to lutes, lute playing, lute history, other old stringed instruments.
How to unsubscribe: Send email message to: lute-request@cs.dartmouth.edu
Archives: All communications are available via ftp and gopher from cs.dartmouth.edu
Related files: Lute tablature typesetting software and music available via ftp/gopher from cs.dartmouth.edu
Gopher accessibility: Yes

MAAMAW BLACKBOARD (MODELING AUTONOMOUS AGENTS IN A MULTI-AGENT WORLD)

Description: MAAMAW Blackboard is a list centering on artificial intelligence and related studies.
Subjects covered: artificial intelligence
Net address for questions or submissions: maamaw@lifia.imag.fr
How to access: Send requests to demazeau@lifia.imag.fr
How to submit: Send submissions to maamaw@lifia.imag.fr

MAC-SUPPORTERS

Description: MAC-SUPPORTERS is intended for all Apple Macintosh systems support staff in higher education institutions in the U.K. Most postings request information on system and software problems, availability of software solutions, or provide info on software titles particularly useful to the academic community. The list is complementary to MAC-ADEMIC-UK@mailbase.ac.uk (an open LIST for Apple Macintosh end-users).
Net address for operations: MAILBASE@MAILBASE.AC.UK
Net address for questions or submissions: MAC-SUPPORTERS@MAILBASE.AC.UK
Established: October 1990
Subscribers: 250+
Sponsor: Goldsmiths' College, New Cross, London SE14 6NW, UK.
List moderated: No.
Editorial contact: David Riddle
Goldsmiths' College, Computing Service, New Cross, London SE14 6NW, UK.
Tel: 081 694 2574
Fax: 081 692 5018
Internet: dpr@gold.ac.uk
How to access: To join this list send the command: join listname firstname lastname as the only text of an e-mail mes-

sage to: mailbase@uk.ac.mailbase (Remember to replace firstname and lastname with your first name and last name).
Access policy: Members must have a 'support' role in respect of a nominal 10 Apple Macintosh computer systems at a U.K. academic institution with access to the Internet. Members may be either departmental or computing service based.
How to unsubscribe: To leave this list send the command: leave listname firstname lastname as the only text of an e-mail message to: mailbase@uk.ac.mailbase (Remember to replace firstname and lastname with your first name and last name).
How to submit: Must be a registered subscriber to the LIST.
Submission policy: Attempts by non-members to submit to the LIST are rejected.
Archives: Automatic archive and archive deletion (about a year of messages kept in store).
Related files: Yes. A limited number of HyperCard stacks, shareware utilities and summaries of responses to questions, are available.

MACPROG@WUVMD.WUSTL.EDU
Description: MACPROG@WUVMD is a discussion list on programming languages.
Subjects covered: computer science; computer hardware and software
List moderated: No.
Editorial contact: Bill Brandt
Internet: wbrandt@cms.cc.wayne.edu
Bitnet: wbrandt@waynest1
How to access: Send subscribe message to listserv@wuvmd or listserv@wuvmd.wustl.edu
How to unsubscribe: Send unsubscribe message to listserv@wuvmd or listserv@wuvmd.wustl.edu

MACPSYCH
Description: MacPsych covers discussion of how to use the Macintosh computer in teaching and research in academic psychology.
Subjects covered: psychology; computer hardware and software
Net address for operations: macpsych-request@stolaf.edu
Net address for questions or submissions: macpsych-request@stolaf.edu
Established: December 1990
Subscribers: 405
Sponsor: SCiP sponsors the list, BRMIC sponsors the archive. For information on SCiP, contact: Doug Eamon, Society for Computers in Psychology, University of Wisconsin at Whitewater, Whitewater, WI 53190; EAMOND@UWWVAX.UWW.EDU. Behavior Research Methods, Instruments, & Computers, A Journal of the Psychonomic Society, Psychonomic Society Publications, 1710 Fortview Road, Austin, TX 78704.
Host: St. Olaf College, 1420 St. Olaf Avenue, Northfield, MN 55057.
List moderated: Yes.
Moderation procedure: Members send contributions to macpsych@stolaf.edu and moderator screens them for relevance to psychology and the use of macintosh computers. They are then sent to the list.
Editorial contact: Chuck Huff
Psychology Department
Tel: (507) 646-3625
Fax: (507) 646-3549

Internet: huff@stolaf.edu
Review: Reviews have appeared in: Huff, C. W., & Sobiloff, B. (1993). MacPsych: A Discussion List and Archive for Psychology on the Macintosh. Behavior Research Methods, Instruments, and Computers, 25(1), 60-64; Huff, C. W. (1992). Psychology: Keeping up with the state of the art in computing. Social Science Computer Review, 10(4), 523-530.
How to access: Send a message to macpsych-request@stolaf.edu
How to unsubscribe: Send a message to macpsych-request@stolaf.edu
How to submit: Send a message to macpsych@stolaf.edu
Submission policy: Send a message to macpsych@stolaf.edu
Archives: Software and documents written by list members or made available by other interested parties. Some have been described in the journal ''Behavior Research Methods, Instruments, & Computers,'' a methdological journal of the Psychonomic Society. Anonymous ftp to ftp.stolaf.edu in the directory pub/macpsych
Gopher accessibility: Gopher and WAIS accessible both for software archive and list comments.

MAGAZINE@RPITSVM
Description: MAGAZINE@RPITSVM is a forum for discussing topics related magazine editing and publishing.
Subjects covered: journalism
Host: Comserve
List moderated: Yes.
Editorial contact: Comserve Staff
Internet: support@vm.its.vpi.edu
Bitnet: support@rpitsvm
How to access: Send subscribe message to comserve@rpitsvm or comserve@vm.its.vpi.edu
How to unsubscribe: Send subscribe message to comserve@rpitsvm or comserve@vm.its.vpi.edu

MAIL-BBONES@YORKU.CA
Description: MAIL-BBONES is a forum on the construction of enterprise-wide e-mail backbones.
Subjects covered: electronic networking; campus-wide information systems
List moderated: No.
Internet: MAIL-BBONES-REQUEST@YORKU.CA
How to access: Contact the Editor
How to unsubscribe: Contact the Editor

MAIL-MEN
Description: MAIL-MEN is a discussion group focusing on men's issues and gender studies.
Subjects covered: gender studies; feminism; women's studies; men's studies
Net address for operations: MAIL-MEN-REQUEST@ATTUNIX.ATT.COM
List moderated: No.
How to access: Send subscription requests to MAIL-MEN-REQUEST@ATTUNIX.ATT.COM (Internet).

MAILJC NETWORK
Description: MailJC Network is an electronic non-hostile environment for discussion among christians. Non-christians may

join the list and "listen-in," but full blown debates between Christians and non-Christians are best carried out in soc.religion.christian or talk.religion newsgroups (those are Usenet groups).
Subjects covered: religion; Christianity
Net address for operations: mailjc-request@cps.altadena.ca.us
Net address for questions or submissions: mailjc@cps.altadena.ca.us
Established: 1984
Subscribers: 550
Sponsor: College Park Software, 461 W. Loma Alta Dr., Altadena, CA 91001-3841; 818-791-9153.
List moderated: Yes.
Moderation procedure: Moderator collects submissions and re-mails appropriate ones to list in digest form. New authors submit introductions first.
Editorial contact: Liz Allen
College Park Software, 461 W. Loma Alta Dr., Altadena, CA 91001-3841.
Tel: 818-791-9153
Fax: 818-791-1755
Internet: liz@cps.altadena.ca.us
How to access: Email to mailjc-request@cps.altadena.ca.us
How to unsubscribe: Email to mailjc-request@cps.altadena.ca.us
How to submit: Email to mailjc@cps.altadena.ca.us To submit
Submission policy: Policy issues are handled via informal discussion with moderator with occasional requests for feedback in the digest itself.
Archives: Archives are available; contact listowner for details.

MAPS-L
Description: MAPS-L is a discussion and information list for map librarians, cartographers, geographers, map producers, map sellers, and all who are interested in cartographic information (where cartographic information is seen is its widest sense--spatial data of all types). The list is heavily academic and map librarian oriented, but with many subscribers from areas such as federal and state agencies and others interested in spatial data. The list runs around 10 messages a day.
Subjects covered: cartography; geography; geographic information systems; library and information science
Net address for operations: Listserv@uga Network
Net address for questions or submissions: Maps-l@uga
Subscribers: 582
Sponsor: University of Georgia Libraries
Athens, GA 30602
Host: University of Georgia
Athens, GA 30602
List moderated: Yes.
Moderation procedure: All mail sent to the list is forwarded to the Moderator by the listserv. The Moderator looks at the messages and edits as needed before sending messages back to the listserv for forwarding to all subscribers of the list. The list moderator tries to keep the list on subject and tries to reroute traffic where needed. Rejected mail is sent back to the sender with reasons and suggestions for reasonable changes.
Editorial contact: John Sutherland
Map Collection, Science Library, University of Georgia Libraries, Athens, GA 30602
Tel: (706) 542-0690
Fax: (706) 542-6523
Internet: JSUTHERL@UGA.CC.UGA.EDU

Bitnet: JSUTHERL@UGA
Technical contact: Jean Snow
Computer Center, University of Georgia, Athens, GA 30605
Internet: JEAN@UGA.CC.UGA.EDU
Bitnet: JEAN@UGA
Copyright statement: No copyright statement. General rules include: 1. Ask permission before citing; 2. Quote the source (the author of the message and the name of the list: Maps-L; 3. Individual message author retains the right to not allow reproduction; 4. Maps-L retains the rights to all traffic through the list but allows the reproduction of the traffic for noncommercial, fair use reproduction. 5. The list is an attempt to provide a means of cartographic information flow between the subscribers.
How to access: Send a message to: LISTSERV@UGA
Access policy: Open to all subscribers who are interested in cartographic information. The moderator reserves the right to decide what is outside the topic and the right to limit messages and subscribers who do not adhere to the topic.
How to unsubscribe: Send a message to: LISTSERV@UGA
Say in the message: UNSUBSCRIBE MAPS-L
How to submit: Send the message to: MAPS-L@UGA
Submission policy: We would prefer that you put the subject of the message in the subject header line. Messages should be on the topic of the list, cartographic information. Do not use the list to send messages to one person, rather send the message direct to that person. If the moderator has a problem with sending a message out over MAPS-L, the message will be sent to the sender so the problem can be discussed and fixed. The moderator may edit messages into a digest message when there are several messages on the same topic. The moderator will not serve as a censor but rather as a moderator to keep the list on track.
Archives: The list messages are archived by the listserv@uga.
Related files: Currently there are no files, other documents, or a FAQ (Frequently Asked Questions list) available. Some may be available in the future.
Gopher accessibility: Not as established by the moderator.

MARINE-L
Description: Marine-L is a forum of marine-related studies.
Subjects covered: marine biology; aquaculture
List moderated: No.
Editorial contact: Ted White
Internet: zoowhite@vm.uoguelph.ca
Bitnet: zoowhite@uoguelph
How to access: Send subscribe message to listserv@uoguelph or listserv@vm.uoguelph.ca
How to unsubscribe: Send unsubscribe message to listserv@uoguelph or listserv@vm.uoguelph.ca
Archives: Archives are developed monthly; apply to listowner for details.

MARINE-TECH@MAILBASE.AC.UK
Description: MARINE-TECH@MAILBASE.AC.UK is a discussion forum on marine technology.
Subjects covered: marine biology
List moderated: No.
Internet: marine-tech-request@mailbase.ac.uk
How to access: Send subscribe message to mailbase@mailbase.ac.uk in the following format: join marine-tech Yourfirstname Yourlastname

Archives: Archives are developed monthly; apply to listowner for details.

MARK TWAIN FORUM
Description: The Mark Twain Forum is an electronic discussion group for persons having a scholarly interest in the life and writings of Mark Twain. Postings may include queries, discussion, conference announcements, calls for papers, information on new publications, or anything else that is related to Mark Twain studies.
Subjects covered: Twain, Mark (Samuel Clemens); American literature and language; Clemens, Samuel (Mark Twain)
Net address for operations: LISTSERV@VM1.YORKU.CA or LISTSERV@YORKVM1.BITNET
Net address for questions or submissions: TWAIN-L@VM1.YORKU.CA or TWAIN-L@YORKVM1.BITNET
Established: March 1992
Subscribers: 131
Sponsor: York University, North York, Ontario, Canada M3J 1P3.
List moderated: No.
Editorial contact: Taylor Roberts
Linguistics Department C369 - 1866 Main Mall, University of British Columbia, Vancouver, B.C., Canada V6T 1W5
Internet: ROBERTST@UNIXG.UBC.CA
How to access: Send the command "SUBSCRIBE TWAIN-L your-full-name" to either <LISTSERV@VM1.YORKU.CA> or <LISTSERV@YORKVM1.BITNET>. For example: SUBSCRIBE TWAIN-L Mulberry Sellers. Listserv will send you a confirmation of your subscription, and you'll begin receiving postings immediately, i.e., whenever another subscriber posts a message to the Forum.
How to unsubscribe: Send the command "SIGNOFF TWAIN-L" to either <LISTSERV@VM1.YORKU.CA> or <LISTSERV@YORKVM1.BITNET>.
How to submit: Send your posting to either <TWAIN-L@VM1.YORKU.CA> or <TWAIN-L@YORKVM1.BITNET>. It will automatically be redistributed to the other subscribers. You will receive a copy of your own posting as confirmation that it was successfully distributed.
Archives: Every message posted to TWAIN-L is automatically stored in a log file on LISTSERV. A new file begins every month. To get an index of the files available, send the command "INDEX TWAIN-L" to either <LISTSERV@VM1.YORKU.CA> or <LISTSERV@YORKVM1.BITNET>. LISTSERV will send you an index of the filenames and their start dates. The filenames take the form "TWAIN-L LOG9207", where "92" represents the year, and "07" represents the month, i.e., July. To retrieve this file, you would issue the command "GET TWAIN-L LOG9207". The file that is sent contains all the messages that were posted to the Mark Twain Forum in July 1992.
Related files: In addition to the monthly log files, the TWAIN-L FILELIST has a few other items that may be retrieved individually. To see the list of items, send the command "INDEX TWAIN-L" to either <LISTSERV@VM1.YORKU.CA> or <LISTSERV@YORKVM1.BITNET>. LISTSERV will send you an index of the filenames. To retrieve individual files, use the syntax "GET FILENAME FILETYPE". For example, to get the file about the Mark Twain Project, send the command "GET MTP INFO". As public domain electronic texts of

Twain's writings become available, these will be placed on the Forum filelist.

MARKET-L
Description: Market-L is a forum for marketing teachers.
Subjects covered: business
List moderated: No.
Editorial contact: Charles Hofacker
Internet: chofack@acvm.cc.fsu.edu
How to access: Send subscribe message to listserv@ucf1vm
How to unsubscribe: Send unsubscribe message to listserv@ucf1vm
Archives: Archives are developed monthly; apply to listowner for details.

MASONIC@ASGARD.BBN.COM
Description: MASONIC@ASGARD.BBN.COM is a forum discussing freemasonry.
Subjects covered: philosophy; freemasonry
List moderated: Yes.
Editorial contact: Peter Trei
Internet: ptrei@asgard.bbn.com
How to access: Send subscribe message to PTREI@ASGARD.BBN.COM
How to unsubscribe: Send unsubscribe message to PTREI@ASGARD.BBN.COM

MASSCOMM
Description: MassComm is a discussion list in the Comserve group dealing with mass communications.
Subjects covered: communications; sociology
Net address for operations: COMSERVE@RPIECS
Subscribers: 320+
Editorial contact: Timothy Stephen
Bitnet: STEPHEN@RPIECS
Review: Reviewed by List Review Service edited by Raleigh Muns: see appendix.
How to access: Send an email message with a blank subject line to COMSERVE@RPIECS or COMSERVE@RPIECS.VM.ECS.RPI.EDU. The message should consist solely of the line: JOIN MASSCOMM your_name.

MAT-DSGN@JPNTOHOK
Description: MAT-DSGN@JPNTOHOK is a conference on computer-based materials design.
Subjects covered: chemistry
List moderated: No.
How to access: Send subscribe message to listserv@jpntohok
How to unsubscribe: Send unsubscribe message to listserv@jpntohok

MATERI-L
Description: Materi-L is a forum for material science in Israel.
Subjects covered: chemistry
List moderated: Yes.
Editorial contact: Dr. M. Wolff
Bitnet: wolff@ilncrd

How to access: Send subscribe message to listserv@taunivm or listserv@taunivm.tau.ac.il
How to unsubscribe: Send unsubscribe message to listserv@taunivm or listserv@taunivm.tau.ac.il

MATH-L

Description: Math-L is a list dealing with mathematical documents.
Subjects covered: mathematics
List moderated: No.
How to access: Send subscribe message to listserv@yalevm or listserv@yalevm.ycc.yale.edu
How to unsubscribe: Send unsubscribe message to listserv@yalevm or listserv@yalevm.ycc.yale.edu

MBA-L

Description: MBA-L is a forum with news and information on MBA programs.
Subjects covered: education; business
List moderated: No.
Editorial contact: A. Harry Williams
Bitnet: harry@marist
How to access: Send subscribe message to listserv@marist or listserv@marstvm.marist.edu
How to unsubscribe: Send unsubscribe message to listserv@marist or listserv@marstvm.marist.edu
Archives: Archives are developed monthly; apply to listowner for details.

MBU-L

Description: Mbu-L is a discussion of computers and writing.
Subjects covered: writing; computer science
List moderated: No.
Editorial contact: Fred Kemp
Internet: ykfok@ttacs1.ttu.edu
Bitnet: ykfok@ttacs
How to access: Send subscribe message to listserv@ttuvm1 or listserv@ttuvm1.ttu.edu
How to unsubscribe: Send unsubscribe message to listserv@ttuvm1 or listserv@ttuvm1.ttu.edu

MCLR-L

Description: Mclr-L is a forum for discussion of issues and research topics on Latinos.
Subjects covered: Latin America
List moderated: Yes.
Editorial contact: Ramiro Gonzales
Bitnet: ramirog@msu
How to access: Send subscribe message to listserv@msu or listserv%msu.bitnet@vm1.nodak.edu
How to unsubscribe: Send unsubscribe message to listserv@msu or listserv%msu.bitnet@vm1.nodak.edu
Archives: Archives are developed monthly; apply to listowner for details.

MCRIT-L

Description: Mcrit-L is a conference with a multi-criteria format.

Subjects covered: general interest
List moderated: No.
Bitnet: mcrit@hroeuri
How to access: Send subscribe message to listserv@hearn
How to unsubscribe: Send unsubscribe message to listserv@hearn

MECH-L

Description: Mech-L offers discussion on topics related to mechanical engineering, including structure mechanics, composite materials, heat transfer, computer application, fluid mechanics, finite element method, etc.
Subjects covered: mechanical engineering; engineering
Net address for questions or submissions: Mech-L@UTARLVM1.bitnet
Established: 1988
Subscribers: 200
Sponsor: University of Texas at Arlington, Box 19023, Arlington, TX 76019-0023
Host: University of Texas at Arlington, Box 19023, Arlington, TX 76019-0023
Editorial contact: Seiichi Nomura
Box 19023, Arlington, Texas 76019-0023
Tel: (817) 273-2012
Fax: (817) 273-2952
Internet: nomura@zen.uta.edu
Bitnet: b460nom@utarlg
How to access: Send mail to LISTSERV@UTARLVM1 (or listserv@utarlvm1.uta.edu) with one line message as SUB MECH-L FIRST__LASTNAME
How to unsubscribe: Send mail to LISTSERV@UTARLVM1 (or listserv@utarlvm1.uta.edu) with one line message as SINGOFF MECH-L
How to submit: Send mail to MECH-L@UTARLVM1 (or mech-l@utarlvm1.uta.edu)
Archives: Past messages are archived monthly.
Related files: Some of software discussed on the list (i.e. mechanical engineering related software) can be retrieved via anonymous ftp from me.uta.edu under /pub/science

MED-AND-REN-MUSIC

Description: med-and-ren-music carries research questions and conference, library, and other useful information for bona fide researchers into any aspect of medieval or renaissance music.
Subjects covered: music; fine arts; Medieval studies; Renaissance studies
Net address for operations: mailbase@mailbase.ac.uk
Net address for questions or submissions: med-and-ren-music@mailbase.ac.uk
Established: December 1992
Subscribers: 155
Sponsor: JNT Networked Information Services Project, Computing Service, The University, Newcastle upon Tyne NE1 7RU, UK.
Host: Dept. of Music, The University, Newcastle upon Tyne NE1 7RU, UK.
List moderated: No.
Editorial contact: Dr Isobel Preece
Dept. of Music, The University, Newcastle upon Tyne NE1 7RU, UK.
Tel: +44-91-222-6752
Fax: +44-91-261-1182

Internet: Isobel.Preece@newcastle.ac.uk
Technical contact: JNT Networked Information Services Project Computing Service, The University, Newcastle upon Tyne NE1 7RU, UK.
Tel: +44-91-222-8080
Fax: +44-91-222-8765
Internet: mailbase-helpline@mailbase.ac.uk
How to access: Send a message to mailbase@mailbase.ac.uk consisting only of the command: join med-and-ren-music firstname lastname replacing 'firstname, lastname' with your own first name and last name (no middle initials)
Access policy: Anyone with an e-mail address reachable by mailbase may join.
How to unsubscribe: Send a message to mailbase@mailbase.ac.uk consisting only of the command: leave med-and-ren-music
How to submit: Mail submissions to med-and-ren-music@mailbase.ac.uk
Submission policy: Only questions and information useful to bona fide researchers into any aspect of medieval and renaissance music. This list is a research tool, not a chat line.
Archives: Archives are available by on-line service, ftp, and gopher.
Related files: Related files are accessible by on-line service, ftp, and gopher.

MEDCONS@FINHUTC

Description: MEDCONS@FINHUTC is a conference on medical consulting issues.
Subjects covered: medicine
List moderated: Yes.
Editorial contact: Dr. Mikael Peder
Internet: peder@finuh
How to access: Send subscribe message to listserv@finhutc or listserv%finhutc.bitnet@vm1.nodak.edu
How to unsubscribe: Send unsubscribe message to listserv@finhutc or listserv%finhutc.bitnet@vm1.nodak.edu
Archives: Archives are developed monthly; apply to listowner for details.

MEDEVLIT MEDIEVAL ENGLISH LITERATURE DISCUSSION LIST

Description: MEDEVLIT is an electronic mailing list carrying informal discussion on Medieval English Literature and related topics.
Subjects covered: English language and literature; Medieval studies; language and literature
Net address for operations: LISTSERV@siucvmb.siu.edu
Net address for questions or submissions: MEDEVLIT@siucvmb.siu.edu
Established: October 1992
Subscribers: 152
Sponsor: Dept. of English, Southern Illinois University at Carbondale, Carbondale, IL 62901.
List moderated: No.
Editorial contact: Jefferey H. Taylor
R 2 Box 596, Makanda, IL 62958.
Tel: 618/ 529-5026
Internet: gr4302@siucvmb.siu.edu
Bitnet: GR4302@SIUCVMB

How to access: Send to listserv the message: sub MEDEVLIT full name
Access policy: Subscriptions are open to everybody.
How to unsubscribe: Send to listserv the message: unsub MEDEVLIT
How to submit: Send submissions to MEDEVLIT@siucvmb.siu.edu
Submission policy: There is open submission, but please stay on related topics.
Archives: Log files are available through LISTSERV@siucvmb.siu.edu

MEDFEM-L

Description: MEDFEM-L is a list for feminist medievalists. It deals with "any aspect of medieval studies that touches on...feminist studies, women's studies, and gay and lesbian studies."
Subjects covered: Medieval studies; feminism; women's studies; gay and lesbian topics
Net address for operations: LISTSERV@INDYCMS, LISTSERV@INDYCMS.IUPUI.EDU
List moderated: Yes.
How to access: Send subscription messages to LISTSERV@INDYCMS (Bitnet) or LISTSERV@INDYCMS.IUPUI.EDU (Internet).

MEDIA-L

Description: Media-L focuses on the use of media in education.
Subjects covered: education
List moderated: No.
Editorial contact: Jeff Donahue
Bitnet: jdonahue@bingvaxc
How to access: Send subscribe message to listserv@bingvm or listserv%bingvm.bitnet@cunyvm.cuny.edu
How to unsubscribe: Send unsubscribe message to listserv@bingvm or listserv%bingvm.bitnet@cunyvm.cuny.edu

MEDIEV-L

Description: Mediev-L is an electronic conference discussing the Middle Ages.
Subjects covered: history; Medieval era
Host: International History Network
List moderated: Yes.
Editorial contact: Jeff Gardner
Internet: jgardner@ukanvm.ukans.edu
Bitnet: jgardner@ukanvm
How to access: Send subscribe message to listserv@ukanvm or listserv@ukanvm.cc.ukans.edu
How to unsubscribe: Send unsubscribe message to listserv@ukanvm or listserv@ukanvm.cc.ukans.edu
Archives: Yes; Monthly, Send anonymous FTP to: kuhub.cc.ukans.edu and cd MALIN

MEDIMAGE@POLYGRAF

Description: MEDIMAGE@POLYGRAF is a conference on medical imaging technology.
Subjects covered: science and technology; medicine
List moderated: No.
Editorial contact: Michael Smith
Bitnet: mnsmith@umaecs

How to access: Send subscribe message to listserv@polygraf or listserv%polygraf.bitnet@mitvma.mit.edu
How to unsubscribe: Send unsubscribe message to listserv@polygraf or listserv%polygraf.bitnet@mitvma.mit.edu

MEDINF-L

Description: Medinf-L is a conference covering medical informatics.
Subjects covered: medicine
List moderated: Yes.
Editorial contact: Prof. Dr. Claus O. Koehler
Internet: dok205@saver.inet.dkfz-heidelberg.de
How to access: Send subscribe message to listserv@dearn
How to unsubscribe: Send unsubscribe message to listserv@dearn

MEDLIB-L

Description: Medlib-L discusses issues related to medical and health sciences libraries.
Subjects covered: library and information science; medicine; health sciences
Host: Medical School Libraries Section, Medical Library Association
List moderated: No.
Editorial contact: Nancy Start
Internet: hslstart@ubvm.cc.buffalo.edu
Bitnet: hslstart@ubvm
How to access: Send subscribe message to listserv@ubvm or listserv@ubvm.cc.buffalo.edu
How to unsubscribe: Send unsubscribe message to listserv@ubvm or listserv@ubvm.cc.buffalo.edu
Archives: Archives are developed monthly; apply to listowner for details.

MEDNETS@NDSUVM1

Description: MEDNETS@NDSUVM1 is a forum on medical information networks.
Subjects covered: telecommunications; medicine
List moderated: No.
Editorial contact: Marty Hoag
Internet: nu021172@vm1.nodak.edu
Bitnet: nu021172@ndsuvm1
How to access: Send subscribe message to listserv@ndsuvm1 or listserv@vm1.nodak.edu
How to unsubscribe: Send unsubscribe message to listserv@ndsuvm1 or listserv@vm1.nodak.edu
Archives: Archives are developed weekly; apply to listowner for details.

MEDPHYS@RADONC.DUKE.EDU

Description: MEDPHYS@RADONC.DUKE.EDU is a forum on use of radiation in medicine.
Subjects covered: medicine
List moderated: No.
Internet: medphys-request@radonc.duke.edu
How to access: Contact the Editor
How to unsubscribe: Contact the Editor

MEDSCI-L

Description: MedSci-L is a discussion list covering medieval and Renaissance science.
Subjects covered: Medieval studies; science and technology; history of science; Renaissance studies
Net address for operations: Listserv@brownvm
Net address for questions or submissions: MedSci-L@brownvm
How to access: Send message to listserv: SUBSCRIBE <listname> <your name>

MEDSTAT

Description: MEDSTAT is a broadcast system for the UK statistical community. The list is operated by the "Computers In Teaching Initiative" Centre for Statistics, although the broadcasts need not be concerned with teaching.
Subjects covered: statistics; medicine; education; mathematics
Net address for operations: mailbase@mailbase.ac.uk
Net address for questions or submissions: medstat@mailbase.ac.uk
Established: 1988
Subscribers: 351
Sponsor: Joint Information Systems Committee of the UK Higher Education Funding Councils.
Host: University of Newcastle Upon Tyne, UK.
List moderated: No.
Editorial contact: Stuart G. Young
Dept of Statistics, Mathematics Building, University of Glasgow, GLASGOW G12 8QQ Scotland.
Tel: 041-339-8855, ext. 4386
Fax: 041-330-4814
Internet: stuart@stats.gla.ac.uk
How to access: Send message to mailbase@mailbase.ac.uk containing the single line join medstat <firstname> <lastname> where <firstname> and <lastname> should be replaced with your first and last names
How to unsubscribe: Send message to mailbase@mailbase.ac.uk containing the single line leave medstat
How to submit: Send your message to medstat@mailbase.ac.uk
Archives: Message archive files are stored as MM-YYYY where MM is the month number and YYYY is the year number. These can be retrieved by anonymous ftp or by sending a message to mailbase@mailbase.ac.uk containing the line send medstat <filename> where <filename> should be replaced by the name of the file required.
Gopher accessibility: Mailbase can be accessed by gopher.

MEDSTU-L

Description: Medstu-L is a forum for medical students.
Subjects covered: medicine; education
Host: University of New Mexico
List moderated: No.
Editorial contact: Art St. George
Internet: stgeorge@bootes.unm.edu
Bitnet: stgeorge@unmb
How to access: Send subscribe message to listserv@unmvm or listserv@unmvm.edu
How to unsubscribe: Send unsubscribe message to listserv@unmvm or listserv@unmvm.edu
Archives: Archives are developed monthly (for current month only); apply to listowner for details.

MEDTEXTL@UIUCVMD

Description: MEDTEXTL@UIUCVMD is a discussion on the linguistic analysis of medieval texts.
Subjects covered: linguistics; philology; Medieval studies
List moderated: No.
Editorial contact: James Marchand
Internet: marchand@ux1.cso.uiuc.edu
How to access: Send subscribe message to listserv@uiucvmd or listserv@vmd.cso.uiuc.edu
How to unsubscribe: Send unsubscribe message to listserv@uiucvmd or listserv@vmd.cso.uiuc.edu
Archives: Archives are developed monthly; apply to listowner for details.

MEGABYTE UNIVERSITY

Description: Megabyte University is a discussion list centering on computers and writing issues, with emphasis concerning theory, pedagogy, and administration of computer-based writing instruction.
Subjects covered: pedagogy; computer-assisted instruction (CAI)
Net address for operations: listserv@ttuvm1
Net address for questions or submissions: MBU-L@TTUVM1
Established: Summer of 1989
Subscribers: 308
Sponsor: Texas Tech University, Lubbock, TX 79409
List moderated: No.
Editorial contact: Fred Kemp
Department of English, Texas Tech University, Lubbock, TX 79409-3091
Tel: 806-742-2501
Fax: 806-742-0989
Internet: ykfok@ttacs1.ttu.edu
Bitnet: ykfok@ttacs
Technical contact: John Halbert
University Computing Facility, 9 Computer Center, Texas Tech University, Lubbock, TX 79409-3051
Tel: (806) 742-3619
Internet: SNAHAL@TTUVM1.TTU.EDU
Bitnet: SNHAL@TTUVM1.TTU.EDU
How to access: Send the email message: subscribe mbu-l yourfirstname yourlastname to listserv@ttuvm1
Access policy: MBU-L accepts all subscribers interested in computers and writing and willing to maintain reasonable network decorum. Subscription is open and all submissions are accepted.
How to unsubscribe: Send the email message: signoff mbu-l to listserv@ttuvm1
How to submit: Send e-mail to mbu-l@ttuvm1
Submission policy: All e-mail is accepted automatically.

MELLON-L

Description: Mellon-L is a list for Mellon Fellowship holders and other interested parties. Topics of conversation include upcoming Mellon gatherings, teaching in the humanities, graduate student life, and conferences in the humanities. Mellon-L is a very low-volume list.
Subjects covered: conferences and conference listings; Mellon Fellowship; humanities
Net address for operations: listserv@vm1.yorku.ca
Net address for questions or submissions: mellon-l@vm1.yorku.ca or mellon-l@yorkvm1.bitnet

Established: 1990
Subscribers: 172
Sponsor: Andrew W. Mellon Foundation, Princeton NJ
Host: York University, Toronto, Canada
List moderated: No.
Editorial contact: Robert Stainton
Linguistics & Philosophy M.I.T. -- Room 20D-213 Cambridge, MA 02139
Tel: (617) 776-4512 (home) (617) 253-2690 (office)
Fax: (617) 253-8000
Internet: stainton@athena.mit.edu or GL250264@orion.yorku.ca
How to access: Send a message to listserv@vm1.yorku.ca or listserv@yorkvm1.bitnet containing the following line -- sub mellon-l <yourfullname>
How to unsubscribe: Send a message to the above address saying -- unsub mellon-l
How to submit: Send your message to mellon-l@vm1.yorku.ca or mellon-l@yorkvm1.bitnet

MENDELE

Description: Mendele is a list featuring discussion of Yiddish and Yiddish-related topics.
Subjects covered: Yiddish language and literature
Net address for operations: mendele@yalevm.ycc.yale.edu
Established: May 15, 1991
Subscribers: 260
Sponsor: Trinity College, Yale University
Host: Trinity College, Yale University
List moderated: Yes.
Moderation procedure: Posts are saved and edited. Each issue comprises about 5000 bytes.
Editorial contact: Noyekh Miller
53 Lawton St., Brookline, MA 02146
Tel: (617) 566-6208
Internet: nmiller@dot.trincoll.edu
How to access: Send message to nmiller@dot.trincoll.edu
Archives: ftp.pub.mendele cd /files

MERSENNE@MAILBASE.AC.UK

Description: MERSENNE is a mailbase discussion forum in science, technology, and medicine.
Subjects covered: science and technology; medicine
List moderated: No.
Internet: mersenne-request@mailbase.ac.uk
How to access: Send subscribe message to mailbase@mailbase.ac.uk in the following format: join mersenne Yourfirstname Yourlastname
Archives: Archives are developed monthly; apply to listowner for details.

METHO@UQUEBEC

Description: METHO is a list covering sociology methods.
Subjects covered: sociology
List moderated: Yes.
Editorial contact: Simon Langlois
Bitnet: langlois@lavalvm1
How to access: Send subscribe message to listserv@uquebec
How to unsubscribe: Send unsubscribe message to listserv@uquebec

Archives: Archives are developed monthly; apply to listowner for details.

METHODS@IRLEARN
Description: METHODS@IRLEARN is a forum focusing on research methodology in medicine.
Subjects covered: medicine; health sciences
Host: Comserve
List moderated: Yes.
Editorial contact: Comserve support staff
Bitnet: support@rpitsvm
How to access: Send subscribe message to COMSERVE@RPITSVM
How to unsubscribe: Send unsubscribe message to COMSERVE@RPITSVM

MEXICO-L
Description: Mexico-L is a forum listing information about Mexico.
Subjects covered: Mexico; travel and tourism
List moderated: No.
Editorial contact: Marco A. Pinones
Bitnet: pl1190827@tecmtyvm
How to access: Send subscribe message to listserv@tecmtyvm or listserv@tecmtyvm.mty.itesm.mx
How to unsubscribe: Send unsubscribe message to listserv@tecmtyvm or listserv@tecmtyvm.mty.itesm.mx
Archives: Archives are developed weekly; apply to listowner for details.

MHCARE-L
Description: MHCARE-L is a list centering on discussion of and information about managed health care.
Subjects covered: health sciences; quality management
Net address for operations: listserv@mizzou1.missouri.edu
Net address for questions or submissions: mhcare@mizzou1.missouri.edu
Established: 1993
Subscribers: 50
Sponsor: University of Missouri, Health Services Mgmt
Host: University of Missouri
List moderated: Yes.
Editorial contact: E. Andrew Balas
University of Missouri-Columbia, 324 Clark Hall, Columbia, MO
Tel: (314) 882-8416
Internet: medinfab@mizzou1.missouri.edu
Bitnet: medinfab@mizzou1
How to access: Send the message: sub mhcare-l your name to the listserv.
How to unsubscribe: Send the message: signoff mhcare-l your name to the listserv
How to submit: mhcare-l@mizzou1
Submission policy: medinfab@mizzou1

MHSNEWS@ICS.UCI.EDU
Description: MHSNEWS is a forum for discussing issues related to the implementation of message handling protocols.
Subjects covered: computer science; electronic networking
List moderated: No.

Editorial contact: Tim Kehres
Internet: kehres@tis.llnl.gov
How to access: Send subscribe message to mhsnews-request@ICS.UCI.EDU
How to unsubscribe: Send subscribe message to mhsnews-request@ICS.UCI.EDU

MICRO-EL@TAUNIVM
Description: MICRO-EL is a discussion forum for members of the Israeli microelectronics research community.
Subjects covered: science and technology
List moderated: Yes.
Editorial contact: Joseph van Zwaren
Internet: jo%ilncrd.bitnet@cunyvm.cuny.edu
Bitnet: jo@ilncrd
How to access: Send subscribe message to listserv@taunivm or listserv@taunivm.tau.ac.il
How to unsubscribe: Send unsubscribe message to listserv@taunivm or listserv@taunivm.tau.ac.il

MICRONET@UOGUELPH
Description: MICRONET@UOGUELPH is a forum for the discussion of issues related to fungus.
Subjects covered: agriculture; plant biology
List moderated: Yes.
Editorial contact: Lewis Melville
Internet: botlew@vm.uoguelph.ca
Bitnet: botlew@uoguelph
How to access: Send subscribe message to listserv@uoguelph or listserv@vm.uoguelph.ca
How to unsubscribe: Send unsubscribe message to listserv@uoguelph or listserv@vm.uoguelph.ca
Archives: Archives are developed monthly; apply to listowner for details.

MIDEUR-L
Description: MIDEUR-L is a discussion list focusing on Central European topics.
Subjects covered: Central Europe; political science; current events
Net address for operations: LISTSERV@UBVM, LISTSERV@UBVM.CC.BUFFALO.EDU
How to access: Send standard subscribe request to the listserv.
How to unsubscribe: Send standard unsubscribe request to the listserv.

MILHST-L
Description: MILHST-L is a discussion list covering all aspects of military history
Subjects covered: military history; history
How to access: Send a subscribe message to listserv@UKANVM.bitnet

MILITARY@ATT.ATT.COM
Description: MILITARY is a forum on military technology.
Subjects covered: engineering; science and technology
List moderated: Yes.
Editorial contact: Bill Thacker

Internet: military@att.att.com or military@cbnews.att.com
How to access: Send subscribe message to MILITARY-RE-QUEST@ATT.ATT.COM
How to unsubscribe: Send unsubscribe message to MILI-TARY-REQUEST@ATT.ATT.COM
Archives: Yes; Apply to listowner for details

MILTON-L
Description: Milton-L is a discussion group centering on the life and works of English poet John Milton.
Subjects covered: literary theory and criticism; poetry; Milton, John; English language and literature
Net address for operations: Milton-request@urvax.urich.edu or Milton-request@urvax.bitnet
Net address for questions or submissions: Milton-L@urvax.urich.edu or Milton-L@urvax.bitnet
Established: June 1991
Subscribers: 78
Sponsor: University of Richmond, Richmond, VA 23173.
List moderated: Yes.
Moderation procedure: Posts are combined into one issue per day and cleaned up if necessary.
Editorial contact: Kevin J.T. Creamer
Office of the Registrar
Tel: (804) 289-8399
Internet: Creamer@urvax.urich.edu
Bitnet: Creamer@urvax.bitnet
Technical contact: John Lundin
Regional Data Center
Tel: (804) 289-8779
Internet: Lundin@urvax.urich.edu
Bitnet: Creamer@urvax.bitnet
How to access: Send your request to Milton-request@urvax.urich.edu or Milton-request@urvax.bitnet. Milton-L is not maintained by a LISTSERV.
Access policy: To better facilitate discussion on the list, subscribers to Milton-L are asked to fill in a brief biography form. Members are subscribed to the list upon reciept of the biography.
How to unsubscribe: Send your request to Milton-request@urvax.urich.edu or Milton-request@urvax.bitnet
How to submit: Send email to Milton-L@urvax.urich.edu or Milton-L@urvax.bitnet
Submission policy: All letters are welcome.
Archives: Archives are maintained at the University of Richmond and will be sent upon request. Archives are also available via anonymous FTP.
Related files: Milton-L archives, biographies and the Project Gutenberg version of Paradise Lost (the original 10 book version) are available via anonymous FTP to urvax.urich.edu. Files are kept in the ANONYMOUS.MILTON directory.
Additional information: We welcome all Milton enthusiasts and students. Current list membership ranges from high school students to Milton scholars from around the world.

MINISTRY-L
Description: Ministry-L is a forum for discussion of the religious ministry.
Subjects covered: religion
List moderated: No.
Editorial contact: Charles Piehl
Bitnet: underhill@gacvax1

How to access: Send subscribe message to listserv@gacvax1
How to unsubscribe: Send unsubscribe message to listserv@gacvax1

MISC
Description: MISC is a discussion list covering various questions and requests, including private requests.
Subjects covered: general interest
Net address for operations: LISTSERV@TREARN.BITNET
Net address for questions or submissions: MISC@TREARN.BITNET
Established: 1992
Subscribers: 127
Sponsor: Ege Univ. Bilgisayar Ar. ve Uyg. Mrk.35100 Bo
Host: Same as above
List moderated: No.
Editorial contact: Esra Delen
Ege Univ. Bilgisayar Ar. ve Uyg. Mrk. 35100 Bornova Izmir Turkey
Tel: 90-51-887221
Fax: 90-51-887230
Internet: ESRA@EGE.EDU.TR
Bitnet: ESRA@TREARN
How to access: Tell listserv at TREARN SUB MISC fullname
How to unsubscribe: Tell listserv at TREARN SIGNOFF MISC
How to submit: By mailing to MISC@TREARN
Archives: Available via LOG files on LISTSERV

MISG-L
Description: Misg-L is forum mostly in the Malayan language on Islamic Studies.
Subjects covered: Islamic studies
List moderated: No.
Editorial contact: Azmi Hashim
Internet: axh113@psuvm.psu.edu
Bitnet: axh113@psuvm
How to access: Send subscribe message to ahx113@psuvm, mmz103@psuvm, ahx113@psuvm.psu.edu or mmz103@psuvm.psu.edu
How to unsubscribe: Send unsubscribe message to ahx113@psuvm, mmz103@psuvm, ahx113@psuvm.psu.edu or mmz103@psuvm.psu.edu
Archives: Archives are developed monthly; apply to listowner for details.

MLA-L
Description: MLA-L is the Music Library Association discussion list.
Subjects covered: library and information science; music
Host: Music Library Association
List moderated: No.
Editorial contact: Richard Griscom
Internet: rwgris01@ulkyvm.louisville.edu
Bitnet: rwgris01@ulkyvm
How to access: Send subscribe message to listserv@iubvm or listserv@iubvm.ucs.indiana.edu
How to unsubscribe: Send unsubscribe message to listserv@iubvm or listserv@iubvm.ucs.indiana.edu
Archives: Archives are developed monthly; apply to listowner for details.

MLHST-L

Description: Mlhst-L is a forum focusing on military history.
Subjects covered: history; military history
List moderated: No.
Editorial contact: Patrick Hughes
Internet: jphughes@ukanvm.cc.ukans.edu
Bitnet: jphughes@ukanvm
How to access: Send subscribe message to listserv@ukanvm or listserv@ukanvm.cc.ukans.edu
How to unsubscribe: Send unsubscribe message to listserv@ukanvm or listserv@ukanvm.cc.ukans.edu

MMEDIA-L

Description: Mmedia-L focuses on the use of multimedia technologies in education and training.
Subjects covered: education; multimedia computing; multimedia; education
List moderated: No.
Editorial contact: Alejandro S. Kurczyn
Bitnet: 499229@vmtecmex
How to access: Send subscribe message to listserv@vmtecmex
How to unsubscribe: Send unsubscribe message to listserv@vmtecmex
Archives: Archives are developed monthly; apply to listowner for details.

MODBRITS NETWORK

Description: ModBrits is an electronic mailing list covering modern British and Irish literature (1895-1955), with the conversation focusing on teaching and research, announcements, bulletins, notes, queries, and scholarly papers.
Subjects covered: English language and literature; Irish language and literature; literary theory and criticism
Net address for operations: LISTSERV@KENTVM.Kent.Edu
Net address for questions or submissions: ModBrits@KentVM.KENT.EDU
Established: January 1992
Subscribers: 150
Sponsor: Center for Conrad Studies, Institute for Bibliography & Editing, Kent State Univ., Kent, Ohio 44242.
Host: Kent State University, Kent, Ohio 44242.
List moderated: Yes.
Moderation procedure: Moderated by an editorial team (faculty of the English Department) that organizes messages by subject matter and packages them for the members' convenience.
Editorial contact: S. W. Reid
Center for Conrad Studies, Institute for Bibliography & Editing, Kent State Univ., Kent, Ohio 44242.
Tel: 216-672-2603
Internet: ModBreds@KentVM.KENT.EDU
Bitnet: ModBreds@KentVM
Technical contact: Christine Shih
Computer Services, Kent State Univ., Kent, Ohio 44242.
Internet: SHIH@KentVM.KENT.EDU
Bitnet: SHIH@KentVM
How to access: Send the message sub ModBrits [your name] to LISTSERV
Access policy: A short statement of information is requested upon receipt of initial inquiry.
How to unsubscribe: Send the message signoff ModBrits to LISTSERV

How to submit: Send e-mail on BITNET/INTERNET to ModBrits
Submission policy: Submissions are welcome from members; full instructions given during subscription process.
Additional information: Additional editor: Bruce Harkness, Center for Conrad Studies, Institute for Bibliography & Editing, Kent State Univ., Kent, Ohio 44242; 216-672-2092; Internet: ModBreds@KentVM.KENT.EDU; Bitnet: ModBreds@KentVM

MOPOLY-L

Description: Mopoly-L is a forum for the discussion of political issues relevant to Missouri.
Subjects covered: political science
List moderated: No.
Editorial contact: Len Rugen
Internet: c43221r@umvma
Bitnet: c43221r@umvma,umsystem.edu
How to access: Send subscribe message to listserv@mizzou1 or listserv@mizzou1.missouri.edu
How to unsubscribe: Send unsubscribe message to listserv@mizzou1 or listserv@mizzou1.missouri.edu
Archives: Archives are developed monthly; apply to listowner for details.

MORPHMET@CUNYVM

Description: MORPHMET@CUNYVM is a forum on the science of morphometrics.
Subjects covered: biology; biophysics
List moderated: No.
Editorial contact: Leslie F. Marcus
Bitnet: lamqc@cunyvm
How to access: Send subscribe message to listserv@cunyvm or listserv@cunyvm.cuny.edu
How to unsubscribe: Send unsubscribe message to listserv@cunyvm or listserv@cunyvm.cuny.edu
Archives: Archives are developed monthly; apply to listowner for details.

MOSSBA@USACHVM1

Description: MOSSBA@USACHVM1 is a forum on Mossbauer spectroscopy and software.
Subjects covered: chemistry; computer science
List moderated: Yes.
Editorial contact: Rafael Venegas
Bitnet: rvenegas@usachvm1
How to access: Send subscribe message to listserv@usachvm1
How to unsubscribe: Send unsubscribe message to listserv@usachvm1
Archives: Archives are developed monthly; apply to listowner for details.

MPSYCH-L

Description: MPSYCH-L carries announcements of interest to mathematical psychologists, whether or not they are members of the Society for Mathematical Psychology; e.g., notices of meetings, calls for papers, and other documents.
Subjects covered: mathematics; psychology
Net address for operations: brownvm.brown.edu
Net address for questions or submissions: mpsych-l@brownvm.brown.edu

Established: March 1991
Subscribers: 274
Sponsor: Facilities donated to the Society for Mathematical Psychology by Brown University, Providence, Rhode Island.
Host: Brown University, Providence, Rhode Island
List moderated: Yes.
Moderation procedure: MPSYCH-L distributes both announcements from the Society for Mathematical Psychology and other items submitted by members and non-members. Submitted items are usually announcements or inquiries. The moderator distributes submissions according to a liberal criterion of whether they are of interest to the members of the Society for Mathematical Psychology.
Editorial contact: Robert Stout
Society for Mathematical Psychology, Butler Hospital, 345 Blackstone Blvd., Providence, RI 02906
Tel: (401) 455-6304
Fax: (401) 455-6293
Internet: BI599088@Brownvm.brown.edu
Bitnet: BI599088@BROWNVM
Technical contact: Mary Ann Metzger
Department of Psychology, University of Maryland, UMBC, Baltmore, MD 21228.
Tel: (410)455-2657
Fax: (410)455-1055
Internet: metzger@umbc.edu
Bitnet: metzger@umbc
How to access: Send command to listserv@brownvm or to listserv@brownvm.brown.edu command: subscribe mpsych-l Your Name Here
Access policy: Requests for subscriptions are reviewed by owner. Both members and non-members of the Society for Mathematical Psychology are accepted.
How to unsubscribe: Send command to listserv@brownvm or to listserv@brownvm.brown.edu command: signoff mpsych-l Your Name Here
How to submit: Send contribution via e-mail to MPSYCH-L@brownv or to MPSYCH-L@brownvm.brown.edu
Submission policy: Announcements and inquiries of interest to the members of the Society for Mathematical Psychology will be distributed.
Archives: Distributed items are retained in listserv archives at brownvm. Additional archives of text and software written by members of the Society for Mathematical Psychology. Retrieval instructions are available from the moderator.

MSP-L

Description: MSP-L is a forum on network messaging protocols.
Subjects covered: computer science; electronic networking
List moderated: No.
How to access: Send subscribe message to listserv@albany or listserv@albany.edu
How to unsubscribe: Send unsubscribe message to listserv@albany or listserv@albany.edu

MUCO-FR@FRMOP11

Description: MUCO-FR@FRMOP11 is a forum on cystic fibrosis.
Subjects covered: medicine
List moderated: No.
Editorial contact: Michael Jorda

Bitnet: jorda@frsun12
How to access: Send subscribe message to listserv%frmop11.bitnet@vm1.nodak.edu or listserv@frmop11
How to unsubscribe: Send unsubscribe message to listserv%frmop11.bitnet@vm1.nodak.edu or listserv@frmop11
Archives: Archives are developed monthly; apply to listowner for details.

MULTI-L

Description: Multi-L is a forum on minority language education.
Subjects covered: linguistics; education
Host: Scientific Commission on Language and Education in Multilingual Settings, International Association of Applied Linguistics (AILA)
List moderated: Yes.
Editorial contact: Bernard Spolsky
Bitnet: f24030@barilvm
How to access: Send subscribe message to listserv@barilvm
How to unsubscribe: Send subscribe message to listserv@barilvm
Archives: Archives are developed monthly; apply to listowner for details.

MULTICAST@ARIZONA.EDU

Description: MULTICAST@ARIZONA.EDU covers issues of multicasting and broadcasting.
Subjects covered: computer science
List moderated: No.
Editorial contact: Joel Snyder
Internet: multicast-request@arizona.edu
How to access: Contact the Editor
How to unsubscribe: Contact the Editor
Archives: Yes.

MULTILIS@ALBNYVM1

Description: MULTILIS@ALBNYVM1 is a discussion forum for users of MULTILIS software.
Subjects covered: library and information science; computer hardware and software
List moderated: No.
Editorial contact: Roger D. Gifford
Bitnet: rdg28@albnyvm1
How to access: Send subscribe message to listserv@albnyvm1
How to unsubscribe: Send unsubscribe message to listserv@albnyvm1
Archives: Yes; Yearly, Private

MULTIMEDIA INFORMATION SERVICES

Description: MMIS is a mailing list whose objectives are to determine user requirements for multimedia information services; to characterise the quality of service requirements from the perspectives of the service user and the information provider; to identify and recommend existing tools which may be used to provide these services; to identify areas where existing tools do not satisfy requirements, and to propose how these gaps might be filled; and to publicise the facilities available and to encourage their use. Among topics discussed are architecture and protocols for remote access to multimedia information; the promotion and development of specific applications in the area

of networked multimedia information services; and the development of human-computer interface tools for multimedia information systems.
Subjects covered: multimedia computing; computer hardware and software; electronic networking
Net address for operations: mailbase@mailbase.ac.uk
Net address for questions or submissions:
mmis@mailbase.ac.uk
Established: March 1993
Subscribers: 97
Sponsor: RARE
Host: Mailbase service, Newcastle University
List moderated: No.
Editorial contact: Chris Adie
Edinburgh University Computing Service, Main Library, George Square, Edinburgh, EH8 9LJ UK.
Tel: +44 31 650 3363
Fax: +44 31 662 4809
Internet: C.J.Adie@ed.ac.uk
How to access: Send the message JOIN MMIS yourfirstname yourlastname to mailbase@mailbase.ac.uk
How to unsubscribe: Send the message LEAVE MMIS to mailbase@mailbase.ac.uk
How to submit: Send a message to mmis@mailbase.ac.uk
Archives: Available by gopher or FTP.
Related files: Gopher or FTP to mailbase.ac.uk See directory pub/mmis
Gopher accessibility: Gopher to mailbase.ac.uk

MUSEUM-L

Description: Museum-L is an electronic forum for discussion of museum management topics.
Subjects covered: management; art; museums
List moderated: No.
Editorial contact: John Chadwick
Internet: chadwick@bootes.unm.edu
Bitnet: chadwick@unmb
How to access: Send subscribe message to listserv@unmvma or listserv@unmvma.unm.edu
How to unsubscribe: Send unsubscribe message to listserv@unmvma or listserv@unmvma.unm.edu

MUSIC-ED@UMINN1

Description: MUSIC-ED@UMINN1 is a forum on music education.
Subjects covered: music; education
List moderated: Yes.
Editorial contact: Dave Schempp
Bitnet: idav@uminn1
How to access: Send subscribe message to listserv@uminn1
How to unsubscribe: Send unsubscribe message to listserv@uminn1
Archives: Archives are developed monthly; apply to listowner for details.

MUSIC-RESEARCH DIGEST

Description: Music-Research Digest is a discussion group established for people whose chief interests concern computers and their applications to music representation systems, information retrieval systems for musical scores, music printing, music analysis, musicology and ethnomusicology, and tertiary music education. The following areas are not the principal concern of this list, although overlapping subjects may well be interesting: primary and secondary education; sound generation techniques; and composition. The restriction on subject matter has frequently been reaffirmed: many readers have asked the Moderator to reject articles on electronic music, and especially electronic musical instruments (MIDI, synthesizers, "how do I make the frobnyx box work on my Commodore 12399XL+??", and so on). Such areas are covered elsewhere in the electronic mail and network world. For example, there is a mailing list specifically on these subjects which can be joined by sending a message containing "SUBSCRIBE EMUSIC-D <your fullname>" to LISTSERV@AUVM.BITNET.
There are Usenet News groups which deal with electronic music also. The best-known is the group rec.music.synth. If you are on a site which has access to News, we recommend exploring these groups if you are interested in MIDI and related topics.
Subjects covered: music
Net address for operations: music-research-request@prg.oxford.ac.uk (this is a human, not a LISTSERV)
Net address for questions or submissions: music-research@prg.oxford.ac.uk
Established: 1986
Subscribers: Unknown (fan-out lists hide numbers); probably in excess of 400.
Sponsor: System facilities are kindly provided by the Computing Laboratory, University of Oxford.
List moderated: Yes.
Moderation procedure: Submissions are checked by the moderator for adherence to the content guidelines.
Editorial contact: Dr. Stephen Page
Andersen Consulting, 2 Arundel Street, London WC2R 3LT, UK
Tel: +44-71-438 5074
Fax: +44-71-831 1133
Internet: music-research-request@prg.oxford.ac.uk
How to access: Send a message to the list administrators at music-research-request@prg.oxford.ac.uk, including your full Internet address.
How to unsubscribe: Ask the list administrators.
How to submit: Mail submissions to music-research@prg.oxford.ac.uk.
Submission policy: Ensure that your contribution is within the content guidelines. In particular, we do not publish articles about music in general, or about MIDI and electronic music. Please feel free to submit relevant contributions at any time. Remember, without contributions there will be no Digest! We especially welcome reports of conferences, book reviews, or pointers to key research activities.
Archives: We maintain an archive which contains back issues of the Digest and other interesting files (e.g. conference reports, bits of software, standards, etc.) The Music-Research Digest archive is available via anonymous ftp to ftp.comlab.ox.ac.uk and look in the directory Music-Research to find the archive. Start with the README file for a description of the archive.

MUTEX

Description: MuTeX is a mailing list focusing on discussion of the music software MuTeX. There are also many music software programs available through ftp.
Subjects covered: computer hardware and software; music; electronic music

Net address for questions or submissions: mutex-request@stolaf.edu
Established: November 25, 1991
Subscribers: 195
List moderated: No.
How to access: To participate in mutex and musictex discussions, you can subscribe to (or unsubscribe from) the "mutex" mailing list at the address: mutex-request@stolaf.edu To send a question to the entire membership of the mutex mailing list, use the address: mutex@stolaf.edu
How to submit: Submissions can be sent to mutex@stolaf.edu
Archives: Archives for the MuTeX mailing list are available via anonymous FTP from: ftp.stolaf.edu:/pub/mutex/archive

NA-NET@NA-NET.ORNL.GOV
Description: NA-NET is an electronic conference on numerical analysis.
Subjects covered: mathematics
Host: Oak Ridge National Laboratories
List moderated: Yes.
Editorial contact: Gene Golub
Internet: golub@sccm.stanford.edu
How to access: Send subscribe message to NA.JOIN@NA-NET.ORNL.GOV
How to unsubscribe: Send unsubscribe message to NA.JOIN@NA-NET.ORNL.GOV
Archives: Yes; In NETLIB

NAC@NDSUVM1
Description: NAC@NDSUVM1 is a periodic listing of conference announcements.
Subjects covered: colleges and universities; conferences and conference listings
List moderated: Yes.
Editorial contact: Marty Hoag
Bitnet: info@ndsuvm1
How to access: Send subscribe message to listserv@ndsuvm1 or listserv@vm1.nodak.edu
How to unsubscribe: Send unsubscribe message to listserv@ndsuvm1 or listserv@vm1.nodak.edu
Archives: Archives are developed weekly; apply to listowner for details.

NACUBO@BITNIC
Description: NACUBO is a forum on the financial administration of colleges and universities.
Subjects covered: colleges and universities; business
Host: National Association of College and University Business Officers
List moderated: Yes.
Editorial contact: Janet Chayes
Internet: chayes@ccsua.ctstateu.edu
How to access: Send subscribe message to listserv@bitnic or listserv@bitnic.educom.edu
How to unsubscribe: Send unsubscribe message to listserv@bitnic or listserv@bitnic.educom.edu
Archives: Yes, archives are available. Contact listowner for details.

NAFIPS-L
Description: NAFIPS-L is the discussion list of the North American Fuzzy Information Processing Society.
Subjects covered: computer science; fuzzy logic; artificial intelligence
Net address for operations: LISTSERV@GSUVM1.BITNET
Net address for questions or submissions: NAFIPS-L@gsuvm1.gsu.edu
How to access: Send the following command to LISTSERV@GSUVM1.BITNET:
SUB NAFIPS-L your_full_name where "your_full_name" is your real name, not your login Id. Non-BitNet users can join by sending the above command as the only line in the text/body of a message to LISTSERV@GSUVM1.GSU.EDU

NAHUAT-L
Description: Nahuat-L is a conference for discussing Aztec studies.
Subjects covered: anthropology; archaeology; Aztec studies
List moderated: No.
Editorial contact: J. F. Schwaller
Internet: schwallr@acc.fau.edu
Bitnet: schwallr@fauvax
How to access: Send subscribe message to listserv@fauvax or listserv@acc.fau.edu
How to unsubscribe: Send unsubscribe message to listserv@fauvax or listserv@acc.fau.edu

NAITLIST
Description: NAITLIST is a discussion list posting messages on subjects of interest to students, professors, and employers in industrial
technology and related fields.
Subjects covered: industrial technology; science and technology
Net address for operations: listserv@ra.msstate.edu
Net address for questions or submissions: naitlist@ra.msstate.edu
Established: October 26, 1992
Subscribers: 41
Sponsor: Mississippi State Univ. chapter of N.A.I.T. (National Association of Industrial Technology), N.A.I.T. Dept. of Technology, P.O. Drawer NU, Miss State, MS 39762
List moderated: Yes.
Moderation procedure: Moderator reviews all messages before posting and approves all subscriptions (no subscribers are refused).
Editorial contact: Cam Proctor
The Pines Mobile Home Community, Box 61, Starkville, MS 39759
Tel: (601)-324-7010
Internet: bcp1@ra.msstate.edu
Bitnet: BCP1@MSSTATE.BITNET
How to access: Email the listserv@ra.msstate.edu and in the body of the letter type: subscribe naitlist [Your full name]
How to unsubscribe: Email the listserv@ra.msstate.edu and in the body of the letter type: unsubscribe naitlist
How to submit: Mail submissions to naitlist@ra.msstate.edu
Submission policy: All posts are approved by the moderator prior to public mailing.
Archives: Copies of previous posts are kept by the moderator. As of May 14, 1993, all of naitlist's previous posts are available via email to the moderator.

NAMEDROPPERS@NIC.DDN.MIL

Description: NAMEDROPPERS is a conference on network domain style names.
Subjects covered: computer science; electronic networking
List moderated: No.
Internet: hostmaster@nic.ddn.mil
How to access: Send subscribe message to NAMEDROPPERS-REQUEST@NIC.DDN.MIL
How to unsubscribe: Send unsubscribe message to NAMEDROPPERS-REQUEST@NIC.DDN.MIL
Archives: Yes; Send anonymous FTP to NAMEDROPPERS:NAMEDROPPERS.yymmdd

NAT-1492@TAMVM1

Description: NAT-1492@TAMVM1 is a forum for discussion about the Columbus Anniversary.
Subjects covered: Columbus, Christopher; history; anthropology
List moderated: Yes.
Editorial contact: Gary S. Trujillo
Internet: gst@gnosys.svle.ma.us
How to access: Send subscribe message to LISTSERV@TAMVM1
How to unsubscribe: Send unsubscribe message to LISTSERV@TAMVM1
Archives: Archives are developed weekly; apply to listowner for details.

NAT-EDU@INDYCMS

Description: NAT-EDU@INDYCMS is a forum on indigenous peoples and education.
Subjects covered: education; anthropology
List moderated: Yes.
Editorial contact: Gary S. Trujillo
Internet: gst@gnosys.svle.ma.us
How to access: Send subscribe message to LISTSERV@INDYCMS
How to unsubscribe: Send unsubscribe message to LISTSERV@INDYCMS
Archives: Archives are developed weekly; apply to listowner for details.

NATCHAT@TAMVM1

Description: NATCHAT@TAMVM1 is a forum for the discussion of indigenous peoples.
Subjects covered: anthropology
List moderated: Yes.
Editorial contact: Gary S. Trujillo
Internet: gst@gnosys.svle.ma.us
How to access: Send subscribe message to LISTSERV@TAMVM1
How to unsubscribe: Send unsubscribe message to LISTSERV@TAMVM1
Archives: Archives are developed weekly; apply to listowner for details.

NATIONAL COMMUNICATION COORDINATOR DISCUSSION LIST

Description: NCC-L exists to transact business and discuss topics of national or regional importance for National Communication Coordinators. A full range of topics are discussed, from residence hall policy formation and review, to program and service delivery, to theoretical aspects of leadership and student governance on campus.
Subjects covered: colleges and universities; student government; residence hall government
Net address for operations: Tamvm1.TAMU.Edu
Net address for questions or submissions: NCC-L@Tamvm1.TAMU.Edu
Established: April 1992
Subscribers: 26
Sponsor: Texas A&M University, 110 YMCA Bldg., College Station, TX 77843-1257.
List moderated: No.
Editorial contact: Michael D. Osterbuhr
110 YMCA Bldg., Texas A&M University, College Station, TX 77843-1257.
Tel: (409) 845-4768
Fax: (409) 862-2434
Internet: N018GH@Tamvm1.TAMU.Edu
Bitnet: N018GH@Tamvm1.Bitnet
How to access: Send a SUBSCRIBE command per your usual machine protocal, to NCC-L@Tamvm1.TAMU.Edu or NCC-L@Tamvm1.Bitnet
Access policy: NCC-L subscription is open, but suggested only for National Communication Coordinators or advisor, for NCC business.
How to submit: Mail to NCC-L@Tamvm1.TAMU.Edu or NCC-L@Tamvm1.Bitnet
Submission policy: Discussion is fairly informal, however, some topics have become so narrow that subscribers were asked to continue their discussions on E-mail. In general, any questions may be raised on the list and may be continued as long as sufficient interest by subscribers carries the discussion forward.
Archives: Open for review by all subscribers; mostly statistics and discussion logs.

NATIVE-L

Description: Native-L is a forum for the discussion of indigenous peoples.
Subjects covered: anthropology
List moderated: Yes.
Editorial contact: Gary S. Trujillo
Internet: gst@gnosys.svle.ma.us
How to access: Send subscribe message to LISTSERV@TAMVM1
How to unsubscribe: Send unsubscribe message to LISTSERV@TAMVM1
Archives: Archives are developed weekly; apply to listowner for details.

NATODATA@CC1.KULEUVEN.AC.BE

Description: NATODATA distributes press releases, speeches, articles, and other information about NATO (North Atlantic Treaty Organization).
Subjects covered: current events; NATO
Host: NATO Defence Support Division, Brussels, Belgium
List moderated: Yes.

Editorial contact: Chris Scheurweghs
Internet: scheurwe@stc.nato.int
How to access: Send subscribe message to listserv@cc1.kuleuven.ac.be
How to unsubscribe: Send unsubscribe message to listserv@cc1.kuleuven.ac.be

NATRESLIB-L (NATURAL RESOURCES LIBRARIANS AND INFORMATION SPECIALISTS DISCUSSION GROUP)
Description: NatResLib-L exists to provide a medium for interaction between Natural Resource Librarians and Information Specialists. All issues, questions, brainstorming, or discussions pertaining to natural resources librarianship are welcome on this unmoderated list.
Subjects covered: library and information science
Net address for questions or submissions: NatResLib-L@cc.usu.edu
Editorial contact: Anne Hedrich
Merrill Library, Utah State University, Logan, Utah 84322-3000.
Internet: annhed@cc.usu.edu
How to access: This is not a listserv discussion group at present. All routine matters, such as signing on to the list, should be done through the list owner at annhed@cc.usu.edu. Any postings to the list should be sent to NatResLib-L@cc.usu.edu.

NATURA-L
Description: Natura-L covers ecological issues in Chile and Latin America.
Subjects covered: environmental studies; Chile; Latin America
List moderated: No.
How to access: Send subscribe message to listserv@uchcecvm
How to unsubscribe: Send unsubscribe message to listserv@uchcecvm
Archives: Archives are developed monthly; apply to listowner for details.

NAVNEWS@NCTAMSLANT.NAVY.MIL
Description: NAVNEWS is a distribution list for the US Navy news service.
Subjects covered: current events; U.S. Navy
Host: United States Navy
List moderated: Yes.
Internet: CLFPAO@NCTAMSLANT.NAVY.MIL
How to access: Contact the Editor
How to unsubscribe: Contact the Editor

NCS-L
Description: Ncs-L is a discussion focusing on the National Crime Survey.
Subjects covered: law and legal studies
List moderated: No.
Editorial contact: Brian Wiersema
Bitnet: brianw@umdd
How to access: Send subscribe message to listserv@umdd or listserv@umdd.umd.edu
How to unsubscribe: Send unsubscribe message to listserv@umdd or listserv@umdd.umd.edu

NDRG-L
Description: NDRG-L is a discussion list on nonlinear dynamics.
Subjects covered: physics
List moderated: No.
Editorial contact: Charles Jaffe
Bitnet: u0d96@wvnvm
How to access: Send subscribe message to listserv@wvnvm or listserv@wvnvm.wvnet.edu
How to unsubscribe: Send unsubscribe message to listserv@wvnvm or listserv@wvnvm.wvnet.edu

NEARNET-TECH@NIC.NEAR.NET
Description: NEARNET-TECH@NIC.NEAR.NET discusses technical issues of the New England Academic and Research Network.
Subjects covered: electronic networking; colleges and universities
Host: New England Academic and Research Network
List moderated: No.
Editorial contact: NEARnet Staff
Internet: nearnet-staff@nic.near.net
How to access: Send subscribe message to NEARNET-TECH-REQUEST@NIC.NEAR.NET
How to unsubscribe: Send unsubscribe message to NEARNET-TECH-REQUEST@NIC.NEAR.NET
Archives: Yes; Send anonymous FTP to NIC.NEAR.NET and cd mail-archives

NEARNET@NIC.NEAR.NET
Description: NEARNET@NIC.NEAR.NET is a forum of the New England Academic and Research Network.
Subjects covered: electronic networking; colleges and universities
Host: New England Academic and Research Network
List moderated: No.
Editorial contact: NEARnet Staff
Internet: nearnet-staff@nic.near.net
How to access: Send subscribe message to NEARNET-REQUEST@NIC.NEAR.NET
How to unsubscribe: Send unsubscribe message to NEARNET-REQUEST@NIC.NEAR.NET
Archives: Yes; Send anonymous FTP to NIC.NEAR.NET and cd mail-archives

NEDER-L
Description: Neder-L is an electronic distribution list for the study of the Dutch language.
Subjects covered: Dutch language and literature; Netherlands
List moderated: Yes.
Editorial contact: Ben Salemans
Internet: u216013@hnykun11
How to access: Send subscribe message to listserv@hearn or listserv@nic.surfnet.nl
How to unsubscribe: Send unsubscribe message to listserv@hearn or listserv@nic.surfnet.nl
Archives: Archives are developed monthly; apply to listowner for details.

NEII@CNI.ORG

Description: NEII@CNI.ORG if the discussion list of the National Engineering Information Initiative.
Subjects covered: engineering
Host: Association of Research Libraries; Library of Congress; Council on Library Resources
List moderated: No.
Editorial contact: William Ellis
Internet: well@seq1.loc.gov
How to access: Send subscribe message to listserv@cni.org
How to unsubscribe: Send unsubscribe message to listserv@cni.org

NESFAD

Description: NESFAD is a list of e-addresses of sci-fi fans in Nordic countries.
Subjects covered: science fiction
List moderated: Yes.
Editorial contact: Ahrvid Engholm
Internet: ahrvid@sfbbs.edvina.se
How to access: Contact the Editor
How to unsubscribe: Contact the Editor

NETSCOUT@VMTECMEX

Description: NETSCOUT is a server discussion about new resources for Bitnet and Internet users.
Subjects covered: Internet; information technology; Bitnet; resource guides
List moderated: No.
Editorial contact: Alejandro S. Kurczyn
Bitnet: 499229@vmtecmex
How to access: Send subscribe message to listserv@vmtecmex or listserv%vmtecmex.bitnet@cunyvm.cuny.edu
How to unsubscribe: Send unsubscribe message to listserv@vmtecmex or listserv%vmtecmex.bitnet@cunyvm.cuny.edu

NETTRAIN@UBVM

Description: NETTRAIN@UBVM is a forum for networking instructors.
Subjects covered: electronic networking; library and information science; Internet; Bitnet
List moderated: Yes.
Editorial contact: Jim Milles
Internet: millesjg@sluvca.slu.edu
How to access: Send subscribe message to listserv@ubvm or listserv@ubvm.cc.buffalo.edu
Message is SUBSCRIBE NETTRAIN Yourfirstname Yourlastname
How to unsubscribe: Send unsubscribe message to listserv@ubvm or listserv@ubvm.cc.buffalo.edu
Message is UNSUBSCRIBE Yourfirstname Yourlastname
Archives: Archives are developed monthly; apply to listowner for details.

NEURO1-L

Description: Neuro1-L is a discussion list on neuroscience research.
Subjects covered: medicine

List moderated: No.
Bitnet: #m01ejn@luccpua
How to access: Send subscribe message to listserv@uicvm or listserv@uicvm.uic.edu
How to unsubscribe: Send unsubscribe message to listserv@uicvm or listserv@uicvm.uic.edu
Archives: Archives are developed monthly; apply to listowner for details.

NEURON DIGEST

Description: Neuron-Digest is a list (in digest form) dealing with all aspects of neural networks (and any type of network or neuromorphic system).
Subjects covered: neural networks; medicine
Net address for operations: neuron-request@cattell.psych.upenn.edu
Net address for questions or submissions: neuron@cattell.psych.upenn.edu
Established: December 1, 1986
Subscribers: 1700
Sponsor: Courtesy of the Psychology Department, University of Pennsylvania 3815 Walnut St., Philadelphia, PA 19104.
List moderated: Yes.
Moderation procedure: Submissions are collected into Digest form, usually by topic or type of submission (e.g., conference announcements, paper announcements, discussion), lightly edited by the moderator, and sent out at least once per week. Entries far off-topic or of a substantially commercial nature are rejected, but otherwise the editorial policy is very liberal.
Editorial contact: Peter Marvit
Psychology Department, University of Pennsylvania, 3815 Walnut St., Philadelphia, PA 19104.
Tel: 215/898-6274 (work); 215/387-6433 (home)
Internet: neuron-request@cattell.psych.upenn.edu
How to access: All requests to be added to or deleted from this list, problems, questions, etc., should be sent to neuron-request@cattell.psych.upenn.edu.
How to submit: Submissions may be sent to neuron@cattell.psych.upenn.edu
Archives: Archived files/messages will be available with anonymous ftp from the machine cattell.psych.upenn.edu (130.91.68.31) in the directory pub/Neuron-Digest. That directory contains back issues with the names vol-nn-no-mm (e.g., vol-3-no-02). I'm also collecting simulation software in pub/Neuron-Software. Contributions are welcome.

NEURON-UK@MAILBASE.AC.UK

Description: NEURON-UK is a mailbase distribution list for information on neural networks.
Subjects covered: electronic networking; computer science
List moderated: No.
Internet: neuron-uk-request@mailbase.ac.uk
How to access: Send subscribe message to mailbase@mailbase.ac.uk in the following format: join neuron-uk Yourfirstname Yourlastname
Archives: Archives are developed monthly; apply to listowner for details.

THE NEW YORK - ISRAEL PROJECT

Description: The New York - Israel Project provides databases, listservs, and archives of material of interest to the Jewish community. It also provides Internet access to Jewish organizations.
Subjects covered: Judaica
Net address for operations: chaim@israel.nysernet.org
Net address for questions or submissions: israelinfo@israel.nysernet.org
Established: January 1992
Fee: Accounts are $200/year for unlimited access. If you have an account on another system then access to us is free but we request a donation of any amount. Pay by check.
Sponsor: NYSERNet
Commercial organization: Non-profit
Editorial contact: Dr. Chaim Dworkin
Chai Computer Associates, 115 East Mt. Airy Avenue, Philadelphia, PA 19119-1715
Internet: chaim@israel.nysernet.org
How to access: Send message to chaim@israel.nysernet.org
Gopher accessibility: gopher to israel.nysernet.org 71

NEW-LIST

Description: NEW-LIST has been established as a clearinghouse for the announcements of new e-mail mailing lists. Many compilers of various lists of lists subscribe to new-list. Once a new list has been announced we try to limit further items about that list to substantive changes (to avoid the extra traffic and confusion). Besides announcements of new lists, the new-list list may be used as a "list of last resort" for searching for a list on a specific topic. The Subject: field of the list mail items is used to indicate the type of item distributed: (eg. Subject NEW: xyz list on xyzology) NEWAnnouncement of NEW lists CHANGE Announcement of CHANGE to a list (ie. host location, subscription address or procedures) SEARCHA list search item.
Subjects covered: Internet; Bitnet; electronic networking; resource guides
Net address for operations: LISTSERV@vm1.nodak.edu or LISTSERV@NDSUVM1.BITNET
Net address for questions or submissions: new-list@vm1.nodak.edu or new-list@NDSUVM1.BITNET
Established: January 1989
Subscribers: 5033
Sponsor: North Dakota State University, Computer Center, PO Box 5164, Fargo, ND 58105.
List moderated: Yes.
Moderation procedure: Items are screened and edited for consistency in format. They are also categorized as to whether they are a new list announcement, changed list information, or list search.
Editorial contact: Marty Hoag
NDSU Computer Center, PO Box 5164, Fargo, ND 58105.
Tel: 701 237-8639
Fax: 701 237-8541
Internet: hoag@vm1.nodak.edu
Bitnet: nu021172@NDSUVM1
How to access: Send e-mail to listserv@vm1.nodak.edu (or LISTSERV@NDSUVM1 on BITNET) with the command SUB NEW-LIST yourfirstname yourlastname in the BODY of the mail. For example: sub new-list Ima Reader
Access policy: Subscriptions are open to anyone.
How to unsubscribe: Send e-mail to listserv@vm1.nodak.edu (or LISTSERV@NDSUVM1 on BITNET) with the command SIGNOFF NEW-LIST in the BODY of the e-mail. If your ad-

dress has changed since subscribing and you are no longer "recognized", send e-mail to new-list-request@vm1.nodak.edu with explicit instructions on what needs to be done (please include the list name).
How to submit: For new list announcements please refer to the file "NEW-LIST FORMAT" before submitting an announcement. To get a copy of this file send e-mail to listserv@vm1.nodak.edu (or LISTSERV@NDSUVM1.BITNET) with the command GET NEW-LIST FORMAT in the BODY of the e-mail. Then send your announcement to new-list@vm1.nodak.edu or on BITNET to NEW-LIST@NDSUVM1.
Submission policy: Any list owner or operator may list an announcement of a new list. We try to verify (but don't guarantee) that the announcements come from an authoritative source to avoid announcement of lists which the owner does not want announced! If you see an announcement of a new which might be appropriate for "new-list", please contact the owner of the new list and let her or him know about "new-list".
Archives: Automatic archives of past list announcements are kept on the host system. You may obtain a list of files via e-mail by sending mail to listserv@vm1.nodak.edu (or LISTSERV@NDSUVM1.BITNET) with the BODY containing INDEX NEW-LIST and may obtain any of the monthy archives by including the command GET NEW-LIST LOG9305 (for the May 1993 archive for example). Archives may also be searched using the LISTSERV database facilities. For more information send LISTSERV the command INFO DATABASE The archives are also available via anonymous FTP to vm1.nodak.edu. Once connected enter CD NEW-LIST and DIR NEW-LIST.* for a list of the files.
Related files: A collection of hints as well as pointers to other documents on finding lists of interest is contained in the file LISTSOF LISTS (via LISTSERV or listsof.lists via anonymous ftp). To receive the file send e-mail to listserv@vm1.nodak.edu (or LISTSERV@NDSUVM1.BITNET) with the command GET LISTSOF LISTS in the body. You may also obtain information on setting up a list with GET NEW-LIST CREATE Other documents are available. For a list of all the files enter INDEX NEW-LIST in the BODY of the mail.

NEW-LISTS@MAILBASE.AC.UK

Description: NEW-LISTS@MAILBASE.AC.UK lists newly opened mailing lists posted on the Mailbase server.
Subjects covered: Internet; resource guides; Mailbase
List moderated: Yes.
Internet: new-lists-request@mailbase.ac.uk
How to access: Send subscribe message to mailbase@mailbase.ac.uk in the following format: join new-lists Yourfirstname Yourlastname
Archives: Archives are developed monthly; apply to listowner for details.

NEWBOOKS@RPITSVM

Description: NEWBOOKS@RPITSVM covers communication studies.
Subjects covered: communications
Host: Comserve
List moderated: No.
Editorial contact: Comserve Support Staff
Internet: support@vm.its.vpi.edu
Bitnet: support@rpitsvm

How to access: Send subscribe message to comserve@rpitsvm or comserve@vm.its.vpi.edu
How to unsubscribe: Send unsubscribe message to comserve@rpitsvm or comserve@vm.its.vpi.edu

NEWCROPS@PURCCVM

Description: NEWCROPS@PURCCVM is a forum on crop biology.
Subjects covered: agriculture; plant biology
List moderated: No.
Editorial contact: Anna Whipkey
Bitnet: simon@purccvm
How to access: Send subscribe message to listserv@purccvm
How to unsubscribe: Send unsubscribe message to listserv@purccvm

NEWEDU-L

Description: NEWEDU-L is an electronic list focusing on the use of technology in education and distance education.
Subjects covered: computer-assisted instruction; education; distance education
Net address for operations: listserv@uscvm.bitnet
How to access: Send standard subscribe request to listserv.
How to unsubscribe: Send standard unsubscribe request to listserv.

NEWJOUR-L

Description: NewJour-L is the place to announce your own (or to forward information about others') newly planned, newly issued, or revised ELECTRONIC NETWORKED journal or newsletter. It is specially dedicated for those who wish to share information in the planning, gleam-in-the-eye stage or at a more mature stage of publication development and availability. It is also the place to announce availability of paper journals and newsletters as they become available on electronic networks. Scholarly discussion lists which regularly and continuously maintain supporting files of substantive articles or preprints may also be reported, for those journal-like sections. We hope that those who see announcements on Bitnet, Internet, Usenet or other media will forward them to NewJour-L, but this does run a significant risk of boring subscribers with a number of duplicate messages. Therefore, NewJour-L is filtered through a moderator to eliminate this type of duplication. It does not attempt to cover areas that are already covered by other lists. For example, sources like NEW-LIST describe new discussion lists; ARACHNET deals with social and cultural issues of e-publishing; VPIEJ-L handles many matters related to electronic publishing of journals. SERIALST discusses the technical aspects of all kinds of serials. You should continue to subscribe to these as you have done before, and contribute to them.
Subjects covered: Internet; electronic journals
Net address for operations: LISTSERV@e-math.ams.org
Net address for questions or submissions: NewJour-L@e-math.ams.org
Established: September 1993
Sponsor: The Association of Research Libraries, Office of Scientific & Academic Publishing, 21 Dupont Circle, Suite 800, Washington, DC 20036.
List moderated: Yes.
Moderation procedure: Postings are filtered through the moderator to avoid duplication.

Editorial contact: Ann Okerson
The Association of Research Libraries, Office of Scientific & Academic Publishing, 21 Dupont Circle, Suite 800, Washington, DC 20036
Internet: osap@cni.org
How to access: Send a message to: LISTSERV@e-math.ams.org
Leave the subject line blank. In the body, type: SUBSCRIBE NewJour-L FirstName LastName
You will have to subscribe in order to post messages to this list.
How to unsubscribe: Use the standard LISTSERV (Internet) directions.

NIS@CERF.NET

Description: NIS@CERF.NET is a compendium of all network information services announcements.
Subjects covered: electronic networking; campus-wide information systems
Host: CERFnet
List moderated: Yes.
Editorial contact: Susan Calcari
Internet: calcaris@cerf.net
How to access: Send subscribe message to listserv@cerf.net
How to unsubscribe: Send unsubscribe message to listserv@cerf.net

NISO-L

Description: NISO-L is a discussion group of the National Information Standards Organization.
Subjects covered: computer hardware and software; library and information science; information technology
Net address for questions or submissions: LISTSERV@NERVM
How to access: Send subscribe message to LISTSERV@NERVM
How to unsubscribe: Send unsubscribe message to LISTSERV@NERVM

NL-KR@CS.RPI.EDU

Description: NL-KR@CS.RPI.EDU is a discussion list on natural language and knowledge representation.
Subjects covered: computer science; linguistics; artificial intelligence
List moderated: Yes.
Editorial contact: Christopher Welty
Internet: weltyc@cs.rpi.edu
How to access: Send subscribe message to NL-KR-REQUEST@cs.rpi.edu
How to unsubscribe: Send unsubscribe message to NL-KR-REQUEST@cs.rpi.edu

NMBRTHRY@NDSUVM1

Description: NMBRTHRY is a list on number theory.
Subjects covered: mathematics
List moderated: Yes.
Editorial contact: Victor S. Miller
Internet: theorynt@watson.ibm.com
Review: Reviewed by List Review Service edited by Raleigh Muns: see appendix
How to access: Send subscribe message to listserv@ndsuvm1

How to unsubscribe: Send unsubscribe message to listserv@ndsuvm1
Archives: Archives are developed monthly; apply to listowner for details.

NNEWS@NDSUVM1
Description: NNEWS@NDSUVM1 is a list that focuses on Internet information resources.
Subjects covered: library and information science; Internet; resource guides
List moderated: Yes.
Editorial contact: Dana Noonan
Internet: noonan@msus1.msus.edu
How to access: Send subscribe message to listserv@ndsuvm1 or listserv@vm1.nodak.edu
How to unsubscribe: Send unsubscribe message to listserv@ndsuvm1 or listserv@vm1.nodak.edu
Archives: Archives are developed weekly; apply to listowner for details.

NNMVS-L
Description: NNMVS-L is a discussion forum for the MVS/TSO NNTP news reader software.
Subjects covered: computer hardware and software
List moderated: No.
Editorial contact: Leonard D. Woren
Internet: ldw@mvsa.usc.edu
Bitnet: ldw@uscmvsa
How to access: Send subscribe message to listserv@uscvm or listserv@vm.usc.edu
How to unsubscribe: Send unsubscribe message to listserv@uscvm or listserv@vm.usc.edu
Archives: Yes.

NOGLSTP
Description: NOGLSTP is the list of the National Organization of Gay and Lesbian Scientists and Technical Professionals.
Subjects covered: gay and lesbian topics; science and technology
Net address for questions or submissions: NOGLSTP-REQUEST@ELROY.JPL.NASA.GOV
List moderated: Yes.
How to access: Send subscription messages to NOGLSTP-REQUEST@ELROY.JPL.NASA.GOV

NOTABENE@TAUNIVM
Description: NOTABENE@TAUNIVM is an information forum for users of Nota Bene word processing software.
Subjects covered: computer hardware and software
List moderated: No.
Editorial contact: Itamar Even-Zohar
Bitnet: b10@taunivm
How to access: Send subscribe message to listserv@taunivm or listserv@taunivm.tau.ac.il

How to unsubscribe: Send unsubscribe message to listserv@taunivm or listserv@taunivm.tau.ac.il
Archives: Archives are developed weekly; apply to listowner for details.

NOTIS-L
Description: Notis-L is a discussion on NOTIS/DOBIS system software.
Subjects covered: library and information science
List moderated: No.
Editorial contact: Tulane Service Account
Bitnet: lsvmaint@tcsvm
How to access: Send subscribe message to listserv@tcsvm
How to unsubscribe: Send unsubscribe message to listserv@tcsvm
Archives: Archives are developed weekly; apply to listowner for details.

NOTISACQ@CUVMB
Description: NOTISACQ@CUVMB is a discussion group for NOTIS acquisitions software.
Subjects covered: library and information science
List moderated: Yes.
Editorial contact: Joyce G. McDonough
Internet: jm86@cunixf.cc.columbia.edu
How to access: Send subscribe message to listserv@cuvmb
How to unsubscribe: Send unsubscribe message to listserv@cuvmb

NOTMUS-L
Description: Notmus-L is a discussion on NOTIS software in music libraries.
Subjects covered: library and information science; music
List moderated: No.
Editorial contact: Chuck Dunn
Bitnet: chuck@ubvm
How to access: Send subscribe message to listserv@ubvm or listserv@ubvm.cc.buffalo.edu
How to unsubscribe: Send unsubscribe message to listserv@ubvm or listserv@ubvm.cc.buffalo.edu
Archives: Archives are developed monthly; apply to listowner for details.

NREN-DISC@PSI.COM
Description: NREN-DISC is a list covering discussion of the National Research and Education Network
Subjects covered: Internet; NREN
List moderated: No.
Editorial contact: Jim Cerny
Internet: j__cerny@unhh.unh.edu

How to access: Send subscribe message to NREN-DISCUSS-REQUEST@PSI.COM

How to unsubscribe: Send unsubscribe message to NREN-DIS-CUSS-REQUEST@PSI.COM

Archives: Yes; Send anonymous FTP to uu.psi.com in archive/nren-discuss

NRSING-L

Description: NRSING-L is a discussion list centering on nursing and health care informatics, computer-assisted learning, and various other nursing and health care related topics.

Subjects covered: health sciences; computer-assisted instruction (CAI); nursing

Net address for operations: listserv@nic.umass.edu

Net address for questions or submissions: nrsing-l@nic.umass.edu

Established: 1991

Subscribers: Approximately 350 representing many countries/today.

Sponsor: University of Massachusetts Medical Center, 55 Lake Ave North, Worcester, MA 01655

Host: University of Massachusetts-Amherst, Amherst, MA

List moderated: No.

Editorial contact: Gordon Larrivee, MS, RN
UMass Med Center, Nsg Admin, 55 Lake Ave., North Worcester, MA 01655

Tel: (508)856-0011

Internet: larivee@umassmed.ummed.edu

Bitnet: larrivee@umssmdvm.bitnet

How to access: Email listserv@nic.umass.edu and in the body type subscribe nrsing-l (your real name)

Access policy: No restrictions on subscription

How to unsubscribe: Send to listserv@nic.umass.edu and in the body type unsub nrsing-l

How to submit: nrsing-l@nic.umass.edu

Submission policy: No restrictions on submissions with use of proper 'netiquette.'

Archives: Archives saved monthly as MM/YY beginning 05/93. Previous archives were lost during list conversion to new UNIX listserv. To receive a complete index mail to: listserv@nic.umass.edu body: index nrsing-l

Additional information: This is UNIX listserv version 6.0 To get help mail to: listserv@nic.umass.edu and in the body type help

NSP-L

Description: NSP-L (Noble Savage Philosophers) is a forum for the discussion of philosophy.

Subjects covered: philosophy

Host: Comserve

List moderated: No.

Editorial contact: Barry B. Floyd

Bitnet: userf98f@rpitsvm

How to access: Send subscribe message to comserve@rpitsvm or comserve@vm.its.vpi.edu

How to unsubscribe: Send unsubscribe message to comserve@rpitsvm or comserve@vm.its.vpi.edu

Archives: Archives are developed monthly; apply to listowner for details.

NT-GREEK (NEW TESTAMENT GREEK STUDIES) CONFERENCE

Description: NT-GREEK is an electronic conference designed to foster communication concerning the scholarly study of the Greek New Testament. Anyone interested in New Testament Studies is invited to subscribe, but the list will assume at least a working knowledge of Biblical Greek. Those interested in learning to study the Bible more personally and less exclusively academic should join the BIBLE list (BIBLE-REQUEST@VIRGINIA.EDU).

Subjects covered: Greek New Testament; Bible studies; religion; Greek language and literature

Net address for operations: djm5g@virginia.edu or djm5g@virginia

Net address for questions or submissions: djm5g@virginia.edu or djm5g@virginia

Sponsor: The list is supported by the University of Virginia. The list is sponsored by the the Center for Christian Study, an independent Christian ministry at the University of Virginia. For more information about the Center for Christian Study contact: The Center for Christian Study, 128 Chancellor Street, Charlottesville, VA 22903 (804) 295-2471.

Editorial contact: David John Marotta
The Center for Christian Study, 128 Chancellor Street, Charlottesville, VA 22903

Tel: (804) 982-3718; (804) 924-5261

Fax: (804) 296-7209

Internet: djm5g@virginia.edu

Bitnet: djm5g@virginia

How to access: You may subscribe by sending an e-mail message to NT-GREEK-REQUEST@VIRGINIA.EDU NTGRKREQ@VIRGINIA.BITNET if your account is on the internet, with the following request as the text of the message. SUB NT-GREEK YourFirstname YourLastname This, the 'SUB ...,' must be part of the message; the subject line will be ignored. Remember two simple rules-of-thumb: If it's a request (SUBscribe, UNSUBscribe), send it to the list requester: NT-GREEK-REQUEST@VIRGINIA.EDU (Internet) NTGRKREQ@VIRGINIA.BITNET (Bitnet) If it's a message for general distribution to the members of the list, send it to the list: NT-GREEK@VIRGINIA.EDU(Internet); NT-GREEK@VIRGINIA.BITNET(Bitnet).

Access policy: Subscription to this conference is open to anyone interested.

How to unsubscribe: You may leave the list at any time by sending a "UNSUBscribe NT-GREEK" request to NT-GREEK-REQUEST@VIRGINIA.EDU. Please note that this request must not be sent to the list address (NT-GREEK@VIRGINIA.EDU) but to the REQUEST address (NT-GREEK-REQUEST@VIRGINIA.EDU).

NUNTIUS-L

Description: Nuntius-L is a discussion forum on the Macintosh NNTP client Nuntius.

Subjects covered: computer hardware and software

List moderated: No.

Editorial contact: Aaron Freimark

Internet: abf1@cornell.edu

How to access: Send subscribe message to listserv@cornell.edu

How to unsubscribe: Send unsubscribe message to listserv@cornell.edu

Archives: Yes.

NUTEPI (NUTRITIONAL EPIDEMIOLOGY)

Description: NUTEPI is an electronic mailing list carrying information about nutritional epidemiologic issues and announcements of meetings of the WHO-CC, and other relevant issues.

Subjects covered: epidemiology; health sciences; medicine

Net address for operations: LISTSERV@tubvm.cs.tu-berlin.de (LISTSERV@DB0TUI11)

Net address for questions or submissions: NUTEPI@tubvm.cs.tu-berlin.de (NUTEPI@DB0TUI11)

Established: April 1991

Subscribers: 65

Sponsor: WHO-CC on Nutritional Epidemiology Institute for Social Medicine and Epidemiology, Federal Health Office, General Pape Strasse 62-66, 12101 Berlin, Germany.

Host: Technical University, Berlin.

List moderated: No.

Editorial contact: Gert Mensink
General Pape Strasse 62-66, 12101 Berlin, Germany.

Tel: + 30 78007 216

Fax: + 30 78007 109

Internet: MENSINK@tubvm.cs.tu-berlin.de

Bitnet: MENSINK@DB0TUI11

How to access: Mail to LISTSERV@tubvm.cs.tu-berlin.de the message ''subscribe NUTEPI''

How to unsubscribe: Mail to LISTSERV@tubvm.cs.tu-berlin.de the message ''signoff NUTEPI''

How to submit: Mail to NUTEPI@tubvm.cs.tu-berlin.de

Archives: There is a monthly archive.

NYSO-L

Description: NYSO-L is the New York State/Ontario chapter of the Music Library Association's discussion list.

Subjects covered: library and information science; music

Host: Music Library Association

List moderated: No.

Editorial contact: Rick McRae

Internet: mmlrick@ubvm.cc.buffalo.edu

Bitnet: mmlrick@ubvm

How to access: Send subscribe message to listserv@ubvm or listserv@ubvm.cc.buffalo.edu

How to unsubscribe: Send unsubscribe message to listserv@ubvm or listserv@ubvm.cc.buffalo.edu

Archives: Archives are developed weekly; apply to listowner for details.

OBJ-REL@EMUVM1.CC.EMORY.EDU

Description: OBJ-REL@EMUVM1.CC.EMORY.EDU is a discussion forum on religion.

Subjects covered: religion

List moderated: No.

Editorial contact: Bert Bruner

Internet: osakb@emuvm1.cc.emory.edu

Bitnet: osakb@emuvm1

How to access: Send subscribe message to listserv@emuvm1 or listserv@emuvm1.cc.emory.edu

How to unsubscribe: Send unsubscribe message to listserv@emuvm1 or listserv@emuvm1.cc.emory.edu

OBJECTIVISM-PHILOSOPHY@TWWELLS.COM

Description: OBJECTIVISM-PHILOSOPHY@TWWELLS.COM is a forum for the discussion of the philosophy of Objectivism.

Subjects covered: philosophy

List moderated: No.

Editorial contact: T. William Wells

Internet: objectivism-request@twwells

How to access: Send subscribe message to OBJECTIVISM-PHILOSOPHY-REQUEST@TWWELLS.COM

How to unsubscribe: Send unsubscribe message to OBJECTIVISM-PHILOSOPHY-REQUEST@TWWELLS.COM

OBJECTIVISM@VIX.COM

Description: OBJECTIVISM@VIX.COM is a forum for the discussion of the philosophy of Objectivism.

Subjects covered: philosophy

List moderated: No.

Editorial contact: Paul Vixie

Internet: objectivism-request@vix.com

How to access: Contact the Editor

How to unsubscribe: Contact the Editor

OCLC-JOURNALS

Description: OCLC-journals is a discussion list carrying machine-readable news articles and information about OCLC electronic publishing, including the Online Journal of Current Clinical Trials.

Subjects covered: electronic publishing; OCLC; computer hardware and software; library and information science

Net address for operations: listserv@oclc.org

Net address for questions or submissions: This list is for dissemination of information only; submissions are not accepted.

Established: November 1992

Subscribers: 53 4

Host: OCLC, Inc., 6565 Frantz Road, Dublin, OH 43017; (614) 764-6000; fax: (614) 764-6096.

List moderated: Yes.

Moderation procedure: Submissions from subscribers are not redistributed to the list.

Editorial contact: Deb Bendig
OCLC, Inc., 6565 Frantz Road, Dublin, OH 43017.

Tel: (614) 761-5016

Fax: (614) 761-5016

Internet: e-pub@oclc.org

Technical contact: Laura Toms
OCLC, Inc., 6565 Frantz Road, Dublin, OH 43017.

Tel: (614) 761-5016

Fax: (614) 761-5047

Internet: ltoms@oclc.org

How to access: Send a message to listserv@oclc.org and include the following string in the messae body: subscribe oclc-journals Your Name replacing ''Your Name'' with the subscriber's name.

Access policy: Anyone may subscribe: no approval is required.

How to unsubscribe: Send a message to listserv@oclc.org and include the following string in the message body: unsubscribe oclc-journals

Submission policy: Submissions are ignored and are not redistributed to the list. This list will probably become a discussion

list and accept submissions from subscribers at some future date.
Archives: Information files as ASCII text.
Additional information: Second technical contact: George Pallas, OCLC, Inc., 6565 Frantz Road, Dublin, OH 43017. tel (614) 764-6301 Fax (614) 761-5047. List service provided by UNIX-LISTSERVER version 5.5.

OCLC-NEWS

Description: OCLC-news is an electronic mailing list carrying press releases from OCLC, Inc.
Subjects covered: computer hardware and software; electronic publishing; OCLC; library and information science
Net address for operations: listserv@oclc.org
Net address for questions or submissions: This list is for dissemination of information only; submissions are not accepted.
Established: September 1992
Subscribers: 985
Host: OCLC, Inc., 6565 Frantz Road, Dublin, OH 43017; (614) 764-6000; fax: (614) 764-6096.
List moderated: Yes.
Moderation procedure: Submissions from subscribers are not redistributed to the list.
Editorial contact: Marifay Makssour
OCLC, Inc., 6565 Frantz Road, Dublin, OH 43017.
Tel: (614) 761-5016
Fax: (614) 761-5016
Internet: e-pub@oclc.org
Technical contact: Laura Toms
OCLC, Inc., 6565 Frantz Road, Dublin, OH 43017.
Tel: (614) 761-5016
Fax: (614) 761-5047
Internet: ltoms@oclc.org
How to access: Send a mesage to listserv@oclc.org and include the following string in the message body: subscribe oclc-journals Your Name replacing ''Your Name'' with the subscriber's name.
Access policy: Anyone may subscribe; no approval is required.
How to unsubscribe: Send a message to listserv@oclc.org and include the following string in the message body: unsubscribe oclc journals
Submission policy: Submissions are ignored and are not redistributed to the list. This list will probably become a discussion list and accept submissions from subscribers at some future date.
Archives: Information files as ASCII text
Additional information: Second technical contact: George Pallas, OCLC, Inc., 6565 Frantz Road, Dublin, OH 43017. tel (614) 764-6301 Fax (614) 761-5047. List service provided by UNIX-LISTSERVER version 5.5.

ODP-L

Description: ODP-L provides reports from the Ocean Drilling Program.
Subjects covered: environmental studies
List moderated: Yes.
Editorial contact: Linda Weatherford
Bitnet: weatherf@tamodp
How to access: Send subscribe message to listserv@tamvm1 or listserv@tamvm1.tamu.edu
How to unsubscribe: Send unsubscribe message to listserv@tamvm1 or listserv@tamvm1.tamu.edu

OFFCAMP@WAYNEST1

Description: OFFCAMP@WAYNEST1 is a discussion list on off-campus library services.
Subjects covered: library and information science
List moderated: No.
Editorial contact: Barton Lessin
Bitnet: blessin@waynest1
How to access: Send subscribe message to listserv@waynest1
How to unsubscribe: Send unsubscribe message to listserv@waynest1

OH-MOTSS

Description: OH-MOTSS is a discussion group for members of the same sex living in Ohio.
Subjects covered: gay and lesbian topics
How to access: Send message to OH-MOTSS-REQUEST@CPS.UDYTON.EDU

OPERA-L

Description: Opera-L is a forum for opera.
Subjects covered: music
List moderated: No.
Editorial contact: Antonio de M. A. Doria
Internet: doria@suwatson.stanford.edu
Bitnet: doria@suwatson
How to access: Send subscribe message to mailserv@brfapq or mailserv%brfapq.bitnet@vm1.nodak.edu
How to unsubscribe: Send unsubscribe message to mailserv@brfapq or mailserv%brfapq.bitnet@vm1.nodak.edu

OPERS-L (MAINFRAME OPERATIONS DISCUSSION LIST)

Description: OPERS-L is a discussion group about mainframe computer operations for computer operators, lead operators, and supervisors. Topics include operator training, tips on operating the various computer systems and I/O gear, software packages available to help day to day computer operations (such as job scheduling, disk and tape management, etc.), problems caused by working night shift, weekends and holidays, education and career advancement issues, war stories about hardware and software problems, health concerns (eye strain and related VDT concerns; carpel tunnel problems), pros and cons on shift rotation vs. permanent shifts, and other issues.
Subjects covered: computer hardware and software
Net address for operations: AKRONVM.BITNET (Bitnet) VM1.CC.UAKRON.EDU
Net address for questions or submissions: AKRONVM.BITNET (Bitnet) VM1.CC.UAKRON.EDU
Established: May, 1991
Subscribers: 400
Sponsor: The University of Akron
Host: 185 Carroll St., Akron, Ohio 44325
List moderated: No.
Editorial contact: Tom Evert
185 Carroll St., Akron, Ohio 44325
Tel: (216) 972-7187
Fax: (216) 972-5238
Internet: O1EVERT@VM1.CC.UAKRON.EDU
Bitnet: O1EVERT@AKRONVM.BITNET

How to access: Send an interactive message or mail to: LISTSERV@AKRONVM SUBscribe OPERS-L Your Name
Access policy: Currently accepting subscriptions.
How to unsubscribe: Send an interactive message or mail to: LISTSERV@AKRONVM UNSUBscribe OPERS-L
How to submit: Send E-mail to OPERS-L@AKRONVM.BITNET
Submission policy: Any Mainframe Computer operations or related submission is welcomed.
Archives: Archive information (past documents, etc.): Previous monthly logs are available. Send an interactive command or mail to: LISTSERV@AKRONVM GET OPERS-L LOGYYMM (where yy = year and mm = month) Currently the logs are available from May '91 (9105) to the present.
Additional information: Peer site is PCCVMs for discussion of any aspect of mainframe computer operations.

OPT-PROC@TAUNIVM
Description: OPT-PROC@TAUNIVM is a forum on holography and other optical computing fields.
Subjects covered: computer science
List moderated: Yes.
Editorial contact: Shelly Glaser
Internet: feglaser@weizmann.weizmann.ac.il
Bitnet: glaser@uscvm
How to access: Send subscribe message to listserv@taunivm or listserv@taunivm.tau.ac.il
How to unsubscribe: Send unsubscribe message to listserv@taunivm or listserv@taunivm.tau.ac.il

OPTICS-L
Description: Optics-L is a forum for Israeli-based work in optics, electro-optics, and laser technologies.
Subjects covered: physics
List moderated: Yes.
Editorial contact: Joseph van Zwaren
Internet: jo%ilncrd.bitnet@cunyvm.cuny.edu
Bitnet: jo@ilncrd
How to access: Send subscribe message to listserv@taunivm or listserv@taunivm.tau.ac.il
How to unsubscribe: Send unsubscribe message to listserv@taunivm or listserv@taunivm.tau.ac.il

OR-L
Description: Or-L is a forum covering political and social research.
Subjects covered: sociology; political science
Host: Inter-university Consortium for Political and Social Research.
List moderated: No.
Editorial contact: Chuck Humphrey
Bitnet: chumphre@ualtavm
How to access: Contact the Editor
How to unsubscribe: Contact the Editor
Archives: Archives are developed yearly; apply to listowner for details.

ORCHIDS@SCU
Description: ORCHIDS is a forum for orchid growers.
Subjects covered: horticulture

List moderated: No.
Editorial contact: Willis Dair
Internet: dair%scu.bitnet@cunyvm.cuny.edu
Bitnet: dair@scu
How to access: Send subscribe message to mailserv@scu or mailserv%scu.bitnet@cunyvm.cuny.edu
How to unsubscribe: Send unsubscribe message to mailserv@scu or mailserv%scu.bitnet@cunyvm.cuny.edu

ORCS-L
Description: ORCS-L is a forum for discussion of management science.
Subjects covered: education; business
List moderated: Yes.
Editorial contact: Ramesh Sharda
Bitnet: mgmtrsh@osuvml
How to access: Send subscribe message to listserv@osuvml
How to unsubscribe: Send unsubscribe message to listserv@osuvml
Archives: Archives are developed monthly; apply to listowner for details.

ORG-GEOCHEM
Description: ORG-GEOCHEM is a conference covering organic geochemistry.
Subjects covered: geology; chemistry
List moderated: No.
Internet: org-geochem-request@mailbase.ac.uk
How to access: Send subscribe message to mailbase@mailbase.ac.uk in the following format: join org-geochem Yourfirstname Yourlastname
Archives: Archives are developed monthly; apply to listowner for details.

ORGCHE-L
Description: Orgche-L is a forum for organic chemistry.
Subjects covered: chemistry
Host: Comserve
List moderated: No.
Editorial contact: Asuncion Valles
Internet: d3qoavc0%eb0ub011.bitnet@cunyvm.cuny.edu
Bitnet: d3qoavc0@eb0ub011
How to access: Send subscribe message to comserve@rpitsvm or comserve@@vm.its.vpi.edu
How to unsubscribe: Send unsubscribe message to comserve@rpitsvm or comserve@@vm.its.vpi.edu

ORIGAMI-L
Description: Origami-L covers all aspects of the Japanese paper folding art of origami.
Subjects covered: art
List moderated: No.
Editorial contact: Maarten van Gelder
Internet: ORIGAMI-REQUEST@NSTN.NS.CA
How to access: Send subscribe message to ORIGAMI-REQUEST@NSTN.NS.CA
How to unsubscribe: Send unsubscribe message to ORIGAMI-REQUEST@NSTN.NS.CA
Archives: Yes, archives are available through anonymous FTP to RUGCIS.RUG.Nl

ORTHODOX@INDYCMS

Description: ORTHODOX@INDYCMS is a forum for discussion of Orthodox Christianity.
Subjects covered: religion; Christianity
List moderated: Yes.
Editorial contact: John B. Harlan
Internet: ijbh200@indyvax.iupui.edu
How to access: Send subscribe message to listserv@indycms or listserv@indycms.iupui.edu
How to unsubscribe: Send unsubscribe message to listserv@indycms or listserv@indycms.iupui.edu
Archives: Yes.

ORTRAD-L

Description: Ortrad-Lis a forum for discussing oral tradition and related topics.
Subjects covered: language and literature; literature; folklore; anthropology
Host: Center for Studies in Oral Tradition, 301 Read Hall, University of Missouri, Columbia, MO 65211
List moderated: No.
Editorial contact: John Foley
Internet: csottime@mizzoui.missouri.edu
Bitnet: csottime@mizzoui
How to access: Send subscribe message to listserv@mizzoui or listserv@mizzoui.edu
How to unsubscribe: Send unsubscribe message to listserv@mizzoui or listserv@mizzoui.edu

OT-HEBREW (OLD TESTAMENT HEBREW STUDIES)

Description: OT-HEBREW is an electronic conference designed to foster communication concerning the scholarly study of the Hebrew Old Testament. Anyone interested in Old Testament Studies is invited to subscribe, but the list will assume at least a working knowledge of Biblical Hebrew and Aramaic. Those interested in learning to study the Bible more personally and less exclusively academic should join the BIBLE list (BIBLE-REQUEST@VIRGINIA.EDU).
Subjects covered: Hebrew Old Testament; Bible studies; religion; Hebrew language and literature
Net address for operations: OT-HEBREW on OT-HEBREW-REQUEST@VIRGINIA.EDU
OTHEBREW on OTHEBREQ@VIRGINIA.BITNET (Bitnet)
Net address for questions or submissions:
djm5g@virginia.edu or djm5g@virginia
Sponsor: The list is supported by the University of Virginia. The list is sponsored by the the Center for Christian Study, an independent Christian ministry at the University of Virginia. For more information about the Center for Christian Study contact: The Center for Christian Study, 128 Chancellor Street, Charlottesville, VA 22903 (804) 295-2471.
List moderated: No.
Editorial contact: David John Marotta
The Center for Christian Study, 128 Chancellor Street, Charlottesville, VA 22903
Tel: (804) 982-3718; (804) 924-5261
Fax: (804) 296-7209
Internet: djm5g@virginia.edu
Bitnet: djm5g@virginia
How to access: Send an e-mail message to OT-HEBREW-REQUEST@VIRGINIA.EDU if you are on the Internet, or

OTHEBREQ@VIRGINIA.BITNET if you are on Bitnet with the following request as the text of the message. SUB OT-HEBREW YourFirstname YourLastname This, the 'SUB ...,' must be part of the message; the subject line will be ignored. Remember two simple rules-of-thumb: If it's a request (SUBscribe, UNSUBscribe), send it to the list requester: OT-HEBREW-REQUEST@VIRGINIA.EDU (Internet) OT-HEBREQ@VIRGINIA.BITNET (Bitnet) If it's a message for general distribution to the members of the list, send it to the list: OT-HEBREW@VIRGINIA.EDU(Internet); OTHEBREW@VIRGINIA.BITNET(Bitnet) Contributions sent to this list are automatically broadcast to everyone else on the list. If you wish to reply to an individual member of the list please send that person mail directly. If you use your systems automatic REPLY feature your message will get sent only to the individual member and not broadcast to the entire list.
Access policy: Subscription to this conference is open to anyone interested.
Additional information: The list is NOT on a listserver, all requests (e.g. SUBscribe or UNSUBscribe) are simply forwarded to the list owner and handled manually. Therefore list server commands such as INDEX do not work. The ridge format of commands is for the sake of consistancy and some automation of requests.

OTS-L

Description: OTS-L is an electronic conference on tropical environmental studies. Postings range from news and queries to job and meeting announcements.
Subjects covered: tropical studies; environmental studies
Net address for operations: listserv@yalevm.ycc.yale.edu
Net address for questions or submissions: ots-L@yalevm.ycc.yale.edu
Established: 1988
Subscribers: 180
Sponsor: Organization for Tropical Studies, Box DM, Duke University, Durham, NC 27706
Editorial contact: Phillip Sollins
Organization for Tropical Studies, Box DM, Duke University, Durham, NC 27706
Tel: 503-737-6582
Fax: 503-737-1393
Bitnet: sollins@fsl.orst.edu
Internet: postmaster@yalevm.ycc.yale.edu
How to access: To subscribe (technical): send "sub OTS-L Your Name" to listserv@yalevm.ycc.yale.edu
Access policy: Subscriptions are open to anyone. Postings can only be made by a subscriber.
How to unsubscribe: Send "unsub OTS-L" to listserv@yalevm.ycc.yale.edu
Archives: Yes, at listserv@yalevm.ycc.yale.edu.

PACARC-L

Description: Pacarc-L is a forum for the discussion of Archaeology in the Pacific Rim.
Subjects covered: archaeology
List moderated: No.
Editorial contact: Dale Croes
Bitnet: croes@wsuvm1
How to access: Send subscribe message to listserv@wsuvm1 or listserv@wsuvm1.bitnet@cunyvm.cuny.edu

How to unsubscribe: Send unsubscribe message to listserv@wsuvm1 or listserv@wsuvm1.bitnet@cunyvm.cuny.edu
Archives: Archives are developed monthly; apply to listowner for details.

PACES-L (PUBLICATIONS ASSOCIATION OF ENGINEERING STUDENTS FORUM)

Description: PACES-L provides a forum for discussion of topics relating to Student Engineering Publications (newspapers, newsletters, handbooks, etc.). Publication Editors and other interested people are invited to participate. Presently PACES-L is being used to help in the evolution of PACES, which is one of the many branches of the Canadaian Federation of Engineering Students. All students in accredited engineering institutions are members of the Canadian Federation of Students (CFES). The CFES provides a voice for all engineering students.
Subjects covered: science and technology; engineering; education; journalism
Net address for operations: LISTSERV@UNB.CA
Net address for questions or submissions: PACES-L@UNB.CA
Established: January 1993
Subscribers: 25
Sponsor: University of New Brunswick, Fredericton, New Brunswick, Canada.
List moderated: List is unmoderated, but is monitored by the Canadian Federation of Engineering Student's Commissioner of Electronic Communication.
Editorial contact: Troy Morehouse, CFES Commissioner of Electronic Communication
Room H-223, Sir Edmund Head Hall, University of New Brunswick, Fredericton, New Brunswick, Canada.
Tel: (506) 453-3534
Fax: (506) 453-4569
Internet: cfes@jupiter.sun.csd.unb.ca
Bitnet: cfes@unb.ca
Technical contact: Same as above
How to access: Send the following one line e-mail message to LISTSERV@UNB.CA
SUB PACES-L your-name-and/or-affilliation
Access policy: Anybody who is interested in engineering and engineering education are invited to participate (being involved with an engineering student publication is not a pre-requisite).
How to unsubscribe: Send the following one line e-mail message to LISTSERV@UNB.CA SIGNOFF PACES-L
How to submit: Send any submissions (postings) to PACES-L@UNB.CA
Submission policy: Postings of a slanderous, sexist, racist, or homophobic nature will not be tolerated on PACES-L. Doing so will result in immediate removal from subscription.
Archives: No currently provided, but may be in the future.
Related files: CFES and PACES-L have related documentation (i.e. minutes, policy manuals, bylaws, logos, addresses, articles, stories, press releases, etc) available via anonymous FTP at jupiter.sun.csd.unb.ca, and can be found in the /pub/cfes directory. An incoming directory is provided for site submissions.

PACIFIC@BRUFPB

Description: PACIFIC@BRUFPB is a conference on the Pacific Rim and Basin.
Subjects covered: communications
List moderated: No.

Editorial contact: Carlos Fernando Nogueira
Bitnet: ctedtc09@brufpb
How to access: Send subscribe message to listserv@brufpb
How to unsubscribe: Send unsubscribe message to listserv@brufpb

PACKET-RADIO@WSMR-SIMTEL20.ARMY.MIL

Description: PACKET-RADIO is a discussion forum on packet radio systems.
Subjects covered: computer hardware and software
List moderated: Yes.
Editorial contact: Keith Petersen
Internet: W8SDZ@WSMR-SIMTEL20.ARMY.MIL
How to access: Send subscribe message to PACKET-RADIO-REQUEST@WSMR-SIMTEL20.ARMY.MIL
How to unsubscribe: Send unsubscribe message to PACKET-RADIO-REQUEST@WSMR-SIMTEL20.ARMY.MIL
Archives: Yes; Send anonymous FTP to WSMR-SIMTEL20.ARMY.MIL

PACS-L

Description: The Public-Access Computer Systems Forum (PACS-L) is a computer conference that deals with all computer systems that libraries make available to their patrons. Utilizing PACS-L, users discuss topics such as CD-ROM databases, expert systems, hypertext programs, microcomputer labs, locally-mounted databases, network-based information resources, and OPACs. The conference does not deal with staff-oriented functions in integrated library systems (e.g., acquisitions, cataloging, circulation, and serials control), staff-oriented microcomputer use (e.g., spreadsheets and word processing), or mediated online searching. While many users are librarians, PACS-L also serves computer specialists, faculty members, and others. The conference was founded in June 1989 by Charles W. Bailey, Jr. Currently, there are over 6,330 users in 56 countries. The conference is moderated by Dana Rooks and Jill Hackenberg. The Information Technology Division of the University of Houston provides technical support for the conference.
Subjects covered: library and information science; information technology
Host: University of Houston, Univ. Libs. and Info. Tech. Division. The University of Houston Libraries provides PACS-L as a public service. It does not verify the accuracy of submitted messages nor does it endorse the opinions expressed by message authors. Authors of PACS-L messages are solely responsible for content of their messages.
List moderated: Yes.
Moderation procedure: Messages sent to PACS-L are reviewed by the conference moderators, who distribute messages on appropriate topics to conference participants. PACS-L moderators reserve the right to reject any posting that we feel is not appropriate for PACS-L. Normally, PACS-L users receive 5-15 messages per day. Please do not send messages longer than about 250 lines; break long messages up into multiple shorter messages.
Editorial contact: Dana Rooks
Assistant Director for Administration, University Libraries, University of Houston, Houston, TX 77204-2091.
Tel: (713) 743-9807
Fax: (713) 743-9748
Bitnet: LIBL@UHUPVM1

Review: Reviewed by List Review Service edited by Raleigh Muns: see appendix.

How to access: To join PACS-L, send the following e-mail message to LISTSERV@UHUPVM1: SUBSCRIBE PACS-L First Name Last Name. (The UH list server also has an Internet address: LISTSERV@UHUPVM1.UH.EDU.)

How to unsubscribe: To sign off PACS-L, send the following e-mail message to LISTSERV@UHUPVM1: UNSUBSCRIBE PACS-L.

Archives: All messages to the conference are automatically archived. Users can search the message database for specific information using complex Boolean queries. The most reliable method of searching the database is to submit batch search jobs to the list server via e-mail messages. Search features include nested Boolean expressions, search limitation by date and time, and SOUNDEX searches.

Related files: An electronic journal, The Public-Access Computer Systems Review, was established in September 1989. The first issue was published in January 1990. The journal became refereed in November 1991. Articles are stored as individual files on the list server, and an annotated table of contents for each issue is sent out as an e-mail message to all PACS-L users. After looking over the table of contents, users can retrieve article files of interest. The journal is cataloged on OCLC and RLIN. A second list, PACS-P, was established in January 1991 for users that want to receive PACS-L publications, but do not want to receive messages from PACS-L users. PACS-P serves over 1,350 users in 42 countries.

Additional information: For More Information About PACS-L: Bailey, Jr., Charles W. "Electronic (Online) Publishing in Action . . . The Public-Access Computer Systems Review and Other Electronic Serials." Online 15 (January 1991): 28-35. Bailey, Jr., Charles W. "The Public-Access Computer Systems Forum: A Computer Conference on BITNET." Library Software Review 9 (March-April 1990): 71-74.

PACS-P@UHUPVM1

Description: PACS-P is the publication distribution list of PACS-L.

Subjects covered: computer hardware and software; library and information science; information technology

Net address for questions or submissions: LISTSERV@UHUPVM1

How to access: To receive the PACS-L publications only (no messages from PACS-L users), send the following message to LISTSERV@UHUPVM1: SUBSCRIBE PACS-P First Name Last Name. Do NOT subscribe to both PACS-L and PACS-P; PACS-L users receive all publications as part of their subscription.

How to unsubscribe: Send unsubscribe message to LISTSERV@UHUPVM1

PAGAN@DRYCAS.CLUB.CC.CMU.EDU

Description: PAGAN@DRYCAS.CLUB.CC.CMU.EDU is a discussion list covering paganism.

Subjects covered: religion

List moderated: Yes.

Editorial contact: Uther Locksley

Internet: uther@drycas.club.cc.cmu.edu

How to access: Send subscribe message to pagan-request@drycas or pagan-request@drycas.club.cc.cmu.edu

How to unsubscribe: Send unsubscribe message to pagan-request@drycas or pagan-request@drycas.club.cc.cmu.edu

Archives: Yes; Send anonymous FTP to: DRYCAS.CLUB.CC.CMU.EDU and cd anonymous/pagarchive

PALS-L

Description: PALS-L covers discussion of the MSUS/Unisys/PALS Library automation system.

Subjects covered: library and information science

List moderated: No.

Editorial contact: David Robinson

Internet: robinson@mtsu.edu

How to access: Send subscribe message to listserv@knuth.mtsu.edu

How to unsubscribe: Send unsubscribe message to listserv@knuth.mtsu.edu

PAMNET

Description: PAMNET is a discussion forum for physics, astronomy, and mathematics librarians.

Subjects covered: physics; astronomy; mathematics; library and information science

How to access: Send subscription requests to Joanne Goode at JMGOODE@UKCC.UKY.EDU

PANET-L

Description: Panet-L is a conference on medical education.

Subjects covered: medicine; education

Host: Panamerican Federation of Associations of Medical Schools (PAFAMS)

List moderated: No.

Editorial contact: Wendy Steele

Internet: steele@mcs.nlm.nih.gov

Bitnet: pafams@yalevm

How to access: Send subscribe message to listserv@yalevm or listserv@yalevm.ycc.yale.edu

How to unsubscribe: Send unsubscribe message to listserv@yalevm or listserv@yalevm.ycc.yale.edu

Archives: Archives are developed monthly; apply to listowner for details.

PARA-DAP@IRLEARN

Description: PARA-DAP is a forum covering different types of data processing.

Subjects covered: computer science

List moderated: No.

Editorial contact: Roton Hanrahan

Internet: hanrah88@irlearn.ucd.ie

Bitnet: hanrah88@irlearn

How to access: Send subscribe message to listserv@irlearn or listserv@irlearn.ucd.ie

How to unsubscribe: Send unsubscribe message to listserv@irlearn or listserv@irlearn.ucd.ie

Archives: Yes.

PBLIST

Description: PBLIST is dedicated to the discussion of problem-based learning in health science education. Topics may include

case-writing, teaching and training of teachers, research and collaboration between departments and institutions, student perspectives on PBL, research and experiences with PBL in various courses and institutional settings, evaluations, and the fostering of collegial relationships in support of these goals.
Subjects covered: problem-based learning; health sciences; education
Net address for operations: MAILSERV@UTHSCSA.EDU
Net address for questions or submissions: PBLIST@UTHSCSA.EDU or PBLIST@UTHSCSA.BITNET
Sponsor: The University of Texas Health Science Center at San Antonio, 7703 Floyd Curl Drive, San Antonio, TX 78284.
List moderated: Yes.
Moderation procedure: List moderated only to exclude messages not related to the mission of the list, or messages that are offensive.
Editorial contact: S. Thomas Deahl DMD PhD
7703 Floyd Curl Drive, San Antonio, TX 78284-7919.
Tel: (210) 567-3333
Fax: (210) 567-2281
Internet: hendricson@uthscsa.edu
Bitnet: hendricson@uthscsa.bitnet
How to access: Send the command SUBSCRIBE within the body of a message to PBLIST@UTHSCSA.EDU or PBLIST@UTHSCSA.BITNET.
How to unsubscribe: Send the command UNSUBSCRIBE within the body of a message to PBLIST@UTHSCSA.EDU or PBLIST@UTHSCSA.BITNET.

PCIP@UDEL.EDU

Description: PCIP@UDEL.EDU discusses TCP/IP setups for personal computers.
Subjects covered: computer hardware and software; telecommunications; electronic networking; Internet
List moderated: Yes.
Editorial contact: James Galvin
Internet: galvin@udel.edu
How to access: Send subscribe message to PCIP-REQUEST@UDEL.EDU
How to unsubscribe: Send unsubscribe message to PCIP-REQUEST@UDEL.EDU

PCORPS-L

Description: PCORPS-L is a discussion list for U. S. Peace Corps volunteers and other international volunteers.
Subjects covered: political activism; Peace Corps
Net address for operations: LISTSERV@CMUVM.CSV.CMICH.EDU
Net address for questions or submissions: PCORPS-L@CMUVM.CSV.CMICH.EDU
Established: October 1992
Subscribers: 93
Sponsor: Central Michigan University, Mt. Pleasant, MI 48859.
List moderated: No.
Editorial contact: Elliott Parker
Journalism Dept., Central Michigan University, Mt. Pleasant, MI 48859.
Tel: (517) 774-3196
Fax: (517) 774-7805
Internet: 3ZLUFUR@CMUVM.CSV.CMICH.EDU
Bitnet: 3ZLUFUR@CMUVM

How to access: Email to LISTSERV@CMUVM.CSV.CMICH.EDU with the message SUB PCORPS-L <real__name>
Access policy: Open to all interested parties.
How to unsubscribe: Email to LISTSERV@CMUVM.CSV.CMICH.EDU with the message SIGNOFF PCORPS-L
How to submit: PCORPS-L@CMUVM.CSV.CMICH.EDU
Submission policy: Open to all interested parties.
Archives: Full archives are available.

PCSUPT-L

Description: PCSUPT-L is a forum for support issues related to IBM-compatible computers.
Subjects covered: computer hardware and software; IBM
List moderated: No.
Editorial contact: Bob Boyd
Internet: BWBOYD@YALEVM
How to access: Send subscribe message to listserv@yalevm or listserv@yalevm.ycc.yale.edu
How to unsubscribe: Send unsubscribe message to listserv@yalevm or listserv@yalevm.ycc.yale.edu

PEDIATRIC-PAIN

Description: PEDIATRIC-PAIN provides an informal discussion of any topic related to pain in children, including, but not restricted to, clinical problems or questions, research problems or proposals, announcements of meetings, book reviews, and educational, political, or administrative aspects of children's pain management and prevention.
Subjects covered: children; medicine; health sciences
Net address for operations: MAILSERV@ac.dal.ca
Net address for questions or submissions: PEDIATRIC-PAIN@ac.dal.ca
Established: June 25, 1993
Subscribers: 65
Sponsor: Dalhousie University, Halifax, NS, Canada.
List moderated: No.
Editorial contact: G. Allen Finley MD FRCPC
IWK Children's Hospital, Halifax, NS B3J 3G9
Tel: 902-428-8111 or 428-8251
Fax: 902-428-8826
Internet: gafinley@ac.dal.ca
How to access: Send e-mail to MAILSERV@ac.dal.ca
The first line of the body of the message should read: subscribe PEDIATRIC-PAIN
Access policy: Open to any professional (or parent or child!) with interest or expertise in the area.
How to unsubscribe: Send to MAILSERV@ac.dal.ca
How to submit: Send messages to PEDIATRIC-PAIN@ac.dal.ca
Submission policy: Currently no restrictions, but the listowner reserves the right to unsubscribe persons abusing the list.
Archives: Available (to subscribers) as monthly archives. Send message to MAILSERV@ac.dal.ca as follows: send PEDIATRIC-PAIN.yyyymm where PEDIATRIC-PAIN.199306 would be June 1993.

PERFORM

Description: PERFORM is an open forum for discussion and queries regarding any aspect of Medieval or Renaissance performance. Topics have included (but are not limited to) theoretical and practical considerations of drama, entertainments, festivals and rituals. We welcome announcements for all related academic activities (conferences, research projects, etc.) and dramatic events. PERFORM maintains an informal relationship with both the Medieval and Renaissance Drama Society (MRDS) and the Societe Internationale pour l'etude du Theatre Medieval (SITM). PERFORM is open to all interested parties.

Subjects covered: language and literature; performance studies
Net address for operations: LISTSERV@IUBVM
Net address for questions or submissions: PERFORM@IUBVM
Established: May 1992
Subscribers: 105
Host: Indiana University, Bloomington, IN 47405.
List moderated: No.
Editorial contact: Jesse D. Hurlbut
1153 Patterson Office Tower, Lexington, KY 40506-0027.
Tel: (606) 257-8450
Internet: frejdh@ukcc.uky.edu
Bitnet: frejdh@ukcc
Indexed or abstracted: Medieval studies
How to access: Send the message 'SUB PERFORM your name' to LISTSERV@IUBVM >
Access policy: All interested parties are welcome.
How to unsubscribe: Send the message 'UNSUB PERFORM' to LISTSERV@IUBVM
How to submit: Send letters to PERFORM@IUBVM send longer documents (articles, etc.) to FLANIGAN@IUBVM
Submission policy: Discussion on the list is not moderated. Any communication related to PERFORM's topics and objectives may be sent directly to the list. Articles, papers, bibliographies, or course syllabi may be kept on the file server and should be submitted to FLANIGAN@IUBVM.
Archives: The first six months of list activity are archived in a single file. All subsequent activity logged monthly.
Related files: ''From Functional Feast to Frivolous Funhouse: Two Ideals of Play in the Burgundian Court'' by Jesse D. Hurlbut is available by sending the message 'GET HURLBUT PAPER' to LISTSERV@IUBVM By September 1993, there will be a series of scanned images from the 14th-century manuscript of the 'Jour dou jugement' mystery play made available via ftp and WWW.
Additional information: Co-owner:C. Clifford Flanigan, 405 Ballantine Hall, Bloomington, IN 47405; Internetflanigan@iubacs.ucs.indiana.edu; Bitnetflanigan@iubacs

PERFORM-L

Description: PERFORM-L is dedicatd to issues related to the study of performance. The discipline of performance studies includes analysis and theory of traditional theatrical events as well as popular culture, ritual, and sports.
Subjects covered: popular culture; performance studies; cultural studies
Net address for operations: LISTSERV@ACFCLUSTER.NYU.EDU
Net address for questions or submissions: PERFORM-L@ACFCLUSTER.NYU.EDU
Established: September 1992
Subscribers: 170
Sponsor: Performance Studies, Tisch School of the Arts, New York University, 701 Broadway, 6th Floor, New York, NY 10003.

List moderated: No.
Editorial contact: Dr. Sharon Mazer
Undergraduate Drama, Tisch School of hte Arts, New York University, 701 Broadway, 3rd Floor, New York, NY 10003.
Tel: 212/998-1850 (NYU) or 212/496-8021 (home)
Fax: 212/998-1855
Internet: MAZERS@ACFCLUSTER.NYU.EDU
How to access: Mail to LISTSERV@ACFCLUSTER.NYU.EDU leave subject area blank, erase any automatic headers/footers, and type SUBSCRIBE PERFORM-L <Your Name>
Access policy: This list is open to all interested users.
How to unsubscribe: Follow procedure for subscribing, substituting UNSUBSCRIBE
How to submit: Send submissions to PERFORM-L@ACFCLUSTER.NYU.EDU
Submission policy: Submissions should be focused on issues related to the study of performance.

PERL-USERS@VIRGINIA.EDU

Description: PERL-USERS is a discussion forum on the Practical Extraction and Report Language.
Subjects covered: computer hardware and software
List moderated: No.
Editorial contact: Marc Rouleau
Internet: mer6g@VIRGINIA.EDU
How to access: Send subscribe message to perl-req@virginia or perl-users-request@virgina.edu
How to unsubscribe: Send unsubscribe message to perl-req@virginia or perl-users-request@virgina.edu

PERU@ATHENA.MIT.EDU

Description: PERU@ATHENA.MIT.EDU is an electronic conference on topics related to Peru.
Subjects covered: Peru
List moderated: No.
Editorial contact: Carlos Reategui
Internet: tbandit@athena.mit.edu
How to access: Send subscribe message to OWNER-PERU@ATHENA.MIT.EDU
How to unsubscribe: Send unsubscribe message to OWNER-PERU@ATHENA.MIT.EDU

PET-L

Description: Pet-L is a discussion list about positron emission tomography (PET).
Subjects covered: physics
List moderated: No.
How to access: Send subscribe message to listserv@ualtavm or listserv@vm.ucs.ualberta.ca
How to unsubscribe: Send unsubscribe message to listserv@ualtavm or listserv@vm.ucs.ualberta.ca

PFERDE@DLRVM

Description: PFERDE@DLRVM is a German language forum covering horsemanship.
Subjects covered: horses; zoology
List moderated: No.
Editorial contact: Heike Mueller
Internet: rz4p@hujiagri

How to access: Send subscribe message to LISTSERV@DLRVM
How to unsubscribe: Send unsubscribe message to LISTSERV@DLRVM
Archives: Archives are developed monthly; apply to listowner for details.

PHARMA@DMU.AC.UK
Description: PHARMA@DMU.AC.UK is a forum for pharmacologists.
Subjects covered: medicine; pharmacology
Host: Dept. of Pharmacy, De Montfort Univ., Leicester, UK
List moderated: No.
Editorial contact: Paul Hodgkinson, FSc. T.
Internet: phh@dmu.ac.uk
How to access: Send subscribe message to PHARM-RE-QUEST@DMU.AC.UK
How to unsubscribe: Send unsubscribe message to PHARM-REQUEST@DMU.AC.UK
Archives: Archives are developed monthly

PHILCOMM@RPITSVM
Description: PHILCOMM@RPITSVM discusses the philosophy of communication.
Subjects covered: philosophy; communications
Host: Comserve
List moderated: No.
Editorial contact: Comserve Support Staff
Internet: support@vm.its.vpi.edu
Bitnet: support@rpitsvm
How to access: Send subscribe message to comserve@rpitsvm or comserve@vm.its.vpi.edu
How to unsubscribe: Send unsubscribe message to comserve@rpitsvm or comserve@vm.its.vpi.edu

PHILOS-L
Description: PHILOS-L is an electronic discussion group on philosophical topics.
Subjects covered: philosophy
Net address for operations: LISTSERV@LIVERPOOL.AC.UK
Net address for questions or submissions: PHILOS-L@LIVERPOOL.AC.UK
Established: 1989
Subscribers: 330
Sponsor: Dept of Philosophy, Liverpool University, PO Box 147, Liverpool L69 3BX UK
Host: Liverpool University
List moderated: No.
Moderation procedure: The list is controlled by occasional interventions of moderator, Stephen R.L. Clark.
Editorial contact: Stephen R.L. Clark
Dept of Philosophy, Liverpool University, P.O. Box 147, Liverpool, L69 3BX UK
Tel: 051 794 2788
Fax: 051 794 2789
Internet: srlclark@liverpool.ac.uk
Technical contact: Alan Thew
Computer Services Dept, Liverpool University, Liverpool, L69 3BX UK
Tel: 051 794 3735

Internet: Alan.Thew@liverpool.ac.uk
How to access: Send the message SUBSCRIBE PHILOS-L to LISTSERV@liverpool.ac.uk
Access policy: Submit queries to srlclark@liverpool.ac.uk. Any philosophically interested persons are welcome; the list is chiefly for UK and other European philosophers.
How to unsubscribe: Send the email message SIGNOFF PHIL-OS-L to listserv@liverpool.ac.uk
How to submit: Send messages to PHILOS-L@liverpool.ac.uk
Submission policy: Postings can be about anything philosophical, although threads shouldn't be kept going for too long.
Archives: Send the message INDEX PHILOS-L to the listserv to receive information about archives.
Additional information: Philos-l acts as a filter and > forwarding service for UK/European philosophers (and others) who don't want to be on too many other lists.

PHILOSED-L
Description: Philosed-L is a forum covering education philosophies.
Subjects covered: philosophy; education
List moderated: No.
Editorial contact: Thomas F. Green
Bitnet: tfgreen@suvm
How to access: Send subscribe message to listserv@suvm
How to unsubscribe: Send unsubscribe message to listserv@suvm

PHILOSOP@YORKVM1
Description: PHILOSOP@YORKVM1 is a list covering academic philosophies.
Subjects covered: philosophy; colleges and universities
List moderated: No.
Editorial contact: P. A. Danielson
Internet: danielsn@unixg.ubc.ca
How to access: Send subscribe message to listserv@yorkvm1 or listserv@vm1.yorku.ca
How to unsubscribe: Send unsubscribe message to listserv@yorkvm1 or listserv@vm1.yorku.ca
Archives: Archives are developed monthly; apply to listowner for details.

PHOTO-L
Description: Photo-L is a forum for dicussion of photography.
Subjects covered: photography
List moderated: No.
How to access: Send subscribe message to listserv@buacca or listserv@buacca.bitnet@cunyvm.cuny.edu
How to unsubscribe: Send unsubscribe message to listserv@buacca or listserv@buacca.bitnet@cunyvm.cuny.edu
Archives: Archives are developed weekly; apply to listowner for details.

PHOTOSYNTHESIS RESEARCHERS' LIST
Description: Photosynthesis Researchers' List is a discussion group coverng all matters concerning photosynthesis.
Subjects covered: photosynthesis; plant biology
Net address for operations: Biosci@net.bio.net
Biosci@daresbury.ac.uk

Net address for questions or submissions: Usenet News (NNTP): bionet.photosynthesis
Email: Photosyn@net.bio.net,
Photosyn@daresbury.ac.uk
Established: On Listserv@vm.tau.ac.il in Aug 1990, Moved to Biosci/Bionet in May 1993
Subscribers: 298
List moderated: No.
Editorial contact: Jonathan B. Marder
Department of Agricultural Botany, The Hebrew University of Jerusalem, Faculty of Agriculture, P.O. Box 12, Rehovot 76100, ISRAEL
Tel: (08 or +9728) 481918
Fax: (08 or +9728) 467763
Internet: MARDER@AGRI.HUJI.AC.IL
Bitnet: MARDER@HUJIAGRI
Technical contact: David Kristofferson (Biosci manager)
Internet: Kristoff@net.bio.net
How to access: For the Americas and the Pacific rim, contact Biosci@net.bio.net. For Europe, Africa, and Central Asia, contact Biosci@daresbury.ac.uk
Access policy: Subscriptions are open to anyone.
How to unsubscribe: For the Americas and the Pacific rim, contact Biosci@net.bio.net. For Europe, Africa, and Central Asia, contact Biosci@daresbury.ac.uk
Submission policy: Any item of general interest to photosynthesis researchers.
Archives: None at the moment. Future items archived at NET.BIO.NET in directory pub/BIOSCI/PHOTOSYNTHESIS
Related files: PHOTOSYNTHESIS GUIDE from LISTSERV@VM.TAU.AC.IL (send message saying "GET PHOTOSYN GUIDE") PHOTOSYN NICELIST (email address list) from LISTSERV@VM.TAU.AC.IL (send message saying "GET PHOTOSYN GUIDE")
Gopher accessibility: Via News Gateways
WAIS accessibility: WAIS indexed with other Biosci groups.
Additional information: USENET news post to bionet.photosynthesis

PHOTREAC@JPNTOHOK

Description: PHOTREAC is a discussion list on electro- and photo-nuclear reaction.
Subjects covered: physics
List moderated: No.
How to access: Send subscribe message to listserv@jpntohok
How to unsubscribe: Send unsubscribe message to listserv@jpntohok

PHYS-L

Description: PHYS-L is a discussion list covering Items of interest to physics educators. It contains postings on lecture demos, educational approaches, textbooks, curricula, grading procedures, physics explanations, and other material.
Subjects covered: physics; education
Net address for operations: LISTSERV@UWF.CC.UWF.EDU or LISTSERV@UWF
Net address for questions or submissions: PHYS-L@UWF.CC.UWF.EDU or LISTSERV@UWF
Established: 1987
Subscribers: 400
Sponsor: University of West Florida,
11000 University Parkway, Pensacola, FL 32514.

Host: University of West Florida, 11000 University Parkway, Pensacola, FL 32514.
List moderated: No.
Editorial contact: Dick Smith
Department of Physics, University of West Florida, 11000 University Parkway, Pensacola, FL 32514.
Tel: (904) 474-2269
Fax: (904) 474-3131
Internet: RSMITH@UWF.CC.UWF.EDU
Bitnet: RSMITH@UWF
Technical contact: Craig Holbert
Computer Services, University of West Florida, 11000 University Parkway, Pensacola, FL 32514.
Tel: (904) 474-2972
Fax: (904) 474-3129
Internet: CRAIG@UWF.CC.UWF.EDU
Bitnet: CRAIG@UWF
How to access: Send mail or interactive command to LISTSERV@UWF: SUBSCRIBE PHYS-L Yourname
Access policy: Open to public subscription.
How to unsubscribe: Send mail or interactive command to LISTSERV@UWF: SIGNOFF PHYS-L
How to submit: Send mail to PHYS-L@UWF
Submission policy: Open to public.
Archives: Most recent two years are archived on disk by monthly file, and can be obtained by sending the following instruction to LISTSERV@UWF:
GET PHYS-L LOGyymm
Related files: No files available via FTP. Many documents and physics-related programs available. These are indexed in PHYSICS FILELIST, which can be obtained by sending the following to LISTSERV@UWF: GET PHYSICS FILELIST

PHYSIC-L

Description: Physic-L is a forum for information on physics for Israeli scientists.
Subjects covered: physics
List moderated: Yes.
Editorial contact: Joseph van Zwaren
Internet: jo%ilncrd.bitnet@cunyvm.cuny.edu
Bitnet: jo@ilncrd
How to access: Send subscribe message to listserv@taunivm or listserv@taunivm.tau.ac.il
How to unsubscribe: Send unsubscribe message to listserv@taunivm or listserv@taunivm.tau.ac.il

PHYSICS@MIAMIU

Description: PHYSICS is a discussion list about physics.
Subjects covered: physics
List moderated: No.
How to access: Send subscribe message to listserv@miamiu
How to unsubscribe: Send unsubscribe message to listserv@miamiu

PHYSICS@QEDQCD.RYE.NY.US

Description: PHYSICS@QEDQCD.RYE.NY.US is a forum on developments in experimental physics.
Subjects covered: physics
List moderated: No.
Editorial contact: Mike Miskulin
Internet: physics-request@qedqcd.rye.ny.us

How to access: Contact the Editor
How to unsubscribe: Contact the Editor

PHYSIO

Subjects covered: science and technology; education
Net address for operations: mailbase@mailbase.ac.uk
Net address for questions or submissions:
physio@mailbase.ac.uk
Established: January 11, 1993
Subscribers: 76
Sponsor: Queen Margaret College, Clerwood Terrace, Edinburgh, Scotland EH12 8TS, UK.
Host: The NISP Project, Computing Service, The University of Newcastle upon Tyne NE1 7RU, UK.
List moderated: No.
Editorial contact: George McMurdo
Department of Communication & Information Studies, Queen Margaret College, Clerwood Terrace, Edinburgh, Scotland EH12 8TS.
Tel: (4431) 031 317 3505
Fax: (4431) 031 316 4165
Internet: cimmu@cis.qmced.ac.uk, geo__mcmurdo@hicom.org
Review: UPFIELD, Heather & MCMURDO, George, Physiotherapists in the Global Village Physiotherapy - the Journal of the Chartered Society of Physiotherapy (ISSN 0031 9406) vol 79 no 5, May 1993, pp 338-9.
How to access: To mailbase@mailbase.ac.uk send the message join physio <firstname> <surname>
How to unsubscribe: To mailbase@mailbase.ac.uk send the message leave physio
How to submit: To physio@mailbase.ac.uk send a message.
Archives: Messages to the list are archived monthly and may be retrieved by e-mail. For an index of available e-mail archives (and other files associated with the PHYSIO list ...) To mailbase@mailbase.ac.uk send the message index physio To obtain a file in the filelist returned by the INDEX command: to mailbase@mailbase.ac.uk send the message send physio <name-of-file-wanted>
Related files: The Mailbase system on JANET, through which PHYSIO is provided, is also an online service, and details of lists, archived e-mail, and files associated with lists, can be browsed interactively ... Telnet to:mailbase.ac.uk (or 128.240.2.118) Login as:guest Password:mailbase The Mailbase system now also has a Gopher interface ... Name = Mailbase Gopher Type = 1 Host = mailbase.ac.uk Port = 70 Path =
Additional information: Additional editors: Heather Upfield, Department of Physiotherapy, Queen Margaret College, Clerwood Terrace, Edinburgh, Scotland EH12 8TS; Brian Durward; Departmentof Physiotherapy; Queen Margaret College, Clerwood Terrace, Edinburgh, Scotland EH12 8TS; tel (4431) 031 317 3644; fax (4431) 031 317 3256; Internetphdurw@main.qmced.ac.uk

PIADAS

Description: A discussion group of Portuguese humor.
Subjects covered: humor; Portuguese language and literature
Technical contact: Walter Morales
Internet: walter@psg.com
How to access: Send message to listserv@pccvm.bitnet one single line: sub piadas <your name>
How to unsubscribe: Send message to listserv@pccvm.bitnet unsub piadas

PINHOLE@MINTIR.FIDONET.ORG

Description: PINHOLE covers pinhole photography.
Subjects covered: photography
List moderated: No,
Editorial contact: Richard R. Vallon, Jr.
Internet: rvallon@mintir!rvallon
How to access: Send subscribe message to PINHOLE-REQUEST@MINTIR.FIDONET.ORG
How to unsubscribe: Send unsubscribe message to PINHOLE-REQUEST@MINTIR.FIDONET.ORG

PIPORG-L

Description: Piporg-L discusses pipe organs and topics of similar focus.
Subjects covered: music; musical instruments
List moderated: No.
Editorial contact: Dave
Internet: schuttschutt@netcom.com
How to access: Send subscribe message to listserv@albany or listserv@albany.edu
How to unsubscribe: Send unsubscribe message to listserv@albany or listserv@albany.edu

PIR-BB@IRLEARN

Description: PIR-BB@IRLEARN is a conference covering medical topics.
Subjects covered: medicine
List moderated: No.
How to access: Send subscribe message to listserv@irlearn or listserv@irlearn.ucd.ie
How to unsubscribe: Send unsubscribe message to listserv@irlearn or listserv@irlearn.ucd.ie

PISMA BRALCEV

Description: Pisma bralcev is an edited but not moderated mailing list which provides the possibility of publishing readers' opinions, questions, inquiries for help, answers, etc. There are also published travel tips and book reviews. Anybody can send a letter to the editor and it will be published on the list under his name. The author can request the anonymity and it will be respected entirely. The frequency of publishing is about one issue per day or less. The language is originally Slovene, but other languages appear as well. The list is also member of "KRPAN, The Slovene Worldwide Computer Network."
Subjects covered: travel and tourism; Slovenia
Net address for operations: Pisma.bralcev@Uni-Lj.SI Pisma-bralcev@IJS.SI
Established: December 1989
Subscribers: 101
List moderated: No.
Moderation procedure: The editor reformats the contributions and puts them together. The editor also adds the table of contents and numbers the issues.
Editorial contact: Andrej Brodnik
University of Waterloo, Waterloo, Ontario, Canada; Jozef Stefan Institute, Ljubljana, Slovenia.
Internet: ABrodnik@WatDragon.UWaterloo.CA, Andrej.Brodnik@IJS.SI, Andrej.Brodnik@Uni-Lj.SI
How to access: Send mail to the list address.
Access policy: There are no restrictions.
How to unsubscribe: Send mail to the list address.

How to submit: Send contribution to the list address.
Submission policy: No restrictions on submitting. Anonymous contributions are also acceptable.
Archives: Archive is kept by the editor and is available on demand.

PJAL

Description: The Progressive Jewish Activism List (PJAL@UTXVM.BITNET) is a forum for organizing and activism-oriented discussion by progressive Jews working for peace and social justice. PJAL is an outgrowth of the Progressive Jewish Mailing List (PJML), an unmoderated discussion forum for progressive Jews. PJAL is a moderated list, which means that list moderators reserve the right to determine the direction and integrity of submissions posted to PJAL. For unmoderated discussions, subscribers are encouraged to join PJML. Posting and list review on PJAL are restricted to list subscribers.
Subjects covered: political activism; political science; Israel; Judaica
Net address for operations: LISTSERV@UTXVM.CC.UTEXAS.EDU
Net address for questions or submissions: PJML@UTXVM.CC.UTEXAS.EDU
Established: 1991
Subscribers: 49
Host: University of Texas at Austin, Austin, TX
List moderated: Yes.
Editorial contact: Steve Carr
3911-A Ave. F., Austin, TX 78751
Tel: (512) 453-8540 or (512) 471-4071 (b)
Internet: CARR@UTXVM.CC.UTEXAS.EDU
How to access: To subscribe to PJAL, please apply to one of the list owners, Steve Carr or Seth Grimes. In your application, please describe your background, state your willingness to adhere to all of the PJAL principles outlined and your acceptance of the moderated format of the list.
Additional information: Second editor is: Seth Grimes, 79bis Bd. de Picpus, 75012 Paris, France; GRIMES@ACCESS; (33-1) 40.19.99.57

PJML

Description: The Progressive Jewish Mailing List (PJML) is an unmoderated discussion forum for progressive Jews.
Subjects covered: political activism; Judaica
Net address for operations: LISTSERV@UTXVM.CC.UTEXAS.EDU
Net address for questions or submissions: PJML@UTXVM.CC.UTEXAS.EDU
Established: 1991
Subscribers: 147
Host: University of Texas at Austin, Austin, TX.
List moderated: No.
Editorial contact: Steve Carr
3911-A Avenue. F, Austin, TX 78751.
Tel: (512) 471-4071
Internet: CARR@UTXVM.CC.UTEXAS.EDU
Bitnet: CARR@UTXVM
How to access: Send the following message to LISTSERV@UTXVM.BITNET or LISTSERV@UTXVM.CC.UTEXAS.EDU: SUB PJML <your first name> <your last name>

Related files: See PJAL mailing list.
Additional information: Additional listowner: Seth Grimes, 79 bis Bd. de Picpus, 75012 Paris, France; (33-1) 40.19.99.57; GRIMES@ACCESS.DIGEX.NET.

PLANT-TAXONOMY@MAILBASE.AC.UK

Description: PLANT-TAXONOMYis a forum on plant taxonomy.
Subjects covered: horticulture; plant biology
List moderated: No.
Internet: plant-taxonomy-request@mailbase.ac.uk
How to access: Send subscribe message to mailbase@mailbase.ac.uk in the following format: join plant-taxonomy Yourfirstname Yourlastname
Archives: Archives are developed monthly; apply to listowner for details.

PMC-MOO

Description: PMC-MOO is a new service offered (free of charge) by the ejournal Postmodern Culture. PMC-MOO is a real-time, text-based, virtual reality environment in which you can interact with other subscribers of the e-journal and participate in live conferences. PMC-MOO will also provide access to texts generated by the journal and by PMC- TALK, and it will provide the opportunity to experience (or help to design) programs which simulate object-lessons in postmodern theory.
PMC-MOO is based on the LambdaMOO program, freeware by Pavel Curtis.
Subjects covered: cultural studies; literary theory and criticism; music; virtual reality
Editorial contact: Eyal Amiran
Box 8105, NC State University, Raleigh, North Carolina 27607
How to access: To connect to PMC-MOO, you must be on the Internet. If you have an internet account, you can make a direct connection by typing the command telnet dewey.lib.ncsu.edu 7777 at your command prompt. Once you've connected to the server, you will receive onscreen instructions on how to log in to PMC-MOO. If you have problems connecting to PMC-MOO or would like more information, contact pmc@unity.ncsu.edu by e-mail.

PMC-TALK

Description: PMC-TALK is a discussion group carrying various postings on postmodernism, theory, pedagogy, conferences, etc.
Subjects covered: language and literature; literary theory and criticism; cultural studies
Net address for operations: LISTSERV@LISTSERV.NCSU.EDU
Net address for questions or submissions: PMC-TALK@UNITY.NCSU.EDU
Established: 1990
Subscribers: 750
Sponsor: North Carolina State U., Raleigh, NC and Oxford University Press
Host: North Carolina State U., Raleigh, NC
List moderated: Yes.
Moderation procedure: All entries of any relevance are formatted and posted
Editorial contact: Chris Barrett
Box 8105, English Department, NCSU, Raleigh, NY 27695
Fax: (919) 515-3628

Internet: PMC-TALK@UNITY.NCSU.EDU
Copyright statement: PMC-TALK is not copyrighted.
How to access: Send to listserv address or write to editor; message should read: SUB PMC-TALK YOUR NAME
How to unsubscribe: Send to listserv address or write to editor; message should read: UNSUB PMC-TALK YOUR NAME
How to submit: Send mail to: PMC-TALK@UNITY.NCSU.EDU
Submission policy: Send anything relevant to postmodern concerns.
Archives: Selected back files are available; information is sent to subscribers about their retrieval.

PNWCSC@UWAVM
Description: PNWCSC@UWAVM is a forum for discussion of topics related to the Pacific Northwest Canadian Studies Consortium.
Subjects covered: library and information science
List moderated: Yes.
Internet: ldibiase@milton.u.washington.edu
How to access: Send subscribe message to listserv@uwavm
How to unsubscribe: Send unsubscribe message to listserv@uwavm
Archives: Yes; Monthly, Private

POLAND-L
Description: Poland-L focuses on the culture and events of Poland.
Subjects covered: Poland; current events; political science
Net address for operations: LISTSERV@UBVM, LISTSERV@UBVM.CC.BUFFALO.EDU
List moderated: No.
Editorial contact: Michael Prussak
Internet: michal@gs58.sp.cs.cmu.edu
How to access: Send subscribe message to listserv@ubvm or listserv@ubvm.cc.buffalo.edu
How to unsubscribe: Send unsubscribe message to listserv@ubvm or listserv@ubvm.cc.buffalo.edu
Archives: Archives are developed weekly; apply to listowner for details.

POLAND@NDCVX.CC.ND.EDU
Description: POLAND@NDCVX.CC.ND.EDU covers news bulletins from Poland.
Subjects covered: Poland; communications; current events; political science
List moderated: No.
Internet: przemek@ndcvx.cc.nd.edu

POLCAN@YORKVM1
Description: POLCAN@YORKVM1 is a forum for Canadian political scientists.
Subjects covered: Canada; political science
Host: Canadian Political Science Association
List moderated: Yes.
Editorial contact: Ian Greene
Internet: yfps0013@vm1.yorku.ca
Bitnet: yfps0013@yorkvm1
How to access: Send subscribe message to listserv@yorkvm1 or listserv@vm1.yorku.ca

How to unsubscribe: Send unsubscribe message to listserv@yorkvm1 or listserv@vm1.yorku.ca
Archives: Yes.

POLCOMM@RPITSVM
Description: POLCOMM@RPITSVM is a forum covering political communication.
Subjects covered: communications; political science
Host: Comserve
List moderated: Yes.
Editorial contact: Comserve Staff
Internet: support@vm.its.vpi.edu
Bitnet: support@rpitsvm
How to access: Send subscribe message to comserve@rpitsvm or comserve@vm.its.vpi.edu
How to unsubscribe: Send unsubscribe message to comserve@rpitsvm or comserve@vm.its.vpi.edu

POLI-SCI@RUTVM1
Description: POLI-SCI@RUTVM1 is a forum for discussing the political history of the US in the 1970s.
Subjects covered: political science
List moderated: Yes.
Editorial contact: Charles McGrew
Internet: mcgrew@aramis.rutgers.edu
How to access: Send subscribe message to listserv@rutvm1 or listserv@rutgers.edu
How to unsubscribe: Send unsubscribe message to listserv@rutvm1 or listserv@rutgers.edu

POLITICA@UFRJ
Description: POLITICA@UFRJ is a forum for discussion of the politics in Brazil.
Subjects covered: political science; Brazil
List moderated: No.
Editorial contact: Nilson Theobald Barbosa
Bitnet: nilson@ufrj
How to access: Send subscribe message to listserv@ufrj or listserv%ufrj.bitnet@cunyvm.cuny.edu
How to unsubscribe: Send unsubscribe message to listserv@ufrj or listserv%ufrj.bitnet@cunyvm.cuny.edu
Archives: Archives are developed monthly; apply to listowner for details.

POLITICS@UCF1VM
Description: POLITICS@UCF1VM is a forum for the discussion of politics.
Subjects covered: political science
Host: University of Central Florida
List moderated: No.
Editorial contact: Eric Anderson
Bitnet: anderson@ucf1vm
How to access: Send subscribe message to listserv@ucf1vm or listserv%ucf1vm.bitnet@mitvma.mit.edu
How to unsubscribe: Send unsubscribe message to listserv@ucf1vm or listserv%ucf1vm.bitnet@mitvma.mit.edu
Archives: Archives are developed weekly; apply to listowner for details.

POLYMERP@RUTVM1
Description: POLYMERP@RUTVM1 is a discussion on polymer physics.
Subjects covered: physics
List moderated: No.
Editorial contact: Peter Barneveld
Internet: peter@fenk.wau.nl
How to access: Send subscribe message to listserv@rutvm1 or listserv@rutgers.edu
How to unsubscribe: Send unsubscribe message to listserv@rutvm1 or listserv@rutgers.edu
Archives: Archives are developed monthly; apply to listowner for details.

PORIFERA
Description: PORIFERA is a list providing contacts between scientists working on sponge biology or sponge chemistry. The decision for the creation of the list was taken during the last International Porifera Symposium ("Sponges in Time and Space"), held in Amsterdam in April 1993.
Subjects covered: sponges; porifera; chemistry; plant biology
Net address for operations:
MAILBASE@UK.AC.MAILBASE
Net address for questions or submissions:
PORIFERA@UK.AC.MAILBASE
Established: April 1993
Subscribers: 23
Sponsor: UK's Information Systems Committee, University of Newcastle Funding Council.
Host: University of Newcastle, Newcastle, UK.
List moderated: No.
Editorial contact: Antonio M. Sole-Cava
Plymouth Marine Laboratory, Citadel Hill, Plymouth PL1 2PB, UK.
Tel: 44 752 222 772
Fax: 44 752 226 865
Internet: AMS@UK.AC.NERC-PML.IBMA
How to access: Send message "JOIN PORIFERA surname name" to MAILBASE@MAILBASE.AC.UK
Access policy: PORIFERA is an open list.
How to unsubscribe: Send message "LEAVE PORIFERA" to MAILBASE@MAILBASE.AC.UK
How to submit: Send text to PORIFERA@MAILBASE.AC.UK

POSIX-ADA@GREBYN.COM
Description: POSIX-ADA is a forum for IEEE 1003.5 workgroup members.
Subjects covered: computer science
Host: IEEE
List moderated: No.
Editorial contact: Karl Nyberg
Internet: karl@grebyn.com
How to access: Send subscribe message to posix-ada-request@grebyn.com
How to unsubscribe: Send unsubscribe message to posix-ada-request@grebyn.com

POSIX-FORTRAN@SANDIA.GOV
Description: POSIX-FORTRAN is a forum for IEEE members working in FORTRAN on the IEEE POSIX specification.
Subjects covered: computer science
Host: IEEE
List moderated: No.
Editorial contact: Michael J. Hannah
Internet: mjhanna@sandia.gov
How to access: Send subscribe message to POSIX-FORTRAN-REQUEST@SANDIA.GOV
How to unsubscribe: Send unsubscribe message to POSIX-FORTRAN-REQUEST@SANDIA.GOV

POSIX-TESTING@MINDCRAFT.COM
Description: POSIX-TESTING is a forum on testing operating systems for conformance to POSIX standards.
Subjects covered: computer science
Host: IEEE
List moderated: No.
Editorial contact: Chuck Karish
Internet: posix-testing-request@mindcraft.com
How to access: Contact the Editor
How to unsubscribe: Contact the Editor

PRENAT-L
Description: Prenat-L is a conference on prenatal health data for New York State.
Subjects covered: medicine
List moderated: Yes.
Editorial contact: Colene Byrne
Bitnet: cmb04@albnydh2
How to access: Send subscribe message to listserv@albnydh2
How to unsubscribe: Send unsubscribe message to listserv@albnydh2
Archives: Archives are developed weekly; apply to listowner for details.

PREZHIST@KASEY.UMKC.EDU
Description: PrezHist@kasey is a discussion list covering the history or the US Presidents from 1789 to the present.
Subjects covered: U.S. Presidents; history
Net address for operations: Listserv@kasey.umkc.edu
Net address for questions or submissions:
PrezHist@kasey.umkc.edu
How to access: Send message to listserv: SUBSCRIBE <listname> <your name>

PRION@ACC.STOLAF.EDU
Description: PRION is an electronic digest of material related to slow virus infection.
Subjects covered: medicine
List moderated: No.
Editorial contact: Chris Swanson
Internet: swansonc@acc.stolaf.edu
How to access: Send subscribe message to PRION-REQUEST@ACC.STOLAF.EDU
How to unsubscribe: Send unsubscribe message to PRION-REQUEST@ACC.STOLAF.EDU
Archives: Yes; Send anonymous FTP to:
BEOWULF.ACC.STOLAF.EDU (130.71.192.20) cd pub/prion

PRISON-L

Description: Prison-L provides a forum for education in prisons.

Subjects covered: education

List moderated: Yes.

Editorial contact: Patricia B. McRae

Bitnet: t350134@univscvm

How to access: Send subscribe message to listserv@dartcms1 or listserv@dartcms1.dartmouth.edu

How to unsubscribe: Send unsubscribe message to listserv@dartcms1 or listserv@dartcms1.dartmouth.edu

PRNCYB-L

Description: PRNCYB-L is a private discussion list and constitutes the official daily communication channel for the Principia Cybernetica Project (PCP). PCP is a computer-supported collaborative attempt to develop an integrated evolutionary-systemic philosophy or world view. Its contributors are distributed over the 5 continents. The main file repository is the ftp site is1.vub.ac.be:/pub/projects/Principia__Cybernetica. Members keep contact mainly by electronic mail (this list), by annual meetings, the printed (and electronic) Newsletter, and postal mail. The PCP philosophy starts from the self-organization of multi-level systems through blind variation and natural selection. This leads to a process metaphysics, a constructive-selectionist epistemology, and an evolutionary ethics. PCP focuses on the clear formulation of basic concepts and principles of the cybernetic approach. This should lead to a semantic network of concepts and links, implemented as a distributed hypertext. The ftp site is the first stage of the worldwide electronic publication of this network of linked texts, which are meant to define and illustrate the fundamental concepts of a transdisciplinary philosophy for the cyber-age.

Subjects covered: science and technology; computer science; cybernetics; metaphysics

Net address for operations: LISTSERV@BINGVMB.BITNET

Net address for questions or submissions: PRNCYB-L@BINGVMB.BITNET

Established: 1992

Subscribers: 48

Sponsor: SUNY-Binghamton

Host: Systems Science SUNY-Binghamton, Binghamton, NY 13902.

List moderated: No.

Editorial contact: Cliff Joslyn

327 Spring St., # 2, Portland, ME 04102.

Internet: cybsys@bingsuns.cc.binghamton.edu

How to access: Private list

Access policy: Application required. Retrieve application by anonymous ftp from: is1.vub.ac.be:/pub/projects/Principia__Cybernetica/Notes__on__PCP.txt or by email request to fheyligh@vnet3.vub.ac.be

How to unsubscribe: Message "unsub PRNCYB-L" to LISTSERV@BINGVMB.BITNET

How to submit: Mail message to PRNCYB-L@BINGVMB.BITNET

Archives: The last year's discussions are stored on LISTSERV@BINGVMB.BITNET

Related files: ftp site for PCP is1.vub.ac.be:/pub/projects/Principia__Cybernetica The ftp site is the first stage of the worldwide electronic publication of this network of linked texts, which are meant to define and illustrate the fundamental concepts of a transdisciplinary philosophy for the cyber-age.

PRO-CITE

Description: PRO-CITE has been established as an international electronic forum for anyone using or interested in using the bibliographic textbase software program PRO-CITE and its companion BIBLIO-LINK programs published by Personal Bibliographic Software. These software programs provide the means to automate a wide variety of scholarly tasks related to the retrieval, organization, and use of bibliographic data. They operate on both MS-DOS and Macintosh platforms. With the much enhanced version 2.0 of Pro-Cite now available for both systems, it seemed like a good time to establish a Bitnet discussion group, whose existence could facilitate the rapid sharing of concerns, interests, problems and solutions among members at all levels of use.

Subjects covered: Pro-Cite; computer hardware and software; Personal Bibliographic Software

Net address for questions or submissions: PRO-CITE@IUBVM

Established: April 14, 1992

Subscribers: 565

List moderated: No.

Editorial contact: Mark T. Day

Assoc. Librarian, Reference, Indiana University Library, Room E159, Bloomington, IN 47405

Tel: (812) 855-8028 or 855-0100

Fax: DAYM@IUBACS.BITNET

Internet: DAYM@UCS.INDIANA.EDU

How to access: Send the following one line e-mail message: SUBSCRIBE PRO-CITE LastName, FirstName via BITNET to: LISTSERV@IUBVM or via INTERNET to: LISTSERV@IUBVM.UCS.INDIANA.EDU

How to unsubscribe: Send the following one line message: UNSUBSCRIBE PRO-CITE to the same address you used to subscribe (item #1 above) [to re-subscribe, follow procedure "1)" above]

How to submit: Send messages for posting on the PRO-CITE list: via BITNET to: PRO-CITE@IUBVM or via INTERNET to: PRO-CITE@IUBVM.UCS.INDIANA.EDU

Archives: You can obtain a list of available archive files by sending an INDEX PRO-CITE command to LISTSERV@IUBVM. 2) Such files can be retrieved by issuing a GET PRO-CITE LOGYYMM command, where "YY" stands for the year and "MM" stands for the month. 3) If you are curious about who your fellow subscribers to this list are, send the message REVIEW PRO-CITE to LISTSERV@IUBVM.

PRO-FEMINIST MEN'S ISSUES MAILING LIST

Description: PRO-FEMINIST MEN'S ISSUES MAILING LIST is a discussion forum covering issues pertaining to being men and being pro-feminist.

Subjects covered: gender studies; feminism; communications; men's studies

Net address for operations: JYANOWITZ@HAMP.HAMPSHIRE.EDU

List moderated: No.

How to access: For more information or to join, contact JYANOWITZ@HAMP.HAMPSHIRE.EDU

PROFESSIONAL ORGANIZATIONAL DEVELOPMENT

Description: Professional Organizational Development (POD) is a list discussing professional development issues in higher education.
Subjects covered: colleges and universities; education
Net address for operations: listserv@lists.acs.ohio-state.edu
How to access: Send standard subscribe request to listserv.
How to unsubscribe: Send standard unsubscribe request to listserv.

PROFSALT@UCCVMA

Description: PROFSALT@UCCVMA is a forum offering assistance for Profs sites.
Subjects covered: campus-wide information services; colleges and universities; electronic networking
Host: University of California
List moderated: No.
Editorial contact: Rich Hintz
Internet: opsrjh@uccvma.bitnet
How to access: Send subscribe message to listserv@uccvma or listserv@uccvma.ucop.edu
How to unsubscribe: Send unsubscribe message to listserv@uccvma or listserv@uccvma.ucop.edu

PROJECT H

Description: Project H is a group of more than 120 enthusiastic people who are collaborating on a quantitative study of electronic discussions. Pertinent to the current thread is that the project emerged from discussions on scholarly lists; many of the project members are members of IPCT-L; and the coordinators, Sheizaf Rafaeli and Fay Sudweeks, "met" on IPCT-L and CMC lists. The CMC literature abounds with laboratory experiments, surveys and, of course, studies of single e-groups such as the one by Mr. Lewenstein. What we found lacking in CMC studies is empirical research to support statements about a broad range of e-groups. We believe our project is pioneering research in filling this gap.
Subjects covered: computer hardware and software; telecommunications; Internet
Editorial contact: Sheizaf Rafaeli
Internet: sheizafr@shum.cc.huji.ac.il
Bitnet: su.edu.au
Copyright statement: We are concerned with the ethical implications of our study. Issues raised include informed consent, the violation of privacy and copyright, the integrity and autonomy of scholarship and inquiry. The quantitative analysis of the aggregate of publicly available, archived content of large group discussions that occurred voluntarily is subject to fewer of the ethical concerns. Nevertheless, groups of us have written up documents on ethics and copyright policies, that are informed by legal knowledge, human-subjects' committees positions, and opinions of members of the group. Individual researchers participating in this study will seek their own universities' human subject committees approval for their role in the study.
How to access: Contact Sheizaf (sheizafr@shum.cc.huji.ac.il) or Fay Sudweeks fays@archsci.arch.su.edu.au for instructions on how to join.
Related files: Key documents and coding formats are stored on an FTP site and available via anonymous FTP. These include the bibliography, biographies of participants, records of discussions in subcommittees, policy statments regarding copyright,

reliability, and sampling, codebooks, message corpora, coding tools, and more. In part, we use ftp availability of our materials to enhance the public nature of this project, and to underscore the 'on stage' nature of our efforts. We also use other computer-mediated communication means. Subsets of us have used synchronous tools, such as "talk", IRC, etc. All of our group discussions are archived and available for public scrutiny.
Additional information: Second editor: Fay Sudweeks, fays@archsci.arch

PROLOG@SUSHI.STANFORD.EDU

Description: PROLOG@SUSHI is a list for Prolog programmers.
Subjects covered: computer science
List moderated: No.
Editorial contact: Chuck Restivo
Internet: restivo@sushi.stanford.edu
How to access: Send subscribe message to PROLOG-REQUEST@SUSHI.STANFORD.EDU or PROLOG-HACKERS-REQUEST@SUSHI.STANFORD.EDU
How to unsubscribe: Send unsubscribe message to PROLOG-REQUEST@SUSHI.STANFORD.EDU or PROLOG-HACKERS-REQUEST@SUSHI.STANFORD.EDU
Archives: Yes.

PROTOCOL@VMD.CSO.UIUC.EDU

Description: PROTOCOL discusses formats used in data transfer over computer networks.
Subjects covered: computer science; electronic networking
List moderated: No.
Editorial contact: Phil Howard
Internet: phil@ux1.cso.uiuc.edu
How to access: Send subscribe message to listserv@uiucvmd or listserv@vmd.cso.uiuc.edu
How to unsubscribe: Send unsubscribe message to listserv@uiucvmd or listserv@vmd.cso.uiuc.edu

PSATC-L

Description: Psatc-L covers problem solving techniques in educational curricula.
Subjects covered: education
List moderated: No.
Editorial contact: Jim Gerland
Bitnet: gerland@ubvms
How to access: Send subscribe message to listserv@ubvm or listserv@ubvm.cc.buffalo.edu
How to unsubscribe: Send unsubscribe message to listserv@ubvm or listserv@ubvm.cc.buffalo.edu
Archives: Archives are developed weekly; apply to listowner for details.

PSI-L

Description: Psi-L is a forum covering parapsychology.
Subjects covered: psychology
List moderated: No.
Editorial contact: Lusi N. Altman
Bitnet: lnaqc@cunyvm
How to access: Send subscribe message to listserv@cunyvm or listserv@cunyvm.cuny.edu

How to unsubscribe: Send unsubscribe message to listserv@cunyvm or listserv@cunyvm.cuny.edu
Archives: Archives are developed weekly; apply to listowner for details.

PSRT-L

Description: PSRT-L is a forum for political science research and training.
Subjects covered: political science
List moderated: Yes.
Editorial contact: Bill Ball and Michael Malaby
Bitnet: polpsrt@mizzou11
How to access: Send subscribe message to listserv@mizzou11
How to unsubscribe: Send unsubscribe message to listserv@mizzou11
Archives: Archives are developed monthly; apply to listowner for details.

PSTAT-L

Description: PSTAT-L is a forum focusing on the statistical software P-STAT.
Subjects covered: mathematics; statistics; computer hardware and software
List moderated: No.
Editorial contact: Peter Flynn
Bitnet: cbts8001@iruccvax
How to access: Send subscribe message to listserv@irlearn or listserv@irlearn.ucd.ie
How to unsubscribe: Send unsubscribe message to listserv@irlearn or listserv@irlearn.ucd.ie
Archives: Archives are developed monthly; apply to listowner for details.

PSYART

Description: PSYART is an electronic discussion group centering around literature and psychology topics.
Subjects covered: language and literature; fine arts; psychoanalysis; psychology
Net address for operations: LISTSERV@nervm.nerdc.ufl.edu
Net address for questions or submissions:
nnh@nervm.nerdc.ufl.edu
Established: May 26, 1994
Subscribers: 47
Sponsor: Institute for Psychological Study of the Art,
Dept. of English, University of Florida, Gainesville, FL 32611.
List moderated: Yes.
Moderation procedure: Informal by owner.
Editorial contact: Norman N. Holland
Dept. of English, Univ. of Florida, Gainesville, FL 32611
Tel: (904) 377-0096
Fax: (904) 392-3584
Internet: nnh@nervm.nerdc.ufl.edu
Bitnet: nnh@nervm
How to access: Send the following message to the listserv:
SUBSCRIBE PSYART firstname lastname

PSYCGRAD@UOTTAWA (PSYCHOLOGY GRADUATE STUDENTS DISCUSSION LIST)

Description: PSYCGRAD@UOTTAWA (Psychology Graduate Students Discussion List) posts discussions on topics in psychology.
Subjects covered: psychology; psychobiology; psychotherapy
Net address for operations: listserv@acadvm1.uottawa.ca
listserv@uottawa.bitnet
Net address for questions or submissions:
psycgrad@acadvm1.uottawa.ca
psycgrad@uottawa.bitnet
Established: August 1991
Subscribers: 570
Sponsor: Matthew Simpson Productions
Host: School of Psychology, University of Ottawa, Ottawa, Ontario K1N 6N5.
List moderated: No.
Technical contact: Matthew Simpson
University of Ottawa, Ottawa, Ontario K1N 6N5
Tel: (613) 564-2964
Fax: (613) 564-9569
Internet: 054340@acadvm1.uottawa.ca
Bitnet: 054340@uottawa.bitnet
How to access: Subscriptions can be sent to
LISTSERV@UOTTAWA.BITNET or
LISTSERV@ACADVM1.UOTTAWA.CA
To subscribe, send one of the commands:
SUB PSYCGRAD Yourfirstname Yourlastname or SUB PSYCGRAD Yourfirstname Yourlastname
SET PSYCGRAD DIGEST or SUB PSYGRD-J Yourfirstname Yourlastname
After you have subscribed, postings to the project can be sent to
PSYCGRAD@UOTTAWA.BITNET or
PSYCGRAD@ACADVM1.UOTTAWA.CA.
Access policy: Graduate students studying in a psychology-related field.
How to unsubscribe: SIGNOFF PSYCGRAD
How to submit: Send email to psycgrad@acadvm1.uottawa.ca or psycgrad@uottawa.bitnet
Submission policy: Must be a graduate student studying in psychology.
Archives: Archvies available at listserv@acadvm1.uottawa.ca
listserv@bitnet
Gopher accessibility: panda1.uottawa.ca (The PSYCGRAD Gopher) gopher panda1.uottawa.ca
ftp aix1.uottawa.ca
/u/ftp/pub/psycgrad/The.PSYCGRAD.Digest
Netnews bit.listserv.psycgrad
Additional information: The main purpose of The PSYCGRAD Project is two-fold. The first is to provide a standard of communication among psychology graduate students. The second is to publish, from the graduate student perspective, professional articles in the field of psychology.

PSYCH-DEV-EUROPE@MAILBASE.AC.UK

Description: PSYCH-DEV-EUROPE@MAILBASE.AC.UK is a list for European developmental psychologists.
Subjects covered: psychology
List moderated: No.
Internet: psych-dev-europe-request@mailbase.ac.uk

How to access: Send subscribe message to mailbase@mailbase.ac.uk in the following format: join psych-dev-europe Yourfirstname Yourlastname
Archives: Archives are developed monthly; apply to listowner for details.

PSYCH-EXPTS@MAILBASE.AC.UK
Description: PSYCH-EXPTS@MAILBASE.AC.UK is a list for European psychologists.
Subjects covered: psychology
List moderated: No.
Internet: psych-expts-request@mailbase.ac.uk
How to access: Send subscribe message to mailbase@mailbase.ac.uk in the following format: join psych-expts Yourfirstname Yourlastname
Archives: Archives are developed monthly; apply to listowner for details.

PTG-FORUM@MAILBASE.AC.UK
Description: PTG-FORUM is a list for members of the Plant Transport Group.
Subjects covered: horticulture
Host: Plant Transport Group, Society of Experimental Biology
List moderated: No.
Internet: ptg-forum-request@mailbase.ac.uk
How to access: Send subscribe message to mailbase@mailbase.ac.uk in the following format: join ptg-forum Yourfirstname Yourlastname
Archives: Archives are developed monthly; apply to listowner for details.

PUBLHIST
Description: PUBLHIST is a discussion list covering topics related to public history.
Subjects covered: public history; history
Net address for questions or submissions: MAILSERV@HUSC2.HARVARD.EDU
How to access: Send message to MAILSERV@HUSC3.HARVARD.EDU with the following message: SUBSCRIBE PUBLHIST Firstname Lastname

PUBLIB
Description: PUBLIB is a general issue public library discussion list that includes net related topics.
Subjects covered: library and information science; public libraries
Established: May, 1993
Editorial contact: Jean Armour Polly
NYSERNet, Inc., 200 Elwood Davis Rd., Suite 103, Liverpool, NY 13088-6147.
Tel: (315) 453-2912 ext. 224
Fax: (315) 453-3052
Internet: jpolly@nysernet.org
How to access: To join the list and receive the mailings from PUBLIB-NET: Send a message to LISTSERV@nysernet.org (no subject necessary) saying: subscribe PUBLIB-NET "your full name here" For example: To:LISTSERV@nysernet.org Subject: Message: subscribe PUBLIB-NET Melvil Dewey

PUBLIB-NET
Description: PUBLIB-NET is a focused discussion list concerned with the use of the Internet in public libraries. All discussions on PUBLIB-NET will also be posted to PUBLIB, which is now a general issue public library discussion list that includes net related topics.
Subjects covered: public libraries; library and information science; telecommunications; computer hardware and software
Established: May, 1993
Editorial contact: Jean Armour Polly
NYSERNet, Inc., 200 Elwood Davis Rd., Suite 103, Liverpool, NY 13088-6147.
Tel: (315) 453-2912 ext. 224
Fax: (315) 453-3052
Internet: jpolly@nysernet.org
How to access: Send a message to LISTSERV@nysernet.org (no subject necessary) saying: subscribe PUBLIB "your full name here" For example: To:LISTSERV@nysernet.org Subject: Message: subscribe PUBLIB Melvil Dewey

PUBLIC OPINION RESEARCH
Description: Public Opinion Research is an online discussion list for academics and professionals interested in public opinion research. This list appeals to researchers currently conducting survey research projects as well as to educators familiar with the public opinion literature. Topics relevant to the list include brief postings of recent poll results, announcements of research projects, methodological and substantive queries, professional news, and job listings.
Subjects covered: public opinion; sociology
Net address for operations: listserv@unc.edu
Net address for questions or submissions: por@unc.edu
List moderated: No.
Editorial contact: Jim Cassell
Institute for Research in Social Science, University of North Carolina-Chapel Hill, Chapel Hill, NC 27599-3355.
Tel: 919-962-0782
Fax: 919-962-4777
Internet: Jim__Cassell@UNC.EDU
How to access: Send the command: subscribe por Jill Doe to listserv@unc.edu, replacing Jill Doe with your own name.
How to unsubscribe: Send an e-mail message to listserv@unc.edu containing the command: unsubscribe por in the body of the message.
How to submit: To send a message to all por subscribers, simply send an e-mail message to: por@unc.edu
Archives: All messages to por are automatically archived. Users may search and retrieve archive files by sending commands to listserv@unc.edu as described above. Sending the command: index por will return a list of all archive files. You may search all por archives for a given text string. The command: search por 'vietnam' & 'mortality' will return a list of all archive files containing the words vietnam and mortality. The lines where these strings occur in the file will be printed. You can retrieve one or more of these files by sending the command: get por file__id replacing file__id with a file name from the output returned from your index or search commands.

PUBLIC-HEALTH
Description: public-health is an electronic forum for discussion of medical and health-related issues.
Subjects covered: public health; health sciences; medicine

Net address for operations: mailbase@mailbase.ac.uk
Net address for questions or submissions: public-health@mailbase.ac.uk
Established: January 1993
Subscribers: 120
Sponsor: Joint Information Systems Committee of the UK Higher Education Funding Councils.
Host: University of Newcastle Upon Tyne, Computing Laboratory, University of Newcastle upon Tyne, Newcastle upon Tyne, UK.
List moderated: No.
Editorial contact: Dr. D W Parkin
Department of Epidemiology & Public Health, The Medical School, University of Newcastle Upon Tyne, Newcastle Upon Tyne NE2 4HH UK.
Tel: +44 91 222 6000, ext 7375
Fax: +44 91 222 8211
Copyright statement: Authors of accepted contributions assign to public-health the right to publish the text electronically in screen-readable ASCII and to make it available permanently in electronic archives. Authors do, however, retain copyright to their contributions and may republish them in any form that they choose, so long as they clearly acknowledge public-health@mailbase.ac.uk as the original source of publication.
How to access: Send message to mailbase@mailbase.ac.uk containing the single line join public-health <firstname> <lastname> where <firstname> and <lastname> should be replaced with your first and last names
How to unsubscribe: Send message to mailbase@mailbase.ac.uk containing the single line leave public-health
How to submit: Send your message to public-health@mailbase.ac.uk
Archives: Message archive files are stored as MM-YYYY where MM is the month number and YYYY is the year number. These can be retrieved by anonymous ftp or by sending a message to mailbase@mailbase.ac.uk containing the line send public-health <filename> where <filename> should be replaced by the name of the file required.
Related files: Additional files stored with the list can be retrieved in the same way as the archive files. An index to files stored with the list can be retrieved by sending a message to mailbase@mailbase.ac.uk containing the single line index public-health
Gopher accessibility: Mailbase can be accessed by gophering to mailbase.ac.uk

PUBNET@CHINACAT.UNICOM.COM
Description: PUBNET@CHINACAT is a forum on pblic access systems administration and use.
Subjects covered: telecommunications; Internet; administration
List moderated: No.
Editorial contact: Chip Rosenthal
Internet: pubnet-request@chinacat.unicom.com
How to access: Contact the Editor
How to unsubscribe: Contact the Editor

PUBYAC CHILDREN AND YOUNG ADULT SERVICES IN PUBLIC LIBRARIES
Description: The PUBYAC discussion group is intended to be one of practical appeal, focusing on programming ideas, outreach and literacy programs for children and caregivers, cen-

sorship issues, children and young adult collection development, administrative considerations, job openings, professional development, and other pertinent services or issues.
Subjects covered: library and information science; public libraries; children
Net address for operations: LISTSERV@lis.pitt.edu
Net address for questions or submissions: PUBYAC@lis.pitt.edu
Established: June 1, 1993
Subscribers: 28
Sponsor: School of Library and Information Science, University of Pittsburgh, Pittsburgh, PA 15260.
List moderated: Yes.
Moderation procedure: Postings are saved to an account from which the moderator reads, then approves or discards. Moderator is a facilitator and administrator of the list, catching mistakes.
Editorial contact: Shannon L. VanHemert
School of Library and Information Science, University of Pittsburgh, Pittsburgh, PA 15260.
Tel: (412) 362-4612
Internet: senti@lis.pitt.edu
Technical contact: Mark Steggert
Internet: mark@lis.pitt.edu
How to access: To listserv@lis.pitt.edu send the message subscribe pubyac Firstname Lastname
Access policy: Open subscriptions.
How to unsubscribe: To listserv@lis.pitt.edu send the message signoff pubyac OR unsubscribe pubyac
How to submit: To pubyac@lis.pitt.edu send a brief message.
Additional information: Additional Editor: Margaret Mary Kimmel, School of Library and Information Science, University of Pittsburgh, Pittsburgh, PA 15260; tel (412) 624-9436; fax (412) 648-7001; Internetkimmel@lis.pitt.edu

PURTOPOI@PURCCVM
Description: PURTOPOI@PURCCVM is a forum on writing.
Subjects covered: writing
List moderated: No.
Editorial contact: Tharon Howard
Internet: ucc@mace.cc.purdue.edu
Bitnet: xucc@purccvm
How to access: Contact the Editor
How to unsubscribe: Contact the Editor
Archives: Archives are developed monthly; apply to listowner for details.

PYNCHON@SFU
Description: PYNCHON@SFU is a forum for discussing the works of Thomas Pynchon.
Subjects covered: American language and literature; fiction; Pynchon, Thomas
List moderated: No.
Editorial contact: Jody Gilbert
Internet: userdog1@cc.sfu.ca
Bitnet: userdog1@sfu
How to access: Send subscribe message to USERDOG1@CC.SFU.CA
How to unsubscribe: Send unsubscribe message to USERDOG1@CC.SFU.CA

PYSCHE-D

Description: PSYCHE-D is an unmoderated discussion group dedicated to supporting an interdisciplinary exploration of the nature of consciousness and its relation to the brain. Relevant perspectives are expected to come from, though not exclusively, disciplines as diverse as Cognitive Science, Philosophy, Psychology, Neuroscience, Artificial Intelligence and Anthropology. Interdisciplinary discussions are particularly encouraged.
Subjects covered: philosophy; psychology; anthropology; artificial intelligence
Net address for operations: LISTSERV@NKI.BITNET
Net address for questions or submissions: PSYCHE-D@nki.bitnet
Established: April 1993
Subscribers: 470
List moderated: Yes.
Moderation procedure: All messages are passed on to the moderator to assess for suitablility.
Editorial contact: Patrick Wilken
Royal Melbourne Institute of Technology,
Bundoora, Victoria, 3083 Australia.
Internet: x91007@pitvax.xx.rmit.edu.au
How to access: Subscriptions to PSYCHE-D may be initiated by sending the one-line message "SUBSCRIBE PSYCHE-D FirstName LastName" to LISTSERV@NKI.BITNET.
How to unsubscribe: Subscriptions to PSYCHE-D may be cancelled by sending the one-line message "UNSUBSCRIBE PSYCHE-D FirstName LastName" to LISTSERV@NKI.BITNET.
How to submit: Post submissions to: PSYCHE-D@NKI.BITNET

Q-METHOD

Description: Q-Method is an electronic discussion group centering on discussion of the theory and application of Q methodology, a philosophy and set of principles and procedures for a science of subjectivity. Among recent topics of discussion are measurement issues (e.g., correlation, factor analysis, analysis of variance), philosophical issues (e.g., the nature of subjectivity, connection to quantum theory, distinctions between Q and R), summaries of pertinent books and articles, and announcements of related conferences.
Subjects covered: Q methodology; physics; measurement studies
Net address for operations: Listserv@kentvm
Net address for questions or submissions: Q-Method@kentvm
Established: Begun as QTemp on 14 Jan 1991; renamed Q-Method on March 1, 1992.
Subscribers: 124
Sponsor: Unsponsored, but loosely associated with the International Society for the Scientific Study of Subjectivity and the print journal Operant Subjectivity.
Host: Kent State University, Kent, OH 44242-0001
List moderated: No.
Editorial contact: Steven R. Brown
Department of Political Science, Kent State
University, Kent, OH 44242-0001
Bitnet: sbrown@kentvm
Technical contact: Christine Shih (postmaster@kentvm)
Computer Services, Kent State University, Kent, OH 44242-0001
Tel: (216) 672-2736
Internet: shih@kentvm.kent.edu
Bitnet: shih@kentvm

How to access: Send command SUB Q-METHOD <YOUR NAME> in email message to LISTSERV@KENTVM
Access policy: Subscription requests should be sent to the listowner, who automatically enrolls subscribers and sends a formal welcome, an index of prior postings, and instructions for obtaining backlogs.
How to unsubscribe: Send the command UNSUB Q-METHOD in an email message to LISTSERV@KENTVM
How to submit: Send an email message to Q-METHOD@KENTVM
Archives: Subscribers are provided with an index of topics posted on a monthly basis, and a cumulative list of posts every three months. Backlogs for most recent six months are available with a GET command from LISTSERV@KENTVM (e.g., GET Q-METHOD LOG9305). Older archives available on request from listowner.

QN

Description: QN, or Queer Nation, is a discussion list covering gay and lesbian issues.
Subjects covered: gay and lesbian topics
How to access: Send message to QN-REQUEST@ATHENA.MIT.EDU

QUAKE-L

Description: Quake-L is an e-conference on earthquakes.
Subjects covered: geology; earthquakes
List moderated: No.
Editorial contact: Marty Hoag
Internet: nu021172@vm1.nodak.edu
Bitnet: nu021172@ndsuvm1
How to access: Send subscribe message to listserv@ndsuvm1 or listserv@vm1.nodak.edu
How to unsubscribe: Send unsubscribe message to listserv@ndsuvm1 or listserv@vm1.nodak.edu
Archives: Archives are developed weekly; apply to listowner for details.

QUAKER-L

Description: Quaker-L is a forum discussing Quakerism.
Subjects covered: religion
List moderated: No.
Editorial contact: Bruce Dienes
Internet: bdienes@psyc.uiuc.edu
How to access: Send subscribe message to listserv@uicvmd or listserv@vmd.cso.uiuc.edu
How to unsubscribe: Send unsubscribe message to listserv@uicvmd or listserv@vmd.cso.uiuc.edu
Archives: Archives are developed weekly; apply to listowner for details.

QUALRS-L

Description: QUALRS-L is a list on Qualitative Research for the Human Sciences.
Subjects covered: education
Net address for operations: listserv@uga.bitnet
How to access: Send standard subscribe request to listserv.
How to unsubscribe: Send standard unsubscribe request to listserv.

RADSIG@UWAVM

Description: RADSIG@UWAVM is a forum discussing radiology.
Subjects covered: medicine; radiology
List moderated: Yes.
Editorial contact: Alan Rowberg
Internet: rowberg@locke.hs.washington.edu
Bitnet: rowberg@uwalocke
How to access: Send subscribe message to listserv@uwavm
How to unsubscribe: Send unsubscribe message to listserv@uwavm
Archives: Archives are developed monthly; apply to listowner for details.

RE-FORUM@UTARLVM1

Description: RE-FORUM@UTARLVM1 is a research forum in real estate.
Subjects covered: business; education
List moderated: No.
Editorial contact: Hans Isakson
Internet: isakson@iscsvax.uni.edu
How to access: Send subscribe message to listserv@utarlvm1 or listserv@utarlvm1.bitnet@vm1.nodak.edu
How to unsubscribe: Send unsubscribe message to listserv@utarlvm1 or listserv@utarlvm1.bitnet@vm1.nodak.edu
Archives: Yes.

RECYCLE@UMAB

Description: RECYCLE@UMAB is a forum on recycling.
Subjects covered: environmental studies
List moderated: No.
Editorial contact: Elizabeth Brindley
Bitnet: ebrindle@umab
How to access: Send subscribe message to listserv@umab or listserv@umab.umd.edu
How to unsubscribe: Send unsubscribe message to listserv@umab or listserv@umab.umd.edu

REDALC@FRMOP11

Description: REDALC@FRMOP11 discusses issues related to creation of Latin American and Carribean networks.
Subjects covered: electronic networking; Latin America
List moderated: No.
Editorial contact: Christian Matias
Internet: ulat-rd@frmop11.cnusc.fr
Bitnet: ulat-rd@frmop11
How to access: Send subscribe message to listserv@frmop11 or listserv@frmop11.cnusc.fr
How to unsubscribe: Send unsubscribe message to listserv@frmop11 or listserv@frmop11.cnusc.fr
Archives: Archives are developed monthly; apply to listowner for details.

REED-L

Description: REED-L is a discussion list focusing on activities of the Records of Early English Drama project at Victoria College at the University of Toronto.
Subjects covered: English language and literature; language and literature; Early English; drama

Net address for operations: LISTSERV@UTORONTO.BITNET, LISTSERV@VM.UTCC.UTORONTO.CA
Net address for questions or submissions: REED-L@UTORONTO.BITNET, REED-L@VM.UTCC.UTORONTO.CA
Established: November 22, 1988
Subscribers: 118
Sponsor: Records of Early English Drama, Victoria College, University of Toronto.
Host: University of Toronto, Toronto, Ontario Canada.
List moderated: Not for postings. However, the moderator does manually add subscribers upon request.
Editorial contact: Abigail Ann Young
Records of Early English Drama, 150 Charles Street West, Toronto, Ontario, Canada M5S 1K9.
Tel: 416-585-4504
Fax: 416-585-4594
Internet: REED@EPAS.UTORONTO.CA, YOUNG@EPAS.UTORONTO.CA
Technical contact: Steve Younker
University of Toronto, Computer and Communications / Technology Support, 255 Huron Street, Room 350, Toronto, Ontario Canada M5S 1A1.
Tel: (416) 978-6281
Fax: (416) 971-2085
Internet: MAINTLSV@VM.UTCC.UTORONTO.CA
Bitnet: MAINTLSV@UTORVM
How to access: Either send e-mail to Abigail Ann Young (YOUNG@EPAS.UTORONTO.CA) or send the following message with no subject header to LISTSERV@VM.UTCC.UTORONTO.CA: SUBSCRIBE REED-L your-actual-name
Access policy: Subscription is open to anyone with an interest in the field of drama, music, or ceremony before 1642, especially those interested in English drama and the work of Records of Early English Drama (REED).
How to unsubscribe: Either send e-mail to Abigail Ann Young (YOUNG@EPAS.UTORONTO.CA) or send the following message with no subject header to LISTSERV@VM.UTCC.UTORONTO.CA: UNSUBSCRIBE REED-L
How to submit: Send email to REED-L@VM.UTCC.UTORONTO.CA
Submission policy: All submissions which conform to Net guidelines and the group topic are welcome. Subscribers are asked, however, to consult with the listowner before sending in excessively long submissions.
Archives: Monthly LOG files are available from LISTSERV@VM.UTCC.UTORONTO.CA.

REGISTRAR-L

Description: Registrar-L is a discussion of college and university registration issues.
Subjects covered: colleges and universities
List moderated: No.
Editorial contact: Paul Aucoin
Internet: paul_aucoin@cornell.edu
Bitnet: p22@cornellc
How to access: Send subscribe message to REGISTRAR-L-REQUEST@CORNELL.EDU

RELATIV1@UWF
Description: RELATIV1 is a discussion forum for Group 1-Special Relativity topics.
Subjects covered: physics
List moderated: No.
Editorial contact: Dick Smith
Bitnet: spacemgr@uwf
How to access: Send subscribe message to listserv@uwf or listserv%uwf.bitnet@cunyvm.cuny.edu
How to unsubscribe: Send unsubscribe message to listserv@uwf or listserv%uwf.bitnet@cunyvm.cuny.edu
Archives: Archives are developed monthly; apply to listowner for details.

RELATIV2@UWF
Description: RELATIV2 is a discussion forum for Group 2-Special Relativity topics.
Subjects covered: physics
List moderated: No.
Editorial contact: Dick Smith
Bitnet: spacemgr@uwf
How to access: Send subscribe message to listserv@uwf or listserv%uwf.bitnet@cunyvm.cuny.edu
How to unsubscribe: Send unsubscribe message to listserv@uwf or listserv%uwf.bitnet@cunyvm.cuny.edu
Archives: Archives are developed monthly; apply to listowner for details.

RELEVANT-LOGIC@EXETER.AC.UK
Description: RELEVANT-LOGIC@EXETER.AC.UK is a forum covering philosophies of logic.
Subjects covered: philosophy
Host: Unioversity of Exeter, Devon, England
List moderated: Yes.
Editorial contact: Geoff B. Keene
Internet: g.b.keene@exeter.ac.uk
How to access: Contact the Editor
How to unsubscribe: Contact the Editor

RELIGCOM
Description: RELIGCOM is a discussion group with postings regarding religious communication.
Subjects covered: religion; communications
Net address for operations: LISTSERV@UKCC.BITNET
Net address for questions or submissions: RELIGCOM@UKCC.BITNET
Established: October 24, 1990
Subscribers: 128
Host: University of Kentucky, Lexington, KY
List moderated: No.
Editorial contact: David D. Tukey
Northern Kentucky University, Highland Heights, KY 41099-6300
Tel: (606) 572-6601
Bitnet: TUKEY@NKUVAX
How to access: Send the following message to LISTSERV@UKCC.BITNET
SUBSCRIBE RELIGCOM <full name>
How to unsubscribe: Send the following message to LISTSERV@UKCC.BITNET
SIGNOFF RELIGCOM

Archives: Postings are archived. Apply for further information to the moderator.

RELIGION@HARVARDA
Description: RELIGION@HARVARDA is a discussion forum on religion.
Subjects covered: religion
List moderated: Yes.
Bitnet: tbry@harvarda
How to access: Send subscribe message to listserv@harvarda or listserv@harvarda.harvard.edu
How to unsubscribe: Send unsubscribe message to listserv@harvarda or listserv@harvarda.harvard.edu
Archives: Archives are developed monthly; apply to listowner for details.

RENAIS-L
Description: Renais-L is a forum for study of the Renaissance.
Subjects covered: history; Renaissance studies
Host: The University of Louisville
List moderated: No.
Editorial contact: James A. Cocks
Internet: jacock01@ulkyvm.louisville.edu
Bitnet: jacock01@ulkyvm
How to access: Send subscribe message to listserv@ulkyvm or listserv@ulkyvm.louisville.edu
How to unsubscribe: Send unsubscribe message to listserv@ulkyvm or listserv@ulkyvm.louisville.edu
Archives: Yes; Single

RES-COMP@NKI
Description: RES-COMP is a forum on computing in research environments.
Subjects covered: computer science
List moderated: No.
Editorial contact: Bill Alexander
Bitnet: alex@nki
How to access: Send subscribe message to listserv@nki
How to unsubscribe: Send unsubscribe message to listserv@nki
Archives: Archives are developed monthly; apply to listowner for details.

RESEARCH
Description: RESEARCH is a list focusing on research funding.
Subjects covered: colleges and universities; education; grants and funding
Net address for operations: listserv@templevm.bitnet
How to access: Send standard subscribe request to listserv.
How to unsubscribe: Send standard unsubscribe request to listserv.

RESIDENCE HALL ASSOCIATION DISCUSSION LIST
Description: RHA-L exists to facilitate an open discussion of topics of interest for resident student government. A full range of issues are discussed, from residence hall policy formation and

review, to program and service delivery, to theoretical aspects of leadership and student governance on campus.

Subjects covered: colleges and universities; student government; residence hall government

Net address for operations: Tamvm1.TAMU.Edu

Net address for questions or submissions: RHA-L@Tamvm1.TAMU.Edu

Established: April 1991

Subscribers: 94

Sponsor: Texas A&M University, 110 YMCA Bldg., College Station, TX 77843-1257.

List moderated: No.

Editorial contact: Michael D. Osterbuhr

110 YMCA Bldg., Texas A&M University, College Station, TX 77843-1257.

Tel: (409) 845-4768

Fax: (409) 862-2434

Internet: N018GH@Tamvm1.TAMU.Edu

Bitnet: N018GH@Tamvm1.Bitnet

How to access: Send a SUBSCRIBE command per your usual machine protocal, to Listserv@Tamvm1.TAMU.Edu or Listserv@Tamvm1.Bitnet

Access policy: RHA-L subscription is open to any interested persons. NCC-L subscription is open, but suggested only for National Communication Coordinators or advisor, for NCC business.

How to submit: Mail to RHA-L@Tamvm1.TAMU.Edu, RHA-L@Tamvm1. Bitnet

Submission policy: Discussion is fairly informal, however, some topics have become so narrow that subscribers were asked to continue their discussions on E-mail. In general, any questions may be raised on the list and may be continued as long as sufficient interest by subscribers carries the discussion forward.

Archives: Open for review by all subscribers; mostly statistics and discussion logs.

REVES@FRMOP11

Description: REVES@FRMOP11 is a conference on health expectancy.

Subjects covered: medicine; health sciences

List moderated: Yes.

Editorial contact: Nicholas Brouard

Bitnet: brouard@frined51

How to access: Send subscribe message to listserv%frmop11.bitnet@vm1.nodak.edu or listserv@frmop11

How to unsubscribe: Send unsubscribe message to listserv%frmop11.bitnet@vm1.nodak.edu or listserv@frmop11

Archives: Archives are developed monthly; apply to listowner for details.

REVIEW-L

Description: Review-L is a list publishing updates from the Religious Studies Publications Journal.

Subjects covered: religion

List moderated: Yes.

Editorial contact: Michael Strangelove

Internet: 441495@acadvm1.uottowa.ca

Bitnet: 441495@uottowa

How to access: Send subscribe message to listserv@uottowa or listserv@acadvm1.uottowa.ca

How to unsubscribe: Send unsubscribe message to listserv@uottowa or listserv@acadvm1.uottowa.ca

Archives: Archives are developed monthly; apply to listowner for details.

RFC@NIC.DDN.MIL

Description: RFC@NIC.DDN.MIL is a distribution list for all new Internet-related Requests for Comments.

Subjects covered: computer science; Internet; electronic networking

List moderated: No.

Internet: RFC-REQUEST@NIC.DDN.MIL

How to access: Send subscribe message to RFC-REQUEST@NIC.DDN.MIL

How to unsubscribe: Send unsubscribe message to RFC-REQUEST@NIC.DDN.MIL

RFE/RL-L

Description: The RFE/RL Daily Report is a digest of the latest developments in Russia, Transcaucasia and Central Asia, and Central and Eastern Europe. It is published Monday through Friday (except German holidays) by the RFE/RL Research Institute (a division of Radio Free Europe/Radio Liberty, Inc.). It is not a free discussion list.

Subjects covered: Central Asia; Central Europe; Russia; political science

Net address for operations: listserv@ubvm.cc.buffalo.edu

Net address for questions or submissions: listserv@ubvm.cc.buffalo.edu

Established: September 1, 1992

Subscribers: 4000

Host: SUNY Buffalo, Buffalo, NY

List moderated: Yes.

Moderation procedure: Only postings of the RFE/RL Research Institute Daily Report are allowed.This list is not a discussion list.

Editorial contact: Dawn Mann

RFE/RL Research Institute, Oettingenstr. 67, 8000 Munich 80 Germany

Tel: (49) (89) 2102-0

Fax: (49) (89) 2102-3259

Internet: mannd@rferl.org

Copyright statement: Copyright 1993 RFE/RL, Inc.

How to access: Send usual listserv subscribe command.

Access policy: Subscription is open to all.

How to unsubscribe: Send usual listserv unsub command.

Archives: Notebook files are created weekly.

Additional information: RFE/RL Research Report articles are released each week to Sovset', whose members can download them. Sovset' address for Operations: support@sovset.org.

RHETORIC@RPITSVM

Description: RHETORIC@RPITSVM is a forum focusing on the use of rhetoric in writing.

Subjects covered: writing

Host: Comserve

List moderated: No.

Editorial contact: Comserve Staff

Internet: support@vm.its.vpi.edu

Bitnet: support@rpitsvm

How to access: Send subscribe message to comserve@rpitsvm or comserve@vm.its.vpi.edu

How to unsubscribe: Send unsubscribe message to
comserve@rpitsvm or comserve@vm.its.vpi.edu

RIPE-MAP@NIC.EU.NET
Description: RIPE-MAP is a forum for discussion of network mapping and visualization issues.
Subjects covered: electronic networking; computer science
List moderated: No.
How to access: Send subscribe message to RIPE-MAP-RE-QUEST@NIC.EU.NET
How to unsubscribe: Send unsubscribe message to RIPE-MAP-REQUEST@NIC.EU.NET
Archives: Yes; Send anonymous FTP to: mcsun.eu.net and cd ftp/ripe/archives/ripe-map

RISKNET
Description: RISKNet is an electronic discussion list covering corporate risk management, insurance markets, and other related issues.
Subjects covered: insurance; business; management
Editorial contact: James R. Garven
Internet: jgarven@mcl.cc.utexas.edu
How to access: Send an email message to majordomo@bongo.cc.utexas.edu. In the body of the message type Subscribe RISKNet <your email address> <your first and last name>

RISKS-L
Description: RISKS-L is a discussion forum on the risks to the public in the use of computers and related systems.
Subjects covered: computer privacy; computer health risks; health sciences
Net address for operations: risks-request@csl.sri.com
Net address for questions or submissions: risks@csl.sri.com
Established: August 1, 1985
Subscribers: Tens of thousands of readers.
Sponsor: ACM, 1515 Broadway, NY, NY 10036
Host: SRI International, Menlo Park, CA 94052-3493
List moderated: Yes.
Editorial contact: Peter G. Neumann
Computer Science Lab, SRI International, EL-243
Tel: 415-859-2375
Fax: 415-859-2844
Internet: neumann@csl.sri.com
Copyright statement: All statements are personal statements, all standard disclaimers apply. Reuse in publications requires approval of the author, except for highlights that appear in the ACM SIGSOFT Software Engineering Notes. Issues may be freely distributed on-line for noncommercial purposes.
How to access: Send mail to risks-request@csl.sri.com or use BITNET listserv, subscribe RISKS
Access policy: The list is open to anyone with internet access. For information regarding delivery of RISKS by FAX, phone 310-455-9300 (or send FAX to RISKS at 310-455-2364, or EMail to risks-fax@vortex.com).
How to unsubscribe: Send mail to risks-request@csl.sri.com or use BITNET listserv if that is how you subscribed.
How to submit: Send mail to risks@csl.sri.com
Submission policy: The masthead guidelines are as follows: Contributions should be relevant, sound, in good taste, objective,

cogent, coherent, concise, and nonrepetitious. Diversity is welcome.
Archives: Vol i issue j, type "FTP CRVAX.SRI.COM<CR>login anony-mous<CR>AnyNonNullPW<CR> CD RISKS:<CR>GET RISKS-i.j<CR>" (where i=1 to 14, j always TWO digits). Vol i summaries in j=00; "dir risks-*.*<CR>" gives directory; "bye<CR>" logs out. The COLON in "CD RISKS:" is essential. "CRVAX.SRI.COM" = "128.18.10.1". <CR>=CarriageReturn; FTPs may differ; UNIX prompts for username, password.
Gopher accessibility: Yes, but not under RISKS control.

RLIN-L
Description: RLIN-L discusses the use of the Research Library Information Network.
Subjects covered: library and information science
Host: Research Libraries Group
List moderated: No.
Editorial contact: John Eilts
Bitnet: bl.tss@rlg
How to access: Send subscribe message to listserv@rutvm1
How to unsubscribe: Send unsubscribe message to listserv@rutvm1
Archives: Archives are developed monthly; apply to listowner for details.

RMUSIC-L
Description: Rmusic-L is a forum for discussion of the professional music industry.
Subjects covered: music
List moderated: No.
Editorial contact: Paul Harris
Bitnet: pharris@umkcvax1
How to access: Send subscribe message to listserv@gitvm1
How to unsubscribe: Send unsubscribe message to listserv@gitvm1
Archives: Archives are developed weekly; apply to listowner for details.

RNA
Description: RNA is a Neural Net list in Spanish.
Subjects covered: artificial intelligence
Net address for operations: LISTSERV@UTFSM.BITNET
How to access: Send a message to LISTSERV@UTFSM.BITNET: SUB RNA <your name>

ROMANIANS
Description: ROMANIANS is a Romanian language forum for distribution of news and information.
Subjects covered: current events; Romania
List moderated: No.
Editorial contact: Mihai Popovici
Internet: romanians@sep.stanford.edu
How to access: Contact the Editor
How to unsubscribe: Contact the Editor

ROOTS-L

Description: Roots-L is a discussion list covering genealogy.
Subjects covered: genealogy; history; immigration; ethnicity
Net address for operations: Listserv@NDSUVM1
Net address for questions or submissions: Roots-L@NDSUVM1
How to access: Send message to listserv: SUBSCRIBE <listname> <your name>

RQSS@UQUEBEC

Description: RQSS@UQUEBEC is a forum covering social science in Quebec.
Subjects covered: sociology
List moderated: Yes.
Editorial contact: Pierre J. Hamel
Internet: hamel@inrs-urb.uquebec.ca
Bitnet: hamel@uquebec
How to access: Send subscribe message to listserv@uquebec or listserv@inrs-urb.uquebec.ca
How to unsubscribe: Send unsubscribe message to listserv@uquebec or listserv@inrs-urb.uquebec.ca
Archives: Archives are developed monthly; apply to listowner for details.

RRA-L

Description: RRA-L is a discussion list for readers of romance literature.
Subjects covered: English language and literature; romance literature
Net address for operations: listserv@kentvm
Net address for questions or submissions: rra-l@kentvm
Established: February 1992
Subscribers: 200
List moderated: Yes.
Moderation procedure: Messages sent to moderator to ensure it is appropriate for the list. If appropriate, it is sent to the list.
Editorial contact: Leslie Haas
Kent State University Library, Kent, OH 44242-0001.
Tel: 216-672-3045
Fax: 216-672-2265
Internet: lhaas@kentvm.kent.edu
Bitnet: lhaas@kentvm
How to access: Mail message to listserv@kentvm in message area say subscribe your name.
Access policy: Open to anyone.
How to unsubscribe: Mail listserv@kentvm mssg. unsub your name
How to submit: Mail message to rra-l@listserv
Submission policy: Send message to list and it will be forwarded if appropriate.
Archives: Yes, archives are available; apply to listowner.
Additional information: Additional editor: Kara Robinson, Kent State University Library, Kent, OH 44242-0001; tel 216-672-3045; fax 216-672-2265; Internet Krobinso@kentvm.kent.edu; Bitnet Krobinso@kentvm

RRL-DIRECTORS

Description: RRL-DIRECTORS is a closed list available only to the Directors and Senior Members of the Regional Research Laboratories (RRLs). There are other RRL-specific lists available to the public.

Subjects covered: management; science and technology; administration
Net address for operations: RRL-DIRECTORS@mailbase.ac.uk
Net address for questions or submissions: RRL-DIRECTORS@mailbase.ac.uk
Established: April 1992
Subscribers: 15
Sponsor: The JNT Networked Information Services, Project 1992, The Computing Service, University of Newcastle upon Tyne, Newcastle, UK NE1 7RU.
Host: Networked Information Services Project (NISP,) University of Newcastle upon Tyne, Newcastle, UK NE1 7RU.
List moderated: Yes.
Moderation procedure: Mail sent to this list is automatically forwarded to the list members. Only members of this closed list may submit to it.
Editorial contact: Christine Hobson
Dept of Town and Regional Planning, University of Sheffield, Western Bank, Sheffield, UK S10 2TN.
Tel: 44 742 826185
Fax: 44 742 722199
Internet: c.hobson@sheffield.ac.uk
Technical contact: Cliff Spencer
The Computing Service, University of Newcastle upon Tyne, Newcastle, UK, NE1 7RU.
Tel: 44 91 222 6000
Internet: mailbase-helpline@mailbase.ac.uk
How to access: This is not possible for members of the public.
How to unsubscribe: Send message to listserv: leave <listname> e.g. leave RRL-DIRECTORS
How to submit: If you are a member, just send an email with your submission to RRL-DIRECTORS@mailbase.ac.uk
Submission policy: The submission will be scanned for libellous statements. Then it will either be forwarded to the most appropriate list, or returned to the sender.
Archives: Available only to members.
Related files: All available by using the Index command - index <listname>
Gopher accessibility: Gopher to mailbase@ac.uk

RRL-NEWS

Description: RRL-NEWS provides news about the Regional Research Laboratories (RRLs) GIS Network 1992-95. Anyone interested in GIS may join. How ever, only approx. 15% of non-UK membership is allowed.
Subjects covered: science and technology; geography; geographic information systems
Net address for operations: RRL-NEWS@mailbase.ac.uk
Net address for questions or submissions: RRL-NEWS@mailbase.ac.uk
Established: April 1992
Subscribers: 64
Sponsor: The JNT Networked Information Services, Project 1992, The Computing Service, University of Newcastle upon Tyne, Newcastle, UK NE1 7RU.
Host: Networked Information Services Project (NISP,) University of Newcastle upon Tyne, Newcastle, UK NE1 7RU.
List moderated: Yes.
Moderation procedure: Mail sent to this list is automatically forwarded to the list owner. Listowner decides whether this particular list is the right one for the type of message, or whether

to suggest one of the sub lists. Listowner either forwards it to the list or returns it to the sender.

Editorial contact: Christine Hobson
Dept of Town and Regional Planning, University of Sheffield, Western Bank, Sheffield, UK S10 2TN.

Tel: 44 742 826185
Fax: 44 742 722199
Internet: c.hobson@sheffield.ac.uk
Technical contact: Cliff Spencer
The Computing Service, University of Newcastle upon Tyne, Newcastle, UK, NE1 7RU.

Internet: mailbase-helpline@mailbase.ac.uk
How to access: Send message: join <listname> <your-email-name> <your firstname> <your lastname> E.g. join RRL-NEWS 123abc@univ.sysa Chris Hobson
How to unsubscribe: Send an email to RRL-NEWS@mailbase.ac.uk with the following command: leave <listname> e.g. leave RRL-NEWS
How to submit: Just send an email with your submission to RRL-NEWS@mailbase.ac.uk
Submission policy: The submission will be scanned by the list owner. It will either be forwarded to the list, or returned to the sender.
Archives: All archive files are kept for one year by date order. Files which have been submitted using the list owners' template will be avai lable by requesting the named file. (The list owner can forward fil es on behalf of the list members). To receive an archive file, send an email to RRL-NEWS@mailbase.ac.uk with the command: send <listname> <filename> E.g. send RRL-NEWS 05-1993 or send RRL-NEWS introduction
Related files: All available by using the Index command - index <listname>
Gopher accessibility: Gopher to mailbase@ac.uk

RRL-PUBLICATIONS

Description: RRL-PUBLICATIONS contains details of RRL research reports and other related publications. Some of these are available in ASCII format and can be downloaded from the list.
Subjects covered: demographics; epidemiology; transportation; science and technology
Net address for operations: RRL-PUBLICA-TIONS@mailbase.ac.uk
Net address for questions or submissions: RRL-PUBLICA-TIONS@mailbase.ac.uk
Established: April 1992
Subscribers: 23
Sponsor: The JNT Networked Information Services, Project 1992, The Computing Service, University of Newcastle upon Tyne, Newcastle, UK NE1 7RU.
Host: Networked Information Services Project (NISP,) University of Newcastle upon Tyne, Newcastle, UK NE1 7RU.
List moderated: Yes.
Moderation procedure: Mail sent to this list is automatically forwarded to the list owner who can either forward it to the list or return it to the sender.
Editorial contact: Christine Hobson
Dept of Town and Regional Planning, University of Sheffield, Western Bank, Sheffield, UK S10 2TN.
Tel: 44 91 222 6000
Internet: mailbase-helpline@mailbase.ac.uk
How to access: Send an email to RRL-PUBLICA-TIONS@mailbase.ac.uk with the following command: join <listname> <your-email-name> <your firstname> <your

lastname> E.g. join RRL-PUBLICATIONS 123abc@univ.sysa Chris Hobson
How to unsubscribe: Send email to RRL-PUBLICA-TIONS@mailbase.ac.uk with the following command: leave <listname> E.g. leave RRL-PUBLICATIONS
How to submit: Just send an email with your submission to RRL-PUBLICATIONS@mailbase.ac.uk
Submission policy: The submission will be scanned for suitability. Then it will either be forwarded to the most appropriate list, or returned to the s ender. Non-RRL reports may be discussed under the GIS-ARTICLES discussion list.
Archives: All archive files are kept for one year by date order. Files which have been submitted using the list owners' template will be avai lable by requesting the named file. (The list owner can forward fil es on behalf of the list members). To receive an archive file, send an email to RRL-PUBLICA-TIONS@mailbase.ac.uk with the command: send <listname> <filename> E.g. send RRL-PUBLICATIONS 05-1993 or send RRL-PUBLICATIONS introduction
Related files: All available by using the Index command - index <listname>
Gopher accessibility: Gopher to mailbase@ac.uk
Additional information: It would be useful for new members to request the following files: send mailbase overview send mailbase user-guide send mailbase on-line-guide

RURALAM

Description: RURALAM contains discussions related to rural development. This discussion list is used sparingly by participants to alert one another to events, new resources, and information needs.
Subjects covered: rural health; travel and tourism; health sciences
Net address for operations: RURALAM@MSU.EDU or RURALAM@MSU.BITNET
Net address for questions or submissions: RURALAM@MSU.EDU or RURALAM@MSU.BITNET
Established: May 1992
Sponsor: Department of Resource Development, Michigan State University, 323 Natural Resources, Bldg. East Lansing, 48824-1222
Host: Department of Resource Development, Michigan State University, 323 Natural Resources, Bldg. East Lansing, 48824-1222
List moderated: No.
Editorial contact: Shawn Lock
Department of Resource Development, Michigan State University, 323 Natural Resources, Bldg. East Lansing, 48824-1222
Tel: 517-336-1866
Fax: 517-353-8994
Internet: 22331mom@msu.edu
Bitnet: 22331mom@msu.bitnet
How to access: Send a message to LISTSERV@MSU.EDU (OR LISTSERV@MSU.BITNET) with the message: subscribe ruralam firstname lastname
Access policy: Subscription is monitored. Listowner approves all subscriptions. This is done mostly as a maintenance and information measure to determine the makeup of participants. No one has ever been denied subscription.

How to unsubscribe: To unsubscribe, send a message to LISTSERV@MSU.EDU (OR LISTSERV@MSU.BITNET) with the message: unsubsribe ruralam firstname lastname
How to submit: Submissions are not moderated. Send posting to RURALAM@MSU.EDU (OR RURALAM@MSU.BITNET).
Submission policy: Normal Internet discussion list etiquette applies.

RURALDEV@KSUVM

Description: RURALDEV@KSUVM is a forum on rural economic issues.
Subjects covered: economics
List moderated: No.
Bitnet: RCYOUNG@KSUVM
How to access: Send subscribe message to listserv@ksuvm
How to unsubscribe: Send unsubscribe message to listserv@ksuvm
Archives: Archives are developed monthly; apply to listowner for details.

RUSHIST@USCVM

Description: RUSHIST is a discussion list focusing on the history of Russia.
Subjects covered: Russia; political science; history
Net address for questions or submissions: RUSHIST@USCVM or RUSHIST@DOSUNI1 or RUSHIST@CSEARN
How to access: Send standard subscribe request to the listserv.
How to unsubscribe: Send standard unsubscribe request to the listserv.

RUSSIA@ARIZVM1

Description: RUSSIA@ARIZVM1 is a list focusing on the new political state of the former Soviet Union and its neighboring countries.
Subjects covered: Russia; Soviet Union; political science
Net address for operations: LISTSERV@ARIZVM1.CCIT.ARIZONA.EDU
Net address for questions or submissions: RUSSIA@ARIZVM1.CCIT.ARIZONA.EDU, RUSSIA@ARIZVM1.BITNET
How to access: Send a standard subscribe request to the listserv.
How to unsubscribe: Send a standard unsubscribe request to the listserv.

RUSTEX-L

Description: RUSTEX-L is a discussion list focusing on the use of Cyrillic characters in computing.
Subjects covered: Russia; Cyrillic characters; computer hardware and software
Net address for operations: LISTSERV@UBVM
Net address for questions or submissions: RUSTEX-L@UBVM
How to access: Send standard subscribe request to the listserv.
How to unsubscribe: Send standard unsubscribe request to the listserv.

S-PRESS@DCZTU1

Description: S-PRESS@DCZTU1 is a German-language forum for German student press organizations.
Subjects covered: journalism
List moderated: No.
Editorial contact: ''Red. Wurzelmaennnchen''
Internet: ptwurzel@ibm.rx.tu-clausthal.de
Bitnet: ptwurzel@dcztu1
How to access: Send subscribe message to listserv@dcztu1 or listserv@ibm.rx.tu-clausthal.de
How to unsubscribe: Send unsubscribe message to listserv@dcztu1 or listserv@ibm.rx.tu-clausthal.de

SABBATH

Description: Sabbath is a list featuring discussions about the rock group Black Sabbath and its former members.
Subjects covered: Black Sabbath; music; rock music
Net address for operations: sabbath-request@fa.disney.com
Net address for questions or submissions: sabbath@fa.disney.com
List moderated: Yes.
Moderation procedure: Moderator digests the contributions and sends them out to subscription list.
Editorial contact: Michael Sullivan
Walt Disney Feature Animation, 1400 Flower St., Glendale, CA 91221.
Tel: (818) 544-2683
Fax: (818) 544 4579
Internet: sullivan@fa.disney.com
How to access: Send your name and email address to sabbath-request@fa.disney.com and ask to be added to the list.
Access policy: Anybody can subscribe.
How to unsubscribe: Send your name and email address to sabbath-request@fa.disney.com and ask to be taken off the list.
How to submit: Send contributions to sabbath@fa.disney.com
Submission policy: All contributions relating to Black Sabbath are welcome. Discussions about former members current projects should be brief.

SAFETY

Description: SAFETY is a discussion list on environmental health and safety issues, particularly as they affect college campuses.
Subjects covered: environmental studies; hazardous waste management; radiation safety; colleges and universities
Net address for operations: LISTSERV@UVMVM.UVM.EDU
Net address for questions or submissions: SAFETY@UVMVM.UVM.EDU
Established: December, 1989
Subscribers: 420
Sponsor: Risk Management Dept., University of Vermont, Burlington, VT, USA
Editorial contact: Ralph Stuart
109 S. Prospect St., Burlington, VT 05405
Tel: (802)656-3068
Fax: (802)656-8682
Internet: rstuart@moose.uvm.edu
Bitnet: rmgtrbs@uvmadmin.bitnet
How to access: Send the message SUB SAFETY <your name> to LISTSERV@UVMVM.UVM.EDU
Access policy: Open to all.

How to unsubscribe: Send the message UNSUB SAFETY to LISTSERV@UVMVM.UVM.EDU
How to submit: E-mail to SAFETY@UVMVM.UVM.EDU
Submission policy: Open to all.
Archives: Monthly log files, searchable by LDBASE
Related files: FILESERV files available, currently: LAB STANDARD OSHA 1910.1450 (Lab Standard); LABSTAND APPEND OSHA 1910.1450 Appendixes; SAFETY EMAIL 1989 Article: E-MAIL for safety people; RTKLAB CSA 1989 Article: Implementing lab standard; LESSIS BETTER Complete text of ACS pamphlet; AUDIT HAZMIN Lab waste minimization audit form; SURVEY HAZMIN Lab waste minimization survey form; 101WAYS HAZMIN 101 ways to minimize lab waste; SAFETY CULTURE Developing a Safety Culture in Academia; EPA BBS List of EPA-sponsored bulletin boards.
Gopher accessibility: File accessibility coming.

SAIS-L: SCIENCE AWARENESS AND PROMOTION DISCUSSION

Description: SAIS-L@UNB.CA was formed in the hopes of linking those who are interested in helping promote science to students. Discussions of any aspect of science promotion are welcome as this list is unmoderated. We strongly encourage participation of the list members.
Subjects covered: science and technology; education
Net address for operations: LISTSERV@UNB.CA
Net address for questions or submissions: SAIS-L@UNB.CA
Established: April 11, 1991
Subscribers: 216
Sponsor: University of New Brunswick, P.O. Box 4400, Fredericton, New Brunswick E3B 5A3, CANADA.
Host: University of New Brunswick, P.O. Box 4400, Fredericton, New Brunswick E3B 5A3, CANADA.
List moderated: No.
Editorial contact: Keith W. Wilson
Dept. of Psychology, University of Aberdeen, Aberdeen, Scotland AB9 2UB.
Tel: (011-44) 224 272239
Fax: (011-44) 224 487048
Internet: k.wilson@aberdeen.ac.uk
Technical contact: Brian Lesser
Computing Services, University of New Brunswick, P.O. Box 4400, Fredericton, New Brunswick E3B 5A3, CANADA.
Tel: (506) 453-4573
Fax: (506) 453-3590
Internet: bcl@unb.ca
Copyright statement: Copyright of articles posted to SAIS-L remain with the person posting. Articles posted do not necessarily reflect the views of the list owner or SAIS (Student Awareness In Science).
How to access: Send the following command to: LISTSERV@UNB.CA: sub sais-l <your full name>
Subscriptions are not automatic and therefore may take a day or two to be added.
Access policy: SAIS-L subscription is open to all those interested in science and its promotion.
How to unsubscribe: Send the following command to LISTSERV@UNB.CA: unsub sais-l
How to submit: Articles for submission to SAIS-L should be mailed to SAIS-L@UNB.CA
Submission policy: This list is unmoderated and thus any article may be posted, however please try to keep the subject of science.

Archives: To retrieve past documents, send to LISTSERV@UNB.CA the following command in order to obtain an index of files available: index SAIS-L
To obtain files, send the following to LISTSERV@UNB.CA: get SAIS-L <filename>
Additional information: Additional information pertaining to SAIS-L or SAIS (Student Awareness In Science, a non-profit organization based in Atlantic Canada for the promotion of science) may be obtained from Keith Wilson (k.wilson@aberdeen.ac.uk).

SAME@FRULM11

Description: SAME@FRULM11 is a forum on symbolic and algebraic manipulation.
Subjects covered: mathematics
List moderated: No.
Editorial contact: Daniel Lazard
Bitnet: dl@frunip11
How to access: Send subscribe message to listserv@frulm11
How to unsubscribe: Send unsubscribe message to listserv@frulm11
Archives: Archives are developed monthly; apply to listowner for details.

SAN-LINK

Description: SAN-Link is an electronic forum for discussion of sustainable agriculture. The Sustainable Agriculture Network (SAN) was formed in 1990 to extend a community that encourages and supports its members searching for alternative agricultural solutions. SAN is a cooperative effort of organizations as diverse as the National Agricultural Library, CENEX Land O' Lakes, Utah State University's Agricultural Systems Technology and ATTRA (Appropriate Technology Transfer for Rural Areas). It was developed by a "SAN-Link" Committee with support from the United States Department of Agriculture's (USDA) Sustainable Agriculture Research and Education (SARE) program.
Subjects covered: sustainable agriculture; agriculture
Editorial contact: Gabriel A. Hegyes
SAN-Link Coordinator, c/o Alternative Farming Systems, Information Center, Rm. 304 National Agricultural Library, 10301 Baltimore Blvd. Beltsvilld, MD 20705-2351.
Tel: (301) 504-6425
Fax: (301) 504-6409
Internet: ghegyes@nalusda.gov
Review: Chuck Francis and Garth Youngberg write, "Sustainable Agriculture is a philosophy based on human goals and on understanding the long-term impact of our activities on the environment and on other species. Use of this philosophy guides our application of prior experience and the latest scientific farm systems. These systems reduce environmental degradation, maintain agricultural productivity, promote economic viability in both the short and long term and maintain stable rural... quality of life."
How to access: Send an email message to ghegyes@nalusda.gov
Related files: A calendar of sustainable agriculture meetings and events is updated monthly by Gabriel Hegyes, SAN-Link Coordinator. The calendar is broadcast over SANET-mg, or can be retrieved through the Almanac at North Carolina State University, or through FTP. SAN has an electronic mail group "sanet-mg" with over 200 individuals interested in, and knowledgeable about, sustainable agriculture. Members of the group

share sources of information and help answer each others' questions. ECONET, a non-profit electronic service runs a mirror of the conference expanding participation.

Gopher accessibility: SAN has an increasing number of data-bases available for searching at the North Carolina State University Almanac site. They include: * SARE/ACE projects (summaries of the projects funded by the USDA SARE program and the EPA/USDA Agriculture in Concert with the Environment (ACE) program). * "The Showcase" (annotated bibliography of educational and informational materials, emphasizing information readily useful to farmers). *"The Yellow Pages" (The Directory of Sustainable Agriculture Experts and Expertise). These catalogs can be searched through Gopher or WAIS by telneting to twosocks.ces.ncsu.edu and logging in as "gopher". In addition, with simple email commands these publications are available to be searched like a database, and ordered by filename or as whole publications. File Transfer Protocol (FTP) access is also available.

SAPPHO

Description: SAPPHO is an electronic discussion group on topics of concern to gay and bisexual women.
Subjects covered: gay and lesbian topics
Net address for operations: SAPPHO-RE-QUEST@MC.LCS.MIT.EDU
List moderated: Yes.
How to access: Send subscription messages to NOGLSTP-RE-QUEST@ELROY.JPL.NASA.GOV

SASH—SOCIOLOGISTS AGAINST SEXUAL HARASSMENT

Description: SASH is a moderated list focusing on sexual harassment.
Subjects covered: sociology; feminism; women's studies; workplace studies
Net address for questions or submissions: AZPXS@ASUACAD, AZPXS@ASUVM.INRE.ASU.EDU
List moderated: Yes.
How to access: For more information or to subscribe, write to Phoebe M. Stambaugh, AZPXS@ASUACAD (Bitnet) or AZPXS@ASUVM.INRE.ASU.EDU (Internet).

SAVEIT-L

Description: SAVEIT-L is an online users group for the software package SAVEIT. SAVEIT manages a library's interlibrary loan statistics. Discussion focuses on strengths and weaknesses of the program, its day to day usage, the managerial use of its data, technical problems and upgrades, how the program interacts with other library software, and how it compares to other statistical packages.
Subjects covered: computer hardware and software
Net address for operations: LISTSERV@VM.USC.EDU or LISTSERV@USCVM.BITNET
Net address for questions or submissions: SAVEIT-L@VM.USC.EDU or SAVEIT-L@USCVM.BITNET
Established: November 1992
Subscribers: 220
Sponsor: University of Southern California
Host: University of Southern California
List moderated: Yes.

Moderation procedure: Forum is open, but moderators resolve mail delivery problems, watch for mail abusers, and try to facilitate discussion, by keeping it focused to the topic.
Editorial contact: Mary Hollerich
Doheny Memorial Library, University of Southern California, Los Angeles, CA 90089-0182.
Tel: 213-740-7612
Fax: 213-749-1045
Internet: MARYH@CALVIN.USC.EDU
Technical contact: John Riehl
Bitnet: Internet Rhiel@VM.USC.EDU
How to access: Send a note to the LISTSERV addresses above, include no subject line, but put this command in the body of the message: SUBSCRIBE SAVEIT-L (first name) (last name) Omit the parentheses.
Access policy: Subscription is open to interested parties. However, moderators will remove members who abuse the privileges of the list, or whose mail addresses create consistent delivery problems.
How to unsubscribe: Send a note to the LISTSERV addresses above, include no subject line, but put this command in the body of the message UNSUBSCRIBE SAVEIT-L
How to submit: Send mail to SAVEIT-L@VM.USC.EDU
Submission policy: Types of submissions are limited only by the scope of the discussion group. They may range from technical queries, like software bugs, to operations aspects, like "how to do it", to ethical questions like confidentiality or copyright. Nonmembers may also submit queries to the list.
Additional information: Additional editors: James W. Pool, McFarlin Library, 2933 E. 6th St., Tulsa, OK 74104-3123; tel (918) 631-3485; fax (918) 631-3791; Internet: JWP@VAX2.UTULSA.EDU
Nina Chambers, University of Washington Libraries, Seattle, WA 98195 ; tel (206) 543-1899; fax (206) 685-8049; Internet CHAMBERS@U.WASHINGTON.EDU
Dan Gottlieb, University of Cincinnati Libraries, ILL, 480 Langsam Library, Cincinnati, Ohio 45221-0033; tel (513) 556-1525; fax (513) 556-2161; Internet GOT-TLIEB@UCBEH.SAN.UC.EDU

SBNC-L

Description: SBNC-L is a forum for members of the Brazil Society for Neuroscience.
Subjects covered: medicine; Brazil
Host: Brazil Society for Neuroscience
List moderated: No.
Editorial contact: Dora Ventura
Bitnet: dventura@bruspvm or dventura@brusp
How to access: Send subscribe message to listserv@bruspvm
How to unsubscribe: Send unsubscribe message to listserv@bruspvm
Archives: Archives are developed monthly; apply to listowner for details.

SBRHYM-L

Description: Sbrhym-L is a literary discussion list from SUNY/Stony Brook.
Subjects covered: literature; fiction; poetry
List moderated: No.
Editorial contact: Stefanas Maniatis
Bitnet: smaniati@sbccvm
How to access: Send subscribe message to listserv@sbccvm

How to unsubscribe: Send unsubscribe message to
listserv@sbccvm
Archives: Yes; apply to listowner for details.

SBSWE-L

Description: SBSWE-L is a forum for the Stony Brook Society
of Women Engineers.
Subjects covered: engineering
Host: Society of Women Engineers
List moderated: No.
Internet: BRONWEN@SBCCVM
How to access: Send subscribe message to listserv@sbccvm
How to unsubscribe: Send unsubscribe message to
listserv@sbccvm
Archives: Yes; Apply to listowner for details

SCHOLAR@CUNYVM

Description: SCHOLAR@CUNYVM is a discussion group
covering natural language processing.
Subjects covered: linguistics
List moderated: Yes.
Editorial contact: Joseph Raben
Bitnet: jqrqc@cunyvm
How to access: Send subscribe message to listserv@cunyvm or
listserv@cunyvm.cuny.edu
How to unsubscribe: Send unsubscribe message to
listserv@cunyvm or listserv@cunyvm.cuny.edu
Archives: Archives are developed monthly; apply to listowner
for details.

SCHOOL-L

Description: School-L is a list centering on schools.
Subjects covered: education
List moderated: No.
Editorial contact: Mike Norris
Bitnet: mnorris@irlearn
How to access: Send subscribe message to listserv@irlearn or
listserv@irlearn.ucd.ie
How to unsubscribe: Send unsubscribe message to
listserv@irlearn or listserv@irlearn.ucd.ie

SCI-AND-TECH-HUMAN-RESOURCES@MAILBASE.AC.UK

Description: SCI-AND-TECH-HUMAN-RESOURCES is a
mailbase forum on human resources in the science and technol-
ogy labor force.
Subjects covered: science and technology
Host: SPSG
List moderated: No.
Internet: sci-and-tech-human-resources-request@mailbase.ac.uk
How to access: Send subscribe message to
mailbase@mailbase.ac.uk in the following format: join sci-and-
tech-human-resources Yourfirstname Yourlastname
Archives: Archives are developed monthly; apply to listowner
for details.

SCI.MILITARY

Description: Sci.military is a discussion list featuring topics re-
lated to military history and technology.
Subjects covered: military history; science and technology
Net address for operations: military.request@daytonoh.ncr.com
or mil-req@law7.daytonoh.ncr.com
Net address for questions or submissions:
sci.military@daytonoh.ncr.com or mili-
tary@law7.daytonoh.ncr.com
Established: 1985
Subscribers: 30,000 readers world wide
List moderated: Yes.
Moderation procedure: News postings are e-mailed to the
moderator (me) for approval and posting.
Editorial contact: Steve Bridges
NCR Corporation Law Department, WHQ-B
1700 S. Patterson Blvd Dayton OH 45479
Tel: (513) 445-4486
Fax: (513) 445-1933
Internet: steve@law7.daytonoh.ncr.com or
steve.bridges@daytonoh.ncr.com
How to access: Check with local sys admin.
Access policy: Check with local sys admin.
How to unsubscribe: Check with local sys admin.
How to submit: Post article to sci.military.
Additional information: sci.military is simply a moderated
USENET newsgroup. The mailing list that used to exist for it
was discontinued December 1992.

SCIFRAUD@ALBNYVM1

Description: SCIFRAUD@ALBNYVM1 is a forum for the dis-
cussion of scientific fraud.
Subjects covered: ethics; philosophy; science and technology;
law and legal studies
List moderated: No.
Editorial contact: Al Higgins
Bitnet: ach13@albnyvms
How to access: Send subscribe message to listserv@albnyvm1
or listserv@uacsc2.albany.edu
How to unsubscribe: Send unsubscribe message to
listserv@albnyvm1 or listserv@uacsc2.albany.edu
Archives: Archives are developed monthly; apply to listowner
for details.

SCIT-L

Description: Scit-L provides a forum for issues related to com-
munications and information technology.
Subjects covered: communications; technology education
Moderation procedure: Yes.
Editorial contact: Elia Zureik
Bitnet: scitdoc@qucdn
How to access: Send subscribe message to listserv@qucdn
How to unsubscribe: Send unsubscribe message to
listserv@qucdn

SCOLT

Description: SCOLT, The Southern Conference on Language
Teaching, offers a new discussion list as a service to all its
constituents who are interested in foreign language education.
Individuals in foreign language education may subscribe.
Subjects covered: language and literature; education

Net address for operations:
Listserv@catfish.valdosta.peachnet.edu
Net address for questions or submissions:
SCOLT@catfish.valdosta.peachnet.edu
Established: November 1992
Subscribers: 125
Sponsor: Southern Conference on Language Teaching (SCOLT)
Valdosta State University Valdosta, GA 31698
Host: Valdosta State University Valdosta, GA 31698
List moderated: No.
Editorial contact: Lee Bradley
Executive Director, SCOLT
Valdosta State University, Valdosta, GA 31698
Tel: (912) 333-7358
Fax: (912) 333-7389
Internet: lbradley@grits.valdosta.peachnet.edu
How to access: SUB SCOLT <Your Name> sent to
LISTSERV@catfish.valdosta.peachnet.edu
Access policy: Anyone is free to use this service for disseminating professional announcements, presentations, special programs, job availabilities, questions, inquiries, searches, informal article reviews, etc. The SCOLT List is not, however, a forum for personal communications. Remember that messages on a List are distributed to all subscribers!
How to unsubscribe: UNSUB SCOLT sent to
LISTSERV@catfish.valdosta.peachnet.edu
How to submit: Once you are subscribed, mail to the list is addressed to SCOLT@catfish.valdosta.peachnet.edu. Please include a ''signature block'' (name, full address, phone, fax) at the end of your messages sent to the list.
Archives: The message GET SCOLT ARCHIVE sent to the LISTSERV will retrieve archives of SCOLT.

SCR-L

Description: Scr-L is a forum for the study of brain-injury related rehabilitation.
Subjects covered: psychology
List moderated: No.
Editorial contact: Joe Silsby
Bitnet: birpjoe@mizzou1
How to access: Send subscribe message to listserv@mizzou1
How to unsubscribe: Send unsubscribe message to
listserv@mizzou1
Archives: Archives are developed monthly; apply to listowner for details.

SCREEN-L

Description: SCREEN-L is an unmoderated list for all who study, teach, theorize about or research film and television-- mostly in an academic setting, but not necessarily so. SCREEN-L ranges from the abstract (post- post-structuralism) to the concrete (roommate match-ups for the next conference).
Subjects covered: filmmaking; communications; popular culture
Net address for operations: LISTSERV@UA1VM.UA.EDU
Net address for questions or submissions: SCREEN-L@UA1VM.UA.EDU
Established: March 15, 1991
Subscribers: 427
Sponsor: Telecommunication and Film Department, The University of Alabama, P.O. Box 870152, Tuscaloosa, AL 35487-0152.
Host: Seebeck Computer Center, The University of Alabama.

List moderated: No.
Editorial contact: Jeremy Butler
P.O. Box 870152, Tuscaloosa, AL 35487-0152.
Tel: (205) 348-6350
Fax: (205) 348-6213
Internet: JBUTLER@UA1VM.UA.EDU
Bitnet: JBUTLER@UA1VM
Review: Reviewed by List Review Service edited by Raleigh Muns: see appendix.
How to access: Send the following command to LISTSERV@UA1VM.UA.EDU: SUB SCREEN-L <your name>
Access policy: Subscription to SCREEN-L is completely open. Anyone may join.
How to unsubscribe: Send the following command to LISTSERV@UA1VM.UA.EDU: UNSUB SCREEN-L
How to submit: Send submissions to SCREEN-L@UA1VM.UA.EDU.
Submission policy: SCREEN-L is an unmoderated, open list. Anyone may post messages to it, even if they do not belong to the list.
Archives: Monthly archives of all SCREEN-L postings are kept in SCREEN-L FILELIST, accessible through LISTSERV@UA1VM.UA.EDU.
Related files: SCREEN-L FILELIST contains a few text files related to the study of film and television.

SCRNWRIT@TAMVM1

Description: SCRNWRIT@TAMVM1 is a forum for discussing screenwriting.
Subjects covered: writing; cinema studies; television
List moderated: No.
Editorial contact: Jack Stanley
Bitnet: jrs4284@panam
How to access: Send subscribe message to listserv@tamvm1
How to unsubscribe: Send unsubscribe message to listserv@tamvm1
Archives: Archives are developed monthly; apply to listowner for details.

SCS-L

Description: SCS-L is a discussion list focusing on cultural and political issues in the former Soviet Union.
Subjects covered: Former Soviet Union; current events; political science
Net address for operations: LISTSERV@INDYCMS
How to access: Send standard subscribe request to the listserv.
How to unsubscribe: Send standard unsubscribe request to the listserv.

SEACNET

Description: SEACnet is a moderated distribution list of environmental news, information, actions, etc., related to EnviroGopher.
Subjects covered: environmental studies
Net address for operations: env-link+forms@andrew.cmu.edu
Net address for questions or submissions: env-link+@andrew.cmu.edu
Established: September 1991
Method of issuance: Postings are issued via e-mail.

Postings are announced on Usenet groups as well as every major computer network.
Available in other media: Yes. EnviroDisk and Printouts available (call for more info).
Subscribers: 430,000 people, 93 countries
Sponsor: The EnviroLink Network, 4551 Forbes Ave., 3rd Floor, Pittsburgh, PA 15213.
List moderated: Yes.
Editorial contact: Josh Knauer
4551 Forbes Ave., 3rd Floor, Pittsburgh, PA15213.
Tel: (412) 681-9608
Fax: (412) 681-6707
Internet: jk71 + @andrew.cmu.edu
Indexed or abstracted: Yes, EnviroGopher
(envirolink.hss.cmu.edu)
How to access: Send a request to:
seac + forms@andrew.cmu.edu and list your region number.
Access policy: Anyone can subscribe.
How to unsubscribe: Same as above
How to submit: Send mail to seac + forms@andrew.cmu.edu
Archives: To read our archives on EnviroGopher, telnet to:
envirolink.hss.cmu.edu login: gopher password: envirolink *send mail to: admin@envirolink.hss.cmu.edu*
Related files: Telnet to: envirolink.hss.cmu.edu login id: gopher password: envirolink
Gopher accessibility: Yes, these files are accessible on EnviroGopher.

SEASIA-L
Description: SEASIA-L carries news and information of Southeast Asian Studies.
Subjects covered: South Asia; political science
Net address for operations: LISTSERV@MSU.EDU
Net address for questions or submissions: SEASIA-L@MSU.EDU
Established: February 1992
Subscribers: 717
Sponsor: Center for Asian Studies, Mich. State U., E. Lansing, MI
Host: Michigan State University
List moderated: No.
Editorial contact: Elliott Parker
Journalism Dept., Central Michigan University, Mt. Pleasant, MI 48859.
Tel: 517.774.3196
Fax: 517.774.7805
Internet: 3ZLUFUR@CMU.CSV.CMICH.EDU
Bitnet: ZLUFUR@CMUVM
How to access: Send the following command to the listserv address above: SUB SEASIA-L
Access policy: This list is open to all interested parties.
How to unsubscribe: Send the following command to the listserv address above: SIGNOFF SEASIA-L
How to submit: Send message to: SEASIA-L@MSU.EDU
Archives: Weekly notebooks are archived by the listserv for last 3-4 months.
Related files: Bibliographies, papers, etc., are available on the SEASIA-L filelist.

SECULAR-HUMANIST@SUGAR.NEOSOFT.COM
Description: SECULAR-HUMANIST@SUGAR.NEOSOFT.COM is a forum for discussion of secular lifestyles.
Subjects covered: religion
List moderated: Yes.
Editorial contact: Jim Thompson
Internet: secular-humanist-request@sugar.neosoft.com
How to access: Send subscribe message to SECULAR-HUMANIST-REQUEST@SUGAR.NEOSOFT.COM
How to unsubscribe: Send unsubscribe message to SECULAR-HUMANIST-REQUEST@SUGAR.NEOSOFT.COM

SECURITY@AIM.RUTGERS.EDU
Description: SECURITY@AIM.RUTGERS.EDU offers a general discussion on any and all types of security.
Subjects covered: security; computer privacy; law and legal issues
List moderated: No.
Editorial contact: *Hobbit*
Internet: hobbit@aim.rutgers.edu
How to access: Send unsubscribe message to listserv@bitnic or security-request@aim.rutgers.edu
How to unsubscribe: Send subscribe message to listserv@bitnic or security-request@aim.rutgers.edu

SEDIT-L
Description: SEdit-L is a discussion list for editors of scholarly editions.
Subjects covered: language and literature; history; writing; editing
Net address for operations: Listserv@UMDD
Net address for questions or submissions: SEdit-L@UMDD
How to access: Send message to listserv: SUBSCRIBE <listname> <your name>

SEDS-L
Description: SEDS-L is a conference for Students for Exploration and Development of Space.
Subjects covered: astronomy; space and space exploration
List moderated: No.
Editorial contact: H. Alan Montgomery
Bitnet: fhd@tamvml
How to access: Send subscribe message to listserv@tamvml or listserv@tamvml.tamu.edu
How to unsubscribe: Send unsubscribe message to listserv@tamvml or listserv@tamvml.tamu.edu
Archives: Archives are developed weekly; apply to listowner for details.

SEDSNEWS@TAMVM1
Description: SEDSNEWS@TAMVM1 is a forum featuring news about space and space exploration.
Subjects covered: astronomy; space and space exploration
List moderated: No.
Editorial contact: H. Alan Montgomery
Bitnet: fhd@tamvml

How to access: Send subscribe message to listserv@tamvm1 or listserv@tamvm1.tamu.edu
How to unsubscribe: Send unsubscribe message to listserv@tamvm1 or listserv@tamvm1.tamu.edu
Archives: Archives are developed weekly; apply to listowner for details.

SEELANGS@CUNYVM

Description: SEELANGS@CUNYVM is the list covering discussion of Slavic and East European languages.
Subjects covered: Former Soviet Union; Eastern Europe; language and literature
Net address for operations: LISTSERV@CUNYVM
How to access: Send standard subscribe request to the listserv.
How to unsubscribe: Send standard unsubscribe request to the listserv.

SEENET (THE SOCIETY FOR EARLY ENGLISH AND NORSE ELECTRONIC TEXTS)

Description: SEENET has been formed to obtain, produce, and disseminate scholarly electronic editions of texts in Old Norse, Old English, and Middle English.
Subjects covered: Old Norse language and literature; Old English language and literature; Middle English language and literature; language and literature
Fee: Annual fee--not yet set--in return for one text on floppy disk, CD-ROM, or tape. The group is seeking sponsorship from an academic press.
Editorial contact: Hoyt N. Duggan Department of English, University of Virginia, Charlottesville, VA 22903.
Department of English, University of Virginia, Charlottesville, VA 22903.
Internet: HND@VIRGINIA.EDU
How to access: Send an email message to HND@VIRGINIA.EDU for more information

SEISMD-L

Description: Seismd-L is a conference covering earthquakes and seismological topics.
Subjects covered: geology; earthquakes
List moderated: Yes.
Editorial contact: Francis Wu
Bitnet: fwu@bingvmb
How to access: Send subscribe message to listserv@bingvmb or listserv%bingvmb.cunyvm.cuny.edu
How to unsubscribe: Send unsubscribe message to listserv@bingvmb or listserv%bingvmb.cunyvm.cuny.edu

SEMIGROUPS

Description: SEMIGROUPS is a discussion list for mathematicians interested in any aspect of semigroup theory or related topics.
Subjects covered: mathematics
Net address for operations: mailbase@mailbase.ac.uk
Net address for questions or submissions: semigroups@mailbase.ac.uk
Established: August 1992
Subscribers: 29

Sponsor: Joint Information Systems Committee of the UK Higher Education Funding Councils
Host: University of newcastle Upon Tyne, UK
List moderated: No.
Editorial contact: Dr. JH Renshaw
Faculty of Mathematical Studies, University of Southampton, England.
Tel: (0703) 593673
Fax: (0703) 593939
Internet: jhr@maths.soton.ac.uk
Copyright statement: Authors of accepted contributions assign to semigroups the right to publish the text electronically in screen-readable ASCII and to make it available permanently in electronic archives. Authors do, however, retain copyright to their contributions and may republish them in any form that they choose, so long as they clearly acknowledge semigroups@mailbase.ac.uk as the original source of publication.
How to access: Send message to mailbase@mailbase.ac.uk containing the single line: join semigroups <firstname> <lastname> where <firstname> and <lastname> should be replaced with your first and last names.
How to unsubscribe: Send message to mailbase@mailbase.ac.uk containing the single line: leave semigroups
How to submit: Send your message to semigroups@mailbase.ac.uk
Archives: Message archive files are stored as MM-YYYY where MM is the month number and YYYY is the year number. These can be retrieved by anonymous ftp, gopher or by sending a message to mailbase@mailbase.ac.uk containing the line send semigroups <filename> where <filename> should be replaced by the name of the file required.
Related files: Additional files stored with the list can be retrieved in the same way as the archive files. An index to files stored with the list can be retrieved by sending a message to mailbase@mailbase.ac.uk containing the single line: index semigroups
Gopher accessibility: Mailbase can be accessed by gophering to mailbase.ac.uk

SEMIOS-L

Description: Semios-L is a forum for discussions pertaining to both verbal and non-verbal communication.
Subjects covered: communications
List moderated: No.
Editorial contact: Steven Skaggs
Internet: soskago1@ulkyvm.louisville.edu
How to access: Send subscribe message to listserv@ulkyvm or listserv@ulkyvm.louisville.edu
How to unsubscribe: Send unsubscribe message to listserv@ulkyvm or listserv@ulkyvm.louisville.edu
Archives: Archives are developed monthly; apply to listowner for details.

SENIOR@INDYCMS

Description: SENIOR@INDYCMS is a conference on health for senior citizens.
Subjects covered: medicine
List moderated: No.
Editorial contact: John B. Harlan
Internet: jbharlan@indyvax.iupui.edu

Bitnet: jbharlan@indyvax
How to access: Send subscribe message to listserv@indycms or listserv@indycms.iupui.edu
How to unsubscribe: Send unsubscribe message to listserv@indycms or listserv@indycms.iupui.edu
Archives: Archives are developed monthly; apply to listowner for details.

SERIALS@UVMVM

Description: SERIALS@UVMVM is a forum for discussion of serials librarianship.
Subjects covered: library and information science
List moderated: Yes.
Editorial contact: Birdie MacLennan
Internet: bmaclenn@uvmvm.uvm.edu
Bitnet: bmaclenn@uvmvm
How to access: Send subscribe message to listserv@uvmvm or listserv@uvmvmuvm.edu
How to unsubscribe: Send unsubscribe message to listserv@uvmvm or listserv@uvmvmuvm.edu
Archives: Archives are developed monthly; apply to listowner for details.

SERIALST

Description: SERIALST serves as an informal electronic forum for most aspects of serials processing in libraries. Appropriate topics include: cataloging, acquisitions, collection management, serials budgets and pricing issues, binding, preservation, microfilm and other non print serials media, union list activities, announcements, news, and job postings that may be of interest to the serials community.
Subjects covered: library collection development; library and information science; serials librarianship
Net address for operations:
LISTSERV@UVMVM.UVMVM.EDU or
LISTSERV@UVMVM.BITNET
Net address for questions or submissions:
SERIALST@UVMVM.UVM.EDU or SERIALST@UVMVM.BITNET
Established: October 18, 1990
Subscribers: 1350
Sponsor: University of Vermont, Burlington, Vermont 05405.
Host: University of Vermont, Burlington, Vermont 05405.
List moderated: Yes.
Moderation procedure: Incoming mail is sent to the moderators, who then screen for misdirected mail and forward messages on appropriate topics to the list of subscribers.
Editorial contact: Birdie MacLennan
University of Vermont, Bailey/Howe Library
Burlington, VT 05405.
Tel: 802-656-2016
Fax: 802-656-4038
Internet: BMACLENN@UVMVM.UVM.EDU
Bitnet: BMACLENN@UVMVM.BITNET
Technical contact: Listserv manager
Bitnet: POSTMASTER@UVMVM.UVM.EDU Bitnet:
POSTMASTER@UVMVM.BITNET
Review: Not reviewed, but noted in Serials Review, 17:3 (1991), Editorial Serials Librarian, 23:1/2 (1992), p. 23 Library Resources & Technical Services, 35:4 (Oct. 1991), p. 507.
How to access: Send an e-mail message to:
LISTSERV@UVMVM.UVM.EDU or:

LISTSERV@UVMVM.BITNET ignore the subject line; the body of the message should read: SUBSCRIBE SERIALST <your full name>
Access policy: Open subscription; anyone with access to BITNET or Internet may subscribe themselves.
How to unsubscribe: Send an e-mail message to:
LISTSERV@UVMVM.UVM.EDU or:
LISTSERV@UVMVM.BITNET ignore the subject line; the body of your message should read: UNSUBSCRIBE SERIALST (or alternately) SIGNOFF SERIALST
How to submit: Send SERIALST messages to: SERIALST@UVMVM.UVM.EDU or, SERIALST@UVMVM.BITNET
Archives: Message database is archived on LISTSERV@UVMVM and is retrievable by monthly log and/or via LISTSERV (LDBASE) database search protocols. Contact the listowner for additional information.
Additional information: Additional editors: Marcia Tuttle, Associate Moderator, University of North Carolina, Chapel Hill; Internet: TUTTLE@GIBBS.OIT.UNC.EDU
Ann Ercelawn, Associate Moderator, Vanderbilt University; Internet: ERCELAA@CTRVAX.VANDERBILT.EDU; Bitnet: ERCELAA@VUCTRVAX

SF-LOVERS DIGEST

Description: SF-Lovers Digest has discussed many topics, all of them related in some way to the theme of science fiction or fantasy. The topics have ranged very widely from rewritten stories, SF and fantasy books, SF movies, and SF conventions to reviews of books, movies and television shows. The range of topics is quite wide and anyone is welcome to submit material on these or other topics of interest in this general area. The digest has a very large number of readers, and trivial messages are strongly discouraged due to the heavy load SF-Lovers puts on the host's CPU and disk space. Messages to SF-Lovers are batched and broadcast periodically.
Subjects covered: science fiction; language and literature
Net address for operations: sf-lovers-request@rutgers.edu
Net address for questions or submissions: Written SF: sf-lovers-written@rutgers.edu
Sf on Television: sf-lovers-tv@rutgers.edu
Sf Films: sf-lovers-movies@rutgers.edu
SF Conventions: ssf-lovers-cons@rutgers.edu
General discussions that don't fit specifically in the other topic headings sf-lovers-misc@rutgers.edu
Established: 1980
Subscribers: Unknown. Distribution includes a number of other bulletin boards, redistribution points, etc. Estimates are anywhere from 1500 to 200,000.
Host: Rutgers University, New Brunswick, NJ
List moderated: Yes.
Moderation procedure: All messages sent to the above submission address as well as to the corresponding Usenet newsgroups are forwarded to a separate mail address where I collate, select submissions for each issue, and edit them for spelling, punctuation and readability.
Editorial contact: Saul Jaffe
Rutgers University, P.O. Box 879, Hill Center, Busch Campus, Piscataway, NJ. 08855.
Tel: (908) 932-4207
Fax: (908) 932-2968
Internet: sf-lovers-request@rutgers.edu

Sample contents: All subjects related to science fiction in all media.
Copyright statement: SF-Lovers Digest is a copyrighted publication. It may be freely printed, copied or redistributed as long as it is copied in its entirety with all headers, trailers, credits, copyright notices and other identifying information completely intact. All rights to all material published within the Digest belong to the author of that material and may not be used in any other publication without permission of the author.
How to access: sf-lovers-request@rutgers.edu
Submission policy: Written SF: sf-lovers-written@rutgers.edu
Sf on Television: sf-lovers-tv@rutgers.edu
Sf Films: sf-lovers-movies@rutgers.edu
SF Conventions: sf-lovers-cons@rutgers.edu
General discussions that don't fit specifically in the other topic headings sf-lovers-misc@rutgers.edu
Archives: As part of the services provided by SF-LOVERS, a complete archive of back volumes is maintained on gandalf.rutgers.edu and is available via FTP (for help on FTP, you may send email to sf-lovers-ftp@gandalf.rutgers.edu with the command ''help'' in the body of the message). Also in the archives are a variety of episode guides, author bibliographies and text files that are of interest to readers of SF/Fantasy. There is also a list of SF/Fantasy conventions that is updated periodically (usually every two months) sorted by geographic region and by date.
Gopher accessibility: There is no Gopher access at the moment, though there are plans to add it.

SGANET@VTM1
Description: SGANET (Student Government Global Mail Network) is a list for members of student governments.
Subjects covered: colleges and universities
List moderated: No.
Editorial contact: Brian McConnell
Internet: bmcconne@vtssi.vt.edu
How to access: Send subscribe message to listserv@vtm1
How to unsubscribe: Send unsubscribe message to listserv@vtm1

SGML-MATH@MATH.AMS.ORG
Description: SGML-MATH@MATH.AMS.ORG discusses all aspects of SGML text coding related to mathematics.
Subjects covered: mathematics; computer hardware and software
List moderated: No.
Editorial contact: David L. Rogers
Internet: dlr@e-math.ams.org
How to access: Send subscribe message to support@e-math.ams.org
How to unsubscribe: Send unsubscribe message to support@e-math.ams.org
How to submit: Send message to support@e-math.ams.org

SGML-TABLE@MATH.AMS.ORG
Description: SGML-TABLE@MATH.AMS.ORG discusses all aspects of SGML related to mathematics.
Subjects covered: mathematics; computer hardware and software
List moderated: No.
Editorial contact: David L. Rogers

Internet: dlr@e-math.ams.org
How to access: Send subscribe message to support@e-math.ams.org
How to unsubscribe: Send unsubscribe message to support@e-math.ams.org
How to submit: Send message to support@e-math.ams.org

SGML@MAILBASE.AC.UK
Description: SGML@MAILBASE.AC.UK is a discussion on all related aspects of SGML text coding.
Subjects covered: computer hardware and software
List moderated: No.
Internet: sgml-request@mailbase.ac.uk
How to access: Send subscribe message to mailbase@mailbase.ac.uk in the following format: join sgml Yourfirstname Yourlastname
Archives: Archives are developed monthly; apply to listowner for details.

SHAKER
Description: The Shaker forum is an avenue for the discussion of the history, sociology, material culture, and spiritualism of the Shaker (United Society of Believers in Christ's Second Appearance) movement in America. Also, discussions of other utopian communities (Oneida, New Harmony, Amana, etc.) are welcome.
Subjects covered: history; religion; Shakers
Net address for operations: Listserv@ukcc.uky.edu (or ukcc.bitnet)
Net address for questions or submissions: Listserv@ukcc.uky.edu (or ukcc.bitnet)
Established: 1990
Subscribers: 120
Sponsor: University of Kentucky, Lexington, KY 40506.
List moderated: No.
Editorial contact: Marc A. Rhorer
105 Grehan-Journalism Bldg, Univ. of Kentucky, Lexington, KY 40506-0042.
Tel: 606-257-4839
Fax: 606-257-7818
Internet: rhorer@ukcc.uky.edu
Bitnet: rhorer@ukcc
Technical contact: Marc A. Rhorer
How to access: One subscribes like for other listserv lists, by sending mail to listserv@ukcc.uky.edu (or others) saying SUBSCRIBE SHAKER your full name
Archives: Archives are available from Listserv@ukcc.uky.edu

SHAKSPER@UTORONTO
Description: SHAKSPER@UTORONTO is a forum on the works of William Shakespeare.
Subjects covered: English language and literature; Shakespeare, William
List moderated: Yes.
Editorial contact: Hardy Cook
Internet: hmcook@boe00.minc.umd.edu
How to access: Send subscribe message to listserv@utoronto or listserv@epas.utoronto.ca
How to unsubscribe: Send unsubscribe message to listserv@utoronto or listserv@epas.utoronto.ca

Archives: Archives are developed monthly; apply to listowner for details.

SHARE-L
Description: Share-L is a discussion on spectroscopic events.
Subjects covered: chemistry
List moderated: No.
Editorial contact: Dr. Michael F. Reid
Bitnet: mfreid@hkucc
How to access: Send subscribe message to listserv@frors12
How to unsubscribe: Send unsubscribe message to listserv@frors12
Archives: Archives are developed monthly; apply to listowner for details.

SHARP-L
Description: SHARP-L is the discussion list of SHARP, an organization bringing together scholars now working in a wide variety of disciplines and departments--literary scholars, historians, archivists, bibliographers, publishing professionals, and so on-who share a common interest in the history of books, newspapers, and periodicals.
Subjects covered: humanities; publishing; history
Net address for operations: LISTSERV@IUBVM (Bitnet) or LISTSERV@IUBVM.UCS.INDIANA.EDU
Established: 1993
Editorial contact: Patrick Leary
Internet: pleary@ucs.indiana.edu
Bitnet: pleary@iubacs
How to access: Subscriptions should be placed to LISTSERV@IUBVM (Bitnet) or LISTSERV@IUBVM.UCS.INDIANA.EDU, with the command SUB SHARP-L [your name].

SHOTHC-L
Description: SHOTHC-L is a discussion group of the Society for History of Technology.
Subjects covered: science and technology; computer science
Host: Society for History of Technology
List moderated: No.
Editorial contact: Dr. Paul Ceruzzi
Bitnet: nasem001@sivm
How to access: Send subscribe message to listserv@sivm
How to unsubscribe: Send unsubscribe message to listserv@sivm
Archives: Archives are developed monthly; apply to listowner for details.

SIIN-L
Description: Siin-L is an information network covering small islands.
Subjects covered: communications; islands
List moderated: No.
Editorial contact: Catherine Edward
Internet: edward@upei.ca
How to access: Send subscribe message to listserv@unbvm1 or listserv@unb.ca
How to unsubscribe: Send unsubscribe message to listserv@unbvm1 or listserv@unb.ca

Archives: Archives are developed monthly; apply to listowner for details.

SIMULA@BITNIC
Description: SIMULA@BITNIC is a forum for discussions of the SIMULA programming language.
Subjects covered: computer science
List moderated: No.
How to access: Send subscribe message to listserv@bitnic or listserv@bitnic.educom.edu
How to unsubscribe: Send unsubscribe message to listserv@bitnic or listserv@bitnic.educom.edu
Archives: Archives are developed monthly; apply to listowner for details.

SIMULATED ANNEALING MAILING LIST
Description: Simulated Annealing Mailing List is an electronic discussion group covering the combinatorial optimization technique known as simulated annealing. This technique uses random moves and a statistical selection method very close to the behavior of particles in a thermodynamic system. The list discusses this algorithm and related algorithms, such as ''TABU Search'', genetic algorithms, etc.
Subjects covered: simulated annealing; mathematics; genetic algorithms; thermodynamics
Net address for operations: anneal-request@cs.ucla.edu
Net address for questions or submissions: anneal@cs.ucla.edu
Established: February 1990
Subscribers: 204
Sponsor: UCLA Computer Science Department
List moderated: No.
Editorial contact: Dan R. Greening
Software Transformation, Inc., Suite 100, 1601 Saratoga-Sunnyvale Rd., Cupertino, CA 95014
Tel: (408) 973-8081 x313
Fax: (408) 973-0989
Internet: dgreen@cs.ucla.edu
Technical contact: Dan R. Greening
Software Transformation, Inc., Suite 100, 1601 Saratoga-Sunnyvale Rd., Cupertino, CA 95014.
Tel: (408) 973-8081 x313
Fax: (408) 973-0989
Internet: dgreen@cs.ucla.edu
How to access: Send the following text to majordomo@sti.com: subscribe anneal
Access policy: No policy forum available.
How to unsubscribe: Send the following text to majordomo@sti.com: unsubscribe anneal
How to submit: Send the article as an e-mail message to anneal@cs.ucla.edu.
Submission policy: No policy forum available.
Archives: Archives are not currently retained. An offer of an Internet-accessible archive site would be welcome.

SIMULATION@UFL.EDU
Description: SIMULATION is a conference covering computer simulation.
Subjects covered: computer science
List moderated: No.
Editorial contact: Paul Fishwick

Internet: fishwick@fish.cis.ufl.edu or
fishwick@uflorida.cis.ufl.edu
How to access: Send subscribe message to SIMULATION-RE-
QUEST@UFL.EDU
How to unsubscribe: Send unsubscribe message to SIMULA-
TION-REQUEST@UFL.EDU

SIMULATOR-BUGS@CS.ROCHESTER.EDU

Description: simulator-bugs@cs.rochester.edu is a mailing list
for users of the Rochester Connectionist Simulator.
Subjects covered: artificial intelligence
How to access: All requests to be added to or deleted from this
list, problems, questions, etc., should be sent to simulator-re-
quest@cs.rochester.edu.
Related files: The simulator is available in cs.rochester.edu:/
pub/simulator

SIMULATOR-USERS@CS.ROCHESTER.EDU

Description: simulator-users@cs.rochester.edu is a mailing list
for users of the Rochester Connectionist Simulator.
Subjects covered: artificial intelligence
How to access: All requests to be added to or deleted from this
list, problems, questions, etc., should be sent to simulator-re-
quest@cs.rochester.edu.
Related files: The simulator is available in cs.rochester.edu:/
pub/simulator

SIR-USERS

Description: SIR is a data management system for research
data. The sir-users list is a forum for technical discussion related
to SIR and for user group issues to be raised and discussed. The
developers of SIR will not necessarily be members but are
aware of its existence and may perhaps contribute.
Subjects covered: computer hardware and software; computer
science
Net address for operations: mailbase@mailbase.ac.uk
Net address for questions or submissions: sir-
users@mailbase.ac.uk
Established: February 1993
Subscribers: 25
Sponsor: Joint Information Systems Committee of the UK
Higher Education Funding Councils.
Host: University of Newcastle Upon Tyne, UK
List moderated: No.
Editorial contact: John S. Lemon Aberdeen
University Computing Centre, Edward Wright Building, Dunbar
Street, Aberdeen AB 9 2TY, Scotland.
Tel: +44 (224) 273350
Fax: +44 (224) 273372
Internet: j.s.lemon@aberdeen.ac.uk
Technical contact: John S. Lemon
How to access: Send message to mailbase@mailbase.ac.uk con-
taining the single line join sir-users <firstname> <lastname>
where <firstname> and <lastname> should be replaced with
your first and last names.
How to unsubscribe: Send message to
mailbase@mailbase.ac.uk containing the single line leave sir-
users

How to submit: Send your message to sir-
users@mailbase.ac.uk
Archives: Archive information (past documents, etc.): Message
archive files are stored as MM-YYYY where MM is the month
number and YYYY is the year number. These can be retrieved
by anonymous ftp or by sending a message to
mailbase@mailbase.ac.uk containing the line send sir-users
<filename> where <filename> should be replaced by the
name of the file required.
Related files: Additional files stored with the list can be retrieved in the same way as the archive files. An index to files
stored with the list can be retrieved by sending a message to
mailbase@mailbase.ac.uk containing the single line index sir-
users
Gopher accessibility: Mailbase can be accessed by gophering
to mailbase.ac.uk

SIRIAC-L

Description: Siriac-L is a discussion list on Latin America and
the Caribbean.
Subjects covered: Latin America; Caribbean
Host: Sistema Integrado de Recursos Informaticos y Cientificos
Universidad de Puerto Rico.
List moderated: No.
Editorial contact: Roberto Loran
Internet: r—loran@racin.clu.net
How to access: Send subscribe message to listserv@enlace
How to unsubscribe: Send unsubscribe message to
listserv@enlace
Archives: Archives are developed monthly; apply to listowner
for details.

SIS@MAILBASE.AC.UK

Description: SIS@MAILBASE.AC.UK is a forum for discus-
sion of information systems.
Subjects covered: business
List moderated: No.
Internet: sis-request@mailbase.ac.uk
How to access: Send subscribe message to
mailbase@mailbase.ac.uk in the following format: join sis
Yourfirstname Yourlastname
Archives: Archives are developed monthly; apply to listowner
for details.

SKEPTIC@YORKVM1

Description: SKEPTIC@YORKVM1 is a forum for discussion
of philosophical skepticism.
Subjects covered: philosophy
List moderated: No.
Editorial contact: Norman R. Gall
Bitnet: gall@yunexus
How to access: Send subscribe message to listserv@yorkvm1 or
listserv@vm1.yorku.ca
How to unsubscribe: Send unsubscribe message to
listserv@yorkvm1 or listserv@vm1.yorku.ca
Archives: Archives are developed weekly; apply to listowner
for details.

SLAJOB

Description: SLAJOB is an electronic discussion group featuring job vacancy announcements for the information professional including all types of special libraries, as well as other related occupations for which the information professional (MLS candidate) would be able to fulfill. The SLAJOB list is a service provided by the Indiana Center for Database Systems and the student chapter of the Special Libraries Association (SLA) at Indiana University.

Subjects covered: career opportunities; Special Libraries Association; library and information science

Net address for operations: listserv@iubvm

Net address for questions or submissions: listserv@iubvm or listserv@iubvm.ucs.indiana.edu

Established: November 20, 1992

Subscribers: 1,300

Sponsor: Indiana Center for Database Systems, 401 Lindley Hall, Bloomington, IN 47405; dorchard@ucs.indiana.edu

Host: Indiana University, UCS, Bloomington, IN 47405; listmast@iubvm

List moderated: Yes.

Moderation procedure: Subscribers (or nonsubscribers) send a job vacancy notice with job description to "slajob@iubvm or slajob@iubvm.ucs.indiana.edu" and the editors determine whether the notice is appropriate for the listserv. Jobs must be something in which the MLS information professional would find interesting.

Editorial contact: Douglas L. Orchard
3315 Longview #76
Bloomington, IN 47405

Tel: (812) 855-2490

Fax: (812) 855-4829

Internet: dorchard@ucs.indiana.edu

Bitnet: clmonnie@iubacs

Technical contact: Cindy Monnie
School of Library and Information Science,
Indiana University, Bloomington, IN 47405.

Tel: (812) 334-7684

Internet: clmonnie@ucs.indiana.edu

Bitnet: clmonnie@iubacs

How to access: Internet: send message to: listserv@iubvm.ucs.indiana.edu leave subject line blank, type the following in the text: subscribe slajob firstname lastname. Bitnet: send message to: listserv@iubvm leave subject line blank, type the following in the text: subscribe slajob firstname lastname

Access policy: No policy. Anyone can subscribe.

How to unsubscribe: Internet: send message to: listserv@iubvm.ucs.indiana.edu leave subject line blank, type the following in the text: signoff slajob Bitnet: send message to: listserv@iubvm leave subject line blank type the following in the text signoff slajob

How to submit: Send message to: slajob@iubvm.ucs.indiana.edu type position title in subject line enter job description in text

Submission policy: Must be a position for a special library as defined by the Special Libraries Association or a position for which a member of SLA or person who holds an MLS degree would be interested.

Archives: All positions are immediately archived for one month. Directions on how to access archived information are given with the subscription notice.

SLART-L (SECOND LANGUAGE ACQUISITON, RESEARCH, AND TEACHING)

Description: SLART-L (Second Language Acquisiton, Research, and Teaching) is an electronic discussion forum for topics related to second language acquisition, research, and teaching.

Subjects covered: language and literature; education

Net address for operations: LISTSERV2CUNYVM.CUNY.EDU

Net address for questions or submissions: SLART-L@CUNYVM.CUNY.EDU

Established: 1990

Subscribers: 550

Sponsor: City University of New York

Host: City University of New York

List moderated: No.

Editorial contact: Anthea Tillyer
Hunter College/ELI, 695 Park Avenue (10th Fl. East).

Tel: (212) 757-5741

Fax: (212) 489-368

Internet: ABTHC@CUNYVM.CUNY.EDU

Bitnet: ABTHC@CUNYVM.BITNET

Technical contact: Bill Gruber
UCC/CUNY, 555 West 57th Street, New York, NY 10019.

Tel: (212) 903-3688

Internet: BIGCU@CUNYVM.CUNY.EDU

Bitnet: BIGCU@CUNYVM.BITNET

Copyright statement: See statement under TESLCS-L.

How to access: LISTSERV@CUNYVM.CUNY.EDU SUB SLART-L <subscriber's full name>

Access policy: Subscription open.

How to unsubscribe: Mail to LISTSERV@CUNYVM.CUNY.EDU UNSUB SLART-L

How to submit: All members of SLART-L (but only members) may submit.

Archives: Logs archived monthly, public.

SLEEP-L

Description: SLEEP-L carries notices, consultation requests, research reports, and book reviews, pertaining to all aspects of sleep, both normal and pathological.

Subjects covered: sleep; psychology

Net address for operations: LISTSERV@QUCDN

Net address for questions or submissions: SLEEP-L@QUCDN

Established: July 1991

Subscribers: 118

Sponsor: Kingston Psychiatric Hospital, P.O. Bag 603, Kingston, Ontario, Canada K7L 4X3.

Host: Queen's University Kingston, Ontario, Canada.

List moderated: Yes.

Moderation procedure: List membership restricted to those actively involved in sleep disorders medicine, related areas of research and those in training in related fields. Submissions are forwarded unedited, but screened in order to insure a professional level of discourse.

Editorial contact: Dr. Steve Southmayd
Dept. of Psychology, Kingston Psychiatric Hospital, P.O. Bag 603, Kingston, Ontario, Canada K7L 4X3.

Tel: (613) 546-1101

Fax: (613) 548-5588

Internet: Steve.E.Southmayd@Queen'sU.Ca

Bitnet: SOUTHMAY@QUCDN
Review: Southmayd S.E. Computer Network Communications: SLEEP-L@QUCDN, Newsletter of the Association of Professional Sleep Societies, spring 1993, 20-21.
Copyright statement: Copyright rests with the original contributor. Re-distribution of previously published material is by explicit consent of the organization to which copyright has been granted at the time of publication, only. It is requested that material first appearing on SLEEP-L be re-distributed only with the explicit consent of the original contributor.
How to access: Mail to listserv@QUCDN with the message: sub sleep-l
Access policy: Membership is restricted. Please provide area of interest and institutional affiliation in request to subscribe.
How to unsubscribe: Mail to listserv@QUCDN with the message: unsub sleep-l
How to submit: Mail to list (SLEEP-L@QUCDN) or moderator
Submission policy: Submissions forwarded in unedited form provided they conform to acceptable standards of professional discourse and respect patient confidentiality.
Archives: Archive logs and notebooks are available. Apply to moderator for details.

SLOVAK-L

Description: SLOVAK-L is a discussion list covering current events and political developments in the Slovak Republic.
Subjects covered: Slovak Republic; current events; political science
Net address for operations: LISTSERV@UBVM
Review: Reviewed by List Review Service edited by Raleigh Muns: see appendix.
How to access: Send standard subscribe request to the listserv.
How to unsubscribe: Send standard unsubscribe request to the listserv.

SM-RUM@ICNUCEVM

Description: SM-RUM@ICNUCEVM is a list covering discussion of small ruminant mammals.
Subjects covered: zoology; agriculture
List moderated: No.
Editorial contact: Alessio Valentini
Bitnet: tusciazo@icnucevm
How to access: Send subscribe message to listserv@icnucevm
How to unsubscribe: Send unsubscribe message to listserv@icnucevm
Archives: Archives are developed yearly; apply to listowner for details.

SMDM-L

Description: SMDM-L is a conference on medical decision making.
Subjects covered: medicine
Host: Society for Medical Decision-Making
List moderated: Yes.
Editorial contact: James Levin, MD, Ph.D.
Bitnet: jlevin@simvax
How to access: Send subscribe message to listserv@dartcms1 or listserv@dartcms1.dartmouth.edu
How to unsubscribe: Send unsubscribe message to listserv@dartcms1 or listserv@dartcms1.dartmouth.edu

Archives: Archives are developed monthly; apply to listowner for details.

SMS-SNUG@UNCVM1

Description: SMS-SNUG@UNCVM1 is a conference on shared medical systems.
Subjects covered: medicine
Host: Hospitals Information Systems Division, University of North Carolina
List moderated: No.
Editorial contact: Lyman Ripperton
Internet: lyman@unchmvs.unch.unc.edu
How to access: Send subscribe message to listserv@uncvm1 or listserv@uncvm1oit.unc.edu
How to unsubscribe: Send unsubscribe message to listserv@uncvm1 or listserv@uncvm1oit.unc.edu
Archives: Archives are developed monthly; apply to listowner for details.

SMT-LIST

Description: SMT-LIST offers discussion of issues of interest to professional and pre-professional academic music theorists, musicologists, composers, and performers.
Subjects covered: music
Net address for operations: smt-request@husc.harvard.edu
Net address for questions or submissions: given only on subscription
Established: January, 1990
Subscribers: 200
Sponsor: Society for Music Theory (SMT)
Host: Harvard University, Harvard Arts and Sciences, Computer Services (HASCS), Science Center, Cambridge, MA 02138
Editorial contact: Lee A. Rothfarb
Harvard University, Music Dept., Cambridge, MA 02138
Tel: (617) 495-2791
Fax: (617) 496-8081
Internet: rothfarb@husc.harvard.edu
Bitnet: rothfarb@husc.bitnet
Technical contact: Tom Heft
Harvard University, Harvard Arts and Sciences
Computer Services (HASCS), Science Center, Cambridge, MA 02138
Tel: (617) 495-1273
Internet: heft@husc.harvard.edu
Bitnet: rothfarb@husc.bitnet
How to access: Send message to smt-request@husc.harvard.edu (or smt-request@husc.bitnet); in "Subject:" field, type the word ADD; in the message: name, snailmail and email addresses, tel. no., institutional affiliation, interest in/connection with music theory.
Access policy: Users must have sufficient background in music theory to follow and contribute to discussions on a professional level.
How to unsubscribe: Send a message to smt-request@husc.harvard.edu (or smt-request@husc.bitnet); in "Subject:" field, type the word REMOVE
How to submit: An address is given to the subscriber upon subscription.
Archives: Each month's messages are archived in a collection file called smt-list.current, available through anonymous FTP (site: husc4.harvard.edu; directory: /pub/smt/smt-list

Related files: smt-list.current contains messages for the current month; path months' messages in files named by month, e.g. smt-list.april93

SNNS@INFORMATIK.UNI-STUTTGART.DE

Description: snns@informatik.uni-stuttgart.de is a mailing list for users of the Stuttgart Neural Network Simulator.
Subjects covered: artificial intelligence
How to access: Send a message to listserv@informatik.uni-stuttgart.de with subscribe snns <Your Full Name> in the message body.
Related files: The simulator is available in ifi.informatik.uni-stuttgart.de:/pub/SNNS/SNNSv2.1.tar.Z [129.69.211.1]

SOC-CULTURE-GREEK-POST@CS.WISC.EDU

Description: SOC-CULTURE discusses Greek culture and society.
Subjects covered: Greek culture
List moderated: No.
Editorial contact: Manolis Tsangaris
Internet: mt@cs.wisc.edu
How to access: Send subscribe message to SOC-CULTURE-GREEK-REQUEST@CS.WISC.EDU
How to unsubscribe: Send unsubscribe message to SOC-CUL-TURE-GREEK-REQUEST@CS.WISC.EDU
How to submit: Send message to soc-culture-greek-request@cs.wisc.edu

SOC.CULTURE.LATIN-AMERICA

Description: SOC.CULTURE.LATIN-AMERICA is a Usenet newsgroup covering social and cultural issues for Latin America.
Subjects covered: Latin America
List moderated: No.
How to access: Ask your system manager whether this service is accessed through your facility.

SOC.MOTSS

Description: SOC-MOTSS is a Usenet newsgroup for members of the same sex.
Subjects covered: gay and lesbian topics
How to access: Usenet address is soc.motss

SOCHIFI@PUCING

Description: SOCHIFI@PUCING is a forum for the Chilean Society of Physics.
Subjects covered: physics
Host: Chilean Society of Physics
List moderated: No.
How to access: Send subscribe message to listserv@pucing
How to unsubscribe: Send unsubscribe message to listserv@pucing

SOCHIST@USCVM

Description: SOCHIST@USCVM is a forum covering social history disciplines.

Subjects covered: history; social history; cultural studies
List moderated: No.
Editorial contact: Bob Pasker
Internet: bob@halfdome.sf.ca.us
How to access: Send subscribe message to listserv@uscvm or listserv@vm.usc.edu
How to unsubscribe: Send unsubscribe message to listserv@uscvm or listserv@vm.usc.edu

SOCORG-K@UTORONTO

Description: SOCORG-K@UTORONTO is a forum covering sociological issues.
Subjects covered: sociology
List moderated: Yes.
Editorial contact: Dr. Allison Griffith
Internet: aigel@canal.crc.uno.edu
Bitnet: aigel@uno
How to access: Send subscribe message to listserv@utoronto or listserv@vm.epas.utoronto.ca
How to unsubscribe: Send unsubscribe message to listserv@utoronto or listserv@vm.epas.utoronto.ca
Archives: Archives are developed weekly; apply to listowner for details.

SOCWORK

Description: SOCWORK is a discussion group centering on matters of interest to practitioners in social welfare and social work.
Subjects covered: social work
Net address for operations: LISTSERV@UMAB
Established: 1987
Subscribers: 150
Sponsor: University of Maryland School of Social Work
List moderated: Yes.
Moderation procedure: Moderator mainly takes care of adds and drops to the list.
Editorial contact: Harris Chaiklin
U. Md. School of Social Work, 525 W. Redwood St., Baltimore, MD 21201
Tel: (410) 706-7746
Fax: (410) 706-6046
Internet: HCHAIKLI@SSW02/AB.UMD.EDU
How to access: Tell listserv at UMAB SUBSCRIBE SOCWORK (FULL NAME) or send note to listserve at UMAB with SUBSCRIBE SOCWORK (FULL NAME)
Access policy: Anyone can join.
How to unsubscribe: Tell listserv at UMAB SIGNOFF SOCWORK or send a note to listserv at UMAB saying SIGNOFF SOCWORK
How to submit: Send a note to list to submit.
Gopher accessibility: Yes, this list is accessible through a Gopher server.

SOFT-ENG@MWUNIX.MITRE.ORG

Description: SOFT-ENG is a forum on software engineering and related topics.
Subjects covered: computer science; engineering
List moderated: No.
Editorial contact: Alok C. Nigam
Internet: nigam@MWUNIX.MITRE.ORG

How to access: Send subscribe message to SOFT-ENG-RE-QUEST@MWUNIX.MITRE.ORG
How to unsubscribe: Send unsubscribe message to SOFT-ENG-REQUEST@MWUNIX.MITRE.ORG

SOFTPATS@UVMVM.UVM.EDU

Description: SOFTPATS@UVMVM.UVM.EDU discusses software patents.
Subjects covered: computer hardware and software
List moderated: No.
Editorial contact: Garrett A. Wollman
Internet: wollman@emily.uvm.edu
How to access: Send subscribe message to listserv@uvmvm or listserv@uvmvm.uvm.edu
How to unsubscribe: Send unsubscribe message to listserv@uvmvm or listserv@uvmvm.uvm.edu

SOFTREVU@BROWNVM.BROWN.EDU

Description: SOFTREVU is a forum for discussion of software packages.
Subjects covered: computer hardware and software
List moderated: Yes.
Editorial contact: Jamie Donnelly, IV
How to access: Send subscribe message to listserv@brownvm or listserv@brownvm.brown.edu
How to unsubscribe: Send unsubscribe message to listserv@brownvm or listserv@brownvm.brown.edu

SOFTWARE-MEASUREMENT@MAILBASE.AC.UK

Description: SOFTWARE-MEASUREMENT is a mailbase list covering software metrics.
Subjects covered: computer science; engineering
List moderated: No.
Internet: software-measurement-request@mailbase.ac.uk
How to access: Send subscribe message to mailbase@mailbase.ac.uk in the following format: join software-measurement Yourfirstname Yourlastname
Archives: Archives are developed monthly; apply to listowner for details.

SOFTWARE-TESTING@MAILBASE.AC.UK

Description: SOFTWARE-TESTING is a mailbase discussion list on the testing of software.
Subjects covered: computer science; engineering
List moderated: No.
Internet: software-testing-request@mailbase.ac.uk
How to access: Send subscribe message to mailbase@mailbase.ac.uk in the following format: join software-testing Yourfirstname Yourlastname
Archives: Archives are developed monthly; apply to listowner for details.

SOMACHI@PUCING

Description: SOMACHI@PUCING is a list for the Sociedad Matematica de Chile.
Subjects covered: mathematics
Host: Sociedad Matematica de Chile

List moderated: No.
Editorial contact: Carlos O'Ryan
Bitnet: coryan@pucing
How to access: Send subscribe message to listserv@pucing
How to unsubscribe: Send unsubscribe message to listserv@pucing
Archives: Archives are developed monthly; apply to listowner for details.

SOS-DATA@UNCVM1

Description: SOS-DATA@UNCVM1 is a list focusing on social science data.
Subjects covered: sociology
List moderated: No.
Editorial contact: Jim Cassell
Bitnet: cassell@uncvm1
How to access: Send subscribe message to listserv@uncvm1 or listserv@uncvm1.oit.unc.edu
How to unsubscribe: Send unsubscribe message to listserv@uncvm1 or listserv@uncvm1.oit.unc.edu
Archives: Archives are developed monthly; apply to listowner for details.

SOUTH ASIAN WOMEN'S NET

Description: SOUTH ASIAN WOMEN'S NET is a discussion group for women from South Asian countries and for those interested in their concerns. Open only to women.
Subjects covered: South Asia; feminism; women's studies
Net address for operations: LISTSERV@TAMVM1, LISTSERV@TAMVM1.TAMU.EDU
List moderated: No.
How to access: To subscribe, write to USUBRAMA@MAGNUS.ACS.OHIO-STATE.EDU or to SUSANC@HELIX.NIH.GO
Access policy: Open only to women.

SOVHIST@USCVM

Description: SOVHIST@USCVM is a discussion list covering the history of the Soviet Union.
Subjects covered: Soviet Union; history; political science
Net address for operations: LISTSERV@USCVM or LISTSERV@DOSUNI1 or LISTSERV@CSEARN
How to access: Send standard subscribe request to the listserv.
How to unsubscribe: Send standard unsubscribe request to the listserv.

SPACE DIGEST

Description: Space Digest is a public forum for discussing all types of space-related topics. Email to the digest is collected during the day, and the condensed collection (sorted by Subject) is distributed at night. Three to four digests will be mailed on a typical day. Technically, Space Digest mirrors the Usenet newsgroup sci.space; all posts made to sci.space will appear in Space Digest, and vice versa. So if you have access to the sci.space newsgroup you do not need to subscribe to Space Digest. Space Digest is umoderated. That means nothing and no one will be censored, so it's up to everybody to observe proper netiquette (e.g., read the Frequently-Asked-Questions list before posting a common question, and don't flood the list with lots of email).

Subjects covered: space and space exporation; astronomy
Net address for operations: listserv@uga or
listserv@uga.cc.uga.edu orspace-request@isu.isunet.edu
Net address for questions or submissions: space@uga or
space@isu.isunet.edu
Established: November 1980
Subscribers: Believed to be > 2000 for the mailing list as of
July 1992, but unknown (> 50000 ?) for the newsgroup.
Sponsor: Computer Resources Director, International Space
University, 955 Massachusetts Avenue, Cambridge, MA 02139.
List moderated: No.
Editorial contact: Steve Abrams
International Space University, 955 Massachusetts Avenue,
Cambridge, MA 02139.
Tel: +1 (617) 354 -1987
Fax: +1 (617) 354 -7666
Internet: steve@isu.isunet.edu
Copyright statement: Please do not submit copyrighted mate-
rial! Messages posted to Space Digest are assumed to be in the
public domain.
How to access: Send a subscribe <your name> message in the
body, not subject of your email to one of these addresses:
BITNET:listserv@uga Internet: listserv@uga.cc.uga.edu or
space-request@isu.isunet.edu
Access policy: Anyone may subscribe to Space Digest. However, people with access to the USENET newsgroup sci.space
need not subscribe, since Space Digest is a (nearly) exact copy
of that newsgroup.
How to unsubscribe: Send the message signoff to one of the
addresses listed above.
How to submit: Send your submissions (which will be read by
thousands of people, so keep it short and to the point!) to:
space@isu.isunet.edu
Submission policy: Send any policy questions to space-re-
quest@isu.isunet.edu. Please do not send policy requests (like
''subscribe'' and ''signoff'') to the submission address. No one
else wants to read it!
Archives: Archives of Space Digest are available by anonymous
FTP and by listserv ''get index'' mechanisms. Recent issues can
be obtained via the LISTSERV at uga.cc.uga.edu or by anonymous FTP to isu.isunet.edu (192.131.110.15), in directory pub/
space/V# [where ''#'' is the volume number]. Past archives are
available by anonymous FTP to julius.cs.qub.AC.UK
(143.117.5.6), in directory pub/SpaceDigestArchive.
Related files: The Frequently Asked Questions (FAQ) List for
the sci.space newsgroup (and therefore also Space Digest) is
available via anonymous FTP from many sites, including
ames.arc.nasa.gov (128.102.18.3) in directory pub/SPACE/FAQ
and rtfm.mit.edu (currently 18.70.0.224) in directory pub/usenet/
sci.space. There are lots of interesting things (images, software,
NASA Press Kits) in the NASA Ames Center archive (also under pub/SPACE), and also in the JPL (NASA/Caltech Jet Pro-
pulsion Laboratories) archive at pubinfo.jpl.nasa.gov
(128.149.6.2), in the top-level directory.
Additional information: Additional editors: Mark Maimone,
Computer Science Department, Carnegie Mellon University,
5000 Forbes Avenue, Pittsburgh, PA 15213-3891; (412) 268 -
7698; mwm@cmu.edu

SPACE-IL@TAUNIVM

Description: SPACE-IL@TAUNIVM is a list of the Israeli
Space and Remote Sensing Bulletin.
Subjects covered: astronomy; space and space exploration

Host: Israeli Space Agency
List moderated: Yes.
Editorial contact: Roby Gilead
Bitnet: roby@taunivm
How to access: Send subscribe message to listserv@taunivm or
listserv@taunivm.tau.ac.il
How to unsubscribe: Send unsubscribe message to
listserv@taunivm or listserv@taunivm.tau.ac.il
Archives: Archives are developed monthly; apply to listowner
for details.

SPACE-INVESTORS@CS.CMU.EDU

Description: SPACE-INVESTORS is a forum about investing
in the aerospace industry.
Subjects covered: business; space and space exploration
List moderated: No.
Editorial contact: Vince Cate
Internet: vac@cs.cmu.edu
How to access: Send subscribe message to SPACE-INVES-
TORS-REQUEST@CS.CMU.EDU
How to unsubscribe: Send unsubscribe message to SPACE-IN-
VESTORS-REQUEST@CS.CMU.EDU

SPACE@ANDREW.CMU.EDU

Description: SPACE@ANDREW.CMU.EDU is a forum for
discussion of space.
Subjects covered: astronomy; space and space exploration
List moderated: No.
Editorial contact: Owen T. Anderson
Internet: ota@andrew.cmu.edu
How to access: Send subscribe message to SPACE-RE-
QUEST@ANDREW.CMU.EDU
How to unsubscribe: Send unsubscribe message to SPACE-RE-
QUEST@ANDREW.CMU.EDU

SPACE@FINHUTC

Description: SPACE@FINHUTC is a forum for discussions on
space.
Subjects covered: astronomy; space and space exploration
List moderated: Yes.
Editorial contact: Harri Salminen
Bitnet: postmast@finhutc
How to access: Send subscribe message to listserv@finhutc
How to unsubscribe: Send unsubscribe message to
listserv@finhutc
Archives: Yes; Send all requests to SPACE-RE-
QUEST@ANGBAND.S1.GOV

SPILIB-L

Description: Spilib-L features discussion of SPIRES.
Subjects covered: library and information science
List moderated: No.
Editorial contact: Bhaskaran Balakrishnan
Bitnet: bbalakri@suvm
How to access: Send subscribe message to listserv@suvm
How to unsubscribe: Send unsubscribe message to
listserv@suvm
Archives: Archives are developed monthly; apply to listowner
for details.

SPORTPSY@TEMPLEVM
Description: SPORTPSY@TEMPLEVM is a forum for sports psychology.
Subjects covered: psychology
List moderated: No.
Editorial contact: Michael Sachs
Bitnet: v5289e@templevm
How to access: Send subscribe message to listserv@templevm or listserv%templevm.bitnet@vm1.nodak.edu
How to unsubscribe: Send unsubscribe message to listserv@templevm or listserv%templevm.bitnet@vm1.nodak.edu
Archives: Archives are developed monthly; apply to listowner for details.

SPSSX-L
Description: SPSSX-L is an electronic forum for discussion of the statistical program SPSSX.
Subjects covered: statistics; education; computer hardware and software
Net address for operations: listserv@uga.bitnet
How to access: Send standard subscribe request to listserv.
How to unsubscribe: Send standard unsubscribe request to listserv.

SQSP@UQUEBEC
Description: SQSP@UQUEBEC is a forum for political science at the University of Quebec.
Subjects covered: political science
List moderated: Yes.
Editorial contact: Pierre J. Hamel
Internet: hamel@inrs-urbb.uquebec.ca
Bitnet: hamel@uquebec
How to access: Send subscribe message to listserv@uquebec
How to unsubscribe: Send unsubscribe message to listserv@uquebec
Archives: Archives are developed monthly; apply to listowner for details.

SRVREQ-L
Description: SRVREQ-L is a forum for discussion of network servers and workstations.
Subjects covered: electronic networking; computer hardware and software
List moderated: No.
Editorial contact: Manjit Trehan
Bitnet: itms400@indycms
How to access: Send subscribe message to listserv@indycms
How to unsubscribe: Send unsubscribe message to listserv@indycms

SSSSTALK
Description: SSSSTALK is a discussion list centered on sexuality. Professional researchers, clinicians, educators, and students in the field of sexuality are invited to communicate to this list.
Subjects covered: sexuality; feminism; women's studies
Net address for operations: LISTSERV@TAMVM1, LISTSERV@TAMVM1.TAMU.EDU
List moderated: No.

How to access: Send subscription messages to LISTSERV@TAMVM1 (Bitnet) or LISTSERV@TAMVM1.TAMU.EDU (Internet).

ST-AUDIT@UWF
Description: ST-AUDIT@UWF is a list covering spacetime topics.
Subjects covered: astronomy; space and space exploration
List moderated: No.
Editorial contact: Dick Smith
Bitnet: spacemgr@uwf
How to access: Send subscribe message to listserv@uwf or listserv%uwf.bitnet@cunyvm.cuny.edu
How to unsubscribe: Send unsubscribe message to listserv@uwf or listserv%uwf.bitnet@cunyvm.cuny.edu

STARDATA@HASARA11
Description: STARDATA covers social research and sociological issues.
Subjects covered: sociology; demographics
List moderated: Yes.
Editorial contact: Paul de Guchteneire
Bitnet: a9530005@hasara11
How to access: Send subscribe message to listserv@hasara11
How to unsubscribe: Send unsubscribe message to listserv@hasara11
Archives: Yes; Apply to listowner for details.

STAT-GEO@UFRJ
Description: STAT-GEO@UFRJ is a forum focusing on statistical methods in the geosciences.
Subjects covered: geoscience; science and technology
List moderated: No.
Editorial contact: Hugo Richard
Bitnet: igg02001@ufrj
How to access: Send subscribe message to listserv@ufrj or listserv@ufrj.bitnet@cunyvm.cuny.vm
How to unsubscribe: Send unsubscribe message to listserv@ufrj or listserv@ufrj.bitnet@cunyvm.cuny.vm
Archives: Archives are developed monthly; apply to listowner for details.

STATEPOL@UMAB
Description: STATEPOL@UMAB is a forum discussing state politics in the U.S.
Subjects covered: political science
List moderated: No.
Editorial contact: Jim Hoefler
Bitnet: hoefler@dickinsn
How to access: Send subscribe message to listserv@umab or listserv@umab.umd.edu
How to unsubscribe: Send unsubscribe message to listserv@umab or listserv@umab.umd.edu

STD-UNIX@UUNET.UU.NET
Description: STD-UNIX is a discussion of UNIX standards.
Subjects covered: computer science; electronic networking
Host: IEEE

List moderated: No.
Editorial contact: John Quarterman
Internet: longway!jsq@cs.utexas.edu
How to access: Send subscribe message to STD-UNIX-RE-QUEST@UUNET.UU.NET
How to unsubscribe: Send unsubscribe message to STD-UNIX-REQUEST@UUNET.UU.NET
Archives: Yes; Send anonymous FTP to UUNET.UU.NET and cd ftp/pub/mod.std.unix

STLHE-L

Description: STLHE-L is the list covering learning in higher education generally.
Subjects covered: colleges and universities; education
Net address for operations: listserv@unbvm1.bitnet
How to access: Send standard subscribe request to listserv.
How to unsubscribe: Send standard unsubscribe request to listserv.

STOMP-DEVELOP@MAILBASE.AC.UK

Description: STOMP-DEVELOP is a mailbase forum for developers of SToMP (Software Teaching of Modular Physics) material.
Subjects covered: physics
Host: UFC
List moderated: No.
Internet: stomp-develop-request@mailbase.ac.uk
How to access: Send subscribe message to mailbase@mailbase.ac.uk in the following format: join stomp-develop Yourfirstname Yourlastname
Archives: Archives are developed monthly; apply to listowner for details.

STOMP-MEASURE@MAILBASE.AC.UK

Description: STOMP-MEASURE is a forum for developers of SToMP (Software Teaching of Modular Physics) measurement courseware material.
Subjects covered: physics
List moderated: No.
Internet: stomp-measure-request@mailbase.ac.uk
How to access: Send subscribe message to mailbase@mailbase.ac.uk in the following format: join stomp-measure Yourfirstname Yourlastname
Archives: Archives are developed monthly; apply to listowner for details.

STOMP-SYSTEM@MAILBASE.AC.UK

Description: STOMP-SYSTEM is a forum covering work related to SToMP (Software Teaching of Modular Physics).
Subjects covered: physics
List moderated: No.
Internet: stomp-system-request@mailbase.ac.uk
How to access: Send subscribe message to mailbase@mailbase.ac.uk in the following format: join stomp-system Yourfirstname Yourlastname
Archives: Archives are developed monthly; apply to listowner for details.

STOMP-WAVES@MAILBASE.AC.UK

Description: STOMP-WAVES is a forum for SToMP developers working with wavs and vibration courseware.
Subjects covered: physics
List moderated: No.
Internet: stomp-waves-request@mailbase.ac.uk
How to access: Send subscribe message to mailbase@mailbase.ac.uk in the following format: join stomp-waves Yourfirstname Yourlastname
Archives: Archives are developed monthly; apply to listowner for details.

STOPRAPE

Description: STOPRAPE is a sexual assault activist list.
Subjects covered: sexuality; feminism; women's studies; activism
Net address for operations: LISTSERV@BROWNVM, LISTSERV@BROWNVM.BROWN.EDU
List moderated: No.
How to access: Send subscription messages to LISTSERV@BROWNVM (Bitnet) or LISTSERV@BROWNVM.BROWN.EDU (Internet).

STUMPERS-L

Description: STUMPERS-L is a networking resource for reference questions that have people, in essence, stumped! Should the usual library reference sources provide no satisfactory information for your query, turn to the people on STUMPERS-L. STUMPERS-L has a moderator who performs maintenance duties to its electronic message waves, however, STUMPERS-L is a self-monitored list for the people by the people. The SUB-SCRIBERS make it run! STUMPERS-L is an e-mail based electronic conference that operates across computer networks all over the world. It is a mailing list rather than a bulletin board in that MAILSERV's function, as far as STUMPERS-L is concerned, is to forward e-correspondence to subscribers.
Subjects covered: Internet; library and information science
Editorial contact: Joann M. Wleklinski
Rosary College, 7900 West Division Street, River Forest, IL 60305.
Internet: ROSLIBREFRC@CRF.CUIS.EDU
How to access: Send a subscribe message to STUMPERS-L@CRF.CUIS.EDU
How to unsubscribe: Send the message "UNSUBSCRIBE STUMPERS-L <the-e-mail-address-you-subscribed-with>" to the following address: MAILSERV@CRF.CUIS.EDU Please REMEMBER to use the EXACT e-mail address that you had used to subscribe to STUMPERS-L.
How to submit: The address to send e-mail to the STUMPERS-L list is: STUMPERS-LIST@CRF.CUIS.EDU

STUTT-L

Description: Stutt-L provides a forum to study the problem of stuttering.
Subjects covered: disabilities; speech studies
List moderated: No.
Editorial contact: Woody Starkweather
Bitnet: v5002e@templevm
How to access: Send subscribe message to listserv@templevm or listserv%templevm.bitnet@vm1.nodak.edu

How to unsubscribe: Send unsubscribe message to listserv@templevm or listserv%templevm.bitnet@vm1.nodak.edu
Archives: Archives are developed monthly; apply to listowner for details.

STUXCH-L

Description: Stuxch-L is a student exchange network for students in the art, architecture, and design fields.
Subjects covered: art; architecture; colleges and universities
List moderated: No.
Editorial contact: Harold R. Lawrence
Bitnet: hrl@psuarch
How to access: Send subscribe message to listserv@psuvm or listserv@psuvm.psu.edu
How to unsubscribe: Send unsubscribe message to listserv@psuvm or listserv@psuvm.psu.edu
Archives: Archives are developed monthly; apply to listowner for details.

SUEARN-L

Description: SUEARN-L discusses issues of Internet connections with the republics of the former USSR.
Subjects covered: Internet; Russia
List moderated: Yes.
Editorial contact: Mike Meystel
Internet: meystma@duvm
How to access: Send subscribe message to listserv@ubvm or listserv@ubvm.cc.buffalo.edu
How to unsubscribe: Send unsubscribe message to listserv@ubvm or listserv@ubvm.cc.buffalo.edu

SUNYLA-L

Description: Sunyla-L is a discussion list for the SUNY Library Association.
Subjects covered: library and information science
Host: State University of New York Library Association.
List moderated: No.
Editorial contact: Frank Mols
Bitnet: fmols@bingvmb
How to access: Send subscribe message to listserv@bingvmb or listserv%bingvmb.bitnet@cunyvm.cuny.edu
How to unsubscribe: Send unsubscribe message to listserv@bingvmb or listserv%bingvmb.bitnet@cunyvm.cuny.edu

SUP-COND@TAUNIVM

Description: SUP-COND@TAUNIVM is a forum on superconductivity.
Subjects covered: chemistry
List moderated: Yes.
Editorial contact: Joseph van Zwaren
Internet: jo%ilncrd.bitnet@cunyvm.cuny.edu
Bitnet: jo@ilncrd
How to access: Send subscribe message to listserv@taunivm or listserv@taunivm.tau.ac.il
How to unsubscribe: Send unsubscribe message to listserv@taunivm or listserv@taunivm.tau.ac.il

SUPERC@FRMOP11

Description: SUPERC is a forum on superconductivity.
Subjects covered: engineering
List moderated: No.
How to access: Send subscribe message to listserv@frmop11 or listserv@frmop11,bitnet@vm1.nodak.edu
How to unsubscribe: Send unsubscribe message to listserv@frmop11 or listserv@frmop11,bitnet@vm1.nodak.edu

SUPERGUY@UCG1VM

Description: SUPERGUY@UCG1VM is a forum covering superhero genre forms of literature.
Subjects covered: literature; science fiction
List moderated: No.
Editorial contact: Tad Simmons
Internet: simmons@ucf1vm.cc.ucf.edu
Bitnet: simmons@ucf1vm
How to access: Send subscribe message to listserv@ucf1vm or listserv@ucf1vm.cc.ucf.edu
How to unsubscribe: Send unsubscribe message to listserv@ucf1vm or listserv@ucf1vm.cc.ucf.edu
Archives: Archives are developed weekly; apply to listowner for details.

SWIP-L

Description: SWIP-L is an information and discussion list for members of the Society for Women in Philosophy and others interested in feminist philosophy.
Subjects covered: philosophy; feminism; women's studies
Net address for operations: LISTSERV@CFRVM, LISTSERV@CFRVM.CFR.USF.EDU
List moderated: No.
How to access: Send subscription messages to LISTSERV@CFRVM (Bitnet) or LISTSERV@CFRVM.CFR.USF.EDU (Internet).

SYMBOLIC MATH

Description: SYMBOLIC MATH is an e-conference on symbolic math languages.
Subjects covered: mathematics
List moderated: No.
Editorial contact: Laurence Leff
Internet: leff@smu.uucp
How to access: Send subscribe message to leff@smu.uucp
How to unsubscribe: Send unsubscribe message to leff@smu.uucp

SYSTERS

Description: SYSTERS is designed for professional women in computer science. Among other items, the list includes job listings, book reviews, information about discrimination, etc. "It is also a place to organize efforts to change or influence policies affecting women in computer science."
Subjects covered: computer science; feminism; women's studies
Net address for questions or submissions: SYSTERS-REQUEST@DECWRL.DEC.COM
List moderated: No.
Editorial contact: Anita Borg

Internet: SYSTERS-REQUEST@DECWRL.DEC.COM
How to access: Send subscription messages to Anita Borg at SYSTERS-REQUEST@DECWRL.DEC.COM

T-ASSIST@UNMVMA

Description: T-Assist@UNMVMA is a discussion list for teaching assistants.
Subjects covered: education; graduate students
Net address for operations: Listserv@UNMVMA
Net address for questions or submissions: T-Assist@UNMVMA
How to access: Send message to listserv: SUBSCRIBE <listname> <your name>

TAG-L

Description: Tag-L focuses on talented and gifted education programs.
Subjects covered: education
List moderated: No.
Editorial contact: Jolene Richardson
Internet: nu172504@vm1.nodak.edu
Bitnet: nu172504@ndsuvm1
How to access: Send subscribe message to listserv@ndsuvm1 or listserv@vm1.nodak.edu
How to unsubscribe: Send unsubscribe message to listserv@ndsuvm1 or listserv@vm1.nodak.edu

TAMIL-L

Description: Tamil-L is a forum for Tamil Studies.
Subjects covered: cultural studies
List moderated: No.
Editorial contact: Thomas Malten
Internet: d87@@vm.urz.uni-heidelberg.de
How to access: Send subscribe message to listserv@dhdurz1
How to unsubscribe: Send unsubscribe message to listserv@dhdurz1

TCP-IP@NIC.DDN.MIL

Description: TCP-IP@NIC.DDN.MIL is a forum on Internet TCP-IP communication protocols.
Subjects covered: electronic networking; computer science
List moderated: No.
How to access: Send subscribe message to TCP-IP-REQUEST@NIC.DDN.MIL
How to unsubscribe: Send unsubscribe message to TCP-IP-REQUEST@NIC.DDN.MIL

TEACHEFT

Description: TEACHEFT is a list centering on discussion of teacher effectiveness.
Subjects covered: education
Net address for operations: listserv@wcu.bitnet
How to access: Send standard subscribe request to listserv.
How to unsubscribe: Send standard unsubscribe request to listserv.

TECHBUL-L

Description: Techbul-l is an electronic mailng list carrying announcements of new OCLC Technical Bulletins. The Technical Bulletins themselves are available from the list's archives.
Subjects covered: OCLC; computer hardware and software; library and information science
Net address for operations: listserv@oclc.org
Net address for questions or submissions: This list is for dissemination of information only; submissions are not accepted.
Established: March 1993
Subscribers: 288
Host: OCLC, Inc., 6565 Frantz Road, Dublin, OH 43017; (614) 764-6000; fax: (614) 764-6096.
List moderated: Yes.
Moderation procedure: Submissions from subscribers are not redistributed to the list.
Editorial contact: Lois Yoakam
OCLC, Inc. 6565 Frantz Road, Dublin, OH 43017.
Tel: (614) 764-6000
Fax: (614) 764-6096
Internet: lois__yoakam@oclc.org
Technical contact: Laura Toms
OCLC, Inc., 6565 Frantz Road, Dublin, OH 43017.
Tel: (614) 761-5016
Fax: (614) 761-5047
Internet: ltoms@oclc.org
How to access: Send a message to listserv@oclc,org and include the following string in the message body: subscribe techbul-l Your Name replacing "Your Name" with the subscriber's name.
Access policy: Anyone may subscribe; no approval is needed.
How to unsubscribe: Send a message to listserv@oclc.org and include the following string in the message body: unsubscribe techbul-l.
Submission policy: Submissions are ignored and are not redistributed to the list.
Archives: OCLC Technical Bulletins in machine-readable format. Non-subscribers as well as subscribers may request documents from the archive. Subscribers receive announcement of new Technical Bulletins.
Additional information: Second technical contact: George Pallas, OCLC, Inc., 6565 Frantz Road, Dublin, OH 43017. tel (614) 764-6301 Fax (614) 761-5047; List service provided by UNIX-LISTSERVER version 5.5.

TECHED-L

Description: Teched-L focuses on training for educators.
Subjects covered: education
List moderated: No.
How to access: Send subscribe message to listserv@psuvm or listserv@psuvm.psu.edu
How to unsubscribe: Send unsubscribe message to listserv@psuvm or listserv@psuvm.psu.edu

TECHNOLOGY-TRANSFER-LIST@SEI.CMU.EDU

Description: TECHNOLOGY-TRANSFER-LIST is a discussion on innovation and technology transfer.
Subjects covered: science and technology; technology transfer
Host: Technology Applications Group, Software Engineering Institute
List moderated: No.

How to access: Send subscribe message to TECHNOLOGY-TRANSFER-LIST-REQUEST@SEI.CMU.EDU
How to unsubscribe: Send unsubscribe message to TECHNOLOGY-TRANSFER-LIST-REQUEST@SEI.CMU.EDU

TECHSERV@NIST.GOV
Description: TECHSERV is a forum of the Technology Services Unit of the National Institute of Standards and Technology.
Subjects covered: engineering; science and technology
Host: National Institute of Standards and Technology
List moderated: No.
Editorial contact: John Makulowich
Internet: johnjohn@micf.nist.gov
Bitnet: johnjohn@nbsmicf
How to access: Send subscribe message to TECHSERV-REQUEST@NIST.GOV
How to unsubscribe: Send unsubscribe message to TECHSERV-REQUEST@NIST.GOV
Archives: Yes; Send anonymous FTP to: ENH.NIST.GOV (129.6.16.1) and cd archives.

TECHTALK-L
Description: TECHTALK-L is a list to encourage a dialogue between the people responsible for technical aspects of computer-supported communication facilities to discuss issues of technical, political, and organizational interest with faculty who work in and administer these labs.
Subjects covered: computer hardware and software; electronic publishing; science and technology; telecommunications
Net address for operations: majordomo@mtu.edu
Net address for questions or submissions: techtalk-l@mtu.edu
Established: 1992
Subscribers: 25
Sponsor: Michigan Technological University, 1400 Townsend, Houghton, MI 49931.
List moderated: No.
Editorial contact: Dickie Selfe
138 Walker, MTU-Humanities Dept., Houghton, MI 49931.
Tel: (906) 487-3225
Internet: rselfe@mtu.edu
Technical contact: Mark Mach
113 Walker, MTU-Humanities Dept., Houghton, MI 49931.
Tel: (906) 487-2582
Internet: mrmach@mtu.edu
Copyright statement: Please do not quote any posting without authorization of author that has been forwarded to the list manager.
How to access: Send ''subscribe_techtalk-l'' <your e-mail address>'' to ''majordomo@mtu.edu''
Access policy: Open to anyone.
How to unsubscribe: Send ''unsubscribe_techtalk-l'' <your e-mail address>'' to ''majordomo@mtu.edu''
How to submit: Send mail to ''techtalk-l@mtu.edu''

TECNET
Description: TECnet is an electronic discussion forum for topics related to intercultural communication, especially in the teaching of English as a second or foreign language.
Subjects covered: communications; English as a second language; education; adult education

Net address for operations: LISTSERV@CUNYVM.CUNY.EDU
Net address for questions or submissions: TESLFF-L@CUNYVM.CUNY.EDU
Established: November 1992
Subscribers: 120
Sponsor: City University of New York
Host: City University of New York
List moderated: No.
Editorial contact: Anthea Tillyer
Hunter College/IELI, 695 Park Avenue (10th Fl. East,), New York, NY 10021.
Tel: (212) 757-5741
Fax: (212) 489-3687
Internet: ABTHC@CUNYVM.CUNY.EDU
Bitnet: ABTHC@CUNYVM.BITNET
Technical contact: Bill Gruber
UCC/CUNY, 555 West 57th Street, New York, NY 10019.
Tel: (212) 903-3688
Internet: BIGCU@CUNYVM.BITNET or BIGCU@CUNYVM.CUNY.EDU
Copyright statement: All electronic postings of personal questions and/or comments are con- sidered the private property of the writer. They are protected by copyright. Therefore, no one may re-post on another network anything that is written on TESL-L or its branches without first obtaining the written permission of the original writer, nor may TESL-Lers repost on TESL-L items that have been on other nets or in other media without the written authorization of the original author, or a proper citation (if it is a quotation). Furthermore, items posted on TESL-L may not be published or reprinted in any other medium without the permission of the writer. Our database is also subject to copyright laws. If you submit (and we hope you do) copies of your previously-published articles, we must get the permission of the original publisher to include your article in our database. It is also the practice of TESL-L (although publishers do not require it) that we get explicit written permission from all the writers involved in the article, even when one of them submitted the item to us for inclusion in the database.
How to access: Email to LISTSERV@CUNYVM.CUNY.EDU ''SUB TESLIC-L''
Access policy: Subscription open to members of TESL-L only.
How to unsubscribe: Email to LISTSERV@CUNYVM.CUNY.EDU ''UNSUB TESLIC-L''
How to submit: Email to TESLIC-L@CUNYVM.CUNY.EDU
Submission policy: All members of TESLIC-L may submit.
Archives: Logs are archived monthly.
Related files: Extensive database of materials related to the field. Apply to listowner for details.

TECNET BBS
Description: TECnet is a BBS serving small and medium-sized manufacturers and agencies providing technical assistance on computer-aided design and database software.
Subjects covered: computer-assisted design (CAD); computer hardware and software
Net address for questions or submissions: info@tecnet.me.tufts.edu
Established: 1989
Fee: $95 one time fee.
Sponsor: Tufts University Manufacturing Resource Center
Editorial contact: Dr. Leslie Schneider

Tufts University College of Engineering, Anderson Hall, Room 204, Medford, MA 02155.
Tel: (617) 627-3818
Fax: (617) 623-1420
Internet: leslie@tecnet.me.tufts.edu
Technical contact: Charlie Rosenberg
Tufts University College of Engineering, Anderson Hall, Room 204, Medford, MA 02155.
Tel: (617) 627-3818
Fax: (617) 623-1420
Internet: charlie@tecnet.me.tufts.edu
Sample contents: Information Services, Databases and Conferences on TECnet include: CAD selection tool; CAD utility software; Chemical safety data; Commerce Business Daily; Directory of Business and Financial Assistance; Federal Register; ISO 9000 reference materials; Military Specifications Index; QUICKVIEW business practices assessment tool; Used industrial equipment directory; Business news briefs; CAD software support conference; Database software support conference; IBM-PC support conference; Manufacturing networks conference; Spreadsheet software support conference.
Review: New Technology Week, Volume 7, Number 15, April 12, 1993, page 11, ''Electronic Net Aimed at Manufacturing May Ride NIST Wavecrest''.
How to access: info@tecnet.me.tufts.edu
How to unsubscribe: info@tecnet.me.tufts.edu

TEI-ANA@UICVM

Description: TEI-ANA@UICVM covers text coding and analysis.
Subjects covered: linguistics; computer hardware and software
List moderated: No.
Editorial contact: Terry Langendoen
Bitnet: langendt@arizvm1
How to access: Send subscribe message to listserv@uicvm or listserv@uicvm.uic.edu
How to unsubscribe: Send unsubscribe message to listserv@uicvm or listserv@uicvm.uic.edu
Archives: Archives are developed monthly; apply to listowner for details.

TEI-L

Description: TEI-L is a discussion list on text coding and analysis.
Subjects covered: linguistics; computer hardware and software
Host: Text Encoding Initiative
List moderated: Yes.
Internet: lov@vax.oxford.ac.uk
Bitnet: v35395@uicvm
How to access: Send subscribe message to listserv@uicvm or listserv@uicvm.uic.edu
How to unsubscribe: Send unsubscribe message to listserv@uicvm or listserv@uicvm.uic.edu
Archives: Archives are developed monthly; apply to listowner for details.

TEI-META@UICVM

Description: TEI-META@UICVM is a forum for the Text Encoding Initiative - Metalanguage Committee.
Subjects covered: linguistics
Host: Text Encoding Initiative

List moderated: Yes.
Internet: barnard@qucis.queenu.ca
Bitnet: v35395@uicvm
How to access: Send subscribe message to listserv@uicvm or listserv@uicvm.uic.edu
How to unsubscribe: Send unsubscribe message to listserv@uicvm or listserv@uicvm.uic.edu
Archives: Archives are developed monthly; apply to listowner for details.

TEI-REP@UICVM

Description: TEI-REP@UICVM covers the Text Encoding Initiative.
Subjects covered: linguistics
Host: Text Encoding Initiative
List moderated: No.
Editorial contact: Terry Langendoen
Bitnet: langendt@arizvm1
How to access: Send subscribe message to listserv@uicvm or listserv@uicvm.uic.edu
How to unsubscribe: Send unsubscribe message to listserv@uicvm or listserv@uicvm.uic.edu
Archives: Archives are developed monthly; apply to listowner for details.

TEL@USCVM

Description: TEL@USCVM is a forum for Turkish scientists around the world.
Subjects covered: science and technology
List moderated: No.
Editorial contact: Metin Akbil
Internet: umzakbi@vax1.cc.lehigh.edu
How to access: Send subscribe message to listserv@uscvm or listserv@vm.usc.edu
How to unsubscribe: Send unsubscribe message to listserv@uscvm or listserv@vm.usc.edu

TELECOM-PRIV@PICA.ARMY.MIL

Description: TELECOM-PRIV discusses telecommunications privacy issues.
Subjects covered: telecommunications; information technology; computer privacy
List moderated: Yes.
Editorial contact: Dennis Rears
Internet: drears@pica.army.mil
How to access: Send subscribe message to TELECOM-PRIV-REQUEST@PICA.ARMY.MIL
How to unsubscribe: Send unsubscribe message to TELECOM-PRIV-REQUEST@PICA.ARMY.MIL
Archives: Yes; Send anonymous FTP to pica.army.mil [129.139.160.200]

TELECOM@EECS.NWU.EDU

Description: TELECOM@EECS.NWU.EDU is a forum on telecommunications technology
Subjects covered: telecommunications; information technology
List moderated: No.
Editorial contact: Patrick Townson
Internet: ptownson@eecs.nwu.edu

How to access: Send subscribe message to TELECOM-RE-QUEST@EECS.NWU.EDU
How to unsubscribe: Send unsubscribe message to TELECOM-REQUEST@EECS.NWU.EDU
Archives: Yes; Send anonymous FTP to lcs.mit.edu and cd telecom-archives

TELEMED@FRMOP11

Description: TELEMED@FRMOP11 is a conference for members of the TELEMED Project.
Subjects covered: medicine
List moderated: Yes.
Editorial contact: Jacques Brunerie
Bitnet: bruneri@frmop11
How to access: Send subscribe message to listserv%frmop11.bitnet@vm1.nodak.edu or listserv@frmop11
How to unsubscribe: Send unsubscribe message to listserv%frmop11.bitnet@vm1.nodak.edu or listserv@frmop11
Archives: Archives are developed monthly; apply to listowner for details.

TESL-L

Description: TESL-L is a discussion group for teachers of English as a second or foreign language around the world.
Subjects covered: English as a second language; education; adult education
Net address for operations: LISTSERV@CUNYVM.CUNY.EDU
Net address for questions or submissions: TESL-L@CUNYVM.CUNY.EDU
Established: MAY 1991
Subscribers: 1700
Sponsor: TESL-L is supported by a grant from the US Department of Education's Fund for the Improvement of Post-Secondary Education (FIPSE), Anthea Tillyer, Project Director. Sponsoring institution is the City University of New York.
Host: CUNYVM
Editorial contact: Anthea Tillyer
Anthea Tillyer, Hunter College/IELI, 695 Park Avenue (10th fl. East), New York, NY 10021.
Tel: (212) 757-5741
Fax: (212) 489-3687
Internet: ABTHC@CUNYVM.CUNY.EDU
Bitnet: ABTHC@CUNYVM.BITNET
Technical contact: Bill Gruber
UCC/CUNY, 555 West 57th Street, New York, NY 10019.
Tel: (212) 903-3688
Internet: BIGCU@CUNYVM.CUNY.EDU
Bitnet: BIGCU@CUNYVM.BITNET
Copyright statement: Copyright Anthea TILLYER
How to access: Email to listserv@cunyvm.cuny.edu ''SUB tesl-l''
Access policy: Open subscription.
How to unsubscribe: Email to listserv@cunyvm.cuny.edu ''UNSUB TESL-L
How to submit: TESL-L@CUNYVM.CUNY.EDU
Submission policy: Submissions by TESL-L members only.
Archives: Logs, weekly, public.
Related files: Extensive database of materials related to English as a second or foreign language teaching. Apply to listowner for details.

Additional information: TESL-L has eight ''branches'' or sub-lists.

TESLA@NERVM

Description: TESLA@NERVM is a discussion forum on library technical standards.
Subjects covered: library and information science
List moderated: Yes.
Editorial contact: Mark Hinnebusch
Bitnet: fclmth@nervm
How to access: Send subscribe message to listserv@nervm
How to unsubscribe: Send unsubscribe message to listserv@nervm

TESLCA-L (COMPUTER-ASSISTED LEARNING SUB-LIST OF TESL-L)

Description: TESLCA-L (Computer-Assisted Learning Sub-List of TESL-L) is an electronic discussion forum for topics related to computer-assisted language learning (Call) in the field of teaching English to speakers of other languages.
Subjects covered: computer-assisted instruction (CAI); education; language and literature; English as a second language
Net address for operations: LISTSERV@CUNYVM.CUNY.EDU
Net address for questions or submissions: TESCLA-L2CUNYVM.CUNY.EDU
Established: November 1992
Subscribers: 250
Sponsor: City University of New York
Host: City University of New York
List moderated: No.
Editorial contact: Anthea Tillyer
Hunter College/ELI, 695 Park Avenue (10th Fl. East).
Tel: (212) 757-5741
Fax: (212) 489-3687
Internet: ABTHC@CUNYVM.CUNY.EDU
Bitnet: ABTHC@CUNYVM.BITNET
Technical contact: Bill Gruber
UCC/CUNY,555 West 57th Street, New York, NY 10019.
Tel: (212) 903-3688
Internet: BIGCU@CUNYVM.CUNY.EDU
Bitnet: BIGCU@CUNYVM.BITNET
Copyright statement: All electronic postings of personal questions and/or comments are considered the private property of the writer. They are protected by copyright. Therefore, no one may re-post on another network anything that is written on TESL-L or its branches without first obtaining the written permission of the original writer, nor may TESL-Lers repost on TESL-L items that have been on other nets or in other media without the written authorization of the original author, or a proper citation (if it is a quotation). Furthermore, items posted on TESL-L may not be published or reprinted in any other medium without the permission of the writer. Our database is also subject to copyright laws. If you submit (and we hope you do) copies of your previously-published articles, we must get the permission of the original publisher to include your article in our database. It is also the practice of TESL-L (although publishers do not require it) that we get explicit written permission from all the writers involved in the article, even when one of them submitted the item for us for inclusion in the database.
How to access: Mail to LISTSERV@CUNYVM.CUNY.EDU SUB TESLCA-L <subscriber's full name>

Access policy: Subscription open to members of TESL-L only.
How to unsubscribe: Mail to
LISTSERV@CUNYVM.CUNY.EDU UNSUB TESLCA-L
How to submit: Mail to TESLCA-L@CUNYVM.CUNY.EDU
Submission policy: All members of TESLCA-L may submit.
Archives: Logs archives monthly, public.
Related files: Extensive database of materials related to the field.
Additional information: This list is a "branch" of TESL-L and only TESL-L members are eligible to join it.

TESLEC-L

Description: Teslec-L is a forum that examines the use of electronic communication in language instruction.
Subjects covered: education
Sponsor: U.S. Department of Education Fund for the Improvement of Post-Secondary Education
List moderated: No.
Editorial contact: Anthea Tillyer
Internet: abthc@cunyvm.cuny.edu
Bitnet: abthc@cunyvm
How to access: Send subscribe message to listserv@psuvm or listserv@cunyvm or listserv@cunyvm.cuny.edu
How to unsubscribe: Send unsubscribe message to listserv@psuvm or listserv@cunyvm or listserv@cunyvm.cuny.edu
Archives: Archives are developed weekly; apply to listowner for details.

TESLFF-L

Description: TESLFF-L is an electronic discussion forum for topics related to whole language and fluency first appraoches to the teaching of English as a second or foreign language.
Subjects covered: English as a second language; whole language; education; adult education
Net address for operations:
LISTSERV@CUNYVM.CUNY.EDU
Net address for questions or submissions: TESLIT-L@CUNYVM.CUNY.EDU
Established: November, 1992
Subscribers: 150
Sponsor: City University of New York
Host: City University of New York
List moderated: No.
Editorial contact: Anthea Tillyer
Hunter College/IELI, 695 Park Avenue (10th Fl. East,), New York, NY 10021.
Tel: (212) 757-5741
Fax: (212) 489-3687
Internet: ABTHC@CUNYVM.CUNY.EDU
Bitnet: ABTHC@CUNYVM.BITNET
Technical contact: Bill Gruber
UCC/CUNY, 555 West 57th Street, New York, NY 10019.
Tel: (212) 903-3688
Internet: BIGCU@CUNYVM.CUNY.EDU
Copyright statement: All electronic postings of personal questions and/or comments are considered the private property of the writer. They are protected by copyright. Therefore, no one may re-post on another network anything that is written on TESL-L or its branches without first obtaining the written permission of the original writer, nor may TESL-Lers repost on TESL-L items that have been on other nets or in other media without the writ-

ten authorization of the original author, or a proper citation (if it is a quotation). Furthermore, items posted on TESL-L may not be published or reprinted in any other medium without the permission of the writer. Our database is also subject to copyright laws. If you submit (and we hope you do) copies of your previously-published articles, we must get the permission of the original publisher to include your article in our database. It is also the practice of TESL-L (although publishers do not require it) that we get explicit written permission from all the writers involved in the article, even when one of them submitted the item to us for inclusion in the database.
How to access: Email to LISTSERV@CUNYVM.CUNY.EDU "SUB TESLFF-L"
Access policy: Subscription open to members of TESL-L only.
How to unsubscribe: Email to
LISTSERV@CUNYVM.CUNY.EDU "UNSUB TESLFF-L"
How to submit: Email to TESLIT-L@CUNYVM.CUNY.EDU
Submission policy: All members of TESLFF-L may submit.
Archives: Logs are archived monthly.
Related files: Extensive database of materials related to the field. Apply to listowner for details.

TESLIC-L

Description: Teslic-L is a forum that examines intercultural communication in education.
Subjects covered: cultural studies
Sponsor: U.S. Department of Education Fund for the Improvement of Post-Secondary Education
List moderated: No.
Editorial contact: Anthea Tillyer
Internet: abthc@cunyvm.cuny.edu
Bitnet: abthc@cunyvm
How to access: Send subscribe message to listserv@psuvm or listserv@cunyvm or listserv@cunyvm.cuny.edu
How to unsubscribe: Send unsubscribe message to listserv@psuvm or listserv@cunyvm or listserv@cunyvm.cuny.edu
Archives: Archives are developed weekly; apply to listowner for details.

TESLIE-L

Description: TESLIE-L is an electronic discussion forum for topics related to the administration of intensive English language programs in the US and around the world.
Subjects covered: English as a second language; education; adult education
Net address for operations:
LISTSERV@CUNYVM.CUNY.EDU
Net address for questions or submissions: TESLIE-L@CUNYVM.CUNY.EDU
Established: October, 1992
Subscribers: 250
Sponsor: City University of New York
Host: City University of New York
List moderated: No.
Editorial contact: Anthea Tillyer
Hunter College/IELI, 695 Park Avenue (10th Fl. East,), New York, NY 10021.
Tel: (212) 757-5741
Fax: (212) 489-3687
Internet: ABTHC@CUNYVM.CUNY.EDU
Bitnet: ABTHC@CUNYVM.BITNET

Technical contact: Bill Gruber
UCC/CUNY, 555 West 57th Street, New York, NY 10019.
Tel: (212) 903-3688
Internet: BIGCU@CUNYVM.CUNY.EDU
Bitnet: BIGCU@CUNYVM.BITNET
Copyright statement: All electronic postings of personal questions and/or comments are considered the private property of the writer. They are protected by copyright. Therefore, no one may re-post on another network anything that is written on TESL-L or its branches without first obtaining the written permission of the original writer, nor may TESL-Lers repost on TESL-L items that have been on other nets or in other media without the written authorization of the original author, or a proper citation (if it is a quotation). Furthermore, items posted on TESL-L may not be published or reprinted in any other medium without the permission of the writer. Our database is also subject to copyright laws. If you submit (and we hope you do) copies of your previously-published articles, we must get the permission of the original publisher to include your article in our database. It is also the practice of TESL-L (although publishers do not require it) that we get explicit written permission from all the writers involved in the article, even when one of them submitted the item to us for inclusion in the database.
How to access: Email to LISTSERV@CUNYVM.CUNY.EDU "SUB TESLIE-L"
Access policy: Subscription open to members of TESL-L only.
How to unsubscribe: Email to LISTSERV@CUNYVM.CUNY.EDU "UNSUB TESLIE-L"
How to submit: Email to TESLIE-L@CUNYVM.CUNY.EDU
Submission policy: All members of TESLIE-L may submit.
Archives: Logs are archived monthly.
Related files: Extensive database of materials related to the field. Apply to listowner for details.
Additional information: This list is a "branch" of TESL-L and only TESL-L members are eligible to join it.

TESLIT-L

Description: TESLIT-L is an electronic discussion forum for topics related to adult education and literacy issues, particularly in the teaching of English as a second or foreign language.
Subjects covered: adult education; literacy; English as a second language; education
Net address for operations:
LISTSERV@CUNYVM.CUNY.EDU
Net address for questions or submissions: TESLJB-L@CUNYVM.CUNY.EDU
Established: November, 1992
Subscribers: 150
Sponsor: City University of New York
Host: City University of New York
List moderated: No.
Editorial contact: Anthea Tillyer
Hunter College/IELI, 695 Park Avenue (10th Fl. East,), New York, NY 10021.
Tel: (212) 757-5741
Fax: (212) 489-3687
Internet: ABTHC@CUNYVM.CUNY.EDU
Bitnet: ABTHC@CUNYVM.BITNET
Technical contact: Bill Gruber
UCC/CUNY, 555 West 57th Street, New York, NY 10019.
Tel: (212) 903-3688
Internet: BIGCU@CUNYVM.CUNY.EDU
Bitnet: BIGCU@CUNYVM.BITNET

Copyright statement: All electronic postings of personal questions and/or comments are considered the private property of the writer. They are protected by copyright. Therefore, no one may re-post on another network anything that is written on TESL-L or its branches without first obtaining the written permission of the original writer, nor may TESL-Lers repost on TESL-L items that have been on other nets or in other media without the written authorization of the original author, or a proper citation (if it is a quotation). Furthermore, items posted on TESL-L may not be published or reprinted in any other medium without the permission of the writer. Our database is also subject to copyright laws. If you submit (and we hope you do) copies of your previously-published articles, we must get the permission of the original publisher to include your article in our database. It is also the practice of TESL-L (although publishers do not require it) that we get explicit written permission from all the writers involved in the article, even when one of them submitted the item to us for inclusion in the database.
How to access: Email to LISTSERV@CUNYVM.CUNY.EDU "SUB TESLIT-L"
Access policy: Subscription open to members of TESL-L only.
How to unsubscribe: Email to LISTSERV@CUNYVM.CUNY.EDU "UNSUB TESLIT-L"
How to submit: Email to TESLIT-L@CUNYVM.CUNY.EDU
Submission policy: All members of TESLIT-L may submit.
Archives: Logs are archived monthly.
Related files: Extensive database of materials related to the field. Apply to listowner for details.

TESLJB-L

Description: TESLJB-L is an electronic discussion forum for topics related to jobs and employment issues in the field of teaching English as a second or foreign language.
Subjects covered: English as a second language; career opportunities; education; adult education
Net address for operations:
LISTSERV@CUNYVM.CUNY.EDU
Net address for questions or submissions: TESLJB-L@CUNYVM.CUNY.EDU
Established: November 1992
Subscribers: 150
List moderated: No.
Editorial contact: Anthea Tillyer
Hunter College/IELI, 695 Park Avenue (10th Fl. East,), New York, NY 10021.
Tel: (212) 757-5741
Fax: (212) 489-3687
Internet: ABTHC@CUNYVM.CUNY.EDU
Bitnet: ABTHC@CUNYVM.BITNET
Technical contact: Bill Gruber
UCC/CUNY, 555 West 57th Street, New York, NY 10019.
Tel: (212) 903-3688
Internet: BIGCU@CUNYVM.CUNY.EDU
Bitnet: BIGCU@CUNYVM.BITNET
Copyright statement: All electronic postings of personal questions and/or comments are considered the private property of the writer. They are protected by copyright. Therefore, no one may re-post on another network anything that is written on TESL-L or its branches without first obtaining the written permission of the original writer, nor may TESL-Lers repost on TESL-L items that have been on other nets or in other media without the written authorization of the original author, or a proper citation (if it is a quotation). Furthermore, items posted on TESL-L may not

be published or reprinted in any other medium without the permission of the writer. Our database is also subject to copyright laws. If you submit (and we hope you do) copies of your previously-published articles, we must get the permission of the original publisher to include your article in our database. It is also the practice of TESL-L (although publishers do not require it) that we get explicit written permission from all the writers involved in the article, even when one of them submitted the item to us for inclusion in the database.
How to access: Email to LISTSERV@CUNYVM.CUNY.EDU "SUB TESLJB-L"
Access policy: Subscription open to members of TESL-L only.
How to unsubscribe: Email to LISTSERV@CUNYVM.CUNY.EDU "UNSUB TESLJB-L"
How to submit: Email to TESLJB-L@CUNYVM.CUNY.EDU
Submission policy: All members of TESLJB-L may submit.
Archives: Logs are archived monthly.
Additional information: This list is a "branch" of TESL-L and only TESL-L members are eligible to join it.

TESLMW-L (MATERIALS WRITERS SUB-LIST OF TESL-L)

Description: TESLMW-L (Materials Writers Sub-List of TESL-L) is an electronic discussion forum for writers of books and materials for use in the teaching of English as a second foreign language.
Subjects covered: education; English as a second language; language and literature
Net address for operations: LISTSERV@CUNYVM.CUNY.EDU
Net address for questions or submissions: TESLMW-L@CUNYVM.CUNY.EDU
Established: November 1992
Subscribers: 150
Sponsor: City University of New York
Host: City University of New York
List moderated: No.
Editorial contact: Anthea Tillyer
Hunter College/ELI, 695 Park Avenue (10th Fl. East).
Tel: (212) 757-5741
Fax: (212) 489-3687
Internet: ABTHC@CUNYVM.CUNY.EDU
Bitnet: ABTHC@CUNYVM.BITNET
Technical contact: Bill Gruber
UCC/CUNY, 555 West 57th Street, New York, NY 10019.
Tel: (212) 903-3688
Internet: BIGCU@CUNYVM.CUNY.EDU
Bitnet: BIGCU@CUNYVM.BITNET
Copyright statement: See statement under TESLCS-L.
How to access: Mail to LISTSERV@CUNYVM.CUNY.EDU SUB TESLMW-L <subscriber's full name>
Access policy: Subscription open to members of TESL-L only.
How to unsubscribe: Mail to LISTSERV@CUNYVM.CUNY.EDU
How to submit: Mail to TESLMW-L@CUNYVM.CUNY.EDU
Submission policy: All members of TESLMW-L may submit.
Archives: Logs archives monthly, public.
Related files: Extensive database of materials related to the field.

TESTING-ARCHIVE@ERNIE.CS.UIUC.EDU

Description: TESTING-ARCHIVE is an archive of material on software testing.
Subjects covered: computer science; engineering
List moderated: No.
Editorial contact: Brian Marick
Internet: testing-archive-request@ernie.cs.uiuc.edu
How to access: Send subscribe message to TESTING-ARCHIVE-REQUEST@ERNIE.CS.UIUC.EDU
How to unsubscribe: Send unsubscribe message to TESTING-ARCHIVE-REQUEST@ERNIE.CS.UIUC.EDU
Archives: Yes; Send anonymous FTP to: cs.uiuc.edu and cd /pub/testing/archiveXX

TESTING-RESEARCH@ERNIE.CS.UIUC.EDU

Description: TESTING-RESEARCH is a forum for software testing researchers.
Subjects covered: computer science; engineering
List moderated: No.
Editorial contact: Brian Marick
Internet: testing-archive-request@ernie.cs.uiuc.edu
How to access: Send subscribe message to TESTING-RESEARCH-REQUEST@ERNIE.CS.UIUC.EDU
How to unsubscribe: Send unsubscribe message to TESTING-RESEARCH-REQUEST@ERNIE.CS.UIUC.EDU

TEX-D-L

Description: Tex-d-L is a forum on the German version of the TeX typesetting program.
Subjects covered: computer hardware and software
List moderated: No.
Editorial contact: Joachim Lammarsch
Internet: x92@dhdurz1
How to access: Send subscribe message to listserv@dearn
How to unsubscribe: Send unsubscribe message to listserv@dearn

TEX-PUBS@SHSU

Description: TEX-PUBS@SHSU is a distribution list for TeX-related publications.
Subjects covered: computer hardware and software
List moderated: Yes.
Editorial contact: George D Greenwade, Ph.D.
Internet: bed—gdg@shsu.edu
Bitnet: bed—gdg@shsu
How to access: Send subscribe message to listserv@shsu or listserv@shsu.edu
How to unsubscribe: Send unsubscribe message to listserv@shsu or listserv@shsu.edu
Archives: Yes; Located at fileserv@shsu or fileserv@shsu.edu

TEXHAX DIGEST

Description: TeXhax Digest covers all topics relevant to TeX and its supporting software.
Subjects covered: computer hardware and software; TeX software
Net address for operations: TeXhax-request@tex.ac.uk
Net address for questions or submissions: TeXhax@tex.ac.uk

Established: 1985
Subscribers: 1123
Sponsor: UK TeX Users Group, c/o Information Services, Aston University, Birmingham B4 7ET, UK; TeX Users Group, P.O.Box 869, Santa Barbara, CA 93102.
Host: Aston University, Aston Triangle, Birmingham B4 7ET, UK.
List moderated: Yes.
Moderation procedure: Submissions are sent out in digest format.
Editorial contact: Peter Abbott
Information Services, Aston University, Aston Triangle, Birmingham B4 7ET, UK.
Tel: +44 21 359 3611 ext 4245
Internet: P.Abbott@aston.ac.uk
Bitnet: P.Abbott%uk.ac.aston@ukacrl.bitnet
Copyright statement: TeXhax Digest can be freely copied.
How to access: Send a message in the format "SUBSCRIBE TEX-L <Your name>" to TeXhax-request@tex.ac.uk
Access policy: Anyone can subscribe.
How to unsubscribe: Send a message in the format "UNSUBSCRIBE TEX-L" to TeXhax-request@tex.ac.uk
How to submit: Send contributions to TeXhax@tex.ac.uk
Archives: In UK TeX Archive, ftp.tex.ac.uk (134.151.44.19), in directories below /work/archive/digests/texhax Other archives holding past copies: pip.shsu.edu (192.92.115.10), ftp.uni-stuttgart.de (129.69.1.12).
Gopher accessibility: Gopher to "UK TeX Archive".
Additional information: Additional editors: David Osborne, Cripps Computing Centre, University of Nottingham, University Park, Nottingham NG7 2RD, UK; tel +44 602 515151, ext 8169; Internet cczdao@unicorn.nott.ac.uk; Bitnet cczdao%uk.ac.nott.unicorn@ukacrl.bitnet

TEXHAX@CS.WASHINGTON.EDU
Description: TEXHAX@CS.WASHINGTON.EDU is a forum for TeX and Metafont softwares and related issues.
Subjects covered: computer hardware and software
List moderated: No.
Editorial contact: Pierre MacKay
Internet: mackay@cs.washington.edu
How to access: Send subscribe message to listserv@uwavm.acs.washington.edu or texhax-request@cs.washington.edu
How to unsubscribe: Send unsubscribe message to listserv@uwavm.acs.washington.edu or texhax-request@cs.washington.edu
Archives: Yes; Send anonymous FTP to june.cs.wahington.edu and cd ftp/TeXhax

TEXTCRIT@VAX.OXFORD.AC.UK
Description: TEXTCRIT@VAX.OXFORD.AC.UK covers textual criticism.
Subjects covered: linguistics; language and literature
Host: The Computers and Manuscripts Project, Oxford University Computing Service
List moderated: No.
Editorial contact: Peter Robinson
Internet: textcrit@vax.ox.ac.uk
How to access: Send subscribe message to TEXTCRIT@VAX.OX.AC.UK

How to unsubscribe: Send unsubscribe message to TEXTCRIT@VAX.OX.AC.UK

TEXTILES@TREARN
Description: TEXTILES@TREARN is a discussion on textiles and clothing studies.
Subjects covered: science and technology
List moderated: No.
Editorial contact: Haluk Demirbag
Internet: tex5had@cms1.leeds.ac.uk
How to access: Send subscribe message to listserv@trearn or listserv%trearn.bitnet@cunyvm.cuny.edu
How to unsubscribe: Send unsubscribe message to listserv@trearn or listserv%trearn.bitnet@cunyvm.cuny.edu
Archives: Archives are developed monthly; apply to listowner for details.

THEOLOGY@UICVM
Description: THEOLOGY@UICVM is a forum for discussion of the intellectual aspects of religion.
Subjects covered: religion
List moderated: No.
Editorial contact: Charley Earp
Bitnet: u16481@uicvm
How to access: Contact the Editor
How to unsubscribe: Contact the Editor

THEORYNET@WATSON.IBM.COM
Description: THEORYNET is an electronic conference on theoretical computer science.
Subjects covered: computer science
List moderated: Yes.
Editorial contact: Victor Miller
Internet: theorynet-request@watson.ibm.com
How to access: Send subscribe message to listserv@ndsuvm1 or listserv@request@watson.ibm.com
How to unsubscribe: Send unsubscribe message to listserv@ndsuvm1 or listserv@request@watson.ibm.com
Archives: Yes; Apply to LISTSERV@NDSUVM1 for details.

THPHYSIO@FRMOP11
Description: THPHYSIO@FRMOP11 is a conference on thermal physiology.
Subjects covered: medicine
List moderated: No.
Editorial contact: Michael Jorda
Bitnet: jorda@frsun12
How to access: Send subscribe message to listserv@frmop11 or listserv%frmop11.bitnet@vm1.nodak.edu
How to unsubscribe: Send unsubscribe message to listserv@frmop11 or listserv%frmop11.bitnet@vm1.nodak.edu
Archives: Archives are developed monthly; apply to listowner for details.

TIPS (TEACHING IN THE PSYCHOLOGICAL SCIENCES)

Description: TIPS (TEACHING IN the PSYCHOLOGICAL SCIENCES) is a discussion group covering all topics of interest to the teaching of Pyschology.
Subjects covered: psychology; education
Net address for operations: Internet: LISTSERV@FRE.FSU.UMD.EDU Bitnet: LISTSERV%FRE.FSU.UMD.EDU@CUNYVM.CUNY.EDU
Net address for questions or submissions: Internet: TIPS@FRE.FSU.UMD.EDU BITNET - TIPS%FRE.FSU.UMD.EDU@CUNYVM.CUNY.EDU
Established: June 1, 1992
Subscribers: 450
Sponsor: Frostburg State University, Frostburg, MD 21536
Host: Frostburg State University, Frostburg, MD 21536
List moderated: No.
Editorial contact: Bill Southerly
Dept. of Pyschology, Frostburg State Univ., Frostburg, MD 21532
Tel: (301) 689-4193
Fax: (301) 689-4737
Internet: E2PYTIPS@FRE.FSU.UMD.EDU
Bitnet: E2PYSOU@FRE.TOWSON.EDU
Technical contact: Teresa Feck
Academic Computing, Frostburg State University, Frostburg, MD 21532
Tel: (301) 689-7090
Fax: (301) 689-4737
Internet: D2DCFEC@FRE.FSU.UMD.EDU
Bitnet: D2DCFEC@FRE.TOWSON.EDU
How to access: Send the one line message:
SUBSCRIBE TIPS Yourfirstname Yourlastname to one of the following addresses: Internet: LISTSERV@FRE.FSU.UMD.EDU; Bitnet: LISTSERV%FRE.FSU.UMD.EDU@CUNYVM.CUNY.EDU.
Access policy: Open to all with an interest in teaching.
How to unsubscribe: Send the one line message: UNSUBSCRIBE TIPS
How to submit: Send messages to: Internet: TIPS@FRE.FSU.UMD.EDU; Bitnet: TIPS%FRE.FSU.UMD.EDU@CUNYVM.CUNY.EDU
Submission policy: This list is open to all with an interest in teaching.
Archives: Each month's discussion is available for retrieval by an e-mail message. Instructions are distributed to subscribers when they join the group.
Related files: A file server capability is planned for the summer of 1993; it will be accessible by E-Mail message and possibly FTP.

TITNET

Description: TITNET is the electronic discussion list for The International Tit Society (TITS) and is intended for researchers in the biology of Paridae (tits) and other hole-nesting birds. TITNET is an updated list of researchers (and subscribers to its related electronic periodicals TITNEWS and TITNOTES), which provides the name, institutional affiliation, email address(es), species studied, and topics studied of each researcher in its database. TITNEWS carries announcements (e.g., scientific meetings), exchanges concerning techniques (e.g., software, data-bases), etc., and discussions of various related activities. TITNOTES carries research material (including requests for information) on the biology of tits, titmice, chickadees and other cavity-nesting birds.
Subjects covered: birds; chickadees; titmice; Paridae
Net address for operations: JHailman@MACC.Wisc.edu
Net address for questions or submissions: JHailman@MACC.Wisc.edu
Established: December 1990
Method of issuance: Issues are made available through email transmission to distribution list.
Available in other media: Millicent (Penny) Sigler Ficken edits the TITS hardcopy newsletter, PARUS INTERNATIONAL, which is sent out about twice per year in mid-summer and mid-winter. Contributions to PARUS INTERNATIONAL may be sent directly to her: Dr. M. S. Ficken Cedar-Sauk Area Field Station, 3095 Blue Goose Road, Saukville, WI 53080.
Subscribers: 51
Editorial contact: Jack P. Hailman
Department of Zoology 430 Lincoln Drive, Birge Hall, University of Wisconsin, Madison, WI 53706.
Tel: (608) 262-2636
Internet: JHailman@MACC.Wisc.edu Bitnet
Bitnet: JHailman@WiscMACC.bitnet
Sample contents: Contents of latest issues: TITNET 9: subscriber list as of 5 Feb 1993.
Copyright statement: Titnet does not copyright its transmissions, but
research abstracts appearing in TITNOTES belong by U.S. copyright law to the creating authors.
How to access: Send an email message of inquiry to JHailman@MACC.Wisc.edu
How to unsubscribe: Send an email message of inquiry to JHailman@MACC.Wisc.edu
How to submit: Send an email message of inquiry to JHailman@MACC.Wisc.edu
Archives: Archives are available upon individual request.

TLTP-PSYCLE

Description: TLTP-psycle is a contact and discussion list for members involved in the PsyCLE project, a three year project to design and implement computer-based courseware and resources for Introductory Psychology in UK universities.
Subjects covered: psychology; computer hardware and software
Net address for operations: mailbase@uk.ac.mailbase
Net address for questions or submissions: tltp-psycle@mailbase.ac.uk
Established: 1992
Subscribers: 51
Sponsor: University of York, York YO1 5DD, UK.
Host: University of Newcastle, UK.
List moderated: No.
Editorial contact: Jean McKendree
Department of Psychology, University of York, York YO1 5DD.
Tel: 0904 433139
Fax: 0904 433181
Internet: jm25@uk.ac.york
Technical contact: John Martin
University of Newcastle
How to access: Send join tltp-psycle FirstName LastName to mailbase@uk.ac.mailbase

Access policy: This is an open list, but discussion is meant to be restricted to the members of the PsyCLE consortium. Specific questions from others can be addressed to the list owner.

How to unsubscribe: Send unsubscribe FirstName LastName to mailbase@uk.ac.mailbase

How to submit: Send message to tltp-psycle@uk.ac.mailbase

Submission policy: Basically, the list is meant to be limited to the members of the PsyCLE consortium, though membership is not restricted.

Additional information: As this is a three year project, it is likely that the list may disappear sometime in 1996.

TML-L (THESAURUS MUSICARUM LATINARUM)

Description: TML-L is an electronic discussion list on topics related to Latin music theory of the Middle Ages and Renaissance, but it is primarily used to announce the online availability of new texts. All announcements are maintained in annual Log files. The texts of the TML are available in various filelists and can be requested in any of the normal manners. A parallel set of texts is maintained on the TML-FTP. Additional files include the TML Canon (listing all available texts, their sources, and various vital statistics).

Subjects covered: Latin language and literature; music

Net address for operations: LISTSERV@IUBVM (or LISTSERV@IUBVM.UCS.INDIANA.EDU)

Net address for questions or submissions: TML-L@IUBVM (or TML-L@IUBVM.UCS.INDIANA.EDU)

Established: May 1993

Sponsor: This list is partially funded by a grant from the National Endowment for the Humanities, an independent federal agency.

Host: School of Music, Indiana University, Bloomington, IN 47405

List moderated: Yes, the Project Director of the Thesaurus Musicarum Latinarum maintains the list.

Editorial contact: Thomas J. Mathiesen
Thesaurus Musicarum Latinarum, Dept. of Musicology, School of Music, Indiana University, Bloomington, IN

Tel: (812) 876-3592, 855-5471, 855-6889

Fax: (812) 876-3592

Internet: MATHIESE@UCS.INDIANA.EDU

Bitnet: MATHIESE@INDIANA

Copyright statement: The data contained in the Thesaurus Musicarum Latinarum (hereafter TML) is made available to scholars for non-commercial use and study. It has been compiled from public domain and copyrighted materials. Copyrighted materials have been included in the TML by permission of the copyright holders, who reserve all rights to their materials. The TML claims copyright on the compilation, the Introduction, the TML Canon, and all individual text files created and edited by the TML staff from public domain or manuscript material. The TML believes that non-commercial use of the TML by scholars in searching for words and phrases would constitute "fair use" under the law. Nevertheless, the users of the TML are individually responsible for insuring that their own use of these materials does not violate the rights of any third parties. Neither Indiana University nor the TML Project Director nor any member of the TML staff shall be responsible for any improper or unlawful use of the materials contained in the TML.

How to access: To subscribe, send the following one-line message (do not include anything in the Subject: line of your mainframe's mail utility): SUBSCRIBE TML-L <your full name here> to one of the following addresses: LISTSERV@IUBVM [the Bitnet address] or LISTSERV@IUBVM.UCS.INDIANA.EDU [the Internet address] Since the address to which you send your subscription will specify whether the Listserver regards you as an Internet or a Bitnet subscriber, you should select the network you prefer if you have a choice of addresses.

Access policy: Subscriptions are open to anyone.

How to unsubscribe: To unsubscribe, send the following one-line message (do not include anything in the Subject: line of your mainframe's mail utility): SIGNOFF TML-L to one of the following addresses: LISTSERV@IUBVM [the Bitnet address] or LISTSERV@IUBVM.UCS.INDIANA.EDU [the Internet address] You must select the same network under which your subscription was originally registered.

How to submit: Contact the list manager, as listed above.

Submission policy: Contact the list manager, as listed above.

Archives: Annual log files and all text files of the Thesaurus Musicarum Latinarum.

Related files: A parallel set of text files is available on the TML-FTP (further information about the TML-FTP is contained in the INTRO TEXT, available on the TML-L Filelist). The Thesaurus Musicarum Latinarum text program.

Additional information: See also Thesaurus Musicarum Latinarum text program listed elsewhere in this directory.

TOLKIEN@JHUVM

Description: TOLKIEN@JHUVM is a forum for J.R.R. Tolkien readers.

Subjects covered: English language and literature; Tolkien, J.R.R.

List moderated: No.

Internet: gandalf@malloco.ing.puc.cl

How to access: Send subscribe message to listserv@jhuvm

How to unsubscribe: Send unsubscribe message to listserv@jhuvm

Archives: Archives are developed monthly; apply to listowner for details.

TOLKLANG

Description: TolkLang is an electronic list featuring discussions of the linguistic aspects of J.R.R. Tolkien's works. This covers everything from Elvish vocabulary and grammar to his use of Old English.

Subjects covered: language and literature; linguistics; Tolkien, J.R.R.

Net address for operations: tolklang-request@dcs.ed.ac.uk

Net address for questions or submissions: tolklang@dcs.ed.ac.uk

Established: November 1, 1993

Subscribers: 373

Sponsor: Department of Computer Science, University of Edinburgh, UK.

List moderated: Yes.

Moderation procedure: All posts are reviewed before being sent out; normally no change is made, but off-topic posts may be rejected or simple questions answered.

Editorial contact: Julian Bradfield
Dept of Computer Science, University of Edinburgh, The King's Buildings, Mayfield Road, Edinburgh, United Kingdom EH9 3JZ

Tel: +44 31 650 5998
Fax: +44 31 667 7209
Internet: tolklang-request@dcs.ed.ac.uk Bitnet
How to access: Email to tolklang-request@dcs.ed.ac.uk
How to unsubscribe: Email to tolklang-request@dcs.ed.ac.uk
How to submit: Email to tolklang@dcs.ed.ac.uk
Submission policy: List subscribers only may post to list. Content should be at least vaguely related to Tolkienian linguistics.
Archives: Available by anonymous FTP from ftp.dcs.ed.ac.uk:/export/TolkLang. A mail-server is available for subscribers.
Additional information: The list is also available as a weekly electronic digest.

TPS-L

Description: TPS-L (Talk Politics Soviet) is an electronic discussion list covering political and economic topics in Russia and its neighboring states.
Subjects covered: Soviet Union; Russia; political science; current events
Net address for operations: LISTSERV@INDYCMS
How to access: Send standard subscribe request to the listserv.
How to unsubscribe: Send standard unsubscribe request to the listserv.

TQM-L

Description: TQM-L is a discussion on aspects of total quality management at colleges and universities.
Subjects covered: colleges and universities
List moderated: No.
Editorial contact: Phil Endacott
Bitnet: endacott@ukanvax
How to access: Send subscribe message to listserv@ukanvm or listserv@ukanvm.cc.ukans.edu
How to unsubscribe: Send unsubscribe message to listserv@ukanvm or listserv@ukanvm.cc.ukans.edu
Archives: Archives are developed weekly; apply to listowner for details.

TRANSGEN

Description: TRANSGEN is a discussion list covering transgender, transexual, and transvestite issues.
Subjects covered: gay and lesbian topics; gender studies
How to access: Send subscribe message to LISTSERV@BROWNVM.BITNET

TRAVEL-ADVISORIES

Description: The Travel-Advisories mailing list is the Internet and BITNET distribution point for U.S. State Department Counsular Information Sheets and Travel Warnings. In addition to being distributed in mailing list format, this information is also available via St. Olaf's gopher and WAIS servers.
Subjects covered: government information; travel and tourism
Net address for questions or submissions: travel-advisories-request@stolaf.edu
Established: April 26, 1991
Subscribers: 724
List moderated: No.
How to access: Subscription and unsubscription requests should be sent to: travel-advisories-REQUEST@stolaf.edu

How to unsubscribe: Subscription and unsubscription requests should be sent to: travel-advisories-REQUEST@stolaf.edu
Archives: Messages sent to the travel-advisories mailing list are archived and are available via anonymous FTP from: ftp.stolaf.edu:pub/travel-advisories/archive
contains all messages posted to the list ftp.stolaf.edu:pub/travel-advisories/advisories/country contains the current travel information for a given country. Past postings are also available via electronic mail by sending FTP commands to: ftpbymail@stolaf.edu For more detailed instructions, send the word "HELP" to this address. Or to retrieve an advisory (for example, Peru), mail a note to this address containing the message: cd pub/travel-advisories/advisories get peru You may include the word "ls" to get a list of all available travel information. Take care to use lower-case letters only when specifying a country name.

TRAVEL-L

Description: TRAVEL-L is a list centering on discussion of travel issues and information.
Subjects covered: travel and tourism
Net address for operations: TRAVEL-L@TREARN.BITNET
Established: 1990
Subscribers: 327
Sponsor: Ege Univ. Bilgisayar Ar. ve Uyg. Mrk. 35100 Bornova Izmir Turkey
Host: Same as above
List moderated: No.
Editorial contact: Esra Delen
Ege Univ. Bilgisayar Ar. ve Uyg. Mrk. 35100 Bornova Izmir Turkey
Tel: 90-51-887221
Fax: 90-51-887230
Internet: ESRA@EGE.EDU.TR
Bitnet: ESRA@TREARN
How to access: Tell listserv at TREARN SUB TRAVEL-L fullname
How to unsubscribe: Tell listserv at TREARN SIGNOFF TRAVEL-L
How to submit: By mailing to TRAVEL-L@TREARN
Archives: Available via LOG files on LISTSERV

TRDEV-L

Description: TRDEV-L, the Training and Development List, provides a forum for the exchange of information on the training and development of human resources. The primary focus of this list is to stimulate research collaboration and assistance in training and development for the professional and the academic communities.
Subjects covered: human resources; training and development; colleges and universities
Net address for questions or submissions: PSUVM
Established: Spring 1991
Subscribers: 190
Sponsor: Penn State University, 109A Rackley Building, University Park, PA 16802
List moderated: No.
Editorial contact: Jeff M. Allen
Penn State University, 109A Rackley Building, University Park, PA 16802
Tel: (814)863-2589
Fax: (814)863-7532

Internet: JMA110@PSUVM.PSU.EDU
Bitnet: JMA110@PSUVM.BITNET
How to access: Tell listserve at PSUVM SUB TRDEV-L
yourname
Access policy: Open to persons interested in training and development.
How to unsubscribe: Tell listserv at PSUVM SIGNOFF
TRDEV-L
How to submit: NOTE TRDEV-L@PSUVM
Additional information: Co-editor is David Passmore.

TSCCOM-L
Description: TSCCOM-L is a forum of the Tunisian Scientific
Coordination Committee.
Subjects covered: science and technology
List moderated: No.
How to access: Send subscribe message to listserv@uiucvmd or
listserv@vmd.cso.uiuc.edu
How to unsubscribe: Send unsubscribe message to
listserv@uiucvmd or listserv@vmd.cso.uiuc.edu

TSSNEWS@PSUVM
Description: TSSNEWS@PSUVM is a forum of the Tunisian
Scientific Society.
Subjects covered: science and technology
List moderated: No.
Editorial contact: Bilel N. Jamoussi
Bitnet: bnj@psuecl
How to access: Send subscribe message to listserv@psuvm or
listserv@psuvm.psu.edu
How to unsubscribe: Send unsubscribe message to
listserv@psuvm or listserv@psuvm.psu.edu

TWAIN-L
Description: Twain-L is a forum for discussing the life and
works of Samuel Clemens (Mark Twain).
Subjects covered: literature; Twain, Mark (Samuel Clemens)
List moderated: No.
Editorial contact: Taylor Roberts
Internet: troberts@vm1.yorku.ca
Bitnet: troberts@yorkvm1
How to access: Send subscribe message to listserv@yorkvm1 or
listserv@vm1.yorku.ca
How to unsubscribe: Send unsubscribe message to
listserv@yorkvm1 or listserv@vm1.yorku.ca
Archives: Archives are developed weekly; apply to listowner
for details.

TWINS
Description: TWINS is a discussion list on all aspects of being
a twin or being a parent of twins or other multiples (triplets,
etc.).
Subjects covered: parenting multiples
Net address for operations: owner-twins@athena.mit.edu
Net address for questions or submissions:
twins@athena.mit.edu
Established: April 1993
Subscribers: 73
Host: Massachusetts Institute of Technology
List moderated: No.

Editorial contact: Robyn Kozierok
MIT, 20 Ames St. Rm. 401c, Cambridge, MA
Tel: (617) 253-0116
Fax: (617) 258-6264
Internet: owner-twins@athena.mit.edu
How to access: Email owner-twins@athena.mit.edu
Access policy: Anyone may join -- takes 24 hours to process email owner-twins@athena.mit.edu
How to unsubscribe: Email owner-twins@athena.mit.edu
How to submit: Email twins@athena.mit.edu
Related files: Misc.kids twins FAQ list -- email
tscott@ocsmd.ocs.com

TWUNIV-L
Description: Twuniv-L is a discussion group for Chinese scholars.
Subjects covered: Taiwan; Chinese studies
List moderated: No.
Internet: ncus002@twnmoe10
How to access: Send subscribe message to listserv@twnmoe10
How to unsubscribe: Send unsubscribe message to
listserv@twnmoe10
Archives: Archives are developed monthly; apply to listowner
for details.

TXDXN-L@UHUPVM1
Description: TXDXN-L is a discussion list of the Texas Documents Information Network
Subjects covered: computer hardware and software; library and
information science; information technology
Net address for questions or submissions:
LISTSERV@UHUPVM1
How to access: Send subscribe message to
LISTSERV@UHUPVM1
How to unsubscribe: Send unsubscribe message to
LISTSERV@UHUPVM1

UG-L
Description: UG-L discusses usage/abuse of the Internet.
Subjects covered: Internet
List moderated: No.
Internet: LISTMGRGT@HEARN
How to access: Send subscribe message to listserv@bitnic or
listserv@bitnic.educom.edu
How to unsubscribe: Send unsubscribe message to
listserv@bitnic or listserv@bitnic.educom.edu
Archives: Archives are developed monthly; apply to listowner
for details.

UIGIS-L
Description: UIGIS-L covers geographic information systems.
Subjects covered: geographic information systems
List moderated: No.
Editorial contact: David M. Mark
Internet: gismgr@ubvm.cc.buffalo.edu
Bitnet: gismgr@ubvms
How to access: Send subscribe message to listserv@ubvm or
listserv@ubvm.cc.buffalo.edu
How to unsubscribe: Send unsubscribe message to
listserv@ubvm or listserv@ubvm.cc.buffalo.edu

Archives: Archives are developed weekly; apply to listowner for details.

UK DATA PROTECTION ACT 1984
Description: The UK Data Protection Act 1984 is a discussion group for those people involved with data protection issues in the UK and worldwide.
Subjects covered: data protection; government; political science
Established: March 1993
Subscribers: 60
Sponsor: Newcastle University, United Kingdom
Host: Newcastle University
Editorial contact: Sally Justice
South Bank University, London, UK
Tel: 071 815 6509
Fax: 071 815 8155
Internet: justicsa@vax.sbu.ac.uk
Bitnet: justicsa@vax.sbu.ac.uk
How to access: Send message to mailbase@mailbase.ac.uk: Join data-protection Firstname Lastname
How to unsubscribe: Leave data-protection
How to submit: Send message to data-protection@ mailbase.ac.uk
Submission policy: Send message to justicsa@vax.sbu.ac.uk
Archives: Send message to mailbase@mailbase.ac.uk index data-protection to fetch a file type send data-protection filename

UKRAINE@ARIZVM1
Description: UKRAINE@ARIZVM1 is a list covering the Ukraine and its language and culture.
Subjects covered: Ukraine; language and literature; political science; current events
Net address for operations: LISTSERV@ARIZVM1 or LISTSERV@ARIZVM1.CCIT.ARIZONA.EDU
How to access: Send standard subscribe request to the listserv.
How to unsubscribe: Send standard unsubscribe request to the listserv.

ULTRALITE-LIST
Description: ultra-lite is an electronic forum for discussion of NEC UltraLite computers, models PC-17-01 and PC-17-02 only.
Subjects covered: computer hardware and software; computer science
Net address for operations: listserv@grot.starconn.com
Net address for questions or submissions: ultralite-list@grot.starconn.com
Established: April 4, 1991
Subscribers: 84
List moderated: No.
Editorial contact: Brian Smithson
1104 Burntwood Court, Sunnyvale, CA 94089
Tel: +1 408 738 5939
Fax: +1 408 732 3202
Internet: ultralite-list-owner@grot.starconn.com
Technical contact: Brian Smithson
Same as above
How to access: Send the message "sub ultralite-list firstname lastname" in message body, addressed to listserv@grot.starconn.com
Access policy: There is no explicit policy.

How to unsubscribe: Send the message "unsub ultralite-list firstname lastname" in message body, addressed to listserv@grot.starconn.com
How to submit: Messages should be addressed to ultralite-list@grot.starconn.com
Archives: Digests of articles are available through listserv commands.
Related files: Some UltraLite-specific programs and documents are available, through listserv commands.

UN@INDYCMS
Description: UN@INDYCMS is a forum covering the United Nations.
Subjects covered: political science; United Nations
List moderated: No.
Editorial contact: John B. Harlan
Internet: ijbh200@indyvax.iupui.edu
Bitnet: ijbh200@indyvax
How to access: Send subscribe message to listserv@indycms or listserv@indycms.iupui.edu
How to unsubscribe: Send unsubscribe message to listserv@indycms or listserv@indycms.iupui.edu
Archives: Archives are developed monthly; apply to listowner for details.

UNIANDES@ANDESCOL
Subjects covered: Latin America
List moderated: No.
Editorial contact: Jorge Gutierrez
Bitnet: jgutierr@andescol
How to access: Send subscribe message to listserv@andescol
How to unsubscribe: Send unsubscribe message to listserv@andescol

UNICRN-L
Description: UNICRN-L discusses topics related to SIRSI/UNICORN automated systems.
Subjects covered: library and information science
List moderated: No.
Editorial contact: Fred Dayton
Bitnet: fred@psuorvm
How to access: Send subscribe message to listserv@psuorvm
How to unsubscribe: Send unsubscribe message to listserv@psuorvm
Archives: Archives are developed yearly; apply to listowner for details.

UNIVERSE@NDSUVM1
Description: UNIVERSE@NDSUVM1 is a forum for astronomers in the Midwest US.
Subjects covered: astronomy
List moderated: No.
How to access: Send subscribe message to listserv@ndsuvm1 or listserv@vm1.nodak.edu
How to unsubscribe: Send unsubscribe message to listserv@ndsuvm1 or listserv@vm1.nodak.edu

UNIX-SOURCES@BRL.MIL
Description: UNIX-SOURCES is an Internet distribution list of material from the Usenet Unix newsgroup.
Subjects covered: computer hardware and software; Unix
List moderated: No.
Editorial contact: Chuck Kennedy
Internet: kermit@brl.mil
How to access: Send subscribe message to listserv@ndsuvm1 or listserv@vm1.nodak.edu
How to unsubscribe: Send unsubscribe message to listserv@ndsuvm1 or listserv@vm1.nodak.edu

UNIX-SW@WSMR-SIMTEL20.ARMY.MIL
Description: UNIX-SW is a list of newly available UNIX-C software packages.
Subjects covered: computer hardware and software; Unix
List moderated: No.
Editorial contact: Dave Curry
Internet: DCURRY@WSMR-SIMTEL20.ARMY.MIL
How to access: Send subscribe message to UNIX-SW-RE-QUEST@WSMR-SIMTEL20.ARMY.MIL
How to unsubscribe: Send unsubscribe message to UNIX-SW-REQUEST@WSMR-SIMTEL20.ARMY.MIL
Archives: Yes; Send anonymous FTP to WSMR-SIMTEL20.ARMY.MIL

UNIX-WIZARDS@BRL.MIL
Description: UNIX-WIZARDS is a discussion list on Unix topics.
Subjects covered: computer hardware and software; Unix
List moderated: No.
Editorial contact: Mike Muuss
Internet: mike@brl.mil
How to access: Send subscribe message to listserv@ndsuvm1 or unix-wizards-request@brl.mil
How to unsubscribe: Send unsubscribe message to listserv@ndsuvm1 or unix-wizards-request@brl.mil

URANTIAL@UAFSYSB
Description: URANTIAL@UAFSYSB is a forum for discussion of topics related to URANTIA.
Subjects covered: philosophy
List moderated: No.
How to access: Send subscribe message to listserv@uafsysb
How to unsubscribe: Send unsubscribe message to listserv@uafsysb

URBAN-L
Description: Urban-L is a discussion list on urban planning.
Subjects covered: urban planning
List moderated: No.
How to access: Send subscribe message to listserv@trearn
How to unsubscribe: Send unsubscribe message to listserv@trearn
Archives: Archives are developed yearly; apply to listowner for details.

URBAREG@UQUBEC
Description: URBAREG@UQUBEC is a forum focusing on urban planning.
Subjects covered: urban planning
List moderated: No.
How to access: Send subscribe message to listserv@uquebec
How to unsubscribe: Send unsubscribe message to listserv@uquebec

USENET.HIST@UCSD.EDU
Description: USENET.HIST is a forum on the historical aspects of Usenet.
Subjects covered: Usenet Newsgroups; Internet
List moderated: No.
Editorial contact: Bruce Jones
Internet: bjones@ucsd.edu
How to access: Contact the Editor
How to unsubscribe: Contact the Editor

USMARC-L
Description: USMARC-L is a forum for discussion of USMARC formats.
Subjects covered: library and information science
Host: Library of Congress Network Development; MARC Standards Office
List moderated: Yes.
Editorial contact: Rebecca Guenther
Internet: rgue@seq1.loc.gov
How to access: Send subscribe message to listserv@maine
Archives: Archives are developed monthly; apply to listowner for details.

UUS-L
Description: Uus-L is a forum for Unitarian Universalists.
Subjects covered: religion
List moderated: No.
Editorial contact: Steve Traugott
Internet: uus-lman@terraluna.spacecoast.org
How to access: Send subscribe message to listserv@ubvm or listserv@ubvm.cc.buffalo.edu
How to unsubscribe: Send unsubscribe message to listserv@ubvm or listserv@ubvm.cc.buffalo.edu

VAL-L
Description: VAL-L is a list featuring Michael Valentine Smith's commentary on the current events and political developments of the former Soviet Union.
Subjects covered: Soviet Union; Russia; political science; current events
Net address for operations: LISTSERV@UCF1VM
How to access: Send standard subscribe request to the listserv.
How to unsubscribe: Send standard unsubscribe request to the listserv.

VETCAI-L
Description: Vetcai-L is a forum covering veterinary science
Subjects covered: veterinary; computer-assisted instruction (CAI)

List moderated: Yes.
Editorial contact: John Galland
Bitnet: galland@ksuvm
How to access: Send subscribe message to listserv@ksuvm
How to unsubscribe: Send unsubscribe message to listserv@ksuvm
Archives: Archives are developed monthly; apply to listowner for details.

VETINFO@UCDCVDLS

Description: VETINFO@UCDCVDLS is a forum covering computers and veterinary medicine.
Subjects covered: veterinary science; computer hardware and software
Editorial contact: James T. Case, DVM, Ph.D.
Bitnet: jcase@ucdcvdls
How to access: Send subscribe message to listserv@ucdcvdls
How to unsubscribe: Send unsubscribe message to listserv@ucdcvdls
Archives: Archives are developed monthly; apply to listowner for details.

VETLIB-L

Description: Vetlib-L is a forum for discussing vetrinary medical library issues.
Subjects covered: library and information science; veterinary science
List moderated: No.
Editorial contact: Vicki Kok
Bitnet: kok@vtvm2
How to access: Send subscribe message to listserv@vtvm2
How to unsubscribe: Send unsubscribe message to listserv@vtvm2
Archives: Archives are developed monthly; apply to listowner for details.

VETMED-L

Description: Vetmed-L is a forum for discussion of veterinary medicine
Subjects covered: veterinary science; medicine
List moderated: No.
Editorial contact: Harold Pritchett
Bitnet: harold@uga
How to access: Send subscribe message to listserv@uga or listserv@uga.cc.uga.edu
How to unsubscribe: Send unsubscribe message to listserv@uga or listserv@uga.cc.uga.edu
Archives: Archives are developed monthly; apply to listowner for details.

VICTORIA

Description: Victoria is the electronic conference for Victorian Studies, covering all aspects of 19th-century British history and culture.
Subjects covered: cultural studies; Great Britain; history; art
Net address for operations:
LISTSERV@IUBVM.UCS.INDIANA.EDU or
LISTSERV@IUBVM (Bitnet)

Net address for questions or submissions:
VICTORIA@IUBVM.UCS.INDIANA.EDU
VICTORIA@IUBVM (Bitnet)
Established: March 1993
Subscribers: 350
Host: Indiana University, Bloomington, IN 47405
Editorial contact: Patrick Leary
321 N. Washington #1
Tel: (812) 330-8207
Internet: pleary@ucs.indiana.edu
Bitnet: pleary@iubacs
How to access: Send command SUB VICTORIA to LISTSERV@IUBVM.UCS.INDIANA.EDU
How to unsubscribe: Send command SIGNOFF VICTORIA to LISTSERV@IUBVM.UCS.INDIANA.EDU
How to submit: Send message to VICTORIA@IUBVM.UCS.INDIANA.EDU
Submission policy: Please include your name and e-mail address at the bottom of any message you post.
Archives: Monthly log files of postings; bibliographical material available. Apply to listowner for details.
Additional information: VICTORIA welcomes all scholars, in whatever discipline, interested in sharing information and ideas about Victorian Britain.

VIDPRO-L

Description: Vidpro-L is a forum for discussion of video production.
Subjects covered: cinema studies; television
List moderated: No.
Editorial contact: P. Gordon Sroufe
Internet: cfpgs1@uxa.ecn.bgu.edu
Bitnet: cfpgs1@ecnuxa
How to access: Send subscribe message to listserv@ecnuxa or listserv@uxa.ecn.bgu.edu
How to unsubscribe: Send unsubscribe message to listserv@ecnuxa or listserv@uxa.ecn.bgu.edu

VIFLIS, THE VIRTUAL INTERNATIONAL FACULTY IN LIBRARY AND INFORMATION SCIENCE.

Description: VIFLIS is a LISTSERV conference to promote interaction between faculties and students in library and information science in the United States and abroad. Its purposes are to (1) facilitate student/faculty interaction in a friendly, non-threatening environment, (2) enable students to locate resources and information not available elsewhere, (3) enable students to locate short term advisors on a particular issue or topic to be explored, and (4) to develop a database of faculty expertise on international issues and consulting.
Subjects covered: library and information science; computer hardware and software; colleges and universities; education
Net address for operations: LISTSERV@ARIZVM1
Net address for questions or submissions:
VIFLIS@ARIZVM1
Established: January 1992
Subscribers: 95
Sponsor: American Society for Information Science, Special Interest Group on International Information Issues.
Host: School of Library Science, University of Arizona, 1515 East First St., Tucson, AZ 85719

Editorial contact: Gretchen Whitney, Asst. Prof. address School of Library Science, University of Arizona, 1515 East First Street, Tucson, AZ 85719
Tel: (602) 621-3491
Fax: (602) 621-3279
Internet: GWHITNEY@CCIT.ARIZONA.EDU
Bitnet: GWHITNEY@ARIZVMS
How to access: Send message to listserv@arizvm1.bitnet with no header and only subscribe viflis melvil dewey replacing melvil's name with your own.
Access policy: List is open to anyone.
How to unsubscribe: Send message to listserv@arizvm1.bitnet with no header and only unsubscribe viflis in the message.
How to submit: Send message with meaningful header and whatever text desired to viflis@arizvm1
Archives: This list is archived monthly on listserv@arizvm1.
Additional information: Michel Menou address CIDEGI, 129 AV P Vaillant-Couturier, Gentilly, France F94250 tel 142-537-033 fax 147-358-798 Internet menou@cosy.uoguelph.ca

VIRTU-L

Description: VIRTU-L is an electronic discussion group covering virtual reality and related computing, social, and technological issues. It is a redistribution of the Usenet newsgroup sci.virtual-worlds intended for people who either do not have Usenet access or who want to insure they receive ever message in their personal mailbox. Messages posted to sci.virtual-worlds (which is a moderated newsgroup) are sent to all virtu-l subscribers at the same time as they are released to Usenet. Messages sent to virtu-l are sent to the sci.virtual-worlds moderators at the same time as they are sent to virtu-l subscribers. This means that there may be a slight delay before messages reach the subscribers when crossing email/Usenet boundaries, but usually not more than a day or so.
Subjects covered: virtual reality; computer hardware and software
Net address for operations: virtu-l@vmd.cso.uiuc.edu (or virtu-l@uiucvmd.bitnet)
Net address for questions or submissions: listserv@vmd.cso.uiuc.edu
(or listserv@uiucvmd.bitnet)
Established: Spring 1992
Subscribers: 360 addresses, many of which feed internal redistribution lists or campus newsfeeds -- so the total number of subscribers is unknown, but almost certainly in the thousands.
Sponsor: University of Illinois at Urbana-Champaign
List moderated: Yes.
Moderation procedure: Messages posted wait for the list manager (gbnewby) to be forwarded back to virtu-l. All messages are posted, except for (a) sub/unsub requests and (b) messages very far off the topic (e.g., blanket postings to multiple lists).
Editorial contact: Gregory B. Newby
Grad. School of Library and Information Science, University of Illinois at Urbana-Champaign, Urbana, IL
Tel: (217) 244-7365
Fax: (217) 244-3302
Internet: gbnewby@uiuc.edu
Bitnet: gbnewby@uiucvmd
How to access: Email to listserv@vmd.cso.uiuc.edu (or listserv@uiucvmd.bitnet) with the text: subscribe virtu-l Your Full Name If you have problems subscribing or unsubscribing,

send email to gbnewby@vmd.cso.uiuc.edu or gbnewby@uiucvmd.bitnet.
Access policy: This list is open to all.
How to unsubscribe: Email to listserv@vmd.cso.uiuc.edo (or listserv@uiucvmd.bitnet) with the text:
unsubscribe virtu-l NOTE: this must be done from the SAME email address as you subscribed from.
How to submit: Email to virtu-l@vmd.cso.uiuc.edu (there will be a delay of up to two days until the moderator posts the message. Usually, turnaround is the same day).
Submission policy: This list is open to all.
Archives: VIRTU-L is archived as part of sci.virtual-worlds. Key FTP sites include u.washington.edu:pub/VR/archives.
Related files: Some files, including an FAQ, at u.washington.edu via anon. FTP

VIRUS-L

Description: Virus-L is a forum for discussion of computer viruses.
Subjects covered: computer hardware and software; computer viruses
List moderated: No.
Editorial contact: Kenneth R. van Wyk
Internet: luken@vax1.cc.lehigh.edu
How to access: Send subscribe message to listserv@lehiibm1 or listserv@ibm1.cc.lehigh.edu
How to unsubscribe: Send unsubscribe message to listserv@lehiibm1 or listserv@ibm1.cc.lehigh.edu
Archives: Yes.

VISION-LIST@ADS.COM

Description: VISION-LIST is a forum covering artificial intelligence vision.
Subjects covered: artificial intelligence; computer science
List moderated: No.
Editorial contact: Tod Levitt
Internet: levit@ads.com
How to access: Send subscribe message to VISION-LIST-REQUEST@ADS.COM
How to unsubscribe: Send unsubscribe message to VISION-LIST-REQUEST@ADS.COM
Archives: Yes; Send anonymous FTP to: ADS.COM

VM-UTIL@TRINITY

Description: VM-UTIL@TRINITY discusses and contains utilities for VM/SP and CMS operating systems.
Subjects covered: computer hardware and software
List moderated: No.
Editorial contact: David Young
Internet: dyoung%trinity.bitnet@cunyvm.cuny.edu
How to access: Send subscribe message to listserv@trinity or listserv@ubvm.cc.buffalo.edu
How to unsubscribe: Send unsubscribe message to listserv@trinity or listserv@ubvm.cc.buffalo.edu
Archives: Yes.

VMVIRUS@PCCVM

Description: VMVIRUS@PCCVM is a posting of all VM-based computer viruses.

Subjects covered: computer hardware and software; computer viruses
List moderated: Yes.
Editorial contact: R.N. Hathhorn
Bitnet: sysmaint@pccvm
How to access: Send subscribe message to listserv@pccvm
How to unsubscribe: Send unsubscribe message to listserv@pccvm
Archives: Yes.

VPIEJ-L

Description: Vpiej-L focuses on electronic publishing standards and other issues in the production and editing of scholarly electronic journals.
Subjects covered: library and information science; electronic publishing; publishing
List moderated: Yes.
Editorial contact: James Powell
Internet: jpowell@vtvm1.cc.vt.edu
Bitnet: jpowell@vtvm1
Review: Reviewed by List Review Service edited by Raleigh Muns: see appendix.
How to access: Send subscribe message to listserv@vtvm1 or listserv@vtvm1.cc.vt.edu
How to unsubscribe: Send unsubscribe message to listserv@vtvm1 or listserv@vtvm1.cc.vt.edu
Archives: Archives are developed monthly; apply to listowner for details.

VPLLIST@SUSHI.STANFORD.EDU

Description: VPLLIST@SUSHI is a forum covering visual programming languages.
Subjects covered: computer science
List moderated: No.
Editorial contact: Marvin M. Zauderer
Internet: zauderer@sushi.stanford.edu
How to access: Send subscribe message to vpllist-request@sushi.stanford.edu
How to unsubscribe: Send unsubscribe message to vpllist-request@sushi.stanford.edu
Archives: Yes; Send anonymous FTP to sushi.stanford.edu and cd VPLLISTARCHIVE.

VT-HSNET@VTVM1

Description: VT-HSNET@VTVM1 is a network for Virginia schools grades K-12.
Subjects covered: education
List moderated: No.
Editorial contact: Phil Benchoff
Bitnet: BENCHOFF@VTVM1
How to access: Send subscribe message to listserv@vtvm1
How to unsubscribe: Send unsubscribe message to listserv@vtvm1
Archives: Yes; Monthly, Private

VTCAD-L

Description: Vtcad-L is a forum dedicated to the discussion of computer-aided design and related topics.
Subjects covered: computer-assisted design (CAD)
Host: Virginia Polytechnic University

List moderated: No.
Editorial contact: Darrell A. Early
Internet: bestuur@vtmt2.cc.vt.edu
How to access: Send subscribe message to listserv@vtvm2 or listserv@vtvm2.cc.vt.edu
How to unsubscribe: Send unsubscribe message to listserv@vtvm2 or listserv@vtvm2.cc.vt.edu
Archives: Archives are developed weekly; apply to listowner for details.

VTLSLIST@VTVM1

Description: VTLSLIST@VTVM1 is a list for users of the Virginia Tech Library System integrated software.
Subjects covered: library and information science
List moderated: Yes.
Editorial contact: Buddy Litchfield
Bitnet: buddyl@vtvm1
How to access: Send subscribe message to listserv@vtvm1
How to unsubscribe: Send unsubscribe message to listserv@vtvm1
Archives: Archives are developed monthly; apply to listowner for details.

VTWOMEN

Description: VTWOMEN is an electronic discussion group on women's issues.
Subjects covered: women's studies; gender studies; cultural studies
Net address for operations: LISTSERV@VTVM1
Net address for questions or submissions: VTWOMEN@VTVM1
Established: October 1992
Subscribers: 120
Sponsor: Women's Network at Virginia Tech
Host: Virginia Polytechnic Institute and State University
List moderated: No.
Editorial contact: Sarah Richardson
VPI & SU Blacksburg, VA 24060
Tel: (703) 231-8035
Fax: (703) 231-6673
Internet: srich@vtvm1.cc.vt.edu
Bitnet: srich@vtvm1.bitnet
How to access: Send mail or interactive message to listserv@vtvm1
Access policy: This list is open to anyone.
How to unsubscribe: Send mail or interactive message to listserv@vtvm1
How to submit: Send mail to vtwomen@vtvm1
Submission policy: No restrictions.
Archives: Archives are available through the listserv.

VWAR-L

Description: Vwar-L is a forum for the discussion of topics related to the Vietnam War.
Subjects covered: history; Vietnam War
List moderated: No.
Editorial contact: Lydia Fish
Bitnet: fishlm@snybufva
How to access: Send subscribe message to listserv@ubvm or listserv@ubvm.cc.buffalo.edu

How to unsubscribe: Send unsubscribe message to listserv@ubvm or listserv@ubvm.cc.buffalo.edu
Archives: Archives are developed weekly; apply to listowner for details.

VZLA-L

Description: Vzla-L is a forum for discussion of topics related to Venezuela.
Subjects covered: Venezuela
List moderated: Yes.
Editorial contact: Juan Carlos Guzman
Internet: venezuela-request@athena.mit.edu
Bitnet: guzjuaa@yalevm
How to access: Send subscribe message to listserv@yalevm or listserv@yalevm.ycc.yale.edu
How to unsubscribe: Send unsubscribe message to listserv@yalevm or listserv@yalevm.ycc.yale.edu
Archives: Archives are developed weekly; apply to listowner for details.

WCENTER

Description: WCENTER is a list offering information and discussion on the establishment and administration of English-department writing centers, including learning theory and tutoring practices.
Subjects covered: writing; education
Net address for operations: listserv@ttuvm1
Established: fall, 1991
Subscribers: 180
Sponsor: Texas Tech University, Lubbock, TX 79409
Host: Texas Tech University, Lubbock, TX 79409
List moderated: No.
Editorial contact: Lady Falls Brown
Department of English, Texas Tech University, Lubbock, TX 79409-3091
Tel: (806) 742-2501
Fax: (806) 742-0989
Internet: YKFLB@ttacs1.ttu.edu
Bitnet: YKFLB@ttacs
Technical contact: John Halbert
University Computing Facility, 9 Computer Center, Texas Tech University, Lubbock, TX 79409-3051
Tel: (806) 742-3619
Internet: SNAHAL@TTUVM1.TTU.EDU
Bitnet: SNHAL@TTUVM1.TTU.EDU
How to access: Send the email message: subscribe wcenter yourfirstname yourlastname to listserv@ttuvm1
Access policy: WCENTER welcomes all subscribers interested in writing centers and willing to maintain reasonable network decorum. Subscription is open and all submissions are accepted.
How to unsubscribe: Send the email message: signoff wcenter to listserv@ttuvm1
How to submit: Send e-mail to wcenter@ttuvm1
Submission policy: All e-mail accepted automatically

WEATHER-USERS

Description: weather-users is a list covering computer programs to use and status of Internet weather servers.
Subjects covered: computer science; Internet
Net address for operations: weather-users-request@zorch.sf-bay.org

Net address for questions or submissions: weather-users-zorch.sf-bay.org
Established: June 1992
Subscribers: 210
List moderated: No.
Editorial contact: Scott Hazen Mueller
4108 Killigrew Drive
Tel: (209) 545-9417
Internet: scott@zorch.sf-bay.org
How to access: Send mail to weather-users-request@zorch.sf-bay.org
How to unsubscribe: Send mail to weather-users-request@zorch.sf-bay.org
How to submit: Send mail to weather-users@zorch.sf-bay.org

WEIGHTS

Description: Weights is about anything having to do with the world of lifting weights. Routines, nutrition, injuries, and more. The experiences on the list range from brand new beginners to competetive bodybuilders. Women are well represented on the list as well. We're also international, with members from Australia to Norway. If it is somehow related to the lifting of a weight, it's welcome on the list.
Subjects covered: weight lifting; sports; health sciences
Net address for operations: weights-request@fa.disney.com
Net address for questions or submissions: weights@fa.disney.com
Established: March 7, 1990
Subscribers: 525
List moderated: Yes.
Moderation procedure: Moderator digests contributions and sends out an issue generally every weekday. The only limitations on contributions are as follows: things for sale must be weight-related and not be from a commercial venture, and discussions of illegal drugs (i.e., steroids) cannot be anonymous, and cannot involve how to obtain or use illegal drugs.
Editorial contact: Michael Sullivan
Walt Disney Feature Animation, 1400 Flower St., Glendale, CA 91221
Tel: (818) 544-2683
Fax: (818) 544-4579
Internet: sullivan@fa.disney.com
How to access: Send name and email address to weights-request@fa.disney.com and ask to subscribe.
Access policy: The list is open to all.
How to unsubscribe: Send name and email address to weights-request@fa.disney.com and ask to unsubscribe.
How to submit: Send contributions to weights@fa.disney.com.
Submission policy: All contributions are welcome as long as the follow the guidelines above.
Related files: The index and FAQ can be gotten by sending mail to weights-back-issues@fa.disney.com. Put the word ''index'' or ''frequent'' in the body of the message, one word per line.

WEIRD-L

Description: Weird-L is a list of alternative literature and topics.
Subjects covered: alternative literature
List moderated: Yes.
Editorial contact: Jeremy Bornstein
Internet: jeremy@apple.com

Bitnet: jeremy@brownvm
Review: Reviewed by List Review Service edited by Raleigh
Muns: see appendix.
How to access: Send subscribe message to listserv@brownvm
or listserv@brownvm.brown.edu
How to unsubscribe: Send unsubscribe message to
listserv@brownvm or listserv@brownvm.brown.edu
Archives: Archives are developed monthly; apply to listowner
for details.

WELSH-L

Description: WELSH-L is a Welsh Language bulletin board
aiming to foster the amicable discussion of the Welsh language,
Welsh culture, history, and politics, and to offer a forum for
speakers and learners of the Welsh language. Both Welsh and
English may be used. Users are encouraged to exchange their
opinions in Welsh, if they can, and special consideration may be
given to learners expressing themselves in Welsh. The emphasis
will be on Welsh as a living language, and Welsh culture as
actually lived out in Wales at the present day. Discussions of
Celtic myth in general, the relationship between Celtic paganism
and Anglo-Saxon Wicca, etc. will probably find a more ready
audience on the CELTIC-L bulletin board at
IRLEARN.UCD.IE. If there is an interest in expanding the
range of topics to include discussion in and about the language
and culture of Welsh's close sister languages, Breton and Cor-
nish, WELSH-L will be able to serve as a forum for that as
well.
Subjects covered: Welsh language and literature; Celtic studies;
language and literature
Net address for operations: LISTSERV@IRLEARN(from
BITNET, EARN)
LISTSERV%IRLEARN.UCD.IE@UK.AC.EARN-RELAY(from
JANET)
LISTSERV@IRLEARN.UCD.IE(from Internet)
Net address for questions or submissions: WELSH-
L@IRLEARN(from BITNET, EARN)
WELSH-L%IRLEARN.UCD.IE@UK.AC.EARN-RELAY(from
JANET)
WELSH-L@IRLEARN.UCD.IE(from Internet)
Established: November 1992
Subscribers: 172
Host: University College Dublin, Dublin, Republic of Ireland.
List moderated: No.
Editorial contact: Michael Everson
School of Architecture, UCD, Richview, Clonskeagh, Dublin 14,
Republic of Ireland.
Tel: +353 1 706-2745
Fax: +353 1 283-7778
Internet: EVERSON@IRLEARN.UCD.IE
Bitnet: EVERSON@IRLEARN
Technical contact: Briony Williams
CSTR, 80 South Bridge, Edinburgh EH1 1HN, Scotland, UK.
Tel: +44-31-650-2790 (outside UK); 031-650-2790 (inside UK)
Fax: +44-31-226-2730 (outside UK); 031-226-2730 (inside
UK)
Internet: BRIONY@CSTR.ED.AC.UK
How to access: To subscribe to WELSH-L, send the following
message SUBSCRIBE WELSH-L <your full name> to
LISTSERV by TELL (VM) or by SEND (VAX/VMS) or by
MAIL.
How to unsubscribe: To unsubscribe to WELSH-L, send the
following message UNSUBSCRIBE WELSH-L to LISTSERV

by TELL (VM) or by SEND (VAX/VMS) or by MAIL. If you
send your request by MAIL, send the mail to
LISTSERV@IRLEARNfrom EARN, BITNET, etc.
LISTSERV%IRLEARN.UCD.IE@UK.AC.EARN-RELAYfrom
JANET LISTSERV@IRLEARN.UCD.IEfrom other networks.
How to submit: To submit a posting to WELSH-L, send it by
mail to: WELSH-L@IRLEARNfrom EARN, BITNET, etc.
WELSH-L%IRLEARN.UCD.IE@UK.AC.EARN-RELAYfrom
JANET WELSH-L@IRLEARN.UCD.IEfrom other networks.
Submission policy: 1. Any subject is fair game through the
medium of Welsh. 2. Welsh-related subjects are fair game
through the medium of English. 3. Translations or summaries of
posts can be helpful to learners. They are welcome, but not required. These are guidelines: WELSH-L can offer a great deal
to learners of Welsh. But it does exist first and foremost to
allow speakers who don't wish to communicate in English to do
so.
Archives: Monthly log files are automatically archived in the
WELSH-L directory at IRLEARN: e.g., LOG9301 for January
1993 Send a mail message to LISTSERV saying only GET
WELSH-L LOG9301 (or whichever).
Related files: In the summer of 1993, it is hoped to set up an
electronic library for WELSH-L at IRLEARN, for automatic retrieval of files. In the mean time, the following are available
from briony@cstr.ed.ac.uk. File of information on Welsh lan-
guage learning resources (including some info on Cornish and
Breton activities). File detailing the accenting conventions used
on WELSH-L. File detailing the phonetics of Welsh, and the
ASCII representation of Welsh phonemes.
Additional information: A second technical contact is: Peter
Coghlan, UCD Computing Services, University College, Dub-
lin,Dublin 14, Republic of Ireland.
PCOGHLAN@IRLEARN.UCD.IE Bitnet
PCOGHLAN@IRLEARN.
Only subscribers may post to WELSH-L.

WGAS-L

Description: WGAS-L covers astronomical software.
Subjects covered: astronomy; computer hardware and software
List moderated: No.
How to access: Send subscribe message to listserv@scfvm
How to unsubscribe: Send unsubscribe message to
listserv@scfvm

WHIM@TAMVM1

Description: WHIM is a forum for topics related to the study of
humor.
Subjects covered: humor
List moderated: No.
Editorial contact: Mary L. Rose
Bitnet: rose@panam, rose@panam1, rose@panam2
How to access: Send subscribe message to listserv@tamvm1 or
listserv@tamvm1.tamu.edu
How to unsubscribe: Send unsubscribe message to
listserv@tamvm1 or listserv@tamvm1.tamu.edu
Archives: Yes; apply to listowner for details.

WHIRL (WOMEN'S HISTORY IN RHETORIC AND LANGUAGE)

Description: WHIRL, Women's History in Rhetoric and Language, is a new discussion list formed to promote research,

scholarship, and quality teaching by providing a place for information sharing and collaboration. The focus of discussion includes all kinds of women's rhetorical activities, including argumentation and debate, public speaking and oratory, fiction and non-fiction, and so on. All historical eras are included, from ancient Egypt, Greece and Rome through the rhetorical activities of Barbara Bush and Hilary Clinton.
Subjects covered: women's studies; rhetoric
Net address for operations: listserv@psuvm.psu.edu
How to access: Send the following message to listserv@psuvm
sub whirl your name

WHOORAL-PILOT@MAILBASE.AC.UK
Description: WHOORAL is an electronic discussion list for the exchange of information between researchers in the field of oral health and dental research. This list was set up as part of the COSINE project (Cooperation for Open Computer system inerconnection in Europe) which encouraged the use of electronic communication within the researh community. The Oral Health Services Research Centre, University Dental School, Cork,Ireland, was chosen as one of 10 "special interest groups" to take part in the COSINE project. As a WHO collaborating centre for Oral Health Research, we encouraged the use of Electronic communications between researchers in the field. The WHOORAL-PILOT list was set during the COSINE project, and it is hoped that the service will be continued past the duration of the COSINE project.
Subjects covered: health sciences; dental sciences; medicine
Net address for operations:
MAILBASE@MAILBASE.AC.UK
Net address for questions or submissions:
MAILBASE@MAILBASE.AC
Established: August 1992
Subscribers: 23
Sponsor: Oral Health Services Research Centre, University College, Dental School, Cork, Ireland.
Host: University of Newcastle, Newcastle upon Tyne, UK.
List moderated: No.
Editorial contact: Dr. Ruben Keane
Oral Health Services Research Centre, University College, Dental School, Cork, Ireland.
Tel: +21 276871, ext. 2761
Fax: +21 545391
Internet: IN%'STPD8008@IRUCCVAX.UCC.IE
Technical contact: Ms. Kathryn Neville
Oral Health Services Research Centre, University College, Dental School, Cork, Ireland.
Tel: +21 276871, ext. 2761
Fax: +21 545391
Internet: IN%'STPD8008@IRUCCVAX.UCC.IE
How to access: Send the following commands to MAILBASE@MAILBASE.AC.UK : JOIN WHOORAL-PILOT <firstname secondname>
How to unsubscribe: Send the following commands to MAILBASE@MAILBASE.AC.UK : LEAVE WHOORAL-PI-LOT <firstname secondname>
How to submit: Messages for distribution via the list should be sent to IN%'WHOORAL-PILOT@MAILBASE.AC.UK''

WIML-L (WOMEN'S ISSUES IN MUSIC LIBRARIANSHIP)
Description: WIML-L is a list covering topics related to women in music librarianship.
Subjects covered: library and information science; feminism; women's studies; music
Net address for questions or submissions: LGREEN@IUBVM
List moderated: No.
How to access: Send subscription messages to Laura Gayle Green, LGREEN@IUBVM

WIP@SUVM
Description: WIP@SUVM is a conference for Works in Progress.
Subjects covered: education
List moderated: No.
How to access: Send subscribe message to listserv@suvm
How to unsubscribe: Send unsubscribe message to listserv@suvm

WIPHYS
Description: WIPHYS is a moderated list for issues of concern to women in physics.
Subjects covered: physics; feminism; women's studies
Net address for operations: LISTSERV@NYSERNET.ORG
List moderated: Yes.
How to access: Send subscription messages to LISTSERV@NYSERNET.ORG

WISENET
Description: WISENET is an electronic discussion group covering topics surrounding women in science, engineering, and mathematics.
Subjects covered: engineering; feminism; mathematics; science and technology
Net address for operations: LISTSERV@UICVM, LISTSERV@UICVM.UIC.EDU
List moderated: No.
How to access: Send subscription messages to LISTSERV@UICVM (Bitnet) or LISTSERV@UICVM.UIC.EDU

WITI
Description: WITI is the discussion group of the International Network of Women in Technology.
Subjects covered: science and technology; feminism; women's studies
Net address for questions or submissions: WITI@CUP.PORTAL.COM
List moderated: No.
How to access: Send subscription messages to WITI@CUP.PORTAL.COM

WITSENDO
Description: WITSENDO on LISTSERV@DARTCMS1 or LISTSERV@dartcms1.dartmouth.edu WITSENDO is a moderated mailing list which discusses all aspects of ENDO-METRIOSIS with particular emphasis on coping with the dis-

ease and its treatment. Anyone with an interest in this disease is welcome to participate whether or not they actually suffer from the disease. The list will act as a clearinghouse for information exchange and to promote discussion of current treatments, research and educational literature. Professional (medical) comments are of course, most welcome. However, the list is primarily dedicated to the women who suffer from this painful and often demoralizing disease, therefore any information should be expressed in lay terms and attempt to exclude professional jargon or at the very least provide adequate references and/or definitions of terms.

Subjects covered: endometriosis; medicine
Net address for operations:
LISTSERV@DARTCMS1.DARTMOUTH.EDU
Net address for questions or submissions:
WITSENDO@DARTCMS1.DARTMOUTH.EDU
Established: May 1992
Subscribers: 100+
Sponsor: Dartmouth College, New Hampshire
Host: Dartmouth College, New Hampshire
List moderated: Yes.
Moderation procedure: All mail not coming from the moderator goes to moderator before posting.
Editorial contact: Martin A. Thompson
Petawawa, Ontario, Canada
Tel: (613) 584-1800 (X4087)
Fax: (613) 584-1800
Internet: roihar@crl.aecl.ca
How to access: Send mail to:
LISTSERV@DARTCMS1.BITNET or
LISTSERV@dartcms1.dartmouth.edu with the BODY of the mail (NOT subject) containing the command: SUB WITSENDO yourfullname
Access policy: Anyone may submit or post to this list.
How to unsubscribe: To Unsubscribe to the list, send mail to:
LISTSERV@DARTCMS1.BITNET or
LISTSERV@dartcms1.dartmouth.edu
with the BODY of the mail (NOT subject) containing the command: DEL WITSENDO yourfullname To submit (technical):
To post to the list, send mail to:
WITSENDO@DARTCMS1.BITNET or
WITSENDO@dartcms1.dartmouth.edu
Archives: If sent in the body of a message to the listserv INDEX WITSENDO sends you the list of archives. SEND WITSENDO yy-nnnnn sends you the yy-nnnnn archive file shown by the INDEX command.

WKSPHYS

Description: WKSPHYS is an electronic discussion group covering research issues in physics education.
Subjects covered: physics; education
Net address for operations: listserv@idbsu.bitnet
Net address for questions or submissions:
wksphys@idbsu.bitnet
Established: 1988
Subscribers: 83
Host: Boise State University, Boise, ID 83725
Editorial contact: Dewey I. Dykstra, Jr.
Dept of Physics, Boise State University, 1910 University Dr., Boise, ID 83725-1570.
Tel: (208) 385-1934
Fax: (208) 385-4330
Internet: rphdykst@idbsu.idbsu.edu

Bitnet: rphdykst@idbsu.bitnet
Technical contact: Alan Ebel
Center for Data Processing, Boise State University, 1910 University Dr. Boise, ID 83725.
Internet: dosebel@idbsu.idbsu.edu
Bitnet: dosebel@idbsu.bitnet
Copyright statement: Copyright to specific materials that appear on the list is considered to be held by the author of the note in which those materials are found.
How to access: Send request to list-owner. Include information as to experience in research in physics education.
Access policy: Be active in research in physics education.
How to unsubscribe: Send request to list-owner.
How to submit: Be a member of the list and send note to wksphys@idbsu
Submission policy: Discussion should be confined to issues relating to research in learning and teaching physics.
Archives: Standard listserv services.
Additional information: We are planning to change the name of the list (new name not yet determined) and convert it from a listserv private list to a public one. Inquiries should be addressed to the list-owner address above.

WMN-HLTH

Description: WMN-HLTH is a forum of the Women's Health Electronic News Line, begun by the Center for Women's Health Research.
Subjects covered: health sciences; feminism; women's studies
Net address for operations: LISTSERV@UWAVM,
LISTSERV@UWAVM.U.WASHINGTON.EDU
List moderated: No.
How to access: Send subscription messages to
LISTSERV@UWAVM (Bitnet) or
LISTSERV@UWAVM.U.WASHINGTON.EDU

WMST-L (WOMEN'S STUDIES LIST)

Description: WMST-L deals with the academic side of Women's Studies: teaching, research, and program administration. The list also welcomes relevant job and conference announcements and calls for papers.
Subjects covered: women's studies; gender studies
Net address for operations: LISTSERV@UMDD (Bitnet) LISTSERV@UMDD.UMD.EDU (Internet)
Net address for questions or submissions: WMST-L@UMDD (Bitnet) WMST-L@UMDD.UMD.EDU (Internet)
Established: May, 1991
Subscribers: 1770 in 32 countries
Host: UMDD is a mainframe computer at the University of Maryland, College Park, MD 20742.
List moderated: No.
Editorial contact: Joan Korenman
Women's Studies Program, Univ. of Maryland, Baltimore County, Baltimore, MD 21228-5398.
Tel: (410) 455-2040
Fax: (410) 455-1070
Internet: KORENMAN@UMBC2.UMBC.EDU
Bitnet: KORENMAN@UMBC
Review: Raleigh C. Muns' review (List ReviewService, vol. 1 no. 6, Feb. 10, 1992) called WMST-L "...a major resource for practitioners in the field of Women's Studies." The problem of heavymail volume mentioned in Muns' review has been eased by the availability of a digest option (more selective than the

standard listserv digest option). See appendix for entire text of review.

How to access: Send the e-mail message "SUB WMST-L Your Name" (no quotation marks) to LIST SERV@UMDD or LISTSERV@UMDD.UMD.EDU

Access policy: Anyone interested in the academic side of Women's Studies may subscribe.

How to unsubscribe: Send the e-mail message SIGNOFF WMST-L to the same LISTSERV address to which the subscription message was sent.

How to submit: Send messages for distribution to WMST-L@UMDD or WMST-L@UMDD.UMD.EDU

Submission policy: Only subscribers may post messages. Only messages dealing with Women's Studies teaching, research, or program administration (or Women's Studies job and conference announcements) should be sent. Messages dealing with gender-related societal issues or jobs/conferences not related to Women's Studies should be sent to other lists, not WMST-L. Archive information (past documents, etc.): All messages are stored inaccessible, searchable weekly logfiles. Some compilations of messages on specific topics are available as files.

Archives: All messages are stored in accessible, searchable weekly logfiles. Some compilations of messages on specific topics are available as files.

Related files: Course syllabi, feminist film reviews, and other files related to Women's Studies are available from LISTSERV@UMDD. Lists of available files may be obtained by sending the following messages to LISTSERV: INDEX WMST-L (for the general filelist); INDEX SYLLABI (for the syllabus filelist); INDEX FILM (for the feminist film reviews) .

Gopher accessibility: Many (but by no means all) WMST-L files are also located on the WomensStudies section of INFO, a gopher-accessible database at the University of Maryland. The telnet and gopher address is info.umd.edu (listed under /Teaching/WomensStudies).

WOMEN

Description: WOMEN is a discussion list attempting to connect all women's groups and areas of interest for women.

Subjects covered: gender studies; feminism; communications; women's studies

Net address for operations: WOMEN-RE-QUEST@ATHENA.MIT.EDU

List moderated: No.

How to access: To subscribe, write WOMEN-RE-QUEST@ATHENA.MIT.EDU

WON--THE WOMEN'S ONLINE NETWORK

Description: WON, the Women's Online Network, is an electronic discussion group for women. Its political orientation is intended to help in the dissemination of information about and the formation of political strategies for improving the position of women internationally.

Subjects covered: gender studies; feminism; activism; women's studies

Net address for questions or submissions: CARMELA@ECHO.PANIX.COM, HORN@ECHO.PANIX.COM

Fee: Yes: $20 per year, negotiable if necessary.

List moderated: Yes.

How to access: To join, contact the co-founders at CARMELA@ECHO.PANIX.COM or

HORN@ECHO.PANIX.COM (Internet) or by phone at (212) 255-3839 (New York).

WORD-MAC

Description: WORD-MAC is a moderated list that covers the use of Microsoft Word on the Macintosh platform (only).

Subjects covered: Macintosh computers; Microsoft Word; computer hardware and software

Net address for operations: listserv@alsvid.une.edu.au

Net address for questions or submissions: word-mac@alsvid.une.edu.au

Subscribers: 820

Sponsor: University of New England-Northern Rivers, PO Box 157, Lismore, NSW 480, Australia

List moderated: All posts to word-mac are moderated.

Editorial contact: Roger Debreceny

Tel: 61-66-20-3837

Fax: 61-66-22-1237

Internet: mmacword@alsvid.une.edu.au or word-mac-request@alsvid.une.edu.au

How to access: Send a message to: listserv@alsvid.une.edu.au with the text subscribe word-mac your_first_name your_surname in the body of the message. If a subscriber wishes to receive the mail as a digest (and most list members do) send the following message to listserv: set word-mac mail digest

How to unsubscribe: To unsubscribe send a message to: listserv@alsvid.une.edu.au with the text unsubscribe word-mac or signoff word-mac in the body of the message

How to submit: Send your message to: word-mac@alsvid.une.edu.au

Archives: Archives of the list are held on alsvid.une.edu.au. Either gopher off to alsvid.une.edu.au (port 70) and go to the pub/archive/word-mac/digests directory or alternatively do an anonymous FTP to alsvid.une.edu.au in the same directory.

WORKS-L

Description: Works-L is a sub-group of the WRITERS discussion group used for submitting longer works.

Subjects covered: writing

List moderated: Yes.

Editorial contact: Pat Carey

Internet: carey@plains.nodak.edu

Bitnet: carey@ndsuvm1

How to access: Send subscribe message to LISTSERV@NDSUVM1 or LISTSERV@VM1.NODAK.EDU

How to unsubscribe: Send unsubscribe message to LISTSERV@NDSUVM1 or LISTSERV@VM1.NODAK.EDU

Archives: Yes; Apply to listowner for details

WORKS@RUTGERS.EDU

Description: WORKS@RUTGERS.EDU is a discussion on workstation computers.

Subjects covered: computer hardware and software

Editorial contact: Dave Steiner

Internet: steiner@rutgers.edu

How to access: Send subscribe message to listserv@rutvm1 or works-request@rutgers.edu

How to unsubscribe: Send unsubscribe message to listserv@rutvm1 or works-request@rutgers.edu

Archives: Yes.

WORLD-L

Description: World-L is a forum for discussing world history from a non-eurocentric perspective.
Subjects covered: history
List moderated: No.
Editorial contact: Haines Brown
Internet: brownh@ccsva@ctstateu.edu
Bitnet: brownh@ctstateu
How to access: Send subscribe message to listserv@ubvm or listserv@ubvm.cc.buffalo.edu
How to unsubscribe: Send unsubscribe message to listserv@ubvm or listserv@ubvm.cc.buffalo.edu

WRITERS@NDSUVM1

Description: WRITERS@NDSUVM1 is a forum on the business of writing.
Subjects covered: writing
List moderated: No.
Editorial contact: Pat Corey
Internet: corey@plains.nodak.edu
How to access: Send subscribe message to listserv@ndsuvm1 or listserv@vm1.nodak.edu
How to unsubscribe: Send unsubscribe message to listserv@ndsuvm1 or listserv@vm1.nodak.edu
Archives: Archives are developed weekly; apply to listowner for details.

WWII-L

Description: WWII-L is a forum for discussing the Second Word War.
Subjects covered: history; World War II
List moderated: No.
Editorial contact: Larry W. Jewell
Internet: jewell@mace.cc.purdue.edu
How to access: Send subscribe message to listserv@ubvm or listserv@ubvm.cc.buffalo.edu
How to unsubscribe: Send unsubscribe message to listserv@ubvm or listserv@ubvm.cc.buffalo.edu
Archives: Archives are developed weekly; apply to listowner for details.

WWP-L (WOMEN WRITERS PROJECT LIST)

Description: The Women Writers Project at Brown University has compiled an electronic textbase of nearly 400 texts by women in English before the Victorian Period. The goals of the WWP-L list are to disseminate information about the WWP itself; to encourage discussion between those working on, studying, and teaching early texts by women; to share other information useful to scholars of the early modern periods, including book announcements, conference schedules and calls for papers; to announce particular projects that include or involve writers whose works may be included in the textbase now or later; and to discuss any other topics considered appropriate by its scholarly members.
Subjects covered: women's studies; writing; English language and literature
Host: Brown University
Editorial contact: Elaine Brennan

Brown Women Writers Project, Box 1841, Brown University, Providence, RI 02912.
Tel: 401/863-3619
Internet: Elaine__Brennan@brown.edu
How to access: Contact editor at Elaine__Brennan@brown.edu

WX-LSR@UIUCVMD

Description: WX-LSR contains weather data.
Subjects covered: meteorology; computer hardware and software
List moderated: No.
Editorial contact: Chis Novy
Internet: axvsccn@uicvmc.aiss.uiuc.edu
Bitnet: axvsccn@uiucvmc
How to access: Send subscribe message to listserv@uiucvmd or listserv@vmd.cso.uiuc.edu
How to unsubscribe: Send unsubscribe message to listserv@uiucvmd or listserv@vmd.cso.uiuc.edu
Archives: Archives are developed weekly; apply to listowner for details.

WX-MISC@UIUCVMD

Description: WX-MISC is a forum containing information on miscellaneous WX software products.
Subjects covered: meteorology; computer hardware and software
List moderated: No.
Editorial contact: Chis Novy
Internet: axvsccn@uicvmc.aiss.uiuc.edu
Bitnet: axvsccn@uiucvmc
How to access: Send subscribe message to listserv@uiucvmd or listserv@vmd.cso.uiuc.edu
How to unsubscribe: Send unsubscribe message to listserv@uiucvmd or listserv@vmd.cso.uiuc.edu
Archives: Archives are developed weekly; apply to listowner for details.

WX-NATNL@UIUCVMD

Description: WX-NATNL is a forum containing information on national WX summaries.
Subjects covered: meteorology; computer hardware and software
List moderated: No.
Editorial contact: Chis Novy
Internet: axvsccn@uicvmc.aiss.uiuc.edu
Bitnet: axvsccn@uiucvmc
How to access: Send subscribe message to listserv@uiucvmd or listserv@vmd.cso.uiuc.edu
How to unsubscribe: Send unsubscribe message to listserv@uiucvmd or listserv@vmd.cso.uiuc.edu
Archives: Archives are developed weekly; apply to listowner for details.

WX-PCPN@UIUCVMD

Description: WX-PCPN is a forum containing information on precipitation WX products.
Subjects covered: meteorology; computer hardware and software
List moderated: No.
Editorial contact: Chis Novy

Internet: axvsccn@uicvmc.aiss.uiuc.edu
Bitnet: axvsccn@uiucvmc
How to access: Send subscribe message to listserv@uiucvmd or listserv@vmd.cso.uiuc.edu
How to unsubscribe: Send unsubscribe message to listserv@uiucvmd or listserv@vmd.cso.uiuc.edu
Archives: Archives are developed weekly; apply to listowner for details.

WX-STLT@UIUCVMD

Description: WX-STLT is a forum containing information on satellite weather-related messages.
Subjects covered: meteorology; computer hardware and software
List moderated: No.
Editorial contact: Chis Novy
Internet: axvsccn@uicvmc.aiss.uiuc.edu
Bitnet: axvsccn@uiucvmc
How to access: Send subscribe message to listserv@uiucvmd or listserv@vmd.cso.uiuc.edu
How to unsubscribe: Send unsubscribe message to listserv@uiucvmd or listserv@vmd.cso.uiuc.edu
Archives: Archives are developed weekly; apply to listowner for details.

WX-SWO@UIUCVMD

Description: WX-SWO is a forum containing information on severe weather projections.
Subjects covered: meteorology; computer hardware and software
List moderated: No.
Editorial contact: Chis Novy
Internet: axvsccn@uicvmc.aiss.uiuc.edu
Bitnet: axvsccn@uiucvmc
How to access: Send subscribe message to listserv@uiucvmd or listserv@vmd.cso.uiuc.edu
How to unsubscribe: Send unsubscribe message to listserv@uiucvmd or listserv@vmd.cso.uiuc.edu
Archives: Archives are developed weekly; apply to listowner for details.

WX-TALK@UIUCVMD

Description: WX-TALK is a discussion forum focusing on weather-related phenomena.
Subjects covered: meteorology; computer hardware and software
List moderated: No.
Editorial contact: Chis Novy
Internet: axvsccn@uicvmc.aiss.uiuc.edu
Bitnet: axvsccn@uiucvmc
How to access: Send subscribe message to listserv@uiucvmd or listserv@vmd.cso.uiuc.edu
How to unsubscribe: Send unsubscribe message to listserv@uiucvmd or listserv@vmd.cso.uiuc.edu
Archives: Archives are developed weekly; apply to listowner for details.

WX-TROPL@UIUCVMD

Description: WX-TROPL is a forum containing information on hurricane and tropical storm WX products.

Subjects covered: meteorology; computer hardware and software
List moderated: No.
Editorial contact: Chis Novy
Internet: axvsccn@uicvmc.aiss.uiuc.edu
Bitnet: axvsccn@uiucvmc
How to access: Send subscribe message to listserv@uiucvmd or listserv@vmd.cso.uiuc.edu
How to unsubscribe: Send unsubscribe message to listserv@uiucvmd or listserv@vmd.cso.uiuc.edu
Archives: Archives are developed weekly; apply to listowner for details.

WX-WATCH@UIUCVMD

Description: WX-WATCH is a forum containing information on WX watches/cancellations.
Subjects covered: meteorology; computer hardware and software
List moderated: No.
Editorial contact: Chis Novy
Internet: axvsccn@uicvmc.aiss.uiuc.edu
Bitnet: axvsccn@uiucvmc
How to access: Send subscribe message to listserv@uiucvmd or listserv@vmd.cso.uiuc.edu
How to unsubscribe: Send unsubscribe message to listserv@uiucvmd or listserv@vmd.cso.uiuc.edu
Archives: Archives are developed weekly; apply to listowner for details.

WX-WSTAT@UIUCVMD

Description: WX-WSTAT is a forum containing information on WX Watch status and storm reporting.
Subjects covered: meteorology; computer hardware and software
List moderated: No.
Editorial contact: Chis Novy
Internet: axvsccn@uicvmc.aiss.uiuc.edu
Bitnet: axvsccn@uiucvmc
How to access: Send subscribe message to listserv@uiucvmd or listserv@vmd.cso.uiuc.edu
How to unsubscribe: Send unsubscribe message to listserv@uiucvmd or listserv@vmd.cso.uiuc.edu
Archives: Archives are developed weekly; apply to listowner for details.

WXSPOT-L@UIUCVMD

Description: WXSPOT-L is a forum containing information on severe storm spotter training.
Subjects covered: meteorology; computer hardware and software
List moderated: No.
Editorial contact: Chis Novy
Internet: axvsccn@uicvmc.aiss.uiuc.edu
Bitnet: axvsccn@uiucvmc
How to access: Send subscribe message to listserv@uiucvmd or listserv@vmd.cso.uiuc.edu
How to unsubscribe: Send unsubscribe message to listserv@uiucvmd or listserv@vmd.cso.uiuc.edu
Archives: Archives are developed weekly; apply to listowner for details.

X-ADA@EXPO.LCS.MIT.EDU

Description: X-ADA is a discussion on standards related to X Window System with Ada.
Subjects covered: computer science; electronic networking
List moderated: No.
Editorial contact: X Consortium Staff
Internet: lists-request@expo.lcs.mit.edu
How to access: Send subscribe message to X-ADA-REQUEST@EXPO.LCS.MIT.EDU
How to unsubscribe: Send unsubscribe message to X-ADA-REQUEST@EXPO.LCS.MIT.EDU

X-SERIAL@LLL-CRG.LLNL.GOV

Description: X-SERIAL is a discussion on low bandwidth media.
Subjects covered: computer science
List moderated: No.
Editorial contact: Casey Leedom
Internet: CASEY@GAUSS.LLNL.GOV
How to access: Send subscribe message to X-SERIAL-REQUEST@LLL-CRG.LLNL.GOV
How to unsubscribe: Send unsubscribe message to X-SERIAL-REQUEST@LLL-CRG.LLNL.GOV
Archives: Yes; Send request to X-SERIAL-REQUEST@LLL-CRG.LLNL.GOV

X11-3D@ATHENA.MIT.EDU

Description: X11-3D is a forum on 3-D extensions to the X Window system.
Subjects covered: computer science; electronic networking
List moderated: No.
Editorial contact: X Consortium Staff
Internet: lists-request@expo.lcs.mit.edu
How to access: Send subscribe message to X11-3D-REQUEST@ATHENA.MIT.EDU
How to unsubscribe: Send unsubscribe message to X11-3D-REQUEST@ATHENA.MIT.EDU

X500-EXCHANGE@CNI.ORG

Description: X500-EXCHANGE is a forum for CNI/IETF X.500 service developers.
Subjects covered: computer science; electronic networking
Host: Coalition for Networked Information; Internet Engineering Task Force
List moderated: No.
Editorial contact: Tim Howes
Internet: tim@terminator.cc.umich.edu
How to access: Send subscribe message to listserv@cni.org
How to unsubscribe: Send unsubscribe message to listserv@cni.org

XCULT-X@UMRVMB

Description: Xcult-X@UMRVMB is a forum for discussion of global communication philosophy.
Subjects covered: communications
List moderated: No.
Editorial contact: Lance Haynes
Bitnet: lance@umrvmb

How to access: Send subscribe message to listserv@umrvmb or listserv@umrvmb.umr.edu
How to unsubscribe: Send unsubscribe message to listserv@umrvmb or listserv@umrvmb.umr.edu
Archives: Archives are developed monthly; apply to listowner for details.

XGKS@UNIDATA.UCAR.EDU

Description: XGKS@UNIDATA is a forum on the uses of the XGKS protocol system.
Subjects covered: computer science; electronic networking
List moderated: No.
Editorial contact: Steve Emmerson
Internet: xgks-request@unidata.ucar.edu
How to access: Send subscribe message to XGKS-REQUEST@UNIDATA.UCAR.EDU
How to unsubscribe: Send unsubscribe message to XGKS-REQUEST@UNIDATA.UCAR.EDU

XIMAGE@EXPO.LCS.MIT.EDU

Description: XIMAGE@EXPO.LCS.MIT.EDU covers image processing in an X Window System.
Subjects covered: computer science
List moderated: No.
Editorial contact: X Consortium Staff
Internet: lists-request@expo.lcs.mit.edu
How to access: Send subscribe message to XIMAGE-REQUEST@EXPO.LCS.MIT.EDU
How to unsubscribe: Send unsubscribe message to XIMAGE-REQUEST@EXPO.LCS.MIT.EDU

XPERT@EXPO.LCS.MIT.EDU

Description: XPERT@EXPO is a discussion forum about the X Window System.
Subjects covered: computer science
List moderated: No.
Editorial contact: Keith Packard
Internet: keith@expo.lcs.mit.edu
How to access: Send subscribe message to XPERT-REQUEST@ATHENA.MIT.EDU
How to unsubscribe: Send unsubscribe message to XPERT-REQUEST@ATHENA.MIT.EDU

XPRESS-LIST@CSD.MOT.COM

Description: XPRESS-LIST@CSD.MOT.COM is a forum for discussion of the X-Press Information Service and related topics about cable television systems.
Subjects covered: communications; information technology
List moderated: No.
Editorial contact: Brian Smithson
Internet: brian@csd.mot.com
How to access: Send subscribe message to XPRESS-LIST-REQUEST@CSD.MOT.COM
How to unsubscribe: Send unsubscribe message to XPRESS-LIST-REQUEST@CSD.MOT.COM

XVIDEO@EXPO.LCS.MIT.EDU

Description: XVIDEO@EXPO is a forum on using still and full motion video within the X Window System.
Subjects covered: computer science
List moderated: No.
Editorial contact: X Consortium Staff
Internet: lists-request@expo.lcs.mit.edu
How to access: Send subscribe message to XVIDEO-RE-QUEST@EXPO.LCS.MIT.EDU
How to unsubscribe: Send unsubscribe message to XVIDEO-REQUEST@EXPO.LCS.MIT.EDU

XXI@CHCECVM

Description: XXI@CHCECVM is a multi-lingual discussion on science and technology.
Subjects covered: science and technology
List moderated: Yes.
Editorial contact: Nicolas Luco
Bitnet: nluco@uchcecvm
How to access: Send subscribe message to listserv@uchcecvm
How to unsubscribe: Send unsubscribe message to listserv@uchcecvm
Archives: Archives are developed weekly; apply to listowner for details.

Y-RIGHTS@SJUVM.BITNET

Description: The Y-RIGHTS list covers discussion of the rights of children and teenagers (called Y-Rights for ''Youth Rights'', or ''Youngster's Rights'' or ''Why Rights?'' It's a very open list, and everyone is welcome to participate on it, whether you are a teacher, a professional, a student, or a kid or teenager yourself.
Subjects covered: children; children's rights; human rights
Net address for operations: LISTSERV@SJUVM.BITNET
Net address for questions or submissions: Y-RIGHTS@SJUVM.BITNET
Established: March 1991 as child@hamp.hampshire.edu Moved to Y-RIGHTS@SJUVM.BITNET on Friday, November 8th, 1991
Subscribers: 107
Sponsor: SJUVM.BITNET
Host: SJUVM.BITNET
List moderated: No.
Editorial contact: Kenneth Udut
170 East Clay Avenue
Tel: 908 241 6246
Fax: 908 241 8528
Internet: kudut@hamp.hampshire.edu
Bitnet: kudut@hampvms.bitnet
Copyright statement: All posts to the children's rights list (currently Y-RIGHTS@SJUVM.BITNET, previously child@hamp.hampshire.edu) and any archives of the children's rights list kept at LISTSERV@SJUVM.BITNET and elsewhere, are hereby released into the public domain, both past and future. While we (Y-RIGHTS) would like to receive credit for anything we or our members produce during the process of discussion and action, it is not a requirement.
How to access: Send email to LISTSERV@SJUVM with the message SUB Y-RIGHTS Firstname Lastname
Access policy: You must use a first name and a last name.

How to unsubscribe: Send E-Mail to LISTSERV@SJUVM.BITNET with the message UNSUB Y-RIGHTS
How to submit: Send E-Mail to Y-RIGHTS@SJUVM.BITNET. This message will go directly to the list members.
Archives: The Weekly Notebooks are kept at LISTSERV@SJUVM.BITNET. The ''Y-RIGHTS DIGEST'' is simply an automated distribution of each notebook as it is completed and written. To subscribe to the children's rights digest (Y-RIGHTS DIGEST) send e-mail to LISTSERV@SJUVM.BITNET with the message: AFD ADD Y-RIGHTS DIGEST To stop receiving the Y-RIGHTS DIGEST, send e-mail to LISTSERV@SJUVM.BITNET with the message: AFD DEL Y-RIGHTS DIGEST from the account that originally subscribed to it. If you can't successfully delete yourself from the digest, e-mail a regular message to KUDUT@HAMP.HAMPSHIRE.EDU and Ken will manually remove you from the automatic file distribution.
Related files: All Y-RIGHTS archives are stored at LISTSERV@SJUVM.BITNET. Any other texts directly related will be stored there. If any texts are found in relation to the rights of children and teenagers please send them to KUDUT@HAMP.HAMPSHIRE.EDU. You will receive credit for your contribution.

YES-CAMPS (YOUTH ENGINEERING AND SCIENCE CAMPS OF CANADA)

Description: YES-CAMPS provides a forum for discussion for the various YES Camp directors and vounteers. YESCAMP allows subscribers to discuss problems, ideas, suggestions, etc., regarding the operation of weekly summer science and engineering camps across Canada. YESCAMP is one of the many branches of the Canadian Federation of Engineering Students. All students in accredited engineering institutions are members of the Canadian Federation of Students (CFES). The CFES provides a voice for all engineering students.
Subjects covered: science and technology; engineering; education
Net address for operations: LISTSERV@UNB.CA
Net address for questions or submissions: YESCAMP@UNB.CA
Established: January 1993
Subscribers: 25
Sponsor: University of New Brunswick Fredericton, New Brunswick, Canada.
Host: University of New Brunswick Fredericton, New Brunswick, Canada.
List moderated: List is unmoderated, but is monitored by the Canadian Federation of Engineering Student's Commissioner of Electronic Communication.
Editorial contact: Troy Morehouse
CFES Commissioner of Electronic Communication, Room H-223, Sir Edmund Head Hall, University of New Brunswick, Fredericton, New Brunswick, Canada.
Tel: (506) 453-3534
Fax: (506) 453-4569
Internet: cfes@jupiter.sun.csd.unb.ca
Bitnet: cfes@unb.ca
How to access: Send the following one line e-mail message to LISTSERV@UNB.CA SUB YESCAMP your-name-and/or-af-filliation

Access policy: Anybody who is interested in engineering and engineering education are invited to participate (being an engineering student is not a pre-requisite).
How to unsubscribe: Send e-mail message to LISTSERV@UNB.CA
How to submit: Send any submissions (postings) to YESCAMP@UNB.CA
Submission policy: Postings of a slanderous, sexist, racist, or homophobic nature will not be tolerated on YESCAMP. Doing so will result in immediate removal from subscription.
Archives: No currently provided, but may be in the future. Related (ftp) files and other documents accessible (electronic texts, etc): CFES and YESCAMP have related documentation (i.e. minutes, policy manuals, bylaws, logos, addresses, etc) available via anonymous FTP at jupiter.sun.csd.unb.ca, and can be found in the /pub/cfes directory. An incoming directory is provided for site submissions.

YORK-COLLAB-WORK@MAILBASE.AC.UK
Description: YORK-COLLAB-WORK covers distance education.
Subjects covered: education; distance education
List moderated: No.
Internet: york-collab-work-request@mailbase.ac.uk
How to access: Send subscribe message to mailbase@mailbase.ac.uk in the following format: join york-collab-work Yourfirstname Yourlastname
Archives: Archives are developed monthly; apply to listowner for details.

YTERM-L
Description: YTERM-L is a forum for the Yale Terminal Emulation telecommunications software.
Subjects covered: computer hardware and software; telecommunications

List moderated: No.
Editorial contact: Susan Barmhall
Internet: susan@yalevm.ycc.yale.edu
Bitnet: susan@yalevm
How to access: Send subscribe message to listserv@yalevm or listserv@yalevm.ycc.yale.edu
How to unsubscribe: Send unsubscribe message to listserv@yalevm or listserv@yalevm.ycc.yale.edu

YUNUS@TRMETU
Description: YUNUS is a discussion of the TeX typesetting system software.
Subjects covered: computer hardware and software
List moderated: No.
Editorial contact: Mustafa Akgul
Internet: akgul@trbilun
How to access: Send subscribe message to listserv@trmetu
How to unsubscribe: Send unsubscribe message to listserv@trmetu
Archives: Archives are developed monthly; apply to listowner for details.

Z3950IW@NERVM
Description: Z3950IW@NERVM is a workshop for implementors of the ANSI Z39.50 data transfer protocol.
Subjects covered: computer science
List moderated: No.
Editorial contact: Mark Hinnebusch
Bitnet: fclmth@nervm
How to access: Send subscribe message to listserv@nervm
How to unsubscribe: Send unsubscribe message to listserv@nervm
Archives: Archives are developed monthly; apply to listowner for details.

Section 2. Electronic Journals and Newsletters

A & G INFORMATION SERVICES

Description: A & G Information Services provides information regularly on St. Petersburg, Russia
Subjects covered: Russia
Frequency: Weekly
Established: August 1991
Method of issuance: Issues are emailed to subscribers as published.
Fee: Yes
Journal refereed: No
Editorial contact: Elena Artemova
P.O. Box 589, 199000 St. Petersburg, Russia.
Internet: esa@cfea.ecc.spb.su or spbeac@sovamsu.sovusa.com
How to access: Mail inquiries to editor's address listed above.

ACADEME THIS WEEK (THE CHRONICLE OF HIGHER EDUCATION)

Description: Academe This Week is a free service offered by the Chronicle of Higher Education. Posted at noon each Tuesday, it includes a guide to the news in the current week's Chronicle, a calendar of events in Academe for the next two weeks, a schedule of Congressional hearings of interest to the men and women of Academe, important deadlines for fellowships, grant applications, exchange programs, and more, a list of best-selling books on campuses, a listing of hundreds of job openings in Academe from the current week's Bulletin Board pages of the Chronicle.
Subjects covered: higher education; career opportunities; colleges and universities; current events
Net address for operations: help@chronicle.merit.edu (or with gopher, point to chronicle.merit.edu, port 70)
Net address for questions or submissions: editor@chronicle.merit.edu
Frequency: Weekly
Established: April 14, 1993
Number of issues published to date: 49 per year
Method of issuance: Issues sent via email or are gopher accessible. Issues are announced in the Chronicle of Higher Education weekly.
Commercial organization: The Chronicle of Higher Education, 1255 23rd Street, NW, Washington, DC 20037; (202) 466-1000.
Editorial contact: Corbin Gwaltney
The Chronicle of Higher Education, 1255 23rd Street, NW, Washington, DC 20037.
Tel: 202-466-1000
Fax: 202-296-2691
Internet: editor@chronicle.merit.edu
Technical contact: Judith Axler Turner

The Chronicle of Higher Education, 1255 23rd Street, NW, Washington, DC 20037.
Tel: 202-466-1000
Fax: 202-296-2691
Internet: judith@page1.com
Copyright statement: You may save or print the result of your searches on Academe This Week for personal use whenever you like. Permission from The Chronicle is required for other uses. All information is copyright 1993 by The Chronicle of Higher Education, Inc.
Gopher accessibility: Academe This Week is available through Gopher under "All the Gopher Servers in the World." It is also available on more than 60 campus Gopher-based networks.

ACCESS!

Description: ACCESS! is an electronic newsletter devoted to the issues of concern to library science graduates entering the job market.
Subjects covered: library and information science; career opportunities
Established: October 11, 1993
Recent issue published: Premier issue
Editorial contact: Donald M. Schwartz
Internet: donald_m_schwartz@mts.cc.wayne.edu
Bitnet: donald_m_schwartz@waynemts.bitnet
How to access: Send email message to editor at donald_m_schwartz@mts.cc.wayne.edu or donald_m_schwartz@waynemts.bitnet
How to unsubscribe: Send email message to editor at donald_m_schwartz@mts.cc.wayne.edu or donald_m_schwartz@waynemts.bitnet

ACQUISITIONS LIBRARIANS ELECTRONIC NETWORK (ACQNET)

ISSN: 1057-5308
Description: ACQNET is an electronic newsletter for library professionals.
Subjects covered: library and information science; library collection development
Frequency: Irregular
Established: December 1991
Method of issuance: Issues are emailed to subscribers as published.
Editorial contact: Christian M. Boissonnas
Cornell University Library, 110 A Olin Library, Ithaca, NY 14853-5301.
Tel: (607) 255-4960
Fax: (607) 255-9346

Internet: cri@cornellc.cit.cornell.edu
Bitnet: cri@cornellc

AIDEVAISB.ED.AC.UK

Description: aidevaisb.ed.ac.uk is described as an occasional newsletter for those interested in artificial intelligence applications in and for developing countries. The newsletter is sent to the mailing list and to the newsgroup comp.society.development.
Subjects covered: artificial intelligence
How to access: Send requests to be added to the mailing list to Kathleen King <kk@aisb.ed.ac.uk>

AIDS BOOK REVIEW JOURNAL

Description: AIDS Book Review Journal is an electronic review of books and other information about Aquired Immune Deficiency Syndrome and related issues.
Subjects covered: AIDS/HIV studies; medicine; health science
Frequency: Monthly, or more frequent.
Established: 1993
Method of issuance: Issues are emailed to subscribers as published.
Journal refereed: No.
Editorial contact: H. Robert Malinowsky
Bitnet: u50095@uicvm
How to access: Send the message SUBSCRIBE AIDSBKRV to listserv@uicvm or listserv@uicvm.uic.edu
Archives: Back issues are available by sending the message INDEX AIDSBKRV to listserv@uicvm or listserv@uicvm.uic.edu

ALAWON: THE ALA WASHINGTON OFFICE NEWSLINE

Description: ALAWON is the newsletter of the American Library Association's Washington, DC, office; it focuses on legislation impacting the library profession.
Subjects covered: American Library Association; library and information science
Frequency: Irregular
Established: 1992
Method of issuance: Issues are emailed to subscribers as published.
Host: American Library Association
Journal refereed: No
Editorial contact: Fred King
ALA Washington Office, 110 Maryland Avenue, NE, Washington, DC 20002-5675
Tel: 202-547-4440
Fax: 202-547-7363
Internet: fdk@alawash.org
Sample contents: CLINTON'S BUDGET RECONCILIATION MEASURE SQUEAKS THROUGH; FURTHER INFORMATION ON LIBRARY APPROPRIATIONS NOT YET AVAILABLE; POSTAL REVENUE FORGONE - ACTION NEEDED; COPYRIGHT OFFICE TO HOLD HEARING; FAMILY ENGLISH LITERACY GRANTS AVAILABLE; DEPT. OF EDUCATION ACCEPTING APPLICATIONS FOR FY94 GRANTS; HACKNEY AND PAYZANT CONFIRMED BY SENATE.
Copyright statement: All or part of ALAWON may be redistributed, with appropriate credits.
How to access: Send the message "subscribe ala-wo [your name]" to listserv@uicvm (Bitnet) or listserv@uicvm.uic.edu (internet)

Archives: Back issues of ALAWON are available from the list server. To find out what's available, send the message "send ala-wo filelist" to the listserv. The ALA-WO filelist contains the list of files with the exact filename and filetype. To get a particular file, issue the command "send filename filetype" to the listserv. Do not include the quotes in your commands.

ALCTS NETWORK NEWS

ISSN: 1056-6694
Description: ALCTS NETWORK NEWS is an electronic newsletter published irregularly by the Association for Library Collections & Technical Services, a division of the American Library Association. Topics in the newsletter center on library collection development and other, related technical service issues.
Subjects covered: library collection development; library and information science
Net address for operations: listserv@uicvm
Net address for questions or submissions: u34261@uicvm
Frequency: irregular
Established: May 13, 1991
Number of issues published to date: 5 volumes
Method of issuance: Issues are distributed via email as published.
Recent issue published: v5., no. 27 (May 13, 1993)
Subscribers: 1900
Sponsor: Association for Library Collections & Technical Services
Host: 50 E. Huron St., Chicago, IL 60611
Editorial contact: Karen Whittlesey
ALCTS, 50 E. Huron St., Chicago, IL 60611
Tel: (312) 280-5034
Copyright statement: All materials in the newsletter subject to copyright by the American Library Association may be reprinted or redistributed for the noncommercial purpose of scientific or education advancement granted by Sections 107 and 108 of the Copyright Revision Act of 1976. For other reprinting or redistribution or translations, address requests to the ALA Office of Rights and Permissions, 50 E. Huron Street, Chicago, IL 60611.
How to access: To subscribe, issue the network command "tell listserv@uicvm sub alcts [your name]."
How to submit: News items should be sent to the editor at Bitnet address u34261@uicvm.
Submission policy: Send questions about membership in ALCTS to the ALCTS Office, u34261@uicvm.
Archives: Back issues of AN2 are available through the listserver. To find out what's available, send the following command to LISTSERV@UICVM: send alcts filelist The ALCTS FILELIST contains the list of files with the EXACT filename and filetype. To get a particular file, issue this command to the LISTSERV@UICVM: send filename filetype.

ALGEBRAIC GEOMETRY E-PRINTS

Description: ALGEBRAIC GEOMETRY E-PRINTS distributes abstracts of mathematical papers. On request any paper can be obtained (Subj: get paper #).
Subjects covered: algebraic geometry; mathematics
Net address for operations: alg-geom@publications.math.duke.edu
Net address for questions or submissions: alg-geom@publications.math.duke.edu
Frequency: Daily

Established: February 6, 1992
Method of issuance: E-prints are issued daily through e-mail.
Available in other media: No, but print copies can be easily obtained using Tex.
Subscribers: 947
Sample contents: Three abstracts + informations about the system used (Latex, AMS-Tex`ots).

AM/FM ONLINE EDITION

Description: AM/FM Online Edition is an electronic digest of news from a variety of radio sources in the UK.
Subjects covered: radio
Frequency: Monthly
Established: July 1992
Method of issuance: Issues are emailed to subscribers as published.
Journal refereed: No
Editorial contact: Stephen Hebditch
Internet: steveh@orbital.demon.co.uk
How to access: Send the message SUBSCRIBE AMFM to listserv@orbital.demon.co.uk An index is also available by sending the message INDEX AMFM to listserv@orbital.demon.co.uk

AMATEUR COMPUTERIST

Description: Amateur Computerist is an electronic publication focusing on the novice computer user.
Subjects covered: computer hardware and software; computer science; information technology
Established: 1992
Method of issuance: Issues are emailed to subscribers as published. Issues are also available via FTP and through USENET.
Journal refereed: No
Editorial contact: Ronda Hauben
P.O. Box 4344, Dearborn, MI 48126.
Internet: au329@cleveland.freenet.edu, ae547@yfn.ysu.edu
How to access: Email subscription request to: hauben@cunixf.cc.columbia.edu or au329@cleveland.freenet.edu Also available via FTP to wuarchive.wustl.edu The directory is /doc/misc/acn/
Related files: Also available as the Usenet newsgroup alt.amateur-comp

AMAZONS INTERNATIONAL

Description: Amazons International is an electronic newsletter focusing on assertivness in women.
Subjects covered: women's studies
Frequency: Monthly, possibly irregular.
Established: April 1991
Method of issuance: Issues are emailed to subscribers as published.
Journal refereed: No
Editorial contact: Thomas Gramstad
Internet: thomas@smaug.uio.no
How to access: Email to thomas@smaug.uio.no

AMERICAN ARAB SCIENTIFIC SOCIETY NEWSLETTER

Description: The American Arab Scientific Society Newsletter covers economic and technological issues of Arab communities.

Subjects covered: Arab studies; science and technology
Frequency: Quarterly
Established: 1992
Method of issuance: Issues are available via FTP.
Journal refereed: No
Editorial contact: Abdelsalam Heddaya
Internet: amass-request@cs.bu.edu
How to access: FTP to cs.bu.edu
The directory is: /amass/newsletters/

AMERICAN PSYCHOLOGICAL ASSOCIATION'S RESEARCH FUNDING BULLETIN

Description: The APA's Research Funding Bulletin provides a compilation of information on research grants.
Subjects covered: grants and funding; American Psychological Association
Frequency: Twice-monthly
Established: February 1989
Method of issuance: Issues are emailed to subscribers as published.
Host: American Psychological Association
Journal refereed: No
Editorial contact: Cheri Fullerton
American Psychological Association, Science Directorate, 750 First Street, NE, Washington, DC 20002-4242.
Internet: apasdcf@gwuvm.bitnet
How to access: Send the message SUBSCRIBE APASD-L to listserv@vtvm2

ANDREW VIEW

Description: Andrew View publishes information about the Andrew Consortium and Andrew-based software developments.
Subjects covered: computer science; computer hardware and software
Frequency: Quarterly
Established: 1982
Method of issuance: Issues are emailed to subscribers as published.
Host: Carnegie-Mellon University
Journal refereed: No
Editorial contact: Fred Hansen
Internet: wilfred.hansen@cs.cmu.edu, wjh+@cmu.edu
How to access: Send the message SUBSCRIBE ANDREW to info-andrew-request@andrew.cmu.edu

ARCHITRONIC: THE ELECTRONIC JOURNAL OF ARCHITECTURE

ISSN: 1066-6516
Description: Architronic is an electronic forum for the study of architecture, including research and critical analysis.
Subjects covered: architecture; environmental studies; design
Frequency: Three issues per year.
Established: December 1992
Method of issuance: Issues are emailed to subscribers as published.
Fee: None.
Host: School of Architecture and Environmental Design
Journal refereed: Yes.

School of Architecture and Environmental Design, Kent State Unversity, P.O. Box 5190, Kent, OH 44242.
Tel: (206) 672-2869
Fax: (216) 672-4706
Internet: arcitron@kentvm.kent.edu
Bitnet: arcitron@kentvm
How to access: Send the message SUBSCRIBE ARCITRON to listserv@kentvm.kent.edu or listserv@kentvm
Archives: Back issues are available via ftp to ksuvxa.kent.edu. Login as ARCHITECTURE and use the password ARCHIVES. To retrieve, type the message GETf v1n1.txt

ARM THE SPIRIT

Description: Arm The Spirit is a anti-imperialist/autonomist collective that disseminates information about liberation struggles in advanced capitalist countries and in the so-called 'Third World.' Our focus is on armed struggle and other forms of militant resistance but we do not limit ourselves to this. In Arm The Spirit you can find news on political prisoners in North America and Europe, information on the struggles of Indigenous peoples in the Americas, communiques from guerrilla groups, debate and discussion on armed struggle and much more. We also attempt to cover anti-colonial national liberation struggles in Kurdistan, Puerto Rico, Euskadi and elsewhere.
Subjects covered: political activism; alternative literature; current events
Frequency: Bi-monthly
Established: 1992
Method of issuance: Issues are emailed to subscribers as published.
Journal refereed: No
Arm the Spirit, c/o Wild Seed Press, P.O. Box 57584, Jackson Stn., Hamilton, Ontario
L8P 4X3 Canada; or: Arm the Spirit, c/o Autonome Forum, P.O. Box 1242, Burlington, VT 05402-1242.
Internet: aforum@moose.uvm.edu
How to access: Send a message with the header ''ATS: e-mail request'' to: aforum@moose.uvm.edu

ARMADILLO CULTURE: THE JOURNAL OF MODERN DASYPODIDAE

Description: Armadillo Culture is an electronic magazine publishing poetry and fiction and covering cultural events in the Washington, DC, area.
Subjects covered: current events; alternative literature; fiction; poetry
Frequency: Quarterly
Established: 1991
Method of issuance: Issues are emailed to subscribers as published.
Journal refereed: No
Editorial contact: Steve Okay
Armadillo Culture, 2857 Foxmill Rd., Herndon, VA 22071.
Internet: sokay@cyclone.mitre.org
How to access: Send a message to sokay@cyclone.mitre.org
Gopher accessibility: Gopher accessible at: etext.archive.umich.edu

ARTCOM

Description: ARTCOM is a forum dedicated to the interface of contemporary art and new communication technologies.''

Subjects covered: art; fine arts; communications
Method of issuance: Issues are emailed to subscribers as published; also available as the Usenet newsgroup, alt.artcom
Journal refereed: No.
Editorial contact: Carl Loeffler
Internet: cel@andrew.cmu.edu
Technical contact: Fred Truck
Internet: fjt@well.sf.ca.us
How to access: Send email message to artcomtv@well.sf.ca.us
How to unsubscribe: Send email message to artcomtv@well.sf.ca.us
How to submit: Send email message to artcomtv@well.sf.ca.us
Submission policy: Send email message to artcomtv@well.sf.ca.us
Archives: Back issues of ART COM are available on the ARTCOM Electronic Network (ACEN) on the WELL, and available through the CompuServe Packet Network and PC Pursuit.
Additional information: ARTCOM is available via the Well by entering the following messages at the OK prompt: g acen.

ASTRO-PH@BABBAGE.SISSA.IT

Description: astro-ph@babbage.sissa.it is an electronic journal on astrophysics and related topics.
Subjects covered: astrophysics

AUTOMATOME

Description: Automatome is a newsletter published by the American Association of Law Libraries' Automation and Scientific Development Special Interest Section.
Subjects covered: computer hardware and software; library and information science; law and legal studies
Method of issuance: Issues are emailed to subscribers as published.
Host: American Association of Law Libraries
Journal refereed: No
Editorial contact: Anna Belle Leiserson
Internet: leiserab@ctrvax.vanderbilt.edu
How to access: Send a message to law-lib@ucdavis.edu

AXE: REVUE ELECTRONIQUE DE LA LITTERATURE QUEBECOISE ET FRANCOPHONE

Description: AXE covers world literature in French.
Subjects covered: French language and literature
Frequency: Three issues per year
Established: January 1993
Method of issuance: Issues are emailed to subscribers as published.
Host: McGill University
Journal refereed: No
Editorial contact: Janusz Przychodzen
Departement de langue et litterature francaises, University McGill, 3460, rue McTavish, Montreal, H3A 1X9, Quebec, Canada.
Internet: cxzn@musica. mcgill.ca
How to access: Send the message SUBSCRIBE AXE-LIST to listserv@vm1. mcgill.ca
Archives: Back issues are available via listserv@vm1.mcgill.ca.

Related files: A related discussion group is AXE-TALK, located at listserv@vm1.mcgill.ca

BEAN BAG
Description: Bean Bag is a twice-yearly publication covering legume systematics.
Subjects covered: legumes; plant biology; botany
Frequency: Twice yearly
Established: May 1987
Method of issuance: Issues are emailed to subscribers as published.
Host: US Department of Agriculture
Journal refereed: No.
Editorial contact: Joseph H. Kirkbride
USDA, Agricultural Research Service, Systematic Botany and Mycology Laboratory, Building 265, BARC-East, Beltsville, MD 20705-2350.
Tel: (301) 504-9447
Internet: jkirkbride@asrr.arsusda.gov
How to access: May be accessed through gopher via huh.harvard.edu

BETWEEN THE LINES - A DEBBIE GIBSON DISCUSSION FORUM
Description: Between the Lines - A Debbie Gibson Discussion Forum posts reviews, opinions, information, and transcriptions in reference to the young music artist Debbie Gibson.
Subjects covered: Gibson, Debbie; music
Frequency: Irregular: based on amount/frequency of information and submissions.
Established: March 1989
Number of issues published to date: 59
Method of issuance: Issues are distributed through e-mail; some postal mail distribution. Issues are announced on Usenet Newsgroups: rec.music.info and rec.music.misc
Available in other media: Yes, on paper. Issues are computer printed and sent to postal mail subscribers.
Recent issue published: Volume 5, Issue 9
Subscribers: 275
Fee: Free via email, $0.65/issue via postal mail. By cheque/money order.
Journal refereed: Article submissions are screened and proofread. Most are printed.
Editorial contact: Myra Wong
Internet: mkwong@scf.nmsu.edu
Bitnet: mkwong@ucsd.bitnet
Technical contact: Myra Wong
Internet: mkwong@scf.nmsu.edu
Bitnet: mkwong@ucsd.bitnet
Sample contents: Album reviews, television appearance summary, updated information, introductions by members.
Indexed or abstracted: Index currently being compiled.
How to access: Send request to: mkwong@scf.nmsu.edu
Access policy: In email request, please indicate that you wish to subscribe to the BtL mailing list.
How to unsubscribe: Send request to: mkwong@scf.nmsu.edu
How to submit: Send to: mkwong@scf.nmsu.edu
Submission policy: Please proofread your articles and they will be considered for an upcoming issue.
Archives: Available from FTP site ftp.uwp.edu in the directory /pub/music/lists/btl/archives and by email from Myra Wong (mkwong@scf.nmsu.edu)

Related files: Lyrics, GIFs, transcriptions about Debbie Gibson.
Additional information: Second editor: Felix Ng, 2137 Qualicum Drive, Vancouver, B.C., V5P 2M3, CANADA TEL.(604)322-5936; fng@acca.nmsu.edu

BIOMEDICAL LIBRARY ACQUISITIONS BULLETIN (BLAB)
ISSN: 1064-699X
Description: BLAB is an electronic publication covering biomedical libraries and librarians.
Subjects covered: library and information science; medicine; health sciences
Frequency: Monthly
Established: April 1992
Method of issuance: Issues are emailed to subscribers as published.
Host: Norris Medical Library, University of Southern California.
Journal refereed: No
Editorial contact: David H. Morse
USC Norris Medical Library, 2003 Zonal Ave., Los Angeles, CA 90033.
Tel: (213) 342-1134
Internet: dmorse@hsc.usc.edu
How to access: Send an email to dmorse@hsc.usc.edu

BITS AND BYTES ONLINE
Description: Bits and Bytes Online is a weekly ejournal reviewing new product developments in the computer field.
Subjects covered: computer hardware and software
Frequency: Weekly
Editorial contact: Jay Machado
How to access: Send email to slakmaster@aol.com

BLIND NEWS DIGEST
Description: Blind News Digest compiles information about visual handicaps. Formerly titled the Handicap Digest.
Subjects covered: disabilities; blindness
Frequency: Irregular
Established: September 1992
Method of issuance: Issues are emailed to subscribers as published.
Journal refereed: No
Editorial contact: Bill McGarry
Olivetti North America, 2 Enterprise Drive, Shelton, CT 06484.
Internet: wtm@bunker.afd.olivetti.com
How to access: Send the message SUBSCRIBE BLINDNWS to listserv@ndsuvm1 or listserv@vm1.nodak.edu

BLINK
Description: BLINK would like to be a forum for the issues surrounding the intersection of consciousness and technology. This is our best defense against postmodern angst: to critically look at and anticipate the cultural and social changes spurred by the rapid development of technology.
Subjects covered: cultural studies; alternative literature; popular culture
Editorial contact: Justin Kerr
Internet: ratsbats@casbah.acns.nwu.edu

How to access: Gopher accessible at: gopher.well.sf.ca.us

BOSNET
Description: Bosnet is an electronic daily covering current events in Bosnia and Herzegovina.
Subjects covered: Eastern Europe; Bosnia; current events; political science
How to access: Send message to editor at HOZO@MATH.LSA.UMICH.EDU
How to unsubscribe: Send message to editor at HOZO@MATH.LSA.UMICH.EDU

BOTANICAL ELECTRONIC NEWS
ISSN: 1188-603X
Description: Botanical Electronic News publishes information about plant biology and botany worldwide.
Subjects covered: botany; plant biology; environmental studies
Frequency: Monthly, or more frequently.
Established: Spring 1991
Method of issuance: Issues are emailed to subscribers as published.
Journal refereed: No.
Editorial contact: Dr. Adolf Ceska
P.O. Box 8546, Victoria, BC, Canada V8W 3S2.
Tel: (604) 477-1211
Internet: aceska@cue.bc.ca
How to access: Send a message to aceska@cue.bc.ca

BRAILLE FORUM
Description: Braille Forum, a publication of the American Council of the Blind, covers topics related to Braille.
Subjects covered: blindness; Braille; disabilities
Frequency: Bimonthly
Established: 1990
Method of issuance: Available via FTP (.zip files)
Host: American Council of the Blind
Journal refereed: No
How to access: FTP to handicap.shel.isc-br.com
The directory is: /pub/forum/

BRAILLE MONITOR
ISSN: 0006-8829
Description: Braille Monitor covers topics related to Braille.
Subjects covered: blindness; Braille; disabilities
Frequency: Monthly
Established: 1990
Method of issuance: Available via FTP (.zip files)
Journal refereed: No
How to access: FTP to handicap.shel.isc-br.com
directory: /pub/monitor/

THE BUFFER
Description: The Buffer is an electronic journal covering a wide range of computer-related topics, including, in a recent issue, DOS 6.0, email to the White House, OMGATE in Romania, multimedia psychology, etc.
Subjects covered: computer hardware and software; colleges and universities

Frequency: Monthly
Established: 1986
Recent issue published: Volume 28, Number 6
Subscribers: 1250
Fee: Free electronically; $12 annually in print if off campus. Paid by check or money order.
Sponsor: University of Denver
Host: Computing and Information Resources, University of Denver, Denver, CO 80208
Journal refereed: Yes. It is necessary to submit an article to Buffer and the article will be reviewed by the editorial staff. If appropriate for the Buffer, any changes will be sent to author prior to publication.
Editorial contact: Rebecca Rowe
University of Denver, Computing and Info Resources, 2020 So. Race St., Denver, Colorado 80208.
Tel: (303) 871-4506
Internet: buffer@du.edu
Bitnet: buffer@ducair
Indexed or abstracted: Index available for past 3 years published in every DECEMBER issue of the Buffer. Under subject and chronologically.
Copyright statement: Copyright 1993 by the University of Denver. Unless otherwise indicated, permission is granted to reprint articles from the BUFFER for noncommercial purposes, provided the author and source are credited.
How to access: Send email message to buffer@du.edu or buffer@ducair
Access policy: Send email message to buffer@du.edu or buffer@ducair
How to unsubscribe: Send email message to buffer@du.edu or buffer@ducair
How to submit: Send email message to buffer@du.edu or buffer@ducair

BULLETIN OF THE GENERAL THEOLOGICAL LIBRARY OF BANGOR
ISSN: 1052-8202
Description: The Bulletin reports on new acquisitions to the Library.
Subjects covered: library collection development; religion; library and information science
Frequency: Quarterly
Established: 1992
Method of issuance: Issues are emailed to subscribers as published.
Journal refereed: No
Editorial contact: Mark Stoffan
Bangor Theological Seminary, 159 State Street, Portland, ME, 04101.
Internet: mark@btsgatep.caps.maine.edu
How to access: FTP to panda1.uottawa.ca
The directory is: /pub/religion/

A BYTE OF TORAH
Description: A Byte of Torah is a weekly electronic newsletter regarding the Torah, the five founding books of the Hebrew religion.
Subjects covered: religion; Torah; Hebrew language and literature
Frequency: Weekly
Established: 1991

Method of issuance: Issues are emailed to subscribers as published.
Journal refereed: No.
Editorial contact: Zev S. Itzkowitz
Internet: bytetorah@israwl.nysernet.org
How to access: FTP to israel.nysernet.org
The directory is: /israel/tanach/commentary/
bytetorah/
Or send the message SUBSCRIBE BYTETORAH to
listserv@israwl.nysernet.org

CACHE UPDATE
Description: Cache Update is an electronic publication covering the Andrew File System.
Subjects covered: computer science; computer hardware and software; information technology
Method of issuance: Issued by FTP
Journal refereed: No
How to access: FTP to grand.cantral.org
The directory is: /pub/cache.update

CACTUS NEWSLETTER
Description: The CACTUS Newsletter is an electronic publication of the Capital Area Central Texas Unix Society, covering aspects of Unix programming and development.
Subjects covered: Unix; computer science; computer hardware and software
Frequency: Monthly
Method of issuance: Issues are emailed to subscribers as published. Hardcopy also available.
Host: Capital Area Central Texas Unix Society
Journal refereed: No
Internet: newsletter@cactus.org, officers@cactus.org

CAMPUS COMPUTING NEWSLETTER
Description: The Campus Computing Newsletter covers activities at the University of Missouri in Columbia.
Subjects covered: University of Missouri, Columbia; colleges and universities; computer hardware and software
Frequency: Monthly during academic year
Established: 1991
Host: University of Missouri, Columbia
Journal refereed: No
Editorial contact: Molly Crozier
University of Missouri, Columbia, Campus Computing, 200 Heinkel Building, Columbia, MO 65211.
Internet: ccmolly@mizzou1.missouri.edu
How to access: Send requests to
ccmolly@mizzou1.missouri.edu

CAROLINA
Description: Carolina is an electronic news weekly covering politcal and social developments in the Czech Republic.
Subjects covered: Czech Republic; current events; political science
Frequency: Weekly
Method of issuance: Issues are emailed to subscribers as published.
Journal refereed: No
Editorial contact: Vaclav Trojan

Internet: carolina@n.fs.cuni.cs, trojan@csearn.bitnet
How to access: Send the message SUBSCRIBE CAR-CS to
listserv@csearn.bitnet

CATALYST: THE COMMUNITY SERVICES CATALYST
ISSN: 0739-9227
Description: Catalyst is an electronic journal covering community colleges.
Subjects covered: colleges and universities; administration
Frequency: Quarterly
Established: Fall 1991
Method of issuance: Issues are emailed to subscribers as published. Also available through FTP, WAIS, hardcopy, microfiche, or microfilm.
Host: National Council on Community Services & Continuing Education
Journal refereed: Yes
Editorial contact: Lon Savage
Bitnet: savage@vtvm1
How to access: Send the message SUBSCRIBE CATALYST to listserv@vtvm1 or listserv@vtvm1.cc.vt.edu. Or FTP to borg.lib.vt.edu The directory is: /pub/CATALYST/

CCNEWS - CAMPUS COMPUTING NEWSLETTER
Description: CCNEWS covers campus computing and editors and staff of publications dealing with campus computing.
Subjects covered: campus-wide information systems; technology education; colleges and universities; writing
Frequency: Biweekly
Method of issuance: Issues are emailed to subscribers as published.
Journal refereed: No
Bitnet: ccnews@educom
How to access: Send the message SUBSCRIBE CCNEWS to
listserv@bitnic

CERFNET NEWS
Description: CERFNet News covers issues of interest to institutions linked through the CERFNet regional Internet network.
Subjects covered: Internet; electronic networking; computer science; telecommunications
Frequency: Bimonthly
Established: January 1989
Method of issuance: Issues emailed to subscribers as published. Also available via FTP and hardcopy.
Host: California Education & Research Federation Network (CERFnet)
Journal refereed: No
Internet: help@cerf.net
How to access: Send the message SUBSCRIBE CERF-NEWS to listserv@cerf.net

CFS-NEWS (CHRONIC FATIGUE SYNDROME ELECTRONIC NEWSLETTER)

ISSN: 1066-8152

Description: CFS-NEWS (Chronic Fatigue Syndrome Electronic Newsletter) is an independent newsletter seeking to serve the CFS community by quickly disseminating information about current medical research on CFS. It will be issued between 1 and 4 times each month to give updates on these developments. Other CFS topics of interest to the readership will also be covered. Advice and contributions of news items are welcome. Chronic fatigue syndrome is an illness characterized by debilitating fatigue and a variety of flu-like symptoms. The condition is also known as chronic fatigue immune deficiency syndrome (CFIDS), myalgic encephalomyelitis (ME) and by other names, and in the past has been known as chronic Epstein-Barr virus (CEBV).

Subjects covered: chronic fatigue syndrome; myalgic encephalomyelitis; health sciences; medicine

Net address for operations: LISTSERV@LIST.NIH.GOV or LISTSERV@NIHLIST.BITNET

Net address for questions or submissions: CFS-NEWS@LIST.NIH.GOV

Frequency: Irregular

Established: August 1992

Number of issues published to date: 19

Method of issuance: Issues are distributed in three ways: 1) on the Internet, by subscription through LISTSERV; 2) on USENET, as newsgroup bit.listserv.cfs.newsletter; and 3) on Fidonet, through the CFS Echo.

Subscribers: Internet, 470 (May 1993); Fidonet, sent through CFS echo to 91 BBSs, number of readers unknown.

Editorial contact: Roger Burns
2800 Quebec St. NW, #1242, Washington, DC 20008.

Tel: (202) 966-8738

Internet: cfs-news@list.nih.gov

Bitnet: cfs-news@nihlist Fidonet: 1:109/432

Sample contents: Contents of latest issue: 1. New edition "Living With M.E." by Dr. Charles Shepherd; 2. May 12 (Awareness Day) Update; 3. USA budget hearings: clarification; 4. Networking News.

Indexed or abstracted: The last issue of each half-year contains an index of the issues for that half-year.

Copyright statement: Copyright (c) 1993 by Roger Burns. Permission is granted to excerpt this document if the source (CFS-NEWS) is cited. Permission is also granted to reproduce the entirety of this document unaltered. This notice does not diminish the rights of others whose copyrighted material as so noted may be quoted herein. Note that Fido and Fidonet are registered marks of Tom Jennings and Fido Software.

How to access: Send the command SUB CFS-NEWS <your> <name> to the Internet address LISTSERV@LIST.NIH.GOV or to BITNET address LISTSERV@NIHLIST

Access policy: Subscriptions are open to all.

How to unsubscribe: Send the command UNSUB CFS-NEWS to either of the LISTSERV addresses described above.

How to submit: cfs-news@list.nih.gov

Archives: Internet/BITNET: Send command GET CFS-NEWS ### where ### = 001 for issue # 1, = 002 for issue #2, etc., to the Albany LISTSERV at address LISTSERV@ALBNYDH2 on BITNET or Internet address LISTSERV%ALBNYDH2.BITNET@ALBANY.EDU. Fidonet: can be FREQ'd from node 1:279/14 or dial Project ENABLE BBS, telephone 1-304-766-7842, file area 22.

Other systems: Compuserve, GOODHEALTH forum, filenames CFSNEW.### where ### = 001 etc.; GEnie, page 970, file area 18; USA CFIDS/CFS BBS, telephone 1-207-623-8486, file area H; Tucson CFS BBS, telephone 1-602-790-7420; Shaking Hands BBS (Britain), telephone 44-252-626233.

Related files: There are many files about CFS available at the Albany LISTSERV described above. Send the command GET CFS-D FILELIST by e-mail to the LISTSERV address in order to obtain a listing of files currently available. There are also many CFS files available at the Project ENABLE BBS in file area 22, telephone 1-304-766-7842.

Additional information: Note Internet lists CFS-L (general discussion), CFS-D (notice of updates to CFS information files at Albany LISTSERV), and CFS-MED (medical discussion). The file CFS-RES.TXT describes most electronic sources of CFS information. Send the command GET CFS-RES TXT to the Albany LISTSERV (addresses given above under "Back issues" section); also as filename CFS-RES.TXT on Project Enable BBS (see above); filename CFSRES.TXT on Compuserve's GOODHEALTH forum.

CHAOS CORNER

Description: Chaos Corner contains random pieces of information I have found interesting during the time I spend roaming the Internet. Sometimes I give pointers to files available via ftp, other times I supply files on request (it's a way to get feedback on what people find interesting).

Subjects covered: computer hardware and software; Internet; telecommunications; science and technology

Net address for operations: chaos-request@pelican.cit.cornell.edu

Net address for questions or submissions: chaos-request@pelican.cit.cornell.edu

Frequency: Irregular: 3-9 weeks between issues.

Established: June 1991

Number of issues published to date: 24

Method of issuance: Issues are distributed via e-mail, Usenet, and CompuServe.

Available in other media: The issues are faxed to several subscribers upon publication.

Recent issue published: Volume 03 Number 3

Subscribers: 650+

Sponsor: Cornell Information Technologies, 325 CCC, Garden Avenue, Ithaca, NY 14853.

Editorial contact: Bob Cowles (aka Dr. Chaos)
325 CCC, Garden Ave., Ithaca, NY 14853.

Tel: (607) 255-7572

Fax: (607) 254-5222

Internet: Bob.Cowles@cornell.edu

Bitnet: rdc@cornella

Sample contents: Mailbag -- Chaos Corner now World Readable? Mailbag -- Earthquake Information New Job Titles Amateur Radio Information available Ham Radio CD-ROm available and Other CD-ROMs Trying to locate files? - New version of Xarchie available Sound Blaster support and Internet Talk Radio WUARCHIVE ftp Server is available THE - a free clone of Xedit or Kedit Maps of the Internet and other places Want to know more about Fractals? -- Get the Fractal FAQ IBM MONITOR REPAIR: Models 8512, 8513, ... Would you like to visit an Electronic Art Gallery? List of Bulletin Board Systems accessible from the Internet The Official Word from the White House Answer to the question, "What is the Internet?" Special until July 1! Quality PC Utilities Wrapup of V03 N03.

Indexed or abstracted: Each year I have published a text and PostScript version of the collected issues for the year, along with an index, in both electronic (free) and hardcopy ($3) form. The index for the year's issues is also available as a separate file.

Copyright statement: Copyright 1993 by Robert D. Cowles. Permission is hereby granted to republish complete issues in unaltered form. Republication of partial issues must reference source and state that subscriptions to Chaos Corner are available (free) by sending electronic mail to chaos-request@pelican.cit.cornell.edu.

How to access: E-mail to chaos-request@pelican.cit.cornell.edu

How to unsubscribe: E-mail to chaos-request@pelican.cit.cornell.edu

How to submit: E-mail to chaos-request@pelican.cit.cornell.edu

Archives: Yes, all texts are available. Apply to contact name above for more information.

Related files: Many files referenced in the earier volumes are still available by request. All back issues are available via anonymous ftp.

Gopher accessibility: Gopher and WAIS availability for searching for individual articles is expected by the end of the summer.

CHAOS DIGEST (CHAOSD)

Description: Chaos Digest covers computer-related activities in French-speaking countries.

Subjects covered: computer hardware and software; telecommunications; French language and literature

Frequency: Weekly

Established: 1993

Method of issuance: Issues emailed to subscribers as published.

Journal refereed: No

Editorial contact: Jean-Bernard Condat

Chaos Computer Club France, B.P. 8005, 69351, Lyon cedex 08, France.

Tel: +33 1 47874083

Fax: +33 1 47877070

Internet: jbcondat@attmail.com

How to access: Send email message to jbcondat@attmail.com

CHE ELECTRONIC NEWSLETTER

Description: The ChE Electronic Newsletter covers topics related to chemical engineering.

Subjects covered: chemical engineering; chemistry

Frequency: Twice monthly

Established: 1991

Method of issuance: Issues emailed to subscribers as published.

Journal refereed: No

Editorial contact: Dr. Martyn S. Ray

Curtin University of Technology, GPO Box U1987, Perth 6001, Western Australia.

Tel: 09-351-77-2

Fax: 09-351-2681

Internet: trayms@cc.curtin.edu.au

How to access: Send email to trayms@cc.curtin.edu.au

CHEM-ENG

Description: CHEM-ENG is an electronic journal on chemical engineering.

Subjects covered: chemistry

Editorial contact: Martyn Ray

Internet: trayms@cc.curtin.edu.au

How to access: Send email message to trayms@cc.curtin.edu.au

How to submit: Send email message to trayms@cc.curtin.edu.au

CHILE NEWS DATABASE

Description: The Chile News Database is a digest of news from Chile.

Subjects covered: Chile; current events; political science

Method of issuance: Issues mailed via Telnet

Journal refereed: No

How to access: Telnet to pucc.princeton.edu. Logon: folio.

CHINA NEWS DIGEST

Description: The China News Digest covers contemporary Chinese political and cultural life.

Subjects covered: China

Frequency: Weekly

Established: June 1989

Method of issuance: Issues are emailed to subscribers as published.

Journal refereed: No

Editorial contact: Zuofeng Li cnd-editor@sdsc.edu

cnd-manager@sdsc.edu

cnd-tech@sdsc.edu

cnd-cm@sdsc.edu

How to access: Send the message SUBSCRIBE CHINA-ND to listserv@kentvm.bitnet

Related files: A companion discussion list, CCMAN-L is available listserv@uga.uga.edu

Additional information: Additional editors: Wei Lin, Chuseng Lin, and Ming Zhang.

CHIP Q POLITICAL, ENVIRONMENTAL, ECONOMIC AND HUMAN RIGHTS NEWS CHILE INFORMATION PROJECT

Description: CHIP is an electronic publication focusing on political and social developments in Chile.

Subjects covered: Chile; political science

Frequency: Daily

Established: 1990

Method of issuance: Issues are emailed to subscribers as published.

Journal refereed: No.

Editorial contact: Steve Anderson

P.O. Box 53331, Central Post Office, Santiago, Chile.

Tel: (562)777-5376

Fax: (562)735-2267

Internet: anderson %chip.mic.cl@cunyvm.cuny.edu

How to access: Send email to: anderson@chip.mic.cl or uchdcc!chip!anderson@unnet.uu.net or anderson%dchip.mic.cl@cunyvm.cuny.edu

CHRISTIAN LIFE IN THE COMPUTER ERA

Description: Christian LIFE is an electronic monthly newsletter focusing on modern life.

Subjects covered: religion; computer science; cultural studies

Frequency: Monthly

Established: 1992

Method of issuance: Issues are emailed to subscribers as published.
Journal refereed: No
Editorial contact: Tony McGregor
Internet: tony.mcgregor@rdt.monash.edu.au
How to access: Send email to
tony.mcgregor@rdt.monash.edu.au

CITATIONS FOR SERIAL LITERATURE
ISSN: 1061-7434
Description: Citations for Serial Literature was created in February 1992 with a threefold purpose: to identify literature related to the serial information chain, to disseminate this information in a timely manner, and to create an index in this field with electronic searching capabilities. To achieve these goals, Citations for Serial Literature publishes tables of contents, and abstracts when they are available, for a variety of journals which address issues of concern to serials librarians, vendors, and publishers.
Subjects covered: library and information science; serials librarianship; scholarly communication
Net address for operations: listserv@mitvma or listserv@mitvma.mit.edu
Net address for questions or submissions: sercites@mitvma, sercites@mitvma.mit.edu, or mgeller@athena.mit.edu
Frequency: Irregular
Established: February 20, 1992
Number of issues published to date: 43
Method of issuance: Issues are distributed through the Bitnet Listserv.
Recent issue published: Vol. 2, No. 6 (May 9, 1993)
Subscribers: 374
Editorial contact: Marilyn Geller
MIT Libraries, Room 14E-210A, Cambridge, MA 02139-4307.
Tel: (617) 253-0587
Fax: (617) 253-2464
Internet: mgeller@athena.mit.edu
Sample contents: Complete tables of contents are included for the following titles: Advances in Serials Management; Newsletter on Serials Pricing Issues; Serials; and Serials Review. In addition, selective table of contents are included for the following titles: Information Standards Quarterly; Issues in Science and Technology Librarianship; and Library Acquisitions: Practice and Theory. The editor is always interested in discussing the inclusion of other titles in an effort to provide more comprehensive coverage.
Review: ''All complete and selective table of contents materials in Citations for Serial Literature are reproduced with the permission of the original publisher. The section of this ejournal entitled 'Serendipitous citings' includes relevant citations from journals not generally indexed here. These citations are contributed by users.''
How to access: Send a message to listserv@mitvma or listserv@mitvma.mit.edu that reads: subscribe sercites <your name>
Access policy: Subscription is open to anyone with access to the Internet or BITNET.
How to unsubscribe: Send a message to listserv@mitvma or listserv@mitvma.mit.edu that reads: unsubscribe sercites
How to submit: sercites@mitvma, sercites@mitvma.mit.edu, or mgeller@athena.mit.edu
Submission policy: Citations for Serial Literature has a section entitled ''Serendipitous citings'' which includes relevant citations from journals not generally covered in this index. Everyone is welcome to contribute to this section. In addition, editors and publishers of journals related to the serials information chain who are interested in participating in this project, are encouraged to contact the editor to discuss the possibility.
Gopher accessibility: Complete holdings available in the North Carolina State University Gopher (dewey.lib.ncsu.edu)

CLASS FOUR RELAY MAGAZINE
Description: Class Four Relay Magazine is a publication for the relay community.
Subjects covered: computer science; information technology
Editorial contact: Joey J. Stanford
Internet: stjs@vm.marist.edu
Bitnet: stjs@marist
How to access: Send email message to stjs@vm.marist.edu

CLIONET
Description: CLIONET is an Australian history monthly ejournal.
Subjects covered: Australia; history
Net address for operations: hnsource.cc.ukans.edu
Frequency: Monthly
How to access: Telnet to the HNSource history gopher at the University of Kansas: telnet to hnsource.cc.ukans.edu, and try the menu option HNSOURCE DOCUMENTS ARCHIVE

COMP-SCI@ILNCRD
Description: COMP-SCI@ILNCRD is an electronic newsletter covering computer science in Israel.
Subjects covered: computer science
Editorial contact: Joseph van Zwaren
Bitnet: jo@ilncrd
How to access: Send subscribe message to listserv@taunivm or listserv@taunivm.tau.ac.il
How to unsubscribe: Send unsubscribe message to listserv@taunivm or listserv@taunivm.tau.ac.il

COMPU-ECON (COMPUTATIONAL ECONOMICS)
ISSN: 0927-7099
Description: COMPU-ECON is an electronic journal covering all fields of numerical analysis in economics.
Subjects covered: economics; numerical analysis; econometrics
Net address for operations: listserv@hasara11.bitnet
Net address for questions or submissions: csem@sara.nl
Frequency: quarterly
Established: 1988
Issues are announced through csemlist, gopher,sara.nl
Available in other media: Issues are published also in aper + postscript (in preparation)
Recent issue published: Volume 6
Fee: $216 library $50 private
Commercial organization: Kluwer Academic
Journal refereed: Yes, peer reviewed.
Editorial contact: Hans Amman
Dept Macroeconomics, University of Amsterdam, Roeterstraat 11, E1 911,

1018 WB Amsterdam, the Netherlands
Tel: 31-20-5254203
Fax: 31-20-5255280
Internet: amman@sara.nl
Bitnet: a608hans@hasara11
Technical contact: same as above
Indexed or abstracted: Journal Economic Lit.
Copyright statement: Kluwer Academic Publishers, the Netherlands
How to access: Send mail to amman@sara.nl
How to unsubscribe: Send mail to amman@sara.nl
How to submit: Send mail to amman@sara.nl
Submission policy: Send mail to amman@sara.nl
Archives: Yes, only on paper. Contact amman@sara.nl
Gopher accessibility: gopher.sara.nl

COMPUTER SCIENCE CENTER LINK

Description: Computer Science Center Link discusses academic and enterprise computing.
Subjects covered: colleges and universities; telecommunications; computer hardware and software; academic computing
Frequency: Five times yearly
Method of issuance: Issues are emailed to subscribers as published.
Host: University of Maryland
Journal refereed: No
How to access: Send mail to Link Editor, Computer Science Center, University of Maryland, College Park, MD 20742.

COMPUTER UNDERGROUND DIGEST (CUD OR CU-DIGEST)

ISSN: 1004-042X
Description: Computer Underground Digest is an open forum dedicated to sharing information among computerists and to the presentation and debate of diverse views.
Subjects covered: computer science; information technology
Frequency: Weekly
Established: 1990
Method of issuance: Issues are emailed to subscribers as published. Also available as a Usenet newsgroup, or through commercial networks, and bulletin boards.
Journal refereed: No
Editorial contact: Jim Thomas
Department of Sociology, NIU, DeKalb, IL 60115.
Internet: tk0jut2@mvs.cso.niu.edu
Bitnet: TK0JUT2@NIU.BITNET
How to access: Send an email message to tk0jut2@mvs.cso.niu.edu or cudigest@mindvox.phantom.com
Gopher accessibility: Gopher accessible at: etext.archive.umich.edu
Additional information: Additional editor: Gordon Meyer

COMPUTING AND NETWORK NEWS

Description: Computing and Network News covers electronic networking and use of computers at Kansas State University.
Subjects covered: Kansas State University; computer hardware and software; electronic networking; information technology
Frequency: Monthly
Established: 1991

Method of issuance: Issues are emailed to subscribers as published.
Host: Kansas State University
Journal refereed: No
Editorial contact: Betsy Edwards
Internet: betsy@ksuvm.bitnet, betsy@ksuvm.ksu.edu
How to access: Send an email to editor@ksuvm.bitnet or editor@ksuvm.ksu.edu

COMPUTISTS' COMMUNIQUE

Description: Computists' International is a mutual-aid association for AI/IS/CS researchers. The Communique is a weekly online news service, available to members at no additional charge. Topics covered include artificial intelligence research, advanced algorithms, research news, grant sources, job ads, and resource leads.
Subjects covered: computer hardware and software; artificial intelligence
Net address for operations: laws@ai.sri.com
Net address for questions or submissions: laws@ai.sri.com
Established: April 1, 1991
Available in other media: Issues are also available in print.
Fee: Membership is $135 for professionals, $55 for students, free to unemployed computer scientists; group rates follow a log2 rule. 50% discount outside the US. 10% discount on renewals. Either prepaid or billed.
Commercial organization: Computists International, 4064 Sutherland Drive, Palo Alto, CA 94303.
Editorial contact: Dr. Kenneth I. Laws
Computists International, 4064 Sutherland Drive, Palo Alto, CA 94303.
Tel: (415) 493-7390
Internet: laws@ai.sri.com
Copyright statement: Members are permitted to print a copy of each Communique and to keep a backup series. Additional copies may be shared with students or others whom you directly mentor, and occasional copies may be circulated for recruiting purposes. Occasional articles may be clipped if attribution is given. You may also pass around your own copy of the Communique as you would any printed newsletter, so long as additional copies are not made. (Don't post it to an electronic bboard, please, unless you've arranged group membership.)
Archives: Back issues of the news weekly are available.
Related files: Additional job ads and research software announcements related to this service are available by request from contact above.
Additional information: There is a full money-back guarantee. Interested persons may receive a free sample issue of Computists' Communique.

COND-MAT@BABBAGE.SISSA.IT

Description: cond-mat@babbage.sissa.it is an electronic journal on condensed matter and related topics.
Subjects covered: physics

CONSORTIUM UPDATE

Description: A newsletter which publishes current events regarding the SPIRES Consortium.
Subjects covered: SPIRES Consortium
Frequency: Quarterly

Method of issuance: Issues are emailed to subscribers as published.
Journal refereed: No
SPIRES Consortium Office, 115 Polya Hall, Stanford University, Stanford, CA 94305.
Internet: consortium@forsythe.stanford.edu, consortium@stanford.bitnet

COPT-NET NEWSLETTER

Description: The Copt-Net Newsletter covers topics related to the Coptic Orthodox Church.
Subjects covered: religion; Coptic Orthodox Church
Frequency: Irregular
Established: 1992
Method of issuance: Issues are emailed to subscribers as published. Also accessible via Gopher; apply to editor for more information.
Journal refereed: Yes
Editorial contact: Amgad Bassili
Internet: bassili@cs.arizona.edu
How to access: Send a message to gopher.cic.net or FTP to cs.bu.edu with the directory: /CN/newsletters/

CORE

ISSN: 1062-6697
Description: CORE is an electronic journal of poetry, fiction, essays, and criticism.
Subjects covered: language and literature; poetry
Net address for operations: core-journal@eff.org
Net address for questions or submissions: core-journals@eff.org
Frequency: Monthly, roughly. Sometimes a month is skipped if I don't have enough material.
Established: August 1991
Number of issues published to date: 12
Method of issuance: Issues available via e-mail, ftp, gopher, newsgroups. Issue availability is announced on rec.arts.books, rec.arts.poems, alt.prose, misc.writing, rec.mag, alt.zine.
Available in other media: No
Recent issue published: Volume 2, Number 4
Subscribers: 300
Journal refereed: No
Editorial contact: Rita Rouvalis
30 Norfolk St., Cambridge, MA 02139
Tel: (617) 864-1440
Internet: rita@village.com; rita@eff.org; rita@world.std.com
Technical contact: Rita Rouvalis
30 Norfolk St., Cambridge, MA 02139
Tel: (617) 864-1440
Sample contents: 9 sestinas
Indexed or abstracted: ftp.eff.org
Copyright statement: Please feel free to reproduce CORE in its entirety only throughout Cyberspace. To reproduce articles individually, please contact the author.
How to access: Send e-mail to core-journal@eff.org; including your e-mail address on a line by itself at the left margin is appreciated.
Access policy: Subscriptions open to anyone.
How to unsubscribe: Send e-mail to core-journal@eff.org to unsubscribe
Submission policy: No more than 3 poems or one work of prose at a time, please. Must be in ASCII, without tabs.

Archives: Back issues are available via anonymous ftp from ftp.eff.org from the /pub/journals directory, and in the Electronic Frontier Foundation Gopher Space on the Instant Karma Zine Stand.
Gopher accessibility: Gopher available through Electronic Frontier
Foundation/ Instant Karma Zine Stand.

COSMIC UPDATE

Description: Cosmic Update provides information on new NASA software.
Subjects covered: NASA; computer hardware and software; astronomy; space and space exploration
Frequency: Monthly
Established: 1993
Method of issuance: Issues are emailed to subscribers as published.
Journal refereed: No
COSMIC, University of Georgia, 382 E. Broad Street, Athens, GA 30602.
Tel: (404) 542-3265
Fax: (404) 542-4807
Internet: service@cossack.cosmic.uga.edu
How to access: Send email to service@cossack.cosmic.uga.edu

COUSINS

Description: Cousins is an electronic journal of alternative literature.
Subjects covered: alternative literature
How to access: Gopher accessible at: etext.archive.umich.edu

CPSR/PDX NEWSLETTER

Description: The CPRS/PDX Newsletter is sponsored by Computer Professionals for Social Responsibility.
Subjects covered: computer science; computer hardware and software
Frequency: Monthly
Established: 1988
Method of issuance: Issues are emailed to subscribers as published.
Journal refereed: No
Editorial contact: Erik Nilsson
Internet: erikn@boa.mitron.tek.com
How to access: Send message to erikn@boa.mitron.tek.com

CRASH

Description: Crash is a ''guide to traveling through the underground, featuring alternative travel stories, hints, and tips.''
Subjects covered: travel and tourism; alternative literature
Editorial contact: John Labovitz
Internet: johnl@netcom.com
How to access: ftp to netcom.com and change directory to /pub/johnl/zines/crash

CRTNET (COMMUNICATION RESEARCH AND THEORY NETWORK)

Description: CRTNET (Communication Research and Theory Network), an electronic journal, is an open forum for discussion

among members on subjects relevant to the study of human communication, speech, and rhetoric. We also publish bulletins, announcements, documents, research queries, and so on.
Subjects covered: communications; speech studies; rhetoric
Net address for operations: LISTSERV@PSUVM.BITNET
Established: July 1985
Subscribers: 950
Editorial contact: Tom Benson
Edwin Erle Sparks Professor of Rhetoric Dept. of Speech Communication, 227 Sparks Building, Penn State University, University Park, PA 16802 USA
Tel: (814) 238-5277 (home); (814) 865-4201 (office); (814) 865-3461 (secretary)
Fax: 814-863-7986
Internet: t3b@psuvm.psu.edu
Bitnet: T3B@PSUVM
Technical contact: Bill Verity
Bitnet: WHV@PSUVM
How to access: TELL LISTSERV@PSUVM SUB CRTNET <firstname> <lastname> or send email to CRTNET@PSUVM requesting a subscription; give full name and email address.
Access policy: All are welcome to subscribe.
How to unsubscribe: TELL LISTSERV@PSUVM UNSUB CRTNET
How to submit: Send email note to CRTNET@PSUVM or to the editor.
Submission policy: All are welcome to participate, within general guidelines of relevance and civility. Please include a clear SUBJECT: line; no left margin; space between paragraphs; 0-60 column lines; include author's name and email address at bottom of message.
Archives: Past issues are archived on LISTSERV@PSUVM and by COMSERVE@RPITSVM.

CTHEORY--VIRTUAL REVIEW OF BOOKS FOR POST-MODERN THEORY

Description: CTHEORY is a new international, electronic review of books on theory, technology and culture. Reviews are posted monthly of key books in contemporary discourse as well as theorisations of major 'event-scenes' in the mediascape. Editors and contributors include: Kathy Acker, Jean Baudrillard, Bruce Sterling, Arthur and Marilouise Kroker, Deena and Michael Weinstein. CTHEORY will also offer the possibility of interactive discussions among its subscribers in the electronic theory 'sim-posium/salon.'
Subjects covered: science and technology; computer science; book reviews
How to access: Send email to: LISTSERV@VM1.MCGILL.CA with text body: "SUBSCRIBE CTHEORY <full-name>

CTT-DIGEST

Description: ctt-Digest is a compilation of postings from the Usenet newsgroup comp.text.tex, dealing with TEX-related topics.
Subjects covered: computer science; computer hardware and software
Frequency: Daily
Method of issuance: Issues are emailed to subscribers as published.
Journal refereed: No
Editorial contact: George D. Greenwade

Department of Economics and Business Analysis, College of Business Administration, P.O. Box 2118, Sam Houston State University, Huntsville, TX 77341.
Tel: (409) 294-1266
Fax: (409) 294-3612
Internet: bed__gdg@shsu
Bitnet: bed__gdg@shsu.edu
How to access: Send the message SUBSCRIBE CTT-DIGEST to listserv@shsu.bitnet or listserv@shsu.edu

CULT OF THE DEAD COW

Description: Cult of the Dead Cow is an electronic newsletter publishing a wide variety of alternative literature.
Subjects covered: poetry; American literature and language
Frequency: Irregular
Method of issuance: Issues are emailed to subscribers as published.
Journal refereed: No
Editorial contact: Paul Leonard
Internet: obscure@mindvox.phantom.com
How to access: Send message to obscure@mindvox.phantom.com

CURRENT CITES

ISSN: 1060-2356
Description: Current Cites scans over 30 journals in library and information technology for selected articles on optical disk technologies, computer networks and networking, information transfer, expert systems and artificial intelligence, electronic publishing, and hypermedia and multimedia. Brief annotations accompany most of the citations.
Subjects covered: optical disk technologies; electronic publishing; artificial intelligence; hypermedia
Net address for operations: drobison@library.berkeley.edu and/or LISTSERV@UHUPVM1.BITNET
Frequency: Monthly
Established: August 1990
Number of issues published to date: 34
Method of issuance: New issues are sent to subscribers via email as published. Issues are reprinted in Computers in Libraries magazine.
Recent issue published: vol. 4, no.5
Subscribers: 185 direct, 6,140 via PACS-L, and 1,260 via PACS-P
Sponsor: Information Systems Instruction & Support, The Library, The University of California at Berkeley, Berkeley, CA 94720
Journal refereed: No
Editorial contact: David F. W. Robison
ISIS Rm. 130 Main Library UC Berkeley Berkeley, CA 94720
Tel: (510) 643-9494
Fax: (510) 643-6135
Internet: drobison@library.berkeley.edu
Bitnet: drobison@ucblibra
Technical contact: Same as above
Copyright statement: Copyright (C) 1993 by the Library, University of California, Berkeley. All rights reserved. All product names are trademarks or registered trademarks of their respective holders. Mention of a product in this publication does not necessarily imply endorsement of the product. Copying is permitted for noncommercial use by computerized bulletin board/conference systems, individual scholars, and libraries. Libraries

are authorized to add the journal to their collections at no cost. This message must appear on copied material. All commercial use requires permission from the editor, who may be reached in the following ways: drobison@library.berkeley.edu // drobison@ucblibra // (510)643-9494

How to access: Send an e-mail message to the editor: drobison@library.berkeley.edu // drobison@ucblibra

Access policy: Open to anyone.

How to unsubscribe: Send an e-mail message to the editor: drobison@library.berkeley.edu // drobison@ucblibra

How to submit: Send an e-mail message to the editor: drobison@library.berkeley.edu // drobison@ucblibra

Submission policy: Submissions accepted for review. We attempt to answer all questions.

Archives: Yes, via ftp (ftp.lib.berkeley.edu in directory /pub/ Current.Cites), WAIS, and Gopher.

Gopher accessibility: Yes

WAIS accessibility: Yes

WorldWideWeb accessibility: Yes

CYBERSPACE VANGUARD MAGAZINE

Description: Cyberspace Vanguard Magazine published information of interest to science fiction readers and writers.

Subjects covered: science fiction; current events; alternative literature

Frequency: Monthly

Established: January 1993

Method of issuance: Issues are emailed to subscribers as published.

Journal refereed: No

Editorial contact: T. J. Goldstein
Cyberspace Vanguard, P.O. Box 25704, Garfield Heights, OH 44125.

Internet: cn577@Cleveland.Freenet.Edu or tlg4@po.cwru.edu

How to access: Send email to cn577@Cleveland.Freenet.edu

Related files: Hardcopies of the magazine are available from: P.O. Box 25704, Garfield Hts. OH 44125.

DARGONZINE Q: THE MAGAZINE OF THE DARGON PROJECT

Description: Dargonzine publishes stories related to the multiple-authored Dargon Project, a fantasy collaboration.

Subjects covered: fantasy fiction

Frequency: Irregular

Established: 1988

Method of issuance: Issues are emailed to subscribers as published.

Journal refereed: No

Editorial contact: Dafydd

Bitnet: whit@duvm.bitnet

How to access: Send email to whit@duvm.bitnet

DATA ENTRIES

Description: DATA ENTRIES is an electronic newsletter covering the Mary Evelyn Glagg-Huey Library in Texas. Today, the Woman's Collection, housed at the Mary Evelyn Blagg-Huey Library on the TWU campus, contains more than 42,000 books and periodicals, 2500 feet of manuscript and archival records, and approximately 20,000 photographs. In addition, the library acquires many of the large microfilm editions of manuscripts

and printed collections published by other libraries and boasts a woman's clothing and textile collection.

Subjects covered: women's studies; library and information science

Frequency: Irregular

Established: 1992

Method of issuance: Issues are emailed to subscribers as published.

Host: Mary Evelyn Blagg-Huey Library, Denton, TX

Journal refereed: No

Editorial contact: Joe Natale

Internet: s__natale@twu, s__natale@twu.edu

How to access: Send message to s__natale@twu or s__ natale@twu.edu

Related files: To access the Texas Woman's University Library Collections via Internet: 1. TELNET to TWU.EDU; 2. At the USERNAME: prompt enter IRIS; 3. At the login: prompt press ENTER; 4. At the ONLINE CATALOG Menu enter 1; To exit enter E from the Main Menu, then enter 3.

Additional information: TWU, the largest university primarily for women in the U.S, has approximately 10,000 students and is located 35 miles north of the Dallas-Fort Worth metroplex. The Library houses more than three-quarters of a million items. For questions about the Woman's Collection, contact Dawn Letson 817-898-3754 or at s__letson@twu.edu (Internet).

DATELINE: STARFLEET

Description: Dateline-Starfleet publishes information of interest to fans of Star Trek.

Subjects covered: Star Trek; science fiction

Frequency: Monthly

Established: 1990

Method of issuance: Available from the America Online computer network.

Journal refereed: No

Editorial contact: Bill Mason

Internet: data1701d@al1.com

How to access: FTP to sumex-aim.stanford.edu

DDN MANAGEMENT BULLETIN

Description: DDN Management Bulletin provides information to administrators of Defense Data Network installations.

Subjects covered: military studies; computer hardware and software; information technology

Frequency: Irregular

Established: 1984

Method of issuance: Issues are vailable via FTP.

Host: Defense Data Network Information Center

Journal refereed: No

DDN Network Info Center

Tel: (800) 365-3642

Internet: nic@nic.ddn.mil

DECNEWS FOR EDUCATION AND RESEARCH

Description: DECNEWS for Education and Research is a monthly electronic publication from Digital Equipment Corp.'s Education Business Unit for the education and research communities worldwide. Included are product announcements, customer news, and resource information on courses, the Internet, etc.

Subjects covered: computer hardware and software; Digital Equipment Corporation; education
Net address for operations: Listserv@ubvm.cc.buffalo.edu
Net address for questions or submissions:
decnews@akocoa.enet.dec.com
Frequency: Monthly
Established: March 1992
Number of issues published to date: 24+
Method of issuance: Issues are sent via Internet and Bitnet subscription lists. Issues are announced on Digital newsgroups.
Recent issue published: Vol 2, No. 6
Subscribers: 3000+
Sponsor: Digital Equipment Corp.
Commercial organization: Yes.
Editorial contact: Betsy Carroll
50 Nagog Park, AK02-2/D8, Acton, MA 01720
Tel: (508) 264-7698
Internet: bcarroll@akocoa.enet.dec.com
Copyright statement: Copyright 1993 by Digital Equipment Corporation.
How to access: Send a message to
Listserv@ubvm.cc.buffalo.edu.
Access policy: DECNEWS is open to all.
How to unsubscribe: Send the following message to
listserv@ubvm.cc.buffalo.edu delete decnews firstname lastname
How to submit: bcarroll@akocoa.enet.dec.com
Archives: Yes, including WorldWideWeb (WWW) information server access; instructions provided at the end of each issue.
Related files: Full text documents such as press releases, product fact sheets, information sheet, white papers, etc., are available.

DELAWARE VALLEY RAIL PASSENGER

Description: Delaware Valley Rail Passenger offers information on railroading and transportation in the greater Philadelphia vicinity.
Subjects covered: railroads; transportation
Frequency: Monthly
Established: 1992
Host: Delaware Valley Association of Railroad Passengers
Journal refereed: No
Editorial contact: Matthew Mitchell
Internet: iekp898@tjuvm.bitnet, iekp898@tjuvm.tju.edu
How to access: Send the message RINDEX RAILROADS to
listserv@cunyvm

DEVELOPNET NEWS

Description: DevelopNet News is an electronic newsletter covering technology transfer.
Subjects covered: technology transfer; computer hardware and software; information technology
Frequency: Monthly
Method of issuance: Issues are emailed to subscribers as published.
Host: Volunteers in Technical Assistance
Journal refereed: No
Editorial contact: R.R. Ronkin
Internet: vita@gmuvax.gmu.edu
Bitnet: vita@gmuvax
How to access: Send email to vita@gmuvax or
vita@gmuvax.gmu.edu

DISASTER RESEARCH

Description: Disaster Research is an electronic publication covering information related to disasters and hazards.
Subjects covered: disaster studies
Frequency: Monthly or more frequently
Established: 1989
Method of issuance: Issues are mailserved to subscribers.
Journal refereed: No
Editorial contact: David Butler
Natural Hazards Information Center, IBS #6, Campus Box 482, University of Colorado, Boulder, CO 80309-0482.
Tel: (303) 492-6818
Fax: (303) 492-6924
Internet: hazards@vaxf.colorado.edu
How to access: Send the message SUBSCRIBE HAZARDS to mailserv@colorado or mailserv@vaxf.colorado.edu

DISTANCE EDUCATION ONLINE SYMPOSIUM (DEOSNEWS)

ISSN: 1062-9416
Description: Distance Education Online Symposium is an electronic publication covering a range of topcs related to distance education and technology.
Subjects covered: distance education; computer-assisted instruction (CAI); information technology
Frequency: Biweekly
Established: April 25, 1991
Method of issuance: Issues are emailed to subscribers as published.
Host: American Center for the Study of Distance Education, Pennsylvania State University.
Journal refereed: No
Editorial contact: Morten Flate Paulsen
NKI, Box 111, 1341 Bekkestua, Norway.
Internet: morten@nki.no
How to access: Send the message SUBSCRIBE DEOSNEWS to listserv@psuvm.psu.edu

DISTED: THE ONLINE JOURNAL OF DISTANCE EDUCATION

Description: DISTED is an electronic journal covering topics related to distance education, computer-mediated learning, and electronic networking.
Subjects covered: education; distance education; telecommunications
Net address for operations: LISTSERV@UWAVM.Bitnet
Net address for questions or submissions:
JADIST@ALASKA.Bitnet
Editorial contact: Jason B. Ohler
Bitnet: JFJBO@ALASKA.Bitnet
Technical contact: Paul J. Coffin
Bitnet: SPJC@ALASKA.Bitnet
How to access: Send the email message SUB DISTED your_full_name to LISTSERV@UWAVM.Bitnet
How to unsubscribe: Send the email message UNSUB DISTED your_full_name to LISTSERV@UWAVM.Bitnet

DONOSY (ENGLISH EDITION)

ISSN: 1059-4027
Description: Donosy (English edition) is an electronic newsletter covering Polish news and cultural events.
Subjects covered: Polish language and literature; international studies; political science; cultural studies
Net address for operations: donosy@fuw.edu.pl
Net address for questions or submissions: przemek@ndcvx.cc.nd.edu
Frequency: Weekly
Established: 1990
Number of issues published to date: 300
Method of issuance: Issues are sent via e-mail to the subscription list.
Recent issue published: 1083-1088 (the issue of the English version covers 6 editions of the Polish version, and the issue numbering reflects that).
Subscribers: 340
Sponsor: Warsaw University, Notre Dame University
Editorial contact: Xawery Stojda
Bajonska 3, 03-963 Warszawa
Tel: (48-22) 17 79 85
Internet: donosy@fuw.edu.p
Technical contact: Przemek Klosowski
Internet: przemek@ndcvx.cc.nd.edu
How to access: Contact przemek@ndcvx.cc.nd.edu
Archives: Archives are available using anonymous ftp at tirana.berkeley.edu

DONOSY (POLISH EDITION)

ISSN: 0867-6860
Description: Donosy (Polish edition) is an electronic daily newsletter about all topics related to Poland and Polish affairs. "Donosy" are texts entirely written in Polish.
Subjects covered: Polish language and literature; international studies; political science; cultural studies
Net address for operations: donosy@fuw.edu.pl
Net address for questions or submissions: donosy@fuw.edu.pl
Frequency: Daily (except Sundays)
Established: August 1989
Number of issues published to date: 1099
Method of issuance: Issues are sent via Listerv DISTRIBUTE system.
Available in other media: Yes, Donosy are read in Polish radio programmes, in many Polish emigration centers. In some places Donosy are printed. Reprints of Donosy are the constant parts of several Polish-language journals and newspapers abroad.
Subscribers: 4032 e-mail; about 5000 printed copies
Sponsor: Warsaw University, Physics Department
Editorial contact: Kwasery Stojda
Gorczewska 88a m 11 PL-01-117 Warsaw
Tel: (48-22) 17 79 85
Internet: xawer@fuw.edu.pl Bitnet
Technical contact: Michal Jankowski
Tel: (048) (2) 628-30-31 x 198
Internet: michalj@fuw.edu.pl
Sample contents: Special issue about fall of the Polish government.
Indexed or abstracted: Library of Congress, Biblioteka Narodowa (Polish National Library).
Copyright statement: Copyright (c) 1993 by Ksawery Stojda "Donosy" objete sa copyrightem. Regularne FORWARD-

owanie bez zgody redakcji zabronione. Dopuszczamy obrot pojedynczymi numerami archiwalnymi.
How to access: Send mail to donosy@fuw.edu.pl and wait patiently several days. No automatic sub/unsub procedures are available.
How to unsubscribe: Send an email message to donosy@fuw.edu.pl and wait patiently several days. No automatic sub/unsub procedures are available.
How to submit: Send an email message to donosy@fuw.edu.pl and wait patiently several days. No automatic sub/unsub procedures are available.
Archives: Available through e-mail (on request.)
Related files: HEPNET: 13411::DUA1:[XAWER.DONOSY.DONOSYyy]yymmdd.nnn[n] where yy = year, mm = month, dd = day, nnn/nnnn = issue no.

DROSOPHILA INFORMATION NEWSLETTER

Description: Drosophila Information Newsletter covers the biology of drosophila (flies).
Subjects covered: flies; biology; drosophila
Frequency: Quarterly
Established: 1990
Method of issuance: Issues are emailed to subscribers as published.
Journal refereed: No
Editorial contact: Kathy Matthews
Department of Biology, Indiana University, Bloomington, IN 47405.
Tel: (812) 855-5782
Fax: (812) 855-2577
Internet: matthewk@ucs.indiana.edu
Bitnet: matthewk@iubacs
How to access: Send the message SUBSCRIBE DIS-L to listserv@iubvm or listserv@iubvm.ucs.indiana.edu

DRUM

Description: Drum is an electronic journal of alternative literature.
Subjects covered: alternative literature
Editorial contact: R. Patrick Jones
Internet: dh644@cleveland.Freenet.edu
How to access: Gopher accessible at: gopher.well.sf.ca.us

DRYDYMALKI

ISSN: 1064-9794
Description: DRYDYMALKI is a compilation of stories from the Polish press.
Subjects covered: Poland; current events
Frequency: Biweekly
Established: 1991
Method of issuance: Issues are emailed to subscribers as published.
Journal refereed: No
Editorial contact: Zbigniew J. Pasek
Internet: zbigniew@engin.umich.edu
How to access: Send email to: zbigniew@engin.umich.edu

DUPONT CIRCLE REPORTER

Description: The Dupont Circle Reporter: An Informal Newsletter for the Federal Depository Library Community covers government documents librarianship and the distribution of documents to depository libraries.
Subjects covered: government information; library and information science
How to access: Subscribers to GOVDOC-L, MAPS-L, or LAW-LIB automatically receive this newsletter.

EDPOLYAR (EDUCATION POLICY ANALYSIS ARCHIVES)

ISSN: 1068-2341
Description: EDPOLYAR is an electronic serial covering policy analysis of education issues.
Subjects covered: education; colleges and universities; administration; comparative education
Net address for operations: LISTSERV@ASUACAD.BITNET
Net address for questions or submissions: Glass@asu.edu
Frequency: Irregular, as articles are published
Established: January 13, 1993
Number of issues published to date: 6
Method of issuance: Through email to subscription lists. Issues are announced on various listservs.
Recent issue published: Vol. 1, No. 6
Subscribers: 700
Sponsor: Arizona State University, Tempe, AZ 85287.
Host: Arizona State University, Tempe, AZ 85287.
Journal refereed: Yes. There is a standing editorial board, and blind reviewng of texts by two board members.
Editorial contact: Gene V. Glass
College of Education, Arizona State University, Tempe, AZ 85287-2411.
Tel: (602) 965-2692
Internet: Glass@asu.edu
Bitnet: Glass@asu
Sample contents: Articles on anti-intellectualism among teachers.
Copyright statement: ''Articles may be reproduced for educational, noncommercial uses.''
How to access: LISTSERV@ASUACAD.BITNET SUB EDPOLYAR name
How to unsubscribe: Send message to LISTSERV@ASUACAD.BITNET SIGNOFF EDPOLYAR
How to submit: Glass@asu.edu
Archives: Send to LISTSERV@ASUACAD.BITNET INDEX EDPOLYAR
Gopher accessibility: Gopher accessible via telnet to INFO.ASU.EDU

EDUPAGE

Description: EDUPAGE is a weekly electronic news digest of the information technology industry as it relates to the field of education.
Subjects covered: education; computer-assisted instruction (CAI); information technology
Frequency: Weekly
Established: 1993
Method of issuance: Issues are emailed to subscribers as published.
Host: EDUCOM, Washington DC
Journal refereed: No

Internet: edupage@educom.edu
How to access: Send a message to: edupage@educom.edu with name, institution name and email address.

EFFECTOR ONLINE

ISSN: 1062-9424
Description: EFFector Online is a publication of the Electronic Fronter Foudation, Inc., covering Internet policy and developments.
Subjects covered: Internet; electronic networking; information technology
Frequency: Semi-monthly
Established: 1990
Method of issuance: Issues are emailed to subscribers as published.
Host: Electronic Frontier Foundation
Journal refereed: No
Electronic Frontier Foundation, 238 Main Street, Cambridge, MA 02142.
Tel: (617) 547-4500
Fax: (617) 547-4520
Internet: editors@eff.org
How to access: FTP to ftp.eff.org
The directory is: /pub/EFF/newsletters/
Send email to: eff-request@eff.org
Also available as USENET newsgroup comp.org.eff.news

EGO PROJECT

Description: Ego Project is an electronic magazine featuring reviews of music recordings, movies, and books.
Subjects covered: music; book reviews; alternative literature
Editorial contact: Corey Nelson
Ego Project, 1717 Monroe #b, Bellingham, WA 98225.
Internet: ieya@byron.well.sf.ca.us
How to access: Send message to ieya@byron.well.sf.ca.us

EJASA (THE ELECTRONIC JOURNAL OF THE ASTRONOMICAL SOCIETY OF THE ATLANTIC)

Description: EJASA (The Electronic Journal of the Astronomical Society of the Atlantic) publishes information on astronomy and space exploration issues.
Subjects covered: astronomy; space and space exploration
Net address for questions or submissions:
klaes@verga.enet.dec.com
Frequency: Irregular
Established: August 1989
Number of issues published to date: 46
Method of issuance: Internet (USENET) space-related newsgroups, some E-Mail Issues are announced on the Internet and through email.
Available in other media: Yes. Hardcopies are mailed on request.
Recent issue published: Volume 4, Number 10 (May 1993)
Subscribers: 70
Sponsor: Astronomical Society of the Atlantic
Host: Astronomical Society of the Atlantic (ASA) P. O. Box 15038 Atlanta, Georgia 30333-9998; asa@chara.gsu.edu; ASA BBS: (404) 321-5904, 300/1200/2400 Baud or telephone the So-

ciety Recording at (404) 264-0451 to leave your address and/or receive the latest Society news.

Journal refereed: Not at present.

Editorial contact: Larry Klaes
95 Fairmont Street, Arlington, MA 02174

Tel: (617) 643-4927

Internet: klaes@verga.enet.dec.com

Sample contents: Fade to White: The Loss of the Night Sky, by Robert Bunge; Recent Soviet Lunar and Planetary Program Revelations, by Andrew J. LePage; by Grand Canyon Star Party, Courtesy of Paul Dickson.

Indexed or abstracted: Yes, at anonymous ASA FTP site chara.gsu.edu (131.96.5.29).

Copyright statement: Articles submitted, unless otherwise stated, become the property of the Astronomical Society of the Atlantic, Incorporated. Though the articles will not be used for profit, they are subject to editing, abridgment, and other changes. Copying or reprinting of the EJASA, in part or in whole, is encouraged, provided clear attribution is made to the Astronomical Society of the Atlantic, the Electronic Journal, and the author(s). Opinions expressed in the EJASA are those of the authors' and not necessarily those of the ASA. This Journal is Copyright (c) 1993 by the Astronomical Society of the Atlantic, Incorporated.

How to access: Either pick up a copy from USENET or write to Larry Klaes at: klaes@verga.enet.dec.com or -...!decwrl!verga.enet.dec.com!klaes or - klaes%verga.dec@decwrl.enet.dec.com or - klaes%verga.enet.dec.com@uunet.uu.net

How to unsubscribe: Same as technical

How to submit: Same as above

Submission policy: Submissions are welcome for consideration.

Archives: Yes, at ASA FTP site (See above)

EJOURNAL

ISSN: 1054-1055

Description: EJournal is an all-electronic, Matrix distributed, peer-reviewed, academic periodical. We are particularly interested in theory and practice surrounding the creation, transmission, storage, interpretation, alteration and replication of electronic text. We are also interested in the broader social, psychological, literary, economic and pedagogical implications of computer-mediated networks. The journal's essays are delivered free to Bitnet/Internet/ Usenet addressees. Recipients may make paper copies; EJournal will provide authenticated paper copy from our read-only archive for use by academic deans or others. Individual essays, reviews, stories-- texts --sent to us will be disseminated to subscribers as soon as they have been through the editorial process, which will also be "paperless." We expect to offer access through libraries to our electronic Contents and Abstracts, and to be indexed and abstracted in appropriate places.

Subjects covered: Internet; virtual culture; telecommunications; communications

Net address for operations: LISTSERV@ALBANY.bitnet

Net address for questions or submissions: EJOURNAL@ALBANY.bitnet

Frequency: Irregular

Established: Begun 1989; first issue 1991

Number of issues published to date: 11

Method of issuance: Issues are distributed via Listserv. Issues are announced on various related discussion lists.

Recent issue published: Volume 2, Number 5

Subscribers: 3010

Sponsor: Department of English, University at Albany, Albany, NY 12222.

Host: Department of English, University at Albany, Albany, NY 12222.

Journal refereed: Yes; editors review and report on submissions. A consensus is inferred in publication.

Editorial contact: Edward M. (Ted) Jennings
Department of English, University at Albany, Albany, NY 12222.

Tel: (518) 442-4091

Fax: (518) 442-4599

Bitnet: JENNINGS@ALBANY or jennings@albnyvm1 or jennings@albnyvms

Sample contents: For contents (and abstracts), send the message GET EJRNL CONTENTS to LISTSERV@ALBANY.bitnet . Latest issue: "Virtual Authors and Network Community" by David Sewall.

Copyright statement: This electronic publication and its contents are (c) copyright by EJournal. Permission is hereby granted to give away the journal and its contents, but no one may "own" it. Any and all financial interest is hereby assigned to the acknowledged authors of individual texts. This notification must accompany all distribution of EJournal.

How to access: Send the e-mail message SUB EJRNL subscriber's name to LISTSERV@ALBANY.bitnet

How to unsubscribe: Send the message UNSUB EJRNL to LISTSERV@ALBANY.bitnet

Gopher accessibility: EJournal can be found via Gopher, Archie, and so forth.

Additional information: Writers who think their texts might be appreciated by EJournal's audience are invited to forward files to EJOURNAL@ALBANY.bitnet. If you are wondering about starting to write a piece for to us, feel free to ask if it sounds appropriate. There are no "styling" guidelines; we try to be a little more direct and lively than many paper publications, and considerably less hasty and ephemeral than most postings to unreviewed electronic spaces. We read ASCII; we look forward to experimenting with other transmission and display formats and protocols. Board of Advisors: Stevan Harnad, Princeton University; Dick Lanham, University of California at L.A.; Ann Okerson, Association of Research Libraries; Joe Raben, City University of New York; Bob Scholes, Brown University; Harry Whitaker, University of Quebec at Montreal.

EJVC (ELECTRONIC JOURNAL OF VIRTUAL CULTURE)

Description: The Electronic Journal on Virtual Culture (EJVC) is a refereed scholarly journal that fosters, encourages, advances and communicates scholarly thought on virtual culture. Virtual culture is computer-mediated experience, behavior, action, interaction and thought, including electronic conferences, electronic journals, networked information systems, the construction and visualization of models of reality, and global connectivity.

Subjects covered: computer hardware and software; cyberspace; Internet; virtual culture

Net address for operations: LISTSERV@KENTVM or LISTSERV@KENTVM.KENT.EDU

Journal refereed: Yes. An article may be submitted at any time to the EJVC for peer-review with the understanding that the peer-review requires time. Acknowledgements of the arrival of any article shall be made within 24 hours of arrival. Notification of acceptance or rejection shall be sent to authors within 30 days of the arrival of the submission. Submissions are accept-

able only by electronic mail or send/file. Submissions may be made to either the Editor-in-Chief or the Co-Editor.
Editorial contact: Ermel Stepp, Editor
Internet: M034050@MARSHALL.WVNET.EDU
Bitnet: M034050@MARSHALL
Copyright statement: Copyright of articles published by Electronic Journal on Virtual Culture is held by the author of a given article. If an article is re-published elsewhere it must include a statement that it was originally published by Electronic Journal on Virtual Culture.
How to access: Send e-mail to LISTSERV@KENTVM or LISTSERV@KENTVM.KENT.EDU with no other lines in the heading and the following sole line of text: subscribe EJVC-L YourFullName where YourFullName is your real name.
How to submit: Prospective articles may be submitted to the EJVC by email or sendfile (or send/file) to the Editor-in-Chief or the Co-Editor.
Archives: FTP and LISTSERV archives of the EJVC are maintained. The archives of the EJVC may be accessed by anonymous FTP and by email or interactive commands. Anonymous FTP Instructions: ftp byrd.mu.wvnet.edu login anonymous password: user's electronic address cd /pub/ejvc type EJVC.INDEX.FTP get filename (where filename = exact name of file in INDEX) quit
Additional information: Co-editor: Diane Kovacs, Kent State Universtiy; DKOVACS@KENTVM.KENT.EDU or DKOVACS@KENTVM

THE ELECTRIC ECLECTIC

Description: The Electric Eclectic is a multimedia Internet magazine, featuring sound and image files in addition to text files.
Subjects covered: Internet; multimedia computing
Editorial contact: Nathaniel Borenstein
Bellcore Corp., Morristown, NJ
Related files: A discussion list on the topic of the Electric Eclectic has been formed. Send an email message to ee-discuss-request@eitech.com, with the word subscribe in the subject line of the message.

THE ELECTRIC MYSTIC'S GUIDE TO THE INTERNET

Description: The Electric Mystic's Guide is a non-technical survey of all major documents, archives and services of relevance to Religious Studies and related fields that are available through the international, academic computer networks commonly referred to as the Net (BITNET, Internet and affiliated networks). This includes networked papers, reviews, book notes, dissertations, major sacred texts, software programs, electronic mail address collections, general information files, data banks, electronic journals, newsletters, online discussion groups, specialized commercial and public networks, and relevant networked organizations, associations, institutions and companies. It should be noted that the Electric Mystic's Guide is not meant to be a handbook on how to use the Net, and thus assumes a certain level of familiarity with FTP, Telnet, LISTSERV and other Net operating programs. Nonetheless, extensive instructions have been included in the guide to ensure that readers will be able to access the material documented herein.
Journal refereed: No
Editorial contact: Michael Strangelove
How to access: ftp to pandal.uottawa.ca and change directories to /pub/religion. The filename is electric-mystics-guide.ps.z.

ELECTRONIC AIR

Description: Electronic Air centers on institutional research, planning, and policy analysis at colleges and universities. It welcomes news items, comments about recent publications, job announcements, requests for help or suggestions from our readers, announcements of professional meetings and conferences, abstracts of papers which authors are willing to share, persons relocating or promoting to new IR jobs or retiring, etc. All such items should be relevant to the concerns of professionals in insitutional research, planning, or policy analysis.
Subjects covered: colleges and universities; policy planning and analysis
Net address for operations: LISTSERV@VTVM1
Net address for questions or submissions: NELSON__L@PLU.BITNET
Frequency: Bi-weekly
Established: October 22, 1986
Number of issues published to date: 167
Method of issuance: Sent to listmembers via listserv.
Available in other media: No, not in an organized way.
Recent issue published: v. 13, no. 9
Subscribers: 1044 subscribers
Sponsor: Assn. for Institutional Research, 314 Stone Building, Florida State University, Tallahassee, FL 32306-3038
Host: Pacific Lutheran University,Tacoma, WA 98447
Editorial contact: LARRY W. NELSON, Director, Institutional Research and Planning
Hauge Administration Building 100, Pacific Lutheran University, Tacoma, Washington 98477
Tel: (206) 535-8320
Fax: (206) 535-8320
Internet: NELSON__L@PLU
Technical contact: Greg Kroll
VA Polytechd Inst. & St. U.
Blacksburg, VA 24061-0157
Bitnet: VA Polytechd Inst. & St. U.
Blacksburg, VA 24061-0157
Sample contents: Editor's Note: AIR Forum and Preventing E-Mail Pile-ups; The Changing Scene; News - Community College Fee Increase Studies; Call for Proposals: 1993 CAIR Annual Conference; Occupational & Educational Outcomes Report for Recent Grads; U.S. Government Publications Available; OERI Telephone Numbers Listed; Help - Requiring Students to Have Laptop Computers; Multiple Regression Faculty Salary Studies; Recommended Reading on Planning, Assessment, Qual. Imprvmt.; Financial Analyst/Planner Position Series Ideas Sought; Clarifying Student Right-to-Know Reporting Categories; Evaluation Process for Counseling Services; Conference - TQM in Higher Ed. Conf. June 21-22; Position Listings - University of Alabama; Brookdale Community College, New Jersey; St. Olaf College, Northfield, MN; Parting Thought
How to access: Send to LISTSERV@VTVM1 a message saying SUB AIR-L your__first__name your__last__name or Send to NELSON__L@PLU.BITNET a message indicating your wish to subscribe to The Electronic AIR. Include your full name, your institution's name, and its state our country.
Access policy: All subscription requests are accepted.
How to unsubscribe: Send to LISTSERV@VTVM1 a message saying UNSUB AIR-L or Send to NELSON__L@PLU.BITNET a message indicating your wish to unsubscribe from The Electronic AIR.
How to submit: Send to LISTSERV@VTVM1 a message saying UNSUB AIR-L or Send to NELSON__L@PLU.BITNET a

message indicating your wish to unsubscribe from The Electronic AIR.

Submission policy: AIR-L is a moderated list where all items are distributed bi-weekly in edited newsletter form. Submissions are reviewed by the editor for relevance to the readership and stated purposes, length, grammatical usage, etc. Some messages are editorially modified and some are returned to senders for extensive editing or with an indication that they will not be published because they fall outside the publication's scope. All messages are edited to comply with a consistent style and appearance.

Archives: Single back issues are available by submitting a request to the editor.

ELECTRONIC HEBREW USERS NEWSLETTER (E-HUG)

Description: E-Hug is an electronic newsletter covering all aspects of using computers in the analysis of Hebrew and related languages.

Subjects covered: Hebrew language and literature; computer science

Frequency: Weekly or biweekly

Method of issuance: Issues are emailed to subscribers as published.

Journal refereed: No

Editorial contact: Ari Davidow

Internet: well!ari@apple.com

How to access: Send the message SUBSCRIBE E-HUG to listserv@dartcms1 or listserv@dartcms1.bitnet

THE ELECTRONIC JOURNAL OF COMMUNICATION/LA REVUE ELECTRONIQUE DE COMMUNICATION

ISSN: 1183-5656

Description: EJC/REC is devoted to the study of communication theory, research, practice, and policy. Manuscripts reporting original research, methodologies relevant to the study of human communication, critical syntheses of research, and theoretical and philosphical perspectives on communication, are encouraged. Seeking an international audience, the Journal publishes abstracts of all articles and the introduction to each topic-oriented issue in French as well as English.

Subjects covered: social sciences; computer science; communications

Net address for operations: Support@Rpitsvm (bitnet); Support@Vm.Its.Rpi.Edu (Internet)

Net address for questions or submissions: Support@Rpitsvm, Support@Vm.Its.Rpi.Edu, or e-mail address for the special issue editor

Frequency: Quarterly

Established: 1990

Number of issues published to date: 5

Method of issuance: The journal is distributed through international academic computer networks. Subscribers belong to an electronic conference serving as the distribution channel for the journal. New issues are announced by distributing a "table of contents" file, which contains a table of contents, an introduction to the issue, and abstracts of all articles appearing within that issue. Interested readers may then obtain the electronic files containing the text of articles in which they are interested by sending the appropriate command to the database in which the

articles are stored. Articles may be retrieved by using the "send" command and the appropriate file name in electronic mail messages sent to Comserve@Rpitsvm or Comserve@Vm.Its.Rpi.Edu, as in: Send Maule V3N293. No other words or symbols should appear in the mail messages. Issue availability is announed on electronic conference EJCREC@Rpitsvm or EJCREC@Vm.Its.Rpi.Edu

Available in other media: No (but plans are underway to distribute a pc based version).

Recent issue published: Volume 3, Number 2

Subscribers: 690

Sponsor: Communication Institute for Online Scholarship, P. O. Box 57, Rotterdam Junction, NY 12150.

Host: Rensselaer Polytechnic Institute, Troy, NY 12180.

Journal refereed: Yes. Issues are organized around specific topics or themes and guest edited by scholars with a particular interest and expertise in the issue's focus. Each guest editor selects an editorial board, the members of which serve as referees for manuscripts submitted for the issue.

Editorial contact: Teresa M. Harrison, Managing Editor Dept. of Language, Literature, & Communication, Rensselaer Polytechnic Institute, Troy, NY 12180.

Tel: (518) 276-8261

Internet: Harrison@Vm.Its.Rpi.Edu

Bitnet: Harrison@Rpitsvm

Technical contact: Teresa M. Harrison, Managing Editor Dept. of Language, Literature, & Communication, Rensselaer Polytechnic Institute, Troy, NY 12180.

Tel: (518) 276-8261

Internet: Harrison@Vm.Its.Rpi.Edu

Bitnet: Harrison@Rpitsvm

Sample contents: (1) Editor's Introduction: Computer-Mediated Communication/ Introduction de l'editeur: La communication informatisee, Thomas W. Benson Pennsylvania State University; (2) CMC: The Medium and the Message/Communication informatisee: Support et message, Norman Coombs Rochester Institute of Technology, Filename: Coombs V3N293; (3) Using Computer Mediated Communication in an Educational Context: Educational Outcomes and Pedagogical Lessons/La communication informatisee dans un contexte pedagogique: Les resultats et les lecons pedagogiques de la teleconference informatisee, Ray Archee University of Western Sydney, Nepean Filename: Archee V3N293; (4) Computer-Mediated Communication to Facilitate Seminar Participation and Active Thinking: A Case Study/Une etude de cas: La communication informatisee comme moyen de faciliter la participation et la reflexion en classe de travaux pratiques, Leonard J. Shedletsky University of Southern Maine, Filename: Shedlet V3N293; (5) Strategic Uses of Electronic Mail in Organizations/Les utilisations strategiques du courrier electronique dans les organisations, Steven R. Phillips University of Montana, Eric M. Eisenberg University of Southern California Filename: Phillips V3N293; (6) Electronic Mail as a Media Choice for Managers/Le courrier electronique comme choix de media pour les administrateurs, Allison M. Loperfido Cornell University Filename: Loperfid V3N293; (7) Gender and Democracy in Computer-Mediated Communication/ Sexe et democratie dans la communication informatisee, Susan C. Herring University of Texas at Arlington Filename: Herring V3N293; (8) Individual Differences and Computer Mediated Communication: The Role of Perception/Les differences individuelles et la communication informatisee: Le role de la perception, Bolanle A. Olaniran Texas Tech University Filename: Olaniran V3N293; (9) Precis of "Behavioral and Perceptua

Review: For an historical description of the development of EJC/REC, see: Harrison, T., Stephen, T., & Winter, J. (1991). "Online Journals: Disciplinary Designs for Electronic Scholarship." *Public Access Computer Review*, 2(1), 25-38.

Indexed or abstracted: ComIndex (pc based index of 37 communication journals)

How to access: Send the following command in an electronic mail message to Comserve@Rpitsvm (bitnet) or Comserve@Vm.Its.Rpi.Edu (internet): Subscribe EJCREC Your Name as in: Subscribe EJCREC Mary Smith

How to unsubscribe: Send the following command in an electronic mail message to Comserve@Rpitsvm (bitnet) or Comserve@Vm.Its.Rpi.Edu (internet): UnSubscribe EJCREC

How to submit: Contact editor

Submission policy: Contact editor

Archives: A directory of all EJC/REC articles is available. To obtain the directory, send the following command to Comserve@Rpitsvm or Comserve@Vm.Its.Rpi.Edu: Send EJCREC Directry. The directory contains information about how to get the files comprising back issues.

ELECTRONIC JOURNAL OF DIFFERENTIAL EQUATIONS

Description: The Electronic Journal of Differential Equations is a joint venture of mathematicians at the University of North Texas and Southwest Texas State University. It is peer reviewed and will be indexed and reviewed in Mathematical Reviews.

Subjects covered: mathematics; differential equations

Editorial contact: Nikie Cotter
Reference Librarian, Science and Technology Library, University of North Texas, Denton Texas.

Internet: ncotter@library.unt.edu

How to access: Telnet to ejde.math.unt.edu or ejde.math.swt.edu and login as ejde (lower case). Because of the problems inherent in printing mathematical equations, there are three files of each article available. One goes to an Xterminal (this is the fanciest way and I have only seen one terminal that is actually used except for the ones at demos), the second is written with TeX and requires the software that translates (if the library doesn't have it, the math department probably does) and the third file is a Postscript file, which requires only a Postscript printer. If none of these methods are available, we are going to keep a print copy that will be available for interlibrary loan.

ELECTRONIC PUBLIC INFORMATION NEWSLETTER

Description: The Electronic Public Information Newsletter is an occasional publication surveying Internet related information.

Subjects covered: Internet; electronic networking

Editorial contact: James McDonough

Internet: epin@access.digex.com

How to access: Send message to editor at epin@access.digex.com

ELECTRONICS LETTERS ONLINE

Description: Electronics Letters Online is published by the Institution of Electrical Engineers (IEE) and distributed to subscribers by OCLC Online Computer Library Center via the Internet and dial-up telecommunications networks. The new electronic journal will carry the same 1,400 to 1,500 articles per year as the print version but will display them through the GUIDON interface, a Windows-based graphical user interface developed by OCLC. GUIDON supports full-text searching by subject, title, author, keyword, date, and a full range of Boolean and proximity operators. It displays full text, figures, tables, and equations in quality that rivals the printed page. GUIDON operates in the Microsoft Windows environment on an 80286 or higher PC. Electronics Letters Online will also be available with a command-driven ASCII user interface that runs on a terminal or PC with software emulating a VT100 terminal. Through links to IEE's INSPEC database, subscribers to Electronics Letters Online will also have access to abstracts of references cited in the articles. The INSPEC database is the world's largest and most comprehensive source of reference literature in the fields of physics, electrical and control engineering, electronics, and computing.

Subjects covered: electrical engineering; computer science

Established: October 1993 in electronic form; previously only in printed form.

Fee: Yes, contact OCLC for more details.

Sponsor: Institution of electrical engineers and OCLC.

Editorial contact: Professor Peter Clarricoats

How to access: Conact OCLC for more details.

END PROCESS

Description: End Process is a quarterly electronic newsletter of visual data.

Subjects covered: graphics; computer hardware and software

Frequency: Quarterly

Established: 1993

Method of issuance: Issues are emailed to subscribers as published.

Journal refereed: No

Editorial contact: Ed Stastny
9018 Westridge Drive, Omaha, NE, 68124.

Internet: ed@cwis.unomaha.edu

How to access: Send email to: ed@cwis.unomaha.edu

ENERGY IDEAS

Description: Energy Ideas is an electronic publication offering information on the efficient use of energy resources.

Subjects covered: energy studies; environmental studies

Frequency: Monthly

Established: 1992

Method of issuance: Issues are emailed to subscribers as published.

Journal refereed: No

Editorial contact: Jonathan Kleinman

Internet: ei@igc.apc.org

How to access: Subscribe to EcoNet or send a message to ei@igc.apc.org.

ENERGY RESEARCH IN ISRAEL NEWSLETTER

Description: Energy Research in Israel covers the efficient use of energy resources and related issues.

Subjects covered: Israel; energy studies; environmental studies

Frequency: Irregular

Method of issuance: Issues are emailed to subscribers as published.

Journal refereed: No

Editorial contact: Dr. Michael Wolff
Internet: wolff@ilncrd
How to access: Send the message SUBSCRIBE ENERGY-L to listserv@taunivm

ENEWS

Description: ENEWS is subtitled the International Newsletter on Energy Efficiency Issues in the Developing Countries.
Subjects covered: energy studies; environmental studies
Frequency: Three times per year
Established: 1993
Method of issuance: Issues are emailed to subscribers as published.
Journal refereed: Yes
Editorial contact: Gilberto Jannuzzi
Internet: enews@fem.unicamp.br
How to access: Send the message SUBSCRIBE L-ENEWS to listserv@fem.unicamp.br

EROFILE

Description: Erofile covers French and Italian literary topics.
Subjects covered: French language and literature; Italian language and literature
Journal refereed: No
Internet: erofile@ucsbuxa.ucsb.edu
Bitnet: erofile@ucsbuxa.bitnet
How to access: Send email to: erofile@ucsbuxa.bitnet or erofile@ucsbuxa.ucsb.edu

ETHNOMUSICOLOGY RESEARCH DIGEST

ISSN: 1054-1624
Description: Ethnomusicology Research Digest includes news, dissertation abstracts, works-in-progress, obituaries, reviews of print, records, electronic titles.
Subjects covered: ethnomusicology; music; cultural studies
Net address for operations: LISTSERV@UMDD or LISTSERV@UMDD.UMD.EDU
Net address for questions or submissions: ETHMUS-L@UMDD or ETHMUS-L@UMDD.UMD.EDU
Established: December 1989
Number of issues published to date: 114
Method of issuance: Sent to subscribers on listserv list.
Available in other media: Yes. Print available on request from School of Music, University of Washington DN-10, Seattle, WA 98195 U.S.A.
Recent issue published: Vol 4, no 13
Subscribers: 284
Editorial contact: Dr. Karl Signell
Center for Turkish Music, Music Department, University of Maryland, Baltimore County Baltimore, MD 21228
Tel: (410) 455-2489
Fax: (410) 455-1070
Internet: signell@umdd.umd.edu
Bitnet: signell@umdd
Sample contents: New blues list; computer research in musicology.
Indexed or abstracted: INDEX file on INFO.UMD.EDU (see above for subdirectory) and in ARCHIVE INFO file in listserv archive

How to access: See ETHMUS-L listserv list
Archives: See ETHMUS-L listserv list
Related files: See ETHMUS-L

EUITNEWS

Description: EUITNEWS is Educom's electronic newsletter for the EUIT program (Educational Uses of Information Technology). It covers distance education, computer-based instructional technology, and other issues.
Subjects covered: computer-assisted instruction; education
Net address for operations: listserv@bitnic.educom.edu
How to access: Send standard subscribe request to listserv.
How to unsubscribe: Send standard unsubscribe request to listserv.

EUVE: ELECTRONIC NEWSLETTER OF THE EUVE OBSERVATORY

ISSN: 1065-3597
Description: EUVE covers astrophysics, astronomy, and other space-related topics.
Subjects covered: astrophysics; astronomy
Frequency: Weekly to biweekly
Established: 1991
Method of issuance: Issues are mailed to subscribers as published.
Host: Center for Extreme Ultraviolet Astrophysics, University of California at Berkeley.
Journal refereed: No
Internet: carlos@cea.berkeley.edu
How to access: FTP to cea-ftp.cea.berkeley.edu
The directory is: /pub/archive/newsletters

FACTSHEET FIVE

Description: FactSheet Five is an electronic magazine covering a wide variety of alternative topics.
Subjects covered: Star Trek; language and literature; alternative literature
Frequency: Monthly or more frequently.
Established: 1992
Method of issuance: Issues are emailed to subscribers as published.
Journal refereed: No
Editorial contact: Jerod Pore
FactSheet Five, 1800 Market Street, San Francisco, CA 94102.
Internet: jerod23@well.sf.ca.us
How to access: Send email to jerod23@well.sf.ca.us.

FARNET GAZETTE

Description: FARNet Gazette provides information to electronic networking specialists.
Subjects covered: electronic networking; information technology; computer hardware and software
Frequency: Irregular
Method of issuance: Issues are emailed to subscribers as published.
Host: FARNet
Journal refereed: No
Editorial contact: Laura Breeden
Internet: breeden@farnet.org

How to access: Send email to gazette-request@farnet.org
Additional information: Additional editor: Carlos Robles, roblesc@farnet.org

FATHERS AND CHILDREN FOR EQUALITY NEWSLETTER

Description: FACE covers topics related to non-custodial parents' rights.
Subjects covered: parents' rights; parenting; family studies
Frequency: Monthly
Established: 1992
Method of issuance: Issues are emailed to subscribers as published.
Host: Fathers and Children for Equality
Journal refereed: No
Editorial contact: Aaron L. Hoffmeyer
FACE (Fathers and Children for Equality), P.O. Box 18022, Columbus, OH 43218.
Internet: tr@cbnea.att.com
How to access: Subscribe to the FREE-L Listserv mailing list, using standard listserv request commands: listserv@iupui.edu or listserv@indycms.iupui.edu

FEDERAL INFORMATION NEWS SYNDICATE

Description: Federal Information News Syndicate is a newsletter focusing on information technology and futurism.
Subjects covered: futurism; information technology
Frequency: Biweekly
Established: 1993
Method of issuance: Issues are emailed to subscribers as published. Also available in printed form; apply to editor for details.
Journal refereed: No
Internet: fins@access.digex.com
How to access: Send email to fins@access.digex.com

FINEART FORUM

Description: FineArt Forum is an electronic journal offering announcements and news of interest to artists using technology.
Subjects covered: art; science and technology; computer hardware and software; fine arts
Net address for operations: fineart@erc.msstate.edu
Net address for questions or submissions: fineart@erc.msstate.edu
Frequency: Monthly: distributed on the 1st of the month
Established: 1987
Method of issuance: Issues are distributed as email postings. Issues are announced on several lists; apply for details.
Available in other media: Yes. Paper copies are available from our distributors.
Recent issue published: Vol. 7, No. 6
Fee: Electronic version is free; paper copies cost $65.
Sponsor: FineArt Forum is published by the Mississippi State University National Science Foundation Engineering Research Center for Computational Field Simulation, PO Box 6176, Mississippi State MS 39762. 601 325 8814 voice, 601 325 7692 fax. fineart@erc.msstate.edu
Host: It is distributed by ISAST, 672 South Van Ness, San Francisco CA 94110. fast@garnet.berkeley.edu It is the newsletter of the Art, Science, Technology Network President Annick

Bureaud, ASTN, 57 Rue Falguiere, Paris France. bureaud@altern.com
Editorial contact: Paul Brown
MSU/NSF ERC, PO Box 6176,
Mississippi State, MS 39762.
Tel: (601) 325 8814
Fax: (601) 325 7692
Internet: brown@erc.msstate.edu
Sample contents: Call for Backissues: Paul Brown; VR-SOUND-DATABASE: Christian Huebler; AUTOCAD list moved to JHUVM: ID FORUM Hypertext project: Tim Mclaughlin; MULTIMEDIA CONFERENCE: Suzy Turner; COMPUTER CONFERENCING IN HIGHER EDUCATION: S.A. Rae; COMPUGRAPHICS '93: Harold P. Santo; Network Services Conference: David Sitman; FAX ART: Daniel Smith; FTP of hypertext: Raleigh Muns; L O C I S: Don Mabry; Call for Reviewers - LOD: Raymond Lauzzana; Lighting Distribution List: Clay Belcher; Multimedia Shows: Amatul Hannan; Music-research Information: Leard Reed; Altemus III NOMAD: Michael W. Smith; OTIS update: Ed Stastny; Oberlin workshops: Gary Lee Nelson; XEROX PARC Mail Art: Marshall Bern; PMC-MOO: Diane Kovacs; Interactive Poetry: Judith B. Kerman; Composer Residence Program: John Bischoff; LES MIRADORS DE LA PAIX: Annick Bureaud; Inherent Rights: Annick Bureaud; Job announcement: Cynthia Rubin; SigGraph Stuff: Philip Galanter; Symposium on Public Graphics: DESIGN-L; Diaspar VR Network: Wyatt Miler; Wax on Internet: Artist #1; VPANET: Mike Butler; Positions Available: Patty Seger.
How to access: Send an email message to:
fast@garnet.berkeley.edu with the content:
SUBSCRIBE FINEART <your name, address and email details> NOTE that ALL OTHER correspondence should go via our editorial address as below.
Access policy: Everyone is welcome.
How to unsubscribe: Send a message to
fast@garnet.berkeley.edu
with the content: SIGNOFF FINEART <your name, address and email details>
How to submit: Send mail to fineart@erc.msstate.edu
Archives: Send mail to fineart@erc.msstate.edu
Related files: FineArt_Online is in service as of July 1,1993. It will include a Directory of Network Services of interest to artists and designers and a general news and information area. We plan to include a bibliography of art & technology soon.
Gopher accessibility: FineArt_Online will have ftp and Gopher access. After 7/1/93 information on how to access FineArt_Online will be avalable by email request from: fineart@erc.msstate.edu

FLORA ONLINE

ISSN: 0892-9106
Description: Flora Online is a refereed electronic journal covering topics related to systematic botany and plant biology.
Subjects covered: plant biology; botany
Frequency: Irregular
Established: 1987
Method of issuance: Issues are available via FTP, BBS, Gopher, or on diskette.
Journal refereed: Yes
Editorial contact: Richard H. Zander
Internet: visbms@ubvms.cc.buffalo.edu
Bitnet: visbms@ubvms.bitnet

How to access: FTP to huh.harvard.edu.
The directory is: /pub/newsletters/flora.online/ Or gopher to: go-pher.cic.net

FLORIDA EXTENSION BEEKEEPING NEWSLETTER

ISSN: 0889-3764
Description: Florida Extension Beekeeping Newsletter covers all aspects of beekeeping.
Subjects covered: beekeeping
Frequency: Monthly
Established: 1984
Method of issuance: Issues are emailed to subscribers as published.
Host: University of Florida
Journal refereed: No
Editorial contact: Dr. Malcolm T. Sanford
Building 970, Box 119620, University of Florida, Gainesville, FL 32611-0620.
Internet: mts@gnv.ifas.ufl.edu
Bitnet: mts@ifasgnv.bitnet
How to access: Subscribe to Bee-L to receive issues, or contact editor at mts@gnv.ifas.ufl.edu or mts@ifasgnv.bitnet

FLORIDA SUNFLASH

Description: Florida SunFlash is an electronic newsletter providing informatoin on Sun Microsystems' products and services.
Subjects covered: computer hardware and software; computer science; Sun Microsystems
Frequency: Irregular
Established: January 1989
Method of issuance: Issues are emailed to subscribers as published.
Host: Sun Microsystems
Journal refereed: No
Editorial contact: John McLaughlin
Internet: flash@sun.com, info-sunflash@sun.com
How to access: Send email to sunflash-request@sun.com.

FOREFRONTS

Description: FOREFRONTS is a newsletter covering research and developments at the Cornell Theory Center's Supercomputing facility.
Subjects covered: computer science; telecommunications
Frequency: Quarterly
Established: 1992
Method of issuance: Issues accessible via Gopher
Host: Cornell Theory Center
Journal refereed: No
Editorial contact: Allison Loperfido
Internet: allison@tc.cornell.edu
How to access: Gopher to gopher.tc.cornell.edu
For hardcopy subscription, send email request to: herzog@tc.cornell.edu

FRENCH LANGUAGE PRESS REVIEW

Description: French Language Press Review is published by the France Ministry of Foreign Affairs in Washington, DC.

Subjects covered: French language and literature; current events
Method of issuance: Issues are emailed to subscribers as published. Also accessible via Gopher.
Host: France Ministry of Foreign Affairs
Journal refereed: No
How to access: Gopher to gopher.cic.net

FULBRIGHT EDUCATIONAL ADVISING NEWSLETTER (FULBNEWS)

Description: FULBNEWS is an electronic newsletter sponsored by the Fulbright Commission of Brazil covering education and related issues.
Subjects covered: education
Frequency: Three times per year
Established: 1993
Method of issuance: Issues are emailed to subscribers as published.
Host: Fulbright Commission
Journal refereed: No
Editorial contact: Rita Monteiro
Internet: fulb@brlncc
How to access: Send the message SUBSCRIBE FULBNEWS to listserv@brlncc

FUNCT-AN@BABBAGE.SISSA.IT

Description: funct-an@babbage.sissa.it is an electronic journal dealing with funtional analysis.
Subjects covered: functional analysis; philosophy; computer science

FUNHOUSE

Description: Funhouse is an electronic magazine ''of degenerate pop culture. Offbeat films, music, literature, and experiences are largely covered, with the one stipulation that articles are attempted to be detailed and well documented, although this is no guarantee of completeness or correctness, so that the interested reader may further pursue something which may spark her interest.''
Subjects covered: alternative literature; book reviews; music; popular culture
Editorial contact: Jeff Dove
Internet: jeffdove@well.sf.ca.us
How to access: Gopher accessible at: etext.archive.umich.edu

FUTURECULTURE FAQ

Description: FutureCulture FAQ is a document updated quarterly covering a variety of information technology, techno-culture, and futurism related topics.
Subjects covered: information technology; futurism; techno-culture
Frequency: Quarterly
Established: 1991
Method of issuance: Issues are emailed to subscribers as published.
Journal refereed: No
Editorial contact: ahawks@nyx.cs.du.edu
How to access: Send the message SEND FAQ to future-request@nyx.cs.du.edu or gopher to gopher.cic.net

GLOSAS NEWS

ISSN: 1188-6307
Description: GLOSAS is an electronic journal publishing contributions dealing with the practical applications of telecommunications in education. We lay particular emphasis on global cooperative gaming, simulations and educational exchanges as well as initiatives to broaden network access on a global scale. Our ultimate objective is to see the establishment of a global (electronic) university which would offer universal access to quality education.
Subjects covered: colleges and universities; education; telecommunications; distance education
Net address for operations: GLOSAS@vm1.mcgill.ca
Net address for questions or submissions: anton@vax2.concordia.ca
Frequency: Bimonthly
Established: November 1991
Number of issues published to date: 13
Method of issuance: Issues are distributed via email and fax.
Recent issue published: Vol.3, No. 1
Subscribers: Approximately 900-1,000
Sponsor: GLOSAS/USA 43-23 Colden Street, Flushing, NY 11355-3998.
Host: McGill University, Montreal, Canada.
Editorial contact: Prof. Anton Ljutic
Champlain College, Montreal
Tel: (514) 672-7360 x280
Fax: (514) 672-9299
Internet: anton@vax2.concordia.ca ; anton@carleton.ca
Sample contents: Part I: 0. About GN; 1. Editorial: About "Teaching on the LAN"; 2. Feature article: Teaching on the LAN, by Dr. Stan Kulikowski II; Part 2: 3. Current news and work in progress at GLOSAS; 4. New global resources; a) SATNEWS; b) The South Scanner Satellite Services Chart; c) An homage to facsimile (on its 150th anniversary); Part 3: 5. Special supplement: From Here to Implicity, by David Boulton.
How to access: There are two GLOSAS News bulletins - Global Education (GN/GE) and Global Peace Gaming (GN/GPG). Both are labelled accordingly on the subject line. For example, an issue of the Global Education bulletin would be labelled GN/GPG/Vxx/Nyy (V = Volume and N = Number). For added convenience, the subject line also shows the approximate size of the file. This is generally kept under 33 Kbytes. GN/GE appears 4-5 times and GN/GPG 5-6 times annually.

GNU'S BULLETIN

Description: GNU's Bulletin is the newsletter of the Free Software Foundation and advocates the free distribution of all software. GNU is an integrated software program (GNU's Not Unix).
Subjects covered: computer hardware and software
Frequency: Semi-annual
Method of issuance: Issues are emailed to subscribers as published.
Host: Free Software Foundation
Journal refereed: No
Free Software Foundation, 675 Massachusetts Avenue, Cambridge, MA 02139.
Tel: (617)876-3298
Internet: gnu@prep.ai.mit.edu
How to access: Send message to gnu@prep.ai.mit.edu

GR-QC@XXX.LANL.GOV

Description: gr-qc@xxx.lanl.gov is an electronic journal focusing on questions of general relativity and quantum cosmology.
Subjects covered: physics; astrophysics

GROCHZ KAPUSTA

Description: Grochz Kapusta is a weekly electronic digest of current events in Poland
Subjects covered: Poland; current events
Frequency: Weekly
Established: 1992
Method of issuance: Issues are emailed to subscribers as published. Also via Gopher and FTP.
Journal refereed: No
Editorial contact: Marian Kuras
Bitnet: eijuras@plkrcy11.bitnet
How to access: Send an email message to bielewcz@uwpg02.uwinnipeg.ca
Related files: Back issues are available by ftp to tirana.berleley.edu in the directory /pub/VARIA/polish/dir__groch

HANDICAP DIGEST

Description: Handicap Digest is an electronic compilation of news and other information concerning people with physical disabilities.
Subjects covered: disabilities; blindness
Established: 1986
Method of issuance: Issues are emailed to subscribers as published.
Journal refereed: No
Editorial contact: Bill McGarry
ISC-Bunker Ramo, 2 Enterprise Drive, Shelton, CT 06484.
Internet: wtm@bunker.afd.olivetti.com
How to access: Send the message SUBSCRIBE L-HCAP to listserv@ndsuvm1 or listserv@vm1.nodak.edu

HEP-LAT@FTP.SCRI.FSU.EDU

Description: hep-lat@ftp.scri.fsu.edu is an ejournal dealing with computational and lattice physics.
Subjects covered: physics; mathematics

HEP-PH@XXX.LANL.GOV

Description: hep-ph@xxx.lanl.gov is an electronic journal on high-energy physics and related topics.
Subjects covered: physics

HEP-TH@XXX.LANL.GOV

Description: hep-th@xxx.lanl.gov is an electronic journal on high-energy physics and related topics.
Subjects covered: physics

HI-REZ

Description: Hi-Rez is described as an "electronic journal for CyberBeatniks."
Subjects covered: alternative literature; popular culture
How to access: Gopher accessible at: etext.archive.umich.edu

HICNET MEDICAL NEWSLETTER

Description: HICNet Medical News contains the latest medical news that can be obtained. Regular columns include the Centers for Disease Control MMWR, news from the FDA, news from the National Institutes of Health, and AIDS Daily Summary.

Subjects covered: medicine; health sciences; AIDS/HIV studies

Net address for operations: listserv@asuvm.inre.asu.edu

Net address for questions or submissions: mednews@stat.com

Frequency: Weekly

Established: 1985

Number of issues published to date: 300

Method of issuance: Distribution via listserv and mailing lists, also posted to usenet sci.med Issues are announced on the hicn-notify-request@stat.com mailing list.

Editorial contact: David S. Dodell, DMD
10250 North 92nd Street, Suite 210, Scottsdale, Arizona 85258-4599.

Tel: (602) 860-1121

Fax: (602) 451-6135

Internet: david@stat.com

Bitnet: ATW1H@ASUACAD

Copyright statement: Compilation Copyright 1993 by David Dodell, D.M.D. All rights Reserved. License is hereby granted to republish on electronic media for which no fees are charged, so long as the text of this copyright notice and license are attached intact to any and all republished portion or portions.

How to access: Send email to listserv@asuacad.bitnet or listserv@asuvm.inre.asu.edu first line of text subscribe MEDNEWS YourFirstName YourLastName

Access policy: Open to everyone.

How to unsubscribe: Same as subscribe except first line of text now reads: unsubscribe MEDNEWS

How to submit: mednews@stat.com

Archives: vml.nodak.edu in HICNEWS directory ftp.uci.edu listserv@asuacad.bitnet

HIGH WEIRDNESS BY EMAIL

Description: High Weirdness is an electronic newsletter offering offbeat literature and alternative texts.

Subjects covered: alternative literature; poetry; American literature and language

Frequency: Irregular

Established: 1992

Method of issuance: Issues are emailed to subscribers as published. Also via USENET and FTP.

Journal refereed: No

Internet: mporter@nyx.cs.du.edu

How to access: FTP to red.css.itd.umich.edu
The directory is: /zines/weirdness/
or FTP to slopoke.mlb.semi.harris.com
The directory is: /pub/weirdness/
Also gopher accessible at: gopher.well.sf.ca.us

HOLY TEMPLE OF MASS CONSUMPTION

Description: Holy Temple of Mass Consumption is an electronic journal of "articles, opinions, reviews, and artwork of a loosely-defined collection of cranks, weirdos, freaks, net.personalities, curmudgeons, and anyone else who turns us on at the time. Commentary on nearly everything, with particular attention to societal decay in general and mass-media conspiracy programming in particular. Or anything else we decide to write about, with strong ties to the finest SubGenius traditions."

Subjects covered: alternative literature; American literature and language; popular culture

Frequency: Monthly

Established: 1990

Method of issuance: Issues are emailed to subscribers as published.

Journal refereed: No

Editorial contact: Wayne Aiken
P.O. Box 30904, Raleigh, NC 27622.

Internet: slack@ncsu.edu

How to access: Send an email message to slack@ncsu.edu Hardcopy is also available from P.O. Box 30904, Raleigh, NC 27622.

HOST

Description: HOST is an electronic journal covering the history of science and technology.

Subjects covered: science and technology; history

Net address for questions or submissions: jsmith@epas.utoronto.ca

How to access: Send message to jsmith@epas.utoronto.ca

HOTT (HOTT OFF THE TREE)

Description: HOTT (Hott off the Tree) contains excerpts and abstracts of articles about current technology that effect or might have impact on libraries and educational institutions.

Subjects covered: science and technology; library and information science; education; computer science

Net address for operations: hott@ucsd.edu

Net address for questions or submissions: sjurist@ucsd.edu

Frequency: weekly (almost)

Established: October 1990

Number of issues published to date: Approximately 125

Method of issuance: By subscription through e-mail via a UCSD listserv (but the "listserv" is restricted so only I can transmit on it)

Recent issue published: 93.05.11

Subscribers: At least 200 people have subscriptions, but many of them also serve as distribution points. HOTT is also available on MEVLYL, the UC Catalog

Sponsor: Technology Watch Information Group, UCSD Libraries

Host: University of California, San Diego, 9500 Gilman Drive, La Jolla, CA 92093-0175

Editorial contact: Susan Jurist
UCSD Library 0175-F, 9500 Gilman Drive, La Jolla, CA 92093-0175

Tel: (619) 534-7193

Fax: (619) 534-0189

Internet: sjurist@ucsd.edu

Review: "HOTT has been cited in several places, but because of time constraints, I can't put my hands on them right now. One was the newsletter Apple sends to computer center types on campuses, and one was a recent issue on Multimedia for educational institutions."

How to access: Send e-mail to listserv@ucsd.edu with message subscribe <full.email.address> hott-list

How to unsubscribe: Send e-mail to listserv@ucsd.edu with message unsubscribe <full.email.address> hott-list

How to submit: hott@ucsd.edu

Submission policy: hott@ucsd.edu

Archives: Back issues available: on InfoPath, the UCSD gopher.

I.S.P.O.B. BULLETIN YSSTI

ISSN: 0353-9334
Description: The I.S.P.O.B. Bulletin is an electronic newsletter covering information science and technology issues in Yugoslavia.
Subjects covered: information technology; library and information science; science and technology
Frequency: Quarterly
Method of issuance: Issues are emailed to subscribers as published.
Host: University of Maribor, Yugoslavia
Journal refereed: No
Editorial contact: Davor Sostaric
University of Maribor, Institute of Information Sciences, Yugoslavia.
Internet: sostaric@uni-mb.ac.mail.yu, sostaric@ean.uni-mb.ac.mail.yu
Bitnet: davor%rcum@yubgef51.bitnet

IBJ: INTERNET BUSINESS JOURNAL

Description: The electronic version of the Internet Business Journal contains only the table of contents, article abstracts, editorial, letter from the publisher, and the column, Access--Ability, by Dr. Norm Coombs. Topics discussed in IBJ include commercialization of the Internet, business opportunities, and resources to be found on the Internet. The e-version is freely available in low ascii text and will soon be available as a PostScript file. The electronic version is roughly 11 pages in length (770 lines, 31238 bytes).
Subjects covered: Internet; business; telecommunications
Sponsor: Wladyslaw Poniecki Foundation
Editorial contact: Christopher Locke, Editor-in-Chief
Internet: chris@avalanche.com
Sample contents: RFC/FYI - Editorial, Christopher Locke; The National Information Infrastructure, Dr. Vinton G. Cerf; The Rise of Commercialization in the Internet, Robert Larribeau, Jr., Benefits of Commercial Use and Commercialization of the Internet, Bill Washburn; Advertising on the Internet, Adam Gaffin; Internet User Survey Results, Thomas J. Cozzolino & Thomas H. Pierce; Corporate Cybrary Networks: An Idea Whose Time Has Come, Michel Bauwens; The Cornell GateDaemon Consortium, Martyne Hallgren; National Science Foundation InterNIC Services; Regular Features: Internet in the UK, Susan Hallam; News From Europe, Michel Bauwens; Internet User Profile Access-Ability: Assistive Technologies and the Net Access-Ability: Assistive Technologies and the Net, Dr. Norm Coombs; Virtual Markets and Network Niches; Resources for Networked Business, Commerce and Industry; Government Online Network; News Network; The Internet in Print.
How to access: To access Volume One, Number One (June-July, 1993): Via LISTSERV send the command: get ibj-l ibj-1993.jun-jul to LISTSERV@poniecki.berkeley.edu Send the command in the body of the message, NOT in the subject line. DO NOT USE THE REPLY KEY TO SEND THIS COMMAND. NOTE: Only IBJ-L subscribers will be able to retrieve the LISTSERV copy. To subscribe to IBJ-L, send the command: SUB IBJ-L YOUR NAME to Listserv@poniecki.berkeley.edu Via anonymous FTP: FTP to poniecki.berkeley.edu cd pub/ibj get ibj-1993.jun-jul Via Gopher: gopher poniecki.berkeley.edu

70 select Info Services
Additional information: Queries regarding The Internet Business Journal should be sent to: Michael Strangelove, Publisher The Internet Business Journal. BITNET: 441495@Uottawa Internet: 441495@Acadvm1.Uottawa.CA Compuserve: 72302,3062 S-Mail: 177 Waller, Ottawa, Ontario, K1N 6N5 CANADA Voice: (613) 747-0642 FAX: (613) 564-6641.

ICS ELECTROZINE: INFORMATION, CONTROL, SUPPLY

Description: ICS Electrozine is an alternative electronic newsletter covering a wide variety of topics, ranging from games to the Internet.
Subjects covered: Internet; games and entertainment; information technology
Frequency: Biweekly
Established: 1993
Method of issuance: Issues are emailed to subscribers as published.
Journal refereed: No
Internet: org__zine@wsc.colorado.edu
How to access: Send an email message to org__zine@wsc.colorado.edu

IHOUSE-L INTERNATIONAL VOICE NEWSLETTER PROTOTYPE LIST

Description: IHOUSE-L International Voice Newsletter is the electronic newsletter of Washington University's International Office. It contains information of interest to foreign students studying at Washington University.
Subjects covered: education; colleges and universities
Frequency: Quarterly
Established: 1991
Method of issuance: Issues are emailed to subscribers as published.
Editorial contact: Doyle Cozadd
Bitnet: c73221dc@wuvmd
How to access: Send the message SUBSCRIBE IHOUSE-L to listserv@wuvmd

ILAS-NET

Description: ILAS-NET is a moderated newsletter for mathematicians from all over the world, dealing with linear algebra.
Subjects covered: linear algebra; mathematics
Net address for operations: LISTSERV@TECHNION.TECHNION.AC.
Net address for questions or submissions: MAR23AA@TECHNION.TECHNION.AC.IL
Established: November 9, 1987
Subscribers: 507
Sponsor: ILAS - The International Linear Algebra Society, Mathematics Department
Technion - Israel Institute of Technology, Haifa 32000 Israel.
Editorial contact: Prof. Daniel Hershkowitz
Mathematics Department, Technion - Israel Institute of Technology, Haifa 32000
Israel
Tel: 972-4-294282
Fax: 972-4-324654
Internet: mar23aa@technion.technion.ac.il

Bitnet: mar23aa@technion
Technical contact: same as above
Review: ILAS operates ILAS-NET, an electronic news service. We transmit announcements of ILAS activities and circulate other notices of interest to linear algebraists.
How to access: Send the message SUB ILAS-NET to LISTSERV@TECHNION.TE
Access policy: This electronic newsletter is open to all.
How to unsubscribe: Send the message SIGNOFF ILAS-NET to LISTSERV@TECHN
How to submit: Send submissions to mar23aa@technion.technion.ac.il
Submission policy: This newsletter publishes notices of interest to linear algebraists.
Archives: Ask from mar23aa@technion.technion.

INFOBITS
Description: INFOBITS is a monthly information service provided by the Institute for Academic Technology's Information Resources Group. It covers information and instructional technologies.
Subjects covered: information technology; computer-assisted instruction (CAI)
Net address for operations: listserv@gibbs.oit.unc.edu
How to access: Send email to listserv@gibbs.oit.unc.edu with the following message: SUBSCRIBE INFOBITS Firstname Lastname

INFORMATION NETWORKING NEWS
ISSN: 0966-2774
Description: Information Networking News publishes feature articles on CD-ROM networking projects, reviews and evaluations of systems and products, discussions of related topics (e.g., licensing questoins), details of forthcoming conferences, etc.
Subjects covered: library and information science; CD-ROMs; colleges and universities; electronic networking
Net address for operations: CDROMLAN @ IDBSU, CD-ROM-NETWORK @ JNT.AC.UK
Net address for questions or submissions: GARTNER @ VAX.OX.AC.UK
Frequency: Quarterly; irregular
Established: 1992
Number of issues published to date: 5
Method of issuance: New issues are distributed via email.
Available in other media: No.
Recent issue published: 5
Sponsor: Joint Network Team, CD-ROM and Information Networking Group, c/o Michele Shoebridge, University of Birmingham, Edgbaston, Birmingham B15 2TT, UK.
Journal refereed: No.
Editorial contact: Richard Gartner
Bodleian Library, Broad Street, Oxford OX1 3BG, UK.
Tel: +44 865 277060
Fax: +44 865 277182
Internet: GARTNER@VAX.OX.AC.UK
Sample contents: Networking Medline on Hard Disk: CD Plus and SilverPlatter Compared, by John Cox, Royal Free Hospital School of Medicine, London UK; Networking CD-ROMs with NFS: A Brief Review, by Edmund Sutcliffe, University of York, UK; The Library CD-ROM Service at Imperial College, by Janice Yeadon and Harry Gluck, Imperial College of Science and Technology, London, UK; Assessment and Evaluation of

Networked CD-ROMs as Academic Information Sources, by Sarah Ward, University of Manchester Institute of Science & Technology, Manchester, UK; Forthcoming Events and Conferences.
How to access: INFORMATION NETWORKING NEWS is sent to:- 1) the CD-ROM-NETWORK @ UK.AC.JNT discussion list: to add your name to this list, simply send a request to CD-ROM-NETWORK-REQUEST @ UK.AC.JNT 2) the CDROMLAN @ IDBSU mailing list: to join this list send a message to LISTSERV @ IDBSU containing the single line "SUBSCRIBE CDROMLAN Yourfirstname Yourlast name" eg. "SUBSCRIBE CDROMLAN Alan Smith"
How to unsubscribe: 1) the CD-ROM-NETWORK @ UK.AC.JNT discussion list: to remove your name from this list, simply send a request to CD-ROM-NETWORK-REQUEST @ UK.AC.JNT 2) the CDROMLAN @ IDBSU mailing list: to ubsubscribe from this list send a message to LISTSERV @ IDBSU containing the single line "UNSUBSCRIBE CDROMLAN Yourfirstname Yourlast name" eg. "UNSUBSCRIBE CDROMLAN Alan Smith"
How to submit: Email to GARTNER@VAX.OX.AC.UK
Archives: YES Back copies are available by ftp from the LIBSOFT archive at the University of Western Ontario, Canada. To access this archive: FTP to HYDRA.UWO.CA (129.100.2.13). Login as ANONYMOUS, and give your email address as a password. Type CD LIBSOFT to change to the LIBSOFT directory. Type GET + filename to retrieve the file you want (GET INFNETNEWS5.TXT for issue no 5). Type CLOSE to close the connection. Type QUIT to leave the FTP software.
Gopher accessibility: 1) On the BUBL Bulletin Board in the UK: to access this service:- - from JANET, connect to GLA.BUBL (or 00007110004011) - from IXI: connect to 20433450710511 - from Internet: telnet to SUN.NSF.AC.UK, login: janet, hostname: uk.ac.glasgow.bubl 2) Gopher access: available on the Radcliffe Science Library gopher, Oxford, UK. EITHER: telnet to RSL.OX.AC.UK, login: gopher (no password required) OR: point your gopher at:-
Name = Oxford Radcliffe Science Library Type = 1 Port = 70 Path = 1/ Host = rsl.ox.ac.uk
Additional information: Additional editors: Michele Shoebridge, Main Library, University of Birmingham, Edgbaston, Birmingham B15 2TT, UK; tel: +44 21 414 5835; M.I.SHOEBRIDGE.BHAM.AC.UK; Doug Moncur, Computing Service, University of York, Heslington, York YO1 5DD, UK; tel: +44 904 433815; D.MONCUR@YORK.AC.UK; Paul Leman, Computing Service, University of Sheffield, Sheffield, UK; CS1PJL@PRIMEA.SHEFFIELD.AC.UK

INFORMATION TECHNOLOGY TIMES
Description: Information Technology Times is a newsletter focusing on IT concerns at the University of California at Davis.
Subjects covered: information technology; telecommunications; electronic networking; computer hardware and software
Frequency: Quarterly
Method of issuance: Issues are emailed to subscribers as published.
Host: Department of Information Technology, University of California at Davis
Journal refereed: No
Editorial contact: Ivars Balkits
Internet: isbalkits@ucdavis.edu

How to access: FTP to silo.ucdavis.edu The directory is: /it-newsletter/ or Gopher to gopher.ucdavis.edu and choose it-newsletter

INSTANT MATH PREPRINTS (IMP)

Description: Instant Math Preprints is comprised of a database of abstracts of math preprints located at Yale University and the full-text preprints themselves which are available through ftp at a variety of institutions.
Subjects covered: mathematics
Frequency: Irregular
Method of issuance: The database is accessible through telnet.
Host: Yale University Libraries; American Mathematical Society
Journal refereed: No
Editorial contact: Katherine Branch
Head of Science Libraries
Yale University, 219 Prospect Street, New Haven, CT 06511
Tel: (203) 432-3439
Fax: (203) 432-3441
Internet: katherine__branch@quickmail.cis.yale.edu
How to access: Contact katherine__ branch@quickmail.cis.yale.edu

INTERNATIONAL TELETIMES

Description: International Teletimes is a general interest magazine. There are several recurring monthly columns but the rest of the content changes from month to month as new themes are chosen. The goal of Teletimes is to attract a large variety of writers from all over the world so that the readers will be exposed to a great variety of ideas and opinions.
Subjects covered: alternative literature
Editorial contact: Ian Tojtowicz
Internet: ian@breez.wimsey.com
How to access: ftp to sumex-aim.standord.edu and find the directory named /info-mac/per/teletimes-*.hqx

THE INTERNET HUNT

Description: The Internet Hunt is not strictly an electronic journal, although new installments appear regularly, posted to a variety of discussion lists, Usenet newsgroups, and ftp sites. It is a question and answer forum designed to test Internetters' abilities to retrieve items of information using only the Internet.
Subjects covered: Internet; library and information science
Editorial contact: Rick Gates
University of Arizona, Tucson, AZ 85719.
Tel: 602-621-3958
Internet: rgates@nic.cic.net
Archives: Archives are available at ftp.cic.net and ftp.cni.org, among other sites.
Gopher accessibility: New Hunts are gopher-accessible at gopher.cic.net and gopher at gopher.cni.org, among other places.

INTERNET MONTHLY REPORT

Description: The Internet Monthly Report is an electronic newsletter of the Internet Research Group.
Subjects covered: Internet; telecommunications
Frequency: Monthly
Established: 1991

Method of issuance: Issues are emailed to subscribers as published.
Host: Internet Research Group
Journal refereed: No
Internet: imr@isi.edu
How to access: FTP to venera.isi.edu The directory is: /in-notes/imr/ Or send email to rfc-info@isi.edu

INTERTEXT - AN ELECTRONIC FICTION MAGAZINE

Description: Intertext (formerly titled Athene) is an electronic publication featuring fiction, poetry, and other texts related to cybercultural modes of expression.
Subjects covered: science fiction; language and literature; fantasy fiction; horror fiction
Frequency: Bimonthly
Established: 1991
Method of issuance: Issues are emailed to subscribers as published.
Journal refereed: No
Editorial contact: Jason Snell
InterText, 21645 Parrotts Ferry, Sonora, CA 95370.
Internet: jsnell@ocf.berkeley.edu or intertxt@network.ucsd.edu
How to access: Send message to jsnell@ocf.Berkeley.edu
Gopher accessibility: Gopher accessible at: etext.archive.umich.edu

IOUDAIOS REVIEW

ISSN: 1183-9937
Description: IOUDAIOS Review is a review journal for books primarily in the field of early Judaism (200 B.C.E. - 200 C.E.) and secondarily in the relation of early Judaism to Christian origins. It is the electronic journal of the discussion list IOUDAIOS@YORKVM1.
Subjects covered: Judaica; Hebrew language and literature; language and literature; Christianity
Net address for operations: LISTSERV@YORKVM1
Net address for questions or submissions: n51nh301@unity.ncsu.edu
Frequency: Irregular
Established: July 1991
Number of issues published to date: 3 (1 ''issue'' per year)
Method of issuance: Automatic on list IOUD-REV
Issues are announced on IOUDAIOS@YORKVM1
Available in other media: No. Hard copy is lodged in the National Library of Canada (Ottawa).
Recent issue published: 3.015
Subscribers: 240
Sponsor: Wilfrid Laurier University; North Carolina State University
Host: York University, 4700 Keele Street, North York, ON, Canada M3J 1P3
Editorial contact: William Adler, Department of Philosophy and Religion, North Carolina State University, Raleigh, NC, U.S.A. 27695-8103
Tel: (919) 515-3214
Internet: n51nh301@unity.ncsu.edu
Sample contents: Each review appears as a separate number in the annual ''issue.''
Copyright statement: (c) [date] Reproduction beyond fair use only on permission of the editors.

How to access: Send message "SUB IOUD-REV Your Name" to LISTSERV@YORKVM1.
Access policy: Available primarily to members of the discussion list IOUDAIOS.
How to unsubscribe: Send message "UNS IOUD-REV" to LISTSERV@YORKVM1.
How to submit: David Reimer (dreimer@mach1.wlu.ca/ dreimer@vax.ox.ac.uk).
Submission policy: William Adler (n51nh301@unity.ncsu.edu)
Archives: From listserv@yorkvm1; see file IOUD-REV INDEX for list of past reviews.
Related files: Instructors to contributors and conventions used for tagging of e-text available in file IOUD-REV GUIDE.
Gopher accessibility: The editors are currently exploring the possibility of having the archive stored on a gopher site.
Additional information: David Reimer, Regent's Park College, Oxford OX1 2LB England; tel(0865) 59887; Internet dreimer@vax.ox.ac.uk. The editors are considering making available a hard-copy edition of IOUDAIOS Review.

IPCT-J (INTERPERSONAL COMPUTING AND TECHNOLOGY: AN ELECTRONIC JOURNAL FOR THE 21ST CENTURY)
ISSN: 1064-4326
Description: IPCT: An Electronic Journal for the 21st Century is based on the following premises: The electronic journal is the wave of the future. By the year 2000, the bulk of information will be exchanged electronically and the nature of print media will have changed drastically. There are, currently, several barriers to the use of electronic journals as outlets for scholarly research. These include: copyright problems, the problem of co-ordinating with print publication, and especially the validation of the electronic journal as a legitimate outlet for dissemination of scholarly studies, suitable for credit toward promotion and tenure in colleges and universities. IPCT: An Electronic Journal for the 21st Century will attempt to address these three concerns.
Subjects covered: telecommunications; Internet; communications
Net address for operations: LISTSERV@GUVM.GEORGETOWN.EDU
Frequency: Quarterly
Established: January 1993
Number of issues published to date: 3
Method of issuance: Issues emailed to subscribers on list. New issues are announced on IPCT-L, the related list.
Recent issue published: Volume 1, Number 3, July 1993
Subscribers: 800+
Sponsor: Published by the Center for Teaching and Technology, Academic Computer Center, Georgetown University, Washington, DC 10057. Additional support provided by the Center for Academic Computing, The Pennsylvania State University, University Park, PA 16802.
Journal refereed: Yes. All articles will be given at least two blind reviews and published articles will be selected by the editors. In our reviewing process, we will conform to the highest standards of reviewing used in the best print journals. Our associate editors (reviewers) will be selected on criteria of editorial experience and status in their field of expertise.
Editorial contact: Gerald M. Phillips
Internet: gmp@psuvm.psu.edu
Bitnet: GMP@PSUVM.BITNET
Technical contact: Zane Berge

Internet: BERGE@GUVAX.GEORGETOWN.EDU
Bitnet: BERGE@GUVAX
Sample contents: A report of Syracuse University's Computer-Facilitated Learning Program in Adult Education; Using Computers to Teach Journalism: What Some Students Think; Advantages of Group Decision Support Systems; Augmenting a Group Discussion Course with Computer-Mediated Communication in a Small College Setting.
Copyright statement: Copyright 1993 Georgetown University. Copyright of individual >articles in this publication is retained by the individual authors. Copyright of the compilation as a whole is held by Georgetown University. It is asked that any republication of this article state that the article was first published in IPCT-J.
How to access: Send the following one-line message in the body of an email message to LISTSERV@GUVM or LISTSERV@GUVM.GEORGETOWN.EDU; SUBSCRIBE IPCT-J YOURFIRSTNAME YOURLASTNAME
How to unsubscribe: Send the following one line message to LISTSERV@GUVM or LISTSERV@GUVM.GEORGETOWN.EDU as an interactive message or (in the body, not the Subject: line of the email note): SIGNOFF IPCT-J
Archives: Articles are stored as files at LISTSERV@GUVM.BITnet. To retrieve a file interactively, send the GET command given after the article abstract to LISTSERV@GUVM. To retrieve the article as a e-mail message add F=MAIL to your interactive message, or send an e-mail note in the following format: To:listserv@guvm.georgetown.edu GET <FILENAME> IPCTV1N3 . The GET command GET IPCTV1N3 PACKAGE will retrieve the entire issue. [WARNING: This will send all five files with a total of over > 2600 lines.] The listserv's Internet address is LISTSERV@GUVM.GEORGETOWN.EDU Back issues of the journal are stored at LISTSERV@GUVM. To obtain a list of all available files, send the following message to LISTSERV@GUVM: INDEX IPCT-J. The name of each issue's table of contents file begins with the word "CONTENTS". FTP of IPCT-J articles is available. FTP to GUVM.CCF.GEORGETOWN.EDU or 141.161.71.1, logon IPCT-J, password is GUEST. All IPCT-J files are currently ASCII format only. If you experience difficulties with these instructions, please consult your local site administrator for specific instructions that may apply to your system.
Related files: IPCT-L, Interpersonal Computing and Technology List (Subscribers to IPCT-L automatically receive IPCT-J).

IR-LIST DIGEST
ISSN: 1064-6965
Description: IR-LIST Digest contains papers, meeting announcements, information searches, job listings, conference proceedings, bibliographies, dissertation abstracts, and other material about information retrieval. This forum facilitates exchanging ideas, asking and answering questions, and generally sharing information and knowledge on information retrieval theory and technology.
Subjects covered: library and information science; computer hardware and software
Net address for operations: listserv@uccvma
Net address for questions or submissions: ncgur@uccmvsa.bitnet, ir-l@uccvma.bitnet
Frequency: Weekly
Established: 1989

Number of issues published to date: 160
Method of issuance: Issues are mailed to listserv distribution list.
Recent issue published: Volume 10, Number 19, Issue 163
Subscribers: 1375
Sponsor: Library Automation, University of California, Office of the President, 300 Lakeside Drive, 8th floor Oakland, CA 94612-3550.
Host: Library Automation, University of California, Office of the President, 300 Lakeside Drive, 8th floor Oakland, CA 94612-3550.
Journal refereed: No, submissions are organized by topic and emailed weekly in issues generally no longer than 400 lines. Submissions are edited lightly for typographical errors, etc., and are only rejected if the topic is not relevant.
Editorial contact: Clifford A. Lynch
Library Automation, University of California, Office of the President, 300 Lakeside Drive, 8th floor Oakland, CA 94612-3550.
Tel: 510/987-0522
Fax: 510/839-3573
Internet: calur@uccmvsa.ucop.edu
Bitnet: calur@uccmvsa
Technical contact: Nancy Gusack
Library Automation, University of California, Office of the President, 300 Lakeside Drive, 8th floor Oakland, CA 94612-3550.
Tel: 510/987-0565
Fax: 510/839-3573
Internet: ncgur@uccmvsa.ucop.edu
Bitnet: ncgur@uccmvsa
Sample contents: I. NOTICES; A. Meeting Announcements/ Calls for Papers; 1. 4th Int'l. Workshop on Network & Operating System; Support for Digital Audio & Video; 2. 1993 Int'l. Simulation Technology Multiconference; 3. Hypertext '93: Student Volunteers; 4. Towards a Global Expert System in Law; 5. 2nd Int'l. Conference on Arabic & Advanced Computer Technology.
How to access: Send requests to Nancy Gusack at ncgur@uccmvsa.bitnet or ncgur@uccmvsa.ucop.edu
Access policy: This serial is open to anyone.
How to unsubscribe: Send requests to Nancy Gusack at ncgur@uccmvsa.bitnet or ncgur@uccmvsa.ucop.edu
How to submit: Send submissons or questions to Nancy Gusack at ncgur@uccmvsa.bitnet or ncgur@uccmvsa.ucop.edu
Submission policy: Anyone may submit items for the digest.
Archives: Archives are available. Via listserv: Send the message INDEX IR-L to listserv@uccvma.bitnet or listserv@uccvma.ucop.edu. To get a specific issue listed in the Index, send the message GET IR-L LOGYYMM, where YY is the year and MM is the numeric month in which the issue was mailed, to either of those listserv addresses. Using anonymous FTP via the host dla.ucop.edu, the files will be found in the directory pub/irl, stored in subdirectories by year (e.g., /pub/irl/ 1993).
Additional information: Additional editors: Nancy Gusack, Library Automation, University of California, Office of the President, 300 Lakeside Drive, 8th floor Oakland, CA 94612-3550; tel510/987-0565; fax510/839-3573; Internet: ncgur@uccmvsa.ucop.edu; Bitnet: ncgur@uccmvsa; Mary Engle, Library Automation, University of California, Office of the President, 300 Lakeside Drive, 8th floor Oakland, CA 94612-3550; tel510/987-0563; fax510/839-3573; Internet: meeur@uccmvsa.ucop.edu; Bitnet: meeur@uccmvsa

ISSUES IN SCIENCE AND TECHNOLOGY LIBRARIANSHIP

Description: Issues In Science and Technology Librarianship is a publication of the Science and Technology Section of the Association of College and Research Libraries, a division of the American Library Association.
Subjects covered: science and technology; library and information science
Net address for questions or submissions: ACRLSTS@HAL.UNM.EDU
Editorial contact: Harry Llull
How to access: Send email message to ACRLSTS@HAL.UNM.EDU
How to unsubscribe: Send email message to ACRLSTS@HAL.UNM.EDU
Additional information: Editorial Board: Lynn Kaczor, Gregg Sapp, and John Saylor. This publication is produced at the Centennial Science and Engineering Library, University of New Mexico, Albuquerque, New Mexico, and sent out in electronic form only. Send message to ACRLSTS@HAL.UNM.EDU for further details.

JONATHAN'S SPACE REPORT

Description: Jonathan's Space Report is an electronic compilation of space-related news and information on astronomy and space flight.
Subjects covered: astronomy; space and space exploration
Frequency: Irregular
Established: 1989
Method of issuance: Issues are emailed to subscribers as published.
Journal refereed: No
Editorial contact: Jonathan McDowell
Internet: mcdowell@urania.harvard.edu
How to access: Send email to: mcdowell@urania.harvard.edu

JOURNAL OF ARTIFICIAL INTELLIGENCE RESEARCH (JAIR)

Description: JAIR is published by the AI Access Foundation, a nonprofit corporation devoted to the electronic dissemination of scientific results in AI. JAIR is a refereed publication, covering all areas of AI, that will be distributed free of charge over the internet by ftp, electronic mail, and in the newsgroups comp.ai.jair (announcements and abstracts of new papers), comp.ai.jair.ps (postscript versions of papers), comp.ai.jair.text (text versions of papers), comp.ai.jair.code (code and data appendices), and comp.ai.jair.d (unmoderated discussion of published articles).
Subjects covered: artificial intelligence
Available in other media: Each complete volume of JAIR will be published in print by Morgan Kaufmann.
Journal refereed: Yes. JAIR aims to have a review turn-around time of about 5 weeks, with electronic publication occurring immediately after the editor receives the final version of an accepted article.
How to access: Further information regarding submissions can be obtained by sending a request to jair@ptolemy.arc.nasa.gov.

JOURNAL OF COMPUTING IN HIGHER EDUCATION

ISSN: 1042-1726
Description: The Journal of Computing in Higher Education publishes refereed articles on instructional technologies and the use of computer-based systems in education.
Subjects covered: education; computer-assisted instruction (CAI)
Frequency: Biannual
Established: 1989
Method of issuance: Issues are emailed to subscribers as published.
Journal refereed: Yes
Editorial contact: Carol B. MacKnight
Office of Instructional Technology, A115 Lederle Graduate Research Center, Amherst, MA 01003.
Internet: cmacknight@ucs.umass.edu
How to access: Send a message to cmacknight@ucs.umass.edu

JOURNAL OF EXTENSION

ISSN: 0022-0140
Description: Journal of Extension is a peer-reviewed electronic journal dealing with distance learning, adult education, and land-grant educational institutions. Manuscripts submitted for the various Journal sections are subject to peer review by three members of the Editorial Committee. The Journal is the official refereed publication of the Cooperative Extension System. The Journal expands and updates the research and knowledge base for Extension professionals and other adult educators to improve their effectiveness. In addition, the Journal serves as a forum for emerging and contemporary issues affecting Extension education. It is written and edited by Extension professionals, sharing with their colleagues successful educational applications, original and applied research findings, scholarly opinions, educational resources, and challenges on issues of critical importance to Extension educators.
Subjects covered: agriculture; colleges and universities; distance education; adult education
Net address for operations: joe.uwex.edu
Frequency: Quarterly
Established: December 1992 for electronic version, since 1962 for print.
Number of issues published to date: 2 in electronic form, 120 for print
Method of issuance: Email distribution to subscription list. Issues are announced on email via joe@joe.uwex.edu
Available in other media: Print is existing. We are doing a pilot project to evaluate whether Extension county agents will accept an electronic format. Continuation of electronic format (and paper) depends upon the results of this study. During our pilot project, we'll electronically publish five issues (Winter ''92 through Winter '93). Subscribers tp EJOE may request articles in text., PostScript, and Rich Text Formats from current and back issues. EJOE is one of a few E-journals that offers multiple formats to their subscribers.
Recent issue published: 31, Number 1
Subscribers: 500 outside subscribers and 13 states where all Extension personnel with e-mail addresses are subscribed. Est. total 3000.
Sponsor: Extension Journal Inc, Madison WI
Host: University of Wisconsin-Extension
Journal refereed: Yes.
Editorial contact: Ellen Ritter

Room 229, Reed McDonald Building, Texas A&M,College Station, TX 77843-2112
Tel: (409) 845-2211
Internet: e-ritter1@tamu.edu (Ellen Ritter)
Technical contact: Dirk Herr-Hoyman
302 Hiram Smith Hall, 1545 Observatory Dr., University of Wisconsin-Extension, Madison, WI 53706
Tel: (608) 265-3893
Fax: (608) 265-2530
Internet: hoymand@joe.uwex.edu
Indexed or abstracted: We provide contents with abstracts and a full-text search via e-mail and Gopher. There is a yearly index published with the Fall issue. The Journal of Extension is most likely indexed by other services, for example it is found in CARL.
Copyright statement: Copyright (c) 1993 by Extension Journal, Inc. Articles appearing in the Journal become property of the Journal. Single copies of these articles may be reproduced in print or electronic form for use in educational or training activities. However, inclusion of the articles in other publications, electronic sources, or systematic large-scale distribution may be done only with prior written permission of the Journal Editorial Office, 432 N. Lake Street, Madison, Wisconsin 53706.
How to access: Send e-mail to almanac@joe.uwex.edu with message "subscribe joe".
Access policy: Open to all with access to Internet e-mail. Detailed guidelines for contributors are available by emailing editor.
How to unsubscribe: Send e-mail to almanac@joe.uwex.edu with message "unsubscribe joe"
How to submit: Submissions are sent via U.S. Mail to the editor. Send 4 copies and $20 review fee.
Archives: This journal has been archived from Fall 1987. You may send search requests via E-mail that query a collection of over 500 JOE articles published since the Winter 1987 issue.
Related files: We'll support anonymous ftp access to our article collection.
Gopher accessibility: Gopher access is planned for Summer 1993.
WAIS accessibility: WAIS in Fall 1993.
WorldWideWeb accessibility: WWW if EJOE continues past pilot study.
Additional information: Other future enhancements include the use of MIME (Multimedia Internet Mail Extensions), and likely use of Adobe Acrobat's PDF (Portable Document Format).

JOURNAL OF FLUIDS ENGINEERING-- ARCHIVE

Description: The Journal of Fluids Engineering, published by The American Society of Mechanical Engineers, has begun offering its readers the opportunity to obtain electronic files, via the Internet, of the full data on which some of its published research papers are based. It appears that many readers already are using the service. In its two most recent issues (December 1992 and March 1993), the Journal has published a total of five research papers accompanied by extensive research data -- far too voluminous to be included in the print journal; the data are archived electronically in the Newman Library at Virginia Polytechnic Institute and State University and available via the Internet as electronic files. Readers are advised, through notes accompanying each article and instructions at the back of each journal issue, how they can retrieve the files electronically via File Transfer Protocol (ftp). The service was initiated on an experimental basis through the cooperation of the Scholarly Communications Project at Virginia Tech, which publishes several electronic journals, and the University Libraries, which contributed the storage space.

Subjects covered: fluids; engineering; science and technology
Sponsor: The American Society of Mechanical Engineers

JOURNAL OF TECHNOLOGY EDUCATION

ISSN: 1045-1064
Description: The Journal of Technology Education, as its name implies, focuses on research, theory, and practice relating to the field of technology education. Not to be confused with "educational technology," which is all about instructional technologies, technology education is a subject in our public schools that attempts to teach ALL children a a little bit about a lot of different technologies. Technology education content falls within four general areas: Communication, Manufacturing, Transportation, and Construction.
Subjects covered: technology education; communications; manufacturing; transportation
Net address for operations: listserv@vtvm1.cc.vt.edu
Frequency: Twice annually: Fall and Spring issues
Number of issues published to date: 2
Method of issuance: Hard copy and electronic versions.
Available in other media: Yes. Print. There is also a more traditional "hard copy" version of the JTE available at the VERY modest cost of $8/year ($12/year for those outside the United States). If you are interested in the hard copy subscription, send a check (drawn against an American Bank) and your address to: Journal of Technology Education, 144 Smyth Hall, Virginia Tech, Blacksburg, VA 24061-0432.
Recent issue published: Volume 4 #2
Subscribers: 530 hard copy, about 1000 electronic
Fee: Fees are only for hard copy. Electronic version is currently free, though we may soon go to "shareware" billing procedures.
Sponsor: Virginia Tech
Host: Virginia Tech
Journal refereed: Yes. Blind review by three reviewers.
Editorial contact: Mark Sanders
144 Smyth Hall, Virginia Tech, Blacksburg, VA 24061-0432
Tel: I prefer these not be listed.
How to access: To subscribe to the electronic version of the JTE, send the e-mail message below to the address: LISTSERV at VTVM1. The message to send is: SUBSCRIBE JTE-L first name last name where first name and last name is YOUR name, without any punctuation Do not include a subject with your message, as this may cause problems.
Submission policy: Send 5 hard copies of article to the editor
Archives: All issues are electronically archived and available.

JOURNAL OF THE INTERNATIONAL ACADEMY OF HOSPITALITY RESEARCH

ISSN: 1052-6099
Description: The Journal of the International Academy of Hospitality Research is a fee-based, refereed electronic journal covering a wide range of topics in tourism and hospitality research.
Subjects covered: travel and tourism; hospitality research
Frequency: Irregular
Established: 1990
Method of issuance: Individual articles are emailed to subscribers as published.

Fee: Subscriptions: $30 to institutions; $20 to individuals; $10 to students.
Host: International Academy of Hospitality Research, Virginia Polytechnic Institute
Journal refereed: Yes
Internet: jiahred@vtvm1.cc.vt.edu
How to access: Send the message SUBSCRIBE JIAHR-L to listserv@vtvm1.cc.vt.edu
Related files: Send the message INDEX JIAHR-L to listserv@vtvm1.cc.vt.edu or FTP to borg.lib.vt.edu and choose directory: /pub/JIAHR

JOURNAL OF UNDERGRADUATE RESEARCH

Description: The Journal of Undergraduate Research offers research documents on liberal arts and humanities related topics.
Subjects covered: language and literature; humanities
Frequency: Semi-annual
Established: 1993
Method of issuance: Available via FTP or Gopher
Journal refereed: Yes
Internet: fox@csf.colorado.edu
How to access: FTP to spot.colorado.edu
The directory is: /spot/usr/ftp/eforum/honors/journal ugr/
Or gopher to: csf.colorado.edu

KANJI OF THE DAY

Description: Kanji of the Day emails one word of Kanji every day to its subscribers.
Subjects covered: Kanji
Frequency: Daily
Method of issuance: Issues are emailed to subscribers as published.
Journal refereed: No
Internet: stueber@vax.mpiz-koeln.mpg.dbp.de
How to access: Gopher to gopher.cic.net

KIDLINK NEWSLETTER

Description: The KIDLINK Newsletter provides information for educators and other interested parties on the activities of the KIDLINK program to get children involved in telecommunicating with each other worldwide.
Subjects covered: telecommunications; children; Internet
Frequency: Bimonthly
Established: 1990
Method of issuance: Issues are emailed to subscribers as published.
Editorial contact: Odd de Presno
Internet: opresno@extern.uio.no
How to access: Send email to opresno@extern.uio.no

LAW AND POLITICS BOOK REVIEW

ISSN: 1062-7421
Description: Law and Politics Book Review is an electronic journal featuring reviews of current books reporting scholarly research on law and courts; reviews by experts in the field; length ranges generally from 1000 to 2000 words; most reviews are published within 6 months of receipt of book.

Subjects covered: law and legal studies; book reviews; political science
Net address for operations: listserv@mizzou1.missouri.edu
Net address for questions or submissions: psrt-l@mizzou1.missouri1.edu
Frequency: usually once a week
Established: March 1990
Method of issuance: Issues are distributed via e-mail as published.
Recent issue published: Vol. 3, No. 5 (May 1993)
Subscribers: 600
Sponsor: Law & Courts Section, American Political Science Association, 1527 New Hampshire Ave. NW, Washington, DC 20036
Host: Department of Political Science, Northwestern University, 601 University Place, Evanston, IL 60208
Journal refereed: No
Editorial contact: Professor Herbert Jacob
Department of Political Science, Northwestern University, 601 University Place, Evanston, IL 60208
Tel: (708) 491-2648
Fax: (708) 491-8985
Internet: mzltov@nwu.edu
Sample contents: Books reviewed: Robin Fox, Reproduction & Succession: Studies in Anthropology, Law and Society. New Brunswick, N.J: Transaction Press, 1993. Reviewed by William Arens (SUNY Stony Brook); Paul Chevigny, Gigs: Jazz and the Cabaret Laws in New York City. New York: Routledge, 1991. Reviewed by Dennis Coyle (Catholic University of America); Barbara J. Shapiro, Beyond Reasonable Doubt and Probable Cause: Historical Perspectives on the Anglo-American Law of Evidence. Berkeley: University of California Press, 1993. Reviewed by Stephan Landsman (Cleveland-Marshall College of Law); Kitty Calavita, Inside the State: The Bracero Program, Immigration, and the I.N.S.. New York: Routledge, 1992. Reviewed by Peter H. Schuck (Yale Law School); Kermit L. Hall (ed.), The Oxford Companion to the Supreme Court of the United States. New York: Oxford University Press, 1993. Reviewed by Herbert Jacob (Northwestern University); and David G. Barnum, The Supreme Court and American Democracy. New York: St. Martins Press, 1993. Reviewed by Richard Brisbin (West Virginia State University).
Copyright statement: Authors of reviews assign to The Law and Politics Book Review the right to distribute their text electronically and to archive and make it permanently retrievable electronically, but they retain the copyright. After their review has appeared in The Law and Politics Book Review, authors may reproduce their review or authorize others to do so elsewhere. We ask, however, that you credit The Law and Politics Book Review as the source.
How to access: Send message: SUBSCRIBE PSRT-L [YOURNAME] to LISTSERV@MIZZOU1.MISSOURI.EDU
How to unsubscribe: UNSUBSCRIBE PSRT-L to LISTSERV@MIZZOU1.MISSOURI.EDU
How to submit: mzltov@nwu.edu
Archives: To order previously published reviews, send the command GET INDEX LPBR to LISTSERV@MIZZOU1.MISSOURI.EDU and then request individual files from that list. To order ALL past reviews, just send the command GET LPBR PACKAGE to LISTSERV@MIZZOU1.MISSOURI.EDU.

LC CATALOGING NEWSLINE
ISSN: 1066-8829
Description: The LC Cataloging Newsline provides information on the Library of Congress' cataloging activies.
Subjects covered: library and information science; Library of Congress; library collection development
Frequency: Quarterly
Established: 1993
Method of issuance: Issues are emailed to subscribers as published.
Journal refereed: Reviewed by the LCCN Advisory Committee and approved by the Director for Cataloging
Editorial contact: Robert M. Hiatt
Internet: hiatt@mail.loc.gov
How to access: Send the message SUBSCRIBE LCCN to listserv@sun7. loc.gov

LEONARDO ELECTRONIC NEWS
Description: Leonardo Electronic News contains short articles dealing with the uses of science and technology in the arts. Every other issue, which is edited by Judy Malloy is called a WORDS ON WORKS ISSUE, which contains 3-4 writings by artists about a single art piece, installation, project etc. The other issues are either thematic or general issues. Past issues have covered Holography, Sound and Movement and New Technology and Entertainment. Each issue also contains calendar listings for the following month and information about some upcoming opportunities in the arts, sciences and technology.
Subjects covered: science and technology; fine arts; hypermedia; language and literature
Net address for operations: fast@garnet. berkeley.edu.
Net address for questions or submissions: fast@garnet. berkeley.edu.
Frequency: Monthly
Established: November 1991
Method of issuance: Issues are sent via subscription to individuals and exploders.
Available in other media: MIT Press is offering Leonardo Electronic News monthly to subscribers for $25 a year. Current members of Leonardo/ISAST, subscribers to the journal LEONARDO, and our LEN subscribers who have donated money to Leonardo/ISAST to support this activity, will receive their issues gratis. Individuals and organizations subscribing now will receive issues until the end of 1994, providing 16 issues for the price of 12. FineArt Forum subscribers will continue to receive FineArt Forum gratis. To subscribe to Leonardo Electronic News, send your name, address and credit card information to: journals-orders@mit.edu.
Recent issue published: Volume 3, Number 6 to be sent out 6/15
Subscribers: 750
Fee: Currently electronic subscriptions are free of charge, but donations are gladly accepted. Check, money order, credit card.
Sponsor: Leonardo, the International Society for the Arts, Sciences and Technology (ISAT), 672 South Van Ness, San Francisco, CA 94110.
Host: Same as above
Editorial contact: Craig Harris, Executive Editor
Leonardo/ISAT, 672 South Van Ness, San Francisco, CA 94110.
Tel: (415) 431-7414
Fax: (415) 431-5737
Internet: craig@well.sf.ca.us

Technical contact: Annie Lewis
Leonardo/ISAST, 672 Van Ness, San Francicso, CA 94110.
Tel: (415) 431-5737
Internet: fast@garnet.berkeley.edu, isast@well.sf.ca.us
Bitnet: FAST@UCBGARNET.bitnet
Sample contents: The May 15th isssue was a WORDS ON WORKS ISSUE. Table of Contents: WORDS ON WORKS: About Words on Works, by Judy Malloy; Gulf War Memories, by Joseph De Lappe; Paradise Tossed, by Jill Scott; Muto(Scape), by Christopher Burnett; Razor Fabric, by Boris Stuchebrjukov; PROGRAMS, PRODUCTS, REVIEWS: The Telluride Institute, by Richard Lowenberg; FISEA 93, by Roman Verostko; Video Review of Computer Music Research, by Robin Bargar; Notes on Authoring "Word Works," by Judy Malloy; FAST INFORMATION; FAST Updates, by Annie Lewis; FAST Calendar, by Zara Santos.
Review: "The three major on-line electonic journals publishing information through interactive writings are Postmodern Culture, E-Journal, and Leonardo Electronic News. '" NY TImes Book Review, June 21, 1992.
How to access: E-mail requests to fast@garnet.berkely.edu with the message Sub LEN, name, e-mail address, and postal address.
Access policy: Subscriptions only available with receipt of postal address. Status of gratis subscriptions subject to change at any time.
How to unsubscribe: Send E-mail request to fast@garnet.berkeley.edu with message UNSUB LDN, name and e-mail address.
How to submit: Contact Annie Lewis at fast@garnet.berkeley.edu.
Submission policy: All submissions accepted, reproduction is contingent on space available and timing and relevance of material submitted.
Archives: Available for past year only free of charge, contact Leonardo/ISAST for terms of receiving other issues.
Additional information: Second editor: Judy Malloy. Leonardo/ISAT, 672 South Van Neww, San Francisco, CA 94110 USA. Tel. (415) 431-7414; fax (415) 431-5737; Internet jmalloy@well.sf.ca.us Second technical contact: Annie Lewis, Leonardo/ISAST, 672 South Van Ness, San Francisco, CA 94110. tel (415) 431-7414; fax (415) 431-5737; fast@garnet.berkeley.edu or FAST@UCBGARNET.bitnet. Also: The agreement for LEN to be published by MIT Press as their first electronic publication on the internet represents a significant development in the evolution of LEN, the internet delivery system, and publishing in general. LEN will continue to provide such features as Words on Works, profiles of current work at art/science/technology facilities around the world, and bibliographies/abstracts on a variety of current topics of interest. It will expand to include longer feature articles and new columns in a variety of topic areas.

LIBRES (LIBRARY AND INFORMATION SCIENCE RESEARCH ELECTRONIC JOURNAL)

ISSN: 1058-6768
Description: LIBRES is a quarterly, peer-reviewed electronic journal with an editorial board of library and information science scholars. LIBRES communicates scholarly thought on library and information science. Since 1990, LIBRES has published non-refereed articles, reports, and drafts as well as news and discussion of library and information science research, applications, and events. The first regular, quarterly issue which includes the peer-reviewed sections will be on Oct. 15, 1993. When warranted by the volume and flow of scholarship, special and/or supplementary issues on emergent themes will be distributed. LIBRES will have four sections: 1. Research and applications (refereed) Peer-reviewed scholarly articles from multiple sub-disciplines of library and information science on such topics as analysis, evaluation, applications (reports of progress at libraries), and other research. Editor to be Appointed; 2. Essays and opinions (non-refereed) Edited by Diane K. Kovacs; 3. News, letters, Reviews of print and electronic resources and other discussions (non-refereed) Edited by Leslie Haas; 4. Pre-Print and Abstracts Distribution (non-refereed) Editor to be Appointed. LIBRES will be distributed through a listserv fileserver, an ftp site and a gopher server. Subscribers will be made aware of the available issue by distribution of a quarterly table of contents to LIBRES, LIBREF-L, and other e-conferences that request the service. LIBRES will be indexed in the ERIC RIE.
Subjects covered: library and information science
Net address for operations: Listserv@kentvm
Frequency: Quarterly
Established: 1990
Method of issuance: Issues are distributed to list via email. Subscribers will be made aware of the available issue by distribution of a quarterly table of contents to LIBRES, LIBREF-L, and other e-conferences that request the service.
Subscribers: 1542
Sponsor: Kent State University, Kent, OH.
Host: Kent State University, Kent, OH.
Journal refereed:
Editorial contact: Diane Kovacs
Kent State University Library and Media Services, Kent, OH 44242-0001.
Tel: 216-672-2962
Fax: 216-672-2265
Internet: dkovacs@kentvm.kent.edu
Bitnet: dkovacs@kentvm
Sample contents: Article on Humanities Reference available electronically.
How to access: Send mail to listserv@kentvm and in message area type subscribe Your name
Access policy: No restrictions on subscribing to this journal
How to unsubscribe: Send message to listserv@kentvm and in the message area type unsub your name
Gopher accessibility: LIBRES will be distributed through a listserv fileserver, an ftp site and a gopher server.
Additional information: Additional editors: Leslie Haas, Kent State University Libraries and Media Services, Kent, OH 44242-0001; tel 216-672-2962; fax 216-672-2265; Internet dkovacs@kentvm.kent.edu; Bitnet dkovacs@kentvm; Amey Park, Kent State University Libraries and Media Services, Kent, OH 44242-0001; tel 216-672-2962; fax 216-672-2265; Internet Apark @kentvm.kent.edu; Bitnet /apark@kentvm

LIMINAL-LIMINAL EXPLORATIONS

Description: LIMINAL seeks to apply new inter- and transdisciplinary methods, theories, ideas, concepts, and approaches to the study of cultural phenomena as well as the inventive application of existing approaches. The term 'cultural phenomena' is taken to mean, but not limited to, meaning: 1) an activity engaged in by humans as members of a social network, 2) the product(s) of such engagement(s), 3) the motivators of such activities or engagements, 4) the functioning of such social networks themselves.

Subjects covered: alternative literature; philosophy
The Liminal Group, Box 154, BGSU, Bowling Green, OH 43403.
Internet: swilbur@andy.bgsu.edu
How to access: Gopher accessible at: etext.archive.umich.edu

LINK LETTER

Description: Link Letter is the newsletter of the Merit/NSFNET Information Services and provides information on the Internet.
Subjects covered: Internet; telecommunications; information technology
Frequency: Irregular
Established: 1988
Method of issuance: Issues are emailed to subscribers as published.
Host: Merit/NSFNET Information Services
Journal refereed: No
Editorial contact: Patricia Smith
MERIT/NSFNET Information Services, 2901 Hubbard, Pod G, Ann Arbor, MI 48019-2016.
Tel: (800) 66-MERIT
Internet: nsfnet-info@merit.edu
How to access: FTP to nic.metit.edu
The directory is: /newsletters/linkletter/ Or send email to nsfnet-linkletter-request@merit.edu

LIST REVIEW SERVICE

ISSN: 1060-8192
Description: List Review Service is a periodic service providing indepth reviews of Internet and Bitnet discussion lists.
Subjects covered: Internet; discussion lists
Frequency: Irregular
Established: 1991
Method of issuance: Issues are emailed to subscribers as published.
Journal refereed: No
Editorial contact: Raleigh C. Muns
Thomas Jefferson Library, University of Missouri-St. Louis, 8001 Natural Bridge Rd., St. Louis, MO 63121.
Tel: (314) 553-5059
Internet: srcmuns@umslvma.umsl.edu
How to access: Send the message SUBSCRIBE LSTREV-L <your__name> to listserv@umslvma or listserv@umslvma.umsl.edu

LITA NEWSLETTER

Description: LITA Newsletter is the electronic edition of the long-standing paper newsletter of the same title. It contains the same material as the printed version, but without graphics.
Subjects covered: information technology; library and information science; Library and Information Technology Association
Net address for operations: listserv@dartmouth.edu or listserv@dartcms1
Frequency: Quarterly
Established: August 1993
Number of issues published to date: 1
Recent issue published: Volume 14 Number 4
How to access: Send the following message to listserv@dartmouth.edu (or listserv@dartcms1 for bitnet users):

SUBSCRIBE LITANEWS <YourFirstName> <YourLastName>
Archives: Back issues of the Lita Newsletter will be archived on PACS-L.

LPN-L (LABORATORY PRIMATE NEWSLETTER)

ISSN: 0023-6861
Description: LPN-L, the electronic version of the Laboratory Primate Newsletter, offers information on primate research. The Laboratory Primate Newsletter provides a central source of information about nonhuman primates and related matters to scientists who use these animals in their research and those whose work supports such research. The Newsletter (1) provides information on care and breeding of nonhuman primates for laboratory research, (2) disseminates general information and news about the world of primate research (such as announcements of meetings, research projects, sources of information, nomenclature changes), (3) helps meet the special research needs of individual investigators by publishing requests for research material or for information related to specific research problems, and (4) serves the cause of conservation of nonhuman primates by publishing information on that topic. As a rule, research articles or summaries accepted for the Newsletter have some practical implications or provide general information likely to be of interest to investigators in a variety of areas of primate research. However, special consideration will be given to articles containing data on primates not conveniently publishable elsewhere. General descriptions of current research projects on primates will also be welcome.
Subjects covered: primates; biology
Net address for operations: LISTSERV@BROWNVM or LISTSERV@BROWNVM.BROWN.EDU
Net address for questions or submissions: PRIMATE@BROWNVM or PRIMATE@BROWNVM.BROWN.EDU
Frequency: quarterly
Established: LPN-L started in 1991; The Newsletter started in 1962.
Number of issues published to date: 10 electronic; 126 in paper.
Method of issuance: Listserver for electronic; bulk mail for paper. Issues are announced on the mailing list PRIMATE-TALK.
Available in other media: Yes. The Newsletter is an established, but informal, journal.
Recent issue published: 32(2)
Subscribers: 155 electronic; 1100 paper
Fee: None, but foreign paper subscribers pay mail charges. Subscribers outside the United States are asked to pay US$6.00 per year mailing charges (US$12 for air mail). Please make checks payable to Brown University.
Sponsor: Comparative Medicine Program, National Center for Research Resources, National Institutes of Health, Bethesda, MD 20892
Host: Brown University, Providence, RI 02912
Journal refereed: No.
Editorial contact: Judith E. Schrier
Box 1853, Brown University, Providence, RI 02912
Tel: (401) 863-2511
Fax: (401) 863-1300
Internet: primate@brownvm.brown.edu
Bitnet: primate@brownvm

Sample contents: Articles and Notes; Guest Editorial: Primate Well-Being Is Not Promoted by Suit, by C. Crockett; Comments on Baytril@ Antimicrobial Therapy and Considerations for Intramuscular Antibiotic Therapy in Captive Primates, by A. S. Line; Ethics in Primatology, by A. J. Petto & K. D. Russell; Toys as Environmental Enrichment for Captive Juvenile Chimpanzees (Pantroglodytes), by N. Shefferly, J. Fritz, &S. Howell; What Really Happened in Rio? by A. Jolly; Prediction of Affiliation and Sexual Behavior in Rhesus Monkeys with Previous Familiarity, by D. R. Rasmussen; Enrichment for Primates in a Toxicology Facility,
by J. McNulty, etc.
Copyright statement: Welcome to the e-mail edition of the Laboratory Primate Newsletter. All material is copyrighted, but may be circulated electronically, or printed out and reproduced for classroom and other non-commercial purposes, as long as reference is made to the source.
How to access: Readers with access to electronic mail may receive the non-graphics contents of each issue by sending the message ''subscribe LPN-L your-own-name'' to ''listserv@brownvm.brown.edu''
Archives: Yes. Electronic through the listserver, and paper at $3/issue. All back issues are available. For a list of back issues send the command ''get LPN-L filelist'' to ''listserv@brownvm.brown.edu'' You may then obtain the listed files by sending the command ''get <filename>< filetype>'' to the same address.

LYMENET NEWSLETTER
Description: LymeNet Newsletter offers information and news about Lyme disease.
Subjects covered: Lyme disease; medicine; health sciences
Frequency: Biweekly
Established: 1993
Method of issuance: Issues are emailed to subscribers as published.
Journal refereed: No
Editorial contact: Marc Gabriel
Internet: mcg2@lehigh.edu
How to access: Send the message SUBSCRIBE LYMENET-L to listserv@lehigh.edu

MAB NORTHERN SCIENCES NETWORK NEWSLETTER
ISSN: 1014-7470
Description: The Network Newsletter contains information on MAB activities.
Subjects covered: cold regions research; science and technology
Frequency: Semi-annual
Method of issuance: Issues are emailed to subscribers as published.
Host: MAB Northern Sciences Network
Journal refereed: No
Editorial contact: Ms. Anna-Liisa Sippola
Arctic Centre, University of Lapland, P.O. Box 122, 96101 Rovaniemi, Finland.
Internet: sippola@finfun.bitnet
How to access: Send the message SUBSCRIBE NSNNEWS to listserv@finhutc.bitnet

MAGYAR ELECTRONIKUS TOZSDE (HUNGARIAN ELECTRONIC EXCHANGE)
ISSN: 1216-0229
Description: Magyar Electronikus Tozsde is a weekly Hypertex Information Base about the Hungarian stock & commodity exchange.
Subjects covered: economics; business; stock and commodity exchange; Hungary
Net address for operations: h4458orc@ella.hu
Frequency: Weekly
Established: 1990
Number of issues published to date: 123
Method of issuance: Issues are distributed to subscription list as published.
Recent issue published: 1993.III.#22
Host: IIFP Budapest Vicktor Hugo u.
Editorial contact: Zsolt Laszlo Orczan
Budapest PF.311 H1536, Hungary
Tel: 361 252-6697
Fax: 361 156 3482
Internet: orczan@mars.sztaki.hu
Bitnet: IB000EA5@HUEARN
Copyright statement: All rights reserved.
How to access: Send email (subject: MET) to h4458orc@ella.hu Subject: MET <ibusz> with message or question. Editor will reply.
Gopher accessibility: You can read original on Gopher, Path -> Europe -> Hungary -> HIX....

MATERIAL SCIENCE IN ISRAEL NEWSLETTER
Description: Material Science in Israel Newsletter covers information of relevance to researchers in material science,
Subjects covered: material science; science and technology
Frequency: Irregular
Method of issuance: Issues are emailed to subscribers as published.
Journal refereed: No
Editorial contact: Dr. Michael Wolff
Coordinator for the Exact Sciences, National Council for Research and Development.
Bitnet: wolff@ilncrd
How to access: Send the message SUBSCRIBE MATERI-L to listserv@taunivm

MATRIX NEWS
ISSN: 1059-0749
Description: Matrix News is a newsletter covering topics related to the Internet and associated electronic information networks.
Subjects covered: Internet; electronic networking; telecommunications
Frequency: Monthly
Established: 1992
Method of issuance: Issues are emailed to subscribers as published.
Journal refereed: No
Tel: (512) 451-7602
Fax: (512) 450-1436
Internet: mids@tic.com
How to access: Send message to mids@tic.com for information

MC JOURNAL: THE JOURNAL OF ACADEMIC MEDIA LIBRARIANSHIP

ISSN: 1069-6792

Description: MC Journal covers all aspects of academic audio-visual librarianship and media center management.

Subjects covered: computer hardware and software; library and information science; library collection development

Net address for operations: mcjrnl@ubvm.bitnet, mc-jrnl@ubvm.cc.buffalo.edu

Net address for questions or submissions: mcjrnl@ubvm.bitnet, mcjrnl@ubvm.cc.buffalo.edu

Established: November 1992

Number of issues published to date: 3

Method of issuance: e-mail

Recent issue published: Vol.2 #1, Winter 1994

Subscribers: 400

Sponsor: State University of New York at Buffalo, Buffalo, New York 14260.

Journal refereed: Yes, there is a double-blind review process.

Editorial contact: Lori Widzinski
Media Resources Center, Health Sciences Library, Abbott Hall, 3435 Main St., Buffalo, NY 14214-3002.

Tel: 716-829-3614

Fax: 716-829-2211

Internet: HSLLJW@ubvm.cc.buffalo.edu

Bitnet: HSLLJW@ubvm

Technical contact: Jim Gerland
Computing Center, SUNY Buffalo, Buffalo, NY.

Tel: 716-645-3557

Internet: Gerland@ubvm.cc.buffalo.edu

Bitnet: Gerland@ubvm

Copyright statement: Copyright for the texts is retained by the individual authors. MC Journal: The Journal of Academic Media Librarianship (c)1993 has the nonexclusive right to publish the articles in the journal and in future publications. MC Journal may be shared among individuals, noncommercial computer conferences, and libraries. Articles may NOT be republished in any medium without consent from the author(s) and advance written or electronic notification of the editors.

How to access: Send a message to LISTSERV@ubvm.bitnet or LISTSERV@ubvm.cc.buffalo.edu. The message should be this command: SUB MCJRNL Firstname Lastname (e.g., SUB MC-JRNL John Jones). The command is the text of your message; the subject is ignored by LISTSERV.

How to unsubscribe: Send the following message to LISTSERV@ubvm.bitnet or LISTSERV@ubvm.cc.buffalo.edu: Signoff MCJRNL. This is text of your message, not the subject line.

How to submit: Contact editor.

Submission policy: Contact editor.

Archives: Yes, archives are available; contact editor.

MECKJOURNAL

ISSN: 1058-692X

Description: MeckJournal publishes articles, reviews, and news and conference reports taken from its battery of print magazines and newsletters in information technology areas, primarily on Internet-related and electronic networking topics.

Subjects covered: library and information science; computer hardware and software; electronic networking; Internet

Net address for operations: meckler@jvnc.net

Net address for questions or submissions: meckler@jvnc.net

Frequency: Bimonthly

Established: September 1991

Number of issues published to date: 12

Method of issuance: MeckJournal is distributed to its subscription list as new issues are published. Current and back ssues are also available by telneting to nicol.jvnc.net, typing nicol at the login prompt, and selecting Publications from the main menu. Further menus will direct the user to the MeckJournal issue file.

Available in other media: Articles from MeckJournal appear in selected print publications from Mecklermedia, including Computers in Libraries, OCLC Systems and Services, Internet World, Internet Research, and Campus-Wide Information Systems.

Recent issue published: Volume 3, Number 5, September/December 1993

Subscribers: 1200

Sponsor: Mecklermedia, 11 Ferry Lane West, Westport, CT 06880; (203) 226-6967; fax: (203) 454-5840.

Host: Same as above

Commercial organization: Yes.

Journal refereed: No.

Editorial contact: Anthony Abbott
Mecklermedia, 11 Ferry Lane West, Westport, CT 06880

Tel: (203) 226-6967

Fax: (203) 454-5840

Internet: meckler@jvnc.net

Sample contents: News (Selected from Campus-Wide Information Systems, May/June 1993, edited by Milo Nelson); Feature Article: Intel Processor-Based Systems: Buying Today, Planning for Tomorrow, by Eric Flower, Librarian at the University of Hawaii-West Oahu.

Copyright statement: Copyright Mecklermedia. Copying is permitted for noncommercial use by computer conferences, individual scholars, and libraries. Libraries are authorized to add MeckJournal to their collections either in electronic or printed form at no charge. This message must appear on all copied materials. All commercial use requires permission.

How to access: Subscription requests should be sent to the editor at meckler@jvnc.net

Access policy: Subscriptions are open to all.

How to unsubscribe: Send a message to meckler@jvnc.net requesting to unsubscribe.

How to submit: Send all messages to meckler@jvnc.net.

Submission policy: All orignal submissions should concern some aspect of computer-based systems in libraries, industry, the commercial arena, or the home.

Archives: Current and back ssues are also available by telneting to nicol.jvnc.net and typing nicol at the login prompt. No password is needed. Then select Publications from the main menu. Further menus will direct user to MeckJournal issue file.

Related files: MC(2)—Mecklermedia Electronic Publishing Service is available by telneting to nicol.jvnc.net, typing nicol at the login prompt (no password is needed), and selecting from the main menu. The several files found there include Mecklermedia complete catalog of publications, advance information on Mecklermedia conferences, indexes to back issues of Mecklermedia periodicals, and selected temporary files.

Gopher accessibility: MC(2), the service which contains current and back issues of MeckJournal, is accessible through the Internet Gopher at JvNCNet, the regional node of the Internet which maintains Mecklermedia telnet files.

MEDIA RELATIONS NETWORK NEWS (MRN NEWS)

Description: MRN News covers activities in academic public relations.
Subjects covered: colleges and universities; public relations
Frequency: Monthly
Method of issuance: Issues are emailed to subscribers as published.
Journal refereed: No
Editorial contact: Dan Forbush
Internet: daniel.forbush@sunysb.edu
How to access: Send email request to daniel.forbush@sunysb.edu

MEDNEWS@ASUACAD

See HICNET Medical News

A MEGABYTE OF TORAH

Description: A MegaByte of Torah is a monthly electronic publication dealing with topics related to the Jewish month.
Subjects covered: religion; Torah; Hebrew language and literature
Frequency: Monthly
Established: 1991
Method of issuance: Issues are emailed to subscribers as published.
Journal refereed: No
Editorial contact: Zev S. Itzkowitz
Internet: bytetorah@israwl.nysernet.org
How to access: FTP to israel.nysernet.org
The directory is: /israel/tanach/commentary/bytetorah/
Or send the message SUBSCRIBE BYTETORAH to listserv@israwl.nysernet.org

MICHNET NEWS

Description: MichNet News offers information about developments on the Michigan state network.
Subjects covered: Internet; Michigan; electronic networking
Frequency: Quarterly
Method of issuance: Issues are emailed to subscribers as published.
Journal refereed: No
Editorial contact: Pat McGregor
Merit Network, Inc., 1975 Beal Avenue, Ann Arbor, MI 48109-2112.
Tel: (313) 764-9430
Internet: patmcg@merit.edu
Bitnet: userw02v@umichum
How to access: Send a message to mnn-request@merit.edu

MICNEWS

Description: MICnews covers computing information for the UCLA community.
Subjects covered: computer hardware and software
Method of issuance: Issues are emailed to subscribers as published.
Host: Microcomputer Information Center, University of California at Los Angeles.
Journal refereed: No
How to access: Send the message SUBSCRIBE MICNEWS to listserv@uclacn1.ucla.edu

MODAL ANALYSIS

ISSN: 1066-0763
Description: Modal Analysis: The International Journal of Analytical and Experimental Modal Analysis publishes abstracts of papers published in the print journal of the same title.
Subjects covered: modal analysis
Frequency: Quarterly
Established: 1993
Method of issuance: Issues are emailed to subscribers as published.
Host: Society for Experimental Mechanics
Journal refereed: Yes
Editorial contact: Lon Savage
Scholarly Communications Project, Virginia Polytechnic Institute, University Libraries, P.O. Box 90001, Blacksburg, VA 24062-9001.
Internet: savage@vtvm1.cc.vt.edu
Bitnet: savage@vtvm1
How to access: Send the message SUBSCRIBE MODAL to listserv@vtvm1.cc.vt.edu

MUSIC THEORY ONLINE (MTO)

ISSN: 1067-3040
Description: Music Theory Online (MTO) is an electronic publication offering information on music theory; music theoretical and analytical essays; history of music theory; music cognition; and other related information.
Subjects covered: music
Net address for operations: listserv@husc.harvard.edu
Net address for questions or submissions: mto-editor@husc.harvard.edu
Frequency: Bimonthly
Established: February 1993
Number of issues published to date: 3
Method of issuance: User retrieves issues via a FileServer.
Recent issue published: No. 3
Subscribers: 200
Sponsor: Society for Music Theory (SMT)
Host: Harvard University, Harvard Arts and Sciences Computer Services (HASCS)
Journal refereed: Yes, submissions are distributed to three consulting editors for review.
Editorial contact: Lee A. Rothfarb
Harvard Univ., Music Dept., Cambridge, MA 02138
Tel: (617) 495-2791
Fax: (617) 496-8081
Internet: rothfarb@husc.harvard.edu

Bitnet: rothfarb@husc.bitnet
Technical contact: Tom Heft, Unix System Programmer
Harvard Univ., Science Center, Cambridge, MA 02138
Tel: (617) 495-2791
Fax: (617) 496-8081
Internet: heft@husc.harvard.edu
Bitnet: rothfarb@husc.bitnet
Sample contents: An article on perception of rhythm and meter.
Copyright statement: [1] Music Theory Online (MTO) as a whole is Copyright (c) 1993, all rights reserved, by the Society for Music Theory, which is the owner of the journal. Copyrights for individual items published in MTO are held by their authors. Items appearing in MTO may be saved and stored in electronic or paper form, and may be shared among individuals for purposes of scholarly research or discussion, but may *not* be republished in any form, electronic or print, without prior, written permission from the author(s), and advance notification of the editors of MTO. [2] Any redistributed form of items published in MTO must include the following information in a form appropriate to the medium in which the items are to appear. [3] Libraries may archive issues of MTO in electronic or paper form for public access so long as each issue is stored in its entirety, and no access fee is charged. Exceptions to these requirements must be approved in writing by the editors of MTO, who will act in accordance with the decisions of the Society for Music Theory.
How to access: Send message to "listserv@husc.harvard.edu" or to "listserv@husc.bitnet"; contents of message: subscribe mto-j
Access policy: By approval; MTO is a journal for professional and pre-professional music theorists, composers, musicologists, and performers, who have sufficient background in music theory to understand the content of MTO.
How to unsubscribe: Send message to one of the "listserv" addresses; message content: unsubscribe mto-j.
To submit or for questions (technical): message to mto-editor@husc.harvard.edu (or mto-editor@husc.bitnet)
To submit or for questions (policy): should retrieve the document "authors.txt" (guidelines for authors and editorial policy) once subscribed.
Archives: Archives are accessible through anonymous FTP to the site husc4.harvard.edu; back issues can also be retrieved with the MTO FileServer (instructions in the MTO Guide, called "information.txt," which is available through the MTO FileServer.
Gopher accessibility: A gopher is not available yet, but it is under consideration.

NASDAQ FINANCIAL EXECUTIVE JOURNAL (NFEJ)

Description: The Nasdaq Financial Executive Journal is a hypertext version of the print journal of the same name, offering executives key information about the stock market.
Subjects covered: business; economics
How to access: The NFEJ is mounted on the WorldWideWeb on the Legal Information Institute Web serve on fatty.law.cornell.edu, at Port 80. Users may also telnet to fatty.law.cornell.edu and login as WWW. No password is needed. Select NFEJ from the menu.

NAVY NEWS SERVICE (NAVNEWS)

Description: NAVNEWS is an electronic publication of the Navy Internal Relations department, offering news on Navy activities.
Subjects covered: U.S. Navy
Frequency: Weekly
Method of issuance: Issues are emailed to subscribers as published.
Host: Navy Internal Relations, Washington, DC
Journal refereed: No
Editorial contact: CDR Tim Taylor
Internet: navnews@nctamslant.navy.mil
How to access: Send email to navnews@nctamslant.navy.mil. Include your email address in the message.

NEARNET NEWSLETTER

Description: NEARnet Newsletter offers information on electronic networking in the college and university community.
Subjects covered: colleges and universities; Internet; campus-wide information systems
Frequency: Quarterly
Method of issuance: Issues are emailed to subscribers as published.
Journal refereed: No
Editorial contact: NEARnet; Bolt Beranet and Newman, Inc., 10 Moulton Street, Mail Stop 6/3B, Cambridge, MA 02138.
Tel: (617) 873-8730
Internet: nearnet-staff@nic.near.net
How to access: Send email to nearnet-staff@nic.near.net

NEARNET THIS MONTH

Description: NEARnet this Month is an electronic newsletter for NEARnet members.
Subjects covered: Internet; electronic networking
Frequency: Monthly
Host: NEARnet
Journal refereed: No
Internet: nearnet-us@nic.near.net
How to access: FTP to nic.near.net
The directory is: /newsletters/nearnet.this.month/

NEKUDA E-JOURNAL

Description: Nekuda E-Journal is a monthly treatment of political events in Israel.
Frequency: Monthly
Established: 1993
Method of issuance: Issues are emailed to subscribers as published.
Journal refereed: No
Editorial contact: Zvi Lando
Internet: lando@brachot.jct.ac.il
How to access: Send email to lando@brachot.jct.ac.il requesting subscription.

NETWORK AUDIO BITS AND AUDIO SOFTWARE REVIEW

Description: Network Audio Bits is an electronic review of popular music.
Subjects covered: music; popular music

Method of issuance: Issues are emailed to subscribers as published.
Journal refereed: No
Editorial contact: Michael A. Murphy
Bitnet: murph@maine.bitnet
How to access: Send email to murph@maine.bitnet

NETWORK NEWS

Description: Network News: An Update to Libraries and information resources on the Internet, (sometimes called Net-News) is an irregularly published compilation of Internet-related information.
Subjects covered: Internet; electronic networking; computer hardware and software; information technology
Net address for operations: listserv@ndsuvm1.bitnet or listserv@vm1.nodak.edu
Frequency: Irregular
Method of issuance: Issues are emailed to subscribers as published.
Sponsor: Metronet.
Journal refereed: No
Editorial contact: Dana Noonan
Tel: 612-825-9312
Fax: 612-224-4827
Internet: noonan@msus1.msus.edu
Sample contents: A Guide to Internet/Bitnet Update; A Guide to Internet/Bitnet - Online Version; New Online Catalogs; Other New Services; Check the FAQs; Down the Gopher Hole; Recommended Reading; Going Up North; Corrections and Additions; New on MetroLine.
Copyright statement: Copyright: 1993 Dana Noonan. Permission granted to redistribute the unmodified version of this newsletter provided no fee is charged for it.
How to access: Send the message SUBSCRIBE NEWS to listserv@ndsuvm1.bitnet or listserv@vm1.nodak.edu
Archives: Archives are available via listserv or ftp from vm1.nodak.edu in nnews directory

NETWORK Q NOVA SCOTIA'S INDUSTRIAL TECHNOLOGY NEWSLETTER

Description: Network is a technology newsletter covering a variety of computer-related and science topics.
Subjects covered: science and technology; computer hardware and software
Frequency: Bimonthly
Method of issuance: Issues are Gopher accessible.
Journal refereed: No
Editorial contact: Valerie Roma
Technology Associations Secretariat, 1046 Barrington St., Halifax, NS B3H 2R1.
How to access: Send email to vroma@nsatc.ns.ca

NEW HISTORICUS: A KANSAS JOURNAL OF HISTORY

Description: New Historicus publishes articles and bibliographic essays on all periods and geographical areas of history.
Subjects covered: history
How to access: Send an email message to TNP@UKANVM.bitnet

NEW HORIZONS IN ADULT EDUCATION
ISSN: 1062-3183
Description: New Horizons in Adult Education is the refereed electronic journal of the Adult Education Network (AEDNET, an international electronic network. The network is operated through a listserv that enables subscribers to share information. Researchers, practitioners, and graduate students in adult and continuing education are provided with opportunities to discuss important topics and concerns in an online environment. AEDNET is operated by the Adult Education Program of the Programs for Higher Education of the Abraham S. Fischler Center for the Advancement of Education at Nova University located in Fort Lauderdale, Florida. AEDNET activities include network-wide discussions and information exchanges on topics and queries, conferences and special events, of interest to adult and continuing educators.
Subjects covered: adult education; education; distance education
Net address for operations: listserv@alpha.acast.nova.edu
Issues are announced on the Aednet discussion list.
Recent issue published: Volume 7 Number 1 Spring 1993
Journal refereed: Yes.
Sample contents: Editor's Preface; Radical Adult Education With Older Persons; Theory-Based Practice: A Model SDLS Program; The Need for Continuing Education for the Deaf: Are Adult Educators Listening?; Towards an Anti-Racist, Feminist Teaching Method; Cumulative Index to New Horizons.
How to access: The New Horizons journals exist as a set of files maintained in an archive called "horizons." You can request a list of all available journals by sending a message to: listserv@alpha.acast.nova.edu. The subject line can be anything at all. The body of your message should be the request: index horizons. After a few minutes, you should receive a mail message from the listserv showing a list of all New Horizons journals by file name. The journals are named by volume and number. For example, volume 6, number 2 would have the file name vol6n2. Also shown in the list is how many parts make up each journal. For the INDEX of the newsletter or the jobs listing just substitute "aednews" or "aedjobs" for the word horizons. Now that you have seen the names of all the journals, newsletters or jobs listings, you may request one of them be sent to you by sending another email message to: listserv@alpha.acast.nova.edu The subject line can be anything at all. The body of your message should be the request: get horizons vol6n2 After a few minutes you should receive a new mail message. The contents of the message will be the text of volume 6, number 2 of the journal. To obtain the text of a particular newsletter or jobs listing, substitute "aednews" or "aedjobs" for the word horizons and be sure to substitute the appropriate file name for vol6n2. You can send several requests per mail message.
How to submit: Send submissions to horizons@alpha.acast.nova.edu

NEWSBRIEF
Description: Newsbrief offers news about campus events and other information to the community of the University of North Carolina.
Subjects covered: events listings; colleges and universities; University of North Carolina
Frequency: Biweekly
Method of issuance: Issues are emailed to subscribers as published.

Host: Office of Information Technology, University of North Carolina at Chapel Hill.
Journal refereed: No
Editorial contact: Scott Romine
Internet: romine@uncvx1.oit.unc.edu
How to access: Send the message SUBSCRIBE OIT-NEWS to listserv@uncvm1.bitnet

NEWSLETTER ON SERIALS PRICING ISSUES

ISSN: 1046-3410
Description: The Newsletter on Serials Pricing Issues provides information on price changes by major serials publishers and letters and discussion on concerns about increases in the cost of maintaining library collections.
Subjects covered: library collection development; library and information science; publishing
Frequency: Irregular
Established: 1989
Method of issuance: Issues are emailed to subscribers as published.
Journal refereed: No
Editorial contact: Marcia Tuttle Serials Department, CB #3938, Davis Library, University of North Carolina, Chapel Hill, NC 27599-3938.
Tel: (919) 962-1067
Fax: (919) 962-0484
Internet: tuttle@gibbs.oit.unc.edu
How to access: Send the message SUBSCRIBE PRICES to listser@gibbs.oit.unc.edu

NEWSLINE

Description: Newsline offers information about Comserve, an electronic information service in the field of communications studies.
Subjects covered: communications; electronic networking
Frequency: Irregular
Established: 1986
Method of issuance: Issues are emailed to subscribers as published.
Journal refereed: No
Editorial contact: Timothy Stephen
Internet: support@vm.its.rpi.edu
Bitnet: support@rpitsvm
How to access: Send the message SUBSCRIBE NEWSLINE to comserve@rpitsvm or comserve@vm.its.rpi.edu
Additional information: Additional editor: Teresa Harrison

NIBNEWS

Description: NIBNews covers information about Brazilian and Latin American medical research activities.
Subjects covered: medicine; Brazil; health sciences
Frequency: Monthly
Method of issuance: Issues are emailed to subscribers as published.
Journal refereed: No
Editorial contact: Renato M.E. Sabbatini, Ph.D
Center for Biomedical Informatics, State University of Campinas, P.O. Box 6005, Campinas, SP 13081, BRAZIL.
Tel: +55 192 397130
Fax: +55 192 394717

Internet: sabbatini@ccvax.unicamp.br
Bitnet: sabbatini@bruc.Bitnet
How to access: Send email to sabbatini@ccvax.unicamp.br
Related files: Back issues are available through FTP to ccsun.unicamp.br. The directory is: /pub/medicine/documents/

NLSNEWS NEWSLETTER

Description: NLSNews covers labor statistics.
Subjects covered: labor statistics; government information
Frequency: Quarterly
Established: 1987
Method of issuance: Issues are emailed to subscribers as published.
Host: Center for Human Resource Research, Ohio State University.
Journal refereed: No
Editorial contact: Steve McClaskie
Bitnet: mcclaskie@ohsthr
How to access: Send the message SEND SUBSCRIBE.INFO to nlserve@ohsthr

NORDIC ELECTRONIC SCIENCE FICTION DIRECTORY (NESFAD)

Description: Nordic Electronic Science Fiction Directory (NESFAD) contains an updated list of science-fiction fans with E-media access in the Nordic area. Each issue also contains a brief news section. NESFAD is not a list that discusses the subject of science fiction. It is a list of E-addresses to be used as a reference and to create contact between Nordic sf fans.
Subjects covered: science fiction; Nordic studies
Net address for operations: ahrvid@sfbbs.edvina.seor broimola@abo.fi
Net address for questions or submissions: ahrvid@sfbbs.edvina.se or broi mola@abo.fi
Frequency: NESFAD is published 4-5 times yearly
Established: December 1991
Subscribers: 200
Editorial contact: Ahrvid Engholm
Renstiernas Gata 29, S-116 31 Stockholm, Sweden
Tel: 46 8 641 34 05
Internet: ahrvid@sfbbs.edvina.se, ahrvid@stacken.kth.se or ah rvid@cw.se
Technical contact: Ahrvid Engholm
Renstiernas Gata 29, S-116 31 Stockholm, Sweden
Tel: +46 8 641 34 05
Internet: ahrvid@sfbbs.edvina.se, ahrvid@stacken.kth.se or ahrvid@cw.se
How to access: Send mail to ahrvid@sfbbs.edvina.se or broimola@abo.fi, say you want to join the list and include the following info: Name, Internet address,alternate media address (Fido, fax, Memonet, etc), address, telephone number, and finally, a blurb about yourself (two lines, ca 140 characters long). Entries may be edited to make them clearer. Only Nordic residents or Nordic citizens abroad may be on the list. Others may subscribe (without being on the list) and should then send name and Internet-address.
Access policy: Anyone may subscribe, but only Nordic residents or Nordic citizens may be listed in NESFAD.
How to unsubscribe: Write to ahrvid@sfbbs.edvina.se or broimola@abo.fiand with the message that you want to unsubscribe.
Archives: No archive site available yet.

Additional information: Second editor: Ben Roimola, Puistokatu 15b A 5, SF-20100 Turku, Finland tel +358 21 306 0 60; Internet broimola@abo.fi; Bitnet broimola@finabo

NORTHWESTNET NODENEWS

Description: NorthWestNet Node News is an electronic newsletter covering Internet and networking-related topics for the U.S. Northwest.
Subjects covered: Internet
Frequency: Quarterly
Established: 1992
Method of issuance: Issues are emailed to subscribers as published.
Host: NorthWestNet, 15400 SE 30th Place, Suite 202, Bellevue, WA 98007.
Journal refereed: No
Editorial contact: Jan Eveleth
Tel: (206) 562-3000
Internet: eveleth@nwet.net
How to access: Send email requests to info@nwnet.net

OBSCURE ELECTRONIC

Description: OBSCURE is the magazine that profiles the people in this publishing subculture.
Subjects covered: alternative literature
Editorial contact: James P. Romenesko
Internet: obscure@csd4.csd.uwm.edu
How to access: Gopher accessible at: gopher.well.sf.ca.us

OFFLINE

Description: OFFLINE is a newsletter covering issues in the study of religion and biblical texts.
Subjects covered: religion
Frequency: Quarterly
Established: 1988
Method of issuance: Issues are emailed to subscribers as published.
Host: Society of Biblical Literature
Journal refereed: No
Editorial contact: Robert A. Kraft
Box 36, College Hall, University of Pennsylvania, Philadelphia, PA 19104-6303.
Tel: (215) 898 5827
Internet: kraft@ccat.sas.upenn.edu
How to access: FTP to ccat.sas.upenn.edu
The directory is: /pub/offline/
Or gopher to: gopher ccat.sas.upenn.edu

OLD ENGLISH COMPUTER--ASSISTED LANGUAGE LEARNING NEWSLETTER (OE-CALL)

Description: OE-CALL is an electronic newsletter covering the study of Old English language and literature.
Subjects covered: Old English language and literature; language and literature
Frequency: Irregular
Method of issuance: Issues are emailed to subscribers as published.
Journal refereed: No

Bitnet: lees@fordmurh.bitnet, u47c2@wvnvm.bitnet
How to access: Send an email message to u47c2@wvnvm.bitnet

OMHR (ONLINE MODERN HISTORY REVIEW)

Description: OMHR is an ejournal covering topics in modern history.
Subjects covered: history
Net address for questions or submissions: ua832@freenet.victoria.bc.ca
How to access: Send message to editor at ua832@freenet.victoria.bc.ca

ONLINE JOURNAL OF CURRENT CLINICAL TRIALS

ISSN: 1059-2725
Description: The Online Journal of Current Clinical Trials is a refereed multimedia electronic journal covering clinical experimentation. It is published by the American Association for the Advancement of Science in association with OCLC, Inc.
Subjects covered: medicine; health sciences
Frequency: Irregular
Established: July 1992
Method of issuance: Articles are emailed to subscribers as published.
Fee: Yes; apply to AAAS subscription department
Host: American Association for the Advancement of Science (AAAS) and the Online Computer Library Center (OCLC).
Journal refereed: Yes
Editorial contact: Edward J. Huth, M.D., Online Journal of Current Clinical Trials,1333 H Street, NW, Room 1155, Washington, DC 20005; Attention: AAAS Subscription Department.
Tel: (202) 326-6446
How to access: Send request to AAAS subscription department.

OPEN CACSD

Description: OPEN CACSD is the electronic newsletter of the IFAC/IEEE-CSS Working Group on Guidelines for Open Computer-Aided Control Systems Design (CACSD) Software. Items covered include any subject related to the "opening up" of computer-based applications for the analysis, design, simulation and implementation of control systems. Examples of suitable topics would be, data definitions for CACSD, user interfaces for CACSD, system modelling languages, environments for the integration of CACSD tools, how to get CACSD packages to talk to each other, advantages and disadvantages of Matlab, MATRIXx, ACSL etc., examples of good or bad practice in commercial packages.
Subjects covered: computer science; computer hardware and software
Net address for operations: mailbase@mailbase.ac.uk
Net address for questions or submissions: C.P.Jobling@Swansea.ac.uk
Frequency: Irregular
Established: February 1992
Number of issues published to date: 13
Method of issuance: New issues are emailed to subscribers.
Recent issue published: Volume 1 Number 1.
Subscribers: 257

Sponsor: Institution of Electrical and Electronic Engineers (IEEE) Control Systems Society (CSS) and the International Federation of Automatic Control (IFAC) joint working group on guidelines for computer-aided control system design (CACSD) software.
Host: Department of Electrical and Electronic Engineering, University of Wales, University College of Swansea, Singleton Park, Swansea SA2 8PP, Wales, UK.
Journal refereed: No.
Editorial contact: Chris P. Jobling
Department of Electrical and Electronic Engineering, University of Wales, University College of Swansea, Singleton Park, Swansea SA2 8PP, Wales, UK.
Tel: +44-792-295580
Fax: +44-792-295686
Internet: C.P.Jobling@Swansea.ac.uk
How to access: Send an e-mail message to mailbase@mailbase.ac.uk containing the message: join engineering-cace {Your first name} {Your last name}
How to unsubscribe: Send an e-mail message to mailbase@mailbase.ac.uk containing the message: leave engineering-cace
How to submit: To submit articles, send them in text-only format to C.P.Jobling@Swansea.ac.uk clearly marked "for submission to Open CACSD". Articles should be brief and to the point. Longer articles can be submitted but may only be announced in the Open CACSD in which case they will be kept on mailbase@mailbase.ac.uk and the other archive sites at which Open CACSD is archived.
Archives: Yes.
Related files: Back issues and a number of longer articles on topics related to Open CACSD, for example discussion papers and requests for comments on proposed standards, are kept at mailbase.ac.uk. They can be obtained using anonymous ftp from mailbase.ac.uk in directory /pub/engineering-cace. They are also kept at the UK control information database uk.ac.gla.mech.dodo in directory /contents/newsletters/opencacsd and at the SCAD database ftp.utdallas.edu in /pub/scad/cacsdletters.
Gopher accessibility: mailbase is available from Gopher
Additional information: The Open CACSD newsletter is related to the UK mailbase discussion group engineering-cace. New subscribers should register through mailbase as described above. Free discussion of issues related to Open CACSD should use the engineering-cace forum. The editor also keeps an eye on the US ENET group sci.engr.control and may reprint interesting articles in the newsletter.

ORGANIZED THOUGHTS
Description: Organized Thoughts covers libertarianism, socialism, and related political philisphies.
Subjects covered: political science; libertarianism
Frequency: Irregular
Established: 1992
Method of issuance: Issues are emailed to subscribers as published.
Journal refereed: No
Editorial contact: Mike Lepore
RR #1, Box 347 L, Stanfordville, NY 12581.
Internet: mlepore@mcimail.com
How to access: Send the message SUBSCRIBE L-UNION to listserv@uvmvm or listserv@uvmvm.uvm.edu

PARTHENOGENESIS
Description: Parthenogenesis is an electronic journal of alternative literature
Subjects covered: alternative literature; popular culture
Editorial contact: Dan Herrick
Parthenogenesis, 804 S. College, Suite 8363, Ft. Collins, CO 80524.
Internet: dherrick@nyx.cs.du.edu
How to access: Gopher accessible at: etext.archive.umich.edu

PEOPLE POWER UPDATE
Description: People Power Update is the electronic newsletter of the bicycle advocacy group People Power.
Subjects covered: bicycles; environmental studies
Editorial contact: Ron Goodman
People Power, 226 Jeter Street, Santa Cruz, CA 95060.
Tel: (408) 425-8851
Internet: goodman@cats.uscs.edu
How to access: Gopher accessible at: gopher.well.sf.ca.us

PEOPLE'S TRIBUNE (ONLINE EDITION)
Description: The People's Tribune is an alternative political newsletter.
Subjects covered: political science
Method of issuance: Issues are emailed to subscribers as published.
Journal refereed: No
Internet: jdav@igc.org
How to access: Gopher to gopher.cic.net or email to jdav@igc.org with a subscription request.

PHIRST AMENDMENT
Description: Phirst Amendment is an alternative political newsletter.
Subjects covered: political science
Method of issuance: Issues are emailed to subscribers as published.
Journal refereed: No
How to access: Gopher to gopher.cic.net

PIGULKI
ISSN: 1060-9288
Description: PIGULKI is an occasional magazine (electronic) of news and humor relating to Poland and Polish issues, particularly Poland's democratic evolution and its expansion of computer networking internally and to the West. Written in English; intended for audiences both in the West and in Poland.
Subjects covered: Poland; current events; world history; computer science
Frequency: Irregular; (approximately quarterly)
Established: July 15, 1990
Number of issues published to date: 13
Method of issuance: Issues are emailed when published.
Issue availability is announced on bulletin boards of Polish interest: POLAND-L, PLEARN-L, soc.culture.polish
Available in other media: No
Recent issue published: No. 13, April 1, 1993
Subscribers: 405
Journal refereed: No

Editorial contact: Marek Cypryk
Alexandrowska 104 m 54, 91-224 Lodz, Poland
Tel: (48/42) 52-77-84
Internet: mcypryk@plearn.edu.pl
Bitnet: mcypryk@plearn
Technical contact: Marek Zielinski
85-20 67 Ave., Rego Park, NY 11374, USA
Tel: (718) 997-0695
Internet: zielinski@acfcluster.nyu.edu
Bitnet: zielinsk@nyuacf
Sample contents: April 1, 1993, ISSN 1060-9288, Number 13
Po Prostu
UP IN SMOKE by D. Phillips Polish Affairs;
POLAND - THE COUNTRY UNDER RECONSTRUCTION by
J. Drygalski; THE POLISH COMPUTERIZATION PUZZLE by
J. Kryt; A GUIDE TO NETWORK RESOURCES by M.
Zielinski; POLAND - ELECTRONIC CONTACTS by R.
Maszkowski and M. Zielinski; The Back Page; Travelog: AN-
CIENT RITES AND SALUTATIONS by J. Klimkowski
Copyright statement: PIGULKI is distributed free of charge to
masochistic readers who request it from an authorized distributor or ftp site (above). Signed articles are Copyright (c) 1993 by
their authors. PIGULKI may not be copied or retransmitted
without prior permission by the editors and notification of your
local public health authorities. Permission to excerpt is granted
in advance for academic use, provided there is full attribution
and concurrent notification of the editors. Your articles, letters,
threats, denunciations are welcome; please send them to any
editor you can find who'll admit being one. We reserve the right
to edit for brevity.
How to access: Send email request to an authorized distributor:
North America-Dave Phillips (davep@acsu.buffalo.edu);
Oceania-Marek Samoc (mjs111@phys.anu.edu.au); Europe and
Africa-Marke Zielinski (zielinski@acfcluster.nyu.edu). PIGULKI
is also available from the NCU BBS in Torun, located in the
Student Government of the Nicolaus Copernicus University. Its
sysop is Rafal Maszkowski, <sysop%ncubbs@cc.ncu.edu.pl>;
the BBS is accessible 24 hours at 48-56-14252 (2400, N81,
MNP5). PIGULKI is available in ASCII and in printable POST-
SCRIPT forms. The ASCII version is distributed by E-mail, the
Postscript edition is available by anonymous ftp, by E-mail and
using Gopher. For instructions see below under Back Issues.
Submission policy: Articles, letters, threats, denunciations can
be send to any editor. We reserve the right to edit for brevity.
Archives: Back issues available:
ANONYMOUS FTP: The sites at alfa.camk.edu.pl, gal-
axy.uci.agh.edu.pl, info.in2p3.fr, laserspark.anu.edu.au,
poniecki.berkeley.edu and zsku.p.lod.edu.pl store back issues in
subdirectory /pub/pigulki. Log in as 'anonymous' and give your
E-address as password. ASCII files have extension pub, Postscript files have extension ps. MAIL: Send mail to
netlib@alfa.camk.edu.pl with the line 'send index from pigulki'
to obtain the list of available files, and with the line 'send
pigulk13.pub from pigulki' to obtain eg. the current ASCII issue. For Postscript substitute ps for pub. GOPHER: In your Gopher's list of Other Gophers locate ''University of Mining and
Metallurgy, Cracow'', or ''Uniwersytet Kalifornijski, Berkeley'',
and find ''Public access files/pigulki'' or ''Publications/pigulki''
menu entries. Or connect directly to <galaxy.uci.agh.edu.pl> or
<poniecki.berkeley.edu> using your gopher client.
Gopher accessibility: In your Gopher's list of Other Gophers
locate ''University of Mining and Metallurgy, Cracow'', or
''Uniwersytet Kalifornijski, Berkeley'', and find ''Public access
files/pigulki'' or ''Publications/pigulki'' menu entries. Or con-
nect directly to <galaxy.uci.agh.edu.pl> or <poniecki.berke-
ley.edu> using your gopher client. The gopher coverage
changes very rapidly. Ther may be other gopher sites carrying
PIGULKI. Use Veronica to locate them.
Additional information: Additional editors:
Jerzy Klimkowski, Glen Allen, VA
Internet: jleleno@cabell.vcu.edu
Dave Phillips, 2689 Elmwood Av. #2, Kenmore, NY 14217,
USA
(716) 874-9407
Internet: davep@acsu.buffalo.edu
Jacek Ulanski
Wieckowskiego 48 m 19, 90-735 Lodz, Poland
tel(48/42) 32-78-51
Internet: julanski@plearn.edu.pl
Bitnet: julanski@plearn
Marek Zielinski
85-20 67 Ave, Rego Park, NY 11374, USA
(718) 997-0695
Internet: zielinski@acfcluster.nyu.edu
Bitnet: zielinsk@nyuacf

PIRRADAZISH: BULLETIN OF ACHAEMENIAN STUDIES

Description: Pirradazish is an electronic journal covering re-
search into the Achaemenian (Persian) empire, 500-330 BC.
Subjects covered: Achaemenian studies; ancient history
Frequency: Semi-annual
Established: 1993
Method of issuance: Issues emailed to subscribers as published.
Editorial contact: Charles E. Jones
Internet: ce-jones@uchicago.edu
How to access: Send the message GET PERSIA BIB to
listserv@emuvm1 to receive back issues.

PLAY BY EMAIL

Description: Play by EMail is an electronic magazine about
email wargames, featuring reviews, information, and other top-
ics.
Subjects covered: wargames; computer hardware and software;
Internet
Editorial contact: Greg Lindahl
Internet: gl8f@fermi.clas.Virginia.EDU
How to access: Gopher accessible at: gopher.well.sf.ca.us

POSTMODERN CULTURE

ISSN: 1053-1920
Description: Postmodern Culture issues typically include six es-
says, a popular-culture column, book reviews, and at least one
creative work (poetry, script, fiction).
Subjects covered: language and literature; literary theory and
criticism; cultural studies
Net address for operations: listserv@listserv.ncsu.edu
Net address for questions or submissions:
pmc@unity.ncsu.edu
Frequency: 3 times a year
Established: 1990
Number of issues published to date: 8
Method of issuance: Issues available through email, disk, and
fiche. Issue availability is announced to subscribers, on email
discussion groups.

Available in other media: Yes, PMC is available in both disk and fiche formats, primarily for library use
Recent issue published: Volume 3, Number 2
Subscribers: 3000
Fee: None for email/ $15/yr others personal/$30 institutions by check
Sponsor: North Carolina State U., Raleigh, NC and Oxford University Press
Host: North Carolina State U., Raleigh, NC
Journal refereed: Yes. Ms. reviewed by editors, sent to 3 reviewers, two of them from the journal's editorial board, one self-nominated from among our subscribers (screened by editors).
Editorial contact: Eyal Amiran
Box 8105, English Department, NCSU, Raleigh, NY 27695
Tel: (919) 515-4168
Fax: (919) 515 3628
Internet: eaeg@unity.ncsu.edu
Technical contact: Chriss Barrett
Box 8105, English Department, NCSU, Raleigh, NY 27695
Tel: (919) 515-4168
Fax: (919) 515 3628
Internet: zeus8@unity.ncsu.edu
Review: In Times of London, New York Times Book Review, Factsheet Five, Lingua Franca, The Chronicle of Higher Education, The Raleigh News and Observer.
Indexed or abstracted: MLA INDEX
Copyright statement: Essays are copyright to the author.
How to access: Send to LISTSERV@LISTSERV.NCSU.EDU or write the editors. Message: SUB PMC-LIST YOUR NAME
How to unsubscribe: Send to LISTSERV@LISTSERV.NCSU.EDU Message: UNSUB PMC-LIST
Submission policy: Write the editors via email or snail mail.
Archives: Back issues are available; contact editors.
Related files: PMC-TALK is a list centering on discussion of texts appearing in Postmodern Culture. PMC-MOO is a new service offered (free of charge) by Postmodern Culture. PMC-MOO is a real-time, text-based, virtual reality environment in which you can interact with other subscribers of the journal and participate in live conferences. PMC-MOO will also provide access to texts generated by the journal and by PMC- TALK, and it will provide the opportunity to experience (or help to design) programs which simulate object-lessons in postmodern theory. PMC-MOO is based on the LambdaMOO program, freeware by Pavel Curtis. To connect to PMC-MOO, you must be on the internet. If you have an internet account, you can make a direct connection by typing the command: telnet dewey.lib.ncsu.edu 7777 at your command prompt. Once you've connected to the server, you will receive onscreen instructions on how to log in to PMC-MOO. If you have problems connecting to PMC-MOO or would like more information, contact pmc@unity.ncsu.edu by e-mail.
Gopher accessibility: At NCSU
WAIS accessibility: At NCSU
WorldWideWeb accessibility: At NCSU
Additional information: Additional editor: John Unsworth, Box 8105, English Department, NCSU, Raleigh, NC 27695; (919) 515-4138; fax (919) 515-3628; jmueg@unity.ncsu.edu

POSTMODERN JEWISH PHILOSOPHY
Description: Postmodern Jewish Philosphy covers topics related to the interpretation of Jewish theologies in modern life.

Subjects covered: philosophy; Judaica
Frequency: Irregular
Established: 1991
Method of issuance: Issues are emailed to subscribers as published.
Journal refereed: No
Editorial contact: Peter Ochs
Department of Religion, Drew University, Madison, NJ 07940.
Tel: (201) 408-3222
Internet: pochs@drew.drew.edu
Bitnet: pochs@drew
How to access: Send a message to pochs@drew.bitnet

POWDERKEG
Description: PowderKeg is a newsletter covering original fiction and poetry.
Subjects covered: fiction; poetry; American literature and language
Method of issuance: Issues are accessible through FTP only.
Journal refereed: No
How to access: FTP to nebula.lib.vt.edu

PRACTICAL ANARCHY ONLINE
Description: Practical Anarchy Online is an electronic newsletter covering anarchy and related political philosophies.
Subjects covered: anarchy; political science; philosophy
Frequency: Bimonthly
Method of issuance: Issues are emailed to subscribers as published.
Journal refereed: No
Editorial contact: Chuck Munson
Internet: ctmunson@macc.wisc.edu
How to access: Send email to cardell@lysator.liu.se or ctmunson@macc.wisc.edu
Gopher accessibility: Gopher accessible at: gopher.well.sf.ca.us

PRINCIPIA CYBERNETICA NEWSLETTER
Description: Principia Cybernetica covers a wide range of theoretical issues related to the development of a cybernetic world view.
Subjects covered: philosophy; computer science
Frequency: Annual
Established: 1990
Method of issuance: Issues are emailed to subscribers as published.
Journal refereed: No
Editorial contact: Dr. Francis Heylighen
PO, Free university of Brussels, Pleinlaan 2, B-1050 Brussels, Belgium.
Tel: +32-2-6412525
Fax: +32-2-6412489
Internet: fheyligh@vnet3.vub.ac.be
How to access: Send email to editor at: fheyligh@vnet3.vub.ac.be

PROJECT GUTENBERG NEWSLETTER
Description: The Project Gutenberg Newsletter updates activities of the Project Gutenberg text program, an independent program to make electronic versions of literary classics and other works easily available.

Frequency: Monthly
Established: 1988
Method of issuance: Issues are emailed to subscribers as published.
Journal refereed: No
Editorial contact: Michael Hart
National Clearinghouse for Machine Readable Texts
Internet: dircompg@ux1.cso.uiuc.edu
How to access: Send the message SUBSCRIBE GUTNBERG to listserv@uiucvmd.bitnet or listserv@vmd.cso.uiuc.edu

PROMPT

Description: Prompt news briefs and tips from the NCSU Computing Center, provides timely news and briefs related to computing for the NCSU community.
Subjects covered: North Carolina State University; computer hardware and software
Net address for operations: listserv@listserv.ncsu.edu
Net address for questions or submissions: noell@unity.ncsu.edu
Established: 1991
Method of issuance: Issues are emailed to subscription list.
Available in other media: Available in print.
Recent issue published: May 10, 1993
Subscribers: 650 electronic
Sponsor: NCSU Computing Center, Raleigh NC.
Journal refereed: No.
Editorial contact: Sarah Noell
North Carolina State University, Box 7109, Raleigh, NC 27695.
Tel: 919-515-5420
Fax: 919-515-3787
Internet: noell@unity.ncsu.edu
How to access: To listserv send the following message: sub prompt-l your name
How to unsubscribe: Mail to listserv@listserv.ncsu.edu
How to submit: Mail to noell@unity.ncsu.edu
Submission policy: Mail to noell@unity.ncsu.edu
Gopher accessibility: Available on Gopher server maintained by ncsu (gopher.ncsu.edu); and on our CWIS, callend Happenings! (telnet ccvax1.cc.ncsu.edu; logon as info)
Additional information:

PROXIMITY

Description: PROXIMITY is a new e-journal just started by the Professional Writing Program at Towson State University. It will publish creative and general non-fiction writing. Our first regular issue is due out in September 1993. We welcome queries from writers.
Subjects covered: writing; American literature and language
Net address for operations: prox@toe.towson.edu
Net address for questions or submissions: prox@toe.towson.edu
Established: September 1993
Number of issues published to date: 1
Subscribers: 35
Sponsor: Towson State University, Towson, MD 21204.
Journal refereed: No.
Editorial contact: Prof. Paul Miers
Eng. Department, Towson State University, Towson, MD 21204.
Tel: 410-830-2855
Internet: e7e4mie@toe.towson.edu

Bitnet: e7e4mie@towsonvx
Copyright statement: Writers retain copyright and are asked to acknowledge electronic publication.
How to access: prox@toe.towson.edu
How to unsubscribe: prox@toe.towson.edu
How to submit: prox@toe.towson.edu
Archives: Send request to prox@toe.towson.edu
Additional information:

THE PSYCGRAD JOURNAL (PSYCHOLOGY GRADUATE STUDENT JOURNAL)

ISSN: APPLIED FOR.
Description: The PSYCGRAD Journal (Psychology Graduate Student Journal) is an electronic journal containing papers written by graduate students studying in the field of psychology. Among topics discussed are aging, cognitive psychology, comparative and developmental psychobiology, developmental psychology, educational psychology, human sexuality, industrial/organizational psychology, graduate student issues, motivation and emotion, neuroscience, personality, psycholinguistics, psychological sssessment, psychopathology-nosology-etiology, psychophysics and perception, psychosomatics, psychotherapy, school counseling, social cognition, and social psychology.
Subjects covered: psychology; psychobiology; psychotherapy
Net address for questions or submissions: psygrd-j@acadvm1.uottawa.ca or psygrd-j@uottawa.bitnet
Established: January 1993
Number of issues published to date: Several papers in submission
Method of issuance: Issues are sent via electronic mail as published.
Subscribers: 290
Sponsor: Matthew Simpson Productions Ltd.
Host: School of Psychology, University of Ottawa, Ottawa, Ontario K1N 6N5
Journal refereed: Yes. Each editor is responsible for compiling topic-specific volumes. Submissions are sent to the volume editors.
Editorial contact: Matthew Simpson, School of Pyschology, 145 Jean Jacques Lussier, University of Ottawa, Ottawa, Ontario, Canada K1N 6N5
School of Pyschology, University of Ottawa, Ontario, Canada
Tel: (613) 564-2964
Fax: (fax) (613) 564-9569
Internet: 054340@acadvm1.uottawa.ca
Bitnet: 054340@uottawa.bitnet
Technical contact: Matthew Simpson
School of Psychology
University of Ottawa Ottawa, Ontario K1S 5L5
Tel: (613) 564-2964 (w)
Fax: (613) 564-9569
Internet: 054340@acadvm1.uottawa.ca
Bitnet: 054340@uottawa.bitnet
Copyright statement: The Psychology Graduate Student Journal: The PSYCGRAD Journal (c) is copyrighted by Matthew Simpson (054340@ acadvm1.uottawa.ca). As such, all replications of this material must maintain this statement within its content. Each individual author maintains the copyright over the article. Articles may be reproduced in another journal only with the permission of the Executive Editor of The PSYCGRAD Journal (Matthew Simpson) if the editor of the secondary journal is notified of the previous publication and if The

PSYCGRAD Journal is cited in any secondary publication as the source of original publication. The Psychology Graduate Student Journal: The PSYCGRAD Journal is a voluntary production of The PSYCGRAD Project. The PSYCGRAD Project maintains the right to replicate its contents for its purposes.

How to access: Send the following commands to listserv@acadvm1.uottawa.ca or listserv@uottawa.bitnet SUB PSYGRD-J Yourfirstname Yourlastname

Access policy: Anyone interested in the field of psychology can subscribe.

How to submit: Requirements for Submission: 1. All submitted articles should be in text format. 2. All articles should contain a table of contents outlined according to 0.0 Abstract 1 Main topic number one 1.1 First sub-topic of main topic one 1.1.1 First sub-sub-topic of main topic one 1.2 Second sub-topic of main topic one 2 Second main topic etc... 3. Each paragraph should begin with the appropriate number outlined in the table of contents. (Items 2 and 3, mentioned above, are necessary because bold and italic fonts are not recognized on most electronic-mail systems). 4. Each line should be no greater than 70 columns in width. This is necessary to decrease line-wrapping across systems. 5. APA guidelines must be adhered to (except where otherwise inconvenienced by electronic format, eg. items above). 6. The author of the article maintains full copyright. However, The PSYCGRAD Journal retains the right, for its purposes, to replicate and distribute the article. 7. Articles must not have been published elsewhere in written form. (Not published in journals; May ?? have been posters or talks at conferences.) Articles accepted for publication in The PSYCGRAD Journal may be published elsewhere at a later date with the permission of the Executive Editor if the editor(s) of the second journal are notified of this publication, and it is noted in any subsequent publication that the article was originally published in The PSYCGRAD Journal. 8. After the title of each article, the author's name, postal address, e-mail address, and affiliated institution must appear. 9. A list of keywords must also be provided. PSYGRD-J Subscriptions are open to the public. The journal is currently being maintained by a program called Listserv, and is distributed to the Internet and Bitnet electronic community. It is intended that with time, the journal will obtain ISSN classification.

Archives: Yes, gopher, ftp. gopher panda1.uottawa.ca ftp aix1.uottawa.ca /u/ftp/pub/psycgrad/The.PSYCGRAD.Journal

Gopher accessibility: Gopher panda1.uottawa.ca

PSYCHE: AN INTERDISCIPLINARY JOURNAL OF RESEARCH ON CONSCIOUSNESS

ISSN: 1039-723X

Description: PSYCHE is a refereed electronic journal dedicated to supporting the interdisciplinary exploration of the nature of consciousness and its relation to the brain. PSYCHE publishes material relevant to that exploration from the perspectives afforded by the disciplines of Cognitive Science, Philosophy, Psychology, Neuroscience, Artificial Intelligence and Anthropology. Interdisciplinary discussions are particularly encouraged.

Subjects covered: philosophy; psychology; anthropology; artificial intelligence

Net address for operations: LISTSERV@NKI.BITNET

Net address for questions or submissions: x91007@pitvax.xx.rmit.edu.au

Frequency: Quarterly

Established: December 1992

Method of issuance: Via the e-list PSYCHE-L

Available in other media: Still to be determined.

Recent issue published: 1(1) [Late June 1993]

Subscribers: 1400

Host: Royal Melbourne Institute of Technology, Bundoora, Victoria, 3083 Australia.

Journal refereed: Yes. Unsolicited submissions of original works within any of the above categories are welcome. Prospective authors should send articles directly to the executive editor. Submissions should be in a single copy of plain (ASCII) text if submitted electronically or four (4) copies if submitted by mail. Submitted matter should be preceded by: the author's name; address; affiliation; telephone number; electronic mail address. Any submission to be peer reviewed should be preceded by a 100-200 word abstract as well. Note that peer review will be blind, meaning that the prefatory material will not be made available to the referees. In the event that an article needs to be shortened for publication in the print version of PSYCHE the author will be responsible for making any alterations requested by the editors.

Editorial contact: Patrick Wilken Royal Melbourne Institute of Technology, Bundoora, Victoria, 3083 Australia.

Internet: x91007@pitvax.xx.rmit.edu.au

Copyright statement: Authors of accepted articles assign to PSYCHE the right to publish the text both electronically and as printed matter and to make it available permanently in an electronic archive. Authors will, however, retain copyright to their articles and may republish them in any forum they want so long as they clearly acknowledge PSYCHE as the original source of publication.

How to access: Subscriptions to the electronic version of PSYCHE may be initiated by sending the "SUBSCRIBE PSYCHE-L Your Name" one-line command (without quotes) in the body of an electronic mail message to LISTSERV@NKI.BITNET (or LISTSERV%NKI.BITNET@cunyvm.cuny.edu). Subscriptions to the print version may be initiated by contacting the executive editor; a nominal fee will be required to cover printing and mailing costs.

Access policy: No restriction on subscription.

How to unsubscribe: Sending the "UNSUBSCRIBE PSYCHE-L Your Name" one-line command (without quotes) in the body of an electronic mail message to LISTSERV@NKI.BITNET (or LISTSERV%NKI.BITNET@cunyvm.cuny.edu).

How to submit: Send all queries and submissions to the Executive Editor Patrick Wilken <email: x91007@pitvax.xx.rmit.edu.au>.

Additional information: Associate Editors include: George Buckner, Martin Marietta Corp., 79 Alexander Drive, Bldg 4501, Research Triangle Park, North Carolina 27709; grb@nccibm1.bitnet; Stephen Jackson, Department of Psychology, UCNW, University of Wales, Bangor, Gwynedd LL57 2DG. UK; pss042@bangor.ac.uk; Kevin B. Korb, Department of Computer Science, Monash University, Clayton, Victoria, 3168 Australia; korb@bruce.cs.monash.edu.au; Juan A. Siguenza, Instituto de Ingenieria del Conocimiento Universidad Autonoma de Madrid, Madrid, Spain; siguenza@emdcci11.bitnet; Stuart Watt, Human Cognition Research Laboratory, Open University, Walton Hall, Milton Keynes, MK7 6AA UK; S.N.K.Watt@open.ac.uk.

PSYCOLOQUY

ISSN: 1055-0143

Description: Psycoloquy is a refereed electronic journal sponsored on an experimental basis by the American Psychological Association and currently estimated to reach a readership of 20,000. Psycoloquy publishes brief reports of new ideas and findings on which the author wishes to solicit rapid peer feedback, international and interdisciplinary (''Scholarly Skywriting''), in all areas of psychology and its related fields (biobehavioral, cognitive, neural, social, etc.) Also included are refereed target articles, commentaries and authors' responses, as well as an unrefereed, unarchived newsletter section with professional notices and queries. All contributions are refereed by members of Psycoloquy's Editorial Board.

Subjects covered: psychology; cognitive science; philosophy; computer science

Net address for operations: listserv@pucc.bitnet or listserv@psyc.princeton.edu (listserv/bitnet version); psyc-request@phoenix.princeton.edu (Usenet version)

Net address for questions or submissions: psyc@pucc.bitnet or psyc@pucc.princeton.edu (listserv/bitnet version) sci.psychology.digest (Usenet) or psyc@phoenix.princeton.edu

Frequency: Irregular

Established: 1985; a refereed journal since 1989

Number of issues published to date: No issues. Articles appear as accepted, after refereeing and editing. In 1992 there were 70 target articles, commentaries and replies in the archived refereed section and about 15 Newsletter sections (not archived).

Method of issuance: Issues sent to the Listerv subscribership (-3000) directly every time an article appears; posted to Usenet (sci.psychology.digest, readership -20,000 by Arbitron estimate). Because PSYCOLOQUY is interdisciplinary, the lists on which its contents are announced vary with subject matter; they include psychology lists, neuroscience lists, biology, linguistics, philosophy, computer science; on Listserv and Usenet. They are sometimes also sent to the 4000-nale list of Behavioral and Brain Sciences (BBS) Associates. BBS is a paper journal of open peer commentary published by Cambridge University Press and edited by me. PSYCOLOQUY is its electronic counterpart, but it is completely independent, and sponsored by the American Psychological Association.

Available in other media: No, but it is permanently archived in several electronic archives. It is our explicit desire and intention NOT to produce a paper version, to encourage electronic-only access, search, retrieval and archiving.

Recent issue published: psyc.93.4.39.language-comprehension.2.powers (i.e. PSYCOLOQUY volume 4 number 39 1993; topic: language comprehension ''thread number'' on that topic: 2 author: Powers)

Subscribers: Bitnet/Listserv: 3112 Usenet/ -20,000 (Arbitron Readership survey estimate)

Sponsor: American Psychological Association, Washington, DC (Psycholoquy subsidized by APA, $15,000 per annum)

Host: Princeton University, Princeton NJ

Journal refereed: Yes. There is an editorial board of 80; submissions are sent to several referees; their reports are transmitted to the author by the editorial, together with his editorial disposition (reject, revise, accept, etc.) with instructions for revision, if any. Peer review is standard, as or paper journal (e.g. BBS).

Editorial contact: Stevan Harnad
Cognitive Science Laboratory, Princeton University, 221 Nassau Street, Princeton, NJ 08542
Tel: (609) 921-7771

Fax: (609) 258-2682
Internet: harnad@princeton.edu
Bitnet: harnad@pucc
Technical contact: Malcolm Bauer
Department of Psychology, Princeton University, Princeton, NJ 08544
Tel: (609) 258-1836
Fax: (609) 258-1836

Sample contents: Latest is the Powers commentary listed above: psyc.93.4.39.language-comprehension.2.powers

Review: There have been many articles and reviews of Psycoloquy. It was selected as one of the 10 best new magazines of 1990: Katz, W. (1991) The ten best magazines of 1990. Library Journal 116: 48 - 51. It was also reviewed and featured in Current Contents: Garfield, E. (1991) Electronic journals and skywriting: A complementary medium for scientific communication? Current Contents 45: 9-11, November 11 1991. And in several of the editor's own papers: Harnad, S. (1990) Scholarly Skywriting and the Prepublication Continuum of Scientific Inquiry. Psychological Science 1: 342 - 343 (reprinted in Current Contents 45: 9-13, November 11 1991). Harnad, S. (1991) Post-Gutenberg Galaxy: The Fourth Revolution in the Means of Production of Knowledge. Public-Access Computer Systems Review 2 (1): 39 - 53 (also reprinted in PACS Annual Review Volume 2 1992; and in R. D. Mason (ed.) Computer Conferencing: The Last Word. Beach Holme Publishers, 1992; and in: M. Strangelove & D. Kovacs: Directory of Electronic Journals, Newsletters, and Academic Discussion Lists (A. Okerson, ed), 2nd edition. Washington, DC, Association of Research Libraries, Office of Scientific & Academic Publishing, 1992). Harnad, S. (1992) Interactive Publication: Extending the American Physical Society's Discipline-Specific Model for Electronic Publishing. Serials Review, Special Issue on Economics Models for Electronic Publishing, pp. 58 - 61.

Indexed or abstracted: Not yet, but it will be by APA, (APA publishes Psychological Abstracts, the largest and most comprehensive Abstract service in this field).

Copyright statement: Authors of accepted manuscripts assign to Psycoloquy the right to publish and distribute their text electronically and to archive and make it permanently retrievable electronically, but they retain the copyright, and after it has appeared in Psycoloquy authors may republish their text in any way they wish -- electronic or print -- as long as they clearly acknowledge Psycoloquy as its original locus of publication. However, except in very special cases, agreed upon in advance, contributions that have already been published or are being considered for publication elsewhere are not eligible to be considered for publication in Psycoloquy.

How to access: There are two ways to access Psycoloquy: (1) To subscribe to Psycoloquy on Bitnet send email to: listserv@pucc.bitnet or listserv@pucc.princeton.edu containing the following one-line message (without a message header or topic, i.e. leave ''Subject'' line blank): sub psyc Firstname Lastname (substituting your first and last name, of course). (These instructions DO work, so please follow them faithfully! If for some reason you still do not succeed, send email to psyc@pucc.bitnet or psyc@pucc.princeton.edu and we will subscribe you by hand.) (2) Psycoloquy can also be accessed on Usenet as the moderated newsgroup sci.psychology.digest but then you will regularly have to check Usenet for new issues, because they are not automatically emailed to you as they are in the Bitnet version (the Listserv access model is individual subscription, the Usenet access model is an institutional library). The Usenet edition is sent to your Institution's Usenet archive, and kept there for a few weeks. After that, it must be retrieved from the permanent Psycoloquy archives in one of several possible ways, as described below.

How to unsubscribe: Send (again to listserv@pucc.bitnet, not to psyc@pucc.bitnet, which is only for submissions) the message:unsub psyc. If you are going away for a while and would like to temporarily halt your subscription, send to listserv@pucc.bitnet the message: set psyc nomail. When you return, send to the same address the message: set psyc mail. Remember not to send these messages to psyc@pucc.bitnet but to listserv@pucc.bitnet.

How to submit: psyc@pucc.bitnet or psyc@pucc.princeton.edu or psyc@phoenix.princeton.edu or sci.psychology.digest (Usenet Newsgroup)

Submission policy: psyc@pucc.bitnet or psyc@pucc.princeton.edu or psyc@phoenix.princeton.edu or sci.psychology.digest (Usenet Newsgroup)

Archives: There are three ways to search and retrieve from the Psycoloquy archives: Psycoloquy is now retrievable both by the standard listserv file retrieval commands on Bitnet and by anonymous ftp (plus some remarkable new tools) on the Internet: (1) Bitnet/Listserv Retrieval of Psycoloquy Archive: Bitnet users can either send the commands shown below as a TELL message to Listserv (TELL LISTSERV AT PUCC) or as email to LISTSERV@PUCC.bitnet. If you use email, your commands should appear in the body of the message and not in the subject line. Remember to send your mail requests to LISTSERV@PUCC.bitnet, not to PSYC@PUCC.bitnet to get a list of all PSYC files: GET PSYC FILELIST. This will send you a file containing the names of all the available files. Then, to order an individual file: GET fname ftype fname and ftype are the CMS Filename and Filetype as listed in the PSYC FILELIST file. (2) Internet/Unix/ftp Retrieval of Psycoloquy Archive: The Psycoloquy archives are available by anonymous ftp, if you have it. To retrieve a file by ftp from a Unix/Internet site, type either: ftp princeton.edu or ftp 128.112.128.1. When you are asked for your login, type: anonymous
Enter password as per instructions (make sure to include the specified @), and then change directories with: cd /pub/harnad To show the available files, type: ls. Next, retrieve the file you want with (for example): get psyc.92.3.15.consciousness.1.bridgeman. When you have the file(s) you want, type: quit. In case of doubt or difficulty, consult your system manager. (3) Easier and more direct and powerful access to the Psycoloquy archives is also available via archie, gopher, veronica and various wais servers, which do all the anonymous ftp search and retrieval for you and allow keyword and even full-text searching. Please ask your system administrator about these remarkable new electronic search and retrieval tools.

Gopher accessibility: Access to the Psycoloquy archives is also available via archie, gopher, veronica and various wais servers, which do all the anonymous ftp search and retrieval for you and allow keyword and even full-text searching. See more information above.

PUBLIC-ACCESS COMPUTER SYSTEMS NEWS

ISSN: 1050-6004
Description: PACS-News is a newsletter covering a wide range of computing related activities relevant to academic libraries.
Subjects covered: colleges and universities; library and information science

Frequency: Irregular
Established: 1990
Method of issuance: Issues are emailed to subscribers of PACS-Las published.
Host: University of Houston Libraries
Journal refereed: No
Editorial contact: Dana Rooks
Bitnet: libpacs@uhupvm1.bitnet
How to access: Send the message SUBSCRIBE PACS-L to listserv@uhupvm1 or listserv@uhupvm1.hh.edu
Related files: Related to PACS-L and PACS-Review

PUBLIC-ACCESS COMPUTER SYSTEMS REVIEW

ISSN: 1048-6542
Description: PACS-Review covers computing topics of interest to the academic library community
Subjects covered: colleges and universities; academic computing; library and information science
Frequency: Irregular
Established: 1990
Method of issuance: Issues are emailed to subscribers of PACS-Las published.
Host: University of Houston Libraries
Journal refereed: Yes
Editorial contact: Charles W. Bailey, Jr.
Assistant Director for Systems, University Libraries, University of Houston, Houston, TX 77204-2091.
Tel: (713) 743-9804
Fax: (713) 743-9748
Internet: lib3@uhupvm1.uh.edu
Bitnet: lib3@uhupvm1
How to access: Send the message SUBSCRIBE PACS-L to listserv@uhupvm1 or listserv@uhupvm1.uh.edu
Related files: Related to PACS-L and PACS-News

PUBS-IAT

Description: Pubs-IAT is the electronic newsletter of the Institute for Academic Technology.
Subjects covered: education; colleges and universities; information technology
Net address for operations: listserv@gibbs.oit.unc.edu
How to access: Send standard subscribe request to listserv.
How to unsubscribe: Send standard unsubscribe request to listserv.

PURPLE THUNDERBOLT OF SPODE (PURPS)

Description: PURPS is an electronic journal carrying a variety of humor, fiction, poetry, and news related to the Otisian faith.
Subjects covered: fiction; poetry; Otisian studies; cultural studies
Frequency: Irregular
Method of issuance: Issues are emailed to subscribers as published.
Journal refereed: No
Internet: hailotis@socpsy.sci.fau.edu, barker@acc.fau.edu
How to access: Send an email to HailOtis@socpsy.sci.fau.edu or barker@acc.fau.edu

QUANTA

ISSN: 1053-8496
Description: Quanta regularly features science fiction short stories and serials.
Subjects covered: language and literature; science fiction
Net address for operations: quanta-request@andrew.cmu.edu
Net address for questions or submissions:
quanta@andrew.cmu.edu
Frequency: 4 to 5 issues yearly
Established: 1989
Number of issues published to date: 17
Method of issuance: Issues available through electronic mail / ftp servers / gopher / compuserve / aol. Availability of new issues is announced on relevant newsgroups.
Available in other media: Yes, available on disk, although this is in the pilot stages currently.
Recent issue published: Volume 5, Number 1
Subscribers: 2200
Sponsor: CMU
Host: CMU
Journal refereed: No
Editorial contact: Daniel K. Applequist
3003 Van Ness St, NW, #S919, Washington, DC 20008
Tel: (202) 364-5953
Internet: dav@visix.com
Sample contents: Article: ''Looking Ahead,'' by Daniel K. Appelquist; Serials: ''The Harrison Chapters,'' by Jim Vassilakos; ''Dr. Tomorrow,'' by Marshall F. Gilula; Stories: ''Marketable Assets,'' by Vicki L. Martin; ''Matrix Error,'' by Charles B. Owen.
Copyright statement: All submissions, request for submission guidelines, requests for back issues, queries concerning subscriptions, letters, comments, or other correspondence should be sent to the Internet address. Copyright 1993 by Daniel K. Appelquist, quanta@andrew.cmu.edu. This magazine may be archived, reproduced and/or distributed provided that it is left intact and that no additions or changes are made to it.
How to access: Subscriptions come in three flavors: Mail subscriptions, where each issue is sent as a series of electronic mail messages; Bitnet subscriptions, where each issue is sent as a file over Bitnet; and FTP subscriptions, where subscribers receive a notification when a new issue has been placed at a designated FTP site.
Archives: Anonymous FTP servers that carry current and back issues of Quanta are: export.acs.cmu.edu (128.2.35.66); ftp.eff.org (192.88.144.4); lth.se (130.235.16.3); catless.newcastle.ac.uk (128.240.150.127). ASCII Quanta issues are available via Gopher server at gopher-srv.acs.cmu.edu, port 70, in the Archives directory. Issues of Quanta are also available on CompuServe in the ''Zines from the Net'' area of the EFF forum (accessed by typing GO EFFSIG).
Gopher accessibility: ASCII issues are available via Gopher server at gopher-srv.acs.cmu.edu, port 70, in the Archives directory.
Additional information: Fiction Submission Guidelines: Quanta publishes anything and everything from short-short pieces to large multi-part novellas or serials. Since Quanta is primarily a magazine of science fiction, there should be some science fiction content in the story, however, for our purposes, 'science fiction' is defined very broadly. The most important factor for any submission is good story telling. A ripping good story with only marginal science-fiction content is much more likely to be printed than a story with heavy SF content that is badly written. Please do not send any stories which use pre-made, possibly copyrighted, characters or settings (such as Star Trek stories, or continuations to the Apprentice Adept series). Stories that don't 'fit in' to a niche, or that are written in an off-beat or otherwise interesting narratorial style are always welcome. Quanta is distributed throughout the world across computer networks (mainly the Internet and BITnet) for free. Since Quanta has no income, it can't currently pay writers for their submissions. However, Quanta currently goes out to over 2200 subscribers, a higher subscriber base than many small-press journals, and this number continues to rise every day. Quanta continues to receive recognition, most recently garnering second runner up in the category of 'Regular Literary Publications' in the Digital Publishing Association's 'Digital Quill' awards (see the March, 1993 issue of Analog magazine for an article describing these awards which also discusses other electronic publishing issues). So what Quanta lacks in ability to reward its contributors monetarily, it makes up for in distribution and recognition. If possible, submissions should be in electronic form (on disk, or by electronic mail). Disks can be of either MS-DOS or Macintosh format. Straight text or RTF files are preferred, although other file formats are acceptable.

QUERY

Description: Query is a magazine covering multimedia and networking related to Apple computers in higher education.
Subjects covered: Internet; multimedia computing; Macintosh computers; education
How to access: Gopher accessible at consultant.micro.umn.edu and other public access gopher points.

RADIO HAVANA CUBA NEWSCAST

Description: Radio Havana Cuba Newscast is an electronic digest of news stories from Cuba, the Caribbean, and Latin America.
Subjects covered: Cuba; current events
Frequency: Daily
Established: 1992
Journal refereed: No
Internet: radiohc@tinored.cu
How to access: Email radiohc@tinored.cu for subscription details.

RD: GRADUATE RESEARCH IN THE ARTS

ISSN: 1188-0708
Description: RD publishes humanities texts by graduate students.
Subjects covered: graduate students; humanities
Frequency: Semi-annual
Method of issuance: Issues are emailed to subscribers as published.
Journal refereed: Yes
Editorial contact: Stephen N. Matsuba
Internet: rd@writer.yorku.ca, eng15105@nexus.yorku.ca
How to access: Send a message to rd@writer.yorku.ca.bitnet

REACH Q RESEARCH AND EDUCATIONAL APPLICATIONS OF COMPUTERS IN THE HUMANITIES

Description: REACH covers humanities computing at the University of California at Santa Barbara.
Subjects covered: University of California at Santa Barbara; colleges and universities; computer hardware and software
Frequency: Quarterly
Established: 1989
Method of issuance: Issues are emailed to subscribers as published.
Host: Humanities Computing, University of California at Santa Barbara.
Journal refereed: No
Editorial contact: Eric Dahlin
Internet: hcfidahl@ucsbuxa.ucsb.edu
Bitnet: hcfidahl@ucsbuxa
How to access: Send the message SUBSCRIBE REACH to listserv@ucsbvm.bitnet

RELIGIOUS STUDIES PUBLICATIONS JOURNAL

ISSN: 1188-5734
Description: Religious Studies Publications Journal publishes bibliographies and research-oriented work.
Subjects covered: religion
Frequency: Irregular
Established: 1992
Method of issuance: Issues are emailed to subscribers as published.
Host: Department of Religious Studies, University of Ottawa; Department of Religious Studies, Carleton University; American Academy of Religion.
Journal refereed: No
Editorial contact: Michael Strangelove
Department of Religious Studies, University of Ottawa, 177 Waller, Ottawa, Ontario, KIN 6N5 Canada.
Tel: (613)564-2300
Fax: (613) 56406641
Internet: 441495@acadvm1.uottawa.ca
Bitnet: 441495@uottawa
How to access: Send the message SUBSCRIBE CONTENTS to listserv@uottawa or listserv@acadvm1.uottawa.ca

RENEWS

Description: ReNews covers the computer industry in Russia.
Subjects covered: Russia; computer hardware and software
Frequency: Weekly in Russian, monthly in English.
Established: 1992
Method of issuance: Issues are emailed to subscribers as published.
Host: RELCOM
Journal refereed: No
Editorial contact: Vladimir Shliemin
RELCOM Corp.
Tel: +7 095 1989510, 1983796 Moscow
Internet: nev@renews.relcom.msk.su
How to access: Send the message SUBSCRIBE RENEWS to nev@renews.relcom.msk.su

REZO

Description: Rezo is the electronic newsletter of the Regroupement Quebecois des Sciences Sociales.
Subjects covered: science and technology
Frequency: Irregular
Established: 1989
Method of issuance: Issues are emailed to subscribers as published.
Host: Regroupement Quebecois des Sciences Sociales
Journal refereed: No
Editorial contact: Pierre J. Hamel
Institut National de la Recherche Scientifique, INRS-Urbanisation, 3465, rue Durocher, Montreal, Quebec H2X 2C6.
Internet: hamelpj@inrs-urb.uquebec.ca
How to access: Send the message SUBSCRIBE RQSS to listserv@uquebec

RFE/RL RESEARCH INSTITUTE DAILY REPORT

Description: RFE/RL is a survey of political development in Russia, Central Asia, and Eastern Europe.
Subjects covered: Russia; Eastern Europe; political science
Frequency: Daily
Established: 1992
Method of issuance: Issues are emailed to subscribers as published.
Host: Radio Free Europe
Journal refereed: No
Editorial contact: Dawn Mann
Information Resources Department, Radio Free Europe.
Internet: mannd@rferl.org
How to access: Send the message SUBSCRIBE RFERL-L to listserv@ubvm or listserv@ubvm.cc.buffalo.edu

RFE/RL RESEARCH INSTITUTE RESEARCH BULLETIN

Description: The Research Bulletin covers information related to Russia, Central Asia, and Eastern Europe.
Subjects covered: Russia; Eastern Europe; political science
Frequency: Weekly
Established: 1989
Method of issuance: Issues are distributed via commercial network.
Host: Radio Free Europe
Journal refereed: No
Editorial contact: Dawn Mann
Information Resources Department, Radio Free Europe
Internet: mannd@rferl.org
How to access: Send message to support@Sovset.org

RIF/T: A JOURNAL OF CONTEMPORARY POETRY AND POETICS

ISSN: (PENDING)
Description: RIF/T: A Journal of Contemporary Poetry and Poetics publishes experimental, avant garde, or language-oriented poetries by poets like Charles Bernstein and Robert Kelly. Also included are short essays on poetics, discussions, and electronic fora.
Subjects covered: poetry; language and literature; American literature and language

Net address for operations: listserv@ubvm.cc.buffalo.edu
Net address for questions or submissions: e-poetry@ubvm.cc.buffalo.edu
Frequency: Bimonthly
Established: Spring 1993
Number of issues published to date: 1
Method of issuance: ASCII TEXT FILE
Recent issue published: No. 1
Subscribers: 200+
Host: SUNY @ Buffalo
Editorial contact: Kenneth Sherwood
Dept. of English, SUNY at Buffalo, Buffalo, NY 14260.
Copyright statement: Copyright by the Editors of RIF/T. All rights revert to authors after initial publication. Contents may be freely distributed in whole or part by electronic means only, and with the provision that this copyright statement be included. Non-electronic reproduction is allowed for personal use only.
How to access: Send the command: subscribe e-poetry your name to listserv@ubvm.cc.buffalo.edu as the first an only line in an e-mail message
How to unsubscribe: Send the command unsubscribe e-poetry to the above address.
How to submit: Send message to e-poetry@ubvm.cc.buffalo.edu
Archives: Archived files will be available through normal Listserv GET procedures in the future.

RISKS-FORUM DIGEST
Description: Risks-Forum Digest covers computer security and related topics.
Subjects covered: computer security; computer science; computer hardware and software
Frequency: Weekly or more frequent
Established: 1985
Method of issuance: Issues are emailed to subscribers as published.
Host: Association for Computing Machinery (ACM)
Journal refereed: No
Editorial contact: Peter G. Neumann
Computer Science Lab, SRI International, EL-243, Menlo Park, CA 94025-3493.
Internet: neumann@csl.sri.com
How to access: Send email to risks-request@csl.sri.com

ROKPRESS
Description: RokPress is a current-events newsletter covering developments in Slovenia.
Subjects covered: current events; political science; Slovenia
How to access: Send request to editor at IBENKO@MAVERICO.UWATERLOO.CA
How to unsubscribe: Send request to editor at IBENKO@MAVERICO.UWATERLOO.CA

RSI NETWORK NEWSLETTER
Description: The RSI Network Newsletter covers repetitive stress injuries.
Subjects covered: medicine; health sciences
Frequency: Quarterly
Established: 1991
Method of issuance: Issues are emailed to subscribers as published.

Journal refereed: No
Editorial contact: Craig O'Donnell
Internet: dadadata@world.std.com, 72511.240@compuserve.com
How to access: Send email to dadadata@world.std.com or 72511.240@compuserve.com

SCHOLAR
ISSN: 1060-7862
Description: SCHOLAR is an electronic journal featuring notes on books, contents pages of journals, notes on hardware and software, notices of job openings, notices of text databases, and a calendar of meetings related to natural language processing.
Subjects covered: natural language processing; book reviews
Net address for operations: listserv@cunyvm.cuny.edu
Net address for questions or submissions: nlpqc@cunyvm.cuny.edu
Frequency: Bimonthly
Established: August 1992
Number of issues published to date: 4
Method of issuance: Issues are emailed to the listserve subscription list. Yes, other listservs announce SCHOLAR issues.
Recent issue published: Release BZ (first release of second year)
Subscribers: 2000 (45 countries)
Host: Queens College Foundation, Flushing, NY 11367
Editorial contact: Joseph Raben, P.O. Box F, New York, NY 10028-0025
Tel: (Sept-May) (212) 628-7846 (June-August) (516) 583-7138
Fax: jqrqc@cunyvm.cuny.edu
Technical contact: Lusi Altman
Internet: lnaqc@cunyvm.cuny.edu
How to access: Mail to listserv@cunyvm.cuny.edu
Access policy: No restrictions.
How to unsubscribe: Mmail to listserv@cunyvm.cuny.edu
How to submit: nlpqc@cunyvm.cuny.edu
Submission policy: No restrictions.
Archives: All related (ftp) files and other documents are accessible. All items accessible by ftp from Johns Hopkins University.
Gopher accessibility: Gopher access is being developed for this journal.

SCIENTIST
ISSN: 0890-3670
Description: The Scientist is a biweekly newspaper for scientists and the research community as a whole. Topics covered include funding, research grants, career opportunities, ethical issues, and other concerns of scientists. Established as a print publication in 1986, the electronic version has been available since November 1992.
Subjects covered: science and technology
Frequency: Biweekly
Established: 1992
Method of issuance: Issues are emailed to subscribers as published.
Journal refereed: No.
Editorial contact: Eugene Garfield
Internet: garfield@aurora.cis.upenn.edu
How to access: FTP to nnsc.nsf.net
The directory is: /the-scientist/
Or send email to info-server@nnsc.nsf.net

Gopher accessibility: Gopher-accessible at internic.net under InterNIC Directory and Database Service; Publicly Accessible Database; THE SCIENTIST-Newsletter

SCOPE NEWS
Description: Scope News is the electronic publication of SUNY Albany's School of Information Science and Policy.
Subjects covered: library and information science
Frequency: Monthly though academic year
Method of issuance: Issues are emailed to subscribers as published.
Host: State University of New York at Albany, School of Information Science & Policy
Journal refereed: No
Editorial contact: Maryhope Tobin
Richard Pugh
Bitnet: mt0296@albynyvms.bitnet, rp0358@albynyvms.bitnet
How to access: Send an email request to mt0296@albynyvms.bitnet or rp0358@albynyvms.bitnet

SCRATCH
Description: Scratch is an electronic magazine of alternative literature.
Subjects covered: alternative literature; popular culture
Editorial contact: James Barnett
28 North Avenue, New Rochelle, NY 10805.
Internet: spingo@Panix.Com
How to access: Gopher accessible at: etext.archive.umich.edu

SCREAM BABY
Description: Scream Baby is a newsletter covering the culture of the computer era.
Subjects covered: computer science; futurism
Frequency: Monthly
Established: 1992
Method of issuance: Issues are emailed to subscribers as published.
Journal refereed: No
Editorial contact: David Smith
Internet: bladex@wixer.cactus.org
How to access: Send email to bladex@wixer.cactus.org

SCREAMS OF ABEL
Description: Screams of Abel is an electronic weekly featuring reviews and news about heavy metal rock music.
Subjects covered: music; popular culture; popular music
Editorial contact: Phil Powell
Internet: Phil.Powell@launchpad.unc.edu
How to access: Gopher accessible at: etext.archive.umich.edu

SCUP EMAIL NEWS
Description: SCUP EMAIL News is the electronic newsletter of the Society for College and University Planning.
Subjects covered: colleges and universities; administration
Frequency: Biweekly
Established: 1987
Method of issuance: Issues are emailed to subscribers as published.

Host: Society for College and University Planning
Journal refereed: No
Editorial contact: Joanne Cate
Internet: budlao@uccvma.ucop.edu
Bitnet: budlao@uccvma
How to access: Send email to budlao@uccvma.ucop.edu or usertd8q@umichum

SENSE OF PLACE
Description: Sense of Place covers environmental topics.
Subjects covered: environmental studies
Frequency: Biweekly
Method of issuance: Issues are emailed to subscribers as published.
Host: Dartmouth College
Journal refereed: No
Internet: sop@dartmouth.edu
How to access: Send email to sop@dartmouth.edu

SHAREDEBATE INTERNATIONAL
ISSN: 1054-0695
Description: ShareDebate International is an electronic journal publishing science fiction.
Subjects covered: science fiction; American literature and language
Frequency: 2-3 times per week
Method of issuance: You can obtain the files through anonymous ftp access from wuarchive.wustl.edu from the directory /archive/doc/publications/ShareDebate. Login as 'anonymous' and your complete e-mail address as your password. A complete ftp sample script is available from Applied Foresight.
Available in other media: ShareDebate is available as a disk-based publication for Macintosh and DOS computers.
Fee: $15 for disk-based archive of all published issues.
Host: Applied Foresight, Inc., P.O. Box 20607 Bloomington MN 55420.
Editorial contact: R. H. Martin
CompuServe 71510,1042
Review: ''ShareDebate International is one of the most interesting developments on the electronic-publishing scene, proving that large circulation and big-name writers are no longer available only to publishers with large corporate backing. The day of grassroots mass-market publishing is here at last.'' --J. Neil Schulman, Prometheus award-winning SF author.
Copyright statement: Copyright 1993 by Applied Foresight Inc. All Rights Reserved. (Material by Individual Authors May Be Copyrighted Differently)

SIMULATION DIGEST
Description: Simulation Digest covers simulation software.
Subjects covered: computer hardware and software
Frequency: Weekly
Method of issuance: Issues are emailed to subscribers as pubished.
Journal refereed: No
Editorial contact: Prof. Paul A. Fishwick
Complex Systems and Simulation Group, Department of Computer Science, University of Florida, Bldg. CSE, Room 301, Gainesville, FL 32611.
Internet: fishwick@cis.ufl.edu

How to access: Send email to simulation-request@cis.ufl.edu or send a Gopher message: gopher gopher.cis.ufl.edu

SIMULATIONS ONLINE
Description: Simulations Online covers military simulation software.
Subjects covered: computer hardware and software
Frequency: Irregular
Method of issuance: Issues are emailed to subscribers as published.
Journal refereed: No
Editorial contact: Peter T. Szymonik
Internet: xorg@cup.portal.com, 72637.2272@compuserve.com
How to access: Send email to xorg@cup.portal.com or 72637.2272@compuserve.com

SLSCK...THE NEWSLETTER
Description: SLSCk is an electronic newsletter providing a communications vehicle for the Library Automation Implementation Program (LAIP) of the State University of New York. SLSCk.. the Newsletter provides a means of communicating current software bugs and workarounds, tips for using the multiLIS library automation software, and announcements/updates on LAIP.
Subjects covered: computer hardware and software; library and information science
Net address for operations: schumaje@slseva.ca.sunycentral.edu
Net address for questions or submissions: schumaje@slseva.ca.sunycentral.edu
Frequency: Biweekly
Established: May 1992
Number of issues published to date: 26
Method of issuance: Issues are distributed to subscriber list as published.
Recent issue published: #41
Subscribers: 200+
Sponsor: State University of New York
Host: SUNY Office of Library Services
Journal refereed: No.
Editorial contact: John Schumacher
166 2nd Ave, Troy, NY 12180
Tel: 518-443-5581
Fax: 518-443-5358
Internet: schumaje@slseva.ca.sunycentral.edu
Sample contents: Description of "front-end" menu set up to provide networked access to SUNY library catalogs, current announcements, information on current status of program.
How to access: Send request to:
schumaje@slseva.ca.sunycentral.edu
Gopher access at slscva.ca.sunycentral.edu
Access policy:
How to unsubscribe: Send request to:
schumaje@slseva.ca.sunycentral.edu
Archives: SUNYLA-L and multiLIS Lists are archived.

SOCJETY JOURNAL
Description: Socjety Journal covers science and technology topics. It originates at the Technical University of Wroclaw, Poland.
Subjects covered: science and technology
Method of issuance: Issues are emailed to subscribers as published.
Journal refereed: No

Editorial contact: Ala Lewanowicz
Bitnet: lewanowi@plwrtu11.bitnet
How to access: Send the message to SUBSCRIBE WROCLAW to listserv@plearn.bitnet

SOLSTICE: AN ELECTRONIC JOURNAL OF GEOGRAPHY AND MATHEMATICS
ISSN: 1059-5325
Description: Solstice: An Electronic Journal of Geography and Mathematics publishes research and other texts on topics involving mathematical geography, geography, or mathematics. Occasional reprints and other education features are also published.
Subjects covered: mathematics; geography
Net address for operations: Solstice@UMICHUM.bitnet; Solstice@um.cc.umich.edu
Net address for questions or submissions: Solstice@UMICHUM.bitnet; Solstice@um.cc.umich.edu
Frequency: Twice yearly, on astronomical solstices.
Established: June 1990
Number of issues published to date: Six issues in three volumes: 1990: Volume I, Numbers 1 and 2; 1991: Volume II, Numbers 1 and 2; 1992: Volume III, Numbers 1 and 2.
Method of issuance: Issues are sent over Bitnet and Internet; hard copy also available.
Issues are announced by listing in the catalogues of the Institute of Mathematical Geography, both electronic catalogues and hard copy catalogues.
Available in other media: Yes, print--each full year volume is printed in monograph series of the Institute of Mathematical Geography. Volume/number of latest issue: Volume III, Number 2, December, 1992. Forthcoming, Volume IV, Number 1, June, 1993.
Subscribers: 80
Fee: Free; hard copy is $15.95 for a volume. Willing to invoice customers for hardcopy.
Sponsor: Institute of Mathematical Geography 2790 Briarcliff St. Ann Arbor, MI 48105
Journal refereed: Yes. Submitted manuscript is sent to either a mathematician or a geographer, whichever content is dominant. Written commentary concerning the correctness, suitability, and timeliness of the article is returned to the Editor. A second referee then has the opportunity to offer an opinion on articles which appear to be suitable. In the case of disagreement, a third is consulted. The method of sending materials to the referees is the choice of the referee; manuscripts may be sent over internet/bitnet, on diskette, or as hard copy.
Editorial contact: Sandra Lach Arlinghaus, 2790 Briarcliff St., Ann Arbor, MI 48105-1429.
Tel: (313) 761-1231
Internet: IMaGe@um.cc.umich.edu
Bitnet: IMaGe@UMICHUM
Sample contents: What Are Mathematical Models and What Should They Be?, by Dr. Frank Harar; Where Are We? Comments on the Concept of the Center of Population, by Prof. Frank Barmore; The Pelt of the Earth: An Essay on Reactive Diffusion, by Dr. Sandra L. Arlinghaus and Prof. John D. Nystuen; Index to previous volumes of Solstice; Other publications of the Institute of Mathematical Geography.
Review: Science, AAAS, Nov. 29, 1991 Science News, January 25, 1992, Vol. 141, no. 4 American Mathematical Monthly, Sept. 1992 cites Solstice as "one of world's first electronic journals, using TeX,..." Association of American Geographers, Newsletter, Vol. 27, Number 6, June 1992. Harvard Technology

Window, 1993, facts of publication unknown Graduating Engineering Magazine, 1993, facts of publication unknown.

Indexed or abstracted: It is in Michael Strangelove's latest listing for the Association of Research Libraries. The hardcopy is assigned an ISBN; thus, it appears in Books In Print (R. R. Bowker). Volume I, ISBN:1-877751-44-8; Volume II, ISBN:1-877751-53-7; Volume III, ISBN:1-877751-54-5.

Copyright statement: Copyright, June 1992, Institute of Mathematical Geography. All rights reserved. (Fill in appropriate date, obviously)

How to access: E-mail a request to Solstice@umichum or Solstice@um.cc.umich.edu

Access policy: Anyone wishing to subscribe may do so, free. Note that it is the TeX-ed ASCII files that are transmitted.

How to unsubscribe: E-mail a request to Solstice@umichum or Solstice@um.cc.umich.edu

How to submit: E-mail Solstice@umichum or Solstice@um.cc.umich.edu

Archives: Yes; as hard copy, on diskette, or on ftp files.

SOMALIA NEWS UPDATE

ISSN: 1103-1999

Description: Somalia News Update covers the political, economic, and social situation in Somalia.

Subjects covered: Somalia; political science; current events

Frequency: Irregular

Method of issuance: Issues are emailed to subscribers as published.

Journal refereed: No

Editorial contact: Dr. Bernhard Helander
Department of Cultural Anthropology, University of Uppsala, Tradgardsgatan 18, S-753 09 Uppsala, Sweden.

Internet: bernhard.helander@antro.uu.se

How to access: Send email to bernhard.helander@antro.uu.se

SONIC VERSE MUSIC MAGAZINE (FORMERLY UPDATE ELECTRONIC MUSIC NEWSLETTER)

Description: Sonic Verse Music Magazine is an electronic journal covering music and music-related topics, including, but not limited to, recordings, reviews, technology used in music, lists of facts/events/history, definitions, humor, opinions, ethical/moral, artwork, etc. Sonic Verse highlights "underground" music and independent and major label artists and companies. Sonic Verse is also attempting to close the popular music gap, or mass music gap, by bringing to the forefront those artists and aspects of the music industry that are struggling to make their voices heard. Sonic Verse is providing artists and other areas of the music industry with an opportunity to have recordings, music products, and/or music services presented directly to a large music audience.

Subjects covered: music

Net address for operations: UPNEWS@MARIST or UPNEWS@VM.MARIST.EDU

Net address for questions or submissions: UPNEWS@MARIST or UPNEWS@VM.MARIST.EDU

Frequency: Monthly

Established: July 1991

Number of issues published to date: 31

Method of issuance: Issues are sent via Internet/Bitnet email.

Available in other media: Printed copies of text made available to solicit music industry interest. Desktop publishing is also being considered.

Recent issue published: Volume 3, Issue 5

Subscribers: 1,626

Sponsor: Marist College, 290 North Rd., Poughkeepsie, NY 12601.

Editorial contact: C.V. DeRobertis
P.O. Box 219, Stormville, NY 12582-0219

Tel: (914) 221-0872

Fax: (914) 221-0872

Internet: UICD@VM.MARIST.EDU or URCD@VM.MARISTC.EDU

Bitnet: UICD@MARIST or URCD@MARISTC

Copyright statement: Sonic Verse Music Magazine is (c) Christopher Vincent DeRobertis. (TM work in progress for name ("Sonic Verse") and potential logo.) Sonic Verse magazine may not be reproduced or transmitted in any form, either in whole or part, without the express written consent of Christopher Vincent DeRobertis. All questions, comments, reproduction requests, and general inquiries can be sent to any of the addresses appearing earlier.

How to access: Tell listserv at Marist SUB UPNEWS <yourname>

How to unsubscribe: Tell listserv at Marist SIGNOFF UPNEWS

How to submit: Send e-mail to one of the e-mail addresses mentioned earlier or to UPNEWS@MARIST or UPNEWS@VM.MARIST.EDU

Archives: Back issues may be retrieved from the listserv nodes at MARIST (Marist College) and BITNIC. To find out what data retrieval and search commands are available at the various listservs, Bitnet users can send the following interactive message to receive a listserv help display: TELL LISTSERV AT <node> HELP. To obtain a file of available commands, Bitnet users should mail to LISTSERV@MARIST, and Internet users should send e-mail to LISTSERV@VM.MARIST.EDU. The body of the mail should only contain the line HELP. Subsequent listserv commands can be issued in either format.

SOUND NEWS AND ARTS

Description: SOUND News and Arts is an arts newsletter for the Omaha and Lincoln, Nebraska, areas.

Subjects covered: events listings; music; art

Frequency: Monthly

Established: 1992

Method of issuance: Issues are emailed to subscribers as published.

Host: University of Nebraska

Journal refereed: No

Editorial contact: Ed Stastny
Sound Publishing, Inc., P.O. Box 31104, Omaha, NE 68132.

Internet: ed@cwis.unomaha.edu

How to access: Send an email request to ed@cwis.unomaha.edu

SOUND NEWSLETTER

Description: The Sound Newsletter covers audio hardware and software.

Subjects covered: computer hardware and software; multimedia

Frequency: Bimonthly

Established: 1990

Journal refereed: No

Editorial contact: Dave Komatsu
Internet: sound@ccb.ucsf.edu
How to access: Available only through FTP. Send to sound@ccb.ucsf.edu for further information.

SOUTH FLORIDA ENVIRONMENTAL READER
ISSN: 1044-3479
Description: South Florida Environmental Reader carries articles pertaining to the South Florida environment.
Subjects covered: environmental studies; Florida
Net address for operations: listserv@ucf1vm.cc.ucf.edu
Net address for questions or submissions: fer-l@ucf1vm.cc.ucf.edu, aem@symbiosis.ahp.com
Frequency: Irregular
Number of issues published to date: 44
Method of issuance: Issues distributed to subscription lists via email.
Subscribers: 100
Sponsor: South Florida Environmental Information Project, P.O. Box 1041, South Miami, Florida 33243-1041.
Editorial contact: Andrew Mossberg
6255 SW 69 St,. South Miami, FL 33143-3355.
Tel: (305) 669-1943
Internet: aem@symbiosis.ahp.com
Copyright statement: Copyright 1990 by Andrew Mossberg. Reproduction and distribution of this newsletter is encouraged. Articles may be freely reproduced provided credit is given. Articles with an explicit copyright may have other restrictions. If in doubt, contact the editor or the author of the article. The South Florida Environmental Reader can be contacted at Post Office Box 1041, South Miami, Florida, 33243-1041. By electronic mail, contact us at aem@symbiosis.ahp.com Peace! Justice! Ecology!
How to access: Send a message to listserv@ucf1vm on bitnet, or listserv@ucf1vm.cc.ucf.edu on Internet containing the line subscribe sfer-l
How to unsubscribe: Send a message to listserv@ucf1vm on bitnet, or listserv@ucf1vm.cc.ucf.edu on internet containing unsub sfer-l
How to submit: aem@symbiosis.ahp.com
Archives: Archives are available via ftp to mthvax.cs.miami.edu, directory pub/sfer or from listserv@ucf1vm.cc.ucf.edu

SOUTH SCANNER SATELLITE SERVICES CHART
Description: South Scanner Satellite Services Chart provides a listing of telecommunications satellites.
Subjects covered: telecommunications
Frequency: Monthly
Method of issuance: Issues are emailed to subscribers as published.
Journal refereed: No
Editorial contact: Robert Smathers
Internet: roberts@triton.unm.edu
How to access: Send an email request to roberts@triton.unm.edu

SPACEVIEWS
Description: SpaceViews offers monhtly information on the US space program and other space-related issues.
Subjects covered: space and space exploration; science and technology
Frequency: Monthly
Established: 1992
Method of issuance: Issues are emailed to subscribers as published.
Host: National Space Society
Journal refereed: No
Editorial contact: Bruce Mackenzie
110 Van Norden Rd., Reading, MA 01867-1246.
Internet: brucem@ptltd.com
How to access: Send an email message to brucem@ptltd.com, or man@labrea.zko.dec.com, or tombaker@world.std.com

SPRINGER-VERLAG SCIENCE JOURNALS PROJECT
Description: Springer-Verlag is offering the tables of contents and BiblioAbstracts of 30 important scientific journals via e-mail before publication of the new issue. Tables of contents are free of charge and BiblioAbstracts are available for an annual token fee.
Subjects covered: science and technology; publishing
Established: March 1, 1993
Method of issuance: The files supplied are in ASCII format, structured in accordance with accepted standards. They can be read on any computer without further processing and but also easily integrated into local databases.
Sponsor: Springer-Verlag GmbH & Co. KG, New Technologies / Product Development, P.O. Box 10 52 80, W-6900 Heidelberg, Germany; fax: +49 6221 487 648.
How to access: For details please send an e-mail message containing the word HELP to SVJPS@DHDSPRI6.BITNET or contact SPRINGER@DHDSPRI6.BITNET

SUEARN-L
Description: SUEARN-L is a digest of information on Eastern Europe. Included are articles on computer networking and information resources available in Russia and Eastern Europe.
Subjects covered: Russia; Eastern Europe; telecommunications; computer hardware and software
Net address for questions or submissions: SUEARN-L@UBVM
How to access: Send standard subscribe request to listserv.
How to unsubscribe: Send standard unsubscribe request to listserv.

SURFACES
ISSN: 1188-2492
Description: Surfaces is a refereed electronic journal in the humanities.
Subjects covered: humanities
Frequency: Irregular
Established: 1991
Host: Department of Comparative Literature, University of Montreal
Journal refereed: Yes

The Editors, Surfaces, Dept. of Comparative Literature, Universite de Montreal, C.P. 6128, succ. "A", Montreal, Quebec, H3C 3J7 Canada.
Tel: (514) 343-5683
Fax: (514)343-5684
Internet: guedon@ere.umontreal.ca
How to access: Send an email message to guedon@ere.umontreal.ca

SURFPUNK TECHNICAL JOURNAL

Description: SURFPUNK is an electronic magazine centering on cyberspace and other technical issues.
Subjects covered: multimedia computing; popular culture; computer science; Internet
Frequency: Daily
Established: 1992
Method of issuance: Issues are emailed to subscribers as published.
Journal refereed: No
Internet: strick@osc.versant.com
How to access: Send an email message to surfpunk-request@osc.versant.com

SYLLABUS

Description: Syllabus is a magazine covering multimedia and networking related to Apple computers in higher education.
Subjects covered: Internet; multimedia computing; Macintosh computers; education
Host: Apple Computer Higher Education Gopher at the University of Minnesota Gopher Server.
How to access: Gopher accessible at consultant.micro.umn.edu and other public access gopher points.

TAPROOT REVIEWS ELECTRONIC EDITION

Description: TapRoot is an electronic publication reviewing experimental text-based arts, including fiction, poetry, and other media. Over 100 reviews are featured in each issue.
Subjects covered: fiction; poetry; popular culture
Frequency: Quarterly
Established: 1992
Method of issuance: Issues are emailed to subscribers as published.
Journal refereed: No
Editorial contact: Luigi-Bob Drake
Burning Press, P.O. Box 585, Lakewood, OH 44107.
Internet: au462@cleveland.freenet.edu
How to access: Send email to au462@cleveland.freenet.edu

TAYLOROLOGY

Description: TAYLOROLOGY is a newsletter focusing on the life and death of William Desmond Taylor, a top film director in early Hollywood who was shot to death on February 1, 1922. His unsolved murder was one of Hollywood's major scandals. This newsletter will deal with: (a) The facts of Taylor's life; (b) The facts and rumors of Taylor's murder; (c) The impact of the Taylor murder on Hollywood and the nation. Primary emphasis will be given toward reprinting, referencing and analyzing source material, and sifting it for accuracy.

Subjects covered: cinema studies; crime
Editorial contact: Bruce Long
Internet: bruce@asu.edu
How to access: Gopher accessible at: etext.archive.umich.edu

TECHMATH-NET

Description: TECHMATH-NET is a moderated newsletter for mathematicians, mainly from Israel.
Subjects covered: mathematics
Net address for operations: LISTSERV@TECHNION.TECHNION.AC.IL
Net address for questions or submissions: MAR23AA@TECHNION.TECHNION.AC.IL
Established: October 24, 1990
Subscribers: 178
Sponsor: Mathematics Department, Technion - Israel Institute of Technology, Haifa 32000, Israel
Host: Same as above
Editorial contact: Prof. Daniel Hershkowitz
Mathematics Department, Technion - Israel Institute of Technology, Haifa 32000, Israel
Tel: 972-4-294282
Fax: 972-4-324654
Internet: mar23aa@technion.technion.ac.il
Bitnet: mar23aa@technion
Sample contents: We circulate announcements of mathematical activities in Israel, as well as other notices of interest to mathematicians in Israel.
How to access: Send the message SUB TECHMATH to LISTSERV@TECHNION.TECHNION.AC.IL
Access policy: This newsletter is open to all.
How to unsubscribe: Send the message SIGNOFF TECHMATH to LISTSERV@TECHNION.TECHNION.AC.IL
How to submit: Send submissions to mar23aa@technion.technion.ac.il
Archives: Ask from mar23aa@technion.technion.ac.il

TEIRESIAS

ISSN: 0381-9361
Description: Teiresias is an electronic newsletter of classical studies.
Subjects covered: classical studies
Frequency: Irregular
Established: 1991
Method of issuance: Issues are emailed to subscribers as published.
Journal refereed: No
Editorial contact: A. Schachter
Department of Classics, McGill University, 855 Sherbrooke St. West, Montreal, Quebec, Canada H3A 2T7.
Internet: czas@musica.mcgill.ca
How to access: Send email to czas@musica.mcgill.ca

TELECOM DIGEST

Description: TELECOM Digest covers topics central to telecommunications.
Subjects covered: telecommunications
Frequency: Daily
Method of issuance: Issues are emailed to subscribers as published.
Journal refereed: No

Editorial contact: Patrick Townson
Internet: telecom@eecs.nwu.edu
How to access: Send the message SUBSCRIBE TO DIGEST to: telecom-request@eecs.nwu.edu.
Related files: FTP to lcs.mit.edu
The directory is: telecom-archives

TELEPUTING HOTLINE AND FIELD COMPUTING SOURCE LETTER

Description: Teleputing Hotline covers international telecommunications.
Subjects covered: telecommunications
Frequency: Weekly
Method of issuance: Issues are emailed to subscribers as published.
Journal refereed: No
Editorial contact: Dana Blankenhorn
Tel: (404) 373-7634
MCI: 409-8960
Fax: (404) 378-0794
Internet: CompuServe: 76200,3025,
76200.3025@compuserve.com
How to access: Send email requests to
76200.3025@compuserve.com

TEMPLE OV PSYCHICK YOUTH ON-LINE TRANSMISSION

Description: Temple ov Psychick Youth covers magic, shamanism, and other occult-related topics.
Subjects covered: occult
Frequency: Monthly
Method of issuance: Issues are emailed to subscribers as published.
Journal refereed: No
Internet: alamut@netcom.com
How to access: Send email to vajra@u.washington.edu
Send an FTP to netcom.com directory:/pub/alamut/

TEMPTATION OF SAINT ANTHONY

ISSN: 1062-3981
Description: Temptation of Saint Anthony is a publication offering humor, fiction, and related texts of a pop nature.
Subjects covered: fiction; popular culture
Established: 1990
Journal refereed: No
Editorial contact: Martin Bormann's Cranial Splints
P.O. Box 8166, Philadelphia, PA 19101-8166.
Internet: mbcs@gradient.cis.upenn.edu
How to access: Send email message to
mbcs@gradient.cis.upenn.edu

TERMINOMETRO ELECTRONICO

Description: Terminometro Electronico is an electronic publication in Spanish, French, Italian, and Portuguese providing information on science and technical terminologies, with translation of terms among the four languages.
Subjects covered: science and technology; dictionaries
Frequency: Monthly
Editorial contact: UNION LATINA - Terminometro

Redaccion y administracion, 14, bd. Arago, 75013 PARIS, France.
Tel: 33 (1) 43.36.14.14
Fax: 33 (1) 45.35.75.01
Bitnet: LATINA@FRMOP11
How to access: Send an email message to LATIN-TE@FRMOP11.bitnet

TEX PUBLICATION DISTRIBUTION LIST

Description: TEX Publication Distribution List covers TEX software.
Subjects covered: TeX software; computer hardware and software
Frequency: Irregular
Established: 1991
Method of issuance: Issues are emailed to subscribers as published.
Journal refereed: No
Editorial contact: George D. Greenwade, Ph.D.
Department of Economics and Business Analysis, Sam Houston State University, Huntsville, TX 77341.
Internet: bed__gdg@SHSU.edu
Bitnet: BED__GDG@SHSU
How to access: Send the message SUBSCRIBE TEX-PUBS to listserv@shsu.bitnet or listserv@shsu.edu

TEXMAG

Description: TEXMAG covers TEX software.
Subjects covered: TeX software; computer hardware and software
Frequency: Monthly
Method of issuance: Issues are emailed to subscribers as published.
Journal refereed: No
Editorial contact: Neil Burleson
Internet: nabtexm@rigel.tamu.edu
Bitnet: nabtexm@tamvenus
How to access: Send the message SUBSCRIBE TEXMAG-L to listserv@uicvm.uic.edu or listserv@uicvm

THINKNET

Description: THINKNET is an electronic publication covering philosophical issues.
Subjects covered: philosophy
Frequency: Irregular
Established: 1990
Method of issuance: Issues are emailed to subscribers as published.
Journal refereed: No
Editorial contact: Kent D. Palmer Ph.D.
P.O. Box 8383, Orange, CA 92664.
Internet: palmer@world.std.com
How to access: Send the message SUBSCRIBE THINKNET to palmer@world.std.com

TIDBITS

Description: TidBITS is a free weekly electronic publication that reports on interesting products and events in the computer industry, currently with an emphasis on the world of the Macintosh. In addition to weekly issues, we occasionally publish formal review issues and special issues focussing on a single topic. We feel that publications like TidBITS will become an important medium of exchange as the world becomes more electronically connected.

Subjects covered: computer hardware and software; Macintosh computers

Net address for operations: LISTSERV@RICEVM1.RICE.EDU

Net address for questions or submissions: info@tidbits.com and sponsors@tidbits.com (informational files on our sponsors' products)

Frequency: Weekly

Established: April 1990

Number of issues published to date: 177

Method of issuance: Issues are sent via email, posting as files. Issues are announced over the Internet, CompuServe, America Online, Delphi, BIX, AppleLink, GEnie, and numerous BBSs.

Available in other media: Subscriptions to TidBITS are available along with a disk set containing all back issues.

Recent issue published: Issue #177

Subscribers: Estimated 50,000. That number could be low by as many as another 50,000 very easily since it ignores all BBSs.

Commercial organization: TidBITS, 1106 North 31st Street, Renton, WA 98056.

Editorial contact: Adam & Tonya Engst
1106 North 31st Street, Renton, WA 98055

Tel: (206) 235-7447

Fax: Call voice number first; (206) 235-8203

Internet: ace@tidbits.com

Bitnet: ace@tidbits.com

Review: Following is an extract of a review (the reviewer's name and address is included): Enter TidBITS. TidBITS is Snickers to my microcomputer sweet tooth. It's my Macintosh Gazette. My weekly fix. I always read it. I never print it. I cut and paste pieces of it into e-mail notes and send them to my colleagues. It's as unlike the way I used to get information as it can be. And (Hallelujah!) it doesn't form stacks! With TidBITS I became all at once a new species of information consumer. I don't remember where I first found TidBITS, but I remember my reaction. "Eureka!" Here is the right information for a semi-pro Macintosh user, and just enough of it. TidBITS comes as e-mail to my desktop computer once a week. In it I read first-hand reports about computer viruses. These come direct from the software engineers who work around the clock during outbreaks to adapt disinfectant software to eradicate them. I read about new Mac software, from neat new public domain utilities, to high-end page layout packages, to the inside scoop on Apple's new system software. And there's hardware news as well. I find out what might happen to my lap if my laptop computer's battery shorts out. (Don't ask!) TidBITS doesn't mess around with hearsay. Well, not all the time, anyway. Many of its contributors are support and engineering people from the major software and hardware corporations. --Mark Sheehan (sheehan@indiana.edu) is technical communications administrator and manager of publications for University Computing Services, Indiana University.

How to access: To subscribe to the TIDBITS LISTSERV at Rice University, send email to one of the two following addresses: Bitnet: LISTSERV@RICEVM1; Internet: LISTSERV@RICEVM1.RICE.EDU. In the body of the mail, put the line: SUBSCRIBE TIDBITS your full name and you will be automatically added. You should also receive an acknowledgment from the listserv so you know that you're on.

Access policy: Anyone may subscribe and all are welcome.

How to unsubscribe: If you are already on the mailing list and need to remove yourself because you are leaving for the summer or you just can't keep up with so much mail, send another mailfile to the address above with this line in the body of the mailfile: SIGNOFF TIDBITS and you will be automatically removed as long as you are sending the SIGNOFF command from the same account you used to SUBSCRIBE. The LISTSERV will let you know if the command is successful or not. Changing Addresses: Many people change email addresses and wish to have TidBITS delivered to their new address. To change your address, simply send a SIGNOFF command (see above) from the old account, then send a SUBSCRIBE command (see above again) from the new account.

How to submit: Please send email to: info@tidbits.com for general information about TidBITS and where to find back issues. For submissions and specific questions, please send email to: ace@tidbits.com

Submission policy: We accept (but may not publish) all submissions, and try to answer all reasonable questions.

Archives: Archives are available via FTP at sumex-aim.stanford.edu in the directory info-mac/digest/tb, although this may change in the near future. Although TidBITS is free, we have disk subscriptions available along with a disk set containing all back issues. Please get the file "subscribe" from the fileserver as outlined below. We recommend that people use Easy View 2.32, a freeware text browser, to read the special setext format our text files are in (it's also readable with any text editor on any platform). Easy View 2.32 is available from sumex-aim.stanford.edu for anonymous FTP as:info-mac/app/easy-view-232.hqx. We also have more information about setext and other TidBITS news on our Internet fileserver. Please send email to: fileserver@tidbits.com with the single word help alone in the Subject line. Body text is ignored.

WAIS accessibility: There is an indexed archive of TidBITS issues on the Internet using WAIS. This means anyone can use WAIS to retrieve any article or group of articles. If you already know how to use WAIS, just use the source "macintosh-tidbits.src" on cmns.think.com. Or, to search not only TidBITS but also the voluminous info-mac archives and comp.sys.mac.programmer digests, use "macintosh-news.src" instead. If your Mac is connected to the Internet and uses MacTCP, you can use Macintosh client software to access WAIS. The software may be FTP'd from think.com; look for WAISta-tion-0-63.sit.hqx. There are also WAIS clients available for a variety of other platforms such as DOS, Sun, and VMS. Check on think.com, or, if you're in Europe, check first on nic.funet.fi in the directory /pub/networking/service/wais. Alternately look for the comp.infosystems.wais Frequently Asked Questions list that specifies where each version may be located. If you don't have a Mac on the Internet but you do have access to an Internet-connected computer that offers telnet services, you can use the screen-based WAIS (swais) service along with a VT100 emulator. Just telnet to quake.think.com and enter the username wais (all lowercase) at the login: prompt. This swais service isn't pretty but works for those of us who don't have real Internet connections for our Macs. Either way, use the source document "macintosh-tidbits.src" located on cmns.think.com, and specify one or more keywords that will enable the WAIS server to find the information buried in TidBITS that you want to see. If you're interested in more details about WAIS, browse through the files available in the /wais directory on think.com via FTP, or skim the articles in the comp.infosystems.wais newsgroup.

Information from: Ephraim Vishniac -- ephraim@think.com comp.infosystems.wais FAQ.

Additional information: TidBITS is supported by corporate sponsorships not unlike those used by Public Broadcasting. We mention the sponsor at the beginning of each sponsored issue and also make files from the sponsor available on our fileserver for the duration of the sponsorship period. Recent sponsors have included Salient Software, Nisus Software, and Dantz Development. Contact ace@tidbits.com for more information.

TITNEWS

Description: TITNEWS is an electronic newsletter of The Internetaional Tit Society (TITS) and contains announcements and discussions of activities such as bibliographic systems, exchanges concerning techniques (e.g., software, databases), etc., and discussions of various related activities on tits (Paridae) and other hole-nesting birds whose lifestyles involve biological problems similar to those of tits, titmice, and chickadees. See related entries, TITNOTES and the TITNET discussion list.

Subjects covered: birds; chickadees; titmice; Paridae
Net address for operations: JHailman@MACC.Wisc.edu
Net address for questions or submissions:
JHailman@MACC.Wisc.edu
Frequency: Irregular.
Established: December 1990
Number of issues published to date: 2
Method of issuance: Issues are made available through email transmission to distribution list.
Available in other media: Millicent (Penny) Sigler Ficken edits the TITS hardcopy newsletter, PARUS INTERNATIONAL, which is sent out about twice per year in mid-summer and mid-winter. Contributions to PARUS INTERNATIONAL may be sent directly to her: Dr. M. S. Ficken, Cedar-Sauk Area Field Station, 3095 Blue Goose Road, Saukville, WI 53080.
Recent issue published: TITNEWS 2
Subscribers: 51
Journal refereed: No.
Editorial contact: Jack P. Hailman
Departrnent of Zoology, 430 Lincoln Drive, Birge Hall, University of Wisconsin, Madison, WI 53706.
Tel: (608) 262-2636
Internet: JHailman@MACC.Wisc.edu Bitnet
Bitnet: JHailman@WiscMACC.bitnet
Copyright statement: Titnet does not copyright its transmissions, but research abstracts appearing belong by U.S. copyright law to the creating authors.
How to access: Send an email message of inquiry to JHailman@MACC.Wisc.edu
How to unsubscribe: Send an email message of inquiry to JHailman@MACC.Wisc.edu
How to submit: Send an email message of inquiry to JHailman@MACC.Wisc.edu
Archives: Archives are available upon individual request.

TITNOTES

Description: TITNOTES is the electronic journal of The Internetaional Tit Society (TITS) and carries research material (including requests for information) on the biology of tits, titmice, chickadees and other cavity-nesting birds. See also related newsletter, TITNEWS, and discussion list TITNET.
Subjects covered: birds; chickadees; titmice; Paridae
Net address for operations: JHailman@MACC.Wisc.edu

Net address for questions or submissions:
JHailman@MACC.Wisc.edu
Frequency: Irregular
Established: December 1990
Number of issues published to date: 4
Method of issuance: Issues are made available through email transmission to distribution list.
Available in other media: Millicent (Penny) Sigler Ficken edits the TITS hardcopy newsletter, PARUS INTERNATIONAL, which is sent out about twice per year in mid-summer and mid-winter. Contributions to PARUS INTERNATIONAL may be sent directly to her: Dr. M. S. Ficken Cedar-Sauk Area Field Station, 3095 Blue Goose Road, Saukville, WI 53080.
Recent issue published: TITNOTES 4
Subscribers: 51
Journal refereed: No
Editorial contact: Jack P. Hailman
Department of Zoology 430 Lincoln Drive, Birge Hall, University of Wisconsin, Madison, WI 53706.
Tel: (608) 262-2636
Internet: JHailman@MACC.Wisc.edu Bitnet
Bitnet: JHailman@WiscMACC.bitnet
Sample contents: Research abstracts.
Copyright statement: Titnet does not copyright its transmissions, but research abstracts appearing in TITNOTES belong by U.S. copyright law to the creating authors.
How to access: Send an email message of inquiry to JHailman@MACC.Wisc.edu
How to unsubscribe: Send an email message of inquiry to JHailman@MACC.Wisc.edu
How to submit: Send an email message of inquiry to JHailman@MACC.Wisc.edu
Archives: Archives are available upon individual request.
Additional information: Titnet is the electronic-mail organ of The International Tit Society (TITS). TITS is an informal, world-wide society formed to promote communication among scientists working on tits (Paridae) and other hole-nesting birds whose lifestyle involves biological problems similar to those of tits, titmice, and chickadees. TITS has no dues, no constitution, no elections and no officers. All work is voluntary on the part of those who have the time and motivation to help.

TREK-REVIEW-L

Description: TREK-REVIEW-L covers a variety of information related to the Star Trek television series and associated movies.
Subjects covered: Star Trek; science fiction; television
Frequency: Irregular
Established: 1993
Method of issuance: Issues are emailed to subscribers as published.
Journal refereed: No
Editorial contact: Michael Shappe
Internet: mss1@cornell.edu
How to access: Send the message SUBSCRIBE TREK-REVIEW-L TO LISTSERV@CORNELL.EDU

TUNISIAN SCIENTIFIC SOCIETY NEWSLETTER

Description: The Tunisian Scientific Society Newsletter offers information on technology transfer in Tunisia.
Subjects covered: technology transfer; science and technology; Tunisia

Frequency: Quarterly
Method of issuance: Issues are emailed to subscribers as published
Journal refereed: No
Editorial contact: Bilel N. Jamoussi
Internet: bnj@ecl.psu.edu
Bitnet: jomaa@utkvx.bitnet
How to access: Send an email message to tssnews@athena.mit.edu

TWENTYNOTHING
Description: Twentynothing is a quarterly electronic magazine of opinions, perspective, and humor. As the name suggests, Twentynothing is written by young and rising writers, all in their twenties, but the articles themselves have a universal appeal. The current fall edition of Twentynothing contains pieces ranging from the effects of capitalism in Spain to a Southerner's view on the death penalty to Generation X's position in the job market, in the dating scence, and in history.
Subjects covered: alternative literature; current events
Frequency: Quarterly
Established: August 1993
Recent issue published: Fall
How to access: Twentynothing currently runs under MS DOS, with future versions planned for Unix, Macintosh, and Amiga computers. You can get your free copy via anonymouse ftp at ftp.uu.net in /published/twentysomething/93fall.exe and at brownvm.brown.edu in andrel.931/magf93.exe

UKUUG NEWSLETTER
ISSN: 0965-9412
Description: The UKUUG Newsletter is sponsored by teh UK Unix User Group.
Subjects covered: Unix; computer hardware and software
Frequency: Bimonthly
Established: 1992
Method of issuance: Issues are mailed via FTP to subscribers as published.
Journal refereed: No
Internet: sue@dcs.bbk.ac.uk
How to access: Send email to ukuug@uknet.ac.uk

ULAM QUARTERLY
Description: The Ulam Quarterly is devoted to studies of the philosopher Stanislaw Ulam.
Subjects covered: philosophy; computer science
Frequency: Quarterly
Host: Ulam Center
Palm Beach Atlantic College
University of Florida
Journal refereed: Yes
Internet: blass@goliath.pbac.edu
How to access: FTP to math.ufl.edu directory:/pub/ulam/

UNDISCOVERED COUNTRY
Description: The Undiscovered Country contains general literary material, poems, "death metal" album reviews, and industrial music commentary.
Subjects. covered: language and literature; music; poetry
Net address for operations: cblanc@pomona.claremont.edu

Net address for questions or submissions: cblanc@pomona.claremont.edu
Frequency: Irregular; usually monthly
Established: November 1992
Number of issues published to date: 4
Method of issuance: Issues are emailed to subscribers when published. Issue availability is announed on the following newsgroups: alt.cyberpunk, alt.thrash, alt.prose
Available in other media: No
Recent issue published: Number 4
Subscribers: 176
Host: pomona.claremont.edu
Commercial organization: No
Journal refereed: No
Editorial contact: S.R. Prozak / L.B. Noire
m-b 274/230, E. Bonita, Claremont, CA 91711
Tel: (909) 398-4558
Internet: cblanc@pomona.claremont.edu; rm09216@nyssa.swt.edu
Bitnet: cblanc@pomona; rm09216@swtnyssa
Technical contact: S.R. Prozak / L.B. Noire
m-b 274/230, E. Bonita, Claremont, CA 91711
Tel: (909) 398-4558
Internet: cblanc@pomona.claremont.edu; rm09216@nyssa.swt.edu
Bitnet: cblanc@pomona; rm09216@swtnyssa
Sample contents: Stoner adventures, a serial; poetry; album reviews; letters from the editor
Copyright statement: (c) copyright 1993 sdi, inc. s.r. prozak & l.b. noire. This file can be reproduced and passed on as long as original author, publication and publisher attributions remain.
How to access: Email cblanc@pomona.claremont.edu with message to subscribe
How to unsubscribe: Email cblanc@pomona.claremont.edu with message to unsubscribe
How to submit: Email cblanc@pomona.claremont.edu with questions
Archives: Archives are available through anonymous ftp: pomona.claremont.edu -- cd po__1995:[cblanc.tuc] ftp.eff.org -- with other publications cs.uwp.edu -- with music journals red.css.itd.umich.edu -- with other 'zines all else email cblanc@pomona.claremont.edu, rm09216@nyssa.swt.edu, or request on alt.thrash.
Gopher accessibility: Through ftp.eff.org

UNIT CIRCLE MAGAZINE
Description: Unit Circle Magazine is an electronic quarterly featuring art, poetry, prose, music, and politics.
Subjects covered: popular culture; music; poetry; fiction
Editorial contact: Kevin Goldsmith
Unit Circle, P.O. Box 640 885, San Francisco, CA 94164.
Internet: kmg@sgi.com
How to access: Gopher accessible at: etext.archive.umich.edu

UNPLASTIC NEWS
Description: Unplastic News offers humor and oddities.
Subjects covered: popular culture; alternative literature
Frequency: Bimonthly
Method of issuance: Issues are emailed to subscribers as published.
Journal refereed: No
Editorial contact: Todd Tibbetts

Internet: tibbetts@hsi.com
How to access: Send an email message to tibbetts@hsi.com
Gopher accessibility: Gopher accessible at: gopher.well.sf.ca.us

UPDATE-ELECTRONIC-MUSIC-NEWS

Description: Update-Electronic-Music-News, or UPNEWS@MARIST is an electronic newsletter covering independent and underground new music.
Subjects covered: music
Net address for questions or submissions: UPNEWS@MARIST
Editorial contact: Christopher DeRobertis
Bitnet: uicd@marist
How to access: Send subscribe message to listserv@marist or listserv@vm.marist.edu
How to unsubscribe: Send unsubscribe message to listserv@marist or listserv@vm.marist.edu
Archives: Archives are developed monthly; apply to listowner for details.

VND (VREME NEWS DIGEST)

Description: VREME NEWS DIGEST is an electronic edition of the Yugoslavian news weekly, VREME.
Subjects covered: Yugoslavia (former); current events; political science
How to access: Send request to DMITRIJE@BUENGA.BU.EDU
How to unsubscribe: Send request to DMITRIJE@BUENGA.BU.EDU

VOICES FROM THE NET

Description: Voices from the Net attempts to sample and explore the different types of ''voices'' produced by different activities on the Internet.
Subjects covered: Internet; alternative literature
How to access: Send an email message to: Voices-request@andy.bgsu.edu and in the Subject line type Voices from the Net and in the body type subscribe

WAC NEWS Q THE WORLD ARCHAEOLOGICAL CONGRESS NEWSLETTER

Description: WAC NEWS covers archaeological topics.
Subjects covered: archaeology
Frequency: No set format
Host: World Archaeological Congress
Journal refereed: No
Editorial contact: Brian L. Molyneaux
Internet: moly@charlie.usd.edu
How to access: Send an email message to moly@charlie.usd.edu
Related files: FTP to sunfish.us.edu
The directory is: /pub/WAC/

WE MAGAZINE

Description: We Magazine is an electronic publication of alternative literature.
Subjects covered: alternative literature

Editorial contact: Stephen Cope
We Press, P. O. Box 1503, Santa Cruz, CA 95061.
How to access: Gopher accessible at: etext.archive.umich.edu

WHOLE EARTH REVIEW

Description: Whole Earth Review is ''dedicated to demystification, to self-teaching, and to encouraging people to think for themselves. Thus our motto: 'ACCESS TO TOOLS AND IDEAS.' Tools in the Whole Earth sense include hammers, books, and computer conferencing systems. Our readers are a community of tool-users who share information with one another. The ideas we make accessible have not often been found in university courses, but are becoming recognized as part of what you need to know to be truly educated. Our readers contribute to the editorial content as well, with both reviews and articles.''
Subjects covered: alternative literature; popular culture
Whole Earth Review, 27 Gate Five Road, Sausalito, CA 94965.
Tel: (415) 332-1716
Fax: (415) 332-3110
How to access: Gopher accessible at: gopher.well.sf.ca.us

WIND ENERGY WEEKLY

ISSN: 0747-5500
Description: Wind Energy Weekly is an electronic report on the outlook for renewable energy, energy-related environmental issues, and renewable energy legislation. It also includes wind industry trade news. The electronic edition normally runs about 10kb in length.
Subjects covered: environmental studies; wind studies
Net address for operations: tgray@igc.apc.org (list owner and editor of Weekly)
Frequency: Weekly
Established: 1982 (print), 1992 (electronic edition)
Number of issues published to date: 545 (print), 40 (electronic)
Recent issue published: 12/543
Subscribers: 475 (electronic only)
Fee: Wind Energy Weekly is available in a hardcopy edition for $225/year (North America) or $255/year (rest of world) from the American Wind Energy Association, 777 North Capitol, NE, Suite 805, Washington, DC 20002, USA. The electronic edition contains excerpts from the hardcopy edition and is published with a three-week delay.
Editorial contact: Thomas O. Gray
PO Box 1008, Norwich, VT 05055
Tel: (802) 649-2112
Fax: (802) 649-2113
Internet: tgray@igc.apc.org
Bitnet: tgray@igc.apc.org
Sample contents: California reviews utility wind payments; Union of Concerned Scientists sees wind as lowest-cost renewable energy option for Midwestern U.S.; SeaWest Energy plans 80-MW windfarm in United Kingdom; etc.
Copyright statement: Wind Energy Weekly's electronic edition is not copyrighted. Permission to reproduce is granted freely provided credit is given to the American Wind Energy Association as the source.
How to access: Send a request to tgray@igc.apc.org stating your name, e-mail address, organization (if any), and reason for desiring a subscription.
How to unsubscribe: Send a request to tgray@igc.apc.org.

How to submit: Write to tgray@igc.apc.org.
Submission policy: Write to tgray@igc.apc.org.
Archives: Back issues (lagged by about three months) are available in the conference (BBS area) 'en.energy' on EcoNet. Write to support@igc.apc.org for EcoNet subscription info.
Gopher accessibility: Some excerpts available on EcoGopher.
Additional information: The Weekly is far and away the best and most regular source of information on renewable energy available in a mailing-list type format (i.e., mailed automatically to subscribers' mailboxes) at the present time.

WINDOWS ONLINE REVIEW

Description: Windows Online Review contains software programs for use on Windows-based PCs.
Subjects covered: Microsoft Windows; computer hardware and software
Journal refereed: No
How to access: FTP to ftp.cica.indiana.edu
The directory is: /pub/pc/win3/uploads/
File: WOLR69.ZIP

WORLD VIEW MAGAZINE

Description: World View offers news on international computing issues.
Subjects covered: computer science; computer hardware and software
Frequency: Bimonthly
Method of issuance: Issues are emailed to subscribers as published.
Journal refereed: No
Editorial contact: Scott A. Davis
Internet: dfox@fennec.com, dfox@wixer.cactus org
How to access: Send an email message to wv-sub@fennec.com

XENOCIDE

Description: Xenocide is an electronic magazine about music.
Subjects covered: music
Editorial contact: Jon Konrath
414 S. Mitchell, Suite 13, Bloomington, IN 47401.
Internet: jkonrath@indiana.edu
How to access: Gopher accessible at: etext.archive.umich.edu

Section 3. Electronic Texts, Text Archives, Selected FTP Sites, and Internet Resource Guides

1492: AN ONGOING VOYAGE: AN EXHIBIT AT THE LIBRARY OF CONGRESS

Location: Library of Congress, Washington, DC 20540-9100.
Description: 1492: AN ONGOING VOYAGE describes both pre- and post-contact America, as well as the Mediterranean world at the same time. Compelling questions are raised, such as: Who lived in the Americas before 1492? Who followed in the wake of Columbus? What was the effect of 1492 for Americans throughout the Western Hemisphere? The Library of Congress's Quincentenary exhibition addresses these questions as well as other related themes, including fifteenth century European navigation, the myths and facts surrounding the figure of Columbus, and the differences and similarities between European and American world views at the time of contact. The exhibit is divided into six (6) sections: What Came To Be Called "America," The Mediterranean World, Christopher Columbus: Man and Myth, Inventing America, Europe Claims America, and Epilogue. The original exhibit included over 300 objects: manuscripts, books, maps, and artifacts such as globes, jewelry, and musical instruments. The online exhibit includes images of 22 objects from the original exhibit, representing each of the 6 sections. Each section consists of its own sub-directory within the /exhibit directory and contains the exhibit text for that section, a single image file with "thumbnail'-size copies of the images in that section, and separate image files for each object. The exhibit will be of interest to historians, students of the Age of Discovery, students of Latin-American and American issues, students of Native American issues, and to librarians and information professionals. Please get the README file (in the /pub/ 1492.exhibit directory) for details on what files this exhibit contains. If you have questions about how to use FTP, speak to your local computer support person. If you have questions or comments about the exhibit, please contact Special Project Officer, K.D. Ellis.
Subjects covered: Renaissance studies; Columbus, Christopher; Native Americans; America
Editorial contact: K.D. Ellis
Special Projects Office, Library of Congress, Washington, DC 20540-9100.
Tel: Internet: kell@seq1.loc.gov
Internet: kell@seq1.loc.gov
How to access: FTP to seq1.loc.gov (140.147.3.12). Log in as anonymous and give your email address as a password. Then issue a cd command to change directory to the /pub directory. From there select 1492.exhibit

ALMANAC ELECTRONIC TEXTS CATALOG

Location: Oregon State University, Extension Service
Description: The Almanac Electronic Texts Catalog at Oregon State University Extension Service includes dozens of popular titles in ascii format, including many from Project Gutenberg, available as email files or through ftp.
Subjects covered: electronic texts; language and literature
List of texts available: List of Almanac Etexts
Topic:doyle
Title:The Complete Sherlock Holmes Mysteries

File:koran
Title:The Holy Koran

Topic:mansfield
Title:The Works of Katherine Mansfield
Abstract:These texts are the works of Katherine Mansfield. All works are in plain text format.

File:moby.tar
Title:Moby Dick
Author:Herman Melville

Topic:shakespeare
Title:The Unabridged Works of Shakespeare
Abstract:These texts are The Unabridged Shakespeare, provided courtesy of Moby Lexical Tools. All works are in plain text format.

Topic:yeats
Title:The Works of William Butler Yeats
Abstract:These texts are the works of William Butler Yeats. All works are in plain text format.

File:aesop
Title:Aesop's Fables
Author:Aesop (tr. by George Fyler Townsend)
Version:1.0

File:aesopa
Title:Aesop's Fables
Author:Aesop
Version:1.0

File:alice
Title:Alice's Adventures in Wonderland
Author:Lewis Carroll
Version:2.9

File:bible
Title:The Holy Bible
Version:1.0

File:break
Title:Hymn Of Breaking Strain
Author:Rudyard Kipling

File:civil
Title:Civil Disobedience
Author:Henry David Thoreau

File:crisis
Title:'Producing the Proper Crisis'' speech
Author:Philip Agee

File:crowd
Title:Far From the Madding Crowd
Author:Thomas Hardy
Version:1.3

File:declar
Title:United States Declaration of Independence

File:desert
Title:Address to the Nation, Jan 16, 1991
Author:George Bush

File:dict
Title:Dictionary

File:douglass
Title:The Narrative of the Life of Frederick Douglass, An American Slave
Author:Frederick Douglass
Version:1.0

File:dream
Title:'I Have a Dream'' speech
Author:Martin Luther King, Jr.

File:feder
Title:The Federalist Papers
Version:1.2

File:flatland
Title:Flatland
Author:Edwin A. Abbott

File:fox-in-socks
Title:Fox in Socks
Author:Dr. Seuss

File:green-eggs
Title:Green Eggs and Ham
Author:Dr. Suess

File:grimm
Title:Grimm's Fairy Tales
Author:The Brothers Grimm

File:heart
Title:Heart of Darkness
Author:Joseph Conrad

File:hisong
Title:The Song of Hiawatha
Author:Henry W. Longfellow
Version:1.2

File:jargon
Title:The Jargon File
Version:296

File:kama-sutra
Title:The Love Teachings of Kama Sutra
Author:Vatasyayana (tr. by Indra Sinha)

File:lglass
Title:Through the Looking Glass
Author:Lewis Carroll
Version:1.6

File:magna
Title:The Magna Carta

File:mandrew
Title:M'Andrew's Hymn
Author:Rudyard Kipling

File:martha
Title:The Sons of Martha
Author:Rudyard Kipling

File:mormon
Title:The Book of Mormon
Version:1.3

File:oedipus
Title:The Oedipus Trilogy
Author:Sophocles
Version:1.0

File:opion
Title:O Pioneers!
Author:Willa Cather
Version:1.1

File:paradise-lost
Title:Paradise Lost
Author:John Milton

File:peru-const
Title:Peru Constitution

File:peter
Title:Peter Pan
Author:James M. Barrie
Version:1.4a

File:pilgrim
Title:A Pilgrim's Way
Author:Rudyard Kipling

File:plboss
Title:Paradise Lost
Author:John Milton
Version:1.1 (transcribed by Judy Boss)

File:plrabn
Title:Paradise Lost
Author:John Milton
Version:1.1 (transcribed by Joseph Raben)

File:pride
Title:Pride and Prejudice
Author:Jane Austen

File:problem
Title:LSD: My Problem Child
Author:Albert Hofmann

File:rights
Title:United States Bill of Rights

File:roget
Title:Roget's Thesaurus (1911)
Version:1.3

File:snark
Title:The Hunting of the Snark

Author:Lewis Carroll

File:starwars
Title:Star Wars IV: A New Hope
Author:George Lucas

File:taiwan-const
Title:Taiwan Constitution

File:terance
Title:Terance, This Is Stupid Stuff
Author:A. E. Houseman

File:thinketh
Title:As A Man Thinketh
Author:James Allen

File:treason
Title:No Treason: The Constitution of No Authority
Author:Lysander Spooner

File:trek-anim
Title:Star Trek Episode Guide (animated series)
Author:Saul Jaffe

File:trek-orig
Title:Star Trek Episode Guide (original series)
Author:Saul Jaffe

File:trek-tng
Title:Star Trek: The Next Generation Episode Guide
Author:Saul Jaffe

File:us-const
Title:United States Constitution

File:uscen90
Title:United States Census, 1990
Version:1.1

File:world90
Title:The World Fact Book (1990)
Author:Central Intelligence Agency
Version:1.2

File:world91a
Title:The World Fact Book (1990)
Author:Central Intelligence Agency

File:wuther
Title:Wuthering Heights
Author:Emily Bronte

File:xmas
Title:The Night Before Christmas
Author:Clement Clarke Moore
How to access: To retrieve these documents, send the following request to almanac@OES.ORST.EDU: send etext <topic> <file> where <topic> is the optional sub-topic and <file> is the file name. If you wish to ftp these documents, they are available on OES.ORST.EDU in /pub/data/etext'. Since Almanac can format documents dynamically, you may not find the desired format in /pub/data/etext. If it is requestable through Almanac (i.e., it is listed here) and you would like to retrieve it via ftp, put the following line before other requests in your e-mail to almanac: mode spool This will format all requested documents and spool them in '/pub/spool'. For more information about the Almanac information server, send the message: send guide

ANONYMOUS FTP LIST
Description: The Anonymous FTP List, compiled and updated by Tom Czarnik and Jon Granrose, contains a comprehensive listing of those Internet resource sites that accept anonymous ftp sessions.
Subjects covered: Internet; resource guides
How to access: ftp to pit-manager.mit.edu and change to the directory called /pub/usenet/news.answers/ftp-list. The filenames are sites1.Z, sites2.Z, and sites3.Z.

ARTFL (AMERICAN AND FRENCH RESEARCH ON THE TREASURY OF THE FRENCH LANGUAGE)
Location: University of Chicago Department of Romance Languages and Literatures
Description: The ARTFL Project: In 1957 the French Government initiated the creation of a new dictionary of the French Language, the Tresor de la Langue Francaise. In order to provide access to a large body of word samples, it was decided to transcribe an extensive selection of French texts for use with a computer. Twenty years later, a corpus totaling some 150 million words had been created, representing a broad range of written French -- from novels and poetry to biology and mathematics -- stretching from the seventeenth to the twentieth centuries. It soon became apparent that this corpus of French texts was an important resource not only for lexicographers, but also for many other types of humanists and social scientists engaged in French studies - on both sides of the Atlantic. The result of this realization was American and French Research on the Treasury of the French Language (ARTFL) -- a cooperative project established in 1981 by the Centre National de la Recherche Scientifique and the University of Chicago. Its objectives over the last eight years have been to restructure this database in such a way as to make it accessible to the research community, and to develop tools for its analysis. At present the corpus consists of nearly 2000 texts, ranging from classic works of French literature to various kinds of non-fiction prose and technical writing. The eighteenth, nineteenth and twentieth centuries are about equally represented, with a smaller selection of seventeenth-century texts as well as some medieval and Renaissance texts. Genres include novels, verse, journalism, essays, correspondence, and treatises. Subjects include literary criticism, biology, history, economics, and philosophy. In most cases standard scholarly editions were used in converting the text into machine-readable form, and the data include page references to these editions.
Subjects covered: French language and literature
Net address for operations: artfl@artfl.uchicago.edu
Fee: Our current rates are $500 per year for PhD granting institutions and $250 per year for non-PhD granting institutions. Subscribing institutions are allowed to have an unlimited number of accounts and unlimited usage for all faculty, staff, students, and researchers attached to the organization. ARTFL does not charge for connect time or result reports. The only potential additional charge to the annual subscription is a 15 cent per page printing charge, if users wish to print at the University of Chicago and have results delivered by surface mail. However, results of searches performed on ARTFL can be delivered for no charge by electronic mail or file transfer programs.
Sponsor: University of Chicago Department of Romance Languages and Literatures, 1050 East 59th Street, Chicago, IL.
Host: University of Chicago Department of Romance Languages and Literatures, 1050 East 59th Street, Chicago, IL.

List of texts available: Over 2000 titles are available. Contact program coordinator for full list. American and French Research on the Treasury of the French Language, University of Chicago Department of Romance Languages and Literatures, 1050 East 59th Street, Chicago, IL 60637.
Tel: (312) 702-8488
Internet: artfl@artfl.uchicago.edu
Technical contact: Mark Olsen
Tel: (312) 702-8488, during office hours
Internet: mark@gide.uchicago.edu
Related files: Also included is the User's Guide to PhiloLogic 2.0, a guide describing the software program used to access the ARTFL database on CD-ROM and by network.

BIG DUMMY'S GUIDE TO THE INTERNET

Description: The Big Dummy's Guide to the Internet is a user guide for novices on all the Internet has to offer. The genesis of the Big Dummy's Guide was a few informal conversations, which included Mitch Kapor of the Electronic Frontier Foundation (EFF) and Steve Cisler of Apple Computers, in June of 1991. With the support of Apple Computers, EFF hired a writer (Adam Gaffin) and actually took on the project in September of 1991. The idea was to write a guide to the Internet for folks who had little or no experience with network communications. The Guide is currently posted to "the 'net" in ASCII and Hypercard (Mac) formats.
Subjects covered: Internet; resource guides
How to access: The Big Dummy's Guide to the Internet can be downloaded by anonymous ftp from ftp.eff.org. The ASCII version is located at /pub/EFF/papers/big-dummys-guide.txt. The Hypercard stack is located at /pub/EFF/papers/big-dummys-guide.sit.hqx

BITNET SERVERS

Description: The Bitnet Servers list, compiled by Christopher Condon, carries updated information on network servers and services.
Subjects covered: Internet; resource guides
How to access: ftp to ftp.syr.edu and change to the directory called /networks/doc. The filename is bitnets.txt. Or you can email to listserv@bitnic.educom.edu and in the body of the message type get bitnet servers.

BITNET/INTERNET HEALTH SCIENCE RESOURCES

Location: SuraNet
Description: This Etext program covers all Internet resources, including listserv lists, databases, newsgroups, ejournals, libraries, agencies, bbs's, gophers, etc.
Subjects covered: Internet; library and information science
Net address for operations: ftp.sura.net
Net address for questions or submissions: Le07144@ukanvm or Le07144@ukanvm.cc.ukans.edu
Established: 1991
Number of texts published to date: 1
Method of text retrieval: Texts are retrieved via ftp.
Total number of texts distributed: 1000 +
Host: University of Kansas, Archie R. Dykes Library.
Selection of texts: Text selection is updated 4-5 times per year.
Texts marked or tagged: No.
Editorial contact: Lee Hancock

3580 Rainbow Blvd., #826, Kansas City, KS 66160-7181.
Tel: (913) 262-2003
Fax: (913) 262-2003
Internet: Le07144@ukanvm.cc.ukans.edu
Bitnet: Le07144@ukanvm
Technical contact: Lee Hancock
The University of Kansas Medical Center, Archie R. Dykes Library, 3901 Rainbow Blvd., Kansas City, KS 66160-7181.
Tel: (913) 588-7144
Fax: (913) 588-7304
Internet: Le07144@ukanvm.cc.ukans.edu
Bitnet: Le07144@ukanvm
Copyright statement: (c) Lee Hancock 1993. This document is copyrighted for non-commercial distribution only. Please retain full credit on any distribution copies.
How to access: ftp from ftp.sura.net. The document medical.resources.xxx is found in the directory /pub/nic, where xxx is the date of the current file.
Access policy: Open to the public
How to submit: Email to Info@sura.net or Le07144@ukanvm
Gopher accessibility: Files available through CAMIS and InterNIC gophers.

BUBL, THE BULLETIN BOARD FOR LIBRARIES

Description: BUBL, The Bulletin Board for Libraries, collects information of interest to network-using librarians and their users. A major aim is to provide librarians with information on services and resources on JANET and other networks (e.g., the European IXI network and the world-wide Internet). However, BUBL also covers items of general interest to librarians. Moreover, it is increasingly used by non-librarians, lecturers, students, and others - for the guidance it provides on finding and using networked resources and services. Most BUBL users are from the U.K. However, there are known users in several other countries, including Sweden, the Netherlands, Canada, Hong Kong, and the U.S.A. BUBL is run by the Universities of Strathclyde and Glasgow on behalf of JUGL, the JANET User Group for Libraries. It is partially supported by the Information Systems Committee of the Universities Funding Council and by private sponsorship, but is run on a mainly voluntary basis by the two universities. The user interface is provided by a software package called 'USERBUL'(copyright Leicester University and NISS). This allows information to be accessed through a series of menus and sub-menus. However, since the hierarchical structure is apparent rather than real, users need not 'climb' or 'descend' through menus in order to reach the files or menus they desire. It also allows users to search large files by keyword, to transfer information to their host machine via electronic mail using the POST command, to send a message to the editor, or to display various kinds of online help. Versions of this software are also used by the humanities bulletin board HUMBUL and by the NISS (National Information on Software and Services) bulletin board. Sections of particular interest are: B - electronic reference works of various kinds, including manuals, guides, descriptions of networked services.
Subjects covered: library and information science
Editorial contact: Dennis Nicholson
Strathclyde University Library, Glasgow, Scotland.
Tel: 041 552 3701, ext 4132/4118
Fax: 041 552 3304
Internet: cijs03@vaxa.strathclyde.ac.uk

How to access: BUBL can be accessed through the 'Bibliographic Services' sub-menu on the NISS gateway. Through Janet directly on a PAD terminal, you would typically type: call gla.bubl or call 00007110004011. To access BUBL from the internet: telnet sun.nsf.ac.uk or 128.86.8.7 login: janet (if asked for a password, press return) At the hostname: prompt type uk.ac.glasgow.bubl At the terminal type prompt enter vt100.
Additional information: You do not need a username/password to access BUBL; you may have to wait a few moments while the software is loaded; to POST files to yourself on the Internet use the instructions in BUBL section A9 - i.e. read these before you use post.

BYRD.MU.WVNET.EDU
Location: Marshall University
Description: BYRD.MU.WVNET.EDU is an ftp site containing a large number of files on world history. For a comprehensive listing of all current files on the FTP site, send a request through email or retrieve the file INDEX from the pub/history subdirectory to Mike McCarthy, History Dept., Marshall University, MMCCARTH@MUVMS6.WVNET.EDU
Subjects covered: history; ftp sites; world history; political science
Net address for operations: BYRD.MU.WVNET.EDU (129.71.32.152)
Method of text retrieval: Anonymous ftp
Editorial contact: Mike McCarthy
Marshall University
Internet: YEA003@Marshall.WVNET.Edu

CANADIAN INTERNET-ACCESSIBLE LIBRARIES
Description: The Candian Internet-Accessible Libraries list contains information on Canadian library public access catalogs available over the Internet.
Subjects covered: Internet; resource guides; online public access catalogs; library and information science
How to access: ftp to csuvax1.csu.murdoch.edu.au and change to the directory named /pub/library. The filename is canadian.libraries.list.

CENTER FOR ELECTRONIC RECORDS
Description: The Center for Electronic Records of the U.S. National Archives and Records Administration has established an FTPable directory. The FTP directory can be accessed by FTPing to FTP.CU.NIH.GOV (128.231.64.7). Log on as an anonymous user; press enter at password prompt. The directory in which this information is stored is CNTR__ELEC__RECS (CD CNTR__ELEC__RECS). Use the FTP GET command to retrieve copies of interested materials. In this directory are four files: a READ.ME file describing the contents of the files in the directory; the partial and preliminary public Title List (TITLE.LIST.APR1693), created by the staff of the Center as a guide to some of the records in the custody of the Center; a file containing a brief description of the Center (CENTER, excerpted from National Archives General Information Leaflet #37, ''Information About Electronic Records in the National Archives for Prospective Researchers'') and a description of the fee based reference services provided by the Center (SERVICES). Please note that the Title List file has a line length of 132 characters and currently has 8,101 lines.

Net address for questions or submissions: tif@cu.nih.gov or TIF@NIHCU
Host: Center for Electronic Records (NSX), ATTN: Reference Staff, National Archives, Washington, DC 20408.
Editorial contact: Theodore J. Hull, Archives Specialist, Archival Services Branch
Center for Electronic Records (NSX), ATTN: Reference Staff, National Archives, Washington, DC 20408.
Tel: (202) 501-5579
Internet: tif@cu.nih.gov
Bitnet: TIF@NIHCU.

CENTER FOR TEXT AND TECHNOLOGY
Location: Georgetown University
Description: The Center for Text and Technology contains an archive of electronic texts and e-text projects.
Subjects covered: electronic texts; fulltext
How to access: Ftp to guvax.georgetown.edu. Change directory to CPET__PROJECTS__IN__ELECTRONIC__TEXT then change directory to DIGESTS__DISCIPLINES. Relevant files are contained there. Contact wilder@guvax.bitnet or wilder@guvax.georgetown.edu for the latest information.

CETH (CENTER FOR ELECTRONIC TEXTS IN THE HUMANITIES)
Description: The Center for Electronic Texts in the Humanities is devoted to studying the bibliographic control of electronic texts, education and information in the area of humanities computing, and the development of an online text collection and search and retrieval software.
Subjects covered: humanities; electronic texts
Net address for operations: listserv@pucc, listserv@pucc.princeton.edu
Established: 1992
Sponsor: Center for Electronic Texts in the Humanities, Rutgers and Princeton Universities, 169 College Avenue, New Brunswick, NJ 08903.
Host: Princeton University, Computing and Information Technology, 87 Prospect Avenue, Princeton, NJ 08544.
Editorial contact: Christine Bohlen
Center for Electronic Texts in the Humanities, 169 College Avenue, New Brunswick, NJ 08903
Tel: (908) 932-1384
Fax: (908) 932-1386
Internet: ceth@zodiac.rutgers.edu
Bitnet: ceth@zodiac
Archives: Contents are archived at the listserv address according to regular LISTSERV software practices.
Related files: CETH has a discussion list for all those interested in learning of its activities. To subscribe send the message subscribe ceth firstname lastname to listserv@pucc or listserv@pucc.princeton.edu
Additional information: CETH has established an open electronic discussion list on electronic text centers, ETEXTCTR@RUTVM1 (see entry elsewhere). More information is available at hoogcarspel@zodiac or hoogcarspel@zodiac.rutgers.edu. CETH maintains an inventory of electronic texts on RLIN (Research Libraries Information Network), the Rutgers Inventory of Machine-Readable Texts in the Humanities. Information about its contents at hoogcarspel@zodiac.rutgers.edu (CETH); information about ac-

cess at bl.ric@rlg or bl.ric@rlg.stanford.edu (RLIN Information Center).

COALITION FOR NETWORKED INFORMATION GOPHER

Description: The Coalition for Networked Information, a joint project of the Association of Research Libraries, CAUSE, and EDUCOM promotes the creation of and access to information resources in networked environments in order to enrich scholarship and to enhance intellectual productivity. Roughly 180 organizations and institutions are members of the Coalition Task Force. The Gopher server allows access to the Coalition's FTP archives, archives of Coalition electronic mail forums, Coalition Task Force and Working Group documentation, Coalition databases, and more is being made available through a Gopher interface.

Subjects covered: Coalition for Networked Information; resource guides; Internet
Editorial contact: Craig Summerhill
Systems Coordinator
Internet: craig@cni.org
How to access: Gopher to gopher.cni.org. Port 70.

COMPUTER LITERACY PROJECT

Description: The Computer Literacy Project is a research project into the development of a computer literacy curriculum for pre-service teacher education. A survey was issued in the Spring of 1993 addressing the computer literacy requirements of pre-service teachers. The results of this survey are gopher accessible.

Subjects covered: education; computer literacy
Editorial contact: George Duckett, School of Education at Launceston, The University of Tasmania, P.O. Box 1214 Launceston, Tasmania 7250, Australia.
Internet: gduckett@deakin.oz.au
How to access: Start your gopher and find: Other Archive, Information and Gopher Services; then find: Al Gopher Servers in the World; look for University of Tasmania. Then look for the following files: Departments/Education/Computer Literacy Project/Computer Literacy Survey. If the University of Tasmania is not on your gopher, use the address info.utas.edu.au Port 70. Dana College in Blair, Nebraska, is a mirror site for the Project: gopher.dana.edu. Also available through ftp: ftp to boombox.micro.umn.edu and look for /pub/gopher/00README. There you will find Gopher for IBM and Mac on file. TurboGopher for the Mac is recommended. Or, ftp to ftp.dana.edu and look in the educ/complit directory.

CWIS LIST

Description: The CWIS List, compiled and updated by Judy Hallman, contains the most comprehensive information on campus-wide information systems, freenets, and other Internet-accessible community information services.

Subjects covered: Internet; resource guides; campus-wide information systems; library and information science
How to access: ftp to sunsite.unc.edu and change to the directory called /pub/academic/library/libsoft. The filename is cwis.txt. This list is also available by ftp to infolib.murdoch.edu.au; directory is named /pub/dir/netinfo; filename is cwis.txt

DARTMOUTH DANTE PROJECT

Location: Dartmouth College
Description: The Dartmouth Dante Project is a database of information, including the text of and hundreds of critical commentaries on Dante's Divine Comedy.
Subjects covered: Dante; electronic texts; fulltext
How to access: Telnet to library.dartmouth.edu. Type connect Dante.

DARTMOUTH LIST OF LISTS

Description: The Dartmouth List of Lists, compiled by David Avery, is a list of listserv-operated and manually operated special interest mailing lists. When last updated, the list contained some 2,200 entries.
Subjects covered: Internet; resource guides; library and information science
How to access: ftp to dartcms1.dartmouth.edu and change to the directory named /siglists. The filename is listserv.lists.

DIRECTORY OF ELECTRONIC JOURNALS AND NEWSLETTERS

Description: The Directory of Electronic Journals and Newsletters, compiled by Michael Strangelove, is an authoritative guide to special interest electronic serials, providing descriptive details and subscription procedures.
Subjects covered: Internet; resource guides; electronic serials; library and information science
How to access: Send email to listserv@uottawa.bitnet or listserv@acadvm1.uottawa.ca with the message:
get ejournl1 directry
get ejournl2 directry

DIRECTORY OF SCHOLARLY ELECTRONIC CONFERENCES, 7TH REVISED EDITION.

Location: Kent State University.
Description: The Directory of Scholarly Electronic Conferences, 7th Revised Edition, contains descriptions of electronic conferences (e-conferences) on topics of interest to scholars. E-conference is the umbrella term that includes discussion lists, interest groups, e-journals, e-newsletters, Usenet newsgroups, forums, etc. We have used our own judgment in deciding what is of scholarly interest, and accept any advice or argument about our decisions.
Subjects covered: directories; Internet discussion lists; discussion lists; Bitnet
Net address for operations: Listserv@kentvm or Listserv@kentvm.kent.edu
Net address for questions or submissions: gbell@kentvm or gbell@kentvm.kent.edu
Established: 1993
Number of texts published to date: 1
Method of text retrieval: Retrieved via FTP.
Available in other media: The Directory is published in paperback by the Associate of Research Libraries, Washington, DC.
Sponsor: Kent State University Libraries, Kent, OH 44242.
Host: Kent State University Libraries, Kent, OH 44242.
Texts marked or tagged: Text is keyword indexed.

Editorial contact: Gladys Smiley Bell
Rm. 161, Library Building, Kent State University, Kent, Ohio
44242.
Tel: 216-672-3045
Fax: 216-672-2265
Internet: gbell@kentvm.kent.edu
Bitnet: gbell@kentvm
Copyright statement: Copyright 1993 by Diane K. Kovacs,
The Directory Team and Kent State University Libraries. Single
copies of this directory from its networked sources, or of spe-
cific entries from their networked sources, may be made for in-
ternal purposes, personal use, or study by an individual, library,
or an educational or research institution. The directory or its
contents may not be otherwise reproduced or republished in excerpt or entirety, in print or electronic form, without permission
from Diane K. Kovacs, Kent State University Libraries.
How to access: The 7th Revision of the Directory of Scholarly
Electronic Conferences is available on the LISTSERV@
KENTVM or LISTSERV@KENTVM.KENT.EDU and via
anonymous FTP to ksuvxa.kent.edu in the library directory. The
Files Available: ACADLIST README (explanatory notes for
the Directory); ACADSTAC.HQX (binhexed, self-decompressing, HYPERCARD Stack of first 7 files - Keyword
searchable); ACADCOMP.HQX (binhexed, self-decompressing,
HYPERCARD Stack of FILE8 and FILE9 - Keyword
searchable); ACADLIST FILE1 (Anthropology- Education) 53k;
ACADLIST FILE2 (Geography-Library and Information Science) 91k; ACADLIST FILE3 (Linguistics-Political Science)
49k; ACADLIST FILE4 (Psychology-Writing) 54k; ACADLIST
FILE5 (Biological Sciences) 43k; ACADLIST FILE6 (Physical
Sciences) 43k; ACADLIST FILE7 (Business, Academia, News)
22k; ACADLIST FILE8 (Computer Science, Social, Cultural
and Political Aspects of Computers and Academic Computing
Support) 104k; ACADWHOL HQX(binhexed self-decompressing Macintosh M.S. Word version of all 8 files);
ACADLIST.CHANGES (this is now empty due to difficulty of
keeping up with the changes this time.) To retrieve files from
LISTSERV@KENTVM: 1. Send an e-mail message addressed
to LISTSERV@KENTVM or
LISTSERV@KENTVM.KENT.EDU. 2. Leave the subject and
other info lines blank. 3. The message must read: GET Filename
Filetype (e.g.,filename = ACADLIST filetype = FILE1 or HQX
or whatever) 4. The files will be sent to you and you must
receive them. 5. If you need assistance receiving, etc., contact
your local Computer Services people. To retreive files via anonymous FTP to KSUVXA.KENT.EDU: 1. type: FTP
KSUVXA.KENT.EDU at your dollar sign prompt (VAX) or
ready screen (IBM). If you are on another kind of system consult with your computer services people to find out the proper
procedure. 2. when prompted for 'USERID,' type ANONY-
MOUS. 3. Your password will be your actual use
Gopher accessibility: Host = gopher.usask.ca; Port = 70;
Type = 1; Name = Directory of Scholarly Electronic Conferences; Path = 1/Computing/Internet Information/Directory of
Scholarly Electronic Conferences
Additional information: The Directory Team: Diane Kovacs-
Team Coordinator (Bitnet) dkovacs@kentvm (Internet)
dkovacs@kentvm.kent.edu; Gladys Bell (Bitnet) gbell@kentvm
(Internet) gbell@kentvm.kent.edu; Paul Fehrmann (Bitnet)
pfehrman@kentvm (Internet) pfehrman@kentvm.kent.edu; Mi-
chael Kovacs (Internet) mkovacs@mcs.kent.edu; Leslie Haas
(Bitnet) lhaas@kentvm (Internet) lhaas@kentvm.kent.edu; Gerald Holmes (Bitnet) gholmes@kentvm (Internet)
gholmes@kentvm.kent.edu; Jeannie Langendorfer (Bitnet)

jlangend@kentvm (Internet) jlangend@kentvm.kent.edu; Amey
Park (Bitnet) apark@kentvm (Internet) apark@kentvm.kent.edu;
Kara Robinson (Bitnet) krobinso@kentvm (Internet)
krobinso@kentvm.kent.edu

ECONOMIC BULLETIN BOARD
Location: Department of Commerce, Washington, DC
Description: The Economic Bulletin Board offers data from the
Departments of Commerce, Labor, and the Treasury, the Federal
Reserve Board, and other agencies. Over 2,000 individual files
are accessible through this service.
Subjects covered: economics; government information
Fee: Access will be chargeable; contact EBB for further infor-
mation.
Tel: (202) 482-1986
Internet: AWILLIAMS@ESA.DOC.GOV
How to access: Telnet to EBB.STATUSA.GOV. At the login
prompt, typeTRIAL.

ELECTRONIC DOCUMENT DISTRIBUTION PROJECT, DEPARTMENT OF INDUSTRY AND SCIENCE, GOVERNMENT OF CANADA
Description: The Electroic Document Distribution project
(EDD) currently makes nine telecommunications-related docu-
ments available in both official languages, English and French.
Subjects covered: science and technology; telecommunications
List of texts available: A Guide for the radiotelephone operator
1986, English 56p / French 58p; Decoding the Law on De-
coding 1991, English 13p / French 13p; Convergence, Competi-
tion and Cooperation 1992, English 287p / French 311p; Tele-
communications in Canada: An overview of the Carriage
Industry 1992, Eng 36p / French 38p; Telecommunications:
New Legislation for Canada 1992, Eng 25p / French 28p; New
Media New Choices 1992, English 43p / French 47p; Telecommunications Privacy Principles 1992, English 8p / French 8p; A
Spectrum Policy Framework for Canada 1992, English 29p /
French 30p; Digital Radio: the sound of the future (I downloaded this 1993, Eng 29p / French 31p.
How to access: All documents are available in ASCII format,
uncompressed via anonymous ftp from: debra.dgbt.doc.ca /pub/
isc/. For the most recent index of files, retrieve ''00readme.''
These files are also available via Listerserv for people with email access only. The address is: listserv@debra.dgbt.doc.ca. To
retrieve the most recent index of documents available send the
following command alone in the body of the message: get isc
00readme

ELECTRONIC GOVERNMENT INFORMATION SERVICE
Description: The Electronic Government Information Service is
a service providing electronic versions of US government re-
ports and other documents.
Subjects covered: government information
Established: September 1993
Host: Syracuse University
How to access: Gopher to ERYX.SYR.EDU or telnet to
HAFNHAF.MICRO.UMN.EDU and type gopher at the prompt.
Once in gopher, the documents are found by selecting Other

Gopher and Information Services/North America/USA/General/ EGIS.

ENVIROGOPHER

Description: EnviroGopher is a Gopher archive of texts relating to environmental issues.
Subjects covered: environmental studies
Net address for operations: admin@envirolink.org
Net address for questions or submissions: admin@envirolink.org
Established: April 1993
Number of texts published to date: Over 8,000 texts.
Method of issuance: Gopher archives. No.
Method of text retrieval: Texts can be retrieved through Gopher.
Total number of texts distributed: Thousands.
Sponsor: The EnviroLink Network, 4551 Forbes Ave., Third Floor, Pittsburgh, PA 15213.
Selection of texts: Texts available through Internet Gopher.
Texts marked or tagged: No.
Editorial contact: Josh Knauer
4551 Forbes Ave., Third Floor, Pittsburgh, PA 15213.
Tel: (412) 681-8300
Internet: josh@envirolink.org
How to access: Set gopher or telnet to: envirolink.org login id: gopher

ETHNOFORUM

Location: University of Maryland, College Park
Description: EthnoFORUM is an electronic text program covering documents in ethnomusicology and musical folklore.
Subjects covered: ethnomusicology; music ; cultural studies
Net address for operations: INFO.UMD.EDU
Net address for questions or submissions: SIGNELL@UMDD or SIGNELL@UMDD.UMD.EDU
Established: 1990
Number of texts published to date: 15-20
Method of issuance: Posting on INFO.UMD.EDU
No
Method of text retrieval: FTP or telnet to INFO.UMD.EDU, subdirectory /ReadingRoom/ NewsLetters/EthnoMusicology.
Sponsor: University of Maryland, College Park, MD 20742
Host: Same as above.
Selection of texts: Texts are chosen by the moderator of the discussion group ETHMUS-L.
List of texts available: A list of titles in the program is available by telneting to INFO.UMD.EDU, subdirectory /ReadingRoom/NewsLetters/EthnoMusicology
Editorial contact: Dr. Karl Signell
Center for Turkish Music, Music Department, University of Maryland, Baltimore County Baltimore, MD 21228
Tel: (410) 455-2489
Fax: (410) 455-1070
Internet: signell@umdd.umd.edu
Bitnet: signell@umdd
Related files: ETHMUS-L@UMDD or ETHMUS-L@UMDD.UMD.EDU >

FAQ: ARTIFICIAL INTELLIGENCE QUESTIONS & ANSWERS

Location: School of Computer Science, Carnegie Mellon University
Description: This series of large documents (56016 bytes) comprises a summary of answers to frequently asked questions about artificial intelligence (see Contents listing below). Certain questions and topics come up frequently in the various network discussion groups devoted to and related to Artificial Intelligence (AI). This file/article is an attempt to gather these questions and their answers into a convenient reference for AI researchers. It is posted on a monthly basis. The hope is that this will cut down on the user time and network bandwidth used to post, read and respond to the same questions over and over, as well as providing education by answering questions some readers may not even have thought to ask. If you think of questions that are appropriate for this FAQ, or would like to improve an answer, please send email to mkant + ai-faq@cs.cmu.edu.
Subjects covered: artificial intelligence
Net address for questions or submissions: mkant + ai-faq@cs.cmu.edu
Method of issuance: FTP or email on request
Host: School of Computer Science, Carnegie Mellon University
Editorial contact: Mark Kantrowitz
Internet: Mark.Kantrowitz@GLINDA.OZ.CS.CMU.EDU
Sample contents: Topics Covered:
Part 1:
[1-0]What is the purpose of this newsgroup? [1-1]AI-related Associations and Journals [1-2]How do I get a copy of the proceedings to conference <x>? [1-4]What are the rules for the game of "Life"? [1-5]What AI competitions exist? [1-8]Commercial AI products. [1-9]Glossary of AI terms. [1-10] What are the top schools in AI? [1-11] How can I get the email address for Joe or Jill Researcher? Part 2 (AI-related Newsgroups and Mailing Lists): List of all known AI-related newsgroups, mailing lists, and electronic bulletin board systems. Part 3 (Bibliography): Bibliography of introductory texts, overviews and references Addresses and phone numbers for major AI publishers. Part 4 (FTP Resources): [4-0]General Information about FTP Resources for AI [4-1]FTP Repositories [4-2]FTP and Other Resources. Part 5 (FTP Resources): [5-1]AI Bibliographies available by FTP [5-2]AI Technical Reports available by FTP [5-3]Where can I get a machine readable dictionary, thesaurus, and other text corpora? [5-4]List of Smalltalk implementations.
How to access: The latest version of this file is available via anonymous FTP from CMU: To obtain the file from CMU, connect by anonymous ftp to any CMU CS machine (e.g., ftp.cs.cmu.edu [128.2.206.173]), using username "anonymous" and password "name@host". The files ai-faq-1.text, ai-faq-2.text, ai-faq-3.text, and ai-faq-4.text are located in the directory /afs/cs.cmu.edu/user/mkant/Public/AI/ [Note: You must cd to this directory in one atomic operation, as some of the superior directories on the path are protected from access by anonymous ftp.] If your site runs the Andrew File System, you can just cp the file directly without bothering with FTP.
Archives: The FAQ postings are also archived in the periodic posting archive on rtfm.mit.edu [18.70.0.226]. Look in the anonymous ftp directory /pub/usenet/news.answers/ in the subdirectory ai-faq/. If you do not have anonymous ftp access, you can access the archive by mail server as well. Send an E-mail message to mail-server@rtfm.mit.edu with "help" and "index" in the body on separate lines for more information.

FEDIX: MINORITY ONLINE INFORMATION SERVICE

Description: FEDIX: MOLIS contains information about minorities in the U.S.
Subjects covered: government information; race relations; family studies
How to access: Telnet to fedix.fie.com. Login as molis

FTP.MCC.AC.UK

Location: Computing Centre, University of Manchester, Manchester M13 9PL.
Description: ftp.mcc.ac.uk is an ftp site containing software falling into three main categories: Unix, DOS, and graphics. 'Official' mirror sites for 386bsd (from agate.berkeley.edu), GNU (from prep.ai.mit.edu), Linux (from nic.funet.fi). Graphical software includes AVS and Nurbs.
Subjects covered: computer hardware and software; ftp sites
Net address for operations: ftp.mcc.ac.uk
Established: September 1988
Method of text retrieval: Anonymous ftp
Total number of texts distributed: 17,000
Sponsor: Computing Centre, University of Manchester, Manchester, M13 9PL
Host: Computing Centre, University of Manchester, Manchester, M13 9PL
Editorial contact: Dr. A. V. Le Blanc
Computing Centre, University of Manchester, Manchester, M13 9PL
Tel: +44 61 275 6035
Fax: +44 61 275 6040
Internet: LeBlanc@mcc.ac.uk
How to access: Anonymous ftp from ftp.mcc.ac.uk

FTP.WARWICK.AC.UK

Description: ftp.warwick.ac.uk is a mirror ftp site for prep (gnu software) and other PD software, and some technical local papers.
Subjects covered: computer hardware and software; ftp sites; technical reports
Net address for questions or submissions: csv.warwick.ac.uk
Established: June 1992
Editorial contact: Denis Martin Anthony
Computing Services, University of Warwick, Coventry, CV4 7AL, Great Britain
Tel: +44 203 523037
Fax: +44 203 523267
Internet: cudma@warwick.ac.uk
Copyright statement: Typical copyright statement on local documents is the gnu standard, which is: This file is a University of Warwick document. Copyright (C) 1993 University of Warwick. Permission is granted to make and distribute verbatim copies of this manual provided the copyright notice and this permission notice are preserved on all copies. Permission is granted to copy and distribute modified versions of this manual under the conditions for verbatim copying, provided also that the sections entitled "Distribution" and "General Public License" are included exactly as in the original, and provided that the entire resulting derived work is distributed under the terms of a permission notice identical to this one. Permission is granted to copy and distribute translations of this manual into another language, under the above conditions for modified versions, except that the sections entitled "Distribution" and "General Public License" may be included in a translation approved by the author instead of in the original English.
How to access: ftp to ftp.warwick.ac.uk
Gopher accessibility: gopher.warwick is being run on an experimental basis. It will be the basis of our local information server.

GNET -- TOWARD A TRULY GLOBAL NETWORK

Description: GNET is an Archive and Electronic Journal for documents pertaining to the effort to bring the net to lesser-developed nations and the poorer parts of developed nations. (Net access is better in many "third world" schools than in South-Central Los Angeles). GNET consists of two parts, an archive directory and a moderated discussion. The archive acts as an electronic text program offering papers dealing with networks and projects, host and user hardware and software connection options and protocols, current and proposed applications, education, using the global net, user and system administrator training, the social, political, or spiritual impact of the net, the economic and environmental impact of the net, politics and funding, free speech, security and privacy, and directories of people and resources. There is a readme file and an index file. The index file contains a record for each paper in the archive. The records contain the title of the paper, author, filename, file size, and acquisition date. Since many of our readers are in less-industrialized nations, with high communication cost, there are two files for each paper, an abstract and the body of the paper. That allows people to read the abstracts before copying the entire paper. The GNET list is limited to discussion of the documents in the archive. It is hoped that document authors will follow this discussion, and update their documents accordingly. If this happens, the archive will become a dynamic journal. Monthly mailings will list new papers added to the archive. We wish broad participation, with papers from nuts-and-bolts to visionary.
Subjects covered: distance education; education; computer hardware and software; Internet
Net address for operations: gnet_request@dhvx20.csudh.edu
Net address for questions or submissions: gnet_request@dhvx20.csudh.edu
Established: September 1992
Method of issuance: Monthly emailing of announcement of new titles and related information.
Method of text retrieval: Texts can be retrieved by ftp or ftp-by-mail.
Sponsor: California State University, Dominguez Hills, 1000 East Victoria Street, Carson, CA 90747.
Host: California State University, Dominguez Hills, 1000 East Victoria Street, Carson, CA 90747.
Texts marked or tagged: No.
Editorial contact: Laurence Press
10726 Esther Avenue Los Angeles, CA 90064
Tel: (310) 475-6515
Fax: (310) 516-3664
Internet: lpress@isi.edu
How to access: To submit a document to the archive or subscribe to the moderated discussion list, use the address gnet_request@dhvx20.csudh.edu.
Archives: Archived documents are available by anonymous ftp from the directory global_net at dhvx20.csudh.edu (155.135.1.1). To conserve bandwidth, the archive contains an abstract of each document, as well as the full document. (Those

without ftp access can contact me for instructions on mail-based retrieval).

Additional information: We wish broad participation, with papers from nut-and-bolts to visionary. Suitable topics include, but are not restricted to: descriptions of networks and projects host and user hardware and software connection options and protocols current and proposed applications education using the global net user and system administrator training social, political or spiritual impact economic and environmental impact politics and funding free speech, security and privacy directories of people and resources.

THE GREAT LAKES HAYLIST

Description: The Great Lakes Haylist is a computer database of hay for sale which is updated daily. The following reports may be requested via e-mail: hay for sale by type and by telephone area code; average price per ton by forage quality and area code; and count of hay-listings by telephone area code. Sellers are located by telephone area codes and type of hay for sale. The database contains only offers to sell hay. Sellers, or their county Extension offices may e-mail, fax or surface mail an official listing form to a central address given on the form. Wisconsin and Minnesota staff enter data from the form and maintain the Great Lakes Haylist software. All listings expire after 21 days. The Haylist uses Almanac software (a de facto Extension standard) to serve e-mail requests. The reports can be viewed interactively using Gopher software as well.

Subjects covered: agriculture

Great Lakes Haylist, 302 Hiram Smith Hall, 1545 Observatory Drive, Madison, WI 53706-1289.

Fax: 608.265.2530

How to access: To request a report from the Great Lakes Haylist, follow the steps below: Step one: Compose an e-mail message to the following address. Subject is optional. almanac@wisplan.uwex.edu

Step two: Type in your request. Type carefully -- requests must match the form: send haylist <area code> <hay type> Examples of valid requests are: send haylist 715 alfalfa, send haylist 608 mixed, send haylist 514.

A GUIDE TO INTERNET/BITNET: A METRO LIBRARY USER NETWORK GUIDE

Description: The Guide to Internet/BITNET: A Metro Library User Network Guide by Dana Noonan contains a variety of information resources about both the Internet and Bitnet, with particular emphasis on Bitnet's listserv command language.

Subjects covered: Internet; resource guides; library and information science

Sponsor: Metropolitan State University.

How to access: ftp to vm1.nodak.edu, login as anonymous, type your Internet address as a password, type cd nnews, type dir, and to retrieve the file type get guide1.nnews. Type bye to exit the system.

GUIDE TO NETWORK RESOURCE TOOLS

Description: The Guide to Network Resource Tools describes the tools available for navigating the Internet and retrieving information resources.

Subjects covered: Internet; resource guides

Sponsor: EARN (European Academic and Research Network)

How to access: Send the message GET NETTOOLS MEMO (for plain text) or GET NETTOOLS PS (for Postscript) to LISTSERV@EARNCC.BITNET. The Guide is also available via ftp from: ds.internic.net at /pub/internet-doc/ EARN.nettools.txt; also from naic.nasa.gov at files/general__ info/earn-resource-tool-guide.txt

HISTORY SOURCES

Location: Marshall University, Huntington, WV.

Description: History Sources is a program of electronic texts in various fields of history, including general history, primarily political, military and diplomatic.

Subjects covered: military history; history; political science

Net address for operations: ftp to byrd.mu.wvnet.edu

Net address for questions or submissions: mmccarth@muvms6.wvnet.edu

Established: March 1993

Method of issuance: Texts are available via ftp.

Sponsor: Marshall University, Department of History.

Host: Marshall University

List of texts available: Retrieve file INDEX from pub/history subdirectory of byrd.mu.wvnet.edu. Hundreds of individual titles available.

Editorial contact: Michael J. McCarthy
Dept. of History, Marshall University
Tel: 304/696-6372
Fax: 304/696-6277
Internet: mmccarth@muvms6.wvnet.edu
Bitnet: mmccarth@muvms6

Copyright statement: Owners of files retain copyrights. Electronic storage does not preclude publication elsewhere.

How to access: Anonymous FTP to byrd.mu.wvnet.edu, pub/history subdirectory

How to submit: PUT submissions in pub/history/submissions subdirectory

Submission policy: All documents subject to manager approval, please include relevant citations or attributions.

Related files: Texts available via HNServer (hnsource.cc.ukans.edu, login as 'history'

Additional information: Second editor: Donna J. Spindel, Dept. of History, Marshall University; tel304/696-2719; Internet hst001@marshall.wvnet.edu; Bitnet hst001@marshall

HYTELNET

Description: HYTELNET version 6.6 is a utility which gives an IBM-PC user instant-access to all Internet-accessible library catalogs, FREE-NETS, CWISs, BBSs, Gophers, WAIS, etc.

Subjects covered: online public access catalogs; computer hardware and software; library and information science

Editorial contact: Peter Scott
324 8th St. E., Saskatoon, SA, Canada, S7H0P5
Tel: 306-244-8761
Internet: aa375@freenet.carleton.ca

How to access: TO RETRIEVE HYTELNET: At your system prompt, enter: ftp ftp.usask.ca or ftp 128.233.3.11. When you receive the Name prompt, enter:anonymous When you receive the password prompt, enter your Internet address When you are at the ftp> prompt, enter: binary. At the next ftp> prompt, enter: cd pub/hytelnet/pc. Then enter: get hyteln66.zip. After the transfer has occurred, enter: quit. Proceed with the instructions below to retrieve the UNZIP utilities (which you need unless you already have them).

The Hytelnet program is archived using a PKZIP.EXE. To unarchive it, you must be able to "unzip" the file. If you have the file PKUNZIP.EXE, it will unarchive the hyteln66.zip file (see below for instructions). If you do not have it, you may retrieve it by following these instructions:

TO RETRIEVE PKUNZIP: Use the above instructions for connecting to oak.oakland.edu. At the ftp> prompt, enter: binary, then enter: cd pub/msdos/zip, then enter: get pkz204g.exe. After the transfer has occurred, enter: quit. You can also un-archive with UNZIP.EXE. To retrieve it follow these instructions: TO RETRIEVE UNZIP: At your system prompt, enter: ftp oak.oakland.edu. When you receive the Name prompt, enter: anonymous. When you receive the password prompt, enter your Internet address. When you are at the ftp> prompt, enter: binary. At the next ftp> prompt, enter: cd pub/msdos/zip, then enter: get unz50p1.exe. TO DOWNLOAD IT TO YOUR PC: Because of the plethora of PC communications programs, I will not attempt to give step-by-step instructions here. You should check the instructions for your software for downloading a *binary* file from your Internet account to your PC. TO UNARCHIVE hyteln66.zip: Make a new directory on your hard disk (e.g., mkdir hytelnet) Copy PKUNZIP.EXE or UNZIP.EXE and hyteln66.zip into the new directory. Make sure you are in that directory, then enter: pkunzip hyteln66.zip.

Related files: For related files, ftp to access.usask.ca Files are stored in the pub/hytelnet/pc directory.

Gopher accessibility: Name = HYTELNET - All new files & updates since Version 6.3 Type = 1 Port = 70
Path = ftp:access.usask.ca@/pub/hytelnet/pc/
Host = access.usask.ca

THE INCOMPLETE GUIDE TO THE INTERNET AND OTHER TELECOMMUNICATIONS OPPORTUNITIES ESPECIALLY FOR TEACHERS AND STUDENTS, K-12

Description: The Incomplete Guide to the Internet is a directory of resources available on the Internet mainly for educators.
Subjects covered: education; Internet; resource guides
Available in other media: Also available in print.
Sponsor: NCSA Education Group, 605 E. Springfield Avenue, Champaign, IL 61820.
Editorial contact: Chuck Farmer
NCSA Education Group, 605 E. Springfield Avenue, Champaign, IL 61820.
Internet: cfarmer@landrew.ncsa.uiuc.edu
How to access: ftp to zaphod.ncsa.uiuc.edu or fpt.ncsa.uiuc.edu and select the directory named /Education/Education Resources/; there select Incomplete__Guide

INFORMATION SOURCES: THE INTERNET AND COMPUTER-MEDIATED COMMUNICATIONS

Description: Information Sources is a compact guide to Internet resources, including information on discussion lists and electronic journals.
Subjects covered: Internet; resource guides
How to access: ftp to ftp.rpi.edu, login as anonymous, type your Internet address as a password, type cd pub/communica-

tions, type dir, and to retrieve the file type get internet-cmc. Type bye to exit the system.

INTEREST GROUPS LIST OF LISTS

Description: The Interest Groups List of Lists contains information on a variety of discussion groups, including a description of the content of the group and subscription procedures.
Subjects covered: Internet; resource guides; library and information science
How to access: ftp to ftp.nisc.sri.com and change directory to /netinfo. The filename is interest-groups. Alternative ftp address is nnsc.nsf.net, directory is /info, filename is interest-groups.

THE INTERNATIONAL PHILOSOPHICAL PREPRINT EXCHANGE

Description: The International Philosophical Preprint Exchange is a new service on the Internet intended to make it easy for philosophers with Internet access of any kind to exchange working papers in all areas of philosophy, and to comment publicly on each other's work. The International Philosophical Preprint Exchange provides storage for working papers, abstracts, and comments, and provides a variety of means by which papers and abstracts may be browsed and downloaded. Use of the International Philosophical Preprint Exchange is free of charge, and open to all. The International Philosophical Preprint Exchange is located at Chiba University, Japan, through the generosity of the Department of Philosophy and of Cognitive and Information Sciences, Chiba University. It is administered by an international volunteer group headed by Richard Reiner. Paper submissions are accepted from all, on the sole condition that papers must be of interest to contemporary academic philosophers. In addition to original papers, comments on papers already available on the system are encouraged.
Subjects covered: philosophy
Net address for operations: phil-preprints.l.chiba-u.ac.jp
Internet: phil-preprints-admin@phil-preprints.l.chiba-u.ac.jp
How to access: Papers and abstracts on the International Philosophical Preprint Exchange can be retrieved by email, by ftp, and by Gopher. If you need detailed help in getting started, send a piece of email to the address phil-preprints-service@phil-preprints.l.chiba-u.ac.jp containing exactly the following four lines of text: begin send getting-started index end and a detailed beginner's guide and a list of files available on the system will be returned to you by email (they will be preceded by a detailed message acknowledging your request).
Archives: ftp to phil-preprints.l.chiba-u.ac.jp (log in as "anonymous" or "ftp"); or point your gopher at apa.oxy.edu or at kasey.umkc.edu (look under "Science Studies"); or send email containing mail-server commands to phil-preprints-service@phil-preprints.l.chiba-u.ac.jp (the command "help" is a good way to begin).

THE INTERNET EXPLORER'S TOOLKIT

Description: The Internet Explorer's Toolkit, compiled by Ernest Perex, is a hypertext tour of the Internet containing a wide variety of information about a full range of sources. Also included is a communications shareware program called PSILink.
Subjects covered: Internet; resource guides; library and information science
How to access: ftp tohydra.uwo.ca and change directory to /libsoft. The filenames are explorer.zip, psilink.zip

INTERNET LIBRARY CATALOG

Location: ariel.unm.edu, subdirectory "library"
Description: The Internet Library Catalog, compiled by Art St. George is a frequently updated and authoritative guide to OPACs, campus-wide information systems, and other library-Internet resources.
Subjects covered: Internet; resource guides; campus-wide information systems; online public access catalogs
Net address for operations: stgeorge@bootes.unm.edu
Established: 1990
Method of issuance: Both print and electronic.
Method of text retrieval: ftp, Gopher and WAIS
Sponsor: Universities of New Mexico and Maryland
Host: 2701 Campus Blvd., NE, Albuquerque, NM 87131.
Editorial contact: Art St. George, CIRT, 2701 Campus Blvd., NE, Albuquerque, NM 87131.
Tel: (505) 277-8406
Fax: (505) 277-8101
Internet: stgeorge@bootes.unm.edu
Bitnet: stgeorge@unmb
Technical contact: Carlos Robles
CERFnet
Tel: (619) 455-3907
Internet: roblesc@cerf.net
Copyright statement: This Catalog may be reproduced only for educational, nonprofit uses.
How to access: ftp to ariel.unm.edu and change to the directory named /library. The filename is internet.library. The file is also available through email to listserv@unmvm. In the body of the message type, get library package.
Gopher accessibility: Yes
WAIS accessibility: Yes

INTERNET RESOURCE GUIDE

Description: The Internet Resource Guide, produced by the NSR Network Service Center, is one of the oldest and most respected of navigational guides to the Internet and is accessible through a variety of methods.
Subjects covered: Internet; resource guides; library and information science
How to access: ftp tonnsc.nsf.net and change directory to /resource-guide. The filename is readme. You can email to resource-guide-request@nnsc.nsf.net to request the Guide, or you may telnet to pac.carl.org and at the appropriate prompts type commands: Information databases Internet Resource Guide.

INTERNET TALK RADIO

Description: Internet Talk Radio is a news and information service about the Internet in which professionally produced programs, including interviews and other news features, are distributed to networks where they can be played on any workstation or PC equipped with speakers and audio software. The programs are comprised of digital data and can be ftp'd and emailed real time.
Subjects covered: Internet; radio
Available in other media: Audiotapes of past programs are available from O'Reilly & Associates, Inc. For more details email to listproc@online.ora.com. Put the following information in the body of the message (ignore Subject line): subscribe tapes <your name your company>. You will begin receiving announcements.
Editorial contact: Carl Malamud

Internet Multicasting Service
Internet: For more information, email to questions@radio.com.
How to access: To receive information about how to download or play the files, send email to info@radio.com. To subscribe to a discussion list announcing the availability of new installments of the program, send mail to announce-request@radio.com. For personal attention, send mail to questions@radio.com. For information on ftp sites carrying Internet Talk Radio, send mail to sites@radio.com

INTERNET TOOLS SUMMARY

Description: The Internet Tools Summary, by John December, is a brief description of the functions of various Internet search tools, including ftp, telnet, finger, and other services.
Subjects covered: Internet; resource guides; library and information science
How to access: ftp to ftp.rpi.edu, login as anonymous, type your Internet address as a password, type pub communications, type dir, and to retrieve the file type get internet-tools. Type bye to exit the system.

INTERNET/BITNET ONLINE HEALTH SCIENCES RESOURCE LIST

Description: The Internet /Bitnet Online Health Sciences Resource List, compiled by Lee Hancock, is a compendium of medical and health sciences information accessible on the net. Included is information on electronic periodicals, discussion lists, databases, and other sources.
Subjects covered: Internet; resource guides; library and information science; health sciences
How to access: ftp to hydra.uwo.ca and change directory to /libsoft. The filename is medical_resources.txt. Another ftp source is ftp.sura.net, directory is /pub/nic, and the filename is medical_resources.6-12

INTERNIC DIRECTORY AND DATABASE SERVICES

Description: The InterNIC is a collaborative effort of three organizations operating under a cooperative agreement with the National Science Foundation. The three organizations and the services they provide are: General Atomics--Information Services; Network Solutions Inc.--Registration Services; and AT&T-- Directory and Database Services. We have made every effort to provide a single point of contact for InterNIC services. In some cases, as with the 800 number hot-line and the Gopher service, the point of contact is a connection that can branch to any of the three organizations. For services that are provided uniquely by a single organization, the point of contact is directly with that organization.
Subjects covered: Internet; resource guides
Net address for operations: ds.internic.net
Sponsor: National Science Foundation (NSF)
Tel: 800-862-0677; 908-668-6587
Internet: admin@ds.internic.net
How to access: You can send your questions via email to the following addresses: info@internic.net; hostmaster@rs.internic.net; or admin@ds.internic.net
Related files: Electronic Mailing Lists: To subscribe to any of the following email lists, send email to listserv@is.internic.net and in the body of the message, type: subscribe listname

firstname lastname where the listnames are: announce (contains InterNic announcements); net-resources(contains new Internet resources); net-happenings (Internet news, 5-10/day); nics(information for NIC personnel). To subscribe to the InterNIC newsletter, InterNIC InterActive, send email to: interactive-request@is.internic.net

Gopher accessibility: The online documents of all three organizations are available through Gopher. The root menu for the InterNIC Gopher server provides connections to each of the databases. Use the command: gopher gopher.internic.net or telnet gopher.internic.net (login:gopher)

Additional information: If you want more detailed instructions on accessing us, listing a resource, or placing your organization in the Directory white pages please send email to admin@ds.internic.net or call 1-800-862-0677 or 1-908-668-6587.

INTERNIC DIRECTORY OF DIRECTORIES

Description: The InterNIC Directory of Directories includes lists of ftp sites, lists of various types of servers available on the Internet, lists of white and yellow page directories, library catalogs, and data archives. It enables the user to obtain references to information resources on the Internet and support a variety of access methods and tools, including WAIS, archie, email, telnet, gopher, and, in the future, x.500.

Subjects covered: Internet; resource guides; online public access catalogs

Net address for operations: ds.internic.net

Sponsor: National Science Foundation (NSF) InterNIC Directory and Database Services, AT&T, 5000 Hadley Road, South Plainfield, NJ 07080.

Tel: 800-862-0677; 908-668-6587

Fax: 908-668-3763

Internet: admin@ds.internic.net

How to access: You can send your questions via email to the following addresses: info@internic.net; hostmaster@rs.internic.net; or admin@ds.internic.net

Related files: Electronic Mailing Lists: To subscribe to any of the following email lists, send email to listserv@is.internic.net and in the body of the message, type: subscribe listname firstname lastname where the listnames are: announce (contains InterNic announcements); net-resources(contains new Internet resources); net-happenings (Internet news, 5-10/day); nics(information for NIC personnel). To subscribe to the InterNIC newsletter, InterNIC InterActive, send email to: interactive-request@is.internic.net

Gopher accessibility: The online documents of all three organizations are available through Gopher. The root menu for the InterNIC Gopher server provides connections to each of the databases. Use the command: gopher gopher.internic.net or telnet gopher.internic.net (login:gopher)

Additional information: If you want more detailed instructions on accessing us, listing a resource, or placing your organization in the Directory white pages please send email to admin@ds.internic.net or call 1-800-862-0677 or 1-908-668-6587.

JEWISHNET--GLOBAL JEWISH NETWORKING

Location: WWW Server at the Hebrew University of Jerusalem

Description: The JewishNet server is a central gathering place and clearinghouse for issues of Jewish concern. We hope to establish a broad based electronic forum where those involved in Jewish issues will have a presence and readily available means to reach significant Jewish resources. The information and pointers gathered here are the result of the work done during the last years of planning and advancing the establishment of a Global Jewish Information Network. One tool in this work has been the Jewishnt conference whose proceedings are reflected in this server. Presenting what is available, will allow us to identify what still needs to be done. This is a joint effort of all who contribute to Jewish Networking. I am gratefull to all who have sent and will continue to send suggestions, corrections, pointers to relevant Jewish material to be included in the server. Direct connection to 36 libraries of Jewish interest; Information on 54 lists on Jewish issues; direct connection to 7 Usenet newsgroups of Jewish interest; direct connection to many files with bibliographies, reading lists and answers to Frequently Asked Question on Jewish issues. Topics covered on this server include JUDAICA, Contemporary Jewry and Jewish Education, Jewish Law, Arab- Israeli Relations, Answers to Frequently Asked Questions on Judaism and the Jewish People, Reading lists and bibliographies, access to Jewish interest lists and libraries, access to Jewish interest Usenet newsgroups, and related matters.

Subjects covered: Judaica; distance education; electronic networking

Net address for operations: vms.huji.ac.il Login: WWW

Net address for questions or submissions: dovw@vms.huji.ac.il, viner@bguvm.bgu.ac.il

Established: June 1993

Method of issuance: Files are made available in the Jewishnet WWW server at the Hebrew University. Announcements of new information ares distributed to relevant Jewish interest list and newsgroups.

Method of text retrieval: Telnet to www.huji.ac.il or to vms.huji.ac.il Login as: WWW The information may be retrieved through screens capture in the case of the libraries connected or through email sent to any location in the networks in the case of files reached through the system.

Sponsor: The project is currently seeking a sponsor.

Host: The Hebrew University of Jerusalem, WWW System, Givat Ram, Jerusalem, Israel.

Selection of texts: All the latest and updated material that may be accessed online is included if relevant to Jewish networking and subjects.

Texts marked or tagged: The text is marked following the HTML hypertext system for CERN's WWW system.

Editorial contact: Dov Winer P.O.B. 151, Dor Haela 99875, Israel.

Tel: (972) 2 - 332286

Fax: (972) 2 - 332286

Internet: dovw@vms.huji.ac.il, viner@bguvm.bgu.ac.il

Bitnet: viner@bguvm.BITNET

Technical contact: Dudu Rashty Hebrew University Computer Centre, Givat Ram, Jerusalem, Israel.

Tel: (972) 2 - 584848

Internet: rashty@vms.huji.ac.il

Bitnet: rashty@hujivms.BITNET

Copyright statement: There is no overall copyright statement for the e-texts. Each of the included texts may have its own copyright statement included. JEWISHNET (s) is a registered service mark by Dov Winer (1988)

How to access: The service may be reached from any computer with full Internet connectivity. No need for a special subscrip-

tion. Telnet to: vms.huji.ac.il Login as: WWW Choose 3 and then 7 in the menu.
How to submit: Send messages to: Dov Winer dovw@vms.huji.ac.il or viner@bguvm.bgu.ac.il
Related files: The following list is related to this server: JEW-ISHNT@bguvm.bgu.ac.il
WorldWideWeb accessibility: JewisNet is part of the services of the WWW server of the Hebrew University of Jerusalem. Accessible from all other WWW servers and from Gopher systems which have included pointers to it.

LEHRSTUHL FUER MATHEMATIK - ALGEBRA

Location: Universitaet Passau, Lehrstuhl fuer Mathematik, 94030 Passau, Germany.
Description: alice.fmi.uni-passau.de is the ftp-server of the Lehrstuhl fuer Mathematik - Algebra at Universitaet Passau. The main purpose of this server is to make software developed here (not e-texts other than software documentation) available, e.g., MAS (Modula-Algebra-System) by H. Kredel.
Subjects covered: ftp sites; computer hardware and software; mathematics
Net address for operations: alice.fmi.uni-passau.de
Net address for questions or submissions: alice.fmi.uni-passau.de
Established: October 17, 1991
Host: Universitaet Passau, Lehrstuhl fuer Mathematik, 94030 Passau, Germany.
Editorial contact: Michael Pesch
Universitaet Passau, Lehrstuhl fuer Mathematik, 94030 Passau, Germany.
Tel: +49/851/509-766
Fax: +49/851/509-171
Internet: pesch@alice.fmi.uni-passau.de

LIBRARY RESOURCES ON THE INTERNET: STRATEGIES FOR SELECTION AND USE

Description: Library Resources on the Internet, edited by Laine Farley of the University of California, is a "travel" guide to the Internet's online public access catalogs.
Subjects covered: Internet; resource guides; online public access catalogs; library and information science
How to access: ftp to ftp.unt.edu, login as anonymous, type your Internet address as a password, type cd library, type dir, and to retrieve the file type get libcat-guide. Type bye to exit the system.

LIBRARY-ORIENTED LISTS AND ELECTRONIC SERIALS

Description: Library-Oriented Lists and Electronic Serials, compiled by Charles W. Bailey, Jr., is a compact descriptive list of Internet resources of interest to a wide variety of practicing librarians.
Subjects covered: Internet; resource guides; library and information science
How to access: ftp to nic.sura.net and change directory to /pub/nic. The filename is library.conferences.

LIST OF ACTIVE NEWSGROUPS

Description: The List of Active Newsgroups, compiled by Gene Spafford, is an ongoing listing of Usenet Newsgroups, with some annotation about the topics relevant to each list.
Subjects covered: Internet; resource guides; Usenet Newsgroups
How to access: ftp to pit-manager.mit.edu and change to directory called /pub/usenet/news.annouce.newusers. The filenames there are List_of_Active_Newsgroups,_Part_I and List_of_Active_Newsgroups,_Part_II.

LIST OF PERIODIC POSTINGS

Description: The List of Periodic Postings, compiled by Jonathan Kamens, is an ongoing compilation of informational articles and other documents about Usenet.
Subjects covered: Internet; resource guides; Usenet Newsgroups
How to access: ftp to pit-manager.mit.edu and change to directory called /pub/usenet/news.annouce.newusers. The filenames there are List_of_Periodic_Informational_Postings,_Part_I, List_of_Periodic_Informational_Postings,_Part_II, and List_of_Periodic_Informational_Postings,_Part_III.

LYRIC AND DISCOGRAPHY ARCHIVE

Description: The Lyric and Discography Archive contains song lyrics and lists of musical performances on record by both popular and classical artists. There are over 250 discographies and 1000 songs and record albums represented in the archive.
Subjects covered: ftp sites; music; popular culture
Host: University of Wisconsin-Parkside.
How to access: ftp vacs.uwp.edu Login is "anonymous" and for the password enter your electronic address. The discography archives are currently available via e-mail request from datta@vacs.uwp.edu and via ftp: vacs.uwp.edu:/pub/music/discog/*. The lyrics files are at the ftp site: vacs.uwp.edu:/pub/music/lyrics/*/*. There is now a musical lyrics area where you can find lyrics to various albums. Look in the /pub/music/lyrics directory. Due to the extreme size of the directory, the index and readme files are in the directory: /pub/music/lyrics and the files are in the directory: /pub/music/lyrics/files. A list of musical mailing lists is currently being stored in the music FTP archives: vacs.uwp.edu:/pub/music/misc/mail.lists.music

MC(2)

Description: MC(2) is Meckler Corporation's Gopher-accesible collection of documents including indexes to Computers in Libraries and CD-ROM Librarian magazines; a complete catalog of Meckler publications; conference programs from Meckler-sponsored conferences (annual Virtual Reality conference and expositions, Internet World, Document Delivery World, Computers in Libraries, Computers in Libraries Canada, and Electronic Books 1993). Articles from the ejournal MeckJournal appear in selected print publications from Meckler Corporation, including Computers in Libraries, OCLC Systems and Services, Internet World, Internet Research, and Campus-Wide Information Systems. MeckJournal publishes articles, reviews, and news and conference reports taken from its battery of print magazines and newsletters in information technology areas, primarily on Internet-related and electronic networking topics.

Subjects covered: library and information science; computer hardware and software; electronic networking
Net address for operations: meckler@jvnc.net
Net address for questions or submissions: meckler@jvnc.net
Established: June 1991
Available in other media: Several files maintained on this Gopher-accesible collection of documents have printed counterparts: indexes to Computers in Libraries and CD-ROM Librarian magazines; catalog of Meckler publications; conference programs from Meckler-sponsored conferences. Articles from the ejournal MeckJournal appear in selected print publications from Meckler Corporation, including Computers in Libraries, OCLC Systems and Services, Internet World, Internet Research, and Campus-Wide Information Systems.
Sponsor: Meckler Corporation, 11 Ferry Lane West, Westport, CT 06880; (203) 226-6967; fax: (203) 454-5840.
Host: Same as above
Commercial organization: Yes.
Editorial contact: Anthony Abbott
Meckler Corporation, 11 Ferry Lane West, Westport, CT 06880
Tel: (203) 226-6967
Fax: (203) 454-5840
Internet: meckler@jvnc.net
Copyright statement: Copyright 1993 Meckler Publishing, the publishing division of Meckler Corporation. All rights reserved. Copying is permitted for noncommercial use by computer conferences, individual scholars, and libraries. Libraries are authorized to add MeckJournal and other files in MC(2) to their collections either in electronic or printed form at no charge. This message must appear on all copied materials. All commercial use requires permission.
How to access: MC(2) is accessible by telneting to nicol.jvnc.net, typing nicol at the login prompt, and selecting from the main menu. No password is needed.
Access policy: Access is open to all.
How to submit: Send all messages to meckler@jvnc.net.
Related files: MeckJournal, Meckler's electronic journal, is also available through subscription. Send a subscribe request to meckler@jvnc.net.
Gopher accessibility: MC(2) is accessible through the Internet Gopher at JvNCNet, the regional Internet node which maintains Meckler's telnet files.

NASA ARCHIVES
Description: The NASA Archives from the Ames Research Center contain a large number of documents about space exploration and the U.S. space program. Included is a large collection of images of the Voyager and shuttle missions.
Subjects covered: ftp sites; space and space exploration
How to access: ftp ames.arc.nasa.gov or 128.102.18.3 ftp> open (to) 128.102.18.3 ames.arc.nasa.gov FTP server (Version 4.129 Tue Nov 1 20:20:51 Name (128.102.18.3:aperry): anonymous 331 Guest login ok, send ident as password. Password: (input complete address, userid@node)
Additional information: Description of codes found on the "SPACE" Directory, which covers past and current shuttle and mission status reports: Items are stored by date, with a one or two letter indicator to identify the report type: 'ss' means Shuttle Status, 'ps' means Payload Status, 'h' means NASA Headline News, 'ms' means Magellan Status, 'gs' means Galileo Status, 'r' means Release (which are not dated, but are ordered by release number), and 'vs' stands for Voyager Status. Other files may have more informative names.

NASA SPACELINK
Description: NASA Spacelink is a database of space-related information from the Marshall Space Flight Center in Huntsville, Alabama. Included are news bulletins about shuttle flights and current NASA activities as well as historical and educational materials serving a wide variety of public and research uses.
Subjects covered: space and space exploration; astronomy; education
How to access: Telnet to spacelink.msfc.nasa.gov or xsl.msfc.nasa.gov
Gopher accessibility: Gopher accessible at among other sites, University of California, Santa Barbara

NATIONAL COUNCIL FOR RESEARCH ON WOMEN, RESEARCH IN PROGRESS DATABASE
Description: The Research in Progress Database contains 4,500 records including prepublication information from journals, work-in-progress notes from researchers, grant and funding information, and other data from a variety of sources dealing with the history of women.
Subjects covered: women's studies; gender studies; history
How to access: The database is accessible through the Research Libraries Information Network (RLIN). Logon to RLIN with your institution's account number and password. At the command prompt, type call rlin (rip) to access this database.

NETWORK KNOWLEDGE FOR THE NEOPHYTE: STUFF YOU NEED TO KNOW IN ORDER TO NAVIGATE THE ELECTRONIC VILLAGE
Description: Network Knowledge for the Neophyte, compiled by Martin Raish, of Binghamton University, is an entry-level introduction to the Internet and its wide range of resources.
Subjects covered: Internet; resource guides
How to access: ftp to hydra.uwo.ca, login as anonymous, type your Internet address as a password, type cd pub/libsoft, type dir, and to retrieve the file type get network_knowledge_for_the_neoph.txt. Type bye to exit the system.

THE NEW INTERNET LIBRARY GUIDE
Description: The New Internet Library Guide is a descriptive list of Internet accessible online public access catalogs worldwide.
Subjects covered: Internet; resource guides; on-line public access catalogs
Editorial contact: Billy Barron
University of Texas at Dallas
Internet: billy@utdallas.edu
How to access: The files are available on ftp.utdallas.edu (129.110.10.1) via anonymous FTP in the /pub/staff/billy/ libguide directory. The files are: libraries.intro- Introduction to the Library Guide; libraries.africa- Libraries in Africa; libraries.americas- Libraries in the Western Hemisphere; libraries.asia- Libraries in Asia; libraries.australia - Libraries in Australia & New Zealand; libraries.europe - Libraries in Europe; libraries.instructions - Instructions on using the various libraries. If you are on BITNET and not the Internet, you can do the following to get the file(s): To use BITFTP, send mail to BITFTP@PUCC.BITNET. The body should be as follows: FTP

FTP.UTDALLAS.EDU [filetype] USER ANONYMOUS your-email-address CD /PUB/STAFF/BILLY/LIBGUIDE GET file-name QUIT
filetype is blank for text, UUENCODE for a UUENCODED version of the file (need UUDECODE to undo), or NETDATA for IBM NETDATA format (may only work for IBM Mainframe BITNET users).
How to submit: Send all new information, updates, and deletions to GOPHLIB@GOPHER.YALE.EDU (more details on first page of guide). If you are using a TELNET/TN3270 package not listed in the appendix, please send me the information on it. Also, if you have instructions for a library software package not yet described, please send them to me and give me at least one example where it is in use.

NOT JUST COWS: A GUIDE TO INTERNET/BITNET RESOURCES IN AGRICULTURE AND RELATED SCIENCES

Description: Not Just Cows, compiled by Wilfred Drew, is an authoritative listing of networked resources in agriculture and related fields of study. Ejournals, discussion groups, databases, and other sources are described.
Subjects covered: Internet; resource guides; library and information science; agriculture
How to access: ftp to hydra.uwo.ca and change directory to /libsoft. The filename is agriculture_internet_guide.txt. Another ftp source is ftp.sura.net, directory is /pub/nic, and the filename is agguide.dos

NYSERNET NEW USER'S GUIDE TO USEFUL AND UNIQUE RESOURCES ON THE INTERNET

Description: The NYSERNet New User's Guide to Useful and Unique Resources on the Internet is a comprehensive and wide-ranging directory of information sources of use to both beginner and experienced net searcher. Included are online library catalogs, campus-wide information systems, a sampling of discussion groups, and other resources.
Subjects covered: Internet; resource guides; library and information science
Sponsor: NYSERNet, Inc., Syracuse, NY.
How to access: ftp to nysernet.org, login as anonymous, type your Internet address as a password, type cd pub/guides, type dir, and to retrieve the file type get new.user.guide.v2.2txt (or later version if available). Type bye to exit the system.

ONLINE BOOK INITIATIVE (OBI)

Description: The Online Book Initiative is an electronic text service.
Subjects covered: electronic texts; fulltext
Host: Apple Computer Higher Education Gopher at the University of Minnesota Gopher Server.
How to access: Gopher to world.std.com.

OPACS IN THE UK: A LIST OF INTERACTIVE LIBRARY CATALOGUES ON JANET

Description: OPACs in the UK, compiled by staff at the University of Sussex Library, provides information on dozens of Janet- and Internet-accessible library catalogs.
Subjects covered: Internet; resource guides; online public access catalogs; library and information science
How to access: ftp to ftp.unt.edu and change to the directory named /library. The filename is uk.lib. The file is also available through email to mailbase@newcastle.ac.uk. In the body of the message type get lis-link janet opacs.

POSTMASTER@CS.MAN.AC.UK

Description: The postmaster@cs.man.ac.uk archive contains some of the technical reports issued by the Department of Computer Science, University of Manchester. A complete list of what is available is found in the file pub/ReportList.tex on the Archive.
Subjects covered: computer hardware and software; ftp sites; technical reports
Established: September 1992
Method of text retrieval: Anonymous ftp
Total number of texts distributed: 16
Fee: Electronic copies are free; paper copies are priced per item. Check in British Pounds Sterling payable to The University of Manchester.
Sponsor: Department of Computer Science, University of Manchester, Oxford Road, Manchester M13 9PL UK.
Host: Department of Computer Science, University of Manchester, Oxford Road, Manchester M13 9PL UK.
Editorial contact: Mrs. J.M.Fleet
Department of Computer Science, University of Manchester, Oxford Road, Manchester M13 9PL, UK.
Tel: +44 61 275 6130
Fax: +44 61 275 6236
Internet: techreports@cs.man.ac.uk
Technical contact: Aidan Loyns
Department of Computer Science, University of Manchester, Oxford Road, Manchester M13 9PL, UK.
Tel: +44 61 275 6119
Fax: +44 61 275 6197
Internet: aidan@cs.man.ac.uk
Copyright statement: Copyright 199?. All Rights reserved. Reproduction of all or part of this work is permitted for educational or research purposes on condition that (1) this copyright notice is included, (2) propoer attribution to the author or authors is made and (3) no commercial gain is involved.
How to access: Anonymous ftp to ftp.cs.man.ac.uk cd to pub/TR get the required files (compressed postscript, so select binary mode).
Submission policy: Retrieve the files README and ReportList.tex for more information.

PRINCIPIA CYBERNETICA PROJECT (PCP)

Location: Brussels, Belgium
Subjects covered: science and technology; computer science; cybernetics; metaphysics
Net address for operations: host: is1.vub.ac.be, directory /pub/projects/Principia_Cybernetica

Net address for questions or submissions:
fheyligh@vnet3.vub.ac.be
Established: March 1993
Number of texts published to date: 40 papers, and many shorter texts.
Method of issuance: Titles available on ftp server. No.
Sponsor: Principia Cybernetica Project c/o F. Heylighen, PESP, Free University of Brussels, Pleinlaan 2, B-1050 Brussels, Belgium.
Host: Computing Center, Free University of Brussels, Pleinlaan 2, B-1050 Brussels, Belgium.
Selection of texts: Those texts (mostly from PCP-contributors) are electronically published that address topics connected to the Principia Cybernetica Project.
Texts marked or tagged: Some texts are in LaTeX, in a later stage we expect to use the HTML or HMML mark-up for hypertexts links as used in World-Wide Web.
List of texts available: The ftp directory /pub/projects/Principia_Cybernetica at the host: is1.vub.ac.be, has the following subdirectories, (with an overview of the texts they contain): /Misc.Info : contains diverse information (reports, bibliography, ...) on non-PCP projects or tools that may be useful for PCP. /News : contains the newsletters distributed about PCP, reports on PCP activities, and PRNCYB-L discussions on different topics. /Nodes : contains preliminary concept definitions developed by the PCP-editors, to be organized as a hypertext, semantic network /Papers_Heylighen : contains papers on PCP themes by PCP-editor Francis Heylighen /Papers_Joslyn : contains papers on PCP themes by PCP-editor Cliff Joslyn /Papers_Turchin : contains papers on PCP themes by PCP-editor Valentin Turchin /Papers_Others : contains papers on PCP by other contributors, who do not belong to the editorial board /Software : contains the "HyperVision" application, a simple hypertext viewer and editor for MS-DOS /Texts_General : contains introductory or overview papers by the editors collectively, and collected contributions of others, including the workbook with short papers and abstracts of the PCP Workshop in Brussels, 1991, and the abstracts for the PCP symposium in Namur, 1992 /WF-issue: contains draft papers contributed by the editors and others for a special issue of "World Futures: the journal of general evolution" devoted to the theory of Metasystem Transitions, which forms the core of the PCP philosophy.
Editorial contact: Francis Heylighen
PO, Free University of Brussels, Pleinlaan 2, B-1050 Brussels, Belgium.
Tel: + 32-2-6412525
Fax: + 32-2-6412489
Internet: fheyligh@vnet3.vub.ac.be
Technical contact: Francis Heylighen
Copyright statement: Copyright 1993 by Principia Cybernetica, Brussels and New York. All rights reserved. Electronic texts may be freely copied for individual use, but may not be further distributed or published without permission from the Principia Cybernetica Editorial Board.
How to access: No subscription is needed for anonymous ftp, everybody with network acces can freely access the files; for subscription to the associated mailing list PRNCYB-L, see entry elsewhere in this directory.
How to submit: PCP contributors may freely add (by ftp) texts to the directory /pub/projects/Principia_Cybernetica/Papers Others, but are requested to send an email message describing the file to Francis Heylighen (fheyligh@vnet3.vub.ac.be). The same address can be used for questions. To submit or for ques-

tions (policy): Submitted texts that are deemed insufficiently relevant to PCP by the PCP-editors will be deleted from the archive.
Related files: PRNCYB-L@BINGVMB.BITNET with associated LISTSERV file server. See full entry elsewhere in this directory.
Additional information: This ftp archive constitutes the electronic repository of the Principia Cybernetica Project (PCP). PCP is a computer-supported collaborative attempt to develop an integrated evolutionary-systemic philosophy or world view. Its contributors are distributed over the 5 continents. They keep contact mainly by electronic mail (mailing list PRNCYB-L), by annual meetings, the printed (and electronic) Newsletter, and postal mail. The PCP philosophy starts from the self-organization of multi-level systems through blind variation and natural selection. This leads to a process metaphysics, a constructive-selectionist epistemology, and an evolutionary ethics. PCP focuses on the clear formulation of basic concepts and principles of the cybernetic approach. This should lead to a semantic network of concepts and links, implemented as a hypertext. The repository is the first stage of the worldwide electronic publication of this network of linked texts, which define and illustrate the basic concepts of a transdisciplinary philosophy for the cyberage. Additional editors: Cliff Joslyn, Systems Science, SUNY Binghamton, 327 Spring St. # 2, Portland ME 04102, USA. tel/fax: 207/774-0029 (Fax after notice by phone) Internet: cjoslyn@bingsuns.cc.binghamton.edu, joslyn@kong.gsfc.nasa.gov: Valentin Turchin, Computer Science, City College of New York, New York NY 10031; Internet: turcc@cunyvm.cuny.edu; Bitnet: TURCC@CUNYVM

PROJECT GUTENBERG
Description: Project Gutenberg is an electronic text program of over 80 texts of classic and modern works available through ftp or email.
Subjects covered: electronic texts; language and literature
Available in other media: The Project Gutenberg database is available on CD-ROM from Walnut Creek CD-ROM, 1547 Palos Verdes, Suite 260, Walnut Creek, CA 94596. Email orders to orders@cdrom.com. Semi annual updates on CD are planned.
List of texts available: Texts are available in directories named by the year of release of the etext.
1993: These 1993 etext releases in> cd /etext/etext93
Do a dir *.zip or dir *.txt to see exact names.
A Princess of Mars (Mars #1) (pmars10x.xxx)
Aladdin and the Magic Lamp (alad10x.xxx)
Anne of the Island (iland10x.xxx)
Black ExperiencesCoombs) (blexp10x.xxx)
Burroughs' Beasts of Tarzan [Tarzan #2][tarz210x.xxx]
Civil Disobedience (Thoreau) (civil10x.xxx)
Clinton's Inaugural Address (clintonx.xxx)
The Communist Manifesto (mani10x.xxx)
The Dawn of Amateur Radio (radio10x.xxx)
Decartes' Reason Discourse (dcart1-x.xxx)
Email 101 by John Goodwin (email025.xxx)
The First 100,000 Primes (prime10x.xxx)
From the Earth to the Moon/Jules Verne [moonxxxx.xxx]
[moon10 has _italics, moon10a does not]
Gods of Mars (Mars #2) (gmars10x.xxx)
House of 7 Gables.Hawthorne (7gabl10x.xxx)
Huck Finn (Wiretap/Twain) hfinn10x.xxx
Ivanhoe/Scott/Wiretap [for US Only now][ivnho10x.xxx]
LOC Workshop on Etexts (locet10x.xxx)

The Marvelous Land of Oz (ozland10.xxx)
Milton's Paradise Regained (rgain10x.xxx)
NAFTA, Treaty, Annexes, Tariffs [naftxxxx.xxx]
NREN, by Jean Armour Polly (nren210x.xxx)
The Number "e" (Natural Log) (ee610xxx.xxx)
The Online World/de Presno [Shareware] [online11.xxx] 80
Pi (circumference/diameter) pimil10x.xxx)
Red Badge of Courage, Crane (badge10x.xxx)
The Scarlet Pimpernel (scarp10x.xxx)
The Square Root of Two (2sqrt10x.xxx)
Surfing the Internet (surf10xx.xxx)
Tarzan of the Apes/Burroughs (tarzn10x.xxx)
Terminal Compromise/NetNovel (termc10x.xxx)
The 32nd Mersenne Prime (32pri10x.xxx)
Thuvia, Maid of Mars (Mars #4) (mmars10x.xxx)
Tom Sawyer (Wiretap/Twain) (sawyr10x.xxx)
Warlord of Mars (Mars #3) (wmars10x.xxx)
What is Man? Mark Twain (wman10x.xxx)
The Wonderful Wizard of Oz (wizoz10x.xxx)
1992: These 1992 etext releases in> cd /etext/etext92
Do a dir *.zip or dir *.txt to see exac
Editorial contact: Michael S. Hart
Executive Director of Project Gutenberg Etext, Illinois Benedictine College, Lisle, IL 60532.
Internet: hart@vmd.cso.uiuc.edu
Bitnet: hart@uiucvmd.bitnet
How to access: ftp mrcnext.cso.uiuc.edu login: anonymous password: yourname@your.machine cd etext cd etext93 get filename (be sure to set bin, if you get the .zip files) get more files quit. If you don't have ftp access you can get etexts via email. To retrieve a file via e-mail, first send the following line by itself to almanac@oes.orst.edu "send gutenberg catalog." This will instruct you how to send further requests, and will list the available files. For example, to retrieve __Alice's Adventures in Wonderland__, send to almanac@oes.orst.edu "send gutenberg alice." For more details see the Project Gutenberg Newsletters. To subscribe, send email to listserv@vmd.cso.uiuc.edu or listserv@uiucvmd.bitnet with the message: sub gutnberg your name. No subject is required.

PROJECT HERMES: U.S. SUPREME COURT OPINIONS

Location: Project Hermes, Case Western Reserve University, 319 Wickenden Building, Cleveland, OH 66106.
Description: Project Hermes is an ftp site archiving the full text of U.S. Supreme Court Opinions. The objective of the project is to rapidly provide copies of the Court's opinions in electronic form to as wide an audience as possible.
Subjects covered: government information; law and legal studies; U.S. Supreme Court
Net address for operations: ftp.cwru.edu
How to access: Anonymous ftp to ftp.cwru.edu. The files relating to the opinions are located in the directory "hermes". This directory contains several readme files and two subdirectories: ascii and atex. The "atex" subdirectory contains the files as directly received from the U.S. Supreme Court in the Atex 8000 Document Processing and Typesetting system format. These files contain 8-bit typesetting codes and are extremely difficult to read on a typical display. Those wishing to copy the Atex files should make sure that they set "image" mode in FTP. The "ascii" subdirectory contains the same files as processed by a locally developed filtering program designed to remove the typesetting codes while retaining as much of the

"look" of the document as possible. These files are in plain ASCII text.
Additional information: Contact Project Hermes via email at 7aa584@cleveland.freenet.edu, by writing: Project Hermes, CWRU, 319 Wickenden Building, Cleveland, OH 66106; (216) 368-2733.

QUEER RESOURCES DIRECTORY
Description: The Queer Resources Directory is concerned with AIDS and related issues, civil rights, legal issues, and other topics related to gay and lesbian concerns.
Subjects covered: gay and lesbian topics
How to access: Ftp to nifty.andres.cmu.edu. At the login prompt type anonymous. The directory is pub/QRD.qrd

REQUEST FOR COMMENTS
Location: DDN Network Information Center
Description: The RFC program is a database of frequently asked questions related to the Internet and to internetworking generally.
Subjects covered: Internet; telecommunications
Net address for operations: SERVICE@nic.ddn.mil
Net address for questions or submissions: NIC@nic.ddn.mil or ACTION@nic.ddn.mil
Established: 1991
Method of issuance: Announced on RFC mailing list when available.
Method of text retrieval: Anonymous FTP or SERVICE@nic.ddn.mil mailer
Sponsor: University of Southern California, Information Sciences Institute, 4676 Admiralty Way, Marina del Rey, CA 90292.
Host: DDN Network Information Center, Suite 200, 14200 Park Meadow Dr., Chantilly, VA 22021.
Editorial contact: Jon Postel
University of Southern California, Information Sciences Institute, 4676 Admiralty Way, Marina del Rey, CA 90292
Tel: (310) 822-1511
Internet: Internet postel@isi.edu
How to access: Send a subscribe message to RFC-REQUEST@nic.ddn.mil to receive announcements.
Access policy: Open to all interested parties.
How to unsubscribe: Send an unsubscribe message to RFC-REQUEST@nic.ddn.mil
Additional information: Additional editor: Joyce Reynolds, University of Southern California, Information Sciences Institute, 4676 Admiralty Way, Marina del Rey, CA 90292; tel(310) 822-1511; Internet: jkrey@isi.edu

REVELATIONS FROM THE RUSSIAN ARCHIVES
Location: Library of Congress, Washington, DC 20540-9100.
Description: Revelations from the Russian Archives is an exhibition of materials at the Library of Congress. Information and data files are available through anonymous ftp.
Subjects covered: Russia; Soviet Union; communism
Special Projects Office, Library of Congress, Washington, DC 20540-9100.
Tel: Internet: kell@seq1.loc.gov
Internet: kell@seq1.loc.gov

How to access: FTP to seq1.loc.gov (140.147.3.12). Log in as anonymous and give your email address as a password. Then issue a cd command to change directory to the /pub directory. From there select soviet.archive

ROME REBORN: THE VATICAN LIBRARY & RENAISSANCE CULTURE

Location: Library of Congress, Washington, DC 20540-9100.
Description: Rome Reborn: The Vatican Library & Renaissance Culture is an exhibition of materials at the Library of Congress. Information and data files are available through anonymous ftp.
Subjects covered: Renaissance studies; religion; Christianity; classical studies
Special Projects Office, Library of Congress, Washington, DC 20540-9100.
Tel: Internet: kell@seq1.loc.gov
Internet: kell@seq1.loc.gov
How to access: FTP to seq1.loc.gov (140.147.3.12). Log in as anonymous and give your email address as a password. Then issue a cd command to change directory to the /pub directory. From there select vatican.exhibit

SCROLLS FROM THE DEAD SEA: THE ANCIENT LIBRARY OF QUMRAN AND MODERN SCHOLARSHIP

Location: Library of Congress, Washington, DC 20540-9100.
Description: Scrolls from the Dead Sea: The Ancient Library of Qumran and Modern Scholarship is an exhibition of materials at the Library of Congress. Information and data files are available through anonymous ftp.
Subjects covered: Dead Sea Scrolls; religion; Christianity
Special Projects Office, Library of Congress, Washington, DC 20540-9100.
Tel: Internet: kell@seq1.loc.gov
Internet: kell@seq1.loc.gov
How to access: FTP to seq1.loc.gov (140.147.3.12). Log in as anonymous and give your email address as a password. Then issue a cd command to change directory to the /pub directory. From there select deadsea.scrolls.exhibit.

SPECIAL INTERNET CONNECTIONS

Description: Special Internet Connections, by Scott Yanoff of the University of Wisconsin, Madison, is a compendium of hundreds of information sources on the Internet, including a listing of archie sites. Topics covered range from agriculture to the White House, from amateur radio to weather maps.
Subjects covered: Internet; resource guides
Editorial contact: Scott Yanoff
Internet: yanoff@csd4.csd.uwm.edu
How to access: ftp to csd4.csd.uwm.edu, login as anonymous, type your Internet address as a password, type cd pub, type dir, and to retrieve the file type get innet.services.txt. Type bye to exit the system. Or, to find other sources of this list, finger yanoff@csd4.csd.uwm.edu.

SURANET GUIDE TO SELECTED INTERNET RESOURCES

Description: The SURAnet Guide to Selected Internet Resources covers directories, network tools, and other resources in detail, providing the user with a sampling of a wide variety of diverse information sources available.
Subjects covered: Internet; resource guides; library and information science
Sponsor: SURAnet Network Information Center, College Park, MD.
How to access: ftp to ftp.sura.net, login as anonymous, type your Internet address as a password, type cd pub/nic, type dir, and to retrieve the file type get infoguide.5-93.txt (or a later version if available). Type bye to exit the system.

SURFING THE INTERNET: AN INTRODUCTION

Description: Surfing the Internet: An Introduction by Jean Armour Polly is a guide to resources on the Internet.
Subjects covered: Internet; resource guides; library and information science
How to access: ftp to nysernet.org, login as anonymous, use your Internet address as the password, type in cd pub/resources.guides, type dir, and to retrieve the file, type get surfing2.02.txt (or a later version if available). Type Bye to exit the system.

THERE'S GOLD IN THEM THAR NETWORKS!

Description: There's Gold in Them Thar Networks! or Searching for Treasure in All the Wrong Places by J. Martin of the Network Working Group at Ohio State University is a resource guide to the Internet, with explanations of how to search for and retrieve information from campus-wide information systems, databases, freenets, and bulletin boards.
Subjects covered: Internet; resource guides
How to access: ftp to nic.merit.edu, login as anonymous, type your Internet address as a password, type cd introducing.the.internet, type dir, and to retrieve the file type get network.gold. Type bye to exit the system.

THESAURUS MUSICARUM LATINARUM

Description: Thesaurus Musicarum Latinarum is an electronic text program publishing texts dealing with Latin music theory in the 4-5th centuries C.E. as well as of the Middle Ages and Renaissance. Announcements of newly available texts are maintained in annual Log files. The texts of the TML are available in various file lists and can be requested in any of the normal manners. A parallel set of texts is maintained on the TML-FTP. Additional files include the TML Canon (listing all available texts, their sources, and various vital statistics).
Subjects covered: Latin language and literature; music
Net address for operations: LISTSERV@IUBVM (or LISTSERV@IUBVM.UCS.INDIANA.EDU) or through an FTP option.
Net address for questions or submissions: MATHIESE@IUBVM.UCS.INDIANA.EDU
Established: 1990
Number of texts published to date: 225
Method of issuance: Online
No
Method of text retrieval: Texts may be requested as Bitnet files or retrieved by using the TML-FTP option.

Sponsor: This program is partially funded by a grant from the National Endowment for the Humanities, an independent federal agency.

Host: School of Music, Indiana University, Bloomington, IN 47405

Selection of texts: All versions of texts--print and manuscript--are projected to be included in the database.

Texts marked or tagged: Basic text, with special TML encoding (documentation available on request).

Editorial contact: Thomas J. Mathiesen

Thesaurus Musicarum Latinarum, Dept. of Musicology, School of Music, Indiana University, Bloomington, IN 47405

Tel: (812) 876-3592, 855-5471, 855-6889

Fax: (812) 876-3592

Internet: MATHIESE@UCS.INDIANA.EDU

Bitnet: MATHIESE@INDIANA

Copyright statement: The data contained in the Thesaurus Musicarum Latinarum (hereafter TML) is made available to scholars for non-commercial use and study. It has been compiled from public domain and copyrighted materials. Copyrighted materials have been included in the TML by permission of the copyright holders, who reserve all rights to their materials. The TML claims copyright on the compilation, the Introduction, the TML Canon, and all individual text files created and edited by the TML staff from public domain or manuscript material. The TML believes that non-commercial use of the TML by scholars in searching for words and phrases would constitute "fair use" under the law. Nevertheless, the users of the TML are individually responsible for insuring that their own use of these materials does not violate the rights of any third parties. Neither Indiana University nor the TML Project Director nor any member of the TML staff shall be responsible for any improper or unlawful use of the materials contained in the TML.

How to access: To subscribe, send the following one-line message (do not include anything in the Subject: line of your mainframe's mail utility): SUBSCRIBE TML-L <your full name here> to one of the following addresses: LISTSERV@IUBVM [the Bitnet address] or LISTSERV@IUBVM.UCS.INDIANA.EDU [the Internet address] Since the address to which you send your subscription will specify whether the Listserver regards you as an Internet or a Bitnet subscriber, you should select the network you prefer if you have a choice of addresses.

Access policy: Subscriptions are open to anyone.

How to unsubscribe: To unsubscribe, send the following one-line message (do not include anything in the Subject: line of your mainframe's mail utility): SIGNOFF TML-L to one of the following addresses: LISTSERV@IUBVM [the Bitnet address] or LISTSERV@IUBVM.UCS.INDIANA.EDU [the Internet address] You must select the same network under which your subscription was originally registered.

How to submit: Contact the editor, as listed above.

Submission policy: Contact the editor, as listed above.

Related files: See also TML-L listed elsewhere in this directory.

U.S. CONGRESS SENATE HEARINGS

Description: The U.S Congress Senate Hearings are available in electronic form.

Subjects covered: government information

How to access: Telnet to NCSUVM.CC.NCSU.EDU and locate the directory named SENATE.

U.S. DEPARTMETN OF AGRICULTURE CHILDREN-YOUTH-FAMILY EDUCATION RESEARCH NETWORK

Description: The Children-Youth-Family Education Research Network contains documents available in electronic form.

Subjects covered: government information; education; family studies

How to access: Gopher accessible at gopher@cyfer.esusda.gov

U.S. FEDERAL DRUG ADMINISTRATION

Description: The U.S. Federal Drug Administration database contains news releases, AIDS information, and consumer information about drugs.

Subjects covered: government information; AIDS/HIV studies; chemistry

How to access: Telnet to fdabbs.fda.gov

U.S. GENERAL ACCOUNTING OFFICE REPORTS ARCHIVE

Description: General Accounting Office Reports Archive is an ftp site containing a wide range of documents produced by the GAO. The site is testing electronic availability of the reports to determine whether there is interest in the research community in obtaining information electronically. The reports are in ascii format and available via anonymous ftp.

Subjects covered: General Accounting Office; government information

Net address for operations: try@cu.nih.gov

Method of text retrieval: Anonymous ftp

Editorial contact: Jack L. Brock, Jr.

Government Information and Financial Management Issues, Information Management and Technology Division, General Accounting Office, Washington, DC.

Sample contents: 1. Computer Security: Governmentwide Planning Process Had Limited Impact, GAO/IMTEC-90-48, May 1990. Assesses the government-wide computer security planning process and extent to which security plans were implemented for 22 systems at 10 civilian agencies. (This report is named REPORT1 and is 55,062 bytes or 1,190 lines long.)
2. Drug-Exposed Infants: A Generation at Risk, GAO/HRD- 90-138, June 1990. Discusses health effects and medical costs of infants born to mothers using drugs, impact on the nation's health and welfare systems, and availability of drug-treatment and prenatal care to drug-addicted pregnant women. (This report is named REPORT2 and is 113,916 bytes or 2,421 lines long.)
3. High-Definition Television: Applications for This New Technology, GAO/IMTEC-90-9FS, December 1989. Provides information on 14 HDTV applications and the key industry officials' views on the effect of an HDTV production standard on potential applications. (This report is named REPORT3 and is 31,947 bytes or 643 lines long.)
4. Home Visiting: A Promising Early Intervention Strategy for At-Risk Families, GAO/HRD-90-83, July 1990. Discusses home visiting as an early intervention strategy to provide health, social, educational, and other services to improve maternal and child health and well-being. (This report is named REPORT4 and is 287,547 bytes or 5,711 lines long.)
5. Meeting the Government's Technology Challenge: Results of a GAO Symposium, GAO/IMTEC-90-23, February 1990. Outlines five principles for effective management of information technology that can provide a framework for integrating infor-

mation technology into the business of government. (This report is named REPORT5 and is 39,017 bytes or 777 lines long.)
6. Strategic Defense System: Stable Design and Adequate Testing Must Precede Decision to Deploy, GAO/IMTEC-90-61, July 1990. Discusses why the Strategic De
How to access: FTP to try@CU.NIH.GOV
The directory is GAO-REPORTS. Use the FTP TEXT download format.
Additional information: For further information on these and other documents, call GAO report distribution at 202/275-6241 (7:30 a.m.-5:30 p.m. EST) or write to GAO, P.O. Box 6015, Gaithersburg, MD 20877.

U.S. SUPREME COURT DECISIONS
Description: The U.S. Supreme Court Decisions database contains decision papers available by docket number.
Subjects covered: government information; law and legal studies
How to access: Telnet to info.umd.edu

UNT'S ACCESSING ONLINE BIBLIOGRAPHIC DATABASES
Description: UNT's Accessing Online Bibliographic Databases, compiled by Billy Barron, is an authoritative directory of Internet-accessible OPACs worldwide.
Subjects covered: Internet; resource guides; online public access catalogs; library and information science
How to access: ftp to ftp.unt.edu and change to the directory named /pub/library. The filename is libraries.txt.

USING NETWORKED INFORMATION RESOURCES: A BIBLIOGRAPHY
Description: Using Networked Information Resources: A Bibliography by Diedre E. Stanton is a bibliography of printed publications, network information documents, and resources, including software.
Subjects covered: Internet; resource guides
How to access: ftp to infolib.murdoch.edu.au, login as anonymous, type your Internet address as a password, type cd pub/bib, type dir, and to retrieve the file type get stanton.bib. Type bye to exit the system.

WORKING PAPER ARCHIVE IN ECONOMICS
Description: Working Paper Archive in Economics is open to anyone, free of charge. The hope is that most of the working papers in economics that are now distributed in hard copy format will be available on this archive to anyone with e-mail, ftp, gopher and even World Wide Webb access.

Subjects covered: economics
Editorial contact: Bob Parks
Tel: (314) 935 5665
Internet: bparks@wuecona.wustl.edu
Copyright statement: Copyrights to papers in the archive remains with the authors or their assignees. Archive users may download papers and produce them for their own personal use, but downloading of papers for any other activity, including reposting to other electronic bulletin boards or archives, may not be done without the written consent of the authors. It is the authors' responsibility to notify the archive managers when they wish to have the paper removed.
How to access: To receive an announcement of how to use the system, begin by sending an empty message to: econ-wp@econwpa.wustl.edu. Subject: get announce (Note: the software looks at the subject line, and ignores the body of the message).
Gopher accessibility: The archive may be accessed via a gopher: gopher econwpa.wustl.edu

ZAMFIELD'S WONDERFULLY INCOMPLETE, COMPLETE INTERNET BBS LIST
Description: Zamfield's Wonderfully Incomplete, Complete Internet BBS List, compiled by Thomas Kreeger, contains information about Internet-accessible bulletin board systems, including descriptions of the topics covered on each board.
Subjects covered: Internet; resource guides
How to access: ftp to hydra.uwo.ca and change to the directory called /libsoft. The filename is internet__bbs.txt.

ZINE LIST
Description: Zine List is a list of electronic fanzines updated periodically and posted to Net__Info@gibbs.oit.unc.edu and Usenet newsgroups, such as alt.zines, alt.etext, alt.internet.services, and rec.mag.
Subjects covered: alternative literature; popular culture
Editorial contact: John Labovitz
Internet: johnl@netcom.com
How to access: This list can also be obtained via anonymous FTP from netcom.com as ''/pub/johnl/zines/e-zine-list'', and via email (either single issues or subscriptions) from e-zines-request@netcom.com.
Additional information: For those of you not acquainted with the zine world, ''zine'' is short for either ''fanzine'' or ''magazine,'' depending on your point of view. Zines are generally produced by one person or a small group of people, done often for fun or personal reasons, and tend to be irreverent, bizarre, and/or esoteric. Zines are not ''mainstream'' publications -- they generally do not contain advertisements (except, sometimes, advertisements for other zines), do not have a large subscriber base, and are generally not produced to make a profit.

Section 4. Freenets and Other Community-based Information Services

AKRON FREE-NET
Subjects covered: freenets; community information services
Editorial contact: Anne S. McFarland
Law Library, University of Akron, Akron, OH 44325-2902
Tel: 216-972-6352
Internet: R1ASM@VM1.CC.UAKRON.EDU
Additional information: Now being organized.

ASTEC COMPUTING
Subjects covered: freenets; community information services
Editorial contact: Joseph A. Askins
Arizona Community Computing, Telecommunication Services, Arizona State University, Box 870201, Tempe, AZ 85287-0201
Tel: 602-965-5985
Internet: JOE.ASKINS@ASU.EDU
Additional information: Now being organized.

BCA FREE-NET
Subjects covered: freenets; community information services
Editorial contact: Fred Janofski
Battle Creek Unlimited, Inc., 10856 East MN Avenue, Galesburg, MI 49053
Tel: 616-961-3676
Internet: FredJ@AOL.COM
Additional information: Now being organized.

BIG SKY TELEGRAPH
Subjects covered: community information services; K-12 information services
Net address for operations: bigsky.bigsky.dillon.mt.us (192.231.192.1); modem: (406) 683-7680; 1200 baud
Editorial contact: Frank Odasz
Internet: franko@bigsky.dillon.mt.us
How to access: Login as bbs.
Additional information: Uses SCO Unix on a 386, running XBBS software.

BUFFALO FREE-NET
Subjects covered: freenets; community information services
Net address for operations: freenet.buffalo.edu (128.205.3.99); modem (716) 645-6128
Fee: None
Editorial contact: James finamore
Tel: (716) 877-8800; ext 451

Internet: finamore@ubvms.cc.buffalo.edu
How to access: Login as freeport
Additional information: Uses Sun OS and Freeport software.

CALIFORNIA ONLINE RESOURCES FOR EDUCATION (CORE)
Subjects covered: community information services; k-12 information services
Net address for operations: eis.calstate.edu
Editorial contact: Keith Vogt
Internet: Kvogt@eis.calstate.edu
How to access: Logon as ctp.
Additional information: Uses a Sun workstation.

CAPACCESS (THE NATIONAL CAPITAL AREA PUBLIC ACCESS NETWORK)
Description: CapAccess carries information files provided by local organizations and individuals, private electronic mail, locally-defined forums (news groups) Internet-linked electronic mail, selected access to Internet resources and sites, and a user directory. Other subjects covered include: K-12 education, library, government, social services, and a wide range of topics and sub-topics of interest to local audience. Much information is also contributed by its members.
Subjects covered: freenets; community information services
Net address for operations: cap.gwu.edu
Net address for questions or submissions: info@cap.gwu.edu
Established: July 1992
1300+
Sponsor: CapAccess is an independent, 501-(c)3 non-profit corporation in the District of Columbia. It was received major support from George Washington University and the Corporation for Public Broadcasting.
Host: George Washington University (technical host)
Editorial contact: Taylor Walsh
c/o George Washington University 2121 Eye St. NW, Suite 503
Washington, DC 20052.
Tel: 202-986-2065
Fax: 202-994-0709
Internet: twalsh@cap.gwu.edu
Copyright statement: All registered users sign an agreement in which they agree not to violate copyright restrictions; in which they acknowledge they have rights to material they post on the service. CapAccess does not copyright anything on the system; in discussion areas, users "own their own words."

How to access: Phone: 202-785-1523 Comm settings: 8-1-none
Full duplex; VT100 preferable Internet (telnet): cap.gwu.edu
Guest access:
login = guest password = visitor
(no email, forums, or Internet services)

CHIPPEWA VALLEY FREE-NET

Subjects covered: freenets; community information services
Editorial contact: Steve Marquardt
McIntyre Library, University of Wisconsin-Eau Claire, 105 Garfield Avenue, Eau Claire, WI 54702-5010
Tel: 715-836-3715
Internet: SMARQUAR@uwec.edu
Additional information: Now being organized.

CIAO! FREE-NET

Description: CIAO! Free-Net covers services similar to existing Free-Nets but with a Canadian bias.
Subjects covered: freenets; community information services
Net address for operations: LISTSERV@CIAO.trail.bc.ca
Net address for questions or submissions:
help@CIAO.trail.bc.ca
Established: September 1993
The system is just developing; no count of users is available.
Fee: None
Sponsor: School District #11 (Trail), 2079 Columbia Ave., Trail, B.C., V1R 1K7 Canada.
Host: School District #11 (Trail), 2079 Columbia Ave., Trail, B.C., V1R 1K7 Canada.
Editorial contact: Ken McClean
School District #11 (Trail), 2079 Columbia Ave., Trail, B.C., V1R 1K7 Canada.
Tel: (604)368-6434
Fax: (604)364-2470
Internet: kmcclean@CIAO.trail.bc.ca
Internet: mshowers@CIAO.trail.bc.ca
Commercial services offered through this Freenet: Yes.
How to access: Access freenet through menu system.
Related files: Mining database to be developed

CLEVELAND FREE-NET

Subjects covered: freenets; community information services
Net address for operations: freenet-in-a.cwru.edu, freenet-in-b.cwru.edu, freenet-in-c.cwru, edu; modem: (216) 368-3888
Sponsor: Case Western Reserve University, Cleveland, OH.
Editorial contact: Jeff Gumpf
Internet: jag@po.cwru.edu
Additional information: Uses Sun 6/690 running FreePort software.

COLUMBIA ONLINE INFORMATION NETWORK (COIN)

Subjects covered: freenets; community information services
Net address for operations: bigcat.missouri.edu
Editorial contact: Bill Mitchell
Internet: ccwam@mizzou1.missouri.edu
How to access: Login as guest
Additional information: Uses a Sun workstation running FreePort, Gopher, Pico, and Pine software.

COMSERVE COMMJOBS

Description: Comserve CommJobs is an electronic news service carrying information career opportunities in communication studies. Comserve is a suite of unique services that together comprise the oldest, largest, and most comprehensive online disciplinary center on the nets. The Comserve database contains over 300 individual files related to communication.
Subjects covered: communications; telecommunications; computer hardware and software
Net address for operations: comserve@vm.ecs.rpi.edu
Net address for questions or submissions: Support@Rpiecs or Support@Vm.Ecs.Rpi.Edu
Sponsor: Comserve
How to access: Send the email message: Join CommJobsYour__First__Name Your__Last__Name to comserve@vm.ecs.rpi.edu or contact Support@Rpiecs or Support@Vm.Ecs.Rpi.Edu
How to submit: Support@Rpiecs or Support@Vm.Ecs.Rpi.Edu

COMSERVE NEWSLINE

Description: Comserve Newsline is an electronic news service carrying information about the field of communication studies. Comserve is a suite of unique services that together comprise the oldest, largest, and most comprehensive online disciplinary center on the nets. The Comserve database contains over 300 individual files related to communication.
Subjects covered: communications; telecommunications; computer hardware and software
Net address for operations: comserve@vm.ecs.rpi.edu
Net address for questions or submissions: Support@Rpiecs or Support@Vm.Ecs.Rpi.Edu
Sponsor: Comserve
How to access: Send the email message: Join Newsline Your__First__Name Your__Last__Name to comserve@vm.ecs.rpi.edu or contact Support@Rpiecs or Support@Vm.Ecs.Rpi.Edu
How to submit: Support@Rpiecs or Support@Vm.Ecs.Rpi.Edu

CONFLICTNET

Description: ConflictNet is part of IGC, the Institute for Global Communications, and provides a wide range and variety of information on peace issues internationally.
Subjects covered: peace studies; international studies; political science
Fee: Yes. Various levels of membership fees are available.
Telnet to igc.org (domain name igc.org), type new at the login prompt and hit return at the password prompt. This brings the user into the registration program.
Commercial organization: Yes, non-profit.
How to access: Telnet igc.org or 192.82.108.1 Enter ''new'' at the ''login'' prompt, then <ENTER/RETURN> at the ''password'' prompt.
Related files: EcoNet, PeaceNet, ConflictNet, and HomeoNet, all part of the Institute for Global Communications' services are accessible if one is a subscribing member of this list.

DAYTON FREE-NET

Subjects covered: freenets; community information services
Editorial contact: Patricia Vendt, 040 Library Annex, Wright State University, Dayton, OH 45435
Tel: 513-873-4035
Internet: pvendt@desire.wright.edu

Additional information: Now being organized.

DENVER FREE-NET

Subjects covered: freenets; community information services
Net address for operations: freenet.hsc.colorado.edu
(140.226.1.8); modem: (303) 270-4865
Editorial contact: Drew Mirque
Tel: (303) 270-4300
Internet: drew@freenet.hsc.colorado.edu
How to access: Login as guest.
Additional information: Uses a Sun workstation running Free-Port software.

ECONET

Description: EcoNet is part of IGC, the Institute for Global Communications, and provides a wide range and variety of information on ecology and environmental issues internationally.
Subjects covered: environmental studies; ecology
Fee: Yes. Various levels of membership fees are available.
Telnet to igc.org (domain name igc.org), type new at the login prompt and hit return at the password prompt. This brings the user into the registration program.
Commercial organization: Yes, non-profit.
How to access: Telnet igc.org or 192.82.108.1 Enter "new" at the "login" prompt, then <ENTER/RETURN> at the "password" prompt.
Related files: EcoNet, PeaceNet, ConflictNet, and HomeoNet, all part of the Instititue for Global Communications' services are accessible if one is a subscribing member of this list.

ERLANGEN FREE-NET

Subjects covered: freenets; community information services
Editorial contact: Walter Kugeman
FIM Psychologie, Maximiliansplatz 3, 8520 Erlangen, Germany
Tel: 09131-85-4735
Additional information: Now being organized.

FREE-NET BAYREUTH

Subjects covered: freenets; community information services
Editorial contact: Wolfgang Kiessling
Universitat Bayreuth, Universitats Str. 30, 8580 Bayreuth, Germany
Tel: 0921/553134
Internet: Wolfgang.Kiessling@Uni-Bayreuth,de
Additional information: Now being organized.

GAINESVILLE FREE-NET

Subjects covered: freenets; community information services
Editorial contact: David R. Pokorney
3131 Southwest First Avenue, Gainesville, FL 32607
Tel: 904-392-2061
Internet: poke@ufl.edu
Additional information: Now being organized.

HEARTLAND FREE-NET

Description: Heartland Free-net (HFN) was designated as a not for profit corporation organized to provide a wide range of community information free of charge to people and organizations of Central Illinois. Our current mission statement also reflects this purpose, "A not for profit organization developed to serve and enrich the public by providing a free non-commercial computer based system through which information and ideas are exchanged." Although primarily aimed at serving Central Illinois, the information can be accessed by any person in the state of Illinois, or the world, who has telephone service. Heartland Free-net carries Central Illinois community Information, including data on the greater Peoria Area and the Bloomington/Normal area. Access to nine other Free-nets and to nine selected Internet databases is also offered. The easy to use, extensive information database of Heartland Free-net is available to the public 24 hours a day. Access to all information is through a computer and modem either from homes, businesses, or public access terminals in 32 sites in Central Illinois. Information currently targets Peoria, Illinois but will soon contain information about the communities of Bloomington/Normal as HFN moves to provide toll-free access to this twin city area 40 miles away from Peoria. Public access sites include 27 Illinois Valley Library System Libraries, Peoria County Courthouse, Friendship House, Goodwill Industries, Boys and Girls Club of Peoria, Independence Village, and Parkhill Medical Complex.
Subjects covered: freenets; community information services
Net address for operations: heartland.bradley.edu
Net address for questions or submissions:
xxadm@heartland.bradley.edu
Established: March 7, 1990
6500
Fee: None
Sponsor: Heartland Free-net, Inc. (a not for profit organization.) Bradley University is Internet Host Only. Historical sources of funding for the Heartland Free-net include Ameritech, Bielfeldt Foundation, Bradley University, Caterpillar, Inc., FOA - Illinois, IBM, Illinois State Bar Assn., Illinois Valley Library System, Peoria Journal Star, and Proctor Community Hospital.
Host: Jobst North, Technology Center #415 C, D
Peoria, IL 61625.
Editorial contact: Karen S. Eggert
Jobst North, Technology Center #415 C, D
Peoria, IL 61625.
Tel: (309) 677-2544
Internet: xxadm@heartland.bradley.edu
Commercial services offered through this Freenet: No.
How to access: To access, dial (309) 674-1100 or (309) 438-3200; both E, 7,1 Internet = heartland.bradley.edu Guest login = bbguest
Additional information: About the information sources available on the Heartland Free-net: The secret to the wide range of information available on HFN is the time and expertise contributed by the community. Organizations all over Illinois contribute information which is difficult or impossible to obtain from any other resources. Information on the network covers a large variety of topics; the listing of the complete menu is in the Administration Building area of the network and is 40 typed pages long. Topics covered include 113 areas of social services; a complete year long community calendar; business help resources and statistical information; extensive Senior information and resources; local government information, including addresses of all elected officials; legal data; medicine including chemical dependency, mental, and hospital health services; tax; primary, secondary, and post secondary educational opportunities; home and garden subjects; historical documents; environment and recycling; personal computer, religion and ethics; and travel infor-

mation. Users also have access to personal electronic mail and editorial areas. Experts in all fields from law to chemical dependency to Ham Radio operations to gardening contribute their time and expertise to respond to questions asked anonymously by the public. Specifically, the following organizations are currently contributing information and expertise to the Heartland Free-net: Mental Health Assn. Bloomington/Normal Visitor's and Convention Bureau Illinois State University Better Business Bureau American Red Cross Chamber of Commerce Peoria County Government Peoria City Government Congressman Robert H. Michel Peoria Park District Economic Development Council Peoria Small Business Develop. Center Proctor First Care Illinois Department of Employ. Security Social Security Administration Internal Revenue Service Illinois Eye Center.

HOMEONET
Description: HomeoNet is part of IGC, the Institute for Global Communications, and provides a wide range and variety of information on international issues.
Subjects covered: political science; international studies
Fee: Yes. Various levels of membership fees are available. Telnet to igc.org (domain name igc.org), type new at the login prompt and hit return at the password prompt. This brings the user into the registration program.
Commercial organization: Yes, non-profit.
How to access: Telnet igc.org or 192.82.108.1 Enter "new" at the "login" prompt, then <ENTER/RETURN> at the "password" prompt.
Related files: EcoNet, PeaceNet, ConflictNet, and HomeoNet, all part of the Instititue for Global Communications' services are accessible if one is a subscribing member of this list.

HORNET NESTS FREE-NET
Subjects covered: freenets; community information services
Editorial contact: Clarence Gibson, Jr.
Charlotte-Mecklenburg Organizing Committe, 4810 Horizon Circle, Charlotte, NC 28215
Tel: 704-532-2227
Internet: C.Givson6@Genie.Geis.Com
Additional information: Now being organized.

HURON VALLEY FREE-NET
Subjects covered: freenets; community information services
Editorial contact: Michael Todd Glazier
Michigan Public Computing Consortium, 819 Brown, Suite 4, Ann Arbor, MI 48104
Tel: 313-662-8374
Internet: michael.todd.glazier@umich.edu
Additional information: Now being organized.

LC MARVEL (LIBRARY OF CONGRESS MACHINE-ASSISTED REALIZATION OF THE VIRTUAL ELECTRONIC LIBRARY)
Description: The Library of Congress Machine-Assisted Realization of the Virtual Electronic Library (LC MARVEL) is now available over the Internet. The goal of LC MARVEL is to serve as the Campus-Wide Information System for the Library of Congress' staff and additionally to offer service to the U.S. Congress and constituents throughout the world.

Subjects covered: library and information science; Library of Congress
Net address for questions or submissions: TELNET TO: marvel.loc.gov
LOGON AS: marvel
Established: 1993
Sponsor: Library of Congress, Washington, DC 20540.
Host: Library of Congress, Washington, DC 20540.
How to access: LC MARVEL uses Gopher software and is therefore most easily accessed from another Gopher server or by using a PC-based Gopher client. POINT TO: marvel.loc.gov PORT 70 (140.147.2.15). Although direct telnet access is available, only 10 simultaneous external connections will be supported initially. We recommend accessing LC MARVEL through other Gopher servers or by using a PC-based Gopher client, because no usage restrictions are imposed. For direct connection, TELNET TO: marvel.loc.gov LOGON AS: marvel
How to submit: Please address all comments and reports of any technical problems experienced when using the system to: lcmarvel@seq1.loc.gov

LOCIS: LIBRARY OF CONGRESS INFORMATION SYSTEM
Description: LOCIS is the Library of Congress' online access catalog. It includes books, serials, maps, and access to subject terms lists. LOCIS is available for on-site researchers during all hours LC is open. For researchers using LOCIS over the Internet, the following hours apply: (all times US eastern; closed national holidays) Mon-Fri: 6:30am-9:30pm Sat: 8:00am-5:00pm Sun: 1:00pm-5:00pm The Library of Congress Information System (LOCIS) consists of two systems: (1) SCORPIO provides browsable indexes, set creation, boolean combinations, advanced limiting features, and individual word searching in some files; (2) MUMS provides searching for individual words, searching on some numbers, left-match "compression key" searching, boolean combinations, and several advanced techniques. You can combine the searching features of both systems. HELP screens exist for most files and commands.
Subjects covered: Library of Congress; online public access catalogs
Net address for operations: LOCIS.LOC.GOV
Established: 1993
How to access: Using telnet to access LOCIS: Most college and university computers have telnet service. Telnet is a way to log onto remote computers (in this case, LOC.GOV = the Library of Congress). To log on, you need an account name (in this case LOCIS). (Usually you need a password too, but not here.) Exactly which procedure you use depends on the type of mainframe you have: VAX ("VMS"), IBM ("VM" or "CMS") or UNIX. Telnet to LOCIS.LOC.GOV or else try TELNET 140.147.254.3 or try TN3270 140.147.254.3 (a) If you get: the telnet> prompt, try: open 140.147.254.3 1

LORAIN COUNTY FREE-NET
Subjects covered: freenets; community information services
Net address for operations: freenet.lorain.oberlin.edu (132.162.32.99); modem (216) 366-9721
Editorial contact: Paul Boguski
Internet: boguski@freenet.lorain.oberlin.edu
How to access: Login as guest.
Additional information: Uses a Sun workstation running Free-Port software.

LOS ANGELES FREE-NET (CENTRAL)

Subjects covered: freenets; community information services
Editorial contact: Malcolm Sharp
University of Southern California, School of Public Administration, Los Angeles, CA 90089-0041
Tel: 213-740-0369
Additional information: Now being organized.

LOS ANGELES FREE-NET (VALLEY)

Subjects covered: freenets; community information services
Editorial contact: Avrum Z. Bluming
Hematology-Oncology Group of the San Fernando Valley, 16311 Ventura Blvd., Suite 780, Encino, CA 91436
Tel: 818-981-3818
Internet: aa359@cleveland.freenet.edu
Additional information: Now being organized.

MEDINA COUNTY FREENET

Description: Medina County FreeNet carries resources that are primarily local in nature. Email; electronic contact to some government agencies, such as Ohio Bureau of Employment, Cooperative Extension Office, County Engineers and our congressional representative Sherrod Brown; Online Library and reference information, Special interest groups such as the Kennel Club, Society for the Handicapped, Computer user groups, etc.; Congressional Record, Hermes Project, USA Today newpaper, Public Kiosk, and other local interest information. The Medina County FreeNet is a county run and operated electronic information system. The system is a 501c3, managed by a board of directors elected by the users. The sysops and coordinators are all volunteers.
Subjects covered: freenets; community information services
Established: April 1990
1780
Fee: None
Sponsor: Medina General Hospital,Medina County, District Library, P.O. Box 427,210 South Broadway, Medina, Ohio 44258-0427.
Host: Medina General Hospital,Medina County, District Library, P.O. Box 427,210 South Broadway, Medina, Ohio 44258-0427.
Editorial contact: Dennis C. Hoops
Medina General Hospital,Medina County, District Library, P.O. Box 427,210 South Broadway, Medina, Ohio 44258-0427.
Tel: 216-722-3732
Fax: 216-725-2053
Internet: ac282@cleveland.freenet.edu
Technical contact: Gary Linden
Medina General Hospital,Medina County, District Library, P.O. Box 427,210 South Broadway, Medina, Ohio 44258-0427.
Tel: 216-722-3732
Fax: 216-722-7008
Commercial services offered through this Freenet: No.
How to access: The system is menu driven. For guest, at the login prompt type in lower case "fnguest" (with out quotations)
Access policy: Policy statements are sent upon registration.

NATIONAL CAPITAL FREENET

Subjects covered: freenets; community information services
Net address for operations: freenet.carleton.ca (134.117.1.25); modem: (613) 780-3733
Editorial contact: David Sutherland
Tel: (613) 788-2600; ext. 3701
Internet: aa001@freenet.carleton.ca
How to access: Login as guest.
Additional information: Uses a Sun workstation running Free-Port software.

NORTH SHORE FREE-NET

Subjects covered: freenets; community information services
Editorial contact: Alan Wilson
4 Bracken Place, Elliot Lake, Ontario, Canada P5A 1L4
Tel: 705-848-5106
Internet: alanwils%vef@canrem.com
Additional information: Now being organized.

NORTH TEXAS FREE-NET

Subjects covered: freenets; community information services
Editorial contact: Ken Loss-Cutler
6440 N. Central Expressway, Suite 501, LB42, Dallas, TX 75206
Tel: 214-368-8987
Internet: bh562@cleveland.freenet.edu
Additional information: Now being organized.

OCEAN STATE FREE-NET

Subjects covered: freenets; community information services
Editorial contact: Howard Boksenbaum
Rhode Island Department of State Library Services, 300 Richmond Street, Providence, RI 02903
Tel: 401-277-2726
Additional information: Now being organized.

OKLAHOMA PUBLIC INFORMATION NETWORK

Subjects covered: freenets; community information services
Editorial contact: Denny Stephens
Oklahoma Library Technology Network/ODL, 200 NE 18th Street, Oklahoma City, OK 73105
Tel: 405-521-2505; ext. 277
Additional information: Now being organized.

ORANGE COUNTY FREE-NET

Subjects covered: freenets; community information services
Editorial contact: Kent D. Palmer
P.O. Box 8383, Orange, CA 92664-8383
Tel: 714-762-8551
Internet: palmer@world.std.com
Additional information: Now being organized.

PAC-NET

Subjects covered: freenets; community information services
Editorial contact: Robert Mathews

The Pacific Network Consortium, 1001 Wilder Avenue, Suite 805, Honolulu, HI 96822-2649
Tel: 808-533-3969
Internet: bm189@cleveland.freenet.edu
Additional information: Now being organized.

PALM BEACH FREE-NET
Subjects covered: freenets; community information services
Editorial contact: C. Bruce McClintic
279 Royal Poinciana Way, Palm Beach, FL 33480
Tel: 407-833-9777
Additional information: Now being organized.

PEACENET
Description: PeaceNet is part of IGC, the Institute for Global Communications, and provides a wide range and variety of information on peace issues internationally.
Subjects covered: peace studies; international studies; political science
Fee: Yes. Various levels of membership fees are available. Telnet to igc.org (domain name igc.org), type new at the login prompt and hit return at the password prompt. This brings the user into the registration program.
Commercial organization: Yes, non-profit.
How to access: Telnet igc.org or 192.82.108.1 Enter "new" at the "login" prompt, then <ENTER/RETURN> at the "password" prompt.
Related files: EcoNet, PeaceNet, ConflictNet, and HomeoNet, all part of the Instititue for Global Communications' services are accessible if one is a subscribing member of this list.

POUDRE-R1 GOPHER INFORMATION SERVICE
Subjects covered: community information services; k-12 information services
Editorial contact: Greg Redder
Internet: redder@lobo.rmh.pr1.k12.co.us
How to access: Gopher to lobo.rmh.pr1.k12.co.us (164.104.30.2) No telnet. Guest login.
Additional information: Uses Gopher software running on an IBM RS/6000 model 320H running the AIX (Unix) operating system.

PRAIRENET
Subjects covered: freenets; community information services
Editorial contact: Ann P. Bishop
Graduate School of Library & Information Science, University of Illinois at Urbana-Champaign, 426 David Kinley Hall, 1407 West Gregory Drive, Urbana, IL 61801
Tel: 217-244-3299
Internet: bishop@alexia.lis.uiuc.edu
Additional information: Now being organized.

SANTA BARBARA RAIN
Subjects covered: freenets; community information services
Editorial contact: Timothy Tyndall
RAIN Coordination Committee, 27 E. Victoria Street, Santa Barbara, CA 93101

Tel: 805-564-5635; 805-967-5153
Internet: rain%engrhub@hub.ucsb.edu
Additional information: Now being organized.

SEATTLE COMMUNITY NETWORK
Subjects covered: freenets; community information services
Editorial contact: Douglas Schuler
Seattle Community Network, P.O. Box 85481, Seattle, WA 98145
Tel: 206-865-3832
Internet: douglas@atc.boeing.com
Additional information: Now being organized.

SENDIT NORTH DAKOTA: NORTH DAKOTA'S K-12 EDUCATION TELECOMMUNICATION NETWORK
Subjects covered: community information services; K-12 information services
Net address for operations: sendit.nodak.edu (134.129.105.1)
Editorial contact: Gleason Sackmann
Internet: sackman@sendit.nodak.edu
How to access: Login as bbs with password sendit2me
Additional information: Uses a NeXT workstation running FreePort software.

SLO COUNTY FREE-NET
Subjects covered: freenets; community information services
Editorial contact: Phil Wagner
1470 Ironbark Street, San Luis Obispo, CA 93401
Tel: 805-544-7328
Internet: pwagner@oboe.calpoly,edu
Additional information: Now being organized.

SUNCOAST FREE-NET
Subjects covered: freenets; community information services
Editorial contact: Marilyn Mulla
Tampa-Hillborough County Public Library, 900 N. Ashley Drive, Tampa, FL 33602
Tel: 813-273-3714
Internet: MULLAM@FIRNVX.FIRN.EDU
Additional information: Now being organized.

TALLAHASSEE FREE-NET
Subjects covered: freenets; community information services
Net address for operations: freenet.fsu.edu (144.174.128.43)
Editorial contact: Hilbert Levitz
Tel: (904) 644-1796
Internet: levitz@cs.fsu.edu
How to access: Login as visitor.
Additional information: Uses an IBM workstation running AIX and their own software (modified from VA PEN).

TENNESSEE VALLEY FREE-NET
Subjects covered: freenets; community information services
Editorial contact: Billy Ray Wilson
P.O. Box 201, Huntsville, AL 35804
Tel: 205-544-3849

Additional information: Now being organized.

TRIANGLE FREE-NET

Description: Triangle Free-Net's mission is to provide free, computer-based services connecting local people to one another and to local information. Triangle Free-Net coordinators are: dan.eddleman@launchpad.unc.edu; (919) 929-7220; judy_ hallman@unc.edu; (919) 962-9107 (w); bill.hutchins@launchpad.unc.edu; (919) 968-4292; jrsunc@uncmvs.oit.unc.edu; (Jeff Surles); (919) 966-2956 (w).
Subjects covered: freenets; community information services
Net address for questions or submissions: Judy_ Hallman@unc.edu
Established: 1993
Fee: None
Editorial contact: Judy Hallman
Office of Information Technology, CB# 3460, 311 Wilson Library, University of North Carolina, Chapel Hill, NC 27599-2460
Tel: (919) 962-9107
Fax: (919) 962-5604
Internet: Judy_Hallman@unc.edu
Technical contact: Bill Hutchins
5605 Brisbane Drive, Chapel Hill, NC 27514.
Tel: (919) 968-4292
Internet: Bill_Hutchins@launchpad.unc.edu
How to access: To subscribe to any of the Triangle lists, send to listserv@gibbs.oit.unc.edu the following message: SUBSCRIBE listname yourfirstname yourlastname
For example, subscribe rtpfreenet Judy Hallman
The subject of the message is not important; it is ignored.
How to unsubscribe: You may unsubscribe at any time by sending to listserv@gibbs.oit.unc.edu the following message: UNSUBSCRIBE listname
Related files: For these lists, the sender does NOT receive a copy of the message from the list, and the lists return a reply to the e-mail address that sent the original message, not everyone on the list. For more information about these discussion groups, please contact: Judy Hallman (judy_hallman@unc.edu), (919) 962-9107 Office of Information Technology, 311 Wilson Library, CB# 3460 University of North Carolina, Chapel Hill, NC 27599-3460. RTPFREENET (list) Messages sent to rtpfreenet@gibbs.oit.unc.edu (or rtpfreenet@unc.edu) go to more than 100 people who are interested in keeping informed about the progress of a Free-Net for the Research Triangle Park area, called the Triangle Free-Net. TRIANGLE.FREENET (news group) Triangle.freenet is a Usenet Network News discussion group. Messages sent to the RTPFREENET listserver are automatically posted to the triangle.freenet news group and vice versa. TF-DATA (list) Messages sent to tf-data@gibbs.oit.unc.edu (or tf-data.unc.edu) go to the individuals who are responsible for identifying and entering into the system the data that will be available in the Triangle Free-Net. Chair: Tom Hocking (starman@unc.edu). Co-Chair: Chris Tully (cptully@med.unc.edu). TF-FUND (list) Messages sent to tf-fund@gibbs.oit.unc.edu (or tf-fund@unc.edu) go to the individuals who are responsible for business and financial planning for the Triangle Free-Net. Chair: Kevin Gamble (kgamble@sire.ces.ncsu.edu) Co-Chair: Dan Eddleman (dan.eddleman@launchpad.unc.edu) TF-OPS (list) Messages sent to tf-ops@gibbs.oit.unc.edu (or tf-ops@unc.edu) go to the individuals responsible for designing the user interface and operating the Triangle Free-Net. Chair: Gregor Kohlbach

(gke@nccibm1.bitnet) Co-Chair: Pat Langelier (pat_ langelier@unc.edu) TF-PUB (list) Messages sent to tf-pub@gibbs.oit.unc.edu (or tf-pub@unc.edu) go to the individuals who are responsible
Gopher accessibility: We plan to use Gopher and WAIS in our initial system, WorldWideWeb a little later.

TRISTATE ONLINE

Description: TSO is a community-accessed bulletin board system with over a hundred subject areas and limited access to the Internet. Subjects range from business, law, government, medical, recreation, science, and technology.
Subjects covered: freenets; community information services
Net address for operations: cbos.uc.edu; modem: (513) 579-1990; 300/1200/2400 baud
Editorial contact: Michael King
TriState Online, 201 E. 4th Street, 102-2000, Cincinnati, OH 45201
Tel: (513) 397-1396
Fax: (513) 721-5147
Internet: sysadmin@cbos.uc.edu
Technical contact: Mark Powers
TriState Online, 201 E. 4th Street, 102-2000, Cincinnati, OH 45201
Fax: (513) 721-5147
Internet: powers@cbos.uc.edu
How to access: At the Enter Choice prompt, type CBOS. Login as visitor, with the PIN 9999, and press return at the password prompt.
Additional information: Uses a Tandem platform, running Guardian operating system with Betex software.

TUSCALOOSA FREE-NET

Subjects covered: freenets; community information services
Editorial contact: David K. Brennan
Tuscaloosa Public Library, 1801 River Road, Tuscaloosa, AL 35401
Tel: 205-345-5820
Additional information: Now being organized.

UMASSK12: UNIVERSITY OF MASSACHUSETTS/AMHERST K-12 INFORMATION SYSTEM

Subjects covered: community information services; K-12 information services
Net address for operations: k12.ucs.umass.edu (128.119.175.2)
Editorial contact: Dan Blanchard
Internet: blanchard@nic.umass.edu
How to access: Login as guest.
Additional information: Uses a DEX-5000/133 running a version of FreePort software.

VICTORIA FREE-NET

Subjects covered: freenets; community information services
Net address for operations: freenet.victoria.bc.ca (134.87.16.100); modem: (604) 595-2300
Editorial contact: Gareth Shearman
Tel: (604) 385-4302
Internet: shearman@freenet.victoria.bc.ca

How to access: Login as guest, or gopher to freenet.victoria.bc.ca.
Additional information: Uses a Sun workstation running Free-Port softrware.

VIRGINIA'S PUBLIC EDUCATION NETWORK (PEN)

Subjects covered: community information services; K-12 information services
Net address for operations: vdoe386.vak12ed.edu
Editorial contact: Harold Cothern
Internet: hcothern@vdoe386.vak12ed.edu
How to access: Login as guest with password guest.
Additional information: Uses a RISC 6000 with AIX running PEN software.

WELLINGTON CITYNET

Subjects covered: community information services; freenets
Net address for operations: kosmos.wcc.govt.nz
(192.54.130.39)
Editorial contact: Richard Naylor
Tel: +64-4-801-3303
Internet: rich@tosh.wcc.govt.nz
How to access: Gopher to gopher.wcc.govt.nz. No telnet. Guest login.
Additional information: Uses gopher software.

YOUNGSTOWN FREE-NET

Description: The Youngstown Free-Net offers e-mail, Usenet news, telnet service, dozens of local special interest groups, full text of dozens of documents, full text of the Federal budget, daily electronic issues of USA-TODAY, and more. There are several hundred electronic texts available, a comprehensive list is not available due to its size and the fact that it changes every week as more material becomes available. Contact Lou Anschuetz.
Subjects covered: freenets; community information services
Net address for operations: lou@yfn.ysu.edu
Net address for questions or submissions: lou@yfn.ysu.edu
Established: 1987
9,500
Fee: None
Sponsor: St. Elizabeth Hospital, 1044 Belmont Ave., Youngstown, OH.
Host: Lou Anschuetz, c/o Computer Center, Youngstown State University, Youngstown, OH 44555.
Editorial contact: Lou Anschuetz
Computer Center, Youngstown State University, Youngstown, OH 44555.
Tel: 216-742-3075
Internet: lou@yfn.ysu.edu
Commercial services offered through this Freenet: Yes.
How to access: Login to yfn.ysu.edu as ''visitor'' - all is menu driven. Local phone access is via 216-742-3072, hit enter several times, login as per internet access.
Related files: We do not support ftp.
Additional information: It should be noted that YFN is the model for ALL Free-Net systems. YFN is also the host site for ACADEMY 1. There are, at last count, some 1500 services, items, etc.

Section 5. Campus-Wide Information Systems

The following is information from the listserver CWIS-L@WUVMD.BITNET, prepared by Judy Hallman (Judy__Hallman@unc.edu), UNC-Chapel Hill, August 20, 1993. The editors of ON INTERNET wish to thank Ms. Hallman for her participation in this project.

Introduction
This list of Internet-accessible campus-wide information systems is updated on a regular basis online. You can retrieve the most updated form of this list by anonymous ftp to sunsite.unc.edu; change directories with the command: cd pub/docs/about-the-net/cwis and retrieve the file with the following command: get cwis-l (that's the letter l). Or you may point your gopher to:

Name = cwis-l list of campus wide information services connectable from the Internet Type = 0 Port = 70 Path = 0/.pub/docs/about-the-net/cwis/cwis-l Host = sunsite.unc.edu

Using UNC's laUNCHpad system or LIBS on the UNC-CH VAX
The laUNCHpad System, offered by UNC-CH, can connect you to many of the information systems in this list. You may access laUNCHpad through telnet, using launchpad.unc.edu as the connection. For "username" type 'launch'. When you get laUNCHpad's menu, select item 3, "On-line Information Systems (LIBTEL)."

Or you can use similar software on the UNC-CH DEC VAX computer's VMS service. Connect to uncvx1.oit.unc.edu; for "username" type LIBTEL. When you get the LIBS menu, select item 3 "Campus-wide Information Systems."

The two systems are quite similar, presenting essentially the same information using different menus. LaUNCHpad automates more of the connection steps.

Gophers
Many CWISs are done in Gopher software (from the University of Minnesota). Once you connect to one gopher, you usually have access to all the others that are registered. If you do not have local access to a gopher, here are just two of many you can telnet to (emulate a vt100):

consultant.micro.umn.edu (134.84.132.3) -- home of the gopher! login as gopher

gopher.unc.edu -- the UNC SunSITE gopher login as gopher

UNITED STATES

1. Appalachian State University conrad.appstate.edu (152.10.1.1) Login as info. Emulate a VT100. Hardware/software: DEC/VTX Contact: Ernest Jones <jonesel@appstate.bitnet>

2. Arizona State University PEGASUS and ASEDD asuvm.inre.asu.edu (192.67.165.36) login as helloasu Use tn3270. Hardware/Software: Running PNN News Network Software under VM/CMS (with Profs and FOCUS). Contact: Joy Kramer <iejxk@asuvm.inre.asu.edu> Contains two databases: PErsonal Guide to ASU Stuff (PEGASUS) and Arizona State Economic Development Database (ASEDD).

3. Clemson University eureka.clemson.edu (130.127.8.3) Login as public. Emulate a VT100. Hardware/software: DEC/VTX Contact: Amy Slankard <amy@clust1.clemson.edu> Contains: Weather for SC, NC, and GA; economics; plants; animals; engineering; food; home, health, family and youth.

4. Clemson University clemson.clemson.edu (130.127.8.105) No login (Press ENTER at the signon screen). Hardware/software: HDS/BRS Search Use TN3270 Select F (DORIS) from the menu Contact: Ches Martin <ches@clemson.clemson.edu> Contains organizational minutes, faculty/staff/student directory, stores catalog, job postings, computer resources.

5. Columbia University columbianet.columbia.edu (128.59.40.154 and also .158) No login required. Emulate nothing in particular (any termcap entry). Hardware/software: Sun (Unix), homegrown cwis software, Oliver Laumann's "screen" for simultaneous viewing of several services, and Don Libes "expect" for automatic logins. Contact: David Millman <dsm@columbia.edu> Contains: events calendar, course information, staff & student & classified directories, library catalogs, encyclopedia, job postings, gateway to departmental timesharing, handbooks, reports, policies, office hours, newswire, weather, student grades (spring '93), student placement interview schedules (summer '93).

Features: localized "menu-scan" skips intermediate menus; several full-text searchable areas; two-way gopher gateway (can get to other gophers, and most of this cwis is one).

Gopher access: gopher.cc.columbia.edu, port 71

Some services require authentication. Some are location-based (i.e., you can't get them from there), and some others require an account & password. But most of the information is publicly available.

6. Cornell CUINFO cuinfo.cornell.edu Connect to port 300. Use telnet or tn3270. Different versions of telnet or tn3270 have different syntax for defining the port. The following are the commonest: TELNET cuinfo.cornell.edu 300 TELNET

cuinfo.cornell.edu::300 or TELNET cuinfo.cornell.edu..300 Hardware/software: VM/CMS; IBM S/370 assembler; locally written Contact: Lynne Personius <jrn@cornellc.bitnet> Contains: Uncle Ezra (Electronic Counselor, first program of its kind, a must see), directories, ski reports, jobs, computing information, descriptions of current patents held by Cornell, various newsletters, weather.

7. Drake University acad.drake.edu Login as DRAKEINFO. Emulate a VT100. Hardware/software: DEC/VTX Contact: George Miller <gmiller@acad.drake.edu>.

8. Drexel University - Drexel Online Gopher to gopher.drexel.edu Hardware/software: Gopher and MIT's TechInfo system. Contact: Chris Swisher <swisher@duvm.ocs.drexel.edu>.

9. Holy Cross hcacad.holycross.edu (192.80.94.49) Login as view; password is view. Emulate (a VT100 or better) Hardware/software: (DEC/VTX) Contact: Ralph Fasano <fasano@hcacad.holycross.edu> Contains: News & Entertainment, Campus Libraries, Athletics, Holy Cross Catalog, About Holy Cross, Directories, Food Services, Academic Programs, Student Handbook, Rights & Rules, Clubs & Organizations, Course Guide, Other Misc Topics: Weather, News, Etc.

10. Hood College - HoodInfo merlin.hood.edu login as hoodinfo Gopher to merlin.hood.edu, port 9999 Hardware/software: VMS-based Contact: Eric Gallagher <egallagher@nimue.hood.edu> Contains: Federal employment database and the Career directory.

11. Lafayette Integrated, Networked Campus - LINC lafibm.lafayette.edu (139.147.8.4) Use telnet or tn3270. When you see the LINC logo, ignore the ALT-L advice and clear the logo by pressing Enter. On next screen, instead of logging on, type DIAL MUSIC (case does not matter). On login screen that appears, use GUEST as ID, and GUEST as password. Hardware/software: IBM 9375 running MUSIC/SP Contact: Patrick Ciriello <ciri@lafayacs.bitnet>.

12. Lehigh University, Bethlehem, PA LUNA ns2.cc.lehigh.edu (128.180.2.33) login as guest password lehigh Emulate VT100 use ESC 1 for F1, ESC 2 for F2, etc. Hardware/software: IBM RS/6000s using LUNA software and Oracle Contact: Timothy Foley <tjf0@lehigh.edu> Contains: Over 350 local bulletin boards and conferences maintained by individual departments throughout the campus, On-line software library of public domain programs, Access to Usenet News, Gopher Server (gopher.cc.lehigh.edu) also available to access LUNA information.

13. Library of Congress Machine-Assisted Realization of the Virtual Electronic Library (LC MARVEL) Telnet: marvel.loc.gov (140.147.2.15) login as marvel (Only 10 simultaneous external connections supported initially) Gopher to: marvel.loc.gov port 70 Gopher access recommended (no simultaneous gopher access restrictions) Content contacts: Elizabeth Miller <emil@seq1.loc.gov> or Cheryl Graunke <cgra@seq1.loc.gov> Technical contact: Tom Littlejohn <tlit@seq1.loc.gov> Comments to: LC MARVEL Design Team <lcmarvel@seq1.loc.gov> Contains: LC MARVEL serves as the Campus-Wide Information System for the Library of Congress' staff and additionally offers service to the U.S. Congress and constituents throughout the world. Included on the

system: calendar of events, information on the reading rooms, online exhibits, arrangement of Internet-available "federal government information," congressional information, access to LOCIS (Library of Congress Information System), archives of USMARC listserv, full text of Z39.50 drafts, unique subject-oriented access to vast Internet resources, job vacancies, and much more. (See also Section 4 in this directory for LC MARVEL listing).

14. Michigan State University Gopher access: gopher.msu.edu, port 70 Contact: Rich Wiggins <rwwmaint@msu.edu> Contains: Basic elements of a CWIS, some in place, some being added. Now holds an online photo gallery, history of MSU, calendar of events, access to library catalog, index of social science database (ICPSR) holdings (index is >1M in size). Also contains information on computing, detailed documents on Gopher, complete Network & Database Resources folder, and an index of Gopher site names as well as a Veronica server.

15. Memphis State University msuvx2.memst.edu (141.225.1.3) Login as info. Emulate a VT100. Hardware/software: DEC/VTX Contact: Lynne Mclawhorn <lmclawhorn@msuvx1.memst.edu>.

16. Mississippi State University (MSUinfo) isis.msstate.edu (130.18.80.11) Login: msuinfo Terminal type: enter yours, most supported Hardware/software: SUN 4/490; UNIX/TechInfo Contact: Bennet George (georgeb@ur.msstate.edu) Contains: announcements, campus events, community events, continuing education offerings, jobs, recent press releases, research funding opportunities, fact book, faculty expertise list, etc.

17. MIT TechInfo (18.72.1.146) Accessible either via telnet, or via a native Macintosh, Unix or CMS client application. DOS and a X-Windows application are currently being tested.

For telnet access: telnet techinfo.mit.edu (18.72.1.146) No username/password is required. Once you're in, you can use upper or lower case commands. To exit the system, use the QUIT command.

For native Macintosh access: anonymous ftp to net-dist.mit.edu, look in the /pub/techinfo directory, fetch techinfo.hqx Binhex4 (public domain tool) required to decode the binary. Requires licensed MacTCP drivers to run.

For more information on our system: 1. Once inside TechInfo, documents in the "About TechInfo" folder will explain all the access methods, how to obtain source code, status of new initiatives, the TechInfo protocol, distributed provider capability and more. 2. Send mail to: techinfo@mit.edu.

18. New Mexico State University NMSU/INFO info.nmsu.edu (128.123.3.7) Login as info. Emulate a VT100. Hardware/software: DEC/VTX Contact: D. Brian Ormand <bormand@nmsuvm1.bitnet> or <bormand@nmsu.edu>.

19. North Carolina State University Happening! and InfoPoint Happenings!: happenings.ncsu.edu or 152.1.13.23 Login as info. Emulate a VT100. Hardware/software: DEC/VTX Contact: Harry Nicholos <harry_nicholos@ncsu.edu> Contains: The University Datebook (campus activities by date or keyword), The University Infobook (information about the University's colleges/schools/departments/admin units, as well as the Univer-

sity Bulletin, NCSU Wellness Program, Faculty & Students Senate Meeting Minutes), Faculty/Staff and Student Telephone Directories, Class/Course listing for both the current semester and the upcoming one, Jobs available at NCSU and the State of N.C., Computing Information, NCSU Libraries Information, and Newsletters and Journals, University Surplus Items, and much more!

InfoPoint gopher server: point gopher client to gopher.ncsu.edu, port 70 Contact: Harry Nicholos, harry_nicholos@ncsu.edu Contains majority of information found on Happenings!, as well as connections to other gopher servers at NCSU and around the world.

20. Northwestern University nuinfo.nwu.edu (129.105.113.241) login: nuinfo Hardware/Software: Sun Sparcstation, gopher server Contact Person: Tamara Iversen <nuinfo@nwu.edu> Contains: NUInfo contains the University's catalog, course descriptions and evaluations, information on housing, campus directories, events calendars, library catalog, local weather forecasts, entertainment and restaurant guides, and an index.

21. Notre Dame NDInfo vma.cc.nd.edu Use tn3270. On the "Command ==>" line, type NDInfo. Contact: ndinfo-l@vma.cc.nd.edu (ndinfo-l is an open listserver, you are welcome to join and send comments.

22. NYU ACF INFO system info.nyu.edu (information.nyu.edu) (128.122.138.142) Emulating a VT100 or better enables some additional suboptions Contact: Stephen Tihor <tihor@ACFcluster.nyu.edu> or <tihor@nyuacf.bitnet>.

23. Ohio State University oasis.acs.ohio-state.edu (128.146.216.15) Login as oasis. Contact: oasis@magnus.acs.ohio-state.edu. Contains: The current limited menu provides a listing of the Master Schedule of Classes for Ohio State. Additional menu items will be added in this non-login service in the near future.

24. Pennsylvania State University psuvm.psu.edu (128.118.56.2) >From a VM system, use TELNET; otherwise TN3270 (or equivalent). Enter EBB on the COMMAND line at logon (no userid or password). Hardware/software: VM/ESA 3090-600S system using Cornell's CUINFO Contact: Bob Fowles <rbf@psuvm.psu.edu> 814 865-4774 Contains: Local information and/or schedules about subjects and facilities such as: academic majors, sports, bookstores, campuses, cultural events, careers, computers, phone directories, food, funding, health, housing, libraries, policies and rules, recreation, religion, meetings, conferences, local events, weather forecasts, and student services.

25. Pennsylvania State University: PENpages College of Agriculture Internet address: psupen.psu.edu Login as: pnotpa No password is required Emulation: VT100 Hardware/software: DEC/VTX Contact: support@psupen.psu.edu Contents and Contributors:

PENpages is a full-text information service containing thousands of research-based fact sheets, news articles, newsletters, and reports. Information is entered by faculty and staff of the Pennsylvania State University, the Pennsylvania Department of Agriculture, the United States Department of Agriculture, the Center for Rural Elderly, and many cooperators nationwide.

Information is agricultural-based and consumer-oriented. Topics include: 4-H and youth development, agricultural education, agronomy; Dairy and animal science, engineering, entomology, family life and resource management, food safety, forest resources, gerontology, horticulture, human nutrition, pesticide education, plant pathology, poultry science, rural development, veterinary science, water quality, and many others. *NLTX PENpages is the home of a collection of national databases including: (1) MAPP-the Family and Economic Well-Being National Database which contains children-at-risk, youth-at-risk, family disrupt dislocation, family financial instability, and dependent elderly information. (2) Senior Series National Database contains gerontology information. (3) International Food and Nutrition Database contains information on disease prevention, food safety, health promotion, nutritional requirements, and eating disorders.

26. Pima Community College pimacc.pima.edu (144.90.1.8) Login as pimainfo. Emulate a VT100. Hardware/software: DEC/VTX Contact: Terry Loftus <tloftus@pimacc.pima.edu> or Al Camberos <acamberos@pimacc.pima.edu>.

27. Princeton News Network PNN pucc.princeton.edu (128.112.129.99) Use telnet or tn3270. When you see the VM 370 logo, clear it, and instead of logging on, enter pnn (case does not matter). Clear the information screen that appears. Hardware/software: VM/CMS -- locally written. A UNIX version and a Mac HyperCard version are up, running, and available. All versions (CMS, UNIX, HyperCard) are available to universities at no cost. Contact: Rita Saltz <rita@pucc.bitnet> System and Development: Howard Strauss <howard@pucc.bitnet>.

28. Purdue University THOR+ gopher to thorplus.lib.purdue.edu port 70 Hardware/software: gopher on SPARC 10 Contact: Carl Snow <gophadm@thorplus.lib.purdue.edu> Contains: THORplus is the top level node for access to Internet Gopher servers at Purdue. Presently under construction, THORplus is changing quite rapidly. Services include a link to the Purdue FTP server, images of the Computer Sciences Department faculty, technical reports of interest to computer scientists, the Purdue on line telephone directory, documents on water quality and livestock from the Purdue Extension Service and subject of pointers to internet resources.

29. Purdue University (SSINFO) oasis.cc.purdue.edu (128.210.7.41) Login as ssinfo Emulates vt52, vt100, vt220, adds, ansi, wyse50, hp150, xterm, reg20, z29 visual Hardware/Software Runs a bunch of C and INFORMIX programs under AIX Ver 3.2 on a RISC System 6000 Contact Balaji Ramakrishnan <barama@oasis.cc.purdue.edu> Contains: Purdue Phone Directory, Student Employment Oppurtunities, Tutor Directory, University Calendars, The Loan Counselor, Off Campus Housing, Final/Evening Examination Schedule, Boiler Connection (Provides information on mental/physical health & other student services), Renewing PUCC accounts.

30. Rutgers University info.rutgers.edu No password required Can be accessed from any microcomputer or terminal Hardware/software: written in lush (a public domain program) plus some own developed software. Ir runs in unix environment on a Sun sparkstation 2. Contact: Leny Struminger <struming@zodiac.rutgers.edu> Contains: university-wide ac-

tivities, courses catalogs, Faculty/Staff and students phone directory, computer services, libraries online catalog, weather, news, bus schedules, Rutgers University Press publications, fellowships and grants, dictionaries, etc.

31. Syracuse University PRISM/SUINFO Hardware/software: PRISM/SPIRES running under VM Contact: Bhaskaran Balakrishnan <bbalakri@suvm.bitnet> or <bbalakri@suvm..acs..syr.edu> For sites with tn3270 emulation:

telnet suvm.acs.syr.edu (128.230.1.47) For non-IBM sites running tn3270, the general format is:

tn3270 suvm.acs.syr.edu (Unix) telnet/tn3270 suvm.acs.syr.edu (VAX VMS)

For sites with only vt100 emulation (i.e, no tn3270):

telnet acsnet.syr.edu (128.230.1.21) Once connected, type: SUVM Enter VT100 for the terminal type At the SUVM logon screen, go to the

COMMAND = = = = > line and enter SUINFO Contains: Campus-Wide Information system: Class Schedule, Graduate and Undergraduate Catalog, Job Opportunities, Housing, Student Employment,.S.U. Art Collection database, Weather, etc. Others: ERIC database, HUMANIST discussion group archive, NOTIS-L discussion group archive.

32. University of Arkansas uafsysb.uark.edu (130.184.7.11) Login as info when prompted, enter terminal ID of 56 Hardware/software: IBM 4381-T92E running VM/ESA and Cornell's CUINFO module Contact: Susan Adkins <sa06037@uafsysb.bitnet> or <sa06037@uafsysb.uark.edu> Contains: Calendar of events, campus e-mail directory, and hours and services, CLASSES (Open academic class info), COMPUTE (Computing Services info), HPER (building hours and services, phsy-ed, recreation center), MUSEUM (University museum info and activities), README (general announcements and responses to Q&A received through system), CHECKS (student refund checks, dates if ready), COMMIT (Uni committees), CREDITU (UARK Federal Credit Union info), JOBS (University job openings), POLICIES (Policies and Prodecures, Fin and Adm), SUGGEST (Comments and Suggestions).

33. University of Chicago -- UCInfo Use a gopher client to access UCInfo at gopher.uchicago.edu port 70 Hardware/software: gopher on a Sun Sparc2 Contact: Don Goldhamer <dgoldhamer@uchicago.edu> Contains: campus directory, job openings, course offerings and other student information and links to numerous on-campus specialized gopher servers (Library, Law, Biological Sciences, etc.).

34. University of Colorado at Boulder culine.colorado.edu 852 (128.138.129.2 852) or culine.colorado.edu, then login as culine Hardware/software: modified version of PNN running on both VMS and Unix Emulate a VT100 Contact: Donna Pattee <pattee@spot.colorado.edu>.

35. University of Denver du.edu (130.253.1.4) Login as atdu Contact: Bob Stocker <bstocker@ducair.bitnet>.

36. University of Iowa panda.uiowa.edu (128.255.40.201) No login required. Hardware/software: Panda, which is compatible with Gopher, but with features added. Contact: isca@umaxc.weeg.uiowa.edu.

37. University of Kansas kufacts.cc.ukans.edu (129.237.1.30) Login as kufacts Several terminal types are supported but tn3270 support has not yet been implemented. Hardware/software: Constructed using a multipurpose hypertext browsing system, called Lynx, by Michael Grobe, Charles Rezac, and Lou Montulli Contact: Michael Grobe <grobe@kuhub.cc.ukans.edu>.

38. University of Maryland info.umd.edu Emulate a VT100 Contact: Janet McLeod <mcleod@umail.umd.edu>.

39. University of Michigan cts.merit.edu (35.1.48.149) Which Host: help Emulate a VT100 Contact: info@merit.edu.

40. University of Minnesota at Duluth ub.d.umn.edu (131.212.32.6) Login as info Emulate a vt100. Contact: Frank Simmons <fsimmons@ub.d.umn.edu> Contains: Over 700 documents ranging from athletic schedules to micro-computer prices to art gallery showing schedules. All commands are displayed at the bottom of each screen and separate on-line help is available. Keyword searching is available, although at this time only words in the titles of documents are used.

41. University of Minnesota Twin Cities (Minneapolis/St. Paul) terminal access: consultant.micro.umn.edu (134.84.132.3)

Login as gopher Emulate a vt100.

gopher client access:

configure your gopher client to use gopher.micro.umn.edu as the root gopher server. Gopher client software is available for Mac, PC, NeXT, Unix, X, VMS, and VM/CMS. Retrieve the software via anonymous ftp from bombox.micro.umn.edu; look in the /pub/gopher directory tree.

Contact: Gopher development team <gopher@bombox.micro.umn.edu>

The internet gopher system at the University of Minnesota contains links to gopher servers at over 120 other sites, as well as providing seamless access to anonymous ftp sites, Archie, and WAIS servers. Campus information for the University of Minnesota is available as are over 7000 computer Q&A items (full text searchable) and the student newspaper (the Minnesota Daily).

42. University of Nebraska-Lincoln crcvms.unl.edu (129.93.1.2) Login as INFO Emulate a VT100 Hardware/Software: DEC/Rdb/FMS Contact: Donna Liss <dliss@unlinfo.unl.edu> Contains: An on-line catalog of the University of Nebraska Press publications; campus calendar of events; organizational information; as well as campus and class information.

43. University of New Hampshire's WILDCAT wildcat.unh.edu (132.177.128.58) USERNAME: student (no password required) Control-z to log off VT100/VT200 terminal emulation Hardware/software: DEC/VTX Contact: Robin Tuttle (r__tuttle@unhh.unh.edu) Contains: phone directories, campus cal-

endar, job listings, off- campus housing list, undergraduate catalog, class schedules, newsletters, services and programs, rights
and rules of conduct, athletics and recreation information, activities and workshops.

44. University of New Mexico UNM_INFO unminfo.unm.edu
(129.24.8.235) Login as unminfo Contact: Art St. George
<stgeorge@unmb.bitnet>.

45. University of North Carolina at Chapel Hill INFO
info.oit.unc.edu (152.2.21.17) Login as info. Emulate a VT100.
Hardware/software: DEC/VTX on a VAX 6620 Or gopher to
gibbs.oit.unc.edu, port 7000 or telnet to gibbs.oit.unc.edu
(152.2.21.2) and login as info Hardware/software: gopher on a
Convex C3840 Contact: Judy Hallman <Judy_
Hallman@unc.edu> Contains: Library-related events, including
international meetings and conferences, as well as local events;
the campus directory; job openings; ''The Independent Study''
catalog (courses people can take by correspondence); the undergraduate catalog; continuing education classes; several newsletters, including _International Dimensions_, a newsletter on
activities and opportunities in international medicine; publications of the Institute for Academic Technology; Human Resources manual; grant and funding opportunities (The Catalog of
Federal Domesetic Assistance, NSF, and NIH); guide to preparation of theses and dissertations; Graduate School handbook.

46. University of North Carolina at Greensboro MINERVA
steffi.acc.uncg.edu (128.109.200.3) Login as info or MINERVA
Emulate a VT100. Hardware/software: DEC/VTX Contact: Norman Hill <hillnr@uncg.bitnet>.

47. University of North Carolina at Wilmington SEABOARD
vxc.uncwil.edu (128.109.221.3) Log in as info Emulate a
VT100. Hardware/software: DEC/VTX Contact: Eddy
Cavenaugh <cavenaughd@uncwil.bitnet> or
<cavenaughd@vxc.uncwil.edu> Contains: class schedule list-
ings, institutional statistics, library services, faculty & staff publications, current university news releases, phone directories, facilities schedules.

48. University of Northern Iowa infosys.uni.edu (134.161.1.21)
Log in as public; password is not required Will ask for terminal
type; press RETURN if using a vtxxx. (If you are using a vtxxx
or any other terminal that the system recognizes, it will page;
otherwise it will scroll) Hardware/software: AT&T 3b2/500;
System V UNIX; local CWIS software Contact: Mike Yohe
<yohe@uni.edu> Contains: Telephone directories; closed class
lists; information about computing services, library, residence
system, theater, public safety, and other aspects of university
life; suggestion box and postings of questions and answers. Additional information under development.

49. University of Pennsylvania -- PennInfo penninfo.upenn.edu
(no login id is needed) University of Pennsylvania -- Gopher
gopher.upenn.edu Emulate a VT100 Hardware/software: MIT's
Techinfo; Gopher software Contact: <penninfo-
admin@dccs.upenn.edu> The PennInfo->Gopher gateway and
the Gopher->PennInfo gateway allow seamless access to Gopher via PennInfo and vice versa. PennInfo contains facts about
the University of Pennsylvania; Programs in Residence and Academic Support Services programs for students; tutoring services;
scholars programs, grants, fellowships, and research resources;
entire Penn course register, course timetable, and final examina-

tion schedule and the latest academic calendar; various schools
and events calendars; campus publications; computing topics;
on-campus directories; faculty and staff information; Penn's 14
libraries; official policies and procedures; Schools information;
listings of student organizations and support facilities and
groups; job listings. New on PennInfo---GIF capability (see images of campus maps, African Studies artifacts, etc.). The Central Penn Gopher contains menu topics that provide access to
information on both local and remote Gopher servers, as well as
to PennInfo.

50. University of Pennsylvania School of Medicine - MEDINFO
penninfo.upenn.edu 9010 (no login required - goes directly to
MEDINFO Main Menu) Contact: king@mscf.upenn.edu.

51. University of Vermont Gopher access: gopher.uvm.edu, port
70 Contact: Stephen J. Cavrak, Jr. <sjc@uvmvm.uvm.edu>
Contains: The University's online information system (InfoCat)
with course schedules, campus event calendars, press releases,
job openings, and general information about the University. The
UVM library catalog and phone directory are also available
through this gopher.

52. University of Virginia Grounds-Wide Information Server
Gopher access: gopher.virginia.edu port 70. If you do not have
access to the Gopher software on computers that you normally
use, then you can use the client software on the machine named
''gwis.virginia.edu'' by logging in as the user ''gwis''. No password is required. Contact: gwis@virginia.edu.

53. University of Wisconsin-Madison -- Double CWIS options:

Option 1: blue.adp.wisc.edu Use TN3270. Select option #5 la-
beled INQUIRE. Type in ''INQUIRE'' or hit F5 to begin a
session. INQUIRE is the name of our full-text mainframe based
search engine, and we have mounted several databases under it.
Option 2: (preferred) Use a gopher client to access the UW-
Madison production GOPHER server (gopher.wisc.edu). The
same databases mounted under the INQUIRE platform are
ported and reindexed under the GOPHER server, additional
other options like the campus telephone book have been implemented. This gopher server provides top level access to the
(currently) 4 other gopher servers that have been implemented
on campus. Contact: Kent Hooker <pkh@ra.adp.wisc.edu> or
<khooker@wiscmacc.bitnet>.

54. Washington University wugate.wustl.edu Login as services
Emulate a VT100 Contact: services@wugate.wustl.edu.

55. Yale E N T E R P R I S E yalevm.ycc.yale.edu Connect to
port 300. Use telnet or tn3270. Different versions of telnet or
tn3270 have different syntax for defining the port. The following are the commonest: TELNET yalevm.ycc.yale.edu 300
TELNET yalevm.ycc.yale.edu::300 or TELNET
yalevm.ycc.yale.edu..300 Hardware/software: IBM 3090 using
the CUInfo software developed at Cornell Contact: Mitchell
Block <mblock@yalevm.ycc.yale.edu> Contains: weather,
campus activities & student newspaper, course listings, syllabi,
tutoring programs, job listings, staff reports, and administrative
service descriptions.

INTERNATIONAL

Australia

56. University of New England-Northern Rivers alsvid.une.edu.au Login as info. Emulate a VT100. Hardware/ software: Gopher on a Decstation Or gopher to alsvid.une.edu.au, port 70 Contact: Jean Lowe <cwis@alsvid.une.edu.au> Contains: Campus and community coming events, course, faculty, student services and learning assistance information; library catalogue and library information. Still under development.

Canada

57. Dalhousie University Computing & Information Services ac.dal.ca (129.173.1.100) Username: dalinfo Hardware/Software: Uses pnn software Contact: dalinfo@ac.dal.ca Information provided by: Peter Scott <scott@sklib.usask.ca>.

58. McGill University, Montreal Canada, InfoMcGill Campus-Wide Info System vm1.mcgill.ca (132.206.27.2) Use telnet or tn3270. When you see the VM logo, hit enter to clear it, enter PF3 (or type "INFO") as the screen will prompt you. No userid/password is required. Hardware/Software: IBM 4381. Uses MUSIC/SP software running under VM. (MUSIC/SP is available from IBM under program number 5750-ACF. It provides the software for the CWIS including hierarchical menu support, full text word searching, the ability of data providers to directly update their own CWIS data, and the ability to get e-mail feedback directly from the viewers of their data.) Contact: Roy Miller <ccrmmus@mcgillm.bitnet> or <ccrmmus@musicm.mcgill.ca> (Internet) Contains: Administrative policies, video tape rental library, staff phone book and e-mail addresses, employment opportunities, library information, computing newsletters, computer store price lists, enrollment numbers, student society handbook, coming events, etc.

59. Universite de Montreal (Quebec, Canada) UDEMATIK udematik.umontreal.ca (132.204.2.22) Supports a wide variety of Ascii terminals (VT100, VT220, televideo, X, etc.) Use telnet, no password required. Contact: <udematik@ere.umontreal.ca> or Joelle stemp <stemp@ere.umontreal.ca> or Sebastien roy <roys@ere.umontreal.ca> Contains: Staff phone/e-mail directory, catalog of courses (7,000), University's complete catalog, program comparing and course matching application, and also information on the following topics: programs, admission (undergraduate, graduate, continuing education, French as a second language for students around the world), and all about University computing resources, services and how to get familiar with Internet.

60. University of New Brunswick, Canada, INFO unbmvs1.csd.unb.ca (131.202.1.2) Login with application id INFO There is no password required. INFO is a full-screen CICS application running under MVS. tn3270 emulation. Contact: Bonita Mockler <bgm@unb.ca> Contains: University Calendar, class timetable, phone/fax numbers for faculty/staff/students, faculty and staff email ids, seminar schedules, minutes, newsletter, etc.

Germany

61. Universitaet Osnabrueck, Osnabrueck (An experimental CWIS.) jupiter.rz.uni-osnabrueck.de (131.173.18.1) Emulate a VT100 userid: rzinfo password: rzinfo. Hardware/software: PNN software under VM/CMS and AIX/370. Contact: Ivo Duentsch <duentsch@dosuni1.bitnet> Contains: Information from the computer center, the library, and a telephone list, and it is steadily growing.

62. University of the University of the Saarland at Saarbruecken Experimental gopher-based CWIS Point your gopher to: pfsparc02.phil15.uni-sb.de (134.96.82.13) port 70 THIS IS NOT AN OFFICIAL CAMPUS INFO SYSTEM OF THE U of SAARBRUECKEN, but contains campus info and perhaps will become officialized. Language: German Contact: Alexander Sigel <alsi@sbustd.stud.uni-sb.de>.

Netherlands

63. Tilburg University, Netherlands, KUBgids kublib.kub.nl (137.56.0.56) Login as KUBGIDS There is no password required. Emulate a VT200. Hardware/software: Digital Standard Mumps, DEC/VTX, Topic, Ingres, Sybase, and locally written. Contact: Thomas Place <place@kub.nl> Contains: the library's online public access catalogue, four databases containing bibliographic references to information carriers in several areas of computer science, two databases for current awareness services, a database on grey literature in the field of economics and business science, a database covering information on the province of Brabant and a campus wide information system. Under development is a module for navigation through the subject fields of the various databases. Some of the services are not available to anonymous users of KUBgids from outside the campus.

Switzerland

64. Rechenzentrum Universitaet Zuerich rzucms.unizh.ch (130.60.64.2) Command: info Emulate a tn3270 Software: Princeton Network News (PNN) Language: German Contact: rzuvo@rzu.unizh.ch (Peter Vollenweider) Contains: The Computing Center of the University of Zurich (RZU) is a university service bureau, providing information processing services to Institutes and Students of the University. The UNIZH-Info-Server provides information on services offered at the University of Zurich, for instance: Campus Phone Book (5000 entries), E-mail addresses of the computing center staff, Calendar and Events (updated weekly), Library Information, Athletics, Computing Resources, Student Shops. Beware: By the end of the year, the info service will be moved onto a UNIX platform, SUN or RS/ 6000: rzusun.unizh.ch or rzuaix.unizh.ch. You may try the experimental version: telnet rzusun.unizh.ch user: inserv Emulate a vt100 terminal.

United Kingdom

To access most universities in the UK, first login into JANET, the Joint Academic Network. Access to JANET follows: Access: telnet sun.nsf.ac.uk Login: janet Hostname: type the address of the University you would like to connect to.

65. Birmingham University info.bham.ac.uk (NOTE: Make a direct Internet connection; not through JANET) Login as info or login as help, if you need it. (No password needed.) Emulate a vt100 (ok with 'dumb' teminals; has experimental X-Windows Interface) Hardware/software: Runs on an IBM RS6000 AIX. Written in KornShell. Contact: Roy 'Baby' Pearce <R.A.Pearce@bham.ac.uk> Contains: Largely information on computing matters. Full documentation can be found under the Menu named INFOSERVERS. Documents (and sub-sets) can be down-loaded using email. Carries sections of nationally-available information such as HENSA/micros & HENSA/unix Indexes, JANET Names/Addresses and the Name Registration Scheme (NRS) etc.

66. Edinburgh University festival.ed.ac.uk (129.215.128.2) Login as edinfo Emulate a VT100. Hardware/software: UNIX/ BRS Search Contact: Arthur Wilson <Arthur.Wilson@ed.ac.uk>.

67. King's College London info.kcl.ac.uk Make a direct Internet connection and log in as info, or log in to JANET first and connect to uk.ac.kcl.info (and log in as info). Emulate a VT100. Hardware/software: VAX 8350, using York Infoserver software, provided by York Computing Services. Contact: Harold Short <h.short@oak.cc.kcl.ac.uk> Contains: General College information, Schools and Academic departments, Students Union, Academic Support departments (Computing Centre, Library and Audio-Visual Services), plus access to selected network services. First-generation CWIS, currently undergoing transition from experimental status. Sections known to be still experimental are flagged. Now looking at second-generation options, with particular interest in Gopher and DEC VTX.

68. University of Bradford - ''BradInfo'' For terminal access: telnet to info.brad.ac.uk (143.53.240.5) login as info (or from JANET, PAD to uk.ac.brad.info) >From a gopher client (preferred): Configure your client to connect to gopher.brad.ac.uk

port 70 Or go through the Minnesota gopher selecting ''Other Gopher & Information Servers'', ''Europe'', ''United Kingdom''. Hardware: Sun Software: Gopher contains campus information (directories, course details, publications); e-mail, usenet and network information; access to other Gopher servers. Contact: Paul Sutton <P.C.Sutton@bradford.ac.uk>.

69. University of Bristol info.bristol.ac.uk Make a direct Internet connection and log in as info, or log in to JANET first and type uk.ac.bristol.info. Best to emulate a vt100. Hardware/software: Sun SparcServer using local sofware written in a subset of C chosen to ease portability. Contact: Ann French <ann.french@bristol.ac.uk> Contains: Information about the University and information of general interest to members of the University; for example, the telephone list, electronic mail addresses, details of courses, information about departments, articles from the student newspaper.

70. University of Hull uk.ac.hull.geac Emulate a VT100 Hardware/software: A Geac 9,000 mainframe using locally written software (in Geacs own ZOPL language). The information system is administered totally by library staff. Contact: Bridget Towler <B.A.Towler@sequent.cc.hull.ac.uk>.

71. University of Southampton Campus Information Service JANET address: uk.ac.soton.info This accesses the local Southampton SpiderGate—respond to request for name/address of service with info). Emulate a VT100. Hardware/software: Sun/ Harwell Computer Power Status (free text retrieval package) Contact: Colin K. Work <C.K.Work@UK.AC.Southampton> Contains: broad coverage of University related information. Includes online versions of significant documents plus shorter news and event items.

(Also included in Hallman's online list are freenets and community-wide and K-12 information systems. Information on these is included in section 4 of this book.)

Section 6. Commercial Services on the Internet

BIOSIS: LIFE SCIENCE NETWORK

Description: BIOSIS is a commercial online bibliographic utility whose databases (including Life Science Network) are searchable through the Internet.
Subjects covered: online utility; library and information science; information technology; biology
Sponsor: BIOSIS, 2100 Arch Street, Philadelphia, PA 19103; (215) 587-4800; (800) 523-4806.
How to access: Telnet to lsn.com or 192.132.57.1. For information call BIOSIS 1-800-523-4806 Note: for password, email biosis@relay.upenn.edu

BOOK STACKS UNLIMITED

Description: Book Stacks Unlimited is an electronic bookstore carrying over 250,000 titles which can be searched by subject, author, title, keyword, or ISBN.
Subjects covered: electronic shopping service
Net address for operations: telnet books.com
Fee: There is no fee to browse; there is a fee to order books. Credit cards.
Sponsor: Book Stacks Unlimited, Inc. 200 Public Square, Suite 26-4600, Cleveland, OH 44114-2301; (216) 861-0467.
How to access: Telnet to books.com; standard modem address is (216) 861-0469.

BRS INFORMATION TECHNOLOGIES

Description: BRS is a commercial online bibliographic utility whose databases are searchable through the Internet.
Subjects covered: online utility; library and information science; information technology
Sponsor: BRS Information Technologies, 8000 Westpark Drive, McLean, VA 22102; (800) 289-4277; (703) 442-0900.
How to access: Telnet to brs.com

COMMERCIAL INFORMATION EXCHANGE

Description: The Commercial Information Exchange allows commercial companies to post prices, press releases, information about product lines, and other service descriptions. Companies in the Exchange pay a fee. Use by readers is without charge.
Subjects covered: Internet; commercial shopping services
Fee: Yes.
Sponsor: Commercial Internet Exchange (CIX).
Editorial contact: Bill Washburn
Internet: washburn@cix.org
How to access: Conact Bill Washburn at washburn@cix.org or gopher to cix.org.

DATA-STAR

Description: Data-Star is a commercial online bibliographic utility whose databases are searchable through the Internet.
Subjects covered: online utility; library and information science; information technology
Sponsor: Data-Star, 485 Devon Park Drive, Wayne, PA 19087; (800) 221-7754; (215) 687-6777; 2087 Landings Drive, Mountain View, CA 94043; (415) 988-9550.
How to access: Telnet to reserve.rs.ch

DENDOCHRONOLGY FORUM FOR THE INTERNATIONAL TREE-RING DATA BANK

Description: The International Tree-Ring Data Bank (ITRDB) is an international collaborative effort among scientists interested in the developement and archiving of tree-ring data for the benefit of others. Tree-ring data are then made available to scientists worldwide who wish to utilize the valuable information that may be obtained from the interpretation of tree-ring data. The Dendrochronology Forum was established to foster communication among dendrochronologists who otherwise would be isolated from the mainstream centers of research. Discussions on the forum are informal, yet informative, and mainly concern: 1) the announcement of newly published articles relevant to tree-ring research; 2) discussions about methods and procedures useful in dendrochronology; and, 3) announcements about upcoming meetings of particular concern to tree-ring researchers.
Subjects covered: dendrochronology; plant biology
Net address for operations: LISTSERV@ASUACAD.BITNET
Net address for questions or submissions: ITRDBFOR@ASUACAD.BITNET
Established: June 22, 1993
Sponsor: Laboratory of Tree-Ring Research, University of Arizona, Tucson, AZ 85721.
Editorial contact: Henri D. Grissino-Mayer
Laboratory of Tree-Ring Research, University of Arizona, Tucson, AZ 85721.
Tel: (602) 621 6463 or (602) 612-7681
Fax: (602) 621-8229
Internet: GRAD1@CCIT.ARIZONA.EDU
Bitnet: GRAD1@ARIZVMS.BITNET
How to access: Send the following interactive message to LISTSERV@ASUACAD.BITNET : SUB ITRDBFOR <First name> <Last name>. The format for sending this message will depend on the system being used by the subscriber (e.g., VAX VMS, Prime, IBM, etc.)
How to unsubscribe: Send the following interactive message to LISTSERV@ASUACAD.BITNET : SIGNOFF ITRDBFOR <First name> <Last name>. The format for sending this mes-

sage will depend on the system being used by the subscriber (e.g., VAX VMS, Prime, IBM, etc.)

How to submit: To submit messages to the forum, send to the following address: ITRDBFOR@ASUACAD.BITNET

Archives: To retrieve past messages, send the following interactive message to LISTSERV@ASUACAD.BITNET: GET ITRDBFOR LOG <year><month>. Fof instance, to retrieve all messages for June of 1993, send GET ITRDBFOR LOG9306

Related files: The entire holdings of the ITRDB, including all tree-ring chronologies and sofware used to display and retrieve these data, may be obtained using anonymous ftp. Instructions, ftp to NGDC1.NGDC.NOAA.GOV. At the USERNAME prompt, type "ANONYMOUS." For a password, type in your usename and complete address. At the ftp prompt, type "BINARY." Then change directories by typing "CD PALEO" followed by "CD TREE-RING" followed by "CD ITRDB." Type "MGET *.ZIP" to transfer all zipped files. After the transfer, type "ASCII" followed by "GET <FILENAME>" to transfer all other files. A directory listing may be obtained by typing "DIR" at the ftp prompt.

Additional information: Co-Editor: Harold C. Fritts, Laboratory of Tree-Ring Research, University of Arizona, Tucson, AZ 85721; tel : (602) 887-7291 or (602) 621-6469; fax : (602) 621-8229; Internet: FRITTS1@CCIT.ARIZONA.EDU; Bitnet : FRITTS1@ARIZVMS.BITNET

DIALOG/KNOWLEDGE INDEX

Description: Dialog is a commercial online bibliographic utility whose databases are searchable through the Internet.

Subjects covered: online utility; library and information science; information technology

Sponsor: Dialog Information Services, Inc., 3460 Hillview Avenue, Palo Alto, CA 94304; (415) 858-7800; (800) 334-2564.

How to access: Telnet to dialog.com or 192.132.3.254

DOW JONES NEWS/RETRIEVAL

Description: Dow Jones News/Retrieval is a commercial online bibliographic utility whose databases are searchable through the Internet.

Subjects covered: online utility; library and information science; information technology; business

Sponsor: Dow Jones News/Retrieval, P.O. Box, 300, Princeton, NJ 08543-0300; (800) 522-3567; (609) 520-4638.

How to access: Telnet to djnr.dowjones.com

ELECTRONIC BOOKSTORE ON INTERNET

Description: Electronic Bookstore on Internet is an experimental program to offer published books in electronic form over the Internet.

Subjects covered: electronic shopping service

Net address for questions or submissions: ebooks-info@digex.net

Ebooks

Tel: (703) 820-0341

Internet: ebooks-info@digex.net

THE ELECTRONIC NEWSSTAND

Description: The Electronic Newsstand includes tables of contents and selected partial or complete contents from a variety of print magazines (The New Yorker, Internet World, The Economist, The New Republic, Foreign Affairs, National Review, Technology Review, Eating Well, Outside Magazine, The Journal of NIH Research, The Source, and New Age Journal), with subscription offers and the ability to register subscriptions electronically.

Subjects covered: electronic shopping service; publishing

Sponsor: The Internet Company, Hudson, MA, and The New Republic, Inc., Washington, DC.

Editorial contact: Paul Vizza

Tel: (202) 331-7494

Internet: infor@enews.com

How to access: Gopher to gopher.netsys.com on port 2100; or telnet to gopher.netsys.com and login as "enews" (no password is needed)

Gopher accessibility: The Electronic Newsstand is initially provided as a gopher server run by the Internet Company. The server is at gopher.netsys.com on port 2100.

EPIC/FIRSTSEARCH

Description: OCLC is a commercial online bibliographic utility whose databases (including EPIC/FirstSearch) are searchable through the Internet.

Subjects covered: online utility; library and information science; information technology

Sponsor: OCLC (Online Computer Library Center), 6565 Frantz Road, Dublin, OH 43017; (800) 848-5878 (US and Canada); (800) 848-8286 (Ohio).

How to access: Telnet to epic.prod.oclc.org or 132.174.100.2

ESA-IRS

Description: ESA-IRA is a commercial online bibliographic utility whose databases are searchable through the Internet.

Subjects covered: online utility; library and information science; information technology

How to access: Telnet to 192.106.252.1

FAXON FINDER/FAXON XPRESS

Description: Faxon Finder is a subscription acquisition and management service offering a table of contents database of over 10,000 serials titles with an integrated document delivery service, Faxon XPress.

Subjects covered: library and information science; serials librarianship; library-vendor relations; Faxon Company

Net address for operations: HELP@FAXON.COM

Net address for questions or submissions: HELP@FAXON.COM

Established: 1991

Available in other media: Yes. Faxon's Guide to Serials (print, microfiche); Faxon's Guide to CD-ROM (print); Serials Renewal and Analysis Tools, Microlinx Serials Control Software (PC diskette); Faxon Finder on Disc (CD-ROM).

Fee: Yes; varies according to service. Varies according to service and institution.

Sponsor: The Faxon Company, 15 Southwest Park, Westwood, MA 02090.

Host: The Faxon Company, 15 Southwest Park, Westwood, MA 02090.

Commercial organization: Yes.
Editorial contact: Karen Roubicek
The Faxon Company, 15 Southwest Park, Westwood, MA
02090.
Tel: 617-329-3350 (x462)
Fax: 617-326-5484
Internet: ROUBICEK@FAXON.COM
Bitnet: ROUBICEK@FAXON
Technical contact: Roger Pruitt
The Faxon Company, 15 Southwest Park, Westwood, MA
02090.
Tel: 617-329-3350 (x502)
Fax: 617-329-9875
Internet: PRUITT@FAXON.COM
Bitnet: PRUITT@FAXON
Copyright statement: Copyright 1991-1993 The Faxon Company, Inc., and Faxon Research Services, Inc. All rights reserved. No portion of this database may be reproduced for any purpose except as permitted by express license of Faxon Research Services.
How to access: To access Faxon services via the Internet, users must have accounts on the Faxon system. For more information about Faxon services, call 1-800-766-0039.
Related files: Faxon FinderFaxon XPress, Faxon Source, and Faxon Quest are related services offered by the Faxon Company.

FAXON QUEST

Description: Faxon Quest is a subscription acquisition and management service offering online location of back-issue and hard-to-find serials.
Subjects covered: library and information science; serials librarianship; library-vendor relations; Faxon Company
Net address for operations: HELP@FAXON.COM
Net address for questions or submissions:
HELP@FAXON.COM
Established: 1991
Available in other media: Yes. Faxon's Guide to Serials (print, microfiche); Faxon's Guide to CD-ROM (print); Serials Renewal and Analysis Tools, Microlinx Serials Control Software (PC diskette); Faxon Finder on Disc (CD-ROM).
Fee: Yes; varies according to service. Varies according to service and institution.
Sponsor: The Faxon Company, 15 Southwest Park, Westwood, MA 02090.
Host: The Faxon Company, 15 Southwest Park, Westwood, MA 02090.
Commercial organization: Yes.
Editorial contact: Karen Roubicek
The Faxon Company, 15 Southwest Park, Westwood, MA
02090.
Tel: 617-329-3350 (x462)
Fax: 617-326-5484
Internet: ROUBICEK@FAXON.COM
Bitnet: ROUBICEK@FAXON
Technical contact: Roger Pruitt
The Faxon Company, 15 Southwest Park, Westwood, MA
02090.
Tel: 617-329-3350 (x502)
Fax: 617-329-9875
Internet: PRUITT@FAXON.COM
Bitnet: PRUITT@FAXON

Copyright statement: Copyright 1991-1993 The Faxon Company, Inc., and Faxon Research Services, Inc. All rights reserved. No portion of this database may be reproduced for any purpose except as permitted by express license of Faxon Research Services.
How to access: To access Faxon services via the Internet, users must have accounts on the Faxon system. For more information about Faxon services, call 1-800-766-0039.
Related files: Faxon Finder, Faxon Source, Faxon XPress, and Faxon Quest are related files offered by the Faxon Company.

FAXON SOURCE

Description: Faxon Source is a subscription acquisition and management service covering more than 200,000 serials, continuations, and CD-ROM titles from domestic and international publishers. Also included are online serials catalogs of current bibliographic and financial data, a renewal and claiming service, and collection management reports.
Subjects covered: library and information science; serials librarianship; library-vendor relations; Faxon Company
Net address for operations: HELP@FAXON.COM
Net address for questions or submissions:
HELP@FAXON.COM
Established: 1991
Available in other media: Yes. Faxon's Guide to Serials (print, microfiche); Faxon's Guide to CD-ROM (print); Serials Renewal and Analysis Tools, Microlinx Serials Control Software (PC diskette); Faxon Finder on Disc (CD-ROM).
Fee: Yes; varies according to service. Varies according to service and institution.
Sponsor: The Faxon Company, 15 Southwest Park, Westwood, MA 02090.
Host: The Faxon Company, 15 Southwest Park, Westwood, MA 02090.
Commercial organization: Yes.
Editorial contact: Karen Roubicek
The Faxon Company, 15 Southwest Park, Westwood, MA
02090.
Tel: 617-329-3350 (x462)
Fax: 617-326-5484
Internet: ROUBICEK@FAXON.COM
Bitnet: ROUBICEK@FAXON
Technical contact: Roger Pruitt
The Faxon Company, 15 Southwest Park, Westwood, MA
02090.
Tel: 617-329-3350 (x502)
Fax: 617-329-9875
Internet: PRUITT@FAXON.COM
Bitnet: PRUITT@FAXON
Copyright statement: Copyright 1991-1993 The Faxon Company, Inc., and Faxon Research Services, Inc. All rights reserved. No portion of this database may be reproduced for any purpose except as permitted by express license of Faxon Research Services.
How to access: To access Faxon services via the Internet, users must have accounts on the Faxon system. For more information about Faxon services, call 1-800-766-0039.
Related files: Faxon Finder, Faxon Source, Faxon XPress, and Faxon Quest are related files offered by the Faxon Company.

FINE ART, SCIENCE, TECHNOLOGY FAST DATABASE

Description: FAST is an electronic collection of distinct databases in fine art, science, and technology, organized by topic. Current FAST subscribers represent a diverse group of artists, musicians, theoreticians, scientists and other members of the art and technology community. Subscribers and readers are also encouraged to contribute articles, listings, and information to the databases.
Subjects covered: music; art; fine arts; science and technology
Net address for operations: isast@well.sf.ca.us, fast@garnet.berkeley.edu
Net address for questions or submissions: isast@well.sf.ca.us, fast@garnet.berkeley.edu
Established: 1988
Fee: Full year $90 non-members, $60 Leonardo/ISAT members, Quarterly updates $35 non-members, $25 Leonardo/ISAST members. Check, money order, Visa or Mastercard to Leonardo/ISAST, 672 South Van ness, San Francisco, CA 94110, USA
Sponsor: Leonardo, the International Society for the Arts, Sciences and Technology
Host: same as above
Editorial contact: Annie Lewis
Leonardo Electronic News 672 Van Ness, San Francisco, CA 94110.
Tel: (415) 431-7414
Fax: (415) 431- 5737
Internet: fast@garnet.berkely,edu, isast@well.sf.ca.us
Sample contents: FAST is regularly expanded and updated and includes: -Artist's Words on Works (WOW), articles by contemporary artists about their current artworks and works in progress. -Leonardo Abstracts Archive, summaries of the articles and notes published in Leonardo, the bimonthly Journal of the International Society for the Arts, Sciences and Technology. -Review of books, software, magazines, journals, audiotapes, videotapes, and films of interest to the art, science and technology community. -Bibliographies and Book Lists on topics of interest, such as Fractals, Video Art, Television and Society, Computers and Electronic Music, Virtual Reality, Multimedia and Women in Art and Technology -Directory of Resources is a directory of grants, artists-in-residence, programs, fellowships, funding organizations and curator. -Speaker's Network, a project of Leonardo/ISAST, is a listing of Leonardo authors and members who are available for lectures and presentations on topics of interest to the art, science and technology community. -Electronic Mail Database and Directory, updated quarterly -Calendar of international conferences and events -Archives of past issues of Leonardo Electronic News and FineArt Forum.
How to access: To subscribe to FAST, users must have a WELL log-on. Contact the well by phone at (415) 332-4335 or e-mail info@well.sf.ca.us. Subscription fees are $40 per yearm $20 for Leonardo/ISAST members.
How to unsubscribe: Contact isast@well.sf.ca.us

FIRST!

Description: First! is described as a current awareness service to individuals and corporations requiring custom tailored news gathering delivered daily via the Internet.
Subjects covered: current events; commercial services; business
Fee: Yes, fee depends on the level of the service, the number of news stories, and the method of delivery.
Sponsor: Individual Inc., 84 Sherman Street, Cambridge, MA 02140; (617) 354-2230; (800) 766-4224; fax: (617) 864-4066.

GLOBAL NETWORK NAVIGATOR (GNN)

Description: The Global Network Navigator is a general-interest interactive guide to information resrouces on the Internet. GNN includes a news service, an online magazine, the Online Whole Internet Catalog, and a global marketplace containing information about products and services. GNN is an application of the WorldWideWeb.
Subjects covered: commercial shopping service; Internet
Established: 1993
Host: O'Reilly & Associates, Inc., 103A Morris Street, Sebastopol, CA 95472; (800) 998-9938; (707) 829-0515.
How to access: The Global Network Navigator is available over the Internet as a subscription service, which is free during the initial launch period. GNN's goal is to encourage people to try out the service and subscribe if they like it. To receive information about a free subscription to the Global Network Navigator, send email to info@gnn.com.

ITTI-NETWORKS

Description: itti-networks is an electronic discussion list relating to network training and to the development of a generic set of materials for use by network trainers in the UK and elsewhere.
Subjects covered: Internet; electronic networking; computer hardware and software; network training
Net address for operations: mailbase@mailbase.ac.uk
Net address for questions or submissions: itti-networks@mailbase.ac.uk
Established: 1992
Sponsor: Networked Information Services Project/Information Technology Training Initiative.
Host: Newcastle Univ. Computing Service.
Editorial contact: Margaret Isaacs
Newcastle Univ. Computing Service, Newcastle upon Tyne NE1 7RU, UK.
Tel: +44 91 222 8069
Fax: +44 91 222 8765
Internet: margaret.isaacs@ncl.ac.uk
How to access: Send to mailbase@mailbase.ac.uk the message: join itti-networks <firstname> <lastname>
Access policy: Subscriptions are open to anyone.
How to unsubscribe: Send to mailbase@mailbase.ac.uk the message:leave itti-networks <firstname> <lastname>
Archives: Monthly files of messages are held in itti-networks directory of mailbase.ac.uk
Related files: For related files see mailbase.ac.uk /pub/itti-networks

MARKETBASE

Description: MarketBase is a commercial service offering a variety of vendors an electronic venue where purchasers may receive information about a wide range of products and services. There is a fee for vendors to list; browsing by purchasers is free.
Subjects covered: electronic shopping service
Net address for operations: info@mb.com
How to access: Telnet to mb.com. Login as mb.

MEAD DATA CENTRAL: LEXIS/NEXIS

Description: Mead Data Central is a commercial online bibliographic utility whose databases (including LEXIS/NEXIS) are searchable through the Internet.

Subjects covered: online utility; library and information science; information technology; law and legal studies

Sponsor: Mead Data Central, 9393 Springboro Pike, P. O. Box 933, Dayton, OH 45401; (80) 227-9597; (513) 865-6800.

How to access: Telnet to lexis.meaddata.com or 192.73.216.20 or 192.73.216.21 terminal type .vt100a Note: if characters do not echo back, you will have to set your terminal to "local" echo.

MEDLARS

Description: Medlars is a commercial online bibliographic utility whose databases are searchable through the Internet.

Subjects covered: online utility; library and information science; information technology

How to access: Telnet to medlars.nlm.nih.gov Note: currently listed as <FUL036>

THE NET ADVERTISER

Description: The Net Advertiser is a mailing list created to give all the Internet community the opportunity to widespread private sales, rent, offer messages. Everybody can find a place in The Net Advertiser digest, even commercial companies. This is a list maintained by the InfoNet Project, a group of computer science experts, students and consultants whose aim is the propagation of all kind of information across the Internet and CREN world. Advertising in the digest is completely free, except for commercial companies which must submit a $75 fee in order to support the InfoNet Project work.

Subjects covered: Internet; advertising; electronic shopping service

Fee: Yes, for commercial companies using the list there is a $75 fee.

How to access: For any information, subscription and submission write to: netad@uds01.unix.st.it

ONLINE EXPRESS

Description: Online Express is an email-based shopping service.

Subjects covered: electronic shopping service

How to access: For information, email to express@msw.metronet.com

ORBIT SEARCH SERVICES

Description: ORBIT Search Services is a commercial online bibliographic utility whose databases are searchable through the Internet.

Subjects covered: online utility; library and information science; information technology

Sponsor: ORBIT Search Services, Maxwell Online, Inc., 800 Westpark Drive, McLean, VA 22102; (800) 456-7248; (703) 422-0900.

How to access: Telnet to orbit.com or 192.188.13.254

PUBLIC DISC

Description: Public Disc is an information sales and distribution service which allows information providers with product literature, technical papers, and software to reach the Internet community. The service contains a broad range of technical materials.

Subjects covered: Internet; computer hardware and software

Net address for operations: info@PublicDisc.com

Net address for questions or submissions: support@PublicDisc.com

Established: March 1993

Fee: No minimum fee. Only pay for documents purchased.

Sponsor: 459 Hamilton Ave., Palo Alto, CA 94301

Editorial contact: Steve Harari

459 Hamilton Ave, Palo Alto, CA 94301

Tel: 415-617-1515

Fax: 415-617-1516

Internet: harari@PublicDisc.com

Technical contact: Allan Schiffman

Public Disc, 459 Hamilton Ave, Palo Alto, CA 94301

Tel: 415-617-1515

Fax: 415-617-1516

Internet: ams@PublicDisc.com

Copyright statement: Providers retain rights to all materials they upload to Public Disc. Therefore, you must respect the rights of others who provide their information to Public Disc. It is illegal and prohibited by Public Disc for you to copy or redistribute information received or acquired via Public Disc in any fashion to others in violation of a provider's copyrights and/or licensing terms.

How to access: info@PublicDisc.com

How to unsubscribe: info@PublicDisc.com

RLIN (RESEARCH LIBRARIES INFORMATION NETWORK)

Description: RLIN is an online bibliographic utility whose databases are searchable through the Internet.

Subjects covered: online utility; library and information science; information technology

Sponsor: Research Libraries Group, Research Library Information Network, 1200 Villa Street, Mountain View, CA 94041-1100; (415) 962-9951.

How to access: Telnet to rlg.stanford.edu or 36.54.0.18 or rlin.stanford.edu or 36.54.0.19 Note: currently listed as <US109>

ROSWELL ELECTRONIC COMPUTER BOOKSTORE

Description: Roswell Computer Books is a walk-in bookstore devoted exclusively to computer books with a database listing over 7000 titles. The selection of books serves all levels of users from the novice to the data processing professional. Books may be ordered by e-mail, phone, or fax. Orders will be charged to Visa or Mastercard. Corporate and Government purchase orders are accepted. The electronic bookstore is arranged by subject; the database can be searched by partial author, title, or ISBN.

Subjects covered: electronic shopping service; computer books

Net address for questions or submissions: roswell@fox.nstn.ns.ca

Editorial contact: Daniel MacKay

NOC Manager, NSTN Operations Centre, Dalhousie University, Halifax, Nova Scotia, Canada.
Tel: 902-494-NSTN
Internet: daniel@nstn.ns.ca >
How to access: The bookstore is accessible via gopher: - Point your gopher at "nstn.ns.ca", - select "Other Gophers in Nova Scotia", - select "Roswell Electronic Computer Bookstore", - browse the bookstore by category, or - search on author, title, or partial keyword using the gopher search item. If you don't have local gopher facilities, telnet to either consultant.micro.umn.edu or gopher.uiuc.edu, log in as "gopher", navigate your way to the NSTN gopher (usually listed in North America/Canada/Nova Scotia) and gopher as above. If you do not have gopher or telnet ability, direct queries to: roswell@fox.nstn.ns.ca

SPONSORED PROGRAMS INFORMATION NETWORK (SPIN)
Description: SPINE is a database of funding opportunities designed to assist faculty and administration at institutions of higher education in the identification of external support for research, education, and development projects.
Subjects covered: education; grants and funding
Established: 1990
Available in other media: SPIN Micro is a floppy-based version of the SPIN database.
Fee: Internet subscription fees: $500 plus $10 per search, or unlimited searches for $3500.Annual fees for the following update schedules on floppy disk: biweekly/$2995; monthly/$1995; quarterly/$1195
Host: InfoEd., Inc. 453 New Karner Road, Albany, NY 12205; office@infoed.org
Editorial contact: Jill Rydberg
InfoEd., Inc., 453 New Karner Road, Albany, NY 12205
Tel: 518-464-0691
Fax: 518-464-0695
Internet: jill@infoed.org
Technical contact: Tricia deMoulpied
InfoEd., Inc., 453 New Karner Road, Albany, NY 12205
Tel: 518-464-0691
Fax: 518-464-0695
Internet: tricia@infoed.org
How to access: Contact Jill Rydberg, jill@infoed.org *F

SPRINGER-VERLAG SCIENCE JOURNALS PROJECT
Description: Springer-Verlag is offering the tables of contents and BiblioAbstracts of 30 important scientific journals via e-mail before publication of the new issue. Tables of contents are free of charge and BiblioAbstracts are available for an annual token fee.
Subjects covered: science and technology; publishing
Established: March 1, 1993
Method of issuance: The files supplied are in ASCII format, structured in accordance with accepted standards. They can be read on any computer without further processing and but also easily integrated into local databases.
Sponsor: Springer-Verlag GmbH & Co. KG, New Technologies / Product Development, P.O. Box 10 52 80, W-6900 Heidelberg, Germany; fax: +49 6221 487 648.
How to access: For details please send an e-mail message containing the word HELP to SVJPS@DHDSPRI6.BITNET or contact SPRINGER@DHDSPRI6.BITNET

STN INTERNATIONAL
Description: STN International is a commercial online bibliographic utility whose databases are searchable through the Internet.
Subjects covered: online utility; library and information science; information technology
Sponsor: STN International, Chemical Abstracts Service, 2540 Olentangy River Road, P.O. Box 3012, Columbus, OH 43210-0012; (614) 447-3600.
How to access: Telnet to stnc.cas.org or 143.243.5.32

TITLEBANK ELECTRONIC CATALOG FOR THE INTERNET
Description: The TitleBank Electronic Catalog is a collection of publishers' catalogs available through Internet gopher. Users can search and view title information and are able to place orders online. Orders placed through the Catalog are routed to publishers.
Subjects covered: publishing; electronic shopping service
Fee: For more information, contact (508) 486-8976.
Sponsor: Inforonics, Inc. 550, Newtown Road, P.O. Box 458, Littleton, MA 01460; (508) 486-8976.
How to access: Gopher accessible at gopher.infor.com. For more information, contact mga@infor.com; (508) 486-8976.

Section 7. Usenet Newsgroups and Other Mailing Lists

A. USENET NEWSGROUPS

The following list of Usenet Newsgroups is authored by Gene Spafford (spaf@cs.purdue.edu) and David C. Lawrence (tale@uunet.uu.net). Reproduced with permission from Gene Spafford and David C. Lawrence. The newsgroup descriptions were authored by Mr. Spafford and Mr. Lawrence.

You can retrieve the latest version of this quickly growing list from the UUNET news.answers archive. Appended is how to use the mailserver; files are under /pub/usenet/news.answers. Or you can ftp to ftp.uu.net:/usenet/news.answers if you have ftp, or do 1-900-GOT-SRCS anonymous UUCP dialup to uunet.

Below, diff files are the changes from the previous edition posted.

Moderators: moderator-list/part1.Z moderator-list/diff1.Z

Active Groups in comp, misc, news, rec, sci, soc, and talk:
active-newsgroups/diff1.Z
active-newsgroups/part1.Z
active-newsgroups/diff2.Z
active-newsgroups/part2.Z

Groups in other worldwide hierarchies:
alt-hierarchies/diff1.Z
alt-hierarchies/part1.Z
alt-hierarchies/diff2.Z
alt-hierarchies/part2.Z

You can get a list of all groups uunet carries from ftp.uu.net (or uunet!- via uucp) under /uunet-info/newsgroups.Z (newsgroups with descriptions) and /uunet/info/active.Z (newsgroups with traffic margins over past two weeks). This includes many hierarchies that the other sets of lists do not.

The following is a list of active USENET newsgroups as of 23 Jul 1993. This list does not include the gatewayed Internet newsgroups (see below). The groups distributed worldwide are divided into seven broad classifications: "news", "soc", "talk", "misc", "sci", "comp" and "rec". Each of these classifications is organized into groups and subgroups according to topic.

"comp"   Topics of interest to both computer professionals and hobbyists, including topics in computer science, software source, and ab information on hardware and software systems.

"sci"   Discussions marked by special and usually practical knowledge, relating to research in or application of the established sciences.

"misc"   Groups addressing themes not easily classified under any of the other headings or which incorporate themes from multiple categories.

"soc"   Groups primarily addressing social issues and socializing.

"talk"   Groups largely debate-oriented and tending to feature long discussions without resolution and without appreciable amounts of generally useful information.

"news"   Groups concerned with the news network and software themselves.

"rec"   Groups oriented towards the arts, hobbies and recreational activities.

These "world" newsgroups are (usually) circulated around the entire USENET -- this implies world-wide distribution. Not all groups actually enjoy such wide distribution, however. Some sites take only a selected subset of the more "technical" groups, and controversial "noise" groups are often not carried by many sites (these groups are often under the "talk" and "soc" classifications). Many sites do not carry some or all of the comp.binaries groups.

There are groups in other subcategories, but they are local: to institutions, to geographic regions, etc. and they are not listed here. Note that these distribution categories can be used to restrict the propagation of news articles. Currently, distributions include:

world   worldwide distribution (default)
can   limited (mostly) to Canada
eunet   limited (mostly) to European sites in EUNet
na   limited (mostly) to North America
usa   limited (mostly) to the United States

There may be other regional and local distribution categories available at your site. Most US states have distribution categories named after the two letter abbreviation for that state or category (e.g., "ga" for Georgia, "nj" for New Jersey). Please use an appropriate distribution category if your article is not likely to be of interest to USENET readers worldwide.

Some groups are moderated or are monitored mailing lists. They can only be posted to by mailing submissions to the coordinator (provided in a companion posting). Some selected sites provide automatic remailing to the moderator in support of B2.11, C news and INN -- posting to one of these groups automatically mails the article for the poster. Some of the moderated groups are gatewayed to USENET from the Internet and appear as newsgroups to facilitate distribution and posting from the Usenet. Some of these gatewayed Internet newsgroups are listed below, and the rest appear in a companion posting that lists alternative newsgroup hierarchies. Other of the "world" groups are bidirectionally gatewayed with Internet mailing lists; items submitted from the Internet side to the digest are split up and submitted to the USENET group, while articles submitted on the USENET side are bundled up and submitted to the mailing list. A complete list of moderated newsgroups, submission addresses and moderators is given in a companion posting.

The following "world" groups have been gatewayed with the listed Internet lists. Some of them may not still be gatewayed due to broken software and/or gateways; such groups are marked with an asterisk (" *") in the list below. Please contact me if you should know of their current status. Also note that the group "comp.lang.forth" is gatewayed with the Bitnet discussion list "um-forth@weizmann.bitnet", comp.lang.apl is gatewayed with APL-L at the unb.ca node, and rec.railroad is run from "rail-road@queens.bitnet". Some of these lists are gated one-way into Usenet groups; those groups have been marked with a ">" symbol in the list below.

If you are reading this article from a site not on the Usenet, you may subscribe to Internet lists by writing to the request address. You form such an address by putting "-request" before the "@" symbol, as in "unix-emacs-request@vm.tcs.tulane.edu". This gets your message directly to the list maintainer instead of broadcasting it to all the readers of the list.

Also note that moderators of Usenet groups may not be in charge of the corresponding mailing list or gateway. For example, the moderator of comp.sources.unix does not have anything to do with the unix-sources mailing list; matters concerning the mailing list should be addressed to unix-sources-request@brl.mil

USENET GROUP = INTERNET LIST

comp.databases.ingres = info-ingres@math.ams.com
comp.dcom.modems = info-modems@wsmr-simtel20.army.mil
comp.dcom.telecom = telecom@eecs.nwu.edu
comp.emacs = unix-emacs@bbn.com
comp.graphics.gnuplot = info-gnuplot@dartmouth.edu
*comp.lang.ada = info-ada@ajpo.sei.cmu.edu
comp.lang.c = info-c@brl.mil
>comp.lang.c++ = info-g++@prep.ai.mit.edu
>comp.lang.c++ = help-g++@prep.ai.mit.edu
comp.lang.modula2 = info-m2@ucf1vm.bitnet
*comp.lang.pascal = info-pascal@brl.mil
*comp.lang.prolog = prolog@score.stanford.edu
comp.mail.mh = mh-users@ics.uci.edu
comp.os.cpm = info-cpm@wsmr-simtel20.army.mil
comp.os.minix = info-minix@udel.edu
comp.os.vms = info-vax@sri.com
comp.protocols.kerberos = kerberos@athena.mit.edu
comp.protocols.tcp-ip = tcp-ip@nic.ddn.mil
comp.society.privacy = comp-privacy@pica.army.mil
comp.sources.misc = unix-sources@brl.mil
comp.sources.unix = unix-sources@brl.mil
comp.specification.z = zforum@comlab.ox.ac.uk
comp.sys.apollo = apollo@umix.cc.umich.edu
comp.sys.apple2 = info-apple@apple.com
comp.sys.atari.8bit = info-atari8-request@naucse.cse.nau.edu

comp.sys.atari.st = info-atari16-request@naucse.cse.nau.edu
comp.sys.misc = info-micro@wsmr-simtel20.army.mil
comp.sys.prime = info-prime@blx-a.prime.com
comp.sys.tahoe = info-tahoe@csd1.milw.wisc.edu
comp.sys.xerox = info-1100@tut.cis.ohio-state.edu
*comp.terminals = info-terms@mc.lcs.mit.edu
>comp.text.tex = texhax@cs.washington.edu
>comp.text.tex = info-tex@shsu.edu
comp.unix.questions = info-unix@brl.mil
comp.unix.internals = unix-wizards@brl.mil
comp.windows.interviews = interviews@interviews.stanford.edu
comp.windows.x = xpert@expo.lcs.mit.edu
*rec.arts.sf.misc = sf-lovers@rutgers.edu
rec.food.recipes = recipes@rigel.dfrt.nasa.gov
rec.games.diplomacy = dipl-l@mitvma.mit.edu
rec.radio.amateur.misc = info-hams@ucsd.edu
rec.radio.amateur.packet = packet-radio@ucsd.edu
rec.radio.amateur.policy = ham-policy@ucsd.edu
rec.radio.broacasting = journal@airwaves.chi.il.us
rec.radio.info = radio-info@ucsd.edu
rec.radio.shortwave = swl-l@cuvma.columbia.edu
rec.music.funky = funky-music@hyper.lap.upenn.edu
rec.music.gdead = dead-flames@virginia.edu
rec.music.phish = phish@virginia.edu
rec.music.makers.synth = synth-l@auvm.auvm.edu
rec.sport.disc = ultimate-list@doe.carleton.ca
rec.video = videotech@wsmr-simtel20.army.mil

*sci.astro = sky-fans@xx.lcs.mit.edu
sci.astro.fits = fitsbits@nrao.edu
sci.physics = physics@unix.sri.com
sci.physics.fusion = fusion@zorch.sf-bay.org
sci.space = space@isu.isunet.edu
soc.roots = roots-l@vm1.nodak.edu

ALTERNATIVE TOPIC NEWSGROUPS

alt.1d One-dimensional imaging, & the thinking behind it.
alt.3d Three-dimensional imaging.
alt.abortion.inequity Sexism comes in many guises.
alt.abuse-recovery ??. (Moderated)
alt.activism Activities for activists.
alt.activism.d A place to discuss issues in alt.activism.
alt.adoption For those involved with or contemplating adoption.
alt.aeffle.und.pferdle German TV cartoon characters.
alt.alien.vampire.flonk.flonk.flonk simoN.
alt.alien.visitors Space Aliens on Earth! Abduction! Gov't Co-verup!
alt.alt Recursive fun.
alt.amateur-comp The Amateur Computerist.
alt.american.automobile.breakdown.breakdown.breakdown ''...then the steering wheel came off in my hands''.
alt.anarchism %SYSTEM-F-ANARCHISM, the operating system is overthrown.
alt.angst Anxiety in the modern world.
alt.angst.xibo.sex Tightening the screws of your existence.
alt.answers As if anyone on alt has the answers. (Moderated)
alt.anybody You talking to me?
alt.appalachian Appalachian regional issues discussion.
alt.archery Robin Hood had the right idea.
alt.architecture Building design/construction and related topics.
alt.artcom Artistic Community, arts & communication.
alt.astrology Twinkle, twinkle, little planet.
alt.atheism Godless heathens.
alt.atheism.moderated Focused Godless heathens. (Moderated)
alt.authorware Discussions on the use of the Authorware package.
alt.autos.antique Discussion of all facets of older automobiles.
alt.autos.rod-n-custom Discussion of souped-up or customised autos.
alt.bacchus The non-profit ''BACCHUS'' organization.
alt.backrubs Lower...to the right...aaaah!
alt.bad.clams Bad clams sneak up behind you and pounce. Bad clams kill.
alt.baldspot Discussions for the hairing impaired.
alt.basement.graveyard Another side of the do-it-yourself movement.
alt.bbs See alt.self-reference.
alt.bbs.internet ??
alt.bbs.unixbbs Bulletin Board Systems under Uniclones.
alt.bbs.unixbbs.uniboard Discussions about the Uniboard BBS.
alt.bbs.uupcb ??.
alt.beadworld We will appease the bead gods.
alt.beer Good for what ales ya.
alt.best.of.internet Sort of an oxymoron.
alt.binaries.multimedia Sound, text and graphics data rolled in one.
alt.binaries.pictures.d Discussions about picture postings.
alt.binaries.pictures.erotica Gigabytes of copyright violations.
alt.binaries.pictures.erotica.d Discussing erotic copyright violations.

alt.binaries.pictures.fine-art.d Discussion about huge image files. (Moderated)
alt.binaries.pictures.fractals Cheaper just to send the program parameters.
alt.binaries.pictures.misc Have we saturated the network yet?
alt.binaries.pictures.supermodels Yet more copyright violations.
alt.binaries.pictures.tasteless ''Eccchh, that last one was sick...''.
alt.binaries.pictures.utilities Discussion of binary posting utilities.
alt.binaries.sounds.d Sounding off.
alt.binaries.sounds.erotica Ngghhh! MMMMMMM! uuuhhhnnnnnOOOOOHHHhhhhh...
alt.binaries.sounds.misc Digitized audio adventures.
alt.birthright Birthright Party propaganda.
alt.bitch.pork Flames in a particular vein.
alt.bite.my.butt One newsgroup under god, with tyranny & malice for all.
alt.bitterness No matter what it's for, you know how it'll turn out.
alt.bizarre Too wierd for the wierdos.
alt.blahblah Iggy? is that you?
alt.bogus.group Nothing is too good for you, is it.
alt.bonsai Zen and the art of little trees.
alt.books.reviews ''If you want to know how it turns out, read it!''.
alt.boomerang Technology and use of the boomerang.
alt.boostagogo ??.
alt.brother-jed The born-again minister touring US campuses.
alt.buddha.short.fat.guy Religion. And not religion. Both. Neither.
alt.business.multi-level Multi-level (network) marketing businesses.
alt.business.multi-level.scam.scam.scam Hey, look! Mikey likes it!
alt.butt-keg.marmalade Typical yanqui analytic humor.
alt.butt.harp There's a group for everything in alt..
alt.buttered.scones You bring the tea.
alt.cable-tv.re-regulate This probably wouldn't fix the content problem.
alt.cad Computer Aided Design.
alt.cad.autocad CAD as practiced by customers of Autodesk.
alt.california The state and the state of mind.
alt.callahans Callahan's bar for puns and fellowship.
alt.cascade Art or litter you decide.
alt.cd-rom Discussions of optical storage media.
alt.censorship Discussion about restricting speech/press.
alt.cesium Your life is ticking away in very precise increments...
alt.chess.bdg The Blackmar-Diemer Gambit.
alt.chess.ics The Internet Chess Server @valkyries.andrew.cmu.edu.
alt.child-support Raising children in a split family.
alt.chinese.text Postings in Chinese; Chinese language software.
alt.clubs.compsci Often computer science is like being conked on the head.
alt.clueless Duh.
alt.co-evolution About the Whole Earth Review and associated lifestyles.
alt.co-ops Discussion about co-operatives.
alt.cobol Relationship between programming and stone axes.
alt.colorguard Marching bands etc.
alt.com ??.
alt.comedy.british British humour.
alt.comics.buffalo-roam A postscript comic strip.
alt.comics.lnh Interactive net.madness in the superhero genre.

alt.comics.superman No one knows it is also alt.clark.kent.

alt.comics.superman.dies.dies.dies I wonder if we can get the
Naked Guy to replace him.

alt.comp.acad-freedom.news Academic freedom issues related to
computers. (Moderated)

alt.comp.acad-freedom.talk Academic freedom issues related to
computers.

alt.conference-ctr Conference center management issues.

alt.config Alternative subnet discussions and connectivity.

alt.consciousness Discussions on consciousness.

alt.conspiracy Be paranoid -- they're out to get you.

alt.conspiracy.jfk The Kennedy assassination.

alt.control-theory Feedback & similar cybernosis.

alt.cosuard Council of Sysops & Users Against Rate Discrimination.

alt.crackers Best when read with alt.cheese.

alt.crackers.saltine No chloresterol, either.

alt.craig.hulsey.rack.rack.rack A pool shark.

alt.cult-movies Movies with a cult following (e.g., Rocky Horror
PS).

alt.culture.alaska Is this where the ice weasels come from?

alt.culture.electric-midget Waiting for the dwarf, or someone
like him.

alt.culture.indonesia Indonesian culture, news, etc.

alt.culture.karnataka Culture and language of the Indian state of
Karnataka.

alt.culture.kerala People of Keralite origin and the malayalam
language.

alt.culture.ny-upstate They have more than snow and Lake Ontario.

alt.culture.oregon Home of legal-discrimination advocates.

alt.culture.tuva Topics related to the Republic of Tannu Tuva.

alt.culture.us.asian-indian Asian Indians in the US and Canada.

alt.culture.usenet A self-referential oxymoron.

alt.current-events.somalia Discussion of the situation in Somalia.

alt.cyb-sys Cybernetics and Systems.

alt.cyberpunk High-tech low-life.

alt.cyberpunk.chatsubo Literary virtual reality in a cyberpunk
hangout.

alt.cyberpunk.movement Cybernizing the Universe.

alt.cyberpunk.tech Cyberspace and Cyberpunk technology.

alt.cyberspace Cyberspace and how it should work.

alt.cybertoon Cyberpunk epic.

alt.dads-rights Rights of fathers trying to win custody in court.

alt.dcom.telecom Discussion of telecommunications technology.

alt.dear.whitehouse When Hints from Heloise aren't enough.

alt.desert-shield.erotica Happiness is a warm gun.

alt.desert-storm The war against Iraq in Kuwait.

alt.desert-storm.facts For factual information on The Gulf War.

alt.desert-thekurds What's happening to the Kurds in Iraq.

alt.desert.storm.its.not.scud.its.al-hussein.dammit So use another
kind of missile.

alt.desert.toppings I'll have just a little more crude oil on that,
please.

alt.destroy.the.earth Deteriorata meets the Space Orphans.

alt.deutsche.bundesbahn.kotz.kotz.kotz Flaming the German rail
system.

alt.dev.null The ultimate in moderated newsgroups. (Moderated)

alt.devilbunnies Probably better left undescribed.

alt.discordia All hail Eris, etc.

alt.discrimination Quotas, affirmative action, bigotry, persecu-
tion.

alt.divination Divination techniques (e.g., I Ching, Tarot, runes).

alt.dragons-inn A computer fantasy environment (like Usenet is).

alt.dreams What do they mean?

alt.drugs Recreational pharmaceuticals and related flames.

alt.drugs.usenet Many things are addictive besides pills.

alt.duke.basketball.sucks.sucks.sucks Nothing to discuss, everybody knows.

alt.earth__summit Another triumph for George Bush.

alt.education.bangkok.cmc A distance-education project.

alt.education.bangkok.databases A distance-education project.

alt.education.bangkok.planning A distance-education project.

alt.education.bangkok.research A distance-education project.

alt.education.bangkok.student A distance-education project.

alt.education.bangkok.theory A distance-education project.

alt.education.disabled Learning experiences for the disabled.

alt.education.distance Learning over nets etc.

alt.elvis.sighting Guess who I saw at K-mart?

alt.emulators.ibmpc.apple2 The blind leading the blind.

alt.emusic Ethnic, exotic, electronic, elaborate, etc. music.

alt.ensign.wesley.die.die.die We just can't get enough of him.

alt.ernie-pook Long live Lynda Barry.

alt.etext Electronic text announcements.

alt.eunuchs.questions Handling user problems in the real world.

alt.evil Tales from the dark side.

alt.exploding.kibo Perhaps just wishful thinking.

alt.fan.BIFF COWABUNGA, DOOD!!! MY BROTHER SEZ
HES AWSUM.

alt.fan.alok.vijayvargia Vote early, and vote often.

alt.fan.amy-fisher Joey's friend.

alt.fan.andrew-beal Usenet is never having to say you're sorry.

alt.fan.asprin Discussing the works of Robert Lynn Asprin.

alt.fan.biafra An ex-Dead Kennedy.

alt.fan.bill-fenner PSU's cute, loveable, and fuzzy news admin.

alt.fan.brian-ellis ??.

alt.fan.bruce-becker ??.

alt.fan.bruce.woodcock ??.

alt.fan.bugtown For fans of the works of Matt Howarth.

alt.fan.chaki.chaki.chaki Chaki's fan club.

alt.fan.charles-lasner Is assembly language better?

alt.fan.chris-elliott Son of the comedian Bob of ''Bob and Ray''
fame.

alt.fan.dale-bass More flames.

alt.fan.dan-quayle For discussion of the US Vice President.

alt.fan.dave__barry Electronic fan club for humorist Dave
Barry.

alt.fan.david-sternlight ??.

alt.fan.debbie.gibson The world's oldest cheerleader.

alt.fan.dice-man Fans of Andrew Dice Clay.

alt.fan.disney.afternoon Disney Afternoon characters & shows.

alt.fan.don.no-soul.simmons From ''Amazon Women On The
Moon'' fame.

alt.fan.douglas-adams Author of ''The Meaning of Liff'', &
other fine works.

alt.fan.ecsd ??.

alt.fan.eddings The works of writer David Eddings.

alt.fan.elvis-presley The King.

alt.fan.eric-dynamic ??.

alt.fan.frank-zappa Is that a Sears poncho?

alt.fan.furry Fans of funny animals, ala Steve Gallacci's book.

alt.fan.gene-scott A late-nite tv bible-thumper.

alt.fan.gooley Fans of Markian Gooley and his followers.

alt.fan.goons Careful Neddy, it's that dastardly Moriarty again.

alt.fan.greaseman Fans of Doug Tracht, the DJ.

alt.fan.harry-mandel ??.

alt.fan.holmes Elementary, my dear Watfor.

alt.fan.howard-stern Fans of the abrasive radio & TV personality.

alt.fan.hurricane.yip ??.

alt.fan.itchy-n-scratchy Bart Simpson's favorite TV cartoon.

alt.fan.james-bond On his Majesty's Secret Service (& secret linen too).

alt.fan.jimmy-buffett A white sports coat and a pink crustacean.

alt.fan.jiro-nakamura Visiting the shaman.

alt.fan.john-palmer Tygra, tygra, burning blight...

alt.fan.ken-johnson Discussion pertaining to the great man himself.

alt.fan.kent-montana Appreciation of the Kent Montana Book Series.

alt.fan.kevin-darcy For Kebbie.

alt.fan.kevin-walsh For Prof Walsh fans.

alt.fan.lemurs Little critters with BIG eyes.

alt.fan.letterman One of the top 10 reasons to get the alt groups.

alt.fan.lightbulbs A hardware problem.

alt.fan.madonna Nice tits, eh... And how about that puppy?

alt.fan.maria-callas An opera singer.

alt.fan.mary-chungs The famous Cambridge, MA restaurant.

alt.fan.matt.welsh I saw a greater need.

alt.fan.max-headroom A famous Canadian.

alt.fan.meredith-tanner ??.

alt.fan.mike-jittlov Electronic fan club for animator Mike Jittlov.

alt.fan.monty-python Electronic fan club for those wacky Brits.

alt.fan.mst3k Mystery Science Theatre 3000 tv show.

alt.fan.mts Michigan Terminal System, a 1970 precursor to TSO.

alt.fan.naked-guy Discussing Andrew Martinez - the Naked Guy.

alt.fan.nathan.brazil Hero of a Jack Chalker novel.

alt.news.macedonia ??.

alt.fan.oingo-boingo ??.

alt.fan.pern Anne McCaffery's s-f oeuvre.

alt.fan.peter.hammill Fans of the avant-garde musician.

alt.fan.piers-anthony For fans of the s-f author Piers Anthony.

alt.fan.poris ??.

alt.fan.pratchett For fans of Terry Pratchett, s-f humor writer.

alt.fan.q The Qmnipotent Qne holds court here.

alt.fan.rama-krishna ??.

alt.fan.rita-rudner A TV comedienne.

alt.fan.robbie.pink.tutu Electronic fan club for Rob "Tutu" Kolstad.

alt.fan.roger.david.carasso Arguments for allowing abortion up to age 21.

alt.fan.rumpole Join us in Pommeroy's for some Chateau Thames Embankment.

alt.fan.run-dmc Walk dis way...

alt.fan.rush-limbaugh Derogation of others for fun and profit.

alt.fan.schwaben A nice part of Germany.

alt.fan.scott-tai ??.

alt.fan.shostakovich Classical music composer.

alt.fan.spinal-tap Down on the sex farm.

alt.fan.steve-zellers He is the solution to the nitrogen equation.

alt.fan.suicide-squid Breathtaking adventure stories.

alt.fan.tania.bedrax Parfum in a small vial.

alt.fan.tna For the college radio show ''T n A''.

alt.fan.tolkien ...and in the dark shall find them.

alt.fan.tom-robbins A novelist of quaint & affecting tales.

alt.fan.tom__peterson Portland, Oregon's favorite son.

alt.fan.vic-reeves Britain's top Light Entertainer and Formation Mollusc.

alt.fan.wal-greenslade This is the BBC Home Service.......<CHING!>

alt.fan.warlord The War Lord of the West Preservation Fan Club.

alt.fan.wodehouse Discussion of the works of humour author P.G. Wodehouse.

alt.fan.woody-allen ''Bananas'', ''Sleeper'', ''The Front'', ''Annie Hall'', ...

alt.fandom.cons Announcements of conventions (SciFi and others).

alt.fandom.misc Other topics for fans of various kinds.

alt.fans.david.davidian.fascist.fascist.fascist Political commentary.

alt.fashion All facets of the fasion industry discussed.

alt.fax.bondage The ancient secrets revealed.

alt.feet Tales too ticklish to tell.

alt.feminism Like soc.feminism, only different.

alt.filepro ??.

alt.flack FubGeniuf ftuff.

alt.flame Alternative, literate, pithy, succinct screaming.

alt.flame.abortion Somewhere to direct followups to.

alt.flame.eternal In heaven... nothing ever happens...

alt.flame.hairy-douchebag.meredith-tanner Typical yanqui non-consensual humor.

alt.flame.hairy-douchebag.roger-david-carasso More flames.

alt.flame.hirai.cs.dork Flaming a Nutty Perfesser.

alt.flame.marshal.perlman.weenie More flames, from Carasso.

alt.flame.mike-steiner ??.

alt.flame.pizza.greasy Surrogate for Domino's delivery vehicles.

alt.flame.psu Penn State gets its own.

alt.flame.sean-ryan An outspoken Alaskan.

alt.flame.spelling Fore andd abowt piple whoe kant spel.

alt.flame.those.nasty.little.hangnails-ouch Worse than torture.

alt.flame.weemba Roasting the one & only Matthew P. Wiener.

alt.folklore.college Collegiate humor.

alt.folklore.computers Stories & anecdotes about computers (some true!).

alt.folklore.ghost-stories Boo!.

alt.folklore.science The folklore of science, not the science of folklore.

alt.folklore.urban Urban legends, ala Jan Harold Brunvand.

alt.fondle.vomit Chia pet replacement.

alt.food Most folks like it.

alt.food.cocacola & Royal Crown, Pepsi, Dr. Pepper, NEHI, etc...

alt.food.dennys A chain of fast food restaurants.

alt.foolish.users Final resting place for the ''idiot-proof'' zealots.

alt.forgery One place for all forgeries--crossposting encouraged.

alt.freedom.of.information.act ''...EXCEPT THAT Congress shall limit...''.

alt.french.captain.borg.borg.borg Picard, you are not yourself lately.

alt.galactic-guide Entries for the actual Hitchhiker's Guide to the Galaxy.

alt.games.frp.live-action Discussion of all forms of live-action gaming.

alt.games.gb The Galactic Bloodshed conquest game.

alt.games.lynx The Atari Lynx.

alt.games.mornington.crescent Discussion of the Crescent game, and playing.

alt.games.omega The computer game Omega.

alt.games.sf2 The video game Street Fighter 2.

alt.games.tiddlywinks All aspects of the game of Tiddlywinks.

alt.games.torg Gateway for TORG mailing list.

alt.games.vga-planets Discussion of Tim Wisseman's VGA Planets.

alt.games.video.classic From early TV remote controls to Space Invaders, etc.

alt.gathering.rainbow For discussing the annual Rainbow Gathering.

alt.geek To fulfill an observed need.

alt.gobment.lones Talk about the thousand points of blight.

alt.good.morning Would you like coffee with that?.

alt.good.news A place for some news that's good news.

alt.gorby.coup.coup.coup Some say he did it to himself.

alt.gorby.gone.gone.gone Some say he did it to himself.

alt.gorets ...is like a crowded theatre full of piggies.

alt.gossip.royalty GIF's of Fergy on page 3...

alt.gothic The gothic movement: things mournful and dark.

alt.gourmand Recipes & cooking info. (Moderated)

alt.grad-student.tenured Most prison terms are finished sooner.

alt.graffiti Usenet spraypainters and their documenters.

alt.graphics Some prefer this to comp.graphics.

alt.graphics.pixutils Discussion of pixmap utilities.

alt.great-lakes Discussions of the Great Lakes and adjacent places.

alt.great.ass.paulina "For a year I get nothing and then this".

alt.great.ass.wheaton More Stardrek.

alt.grins.und.grunz Latu:rnich swachsinn.

alt.guinea.pig.conspiracy They're here for a reason. It's been kept quiet UNTIL NOW.

alt.guitar You axed for it, you got it.

alt.hackers Descriptions of projects currently under development. (Moderated)

alt.hackers.cough.cough.cough ??.

alt.hackers.malicious The really bad guys - don't take candy from them.

alt.half.operating.system.delay.delay.delay 1/2 an OS for 1/2 a computer, twice as late.

alt.happy.birthday.to.me Sing along the dotted line.

alt.hash.house.harriers Running & drinking, now there's a great combination.

alt.hayco.sucks.mud Odd perversion.

alt.heraldry.sca Heraldry in the Society of Creative Anachronism.

alt.hindu The Hindu religion. (Moderated)

alt.hinz.und.grunz Moin ihr flaschen- und kinder-scha:nder.

alt.horror The horror genre.

alt.horror.cthulhu Campus Crusade for Cthulhu, Ctulhu, Ctulu, and the rest.

alt.horror.werewolves They were wolves, now they're something to be wary of.

alt.hotfut Hospital of the Future.

alt.hotrod High speed automobiles. (Moderated)

alt.housing.nontrad Nontraditional housing (see alt.toys.lego).

alt.hurricane.andrew The 1992 hurricane disaster.

alt.hypertext Discussion of hypertext -- uses, transport, etc.

alt.hypnosis When you awaken, you will forget about this newsgroup.

alt.imploding.kibo What goes out must come in.

alt.individualism Philosophies where individual rights are paramount.

alt.industrial The Industrial Computing Society.

alt.industrial.computing The Industrial Computing Society tries again.

alt.inet92 Relating to the Inet '92 conference in Kobe, Japan.

alt.info-science This is really about library science.

alt.info-theory This is really about information theory.

alt.internet.access.wanted "Oh. OK, how about just an MX record for now?"

alt.internet.services Not available in the uucp world, even via email.

alt.iraqi.dictator.bomb.bomb.bomb Keep doing it till you've got it right.

alt.irc Internet Relay Chat material.

alt.irc.bot Discussion of creating irc bots.

alt.irc.corruption Is nowhere safe?

alt.irc.corruption.log.log.log Discussions of corrupted loggers.

alt.irc.ircii I iscussion of the IRC II client program.

alt.irc.recovery Kill your television... er, IRC client.

alt.irc.sleaze Internet Relay Chat flamage.

alt.irc.sleaze.mark More Internet Relay Chat flamage.

alt.iq.endless-discussion ??.

alt.is.too NOT!

alt.isea International Symposia of Electronic Arts.

alt.journalism.gonzo Fans of Hunter S. Thompson.

alt.jubjub Bandersnatchii are welcome here too.

alt.kalbo ??.

alt.karaoke Amazing that so many people know how to sing off-key.

alt.ketchup Whak Whak ...shake... Whak Damn, all over my tie.

alt.kids-talk A place for the pre-college set on the net.

alt.kill.the.whales This newsgroup is evidence for the coming apocalypse.

alt.killfiles A means for modulating your version of usenet reality.

alt.kodak.cd.bitch.bitch.bitch Definitely a challenge to the dedicated hacker.

alt.lang.apl Compact, cryptic, Greek letters -- the perfect language.

alt.lang.asm Assembly languages of various flavors.

alt.lang.awk A handy UNIX interpreted language.

alt.lang.basic The Language That Would Not Die.

alt.lang.cfutures Discussion of the future of the C programming language

alt.lang.intercal A joke language with a real compiler.

alt.lang.ml The ML and SML symbolic languages.

alt.lang.sas The SAS statistical language.

alt.lang.teco The TECO editor language.

alt.lawyers.sue.sue.sue Worse than banana slug fleas.

alt.letter.chain A microcosm of Usenet itself.

alt.letzebuerger Forum for Luxemburgish students.

alt.licker.store Hiccup!

alt.locksmithing You locked your keys in where?

alt.lucid-emacs.bug Bug reports about Lucid Emacs.

alt.lucid-emacs.help Q&A and general discussion of Lucid Emacs.

alt.lwaxana-troi.die.die.die More Stardrek.

alt.lycra For fans of Spandex & similar apparel.

alt.machines.misc ??.

alt.magic For discussion about stage magic.

alt.magnus__and__ketil A sometimes inspired doofus.

alt.maroney This is really, really stupid.

alt.materials.simulation Computer modeling of materials. (Moderated)

alt.mcdonalds Can I get fries with that?

alt.med.cfs Chronic fatigue syndrome information.

alt.meditation.transcendental Contemplation of states beyond the teeth.

alt.messianic Messianic traditions.

alt.mfs A test group, they said. Oh, sure.

alt.military.cadet Preparing for the coming apocalypse.

alt.misanthropy Who asked you, you scum?

alt.mindcontrol You WILL read this group and ENJOY it!

alt.missing-kids Locating missing children.

alt.models Model building, design, etc.

alt.motd Messages Of The Day.

alt.mothers Most people have at least one.

alt.move.michelle.regina Doesn't she realize what that means?

alt.mud.bsx BSX VR system.

alt.mud.t-rev.stomp.stomp.stomp ''Handkerchief?'' ''Yes, you ninny, and quickly!''

alt.music.alternative For groups having 2 or less Platinum-selling albums.

alt.music.category-freak Lips that touch Def Leppard shall never touch mine.

alt.music.enya Gaelic set to spacey music.

alt.music.filk sf/fantasy related folk music.

alt.music.hardcore Could be porno set to music.

alt.music.jewish Music to make you feel guilty.

alt.music.machines.of.loving.grace Another pop group.

alt.music.marillion Another pop group.

alt.music.pop.will.eat.itself Another pop group.

alt.music.progressive Yes, Marillion, Asia, King Crimson, etc.

alt.music.queen He's dead, Jim.

alt.music.rush For Rushheads.

alt.music.ska Discussions of ska (skank) music, bands, and suchlike.

alt.music.the.police Don't stand so close.

alt.music.tmbg Another pop group.

alt.my.crummy.boss Where'd I put my gun?

alt.my.head.hurts I can't believe this is happening AGAIN...

alt.mythology Zeus rules.

alt.national.enquirer Entertaining, utter drek.

alt.native Issues for and about indigenous peoples of the world.

alt.necromicon Yet another sign of the coming apocalypse.

alt.net.personalities A fan group for everybody.

alt.newbie Alt's answer to news.newusers..

alt.newgroup For people who don't like to rmgroup/newgroup things.

alt.news-media Don't believe the hype.

alt.news.members Society for the Propagation of news.members.

alt.newsgroup.creators.dork.dork.dork Feh.

alt.nick.sucks Probably.

alt.nodies Alaskan helpers.

alt.noise BZZZZT! KRAK!! BLAM! %$@#?! etc.

alt.non.sequitur Richard Nixon.

alt.ntc-textile-res ??.

alt.olympics.medal-tally Hey, dude, mine's bigger.

alt.oobe Out Of Body Experiences (but there's some soul left).

alt.org.food-not-bombs Food Not Bombs is an anti-hunger organisation.

alt.org.pugwash Technological issues from a social stance.

alt.os.nachos A snack operating system for teaching.

alt.overlords Office of the Omnipotent Overlords of the Omniverse.

alt.pagan Discussions about paganism & religion.

alt.paranormal Phenomena which are not scientifically explicable.

alt.parents-teens Parent-teenager relationships.

alt.party Parties, celebration and general debauchery.

alt.pave.the.earth One world, one people, one slab of asphalt.

alt.pcnews Discussing PCNews software.

alt.peace.corps Get paid for foreign travel.

alt.peeves Discussion of peeves & related.

alt.personals Do you really want to meet someone this way?

alt.personals.ads Geek seeks Dweeb. Object: low-level interfacing.

alt.personals.bondage Are you tied up this evening?

alt.personals.misc Dweeb seeks Geek. Object: low-level interfacing.

alt.personals.poly Do you multiprocess?

alt.pets.chia ''Well, I've never been bitten by one!''

alt.philosophy.objectivism A product of the Ayn Rand corporation.

alt.planning.urban As if any city is really planned.

alt.politics.british Politics and a real Queen, too.

alt.politics.bush Discussing Mr. Read-My-Lips.

alt.politics.clinton Discussing Slick Willie & Co.

alt.politics.correct A Neil Bush fan club.

alt.politics.democrats.clinton Another view of silly season in the US.

alt.politics.democrats.d Another view of silly season in the US.

alt.politics.ec European community stuff.

alt.politics.economics War = = Poverty, & other discussions.

alt.politics.elections Everyone who votes for Quayle gets a free lollipop.

alt.politics.equality An oxymoron.

alt.politics.europe.misc Misc. discussions on European politics.

alt.politics.greens Green party politics & activities worldwide.

alt.politics.homosexuality As the name implies

alt.politics.italy How they handle cigarette riots & other things.

alt.politics.kibo BOOM. Ka-WHUMP. CRASH. ...oops...

alt.politics.libertarian The libertarian ideology.

alt.politics.marrou Andre Marrou, Libertarian presidential candidate.

alt.politics.media There's lies, damn lies, statistics, and news reports.

alt.politics.org.misc Political organizations.

alt.politics.org.un Politics at the ''United'' Nations.

alt.politics.perot Discussion of the non-candidate.

alt.politics.radical-left Who remains after the radicals left?

alt.politics.reform Political reform.

alt.politics.sex Not a good idea to mix them, sez Marilyn & Profumo.

alt.politics.shelfbutt Typical yanqui racist humor.

alt.politics.usa.constitution U.S. Constitutional politics.

alt.politics.usa.misc Misc. USA politics.

alt.politics.vietnamese Political & social discussions about Vietnam.

alt.polyamory For those who maintain multiple love relationships.

alt.postmodern Postmodernism, semiotics, deconstruction, and the like.

alt.president.clinton Will the CIA undermine his efforts?

alt.privacy Privacy issues in cyberspace.

alt.prose Postings of original writings, fictional & otherwise.

alt.prose.d Discussions about postings in alt.prose.

alt.psychoactives Better living through chemistry.

alt.psychology.personality Personality taxonomy, such as Myers-Briggs.

alt.pub.cloven-shield S-F role-playing.

alt.pub.havens-rest S-F role-playing.

alt.pulp Paperback fiction, newsprint production, orange juice.

alt.puns.joey-buttafuoco The possibilities are almost endless.

alt.ql.creative The ''Quantum Leap'' tv show.

alt.quake About California and other earthquakes.

alt.quotations Another form of sampling.

alt.radio.pirate Hide the gear, here comes the magic station-wagons.

alt.radio.scanner Discussion of scanning radio receivers.

alt.rap For fans of rap music.

alt.rap-gdead Fans of The Grateful Dead and Rap. Really.

alt.rave Techno-culture: music, dancing, drugs, dancing...

alt.recovery For people in recovery programs (e.g., AA, ACA, GA).

alt.recovery.codependency For people in yet more recovery programs.

alt.religion.adm3a Flaming the merits of the Sigler-Lear ADM3A.

alt.religion.all-worlds Grokking the Church of All Worlds from Heinlein's book.

alt.religion.computers People who believe computing is "real life." alt.religion.emacs Emacs. Umacs. We all macs.

alt.religion.kibology He's Fred, Jim.

alt.religion.sabaean Discussing the Sabaean religious order.

alt.religion.santaism Devil-worshipping dyslexics.

alt.religion.scientology He's dead, Jim.

alt.religion.vince No, not him, the other one -- Vince!

alt.revisionism "It CAN'T be that way 'cause here's the FACTS".

alt.revolution.counter Discussions of counter-revolutionary issues.

alt.rhode_island Discussion of the great little state.

alt.rissa Fans (and otherwise) of Patricia O'Tuama.

alt.rmgroup For the people who like to rmgroup/newgroup things.

alt.rock-n-roll Counterpart to alt.sex and alt.drugs.

alt.rock-n-roll.acdc Dirty deeds done dirt cheap.

alt.rock-n-roll.classic Like the Mac classic and the Sparc classic.

alt.rock-n-roll.hard Music where stance is everything.

alt.rock-n-roll.metal For the headbangers on the net.

alt.rock-n-roll.metal.gnr "Axl Rose" is an anagram for "Oral Sex".

alt.rock-n-roll.metal.heavy Non-sissyboy metal bands.

alt.rock-n-roll.metal.ironmaiden Sonic torture methods.

alt.rock-n-roll.metal.metallica Another pop group.

alt.rock-n-roll.symphonic Cognitive dissonance in an orchestral mode.

alt.rodney.dangerfield A newsgroup that don't get no respect.

alt.rodney.king Four of a kind beat a king.

alt.romance Discussion about the romantic side of love.

alt.romance.chat Talk about no sex.

alt.rush-limbaugh Fans of the conservative activist radio announcer.

alt.sadistic.dentists.drill.drill.drill Novocaine won't help you.

alt.satanism Not such a bad dude once you get to know him.

alt.save.the.earth Environmentalist causes.

alt.sci.astro.aips Discussions on the Astronomical Image Processing System.

alt.sci.astro.figaro The Figaro data-reduction package.

alt.sci.image-facility ??.

alt.sci.physics.acoustics Sound advice.

alt.sci.physics.new-theories Scientific theories you won't find in journals.

alt.sci.planetary Studies in planetary science.

alt.sect.ahmadiyya Discussion of the Ahmadiyyat sect of Islam.

alt.security.index Pointers to good stuff in alt,misc.security. (Moderated)

alt.security.keydist Exchange of keys for public key encryption systems.

alt.security.pgp The Pretty Good Privacy package.

alt.security.ripem A secure email system illegal to export from the US.

alt.sega.genesis Another addiction.

alt.self-improve Self-improvement in less than 14 characters.

alt.sewing A group that is not as it seams.

alt.sex Postings of a prurient nature.

alt.sex.NOT For those who've had enough of sex, or else want to.

alt.sex.aluminum.baseball.bat Postings of a very prurient nature.

alt.sex.bestiality Happiness is a warm puppy.

alt.sex.bestiality.hamster.duct-tape That little squeek they make is so cute...

alt.sex.bondage Tie me, whip me, make me read the net!

alt.sex.bondage.particle.physics Extracting yourself from a quagma.

alt.sex.boredom For those who fall asleep BEFORE.

alt.sex.carasso Where Carasso's SO is himself.

alt.sex.carasso.snuggles I can't talk, my mouth is full.

alt.sex.head Tales of certain erotic activities.

alt.sex.ho Gangsta fun.

alt.sex.homosexual As the name implies.

alt.sex.masturbation Where one's SO is oneself.

alt.sex.motss Jesse Helms would not subscribe to this group.

alt.sex.movies Discussing the ins and outs of certain movies.

alt.sex.nudels.me.too ??.

alt.sex.sonja Yesssss....

alt.sex.stories For those who need it NOW.

alt.sex.stories.d For those who talk about needing it NOW

alt.sex.trans Transsexuality.

alt.sex.wanted Requests for erotica, either literary or in the flesh.

alt.sex.wizards Questions for only true Sex wizards.

alt.sex.woody-allen A Mid-Summer's Night Sex Comedy.

alt.sexual.abuse.recovery Helping others deal with traumatic experiences.

alt.sexy.bald.captains More Stardrek.

alt.shenanigans Practical jokes, pranks, randomness, etc.

alt.showbiz.gossip Who's doing what to whom in showbiz.

alt.shrinky.dinks What are they?

alt.sigma2.height Big or small, come one come all.

alt.sigma2.penis The bigger they are, the softer they fall.

alt.silly.group.names.d Eponymy.

alt.skate-board Discussion of all apsects of skate-boarding.

alt.skinheads The skinhead culture/anti-culture.

alt.slack Posting relating to the Church of the Subgenius.

alt.slack.BoB.dirtbag Posting berating to the Church of the Subgenius.

alt.slime Worse than lawyers.

alt.smouldering.dog.zone Explosions and the deity.

alt.snowmobiles High-horsepower sleds in the powder.

alt.society.ati The Activist Times Digest. (Moderated)

alt.society.civil-disob Civil disobedience.

alt.society.civil-liberties Individual rights.

alt.society.etrnl-vigilanc A Barry Goldwater fan club.

alt.society.revolution Discussions on revolution(s).

alt.society.sovereign Independantistes, unite!

alt.soft-sys.tooltalk Forum for ToolTalk related issues.

alt.sources Alternative source code, unmoderated. Caveat Emptor.

alt.sources.amiga Technically-oriented Amiga PC sources.

alt.sources.amiga.d Discussion of technically-oriented Amiga PC sources.

alt.sources.d Discussion of posted sources.

alt.sources.index Pointers to source code in alt.sources.. (Moderated)

alt.sources.patches Reposted patches from non-bugs groups.

alt.sources.wanted Requests for source code.

alt.spam.tin Spam is neither particle nor wave - it is a property.

alt.spleen The spleen is underappreciated...

alt.sport.bowling In the gutter again.

alt.sport.bungee Like alt.suicide with rubber bands.

alt.sport.darts Look what you've done to the wall!

alt.sport.lasertag Indoor splatball with infrared lasers.

alt.sport.photon Light amusement.

alt.sport.pool Knock your balls into your pockets for fun.

alt.stagecraft Technical theatre issues.

alt.startrek.creative Stories and parodies related to Star Trek.

alt.stupid.putz Getting the next-to-the-last word.

alt.stupid.putz.BoB.BoB.BoB ??.

alt.stupid.putz.gritzner ??.

alt.stupidity Discussion about stupid newsgroups.

alt.suburbs Sprawling on the fringes of the city.

alt.suicide.finals Is that last name, first?

alt.suicide.holiday Talk of why suicides increase at holidays.

alt.suit.att-bsdi Is this where David gets Goliath again?

alt.super.nes Discussion of the Super Nintendo video game.

alt.supermodels Discussing famous & beautiful models.

alt.support Dealing with emotional situations & experiences.

alt.support.big-folks Sizeism can be as awful as sexism or racism.

alt.support.cancer Dealing with the Big C.

alt.support.diet Seeking enlightenment through weight loss.

alt.support.mult-sclerosis Discussion about living with multiple sclerosis.

alt.surfing Riding the ocean waves.

alt.sustainable.agriculture Such as the Mekong delta before Agent Orange.

alt.swedish.chef.bork.bork.bork Don't ask.

alt.sys.amiga.demos Code and talk to show off the Amiga.

alt.sys.amiga.uucp AmigaUUCP.

alt.sys.amiga.uucp.patches Patches for AmigaUUCP.

alt.sys.intergraph Support for Intergraph machines.

alt.sys.pdp8 There's an X Windows port in progress...

alt.tarot In this card game you play for keeps...

alt.tasteless Truly disgusting.

alt.tasteless.jokes Sometimes insulting rather than disgusting or humorous.

alt.tasteless.penis Not a recipe group (we hope!).

alt.test Alternative subnetwork testing.

alt.text.dwb Discussion of the AT&T Documenter's WorkBench.

alt.thrash Thrashlife.

alt.timewasters A Dutch computer club; perhaps a microcosm of Usenet...

alt.tla Palindromic fun, or else Three-Letter-Acronyms.

alt.todd.green.likes.it.up.the.butt Typical yanqui sexist humor.

alt.toolkits.xview The X windows XView toolkit.

alt.toon-pics More copyright violations.

alt.toys.lego Snap 'em together.

alt.transgendered Boys will be girls, and vice-versa.

alt.true.crime To balance out all the false crime on the net.

alt.tv.90210 Teenyboppers on tv.

alt.tv.antagonists Fans of the new "The Antagonists" TV show.

alt.tv.babylon-5 Casablanca in space.

alt.tv.beakmans-world Beakman, Josie the kid, and the big rat.

alt.tv.dinosaurs The bigger they are...

alt.tv.fifteen Nickolodeon's show, "Fifteen", etc.

alt.tv.infomercials Yes! Ron Popeil is telling the truth! Depend on it!

alt.tv.la-law For the folks out in la-law land.

alt.tv.liquid-tv Right there on your pitcher tube.

alt.tv.mash Nothing like a good comedy about war and dying.

alt.tv.melrose-place More teenyboppers on tv.

alt.tv.misc Better to talk about it than watch it.

alt.tv.mst3k Hey, you robots! Down in front!.

alt.tv.muppets Miss Piggy on the tube.

alt.tv.northern-exp For the TV show with moss growing on it.

alt.tv.prisoner The Prisoner television series from years ago.

alt.tv.red-dwarf The British sci-fi/comedy show.

alt.tv.ren-n-stimpy Some change from Lassie, eh?

alt.tv.saved-by-the-bell Fans of the clapper.

alt.tv.seinfeld A funny guy.

alt.tv.simpsons Don't have a cow, man!

alt.tv.snl The Saturday Nite Limbaugh ...errr, Live TV show.

alt.tv.tiny-toon Discussion about the "Tiny Toon Adventures" show.

alt.tv.tiny-toon.plucky-duck Discussion about "The Plucky Duck Show".

alt.tv.twin-peaks Discussion about the popular (and unusual) TV show.

alt.usage.english English grammar, word usages, and related topics.

alt.usenet.recovery Reupholster your news reader.

alt.uu.announce Announcements of Usenet University.

alt.uu.comp.misc Computer department of Usenet University.

alt.uu.comp.os.linux.questions UU Linux learning group - the Q&A column.

alt.uu.future Planning the future of Usenet University.

alt.uu.lang.esperanto.misc Study of Esperanto in Usenet University.

alt.uu.lang.misc Language department of Usenet University.

alt.uu.math.misc Math department of Usenet University.

alt.uu.misc.misc Misc. department of Usenet University.

alt.uu.tools Tools for Usenet University and education.

alt.uu.virtual-worlds.misc Study of virtual worlds in Usenet University.

alt.vampyres Discussion of vampires and related writings, films, etc.

alt.vigilantes Lynch those folks in alt.criminals!

alt.visa.us Discussion/information on visas pertaining to US.

alt.wall "5397 miles to Wall Drug". (Moderated)

alt.wanted.mars.women Mars Needs Women!

alt.wanted.moslem.bestiality It won't be too popular with some folks.

alt.wanted.moslem.gay This is not suggested reading for the intolerant.

alt.wanted.moslem.men Does this include Salman Rushdie?

alt.wanted.moslem.women For those so inclined.

alt.war Not just collateral damage.

alt.war.civil.usa Lest we forget...

alt.war.vietnam Lest we forget...

alt.waves ??.

alt.wee.willie.wisner The guy who came in from the cold (for a while, anyway).

alt.weemba Talk & flames about the one & only Weemba.

alt.whine Why me?

alt.who.is.bob Send $11.

alt.wolves Discussing wolves & wolf-mix dogs.

alt.world.taeis The shared-world project "taeis".

alt.wpi.negativland.subgenii.for.rent Not to be missed.

alt.x-headers.overboard RFC-822 may have opened up Pandora's box.

alt.zines Small magazines, mostly noncommercial.

alt.znet.fnet ZNET-related FNET topics & gateway.

alt.znet.pc ZNET International PC, an ASCII-based magazine.

COMPUTER-RELATED GROUPS

comp.admin.policy Discussions of site administration policies.

comp.ai Artificial intelligence discussions.

comp.ai.fuzzy Fuzzy set theory, aka fuzzy logic.

comp.ai.genetic Genetic algorithms in computing.

comp.ai.nat-lang Natural language processing by computers.

comp.ai.neural-nets All aspects of neural networks.

comp.ai.nlang-know-rep Natural Language and Knowledge Representation. (Moderated)

comp.ai.philosophy Philosophical aspects of Artificial Intelligence.

comp.ai.shells Artificial intelligence applied to shells.

comp.answers Repository for periodic USENET articles. (Moderated)

comp.apps.spreadsheets Spreadsheets on various platforms.

comp.arch Computer architecture.

comp.arch.bus.vmebus Hardware and software for VMEbus Systems.

comp.arch.storage Storage system issues, both hardware and software.

comp.archives Descriptions of public access archives. (Moderated)

comp.archives.admin Issues relating to computer archive administration.

comp.archives.msdos.announce Announcements about MSDOS archives. (Moderated)

comp.archives.msdos.d Discussion of materials available in MSDOS archives.

comp.bbs.misc All aspects of computer bulletin board systems.

comp.bbs.waffle The Waffle BBS and USENET system on all platforms.

comp.benchmarks Discussion of benchmarking techniques and results.

comp.binaries.acorn Binary-only postings for Acorn machines. (Moderated)

comp.binaries.amiga Encoded public domain programs in binary. (Moderated)

comp.binaries.apple2 Binary-only postings for the Apple II computer.

comp.binaries.atari.st Binary-only postings for the Atari ST. (Moderated)

comp.binaries.ibm.pc Binary-only postings for IBM PC/MS-DOS. (Moderated)

comp.binaries.ibm.pc.d Discussions about IBM/PC binary postings.

comp.binaries.ibm.pc.wanted Requests for IBM PC and compatible programs.

comp.binaries.mac Encoded Macintosh programs in binary. (Moderated)

comp.binaries.ms-windows Binary programs for Microsoft Windows. (Moderated)

comp.binaries.os2 Binaries for use under the OS/2 ABI. (Moderated)

comp.bugs.2bsd Reports of UNIX * version 2BSD related bugs.

comp.bugs.4bsd Reports of UNIX version 4BSD related bugs.

comp.bugs.4bsd.ucb-fixes Bug reports/fixes for BSD Unix. (Moderated)

comp.bugs.misc General UNIX bug reports and fixes (incl V7, uucp)

comp.bugs.sys5 Reports of USG (System III, V, etc.) bugs.

comp.cad.cadence Users of Cadence Design Systems products.

comp.cad.compass Compass Design Automation EDA tools.

comp.cad.synthesis Research and production in the field of logic synthesis.

comp.client-server Topics relating to client/server technology.

comp.cog-eng Cognitive engineering.

comp.compilers Compiler construction, theory, etc. (Moderated)

comp.compression Data compression algorithms and theory.

comp.compression.research Discussions about data compression research.

comp.databases Database and data management issues and theory.

comp.databases.informix Informix database management software discussions.

comp.databases.ingres Issues relating to INGRES products.

comp.databases.ms-access MS Windows' relational database system, Access.

comp.databases.object Object-oriented paradigms in databases systems.

comp.databases.oracle The SQL database products of the Oracle Corporation.

comp.databases.pick Pick-like, post-relational, database systems.

comp.databases.sybase Implementations of the SQL Server.

comp.databases.theory Discussing advances in database technology.

comp.dcom.cell-relay Forum for discussion of Cell Relay-based products.

comp.dcom.fax Fax hardware, software, and protocols.

comp.dcom.isdn The Integrated Services Digital Network (ISDN).

comp.dcom.lans.ethernet Discussions of the Ethernet/IEEE 802.3 protocols.

comp.dcom.lans.fddi Discussions of the FDDI protocol suite.

comp.dcom.lans.misc Local area network hardware and software.

comp.dcom.lans.token-ring Installing and using token ring networks.

comp.dcom.modems Data communications hardware and software.

comp.dcom.servers Selecting and operating data communications servers.

comp.dcom.sys.cisco Info on Cisco routers and bridges.

comp.dcom.sys.wellfleet Wellfleet bridge & router systems hardware & software.

comp.dcom.telecom Telecommunications digest. (Moderated)

comp.doc Archived public-domain documentation. (Moderated)

comp.doc.techreports Lists of technical reports. (Moderated)

comp.dsp Digital Signal Processing using computers.

comp.edu Computer science education.

comp.emacs EMACS editors of different flavors.

comp.fonts Typefonts -- design, conversion, use, etc.

comp.graphics Computer graphics, art, animation, image processing.

comp.graphics.animation Technical aspects of computer animation.

comp.graphics.avs The Application Visualization System.

comp.graphics.explorer The Explorer Modular Visualisation Environment (MVE).

comp.graphics.gnuplot The GNUPLOT interactive function plotter.

comp.graphics.opengl The OpenGL 3D application programming interface.

comp.graphics.research Highly technical computer graphics discussion. (Moderated)

comp.graphics.visualization Info on scientific visualization.

comp.groupware Software and hardware for shared interactive environments.

comp.human-factors Issues related to human-computer interaction (HCI).

comp.infosystems Any discussion about information systems.

comp.infosystems.gis All aspects of Geographic Information Systems.

comp.infosystems.gopher Discussion of the gopher information service.

comp.infosystems.wais The Z39.50-based WAIS full-text search system.

comp.infosystems.www The World Wide Web information system.

comp.internet.library Discussing electronic libraries. (Moderated)

comp.ivideodisc Interactive videodiscs -- uses, potential, etc.

comp.lang.ada Discussion about Ada *.

comp.lang.apl Discussion about APL.

comp.lang.c Discussion about C.

comp.lang.c++ The object-oriented C++ language.

comp.lang.clos Common Lisp Object System discussions.

comp.lang.dylan For discussion of the Dylan language.

comp.lang.eiffel The object-oriented Eiffel language.

comp.lang.forth Discussion about Forth.

comp.lang.fortran Discussion about FORTRAN.

comp.lang.functional Discussion about functional languages.

comp.lang.hermes The Hermes language for distributed applications.

comp.lang.idl-pvwave IDL and PV-Wave language discussions.

comp.lang.lisp Discussion about LISP.

comp.lang.lisp.mcl Discussing Apple's Macintosh Common Lisp.

comp.lang.logo The Logo teaching and learning language.

comp.lang.misc Different computer languages not specifically listed.

comp.lang.ml ML languages including Standard ML, CAML, Lazy ML, etc. (Moderated)

comp.lang.modula2 Discussion about Modula-2.

comp.lang.modula3 Discussion about the Modula-3 language.

comp.lang.oberon The Oberon language and system.

comp.lang.objective-c The Objective-C language and environment.

comp.lang.pascal Discussion about Pascal.

comp.lang.pop Pop11 and the Plug user group.

comp.lang.postscript The PostScript Page Description Language.

comp.lang.prolog Discussion about PROLOG.

comp.lang.sather The object-oriented computer language Sather.

comp.lang.scheme The Scheme Programming language.

comp.lang.sigplan Info & announcements from ACM SIGPLAN. (Moderated)

comp.lang.smalltalk Discussion about Smalltalk 80.

comp.lang.tcl The Tcl programming language and related tools.

comp.lang.verilog Discussing Verilog and PLI.

comp.lang.vhdl VHSIC Hardware Description Language, IEEE 1076/87.

comp.laser-printers Laser printers, hardware & software. (Moderated)

comp.lsi Large scale integrated circuits.

comp.lsi.testing Testing of electronic circuits.

comp.mail.elm Discussion and fixes for ELM mail system.

comp.mail.headers Gatewayed from the Internet header-people list.

comp.mail.maps Various maps, including UUCP maps. (Moderated)

comp.mail.mh The UCI version of the Rand Message Handling system.

comp.mail.mime Multipurpose Internet Mail Extensions of RFC 1341.

comp.mail.misc General discussions about computer mail.

comp.mail.mush The Mail User's Shell (MUSH).

comp.mail.sendmail Configuring and using the BSD sendmail agent.

comp.mail.uucp Mail in the uucp network environment.

comp.misc General topics about computers not covered elsewhere.

comp.multimedia Interactive multimedia technologies of all kinds.

comp.newprod Announcements of new products of interest. (Moderated)

comp.object Object-oriented programming and languages.

comp.object.logic Integrating object-oriented and logic programming.

comp.org.acm Topics about the Association for Computing Machinery.

comp.org.decus Digital Equipment Computer Users' Society newsgroup.

comp.org.eff.news News from the Electronic Frontiers Foundation. (Moderated)

comp.org.eff.talk Discussion of EFF goals, strategies, etc.

comp.org.fidonet FidoNews digest, official news of FidoNet Assoc. (Moderated)

comp.org.ieee Issues and announcements about the IEEE & its members.

comp.org.issnnet The International Student Society for Neural Networks.

comp.org.sug Talk about/for the The Sun User's Group.

comp.org.usenix USENIX Association events and announcements.

comp.org.usenix.roomshare Finding lodging during Usenix conferences.

comp.os.386bsd.announce Announcements relating to the 386bsd operating system. (Moderated)

comp.os.386bsd.apps Applications which run under 386bsd.

comp.os.386bsd.bugs Bugs and fixes for the 386bsd OS and its clients.

comp.os.386bsd.development Working on 386bsd internals.

comp.os.386bsd.misc General aspects of 386bsd not covered by other groups.

comp.os.386bsd.questions General questions about 386bsd.

comp.os.coherent Discussion and support of the Coherent operating system.

comp.os.cpm Discussion about the CP/M operating system.

comp.os.linux The free UNIX-clone for the 386/486, LINUX.

comp.os.linux.announce Announcements important to the Linux community. (Moderated)

comp.os.mach The MACH OS from CMU & other places.

comp.os.minix Discussion of Tanenbaum's MINIX system.

comp.os.misc General OS-oriented discussion not carried elsewhere.

comp.os.ms-windows.advocacy Speculation and debate about Microsoft Windows.

comp.os.ms-windows.announce Announcements relating to Windows. (Moderated)

comp.os.ms-windows.apps Applications in the Windows environment.

comp.os.ms-windows.misc General discussions about Windows issues.

comp.os.ms-windows.nt.misc General discussion about Windows NT.

comp.os.ms-windows.nt.setup Configuring Windows NT systems.

comp.os.ms-windows.programmer.misc Programming Microsoft Windows.

comp.os.ms-windows.programmer.tools Development tools in Windows.

comp.os.ms-windows.programmer.win32 32-bit Windows programming interfaces.

comp.os.ms-windows.setup Installing and configuring Microsoft Windows.

comp.os.msdos.apps Discussion of applications that run under MS-DOS.

comp.os.msdos.desqview QuarterDeck's Desqview and related products.

comp.os.msdos.mail-news Administering mail & network news systems under MS-DOS.

comp.os.msdos.misc Miscellaneous topics about MS-DOS machines.

comp.os.msdos.pcgeos GeoWorks PC/GEOS and PC/GEOS-based packages.

comp.os.msdos.programmer Programming MS-DOS machines.

comp.os.msdos.programmer.turbovision Borland's text application libraries.

comp.os.os2.advocacy Supporting and flaming OS/2.

comp.os.os2.announce Notable news and announcements related to OS/2. (Moderated)

comp.os.os2.apps Discussions of applications under OS/2.

comp.os.os2.beta All aspects of beta releases of OS/2 systems software.

comp.os.os2.bugs OS/2 system bug reports, fixes and work-arounds.

comp.os.os2.misc Miscellaneous topics about the OS/2 system.

comp.os.os2.multimedia Multi-media on OS/2 systems.

comp.os.os2.networking Networking in OS/2 environments.

comp.os.os2.programmer Programming OS/2 machines.

comp.os.os2.programmer.misc Programming OS/2 machines.

comp.os.os2.programmer.porting Porting software to OS/2 machines.

comp.os.os2.setup Installing and configuring OS/2 systems.

comp.os.os2.ver1x All aspects of OS/2 versions 1.0 through 1.3.

comp.os.os9 Discussions about the os9 operating system.

comp.os.research Operating systems and related areas. (Moderated)

comp.os.vms DEC's VAX * line of computers & VMS.

comp.os.vxworks The VxWorks real-time operating system.

comp.os.xinu The XINU operating system from Purdue (D. Comer).

comp.parallel Massively parallel hardware/software. (Moderated)

comp.parallel.pvm The PVM system of multi-computer parallelization.

comp.patents Discussing patents of computer technology. (Moderated)

comp.periphs Peripheral devices.

comp.periphs.scsi Discussion of SCSI-based peripheral devices.

comp.programming Programming issues that transcend languages and OSs.

comp.protocols.appletalk Applebus hardware & software.

comp.protocols.dicom Digital Imaging and Communications in Medicine.

comp.protocols.ibm Networking with IBM mainframes.

comp.protocols.iso The ISO protocol stack.

comp.protocols.kerberos The Kerberos authentication server.

comp.protocols.kermit Info about the Kermit package. (Moderated)

comp.protocols.misc Various forms and types of FTP protocol.

comp.protocols.nfs Discussion about the Network File System protocol.

comp.protocols.ppp Discussion of the Internet Point to Point Protocol.

comp.protocols.tcp-ip TCP and IP network protocols.

comp.protocols.tcp-ip.ibmpc TCP/IP for IBM(-like) personal computers.

comp.publish.cdrom.hardware Hardware used in publishing with CD-ROM.

comp.publish.cdrom.multimedi Software for multimedia authoring & publishing.

comp.publish.cdrom.software Software used in publishing with CD-ROM.

comp.realtime Issues related to real-time computing.

comp.research.japan The nature of research in Japan. (Moderated)

comp.risks Risks to the public from computers & users. (Moderated)

comp.robotics All aspects of robots and their applications.

comp.security.misc Security issues of computers and networks.

comp.simulation Simulation methods, problems, uses. (Moderated)

comp.society The impact of technology on society. (Moderated)

comp.society.cu-digest The Computer Underground Digest. (Moderated)

comp.society.development Computer technology in developing countries.

comp.society.folklore Computer folklore & culture, past & present. (Moderated)

comp.society.futures Events in technology affecting future computing.

comp.society.privacy Effects of technology on privacy. (Moderated)

comp.soft-sys.khoros The Khoros X11 visualization system.

comp.soft-sys.matlab The MathWorks calculation and visualization package.

comp.soft-sys.sas The SAS statistics package.

comp.soft-sys.shazam The SHAZAM econometrics computer program.

comp.soft-sys.spss The SPSS statistics package.

comp.software-eng Software Engineering and related topics.

comp.software.licensing Software licensing technology.

comp.software.testing All aspects of testing computer systems.

comp.sources.3b1 Source code-only postings for the AT&T 3b1. (Moderated)

comp.sources.acorn Source code-only postings for the Acorn. (Moderated)

comp.sources.amiga Source code-only postings for the Amiga. (Moderated)

comp.sources.apple2 Source code and discussion for the Apple2. (Moderated)

comp.sources.atari.st Source code-only postings for the Atari ST. (Moderated)

comp.sources.bugs Bug reports, fixes, discussion for posted sources.

comp.sources.d For any discussion of source postings.

comp.sources.games Postings of recreational software. (Moderated)

comp.sources.games.bugs Bug reports and fixes for posted game software.

comp.sources.hp48 Programs for the HP48 and HP28 calculators. (Moderated)

comp.sources.mac Software for the Apple Macintosh. (Moderated)

comp.sources.misc Posting of software. (Moderated)

comp.sources.postscript Source code for programs written in PostScript. (Moderated)

comp.sources.reviewed Source code evaluated by peer review. (Moderated)

comp.sources.sun Software for Sun workstations. (Moderated)

comp.sources.testers Finding people to test software.

comp.sources.unix Postings of complete, UNIX-oriented sources. (Moderated)

comp.sources.wanted Requests for software and fixes.

comp.sources.x Software for the X windows system. (Moderated)

comp.specification Languages and methodologies for formal specification.

comp.specification.z Discussion about the formal specification notation Z.

comp.speech Research & applications in speech science & technology.

comp.std.c Discussion about C language standards.

comp.std.c++ Discussion about C++ language, library, standards.

comp.std.internat Discussion about international standards.

comp.std.misc Discussion about various standards.

comp.std.mumps Discussion for the X11.1 committee on Mumps. (Moderated)

comp.std.unix Discussion for the P1003 committee on UNIX. (Moderated)

comp.std.wireless Examining standards for wireless network technology. (Moderated) (Moderated)

comp.sw.components Software components and related technology.

comp.sys.3b1 Discussion and support of AT&T 7300/3B1/UnixPC.

comp.sys.acorn Discussion on Acorn and ARM-based computers.

comp.sys.acorn.advocacy Why Acorn computers and programs are better.

comp.sys.acorn.announce Announcements for Acorn and ARM users. (Moderated)

comp.sys.acorn.tech Software and hardware aspects of Acorn and ARM products.

comp.sys.alliant Info and discussion about Alliant computers.

comp.sys.amiga.advocacy Why an Amiga is better than XYZ.

comp.sys.amiga.announce Announcements about the Amiga. (Moderated)

comp.sys.amiga.applications Miscellaneous applications.

comp.sys.amiga.audio Music, MIDI, speech synthesis, other sounds.

comp.sys.amiga.datacomm Methods of getting bytes in and out.

comp.sys.amiga.emulations Various hardware & software emulators.

comp.sys.amiga.games Discussion of games for the Commodore Amiga.

comp.sys.amiga.graphics Charts, graphs, pictures, etc.

comp.sys.amiga.hardware Amiga computer hardware, Q&A, reviews, etc.

comp.sys.amiga.introduction Group for newcomers to Amigas.

comp.sys.amiga.marketplace Where to find it, prices, etc.

comp.sys.amiga.misc Discussions not falling in another Amiga group.

comp.sys.amiga.multimedia Animations, video, & multimedia.

comp.sys.amiga.programmer Developers & hobbyists discuss code.

comp.sys.amiga.reviews Reviews of Amiga software, hardware. (Moderated)

comp.sys.apollo Apollo computer systems.

comp.sys.apple2 Discussion about Apple II micros.

comp.sys.apple2.comm Apple II data communications.

comp.sys.apple2.gno The AppleIIgs GNO multitasking environment.

comp.sys.apple2.marketplace Buying, selling and trading Apple II equipment.

comp.sys.apple2.programmer Programming on the Apple II.

comp.sys.apple2.usergroups All about Apple II user groups.

comp.sys.atari.8bit Discussion about 8 bit Atari micros.

comp.sys.atari.advocacy Attacking and defending Atari computers.

comp.sys.atari.st Discussion about 16 bit Atari micros.

comp.sys.atari.st.tech Technical discussions of Atari ST hard/software.

comp.sys.att Discussions about AT&T microcomputers.

comp.sys.cbm Discussion about Commodore micros.

comp.sys.concurrent The Concurrent/Masscomp line of computers. (Moderated)

comp.sys.convex Convex computer systems hardware and software.

comp.sys.dec Discussions about DEC computer systems.

comp.sys.dec.micro DEC Micros (Rainbow, Professional 350/380)

comp.sys.encore Encore's MultiMax computers.

comp.sys.harris Harris computer systems, especially real-time systems.

comp.sys.hp Discussion about Hewlett-Packard equipment.

comp.sys.hp48 Hewlett-Packard's HP48 and HP28 calculators.

comp.sys.ibm.pc.demos Demonstration programs which showcase programmer skill.

comp.sys.ibm.pc.digest The IBM PC, PC-XT, and PC-AT. (Moderated)

comp.sys.ibm.pc.games Games for IBM PCs and compatibles.

comp.sys.ibm.pc.games.action Arcade-style games on PCs.

comp.sys.ibm.pc.games.adventure Adventure (non-rpg) games on PCs.

comp.sys.ibm.pc.games.announce Announcements for all PC gamers. (Moderated)

comp.sys.ibm.pc.games.flight-sim Flight simulators on PCs.

comp.sys.ibm.pc.games.misc Games not covered by other PC groups.

comp.sys.ibm.pc.games.rpg Role-playing games on the PC.

comp.sys.ibm.pc.games.strategic Strategy/planning games on PCs.

comp.sys.ibm.pc.hardware XT/AT/EISA hardware, any vendor.

comp.sys.ibm.pc.misc Discussion about IBM personal computers.

comp.sys.ibm.pc.rt Topics related to IBM's RT computer.

comp.sys.ibm.pc.soundcard Hardware and software aspects of PC sound cards.

comp.sys.ibm.ps2.hardware Microchannel hardware, any vendor.

comp.sys.intel Discussions about Intel systems and parts.

comp.sys.isis The ISIS distributed system from Cornell.

comp.sys.laptops Laptop (portable) computers.

comp.sys.m6809 Discussion about 6809's.

comp.sys.m68k Discussion about 68k's.

comp.sys.m68k.pc Discussion about 68k-based PCs. (Moderated) comp.sys.m88k Discussion about 88k-based computers.

comp.sys.mac.advocacy The Macintosh computer family compared to others.

comp.sys.mac.announce Important notices for Macintosh users. (Moderated)

comp.sys.mac.apps Discussions of Macintosh applications.

comp.sys.mac.comm Discussion of Macintosh communications.

comp.sys.mac.databases Database systems for the Apple Macintosh.

comp.sys.mac.digest Apple Macintosh: info&uses, but no programs. (Moderated)

comp.sys.mac.games Discussions of games on the Macintosh.

comp.sys.mac.hardware Macintosh hardware issues & discussions.

comp.sys.mac.hypercard The Macintosh Hypercard: info & uses.

comp.sys.mac.misc General discussions about the Apple Macintosh.

comp.sys.mac.oop.macapp3 Version 3 of the MacApp object oriented system.

comp.sys.mac.oop.misc Object oriented programming issues on the Mac.

comp.sys.mac.oop.tcl Symantec's THINK Class Library for object programming.

comp.sys.mac.portables Discussion particular to laptop Macintoshes.

comp.sys.mac.programmer Discussion by people programming the Apple Macintosh.

comp.sys.mac.scitech Using the Macintosh in scientific & technological work.

comp.sys.mac.system Discussions of Macintosh system software.

comp.sys.mac.wanted Postings of ''I want XYZ for my Mac.''

comp.sys.mentor Mentor Graphics products & the Silicon Compiler System.

comp.sys.mips Systems based on MIPS chips.

comp.sys.misc Discussion about computers of all kinds.

comp.sys.ncr Discussion about NCR computers.

comp.sys.next.advocacy The NeXT religion.

comp.sys.next.announce Announcements related to the NeXT computer system. (Moderated)

comp.sys.next.bugs Discussion and solutions for known NeXT bugs.

comp.sys.next.hardware Discussing the physical aspects of NeXT computers.

comp.sys.next.marketplace NeXT hardware, software and jobs.

comp.sys.next.misc General discussion about the NeXT computer system.

comp.sys.next.programmer NeXT related programming issues.

comp.sys.next.software Function, use and availability of NeXT programs.

comp.sys.next.sysadmin Discussions related to NeXT system administration.

comp.sys.novell Discussion of Novell Netware products.

comp.sys.nsc.32k National Semiconductor 32000 series chips.

comp.sys.palmtops Super-powered calculators the palm of your hand.

comp.sys.pen Interacting with computers through pen gestures.

comp.sys.prime Prime Computer products.

comp.sys.proteon Proteon gateway products.

comp.sys.pyramid Pyramid 90x computers.

comp.sys.ridge Ridge 32 computers and ROS.

comp.sys.sequent Sequent systems, (Balance and Symmetry).

comp.sys.sgi.admin System administration on Silicon Graphics's Irises.

comp.sys.sgi.announce Announcements for the SGI community. (Moderated)

comp.sys.sgi.apps Applications which run on the Iris.

comp.sys.sgi.bugs Bugs found in the IRIX operating system.

comp.sys.sgi.graphics Graphics packages and issues on SGI machines.

comp.sys.sgi.hardware Base systems and peripherals for Iris computers.

comp.sys.sgi.misc General discussion about Silicon Graphics's machines.

comp.sys.stratus Stratus products, incl. System/88, CPS-32, VOS and FTX.

comp.sys.sun.admin Sun system administration issues and questions.

comp.sys.sun.announce Sun announcements and Sunergy mailings. (Moderated)

comp.sys.sun.apps Software applications for Sun computer systems.

comp.sys.sun.hardware Sun Microsystems hardware.

comp.sys.sun.misc Miscellaneous discussions about Sun products.

comp.sys.sun.wanted People looking for Sun products and support.

comp.sys.tahoe CCI 6/32, Harris HCX/7, & Sperry 7000 computers.

comp.sys.tandy Discussion about Tandy computers: new & old.

comp.sys.ti Discussion about Texas Instruments.

comp.sys.transputer The Transputer computer and OCCAM language.

comp.sys.unisys Sperry, Burroughs, Convergent and Unisys * systems.

comp.sys.xerox Xerox 1100 workstations and protocols.

comp.sys.zenith.z100 The Zenith Z-100 (Heath H-100) family of computers.

comp.terminals All sorts of terminals.

comp.text Text processing issues and methods.

comp.text.desktop Technology & techniques of desktop publishing.

comp.text.frame Desktop publishing with FrameMaker.

comp.text.interleaf Applications and use of Interleaf software.

comp.text.sgml ISO 8879 SGML, structured documents, markup languages.

comp.text.tex Discussion about the TeX and LaTeX systems & macros.

comp.theory.info-retrieval Information Retrieval topics. (Moderated)

comp.unix.admin Administering a Unix-based system.

comp.unix.aix IBM's version of UNIX.

comp.unix.amiga Minix, SYSV4 and other *nix on an Amiga.

comp.unix.aux The version of UNIX for Apple Macintosh II computers.

comp.unix.bsd Discussion of Berkeley Software Distribution UNIX.

comp.unix.dos-under-unix MS-DOS running under UNIX by whatever means.

comp.unix.internals Discussions on hacking UNIX internals.

comp.unix.large UNIX on mainframes and in large networks.

comp.unix.misc Various topics that don't fit other groups.

comp.unix.osf.misc Various aspects of Open Software Foundation products.

comp.unix.osf.osf1 The Open Software Foundation's OSF/1.

comp.unix.pc-clone.16bit UNIX on 286 architectures.

comp.unix.pc-clone.32bit UNIX on 386 and 486 architectures.

comp.unix.programmer Q&A for people programming under Unix.

comp.unix.questions UNIX neophytes group.

comp.unix.shell Using and programming the Unix shell.

comp.unix.sys3 System III UNIX discussions.

comp.unix.sys5.misc Versions of System V which predate Release 3.

comp.unix.sys5.r3 Discussing System V Release 3.

comp.unix.sys5.r4 Discussing System V Release 4.

comp.unix.ultrix Discussions about DEC's Ultrix.

comp.unix.wizards Questions for only true Unix wizards.

comp.unix.xenix.misc General discussions regarding XENIX (except SCO).

comp.unix.xenix.sco XENIX versions from the Santa Cruz Operation.

comp.virus Computer viruses & security. (Moderated)

comp.windows.garnet The Garnet user interface development environment.

comp.windows.interviews The InterViews object-oriented windowing system.

comp.windows.misc Various issues about windowing systems.

comp.windows.news Sun Microsystems' NeWS window system.

comp.windows.open-look Discussion about the Open Look GUI.

comp.windows.suit The SUIT user-interface toolkit.

comp.windows.x Discussion about the X Window System.

comp.windows.x.apps Getting and using, not programming, applications for X.

comp.windows.x.i386unix The XFree86 window system and others.

comp.windows.x.intrinsics Discussion of the X toolkit.

comp.windows.x.pex The PHIGS extension of the X Window System.

MISCELLANEOUS GROUPS

misc.activism.progressive Information for Progressive activists. (Moderated)

misc.answers Repository for periodic USENET articles. (Moderated)

misc.books.technical Discussion of books about technical topics.

misc.consumers Consumer interests, product reviews, etc.

misc.consumers.house Discussion about owning and maintaining a house.

misc.education Discussion of the educational system.

misc.emerg-services Forum for paramedics & other first responders.

misc.entrepreneurs Discussion on operating a business.

misc.fitness Physical fitness, exercise, etc.

misc.forsale Short, tasteful postings about items for sale.

misc.forsale.computers.d Discussion of misc.forsale.computers.*.

misc.forsale.computers.mac Apple Macintosh related computer items.

misc.forsale.computers.other Selling miscellaneous computer stuff.

misc.forsale.computers.pc-clone IBM PC related computer items.

misc.forsale.computers.workstation Workstation related computer items.

misc.handicap Items of interest for/about the handicapped. (Moderated)

misc.headlines Current interest: drug testing, terrorism, etc.

misc.health.alternative Alternative, complementary and holistic health care.

misc.health.diabetes Discussion of diabetes management in day to day life.

misc.int-property Discussion of intellectual property rights.

misc.invest Investments and the handling of money.

misc.invest.real-estate Property investments.

misc.invest.technical Analyzing market trends with technical methods.

misc.jobs.contract Discussions about contract labor.

misc.jobs.misc Discussion about employment, workplaces, careers.

misc.jobs.offered Announcements of positions available.

misc.jobs.offered.entry Job listings only for entry-level positions.

misc.jobs.resumes Postings of resumes and "situation wanted" articles.

misc.kids Children, their behavior and activities.

misc.kids.computer The use of computers by children.

misc.legal Legalities and the ethics of law.

misc.legal.computing Discussing the legal climate of the computing world.

misc.misc Various discussions not fitting in any other group.

misc.news.east-europe.rferl Radio Free Europe/Radio Liberty Daily Report. (Moderated)

misc.news.southasia News from Bangladesh, India, Nepal, etc. (Moderated)

misc.rural Devoted to issues concerning rural living.

misc.taxes Tax laws and advice.

misc.test For testing of network software. Very boring.

misc.wanted Requests for things that are needed (NOT software).

misc.writing Discussion of writing in all of its forms.

NEWS ABOUT USENET

news.admin.misc General topics of network news administration.

news.admin.policy Policy issues of USENET.

news.admin.technical Technical aspects of maintaining network news. (Moderated)

news.announce.conferences Calls for papers and conference announcements. (Moderated)

news.announce.important General announcements of interest to all. (Moderated)

news.announce.newgroups Calls for newgroups & announcements of same. (Moderated)

news.announce.newusers Explanatory postings for new users. (Moderated)

news.answers Repository for periodic USENET articles. (Moderated)

news.config Postings of system down times and interruptions.

news.future The future technology of network news systems.

news.groups Discussions and lists of newsgroups.

news.lists News-related statistics and lists. (Moderated)

news.lists.ps-maps Maps relating to USENET traffic flows. (Moderated)

news.misc Discussions of USENET itself.

news.newsites Postings of new site announcements.

news.newusers.questions Q & A for users new to the Usenet.

news.software.anu-news VMS B-news software from Australian National Univ.

news.software.b Discussion about B-news-compatible software.

news.software.nn Discussion about the "nn" news reader package.

news.software.notes Notesfile software from the Univ. of Illinois.

news.software.readers Discussion of software used to read network news.

RECREATIONAL GROUPS

rec.answers Repository for periodic USENET articles. (Moderated)

rec.antiques Discussing antiques and vintage items.

rec.aquaria Keeping fish and aquaria as a hobby.

rec.arts.animation Discussion of various kinds of animation.

rec.arts.anime Japanese animation fen discussion.

rec.arts.anime.info Announcements about Japanese animation. (Moderated)

rec.arts.anime.marketplace Things for sale in the Japanese animation world.

rec.arts.anime.stories All about Japanese comic fanzines. (Moderated)

rec.arts.bodyart Tattoos and body decoration discussions.

rec.arts.bonsai Dwarfish trees and shrubbery.

rec.arts.books Books of all genres, and the publishing industry.

rec.arts.books.tolkien The works of J.R.R. Tolkien.

rec.arts.cinema Discussion of the art of cinema. (Moderated)

rec.arts.comics.info Reviews, convention information and other comics news. (Moderated)

rec.arts.comics.marketplace The exchange of comics and comic related items.

rec.arts.comics.misc Comic books, graphic novels, sequential art.

rec.arts.comics.strips Discussion of short-form comics.

rec.arts.comics.xbooks The Mutant Universe of Marvel Comics.

rec.arts.dance Any aspects of dance not covered in another newsgroup.

rec.arts.disney Discussion of any Disney-related subjects.

rec.arts.drwho Discussion about Dr. Who.

rec.arts.erotica Erotic fiction and verse. (Moderated)

rec.arts.fine Fine arts & artists.

rec.arts.int-fiction Discussions about interactive fiction.

rec.arts.manga All aspects of the Japanese storytelling art form.

rec.arts.marching.drumcorps Drum and bugle corps.

rec.arts.marching.misc Marching-related performance activities.

rec.arts.misc Discussions about the arts not in other groups.

rec.arts.movies Discussions of movies and movie making.

rec.arts.movies.reviews Reviews of movies. (Moderated)

rec.arts.poems For the posting of poems.

rec.arts.prose Short works of prose fiction and followup discussion.

rec.arts.sf.announce Major announcements of the SF world. (Moderated)

rec.arts.sf.fandom Discussions of SF fan activities.

rec.arts.sf.marketplace Personal forsale notices of SF materials.

rec.arts.sf.misc Science fiction lovers' newsgroup.

rec.arts.sf.movies Discussing SF motion pictures.

rec.arts.sf.reviews Reviews of science fiction/fantasy/horror works. (Moderated)

rec.arts.sf.science Real and speculative aspects of SF science.

rec.arts.sf.starwars Discussion of the Star Wars universe.

rec.arts.sf.tv Discussing general television SF.

rec.arts.sf.written Discussion of written science fiction and fantasy.

rec.arts.startrek.current New Star Trek shows, movies and books.

rec.arts.startrek.fandom Star Trek conventions and memorabilia.

rec.arts.startrek.info Information about the universe of Star Trek. (Moderated)

rec.arts.startrek.misc General discussions of Star Trek.

rec.arts.startrek.reviews Reviews of Star Trek books, episodes, films, &c. (Moderated)

rec.arts.startrek.tech Star Trek's depiction of future technologies.

rec.arts.theatre Discussion of all aspects of stage work & theatre.

rec.arts.tv The boob tube, its history, and past and current shows.

rec.arts.tv.soaps Postings about soap operas.

rec.arts.tv.uk Discussions of telly shows from the UK.

rec.arts.wobegon "A Prairie Home Companion" radio show discussion.

rec.audio High fidelity audio.

rec.audio.car Discussions of automobile audio systems.

rec.audio.high-end High-end audio systems. (Moderated)

rec.audio.pro Professional audio recording and studio engineering.

rec.autos Automobiles, automotive products and laws.

rec.autos.antique Discussing all aspects of automobiles over 25 years old.

rec.autos.driving Driving automobiles.

rec.autos.rod-n-custom High performance automobiles.

rec.autos.sport Discussion of organized, legal auto competitions.

rec.autos.tech Technical aspects of automobiles, et. al.

rec.autos.vw Issues pertaining to Volkswagen products.

rec.aviation.announce Events of interest to the aviation community. (Moderated)

rec.aviation.answers Frequently asked questions about aviation. (Moderated)

rec.aviation.homebuilt Selecting, designing, building, and restoring aircraft.

rec.aviation.ifr Flying under Instrument Flight Rules.

rec.aviation.military Military aircraft of the past, present and future.

rec.aviation.misc Miscellaneous topics in aviation.

rec.aviation.owning Information on owning airplanes.

rec.aviation.piloting General discussion for aviators.

rec.aviation.products Reviews and discussion of products useful to pilots.

rec.aviation.simulators Flight simulation on all levels.

rec.aviation.soaring All aspects of sailplanes and hang-gliders.

rec.aviation.stories Anecdotes of flight experiences. (Moderated)

rec.aviation.student Learning to fly.

rec.backcountry Activities in the Great Outdoors.

rec.bicycles.marketplace Buying, selling & reviewing items for cycling.

rec.bicycles.misc General discussion of bicycling.

rec.bicycles.racing Bicycle racing techniques, rules and results.

rec.bicycles.rides Discussions of tours and training or commuting routes.

rec.bicycles.soc Societal issues of bicycling.

rec.bicycles.tech Cycling product design, construction, maintenance, etc.

rec.birds Hobbyists interested in bird watching.

rec.boats Hobbyists interested in boating.

rec.boats.paddle Talk about any boats with oars, paddles, etc.

rec.climbing Climbing techniques, competition announcements, etc.

rec.collecting Discussion among collectors of many things.

rec.collecting.cards Collecting all sorts of sport and non-sport cards.

rec.crafts.brewing The art of making beers and meads.

rec.crafts.metalworking All aspects of working with metal.

rec.crafts.misc Handiwork arts not covered elsewhere.

rec.crafts.textiles Sewing, weaving, knitting and other fiber arts.

rec.equestrian Discussion of things equestrian.

rec.folk-dancing Folk dances, dancers, and dancing.

rec.food.cooking Food, cooking, cookbooks, and recipes.

rec.food.drink Wines and spirits.

rec.food.historic The history of food making arts.

rec.food.recipes Recipes for interesting food and drink. (Moderated)

rec.food.restaurants Discussion of dining out.

rec.food.sourdough Making and baking with sourdough.

rec.food.veg Vegetarians.

rec.gambling Articles on games of chance & betting.

rec.games.abstract Perfect information, pure strategy games.

rec.games.backgammon Discussion of the game of backgammon.

rec.games.board Discussion and hints on board games.

rec.games.board.ce The Cosmic Encounter board game.

rec.games.bridge Hobbyists interested in bridge.

rec.games.chess Chess & computer chess.

rec.games.corewar The Core War computer challenge.

rec.games.design Discussion of game design related issues.

rec.games.diplomacy The conquest game Diplomacy.

rec.games.empire Discussion and hints about Empire.

rec.games.frp.advocacy Flames and rebuttals about various role-playing systems.

rec.games.frp.archives Archivable fantasy stories and other projects. (Moderated)

rec.games.frp.cyber Discussions of cyberpunk related roleplaying games.

rec.games.frp.dnd Fantasy role-playing with TSR's Dungeons and Dragons.

rec.games.frp.marketplace Role-playing game materials wanted and for sale.

rec.games.frp.misc General discussions of role-playing games.

rec.games.go Discussion about Go.

rec.games.hack Discussion, hints, etc. about the Hack game.

rec.games.int-fiction All aspects of interactive fiction games.

rec.games.mecha Giant robot games.

rec.games.miniatures Tabletop wargaming.

rec.games.misc Games and computer games.

rec.games.moria Comments, hints, and info about the Moria game.

rec.games.mud.admin Admnistrative issues of multiuser dungeons.

rec.games.mud.announce Informational articles about multiuser dungeons. (Moderated)

rec.games.mud.diku All about DikuMuds.

rec.games.mud.lp Discussions of the LPMUD computer role playing game.

rec.games.mud.misc Various aspects of multiuser computer games.

rec.games.mud.tiny Discussion about Tiny muds, like MUSH, MUSE and MOO.

rec.games.netrek Discussion of the X window system game Netrek (XtrekII).

rec.games.pbm Discussion about Play by Mail games.

rec.games.pinball Discussing pinball-related issues.

rec.games.programmer Discussion of adventure game programming.

rec.games.rogue Discussion and hints about Rogue.

rec.games.trivia Discussion about trivia.

rec.games.video.arcade Discussions about coin-operated video games.

rec.games.video.classic Older home video entertainment systems.

rec.games.video.marketplace Home video game stuff for sale or trade.

rec.games.video.misc General discussion about home video games.

rec.games.video.nintendo All Nintendo video game systems and software.

rec.games.video.sega All Sega video game systems and software.

rec.games.xtank.play Strategy and tactics for the distributed game Xtank.

rec.games.xtank.programmer Coding the Xtank game and its robots.

rec.gardens Gardening, methods and results.

rec.guns Discussions about firearms. (Moderated)

rec.heraldry Discussion of coats of arms.

rec.humor Jokes and the like. May be somewhat offensive.

rec.humor.d Discussions on the content of rec.humor articles.

rec.humor.funny Jokes that are funny (in the moderator's opinion). (Moderated)

rec.humor.oracle Sagacious advice from the USENET Oracle. (Moderated)

rec.humor.oracle.d Comments about the USENET Oracle's comments.

rec.hunting Discussions about hunting. (Moderated)

rec.juggling Juggling techniques, equipment and events.

rec.kites Talk about kites and kiting.

rec.mag Magazine summaries, tables of contents, etc.

rec.martial-arts Discussion of the various martial art forms.

rec.misc General topics about recreational/participant sports.

rec.models.railroad Model railroads of all scales.

rec.models.rc Radio-controlled models for hobbyists.

rec.models.rockets Model rockets for hobbyists.

rec.models.scale Construction of models.

rec.motorcycles Motorcycles and related products and laws.

rec.motorcycles.dirt Riding motorcycles and ATVs off-road.

rec.motorcycles.harley All aspects of Harley-Davidson motorcycles.

rec.motorcycles.racing Discussion of all aspects of racing motorcycles.

rec.music.a-cappella Vocal music without instrumental accompaniment.

rec.music.afro-latin Music with afro-latin, African and Latin influences.

rec.music.beatles Postings about the Fab Four & their music.

rec.music.bluenote Discussion of jazz, blues, and related types of music.

rec.music.cd CDs -- availability and other discussions.

rec.music.christian Christian music, both contemporary and traditional.

rec.music.classical Discussion about classical music.

rec.music.classical.guitar Classical music performed on guitar.

rec.music.compose Creating musical and lyrical works.

rec.music.country.western C&W music, performers, performances, etc.

rec.music.dementia Discussion of comedy and novelty music.

rec.music.dylan Discussion of Bob's works & music.

rec.music.early Discussion of pre-classical European music.

rec.music.folk Folks discussing folk music of various sorts.

rec.music.funky Funk, rap, hip-hop, house, soul, r&b and related.

rec.music.gaffa Discussion of Kate Bush & other alternative music. (Moderated)

rec.music.gdead A group for (Grateful) Dead-heads.

rec.music.indian.classical Hindustani and Carnatic Indian classical music.

rec.music.indian.misc Discussing Indian music in general.

rec.music.industrial Discussion of all industrial-related music styles.

rec.music.info News and announcements on musical topics. (Moderated)

rec.music.makers For performers and their discussions.

rec.music.makers.bass Upright bass and bass guitar techniques and equipment.

rec.music.makers.guitar Electric and acoustic guitar techniques and equipment.

rec.music.makers.guitar.tablature Guitar tablature/chords.

rec.music.makers.marketplace Buying & selling used music-making equipment.

rec.music.makers.percussion Drum & other percussion techniques & equipment.

rec.music.makers.synth Synthesizers and computer music.

rec.music.marketplace Records, tapes, and CDs: wanted, for sale, etc.

rec.music.misc Music lovers' group.

rec.music.newage "New Age" music discussions.

rec.music.phish Discussing the musical group Phish.

rec.music.reggae Roots, Rockers, Dancehall Reggae.

rec.music.reviews Reviews of music of all genres and mediums. (Moderated)

rec.music.video Discussion of music videos and music video software.

rec.nude Hobbyists interested in naturist/nudist activities.

rec.org.mensa Talking with members of the high IQ society Mensa.

rec.org.sca Society for Creative Anachronism.

rec.outdoors.fishing All aspects of sport and commercial fishing.

rec.pets Pets, pet care, and household animals in general.

rec.pets.birds The culture and care of indoor birds.

rec.pets.cats Discussion about domestic cats.

rec.pets.dogs Any and all subjects relating to dogs as pets.

rec.pets.herp Reptiles, amphibians and other exotic vivarium pets.

rec.photo Hobbyists interested in photography.

rec.puzzles Puzzles, problems, and quizzes.

rec.puzzles.crosswords Making and playing gridded word puzzles.

rec.pyrotechnics Fireworks, rocketry, safety, & other topics.

rec.radio.amateur.antenna Antennas: theory, techniques and construction.

rec.radio.amateur.digital.misc Packet radio and other digital radio modes.

rec.radio.amateur.equipment All about production amateur radio hardware.

rec.radio.amateur.homebrew Amateur radio construction and experimentation.

rec.radio.amateur.misc Amateur radio practices, contests, events, rules, etc.

rec.radio.amateur.packet Discussion about packet radio setups.

rec.radio.amateur.policy Radio use & regulation policy.

rec.radio.amateur.space Amateur radio transmissions through space.

rec.radio.broadcasting Local area broadcast radio. (Moderated)

rec.radio.cb Citizen-band radio.

rec.radio.info Informational postings related to radio. (Moderated)

rec.radio.noncomm Topics relating to noncommercial radio.

rec.radio.shortwave Shortwave radio enthusiasts.

rec.radio.swap Offers to trade and swap radio equipment.

rec.railroad For fans of real trains.

rec.roller-coaster Roller coasters and other amusement park rides.

rec.running Running for enjoyment, sport, exercise, etc.

rec.scouting Scouting youth organizations worldwide.

rec.scuba Hobbyists interested in SCUBA diving.

rec.skate Ice skating and roller skating.

rec.skiing Hobbyists interested in snow skiing.

rec.skydiving Hobbyists interested in skydiving.

rec.sport.baseball Discussion about baseball.

rec.sport.baseball.college Baseball on the collegiate level.

rec.sport.baseball.fantasy Rotisserie (fantasy) baseball play.

rec.sport.basketball.college Hoops on the collegiate level.

rec.sport.basketball.misc Discussion about basketball.

rec.sport.basketball.pro Talk of professional basketball.

rec.sport.cricket Discussion about the sport of cricket.

rec.sport.cricket.scores Scores from cricket matches around the globe. (Moderated)

rec.sport.disc Discussion of flying disc based sports.

rec.sport.fencing All aspects of swordplay.

rec.sport.football.australian Discussion of Australian (Rules) Football.

rec.sport.football.canadian All about Canadian rules football.

rec.sport.football.college US-style college football.

rec.sport.football.misc Discussion about American-style football.

rec.sport.football.pro US-style professional football.

rec.sport.golf Discussion about all aspects of golfing.

rec.sport.hockey Discussion about ice hockey.

rec.sport.hockey.field Discussion of the sport of field hockey.

rec.sport.misc Spectator sports.

rec.sport.olympics All aspects of the Olympic Games.

rec.sport.paintball Discussing all aspects of the survival game paintball.

rec.sport.pro-wrestling Discussion about professional wrestling.

rec.sport.rowing Crew for competition or fitness.

rec.sport.rugby Discussion about the game of rugby.

rec.sport.soccer Discussion about soccer (Association Football).

rec.sport.swimming Training for and competing in swimming events.

rec.sport.table-tennis Things related to table tennis (aka Ping Pong).

rec.sport.tennis Things related to the sport of tennis.

rec.sport.triathlon Discussing all aspects of multi-event sports.

rec.sport.volleyball Discussion about volleyball.

rec.travel Traveling all over the world.

rec.travel.air Airline travel around the world.

rec.travel.marketplace Tickets and accomodations wanted and for sale.

rec.video Video and video components.

rec.video.cable-tv Technical and regulatory issues of cable television.

rec.video.production Making professional quality video productions.

rec.video.releases Pre-recorded video releases on laserdisc and videotape.

rec.video.satellite Getting shows via satellite.

rec.windsurfing Riding the waves as a hobby.

rec.woodworking Hobbyists interested in woodworking.

SCIENCE-RELATED NEWSGROUPS

sci.aeronautics The science of aeronautics & related technology. (Moderated) sci.aeronautics.airliners Airliner technology. (Moderated)

sci.answers Repository for periodic USENET articles. (Moderated)

sci.anthropology All aspects of studying humankind.

sci.aquaria Only scientifically-oriented postings about aquaria.

sci.archaeology Studying antiquities of the world.

sci.astro Astronomy discussions and information.

sci.astro.fits Issues related to the Flexible Image Transport System.

sci.astro.hubble Processing Hubble Space Telescope data. (Moderated)

sci.bio Biology and related sciences.

sci.chem Chemistry and related sciences.

sci.chem.organomet Organometallic chemistry.

sci.classics Studying classical history, languages, art and more.

sci.cognitive Perception, memory, judgement and reasoning.

sci.comp-aided The use of computers as tools in scientific research.

sci.cryonics Theory and practice of biostasis, suspended animation.

sci.crypt Different methods of data en/decryption.

sci.data.formats Modelling, storage and retrieval of scientific data.

sci.econ The science of economics.

sci.econ.research Research in all fields of economics. (Moderated)

sci.edu The science of education.

sci.electronics Circuits, theory, electrons and discussions.

sci.energy Discussions about energy, science & technology.

sci.engr Technical discussions about engineering tasks.

sci.engr.biomed Discussing the field of biomedical engineering.

sci.engr.chem All aspects of chemical engineering.

sci.engr.civil Topics related to civil engineering.

sci.engr.control The engineering of control systems.

sci.engr.manufacturing Manufacturing technology.

sci.engr.mech The field of mechanical engineering.

sci.environment Discussions about the environment and ecology.

sci.fractals Objects of non-integral dimension and other chaos.

sci.geo.fluids Discussion of geophysical fluid dynamics.

sci.geo.geology Discussion of solid earth sciences.

sci.geo.meteorology Discussion of meteorology and related topics.

sci.image.processing Scientific image processing and analysis.

sci.lang Natural languages, communication, etc.

sci.lang.japan The Japanese language, both spoken and written.

sci.life-extension Slowing, stopping or reversing the ageing process.

sci.logic Logic -- math, philosophy & computational aspects.

sci.materials All aspects of materials engineering.

sci.math Mathematical discussions and pursuits.

sci.math.research Discussion of current mathematical research. (Moderated)

sci.math.stat Statistics discussion.

sci.math.symbolic Symbolic algebra discussion.

sci.med Medicine and its related products and regulations.

sci.med.aids AIDS: treatment, pathology/biology of HIV, prevention. (Moderated)

sci.med.dentistry Dentally related topics; all about teeth.

sci.med.nutrition Physiological impacts of diet.

sci.med.occupational Preventing, detecting & treating occupational injuries.

sci.med.pharmacy The teaching and practice of pharmaceutics.

sci.med.physics Issues of physics in medical testing/care.

sci.med.telemedicine Clinical consulting through computer networks.

sci.military Discussion about science & the military. (Moderated)

sci.misc Short-lived discussions on subjects in the sciences.

sci.nanotech Self-reproducing molecular-scale machines. (Moderated)

sci.nonlinear Chaotic systems and other nonlinear scientific study.

sci.optics Discussion relating to the science of optics.

sci.philosophy.tech Technical philosophy: math, science, logic, etc.

sci.physics Physical laws, properties, etc.

sci.physics.fusion Info on fusion, esp. ''cold'' fusion.

sci.physics.research Current physics research. (Moderated)

sci.psychology Topics related to psychology.

sci.psychology.digest PSYCOLOQUY: Refereed Psychology Journal and Newsletter. (Moderated)

sci.research Research methods, funding, ethics, and whatever.

sci.research.careers Issues relevant to careers in scientific research.

sci.skeptic Skeptics discussing pseudo-science.

sci.space Space, space programs, space related research, etc.

sci.space.news Announcements of space-related news items. (Moderated)

sci.space.shuttle The space shuttle and the STS program.

sci.stat.consult Statistical consulting.

sci.stat.edu Statistics education.

sci.stat.math Statistics from a strictly mathematical viewpoint.

sci.systems The theory and application of systems science.

sci.virtual-worlds Modelling the universe. (Moderated)

sci.virtual-worlds.apps Current and future uses of virtual-worlds technology. (Moderated)

SOCIAL AND POLITICAL NEWSGROUPS

soc.answers Repository for periodic USENET articles. (Moderated)

soc.bi Discussions of bisexuality.

soc.college College, college activities, campus life, etc.

soc.college.grad General issues related to graduate schools.

soc.college.gradinfo Information about graduate schools.

soc.college.teaching-asst Issues affecting collegiate teaching assistants.

soc.couples Discussions for couples (cf. soc.singles).

soc.culture.afghanistan Discussion of the Afghan society.

soc.culture.african Discussions about Africa & things African.

soc.culture.african.american Discussions about Afro-American issues.

soc.culture.arabic Technological & cultural issues, *not * politics.

soc.culture.asean Countries of the Assoc. of SE Asian Nations.

soc.culture.asian.american Issues & discussion about Asian-Americans.

soc.culture.australian Australian culture and society.

soc.culture.austria Austria and its people.

soc.culture.baltics People of the Baltic states.

soc.culture.bangladesh Issues & discussion about Bangladesh.

soc.culture.bosna-herzgvna The indepedent state of Bosnia and Herzegovina.

soc.culture.brazil Talking about the people and country of Brazil.

soc.culture.british Issues about Britain & those of British descent.

soc.culture.bulgaria Discussing Bulgarian society.

soc.culture.canada Discussions of Canada and its people.

soc.culture.caribbean Life in the Caribbean.

soc.culture.celtic Irish, Scottish, Breton, Cornish, Manx & Welsh.

soc.culture.china About China and Chinese culture.

soc.culture.croatia The lives of people of Croatia.

soc.culture.czecho-slovak Bohemian, Slovak, Moravian and Silesian life.

soc.culture.europe Discussing all aspects of all-European society.

soc.culture.filipino Group about the Filipino culture.

soc.culture.french French culture, history, and related discussions.

soc.culture.german Discussions about German culture and history.

soc.culture.greek Group about Greeks.

soc.culture.hongkong Discussions pertaining to Hong Kong.

soc.culture.indian Group for discussion about India & things Indian.

soc.culture.indian.telugu The culture of the Telugu people of India.

soc.culture.indonesia All about the Indonesian nation.

soc.culture.iranian Discussions about Iran and things Iranian/Persian.

soc.culture.italian The Italian people and their culture.

soc.culture.japan Everything Japanese, except the Japanese language.

soc.culture.jewish Jewish culture & religion. (cf. talk.politics.mideast)

soc.culture.korean Discussions about Korean & things Korean.

soc.culture.latin-america Topics about Latin-America.

soc.culture.lebanon Discussion about things Lebanese.

soc.culture.maghreb North African society and culture.

soc.culture.magyar The Hungarian people & their culture.

soc.culture.malaysia All about Malaysian society.

soc.culture.mexican Discussion of Mexico's society.

soc.culture.misc Group for discussion about other cultures.

soc.culture.native Aboriginal people around the world.

soc.culture.nepal Discussion of people and things in & from Nepal.

soc.culture.netherlands People from the Netherlands and Belgium.

soc.culture.new-zealand Discussion of topics related to New Zealand.

soc.culture.nordic Discussion about culture up north.

soc.culture.pakistan Topics of discussion about Pakistan.

soc.culture.peru All about the people of Peru.

soc.culture.polish Polish culture, Polish past, and Polish politics.

soc.culture.portuguese Discussion of the people of Portugal.

soc.culture.romanian Discussion of Romanian and Moldavian people.

soc.culture.singapore The past, present and future of Singapore.

soc.culture.soviet Topics relating to Russian or Soviet culture.

soc.culture.spain Discussion of culture on the Iberian peninsula.

soc.culture.sri-lanka Things & people from Sri Lanka.

soc.culture.taiwan Discussion about things Taiwanese.

soc.culture.tamil Tamil language, history and culture.

soc.culture.thai Thai people and their culture.

soc.culture.turkish Discussion about things Turkish.

soc.culture.ukrainian The lives and times of the Ukrainian people.

soc.culture.usa The culture of the United States of America.

soc.culture.venezuela Discussion of topics related to Venezuela.

soc.culture.vietnamese Issues and discussions of Vietnamese culture.

soc.culture.yugoslavia Discussions of Yugoslavia and its people.

soc.feminism Discussion of feminism & feminist issues. (Moderated)

soc.history Discussions of things historical.

soc.libraries.talk Discussing all aspects of libraries.

soc.men Issues related to men, their problems & relationships.

soc.misc Socially-oriented topics not in other groups.

soc.motss Issues pertaining to homosexuality.

soc.net-people Announcements, requests, etc. about people on the net.

soc.penpals In search of net.friendships.

soc.politics Political problems, systems, solutions. (Moderated)

soc.politics.arms-d Arms discussion digest. (Moderated)

soc.religion.bahai Discussion of the Baha'i Faith. (Moderated)

soc.religion.christian Christianity and related topics. (Moderated)

soc.religion.christian.bible-study Examining the Holy Bible. (Moderated)

soc.religion.eastern Discussions of Eastern religions. (Moderated)

soc.religion.islam Discussions of the Islamic faith. (Moderated)

soc.religion.quaker The Religious Society of Friends.

soc.rights.human Human rights & activism (e.g., Amnesty International).

soc.roots Discussing genealogy and genealogical matters.

soc.singles Newsgroup for single people, their activities, etc.

soc.veterans Social issues relating to military veterans.

soc.women Issues related to women, their problems & relationships.

TALK AND DISCUSSION NEWSGROUPS

talk.abortion All sorts of discussions and arguments on abortion.

talk.answers Repository for periodic USENET articles. (Moderated)

talk.bizarre The unusual, bizarre, curious, and often stupid.

talk.environment Discussion the state of the environment & what to do.

talk.origins Evolution versus creationism (sometimes hot!).

talk.philosophy.misc Philosophical musings on all topics.

talk.politics.animals The use and/or abuse of animals.

talk.politics.china Discussion of political issues related to China.

talk.politics.drugs The politics of drug issues.

talk.politics.guns The politics of firearm ownership and (mis)use.

talk.politics.medicine The politics and ethics involved with health care.

talk.politics.mideast Discussion & debate over Middle Eastern events.

talk.politics.misc Political discussions and ravings of all kinds.

talk.politics.soviet Discussion of Soviet politics, domestic and foreign.

talk.politics.space Non-technical issues affecting space exploration.

talk.politics.theory Theory of politics and political systems.

talk.rape Discussions on stopping rape; not to be crossposted.

talk.religion.misc Religious, ethical, & moral implications.

talk.religion.newage Esoteric and minority religions & philosophies.

talk.rumors For the posting of rumors.

UNIX is a registered trademark of UNIX System Laboratories, Inc.; DEC and Ultrix are Trademarks of the Digital Equipment Corporation; VAX is a Trademark of the Digital Equipment Corporation; Ada is a registered Trademark of the Ada Joint Program Office of the United States Department of Defense; Unisys is a registered trademark of Unisys Corporation.

B. CLARINET NEWSGROUPS

The following is a list of Newsgroups sponsored by the ClariNet Communications Corporation, a commercial electronic publishing network service that provides professional news and information, including live UPI wireservice news, in the USENET file format. ClariNet's system provides computer industry news, technology related wirestories, syndicated columns and features, financial information, stock quotes, and more. ClariNet news is provided using the USENET message interchange format, and available via UUCP and other delivery protocols. These formats are supported by a variety of packages for Unix and other systems.

To quote from their promotional material:

"At ClariNet, we license publications of all sorts for electronic distribution. For example, we collect news directly off the UPI wire, classify it and convert it into USENET format. In turn, generated articles are fed out on a regular basis to the UUNET hub machine, Anterior's Bay Area USENET hub, the Performance Systems International Network UUPSI hub and many other distribution points. You pick them up in USENET format and pay a subscription fee based on the number of readers at your site. You read your news using USENET newsreading tools. Small volume publications can also be sent via electronic mail. You can also use our NewsClip programming language. This lets you filter your newsreading as finely as you desire."

For more information, contact: ClariNet Communications Corporation, Box 1479, Cupertino, CA 95015-1479; (408)296-0366; (800) USE-NETS; Fax: (408) 296-1668 E-mail: info@clarinet.com

CURRENT CLARINET NEWGROUPS AND DESCRIPTIONS

clari ClariNet   Electronic Publication Newsgroups
clari.news   ClariNet UPI general news wiregroups
clari.news.hot   Temporary groups for hot news stories
clari.biz   ClariNet UPI business news wiregroups
clari.sports   ClariNet UPI sports wiregroups
clari.tw   ClariNet UPI technology related news wiregroups
clari.nb   ClariNet Newsbytes Information service Newsgroups
clari.newsbytes   ClariNet Newsbytes groups with daily delivery
clari.net   ClariNet non-news newsgroups
clari.canada   ClariNet broadcast style news about Canada
clari.feature   Feature columns and products
clari.local   ClariNet local news
clari.feature.dave_barry   Columns of humourist Dave Barry
clari.feature.mike_royko   Chicago Opinion Columnist Mike Royko
clari.feature.miss_manners   Judith Martin's Humourous Etiquette Advice
clari.canada.newscast   Regular newscast for Canadians
clari.canada.politics   Political and election items
clari.canada.gov   Government related news (all levels)
clari.canada.law   Crimes, the courts and the law.
clari.canada.trouble   Mishaps, accidents and serious problems
clari.canada.features   Alamanac, Ottawa Special, Arts
clari.canada.general   Short items on Canadian News stories
clari.canada.biz   Canadian Business Summaries
clari.tw.aerospace   Aerospace industry and companies
clari.tw.computers   Computer industry, applications and developments
clari.tw.defense   Defense industry issues
clari.tw.education   Stories involving Universities & colleges
clari.tw.electronics   Electronics makers and sellers
clari.tw.environment   Environmental news, hazardous waste, forests
clari.tw.health   Disease, medicine, health care, sick celebs
clari.tw.health.aids   AIDS stories, research, political issues
clari.tw.misc   General technical industry stories
clari.tw.nuclear   Nuclear power & waste
clari.tw.science   General science stories
clari.tw.space   NASA, Astronomy & spaceflight

clari.tw.stocks   Regular reports on computer & technology stock prices
clari.tw.telecom   Phones, Satellites, Media & general Telecom
clari.biz.commodity   Commodity news and price reports
clari.biz.courts   Lawsuits and business related legal matters
clari.biz.economy   Economic news and indicators
clari.biz.economy.world   Economy stories for non-US countries
clari.biz.features   Business feature stories
clari.biz.finance   Finance, currency, Corporate finance
clari.biz.finance.earnings   Earnings & dividend reports
clari.biz.finance.personal   Personal investing & finance
clari.biz.finance.services   Banks and financial industries
clari.biz.invest   News for investors
clari.biz.labor   Strikes, unions and labor relations
clari.biz.market   General stock market news
clari.biz.market.amex   American Stock Exchange reports & news
clari.biz.market.dow   Dow Jones NYSE reports
clari.biz.market.ny   NYSE reports
clari.biz.market.otc   NASDAQ reports
clari.biz.market.report   General market reports, S&P, etc.
clari.biz.mergers   Mergers and acquisitions
clari.biz.misc   Other business news
clari.biz.products   Important new products & services
clari.biz.top   Top business news
clari.biz.urgent   Breaking business news
clari.nb.top   Newsbytes top stories (crossposted)
clari.nb.apple   Newsbytes Apple/Macintosh news
clari.nb.business   Newsbytes business & industry news
clari.nb.general   Newsbytes general computer news
clari.nb.govt   Newsbytes legal and government computer news
clari.nb.ibm   Newsbytes IBM PC World coverage
clari.nb.review   Newsbytes new product reviews
clari.nb.telecom   Newsbytes telecom & online industry news
clari.nb.trends   Newsbytes new developments & trends
clari.nb.unix   Newsbytes Unix news
clari.net.admin   Announcements for news admins at ClariNet sites
clari.net.announce   Announcements for all ClariNet readers ·
clari.net.products   New ClariNet products

clari.net.talk   Discussion of ClariNet -- only unmoderated group

clari.news.almanac   Daily almanac - quotes, 'this date in history' etc.

clari.news.arts   Stage, drama & other fine arts

clari.news.aviation   Aviation industry and mishaps

clari.news.books   Books & publishing

clari.news.briefs   Regular news summaries

clari.news.bulletin   Major breaking stories of the week

clari.news.canada   News related to Canada

clari.news.cast   Regular U.S. news summary

clari.news.children   Stories related to children and parenting

clari.news.consumer   Consumer news, car reviews etc.

clari.news.demonstration   Demonstrations around the world

clari.news.disaster   Major problems, accidents & natural disasters

clari.news.economy   General economic news

clari.news.election   News regarding both US and international elections

clari.news.entertain   Entertainment industry news & features

clari.news.europe   News related to Europe

clari.news.features   Unclassified feature stories

clari.news.fighting   Clashes around the world

clari.news.flash   Ultra-important once-a-year news flashes

clari.news.goodnews   Stories of success and survival

clari.news.gov   General Government related stories

clari.news.gov.agency   Government agencies, FBI etc.

clari.news.gov.budget   Budgets at all levels

clari.news.gov.corrupt   Government corruption, kickbacks etc.

clari.news.gov.international   International government-related stories

clari.news.gov.officials   Government officials & their problems

clari.news.gov.state   State government stories of national importance.

clari.news.gov.taxes   Tax laws, trials etc.

clari.news.gov.usa   US Federal government news. (High volume)

clari.news.group   Special interest groups not covered in their own group

clari.news.group.blacks   News of interest to black people

clari.news.group.gays   Homosexuality & Gay Rights.

clari.news.group.jews   Jews & Jewish interests.

clari.news.group.women   Women's issues and abortion

clari.news.headlines   Hourly list of the top U.S./World headlines

clari.news.hot.east__europe   News from Eastern Europe

clari.news.hot.ussr   News from the Soviet Union

clari.news.interest   Human interest stories

clari.news.interest.animals   Animals in the news

clari.news.interest.history   Human interest stories & history in the making

clari.news.interest.people   Famous people in the news

clari.news.interest.people.column   Daily ''People'' column -- tidbits on celebs

clari.news.interest.quirks   Unusual or funny news stories

clari.news.issues   Stories on major issues not covered in their own group.

clari.news.issues.civil__rights   Freedom, Racism, Civil Rights Issues

clari.news.issues.conflict   Conflict between groups around the world

clari.news.issues.family   Family, Child abuse, etc.

clari.news.labor   Unions, strikes

clari.news.labor.strikes   Strikes

clari.news.law   General group for law related issues

clari.news.law.civil   Civil trials & litigation

clari.news.law.crime   Major crimes

clari.news.law.crime.sex   Sex crimes and trials

clari.news.law.crime.trial   Trials for criminal actions

clari.news.law.crime.violent   Violent crime & criminals

clari.news.law.drugs   Drug related crimes & drug stories

clari.news.law.investigation   Investigation of crimes

clari.news.law.police   Police & law enforcement

clari.news.law.prison   Prisons, prisoners & escapes

clari.news.law.profession   Lawyers, Judges etc.

clari.news.law.supreme   U.S. Supreme court rulings & news

clari.news.lifestyle   Fashion, leisure etc.

clari.news.military   Military equipment, people & issues

clari.news.movies   Reviews, news and stories on movie stars.

clari.news.music   Reviews and issues concerning music & musicians.

clari.news.politics   Politicians & politics.

clari.news.politics.people   Politicians & Political Personalities

clari.news.religion   Religion, religious leaders, televangelists

clari.news.sex   Sexual issues, sex-related political stories

clari.news.terrorism   Terrorist actions & related news around the world

clari.news.top   Top US news stories

clari.news.top.world   Top international news stories

clari.news.trends   Surveys and trends.

clari.news.trouble   Less major accidents, problems & mishaps

clari.news.tv   TV news, reviews & stars.

clari.news.urgent   Major breaking stories of the day

clari.news.weather   Weather and temperature reports

clari.sports.baseball   Baseball scores, stories, games, stats

clari.sports.basketball   Basketball coverage

clari.sports.features   Sports feature stories

clari.sports.football   Pro football coverage

clari.sports.hockey   NHL coverage

clari.sports.misc   Other sports, plus general sports news

clari.sports.motor   Racing, Motor Sports

clari.sports.tennis   Tennis news & scores

clari.sports.olympic   The Olympic Games

clari.sports.top   Top sports news

clari.local.headlines   Various local headline summaries

clari.local.alberta.briefs   Local news Briefs

clari.local.arizona   Local news

clari.local.arizona.briefs   Local news Briefs

clari.local.bc.briefs   Local news Briefs

clari.local.california   Local news

clari.local.california.briefs   Local news Briefs

clari.local.florida   Local news

clari.local.florida.briefs   Local news Briefs

clari.local.georgia   Local news

clari.local.georgia.briefs   Local news Briefs

clari.local.illinois   Local news

clari.local.illinois.briefs   Local news Briefs

clari.local.indiana   Local news

clari.local.indiana.briefs   Local news Briefs

clari.local.iowa   Local news

clari.local.iowa.briefs   Local news Briefs

clari.local.louisiana   Local news

clari.local.manitoba.briefs   Local news Briefs

clari.local.maritimes.briefs   Local news Briefs

clari.local.maryland   Local news

clari.local.maryland.briefs   Local news Briefs
clari.local.massachusetts   Local news
clari.local.massachusetts.briefs   Local news Briefs
clari.local.michigan   Local news
clari.local.michigan.briefs   Local news Briefs
clari.local.minnesota   Local news
clari.local.minnesota.briefs   Local news Briefs
clari.local.missouri   Local news
clari.local.missouri.briefs   Local news Briefs
clari.local.nebraska   Local news
clari.local.nebraska.briefs   Local news Briefs
clari.local.new__england   Local news
clari.local.new__hampshire   Local news
clari.local.new__jersey   Local news
clari.local.new__jersey.briefs   Local news Briefs
clari.local.new__york   Local news
clari.local.new__york.briefs   Local news Briefs
clari.local.ohio   Local news
clari.local.ohio.briefs   Local news Briefs
clari.local.ontario.briefs   Local news Briefs
clari.local.oregon   Local news
clari.local.oregon.briefs   Local news Briefs
clari.local.pennsylvania   Local news
clari.local.pennsylvania.briefs   Local news Briefs
clari.local.saskatchewan.briefs   Local news Briefs
clari.local.texas   Local news
clari.local.texas.briefs   Local news Briefs
clari.local.utah   Local news
clari.local.utah.briefs   Local news Briefs

clari.local.virginia + dc   Local news
clari.local.virginia + dc.briefs   Local news Briefs
clari.local.washington   Local news
clari.local.washington.briefs   Local news Briefs
clari.local.wisconsin   Local news
clari.local.wisconsin.briefs   Local news Briefs
clari.local.chicago   Local news
clari.local.chicago.briefs   Local news Briefs
clari.local.los__angeles   Local news
clari.local.los__angeles.briefs   Local news Briefs
clari.local.nyc   Local news (New York City)
clari.local.nyc.briefs   Local news Briefs
clari.local.sfbay   Stories datelined San Francisco Bay Area
clari.sfbay.general   Main stories for SF Bay Area
clari.sfbay.briefs   Twice daily news roundups for SF Bay Area
clari.sfbay.misc   Shorter general items for SF Bay Area
clari.sfbay.short   Very short items for SF Bay Area
clari.sfbay.police   Stories from the Police Depts. of the SF Bay
clari.sfbay.fire   Stories from Fire Depts. of the SF Bay
clari.sfbay.weather   SF Bay and California Weather reports
clari.sfbay.roads   Reports from Caltrans and the CHP.
clari.sfbay.entertain   Reviews and entertainment news for SF Bay Area
biz.clarinet   Announcements about ClariNet
biz.clarinet.sample   Samples of ClariNet newsgroups for the outside world

Section 8. WAIS-Accessible Databases

The Wide-Area Information Server (WAIS) protocol is a hypertext-based storage and retrieval system allowing natural-language searching across multiple databases structured along similar lines. In this case, the database conformity is based on the ANSI Z39.50 information transfer protocol. Developed by Thinking Machines Corporation, the WAIS client/server program allows users to select from a growing number of compatible databases, construct and conduct search queries using common language terms, and view results rated according to potential usefulness.

Searching WAIS databases is done by first accessing a WAIS client. You may have a WAIS client available to you through the computer system on which you have your Internet account. You can find out by typing wais (or swais for "simple wais," a simpler but more accessible WAIS client) at your system prompt to see if you can connect. If you do not have a client available, you can telnet to a public WAIS client. A convenient one is at quake.think.com. Your login will be "wais". Your password response should be your Internet e-mail address.

Once you have logged in, you will be shown a listing of the data sources available. Typing in a ? or h at this point will give you the following information on key functions:

```
j, down arrow, N     move down one source
k, up arrow, P     move up one source
J, V, D     move down one screen
K, V, U     move up one screen
###     postion to source ##
<space>, <period>     select current source
=     deselect all sources
v, <comma>     view current source info
<return>     perform search
s     select new sources (refresh sources list)
w     select new keywords
X, -     remove current source permanently
o     set and show swais options
h, ?     show this help display
H     display program history
q     leave this program
```

The arrow keys and the spacebar allow you to select items for searching, a w command lets you enter keywords to define your search, and hitting return will perform a search. The results of your keyword search will be a list of documents in the order of how closely they match your keyword parameters. You can then retrieve a document, display it on your screen, keep going with your search, begin a new search, or quit WAIS. The following list of nearly 500 databases represents an edited version of what was retrieved from the wais.com listing of WAIS sources, the most authoritative of the many versions of this quickly growing source list.

1. aarnet-resource-guide.src
:ip-address "139.130.4.6"
:ip-name "archie.au"
:tcp-port 210
:database-name "aarnet-resource-guide"
:maintainer "wais@archie.au"
This server holds a copy of the AARNet Resource Guide. The Guide itself is maintained by G.Huston@jatz.aarnet.edu.au. AARNet is the Australian Academic and Research Network.

2. aas__jobs.src
:ip-address "128.183.36.18"
:ip-name "ndadsb.gsfc.nasa.gov"
:tcp-port 210
:database-name "AAS__jobs"
:maintainer "stelar-info@Hypatia.gsfc.nasa.gov"
This source contains the current listings from the American Astronomical Society Job Register.

3. aas__meeting.src
:ip-name "ndadsb.gsfc.nasa.gov".

:tcp-port 210
:database-name "AAS__meeting"
:maintainer "stelar-info@Hypatia.gsfc.nasa.gov"
This database contains the electronically-submitted abstracts for the most recent of the semi-annual meetings of the American Astronomical Society. The AAS__meeting database is automatically pointed to the most current set of abstracts, so users do not need to retrieve the source file over and over again. The source files for the abstracts from each individual AAS meeting are available by anonymous FTP from hypatia.gsfc.nasa.gov, in the directory /wais-sources. The abstracts in these databases are in LaTeX format, and require the AASTeX macro package for formatting.

4. academic__email__conf.src
:ip-address "130.235.162.11"
:ip-name "munin.ub2.lu.se"
:tcp-port 210
:database-name "academic__email__conf"
:maintainer "anders@munin.ub2.lu.se"
This database contains information on newsgroups and other

electronic conferences. Included are the Directory of Scholarly Electronic Conferences collected by Diane K. Kovacs and a list of newsgroups(/usr/lib/news/newsgroups) with a one line information about each group.

5. acronyms.src
:ip-address ''130.130.64.1''
:ip-name ''wraith.cs.uow.edu.au''
:tcp-port 210
:database-name ''acronyms''
:maintainer ''steve@wraith.cs.uow.edu.au''
A public domain database of acronyms and abbreviations maintained by Dave Sill (de5@ornl.gov). The files of type one__line used in the index were: /shr/lib/wais/wais-sources/acronyms.

6. aeronautics.src
:ip-name ''archive.orst.edu''
:tcp-port 9000
:database-name ''aeronautics''
:maintainer ''wais@archive.orst.edu''
This server has the contents of the aeronautics mailing list ftp area on rascal.ics.utexas.edu. Updated nightly. Comments and questions to archivist@archive.orst.edu.

7. aftp-cs-colorado-edu.src
:ip-address ''128.138.243.151''
:ip-name ''ftp.cs.colorado.edu''
:tcp-port 8000
:database-name ''aftp-cs-colorado-edu''
:maintainer ''hardy@cs.colorado.edu''
You may use this WAIS server to search and retrieve files from the anonymous ftp archive on ftp.cs.colorado.edu [128.138.243.151]. We used Essence, a resource discovery system based on semantic file indexing, to build the WAIS index for this server.

8. agricultural-market-news.src
:ip-address ''128.193.124.4''
:ip-name ''nostromo.oes.orst.edu''
:tcp-port 210
:database-name ''agricultural-market-news''
:maintainer ''wais@nostromo.oes.orst.edu''
This server contains the agricultural commodity market reports compiled by the Agricultural Market News Service of the United States Department of Agriculture. There are approximately 1200 reports from all over the United States. Most of these reports are updated daily. Try searching for 'portland grain.' For more information contact: wais@oes.orst.edu.

9. alt.drugs.src
:ip-name ''archive.orst.edu''
:tcp-port 9000
:database-name ''alt.drugs''
:maintainer ''wais@archive.orst.edu''
These are the contents of the alt.drugs archive. The contents, ideas, methods, thought patterns and anything else in here including the notion of offensitivity about this source are not in any way related to Oregon State University or any of its employees, the Oregon State System of Higher Education, or anyone else you care to hassle. This source will mirror the alt.drugs archive. New documents will be added as they appear. Questions and comments to archivist@archive.orst.edu.

10. alt.gopher.src
:ip-address ''128.109.157.30''
:ip-name ''wais.oit.unc.edu''
:tcp-port 210
:database-name ''altgopher''
:maintainer ''fullton@samba.oit.unc.edu''
News from the gopher newsgroup.

11. alt.sys.sun.src
:ip-address ''152.2.22.81''
:ip-name ''sun-wais.oit.unc.edu''
:tcp-port 210
:database-name ''alt-sys-sun''
:maintainer ''wais@calypso.oit.unc.edu''
Archived news articles from alt.sys.sun. This service is provided by the University of NC at Chapel Hill.

12. alt.wais.src
:ip-address ''128.109.157.30''
:ip-name ''wais.oit.unc.edu''
:tcp-port 210
:database-name ''altwais''
:maintainer ''fullton@samba.oit.unc.edu''
News from the alt.wais newsgroup.

13. amiga-slip.src
:database-name ''/home/wcscps/archive/amiga-slip''
:ip-address ''134.117.1.1''
:ip-name ''alfred.ccs.carleton.ca''
:tcp-port 210
:maintainer ''mcr@ccs.carleton.ca''
The files of type rn used in the index were: /home/wcscps/archive/amiga-slip /home/wcscps/archive/AmigaNOS-faq.

14. amiga__fish__contents.src
:ip-address ''130.235.162.11''
:ip-name ''munin.ub2.lu.se''
:tcp-port 210
:database-name ''amiga__fish__contents''
:maintainer ''hakan@hera.dit.lth.se''
This is an index of the contents of Fred Fish's disks #1-current with a freely distributable AMIGA software library containing an extensive collection of PD, shareware and demo programs.

15. anu-aboriginal-econpolicies.src
:ip-name ''coombs.anu.edu.au''
:ip-address ''150.203.76.2''
:tcp-port 210
:database-name ''ANU-Aboriginal-EconPolicies''
:maintainer ''wais@coombs.anu.edu.au''
Abstracts of discussion papers produced at the Centre for Aboriginal Economic Policy Research (CAEPR), Faculty of Arts, The Australian National University, Canberra ACT 0200, Australia.

16. anu-aboriginal-studies.src
:ip-name ''coombs.anu.edu.au''
:ip-address ''coombs.anu.edu.au''
:tcp-port 210
:database-name ''ANU-Aboriginal-Studies''
:maintainer ''wais@coombs.anu.edu.au''
A loose collection (100Kb) of catalogue records of the Aboriginal Studies Electronic Data Archive (ASEDA) at The Australian Institute of Aboriginal and Torres Strait Islander Studies.

(AIATSIS), Canberra, and of an index to the 14 volumes (1977-90) of the Aboriginal History Journal, Research School of Pacific Studies, The Australian National University. These data were supplemented in April 93 by 64 Kb of other materials derived from the ANU-xxx-xxx Wais series.

17. anu-ancient-dna-studies.src
:ip-name ''coombs.anu.edu.au''
:ip-address ''150.203.76.2''
:tcp-port 210
:database-name ''ANU-Ancient-DNA-Studies''
:maintainer ''wais@coombs.anu.edu.au''
Selected references to the analysis of the ancient DNA.

18. anu-asian-computing.src
:ip-name ''coombs.anu.edu.au''
:ip-address ''coombs.anu.edu.au''
:tcp-port 210
:database-name ''ANU-Asian-Computing''
:maintainer ''wais@coombs.anu.edu.au''
A loose and continuously growing collection of research information, archives, publications, software, fonts, suppliers addresses, notes, solutions and practical hints pertaining to the effective use of Asian and other non-Latin scripts and fonts in the academic computing and text-processing.

19. anu-asian-religions.src
:ip-name ''coombs.anu.edu.au''
:ip-address ''150.203.76.2''
:tcp-port 210
:database-name ''ANU-Asian-Religions''
:maintainer ''wais@coombs.anu.edu.au''
Bibliographic references to the selected (mainly Buddhist) Asian religions.

20. anu-austphilosophyforum-l.src
:ip-name ''coombs.anu.edu.au''
:ip-address ''150.203.76.2''
:tcp-port 210
:database-name ''ANU-AustPhilosophyForum-L''
:maintainer ''wais@coombs.anu.edu.au''
A collection of communications and exchanges submitted since Nov 91 to the AUSTRALASIAN PHILOSOPHY FORUM APF-L on vulcan.anu.edu.au and, subsequently,to APHIL-L listservs.

21. anu-australia-nz-history-l.src
:ip-name ''coombs.anu.edu.au''
:ip-address ''150.203.76.2''
:tcp-port 210
:database-name ''ANU-Australia-NZ-History-L''
:maintainer ''wais@coombs.anu.edu.au''
A collection of communications and exchanges submitted to the Australia-NZ-History-L 'listserv' on the coombs.anu.edu.au machine.

22. anu-australian-economics.src
:ip-name ''coombs.anu.edu.au''
:ip-address ''150.203.76.2''
:tcp-port 210
:database-name ''ANU-Australian-Economics''
:maintainer ''wais@coombs.anu.edu.au''
A bibliographic dbase with details of Discussion Papers 1980-1990 and Conference Publications 1980-1991 prepared at the Centre for Economic Policy Research, Research School of So-

cial Sciences, Australian National University, Canberra, PO. Box 4, ACT 0200 Australia ph. (Intl) + 61 6 249 2247 Fax +61 6 257 1893.

23. anu-canbanthropology-index.src
:ip-name ''coombs.anu.edu.au''
:ip-address ''150.203.76.2''
:tcp-port 210
:database-name ''ANU-CanbAnthropology-Index''
:maintainer ''wais@coombs.anu.edu.au''
INDEX OF CANBERRA ANTHROPOLOGY JOURNAL: 1977-1992.

24. anu-caut-academics.src
:ip-name ''coombs.anu.edu.au''
:ip-address ''150.203.76.2''
:tcp-port 210
:database-name ''ANU-CAUT-Academics''
:maintainer ''wais@coombs.anu.edu.au''
April 1993 register kept by the CAUT - Committee for the Advancement of University Teaching with details of 325 Australian academics working on the teaching development projects.

25. anu-caut-projects.src
:ip-name ''coombs.anu.edu.au''
:ip-address ''coombs.anu.edu.au''
:tcp-port 210
:database-name ''ANU-CAUT-Projects''
:maintainer ''wais@coombs.anu.edu.au''
March 1993 register of 1993 Australian national teaching development projects funded by the CAUT - Committee for the Advancement of University Teaching.

26. anu-coombseminars-listserv.src
:ip-name ''coombs.anu.edu.au''
:ip-address ''150.203.76.2''
:tcp-port 210
:database-name ''ANU-Coombseminars-Listserv''
:maintainer ''wais@coombs.anu.edu.au''
A collection of communications and exchanges submitted to coombseminars list on majordomo@coombs.anu.edu.au.

27. anu-coombspapers-index.src
:ip-name ''coombs.anu.edu.au''
:ip-address ''coombs.anu.edu.au''
:tcp-port 210
:database-name ''ANU-Coombspapers-Index''
:maintainer ''wais@coombs.anu.edu.au''
The annotated index to the Coombspapers Social Sciences Research Data Bank built at the Australian National University. This index is updated at regular intervals, roughly once a fortnight.

28. anu-french-databanks.src
:ip-name ''coombs.anu.edu.au''
:ip-address ''coombs.anu.edu.au''
:tcp-port 210
:database-name ''ANU-French-Databanks''
:maintainer ''wais@coombs.anu.edu.au''
A catalogue (140Kb) of recent French language publications, people, commercial servers (providers), research projects and on-line as well as stand alone data bases available in France which are of relevance to the Humanities, Arts and Social Sciences research.

29. anu-local-waisservers-index.src
:ip-name   "coombs.anu.edu.au"
:ip-address   "150.203.76.2"
:tcp-port   210
:database-name   "ANU-Local-Waiservers-Index"
:maintainer   "wais@coombs.anu.edu.au"
THE CATALOGUE of the ANU＿xxx＿xxx series of WAIS
DATABASES.

30. anu-local-waiservers.src
:ip-name   "coombs.anu.edu.au"
:ip-address   "coombs.anu.edu.au"
:tcp-port   210
:database-name   "ANU-Local-Waiservers"
:maintainer   "wais@coombs.anu.edu.au"
The central (and authoritative) register of sources of the WAIS
servers built at the Australian National University.

31. anu-pacific-archaeology.src
:ip-name   "coombs.anu.edu.au"
:ip-address   "150.203.76.2"
:tcp-port   210
:database-name   "ANU-Pacific-Archaeology"
:maintainer   "wais@coombs.anu.edu.au"
Selected references to the Australian and Pacific archaeology
and prehistory research based on the publications of the Dept. of
Prehistory, Research School of Pacific Studies, Australian National University, Canberra ACT 0200, Australia.

32. anu-pacific-linguistics.src
:ip-name   "coombs.anu.edu.au"
:ip-address   "coombs.anu.edu.au"
:tcp-port   210
:database-name   "ANU-Pacific-Linguistics"
:maintainer   "wais@coombs.anu.edu.au"
A complete catalogue (130Kb) of publications within the PA-
CIFIC LINGUISTICS series published by the Department of
Linguistics, Research School of Pacific Studies, Australian National University.

33. anu-pacific-manuscripts.src
:ip-name   "coombs.anu.edu.au"
:ip-address   "150.203.76.2"
:tcp-port   210
:database-name   "ANU-Pacific-Manuscripts"
:maintainer   "wais@coombs.anu.edu.au"
Complete annotated catalogue of microfilms collection of the
Pacific Manuscripts Bureau (PAMBU), Research School of Pacific Studies, Australian National University, Canberra ACT
0200.

34. anu-pacific-relations.src
:ip-name   "coombs.anu.edu.au"
:ip-address   "coombs.anu.edu.au"
:tcp-port   210
:database-name   "ANU-Pacific-Relations"
:maintainer   "wais@coombs.anu.edu.au"
A melange of excerpts from select working papers, publication
lists and other documents dealing with Australian foreign policies, her neighbours and the Pacific Ocean Region, produced by
the Dept. of International Relations and the Peace Research
Centre at the RSPacS, ANU, phones: ＋61 6 249 2166 (Intl
Relations); ＋61 6 249 3098 (Peace Res. Cent.); fax: ＋61 6
257 1893.

35. anu-philippine-studies-l.src
:ip-name   "coombs.anu.edu.au"
:ip-address   "150.203.76.2"
:tcp-port   210
:database-name   "ANU-Philippine-Studies-L"
:maintainer   "wais@coombs.anu.edu.au"
A collection of communications and exchanges submitted to
philippinestudies-l list on majordomo@coombs.anu.edu.au.

36. anu-philippine-studies.src
:ip-name   "coombs.anu.edu.au"
:ip-address   "150.203.76.2"
:tcp-port   210
:database-name   "ANU-Philippine-Studies"
:maintainer   "wais@coombs.anu.edu.au"
Abstracts of 95 papers delivered at the 4th International Philip-
pine Studies Conference held 1-3 July 1992, on the campus of
the Australian National University, Canberra, ACT 0200.

37. anu-radiocarbon-abstracts.src
:ip-name   "coombs.anu.edu.au"
:ip-address   "150.203.76.2"
:tcp-port   210
:database-name   "ANU-Radiocarbon-Abstracts"
:maintainer   "wais@coombs.anu.edu.au"
This database is an electronic publication of a book by Dilette
POLACH entitled: Radiocarbon Dating Literature: the next 12
years, 1969 - 1980 Annotated Bibliography.

38. anu-shamanism-studies.src
:ip-name   "coombs.anu.edu.au"
:ip-address   "150.203.76.2"
:tcp-port   210
:database-name   "ANU-Shamanism-Studies"
:maintainer   "wais@coombs.anu.edu.au"
BIBLIOGRAPHY ON SHAMANISM by Dr Geoffrey Samuel.

39. anu-socsci-netlore.src
:ip-name   "coombs.anu.edu.au"
:ip-address   "coombs.anu.edu.au"
:tcp-port   210
:database-name   "ANU-SocSci-Netlore"
:maintainer   "wais@coombs.anu.edu.au"
A loose collection (1,030Kb strong) of documents, notes, hints,
solutions, addresses and other net-lore dealing with the information resources, e-mail and networking procedures of significance
to academic researchers in the fields of the Social Sciences, the
Arts and the Humanities.

40. anu-strategic-studies.src
:ip-name   "coombs.anu.edu.au"
:ip-address   "150.203.76.2"
:tcp-port   210
:database-name   "ANU-Strategic-Studies"
:maintainer   "wais@coombs.anu.edu.au"
A bibliography of publications and working papers produced by
the Strategic and Defence Studies Centre, Research School of
Pacific Studies, Australian National University, Canberra, ACT
0200, Australia.

41. anu-taoism-listserv.src
:ip-name   "coombs.anu.edu.au"
:ip-address   "150.203.76.2"
:tcp-port   210

:database-name "ANU-Taoism-Listserv"
:maintainer "wais@coombs.anu.edu.au"
A collection of communications and exchanges submitted to the Taoism-L 'listserv' established on 30 Jul 1993 on the coombs.anu.edu.au machine.

42. anu-thai-yunnan.src
:ip-name "coombs.anu.edu.au"
:ip-address "coombs.anu.edu.au"
:tcp-port 210
:database-name "ANU-Thai-Yunnan"
:maintainer "wais@coombs.anu.edu.au"
Annotated bibliography and the late dr Richard Davis' research notes collection of the Thai-Yunnan Project, Dept. of Anthropology, RSPacS Australian National University, Canberra ACT 0200.

43. anu-theses-abstracts.src
:ip-name "coombs.anu.edu.au"
:ip-address "coombs.anu.edu.au"
:tcp-port 210
:database-name "ANU-Theses-Abstracts"
:maintainer "wais@coombs.anu.edu.au"
The ANU-Theses-Abstracts is a data base of abstracts of the graduate and post-graduate theses produced at the ANU. Although it focuses mainly on the work done since the early 1990s, it also contains abstracts of works written as early as the late 1950s.

44. anu-tropical-archaeobotany.src
:ip-name "coombs.anu.edu.au"
:ip-address "150.203.76.2"
:tcp-port 210
:database-name "ANU-Tropical-Archaeobotany"
:maintainer "wais@coombs.anu.edu.au"
Selected references to the tropical paleo- and archaeobotany research based on the publications of the Dept. of Prehistory, Research School of Pacific Studies, Australian National University, Canberra ACT 0200, Australia.

45. anu-zenbuddhism-calendar.src
:ip-name "coombs.anu.edu.au"
:ip-address "150.203.76.2"
:tcp-port 210
:database-name "ANU-ZenBuddhism-Calendar"
:maintainer "wais@coombs.anu.edu.au"
The ANU-ZenBuddhism-Calendar is a data base of dates, anniversaries and festivals of Zen Buddhism. It has been prepared on the basis of materials collected by Dr. T.M.Ciolek for his planned contemporary Zen Buddhism.

46. anu-zenbuddhims-listserv.src
:ip-name "coombs.anu.edu.au"
:ip-address "150.203.76.2"
:tcp-port 210
:database-name "ANU-ZenBuddhism-Listserv"
:maintainer "wais@coombs.anu.edu.au"
A collection of communications and exchanges submitted to the ZenBuddhism-L 'listserv' on the coombs.anu.edu.au machine.

47. applications-navigator.src
:ip-address "192.31.181.1"
:ip-name "quake.think.com"
:tcp-port 210

:database-name "CM-applications"
:maintainer "wais@quake.think.com"
Connection Machine applications done at Thinking Machines and elsewhere. The author, status, and restrictions are stated along with descriptions of what the application does. Everything from Fluid flow to Artificial life codes are briefly described.

48. arabidopsis-biosci.src
:ip-name "weeds.mgh.harvard.edu"
:ip-address "132.183.190.21"
:tcp-port 210
:database-name "Arabidopsis-BioSci"
:maintainer "curator@frodo.mgh.harvard.edu"
Index of all messages on the BioSci Arabidopsis Genome Electronic Conference. This server includes all messages since March of 1991 from the bionet.genome.arabidopsis usenet newsgroup and the arab-gen@genbank.bio.net mailing list.

49. arabidopsis__thaliana__genome.src
:ip-address "132.183.190.21"
:ip-name "weeds.mgh.harvard.edu"
:tcp-port 210
:database-name "Arabidopsis__thaliana__Genome"
:maintainer "curator@frodo.mgh.harvard.edu"
Arabidopsis is a small flowering plant that is used as a model system for a variety of plant biological research.

50. archaeological__computing.src
:ip-address 134.151.44.19
:ip-name "ftp.tex.ac.uk"
:tcp-port 210
:database-name "archaeological__computing"
:maintainer "spqr@minster.york.ac.uk"
A bibliography of archaeological computing in BibTeX format.

51. archie.au-amiga-readmes.src
:ip-address "139.130.4.6"
:ip-name "archie.au"
:tcp-port 210
:database-name "archie.au-amiga-readmes"
:maintainer "wais@archie.au"
This is an index of the Readme, Index and Contents files for the archive /micros/amiga on the archive site 'archie.au'.

52. archie.au-ls-lrt.src
:ip-address "139.130.4.6"
:ip-name "archie.au"
:tcp-port 210
:database-name "archie.au-ls-lRt"
:maintainer "wais@archie.au"
This is an index of the ls-lRt file for the archive site 'archie.au'.

53. archie.au-mac-readmes.src
:ip-address "139.130.4.6"
:ip-name "archie.au"
:tcp-port 210
:database-name "archie.au-mac-readmes"
:maintainer "wais@archie.au"
This is an index of the Readme, Index and Contents files for the archive /micros/mac on the archive site 'archie.au'.

54. archie.au-pc-readmes.src
:ip-address "139.130.4.6"
:ip-name "archie.au"

:tcp-port   210
:database-name   ''archie.au-pc-readmes''
:maintainer   ''wais@archie.au''
This is an index of the Readme, Index and Contents files for the
archive /micros/pc on the archive site 'archie.au'.

55. askeric-helpsheets.src
:ip-address   ''128.230.34.72''
:ip-name   ''ericir.syr.edu''
:tcp-port   210
:database-name   ''digests''
:maintainer   ''rdlankes@ericir.syr.edu''
This index was created by the AskERIC service. It is a portion
of the AskERIC Library: InfoGuides--Information guides to current topics in education.These files provide Internet resources,
ERIC database search results, and other educational resources.

56. askeric-infoguides.src
:ip-address   ''128.230.34.72''
:ip-name   ''ericir.syr.edu''
:tcp-port   210
:database-name   ''infoguides''
:maintainer   ''rdlankes@ericir.syr.edu''
This server was created by The AskERIC service. It access a
portion of the AskERIC Library: InfoGuides--Information guides
to current topics in education. These files provide Internet resources, ERIC database search results, and other educational resources.

57. askeric-lesson-plans.src
:ip-address   ''128.230.34.72''
:ip-name   ''ericir.syr.edu''
:tcp-port   210
:database-name   ''lessons''
:maintainer   ''rdlankes@ericir.syr.edu''
Part of the AskERIC free library. This database contains over
600 lesson plans on areas such as Math, Language Arts, Science, Social Studies, and misc. Also included are lesson plans
for the PBS series Newton's Apple (10th season).

58. askeric-minisearchers.src
:ip-address   ''128.230.34.72''
:ip-name   ''ericir.syr.edu''
:tcp-port   210
:database-name   ''minisearch''
:maintainer   ''rdlankes@ericir.syr.edu''
This server was created by The AskERIC service. It accesses a
portion of the AskERIC Library: MiniSearches ERIC CD-ROM
database searches on educational topics. Each MiniSearch contains between 10 and 25 citations.

59. askeric-questions.src
:ip-address   ''128.230.34.72''
:ip-name   ''ericir.syr.edu''
:tcp-port   210
:database-name   ''questions''
:maintainer   ''rdlankes@ericir.syr.edu''
This index was created by the AskERIC service. It is a portion
of the AskERIC Library: Q&A--Commonly-asked questions
with their answers. Answers may include ERIC CD-ROM database searches as well as other information resources.

60. astropersons.src
:ip-name   ''ndadsb.gsfc.nasa.gov''

:tcp-port   210
:database-name   ''astropersons''
:maintainer   ''stelar-info@Hypatia.gsfc.nasa.gov''
This database is made available by the STELAR Project, part of
the Astrophysics Data Facility (ADF) at Goddard Space Flight
Center in Greenbelt, MD. It contains the list of electronic mail
addresses compiled by Chris Benn at LaPalma Observatory. It
includes astronomers.

61. astroplaces.src
:ip-address   ''130.167.1.2''
:ip-name   ''stsci.edu''
:tcp-port   210
:database-name   ''astroplaces''
:maintainer   ''reppert@stsci.edu''
Telephone, telex, fax and e-mail addresses for observatories and
astronomy departments worldwide.

62. au-directory-of-servers.src
:ip-address   ''139.130.4.6''
:ip-name   ''archie.au''
:tcp-port   210
:database-name   ''au-directory-of-servers''
:maintainer   ''wais@archie.au''
This is a backup copy of the directory-of-servers which is maintained by brewster@think.com. It is located in Australia and
may provide pointers to local (Australian) copies of international
databases if available.

63. avs__txt__files.src
:database-name   ''/usr1/avs/wais-sources/AVS__TXT__
FILES''
:maintainer   ''avs@doppler.ncsc.org''
:ip-address   ''128.109.178.23''
:ip-name   ''doppler.ncsc.org''
:tcp-port   210
All of the .txt files for Application Visualization System (AVS)
modules freely available on the International AVS Center's
anonymous ftp site have been indexed, as well as informational
files such as AVS__README and FAQ. The anonymous ftp
site can be accessed at avs.ncsc.org.

64. bgrass-l.src
:ip-address   ''128.183.36.18''
:ip-name   ''ndadsb.gsfc.nasa.gov''
:tcp-port   210
:database-name   ''BGRASS-L''
:maintainer   ''warnock@Hypatia.gsfc.nasa.gov''
Archives of the BGRASS-L mailing list, and is dedicated to
sharing an interest in bluegrass music. To join the mailing list,
send a electronic mail to listserv@ukcc.uky.edu. Put HELP in
the contents of the message to receive a list of commands. The
BGRASS-L mailing list is maintained by Frank Godbey
(uka016@ukcc.uky.edu). This server is maintained by Archie
Warnock (warnock@hypatia.gsfc.nasa.gov).

65. bib-appia.src
:ip-address   ''192.68.178.17''
:ip-name   ''wais.fct.unl.pt''
:tcp-port   210
:database-name   ''bib-appia''
:maintainer   ''archive@fct.unl.pt''
This database indexes the bibliographic references of the conferences and Summer schools sponsored by APPIA, the Portuguese

association for artificial intelligence. In the near future, it will also hold references of its members' publications.

66. bib-dmi-ens-fr.src
:ip-address "129.199.104.3"
:ip-name "snekkar.ens.fr"
:tcp-port 210
:database-name "bib-dmi-ens-fr"
:maintainer "chounet@snekkar.ens.fr"
Database of French educational materials.

67. bib-ens-lyon.src
:ip-name "wais-server.ens-lyon.fr"
:tcp-port 210
:database-name "bib-ens-lyon"
:maintainer "moisy@ens.ens-lyon.fr"
Card catalog of the library of the Ecole Normale Superieure de Lyon, France.

68. bib-math-jussieu-fr.src
:ip-address "134.157.13.100"
:ip-name "frmap711.mathp7.jussieu.fr"
:tcp-port 210
:database-name "bib-math-jussieu-fr"
:maintainer "arabia@frmap711.mathp7.jussieu.fr"
Data files of the Bibliotheque Interuniversitaire Scientifique Jussieu, Section Mathematiques-Recherche, Tour 56, 4 place Jussieu, 75252 PARIS cedex 05.

69. bib-paris7.ura-748.src
:ip-address "134.157.13.100"
:ip-name "frmap711.mathp7.jussieu.fr"
:tcp-port 210
:database-name "/usr/home/users/arabia/wais-sources/bib-Paris7.URA-748"
:maintainer "arabia@frmap711.mathp7.jussieu.fr"
Contains bibliographic references from the Bibliotheque de l-Equipe de Theorie des Groupes, Universite de Paris 7.

70. bible-src
:ip-address "131.239.2.100"
:ip-name "cmns-moon.think.com"
:tcp-port 210
:database-name "KJV"
:maintainer "bug-public@think.com"
King James version of the Bible.

71. biblio-maths-info-ens-ulm.src
:ip-name "snekkar.ens.fr"
:tcp-port 210
:database-name "biblio-maths-info-ens-ulm"
:maintainer "chounet@ens.fr"
This source contains a partial list of the scientific works produced at the Department of Mathematics and Computer Science (DMI) at the Ecole Normale Superieure, Paris.

72. bibs-zenon-inria-fr.src
:ip-address "138.96.32.21"
:ip-name "zenon.inria.fr"
:tcp-port 210
:database-name "bibs-zenon-inria-fr"
:maintainer "doc@sophia.inria.fr"
Bibliographic data from the Institut National De La Recherche En Informatique Et En Automatique, France.

73. biologists-addresses.src
:ip-address "134.172.2.69"
:ip-name "net.bio.net"
:tcp-port 210
:database-name "biologists-addresses"
:maintainer "biosci@net.bio.net"
This is an address directory of biologists who use the BIOSCI/ bionet newsgroups dedicated to research in biology/biological sciences.

74. biology-journal-contents.src
:ip-address "134.172.2.69"
:ip-name "net.bio.net"
:tcp-port 210
:database-name "biology-journal-contents"
:maintainer "biosci@net.bio.net"
Original postings come for the BIOSCI / bionet newsgroup bionet.journals.contents. This database is updated daily.

75. biosci.src
:ip-address "134.172.2.69"
:ip-name "net.bio.net"
:tcp-port 210
:database-name "biosci"
:maintainer "biosci@net.bio.net"
Contains a WAIS indexed version of newsgroups of the bionet hierarchy (except for bionet.molbio.genbank.updates) using the master set of files kept on net.bio.net.

76. biowais.src
:ip-address "148.79.64.4"
:ip-name "s-ind2.dl.ac.uk"
:tcp-port 210
:database-name "biowais"
:maintainer "kenton@s-ind2.dl.ac.uk"
A WAIS indexed version of newsgroups of the bionet hierarchy (except for bionet.molbio.genbank.updates) using the master set of files kept by Daresbury Laboratory. This database is updated daily.

77. bit-listserv-novell.src
:ip-address "128.174.64.10"
:ip-name "cyberdyne.ece.uiuc.edu"
:tcp-port 210
:database-name "bit-listserv-novell"
:maintainer "rjoyner@ece.uiuc.edu"
This database contains archives of the discussions found in the Network News group: bit.listserv.novell.

78. bit.listserv.cdromlan.src
:ip-address "130.235.162.11"
:ip-name "munin.ub2.lu.se"
:tcp-port 210
:database-name "bit.listserv.cdromlan"
:maintainer "anders@munin.ub2.lu.se"
An index of the files in the newsgroup bit.listserv.cdromlan. This e-conference will provide an exchange of information on all types of CDROM products, whether they contain indexes, abstracts, full text, statistics, graphics, or other data.

79. bit.listserv.cwis-l.src
:database-name "usenet/bit.listserv.cwis-l"
:ip-name "wais.cic.net"
:maintainer "emv@cic.net"

Index of the CWIS-L LISTSERV. Good source of information about campus-wide information systems, including Gopher, PNN, WAIS, WWW, and any number of others.

80. bit.listserv.pacs-l.src
:ip-address ''130.235.162.11''
:ip-name ''munin.ub2.lu.se''
:tcp-port 210
:database-name ''bit.listserv.pacs-l''
:maintainer ''anders@munin.ub2.lu.se''
Index of the PACS-L LISTSERV. The list deals with all computer systems that libraries make available to their patrons.

81. bitearn.nodes.src
:database-name ''bitnet/bitearn.nodes''
:ip-name ''wais.cic.net''
:tcp-port 210
:maintainer ''emv@cic.net''
BITNET nodes database.

82. book__of__mormon.src
:ip-address ''128.109.157.30''
:ip-name ''wais.oit.unc.edu''
:tcp-port 210
:database-name ''Book__of__Mormon''
:maintainer ''fullton@samba.oit.unc.edu''
The Book or Mormon - Gutenberg version 11.

83. bryn-mawr-clasical-review.src
:ip-name ''orion.lib.Virginia.EDU''
:tcp-port 210
:database-name ''/gopher-data/pub/.indexes/bmcr''
:maintainer ''jpw@orion.lib.Virginia.EDU''
The archives of the Bryn Mawr Classical Review, an ejournal.

84. bush-speeches.src
:ip-address ''152.2.22.81''
:ip-name ''SunSite.unc.edu''
:tcp-port 210
:maintainer ''waiskeeper@sunsite.unc.edu''
:database-name ''bush-speeches''
Not so much speeches as sound bites originating from former president Bush.

85. cacm.src
:ip-address ''192.31.181.1''
:ip-name ''quake.think.com''
:tcp-port 210
:database-name ''cacm''
:maintainer ''wais@quake.think.com''
Communications of the ACM April 89 to April 92 (I think). This is put up with permission from ACM for a limited time test.

86. catalyst.src
:ip-name ''borg.lib.vt.edu''
:tcp-port 210
:database-name ''/LocalLibrary/WAIS/catalyst/catalyst''
Archives of ejournal Catalyst.

87. ccinfo.src
:ip-address ''134.160.52.5''
:ip-name ''fragrans.riken.go.jp''
:tcp-port 210

:database-name ''CCINFO''
:maintainer ''sugawara@viola.riken.go.jp''
World Data Center of Microorganisms (WDC) maintains the World Directory of Culture Collection to support the activities of culture collections and their users. CCINFO is a database of all culture collections whose databases are registered and lodged with WDC.

88. cdbase.src
:ip-address ''131.210.1.4''
:ip-name ''cs.uwp.edu''
:tcp-port 210
:database-name ''cdbase''
:maintainer ''datta@cs.uwp.edu''
A WAIS database of Compact Discs.

89. cell__lines.src
:ip-address ''130.251.201.2''
:ip-name ''istge.ist.unige.it''
:tcp-port 210
:database-name ''Cell__Lines''
:source-name ''/wais/cldb/Cell__Lines''
:maintainer ''wais@istge.ist.unige.it''
At istge.ist.unige.it three databases devoted to availability of biological materials are maintained and updated, in the sphere of the Interlab Project. You can have access to them also by connecting to istge.ist.unige.it using telnet.

90. cerro-l.src
:ip-address ''137.208.3.4''
:ip-name ''wais.wu-wien.ac.at''
:tcp-port 210
:database-name ''cerro-l''
:maintainer ''cerro-l-request@wu-wien.ac.at''
Archives of CERRO-L@AEARN.bitnet. CERRO is the Central European Regional Research Organization.

91. cert-advisories.src
:ip-name ''wais.concert.net''
:tcp-port 8000
:database-name ''cert-advisories''
:maintainer ''abc@concert.net''
CERT advisories mirrored from: cert.sei.cmu.edu:/home/ftp/cert/advisories.

92. cert-clippings.src
:ip-name ''wais.concert.net''
:tcp-port 8000
:database-name ''cert-clippings''
:maintainer ''abc@concert.net''
CERT Clippings. Mirrored from cert.sei.cmu.edu:/home/ftp/cert/clippings.

93. cica-win3.src
:database-name ''archives/cica-win3''
:ip-name ''wais.cic.net''
:tcp-port 210
:maintainer ''emv@cic.net''
This is an index to the win3 Microsoft Windows archive at cica.cica.indiana.edu:/pub/pc/win3/. The WAIS server is provided on an experimental basis to see how useful it is and to suggest further improvements in cataloging and indexing.

94. cicg.bibliotheque.src
:ip-address ''130.190.6.23''
:ip-name ''cicg-communication.grenet.fr''
:tcp-port 210
:database-name ''cicg.bibliotheque''
:maintainer ''cherhal@cicg-communication''
This database contains bibliographic references for the library of CICG (Centre Interuniversitaire de Calcul de Grenoble France) It is a small database concerning books about mainly computer science.

95. cicnet-directory-of-servers.src
:database-name ''cicnet-directory-of-servers''
:ip-name ''wais.cic.net''
:tcp-port 210
:maintainer ''emv@cic.net''
Directory of servers at CICnet. Mirrors the directory at quake.think.com, plus adds information about CICnet servers and also the things running at wais.funet.fi.

96. cicnet-resource-guide.src
:database-name ''cicnet-resource-guide''
:ip-name ''wais.cic.net''
:tcp-port 210
:maintainer ''emv@cedar.cic.net''
This is the CICNet Resource Guide, released in June 1992. The Resource Guide is a guide to some of the resources available on the Internet, with paricular emphasis on the resources available from CICNet members, which include most of the Big 10 universities in the US Midwest.

97. cicnet-wais-servers.src
:ip-name ''wais.cic.net''
:tcp-port 210
:database-name ''INFO''
:maintainer ''emv@cic.net''
WAIS servers that run at the CICnet network information center in Ann Arbor, Michigan, including tools for finding people, archives of discussions, and how to find them, internetworking information, etc.

98. cirm-books.src.src
:ip-name ''cirm5.univ-mrs.fr''
:tcp-port 210
:database-name ''/bases/bibli-cirm/cirm-books.src''
:maintainer ''rolland@cirm5.univ-mrs.fr''
Bibliographic data from the Centre International de Rencontres Mathematiques Bibliotheque Library, Marseille, France.

99. cissites.src
:database-name ''cissites''
:tcp-port 210
:ip-name ''wais.cic.net''
:maintainer ''emv@cedar.cic.net''
A list of contacts for most known organizations in the former Soviet Union who either have or plan to have e-mail connections. Provided by the SUEARN-L list, SUEARN-L@UBVM.BITNET.

100. clinton-speechess.src
:ip-address ''152.2.22.81''
:ip-name ''sunsite.unc.edu''
:tcp-port 210
:database-name ''clinton-speechess''
:maintainer ''waiskeeper@sunsite.unc.edu''
Speeches given by the Bill Clinton, Governor of Arkansas, and the Democratic nominee for thepresidency.

101. cm-applications.src
:ip-address ''192.31.181.1''
:ip-name ''quake.think.com''
:tcp-port 210
:database-name ''CM-applications''
:maintainer ''wais@quake.think.com''
Connection Machine applications done at Thinking Machines and elsewhere. The author, status, and restrictions are stated along with descriptions of what the application does. Everything from Fluid flow to Artificial life codes are briefly described.

102. cm-fortran-manual.src
:ip-address ''131.239.2.100''
:ip-name ''cmns-moon.think.com''
:tcp-port 210
:database-name ''FORT''
:maintainer ''bug-public@think.com''
Connection Machine WAIS server. Documentation for Connection Machine Fortran.

103. cm-images.src
:ip-address ''192.31.181.1''
:ip-name ''quake.think.com''
:tcp-port 210
:database-name ''CM-images''
:maintainer ''blaze@think.com''
Sample Connection Machine images.

104. cm-paris-manual.src
:ip-address ''131.239.2.100''
:ip-name ''cmns-moon.think.com''
:tcp-port 210
:database-name ''PAR''
:maintainer ''bug-public@think.com''
PARIS manual for programming the Connection Machine.

105. cm-star-lisp-docs.src
:ip-address ''131.239.2.100''
:ip-name ''cmns-moon.think.com''
:tcp-port 210
:database-name ''LISP''
:maintainer ''bug-public@think.com''
Connection Machine WAIS server. Thinking Machines Corporation *Lisp Reference Manual.

106. cm-tech-summary.src
:ip-address ''131.239.2.100''
:ip-name ''cmns-moon.think.com''
:tcp-port 210
:database-name ''TS''
:maintainer ''bug-public@think.com''
Connection Machine WAIS server. Thinking Machines Corporation Technical Summary of the Connection Machine System.

107. cm-zenon-inria-fr.src
:ip-address ''138.96.32.21''
:ip-name ''zenon.inria.fr''
:tcp-port 210
:database-name ''cm-zenon-inria-fr''
:maintainer ''wais-admin@zenon.inria.fr''

This source contains all the administrative information to use the Connection Machine located at INRIA Sophia Antipolis.

108. cmfs-documentation.src
:ip-address ''131.239.2.100''
:ip-name ''cmns-moon.think.com''
:tcp-port 210
:database-name ''CMFS''
:maintainer ''bug-public@think.com''
Connection Machine File Server Reference Manual.

109. cnidr-directory-of-servers.src
:ip-address ''128.109.130.57''
:ip-name ''cnidr.org''
:tcp-port 210
:database-name ''directory-of-servers''
:maintainer ''wds@kudzu.cnidr.org''
This directory-of-servers is operated by CNIDR - The Clearinghouse for Networked Information Discovery and Retrieval. This source is updated from freeWAIS waisindexers and also collects new entries from the directory of servers at quake.think.com.

110. cold-fusion.src
:ip-address ''152.2.22.81''
:ip-name ''SunSite.unc.edu''
:tcp-port 210
:database-name ''cold-fusion''
:maintainer ''cfh@sunsite.unc.edu''
This is an annotated bibliography of published materials related to 'Cold Fusion' (the 'Pons & Fleischmann effect').

111. college-email.src
:ip-name ''wais.cic.net''
:tcp-port 210
:database-name ''college-email''
:maintainer ''emv@cic.net''
How to find email addresses for undergraduate and grad students, this source is derived from Mark Kantrowitz's ''College Email Addresses'' survey, which can be found by anonymous FTP from a.gp.cs.cmu.edu:/afs/cs.cmu.edu/user/mkant/Public/college-email.text.

112. com-priv.src
:ip-name ''archive.orst.edu''
:tcp-port 9000
:database-name ''com-priv''
:maintainer ''wais@archive.orst.edu''
This is the com-priv mailing list archive. Updated nightly. Compriv discusses issues related to the commercialization and privatization of the Internet.

113. comp-acad-freedom.src
:ip-address ''192.88.144.4''
:ip-name ''wais.eff.org''
:tcp-port 210
:database-name ''comp-acad-freedom''
:maintainer ''wais@eff.org''
Files relating to the Computers & Academic Freedom lists. Includes computer usage policies, bibliographies, archives of old discussion, and much more.

114. comp-admin.src
:ip-address ''128.109.157.30''
:ip-name ''wais.oit.unc.edu''

:tcp-port 210
:database-name ''comp-admin''
:maintainer ''fullton@samba.oit.unc.edu''
Administrators newsgroups news network.

115. comp.archives.src
:ip-name ''archive.orst.edu''
:tcp-port 9000
:database-name ''comp.archives''
:maintainer ''wais@archive.orst.edu''
This source contains all of comp.archives from the beginning of Ed Vielmetti's work through last night at 7pm.

116. comp.binaries.src
:ip-address ''128.109.157.30''
:ip-name ''wais.oit.unc.edu''
:tcp-port 210
:database-name ''comp-binaries''
:maintainer ''fullton@samba.oit.unc.edu''
Net newsgroup comp.binaries executable programs for a variety of operating systems.

117. comp.cad.cadence.src
:ip-address ''137.207.224.3''
:ip-name ''access.cs.uwindsor.ca''
:tcp-port 210
:database-name ''comp.cad.cadence''
:maintainer ''steve@cs.uwindsor.ca''
This archive contains almost all of the articles posted in the comp.cad.cadence USENET news group. Cadence is a high end VLSI design system.

118. comp.db.src
:ip-address ''128.109.157.30''
:ip-name ''wais.oit.unc.edu''
:tcp-port 210
:database-name ''comp-db''
:maintainer ''fullton@samba.oit.unc.edu''
Ten days' worth of the comp.databases newsgroup news network database.

119. comp.dcom.fax.src
:database-name ''usenet/comp.dcom.fax''
:ip-name ''wais.cic.net''
:tcp-port 210
:maintainer ''emv@cic.net''
For discussion of facsimile hardware, software, and protocols.

120. comp.doc.techreports.src
:ip-address ''130.235.162.11''
:ip-name ''munin.ub2.lu.se''
:tcp-port 210
:database-name ''comp__techreports''
:maintainer ''anders@munin.ub2.lu.se''
This a (start) of a collection of techreports titles, abstracts and availability information collected from comp.doc.techreports as well as from various ftp sites around the world.

121. comp.emacs.src
:ip-address ''128.109.157.30''
:ip-name ''wais.oit.unc.edu''
:tcp-port 210
:database-name ''comp-emacs''
:maintainer ''fullton@samba.oit.unc.edu''

The type of files netnews used in the index were: /usr/spool/
news/comp/emacs

122. comp.internet.library.src
:ip-address "130.235.162.11"
:ip-name "munin.ub2.lu.se"
:tcp-port 210
:database-name "comp.internet.library"
:maintainer "anders@munin.ub2.lu.se"
Index of the newsgroup comp.internet.library discussing electronic libraries.

123. comp.lang.perl.src
:tcp-port 9000
:ip-name "archive.orst.edu"
:database-name "comp.lang.perl"
:maintainer "wais@archive.orst.edu"
This is comp.lang.perl, from 1989 to the present. This archive is
updated daily.

124. comp.lang.tcl.src
:ip-address "128.109.157.30"
:ip-name "wais.oit.unc.edu"
:tcp-port 210
:database-name "comp-lang-tcl"
:maintainer "fullton@samba.oit.unc.edu"
The files of type netnews used in the index were: /usr2/news/
comp/lang/tcl.

125. comp.multi.src
:ip-address "128.109.157.30"
:ip-name "wais.oit.unc.edu"
:tcp-port 210
:database-name "comp-multi"
:maintainer "fullton@samba.oit.unc.edu"
News about multimedia applications.

126. comp.robotics.src
:ip-address "128.148.31.66"
:ip-name "wilma.cs.brown.edu"
:tcp-port 8000
:database-name "comp.robotics"
:maintainer "mlm@cs.brown.edu"
This WAIS server contains all articles posted to the
'comp.robotics' newsgroup. It will be updated daily, at about
6am EST.

127. comp.software-eng.src
:ip-address "130.15.1.93"
:ip-name "ftp.qucis.queensu.ca"
:tcp-port 210
:database-name "software-eng"
:maintainer "dalamb@qucis.queensu.ca"
Database consists of files announced periodically in the FAQ for
the group.

128. comp.sources.src
:ip-address "128.109.157.30"
:ip-name "wais.oit.unc.edu"
:tcp-port 210
:database-name "comp-sources"
:maintainer "fullton@samba.oit.unc.edu"
The files of type netnews used in the index were: /usr/spool/
news/comp/sources.

129. comp.sys.mac.programmer.src
:ip-name "cmns-moon.think.com"
:tcp-port 210
:database-name "CSMP"
:maintainer "ephraim@think.com"
The comp.sys.mac.programmer digest. Info on programming the
Macintosh.

130. comp.sys.mips.src
:ip-address "192.31.153.23"
:ip-name "RANGERSMITH.SDSC.EDU"
:tcp-port 210
:database-name "comp.sys.mips"
:maintainer "hjm@salk-sgi.sdsc.edu"
This database is composed of the back postings of the
comp.sys.mips newsgroup, updated about bi-monthly. The other
SGI subgroups are also freely available via their own WAIS
srcs ie comp.sys.sgi, comp.sys.sgi.misc, comp.sys.sgi.graphics.

131. comp.sys.sgi.admin.src
:ip-address "192.31.153.23"
:ip-name "RANGERSMITH.SDSC.EDU"
:tcp-port 210
:database-name "comp.sys.sgi.admin"
:maintainer "hjm@salk-sgi.sdsc.edu"
This database is composed of the back postings of the
comp.sys.sgi.admin newsgroup, updated about bi-monthly. The
other SGI subgroups are also freely available via their own
WAIS srcs ie comp.sys.mips, comp.sys.sgi, comp.sys.sgi.misc,
comp.sys.sgi.graphics.

132. comp.sys.sgi.announce.src
:ip-address "192.31.153.23"
:ip-name "RANGERSMITH.SDSC.EDU"
:tcp-port 210
:database-name "comp.sys.sgi.announce"
:maintainer "hjm@salk-sgi.sdsc.edu"
This database is composed of the back postings of the
comp.sys.sgi.announce newsgroup, updated about bi-monthly.
The other SGI subgroups are also freely available via their own
WAIS srcs ie comp.sys.mips, comp.sys.sgi, comp.sys.sgi.misc,
comp.sys.sgi.graphics.

133. comp.sys.sgi.apps.src
:ip-address "192.31.153.23"
:ip-name "RANGERSMITH.SDSC.EDU"
:tcp-port 210
:database-name "comp.sys.sgi.apps"
:maintainer "hjm@salk-sgi.sdsc.edu"
This database is composed of the back postings of the
comp.sys.sgi.apps newsgroup, updated about bi-monthly. The
other SGI subgroups are also freely available via their own
WAIS srcs ie comp.sys.mips, comp.sys.sgi, comp.sys.sgi.misc,
comp.sys.sgi.graphics.

134. comp.sys.sgi.bugs.src
:ip-address "192.31.153.23"
:ip-name "RANGERSMITH.SDSC.EDU"
:tcp-port 210
:database-name "comp.sys.sgi.bugs"
:maintainer "hjm@salk-sgi.sdsc.edu"
This database is composed of the back postings of the
comp.sys.sgi.bugs newsgroup, updated about bi-monthly. The
other SGI subgroups are also freely available via their own

WAIS srcs ie comp.sys.mips, comp.sys.sgi, comp.sys.sgi.misc, comp.sys.sgi.graphics.

135. comp.sys.sgi.graphics.src
:ip-address "192.31.153.23"
:ip-name "RANGERSMITH.SDSC.EDU"
:tcp-port 210
:database-name "comp.sys.sgi.graphics"
:maintainer "hjm@salk-sgi.sdsc.edu"
This database is composed of the back postings of the comp.sys.sgi.graphics newsgroup, updated about bi-monthly. The other SGI subgroups are also freely available via their own WAIS srcs ie comp.sys.mips, comp.sys.sgi, comp.sys.sgi.misc, comp.sys.sgi.graphics.

136. comp.sys.sgi.hardware.src
:ip-address "192.31.153.23"
:ip-name "RANGERSMITH.SDSC.EDU"
:tcp-port 210
:database-name "comp.sys.sgi.hardware"
:maintainer "hjm@salk-sgi.sdsc.edu"
This database is composed of the back postings of the comp.sys.sgi.hardware newsgroup, updated about bi-monthly. The other SGI subgroups are also freely available via their own WAIS srcs ie comp.sys.mips, comp.sys.sgi, comp.sys.sgi.misc, comp.sys.sgi.graphics.

137. comp.sys.sgi.misc.src
:ip-address "192.31.153.23"
:ip-name "RANGERSMITH.SDSC.EDU"
:tcp-port 210
:database-name "comp.sys.sgi.misc"
:maintainer "hjm@salk-sgi.sdsc.edu"
This database is composed of the back postings of the comp.sys.sgi.misc newsgroup, updated about bi-monthly. The other SGI subgroups are also freely available via their own WAIS srcs ie comp.sys.mips, comp.sys.sgi, comp.sys.sgi.misc, comp.sys.sgi.graphics.

138. comp.sys.sgi.src
:ip-address "192.31.153.23"
:ip-name "RANGERSMITH.SDSC.EDU"
:tcp-port 210
:database-name "comp.sys.sgi"
:maintainer "hjm@salk-sgi.sdsc.edu"
This database is composed of the back postings of the comp.sys.sgi newsgroup, updated about bi-monthly. The other SGI subgroups are also freely available via their own WAIS srcs ie comp.sys.sgi.mis.

139. comp.sys.src
:ip-address "128.109.157.30"
:ip-name "wais.oit.unc.edu"
:tcp-port 210
:database-name "comp-sys"
:maintainer "fullton@samba.oit.unc.edu"
Ten days of news in the comp.sys newsgroups.

140. comp.text.sgml.src
:ip-name "ifi.uio.no"
:tcp-port 210
:database-name "comp.text.sgml"
:maintainer "anders@ifi.uio.no"
Archive of the comp.text.sgml newsgroup.

141. comp.windows.ms.src
:ip-address "128.109.157.30"
:ip-name "wais.oit.unc.edu"
:tcp-port 210
:database-name "comp-windows-ms"
:maintainer "fullton@samba.oit.unc.edu"
Newsgroup comp.windows.ms featuring information on Microsoft Windows.

142. comp.windows.x.motif.src
:ip-address "137.92.1.12"
:ip-name "services.canberra.edu.au"
:tcp-port 210
:database-name "comp.windows.x.motif"
:maintainer "jan@pandonia.canberra.edu.au"
This is an archive of the comp.windows.x.motif newsgroup as collected by Jan Newmarch (he writes the FAQ).

143. conf.announce.src
:ip-address "198.49.45.10"
:ip-name "ds.internic.net"
:tcp-port 210
:database-name "conf.announce"
:maintainer "admin@ds.internic.net"
A database of conferences and seminars that are announced on the Internet.

144. connection-machine.src
:ip-address "131.239.2.100"
:ip-name "cmns-moon.think.com"
:tcp-port 210
:database-name""
:maintainer "bug-public@think.com"
Connection Machine WAIS server. This source will search all databases on the machine. The databases include: The 1990 World Factbook by the CIA, Patents (just a few), Some biology abstracts, King James Version of the Bible, NIH Guide to Grants and Programs, PARIS manual for programming the Connection Machine, Public mailing lists (activists, and perhaps others, send to server-pub@think.com anything you want to add), Wall Street Journal (couple months).

145. cool-bib.src
:ip-address "36.31.0.7"
:ip-name "aldus.stanford.edu"
:tcp-port 210
:database-name "cool-bib"
:maintainer "waiscool@aldus.stanford.edu"
cool-ref.src contains complete bibliographies on topics pertaining the conservation of library, archives, and museum materials. Conservation OnLine (cool) CoOL is a project of the Preservation Department of Stanford University Libraries.

146. cool-cdr.src
:ip-address "36.31.0.7"
:ip-name "aldus.stanford.edu"
:tcp-port 210
:database-name "cool-cdr"
:maintainer "waiscool@aldus.stanford.edu"
cool-cdr.src contains a directory of people professionally involved with the conservation and preservation of library, archives, and museum materials (conservators, preservation administrators, conservation scientists, archivists, curators, bibliographers, librarians, etc). Conservation OnLine (cool)

CoOL is a project of the Preservation Department of Stanford University Libraries.

147. cool-cfl.src
:ip-address   "36.31.0.7"
:ip-name   "aldus.stanford.edu"
:tcp-port   210
:database-name   "cool-cfl"
:maintainer   "waiscool@aldus.stanford.edu"
cool-cfl.src contains files concerning the conservation of library, archives, and museum materials.

148. cool-directory-of-servers.src
:ip-address   "36.31.0.7"
:ip-name   "aldus.stanford.edu"
:tcp-port   210
:database-name   "cool-directory-of-servers"
:maintainer   "waiscool@aldus.stanford.edu"
cool-directory-of-servers.src is a top level directory for Conservation OnLine (CoOL), a collection of WAIS databases containing information of interest to people involved with the conservation of library, archives and museum materials.

149. cool-lex.src
:ip-address   "36.31.0.7"
:ip-name   "aldus.stanford.edu"
:tcp-port   210
:database-name   "cool-lex"
:maintainer   "waiscool@aldus.stanford.edu"
cool-lex.src contains lexical and classification material pertaining to conservation and preservation, including thesauri (or microthesauri), glossaries, classification schemes, authority lists (descriptors, subject headings), etc. These items are segregated from other CoOL databases in order to avoid false hits in the other databases.

150. cool-net.src
:ip-address   "36.31.0.7"
:ip-name   "aldus.stanford.edu"
:tcp-port   210
:database-name   "cool-net"
:maintainer   "waiscool@aldus.stanford.edu"
cool-net.src contains information on networks, networking, mailing lists, computers, etc, related to Conservation Online.

151. cool-ref.src
:ip-address   "36.31.0.7"
:ip-name   "aldus.stanford.edu"
:tcp-port   210
:database-name   "cool-ref"
:maintainer   "waiscool@aldus.stanford.edu"
cool-ref.src contains bibliographic citations concerning the conservation of library, archives, and museum materials.

152. cool-waac.src
:ip-address   "36.31.0.7"
:ip-name   "aldus.stanford.edu"
:tcp-port   210
:database-name   "cool-waac"
:maintainer   "waiscool@aldus.stanford.edu"
cool-waac contains articles from the WAAC Newsletter (ISSN 1052 0066), a publication of the Western Association for Art Conservation, a nonprofit organization founded in 1974. Published since 1979, WAAC Newsletter publishes ideas, informa-

tion, news, and other material pertaining to the conservation of cultural property, especially matters of interest to conservators in the western United States.

153. cool.src
:ip-address   "36.31.0.7"
:ip-name   "aldus.stanford.edu"
:tcp-port   210
:database-name   "cool"
:maintainer   "waiscool@aldus.stanford.edu"
cool.src contains the archives of the Conservation DistList. Searches will return individual messages (ie undigestified DistList postings). The DistList, a moderated digest, is an electronic forum for discussion of technical and administrative issues of concern to people conservation professionals.

154. cpsr.src
:ip-address   "192.147.248.1"
:ip-name   "wais.cpsr.org"
:tcp-port   210
:database-name   "cpsr"
:maintainer   "listserv-owner@cpsr.org"
This database was created from the CPSR Internet Library files available on-line from ftp.cpsr.org via ftp. These files are also accessible via gopher from gopher.cpsr.org (default port number, i.e. 70) and via a list server for people that only have email. Send a mail message to listserv@cpsr.org with the message HELP - note that the subject is ignored.

155. cs-journal-titles.src
:ip-address   "130.194.74.201"
:ip-name   "daneel.rdt.monash.edu.au"
:tcp-port   210
:database-name   "cs-journal-titles"
:maintainer   "rik.harris@fcit.monash.edu.au"
This database contains a list of journal article titles and authors from approximately 600 computing journals, conference proceedings, books, and seminars.

156. cs-techreport-abstracts.src
:ip-address   "130.194.74.201"
:ip-name   "daneel.rdt.monash.edu.au"
:tcp-port   210
:database-name   "cs-techreport-abstracts"
:maintainer   "rik.harris@fcit.monash.edu.au"
This is a database of titles, and authors of more than 10,000 techreports, preprints, reprints, technical notes, and papers from nearly 100 Universities and research institutes from around the world.

157. cs-techreport-archives.src
:ip-address   "130.194.74.201"
:ip-name   "daneel.rdt.monash.edu.au"
:tcp-port   210
:database-name   "cs-techreport-archives"
:maintainer   "rik.harris@fcit.monash.edu.au"
This is a list of over 210 archive sites that maintain computer science (and similar) technical reports, for public consumption.

158. cscwbib.src
:ip-name   "wais.cpsc.ucalgary.ca"
:tcp-port   210
:database-name   "cscwbib"
:maintainer   "hernadi@cpsc.ucalgary.ca"

This is a comprehensive bibliography of Computer Supported Cooperative Work in refer format. It contains many of the relevant papers from proceedings such as CSCW, ECSCW, CHI; from HCI and related journals; from CSCW-related books; and from technical reports.

159. current.cites.src
:database-name ''current.cites''
:ip-address ''192.131.22.3''
:ip-name ''wais.cic.net''
:tcp-port 210
:maintainer ''emv@cic.net''
Current Cites is a monthly publication of the Library Technology Watch Program -- The Library, University of California at Berkeley . Over 30 journals in librarianship and computer technology are scanned for selected articles. Brief annotations accompany most of the citations.

160. cwis__list.src
:ip-address ''130.235.162.11''
:ip-name ''munin.ub2.lu.se''
:tcp-port 210
:database-name ''cwis__list''
:maintainer ''anders@munin.ub2.lu.se''
List of Campus-Wide Information Systems prepared by Judy Hallman
(hallman@unc.bitnet), UNC-Chapel Hill.

161. ddbs-info.src
:ip-address ''198.49.45.10''
:ip-name ''ds.internic.net''
:tcp-port 210
:database-name ''ddbs-info''
:maintainer ''admin@ds.internic.net''
Information about InterNIC services.

162. directory-grenet-fr.src
:ip-address ''130.190.6.23''
:ip-name ''cicg-communication.grenet.fr''
:tcp-port 210
:database-name ''INFO''
:maintainer ''root@cicg-communication.grenet.fr''
This source is a directory for Wais sources located at: CICG, the Centre Interuniversitaire de Calcul de Grenoble France.

163. directory-irit-fr.src
:ip-address ''141.115.8.1''
:ip-name ''irit.irit.fr''
:tcp-port 210
:database-name ''directory-irit-fr''
:maintainer ''wais-admin@irit.fr''
This source is a directory for Wais sources located at: IRIT, the Institut de Recherche en Informatique Toulouse, France.

164. directory-of-servers.src
:ip-address ''192.31.181.1''
:ip-name ''quake.think.com''
:tcp-port 210
:database-name ''directory-of-servers''
:maintainer ''wais-directory-of-servers@quake.think.com''
This is a White Pages listing of WAIS servers. For more information on WAIS, use the WAIS system on the wais-docs server, or add yourself to the wais-discussion@think.com mailing list, or get the newest software from think.com:/public/wais.

165. directory-zenon-inria-fr.src
:ip-address ''138.96.32.21''
:ip-name ''zenon.inria.fr''
:tcp-port 210
:database-name ''/1/wais/index/directory-zenon-inria-fr''
:maintainer ''wais-admin@zenon.inria.fr''
This source is a directory for Wais sources located at: INRIA, the Institut de Recherche en Informatique et Automatique, France.

166. disco-mm-zenon-inria-fr.src
:ip-address ''138.96.32.21''
:ip-name ''zenon.inria.fr''
:tcp-port 210
:database-name ''disco-mm-zenon-inria-fr''
:maintainer ''djossou@sophia.inria.fr''
Multimedia database of various Compact Disk. The files of this database are in MIME format.

167. disi-catalog.src
:ip-name ''wais.cic.net''
:tcp-port 210
:database-name ''disi-catalog''
:maintainer ''emv@cic.net''
Information about availability and capability of X.500 implementations.

168. dit-library.src
:ip-address ''130.235.162.11''
:ip-name ''munin.ub2.lu.se''
:tcp-port 210
:database-name ''dit-library''
:maintainer ''anders@munin.ub2.lu.se''
Library catalog for Department of Computer Engineering, University of Lund, Lund, Sweden.

169. document__center__catalog.src
:ip-name ''doccenter.com''
:tcp-port 1220
:database-name ''document__center__catalog''
:maintainer ''wais@doccenter.com''
Document Center is a hard copy document delivery service specializing in government and industry specifications and standards.

170. document__center__inventory.src
:ip-name ''doccenter.com''
:tcp-port 1220
:database-name ''document__center__inventory''
:maintainer ''wais@doccenter.com''
Document Center is a hard copy document delivery service specializing in government and industry specifications and standards. Inventory.

171. doe__climate__data.src
:ip-name ''ridgisd.er.usgs.gov''
:tcp-port 210
:database-name ''/usr/opt/wais/db/DOE__Climate__Data''
:maintainer ''tgauslin@ridgisd''
The files of type doe used in the index were: /usr/opt/wais/db/doe/doe.txt.

172. domain-contacts.src
:database-name ''netinfo/domain-contacts''

:ip-name "wais.cic.net"
:tcp-port 210
:maintainer "emv@cic.net"
Internet domains and the listed phone numbers to contact the responsible parties.

173. domain-organizations.src
:database-name "domain-organizations"
:ip-name "wais.cic.net"
:tcp-port 210
:maintainer "emv@cic.net"
This is an index based on Mike Schwartz's __netfind__ seed database as of 15 July, 1992. It matches domain names and acronyms they are based on with the full names of the organizations they belong to. It's useful for answering questions like __ What's the domain name of Foobar Software__ when the answer might be __fbs.com__.

174. dynamic-archie.src
:ip-name "ftp.cs.colorado.edu"
:tcp-port 8000
:database-name "DYNAMIC archie"
:maintainer "hardy@cs.colorado.edu"
This WAIS server performs Archie searches. It uses the wais-server
from the Dynamic WAIS prototype at the University of Colorado in Boulder. To use this WAIS server: supply a keyword for an Archie search.

175. dynamic-netfind.src
:ip-name "ftp.cs.colorado.edu"
:tcp-port 8000
:database-name "DYNAMIC netfind"
:maintainer "hardy@cs.colorado.edu"
This WAIS server performs Netfind searches. It uses the wais-server from the Dynamic WAIS prototype at the University of Colorado in Boulder.

176. earlym-l.src
:ip-address "137.208.3.4"
:ip-name "wais.wu-wien.ac.at"
:tcp-port 210
:database-name "earlym-l"
:maintainer "Gerhard.Gonter@wu-wien.ac.at"
EARLYM-L and the newsgroup rec.music.early are linked.

177. edis.src
:ip-address "140.174.7.1"
:ip-name "kumr.lns.com"
:tcp-port 210
:database-name "edis"
:maintainer "pozar@kumr.lns.com"
State of California's "Emergency Digital Information System" (EDIS). EDIS is a developing protocol and transport service for the broadcast of emergency public information from authorized official agencies to the news media.

178. educom.src
:ip-address "192.52.179.128"
:ip-name "ivory.educom.edu"
:tcp-port 210
:database-name "/usr/local/bin/wais/wais-sources/educom"
:maintainer "root@ivory"
EDUCOM documents, including Review archives, project updates, summaries, and calendar.

179. eff-documents.src
:ip-address "192.88.144.4"
:ip-name "wais.eff.org"
:tcp-port 210
:database-name "eff-documents"
:maintainer "wais@eff.org"
Should generally mirror the EFF ftp archives on ftp.eff.org. Contact wais@eff.org if you have problems. Should be available 24 hours/7 days.

180. eff-talk.src
:ip-address "192.88.144.4"
:ip-name "wais.eff.org"
:tcp-port 210
:database-name "eff-talk"
:maintainer "wais@eff.org"
WAIS-accessible archive of the comp.org.eff.talk newsgroup.

181. elec__journ__newslett.src
:ip-address "130.235.162.11"
:ip-name "munin.ub2.lu.se"
:tcp-port 210
:database-name "elec__journ__newslett"
:maintainer "anders@munin.ub2.lu.se"
Information about electronic journals and newsletters. The main source is: Directory of Electronic Journals and Newsletters by Michael Strangelove.

182. environment-newsgroups.src
:ip-address "130.235.162.11"
:ip-name "munin.ub2.lu.se"
:tcp-port 210
:database-name "environment-newsgroups"
:maintainer "anders@munin.ub2.lu.se"
A number of enivironmental related newsgroups are collected and indexed.

183. eos-ncsu.src
:ip-name "ftp.eos.ncsu.edu"
:tcp-port 8001
:database-name "eos-online-help"
:maintainer "escott@eos.ncsu.edu"
This is an experimental source containing online help for N.C. State University's Project Eos. It descibes Unix, AFS, the TED editor, the MMH Motif Mail Handler, Maple, Matlab, Interleaf, mxrn, dxbook, awman (a Windowing MAN, for Motif), The Xess Motif Spreadsheet, Xfig, Idraw, Gnuplot, and even xclock.

184. eric-archive.src
:ip-name "nic.sura.net"
:tcp-port 210
:database-name "/export/software/nic/wais/databases/ERICarchive"
:maintainer "info@sura.net"
ERIC (Educational Resources Information Center) Digests Information provided by EDUCOM.

185. eric-digests.src
:ip-address "152.2.22.81"
:ip-name "sunSITE.unc.edu"
:tcp-port 210

:database-name ''eric-digests''
:maintainer ''paul＿jones@unc.edu''
This file contains over 1000 ERIC Digests (through 1992).

186. eros-data-center.src
:ip-address ''152.61.192.109''
:ip-name ''sun1.cr.usgs.gov''
:tcp-port 210
:database-name ''eros-data-center''
:maintainer ''tsmith@glis.cr.usgs.gov''
The Earth Resources Observation Systems (EROS) Data Center, located in Sioux Falls, SD is a data management, systems development, and research field center of the U.S. Geological Survey's National Mapping Division.

189. eshic.src
:ip-address ''198.3.227.20''
:ip-name ''romana.crystal.pnl.gov''
:tcp-port 210
:database-name ''eshic''
:maintainer ''eshic@romana.dc.pnl.gov''
ESHIC is an acryonym for Environmental Safety and Health Information Center. The ESHIC is a central repository for the Department of Energy (DOE) Tiger Team Assessment documents, Corrective Action Plans, Progress Assessments; DOE site specific information such as maps, site fact sheets, and site profiles; and other relevant DOE documents concerning compliance, regulations, policy, training, and long-term planning.

188. eurogopher.src
:ip-address ''130.238.98.11''
:ip-name ''pinus.slu.se''
:tcp-port 210
:database-name ''eurogopher''
:maintainer ''larsg@pinus.slu.se''
Indexed archive of the eurogopher mailing list.

189. factsheet-five.src
:database-name ''factsheet-five''
:tcp-port 210
:ip-name ''wais.cic.net''
:maintainer ''emv@msen.com''
FactSheet Five is the central clearinghouse of information about zines, those opinionated publications with press runs of 50 to 5000 (often done through surrepticious use of on-the-job supplies and xerox).

190. falcon3.src
:database-name ''falcon3''
:ip-name ''urbino.mcc.com''
:tcp-port 8000
:maintainer ''knutson@urbino.mcc.com''
This is a collection of most of the mail and news traffic on Falcon 3 since Feb. 1992.

191. fidonet-nodelist.src
:ip-address ''140.174.7.1''
:ip-name ''kumr.lns.com''
:tcp-port 210
:database-name ''nodelist''
:maintainer ''pozar@kumr.lns.com''
The FidoNet(r) NodeList, a listing of the systems within FidoNet.

192. file-archive-uunet.src
:database-name ''uunet''
:ip-name ''wais.cic.net''
:tcp-port 210
:maintainer ''emv@cic.net''
The directory listing of uunet.uu.net, updated nightly.

193. finding-sources.src
:database-name ''faq/finding-sources''
:tcp-port 210
:ip-name ''wais.cic.net''
:maintainer ''emv@cic.net''
Jonathan Kamens' document on how to find sources on the net. Includes information about prospero, archie, comp.archives, the charlie server, and mail-based archive servers.

194. fj.sources.src
:database-name ''usenet/fj.sources''
:ip-name ''wais.cic.net''
:tcp-port 210
:maintainer ''emv@cic.net''
Index to the japanese source group fj.sources.

195. flight＿sim.src
:ip-address ''128.62.25.104''
:ip-name ''urbino.mcc.com''
:tcp-port 8000
:database-name ''flight＿sim''
:maintainer ''knutson@urbino.mcc.com''
This is a collection of postings on various flight simulators. Most are 80x86 based and combat related, but not all.

196. ftp-list.src
:database-name ''ftp-list''
:tcp-port 210
:ip-name ''wais.cic.net''
:maintainer ''emv@cic.net''
This source has Jon Granrose's anonymous FTP list, which is maintained on pilot.njin.net:/pub/ftp-list/.

197. func-prog-abstracts.src
:ip-address ''137.219.17.4''
:ip-name ''coral.cs.jcu.edu.au''
:tcp-port 8000
:database-name ''Func-Prog-Abstracts''
:maintainer ''farrell@coral.cs.jcu.edu.au''
This is a small collection of computer science technical reports, abstracts and papers gathered from ftp sites etc. all over the world.

198. fusion-digest.src
:ip-address ''152.2.22.81''
:ip-name ''sunsite.unc.edu''
:tcp-port 210
:database-name ''fusion-digest''
:maintainer ''cfh@sunsite.unc.edu''
This is an indexed version of the sci.physics.fusion mail digests. The first installation (May 2, 1993) contained the digests from 1/1/93 thru 5/4/93. Updates (past and future) are expected.

199. fyis.src
:ip-address ''198.49.45.10''
:ip-name ''ds.internic.net''
:tcp-port 210

:database-name ''fyis''
:maintainer ''admin@ds.internic.net''
RFCs that are informational in nature.

200. gdb-citation.src
:ip-name ''wais.gdb.org''
:tcp-port 210
:database-name ''gdb-citation''
:maintainer ''help@gdb.org''
Help file for using WAIS to search the Genome Data Base
(GDB). gdb-citation.src (contains GDB Citation Manager information).

201. gdb-contact.src
:ip-name ''wais.gdb.org''
:tcp-port 210
:database-name ''gdb-contact''
:maintainer ''help@gdb.org''
Help file for using WAIS to search the Genome Data Base
(GDB). gdb-contact.src (contains GDB Contact Manager information).

202. gdb-locus.src
:ip-name ''wais.gdb.org''
:tcp-port 210
:database-name ''gdb-locus''
:maintainer ''help@gdb.org''
Help file for using WAIS to search the Genome Data Base
(GDB). gdb-locus.src (contains GDB Locus Manager information).

203. gdb-map.src
:ip-name ''wais.gdb.org''
:tcp-port 210
:database-name ''gdb-map''
:maintainer ''help@gdb.org''
Help file for using WAIS to search the Genome Data Base
(GDB).

204. gdb-map.src
:ip-name ''wais.gdb.org''
:tcp-port 210
:database-name ''gdb-map''
:maintainer ''help@gdb.org''
Help file for using WAIS to search the Genome Data Base
(GDB). gdb-map.src (contains GDB Map Manager information).

205. gdb-mutation.src
:ip-name ''wais.gdb.org''
:tcp-port 210
:database-name ''gdb-mutation''
:maintainer ''help@gdb.org''
Help file for using WAIS to search the Genome Data Base
(GDB). gdb-mutation.src (contains GDB Mutation Manager information).

206. gdb-polym.src
:ip-name ''wais.gdb.org''
:tcp-port 210
:database-name ''gdb-polym''
:maintainer ''help@gdb.org''
Help file for using WAIS to search the Genome Data Base
(GDB). gdb-polym.src (contains GDB Polymorphism Manager
information).

207. gdb-probe.src
:ip-name ''wais.gdb.org''
:tcp-port 210
:database-name ''gdb-probe''
:maintainer ''help@gdb.org''
Help file for using WAIS to search the Genome Data Base
(GDB). gdb-probe.src (contains GDB Probe Manager information).

208. gdb.src
:ip-name ''wais.gdb.org''
:tcp-port 210
:database-name ''gdb''
:maintainer ''help@gdb.org''
Help file for using WAIS to search the Genome Data Base
(GDB). The GDB server gdb.src comprises all of the data
within GDB.

209. genethon__seq.src
:ip-address ''192.70.45.2''
:ip-name ''wais-server.genethon.fr''
:tcp-port 210
:database-name ''genethon__seq''
:maintainer ''Patricia.Rodriguez-Tome@genethon.fr''
This source give access to genethon sequences in embl format.

210. genpept.src
:ip-address ''137.132.9.12''
:ip-name ''nusunix2.nus.sg''
:tcp-port 2100
:database-name ''genpept''
:maintainer ''bchtantw@nuscc.nus.sg''
This is the waisindexed version of the GenPept database, a database of protein sequences translated from genes deposited with
GenBank.

211. genpept.src
:ip-address ''137.132.9.12''
:ip-name ''nusunix2.nus.sg''
:tcp-port 2100
:database-name ''genpept''
:maintainer ''bchtantw@nuscc.nus.sg''
This is the waisindexed version of the GenPept database, a database of protein sequences translated from genes deposited with
GenBank.

212. great-lakes-factsheets.src
:database-name ''great-lakes-factsheets''
:ip-name ''wais.cic.net''
:tcp-port 210
:maintainer ''emv@cic.net''
The Information Service is maintained by The Center for the
Great Lakes, a private non-profit policy research organization
based in Toronto and Chicago. Here you will find Fact Sheets
on a variety of issues and subjects relevant to the Great Lakes/
St. Lawrence River region and ecosystem. The Fact Sheets are
in this directory, and in a subdirectory AOCFACTS.

213. gsa-cfda.src
:ip-address ''128.167.254.179''
:ip-name ''nic.sura.net''
:tcp-port 210
:database-name ''gsa-cfda''
:maintainer ''info@sura.net''

The Catalog of Federal Domestic Assistance is a directory of Federal programs, projects, service and activities which provide assistance or benefits to the American Public. It contains financial and nonfinancial assistance programs administered by departments and establishments of the Federal government.

214. hdb.src
:ip-address   "134.160.52.5"
:ip-name   "fragrans.riken.go.jp"
:tcp-port   210
:database-name   "HDB"
:maintainer   "sugawara@viola.riken.go.jp"
HYBRIDOMA DATABANK (HDB) contains a catalogue of hybridoma cell lines/monoclonal antibodies available throughout the world.

215. higher-education-software.src
:ip-address   "134.7.70.222"
:ip-name   "info.curtin.edu.au"
:tcp-port   210
:database-name   "higher-education-software"
:maintainer   "scor@info.curtin.edu.au"
Software and Courseware On-line Reviews (SCOR) database includes information not just about software suitable for use at the school level, both primary or elementary and secondary, but also about software at the tertiary or higher education level.

216. homebrew.src
:ip-address   "192.31.181.1"
:ip-name   "quake.think.com"
:tcp-port   210
:database-name   "homebrew"
:maintainer   "medlar@adoc.xerox.com"
Indexed archives of the homebrew mailing list and the rec.crafts.homebrew newsgroup. Included files date from 1989, and are reindexed weekly.

217. hst-aec-catalog.src
:ip-address   "130.167.1.2"
:ip-name   "stsci.edu"
:tcp-port   210
:database-name   "hst-aec-catalog"
:maintainer   "reppert@stsci.edu"
The Archived Exposures Catalog (AEC).

218. hst-status.src
:ip-name   "stsci.edu"
:tcp-port   210
:database-name   "/var/spool/uucppublic/.waisindex/hst-status"
:maintainer   "reppert@stsci.edu"
Daily Activity / Instrument Status Reports for Hubble Space Telescope (HST).

219. hst-weekly-summary.src
:ip-name   "stsci.edu"
:tcp-port   210
:database-name "/var/spool/uucppublic/.waisindex/hst-weekly-summary"
:maintainer   "reppert@stsci.edu"
Weekly Summary of Hubble Space Telescope (HST) completed observations.

220. hst-weekly-timeline.src
:ip-name   "stsci.edu"

:tcp-port   210
:database-name "/var/spool/uucppublic/.waisindex/hst-weekly-timeline"
:maintainer   "reppert@stsci.edu"
Weekly Timeline files for current year's Hubble Space Telescope (HST) observations.

221. hyperbole-ml.src
:ip-address   "128.148.31.66"
:ip-name   "wilma.cs.brown.edu"
:tcp-port   8000
:database-name   "hyperbole"
:maintainer   "mlm@cs.brown.edu"
This WAIS server contains all messages sent to the Hyperbole mailing list. Hyperbole is a flexible, information manager built on top of GNU Emacs.

222. hytelnet.src
:ip-address   "129.120.1.42"
:ip-name   "sol.acs.unt.edu"
:tcp-port   210
:database-name   "/usr/local/data/wais/hytelnet"
:maintainer   "billy@unt.edu"
This database contains all the information that is stored in the HYTELNET package by Peter Scott, University of Saskatchewan. This includes library OPACs, BBSes, CWISs, and any other TELNET accessible sites.

223. iat-documents.src
:ip-address   "152.2.22.81"
:ip-name   "sunsite.unc.edu"
:tcp-port   210
:database-name   "/home3/wais/IAT-Documents"
:maintainer   "kotlas@sunsite.unc.edu"
Contains articles from the UNC-CH Institute for Academic Technology newsletter Briefings, copies of papers from the IAT Technology Primers and Technical Papers series, and source lists and bibliographies from the Information Resource Guides series.

224. ibm.pc.faq.src
:ip-address   "128.109.190.3"
:ip-name   "next2.oit.unc.edu"
:tcp-port   210
:database-name   "ibm.pc.FAQ"
:maintainer   "root@next2.oit.unc.edu"
The files of type dash used in the index were: /users/cwis/databases/ibm.pc.alt.FAQ.

225. iesg.src
:ip-address   "198.49.45.10"
:ip-name   "ds.internic.net"
:tcp-port   210
:database-name   "iesg"
:maintainer   "admin@ds.internic.net"
IESG information, working group charters, and meeting minutes.

226. ietf-docs.src
:database-name   "ietf-docs"
:ip-address   "192.87.45.1"
:ip-name   "ns.ripe.net"
:tcp-port   210
:maintainer   "marten@ns.ripe.net"

This WAIS database contains all IETF documents that can be found on ftp.ripe.net, subdirectory ietf.

227. ietf.src
:ip-address   "198.49.45.10"
:ip-name   "ds.internic.net"
:tcp-port   210
:database-name   "ietf"
:maintainer   "admin@ds.internic.net"
IETF information, meeting announcements, working group charters and minutes.

228. ijaema__a.src
:ip-name   "borg.lib.vt.edu"
:tcp-port   210
:database-name   "/LocalLibrary/WAIS/ijaema__a/ijaema__a"
Abstracts: The International journal of analytical and experimental modal analysis.

229. imaj.fr.doc.magazines.src
:ip-address   "130.190.6.23"
:ip-name   "cicg-communication.grenet.fr"
:tcp-port   210
:database-name   "imag.fr.doc.magazines"
:maintainer   "rouverol@cicg-communication"
Archivage du newsgroup francais fr.doc.magazines centre interuniversitaire de calcul de Grenoble, France.

230. imag.ouvrages.src
:ip-address   "130.190.6.23"
:ip-name   "cicg-communication.grenet.fr"
:tcp-port   210
:database-name   "imag.ouvrages"
:maintainer   "rouverol@cicg-communication"
Mediatheque de l'Institut IMAG (Institut d'Informatique et de Mathematiques Appliquees de Grenoble, France).

231. imag.rapports.src
:ip-address   "130.190.6.23"
:ip-name   "cicg-communication.grenet.fr"
:tcp-port   210
:database-name   "imag.rapports"
:maintainer   "rouverol@cicg-communication"
Mediatheque de l'Institut IMAG (Institut d'Informatique et de Mathematiques Appliquees de Grenoble, France).

232. india-infos.src
:ip-name   "enuxhb.eas.asu.edu"
:tcp-port   8000
:database-name   "INFO"
:maintainer   "sridhar@enuxha.eas.asu.edu"
India information and misc. info files mainly lifted off USENET.

233. indian-classical-music.src
:ip-name   "enuxva.eas.asu.edu"
:tcp-port   8000
:database-name   "music"
:maintainer   "sridhar@enuxha.eas.asu.edu"
Database of CDs of Indian Classical Music.

234. inet-libraries.src
:ip-address   "130.235.162.11"
:ip-name   "munin.ub2.lu.se"

:tcp-port   210
:database-name   "inet-libraries"
:maintainer   "anders@munin.ub2.lu.se"
Information on internet accesible libraries collected from various places: UNT's Accessing On-Line Bibliographic Databases by Billy Barron; JANET-OPACS: OPACS in the UK: a list of interactive library catalogues on JANET; and INTERNET LIBRARIES compiled by Dana Noonan.

235. info-afs.src
:ip-address   "134.207.7.4"
:ip-name   "cmsun.cmf.nrl.navy.mil"
:tcp-port   210
:database-name   "info-afs"
:maintainer   "wais-maint@cmf.nrl.navy.mil"
Index of archives of info-afs@transarc.com.

236. info-mac.src
:ip-address   "131.239.2.100"
:ip-name   "cmns-moon.think.com"
:tcp-port   210
:database-name   "MAC"
:maintainer   "bug-public@think.com"
Serves the info-mac usenet list, this is automatically updated, but is not an authorized server of this information.

237. info-nets.src
:ip-address   "131.239.2.100"
:ip-name   "cmns-moon.think.com"
:tcp-port   210
:database-name   "NETS"
:maintainer   "bug-public@think.com"
The info-nets mailing list.

238. info.src
:ip-address   "192.31.181.1"
:ip-name   "quake.think.com"
:tcp-port   210
:database-name   "INFO"
:maintainer   "wais-directory-of-servers@quake.think.com"
This is a White Pages listing of WAIS servers. For more information on WAIS, use the WAIS system on the wais-docs server, or add yourself to the wais-discussion@think.com mailing list, or get the newest software from think.com:/public/wais.

239. internet-intros.src
:ip-address   "35.1.1.48"
:ip-name   "nic.merit.edu"
:tcp-port   210
:database-name   "internet-intros"
:maintainer   "swartz@nic.merit.edu"
This consists of introductory material on the Internet, including bibliographies that point to further sources of information.

240. internet-mail.src
:ip-address   "152.2.22.81"
:ip-name   "sunsite.unc.edu"
:tcp-port   210
:database-name   "internet-mail"
:maintainer   "jem@sunsite.unc.edu"
This file documents methods of sending mail from one network to another. It represents the aggregate knowledge of the readers of comp.mail.misc and many contributors elsewhere.

241. internet-rfcs-europe.src
:ip-name "wais.cnam.fr"
:tcp-port 210
:database-name "RFC"
:maintainer "bortzmeyer@cnam.cnam.fr"
Request For Comments (RFC) of the Internet community. Updated automatically from nic.ddn.mil.

242. internet-standards-merit.src
:ip-address "35.1.1.48"
:ip-name "nic.merit.edu"
:tcp-port 210
:database-name "internet-standards"
:maintainer "swartz@nic.merit.edu"
This is the subset of Internet RFCs that define standards.

243. internet-standards.src
:ip-address "198.49.45.10"
:ip-name "ds.internic.net"
:tcp-port 210
:database-name "stds"
:maintainer "admin@ds.internic.net"
The subset of all the RFCs that have been declared standards by the IETF.

244. internet-user-glossary.src
:ip-address "130.238.98.11"
:ip-name "pinus.slu.se"
:tcp-port 210
:database-name "Internet-user-glossary"
:maintainer "larsg@pinus.slu.se"
Internet Users' Glossary. This glossary concentrates on terms which are specific to the Internet.

245. internet—info.src
:ip-address "130.235.162.11"
:ip-name "munin.ub2.lu.se"
:tcp-port 210
:database-name "internet—info"
:maintainer "anders@munin.ub2.lu.se"
Various introduction texts, guides, help-texts and general information on internet use and etiquette.

246. internet—services.src
:ip-address "130.235.162.11"
:ip-name "munin.ub2.lu.se"
:tcp-port 210
:database-name "internet—services"
:maintainer "anders@munin.ub2.lu.se"
Various documents describing services available on the internet.

247. internic-directory.src
:ip-address "198.49.45.10"
:ip-name "ds.internic.net"
:tcp-port 210
:database-name "resources"
:maintainer "admin@ds.internic.net"
InterNIC Directory of Directories.

248. internic-infosource.src
:ip-address "192.153.156.15"
:ip-name "is.internic.net"
:tcp-port 210
:database-name "internic-infosource"

:maintainer "scout@internic.net"
The Info Source is a collection designed to make finding information about the Internet easier. There are sections for people just getting started on the Internet, for individuals managing midlevel and campus NIC organizations, and for occasional and frequent Internet users.

249. internic-internet-drafts.src
:ip-address "198.49.45.10"
:ip-name "ds.internic.net"
:tcp-port 210
:database-name "internet-drafts"
:maintainer "admin@ds.internic.net"
IETF Internet Draft Documents - ascii text format.

250. internic-whois.src
:ip-address "198.41.0.5"
:ip-name "rs.internic.net"
:tcp-port 210
:database-name "whois"
:maintainer "markk@internic.net"
A wais implementation of the whois database on rs.internic.net. Whois is comprised of root level domains, networks, DNS servers, autonomous system numbers, organizations, and POCs of the domains, networks, servers, and autonomous system numbers.

251. invertpaleodatabase.src
:ip-address "128.32.146.30"
:ip-name "ucmp1.berkeley.edu"
:tcp-port 210
:database-name "/home/ucmp1/gopher-data/mustypes/invert/
.waisindex/paleoiv"
:maintainer "davidp@ucmp1.berkeley.edu"
This free database provides information about all the invertebrate type specimens available in the Museum of Paleontology at the University of California at Berkeley.

252. irtf-rd.src
:database-name "irtf-rd"
:ip-name "wais.cic.net"
:tcp-port 210
:maintainer "emv@cic.net"
This is an archive of the IRTF Resource Discovery mailing list.

253. isoc.src
:ip-address "198.49.45.10"
:ip-name "ds.internic.net"
:tcp-port 210
:database-name "isoc"
:maintainer "admin@ds.internic.net"
Internet Society documents.

254. iubio-arcdocs.src
:ip-address "129.79.224.25"
:ip-name "ftp.bio.indiana.edu"
:tcp-port 210
:database-name "arcdocs"
:maintainer "archive@bio.indiana.edu"
This is an index of abstracts, readme, help and related information on the IUBio Archive of Biology Software and Data. It is updated approximately monthly. Files described in these documents are generally available via ftp or gopher to ftp.bio.indiana.edu.

255. iubio-fly-address.src
:ip-address ''129.79.224.25''
:ip-name ''ftp.bio.indiana.edu''
:tcp-port 210
:database-name ''fly-address''
:maintainer ''archive@bio.indiana.edu''
This is an index of the addresses for Drosophila researchers.

256. iubio-fly-amero.src
:ip-address ''129.79.224.25''
:ip-name ''ftp.bio.indiana.edu''
:tcp-port 210
:database-name ''fly-amero''
:maintainer ''archive@bio.indiana.edu''
Cytological features database. This is a database of polytene chromosome sites that have been found to bind antibodies to particular Drosophila proteins. The database is maintained by Sally Amero and has been formatted by Michael Ashburner.

257. iubio-fly-clones.src
:ip-address ''129.79.224.25''
:ip-name ''ftp.bio.indiana.edu''
:tcp-port 210
:database-name ''fly-clones''
:maintainer ''archive@bio.indiana.edu''
The DROSOPHILA GENMAPS DATABASE is an index to sources of information in Drosophila melanogaster genetics. The subject coverage is limited to genetics research done with molecular biology techniques where genetic information has been localized on the cytogenetic map.

258. iubio-fly-din.src
:ip-address ''129.79.224.25''
:ip-name ''ftp.bio.indiana.edu''
:tcp-port 210
:database-name ''fly-din''
:maintainer ''archive@bio.indiana.edu''
This is an index of the electronic Drosophila Information Newsletter.

259. iubio-flybase.src
:ip-address ''129.79.224.25''
:ip-name ''ftp.bio.indiana.edu''
:tcp-port 210
:database-name ''flybase''
:maintainer ''archive@bio.indiana.edu''
This is an index of the Drosophila database, FlyBase, as maintained by Micheal Ashburner.

260. iubio-flystock-bg.src
:ip-address ''129.79.224.25''
:ip-name ''ftp.bio.indiana.edu''
:tcp-port 210
:database-name ''flystock-bg''
:maintainer ''archive@bio.indiana.edu''
This is an index of the Drosophila fruitfly stocks maintained by the stock center at Bowling Green USA.

261. iubio-flystock-bl.src
:ip-address ''129.79.224.25''
:ip-name ''ftp.bio.indiana.edu''
:tcp-port 210
:database-name ''flystock-bl''
:maintainer ''archive@bio.indiana.edu''

This is an index of the Drosophila fruitfly stocks maintained by the stock center at Bloomington.

262. iubio-flystock-um.src
:ip-address ''129.79.224.25''
:ip-name ''ftp.bio.indiana.edu''
:tcp-port 210
:database-name ''flystock-um''
:maintainer ''archive@bio.indiana.edu''
This is an index of the Drosophila fruitfly stocks maintained by the stock center at Umea Sweden.

263. iubio-gbnew.src
:ip-address ''129.79.224.25''
:ip-name ''ftp.bio.indiana.edu''
:tcp-port 210
:database-name ''gbnew''
:maintainer ''archive@bio.indiana.edu''
This is an index of updates sinces the latest full release of Genbank, the databank of all known gene sequences. It is updated weekly from the update files maintained by NCBI at ncbi.nlm.nih.gov.

264. iubio-genbank.src
:ip-address ''129.79.224.25''
:ip-name ''ftp.bio.indiana.edu''
:tcp-port 210
:database-name ''genbank''
:maintainer ''archive@bio.indiana.edu''
This is an index of the Genbank databank of gene sequences.

265. iubio-info.src
:ip-address ''129.79.224.25''
:ip-name ''ftp.bio.indiana.edu''
:tcp-port 210
:database-name ''INFO''
:maintainer ''archive@bio.indiana.edu''
This WAIS service includes several indexed Biology information sources, including Genbank nucleic acid gene sequence databank, Drosophila genetics BioSci/Bionet network news, and others.

266. iubio-netnews.src
:ip-address ''129.79.224.25''
:ip-name ''ftp.bio.indiana.edu''
:tcp-port 210
:database-name ''netnews''
:maintainer ''archive@bio.indiana.edu''
This is an index of news articles from the BioSci/Bionet newsgroups, as well as the Sci.Bio Usenet group and the bitnet.listserv.info-gcg group.

267. jargon.src
:ip-name ''hal.gnu.ai.mit.edu''
:tcp-port 8000
:database-name ''/src/wais/wais-sources/jargon''
:maintainer ''mycroft@hal.gnu.ai.mit.edu''
This is the latest version of the Jargon File, currently version 2.9.6, roughly what was printed in The New Hacker's Dictionary.

268. jfcc-bacteria.src
:ip-address ''134.160.52.5''
:ip-name ''fragrans.riken.go.jp''

:tcp-port   210
:database-name   "/data/waisguy/src/JFCC-Bacteria"
:maintainer   "sugawara@viola.riken.go.jp"
The Japan Federation for Culture Collections (JFCC) Catalogue of Cultures for bacteria.

269. jfcc-bacteriophages.src
:ip-address   "134.160.52.5"
:ip-name   "fragrans.riken.go.jp"
:tcp-port   210
:database-name   "/data/waisguy/src/JFCC-Bacteriophages"
:maintainer   "sugawara@viola.riken.go.jp"
The Japan Federation for Culture Collections (JFCC) Catalogue of Cultures for bacteriophages.

270. jfcc-fungi-src
:ip-address   "134.160.52.5"
:ip-name   "fragrans.riken.go.jp"
:tcp-port   210
:database-name   "/data/waisguy/src/JFCC-Fungi"
:maintainer   "sugawara@viola.riken.go.jp"
The Japan Federation for Culture Collections (JFCC) Catalogue of Cultures for fungi.

271. jfcc-invertebrate__virus.src
:ip-address   "134.160.52.5"
:ip-name   "fragrans.riken.go.jp"
:tcp-port   210
:database-name   "/data/waisguy/src/JFCC-Invertebrate__virus"
:maintainer   "sugawara@viola.riken.go.jp"
The Japan Federation for Culture Collections (JFCC) Catalogue of Cultures for viruses of invertebrates.

272. jfcc-microalgae.srd
:ip-address   "134.160.52.5"
:ip-name   "fragrans.riken.go.jp"
:tcp-port   210
:database-name   "/data/waisguy/src/JFCC-Microalgae"
:maintainer   "sugawara@viola.riken.go.jp"
The Japan Federation for Culture Collections (JFCC) Catalogue of Cultures for microalgae.

273. jfcc-plant__virus.src
:ip-address   "134.160.52.5"
:ip-name   "fragrans.riken.go.jp"
:tcp-port   210
:database-name   "/data/waisguy/src/JFCC-Plant__virus"
:maintainer   "sugawara@viola.riken.go.jp"
The Japan Federation for Culture Collections (JFCC) Catalogue of Cultures for plant viruses.

274. jfcc-proto.src
:ip-address   "134.160.52.5"
:ip-name   "fragrans.riken.go.jp"
:tcp-port   210
:database-name   "/data/waisguy/src/JFCC-Proto"
:maintainer   "sugawara@viola.riken.go.jp"
The Japan Federation for Culture Collections (JFCC) Catalogue of Cultures for protozoa.

275. jfcc-vertebrate__virus.src
:ip-address   "134.160.52.5"
:ip-name   "fragrans.riken.go.jp"
:tcp-port   210

:database-name   "/data/waisguy/src/JFCC-Vertebrate__virus"
:maintainer   "sugawara@viola.riken.go.jp"
The Japan Federation for Culture Collections (JFCC) Catalogue of Cultures for viruses of vertebrates.

276. jiahr.src
:ip-name   "borg.lib.vt.edu"
:tcp-port   210
:database-name   "/LocalLibrary/WAIS/jiahr/jiahr"
The Journal of the International Academy of Hospitality Research [computer file] : JIAHR.

277. journalism.periodicals.src
:ip-address   "129.100.2.12"
:ip-name   "julian.uwo.ca"
:tcp-port   3041
:database-name   "journalism.periodicals"
:maintainer   "peter@julian.uwo.ca"
The WAIS accessible version of the Journalism Periodicals Index is being made available at no charge as an experiment by the Graduate School of Journalism in Cooperation with CCS at The University of Western Ontario. This server may be restricted in the future to paying customers.

278. jtca__cat.src
:ip-address   "134.160.52.5"
:ip-name   "fragrans.riken.go.jp"
:tcp-port   210
:database-name   "/data/waisguy/src/JTCA__cat"
:maintainer   "sugawara@viola.riken.go.jp"
JTCA Cell Line Database is compiled by the Cell Bank Committee of Japan Tissue Culture Association. It contains a catalogue of cell lines. See also related bibliographic references in JTCA__ref.src.

279. jtca__ref.src
:ip-address   "134.160.52.5"
:ip-name   "fragrans.riken.go.jp"
:tcp-port   210
:database-name   "/data/waisguy/src/JTCA__ref"
:maintainer   "sugawara@viola.riken.go.jp"
JTCA Cell Line Database is compiled by the Cell Bank Committee of Japan Tissue Culture Association. It contains a list of bibliographic references pertaining to the catalogue of cell lines (see JTCA__cat.src).

280. jte.src
:ip-name   "borg.lib.vt.edu"
:tcp-port   210
:database-name   "/LocalLibrary/WAIS/jte/jte"
Journal of technology education.

281. k-12-software.src
:ip-address   "134.7.70.222"
:ip-name   "info.curtin.edu.au"
:tcp-port   210
:database-name   "k-12-software"
:maintainer   "scor@info.curtin.edu.au"
Software and Courseware On-line Reviews (SCOR) database.

282. kidsnet.src
:database-name   "kidsnet"
:ip-name   "wais.cic.net"
:tcp-port   210

:maintainer ''emv@wais.cic.net''
The KIDSNET list was established in May, 1989, to stimulate the development of an international computer network for the use of children and their teachers.

283. linux-addresses.src
:ip-address ''152.2.22.81''
:ip-name ''sunsite.unc.edu''
:tcp-port 210
:database-name ''linux-addresses''
:maintainer ''jem@sunsite.unc.edu''
Here is the latest release of the Linux Address List.

284. linux-faq.src
:ip-address ''152.2.22.81''
:ip-name ''sunSITE.unc.edu''
:tcp-port 210
:database-name ''linux-faq''
:maintainer ''ewt@sunSITE.unc.edu''
This is the Frequently Asked Questions (FAQ) list for the Linux operating system and comp.os.linux newsgroup. Linux is Unix-like operating system for the 386, 486, and 586 available under the terms of the GNU public license.

285. linux-gcc-faq.src
:ip-address ''152.2.22.81''
:ip-name ''sunSITE.unc.edu''
:tcp-port 210
:database-name ''linux-gcc-faq''
:maintainer ''ewt@sunSITE.unc.edu''
This is the Linux FAQ for the Gnu C compiler; it contains answers to frequently asked questions about using GCC under the Linux operating system.

286. linux-mail-faq.src
:ip-address ''152.2.22.81''
:ip-name ''sunSITE.unc.edu''
:tcp-port 210
:database-name ''linux-mail-faq''
:maintainer ''ewt@sunSITE.unc.edu''
These are answers to Frequently Asked Questions about setting up Usenet news and E-Mail under the Linux operating system, using UUCP and SMTP.

287. linux-net-faq.src
:ip-address ''152.2.22.81''
:ip-name ''sunSITE.unc.edu''
:tcp-port 210
:database-name ''linux-net-faq''
:maintainer ''ewt@sunSITE.unc.edu''
This is information on how to set up a computer running Linux operating system on a TCP/IP network.

288. linux-software-map.src
:ip-address ''152.2.22.81''
:ip-name ''sunSITE.unc.edu''
:tcp-port 210
:database-name ''linux-software-map''
:maintainer ''ewt@sunSITE.unc.edu''
The LSM (Linux Software Map) project is an attempt to document all software and other materials for the Linux operating system using a format based upon that proposed by the IAFA working group of the IETF.

289. lists.src
:database-name ''lists''
:tcp-port 210
:ip-name ''wais.cic.net''
:maintainer ''emv@cic.net''
This source has several long lists of Usenet newsgroups, internet and bitnet mailing lists, and electronic serials and journals. There is a fair amount of overlap between the various components used to build this list.

290. livestock.src
:ip-address ''128.46.157.183''
:ip-name ''hermes.ecn.purdue.edu''
:tcp-port 6001
:database-name ''/home/hermes/cems/livestock/wais-sources/livestock''
:maintainer ''cems@ecn.purdue.edu''
Educational materials for livestock production and management.

291. lolita-dator.src
:ip-address ''130.235.162.11''
:ip-name ''munin.ub2.lu.se''
:tcp-port 210
:database-name ''lolita-dator''
:maintainer ''anders@munin.ub2.lu.se''
Lund Unviersity library catalog: a selection of computer-related literature. Some texts in Swedish.

292. lolita-milgo.src
:ip-address ''130.235.162.11''
:ip-name ''munin.ub2.lu.se''
:tcp-port 210
:database-name ''lolita-miljo''
:maintainer ''anders@munin.ub2.lu.se''
Lund Unviersity library catalog: a selection of environmental-related literature. Some texts in Swedish.

293. lp-bibtex-zenon-inria-fr.src
:ip-address ''138.96.32.21''
:ip-name ''zenon.inria.fr''
:tcp-port 210
:database-name ''lp-bibtex-zenon-inria-fr''
:maintainer ''wais-admin@zenon.inria.fr''
This source contains the references to most of the proceedings of the last: ICLP-(International Conference on Logic Programming); SLP-(Symposium on Logic Programming); and NACLP-(North American Conference on Logic Programming) in bibtex format.

294. lp-proceedings.src
:ip-address ''192.68.178.17''
:ip-name ''wais.fct.unl.pt''
:tcp-port 210
:database-name ''lp-proceedings''
:maintainer ''archive@fct.unl.pt''
This resource indexes the BibTeX references of Logic Programming Conferences collected by Ralf Scheidhauer (scheidhr@dfki.uni sb.de).

295. lyrics.src
:ip-address ''131.210.1.4''
:ip-name ''cs.uwp.edu''
:tcp-port 210
:database-name ''lyrics''

:maintainer ''datta@cs.uwp.edu''
The lyrics archives consists of complete lyrics to over 5000 songs made up of over 1100 artists.

296. mac.faq.src
:ip-address ''128.109.190.3''
:ip-name ''next2.oit.unc.edu''
:tcp-port 210
:database-name ''mac.FAQ''
:maintainer ''root@next2.oit.unc.edu''
The files of type dash used in the index were /users/cwis/databases/mac.alt.FAQ.

297. macintosh-news.src
:ip-address ''131.239.2.100''
:ip-name ''cmns-moon.think.com''
:tcp-port 210
:database-name ''MAC CSMP TIDB''
:maintainer ''bug-public@think.com''
This source combines several publications of interest to Macintosh users: The info-mac digest (info-mac@sumex-aim.stanford.edu), Michael Kelly's comp.sys.mac.programmer digest, and Adam Engst's TidBITS electronic magazine for the Macintosh.

298. macintosh-tidbits.src
:ip-address ''131.239.2.100''
:ip-name ''cmns-moon.think.com''
:tcp-port 210
:database-name ''TIDB''
Tidbits electronic magazine for the Macintosh.

299. macpsych.src
:ip-address ''130.71.128.9''
:ip-name ''gopher.stolaf.edu''
:tcp-port 8001
:database-name ''MacPsych''
:maintainer ''macpsych-request@stolaf.edu''
Guidelines for contributors to the MacPsych archive.

300. mailing-lists.src
:database-name ''lists''
:tcp-port 210
:ip-name ''wais.cic.net''
:maintainer ''emv@cic.net''
This source has several long lists of Usenet newsgroups, internet and bitnet mailing lists, and electronic serials and journals.
There is a fair amount of overlap between the various components used to build this list.

301. matrix__news.src
:ip-address ''192.135.128.129''
:ip-name ''ftp.tic.com''
:tcp-port 210
:database-name ''matrix__news''
:maintainer ''jsq@ftp.tic.com''
This directory contains articles, columns, and other information from Matrix News, the monthly newsletter of Matrix Information and Directory Services, Inc. (MIDS).

302. merit-archive-mac.src
:ip-address ''35.1.1.48''
:ip-name ''nic.merit.edu''
:tcp-port 210

:database-name ''merit-archive-mac''
:maintainer ''swartz@nic.merit.edu''
This is an index of the approximately 2000 Macintosh (mac) programs available for anonymous ftp from mac.archive.umich.edu.

303. merit-nsfnet-linkletter.src
:ip-address ''35.1.1.48''
:ip-name ''nic.merit.edu''
:tcp-port 210
:database-name ''merit-nsfnet-linkletter''
:maintainer ''wartz@nic.merit.edu''
Articles from the Merit NSFNET Linkletter (1988 to present), a newsletter containing articles on the NSFNET and the Internet. Each article is indexed separately.

304. meval-bibtex-zenon-inria-fr.src
:ip-address ''138.96.32.21''
:ip-name ''zenon.inria.fr''
:tcp-port 210
:database-name ''meval-bibtex-zenon-inria-fr''
:maintainer ''wais-admin@zenon.inria.fr''
This source contains the bibtex bibliography of the MEVAL project at INRIA Sophia Antipolis, France.

305. michnet-news-src
:ip-address ''35.1.1.48''
:ip-name ''nic.merit.edu''
:tcp-port 210
:database-name ''michnet-news''
:maintainer ''swartz@nic.merit.edu''
The News is the free official newsletter of MichNet, Michigan's regional network, and is published in March, June, September, and December.

306. midi.src
:ip-address ''129.120.1.42''
:ip-name ''sol.acs.unt.edu''
:tcp-port 210
:database-name ''/usr/local/data/wais/midi''
:maintainer ''billy@unt.edu''
MIDI (Musical Instrument Digital Interface) documents. It is commonly used to connect keyboards and sometimes computer together.

307. midwest-weather.src
:database-name ''midwest-weather''
:tcp-port 210
:ip-name ''wais.cic.net''
:maintainer ''emv@cic.net''
National Weather Service forecasts for the states of Michigan, Ohio, Indiana, Illinois, Wisconsin, Iowa, and Minnesota.

308. miljodatabas.src
:ip-address ''130.235.162.11''
:ip-name ''munin.ub2.lu.se''
:tcp-port 210
:database-name ''miljodatabas''
:maintainer ''anders@munin.ub2.lu.se''
A local database on environmental related research projects at Lund University, Sweden. In Swedish.

309. mit-algorithms-bug.src
:ip-address ''18.52.0.92''

:ip-name   "theory.lcs.mit.edu"
:database-name   "/i/wais-index/algorithms-bug"
:tcp-port   210
:maintainer   "ang@theory.lcs.mit.edu"
Algorithms-bug is a collection of bug lists for the book, 'Introduction to Algorithms' by Tom Cormen, Charles Leiserson, and Ron Rivest, all members of Theory of Computation Group, Laboratory for Computer Science, MIT.

310. mit-algorithms-excercise.src
:ip-address   "18.52.0.92"
:ip-name   "theory.lcs.mit.edu"
:database-name   "/i/wais-index/algorithms-exercise"
:tcp-port   210
:maintainer   "ang@theory.lcs.mit.edu"
Algorithms-exercise is a collection of exercises submitted to be used with the book, 'Introduction to Algorithms' by Tom Cormen, Charles Leiserson, and Ron Rivest, all members of Theory of Computation Group, Laboratory for Computer Science, MIT.

311. mit-algorithms-suggest.src
:ip-address   "18.52.0.92"
:ip-name   "theory.lcs.mit.edu"
:tcp-port   210
:database-name   "/i/wais-index/algorithms-suggest"
:maintainer   "ang@theory.lcs.mit.edu"
Algorithms-suggest is a collection of suggestions submitted by readers of the book, 'Introduction to Algorithms' by Tom Cormen, Charles Leiserson, and Ron Rivest, all members of Theory of Computation Group, Laboratory for Computer Science, MIT.

312. monashuni-phonedir.src
:ip-address   "130.194.74.201"
:ip-name   "daneel.rdt.monash.edu.au"
:tcp-port   210
:database-name   "monashuni-phonedir"
:maintainer   "rik.harris@fcit.monash.edu.au"
This is a reasonably up-to-date telephone directory for all campuses of Monash University, Victoria, Australia.

313. movie-lists.src
:ip-address   "128.2.206.11"
:ip-name   "gourd.srv.cs.cmu.edu"
:tcp-port   6000
:database-name   "movie-lists"
:maintainer   "spot@cs.cmu.edu"
This directory contains the latest releases of the USENET rec.arts.movies lists. The lists are intended to provide useful, current references to TV and film credits in an electronic form.

314. music-sruveys.src
:ip-address   "131.210.1.4"
:ip-name   "cs.uwp.edu"
:tcp-port   210
:database-name   "music-surveys"
:maintainer   "datta@cs.uwp.edu"
This server contains the results of the rec.music. Eclectic Music surveys. The surveys are "off the top of the head" comments about musicians and bands. Highly entertaining!

315. mutex.src
:ip-address   "130.71.128.9"

:ip-name   "gopher.stolaf.edu"
:tcp-port   8003
:database-name   "MuTeX"
:maintainer   "mutex-request@stolaf.edu"
The MuTeX package is a set of macros allowing TeX to typeset music. It was written by Andrea Steinbach and Angelika Schofer, as a master's thesis at Rheinische Friedrich-Wilhelms University. MuTeX allows you to typeset single-staff music and lyrics.

316. nafta.src
:ip-address   "152.2.22.81"
:ip-name   "sunsite.unc.edu"
:tcp-port   210
:database-name   "nafta"
:maintainer   "jem@sunsite.unc.edu"
The full text of the North American Free Trade Agreement- that would make eliminate most restrictions on trade, export, and import among the North American countries of Canada, the United States, and Mexico.

317. nasa-directory-of-servers.src
:ip-name   "ndadsb.gsfc.nasa.gov"
:tcp-port   210
:database-name   "NASA-directory-of-servers"
:maintainer   "stelar-info@Hypatia.gsfc.nasa.gov"
This database contains WAIS source files of interest to the NASA community. Some, but not all, are run by the STELAR project at the National Space Science Data Center. Others are here purely as a service to the astronomy, astrophysics, planetary and space physics communities.

318. nasa-larc-abs.src
:ip-name   "techreports.larc.nasa.gov"
:tcp-port   210
:database-name   "nasa-larc-abs"
:maintainer   "M.L.Nelson@LaRC.NASA.GOV"
These reports are available in compressed PostScript format via anonymous ftp from techreports.larc.nasa.gov.

319. national-performance-review.src
:ip-address   "152.2.22.81"
:ip-name   "sunsite.unc.edu"
:tcp-port   210
:database-name   "National-Performance-Review"
:maintainer   "jem@sunsite.unc.edu"
This is the report of the United States "National Performance Review" (NPR), created by a committee headed by Vice-President Albert Gore. It is a series of reccomendations for improving the efficiency of government and reducing waste.

320. nc-supreme-court.src
:ip-address   "152.2.22.81"
:ip-name   "sunsite.unc.edu"
:tcp-port   210
:database-name   "nc-supreme-court"
:maintainer   "jem@sunsite.unc.edu"
Test selection of opinions of the Supreme Court of North Carolina. These Advance Sheets represent information from 332 NC __ No.4 Pages 487-672 dated January 4, 1993.

321. netcdf-group.src
:ip-address   "128.117.140.3"
:ip-name   "wais.unidata.ucar.edu"

:tcp-port   210
:database-name   ''netcdf-group''
:maintainer   ''support@unidata.ucar.edu''
This is the mailing list archive for the
netcdfgroup@unidata.ucar.edu mailing list, containing all the
postings since the mailing list was created on 18 June 1990.
This WAIS index is updated nightly so it might not contain
postings within the last 24 hours.

322. netinfo-docs.src
:ip-address   ''130.95.128.1''
:ip-name   ''uniwa.uwa.oz.au''
:tcp-port   210
:database-name   ''netinfo-docs''
:maintainer   ''root@uniwa''
Various files with information about accessing the internet and
what services are available.

323. netinfo.src
:ip-name   ''wais.concert.net''
:tcp-port   8000
:database-name   ''netinfo''
:maintainer   ''abc@concert.net''
Mirror of netinfo directory on nic.ddn.mil Not all documents
that are mirrored are indexed! Specifically: only .txt files are
indexed.

324. netlib-index.src
:ip-address   ''130.130.64.1''
:ip-name   ''wraith.cs.uow.edu.au''
:tcp-port   210
:database-name   ''netlib-index''
:maintainer   ''steve@cs.uow.edu.au''
This server contains the netlib indexes as they exists on the
Australian netlib server (wraith). Note that this server only contains the indexes of the software available through netlib but not
the software itself. The software can be obtained by mailing to
netlib@cs.uow.edu.au or your local netlib server in the normal
manner.

325. netpolicy.src
:ip-address   ''198.49.45.10''
:ip-name   ''ds.internic.net''
:tcp-port   210
:database-name   ''netpolicy''
:maintainer   ''admin@ds.internic.net''
Network Policies and Procedures.

326. netrek-ftp.src
:ip-address   ''128.2.206.11''
:ip-name   ''gourd.srv.cs.cmu.edu''
:tcp-port   6000
:database-name   ''netrek-ftp''
:maintainer   ''spot@cs.cmu.edu''
This is an archive for information of interest to the Netrek community. The original source was the andrew.games.xtrek bboard
at CMU; later items came from the alt.games.xtrek newsgroup,
and now the rec.games.netrek newsgroup.

327. network-bibliography.src
:ip-address ''130.235.162.11''
:ip-name ''munin.ub2.lu.se''
:tcp-port 210
:database-name ''network-bibliography''

:maintainer   ''anders@munin.ub2.lu.se''
Network related bibliographies.

328. network-tools.src
:ip-name   ''archive.orst.edu''
:tcp-port   9000
:database-name   ''network-tools''
:maintainer   ''wais@archive.orst.edu''
Network tools: readme's, man pages and other useful stuff.

329. neuroprose.src
:database-name   ''neuroprose''
:ip-name   ''wais.cic.net''
:tcp-port   210
:maintainer   ''emv@cic.net''
WAIS index of the neuroprose index at archive.cis.ohio-
state.edu:/pub/neuroprose/INDEX.

330. news-conf.src
:ip-address   ''128.109.157.30''
:ip-name   ''wais.oit.unc.edu''
:tcp-port   210
:database-name   ''news-conf''
:maintainer   ''root@samba.acs.unc.edu''
Conference announcements posted to
news.announce.conferences.

331. news.answers-faqs.src
:ip-name   ''ftp.eunet.ch''
:tcp-port   210
:database-name   ''faqs''
:maintainer   ''archive@eunet.ch''
This server contains all FAQ's from the Usenet newsgroup
news.answers, it is updated daily at 02:30 (GMT + 1).

332. next-managers.src
:ip-address   ''130.71.128.9''
:ip-name   ''gopher.stolaf.edu''
:tcp-port   8004
:database-name   ''NeXT-Managers''
:maintainer   ''next-managers-request@stolaf.edu''
NeXT-Managers contains an archive of all messages posted to
the next-managers mailing list.

333. next.faq.src
:ip-name   ''next2.oit.unc.edu''
:tcp-port   210
:database-name   ''next.FAQ''
:maintainer   ''akers@next2.oit.unc.edu''
Questions about the NeXT computer.

334. nrao.fits.src
:ip-address   ''192.33.115.8''
:ip-name   ''fits.cv.nrao.edu''
:tcp-port   210
:database-name   ''nrao-fits''
:maintainer   ''dwells@fits.cv.nrao.edu''
WAIS Server for FITS Documents.

335. nrao-raps.src
:ip-address   ''192.33.115.65''
:ip-name   ''annie.cv.nrao.edu''
:tcp-port   210
:database-name   ''nrao-raps''

:maintainer   ''library@annie.cv.nrao.edu''
NRAO-RAPS is a bibliographic listing of astronomy and astrophysics preprints received in the Charlottesville library of the National Radio Astronomy Observatory from 1986 forward.

336. nren-bill.src
:database-name   ''nrenbill''
:ip-name   ''wais.cic.net''
:tcp-port   210
:maintainer   ''emv@cic.net''
The High-Performance Computing Act of 1991, otherwise known as the NREN bill.

337. nrenbill.src
:database-name   ''nrenbill''
:ip-name   ''wais.cic.net''
:tcp-port   210
:maintainer   ''emv@cic.net''
The High-Performance Computing Act of 1991, otherwise known as the NREN bill.

338. nsf-awards.src
:ip-address   ''128.150.195.40''
:ip-name   ''stis.nsf.gov''
:tcp-port   210
:database-name   ''nsf-awards''
:maintainer   ''stisop@stis.nsf.gov''
This WAIS database contains award abstracts for awards made by the National Science Foundation. The database covers from the beginning of 1990 to the present (no abstracts are available before 1990).

339. nsf-pubs.src
:ip-address   ''128.150.195.40''
:ip-name   ''stis.nsf.gov''
:tcp-port   210
:database-name   ''nsf-pubs''
:maintainer   ''stisop@stis.nsf.gov''
The nsf-pubs database contains the publications of the National Science Foundation.

340. nsfnet-rfcs.src
:ip-address   ''35.1.1.48''
:ip-name   ''nic.merit.edu''
:tcp-port   210
:database-name   ''nsfnet-rfcs''
:maintainer   ''swartz@nic.merit.edu''
Internet RFCs (Request For Comment) and drafts.

341. ocunix-faq.src
:database-name   ''/home/wcscps/archive/ocunix-faq''
:maintainer   ''wcscps@alfred.ccs.carleton.ca''
:ip-address   ''134.117.1.1''
:ip-name   ''alfred.ccs.carleton.ca''
:tcp-port   210
The Ottawa Carleton Unix Users Group is a co-operative group of basement Unix hackers.

342. oligos.src
:ip-address   ''130.251.201.2''
:ip-name   ''istge.ist.unige.it''
:tcp-port   210
:database-name   ''Oligos''
:source-name   ''/wais/cldb/mpdb''

:maintainer   ''wais@istge.ist.unige.it''
At istge.ist.unige.it three databases devoted to availability of biological materials are maintained and updated, in the sphere of the Interlab Project.

343. online@uunet.ca.src
:database-name   ''online''
:ip-name   ''wais.cic.net''
:tcp-port   210
:maintainer   ''emv@cic.net''
The online@uunet.ca mailing list, for information brokers and other people who search on line databases. Good coverage of commercial, pay per use systems like Dialog, LEXIS, NEXIS, etc. To subscribe send a request to online-request@uunet.ca.

344. oopsla93.src
:ip-name   ''ursamajor.uvic.ca''
:tcp-port   210
:database-name   ''oopsla93''
:maintainer   ''bnfb@cs.uvic.ca''
Registration and attendance information for the 1993 ACM SIGPLAN Conference on Object-Oriented Programming Systems, Languages, and Applications (OOPSLA'93). This server will be maintained through October 1993.

345. open__systems__calendar.src
:ip-address   ''192.31.181.1''
:ip-name   ''quake.think.com''
:tcp-port   210
:database-name   ''open__systems__calendar''
:maintainer   ''jsq@quake.think.com''
These open systems calendar files are collected and posted by Susanne Wilhelm of Windsound Consulting <sws@calvin.wa.com> and John S. Quarterman of Texas Internet Consulting <jsq@tic.com>.

346. oreilly__book__descriptions.src
:ip-name   ''wais.ora.com''
:tcp-port   210
:database-name   ''/online/wais/descriptions/index''
:maintainer   ''wais@wais.ora.com''
Descriptions of books published by O'Reilly & Associates, including the X Window System series, the X Resource, and the Nutshell books.

347. ota.src
:database-name   ''/proj/wais/db/ota/ota''
:ip-address   ''192.31.181.1''
:ip-name   ''quake.think.com''
:tcp-port   210
:maintainer   ''wais@quake.think.com''
This is a test WAIS server for the Congressional Office of Technology Assessment (OTA). It currently (10/92) only contains the partial text of one report on global standards.

348. oz-postcodes.src
:ip-address   ''128.250.186.4''
:ip-name   ''pet1.austin.unimelb.edu.au''
:tcp-port   210
:database-name   ''oz-postcodes''
:maintainer   ''danny@austin.unimelb.edu.au''
This source is an index of Australian Postcodes. Search by placename or by postcode.

349. patent-sampler.src
:ip-address ''131.239.2.100''
:ip-name ''cmns-moon.think.com''
:tcp-port 210
:database-name ''PTNT''
:maintainer ''bug-public@think.com''
About 2 weeks of Patent applications (18MBytes) from the US Patent Office.

350. pegasus-mail-disc.src
:ip-address ''128.174.64.10''
:ip-name ''cyberdyne.ece.uiuc.edu''
:tcp-port 210
:database-name ''pegasus-mail-disc''
:maintainer ''rjoyner@cyberdyne.ece.uiuc.edu''
This database consists of mail sent to all Pegasus Mail Administrators throughout the world. The mail is a discussion of features / bugs in Pegasus Mail and Charon.

351. poetry-index.src
:ip-address 152.2.22.81
:ip-name ''sunsite.unc.edu''
:tcp-port 210
:database-name ''/home3/wais/POETRY-index''
:maintainer ''paul__jones@unc.edu''
This is an index of all the poems and reviews published since volume 151 October 1987 in POETRY magazine of Chicago.

352. poetry.src
:ip-address ''18.85.0.48''
:ip-name ''microworld.media.mit.edu''
:tcp-port 8000
:database-name ''POETRY''
:maintainer ''uriw@microworld.media.mit.edu''
The intention of this server is to collect as many poems as possible. Right now it contains the complete poems of Shakespeare, Yeats, and Elizabeth Sawyer, as well as a smattering of many other poets.

353. posix.1003.2.src
:ip-name ''wais.concert.net''
:tcp-port 8000
:database-name ''POSIX.1003.2''
:maintainer ''abc@concert.net''
Posix 1003.2 Documents from research.att.com.

354. preprints-alg-geom.src
:ip-address ''140.77.241.1''
:ip-name ''enslapp.ens-lyon.fr''
:tcp-port 210
:database-name ''/usr/local/wais-sources/Preprints-alg-geom''
:maintainer ''degio@difool.ens-lyon.fr''
This server contains all titles and abstracts that have been submitted to the alg-geom Preprint server in SISSA.

355. preprints-cond-mat.src
:ip-address ''140.77.241.1''
:ip-name ''enslapp.ens-lyon.fr''
:tcp-port 210
:database-name ''/usr/local/wais-sources/Preprints-cond-mat''
:maintainer ''degio@difool.ens-lyon.src''
This server gives all titles/abstracts on the SISSA preprint server for condensed matter.

356. preprints-gr-qc.src
:ip-address ''140.77.241.1''
:ip-name ''enslapp.ens-lyon.fr''
:tcp-port 210
:database-name ''/usr/local/wais-sources/Preprints-gr-qc''
:maintainer ''degio@difool.ens-lyon.fr''
This server contains all titles/abstracts of papers submitted to the gr-qc server in Los Alamos.

357. preprints-hep-ph.src
:ip-address ''140.77.241.1''
:ip-name ''enslapp.ens-lyon.fr''
:tcp-port 210
:database-name ''Preprints-hep-ph''
:maintainer ''degio@difool.ens-lyon.fr''
This server contains all titles/abstracts emitted by the hep-ph server at babbage.sissa.it. They are all about high energy phenomenology.

358. preprints-hep-th.src
:ip-address ''140.77.241.1''
:ip-name ''enslapp.ens-lyon.fr''
:tcp-port 210
:database-name ''/usr/local/wais-sources/Preprints-hep-th''
:maintainer ''degio@difool.ens-lyon.fr''
This server gives all titles/abstracts on the Los-Alamos Preprint server for theoretical physics.

359. proj-gutenberg.src
:ip-name ''archive.orst.edu''
:tcp-port 9000
:database-name ''proj-gutenburg''
:maintainer ''wais@archive.orst.edu''
This server mirrors the documents produced by Project Gutenberg. The documents themselves are at mrcnext.cso.uiuc.edu: etext/ *.
:ip-address ''137.132.3.3''
:ip-name ''solomon.technet.sg''
:tcp-port 210
:database-name ''prosite''
:maintainer ''waisguy@solomon.technet.sg''
PROSITE: A Dictionary of Protein Sites and Patterns, User Manual, Release 9.10, August 1992.

360. quake.think.com-ftp.src
:ip-address ''192.31.181.1''
:ip-name ''quake.think.com''
:tcp-port 211
:database-name ''anonymous-ftp''
:maintainer ''wais@quake.think.com''
This is a prototype wais-ftp server. This server searches README files throughout the entire FTP directory tree.

361. queer-resources.src
:ip-name ''vector.intercon.com''
:tcp-port 210
:database-name ''/wais/qrd''
:maintainer ''buckmr@vector.intercon.com''
The Queer Resources Directory is a collection of files of interest to the gay community.

362. quran.src
:ip-address ''128.109.157.30''
:ip-name ''wais.oit.unc.edu''

:tcp-port 210
:database-name ''Quran''
:maintainer ''fullton@samba.oit.unc.edu''
The Quran.

363. ra-mime-zenon-inria-fr.src
:ip-address ''138.96.32.21''
:ip-name ''zenon.inria.fr''
:tcp-port 210
:database-name ''ra-mime-zenon-inria-fr''
:maintainer ''doc@sophia.inria.fr''
This source contains whole INRIA reports, especially: Activity
reports for the INRIA Sophia Antipolis center and Technical
and research reports.

364. ra-zenon-inria-fr.src
:ip-address ''138.96.32.21''
:ip-name ''zenon.inria.fr''
:tcp-port 210
:database-name ''ra-zenon-inria-fr''
:maintainer ''doc@sophia.inria.fr''
This source contains INRIA reports in DVI format.

365. rebase__enzymes.src
:ip-address ''192.138.220.2''
:ip-name ''vent.neb.com''
:tcp-port 210
:database-name ''REBASE__enzymes''
:maintainer ''macelis@neb.com''
The Restriction Enzyme Database is a collection of information
about restriction enzymes, methylases, the microorganisms from
which they have been isolated, recognition sequences, cleavage
sites, methylation specificity, the commercial availability of the
enzymes, and references dating back to 1952.

366. rebase__help.src
:ip-address ''192.138.220.2''
:ip-name ''vent.neb.com''
:tcp-port 210
:database-name ''REBASE__help''
:maintainer ''macelis@neb.com''
The Restriction Enzyme Database is a collection of information
about restriction enzymes. This is a description of how to use
the database.

367. rebase__news.src
:ip-address ''192.138.220.2''
:ip-name ''vent.neb.com''
:tcp-port 210
:database-name ''REBASE__news''
:maintainer ''macelis@neb.com''
The Restriction Enzyme Database is a collection of information
about restriction enzymes. This is what's new in REBASE this
month.

368. rebase__references.src
:ip-address ''192.138.220.2''
:ip-name ''vent.neb.com''
:tcp-port 210
:database-name ''REBASE__references''
:maintainer ''macelis@neb.com''
The Restriction Enzyme Database, is a collection of information
about restriction enzymes. These are the published references in
REBASE.

369. rebase__suppliers.src
:ip-address ''192.138.220.2''
:ip-name ''vent.neb.com''
:tcp-port 210
:database-name ''REBASE__suppliers''
:maintainer ''macelis@neb.com''
The Restriction Enzyme Database is a collection of information
about restriction enzymes. This is a list of the commercial suppliers of enzymes.

370. rec.gardens.src
:ip-address ''130.235.162.11''
:ip-name ''munin.ub2.lu.se''
:tcp-port 210
:database-name ''rec.gardens''
:maintainer ''anders@munin.ub2.lu.se''
Index of articles in the newsgroup rec.gardens.

371. rec.music.early.src
:ip-address ''137.208.3.4''
:ip-name ''wais.wu-wien.ac.at''
:tcp-port 210
:database-name ''rec.music.early''
:maintainer ''Gerhard.Gonter@wu-wien.ac.at''
EARLYM-L and the newsgroup rec.music.early are linked.
They were created to provide a forum for exchange of news and
views about medieval, renaissance and baroque music.

372. rec.pets.src
:ip-address ''128.109.157.30''
:ip-name ''wais.oit.unc.edu''
:tcp-port 210
:database-name ''recpets''
:maintainer ''fullton@samba.oit.unc.edu''
Ten days' worth of news in the rec.pets newsgroups.

373. recipes.src
:ip-address ''128.109.157.30''
:ip-name ''wais.oit.unc.edu''
:tcp-port 210
:database-name ''recipes''
:maintainer ''fullton@samba.oit.unc.edu''
Database of recipes.

374. reports-abstracts.src
:ip-address ''131.246.19.3''
:ip-name ''bloch.informatik.uni-kl.de''
:tcp-port 210
:database-name ''reports-abstracts''
:maintainer ''reitherm@informatik.uni-kl.de''
References to technical reports of various origin (refdbms format).

375. research-in-surgery.src
:database-name ''ris''
:ip-name ''gopher.uv.es''
:tcp-port 210
:maintainer ''root@uva.ci.uv.es''
Research in Surgery is published in English three times yearly.
The journal publishes experimental and clinical surgical research
papers.

376. rfc-index.src
:database-name ''rfc-index''

:tcp-port 210
:ip-name "wais.cic.net"
:maintainer "emv@cic.net"
Index to the RFC's. The original source is ftp.nisc.sri.com:/rfc/
rfc-index.txt and it's indexed one paragraph at a time.

377. rfcs.src
:ip-address "198.49.45.10"
:ip-name "ds.internic.net"
:tcp-port 210
:database-name "rfcs"
:maintainer "admin@ds.internic.net"
Request For Comments documents - INTERNET standards and
information.

378. ripe-database.src
:database-name "ripe-database"
:ip-address "192.87.45.1"
:ip-name "ns.ripe.net"
:tcp-port 210
:maintainer "marten@ns.ripe.net"
This WAIS database contains the RIPE Network Management
Database which can be found on ftp.ripe.net, subdirectory ripe/
dbase.

379. ripe-internet-drafts.src
:database-name "internet-drafts"
:ip-address "192.87.45.1"
:ip-name "ns.ripe.net"
:tcp-port 210
:maintainer "marten@ns.ripe.net"
This WAIS database contains all Internet Drafts, that can be
found on ftp.ripe.net, subdirectory internet-drafts.

380. ripe-rfc.src
:database-name "rfc"
:ip-address "192.87.45.1"
:ip-name "ns.ripe.net"
:tcp-port 210
:maintainer "marten@ns.ripe.net"
This WAIS database contains all RFCs that can be found on
ftp.ripe.net, subdirectory rfc.

381. risks-digest.src
:ip-address "131.239.2.100"
:ip-name "cmns-moon.think.com"
:tcp-port 210
:database-name "RISK"
:maintainer "bug-public@think.com"
Risk Digest collection from the arpa-net list, but this is so far an
unofficial archive server. It contains all issues, but is not updated automatically yet.

382. roget-thesaurus.src
:database-name "roget-thesaurus"
:ip-name "wais.cic.net"
:tcp-port 210
:maintainer "emv@cic.net"
Roget's Thesaurus is provided by Project Gutenberg.

383. rpms-pathology.src
:ip-address "146.179.10.3"
:ip-name "mpcc3.rpms.ac.uk"
:tcp-port 210

:database-name "/home/images/pathology/RPMS-pathology"
:maintainer "rmccorkl@rpms.ac.uk"
RPMS (Royal Postgraduate Medical School). This database contains histo-pathological images & documentation on mammalian
endocrine tissues.

384. rsinetwork.src
:ip-address "131.239.2.100"
:ip-name "cmns-moon.think.com"
:tcp-port 210
:database-name "RSI"
:maintainer "bug-public@think.com"
RSInetwork Newsletter For People Concerned About Tendinitis,
Carpal Tunnel Syndrome (CTS), and Other Repetitive Strain
Injuries (RSI).

385. s-archive.src
:database-name "/var/wais/s"
:ip-address "130.95.128.1"
:ip-name "uniwa.uwa.oz.au"
:tcp-port 210
:maintainer "root@uniwa.uwa.oz.au"
S mailing list archive.

386. salk__genome__center.src
:ip-address "192.31.153.23"
:ip-name "RANGERSMITH.SDSC.EDU"
:tcp-port 210
:database-name "Salk__Genome__Center"
:maintainer "romberg@molly.sdsc.edu"
This database contains the results of physical mapping of human
chromosome 11, and other chromosomes, from the San Diego
Genome Center at the Salk Institute.

387. sample-books.src
:tcp-port 210
:ip-address "192.31.181.1"
:ip-name "quake.think.com"
:database-name "sample-books"
:maintainer "wais@quake.think.com"
Sample electronic texts. The files of type text used in the index
were: /usr/spool/ftp/pub/etext/alice-in-wonderland.txt /usr/spool/
ftp/pub/etext/declaration-of-independence.txt /usr/spool/ftp/pub/
etext/hunting-of-the-snark.txt /usr/spool/ftp/pub/etext/night-be-
fore-christmas.txt /usr/spool/ftp/pub/etext/through-the-looking-
glass.txt /usr/spool/ftp/pub/etext/us-constitution.txt.

388. sample-pictures.src
:tcp-port 210
:ip-address "192.31.181.1"
:ip-name "quake.think.com"
:database-name "sample-pictures"
:maintainer "wais@quake.think.com"
Sample pict images. The files of type pict used in the index
were:
/proj/wais/db/picts/Africa-map.mb
/proj/wais/db/picts/Ben-Franklin.mb
/proj/wais/db/picts/Europe-map.mb
/proj/wais/db/picts/Fractal-Brewster.mb
/proj/wais/db/picts/Japanese-Girl.mb
/proj/wais/db/picts/Kenya-map.mb
/proj/wais/db/picts/Opus-Cartoon.mb
/proj/wais/db/picts/US-map.mb
/proj/wais/db/picts/server-Girl.mb.

389. sas-archive.src
:database-name ''/var/wais/sas''
:ip-address ''130.95.128.1''
:ip-name ''uniwa.uwa.oz.au''
:tcp-port 210
:maintainer ''root@uniwa.uwa.oz.au''
sas mailing list archive.

390. sci.astro.hubble.src
:ip-address ''129.219.51.169''
:ip-name ''wfpc3.la.asu.edu''
:tcp-port 210
:database-name ''/disk1/wais/wais-sources/sci.astro.hubble''
:maintainer ''sah@wfpc3.la.asu.edu''
Archive of materials posted to sci.astro.hubble, part of USENET Group Charter - sci.astro.hubble.

391. sci.src
:ip-address ''128.109.157.30''
:ip-name ''wais.oit.unc.edu''
:tcp-port 210
:database-name ''sci''
:maintainer ''fullton@samba.oit.unc.edu''
News from the sci. * newsgroups.

392. scsi-2.src
:ip-address ''131.239.2.100''
:ip-name ''cmns-moon.think.com''
:tcp-port 210
:database-name ''SCSI''
:maintainer ''bug-public@think.com''
This is a draft proposed American National Standard of Accredited Standards Committtee X3.

393. sdsu-directory-of-servers.src
:ip-address ''130.191.224.3''
:ip-name ''wais.sdsu.edu''
:tcp-port 210
:database-name ''SDSU-directory-of-servers''
:maintainer ''wais@wais.sdsu.edu''
This server provides a directory of all San Diego State University wais servers.

394. sdsu__phonebook.src
:ip-address ''130.191.224.3''
:ip-name ''wais.sdsu.edu''
:tcp-port 210
:database-name ''SDSU__PhoneBook''
:maintainer ''wais@wais.sdsu.edu''
This server contains a directory of faculty and staff at San Diego State University.

395. sf-reviews.src
:ip-address ''134.172.2.69''
:ip-name ''net.bio.net''
:tcp-port 210
:database-name ''sf-reviews''
:maintainer ''news@net.bio.net''
This database is an archive of the Usenet newsgroup rec.arts.sf.reviews, which is a forum for reviews of works of interest to fans of science fiction/speculative fiction/fantasy/horror (and sometimes comics).

396. sfsu-phones.src
:ip-address ''130.212.10.102''
:ip-name ''sfsuvax1.sfsu.edu''
:tcp-port 210
:database-name ''phones''
:maintainer ''wais@sfsuvax1.sfsu.edu''
San Francisco State University Telephone Book. Updated as of September 24, 1992.

397. sgml.src
:ip-name ''ifi.uio.no''
:tcp-port 210
:database-name ''SGML''
:maintainer ''anders@ifi.uio.no''
Standard Generalized Markup Language information.

398. sighyper.src
:ip-name ''ifi.uio.no''
:tcp-port 210
:database-name ''SIGHyper''
:maintainer ''anders@ifi.uio.no''
These documents are from the SGML Users' Group's (SGML-UG) Special Interest Group on Hypertext and Multimedia (SIGhyper).

399. silent-tristero.src
:ip-address ''131.239.2.100''
:ip-name ''cmns-moon.think.com''
:tcp-port 210
:database-name ''TRIS''
:maintainer ''bug-public@think.com''
The silent-tristero mailing list, served up by the Public CM WAIS Server.

400. smf-annuaire.src.src
:ip-address ''139.124.3.23''
:ip-name ''cirm5.univ-mrs.fr''
:tcp-port 210
:database-name ''/bases/bibli-cirm/smf-annuaire.src''
:maintainer ''rolland@cirm5.univ-mrs.fr''
Files of the Societe Mathematique de France.

401. smithsonian-pictures.src
:ip-address ''192.216.46.1''
:ip-name ''server.wais.com''
:tcp-port 210
:database-name ''smithsonian-pictures''
:maintainer ''support@wais.com''
These image files have been produced by the Smithsonian Institution's Office of Printing & Photographic Services, and are made available through a generous grant from the Apple Library of Tomorrow Program, under Project Chapman (named for John Chapman, a.k.a. 'Johnny Appleseed').

402. sprintlink.src
:ip-name ''ftp.sprintlink.net''
:tcp-port 210
:database-name ''Sprintlink''
:maintainer ''con@ftp.sprintlink.net''
This is an experimental Gopher.

403. spss-archive.src
:database-name ''/var/wais/spssx''
:ip-address ''130.95.128.1''

:ip-name ''uniwa.uwa.oz.au''
:tcp-port 210
:maintainer ''root@uniwa.uwa.oz.au''
SPSSX mailing list archive.

404. statfaqs.src
:ip-name ''bongo.cc.utexas.edu''
:tcp-port 210
:database-name ''/home/ccix/u13/cc/ssg/wais/statfaqs''
:maintainer ''ssg@bongo.cc.utexas.edu''
List of frequently asked questions and their answers on topics concerning statistics and statistical computing. This list is compiled monthly by the Statistical Services Group, University of Texas at Austin Computation Center.

405. stats-archive.src
:database-name ''/var/wais/stats''
:ip-address ''130.95.128.1''
:ip-name ''uniwa.uwa.oz.au''
:tcp-port 210
:maintainer ''root@uniwa.uwa.oz.au''
stats mailing list archive.

406. strains-bact.src
:ip-address ''134.160.52.5''
:ip-name ''fragrans.riken.go.jp''
:tcp-port 210
:database-name ''STRAINS-bact''
:maintainer ''sugawara@viola.riken.go.jp''
The STRAIN databases, comprising the bacterial, fungi and yeast databases, were developed by the World Data Center for Micro organisms, (WDC) sponsored by UNEP and UNESCO. STRAINS-bact contains a list of bacterial strains preserved in the collections registered in the CCINFO database (see CCINFO.src, STRAINS fungi.src and STRAINS-yeasts.src).

407. strains-fungi.src
:ip-address ''134.160.52.5''
:ip-name ''fragrans.riken.go.jp''
:tcp-port 210
:database-name ''STRAINS-fungi''
:maintainer ''sugawara@viola.riken.go.jp''
STRAINS-fungi contains a list of fungal strains preserved in the collections registered in the CCINFO database (see CCINFO.src, STRAINS-bact.src and STRAINS-yeast.src).

408. strains-yeast.src
:ip-address ''134.160.52.5''
:ip-name ''fragrans.riken.go.jp''
:tcp-port 210
:database-name ''STRAINS-yeast''
:maintainer ''sugawara@viola.riken.go.jp''
STRAINS-yeast contains a list of yeast strains preserved in the collections registered in the CCINFO database (see CCINFO.src, STRAINS-bact.src, STRAINS-fungi.src).

409. stsci-docs.src
:ip-name ''stsci.edu''
:tcp-port 210
:database-name ''/var/spool/uucppublic/.waisindex/stsci-docs''
:maintainer ''reppert@stsci.edu''
User Manuals produced by the Space Telescope Science Institute for use by Hubble Space Telescope (HST) proposers and observers.

410. stsci-preprint-db.src
:ip-address ''130.167.1.2''
:ip-name ''stsci.edu''
:tcp-port 210
:database-name ''stsci-preprint-db''
:maintainer ''reppert@stsci.edu''
STScI-STEP is a bibliographic listing of astronomy and astrophysics preprints received at the Space Telescope Science Institute Library during the last two years, including all HST papers in the refereed literature.

411. sun-admin.src
:ip-address ''152.2.22.81''
:ip-name ''sun-wais.oit.unc.edu''
:tcp-port 210
:database-name ''sun-admin''
:maintainer ''wais@calypso.oit.unc.edu''
This server maintains postings to the comp.sys.sun.admin newsgroup. Articles are archived on sun-wais, with the archives being updated at 6 am EST each day.

412. sun-announce.src
:ip-address ''152.2.22.81''
:ip-name ''sun-wais.oit.unc.edu''
:tcp-port 210
:database-name ''sun-announce''
:maintainer ''wais@calypso.oit.unc.edu''
Archive of comp.sys.sun.announce newsgroup.

413. sun-apps.src
:ip-address ''152.2.22.81''
:ip-name ''sun-wais.oit.unc.edu''
:tcp-port 210
:database-name ''sun-apps''
:maintainer ''wais@calypso.oit.unc.edu''
Archive of comp.sys.sun.apps newsgroup.

414. sun-fixes.src
:ip-name ''wais.vifp.monash.edu.au''
:tcp-port 210
:database-name ''sun-fixes''
:maintainer ''rik.harris@vifp.monash.edu.au''
This is a list of Sun Microsystems bug patches.

415. sun-hardware.stc
:ip-address ''152.2.22.81''
:ip-name ''sun-wais.oit.unc.edu''
:tcp-port 210
:database-name ''sun-hardware''
:maintainer ''wais@calypso.oit.unc.edu''
The files of type netnews used in the index were:
/home2/news-spool/comp/sys/sun/hardware
/home2/newsfeed/comp/sys/sun/hardware.

416. sun-managers-summary.src
:ip-address ''138.47.18.3''
:ip-name ''aurora.latech.edu''
:tcp-port 210
:database-name ''sun-managers-summary''
:maintainer ''dan@engr.latech.edu''
Index of the sun-managers mailing list SUMMARIES *only *, reindexed every morning.

417. sun-misc.src
:ip-address ''152.2.22.81''
:ip-name ''sun-wais.oit.unc.edu''
:tcp-port 210
:database-name ''sun-misc''
:maintainer ''wais@calypso.oit.unc.edu''
Archive of comp.sys.sun.misc newsgroup.

418. sun-openlook.src
:ip-address ''152.2.22.81''
:ip-name ''sun-wais.oit.unc.edu''
:tcp-port 210
:database-name ''sun-openlook''
:maintainer ''wais@sun-wais.oit.unc.edu''
Sun OpenLook newsgroup (comp.windows.open-look).

419. sun-spots.src
:ip-address ''131.239.2.100''
:ip-name ''cmns-moon.think.com''
:tcp-port 210
:database-name ''SNSP SNMN''
:maintainer ''bug-public@think.com''
Sun-Spots Digest and Sun-Managers mailing list.

420. sun-wanted.src
:ip-address ''152.2.22.81''
:ip-name ''sun-wais.oit.unc.edu''
:tcp-port 210
:database-name ''sun-wanted''
:maintainer ''wais@calypso.oit.unc.edu''
Archive of comp.sys.sun.wanted newsgroup.

421. sunflash-1990.src
:ip-address ''152.2.22.81''
:ip-name ''sun-wais.oit.unc.edu''
:tcp-port 210
:database-name ''sunflash-1990''
:maintainer ''wais@sun-wais.oit.unc.edu''
1990 issues of The Florida Sunflash - Sun Microsystems.

422. sunflash-1991.src
:ip-address ''152.2.22.81''
:ip-name ''sun-wais.oit.unc.edu''
:tcp-port 210
:database-name ''sunflash-1991''
:maintainer ''wais@sun-wais.oit.unc.edu''
1991 Issues of the Florida Sunflash - Sun Microsystems
Sunflash Journal.

423. sunflash-1992.src
:ip-address ''152.2.22.81''
:ip-name ''sun-wais.oit.unc.edu''
:tcp-port 210
:database-name ''sunflash-1992''
:maintainer ''wais@sun-wais.oit.unc.edu''
1992 Issues of The Florida Sunflash - Sun Microsystems.

424. sunsite-ftp.src
:ip-address ''152.2.22.81''
:ip-name ''sunsite.unc.edu''
:tcp-port 210
:database-name ''SunSITE-ftp''
:maintainer ''ftpkeeper@sunsite.unc.edu''.

This is an index of all the index and readme files found in the anonymous ftp directory of SunSITE.

425. supreme-court.src
:ip-name ''archive.orst.edu''
:tcp-port 9000
:database-name ''supreme-court''
:maintainer ''wais@archive.orst.edu''
US Supreme Court decisions in full text, courtesy of Project Hermes.

426. sustainable-agriculture.src
:ip-address ''152.2.22.81''
:ip-name ''sunSITE.unc.edu''
:tcp-port 210
:database-name ''/home3/wais/sustainable-agriculture''
:maintainer ''root@sunsite.unc.edu''
Files having to do with sustainable agriculture, appropriate technology, rural living, organic farming, gardening, bulbs, seeds, bees, and the like.

427. tantric-new.src
:ip-address ''152.2.22.81''
:ip-name ''sunsite.unc.edu''
:tcp-port 210
:database-name ''/home3/wais/Tantric-News''
:maintainer ''wais@calypso''
The Society for Tantric Studies.

428. tcl-talk.src
:database-name ''tcl-talk''
:ip-name ''wais.brown.edu''
:tcp-port 210
:maintainer ''Andrew__Gilmartin@Brown.EDU''
The Think Class Library discussion list is for those interested in using Symantec's Think C and Think Pascal object-oriented class library for Macintosh.

429. the-scientist.src
:ip-address ''198.49.45.10''
:ip-name ''ds.internic.net''
:tcp-port 210
:database-name ''the-scientist''
:maintainer ''root@ds.internic.net''
The Scientist, a biweekly newspaper for research scientists, and managers in industry, academia, and government. Focuses on life sciences and biotechology.

430. thesaurus.src
:database-name ''roget-thesaurus''
:ip-name ''wais.cic.net''
:tcp-port 210
:maintainer ''emv@cic.net''
Roget's Thesaurus as provided by Project Gutenberg.

431. tms-technical-reports.src
:ip-address ''192.31.181.1''
:ip-name ''quake.think.com''
:tcp-port 210
:database-name ''tmc-technical-reports''
:maintainer ''blaze@think.com''
There exist currently over 200 technical reports available from Thinking Machines. This is an initial sampling of reports.

432. uc-motif-faq.src
:ip-address ''137.92.1.12''
:ip-name ''services.canberra.edu.au''
:tcp-port 210
:database-name ''UC-motif-FAQ''
:maintainer ''root@services''
The files of type dash used in the index were:
/wais-data/motif/motif-FAQ.

433. ucsc__directory__of__servers.src
:ip-address ''128.114.143.4''
:ip-name ''wais.ucsc.edu''
:tcp-port 210
:database-name ''UCSC__directory__of__servers''
:maintainer ''watkins@scilibx.ucsc.edu''
This source includes all wais sources available at the University of California at Santa Cruz (UCSC).

434. uio__publications.src
:ip-address ''129.240.2.46''
:ip-name ''xantos.uio.no''
:tcp-port 2100
:database-name ''UiO__Publications''
:maintainer ''Geir.Pedersen@use.uio.no''
This server holds bibliographic information on some research publications by faculty at the University of Oslo. The formatting of the bibliographic information is rather non-standard.

435. unc-ch-info.src
:database-name ''/app1/gcc/unc-ch-info''
:ip-name ''gibbs.oit.unc.edu''
:tcp-port 210
:maintainer ''fullton@gibbs.oit.unc.edu''
Most of the database for the University of North Carolina at Chapel Hill (UNC-CH) campus-wide information system (CWIS) called INFO is in the database unc-ch-info.

436. unc-directory-of-servers.src
:ip-address ''128.109.157.30''
:ip-name ''wais.oit.unc.edu''
:tcp-port 210
:database-name ''unc-directory-of-servers''
:maintainer ''fullton@samba.oit.unc.edu''
Directory of servers for the UNC Campus.

437. unced-agenda.src
:ip-address ''192.31.181.1''
:ip-name ''quake.think.com''
:tcp-port 210
:database-name ''/proj/wais/db/sources/unced-agenda''
:maintainer ''wais@quake.think.com''
This is the agenda for the United Nations RIO Summit.

438. unc__bbs__info.src
:ip-address ''128.109.157.30''
:ip-name ''wais.oit.unc.edu''
:tcp-port 210
:database-name ''UNC__BBS__Info''
:maintainer ''fullton@samba.oit.unc.edu''
Documents describing services offered on the UNC Extended Bulletin Board Service.

439. unc__staff__phone.src
:ip-address ''152.2.21.2''

:ip-name ''gibbs.oit.unc.edu''
:tcp-port 210
:database-name ''UNC__Staff__Phone''
:maintainer ''paul__jones@unc.edu''
Telephone listings for Staff members of the University of North Carolina at Chapel Hill.

440. unc__student__phone.src
:ip-address ''152.2.21.2''
:ip-name ''gibbs.oit.unc.edu''
:tcp-port 210
:database-name ''UNC__Student__phone''
:maintainer ''paul__jones@unc.edu''
Directory of Students at the University of North Carolina at Chapel Hill also known as phone numbers mail adddresses email white pages listing.

441. unep-grid.src
:ip-address ''152.61.192.112''
:ip-name ''grid2.cr.usgs.gov''
:tcp-port 210
:database-name ''UNEP-GRID''
:maintainer ''van@grid2.cr.usgs.gov''
The Global Resource Information Database (GRID) is a system of cooperating Centres within the United Nations Environment Programme.

442. unimelb-research.src
:ip-address ''128.250.20.3''
:ip-name ''ariel.its.unimelb.EDU.AU''
:tcp-port 210
:database-name ''unimelb-research''
:maintainer ''rvc@ariel.its.unimelb.EDU.AU''
This server holds a copy of the University of Melbourne Research Report 1990.

443. unix-manual.src
:ip-address ''192.31.181.1''
:ip-name ''quake.think.com''
:tcp-port 210
:database-name ''unix-manual''
Unix user manual.

444. unix.faq.src
:ip-address ''128.109.190.3''
:ip-name ''next2.oit.unc.edu''
:tcp-port 210
:database-name ''unix.FAQ''
:maintainer ''root@next2.oit.unc.edu''
Frequently asked questions about Unix.

445. unl-di-reports.src
:ip-address ''192.68.178.17''
:ip-name ''wais.fct.unl.pt''
:tcp-port 210
:database-name ''unl-di-reports''
:maintainer ''archive@fct.unl.pt''
Departamento de Informatica of Universidade Nova de Lisboa. At this time, the file is neither complete nor accurate.

446. untcomputerdoc.src
:ip-address ''129.120.1.42''
:ip-name ''sol.acs.unt.edu''
:tcp-port 210

:database-name ''/usr/local/data/wais/UNTCompDoc''
:maintainer ''billy@unt.edu''
Documents written by Academic Computing Services of the University of North Texas.

447. us-budget-1993.src
:ip-address ''152.2.22.81''
:ip-name ''sunsite.unc.edu''
:tcp-port 210
:database-name ''US-Budget-1993''
:maintainer ''wais@sunsite.unc.edu''
This is a copy of the Proposed United States of America's federal budget for 1993.

448. us-congress-phone-fax.src
:database-name ''/home3/wais/US-Congress-Phone-Fax''
:ip-address ''152.2.22.81''
:ip-name ''sunsite.unc.edu''
:tcp-port 210
:maintainer ''jem@sunsite.unc.edu''
Telephone numbers and Fax numbers for members of the US Senate and House of Representatives.

449. us-gov-programs.src
:ip-address ''192.31.181.1''
:ip-name ''quake.think.com''
:tcp-port 210
:database-name ''US-Gov-Programs''
:maintainer ''wais@quake.think.com''
The files of type cmapp used in the index were: /proj/wais/db/program-abstracts.text.

450. usace-spk-phonebook.src
:ip-address ''130.165.10.12''
:ip-name ''spk41.usace.mil''
:tcp-port 210
:database-name ''USACE.SPK.Phonebook''
:maintainer ''root@spk41.usace.mil''
This is the district phone book for the US Army Corps of Engineers, Sacramento District.

451. usda-csrs-pwd.src
:ip-address ''192.73.224.111''
:ip-name ''eos.esusda.gov''
:tcp-port 210
:database-name ''usda-csrs-pwd''
:maintainer ''sconn@esusda.gov''
US Department of Agriculture Cooperative State Research Service Directory of Professional Workers in State Agricultural Experiment Stations and Other Cooperating Institutions.

452. usda-rrdb.src
:ip-address ''192.72.224.100''
:ip-name ''es-cit.esusda.gov''
:tcp-port 210
:database-name ''rrdb''
:maintainer ''wais@es-cit.esusda.gov''
The Research Results Database (RRDB) brings together short summaries of recent research results from the USDA's Agricultural Research Service (ARS) and Economic Research Service (ERS).

453. usdacris.src
:ip-address ''128.167.254.179''

:ip-name ''nic.sura.net''
:tcp-port 210
:database-name ''usdacris''
:maintainer ''info@sura.net''
The Current Research Information System (CRIS), established by the U.S. Department of Agriculture (USDA), serves as the USDA documentation and reporting system for publicly supported agricultural, food and nutrition, and forestry research in the United States.

454. usenet-addresses.src
:ip-address ''18.70.0.224''
:ip-name ''rtfm.mit.edu''
:tcp-port 210
:maintainer ''jik@gza.com''
:database-name ''usenet-addresses''
This database contains one-line entries consisting of names and email addresses culled from the Reply-To or From lines of Usenet Usenet postings, as well as a last-seen date associated with each address.

455. usenet-cookbook.src
:ip-address ''131.239.2.100''
:ip-name ''cmns-moon.think.com''
:tcp-port 210
:database-name ''WWP''
:maintainer ''bug-public@think.com''
The USENET Cookbook. Copyright 1991 USENET Community Trust.

456. usenet.src
:ip-address ''18.70.0.224''
:ip-name ''rtfm.mit.edu''
:tcp-port 210
:maintainer ''jik@gza.com''
:database-name ''usenet''
This database contains periodic informational postings (including FAQ postings) from various Usenet newsgroups.

457. ut-research-expertise.src
:ip-address ''129.106.30.1''
:ip-name ''oac.hsc.uth.tmc.edu''
:tcp-port 210
:database-name ''ut_core''
:maintainer ''root@oac.hsc.uth.tmc.edu''
UT CORE - University of Texas Catalog of Research Expertise. The UT_CORE source catalogs the research interests and expertise of the faculty of the University of Texas Health Science Center at Houston.

458. utsun.s.u-tokyo.ac.jp.src
:database-name ''archives/utsun.s.u-tokyo.ac.jp''
:ip-name ''wais.cic.net''
:tcp-port 210
:maintainer ''emv@cic.net''
utsun.s.u-tokyo.ac.jp is a major Japanese anonymous FTP site. It holds archives of the fj. * newsgroups, information about networks in Japan, and a lot of other useful things.

459. uumap.src
:database-name ''uumap''
:ip-name ''wais.cic.net''
:tcp-port 210
:maintainer ''emv@cic.net''

The UUCP mapping project keeps track of UUCP and Usenet sites around the world. This source has the full set of maps.

460. uunet.src
:database-name   "uunet"
:ip-name   "wais.cic.net"
:tcp-port   210
:maintainer   "emv@cic.net"
The directory listing of uunet.uu.net, updated nightly.

461. uxc.cso.uiuc.edu.src
:database-name   "archives/uxc.cso.uiuc.edu"
:ip-name   "wais.cic.net"
:tcp-port   210
:maintainer   "emv@cic.net"
Recursive directory listing of uxc.cso.uiuc.edu.

462. vpiej-l.src
:ip-name   "borg.lib.vt.edu"
:tcp-port   210
:database-name   "/LocalLibrary/WAIS/vpiej-l/vpiej-l"
VPIEJ-L is a discussion list for electronic publishing issues, especially those related to Scholarly Electronic Journals. Topics for discussion include SGML, PostScript, and other e-journal formats; as well as software and hardware considerations for creation of, storage, and access to e-journals.

463. wais-discussion-archives.src
:ip-address   "192.31.181.1"
:ip-name   "quake.think.com"
:tcp-port   210
:database-name   "wais-discussion-archives"
:maintainer   "wais@quake.think.com"
This source provides access to the wais-discussion mailing list's archives.

464. wais-docs.src
:ip-address   "192.31.181.1"
:ip-name   "quake.think.com"
:tcp-port   210
:database-name   "wais-docs"
This is a database containing the text of all the current documentation provided in the WAIS distribution.

465. wais-talk-archives.src
:ip-address   "192.31.181.1"
:ip-name   "quake.think.com"
:tcp-port   210
:database-name   "wais-talk-archives"
:maintainer   "wais@quake.think.com"
The files of type mail used in the index were: /usr/lib/archives/alt-wais-archive; /usr/lib/archives/wais-talk-incoming.

466. water-quality.src
:ip-address   "128.46.157.183"
:ip-name   "hermes.ecn.purdue.edu"
:tcp-port   6001
:database-name   "/home/hermes/cems/water_quality/wais-sources/water-quality"
:maintainer   "cems@ecn.purdue.edu"
Educational materials on water quality assessment, maintenance, and improvement in the United States prepared by the Cooperative Extension System.

467. weather.src
:ip-address   "192.31.181.1"
:ip-name   "quake.think.com"
:tcp-port   210
:database-name   "weather"
:maintainer   "weather-server@quake.think.com"
This is the WEATHER server, brought to you courtesy of the WAIS folks from Thinking Machines, and the weather folks at VMD.CSO.UIUC.EDU and the University of Michigan.

468. welsh.src
:database-name   "/home3/wais/Welsh"
:ip-address   "152.2.22.81"
:ip-name   "sunsite.unc.edu"
:tcp-port   210
This is a WAIS database of the Welsh-l mailing list. The discussion on this list deals with questions concerning Wales and the Welsh language. Much of the discussion is in Welsh.

469. white-house-papers.src
:database-name   "/home3/wais/White-House-Papers"
:ip-address   "152.2.22.81"
:ip-name   "sunsite.unc.edu"
:tcp-port   210
:maintainer   "pjones@sunsite.unc.edu"
These are the White House Press Briefings and other postings dealing with William Jefferson Clinton and Albert Gore as well as members of the President's Cabinet and the first lady Hillary Rodham Clinton, Chelsea, Socks, and others in Washington DC.

470. winsock.src
:ip-address   "152.2.22.81"
:ip-name   "sunsite.unc.edu"
:tcp-port   210
:database-name   "winsock"
:maintainer   "ses@sunsite.unc.edu"
This database contains the complete archives of the windows sockets (winsock) mailing list.

471. world-factbook.src
:ip-address   "131.239.2.100"
:ip-name   "cmns-moon.think.com"
:tcp-port   210
:database-name   "CIA"
:maintainer   "bug-public@think.com"
Factbook by the CIA which contains a good description of every country. The entry for WORLD is also particularly good.

472. world-factbook92.src
:ip-address   "129.100.2.12"
:ip-name   "julian.uwo.ca"
:tcp-port   210
:database-name   "world-factbook92"
:maintainer   "peter@julian.uwo.ca"
CIA World Factbook 1992 (published January 1993) slightly modified from Project Gutenberg sources for WAIS indexing.

473. world91a.src
:ip-address   "192.31.181.1"
:ip-name   "quake.think.com"
:tcp-port   210
:database-name   "/proj/wais/db/sources/world91a"
:maintainer   "jonathan@quake.think.com"
The World Factbook is produced annually by the Central Intelli-

gence Agency for the use of United States Government officials, and the style, format, coverage, and content are designed to meet their specific requirements.

474. wuarchive.src
:database-name ''wuarchive''
:ip-name ''wais.cic.net''
:tcp-port 210
:maintainer ''emv@cic.net''
The directory listing of wuarchive.wustl.edu, updated nightly.

475. x.500.working-group.src
:ip-address ''35.212.224.3''
:ip-name ''wais.cic.net''
:tcp-port 210
:database-name ''disi-catalog''
:maintainer ''emv@cic.net''
This source is derived from the Directory Information Servers Infrastructure Working Group draft 'A Catalog of Available X.500 Implementations', dated November 1991.

476. xgks.src
:ip-address ''128.117.140.3''
:ip-name ''wais.unidata.ucar.edu''
:tcp-port 210
:database-name ''xgks''
:maintainer ''support@unidata.ucar.edu''
This is the mailing list archive for the xgks@unidata.ucar.edu mailing list, containing all the postings since the mailing list was created.

477. zipcodes.src
:ip-address ''192.31.181.1''
:ip-name ''quake.think.com''
:tcp-port 210
:database-name ''/proj/wais/db/sources/zipcodes''
:maintainer ''jonathan@quake.think.com''
WAIS index of USA Zip Code database.

Appendix: List Review Service

Subjecting discussion lists to notice, analysis, and review is an obvious step in developing and legitimizing the efforts of list moderators and editors, whether their lists are on mainstream topics or otherwise. Raleigh Muns of the University of Missouri, St. Louis, Libraries has for the past several years been scrutinizing selected discussion lists, describing their contents, analyzing the message traffic they generate, and otherwise opening up for inspection lists in a variety of subject disciplines that the too-busy Internet user might otherwise have overlooked. His List Review Service is published periodically by The University of Missouri, St. Louis, Libraries. To subscribe to the LIST REVIEW SERVICE send an e-mail message with blank subject line to: LISTSERV@UMSLVMA (Bitnet) or LISTSERV@UMSLVMA.UMSL.EDU (Internet). Message should consist solely of:
SUBSCRIBE LSTREV-L your_name

We are grateful for the editor's permission to reprint his first 25 reviews here. (Copying is permitted for noncommercial use by computerized bulletin board/conference systems, individual scholars, and libraries. Libraries are authorized to add these reviews to their collections at no cost. This message must appear on copied material. All commercial use requires permission. Opinions expressed are solely those of the reviewer and do not represent the views of the University of Missouri, St. Louis. Copyright, Raleigh C. Muns (Reference Librarian), Thomas Jefferson Library, University of Missouri, St. Louis, 8001 Natural Bridge Road, St. Louis, MO 63121 (ph:(314) 553-5059); BITNET: SRCMUNS@UMSLVMA; Internet: SRCMUNS@UMSLVMA.UMSL.EDU.

AFROAM-L (Critical Issues in African American Life and Culture)

LOCATION: AFROAM-L@HARVARDA (Bitnet)
LISTOWNER: Lee D. Baker LDBAKER@HARVARDA
No. of Listserv Subscribers: 190 in 4 countries
REVIEW: Boy did I squirm while reading AFROAM-L. By trade I am a "white male techie," thus, for me, perusing AFROAM-L was like having my feet held very close to some live coals. There's nothing like being inundated with intellectually dense dialogue between African Americans (AA's to adopt the list's own shorthand) to kick all those biases you thought you never had right in the teeth. In other words, reading this list was a blast! Postings on this list included: Issues of the *Somalia News Update* (ISSN 1103-1999). The unabashed diatribes, news stories, and press releases of the "New Liberation News Service" (e-addresses listed were nlns@igc.apc.org and psloh@garnet.berkeley.edu). The "feel" of NLNS is similar to UPI and AP. Dialogue, dialogue, oh wondrous dialogue! People actually talk to each other on AFROAM-L. One heated discussion chewed over the pros and cons of male-only African American schools. Another thread covered the role of the AA community with regards to gays in the military. A third mulled over the environmental rape of poor, predominantly black, communities in the United States. For this latter, Aaron Laramore (alaramor@magnus.acs.ohio-state.edu) suggested Jonathan Kozoll's *Savage Inequalities* (New York: Crown Pub., c1991)) as a good work describing the "environmental racism" applied to, for example, East St. Louis (20 minutes from my office). Having been castigated on an Internet list at one time for bitching about the "Capitalist Monolith" and its strangling effect on certain classes of information, I offer this list as a good place to get an alternative point of view. Americans, white and otherwise, will find a lot of the issues discussed familiar Note: the subjects of the discussions may be familiar, but if you're not tuned in to African American culture, the results will probably not be. Don't stereotype this list in advance. Many of the issues as discussed transcend terms like "left" and "right". Only a handful of non-US accounts were listed as subscribing to this list, which is too bad. I can see some usefulness of AFROAM-L for Europeans attempting to understand the new multi-culturalism of their own countries. We Americans may be all screwed up, but since we've had a lot of practice at it, others might as well take our successes and mistakes to heart. The struggle continues... Oh, yeah. Everyone's the same color in cyberspace. -R. Muns

SYNOPSIS OF ONE WEEK'S ACTIVITY:
Name of List Reviewed: AFROAM-L
Period Monitored: 03 APR 1992 - 09 APR 1993
No. Messages Period Monitored: 96
No. Queries Posted: 05 (05 % of total activity)
No. Non-queries Posted: 91 (95 % of total activity)
Lines Sent (w/o headers): 3591 (app. 156 screens of 23 lines)
Msgs. Posted Last 01 Months: N/A
Searchable Archives: No

SUGGESTED USES FOR LIST:
1) Outstanding resource for ANY ethnic studies program.
2) Says what it does, does what it says - discuss critical issues in African American life and culture.
3) Awareness tool for melanin-deprived individuals.

SUBSCRIPTION INFORMATION :
To subscribe to AFROAM-L, send an e-mail message with blank

subject line to: LISTSERV@HARVARDA (Bitnet address)
Message should consist solely of: SUBSCRIBE AFROAM-L your_name

ANTHRO-L (General Anthropology)

LOCATION: LISTSERV@UBVM (Bitnet)
LISTOWNER: Ezra Zubrow, Hugh Jarvis ANTOWN-ER@UBVM
NUMBER OF SUBSCRIBERS: 409 users in 24 countries
REVIEW: ANTHRO-L, self-described as a "General Anthropology Bulletin Board," focused primarily on issues of an administrative nature during the week monitored. Sample topics were Governmental oversight of academic research. The scheduled demise of the anthropology department at San Diego State University. Queries and answers about the heads of various anthropology departments. More than half of the text received came from a single message via the Asia Watch people regarding the abuse of East Timorese laborers by the Indonesian government. The 608 lines of text supplied chronology, names, and background. The message also contained three appendices consisting of source documents (e.g., statements, petitions, signatories) from Timorese involved in the labor abuse. Such a message is the sort to file away to impress non-net colleagues as to the quality of information available in the aether. Nonetheless, the overall tone of the list failed to arouse my prurient interest. I explored the indices of the list's archives in order to expand my knowledge about the list's subject scope. (Like a restaurant reviewer, I'm aware of the methodological pitfalls in assuming that one bad pizza is representative of the menu each and every day.) Pepperoni and anchovies abound in ANTHRO-L as I found, and explored, in the list's archives the following topics: Excision & Cliterodectomy Liklik tok Pidgin vs. Doodspeak (aka cyberspeak, aka ...) Deviance Syllabus There's nothing like eavesdropping on correspondence on fascinating topics amongst experts in their field to recharge one's fascination with LISTSERVs! Some of the Deviance Syllabus reading list has already been incorporated into my recreational reading plans for the summer. Speaking tentatively as a non-anthropologist, ANTHRO-L looks like a good bet for the unconnected professional to take the computer net-work plunge. Speaking confidently as an information junky, this list is a very, very good read. -R. Muns
SYNOPSIS OF ONE WEEK'S ACTIVITY:
Period Monitored: 13 MAY 92 - 19 MAY 92 (inclusive)
No. Messages Week Monitored: 19
No. Queries Posted: 03 (16 % of total activity)
No. Non-queries Posted: 16 (84 % of total activity)
Lines Sent (w/o headers): 1019 (app. 44 screens of 23 lines)
Note: one message 608 lines long Msgs. Posted Prev. 3 Months: 862 Searchable Archives: Yes
SUGGESTED USES FOR LIST :
1) Eclectic education for undergraduate anthropology students.
2) Contact tool for academic anthropologists.

3) Anthropology problem solving tool (e.g., "Where is ...")
4) Entertainment.
BITNET SUBSCRIPTION INFORMATION:
Send an e-mail message with blank subject line to: LISTSERV@UBVM Message should consist solely of: SUBSCRIBE ANTHRO-L your_name

CD-ROMLAN

LOCATION: LISTSERV@IDBSU.BITNET Boise State Univ., Boise, ID 83725
OWNER OR EDITOR: Dan Lester (ALILESTE@IDBSU.BITNET)
NUMBER OF SUBSCRIBERS: 826 users in 23 countries
REVIEW: These two lists complement each other well (hence this dual review). CDROMLAN supplies detailed technical answers to specific questions about CDROM technology, primarily within Local Area Networks, while CDROM-L is more friendly to the novice. The former dealt more readily with specific problems and specific applications while the latter was excellent at introducing concepts and giving leads to both literature and products. While monitoring both lists simultaneously it was easy to forget which list was active. It's not that there aren't any differences (e.g., see data above) but that taken together a seemingly comprehensive "virtual" list on CD-ROM technology is being produced. Sample discussions on CDROMLAN involved analysis of specific LAN configurations, and a free-for-all on the copyright legality of transferring CD-ROM based data to a hard drive for users in a network to access. Nuggets from CDROM-L contained postings by the list owner (Richard Hintz) outlining the current state of CD-ROM technology, and a nifty lead on the cheapest CD-ROM drive I've heard of yet (the NEC CDR-80 for $229 from DAK).
SYNOPSIS OF ONE WEEK'S ACTIVITY:
Period Monitored: 19 NOV 91 - 25 NOV 91 (inclusive)
Messages Posted: 48
Number of Queries Posted: 19 (40 % of total activity)
Number of Responses Posted: 29 (60 % of total activity)
Lines Sent (w/ headers): 1694 (app. 74 screens of 23 lines)
Lines Sent (w/o headers): 1119 (app. 49 screens of 23 lines)
Searchable Archives: Yes
SUGGESTED USES FOR LIST:
1) Trouble shooting problems with current systems. CDROMLAN was particularly strong in this area.
2) Leads on potential problems and advantages with existing products (both lists).
3) Market analysis by vendors of CD-ROM technology. Subscribers are free with opinions on what's good, what's not, and what they would like to see.
SUBSCRIPTION INFORMATION:
Send an e-mail message with blank subject line to: For CDROMLAN For CDROM-L LISTSERV@IDBSU.BITNET LISTSERV@UCCVMA.BITNET Message should consist solely of: SUBSCRIBE CDROMLAN your_name

COM-SERVE

LOCATION: COMSERVE@RPIEC (Bitnet) COM-SERVE@VM.ECS.RPI.EDU (Internet)
LISTOWNER: Timothy Stephen STEPHEN@RPIECS (Bitnet)
Teresa Harrison HARRISON@RPIECS (Bitnet)
NUMBER OF SUBSCRIBERS: 320
REVIEW: In Italy, "ferragosto" refers to the month of August when the entire population simultaneously goes on vacation. Computer network discussion lists can be italian in this manner, thus this review is less about the Comserve "Hotline" Mass-Comm, and its paltry August activities, than of Comserve itself. The non-profit Communication Institute for Online Study (CIOS) has set up a LISTSERV-like server which administers, among other things, Hotlines, or what most readers of this review would recognize as LISTSERV discussion groups (e.g., LIBREF-L). Comserve Hotlines cover various facets of the field of communications studies, of which MassComm (Mass Communications) is but one. This segmentation into subfields of communications studies effectively cuts down on the noise common in discussion lists of more general natures. Though "Rhetoric" and "Mass Communications" overlap, discussions specific to those areas tend to be cleaner than would happen in a monolithic communications studies group. Don't let the Comserve Octopus scare you. 1. You can send an e-mail message to SUPPORT@RPIECS (Bitnet) or SUPPORT@RPIECS.VM.ECS.RPI.EDU (Internet) asking for help from humans at the outset. 2. You can send the message SHOW HOTLINES to COMSERVE@RPIECS (Bitnet) or COM-SERVE@RPIECS.VM.ECS.RPI.EDU (Internet) to get both a list of Hotlines as well as instructions on how to access them. You can send lots of messages and get lots of help. In practice, I've found that Comserve tends to deliver pretty good end-user documentation automatically to clients trying out a section of the service for the first time. In addition to the Hotlines, Comserve offers database searching of communications journals, a large body of curriculum oriented files (LOTS of bibliographies), a nice NewBooks service notifying subscribers of new publications in the field, and much, much more. Last and MOST DEFINITELY NOT LEAST: If your computer account is on a CMS or VAX machine you can get a menu shell called EASYCOM which makes all of the "where-did-I-put-that-list-of-hotlines-and-just-who-do-I-send-this-request-to-and-by-the-way-what's-the-syntax-for-the-message?" questions disappear. Non-VAXen or CMSters will face nothing worse than what they currently must deal with in the LISTSERV environment. -R. Muns
SYNOPSIS OF ONE WEEK'S ACTIVITY:
Period Monitored: 29 JUL 1992 - 03 SEP 1992 No.
Messages Period Monitored: 17
No. Queries Posted: 12 (70 % of total activity)
No. Non-queries Posted: 05 (30 % of total activity)
Lines Sent (w/o headers): 458 (app. 20 screens of 23 lines)
Msgs. Posted Last 01 Months: 17 Searchable Archives: Yes

SUGGESTED USES FOR LIST:
1) Collection development (see COMSERVE's NewBooks option)
2) Curriculum development (bibliographies, new resources)
3) The usual connections and networking opportunities
SUBSCRIPTION INFORMATION:
Send an e-mail message with blank subject line (or Bitnet TELL) to: COMSERVE@RPIECS (Bitnet address) or COM-SERVE@RPIECS.VM.ECS.RPI.EDU (Internet address) Message should consist solely of: JOIN MASSCOMM your_name

CSE

LOCATION: CSEMLIST@HASARA11
LISTOWNER: Hans M. Amman A608HANS@HASARA11 (Bitnet)
NO. OF LISTSERV SUBSCRIBERS: 198
REVIEW: This e-conference of the Society of Computational Economics aims to provide an online information service for researchers in the field of Computer Science in Economics and Management Science, as well as being an online information service for researchers in the field of "Computational methods in Economics and Econometrics." The list is intended as a bulletin board for exchanging information between researchers. Furthermore, the list gives you an opportunity to raise questions to the subscribers of the list regarding issues or subjects of needed discussions or various viewpoints. I did not receive a lot of postings from this list during the period monitored. The only thing I can assess from this list is that it is a useful tool to those who are interested in the application of computer technology in the field of Economics and Statistics. - P. Wong (Wong is a student in Howard Frederick's "Introduction to NGO Computing" at the University of California, Irvine. Frederick's Internet e-mail address is research@igc.apc.org)
SYNOPSIS OF ONE WEEK'S ACTIVITY:
Period Monitored: 08 MAR 1993 - 24 MAR 1993 No. Messages Period Monitored: 10
No. Queries Posted: 3 (30% of total activity)
No. Non-queries Posted: 7 (70% of total activity)
Searchable Archives: Yes
SUGGESTED USES FOR LIST:
1) Use as an information discussion among researchers in this field.
2) Great place to post questions about issues in this area.
3) Perfect place for a peek into the latest discovery or research in this field.
SUBSCRIPTION INFORMATION:
Send an e-mail with blank subject line to:
LISTSERV@HASARA11 (Bitnet) Message should consist solely of: SUBSCRIBE CSEMLIST firstname lastname

DERRIDA

LOCATION: DERRIDA@CFRVM (Bitnet)
LISTOWNER: David Erben DQFACAA@CFRVM (Bitnet)
NO. OF LISTSERV SUBSCRIBERS: 258 in 20 countries (not one from France!)
REVIEW: When I lived in Los Angeles, cruising among the literati, I was often assailed with the dropped name of Jacques Derrida and his bailiwick, deconstruction. By reviewing the list, DERRIDA, I've at long last had the opportunity to get to the meat behind the Sturm und Drang - and all without having to read a word of Derrida himself! (I confess that I often find myself drawn to the subjects of the list I review after the fact, as is the case here.) Aside from being a comment on the development of my own intellectual facade, this should also be a positive comment on the ongoing dialogue regarding Jacques Derrida taking place on this list. Being ready to discredit a bunch of pompous intellectuals, I instead found legitimate philosophical discourse taking place, and had to immediately discredit my surly predisposition. This list is an Internet classic in that it transparently uses the network medium to explore a rich an¹ complex area of discourse (i.e., the "philosophical, literary, and political importance of French philosopher, Jacques Derrida and deconstruction"). I can unabashedly call this an online scholarly (underline "scholarly") discussion group. The majority of the messages these past two weeks have been about the relationship between writing, meaning, and violence. The layered discussion, which is still evolving on this subject, if followed assiduously is fascinating. I followed three threads: 1) Derrida and phenomenology (is he, or isn't he?), 2) the use of the word "violence" in regards to text, politics, and Derrida, and 3) Derrida's defense of intellectual property rights in the courts and how that affects perceptions of him and his philosophy. I doubt that the range of information and interpretation evidenced by these examples could be generated by an individual. This is not light reading. Prepare to think. -R. Muns
SYNOPSIS OF ACTIVITY:
Period Monitored: 09 MAR 1993 - 22 MAR 1993
No. Messages Period Monitored: 39
No. Queries Posted: 06 (15 % of total activity)
No. Non-queries Posted: 33 (85 % of total activity)
Lines Sent (w/o headers): 1111 (app. 48 screens of 23 lines)
Msgs. Posted During 1993: 264 (current rate = app. 3 msgs/day)
Searchable Archives: Yes
SUGGESTED USES FOR LIST:
1) Get to know Derrida, up close and personal.
2) Use as a paradigm for scholarly online discussions.
3) Improve your word power.
SUBSCRIPTION INFORMATION:
Send an e-mail message with blank subject line to:
LISTSERV@CFRVM (Bitnet address)
LISTSERV@CFRVM.BITNET (Internet address) Message should consist solely of: SUBSCRIBE DERRIDA your_name

Dead Teachers Society

LOCATION: LISTSERV@IUBVM (Bitnet)
LISTOWNER: Scott Anderson BITNET: SOANERS@IUBVM
NUMBER OF SUBSCRIBERS: 109 users in 8 countries 90% USA
REVIEW: A feeling of warm fuzziness stole over me as I monitored this low- key list with the cute name. This is not a list for the intellectual, research-oriented, high-powered network guru. Most Internet/BITNET activity is heavily slanted towards higher education academics and (usually) technically oriented professionals. This list, however, is the ONLY list so far where I have encountered actual high school teachers (what I like to refer to as "real-world types"). This is not to say that the participants are unintellectual, but the environment, the very FEEL of the list, is more relaxed than the academic lists I have encountered to date. The most interesting message posted was from Anne Pemberton of Nottoway High School, Nottoway, VA (APEMBERT@VDOE386.VAK12ED.EDU) who has secured computer network access for her students. She is seeking expert e-correspondents (not "keypals" as she puts it) to be intellectual resources for students in the class. This crack in the ivory tower ghetto of most computer network activity holds fascinating promise and, hopefully, is a portent of even more change in network activity (as if there isn't currently enough volatility in cyberspace!).

As a subscriber, one becomes only "an associate member of the Society of Dead Teachers." By subscribing to the list, you will receive information on how to become a full member. -R. Muns
SYNOPSIS OF ONE WEEK'S ACTIVITY:
Period Monitored: 18 FEB 92 - 24 FEB 92 (inclusive)
Messages Posted: 14
Number of Queries Posted: 03 (21 % of total activity)
Number of Non-queries Posted: 11 (89 % of total activity)
Lines Sent (w/o headers): 201 (app. 9 screens of 23 lines)
Searchable Archives: Yes
SUGGESTED USES FOR LIST:
1) Identify uses for Internet/BITNET in secondary schools.
2) Contact tool for education practitioners.
3) Contact tool for high school students.
4) Empathic environment for shy LISTSERV subscribers.
BITNET SUBSCRIPTION INFORMATION:
Send an e-mail message with blank subject line to: LISTSERV@IUBVM Message should consist solely of: SUBSCRIBE DTS-L your_name

EDPOLYAN

LOCATION: EDPOLYAN@ASUACAD (Bitnet)
LISTOWNER: Gene V. Glass ATGVG@ASUACAD (Bitnet)
NO. OF LISTSERV SUBSCRIBERS: 467 in 13 countries
REVIEW: EDPOLYAN seamlessly mixes the contributions of K-12 instructors and administrators with university level policy

wonks. Postings are terse, dry, and to the point (definitely a compliment). The period in which I monitored EDPOLYAN showed an increase in activity primarily due to the national elections. The rumor mill for Bill Clinton's Secretary of Education frequently mentioned the University of Wisconsin's Chancellor, Donna Shalala (you heard it here second). Several contributors also took it upon themselves to unilaterally post to the list election results from their home states relating to education issues (e.g., Colorado voted against a 1% sales tax increase in support of education). Apparently unmoderated, the group's message stream nonetheless exhibits characteristics of moderated lists in its terseness and ability to maintain discussions relevant to the topic of education. Don't expect entertainment here; do expect utility. EDPOLYAN is one of those rare discussion groups that is exactly what it purports to be. -R. Muns

SYNOPSIS OF ONE WEEK'S ACTIVITY:

Period Monitored: 01 NOV 1992 - 07 NOV 1992

No. Messages Period Monitored: 34

No. Queries Posted: 09 (26 % of total activity)

No. Non-queries Posted: 25 (74 % of total activity)

Lines Sent (w/o headers): 633 (app. 28 screens of 23 lines)

Msgs. Posted Last 01 Months: 64

Searchable Archives: Yes

SUGGESTED USES FOR LIST:

1) Request information about educational institution policies.

2) Explore issues common to different levels of the education hierarchy.

3) Connect with real, practicing educators.

SUBSCRIPTION INFORMATION:

Send an e-mail message with blank subject line to: LISTSERV@ASUACAD (Bitnet address) Message should consist solely of: SUBSCRIBE EDPOLYAN your_name

EQUINE-L (Horse Fanciers)

LOCATION: LISTSERV@PCCVM (Bitnet)

LISTOWNER: W. K. 'Bill' Gorman

BJ496@CLEVELAND.FREENET.EDU

NUMBER OF SUBSCRIBERS: 165 users in 9 countries

REVIEW: "He doth nothing but talk of his horse." -Shakespeare, THE MERCHANT OF VENICE, Act I, Scene ii, Line 43 EQUINE-L is NOT an academic discussion list. A list subscriber can always find things of value in any ongoing electronic discussion, but non-equinophiles will find little of interest by subscribing to a very talkative EQUINE-L. Discourse is extremely civilized and well written. Information ranging from lengthy messages about endurance training, selecting the best horse magazines, or where to send your contributions to save "the Lippizaner of Yugoslavia" are written for true horse fanciers. Not surprising, a large number of messages were posted regarding the lack of coverage of equestrian events in the Olympics, as well as an excellent cooperative effort by subscribers to share what little information was available. Being a regular subscriber to several lists which regularly chew on the problem of intellectual rights in the electronic

universe, I realized I wasn't in Kansas anymore when several messages offering to tape and share the Olympic triplecasts went unchallenged. If you are not a horse fancier (or a social scientist interested in plumbing this particular cyberspace tribe) you will serve neither yourself nor the list by subscribing. The introductory material that subscribers receive should be read carefully before posting any messages. -R. Muns

SYNOPSIS OF ONE WEEK'S ACTIVITY:

Period Monitored: 25 JUL 92 - 31 JUL 92 (inclusive)

No. Messages Week Monitored: 80

No. Queries Posted: 24 (30 % of total activity)

No. Non-queries Posted: 56 (70 % of total activity)

Lines Sent (w/o headers): 1658 (app. 72 screens of 23 lines)

Msgs. Posted Last 01 Months: 405

Searchable Archives: Ye

SUGGESTED USES FOR LIST :

1) Find riding partners.

2) Discuss horse care.

3) Trade training tips.

SUBSCRIPTION INFORMATION:

Send an e-mail message with blank subject line to: LISTSERV@PCCVM (Bitnet address) Message should consist solely of: SUBSCRIBE EQUINE-L your_name

FEDTAX-L

REVIEW: Anyone who would seriously take tax advice from a public forum deserves what they get. This list is not a substitute for a tax specialist. That mandatory caveat given, the range of freely dispensed tax advice tendered on FEDTAX-L is extensive. Most questions, and their subsequent responses, involve esoteric interpretations of specific federal tax situations. Subjects covered during the week monitored included avoiding inheritance taxes, claiming tips, the ubiquitous capital gains distribution problems, and a rousing (and still continuing) sequence of messages pointing out that married people pay more in taxes to the IRS than unwed partners pay. A message from Colleen Wirth (WIRTHC@PORTNOY.SDSC.EDU) on 25 OCT 1991 summed up the list's responses to the "married vs. single" topic thus: married partners, where both work, pay between $800 and $2000 per year more than do single partners; over a 20 year marriage, an average of an extra $28,000 is thus given to the IRS (an organization for which an almost universal disgust is unsurprisingly evinced throughout the postings on the list).

SUGGESTED USES FOR LIST:

1) Instructors of tax courses could monitor FEDTAX-L in order to develop real world questions for students to tackle. Issues and problems too new to be well covered by the tax literature are regularly discussed.

2) Due to the high response rate to queries, FEDTAX-L is a good list for floating your own thorny tax questions. Don't take the advice, but use the information as a stepping-stone for further research. Expect answers.

3) The list has high entertainment value as libertarians and career capitalists tee off on Uncle Sam. The U.S. Government's tax policies and the IRS are regularly slammed by people who seem to know what they're talking about. Nothing may change but you might feel better!

SUBSCRIPTION INFORMATION:

Send an e-mail message with blank subject line to: LISTSERV@SHSU.EDU   Message should consist solely of: SUBSCRIBE FEDTAX-L your_name

FWAKE-L

LOCATION: FWAKE-L@IRLEARN (Bitnet

LISTOWNER: Michael O'Kelly MOKELLY@IRLEARN (Bitnet) No. of Listserv Subscribers: 108 in 9 countries

REVIEW: "His writing is not about something. It is the thing itself." - Samuel Beckett (1906-1989) of James Joyce   Hard core (HARD CORE!!!) scholarship. The byzantine analysis by the _Finnegan's_Wake_ folk becomes transparent in this dense, high-level, incredibly thorough and ongoing discussion of the Joyce opus. I have only read Joyce's _Dubliners_ and don't consider myself an expert. So, as an outsider reading these messages I found myself to be mystified, curious, frustrated, and amused. I felt like I'd walked into a graduate level course totally unprepared. Luckily, I realized I wasn't really "there" and just sat back and enjoyed the discussion, fully expecting blows to eventually be exchanged over the hypothetical placement of a comma. No such luck (yet). Contributor Bill Cadbury (BCADBURY@OREGON.BITNET) posted a number of essays that could have been lectures in an ongoing course. Without contacting him, he may actually have been teaching a course via the list. His, and others, postings tended to be lengthy and wordy, but not fatty. Complex works sometimes require complex analysis. FWAKE-L: Rabid, yes. Vapid, no. Not for the stupid. -R. Muns

SYNOPSIS OF TWO WEEK'S ACTIVITY:

Period Monitored: 01 NOV 1992 - 14 NOV 1992

No. Messages Period Monitored: 16

No. Queries Posted: 02 (12 % of total activity)

No. Non-queries Posted: 14 (88 % of total activity)

Lines Sent (w/o headers): 1640 (app. 71 screens of 23 lines)

Msgs. Posted Last 02 Months: 85

Searchable Archives: Yes

SUGGESTED USES FOR LIST:

1) Print out and pass on messages to those humanist scholars who consider computers to be irrelevant to their pursuits, thus convincing them otherwise.

2) Indispensable tool for any Joyce scholar.

3) Impress people at parties.

SUBSCRIPTION INFORMATION:

Send an e-mail message with blank subject line to: LISTSERV@IRLEARN (Bitnet address) Message should consist solely of: SUBSCRIBE FWAKE-L your_name

GOVDOC-L

LOCATION: LISTSERV@PSUVM.BITNET Pennsylvania State University

MODERATOR: Duncan Aldritch (DUNCAN@EQUINOX.UNR.EDU)

REVIEW: Monitoring GOVDOC-L makes me think of a line in Stanley Kubrick's FULL METAL JACKET: "We are living in a world of doo-doo" (Quote Bowdlerized by editor). There is an awful lot wrong with the U.S. Government's information dissemination activities and this fascinating list is a way to peek in on the doings. More important, any government documents librarian currently not monitoring this list is probably enjoying ignorant bliss. Contributors regularly identify problems in the dissemination procedures of the Government Printing Office (e.g., claiming of unreceived GPO microfiche is an apparent joke), in the documents themselves (e.g., zero percent crime in Minneapolis is due to late reporting), and in the systems devised to catalog and disseminate the rich resources in the field of government information. The most impressive thing upon monitoring the list was the high level of cooperation among the participants. The feeling that "We are living in a world of doo- doo" is counterbalanced by the attitude of "We must all hang together or we shall all hang separately." Participants regularly post receipt of duplicate items available on a first come basis so that others may avoid the less responsive Federal bureaucracy. This biased review does not attempt to explain WHY things seem to be in disarray at the GPO (for example), it is merely a description of the situation as seen by monitoring this list.

SYNOPSIS OF LIST ACTIVITY

Number of Subscribers: 724 users in 8 countries

Period Monitored: 03 DEC 91 - 09 DEC 91 (inclusive)

Messages Posted: 47

Number of Queries Posted: 20 (43 % of total activity)

Number of Non-queries Posted: 27 (57 % of total activity)

Lines Sent (w/ headers): 1902 (app. 83 screens of 23 lines)

Lines Sent (w/o headers): 962 (app. 42 screens of 23 lines)

Searchable Archives: Yes

SUGGESTED USES FOR LIST:

1) Identify current problem areas in government documents librarianship.

 2) Identify missing or desired items in a collection, available as duplicates received by others.

3) Problem solving: e.g., "Where can I get a list of coloring books distributed by the GPO?"

4) Keep abreast of the latest products being disseminated by the government; concurrently, the procedures used to disseminate products.

SUBSCRIPTION INFORMATION:

Send an e-mail message with blank subject line to: LISTSERV@PSUVM.BITNET Message should consist solely of: SUBSCRIBE GOVDOC-L your_name

GRMNHIST: German History Forum

LOCATION: GRMNHIST@VM.USC.EDU;
GRMNHIST@DGOGWDG1 (Bitnet archives)
LISTOWNER: Thomas Zielke; TZIELKE@DGOGWDG1
NO. OF LISTSERV SUBSCRIBERS: 161 subscribers in 12 countries

REVIEW: This list is not for those with just a passing interest in German history. The tone of the list is highly academic and, generally speaking, I think only those with a professional interest in the topic would find any use or enjoyment in it. List members seem to use it mostly as a resource, when facing a roadblock in their personal research. This list is a place to throw out a question and hope for a response that will help clear the jam. The list is dedicated to the discussion of German history, covering all subjects and periods. Questions are asked covering a wide range of historical topics and eras. Various topics in recent posts have concerned finding the proper English idiom when translating material, a request for help in unravelling 18th-Century German territorial bureaucracies and sources on German immigration into Texas in the 19th Century. Many of these postings take the standard form of: "I am beginning\Can anyone help\I am looking for..." These queries do get responses. But, there is very little ongoing discussion on the list. Activity on the list fluctuates considerably; long periods can go by with no postings at all. Mostly it is used as a resource by the list members for specific questions, not for recreation or ongoing conversations. One exception was a request for signatures for a letter to be pub- lished in a German newspaper or magazine in support of the East German writer Christia Wolf. This topic generated many lengthy responses. Eventually, someone commented about one particularly verbose member's remarks. This drew the response, "Well, we must admit - at least this discussion group came alive a bit." (Fred Rump GRMNHIST 19 May 1993) The conversation continued; it developed into an ongoing discussion on the history of the DDR and the role of the Stasi in maintaining the East German state. Over the course of this discussion, several list members took the opportunity to express their personal experiences with the DDR to support their positions. The list is not moderated and actually consists of 2 peered list- servers one in the U.S. and one in Germany. Only the one in Germany maintains a notebook. GRMNHIST is also affiliated with the History Network, a collection of history related files and other resources available on the internet. (Telnet to hnsource.cc.ukans.edu / login: history - no password is required.) The subscribers come from 12 different countries, including Japan and Brazil. -John K. Stemmer (Stemmej@ucbeh.san.uc.edu) Stemmer is the Evening Reference/ILL Librarian at Raymond Walters College (University of Cincinnati).

SYNOPSIS OF ACTIVITY:

Time Period Monitored: 10 MAY 1993 - 07 JUN 1993

No. Messages Period Monitored: 57

No. Queries Posted: 19 (33 % of total activity)

No. Non Queries Posted : 38 (67 % of total activity)

Lines Sent (est.w/o headers): 5200 (app. 227 screens of 23 lines)

Msgs Posted Past 12 Months: N/A

Searchable Archives: Yes

Avg. # msgs day/high/low: 2/12/0

SUBSCRIPTION INFORMATION:

To subscribe to GRMNHIST, send an e-mail message with blank subject line to: LISTSERV@USCVM (Bitnet address) or LISTSERV@VM.USC.EDU (Internet address)Message should consist solely of: SUBSCRIBE GRMNHIST your_name

GUTENBERG

LOCATION: LISTSERV@UIUCVMD (Bitnet)
LISTOWNER: Michael S. Hart BITNET: HART@UIUCVMD
Internet: HART@VMD.CSO.UIUC.EDU
NUMBER OF LISTSERV SUBSCRIBERS: 766 users in 20 countries 84% USA, 6% Canada

REVIEW: "Goal: To Give Away One Trillion Etexts By Year End Of 2001!" List owner Michael Hart has been at this task for approximately 21 years and will probably see the dissemination of his trillion ("texts" not "editions"). List subscribers are regularly notified of the existence, location, and means of retrieval of a wide range of computer readable (ASCII) texts in the public domain. Users typically request information on the existence and locations of specific works. Due to copyright law, the majority of the works predate the 1920's. Items that I have personally downloaded include GRIMM'S FAIRY TALES, NARRATIVES OF FREDERICK DOUGLAS: AN AMERICAN SLAVE, PETER PAN, THE KAMASUTRA (text only!), PARADISE LOST, THE CIA WORLD FACTBOOK (only $129.00 in my Sony Laser Library CD-ROM catalog), and in conjunction with a recent television special, Willa Cather's O PIONEERS! These works DO NOT come with nice, neat search engines to explore them; they consist solely of the text of a given edition. In order to retrieve these, as well as an uncertain and growing number of other works, knowledge of network file transfer procedures is EXTREMELY helpful. Snail mail dissemination appears to be an option for many works. The list owner assiduously keeps subscribers updated on upcoming issues (e.g., THE QURAN). Discussions revolve around issues such as copyright, text format, and a recent exchange of messages decrying the lack of 'definitive and accurately transcribed works from specific editions.' Hart (and I agree with him) is philosophically committed to disseminating texts to the widest possible audience so scholars wishing for bibliographically exact reproductions of specific editions should hesitate to complain after having read this warning. THESE ITEMS ARE FREE!!! Users wishing to contribute time, labor, texts, etc. will benefit from subscribing to this list as well. This is intellectual anarchy at its best: few rules, optimum benefit. -Raleigh C. Muns

SYNOPSIS OF ONE WEEK'S ACTIVITY:

Period Monitored: 29 FEB 92 - 06 MAR 92 (inclusive)

Messages Posted: 21

Number of Queries Posted: 3 (14 % of total activity)

Number of Non-queries Posted: 18 (86 % of total activity)

Lines Sent (w/o headers): 1160 (app. 50 screens of 23 lines)
Searchable Archives: Yes
SUGGESTED USES FOR LIST:
1) Identify public domain electronic texts (primarily in the humanities).
2) Contribute to the common intellectual patrimony of humanity.
3) Collection development for virtual libraries.
BITNET SUBSCRIPTION INFORMATION:
Send an e-mail message with blank subject line to: LISTSERV@UIUCVMD Message should consist solely of: SUBSCRIBE GUTNBERG your_name

History (History Discussion Forum)
LOCATION: HISTORY@PSUVM.PSU.EDU (The largest of the 9 peers making up the HISTORY List) The others are: HISTORY@DGOGWDG1 (ARCHIVES) HISTORY@IRLEARN (ARCHIVES) HISTORY@RUTVM1 (ARCHIVES) HIST-L@UKANVM (ARCHIVES) HISTORY@UMRVMB (ARCHIVES) HISTORY@UBV HISTORY@MCGILL1 HISTORY@CSEARN
LISTOWNER: Thomas Zielke (TZIELKE@DGOGWDG1)
NO. OF LISTSERV SUBSCRIBERS: 480 in 20+ countries

REVIEW: This is a very lively list that lives up to its name. The discussion ranges from the just plain fun and trivial to the serious and scholarly. If you are interested in history, either as a professional or as an avocation, this list is for you. One warning though, it is an extremely busy list - either have plenty of time or be very willing to hit the delete key! Much of it is on the light side. However, scholarly discussion and questions are not uncommon. It is, as one member said, a kind of electronic cocktail party; you can join in the conversation or just sit and "watch." Most of the list is made up of ongoing responses to a question from someone seeking information. New topics appear all the time; basically, whenever someone has suddenly acquired an interest in or idea about something and wants more information on it. Postings to the list, whether scholarly, trivial or in between, generally get prompt and thoughtful responses. However, as are most discussion groups on the Internet, this one is not immune from mudslinging and flame wars. Part of this is academic politics as usual, e.g the proper use of the list itself. But some of it comes from the controversial issues discussed, e.g. the validity of the analogy between slavery and abortion. Recent topics have been very wide ranging.
Examples of some more serious queries would be:
* What to expect when doing research in French archives.
* Placing Freedom of Information Act requests with the FBI.
* Guerrilla movements in the Baltic states after WWII.
* Teaching loads at universities.
Some of the lighter discussions have focused on:
* A request for movies on artists for a fund raiser.
* A request for book titles for summer reading.

* An effort to find a nation that has never been colonized.
(This last thread evolved into an amusing discussion about the qualities of New Jersey and its agricultural products, complete with interstate exit numbers.) Not surprisingly for a list run by historians, the list is archived. However, of the nine peer listservers that support the list, only 5 maintain archives. (See Location) In addition, the HISTORY List is affiliated with the History Network. This is a collection of files and guides to historically related information available on the Internet. The History Network is, by itself, a very valuable resource for anyone interested in history and well worth a look. (Telnet to hnsource.cc.ukans.edu / login: history - no password required) One last point, the list is international. There are members from more than 20 countries, from Estonia to Japan and Brazil to Norway. Whether you are an undergraduate looking for advice, a scholar in need of assistance or just a history buff, HISTORY is a valuable information source and an enjoyable diversion at the same time. John K. Stemmer (Stemmej@ucbeh.san.uc.edu) Stemmer is the Evening Reference/ILL Librarian at Raymond Walters College (University of Cincinnati)
SYNOPSIS OF ACTIVITY:
Total Period Monitored: 21 APR 1993 - 17 MAY 1993 Statistics
Monitoring Period: 21 APR 1993 - 27 APR 1993
No. Messages Period Monitored: 159 (445 for Total Period Monitored)
No. Queries Posted: 49 (31 % of total activity)
No. Non Queries Posted : 110 (69 % of total activity)
Lines Sent (est.): 6400 (app. 278 screens of 23 lines)
Msgs Posted During 1993: ???
Searchable Archives: Yes (see locations)
Avg # of msgs day/high/low: 16/45/0
SUGGESTED USES FOR LIST:
1) Valuable as a resource for advice, suggestions on historically related research, reading, etc.
SUBSCRIPTION INFORMATION :
To subscribe to HISTORY, send an e-mail message with blank subject line to: LISTSERV@PSUVM (Bitnet address) or LISTSERV@PSUVM.PSU.EDU (Internet address) Message should consist solely of: SUBSCRIBE HISTORY your_name

HIT: Highly Imaginative Technology
LOCATION: HIT@UFRJ (Bitnet)
LISTOWNER: Geraldo Xexeo GXEXEO@CERNVM (Bitnet) XEXEO@RIO.COS.UFRJ.BR (Internet) XEXEO@DXCERN.CERN.CH (Internet)
NO. OF LISTSERV SUBSCRIBERS: 322
REVIEW: HIT stands for Highly Imaginative Technology and Science Fiction. This ListSERV group is very casual and relaxed and is more for recreation than anything else. The subscribers carry on here in a casual manner, writing short messages discussing space vehicles, flying cars, and alien creatures. The message density is low with only a few messages coming in on any given day.

A majority of the messages during the week of review revolved around one man's posting of a puzzle. The "Alien Critter" puzzle, posted by George Schaade, was about an alien who visits Earth, proclaiming that there is one creature which is not from Earth but was transplanted from an alien planet. The question: "What is this creature?" This puzzle attracted a lot of proposed answers with justifications. There was even a message posted by a history teacher who had conducted a day of class on the puzzle. Given the subject matter, some of the messages dealing with technology can be a bit tricky to understand. These messages, however, are very few. - A.J. Kim (Kim is a student in Howard Frederick's "Introduction to NGO Computing" at the University of California, Irvine. Frederick's Internet e-mail address is research@igc.apc.org)

SYNOPSIS OF ONE WEEK'S ACTIVITY:

Period Monitored: 19 MAR 1993 - 26 MAR 1993

No. Messages Period Monitored: 35

No. Queries Posted: 06 (17 % of total activity)

No. Non-queries Posted: 29 (83 % of total activity)

Lines Sent (w/o headers): N/A

Msgs. Posted Last 01 Months: N/A

Searchable Archives: Yes

SUGGESTED USES FOR LIST:

1) Good place to chit chat about miscellaneous sci-fi items

SUBSCRIPTION INFORMATION:

To subscribe to HIT, send an e-mail message with blank subject line to: LISTSERV@UFRJ (Bitnet address) Message should consist solely of: SUBSCRIBE HIT your_name

IPCT-L

LOCATION: LISTSERV@GUVM (Bitnet) LISTSERV@GUVM.GEORGETOWN.EDU (Internet)

LISTOWNERS: Zane Berge, Ph.D. BERGE@GUVAX.GEORGETOWN.EDU (Internet)

NUMBER OF SUBSCRIBERS: 566 users in 33 countries

REVIEW: Under the aegis of Georgetown University's Center for Teaching and Technology (CTT), owner Zane Berge describes the purpose of the Interpersonal Computing and Technology List (IPCT-L) as "a forum for the discussion of computing and other technology that can be used to promote learning." Janet Whitaker, a subscriber to IPCT-L referred to some of the other participants (in jest?) as "high fallutin' doctors of whatever." (Janet Whitaker, IPCT-L@GUVM.GEORGETOWN.EDU, 19 June 1992). Indeed! Intellectual warfare at its ivory tower best rages merrily, seriously, and always with great vigor across the face of this issues oriented list. James M. Downey of Salem State College regularly duels Speech Communications Professor Emeritus Gerald M. Phillips of Pennsylvania State University (regularly reduced to "GMP" in postings) over issues of copyright, the role of e-publications in tenure, and whether attempts to regulate the networks constitute implementation of thought police on our still new frontier. I have dubbed them both "Idea and Word Smiths Emeriti" for the quality of their dialogue. Having monitored a growing number of lists, their specific dialogue could serve as a model for how to disagree civilly on the net. Overall, I find a surprising amount of disagreement NOT leading to bitter "but I meant ... be kind ... e-mail is such a difficult way to communicate ideas ..." which is the more common pattern in my cyberspace travels. Dear and gentle readers, read this list to see how "it" is done. The technical details discussed on IPCT-L are philosophical, legal, and sociological in nature, rather than the more typical "Where can I get a copy of MSCDEX for my humanist PC?" This is the place to where I would recommend non-technical discussions of the role of e-communications relocate. Too many other lists degenerate into lesser discussions of "how to discuss what we are discussing." Since this list, in practice, is devoting itself to such matters, a clearer understanding of such issues, either through dialogue or unashamed lurking, can be had by participating. This list does NOT lack in hard nuggets of information. During the week I monitored the list I gleaned specifics on copyright law applied to electronic information, sources covering formats for citing e-mail, and the most outrageous copyright statement I've ever read (Doughbelly Price as cited by John Unsworth, editor of e- journal POSTMODERN CULTURE, in IPCT-L@GUVM.GEORGETOWN.EDU, 17 June 1992). By subscribing to this list, you will have the opportunity to either support or attack GMP's statement, "I am enough of a Jungian to understand that there is a dark side to all of us and we need law and law enforcement to impose civilization on our natural tendency to sybaritism." (Gerald M. Phillips, IPCT-L@GUVM.GEORGETOWN.EDU, 19 June 1992). Sybaritically yours, -R. Muns

SYNOPSIS OF ONE WEEK'S ACTIVITY:

Period Monitored: 15 JUN 92 - 22 JUN 92 (inclusive)

No. Messages Week Monitored: 75

No. Queries Posted: 04 (03 % of total activity)

No. Non-queries Posted: 71 (97 % of total activity)

Lines Sent (w/o headers): 3148 (app. 137 screens of 23 lines)

Msgs. Posted Prev. 3 Months: 1244

Searchable Archives: Yes

SUGGESTED USES FOR LIST:

1) A good place to give ideas rigorous scrutiny.

2) A salon.

3) Exploration of communications issues in the network environment.

SUBSCRIPTION INFORMATION:

Send an e-mail message with blank subject line to: LISTSERV@GUVM (Bitnet address) or LISTSERV@GUVM.GEORGETOWN.EDU (Internet address) Message should consist solely of: SUBSCRIBE IPCT-L your_name

L-HCAP

LOCATION: L-HCAP@NDSUVM1 (Bitnet) L-HCAP@VM1.NODAK.EDU (Internet) BIT.LISTSERV.L-HCAP (Usenet)

LISTOWNER: Bill McGarry L-HCAP@NDSUVM1 (Bitnet) WTM@BUNKER.SHEL-ISC-BR.COM (Internet) UU-NET!BUNKER!WTM (UUCP) 73170,1064 (Compuserve) The Handicap News BBS (141/420) 1-203-337-1607 (Fidonet)

NO. OF LISTSERV SUBSCRIBERS: 230 in 22 countries

REVIEW: Bill McGarry's THE HANDICAP DIGEST is a superb example of computer networking at its best. Drawing messages from the Internet, private bul- etin boards, and commercial e-mail traffic, McGarry produces a tightly edited resource, practically devoid of chatter, and brimming with expo- sition. Subject matter ranges through personal "how I dealt with ..." anecdotes, to announcements of new products (e.g., intelligent prosthe- ses), to extensive bibliographies by experts in their field, such as: Elizabeth H. Dow, Ph.D. (E_DOW@UVMVAX.UVM.EDU), "Bibliography on Pain," THE HANDICAP DIGEST no. 2946, Sep. 29, 1992 (cited as extracted from the Disability Research List, DIS-RES-L@RYERSON.BITNET) The preceding is a thoroughly annotated bibliography on the subject of lower back pain by the information specialist for the Vermont Rehabilitation Engineering Center (what a cool sounding job!). Due to the nature of Handicap Studies (?), there is a strong current of messages requesting, discussing, and presenting medical information. In the issues I reviewed, I also found a healthy mix of humor. "Ever take a spare foot into a shoe store, put it on the counter and asked them if they have anything to fit it in a 1/2" heel?" (DIGEST no. 2946, Sep. 29, 1992). This personal aspect of L-HCAP may be its greatest strength. As an information voyeur I enjoy poking my nose into the various online cultures that are growing in cyberspace. There's something about the black and white of ASCII communication that strips away the awkwardness that often occurs in face-to-face encounters. L-HCAP's amount of message traffic is misleading. McGarry strips out all of that message header gibberish (MHG) we networkers love, leaving a simple e-mail address of sender, and source of message. Of course, you do get MHG with each entire DIGEST. C'est la vie. -R. Muns

SYNOPSIS OF ONE WEEK'S ACTIVITY:
Period Monitored: 27 SEP 1992 - 04 OCT 1992
No. Messages Period Monitored: 42 disseminated in 5 "Digests"
No. Queries Posted: 12 (29 % of total activity)
No. Non-queries Posted: 30 (71 % of total activity)
Lines Sent (w/o headers): 4116 (app. 180 screens of 23 lines)
Msgs. Posted Last 01 Months: 11 "Digests"
Searchable Archives: Yes

SUGGESTED USES FOR LIST:
1) Support tool for physically handicapped humans, friends, and relatives.
2) Nursing and medical students could gain insight into prospective clients (i.e., bedside manner tips).
3) General awareness resource for anyone living on Earth.

SUBSCRIPTION INFORMATION:
Send an e-mail message with blank subject line to: LIST-SERV@NDSUVM1 (Bitnet address) or LIST-SERV@VM1.NODAK.EDU (Internet address) Message should consist solely of: SUBSCRIBE L-HCAP your_name Alterna-

tively, send an e-mail message to list owner, Bill McGarry, at any of the electronic addresses listed above in the SEE SYNOPSIS OF ONE WEEK'S ACTIVITY section, requesting to be added to the subscription list for THE HANDICAP DIGEST.

NMBRTHRY

REVIEW: The low level of activity for this list is not a negative indicator of its value. In order to get a broader view of list activity, I searched the 1991 calendar year archives within which 50 messages were posted. Slow, steady, and concise are adjectives to be applied to list postings. There is minimal information noise coupled with a high response rate to questions in the field of number theory. The body of postings consisted of queries and their subsequent responses, as well as a rare request for papers or a conference notification (3 of the 50 messages). One message notified subscribers of a downloadable software package, version 1.35 of the "Pari package for number theory." Sample topics during the review period were: Carmichael numbers, the rational parameterization of Diophantine equations, and a request for citation on a simple proof of the infinitude of primes (Euler got the credit).

SUGGESTED USES FOR LIST:
1) Problem solving tool in field of number theory.
2) International contact list for mathematicians.
3) Subject awareness tool for mathematically minded academics.

BITNET SUBSCRIPTION INFORMATION:
Send an e-mail message with blank subject line to: LIST-SERV@NDSUVM1 Message should consist solely of: SUB-SCRIBE NMBRTHRY your_name

PACS-L

REVIEW: With more than 3000 subscribers throughout the world, the activity of PACS-L is unsurprisingly high. Most contributors are either librarians or functioning as such and the focus of the list is thus on the issues of the public's access to libraries and their collections. Though the list is moderated (the inaugural LISTSERV REVIEW SERVICE was considered out of scope for PACS-L) the broad subject area covered results in a sometimes frustrating kaleidoscope of messages from which pertinent nuggets must be filtered. The list is officially described as dealing "with all computer systems that libraries make available to their patrons, including CD-ROM databases, computer assisted instruction (CAI or ICAI) programs, expert systems, hypermedia programs, library microcomputer facilities, local databases ..." (see Diane Kovacs' DIRECTORY OF SCHOLARLY ELECTRONIC CONFERENCES, Kent State University, c1991). Typical topics included a discussion of downloading directly to a PC from the Internet, analysis of various CD-ROM products, and a request for German library catalogs searchable via TELNET (promptly responded to by a number of individuals and including pointers to German catalogs of which this TELNET savvy reviewer was previously unaware). As a bonus, two electronic journals regularly appear in PACS-L. PUBLIC ACCESS COMPUTER SYSTEM NEWS (ISSN 1050-6004) is the system-resident journal. An issue posted during the period monitored mentioned that a section of refereed articles would begin appearing. The current and past issues contain short articles covering the range of public access issues generally discussed by the list. CURRENT CITES: LIBRARY TECHNOLOGY WATCH PROGRAM (University of California, David F. W. Robison, editor), lists citations with short abstracts from the library literature on the subject of library technology.

SUGGESTED USES FOR LIST:

1) Monitoring by information professionals for current awareness across a broad range of topics.

2) Useful means to identify librarians world-wide.

3) Good problem-solving tool. Due to number of subscribers, there is a high probability of queries being answered, usually in a number of different ways.

SUBSCRIPTION INFORMATION:

Send an e-mail message with blank subject line to: LIST-SERV@UHUPVM1.BITNET Message should consist solely of: SUBSCRIBE PACS-L your_name

SCREEN-L

LOCATION: LISTSERV@UA1VM (Bitnet) LIST-SERV@UA1VM.UA.EDU (Internet)

LISTOWNER: Jeremy Butler JBUTLER@UA1VM (Bitnet) JBUTLER@UA1VM.UA.EDU (Internet

NUMBER OF SUBSCRIBERS: 296 users in 21 countries

REVIEW: Eclectic, flip, deep, and amusing. SCREEN-L, an unmoderated list, covers film and television studies in a torrent of text bites. Don't let the number of messages keep you from subscribing, though. Most messages are terse and to-the-point missives. Depending upon your e-mail system, the majority of messages should appear on a single screen. A number of postings had the appearance of a Trivial Pursuit game, but with film and television studies so deeply enmeshed in popular culture, many such questions seemingly can only be answered by polling a network audience. I challenge the reference librarian community to come up with information on "the Banana Man," a performer on Captain Kangaroo (query by Rhett Bryson, Bitnet BRY-SON@FRMNVAX1, 92/07/08). Researchers seeking primary materials (e.g., the films of Lester James Peries requested by Rick Provine, Internet REP3S@POE.ACC.VIRGINIA.EDU, 92/07/17), requests for titles covering specific themes (e.g. mannequins, gothic/cyborg, Biblical allegories), and background on the production of various works are just as likely to appear on this list. -R. Muns

SYNOPSIS OF TWO WEEKS ACTIVITY:

Period Monitored: 07 JUL 92 - 20 JUL 92 (inclusive)

No. Messages Last 2 weeks: 42

No. Queries Posted: 16 (38 % of total activity)

No. Non-queries Posted: 26 (62 % of total activity)

Lines Sent (w/o headers): 857 (app. 37 screens of 23 lines)

Msgs. Posted Last 03 Months: 405 (app. 135 messages per month)

Searchable Archives: Yes

SUGGESTED USES FOR LIST:

1) Answer list for normally unanswerable queries about cinema/television/pop culture.

2) A visit to the psyche of a virtual Los Angeles.

3) Current awareness tool for collection development librarians with film and television collections.

SUBSCRIPTION INFORMATION:

Send an e-mail message with blank subject line to: LIST-SERV@UA1VM (Bitnet address) or LIST-SERV@UA1VM.UA.EDU (Internet address) Message should consist solely of: SUBSCRIBE SCREEN-L your_name

SLOVAK-L

LOCATION: SLOVAK-L@UBVM (Bitnet) BIT.LISTSERV.SLOVAK-L (Usenet)

LISTOWNER: Jan George Frajkor GFRAJK-OR@CCS.CARLETON.CA (Internet)

NO. OF LISTSERV SUBSCRIBERS: 193 in 17 countries

REVIEW: One of the enduring fascinations I have with the Internet is its ability to deliver unique and timely points of view. As Czechoslovakia's "Velvet Revolution" segues into its "Velvet Divorce," subscribers to SLOVAK-L can experience geopolitical change virtually firsthand. A sizeable number of messages, if not a majority, come from Czechs and Slovaks, expatriates and citizens, and are mostly in English. Expect occasional untranslated speeches by political dissidents - where else would you get these? Many contributors recognizing the paucity of news about and from Slovakia, have taken it upon themselves to pass on information from the Slovak press as well as Radio Free Europe. Examples of messages consist of Tomas Blazek and Renata Blazeko-va's Slovak language transcription of Jan Carnogursky's Sep. 19, 1992 speech ("Voice of Opposition in Slovakia," BLA-ZEK@MPS.OHIO-STATE.EDU, 12 Jan. 1993), Marian Kubas-ka's list of newly appointed Slovak ambassadors ("Re: embassy," KUBASKA@UAKOM.CS, 13 Jan. 1993), and a raft of comments and complaints about the difficulty many US Post Offices are having with mail addressed to the new country. To my Slovakian friends: Take no offense at this last situation. My spouse has had US Postal officials confused over our attempts to send mail to colleagues in Scotland! -R. Muns

SYNOPSIS OF ONE MONTH'S ACTIVITY:

Period Monitored: 01 JAN 1993 - 28 JAN 1993

No. Messages Period Monitored: 157

No. Queries Posted: 121 (77 % of total activity)

No. Non-queries Posted: 36 (23 % of total activity)

Lines Sent (w/o headers): 8214 (app. 357 screens of 23 lines)

Msgs. Posted During 1992: 1087

Searchable Archives: Yes

SUGGESTED USES FOR LIST :

1) Use to temper the inherent biases of the western press.

2) Great example of real-time global current events source.

3) Take a walk on the Slovak side.

SUBSCRIPTION INFORMATION :

Send an e-mail message with blank subject line to: LIST-SERV@UBVM (Bitnet address) Message should consist solely of: SUBSCRIBE SLOVAK-L your_name

VPIEJ-L

REVIEW: The goal of this list is to discuss the issues of publishing, archiving, and accessing electronic journals (e-journals). I have monitored this list since it was opened to the public in April 1992. The list's postings are extemely Professional (with a capital "P") and I hesitate to recommend it to dilettantes. The subject material posted tends to be esoteric and technical nuts and bolts messages on e-journal production and dissemination. Several postings discussed the philosophical aspects of electronic journals, their role, and their value in scholarly communication. A number of the subjects discussed have been covered on many of the library oriented lists (e.g., PACS-L, LIBREF-L) but this appears to be an appropriate narrowing of subject scope by the list owners. Subscribers to other lists who have regularly plucked out e-journal oriented messages may find it more efficient to subscribe to VPIEJ-L. Sample topics have included: The problems with mixing text and graphics in e-journals. Issue and volume number information in e-journals, specifically in the e-journal PSYCOLOQUY. Announcements of e-journal availability. To date, this has not been a query-dominated "where can I find?" list. Strong contributions by subscribers make this an information dense resource (my euphemism for "really dull unless you are truly interested in the subject matter"). -R. Muns

SUGGESTED USES FOR LIST:

1) Virtual gathering point for e-journal publishers.

2) Increase awareness of the issues surrounding e-journal publication.

3) Input to e-journal publishers from user population.

BITNET SUBSCRIPTION INFORMATION:

Send an e-mail message with blank subject line to: LIST-SERV@VTVM1 Message should consist solely of: SUBSCRIBE VPIEJ-L your_name

WEIRD-L

LOCATION: LISTSERV@BROWNVM (Bitnet)

LISTOWNER: Jeremy Bornstein JEREMY@BROWNVM (Bitnet)

NUMBER OF SUBSCRIBERS: 302 users in 24 countries

REVIEW: WEIRD-L is a list that did not succumb to my usual white male, pseudo-techy analysis. A literary criticism of the irregularly appearing prose and poetry on this list would also be inappropriate since that is not the goal of this service. However, in reading WEIRD-L messages I couldn't help but hear the snapping of fingers in a smoke-filled coffee shop, punctuated by whispered "cools" from beret-wearing, goatee-bedecked denizens of the 1950's. Subscribers will receive 3-5 messages each month on no discernible topic. Posted messages vary in degree of creativity and weirdness (YOU decide). While slogging through e-messages concerning such issues as CD-ROM technology, US Government microfiche distribution, and copyright of electronic journals, I found it an unequivocally interesting experience to suddenly discover in my mailbox, "HOLYSHIT! Another morning where I wake up with charred auto parts sticking out of my torso!" (voodomaster@legba.voodoo.com, "Vodka Induced", WEIRD-L@BROWNVM, April 2, 1992.) Bookkeeping 1 - I had to abandon my electronic dictionaries in order to decipher the mysterious title of this list ("Mmytacist Mmanufacture"), turning to that superior source, WEBSTER'S INTERNATIONAL DICTIONARY OF THE ENGLISH LANGUAGE, UNABRIDGED, 2nd ed. (1934). WEBSTER defines "mytacism" (from which "mmytacist" is apparently derived) thus: my'ta.cism, n [Gr. myta-kismos. Cf. METACISM.] Excessive or wrong use of the letter m, or of the sound it represents, as in writing or in defective speech. Bookkeeping 2 - Listowner Bornstein's description of WEIRD-L (abridged): "weird-l is a list devoted, mainly, to bizarre/disturbing/offensive short stories and ramblings, not humor. You may wish to read   the notebooks before you attempt a posting. The list is edited, and material which is not original with the poster is usually discarded, as are long lists of, for example, cow jokes." Jeremy Bornstein (jeremy@brownvm), from description of list WEIRD-L retrieved from LISTSERV@BROWNVM. -R. Muns

SYNOPSIS OF THREE MONTHS ACTIVITY:

Period Monitored: 01 APR 92 - 05 JUL 92 (inclusive)

No. Messages Last 3 months: 10

No. Queries Posted: 00 (00 % of total activity)

No. Non-queries Posted: 10 (100 % of total activity)

Lines Sent (w/o headers): 512 (app. 22 screens of 23 lines)

Msgs. Posted Last 30 Months: 144 (app. 5 messages per month)

Searchable Archives: Yes

SUGGESTED USES FOR LIST:

1) Scratch the creative writing itch.

2) Anthropological evidence of early network culture.

3) E-mail spice.

SUBSCRIPTION INFORMATION:

Send an e-mail message with blank subject line to: LIST-SERV@BROWNVM (Bitnet address) Message should consist solely of: SUBSCRIBE WEIRD-L your_name

WMST-L

REVIEW: The phrase "drinking from a firehose" has recently been used to describe communication via Internet and BITNET e-mail lists. WMST-L is a likely candidate for the prototype list satisfying the metaphor. WMST-L easily fulfills its charges as set forth by listowner Korenman. The excellent introductory package, including a fine basic LISTSERVER user's guide, highlights WMST-L's role as a major resource for practitioners in the field of Women's Studies. This cataract of data, however, suffers from its own popularity. So much so that instructions are given in the introductory package on how to receive a "WMST-L digest," or a single file of all messages posted on a daily basis. During the time period monitored, it was found that this recently added service was sending files which were too big for many users' e-mail systems. A subsequent message described how to receive packets of files, rather than one single large file. The "good" data consisted of such things as responses to specific questions (e.g., when was the first Women's Studies program in the U.S. initiated?), requests for bibliographic citations, information about specific programs, and my favorite, a number of replys to a questioner looking for films on the theme of family violence. These "good" responses were timely, concise, and explicit. Other "good" data were voluntary postings of articles and letters from the popular media of possible interest to practitioners. The "bad" data consisted of an annoying number of messages self-analyzing the list. In fact, in the finest recursive fashion, there were a couple of messages which complained of the list's discussion of itself! An example which

had me personally rankled for its irrelevancy consisted of an exchange on the inappropriate- ness of writing messages all in capital letters. The "good" data by far outweighs the "bad," and academicians can benefit particularly by subscribing to WMST-L. A daily reader fast with the "delete message" key will have little problem filtering out unwanted messages. The user who is unsure of their e-mail prowess, however, should keep the directions on how to "unsubscribe" handy.

SUGGESTED USES FOR LIST:

1) Curriculum development tool for Women's Studies.

2) Outstanding networking resource for practitioners in the field of Women's Studies.

3) Rich information resource for specific facts in the field.

4) Conference postings

5) Job postings

BITNET/INTERNET SUBSCRIPTION INFORMATION:
Send an e-mail message with blank subject line to: LISTSERV@UMDD <—— BITNET users LISTSERV@UMDD.UMD.EDU <—— INTERNET users Message should consist solely of: SUBSCRIBE WMST-L your_name

Subject Index

This Index covers resources in sections 1, 2, 3, 4, and 6. Numbers in parentheses below indicate: (1) Discussion Lists; (2) Electronic Journals and Newsletters; (3) Electronic Texts, Text Archives, Selected FTP Sites, and Internet Resource Guides; (4) Freenets and Other Community-Based Information Services; and (6) Commercial Services on the Internet.

ABORTION
Choice-Mail (1)

ACADEMIC COMPUTING
Computer Science Center Link (2)
Public-Access Computer Systems Review 1048-6542 (2)

ACADEMIC LIBRARIES
ALF-L (Academic Librarian's Forum) (1)

ACHAEMENIAN STUDIES
Pirradazish: Bulletin of Achaemenian Studies (2)

ACTIVISM
ACTIVIST@ GUVM (1)
ACT-UP@WORLD.STD.COM (1)
AR-ALERTS@NY.NEAVS.COM (1)
Arms-L (1)
BRIDGES (1)
DISARM-D@ALBNYVM1 (1)
FIREARMS0POLITICS@CS.CMU.EDU (1)
STOPRAPE (1)
WON--The Women's Online Network (1)

ADDICTION STUDIES
ADDICT-L (1)

ADMINISTRATION
CADUCEUS--History of Medicine Collections Forum (1)
Catalyst: The Community Services Catalyst 0739-9227 (2)
CUMREC-L (1)
EDPOLYAN (1)
EDPOLYAR (Education Policy Analysis Archives) 1068-2341 (2)
HIM-L (Health Information Management) (1)
LIBADMIN (1)
PUBNET@CHINACAT.UNICOM.COM (1)
RRL-DIRECTORS (1)
SCUP EMAIL News (2)

ADULT EDUCATION
ADLTED-L (1)
AEDNET Discussion List (1)
Journal of Extension 0022-0140 (2)
New Horizons in Adult Education 1062-3183 (2)
TECnet (1)
TESLFF-L (1)
TESLIE-L (1)
TESLIT-L (1)
TESLJB-L (1)
TESL-L (1)

ADVERTISING
The Net Advertiser (6)

AERODYNAMICS
CIT$W (1)

AERONAUTICS
AERONAUTICS@RASCAL.ICS.UTEXAS.EDU (1)

AEROSPACE
AVIATION-THEORY@MC.LCS.MIT.EDU (1)

AFRICA
Africa-L (1)

AFRICAN-AMERICAN STUDIES
AfAm-L (1)
AFAS-L (1)
AFROAM-L (1)

AGRICULTURAL ECONOMICS
DNH-pilot (1)

AGRICULTURE
ag-exp-l (1)
Agric-L (1)
Agris-L (1)
Bnfnet-L (1)
Dairy-L (1)
The Great Lakes Haylist (3)
H-Rural@uicvm (1)
Journal of Extension 0022-0140 (2)
MICRONET@UOGUELPH (1)
NEWCROPS@PURCCVM (1)
Not Just Cows: A Guide to Internet/Bitnet Resources in Agriculture and Related Sciences (3)
SAN-Link (1)
SM-RUM@ICNUCEVM (1)

AIDS/HIV STUDIES
ACT-UP@WORLD.STD.COM (1)
AIDS Book Review Journal (2)
AIDS@RUTVM1 (1)
AIDS-STAT@WUBIOS.WUSTL.EDU (1)
HICNet Medical Newsletter (2)
ICECA@RUTVM1 (1)
U.S. Federal Drug Administration (3)

ALGEBRAIC GEOMETRY
ALGEBRAIC GEOMETRY E-PRINTS (2)

ALGERIA
ALGERIA-NET (1)

ALTERNATIVE LITERATURE
Arm the Spirit (2)
Armadillo Culture: The Journal of Modern Dasypodidae (2)
BLINK (2)
Cousins (2)
Crash (2)
Cyberspace Vanguard Magazine (2)
Drum (2)
Ego Project (2)
FactSheet Five (2)
Funhouse (2)
High Weirdness by Email (2)
Hi-Rez (2)
Holy Temple of Mass Consumption (2)
International TeleTimes (2)
Liminal-Liminal Explorations (2)
Obscure Electronic (2)
Parthenogenesis (2)
Scratch (2)
Twentynothing (2)
Unplastic News (2)
Voices from the Net (2)
We Magazine (2)
Weird-L (1)
Whole Earth Review (2)
Zine List (3)

AMERICA
1492: An Ongoing Voyage: An Exhibit at the Library of
  Congress (3)

AMERICAN CATHOLICISM
AMERCATH (1)

AMERICAN HISTORY
EARAM-L (1)

AMERICAN LANGUAGE AND LITERATURE
PYNCHON@SFU (1)

AMERICAN LIBRARY ASSOCIATION
ALAWON: The ALA Washington Office Newsline (2)

AMERICAN LITERATURE AND LANGUAGE
AMLIT-L (American Literature Discussion List) (1)
Cult of the Dead Cow (2)
High Weirdness by Email (2)
Holy Temple of Mass Consumption (2)
JACK-LONDON@SONOMA.EDU (1)
Mark Twain Forum (1)
PowderKeg (2)
PROXIMITY (2)
RIF/T: A Journal of Contemporary Poetry and Poetics (pending)
  (2)
ShareDebate International 1054-0695 (2)

AMERICAN PSYCHOLOGICAL ASSOCIATION
American Psychological Association's Research Funding
  Bulletin (2)

AMERICAN STUDIES
AMERSTDY@MIAMIU (1)
H-AmStdy@uicvm (1)
H-CivWar@uicvm (1)

ANARCHY
Practical Anarchy Online (2)

ANCIENT HISTORY
Pirradazish: Bulletin of Achaemenian Studies (2)

ANGLICANISM
ANGLICAN (Episcopal Mailing List) (1)

ANIMAL RIGHTS
AR-ALERTS@NY.NEAVS.COM (1)
AR-TALK@THINK.COM (1)

ANIMATION
AGOCG-ANIMATION@MAILBASE.AC.AK (1)
Anime-L (1)

ANTHROPOLOGY
Anthro-L (1)
ETHNOHIS@HEARN (1)
Ethno@RPITSVM (1)
FOLLAC (1)
HumBio-L (1)
HUMEVO@GWUVM (1)
Intercul@RPITSVM (1)
Nahuat-L (1)
NAT-1492@TAMVM1 (1)
NATCHAT@TAMVM1 (1)
NAT-EDU@INDYCMS (1)
Native-L (1)
Ortrad-L (1)
PSYCHE: An Interdisciplinary Journal of Research on
  Consciousness 1039-723X (2)
PYSCHE-D (1)

AQUACULTURE
Aqua-L (1)
Brine-L (1)
Marine-L (1)

ARAB STUDIES
American Arab Scientific Society Newsletter (2)

ARCHAEOLOGY
ANCIEN-L (1)
Arch-L (1)
Nahuat-L (1)
Pacarc-L (1)
WAC NEWS Q The World Archaeological Congress Newsletter
  (2)

ARCHITECTURE
Architronic: The Electronic Journal of Architecture 1066-6516
  (2)
Arclib-L (1)
Design-L (1)
Facxch-L (1)
Stuxch-L (1)

ARCHIVAL THEORY
ARCHIVES@INDYCMS (1)

ARCHIVISM
DISC-NORDLIB (1)

ARGENTINA
ARGENTINA@OIS.DB.TORONTO.EDU (1)

ART
ANSI-ART (1)
ARLIS-L (1)
ARTCOM (2)
ARTCRIT@YORKVM1 (1)
ARTNET@MAILBASE.AC.UK (1)
ART-SUPPORT@MAILBASE.AC.UK (1)
ASCII-ART (1)
Bonsai-L (1)
CLAYART@UKCC (1)
Design-L (1)
DKB-L (1)
ERASMUS@VM.EPAS.UTORONTO.CA (1)
Facxch-L (1)
Fine Art, Science, Technology FAST Database (6)
FineArt Forum (2)
FINEART@RUTVM1 (1)
L-ARTECH@UQAM (1)
Museum-L (1)
Origami-L (1)
SOUND News and Arts (2)
Stuxch-L (1)
Victoria (1)

ART HISTORY
CAAH@PUCC (1)

ARTIFICIAL INTELLIGENCE
AESRG-L (1)
ag-exp-l (1)
AI-CHI@LLL.LLNL.GOV (1)
aidevaisb.ed.ac.uk (2)
AI-ED@SUN.COM (1)
AILIST@DB0TUI11 (1)
AIL-L (1)
AI-medicine (Artificial Intelligence in Medicine) (1)
alife@cognet.ucla.edu (1)
at-finance-board@invnext.worldbank.org (1)
cellular-automata@think.com (1)
CLASS-L (1)
Computists' Communique (2)
connectionists@cs.cmu.edu (1)
Current Cites 1060-2356 (2)
DAI-List (1)
de.sci.ki (1)
de.sci.ki.announce (1)
de.sci.ki.discussion (1)
de.sci.ki.mod-ki (1)
DISTRIBUTED-AI@MAILBASE.AC.UK (1)
EP-List (1)
ESE-L (1)
FAQ: Artificial Intelligence Questions & Answers (3)
FLAIRS@UCF1VM (1)
FUZZY-MAIL (1)
GA-List (1)

IAMEX-L (1)
IE-Digest (1)
Journal of Artificial Intelligence Research (JAIR) (2)
MAAMAW Blackboard (Modeling Autonomous Agents in a
    Multi-Agent World) (1)
NAFIPS-L (1)
NL-KR@CS.RPI.EDU (1)
PSYCHE: An Interdisciplinary Journal of Research on
    Consciousness 1039-723X (2)
PYSCHE-D (1)
RNA (1)
simulator-bugs@cs.rochester.edu (1)
simulator-users@cs.rochester.edu (1)
snns@informatik.uni-stuttgart.de (1)
VISION-LIST@ADS.COM (1)

ASIA-PACIFIC STUDIES
APEX-L (1)

ASTRONOMY
ASTR-O@BRFAPESP (1)
ASTRONOMY@BBN.COM (1)
CANSPACE (Canadian Space Geodesy Forum) (1)
Cosmic Update (2)
EJASA (The Electronic Journal of the Astronomical Society of
    the Atlantic) (2)
EUVE: Electronic Newsletter of the EUVE Observatory 1065-
    3597 (2)
GRAVITY@UWF (1)
HRI-L (1)
ISDS@UIUCVMD (1)
JCMT-L (1)
Jonathan's Space Report (2)
NASA Spacelink (3)
PAMNET (1)
SEDS-L (1)
SEDSNEWS@TAMVM1 (1)
Space Digest (1)
SPACE@ANDREW.CMU.EDU (1)
SPACE@FINHUTC (1)
SPACE-IL@TAUNIVM (1)
ST-AUDIT@UWF (1)
UNIVERSE@NDSUVM1 (1)
WGAS-L (1)

ASTROPHYSICS
astro-ph@babbage.sissa.it (2)
EUVE: Electronic Newsletter of the EUVE Observatory 1065-
    3597 (2)
gr-qc@xxx.lanl.gov (2)

AUSTEN, JANE
Austen-L (1)

AUSTRALIA
CLIONET (2)

AUSTRIA
HABSBURG@PURCCVM (1)

AUTISM
AUTISM (1)

AVIATION
AERONAUTICS@RASCAL.ICS.UTEXAS.EDU (1)

AZTEC STUDIES
Nahuat-L (1)

BARBERSHOP SINGING
Barbershop (1)

BEEKEEPING
Bee-L (1)
Florida Extension Beekeeping Newsletter 0889-3764 (2)

BEER
JudgeNet: the Beer Judge Digest Network (1)

BIBLE STUDIES
Aibi-L (1)
BIBLE (1)
NT-GREEK (New Testament Greek Studies) Conference (1)
OT-HEBREW (Old Testament Hebrew Studies) (1)

BIBLIOGRAPHIC INSTRUCTION
BI-L (Bibliographic Instruction Discussion List) (1)

BICYCLES
People Power Update (2)

BIOCHEMISTRY
CYAN-TOX@GREARN (1)
DIBUG@COMP.BIOZ.UNIIBAS.CH (1)
EBCBCAT@HDETUD1 (1)
FORUMBIO@BNANDP11 (1)
LACTACID@SEARN (1)

BIOLOGY
Biopi-L (1)
BIOSIS: Life Science Network (6)
Color and Vision Network (1)
CYAN-TOX@GREARN (1)
DIS-L (1)
Drosophila Information Newsletter (2)
EMBINFO@IBACSATA (1)
FORUMBIO@BNANDP11 (1)
HumBio-L (1)
HUMEVO@GWUVM (1)
IAMSLIC@UCSD CONFERENCE (1)
INNS-L (1)
LACTACID@SEARN (1)
LPN-L (Laboratory Primate Newsletter) 0023-6861 (2)
MORPHMET@CUNYVM (1)

BIOMEDICINE
ced-courseware (1)

BIOPHYSICS
DIBUG@COMP.BIOZ.UNIIBAS.CH (1)
EBCBCAT@HDETUD1 (1)
FORUMBIO@BNANDP11 (1)
MORPHMET@CUNYVM (1)

BIRDS
TITNET (1)
TITNEWS (2)

TITNOTES (2)

BITNET
Directory of Scholarly Electronic Conferences, 7th Revised
    Edition. (3)
List of Lists (1)
LSTOWN-L (1)
NETSCOUT@VMTECMEX (1)
NETTRAIN@UBVM (1)
NEW-LIST (1)

BLACK SABBATH
Sabbath (1)

BLINDNESS
Blind News Digest (2)
Braille Forum (2)
Braille Monitor 0006-8829 (2)
Handicap Digest (2)

BLUEGRASS MUSIC
BGRASS-L Bluegrass Music Discussion List (1)

BOOK REVIEWS
CTHEORY--Virtual Review of Books for Post-Modern Theory
    (2)
Ego Project (2)
Funhouse (2)
Law and Politics Book Review 1062-7421 (2)
SCHOLAR 1060-7862 (2)

BOSNIA
Bosnet (2)

BOTANY
Bean Bag (2)
Botanical Electronic News 1188-603X (2)
Flora Online 0892-9106 (2)

BRAILLE
Braille Forum (2)
Braille Monitor 0006-8829 (2)

BRAZIL
BR Domain (1)
NIBNews (2)
POLITICA@UFRJ (1)
SBNC-L (1)

BRS INFORMATION TECHNOLOGIES
BRS-L (1)

BUSINESS
AJBS-L (1)
CTI-ACC-AUDIT@MAILBASE.AC.UK (1)
CTI-ACC-BUSINESS@MAILBASE.AC.UK (1)
Dow Jones News/Retrieval (6)
E-EUROPE@PUCC (1)
First! (6)
FLEXWORK@PSUHMC (1)
IBJ: Internet Business Journal (2)
IBJ-L (The Internet Business Journal Distribution List) (1)
JMBA-L (1)
LATCO LIST (1)

CHILDREN
KIDLINK (1)
KIDLINK Newsletter (2)
PEDIATRIC-PAIN (1)
PUBYAC Children and Young Adult Services in Public
 Libraries (1)
Y-RIGHTS@SJUVM.BITNET (1)

CHILDREN'S RIGHTS

CHILE
Chile News Database (2)
Chile-L (1)
CHILENET@UCHCECVM (1)
CHIP Q Political, Environmental, Economic and Human Rights
 News Chile Information Project (2)
EDISTA@USACHVM1 (1)
Natura-L (1)

CHINA
China News Digest (2)
CHINA-ND@KENTVM (1)
CHINA@PUCC (1)
Emedch-L (1)

CHINESE LANGUAGE AND LITERATURE
Chpoem-L (1)

CHINESE STUDIES
Twuniv-L (1)

CHRISTIANITY
BIBLE (1)
ELENCHUS@UOTTOWA (1)
EOCHR (Eastern Orthodox Christian Discussion List) (1)
Histec-L (1)
IOUDAIOS Review 1183-9937 (2)
IOUDAIOS@YORKVM1 (1)
LITURGY (1)
MailJC Network (1)
ORTHODOX@INDYCMS (1)
Rome Reborn: The Vatican Library & Renaissance Culture (3)
Scrolls from the Dead Sea: The Ancient Library of Qumran and
 Modern Scholarship (3)

CHRONIC FATIGUE SYNDROME
CFS-L (Chronic Fatigue Syndrome) (1)
CFS-MED (Chronic Fatigue Syndrome Medical List) (1)
CFS-NEWS (Chronic Fatigue Syndrome Electronic Newsletter)
 1066-8152 (2)

CINEMA STUDIES
Cinema-L (1)
Film-L (1)
H-FILM (1)
HORROR@PACEVM (1)
SCRNWRIT@TAMVM1 (1)
Taylorology (2)
Vidpro-L (1)

CIVIL WAR
H-CivWar@uicvm (1)

CLASSICAL STUDIES
CLASSICS (1)
Contex-L (1)
Rome Reborn: The Vatican Library & Renaissance Culture (3)
Teiresias 0381-9361 (2)

CLEMENS, SAMUEL (MARK TWAIN)
Mark Twain Forum (1)

CLIMATOLOGY
CLIMLIST (1)
ECIXFILES@IGC.ORG (1)

COALITION FOR NETWORKED INFORMATION
Coalition for Networked Information Gopher (3)

COGNITIVE SCIENCE
COG-SCI-L (1)
PSYCOLOQUY 1055-0143 (2)

COLD FUSION
fusion (1)

COLD REGIONS RESEARCH
MAB Northern Sciences Network Newsletter 1014-7470 (2)

COLLEGES AND UNIVERSITIES
AAUA-L (1)
Academe This Week (The Chronicle of Higher Education) (2)
ACES-L (Atlantic Congress of Engineering Students Forum) (1)
Acsoft-L (1)
Advise-L (1)
ALF-L (Academic Librarian's Forum) (1)
AMERICAN-STUDIES@MAILBASE.AC.UK (1)
APEX-L (1)
ASSESS@UKCC (1)
Bras-net (1)
BRUNONIA@BROWNVM (1)
The Buffer (2)
CACI-L (1)
Campus Computing Newsletter (2)
Canadian Association for University Continuing Education
 Electronic Network (1)
Catalyst: The Community Services Catalyst 0739-9227 (2)
CCES-L (Congress of Canadian Engineering Students Forum)
 (1)
CCNEWS - Campus Computing Newsletter (2)
Chairs-L (1)
CNSF-L (1)
COLLIB-L (1)
COMMCOLL (1)
COMP-ACADEMIC-FREEDOM-TALK@EFF.ORG (1)
Computer Science Center Link (2)
Confer-L (1)
CREAD (Latin American & Caribbean Distance and Continuing
 Education) (1)
Crewrt-L (1)
CTI-COMPLIT@MAILBASE.AC.UK (1)
CUMREC-L (1)
CWIS-L (1)
DEOS-L (1)
DJ-L (Campus Radio Disk Jockey Discussion List) (1)
EDPOLYAN (1)

Columbia Online Information Network (COIN) (4)
Dayton Free-Net (4)
Denver Free-Net (4)
Erlangen Free-Net (4)
Free-Net Bayreuth (4)
Gainesville Free-Net (4)
Heartland Free-net (4)
Hornet Nests Free-Net (4)
Huron Valley Free-Net (4)
Lorain County Free-Net (4)
Los Angeles Free-Net (Central) (4)
Los Angeles Free-Net (Valley) (4)
Medina County FreeNet (4)
National Capital Freenet (4)
North Shore Free-Net (4)
North Texas Free-Net (4)
Ocean State Free-Net (4)
Oklahoma Public Information Network (4)
Orange County Free-Net (4)
PAC-NET (4)
Palm Beach Free-Net (4)
Poudre-R1 Gopher Information Service (4)
Prairenet (4)
Santa Barbara RAIN (4)
Seattle Community Network (4)
Sendit North Dakota: North Dakota's K-12 Education
    Telecommunication Network (4)
SLO County Free-Net (4)
Suncoast Free-Net (4)
Tallahassee Free-Net (4)
Tennessee Valley Free-Net (4)
Triangle Free-Net (4)
TriState Online (4)
Tuscaloosa Free-Net (4)
UMassK12: University of Massachusetts/Amherst K-12
    Information System (4)
Victoria Free-Net (4)
Virginia's Public Education Network (PEN) (4)
Wellington Citynet (4)
Youngstown Free-Net (4)

COMPARATIVE EDUCATION
EDPOLYAN (1)
EDPOLYAR (Education Policy Analysis Archives) 1068-2341
    (2)

COMPLEX FLUIDS
Interf-l (1)

COMPUTER BOOKS
Roswell Electronic Computer Bookstore (6)

COMPUTER GRAPHICS
CGE@MARIST (1)
GRAPHICS@OHSTVMA (1)
GRAPHIX@UTFSM (1)
Graph-L (1)
Image-L (1)

COMPUTER HARDWARE AND SOFTWARE
Acsoft-L (1)
ADV-ELI (1)
Adv-Elo (1)
ADV-INFO (1)

ai-kappa-pc (1)
Amateur Computerist (2)
Andrew View (2)
ANSFORTH (1)
ANU-NEWS (1)
ARJUNA@MAILBASE.AC.UK (1)
ASTRA-UG (1)
ATLAS-L (1)
Automatome (2)
BIBSOFT@INDYCMS (1)
Bits and Bytes Online (2)
The Buffer (2)
Cache Update (2)
CACTUS Newsletter (2)
Campus Computing Newsletter (2)
CAP-L (Computer-Aided Publishing) (1)
CARISUSE@SUN1.COGS.NS.CA (1)
CARR-L (1)
CDROM-L (1)
CDROMLAN@IDBSU (1)
CDS-ISIS@HEARN (1)
ced-courseware (1)
Chaos Corner (2)
Chaos Digest (ChaosD) (2)
C + Health@IUBVM (1)
CLU-SW@SEISMO.CSS.GOV (1)
CMSUG-L (1)
CMU-TEK-TCP@CS.CMU.EDU (1)
COCAMED (Computers in Canadian Medical Education) (1)
COMPIL-L (1)
Computational Chemistry List (1)
Computer Science Center Link (2)
Computing and Network News (2)
Computists' Communique (2)
Comserve CommJobs (4)
Comserve Newsline (4)
COMTEN-L (1)
Cosmic Update (2)
CPSR/PDX Newsletter (2)
CRETA-PILOT@MAILBASE.AC.UK (1)
CSP-L (1)
cti-maths (1)
cti-music (1)
ctt-Digest (2)
CUMREC-L (1)
CUPLE-L (1)
CYBSYS-L (1)
DDN Management Bulletin (2)
DECNEWS for Education and Research (2)
DevelopNet News (2)
DISSPLA@TAUNIVM (1)
EBCBCAT@HDETUD1 (1)
EJVC (Electronic Journal of Virtual Culture) (2)
ELEASAI (The Open Forum on Library and Information
    Science Research) (1)
ELLHNIKA@DHDURZ1 (1)
The Embedded Digest (1)
EMULPC-L (1)
EMUSIC-L (1)
End Process (2)
ENDNOTE@UCSBVM (1)
EUEARN-L (1)
FARNet Gazette (2)
FAXONEDI (1)

WGAS-L (1)
Windows Online Review (2)
word-mac (1)
WORKS@RUTGERS.EDU (1)
World View Magazine (2)
WX-LSR@UIUCVMD (1)
WX-MISC@UIUCVMD (1)
WX-NATNL@UIUCVMD (1)
WX-PCPN@UIUCVMD (1)
WXSPOT-L@UIUCVMD (1)
WX-STLT@UIUCVMD (1)
WX-SWO@UIUCVMD (1)
WX-TALK@UIUCVMD (1)
WX-TROPL@UIUCVMD (1)
WX-WATCH@UIUCVMD (1)
WX-WSTAT@UIUCVMD (1)
YTERM-L (1)
YUNUS@TRMETU (1)

COMPUTER HEALTH RISKS
RISKS-L (1)

COMPUTER LANGUAGE PROCESSORS
COMPIL-L (1)

COMPUTER LITERACY
Computer Literacy Project (3)

COMPUTER PRIVACY
COMP-ACADEMIC-FREEDOM-TALK@EFF.ORG (1)
COMP-PRIVACY@PICA.ARMY.MIL (1)
CPSR@GWUVM (1)
FIREWALLS@GREATCIRCLE.COM (1)
RISKS-L (1)
SECURITY@AIM.RUTGERS.EDU (1)
TELECOM-PRIV@PICA.ARMY.MIL (1)

COMPUTER SCIENCE
ABC@CWI.NL (1)
ACM-L (1)
Acsoft-L (1)
ADA-SW@WSMR-SIMTEL20.ARMY.MIL (1)
AESRG-L (1)
ag-exp-l (1)
AHC-L (1)
AI-CHI@LLL.LLNL.GOV (1)
AI-ED@SUN.COM (1)
ai-kappa-pc (1)
AILIST@DB0TUI11 (1)
alife@cognet.ucla.edu (1)
Amateur Computerist (2)
Andrew View (2)
Anest-L (1)
APL-L (1)
ASMICRO-L (1)
ASTRA-UG (1)
BETA@MJOLNER.DK (1)
BIG-DB@MIDWAY.UCHICAGO.EDU (1)
Cache Update (2)
CACTUS Newsletter (2)
Case-L (1)
CERFNet NEWS (2)
Christian LIFE in the Computer Era (2)
CIT$W (1)

Class Four Relay Magazine (2)
CLP.X@XEROX.COM (1)
CNI-ARCH@UCCVMA (1)
COMP-CEN@UCCVMA.UCOP.EDU (1)
COMPIL-L (1)
COMP-SCI@ILNCRD (2)
Computer Underground Digest (CuD or Cu-Digest) 1004-042X
    (2)
Comsoc-L (1)
CPE-LIST@UNCVM1.OIT.UNC.EDU (1)
CPSR/PDX Newsletter (2)
CSP-L (1)
CTF-DISCUSS@CIS.UPENN.EDU (1)
CTHEORY--Virtual Review of Books for Post-Modern Theory
    (2)
CTI-COMPLIT@MAILBASE.AC.UK (1)
ctt-Digest (2)
CW-L (1)
CYBSYS-L (1)
DISTOBJ@HPLB.HP.COM (1)
DISTRIBUTED-AI@MAILBASE.AC.UK (1)
DPMAST-L (1)
ECTL@SNOWHITE.CIS.UOGUELPH.CA (1)
Electronic Hebrew Users Newsletter (E-Hug) (2)
The Electronic Journal of Communication/La Revue
    Electronique de Communication 1183-5656 (2)
Electronics Letters Online (2)
The Embedded Digest (1)
EP-List (1)
ESE-L (1)
Ethics-L (1)
EXPRESS-USERS@CME.NIST.GOV (1)
FASE@CS.UH.EDU (1)
FASTBS-L (1)
FINEART@RUTVM1 (1)
FLAIRS@UCF1VM (1)
Florida SunFlash (2)
FOREFRONTS (2)
FRAC-L (1)
funct-an@babbage.sissa.it (2)
FUZZY-MAIL (1)
GIS-UK (1)
GWMON@SH.CS.NET (1)
HEADER-PEOPLE@MC.LCS.MIT.EDU (1)
HOTT (Hott off the Tree) (2)
HUMBUL (Humanities Bulletin Board) (1)
ICON-GROUP@ARIZONA.EDU (1)
IFIP-DIALUP@ICS.UCI.EDU (1)
IFIP-GTWY@ICS.UCI.EDU (1)
INFO-ADA@AJPO.SEI.CMU.EDU (1)
INFO-C@RESEARCH.ATT.COM (1)
INFO-FRAME@AEROSPACE.AERO.ORG (1)
INFO-FUTURES@ENCORE.COM (1)
INFO-LAW@BRL.MIL (1)
INFO-M2@UCF1VM.CC.UCF.EDU (1)
INFO-ODA + @ANDREW.CMU.EDU (1)
INFO-PASCAL@BRL.MIL (1)
Information Retrieval (1)
info-tandem (1)
INFO-VLSI@THINK.COM (1)
Institute for Computers and Writing (1)
INTERFACES-P-M@CRIM.CA (1)
I-REDES@UTFSM (1)
ISDN@ABALL.IN-BERLIN.DE (1)

ISO10646@JHUVM (1)
ISODE@NIC.DDN.MIL (1)
ISO@NIC.DDN.MIL (1)
LANG-LUCID@CSL.SRI.COM (1)
LITPROG@SHSU.EDU (1)
LN (1)
MACPROG@WUVMD.WUSTL.EDU (1)
Mbu-L (1)
MHSNEWS@ICS.UCI.EDU (1)
MOSSBA@USACHVM1 (1)
MSP-L (1)
MULTICAST@ARIZONA.EDU (1)
NAFIPS-L (1)
NAMEDROPPERS@NIC.DDN.MIL (1)
NEURON-UK@MAILBASE.AC.UK (1)
NL-KR@CS.RPI.EDU (1)
OPEN CACSD (2)
OPT-PROC@TAUNIVM (1)
PARA-DAP@IRLEARN (1)
PIGULKI 1060-9288 (2)
POSIX-ADA@GREBYN.COM (1)
POSIX-FORTRAN@SANDIA.GOV (1)
POSIX-TESTING@MINDCRAFT.COM (1)
Principia Cybernetica Newsletter (2)
Principia Cybernetica Project (PCP) (3)
PRNCYB-L (1)
PROLOG@SUSHI.STANFORD.EDU (1)
PROTOCOL@VMD.CSO.UIUC.EDU (1)
PSYCOLOQUY 1055-0143 (2)
RES-COMP@NKI (1)
RFC@NIC.DDN.MIL (1)
RIPE-MAP@NIC.EU.NET (1)
Risks-Forum Digest (2)
Scream Baby (2)
SHOTHC-L (1)
SIMULA@BITNIC (1)
SIMULATION@UFL.EDU (1)
sir-users (1)
SOFT-ENG@MWUNIX.MITRE.ORG (1)
SOFTWARE-MEASUREMENT@MAILBASE.AC.UK (1)
SOFTWARE-TESTING@MAILBASE.AC.UK (1)
STD-UNIX@UUNET.UU.NET (1)
SURFPUNK Technical Journal (2)
SYSTERS (1)
TCP-IP@NIC.DDN.MIL (1)
TESTING-ARCHIVE@ERNIE.CS.UIUC.EDU (1)
TESTING-RESEARCH@ERNIE.CS.UIUC.EDU (1)
THEORYNET@WATSON.IBM.COM (1)
Ulam Quarterly (2)
ultralite-list (1)
VISION-LIST@ADS.COM (1)
VPLLIST@SUSHI.STANFORD.EDU (1)
weather-users (1)
World View Magazine (2)
X11-3D@ATHENA.MIT.EDU (1)
X500-EXCHANGE@CNI.ORG (1)
X-ADA@EXPO.LCS.MIT.EDU (1)
XGKS@UNIDATA.UCAR.EDU (1)
XIMAGE@EXPO.LCS.MIT.EDU (1)
XPERT@EXPO.LCS.MIT.EDU (1)
X-SERIAL@LLL-CRG.LLNL.GOV (1)
XVIDEO@EXPO.LCS.MIT.EDU (1)
Z3950IW@NERVM (1)

COMPUTER SECURITY
Risks-Forum Digest (2)

COMPUTER VIRUSES
Virus-L (1)
VMVIRUS@PCCVM (1)

COMPUTER-ASSISTED DESIGN (CAD)
ENGINEERING-CASE@MAILBASE.AC.UK (1)
TECnet BBS (1)
Vtcad-L (1)

COMPUTER-ASSISTED INSTRUCTION (CAI)
CBEHIGH@BLEKUL11 (1)
CTI-L (1)
Distance Education Online Symposium (DEOSNEWS) 1062-9416 (2)
ED2000-PILOT@MAILBASE.AC.UK (1)
EDTECH@OHSTVMA (1)
EDUPAGE (2)
EDUTEL@RPITSVM (1)
EUITNEWS (2)
GEOCAL@MAILBASE.AC.UK (1)
HISTORY-TEACHING@MAILBASE.AC.UK (1)
INFED-L (1)
INFOBITS (2)
Intech-L (1)
Journal of Computing in Higher Education 1042-1726 (2)
Megabyte University (1)
NEWEDU-L (1)
nrsing-l (1)
TESLCA-L (Computer-Assisted Learning Sub-List of TESL-L) (1)
Vetcai-L (1)

CONFERENCES AND CONFERENCE LISTINGS
CLP.X@XEROX.COM (1)
GIS-CONFERENCES (1)
KONFER-L (1)
Mellon-L (1)
NAC@NDSUVM1 (1)

CONTESTS AND COMPETITIONS
JudgeNet: the Beer Judge Digest Network (1)

CONTINUING EDUCATION
Canadian Association for University Continuing Education Electronic Network (1)

COPTIC ORTHODOX CHURCH
Copt-Net Newsletter (2)

COPYRIGHT
CNI-COPYRIGHT@CNI.ORG (1)

CRIME
Taylorology (2)

CROATIA
CROATION-NEWS/HRVATSKI-VJESNIK (1)
Cromed-L (1)
CRO-NEWS (1)

CUBA
Radio Havana Cuba Newscast (2)

CULTURAL STUDIES
ALGERIA-NET (1)
AMLIT-L (American Literature Discussion List) (1)
ANCIEN-L (1)
BALZAC-L (1)
BLINK (2)
CATALUNYA@CS.RICE.EDU (1)
Christian LIFE in the Computer Era (2)
DISC-NORDLIB (1)
Donosy (English edition) 1059-4027 (2)
Donosy (Polish edition) 0867-6860 (2)
Electronic College of Theory (1)
EthnoFORUM (3)
Ethnomusicology Research Digest 1054-1624 (2)
F-email (1)
INDIA-L@UKCC (1)
INDIA-L@UTARLVM1 (1)
INDIA-L@UTEMPLEVM (1)
INDIA@PCCVM (1)
INMYLIFE@WKUVX1 (1)
PERFORM-L (1)
PMC-MOO (1)
PMC-TALK (1)
Postmodern Culture 1053-1920 (2)
Purple Thunderbolt of Spode (PURPS) (2)
SOCHIST@USCVM (1)
Tamil-L (1)
Teslic-L (1)
Victoria (1)
VTWOMEN (1)

CURRENT EVENTS
Academe This Week (The Chronicle of Higher Education) (2)
ALGERIA-NET (1)
Arm the Spirit (2)
Armadillo Culture: The Journal of Modern Dasypodidae (2)
Bosnet (2)
Carolina (2)
Cerro-L (1)
Chile News Database (2)
CHINA-ND@KENTVM (1)
CROATION-NEWS/HRVATSKI-VJESNIK (1)
CRO-NEWS (1)
Cyberspace Vanguard Magazine (2)
DRYDYMALKI 1064-9794 (2)
First! (6)
French Language Press Review (2)
Grochz Kapusta (2)
MIDEUR-L (1)
NATODATA@CC1.KULEUVEN.AC.BE (1)
NAVNEWS@NCTAMSLANT.NAVY.MIL (1)
PIGULKI 1060-9288 (2)
POLAND-L (1)
POLAND@NDCVX.CC.ND.EDU (1)
Radio Havana Cuba Newscast (2)
RokPress (2)
ROMANIANS (1)
SCS-L (1)
SLOVAK-L (1)
Somalia News Update 1103-1999 (2)
TPS-L (1)

Twentynothing (2)
UKRAINE@ARIZVM1 (1)
VAL-L (1)
VND (VREME NEWS DIGEST) (2)

CURRICULUM
Disc-L (1)
K12ADMIN (1)

CYBERNETICS
CYBSYS-L (1)
Principia Cybernetica Project (PCP) (3)
PRNCYB-L (1)

CYBERSPACE
EJVC (Electronic Journal of Virtual Culture) (2)
IRVC-L (Forum for Research on Virtual Culture) (1)

CYRILLIC CHARACTERS
RUSTEX-L (1)

CZECH REPUBLIC
Carolina (2)

DANCE
Ballroom (1)
Dance-L (1)

DANTE
Dartmouth Dante Project (3)

DATA ACQUISITION AND ORGANIZATION
IFDO-L (1)

DATA ANALYSIS
CLASS-L (1)

DATA PROTECTION
UK Data Protection Act 1984 (1)

DEAD SEA SCROLLS
Scrolls from the Dead Sea: The Ancient Library of Qumran and Modern Scholarship (3)

DEMOGRAPHICS
ADQ@UQUEBEC (1)
Capdu-L (1)
Casid-L (1)
CENSUS-ANALYSIS@MAILBASE.AC.UK (1)
CENSUS-NEWS@MAILBASE.AC.UK (1)
CENSUS-PUBLICATIONS@MAILBASE.AC.UK (1)
RRL-PUBLICATIONS (1)
STARDATA@HASARA11 (1)

DENDOCHRONOLOGY
Dendochronolgy Forum for the International Tree-Ring Data Bank (6)

DENTAL SCIENCES
Dental-L@irlearn.ucd.ie (1)
WHOORAL-PILOT@MAILBASE.AC.UK (1)

DERRIDA, JACQUES
DERRIDA@CFRVM (1)

ITRDBFOR@ASUACAD (1)

ECONOMETRICS
COMPU-ECON (Computational Economics) 0927-7099 (2)
Corryfee (1)
Csemlist (1)

ECONOMICS
COMPU-ECON (Computational Economics) 0927-7099 (2)
Corryfee (1)
Csemlist (1)
CTI-ECON@MAILBASE.AC.UK (1)
ECONED-L (1)
Economic Bulletin Board (3)
ECONOMY@TECMTYVM (1)
FEMECON-L (1)
HISTORY-ECON@MAILBASE.AC.UK (1)
IE-Digest (1)
IPEnet (International Political Economy) (1)
Magyar Electronikus Tozsde (Hungarian Electronic Exchange)
    1216-0229 (2)
Nasdaq Financial Executive Journal (NFEJ) (2)
RURALDEV@KSUVM (1)
Working Paper Archive in Economics (3)

ECUADOR
ECUADOR@NERS6KI.NCSU.EDU (1)

EDI (ELECTRONIC DATA INTERCHANGE)
FAXONEDI (1)

EDITING
SEdit-L (1)

EDUCATION
ACADV@NDSUVM1 (1)
ACES-L (Atlantic Congress of Engineering Students Forum) (1)
ADLTED-L (1)
AEDNET Discussion List (1)
AI-ED@SUN.COM (1)
allstat (1)
Altlearn (1)
AMERSTDY@MIAMIU (1)
Anet-L (1)
APEX-L (1)
Ashe-L (1)
AskERIC (1)
ASSESS@UKCC (1)
Bicompal (1)
Biopi-L (1)
Bras-net (1)
Canadian Association for University Continuing Education
    Electronic Network (1)
CARR-L (1)
CBEHIGH@BLEKUL11 (1)
CCES-L (Congress of Canadian Engineering Students Forum)
    (1)
CGE@MARIST (1)
Chemed-L (1)
CHINA@PUCC (1)
Civil-L (1)
CLIMLIST (1)
Cneduc-L (1)
COCAMED (Computers in Canadian Medical Education) (1)

Comlaw-L (1)
COMMCOLL (1)
Computer Literacy Project (3)
Crewrt-L (1)
Csrnot-L (1)
CTI-COMPLIT@MAILBASE.AC.UK (1)
CTI-L (1)
cti-maths (1)
cti-music (1)
DECNEWS for Education and Research (2)
DEOS-L (1)
Disc-L (1)
DISTED: The Online Journal of Distance Education (2)
DTS-L (Dead Teachers Society List) (1)
ECONED-L (1)
ECPR-PILOT@MAILBASE.AC.UK (1)
ED2000-EUROPE (1)
ED2000-PILOT@MAILBASE.AC.UK (1)
Edad-L (1)
Edinfo-L (1)
EDISTA@USACHVM1 (1)
EDLAW@UKCC (1)
EDNET (1)
Ednet6-L (1)
EDPOLYAN (1)
EDPOLYAR (Education Policy Analysis Archives) 1068-2341
    (2)
EDSTYLE (1)
EDUCOM-W (1)
EDUC@QUEBEC (1)
EDUPAGE (2)
ELDNET-L (1)
ELEASAI (The Open Forum on Library and Information
    Science Research) (1)
Eric-L (1)
ERL-L (1)
EUITNEWS (2)
Family-L (1)
Fulbright Educational Advising Newsletter (FULBNEWS) (2)
GLOSAS News 1188-6307 (2)
GLOSAS-L (1)
GNET -- Toward a Truly Global Network (3)
GRAD-ADV@ACS.UNC.EDU (1)
HEPROC-L (Higher Education Processes Discussion List) (1)
H-GRAD (1)
HILAT-L (1)
HISTORY-ECON@MAILBASE.AC.UK (1)
HISTORY-TEACHING@MAILBASE.AC.UK (1)
HOME-ED@THINK.COM (1)
HOPOS-L (1)
HOTT (Hott off the Tree) (2)
H-TEACH (1)
Humgrad (1)
HYPERMED@UMAB (1)
IECC: International E-Mail Classroom Connections (1)
IHOUSE-L International Voice Newsletter Prototype List (2)
The Incomplete Guide to the Internet and Other
    Telecommunications Opportunities Especially for Teachers
    and Students, K-12 (3)
INFED-L (1)
Institute for Computers and Writing (1)
The International Health Communication Hotline (1)
JESSE (1)
Journal of Computing in Higher Education 1042-1726 (2)

GWMON@SH.CS.NET (1)
HEADER-PEOPLE@MC.LCS.MIT.EDU (1)
HELPNET@NDSUVM1 (1)
HELP-NET@TEMPLEVM (1)
HY-PEOPLE@ORVILLE.ARC.NASA.GOV (1)
IFIP-DIALUP@ICS.UCI.EDU (1)
IFIP-GTWY@ICS.UCI.EDU (1)
INFO-ANDREW@ANDREW.CMU.EDU (1)
INFO-ANDREW-BUGS@ANDREW.CMU.EDU (1)
INFO-NETS@THINK.COM (1)
Information Networking News 0966-2774 (2)
Information Technology Times (2)
I-REDES@UTFSM (1)
ISDN@ABALL.IN-BERLIN.DE (1)
itti-networks (6)
IUIC-INFS@MAILBASE.AC.UK (1)
IUIC-NEWSLETTER@MAILBASE.AC.UK (1)
JANET@GWUVM (1)
JewishNet--Global Jewish Networking (3)
JEWISHNT-Global Jewish Information Network Project (1)
LSTOWN-L (1)
MAIL-BBONES@YORKU.CA (1)
Matrix News 1059-0749 (2)
MC(2) (3)
MeckJournal 1058-692X (2)
MHSNEWS@ICS.UCI.EDU (1)
MichNet News (2)
MSP-L (1)
MULTIMEDIA INFORMATION SERVICES (1)
NAMEDROPPERS@NIC.DDN.MIL (1)
NEARnet this Month (2)
NEARNET@NIC.NEAR.NET (1)
NEARNET-TECH@NIC.NEAR.NET (1)
NETTRAIN@UBVM (1)
Network News (2)
NEURON-UK@MAILBASE.AC.UK (1)
NEW-LIST (1)
Newsline (2)
NIS@CERF.NET (1)
PCIP@UDEL.EDU (1)
PROFSALT@UCCVMA (1)
PROTOCOL@VMD.CSO.UIUC.EDU (1)
REDALC@FRMOP11 (1)
RFC@NIC.DDN.MIL (1)
RIPE-MAP@NIC.EU.NET (1)
SRVREQ-L (1)
STD-UNIX@UUNET.UU.NET (1)
TCP-IP@NIC.DDN.MIL (1)
X11-3D@ATHENA.MIT.EDU (1)
X500-EXCHANGE@CNI.ORG (1)
X-ADA@EXPO.LCS.MIT.EDU (1)
XGKS@UNIDATA.UCAR.EDU (1)

ELECTRONIC PUBLISHING
ARACHNET@UOTTOWA (1)
CAP-L (Computer-Aided Publishing) (1)
Current Cites 1060-2356 (2)
OCLC-journals (1)
OCLC-news (1)
TECHTALK-L (1)
Vpiej-L (1)

ELECTRONIC SHOPPING SERVICE
Book Stacks Unlimited (6)

Electronic Bookstore on Internet (6)
The Electronic Newsstand (6)
MarketBase (6)
The Net Advertiser (6)
Online Express (6)
Roswell Electronic Computer Bookstore (6)
TitleBank Electronic Catalog for the Internet (6)

ELECTRONIC TEXTS
Almanac Electronic Texts Catalog (3)
Center for Text and Technology (3)
CETH (Center for Electronic Texts in the Humanities) (3)
CETH (Center for Electronic Texts in the Humanities
   Distribution List) (1)
Dartmouth Dante Project (3)
ETEXTCTR@RUTVM1 (1)
GUTNBERG@UIUCVMD (1)
Online Book Initiative (OBI) (3)
Project Gutenberg (3)

ELECTRONICS
ADV-ELI (1)
Adv-Elo (1)

ENDOMETRIOSIS
WITSENDO (1)

ENERGY STUDIES
Energy Ideas (2)
Energy Research in Israel Newsletter (2)
ENEWS (2)

ENGINEERING
ACES-L (Atlantic Congress of Engineering Students Forum) (1)
AELFLOW@TECHNION (1)
AERONAUTICS@RASCAL.ICS.UTEXAS.EDU (1)
ASMICRO-L (1)
AVIATION-THEORY@MC.LCS.MIT.EDU (1)
Case-L (1)
CCES-L (Congress of Canadian Engineering Students Forum)
   (1)
CEC@QUCDN (1)
CEM-L (1)
Circuits-L (1)
CIT$W (1)
Civil-L (1)
CPE-LIST@UNCVM1.OIT.UNC.EDU (1)
CRIN@FRMOP11 (1)
Dynsys-L (1)
ECTL@SNOWHITE.CIS.UOGUELPH.CA (1)
ELDNET-L (1)
Energy-L (1)
ENGINEERING-CASE@MAILBASE.AC.UK (1)
ENGINEERING-DESIGN@MAILBASE.AC.UK (1)
ETHCSE-L (1)
FASE@CS.UH.EDU (1)
feusers (1)
GEODESIC@UBVM (1)
IEEE-L (1)
IEEE@USACHVM1 (1)
INFO-VLSI@THINK.COM (1)
Journal of Fluids Engineering--Archive (2)
Mech-L (1)
MILITARY@ATT.ATT.COM (1)

FAMILY STUDIES
Fathers and Children for Equality Newsletter (2)
FEDIX: Minority Online Information Service (3)
FREE-L (1)
U.S. Departmetn of Agriculture Children-Youth-Family
  Education Research Network (3)

FANTASY FICTION
Dargonzine Q: The Magazine of the Dargon Project (2)
Intertext - An Electronic Fiction Magazine (2)

FAXON COMPANY
Faxon Finder/Faxon XPress (6)
Faxon Quest (6)
Faxon Source (6)
FAXONEDI (1)

FEMINISM
BIFEM-L (1)
BISEXU-L (1)
BRIDGES (1)
EDUCOM-W (1)
FEMAIL (1)
FEMECON-L (1)
FEMINISM-DIGEST (1)
FEMINIST (1)
FEMISA (1)
FEMREL-L (1)
FIST (1)
GENDER (1)
GEOFEM (1)
HELWA-L (1)
H-WOMEN (1)
KOL-ISHA (1)
MAIL-MEN (1)
MEDFEM-L (1)
PRO-FEMINIST MEN'S ISSUES MAILING LIST (1)
SASHSociologists Against Sexual Harassment (1)
South Asian Women's Net (1)
SSSSTALK (1)
STOPRAPE (1)
SWIP-L (1)
SYSTERS (1)
WIML-L (Women's Issues in Music Librarianship) (1)
WIPHYS (1)
WISENET (1)
WITI (1)
WMN-HLTH (1)
WOMEN (1)
WON--The Women's Online Network (1)

FICTION
Armadillo Culture: The Journal of Modern Dasypodidae (2)
PowderKeg (2)
Purple Thunderbolt of Spode (PURPS) (2)
PYNCHON@SFU (1)
Sbrhym-L (1)
TapRoot Reviews Electronic Edition (2)
Temptation of Saint Anthony 1062-3981 (2)
Unit Circle Magazine (2)

FILMMAKING
FILMMAKERS (1)
SCREEN-L (1)

FINE ARTS
ARLIS-L (1)
ARTCOM (2)
Fine Art, Science, Technology FAST Database (6)
FineArt Forum (2)
FINEART@RUTVM1 (1)
HUMBUL (Humanities Bulletin Board) (1)
Leonardo Electronic News (2)
med-and-ren-music (1)
PSYART (1)

FIREARMS
FIREARMS0POLITICS@CS.CMU.EDU (1)

FIRSTSEARCH CATALOG
Firstsearch-L (1)

FLIES
Drosophila Information Newsletter (2)

FLORIDA
South Florida Environmental Reader 1044-3479 (2)

FLORIDA ATLANTIC UNIVERSITY
Fau-L (1)

FLOWERS
Gardens (1)

FLUIDS
Journal of Fluids Engineering--Archive (2)

FOLKLORE
Folklore@TAMVM1 (1)
FOLLAC (1)
Lore@NDSUVM1 (1)
Ortrad-L (1)

FOOD SCIENCE
DNH-pilot (1)
FOODWINE (1)

FORENSIC MEDICINE
Forens-L (1)

FOREVER KNIGHT
FKFIC-L (1)
FORKNI-L (1)

FORMER SOVIET UNION
SCS-L (1)
SEELANGS@CUNYVM (1)

FORTH LANGUAGE STANDARDS
ANSFORTH (1)

FRACTALS
FRAC-L (1)

FRANCE
FranceHS@UWAVM (1)

FREEMASONRY
MASONIC@ASGARD.BBN.COM (1)

LISABEN (1)
MAIL-MEN (1)
National Council for Research on Women, Research in Progress
    Database (3)
PRO-FEMINIST MEN'S ISSUES MAILING LIST (1)
TRANSGEN (1)
VTWOMEN (1)
WMST-L (Women's Studies List) (1)
WOMEN (1)
WON--The Women's Online Network (1)

GENEALOGY
Roots-L (1)

GENERAL ACCOUNTING OFFICE
U.S. General Accounting Office Reports Archive (3)

GENERAL INTEREST
Mcrit-L (1)
MISC (1)

GENETIC ALGORITHMS
Simulated Annealing Mailing List (1)

GENETICS
GA-List (1)
GENETICS@INDYCMS (1)
HumBio-L (1)
info-gcg (1)

GEOGRAPHIC INFORMATION SYSTEMS
CARISUSE@SUN1.COGS.NS.CA (1)
GIS-ARTICLES (1)
GIS-CONFERENCES (1)
GIS-HELP (1)
GIS-JOBS (1)
GIS-L (1)
GIS-NEWS (1)
GIS-UK (1)
IDRISI-UK@MAILBASE.AC.UK (1)
MAPS-L (1)
RRL-NEWS (1)
UIGIS-L (1)

GEOGRAPHY
CTI-GEOG@MAILBASE.AC.UK (1)
GEOCAL@MAILBASE.AC.UK (1)
GEOFEM (1)
GEOGRAPH@FINHUTC (1)
Geonet-L (1)
GIS-ARTICLES (1)
GIS-CONFERENCES (1)
GIS-HELP (1)
GIS-JOBS (1)
GIS-NEWS (1)
GIS-UK (1)
MAPS-L (1)
RRL-NEWS (1)
Solstice: An Electronic Journal of Geography and Mathematics
    1059-5325 (2)

GEOLOGY
ORG-GEOCHEM (1)
Quake-L (1)

Seismd-L (1)

GEOSCIENCE
STAT-GEO@UFRJ (1)

GERMAN LANGUAGE AND LITERATURE
deutsche-liste@ccu.umanitoba.ca (1)
Hesse-L (1)

GERMANY
9NOV-89-L (1)
GRMNHIST: German History Forum (1)

GIBSON, DEBBIE
Between the Lines - A Debbie Gibson Discussion Forum (2)

GOEDEL, KURT
Kurt Goedel Society Mailing List (1)

GOLF
GOLF-L (1)

GOVERNMENT INFORMATION
Capdu-L (1)
CENSUS-ANALYSIS@MAILBASE.AC.UK (1)
CENSUS-NEWS@MAILBASE.AC.UK (1)
CENSUS-PUBLICATIONS@MAILBASE.AC.UK (1)
Dupont Circle Reporter (2)
Economic Bulletin Board (3)
Electronic Government Information Service (3)
FEDIX: Minority Online Information Service (3)
Fedsig-L (1)
FEDTAX-L (1)
FIREARMS0POLITICS@CS.CMU.EDU (1)
Govdoc-L (1)
NLSNews Newsletter (2)
Project Hermes: U.S. Supreme Court Opinions (3)
Travel-Advisories (1)
UK Data Protection Act 1984 (1)
U.S. Congress Senate Hearings (3)
U.S. Departmetn of Agriculture Children-Youth-Family
    Education Research Network (3)
U.S. Federal Drug Administration (3)
U.S. General Accounting Office Reports Archive (3)
U.S. Supreme Court Decisions (3)

GRADUATE EDUCATION
H-GRAD (1)
RD: Graduate Research in the Arts 1188-0708 (2)
T-Assist@UNMVMA (1)

GRANTS AND FUNDING
American Psychological Association's Research Funding
    Bulletin (2)
RESEARCH (1)
Sponsored Programs Information Network (SPIN) (6)

GRAPH THEORY
GRAPHNET (1)

GRAPHICS
AGOCG-ANIMATION@MAILBASE.AC.AK (1)
AGOCG-IP@MAILBASE.AC.AK (1)
Anime-L (1)

ANSI-ART (1)
DKB-L (1)
End Process (2)
GRAPHICS@OHSTVMA (1)
GRAPHIX@UTFSM (1)
Graph-L (1)
Image-L (1)

GREAT BRITAIN
Victoria (1)

GREECE
HELLAS@AUVM (1)
SOC-CULTURE-GREEK-POST@CS.WISC.EDU (1)

GREEK LANGUAGE AND LITERATURE
CLASSICS (1)
ermis (1)
IBYCUS-L@uscvm (1)
NT-GREEK (New Testament Greek Studies) Conference (1)

GREEK POLITICS
ermis (1)

GYMNASTICS
Gymn (1)

HAZARDOUS WASTE MANAGEMENT
SAFETY (1)

HEALTH LEVEL SEVEN
HL-7 (1)

HEALTH SCIENCES
AIDS Book Review Journal (2)
ANCHODD (Australian National Clearinghouse on Drug
   Development) (1)
Anest-L (1)
AROMA-TRIALS@MAILBASE.AC.UK (1)
Biomedical Library Acquisitions Bulletin (BLAB) 1064-699X
   (2)
CFS-L (Chronic Fatigue Syndrome) (1)
CFS-MED (Chronic Fatigue Syndrome Medical List) (1)
CFS-NEWS (Chronic Fatigue Syndrome Electronic Newsletter)
   1066-8152 (2)
C+Health@IUBVM (1)
Dental-L@irlearn.ucd.ie (1)
Health-L (1)
HICNet Medical Newsletter (2)
HIM-L (Health Information Management) (1)
HYPERMED@UMAB (1)
The International Health Communication Hotline (1)
Internet/Bitnet Online Health Sciences Resource List (3)
LIS-MEDICAL@MAILBASE.AC.UK (1)
LymeNet Newsletter (2)
Medlib-L (1)
METHODS@IRLEARN (1)
MHCARE-L (1)
NIBNews (2)
nrsing-l (1)
NUTEPI (Nutritional Epidemiology) (1)
Online Journal of Current Clinical Trials 1059-2725 (2)
PBLIST (1)
PEDIATRIC-PAIN (1)

public-health (1)
REVES@FRMOP11 (1)
RISKS-L (1)
RSI Network Newsletter (2)
RURALAM (1)
Weights (1)
WHOORAL-PILOT@MAILBASE.AC.UK (1)
WMN-HLTH (1)

HEBREW LANGUAGE AND LITERATURE
A Byte of Torah (2)
Electronic Hebrew Users Newsletter (E-Hug) (2)
HEBLANG (1)
IOUDAIOS Review 1183-9937 (2)
IOUDAIOS@YORKVM1 (1)
IVRITEX@TAUNIVM (1)
A MegaByte of Torah (2)
OT-HEBREW (Old Testament Hebrew Studies) (1)

HEGEL G. W. F.
HEGEL@VILLVM (1)

HERBS
Gardens (1)

HESSE, HERMAN
Hesse-L (1)

HIGHER EDUCATION
Academe This Week (The Chronicle of Higher Education) (2)

HISTORY
9NOV-89-L (1)
AfAm-L (1)
AHC-L (1)
Albion-L (1)
AMWEST-H@USCVM (1)
ANCIEN-L (1)
Ansax-L (1)
ASEH-L (1)
BYRD.MU.WVNET.EDU (3)
C18-L (1)
CABOT@SOL.CRD.GE.COM (1)
CHAUCERNET@UNLINFO.UNL.EDU (1)
CLIONET (2)
deutsche-liste@ccu.umanitoba.ca (1)
EARAM-L (1)
Emedch-L (1)
EMHIST-L (1)
ERASMUS@VM.EPAS.UTORONTO.CA (1)
Espora-L (1)
ETHNOHIS@HEARN (1)
FranceHS@UWAVM (1)
GRMNHIST: German History Forum (1)
HABSBURG@PURCCVM (1)
H-AmStdy@uicvm (1)
H-CivWar@uicvm (1)
H-DIPLO (1)
H-Ethnic@uicvm (1)
H-GRAD (1)
History Sources (3)
HISTORYA@UWAVM (1)
HISTORY-ECON@MAILBASE.AC.UK (1)
HISTORY-METHODS@MAILBASE.AC.UK (1)

history@psuvm (1)
HISTORY-VASCO@MAILBASE.AC.UK (1)
HISTOWNR@UBVM (1)
H-Law@uicvm (1)
HLIST@ONEB.ALMANAC.BC.CA (1)
HN-Ask-L (1)
HOLOCAUST@uicvm (1)
HOST (2)
H-POL (1)
H-Rural@uicvm (1)
H-South@uicvm (1)
HTech-L@SIVM (1)
H-Urban (1)
H-WOMEN (1)
IBYCUS-L@uscvm (1)
Interscripta@morgan.ucs.mun.ca (1)
L-CHA@UQAM (1)
Mediev-L (1)
MILHST-L (1)
Mlhst-L (1)
NAT-1492@TAMVM1 (1)
National Council for Research on Women, Research in Progress
    Database (3)
New Historicus: A Kansas Journal of History (2)
OMHR (Online Modern History Review) (2)
PrezHist@kasey.umkc.edu (1)
PUBLHIST (1)
Renais-L (1)
Roots-L (1)
RUSHIST@USCVM (1)
SEdit-L (1)
Shaker (1)
SHARP-L (1)
SOCHIST@USCVM (1)
SOVHIST@USCVM (1)
Victoria (1)
Vwar-L (1)
World-L (1)
WWII-L (1)

HISTORY OF SCIENCE
HOPOS-L (1)
Hpsst-L (1)
MedSci-L (1)

HOLMES, SHERLOCK
Hounds of the Internet (1)

HOLOCAUST STUDIES
HLIST@ONEB.ALMANAC.BC.CA (1)
HOLOCAUST@uicvm (1)

HOME EDUCATION
HOME-ED@THINK.COM (1)

HORROR FICTION
HORROR@PACEVM (1)
Intertext - An Electronic Fiction Magazine (2)

HORSES
PFERDE@DLRVM (1)

HORTICULTURE
Bonsai-L (1)

Hort-L (1)
ORCHIDS@SCU (1)
PLANT-TAXONOMY@MAILBASE.AC.UK (1)
PTG-FORUM@MAILBASE.AC.UK (1)

HOSPITALITY RESEARCH
Journal of the International Academy of Hospitality Research
    1052-6099 (2)

HUMAN RESOURCES
ACADEMIC-INDUSTRY-RELATIONS@MAILBASE.AC.UK
    (1)
HRD-L (1)
HRIS-L (1)
ICEN-L (1)
IOOB-L (1)
TRDEV-L (1)

HUMAN RIGHTS
ACTIV-L (1)
Choice-Mail (1)
IFREEDOM (1)
Y-RIGHTS@SJUVM.BITNET (1)

HUMANITIES
CETH (Center for Electronic Texts in the Humanities) (3)
CETH (Center for Electronic Texts in the Humanities
    Distribution List) (1)
Chug-L (1)
HCFNET@UCSBVM (1)
HUMANIST@BROWNVM (1)
HUMBUL (Humanities Bulletin Board) (1)
Humgrad (1)
Humspc-L (1)
Journal of Undergraduate Research (2)
Mellon-L (1)
RD: Graduate Research in the Arts 1188-0708 (2)
SHARP-L (1)
Surfaces 1188-2492 (2)

HUMOR
PIADAS (1)
WHIM@TAMVM1 (1)

HUNGARY
HUNGARY@GWUVM (1)
Magyar Electronikus Tozsde (Hungarian Electronic Exchange)
    1216-0229 (2)

HYPERMEDIA
Current Cites 1060-2356 (2)
Leonardo Electronic News (2)

IBM
PCSUPT-L (1)

IMAGE PROCESSING
AGOCG-IP@MAILBASE.AC.AK (1)

IMMIGRATION
H-Ethnic@uicvm (1)
Roots-L (1)

SLART-L (Second Language Acquisiton, Research, and
   Teaching) (1)
TESLCA-L (Computer-Assisted Learning Sub-List of TESL-L)
   (1)
TESLMW-L (Materials Writers Sub-List of TESL-L) (1)
TEXTCRIT@VAX.OXFORD.AC.UK (1)
TolkLang (1)
UKRAINE@ARIZVM1 (1)
Undiscovered Country (2)
WELSH-L (1)

LATIN AMERICA
Bras-net (1)
CREAD (Latin American & Caribbean Distance and Continuing
   Education) (1)
FOLLAC (1)
HILAT-L (1)
IBERIAN__ISSUES (1)
LASNET@EMX.UTEXAS.EDU (1)
Laspau-L (1)
LATAM-INFO (1)
LATCO LIST (1)
Mclr-L (1)
Natura-L (1)
REDALC@FRMOP11 (1)
Siriac-L (1)
SOC.CULTURE.LATIN-AMERICA (1)
UNIANDES@ANDESCOL (1)

LATIN LANGUAGE AND LITERATURE
CLASSICS (1)
Thesaurus Musicarum Latinarum (3)
TML-L (Thesaurus Musicarum Latinarum) (1)

LATVIA
BALT-INFO (1)
BALT-L (1)

LAW AND LEGAL STUDIES
AIL-L (1)
Automatome (2)
CALL-L (1)
Cjust-L (1)
Comlaw-L (1)
EDLAW@UKCC (1)
Hislaw-L (1)
H-Law@uicvm (1)
INFO-LAW@BRL.MIL (1)
INT-LAW (1)
Law and Politics Book Review 1062-7421 (2)
LAW-LIB@UCDAVIS.EDU (1)
Lawsch-L (1)
Mead Data Central: LEXIS/NEXIS (6)
Ncs-L (1)
Project Hermes: U.S. Supreme Court Opinions (3)
SCIFRAUD@ALBNYVM1 (1)
SECURITY@AIM.RUTGERS.EDU (1)
U.S. Supreme Court Decisions (3)

LEARNING DISABILITIES
Altlearn (1)

LEGUMES
Bean Bag (2)

LEIBNITZ, GOTTFRIED WILHELM
Kurt Goedel Society Mailing List (1)

LIBERTARIANISM
Libernet (1)
Organized Thoughts (2)

LIBRARY AND INFORMATION SCIENCE
ACCESS! (2)
ACQNET@CORNELLC (1)
Acquisitions Librarians Electronic Network (ACQNET) 1057-
   5308 (2)
Acrlny-L (1)
ADAPT-L@AUVM (1)
Advanc-L (1)
AFAS-L (1)
Agris-L (1)
ALAWON: The ALA Washington Office Newsline (2)
ALCTS NETWORK NEWS 1056-6694 (2)
ALCTS@UICVM (1)
ALEPHINT@TAUNIVM (1)
ALF-L (Academic Librarian's Forum) (1)
ARCHIVES@INDYCMS (1)
Arclib-L (1)
Arie-L (1)
ARLIS-L (1)
ASIS-L (1)
ATLAS-L (1)
AUTOCAT@UVMVM (1)
Automatome (2)
AXSLIB-L@BITNIC (1)
BALT-INFO (1)
BALT-L (1)
BI-L (Bibliographic Instruction Discussion List) (1)
Biomedical Library Acquisitions Bulletin (BLAB) 1064-699X
   (2)
BIOSIS: Life Science Network (6)
BitNet/Internet Health Science Resources (3)
BRS Information Technologies (6)
BRS-L (1)
BRSZ@CNI.ORG (1)
BUBL, The Bulletin Board for Libraries (3)
Bulletin of the General Theological Library of Bangor 1052-
   8202 (2)
Buslib-L (1)
CADUCEUS--History of Medicine Collections Forum (1)
CALL-L (1)
Canadian Internet-Accessible Libraries (3)
CDPLUS-L (1)
CDROM-L (1)
CDS-ISIS@HEARN (1)
CHMINF-L (Chemical Information Sources Discussion List) (1)
CIRCPLUS@IDBSU (1)
Citations for Serial Literature 1061-7434 (2)
COCAMED (Computers in Canadian Medical Education) (1)
COLLIB-L (1)
COMENIUS@CSEARN (1)
CONSALD (1)
Conservation DistList (1)
COOPCAT@NERVM (1)
CWIS List (3)
CWIS-L (1)
Dartmouth List of Lists (3)
DATA ENTRIES (2)

PUBYAC Children and Young Adult Services in Public
  Libraries (1)
RLIN (Research Libraries Information Network) (6)
RLIN-L (1)
Scope News (2)
SERIALST (1)
SERIALS@UVMVM (1)
SLAJOB (1)
SLSCK...the Newsletter (2)
Spilib-L (1)
STN International (6)
Stumpers-L (1)
Sunyla-L (1)
SURAnet Guide to Selected Internet Resources (3)
Surfing the Internet: An Introduction (3)
Techbul-l (1)
TESLA@NERVM (1)
TXDXN-L@UHUPVM1 (1)
UNICRN-L (1)
UNT's Accessing Online Bibliographic Databases (3)
USMARC-L (1)
Vetlib-L (1)
VIFLIS, The Virtual International Faculty in Library and
  Information Science. (1)
Vpiej-L (1)
VTLSLIST@VTVM1 (1)
WIML-L (Women's Issues in Music Librarianship) (1)

LIBRARY AND INFORMATION TECHNOLOGY ASSOCIATION
LITA Newsletter (2)

LIBRARY COLLECTION DEVELOPMENT
Acquisitions Librarians Electronic Network (ACQNET) 1057-
  5308 (2)
ALCTS NETWORK NEWS 1056-6694 (2)
Bulletin of the General Theological Library of Bangor 1052-
  8202 (2)
COLLDV-L (Library Collection Development List) (1)
CONSALD (1)
ILL-L (1)
LC Cataloging Newsline 1066-8829 (2)
MC Journal: The Journal of Academic Media 1069-6792 (2)
Newsletter on Serials Pricing Issues 1046-3410 (2)
SERIALST (1)

LIBRARY MANAGEMENT
COLLDV-L (Library Collection Development List) (1)

LIBRARY OF CONGRESS
LC Cataloging Newsline 1066-8829 (2)
LC MARVEL (Library of Congress Machine-Assisted
  Realization of the Virtual Electronic Library) (4)
LOCIS: Library of Congress Information System (4)

LIBRARY REFERENCE
LIBREF-L (1)

LIBRARY-VENDOR RELATIONS
Faxon Finder/Faxon XPress (6)
Faxon Quest (6)
Faxon Source (6)
FAXONEDI (1)

LINEAR ALGEBRA
ILAS-NET (2)

LINGUISTICS
Aibi-L (1)
CAACSALF@UQUEBEC (1)
Contex-L (1)
CORPORA@400.HD.UIB.NO (1)
DERRIDA@CFRVM (1)
EDMAC@MAILBASE.AC.UK (1)
ELLHNIKA@DHDURZ1 (1)
LANGIT@IVEUNCC (1)
Linguist (1)
MEDTEXTL@UIUCVMD (1)
Multi-L (1)
NL-KR@CS.RPI.EDU (1)
SCHOLAR@CUNYVM (1)
TEI-ANA@UICVM (1)
TEI-L (1)
TEI-META@UICVM (1)
TEI-REP@UICVM (1)
TEXTCRIT@VAX.OXFORD.AC.UK (1)
TolkLang (1)

LITERACY
TESLIT-L (1)

LITERARY THEORY AND CRITICISM
DERRIDA@CFRVM (1)
Electronic College of Theory (1)
EROFILE@UCSBUXA (1)
Milton-L (1)
ModBrits Network (1)
PMC-MOO (1)
PMC-TALK (1)
Postmodern Culture 1053-1920 (2)

LITERATURE
CHICLE@UNMVMA (1)
Litsci-L (1)
Ortrad-L (1)
Sbrhym-L (1)
SUPERGUY@UCG1VM (1)
Twain-L (1)

LITHUANIA
BALT-INFO (1)
BALT-L (1)

LITURGY
LITURGY (1)

LONDON, JACK
JACK-LONDON@SONOMA.EDU (1)

LUTES
Lute (1)

LYME DISEASE
LymeNet Newsletter (2)

MACINTOSH COMPUTERS
Query (2)
Syllabus (2)

Lasmed-L (1)
LIVE-EYE@YORKVM1 (1)
LymeNet Newsletter (2)
MEDCONS@FINHUTC (1)
MEDIMAGE@POLYGRAF (1)
Medinf-L (1)
Medlib-L (1)
MEDNETS@NDSUVM1 (1)
MEDNEWS@ASUACAD (2)
MEDPHYS@RADONC.DUKE.EDU (1)
MEDSTAT (1)
Medstu-L (1)
MERSENNE@MAILBASE.AC.UK (1)
METHODS@IRLEARN (1)
MUCO-FR@FRMOP11 (1)
Neuro1-L (1)
Neuron Digest (1)
NIBNews (2)
NUTEPI (Nutritional Epidemiology) (1)
Online Journal of Current Clinical Trials 1059-2725 (2)
Panet-L (1)
PEDIATRIC-PAIN (1)
PHARMA@DMU.AC.UK (1)
PIR-BB@IRLEARN (1)
Prenat-L (1)
PRION@ACC.STOLAF.EDU (1)
public-health (1)
RADSIG@UWAVM (1)
REVES@FRMOP11 (1)
RSI Network Newsletter (2)
SBNC-L (1)
SENIOR@INDYCMS (1)
SMDM-L (1)
SMS-SNUG@UNCVM1 (1)
TELEMED@FRMOP11 (1)
THPHYSIO@FRMOP11 (1)
Vetmed-L (1)
WHOORAL-PILOT@MAILBASE.AC.UK (1)
WITSENDO (1)

MEDIEVAL STUDIES
CAMELOT@CASTLE.ED.AC.UK (1)
Earlym-L (1)
Interscripta@morgan.ucs.mun.ca (1)
med-and-ren-music (1)
MEDEVLIT Medieval English Literature Discussion List (1)
MEDFEM-L (1)
Mediev-L (1)
MedSci-L (1)
MEDTEXTL@UIUCVMD (1)

MELLON FELLOWSHIP
Mellon-L (1)

MEN'S STUDIES
MAIL-MEN (1)
PRO-FEMINIST MEN'S ISSUES MAILING LIST (1)

METAPHYSICS
Principia Cybernetica Project (PCP) (3)
PRNCYB-L (1)

METEOROLOGY
WX-LSR@UIUCVMD (1)

WX-MISC@UIUCVMD (1)
WX-NATNL@UIUCVMD (1)
WX-PCPN@UIUCVMD (1)
WXSPOT-L@UIUCVMD (1)
WX-STLT@UIUCVMD (1)
WX-SWO@UIUCVMD (1)
WX-TALK@UIUCVMD (1)
WX-TROPL@UIUCVMD (1)
WX-WATCH@UIUCVMD (1)
WX-WSTAT@UIUCVMD (1)

MEXICO
Mexico-L (1)

MICHIGAN
MichNet News (2)

MICROSOFT WINDOWS
ced-courseware (1)
Windows Online Review (2)

MICROSOFT WORD
word-mac (1)

MIDDLE ENGLISH LANGUAGE AND LITERATURE
SEENET (The Society for Early English and Norse Electronic Texts) (1)

MILITARY HISTORY
History Sources (3)
MILHST-L (1)
Mlhst-L (1)
sci.military (1)

MILITARY STUDIES
DDN Management Bulletin (2)

MILTON, JOHN
Milton-L (1)

MODAL ANALYSIS
Modal Analysis 1066-0763 (2)

MOLECULAR MECHANICS
Computational Chemistry List (1)

MULTIMEDIA COMPUTING
The Electric Eclectic (2)
The Electric Eclectic Discussion List (1)
Image-L (1)
Mmedia-L (1)
MULTIMEDIA INFORMATION SERVICES (1)
Query (2)
Sound Newsletter (2)
SURFPUNK Technical Journal (2)
Syllabus (2)

MUSEUMS
Museum-L (1)

MUSIC
78-L (1)
ALLMUSIC@AUVM (1)

OCLC
Firstsearch-L (1)
OCLC-journals (1)
OCLC-news (1)
Techbul-l (1)

OLD ENGLISH LANGUAGE AND LITERATURE
Old English Computer--Assisted Language Learning Newsletter
(OE-CALL) (2)
SEENET (The Society for Early English and Norse Electronic
Texts) (1)

OLD GERMAN LANGUAGE AND LITERATURE
GERLINGL@UIUCVMD (1)

OLD NORSE LANGUAGE AND LITERATURE
SEENET (The Society for Early English and Norse Electronic
Texts) (1)

ONLINE PUBLIC ACCESS CATALOGS
Canadian Internet-Accessible Libraries (3)
HYTEL-L (Hytelnet Updates Distribution List) (1)
HYTELNET (3)
Internet Library Catalog (3)
InterNIC Directory of Directories (3)
KATALIST (1)
Library Resources on the Internet: Strategies for Selection and
Use (3)
LOCIS: Library of Congress Information System (4)
The New Internet Library Guide (3)
OPACs in the UK: A List of Interactive Library Catalogues on
Janet (3)
UNT's Accessing Online Bibliographic Databases (3)

ONLINE UTILITY
BIOSIS: Life Science Network (6)
BRS Information Technologies (6)
Data-Star (6)
Dialog/Knowledge Index (6)
Dow Jones News/Retrieval (6)
EPIC/FirstSearch (6)
ESA-IRS (6)
Mead Data Central: LEXIS/NEXIS (6)
Medlars (6)
ORBIT Search Services (6)
RLIN (Research Libraries Information Network) (6)
STN International (6)

OPTICAL DISK TECHNOLOGIES
Current Cites 1060-2356 (2)

OTISIAN STUDIES
Purple Thunderbolt of Spode (PURPS) (2)

PARENTING
Fathers and Children for Equality Newsletter (2)
FREE-L (1)

PARENTING MULTIPLES
Twins (1)

PARENTS' RIGHTS
Fathers and Children for Equality Newsletter (2)
FREE-L (1)

PARIDAE
TITNET (1)
TITNEWS (2)
TITNOTES (2)

PEACE CORPS
PCORPS-L (1)

PEACE STUDIES
Arms-L (1)
ConflictNet (4)
DISARM-D@ALBNYVM1 (1)
PeaceNet (4)

PEDAGOGY
Megabyte University (1)

PERFORMANCE STUDIES
PERFORM (1)
PERFORM-L (1)

PERSONAL BIBLIOGRAPHIC SOFTWARE
PRO-CITE (1)

PERU
PERU@ATHENA.MIT.EDU (1)

PHARMACOLOGY
ANCHODD (Australian National Clearinghouse on Drug
Development) (1)
De Montfort University (1)
PHARMA@DMU.AC.UK (1)

PHILOLOGY
CLASSICS (1)
GERLINGL@UIUCVMD (1)
MEDTEXTL@UIUCVMD (1)

PHILOSOPHY
APF@VULCAN (1)
ARCANA@UNCCVM (1)
AYN-RAND@UA1VM (1)
BELIEF-L (Personal Ideologies Discussion List) (1)
COMP-SOC@LIMBO.INTUITIVE.COM (1)
Ethics-L (1)
FICINO (1)
Fnord-L (1)
funct-an@babbage.sissa.it (2)
HEGEL@VILLVM (1)
HOPOS-L (1)
Hpsst-L (1)
Intercultural Communication Practicum (1)
The International Philosophical Preprint Exchange (3)
Kurt Goedel Society Mailing List (1)
Libernet (1)
Liminal-Liminal Explorations (2)
MASONIC@ASGARD.BBN.COM (1)
NSP-L (1)
OBJECTIVISM-PHILOSOPHY@TWWELLS.COM (1)
OBJECTIVISM@VIX.COM (1)
PHILCOMM@RPITSVM (1)
Philosed-L (1)
PHILOS-L (1)
PHILOSOP@YORKVM1 (1)

Postmodern Jewish Philosophy (2)
Practical Anarchy Online (2)
Principia Cybernetica Newsletter (2)
PSYCHE: An Interdisciplinary Journal of Research on
    Consciousness 1039-723X (2)
PSYCOLOQUY 1055-0143 (2)
PYSCHE-D (1)
RELEVANT-LOGIC@EXETER.AC.UK (1)
SCIFRAUD@ALBNYVM1 (1)
SKEPTIC@YORKVM1 (1)
SWIP-L (1)
THINKNET (2)
Ulam Quarterly (2)
URANTIAL@UAFSYSB (1)

PHOTOGRAPHY
Photo-L (1)
PINHOLE@MINTIR.FIDONET.ORG (1)

PHOTOSYNTHESIS
Photosynthesis Researchers' List (1)

PHYSICAL SCIENCES
ELDNET-L (1)

PHYSICS
AMP-L (1)
BUILDING-MODELS-COMBINE@MAILBASE.AC.UK (1)
cond-mat@babbage.sissa.it (2)
CUPLE-L (1)
CVNET@YORKVM1 (1)
DASP-L (1)
EPP-L (1)
Fisica-L (1)
fusion (1)
GRAVITY@UWF (1)
gr-qc@xxx.lanl.gov (2)
hep-lat@ftp.scri.fsu.edu (2)
HEPNET-J@JPNKEKVM (1)
hep-ph@xxx.lanl.gov (2)
hep-th@xxx.lanl.gov (2)
NDRG-L (1)
Optics-L (1)
PAMNET (1)
Pet-L (1)
PHOTREAC@JPNTOHOK (1)
Physic-L (1)
PHYSICS@MIAMIU (1)
PHYSICS@QEDQCD.RYE.NY.US (1)
PHYS-L (1)
POLYMERP@RUTVM1 (1)
Q-Method (1)
RELATIV1@UWF (1)
RELATIV2@UWF (1)
SOCHIFI@PUCING (1)
STOMP-DEVELOP@MAILBASE.AC.UK (1)
STOMP-MEASURE@MAILBASE.AC.UK (1)
STOMP-SYSTEM@MAILBASE.AC.UK (1)
STOMP-WAVES@MAILBASE.AC.UK (1)
WIPHYS (1)
WKSPHYS (1)

PLANT BIOLOGY
Bean Bag (2)

Botanical Electronic News 1188-603X (2)
Dendochronolgy Forum for the International Tree-Ring Data
    Bank (6)
Flora Online 0892-9106 (2)
ITRDBFOR@ASUACAD (1)
MICRONET@UOGUELPH (1)
NEWCROPS@PURCCVM (1)
Photosynthesis Researchers' List (1)
PLANT-TAXONOMY@MAILBASE.AC.UK (1)
PORIFERA (1)

POETRY
Armadillo Culture: The Journal of Modern Dasypodidae (2)
Chpoem-L (1)
CORE 1062-6697 (2)
Cult of the Dead Cow (2)
High Weirdness by Email (2)
Milton-L (1)
PowderKeg (2)
Purple Thunderbolt of Spode (PURPS) (2)
RIF/T: A Journal of Contemporary Poetry and Poetics (pending)
    (2)
Sbrhym-L (1)
TapRoot Reviews Electronic Edition (2)
Undiscovered Country (2)
Unit Circle Magazine (2)

POLAND
DRYDYMALKI 1064-9794 (2)
Grochz Kapusta (2)
PIGULKI 1060-9288 (2)
POLAND-L (1)
POLAND@NDCVX.CC.ND.EDU (1)

POLICY PLANNING AND ANALYSIS
ADLTED-L (1)
Electronic AIR (2)

POLISH LANGUAGE AND LITERATURE
Donosy (English edition) 1059-4027 (2)
Donosy (Polish edition) 0867-6860 (2)

POLITICAL ACTIVISM
ACTIV-L (1)
ACTNOW-L (College and Organizational Activism List) (1)
Arm the Spirit (2)
Choice-Mail (1)
PCORPS-L (1)
PJAL (1)
PJML (1)

POLITICAL SCIENCE
9NOV-89-L (1)
ACT-UP@WORLD.STD.COM (1)
Africa-L (1)
ALGERIA-NET (1)
AMERICA (1)
BELIEF-L (Personal Ideologies Discussion List) (1)
Bosnet (2)
BYRD.MU.WVNET.EDU (3)
Carolina (2)
Casid-L (1)
Cerro-L (1)
Chile News Database (2)

CHIP Q Political, Environmental, Economic and Human Rights News Chile Information Project (2)
ConflictNet (4)
Devel-L (1)
Donosy (English edition) 1059-4027 (2)
Donosy (Polish edition) 0867-6860 (2)
EC@INDYCMS (1)
ECPR-ECO (1)
ECPR-PILOT@MAILBASE.AC.UK (1)
FEMISA (1)
H-DIPLO (1)
History Sources (3)
H-Law@uicvm (1)
HomeoNet (4)
H-POL (1)
INFO-RUSS (1)
INMYLIFE@WKUVX1 (1)
IPEnet (International Political Economy) (1)
IRL-POL@IRLEARN (1)
Law and Politics Book Review 1062-7421 (2)
Libernet (1)
MIDEUR-L (1)
Mopoly-L (1)
Organized Thoughts (2)
Or-L (1)
PeaceNet (4)
People's Tribune (Online Edition) (2)
Phirst Amendment (2)
PJAL (1)
POLAND-L (1)
POLAND@NDCVX.CC.ND.EDU (1)
POLCAN@YORKVM1 (1)
POLCOMM@RPITSVM (1)
POLI-SCI@RUTVM1 (1)
POLITICA@UFRJ (1)
POLITICS@UCF1VM (1)
Practical Anarchy Online (2)
PSRT-L (1)
RFE/RL Research Institute Daily Report (2)
RFE/RL Research Institute Research Bulletin (2)
RFE/RL-L (1)
RokPress (2)
RUSHIST@USCVM (1)
RUSSIA@ARIZVM1 (1)
SCS-L (1)
SEASIA-L (1)
SLOVAK-L (1)
Somalia News Update 1103-1999 (2)
SOVHIST@USCVM (1)
SQSP@UQUEBEC (1)
STATEPOL@UMAB (1)
TPS-L (1)
UK Data Protection Act 1984 (1)
UKRAINE@ARIZVM1 (1)
UN@INDYCMS (1)
VAL-L (1)
VND (VREME NEWS DIGEST) (2)

POPULAR CULTURE
BLINK (2)
Funhouse (2)
FUTURE@NYX.CS.DU.EDU (1)
H-FILM (1)
Hi-Rez (2)

Holy Temple of Mass Consumption (2)
INMYLIFE@WKUVX1 (1)
Lyric and Discography Archive (3)
Parthenogenesis (2)
PERFORM-L (1)
Scratch (2)
Screams of Abel (2)
SCREEN-L (1)
SURFPUNK Technical Journal (2)
TapRoot Reviews Electronic Edition (2)
Temptation of Saint Anthony 1062-3981 (2)
Unit Circle Magazine (2)
Unplastic News (2)
Whole Earth Review (2)
Zine List (3)

POPULAR MUSIC
Network Audio Bits and Audio Software Review (2)
Screams of Abel (2)

PORIFERA
PORIFERA (1)

PORTUGAL
Espora-L (1)
HISTORY-VASCO@MAILBASE.AC.UK (1)

PORTUGUESE LANGUAGE AND LITERATURE
PIADAS (1)

POTTERY
CLAYART@UKCC (1)

PRIMATES
LPN-L (1)
LPN-L (Laboratory Primate Newsletter) 0023-6861 (2)

PROBLEM-BASED LEARNING
PBLIST (1)

PRO-CITE
PRO-CITE (1)

PSYCHOANALYSIS
PSYART (1)

PSYCHOBIOLOGY
The PSYCGRAD Journal (Psychology Graduate Student Journal) Applied for. (2)
PSYCGRAD@UOTTAWA (Psychology Graduate Students Discussion List) (1)

PSYCHOLOGY
ACTIVIST@ GUVM (1)
Apasd-L (1)
Apb-L (1)
Apb-ul-L (1)
APSCNET@MCGILL1 (1)
BEHAVIOR@ASUACAD (1)
BRAIN-L (1)
CCHD-L (1)
COGNEURO@PTOLEMY.ARC.NASA.GOV (1)
CREA-CPS@NIC.SURFNET.NL (1)
DIV28@GWUVM (1)

LITURGY (1)
MailJC Network (1)
A MegaByte of Torah (2)
Ministry-L (1)
NT-GREEK (New Testament Greek Studies) Conference (1)
OBJ-REL@EMUVM1.CC.EMORY.EDU (1)
OFFLINE (2)
ORTHODOX@INDYCMS (1)
OT-HEBREW (Old Testament Hebrew Studies) (1)
PAGAN@DRYCAS.CLUB.CC.CMU.EDU (1)
Quaker-L (1)
RELIGCOM (1)
RELIGION@HARVARDA (1)
Religious Studies Publications Journal 1188-5734 (2)
Review-L (1)
Rome Reborn: The Vatican Library & Renaissance Culture (3)
Scrolls from the Dead Sea: The Ancient Library of Qumran and
    Modern Scholarship (3)
SECULAR-HUMANIST@SUGAR.NEOSOFT.COM (1)
Shaker (1)
THEOLOGY@UICVM (1)
Uus-L (1)

RENAISSANCE STUDIES
1492: An Ongoing Voyage: An Exhibit at the Library of
    Congress (3)
Earlym-L (1)
FICINO (1)
med-and-ren-music (1)
MedSci-L (1)
Renais-L (1)
Rome Reborn: The Vatican Library & Renaissance Culture (3)

RESIDENCE HALL GOVERNMENT
National Communication Coordinator Discussion List (1)
Residence Hall Association Discussion List (1)

RESOURCE GUIDES
Anonymous FTP List (3)
Big Dummy's Guide to the Internet (3)
Bitnet Servers (3)
Canadian Internet-Accessible Libraries (3)
Coalition for Networked Information Gopher (3)
CWIS List (3)
Dartmouth List of Lists (3)
Directory of Electronic Journals and Newsletters (3)
A Guide to Internet/BITNET: A Metro Library User Network
    Guide (3)
Guide to Network Resource Tools (3)
The Incomplete Guide to the Internet and Other
    Telecommunications Opportunities Especially for Teachers
    and Students, K-12 (3)
Information Sources: The Internet and Computer-Mediated
    Communications (3)
Interest Groups List of Lists (3)
The Internet Explorer's Toolkit (3)
Internet Library Catalog (3)
Internet Resource Guide (3)
Internet Tools Summary (3)
Internet/Bitnet Online Health Sciences Resource List (3)
InterNIC Directory and Database Services (3)
InterNIC Directory of Directories (3)
Library Resources on the Internet: Strategies for Selection and
    Use (3)

Library-Oriented Lists and Electronic Serials (3)
List of Active Newsgroups (3)
List of Periodic Postings (3)
NETSCOUT@VMTECMEX (1)
Network Knowledge for the Neophyte: Stuff You Need to
    Know in Order to Navigate the Electronic Village (3)
The New Internet Library Guide (3)
NEW-LIST (1)
NEW-LISTS@MAILBASE.AC.UK (1)
NNEWS@NDSUVM1 (1)
Not Just Cows: A Guide to Internet/Bitnet Resources in
    Agriculture and Related Sciences (3)
NYSERNet New User's Guide to Useful and Unique Resources
    on the Internet (3)
OPACs in the UK: A List of Interactive Library Catalogues on
    Janet (3)
Special Internet Connections (3)
SURAnet Guide to Selected Internet Resources (3)
Surfing the Internet: An Introduction (3)
There's Gold in Them Thar Networks! (3)
UNT's Accessing Online Bibliographic Databases (3)
Using Networked Information Resources: A Bibliography (3)
Zamfield's Wonderfully Incomplete, Complete Internet BBS List
    (3)

RHETORIC
CRTNET (Communication Research and Theory Network) (2)
H-RHETORIC (1)
WHIRL (Women's History in Rhetoric and Language) (1)

ROCK MUSIC
Discipline (1)
Sabbath (1)

ROMANCE LITERATURE
RRA-L (1)

ROMANIA
ROMANIANS (1)

RURAL HEALTH
RURALAM (1)

RURAL STUDIES
H-Rural@uicvm (1)
H-South@uicvm (1)

RUSSIA
A & G Information Services (2)
INFO-RUSS (1)
ReNews (2)
Revelations from the Russian Archives (3)
RFE/RL Research Institute Daily Report (2)
RFE/RL Research Institute Research Bulletin (2)
RFE/RL-L (1)
RUSHIST@USCVM (1)
RUSSIA@ARIZVM1 (1)
RUSTEX-L (1)
SUEARN-L (1)
SUEARN-L (2)
TPS-L (1)
VAL-L (1)

A MegaByte of Torah (2)

TRADE AND ECONOMIC DATA
AMERICA (1)
LATCO LIST (1)

TRAINING AND DEVELOPMENT
TRDEV-L (1)

TRANSLATION STUDIES
CRETA-PILOT@MAILBASE.AC.UK (1)
Lantra-L (1)

TRANSPORTATION
Delaware Valley Rail Passenger (2)
Journal of Technology Education 1045-1064 (2)
RRL-PUBLICATIONS (1)

TRAVEL AND TOURISM
Crash (2)
Journal of the International Academy of Hospitality Research
   1052-6099 (2)
Mexico-L (1)
Pisma bralcev (1)
RURALAM (1)
Travel-Advisories (1)
TRAVEL-L (1)

TROPICAL STUDIES
OTS-L (1)

TUNISIA
Tunisian Scientific Society Newsletter (2)

TWAIN, MARK (SAMUEL CLEMENS)
Mark Twain Forum (1)
Twain-L (1)

UKRAINE
UKRAINE@ARIZVM1 (1)

UNITED NATIONS
UN@INDYCMS (1)

UNIVERSITY OF CALIFORNIA AT SANTA BARBARA
REACH Q Research and Educational Applications of Computers
   in the Humanities (2)

UNIVERSITY OF MISSOURI, COLUMBIA
Campus Computing Newsletter (2)

UNIVERSITY OF NORTH CAROLINA
Newsbrief (2)

UNIX
CACTUS Newsletter (2)
UKUUG Newsletter 0965-9412 (2)
UNIX-SOURCES@BRL.MIL (1)
UNIX-SW@WSMR-SIMTEL20.ARMY.MIL (1)
UNIX-WIZARDS@BRL.MIL (1)

URBAN HISTORY
H-Urban (1)

URBAN PLANNING
Urban-L (1)
URBAREG@UQUBEC (1)

US NAVY
NAVNEWS@NCTAMSLANT.NAVY.MIL (1)
Navy News Service (NAVNEWS) (2)

US PRESIDENTS
PrezHist@kasey.umkc.edu (1)

US SUPREME COURT
Project Hermes: U.S. Supreme Court Opinions (3)

USENET NEWSGROUPS
List of Active Newsgroups (3)
List of Periodic Postings (3)
USENET.HIST@UCSD.EDU (1)

VENEZUELA
Vzla-L (1)

VETERINARY SCIENCE
AAVLD-L (1)
COMPMED (1)
Vetcai-L (1)
VETINFO@UCDCVDLS (1)
Vetlib-L (1)
Vetmed-L (1)

VIETNAM WAR
Vwar-L (1)

VIRTUAL CULTURE
Ejournal 1054-1055 (2)
EJVC (Electronic Journal of Virtual Culture) (2)
IRVC-L (Forum for Research on Virtual Culture) (1)

VIRTUAL REALITY
PMC-MOO (1)
VIRTU-L (1)

VISION RESEARCH
Color and Vision Network (1)

WARGAMES
Play by EMail (2)

WASHINGTON, D.C.
dcraves (1)

WEIGHT LIFTING
Weights (1)

WELSH LANGUAGE AND LITERATURE
WELSH-L (1)

WHOLE LANGUAGE
TESLFF-L (1)

WIND STUDIES
Wind Energy Weekly 0747-5500 (2)

These 6 Pocket Guides have been written and designed so that any Internet user can have quick, practical guidance in using the Internet for:

POCKET GUIDES TO THE INTERNET

- **Telnetting**
- **Transferring files with File Transfer Protocol (FTP)**
- **Using and Navigating Usenet**
- **The Internet E-Mail System**
- **Basic Internet Utilities**
- **Terminal Connections**

VOLUME 1
TELNETTING

by Mark Veljkov and George Hartnell

Includes a basic overview of the Internet and an explanation of the Telnet remote logon procedure.
ISBN: 0-88736-943-X
Paper $7.00/£5.00 • Nov. 1993

VOLUME 2
TRANSFERRING FILES WITH FILE TRANSFER PROTOCOL

by Mark Veljkov and George Hartnell

Includes a basic overview of the Internet and an explanation of FTP, the file transfer protocol that allows Internet users to retrieve documents from remote computers.
ISBN: 0-88736-944-8
Paper $7.00/£5.00 • Nov. 1993

VOLUME 3
USING AND NAVIGATING USENET

by Mark Veljkov and George Hartnell

Includes a basic overview of the Internet and an explanation of Usenet Newsgroups, how to logon to them, and the resources available.
ISBN: 0-88736-945-6
Paper $7.00/£5.00 • Nov. 1993

VOLUME 4
THE INTERNET E-MAIL SYSTEM

by Mark Veljkov and George Hartnell

Includes a basic overview of the Internet and an explanation of how to use Internet E-Mail systems, sending and receiving mail and accessing and using mail gateways to commercial mail systems.
ISBN: 0-88736-946-4
Paper $7.00/£5.00 • Nov. 1993

Meckler • 11 Ferry Lane West • Westport, CT 06880 / Fax 203-454-5840
☐ Enter my order for the following *POCKET GUIDES*:

☐ Volume 1 @ $7.00/£5.00   ☐ Volume 4 @ $7.00/£5.00
☐ Volume 2 @ $7.00/£5.00   ☐ Volume 5 @ $7.00/£5.00
☐ Volume 3 @ $7.00/£5.00   ☐ Volume 6 @ $7.00/£5.00
☐ *SAVE!* Enter my order for all 6 volumes for a total price of $35.00/£25.00

My payment is enclosed.   ☐ Check   ☐ VISA   ☐ AMEX   ☐ MC

Card # _____ Exp. Date _____
Signature_____ Phone _____
Name _____
Organization _____
Address_____
City _____ State _____ Zip_____
KPG14

VOLUME 5
BASIC INTERNET UTILITIES

by Mark Veljkov and George Hartnell

Includes a basic overview of the Internet and an explanation of such Internet utilities as Gopher, Archie, Internet White Pages, and other searching aids.
ISBN: 0-88736-947-2
Paper $7.00/£5.00 • Nov. 1993

VOLUME 6
TERMINAL CONNECTIONS

by Mark Veljkov and George Hartnell

Includes a basic overview of the Internet, an explanation of how to logon to a Unix/VMS system, and other basic terminal applications, including working with a variety of telecommunications programs.
ISBN: 0-88736-948-0
Paper $7.00/£5.00 • Nov. 1993

SAVE! Purchase all 6 titles for only $35.00/£25.00